WORD BIBLICAL COMMENTARY

WORD BIBLICAL COMMENTARY

VOLUME 4

Leviticus

JOHN E. HARTLEY

WORD BOOKS, PUBLISHER • DALLAS, TEXAS

Word Biblical Commentary
Leviticus 1–27

Library of Congress Cataloging-in-Publication Data
Main entry under title:

Word biblical commentary.

Includes bibliographies.
1. Bible—Commentaries—Collected Works.
BS491.2.W67 220.7'7 81–71768
ISBN 0–8499–0203–7 (vol. 4) AACR2

Printed in the United States of America

The author's own translation of the Scripture text appears in italic type under the heading *Translation.*

2 3 4 9 AGF 9 8 7 6 5 4 3 2 1

To my daughters
Joyce Ruhamah and Johannah Lynn
two precious blessings from the LORD

Contents

Author's Preface

I find that writing a commentary on a book of the Bible is a humbling experience, for I am always coming up against the obstacle of my limited knowledge. Nevertheless, it is an enriching experience, for I have the great privilege of pondering God's word, line upon line, in order to wrestle from the text its life-giving meaning.

At the center of the Pentateuch stands one of the driest and yet most sublime books of the Bible. It both speaks of mundane matters and leads its readers into the sphere of the holy. Hopefully the insights offered in this volume will help other readers overcome the natural apathy toward this book and enter into its world to discover its riches. Leviticus provides an understanding of holiness-sin-atonement, the essential elements of the divine-human relationship. Furthermore, just as Israel was called to be a holy nation in order to function as a royal priesthood to the nations, the church is called to be a holy people in order that it may serve all the peoples of the world as a royal priesthood. A fuller understanding of both that call and that role is provided by the study of Leviticus.

The format of this series offers the opportunity to investigate the rich message of Leviticus from various perspectives. The author's own literal translation is supported by technical textual and lexical information in the *Notes.* In the *Comment* the meaning of the text is explored in its canonical context. Then the ideas of the passage are recounted from a biblical theological perspective, and these theological themes are pursued into the NT in the *Explanation.* The section called *Form/Structure/Setting* provides the opportunity to look at the structure of each section with special attention to its rhetorical design, since this material was composed for the oral instruction of the congregation. In this section some observations about the literary history of the material are also given, and there is some interaction with traditio-historical work on the passage. Traditio-historical matters are not pursued extensively, however, because of the limitations of space and skill.

I am very grateful to Dr. John D. W. Watts for inviting me to write this volume and for his patient encouragement along the way. At crucial junctures he has provided wise and helpful counsel.

To Dr. Rolf P. Knierim, Professor of Old Testament at the School of Theology at Claremont and Avery Professor of Religion at Claremont Graduate School, I wish to extend my warmest appreciation for his encouragement. He gladly permitted me to attend some of his OT seminars, made available some protocols from those seminars, and has supported my inclusion of material vital to the interpretation of a passage with proper documentation. The structural outlines for chap. 1 and 4:1–5:13 rely heavily on work done in his seminars. In addition, I have learned from Dr. Knierim's work through many of his students. They have proven to be a delightful, most cooperative group. Dr. Henry Sun, who wrote his thesis on the Holiness Code, has been very helpful. Along the way he provided me with extensive bibliographic information. Upon completion of his thesis he provided me a copy, and I have made considerable use of it. He has also been available for exchanging ideas. Mr. William Yarchin penned the history of research in Leviticus, making a significant contribution to this work. He also offered a critique of chaps. 1–14. Dr. Stephen A.

Reed assisted in composing parts of chap. 24, specifically the structure of both sections, material on tending the lampstand and preparing the bread for the table of Presence, and material both on the incident of the person's cursing Yahweh during a fight and on blasphemy in general. He also provided insightful feedback on *Form/Structure/Setting* for chaps. 16–27. One of my colleagues, Dr. Steven Wilkens, assisted in the composition of two excursuses: one on the feasts in chap. 23 and one on the year of Jubilee in chap. 25. A former student, Dr. Timothy Dwyer, prepared a manuscript on Molek which has been edited and augmented for an excursus found in chap. 20. A friend, Dr. Robert Benninger, who has a diploma in Tropical Medicine and Hygiene from the Ross Institute at the University of London, reviewed the material for chaps. 12–15 and offered valuable suggestions from the perspective of a physician. To each of these I extend my hearty thanks.

I am indebted to Mrs. Lark Rilling for careful editorial work on the manuscript. I wish to thank my wife for her hard work in typing the many editions of this work. For the work of the library staff at Azusa Pacific University in locating many important articles and volumes, I am very grateful.

I wish to thank the administration of Azusa Pacific University, particularly Dr. Les Blank, Dean, C. P. Haggard School of Theology, and Dr. Donald Grant, Vice-President for Academic Affairs, for their encouragement in many small and important ways. Many students and colleagues have graciously assisted in a variety of ways, including reading and commenting on portions of this work; I thank Miles Van Pelt for doing many chores. Clifford Anderson has provided some key bibliographic information and copies of significant works.

During the years of writing this manuscript I have experienced a serious illness. I wish to offer praise to the gracious, holy God for providing the strength to bring this task to completion.

Glendora, California JOHN E. HARTLEY

Editorial Preface

The launching of the *Word Biblical Commentary* brings to fulfillment an enterprise of several years' planning. The publishers and the members of the editorial board met in 1977 to explore the possibility of a new commentary on the books of the Bible that would incorporate several distinctive features. Prospective readers of these volumes are entitled to know what such features were intended to be; whether the aims of the commentary have been fully achieved time alone will tell.

First, we have tried to cast a wide net to include as contributors a number of scholars from around the world who not only share our aims, but are in the main engaged in the ministry of teaching in university, college, and seminary. They represent a rich diversity of denominational allegiance. The broad stance of our contributors can rightly be called evangelical, and this term is to be understood in its positive, historic sense of a commitment to Scripture as divine revelation, and to the truth and power of the Christian gospel.

Then, the commentaries in our series are all commissioned and written for the purpose of inclusion in the *Word Biblical Commentary.* Unlike several of our distinguished counterparts in the field of commentary writing, there are no translated works, originally written in a non-English language. Also, our commentators were asked to prepare their own rendering of the original biblical text and to use those languages as the basis of their own comments and exegesis. What may be claimed as distinctive with this series is that it is based on the biblical languages, yet it seeks to make the technical and scholarly approach to a theological understanding of Scripture understandable by—and useful to—the fledgling student, the working minister, and colleagues in the guild of professional scholars and teachers as well.

Finally, a word must be said about the format of the series. The layout, in clearly defined sections, has been consciously devised to assist readers at different levels. Those wishing to learn about the textual witnesses on which the translation is offered are invited to consult the section headed *Notes.* If the readers' concern is with the state of modern scholarship on any given portion of Scripture, they should turn to the sections of *Bibliography* and *Form/Structure/Setting.* For a clear exposition of the passage's meaning and its relevance to the ongoing biblical revelation, the *Comment* and concluding *Explanation* are designed expressly to meet that need. There is therefore something for everyone who may pick up and use these volumes.

If these aims come anywhere near realization, the intention of the editors will have been met, and the labor of our team of contributors rewarded.

General Editors: *David A. Hubbard*
Glenn W. Barker †
Old Testament: *John D. W. Watts*
New Testament: *Ralph P. Martin*

Abbreviations

PERIODICALS, SERIALS AND REFERENCE WORKS

AASOR	Annual of the American Schools of Oriental Research
AB	Anchor Bible
AER	*American Ecclesiastical Review*
AfO	*Archiv für Orientforschung*
AHw	*W. von Soden (ed.), Akkademisches Handwörterbuch* (Wiesbaden: Otto Harrassowitz, 1965–81)
AI	R. de Vaux, *Ancient Israel,* tr. J. McHugh (New York: McGraw-Hill Book Co., 1965)
AJSL	*American Journal of Semitic Languages and Literature*
AJT	*American Journal of Theology*
ALUOS	Annual of Leeds University Oriental Society
AnBib	Analecta biblica
ANET	J. Pritchard (ed.), *Ancient Near Eastern Texts,* 3rd ed. (Princeton: Princeton UP, 1969)
Ang	*Angelicum*
AnOr	Analecta orientalia
AOAT	Alter Orient und Altes Testament
ArOr	*Archiv orientální*
ARW	*Archiv für Religionswissenschaft*
ASOR	American Schools of Oriental Research
ASTI	*Annual of the Swedish Theological Institute*
ATAbh	Alttestamentliche Abhandlungen
ATD	Das Alte Testament Deutsch
ATR	*Anglican Theological Review*
ATSAT	Arbeiten zur Text und Sprache im Alten Testament
AUMSR	Andrews University Monographs, Studies in Religion
AuS	G. H. Dalman, *Arbeit und Sitte in Palästina,* 1928–42 (reprint, Hildesheim: G. Olms, 1987)
AUSS	*Andrews University Seminary Studies*
BA	*Biblical Archaeologist*
BAR	*Biblical Archaeology Review*
BASOR	*Bulletin of the American Schools of Oriental Research*
BBB	Bonner biblische Beiträge
BDB	F. Brown, S. Driver, and C. A. Briggs, *Hebrew and English Lexicon of the Old Testament*
BHS	*Biblia hebraica stuttgartensia*
BHT	Beiträge zur historischen Theologie
Bib	*Biblica*
BibB	Biblische Beiträge
BibOr	Biblica et orientalia
BJRL	*Bulletin of the John Rylands University Library of Manchester*

BKAT	Biblischer Kommentar: Altes Testament
BN	*Biblische Notizen*
BO	*Bibliotheca orientalis*
BSac	*Bibliotheca Sacra*
BT	*The Bible Translator*
BTB	*Biblical Theology Bulletin*
BVC	*Bible et vie chrétienne*
BWANT	Beiträge zur Wissenschaft vom Alten und Neuen Testament
BZ	*Biblische Zeitschrift*
BZAW	Beihefte zur *ZAW*
BZNW	Beihefte zur *ZNW*
CAD	*The Assyrian Dictionary of the Oriental Institute of the University of Chicago*
CB	The Century Bible
CBC	Cambridge Bible Commentary
CBQ	*Catholic Biblical Quarterly*
CJT	*Canadian Journal of Theology*
COT	Gispen commentar
CRAIBL	*Comptes rendus de l'Académie des inscriptions et belles-lettres*
CTM	*Concordia Theological Monthly*
DBAT	*Dielheimer Blätter zum Alten Testament*
DBSup	*Dictionnaire de la Bible, Supplément*
EncJud	*Encyclopaedia judaica (1971)*
ErbAuf	*Erbe und Auftrag*
ETR	*Etudes théologiques et religieuses*
EvQ	*Evangelical Quarterly*
EvT	*Evangelische Theologie*
ExpTim	*Expository Times*
FF	*Forschungen und Fortschritte*
FRLANT	Forschungen zur Religion und Literatur des Alten und Neuen Testaments
GKC	*Gesenius' Hebrew Grammer*, ed. E. Kautzsch, tr. A. E. Cowley
HAR	*Hebrew Annual Review*
HAT	Handbuch zum Alten Testament
HKAT	Handkommentar zum Alten Testament
HR	*History of Religions*
HSAT	Die Heilige Shrift des Alten Testaments
HSM	Harvard Semitic Monographs
HSS	Harvard Semitic Series
HTR	*Harvard Theological Review*
HUCA	*Hebrew Union College Annual*
IBHS	B. Waltke and M. O'Connor, *An Introduction to Biblical Hebrew Syntax* (Winona Lake, IN: Eisenbrauns, 1990)
ICC	International Critical Commentary
IDB	G. A. Buttrick (ed.), *Interpreter's Dictionary of the Bible*
IDBSup	Supplementary volume to *IDB*
IEJ	*Israel Exploration Journal*
ILR	*Israel Law Review*

Int	*Interpretation*
ISBE	G. Bromiley et al. (eds.), *The International Standard Bible Encyclopedia,* revised
JA	*Journal asiatique*
JAAR	*Journal of the American Academy of Religion*
JANESCU	*Journal of the Ancient Near Eastern Society of Columbia University*
JAOS	*Journal of the American Oriental Society*
Jastrow	M. Jastrow, *A Dictionary of the Targumim, the Talmud Babli and Yerushalmi, and the Midrashic Literature,* 2 vols. (Brooklyn, NY: Traditional Press, Inc., n.d.)
JBL	*Journal of Biblical Literature*
JBR	*Journal of Bible and Religion*
JCS	*Journal of Cuneiform Studies*
JJS	*Journal of Jewish Studies*
JNES	*Journal of Near Eastern Studies*
Joüon	P. P. Joüon, *Grammaire de l'hebreu biblique* (Rome: Pontifical Biblical Institute, 1947)
JPOS	*Journal of the Palestine Oriental Society*
JQR	*Jewish Quarterly Review*
JRE	*Journal of Religious Ethics*
JRelS	*Journal of Religious Studies*
JSJ	*Journal for the Study of Judaism*
JSOT	*Journal for the Study of the Old Testament*
JSOTSup	Journal for the Study of the Old Testament Supplement Series
JSS	*Journal of Semitic Studies*
JTS	*Journal of Theological Studies*
KAT	E. Sellin (ed.), Kommentar zum Alten Testament
KB	L. Köhler and W. Baumgartner, *Hebräisches und aramäisches Lexicon zum Alten Testament* (Leiden: Brill, 1967–90)
KD	*Kerygma und Dogma*
KEH	Kurzgefasstes exegetisches Handbuch zum Alten Testament
KHC	Kurzer Hand-Commentar zum Alten Testament
LTQ	*Lexington Theological Quarterly*
MIO	*Mitteilungen des Instituts für Orientforschung*
MRS	Mission de Ras Shamra
MTZ	*Münchener theologische Zeitschrift*
NBC	New Bible Commentary
NCB	New Century Bible
NICOT	New International Commentary on the Old Testament
NRT	*La nouvelle revue théologique*
NT	*Novum Testamentum*
OBT	Overtures to Biblical Theology
OLZ	*Orientalische Literaturzeitung*
Or	*Orientalia* (Rome)
OTL	Old Testament Library
OTS	*Oudtestamentische Studiën*
PAAJR	*Proceedings of the American Academy of Jewish Research*
PEQ	*Palestine Exploration Quarterly*

PG	J. Migne, *Patrologia graeca*
PIR	Preliminary and Interim Report on the Hebrew Old Testament Text Project, vol. 1, Pentateuch, 2nd ed. (New York: United Bible Societies, 1979)
PL	J. Migne, *Patrologia latina*
PLS	D. N. Freedman and K. A. Mathews, *The Paleo-Hebrew Leviticus Scroll (11QpaleoLev)* (American Schools of Oriental Research; Winona Lake, IN: Eisenbrauns, 1985)
POS	Pretoria Oriental Series
RB	*Revue biblique*
RBibIt	*Rivista biblica italiana* (Rome)
REJ	*Revue des études juives*
RevQ	*Revue de Qumran*
RHPR	*Revue d'histoire et de philosophie religieuses*
RHR	*Revue de l'histoire des religions*
RIDA	*Revue Internationale des Droits de l'Antiquité*
RSR	*Recherches des sciences religieuses*
Sal	*Salesianum*
SANT	Studien zum Alten und Neuen Testament
SBLASP	Society of Biblical Literature Abstracts and Seminar Papers
SBLDS	SBL Dissertation Series
SBLMS	SBL Monograph Series
SBS	Stuttgarter Bibelstudien
SBT	Studies in Biblical Theology
ScEc	*Sciences ecclésiastiques*
SCTT	J. Milgrom, *Studies in Cultic Terminology and Theology,* SJLA 36 (Leiden: Brill, 1983)
SJLA	Studies in Judaism in Late Antiquity
SJT	*Scottish Journal of Theology*
ST	*Studia theologica*
StBib	*Studia Biblica et Theologica*
StLit	*Studia liturgica*
StMor	*Studia Moralia*
SWJT	*Southwest Journal of Theology*
TBü	Theologische Bücherei
TDNT	G. Kittel and G. Friedrich (eds.), tr. G.W. Bromiley, *Theological Dictionary of the New Testament*
TDOT	G. Botterweck and H. Ringgren (eds.), tr. D. Green, *Theological Dictionary of the Old Testament*
TGUOS	*Transactions of the Glasgow University Oriental Society*
THAT	E. Jenni and C. Westermann (eds.), *Theologisches Handwörterbuch zum Alten Testament,* 2 vols. (Munich: Kaiser; Zurich: Theologischer Verlag, 1971–76)
TLZ	*Theologische Literaturzeitung*
TOTC	Tyndale Old Testament Commentaries
TQ	*Theologische Quartalschrift*
TRE	G. Krause and G. Müller (eds.), *Theologische Realenzyklopädie* (Berlin: de Gruyter, 1983)

TRu	*Theologische Rundschau*
T Today	*Theology Today*
TWOT	R. L. Harris et al. (eds.), *Theological Wordbook of the Old Testament*, 2 vols. (Chicago: Moody, 1980)
TynBul	*Tyndale Bulletin*
TZ	*Theologische Zeitschrift*
UCOP	University of Cambridge Oriental Publications
UF	*Ugaritische Forschungen*
UT	C. Gordon, *Ugaritic Textbook*
VT	*Vetus Testamentum*
VTSup	*VT* Supplements
WBC	Word Biblical Commentary
WMANT	Wissenschaftliche Monographien zum Alten und Neuen Testament
WZKM	*Wiener Zeitschrift für die Kunde des Morgenlandes*
ZAW	*Zeitschrift für die alttestamentliche Wissenschaft*
ZDPV	*Zeitschrift des deutschen Palästina-vereins*
ZKT	*Zeitshrift für katholische Theologie*
ZLTK	*Zeitschrift für die gesamte lutherische Theologie und Kirche*
ZST	*Zeitschrift für systematische Theologie*
ZTK	*Zeitschrift für Theologie und Kirche*

Hebrew Grammar

abs	absolute	indir obj	indirect object
acc	accusative	inf	infinitive
adj	adjective	masc	masculine
conj	conjunction	niph	niphal
constr	construct	obj	object
dir obj	direct object	pass	passive
fem	feminine	pf	perfect
gen	genitive	pl	plural
hiph	hiphil	prep	preposition
hoph	hophal	ptcp	participle
impf	imperfect	sg	singular
impv	imperative	subj	subject

Textual Notes

Akk	Akkadian	LXX[B]	LXX ms, Vatican Codex
Arab	Arabic	LXX*	LXX ms, original reading
Aram	Aramaic		
Eng	English	ms(s)	manuscript(s)
Eth	Ethiopic	MT	Masoretic Text
Gk.	Greek	Sam	Samaritan Pentateuch
Heb.	Hebrew	Syr	Syriac
LXX	Septuagint	Ugar	Ugaritic
LXX[A]	LXX ms, Alexandrian Codex	Vg	Vulgate

Biblical and Aprocryphal Books

Gen	Genesis
Exod	Exodus
Lev	Leviticus
Num	Numbers
Deut	Deuteronomy
Josh	Joshua
Judg	Judges
Ruth	Ruth
1–2 Sam	1–2 Samuel
1–2 Kgs	1–2 Kings
1–2 Chr	1–2 Chronicles
Ezra	Ezra
Neh	Nehemiah
Esth	Esther
Job	Job
Ps(s)	Psalm(s)
Prov	Proverbs
Eccl	Ecclesiastes
Cant	Canticles, Song of Solomon
Isa	Isaiah
Jer	Jeremiah
Lam	Lamentations
Ezek	Ezekiel
Dan	Daniel
Hos	Hosea
Joel	Joel
Amos	Amos
Obad	Obadiah
Jonah	Jonah
Mic	Micah
Nah	Nahum
Hab	Habakkuk
Zeph	Zephaniah
Hag	Haggai
Zech	Zechariah
Mal	Malachi
Tob	Tobit
Jdt	Judith
Sir	Ecclesiasticus or The Wisdom of Jesus son of Sirach
1–3 Macc	1–3 Maccabees
Matt	Matthew
Mark	Mark
Luke	Luke
John	John
Acts	Acts
Rom	Romans
1–2 Cor	1–2 Corinthians
Gal	Galatians
Eph	Ephesians
Phil	Philippians
Col	Colossians
1–2 Thess	1–2 Thessalonians
1–2 Tim	1–2 Timothy
Titus	Titus
Phlm	Philemon
Heb	Hebrews
Jas	James
1–2 Pet	1–2 Peter
1–3 John	1–3 John
Jude	Jude
Rev	Revelation

Extrabiblical Jewish and Christian Literature

b.	Babylonian Talmud
CD	Cairo Damascus Document
Ḥul.	*Ḥullin*
Jos., *Ant.*	Josephus, *Antiquities*
Jub.	Jubilees
m.	Mishna
Meg.	*Megilla*
Menaḥ.	*Menaḥot*
Neg.	*Negaᶜim*
Nid.	*Niddah*
Pesaḥ.	*Pesaḥim*
1 QS	Manuel of Discipline
11 QpaleoLev	The Paleo-Leviticus Scroll from Cave 11
Qidd.	*Qiddušin*
Sanh.	*Sanhedrin*
Taᶜan.	*Taᶜanit*
T. Gad	*Testament of Gad*
Tg	Targum
Tg. Onq.	*Targum Onqelos*

Tg. Neof.	*Targum Neofiti 1*	*Yebam.*	*Yebamot*
Tg. Ps.-J.	*Targum Pseudo-Jonathan*	*Zebah*	*Zebahim*

MISCELLANEOUS

A.D.	*Anno Domini*	n.	note
ANE	Ancient Near East	n.d.	no date
AV	Authorized Version	NEB	*New English Bible*
B.C.	Before Christ	n.f.	neue folge
chap(s).	chapters(s)	NIV	*New International Version*
cols.	columns	NJPS	New Jewish Publication Society Translation
diss.	dissertation		
ed(s).	edition; edited by; editor(s)	n.s.	new series
		NT	New Testament
E	the Elohistic source	OT	Old Testament
ET	English translation	repr.	reprint
FS	Festschrift	RSV	*Revised Standard Version*
H	Holiness Code	Sem	Semitic
J	the Yahwistic source	tr.	translated; translator
JB	*Jerusalem Bible*	trans.	translation
KJV	King James Version	v(v)	verse(s)
lit.	literally	§	section/paragraph
ms(s)	manuscript(s)	√	root

Commentary Bibliography

Allis, O. T. "Leviticus." In *New Bible Commentary.* Grand Rapids: Eerdmans, 1970. **Baentsch, B.** *Exodus, Leviticus, Numeri.* HKAT. Göttingen: Vandenhoeck & Ruprecht, 1903. **Bamberger, B. J.** *The Torah: A Modern Commentary. III. Leviticus.* New York: Union of American Hebrew Congregations, 1979. **Bertholet, A.** *Leviticus.* KHC. Tübingen/Leipzig: Mohr, 1901. **Bonar, A. A.** *A Commentary on the Book of Leviticus.* Grand Rapids: Baker, 1978. **Calvin, J.** *Commentaries on the Four Last Books of Moses.* Grand Rapids: Eerdmans, reprint of 1852 translation. **Cazelles, H.** *Le Lévitique.* La Bible de Jérusalem. Paris: Cerf, 1958. **Chapman, A. T.**, and **Streane, A. W.** *The Book of Leviticus in the Revised Version.* The Cambridge Bible for Schools and Colleges. Cambridge: UP, 1914. **Clamer, A.** *Le Lévitique.* La Sainte Bible. Paris: Letouzey et Ané, 1940. **Clements, R. E.** "Leviticus." In *The Broadman Bible Commentary.* Ed. C. Allen. Vol 2. Nashville: Broadman, 1970. **Coleman, R. O.** "Leviticus." In *Wycliffe Bible Commentary.* Chicago: Moody, 1962. **Damrosch, D.** "Leviticus." In *The Literary Guide to the Bible.* Ed. R. Alter and F. Kermode. Cambridge, MA: Belknap, 1987. 66–77. **Dillmann, A.** *Das Bucher Exodus und Leviticus* KEH. Leipzig: S. Hirzel, 1880. **Driver, S. R.**, and **White, H. A.** *The Book of Leviticus.* New York: Dodd, Mead, and Co.; Stuttgart: Deutsche Verlags-Anstalt, 1898. **Eerdmans, B. D.** *Alttestamentliche Studien: 4. Das Buch Leviticus.* Giessen: Töpelmann, 1912. **Elliger, K.** *Leviticus.* HAT. Tübingen: Mohr, 1966. **Erdman, C. R.** *The Book of Leviticus.* New York: Revell, 1951. **Faley, R. J.** "Leviticus." In *Jerome Bible Commentary.* Englewood Cliffs, NJ: Prentice Hall, 1968. **Ginsburg, C. D.** "Leviticus." In *Ellicott's Commentary.* Reprint. Grand Rapids: Baker, 1954. **Gispen, W. H.** *Het Boek Leviticus.* Commentaar op het Oude Testament. Kampen: Kok, 1950. **Harris, R. L.** "Leviticus." In *The Expositor's Bible Commentary with the New International Version of the Holy Bible.* Grand Rapids: Regency Reference Library; Zondervan, 1990. 2:499–654. **Harrison, R. K.** *Leviticus: An Introduction and Commentary.* TOTC. Downers Grove, IL: Inter-Varsity, 1980. **Heinisch, P.** *Das Buch Leviticus.* HSAT. Bonn: Hanstein, 1935. **Hertz, J. H.** *Leviticus.* The Pentateuch and Haftorahs. London: Oxford UP, 1932. **Hoffmann, D.** *Das Buch Leviticus I-II.* Berlin: Poppelauer, 1905/06. **Holzinger, H.** "Leviticus." In *Die Heilige Shrift des Alten Testament.* Ed. A. Bertholet. Tübingen, 1922/23. **Keil, C. F.**, and **Delitzsch, F.** *Biblical Commentary on the Old Testament. 2. The Pentateuch.* Tr. J. Martin. Grand Rapids: Eerdmans, 1956. **Kellogg, S.** *Leviticus.* The Expositor's Bible. New York: Funk & Wagnalls, 1900. **Kennedy, A. R. S.** *Leviticus and Numbers.* CB. Edinburgh: T. C. & E. C. Jack; New York: Henry Frowde, 1910. **Kinlaw, D.** "Leviticus." In *Beacon Bible Commentary.* Kansas City: Beacon Hill, 1969. **Knight, G. A. F.** *Leviticus.* Edinburgh: Saint Andrews Press; Philadelphia: Westminster Press, 1981. **Kornfeld, W.** *Das Buch Leviticus.* Die Welt der Bible. Kleinkommentare zur Heiligen Schrift 15. Dusseldorf: Patmos, 1972. ———. *Levitikus.* Die neue Echter-Bibel. Würzburg: Echter, 1983. **Lamparter, H.** "In Gottes Schuld: Ausgewählte Texte aus den dritten und vierten Buch Moses übersetzt und ausgelegt." In *Die Botschaft des Alten Testaments* 7. Stuttgart, 1980. 5–174. **Lange, J. P.**, and **Gardiner, F.** *Leviticus.* Reprint. Grand Rapids: Zondervan, n.d. **Levine, B. A.** *Leviticus* ויקרא. The JPS Torah Commentary. Philadelphia: The Jewish Publication Society, 1989. **Lofthouse, W. F.** "Leviticus." In *A Commentary on the Bible.* Ed. A. Peake. New York: Thomas Nelson and Sons, 1919. **Maarsingh, B.** *Leviticus.* De Prediking van het Oude Testament. Nijkerk: G. F. Callenbach, 1974. **Micklem, N.** "The Book of Leviticus." In *The Interpreter's Bible.* Ed. G. A. Buttrick. New York: Abingdon-Cokesbury Press, 1953. 2:3–134. **Milgrom, J.** "The Book of Leviticus." In *The Interpreter's One Volume Commentary on the Bible.* Ed. C. Laymon. Nashville: Abingdon, 1971. ———. *Leviticus 1–16.* AB 3. New York: Doubleday, 1991. **Noordtzij, A.** *Leviticus.* Bible Student's Commentary. Tr. R. Togtman. Grand Rapids: Zondervan, 1982. **North, C. R.** "Leviticus." In *The Abingdon Bible Commentary.* Ed. F. Eiselen, E. Lewis, and D. Downey. New York: Abingdon, 1929. ———. "Leviticus." In *A Commentary on the Bible.* Ed.

J. Dummelow. New York: MacMillan, 1908. **Noth, M.** *Leviticus: A Commentary.* Philadelphia: Westminster; London: SCM, 1965. **Payne, J. B.** "Leviticus." In *The Biblical Expositor.* Ed. C. Henry. Vol. 1. London: Pickering & Inglis, 1960. **Porter, J. R.** *Leviticus.* CBC. Cambridge: UP, 1976. **Rashi.** *Leviticus: Pentateuch with Targum Onkelos, Haphtaroth and Rashi's Commentary.* Tr. M. Rosenbaum and A. Silbermann. Jerusalem: The Silbermann Family, 1965. **Rendtorff, R.** *Leviticus.* BKAT 3/1. Neukirchen-Vluyn: Neukirchener, 1985. **Saalschutz, J. L.** *Das Mosaische Recht.* 1853; repr. Berlin: Heymann, 1974. **Saydon, P. P.** "Leviticus." In *A Catholic Commentary on Holy Scripture.* Ed. B. Orchard. London: Thomas Nelson and Sons, 1953. 229–44. **Snaith, N. H.** *Leviticus and Numbers.* NCB. London: Oliphants, 1977. **Wenham, G. J.** *The Book of Leviticus.* NICOT. Grand Rapids: Eerdmans, 1979.

Main Bibliography

Texts and Textual Criticism

Angerstorfer, A. "Ist 4QTgLev das Menetekel der neueren Targumforschuung?" *BN* 15 (1981) 55–75. **Birnbaum, S. A.** "The Leviticus Fragments from the Cave." *BASOR* 118 (1950) 20–27. **Callaway, P.** "ʾRBYH in the Temple Scroll XXIV,8." *RevQ* 12/46 (1986) 269–70. **Déaut, R. le.** "A propos d'une leçon du codex *Neofiti 1* (Lev. v 21)." *VT* 17 (1967) 362–63. ———. "Lévitique xxii 26–xxiii 44 dans le Targum palestinien: De l'importance des gloses du *codex Neofiti 1.*" *VT* 18 (1968) 458–71. **Emerton, J. A.** "Unclean Birds and the Origins of the Peshitta." *JSS* 7 (1962) 203–11. **Freedman, D. N.** "Variant Readings in the Leviticus Scroll from Qumran Cave 11." *CBQ* 36 (1974) 525–34. ——— and **Mathews, K. A.** *The Paleo-Hebrew Leviticus Scroll (11 QpaleoLev).* ASOR; Winona Lake, IN: Eisenbrauns, 1985. **Grossfeld, B.** *The Targum Onqelos to Leviticus and the Targum Onqelos to Numbers.* The Aramaic Bible 8. Wilmington, DE: Glazier, 1988. **Kellermann, D.** "Nachlese." *ZAW* 88 (1976) 414–15. **Kornfeld, W.** "Ein unpublizierter Levitikustext." *ZAW* 87 (1975) 211–12. **Lane, D. J.** "'The best words in the best order': Some Comments on the 'Syriacing' of Leviticus." *VT* 39 (1989) 468–79. **Mathews, K. A.** "The Leviticus Scroll (11QpaleoLev) and the Text of the Hebrew Bible." *CBQ* 48 (1986) 171–207. ———. "The Paleo-Hebrew Leviticus Scroll from Qumran." *BA* 50 (1987) 45–54. **Mulder, M. J.**, ed. *Mikra: Text, Translation, Reading and Interpretation of the Hebrew Bible in Ancient Judaism and Early Christianity.* Compendia Rerum Iudaicarum ad Novum Testamentum 2/1. Assen/Maastricht: Van Gorcum; Philadelphia: Fortress, 1988. **Owens, R. J.** "Aphrahat as a Witness to the Early Syriac Text of Leviticus." In *The Peshiṭta: Its Early Text and History. Papers read at the Peshiṭta Symposium held at Leiden 30–31 August 1984.* Ed. P. B. Dirksen and M. J. Mulder. Monographs of the Peshiṭta Institute Leiden 4. Leiden: Brill, 1988. 1–48. **Ploeg, J. P. M. van der.** "Lév ix,23–x,2 dans un texte de Qumran." In *Bibel und Qumran: Beiträge zur Erforschung der Beziehungen zwischen Bibel und Qumranwissenschaft.* Ed. S. Wagner. Berlin: Evangelische Haupt-Bibelgesellschaft zu Berlin, 1968. 153–55. **Puech, É.** "Notes en marge de 11QPaléolévitique: Le fragment L, des fragments inédits et une jarre de la grotte 11 *(Planches I-III).*" *RB* 96 (1989) 161–83. **Rapallo, U.** *Calchi Ebraici nelle Antiche Versioni del «Levitico» (Studio sui Settanta, la Vetus Latina e la Vulgata).* Studi Semitici 39. Rome: Istituto di Studi del Vicion Oriente, Università di Roma, 1971. **Tov, E.** "The Textual Character of the Leviticus Scroll from Qumran Cave 11" (Heb.). *Shnaton la-Mikra* 3 (1978/79) 238–44. **Wevers, J. W.** *Leviticus.* Septuaginta Vetus Testamentum Graecum Auctoritate. Academiae Scientiarum Gottingensis editum. Göttingen: Vandenhoeck & Ruprecht, 1986. ———. *Text History of the Greek Leviticus.* Mitteilungen des Septuaginta-Unternehmens 19. Göttingen: Vandenhoeck & Ruprecht, 1986.

Critical Studies

For an extended bibliography on the Holiness Code, see *Bibliography* for chaps. 17–26.

Allis, O. T. *The Old Testament, Its Claims and Its Critics.* Nutley, NJ: Presbyterian and Reformed, 1972. **Amsler, S.** "Les documents de la loi et la formation du Pentateuque." In *Le Pentateuque en question: Les origines et la composition des cinq premiers livres de la Bible à la lumière des recherches récentes.* Ed. A. Pury. La Monde de la Bible. Genève: Éditions Labor et Fides, 1989. 235–57. **Begrich, J.** "Die priestliche Tora." In *Werden und Wesen des Alten Testaments.* BZAW 66. Berlin: Alfred Töpelmann, 1936. 63–88. **Blenkinsopp, J.** "Structure of P." *CBQ* 38 (1976) 275–92. **Blum, E.** *Studien zur Komposition des Pentateuch.* BZAW 189. Berlin: de

Gruyter, 1990. **Brin, B.** "Concerning Some of the Uses of the Bible in the Temple Scroll." *RevQ* 12 (1987) 519–28. **Cassuto, U.** *The Documentary Hypothesis and the Composition of the Pentateuch.* Jerusalem: Magnes, 1961. **Childs, B. S.** "Die theologische Bedeutung der Endform eines Textes. *TQ* 16 (1987) 242–51. **Clines, D.** *The Theme of the Pentateuch.* JSOTSup 10. Sheffield: University of Sheffield, 1978. **Cross, F. M.** "The Priestly Work." In *Canaanite Myth and Hebrew Epic: Essays in the History of the Religion of Israel.* Cambridge, MA: Harvard UP, 1973. 293–325. **Dussaud, R.** "Du Problème Littéraire au Problème Religieux." *HUCA* 23 (1950/51) 605–10. **Elliger, K.** "Sinn and Ursprung der priesterlichen Geschichtserzählung." *ZTK* 49 (1952) 121–43. **Freedman, D. N.** "Son of Man, Can These Bones Live?" *Int* 29 (1975) 171–86. **Friedman, R. E.** *The Exile and Biblical Narrative: The Formation of the Deuteronomistic and Priestly Works.* HSM 22. Chico, CA: Scholars Press, 1981. **Grelot, P.** "La dernière étape de la rédaction sacerdotale." *VT* 6 (1956) 174–89. **Grintz, J. M.** "'Do not eat on the blood': Reconsiderations in Setting and Dating of the Priestly Code." *ASTI* 8 (1972) 78–105. ————. "Archaic Terms in the Priestly Code" (Heb.). *Leshonenu* 39 (1974/75) 5–20, 163–81; 40 (1975/76) 5–32. **Hals, R. M.** "Is There a Genre of Preached Law?" SBLASP 1 (1973) 1–12. **Haran, M.** "Shiloh and Jerusalem: The Origin of the Priestly Tradition in the Pentateuch." *JBL* 81 (1961) 156–65. ————. "The Idea of Centralization of the Cult in the Priestly Apprehension." *Beer-Sheva* 1 (1973) 114–21. ————. "Behind the Scenes of History: Determining the Date of the Priestly Source." *JBL* 100 (1981) 321–33. ————. "The Character of the Priestly Source: Utopian and Exclusive Features." In *Eighth World Congress of Jewish Studies.* Jerusalem: Magnes, 1983. 131–38. **Henry, M.-L.** *Jahwist und Priesterschrift: Zwei Glaubenszeugnisse des Alten Testaments.* Arbeiten zur Theologie 3. Stuttgart: Calwer, 1960. **Hurvitz, A.** "The Usage of שׁשׁ and בוץ in the Bible and Its Implication for the Date of P." *HTR* 60 (1967) 117–21. ————. "Linguistic Observations on the Biblical Usage of the Priestly Term *ʿEda* (עֵדָה)" (Heb.). *Tarbiz* 40 (1971/72) 261–76; *Immanuel* 1 (1972) 21–23. ————. "The Evidence of Language in Dating the Priestly Code—A Linguistic Study in Technical Idioms and Terminology." *RB* 81 (1974) 24–56. ————. *A Linguistic Study of the Relationship between the Priestly Source and the Book of Ezekiel: A New Approach to an Old Problem.* Cahiers de la RB 20. Paris: J. Gabalda, 1982. ————. "The Language of the Priestly Source and Its Historical Setting—The Case for an Early Date." In *Proceedings of the Eighth World Congress of Jewish Studies.* Jerusalem: World Union of Jewish Studies, 1983. 83–94. **Kapelrud, A. S.** "The Date of the Priestly Code." *ASTI* 3 (1964) 58–64. **Kaufmann, Y.** *The Religion of Israel: From Its Beginnings to the Babylonian Exile.* Tr. M. Greenberg. New York: Schocken Books, 1956. **Kilian, R.** "Die Priesterschrift—Hoffnung auf Heimkehr." In *Wort und Botschaft.* Ed. J. Schreiner. Würzburg, 1967. 226–43. **Kitchen, K. A.** *Ancient Orient and Old Testament.* London: Tyndale, 1966. **Knierim, R. P.** "The Composition of the Pentateuch." SBLASP 24 (1985) 393–415. ————. "Criticism of Literary Features, Form, Tradition, and Redaction." In *The Hebrew Bible and Its Modern Interpreters.* Ed. D. Knight and G. Tucker. Philadelphia: Fortress; Chico, CA: Scholars Press, 1985. 123–65. **Knight, D. A.** *Rediscovering the Traditions of Israel: The Development of the Traditio-Historical Research of the Old Testament, with Special Consideration of Scandinavian Contributions.* SBLDS 9. Missoula, MI: Scholars Press, 1975. ————. "The Pentateuch." In *The Hebrew Bible and Its Modern Interpreters.* Ed. D. Knight and G. Tucker. Philadelphia: Fortress; Chico, CA: Scholars Press, 1985. 263–96. **Koch, K.** "Die Eigenart der priesterschriftlichen Sinaigesetzgebung. *ZTK* 55 (1958) 36–51. ————. *Die Priesterschrift von Exodus 25 bis Leviticus 16: Eine überlieferungsgeschichtliche und literarkritische Untersuchung.* FRLANT 71. Göttingen: Vandenhoeck & Ruprecht, 1959. ————. "P—kein Redaktor! Erinnerung an zwei Eckdaten der Quellenscheidung." *VT* 37 (1987) 446–67. **Kraus, H.-J.** *Geschichte der historisch-kritischen Erforschung des Alten Testaments.* 2d ed. Neukirchen-Vluyn: Neukirchener, 1969. **Kuhl, C.** "Die »Wiederaufnahme«—ein literarkritisches Prinzip?" *ZAW* 64 (1952) 1–11. **Labuschagne, C. J.** "The Pattern of the Divine Speech Formulas in the Pentateuch: The Key to Its Literary Structure." *VT* 32 (1982) 268–96. **Levine, B. A.** "Comments on Some Technical Terms of the Biblical Cult" (Heb.). *Leshonenu* 30 (1965) 3–11. ————. "Priestly Writers." *IDBSup* 683–87. ————.

"To the Study of the Priestly Source: The Linguistic Aspect" (Heb.). *Eretz Israel* 16 (1982) 124–31. ————. "Late Language in the Priestly Source: Some Literary and Historical Observations." In *Proceedings of the Eighth World Congress of Jewish Studies.* Jerusalem: World Union of Jewish Studies, [1983]. 69–82. **Long, B. O.** "Recent Field Studies in Oral Literature and Their Bearing on OT Criticism." *VT* 26 (1976) 187–98. **Lord, A. B.** *The Singer of Tales.* Harvard Studies in Comparative Literature 24. Cambridge: Harvard UP, 1960. **McBride, S. D., Jr.** "The Role of Moses in Old Testament Traditions." *Int* 44 (1990) 229–39. **McEvenue, S. E.** *The Narrative Style of the Priestly Writer.* AnBib 50. Rome: Biblical Institute, 1971. **Millard, A. R.** "The Practice of Writing in Ancient Israel." *BA* 35 (1972) 98–111. **Muilenburg, J.** "A Study of Hebrew Rhetoric: Repetition and Style." VTSup 1 (1953) 1–18. **Neusner, J.** "Translating a Midrash-Compilation: Some New Considerations (Leviticus Rabbah)." *HAR* 7 (1983) 187–201. **Nielsen, E.** *Oral Tradition: A Modern Problem in Old Testament Introduction.* SBT 11. London: SCM Press, 1954. ————. "Moses and the Law." *VT* 32 (1982) 87–98. **Noth, M.** *A History of Pentateuchal Traditions.* Tr. and intro. B. Anderson. Chico, CA: Scholars Press, 1981. **Ploeg, J. van der.** "Le rôle de la tradition orale dans la transmission du texte de l'Ancien Testament." *RB* 54 (1947) 5–41. **Polzin, R.** *Late Biblical Hebrew: Toward an Historical Typology of Biblical Hebrew Prose.* HSM 12. Missoula, MT: Scholars Press, 1976. **Rad, G. von.** *The Problem of the Hexateuch and Other Essays.* Tr. E. Dicken. New York: McGraw-Hill, 1966. **Rendtorff, R.** *Die Gesetze in der Priesterschrift.* FRLANT 62. 2d ed. Göttingen: Vandenhoeck & Ruprecht, 1963. ————. "Traditio-Historical Method and the Documentary Hypothesis." In *Proceeding of the Fifth World Congress of Jewish Studies.* Jerusalem: World Union of Jewish Studies, 1969. 5–11. ————. "Mose als Religionsstifter? Ein Beitrag zur Diskussion über die Anfänge der israelitischen Religion." In *Gesammelte Studien zum Alten Testament.* TBü 57. Munich: Chr. Kaiser, 1975. 152–71. ————. *Das überlieferungsgeschichtliche Problem des Pentateuch.* BZAW 147. Berlin: de Gruyter, 1977 (=*The Problem of the Process of Transmission in the Penteteuch.* Tr. J. Scullion. JSOTSup 89. Sheffield: JSOT, 1990). ———— . *The Old Testament: An Introduction.* Tr. J. Bowden. Philadelphia: Fortress, 1986. **Ringgren, H.** "Oral and Written Transmission in the Old Testament: Some Observations." *ST* 3 (1949) 34–59. **Sæbø, M.** "Priestertheologie und Priesterschrift: Zur Eigenart der priesterlichen Schicht im Pentateuch." VTSup 32 (1981) 357–74. **Sanders, J. A.** *Torah and Canon.* Philadelphia: Fortress, 1978. ————. *Canon and Community: A Guide to Canonical Criticism.* Philadelphia: Fortress, 1984. **Sandmel, S.** "The Haggada within Scripture." *JBL* 80 (1961) 105–22. **Segal, M. H.** "The Composition of the Pentateuch: A Fresh Examination." *Scripta Hierosolymitana* 8 (1961) 68–114. ————. "The Religion of Israel before Sinai." *JQR* 53 (1962/63) 226–56. ————. *The Pentateuch: Its Composition and Its Authorship and Other Biblical Studies.* Jerusalem: Magnes, 1967. **Speiser, E. A.** "Leviticus and the Critics." In *Y. Kaufmann Jubilee Volume.* Ed. M. Haran. Jerusalem: Magnes, 1960. 29–45 (= *Orientale and Biblical Studies.* Philadelphia: University of Pennsylvania Press, 1967. 123–42). **Thompson, R. J.** *Moses and the Law in a Century of Criticism since Graf.* VTSup 19. Leiden: Brill, 1970. **Vaux, R. de.** "A propos du second centenaire d'Astruc réflexions sur l'état actuel de la critique du Pentateuque." VTSup 1 (1953) 182–98 (= *Bible et Orient.* Paris: Cerf, 1967. 41–57). **Vink, J. G.** "The Date and Origin of the Priestly Code in the Old Testament." *OTS* 15 (1969) 1–144. **Wagner, N. E.** "Pentateuchal Criticism: No Clear Future." *CJT* 13 (1967) 225–32. **Weinfeld, M.** "Julius Wellhausen's Understanding of the Law of Ancient Israel and Its Fallacies" (Heb.). *Shnaton la-Miqra* 4 (1980) 81–87. ————. "Social and Cultic Institutions in the Priestly Source against Their Ancient Near Eastern Background." In *Proceedings of the Eighth World Congress of Jewish Studies.* Jerusalem: World Union of Jewish Studies, 1983. 95–129. **Whybray, R. N.** *The Making of the Pentateuch: A Methodological Study.* JSOTSup 53. Sheffield: JSOT Press, 1987. **Winnett, F.** *The Mosaic Tradition.* Toronto: University of Toronto Press, 1949. **Zevit, Z.** "Converging Lines of Evidence Bearing on the Date of P." *ZAW* 94 (1982) 481–510. **Zimmerli, W.** "Sinaibund und Abrahambund: Ein Beitrag zum Verständnis der Priesterschrift." *TZ* 16 (1960) 268–80 (= *Gottes Offenbarung: Gesammelte Aufsätze zum Alten Testament.* TBü 19. Munich: Chr. Kaiser, 1969. 205–16).

CULTURAL AND HISTORICAL STUDIES

For more bibliography on sacrifice see *Bibliography* at chaps. 1–7, on the priesthood at chaps. 8–10, and on ritual purity at chaps. 11–15 and *Excursus* on clean and unclean.

Albright, W. F. "Moses in Historical and Theological Perspective." In *Magnalia Dei: The Mighty Acts of God.* FS G. E. Wright. Ed F. Cross, W. Lemke, and P. Miller, Jr. Garden City, NY: Doubleday, 1976. 120–131. **Amusin, J. D.** "Die Gerim in der sozialen Legislatur des Alten Testaments." *Klio* 63 (1981) 15–23. **Anderson, G. A.** *Sacrifices and Offerings in Ancient Israel: Studies in Their Social and Political Importance.* HSM 41. Atlanta: Scholars Press, 1987. **Brichto, H. C.** "On Slaughter and Sacrifice, Blood and Atonement." *HUCA* 47 (1976) 19–55. **Büchler, A.** *Studies in Sin and Atonement in the Rabbinic Literature of the First Century.* London: Oxford UP, 1928. **Buss, M.** "The Meaning of 'Cult' and the Interpretation of the OT." *JBR* 32 (1964) 317–25. **Clements, R. E.** *God and Temple.* Philadelphia: Fortress, 1965. **Coleman, J. E.** "Origins of the OT Sacrifice." *CBQ* 2 (1940) 13–44. **Cross, F. M.** *Canaanite Myth and Hebrew Epic.* Cambridge, MA: UP, 1973. **Davis, D.** "An Interpretation of Sacrifice in Leviticus." *ZAW* 89 (1977) 387–99. **Douglas, M.** *Purity and Danger.* London: Routledge & Kegan Paul, 1966. **Eberharter, A.** "Das Horn im Kult des Alten Testament." *ZKT* 51 (1927) 394–99. **Fishbane, M.** *Biblical Interpretation in Ancient Israel.* Oxford: Clarendon Press, 1988. **Fretheim, T. E.** "The Priestly Document: Anti-temple?" *VT* 18 (1968) 313–29. **Goodsir, R.** "Animal Sacrifice—Delusion or Deliverance?" In *Studia Biblica 1978. I. Papers on Old Testament and Related Themes.* Ed. E. Livingstone. Sixth International Congress on Biblical Studies, Oxford, 3–7 April 1978. JSOTSup 11. Sheffield: JSOT Press, 1979. 157–60. **Gottwald, N. K.** *The Tribes of Yahweh: A Sociology of the Religion of Liberated Israel 1250–1050 B.C.E.* Maryknoll, NY: Orbis Books, 1979. **Gray, G. B.** *Sacrifice in the Old Testament: Its Theory and Practice.* Oxford: Clarendon, 1925; repr., ed. H. M. Orlinsky, New York: KTAV Publishing House, 1971. **Gray, J.** "Cultic Affinities between Israel and Ras Shamra." *ZAW* 62 (1950) 207–20. **Grayford, S. C.** *Sacrifice and Priesthood: Jewish and Christian.* 2nd ed. London: Methuen, 1953. **Haran, M.** "Priesthood, Temple, Divine Service: Some Observations on Institutions and Practices of Worship." *HAR* 7 (1983) 121–35. ———. *Temples and Temple-Service in Ancient Israel.* Winona Lake, IN: Eisenbrauns, 1985. **Haupt, P.** "Babylonian Elements in the Levitic Ritual." *JBL* 19 (1900) 55–61. **Herbert, A. S.** *Worship in Ancient Israel.* Richmond, VA: John Knox, 1959. **Hermisson, H. J.** *Sprache und Ritus im altisraelitischen Kult.* WMANT 19. Neukirchen-Vluyn: Neukirchener, 1965. **Hurowitz, V.** "The Priestly Account of Building the Tabernacle." *JAOS* 105 (1985) 21–30. **Janowski, B.** *Sühne als Heilsgeschehen: Studien zur Sühnetheologie der Priesterschrift und zur Wurzel KPR im Alten Orient und im Alten Testament.* WMANT 55. Neukirchen-Vluyn: Neukirchener, 1982. **Kaufmann, Y.** *The Religion of Israel.* Tr. and abridged M. Greenberg. Chicago: University of Chicago Press, 1960. **Kennett, R. H.** *Ancient Hebrew Social Life and Custom as Indicated in Law Narrative and Metaphor.* The Schweich Lectures of the British Academy 1931. Munich: Kraus Reprint, 1980. **Knauf, E. A.** "Zur Herkunft und Sozialgeschicte Israels: 'Das Böckchen in der Milch seiner Mutter." *Bib* 69 (1988) 153–69. **Kraus, H.-J.** *Worship in Israel: A Cultic History of the Old Testament.* Tr. G. Buswell. Richmond, VA: John Knox, 1965. **Leach, E. R.** *Culture and Communication, The Logic by Which Symbols Are Connected: An Introduction to the Use of Structuralist Analysis in Social Anthropology.* Cambridge: Cambridge UP, 1976. **Levine, B. A.** *In the Presence of the Lord.* SJLA 5. Leiden: Brill, 1974. **Milgrom, J.** *Studies in Cultic Terminology and Theology.* SJLA 36. Leiden: Brill, 1983. ———. "Day of Atonement." *EncJud* 5:1384–87. ———. 'Kipper.' *EncJud* 10:1039–44. ———. *Cult and Conscience.* SJLA 18. Leiden: Brill, 1976. ———. *Studies in Cultic Theology and Terminology.* SJLA 36. Leiden: Brill, 1983. **Neufeld, E.** "The Socio-economic Background to *Yōbēl* and *Š*^{e}*miṭṭā*." *Rivista degli Studi Orientali* 33 (1958) 53–124. **Neusner, J.** *The Idea of Purity in Ancient Judaism.* Leiden: Brill, 1973. **Obbink, H.** "The Horns of the Altar in the Semitic World, Especially in Jahwism." *JBL* 56 (1937) 45–49. **Pedersen, J.** *Israel Its Life and Culture I-IV.* Copenhagen: Branner OG Korch; London: Geoffrey

Cumberlege, Oxford UP, 1964. **Rendtorff, R.** *Studien zur Geschicte des Opfers im Alten Israel.* WMANT 24. Neukirchen-Vluyn: Neukirchener, 1967. ————. "Der Kultus im Alten Israel." Jahrbuch für Liturgik und Hymnologie 2 (1956) 1–21 (= *Gesammelte Studien zum Alten Testament.* TBü 57. Munich: Chr. Kaiser, 1975. 89–109). **Rigby, P.** "A Structural Analysis of Israelite Sacrifice and Its Other Institutions." *Église et Théologie* 11 (1980) 299–351. **Ringgren, H.** *Israelite Religion.* Tr. D. Green. Philadelphia: Fortress, 1968. **Riviêe, J.** "Satisfactio Vicaria." *RSR* 26 (1952) 221–57. **Rodriguez, A. M.** *Substitution in the Hebrew Cultus.* Andrews University Doctoral Dissertation Series 3. Berrien Springs, MI: Andrews UP, 1979. **Rowley, H. H.** "The Meaning of Sacrifice in the OT." *BJRL* 33 (1950) 74–110. ————. "The Religious Values of Sacrifice." *ExpTim* 58 (1946/48) 69–71. ————. *Worship in Ancient Israel: Its Forms and Meaning.* London: SPCK, 1978. **Schaeffer, H.** *The Social Legislation of the Primitive Semites.* New Haven: Yale UP, 1915. **Smith, W. R.** *The Religion of the Semites: The Fundamental Institutions.* New York: Schocken, 1972. **Snaith, N. H.** "Sacrifices in the OT." *VT* 15 (1965) 73–80. **Thompson, R. J.** *Penitence and Sacrifice in Early Israel outside the Levitical Law.* Leiden: Brill, 1963. **Turner, V. W.** *The Ritual Process.* London: Routledge & Kegan Paul, 1969. **Vaux, R. de.** *Studies in OT Sacrifice.* Cardiff: University of Wales, 1964. ————. *Ancient Israel.* 2 vols. New York: McGraw-Hill, 1965. **Wellhausen, J.** *Prolegomena to the History of Israel.* Preface by W. Smith. Gloucester, MA: Peter Smith, 1973. **Wolff, H. W.** *Anthropology of the Old Testament.* Tr. M. Kohl. Philadelphia: Fortress, 1974. **Yerkes, R. K.** *Sacrifice in Greek and Roman Religion and Early Judiaism.* New York: Scribner, 1952.

Studies in Ancient Israelite Law

Alt, A. "The Origins of Israelite Law." In *Essays on Old Testament History and Religion.* Tr. R. Wilson. Garden City: Doubleday, 1968. 101–71. **Auerbach, E.** "Das Zehngebot—Allgemeine Gesetzes-Form in der Bibel." *VT* 16 (1966) 255–76. **Begrich, J.** "Die priesterliche Tora." In *Werden und Wesen des Alten Testaments.* Ed. P. Volz. BZAW 66. Berlin: Töpelmann, 1936. 63–88 (= *Gesammelte Studien zum Alten Testament.* TBü 21. Munich: Chr. Kaiser, 1964. 232–60). **Boecker, H. J.** *Redeformen des Rechtslebens im Alten Testament.* WMANT 14. Neukirchen: Neukirchener, 1970. ————. *Law and the Administration of Justice in the Old Testament and the Ancient East.* Tr. J. Moiser. Minneapolis: Augsburg, 1980. **Brauner, R. A.** "Some Aspects of Offense and Penalty in the Bible and the Literature of the Ancient Near East." *Gratz College Annual of Jewish Studies* 3 (1974) 9–18. **Buss, M.** "The Distinction between Civil and Criminal Law in Ancient Israel." In *Proceedings of the Sixth World Congress of Jewish Studies I.* Jerusalem: Academic Press, 1977. 51–62. ————. "Logic and Israelite Law." In *Thinking Biblical Law.* Ed. D. Patrick. *Semeia* 45 (1989) 49–65. **Cazelles, H.** "Le sens religieus de la loi." In *Populus Dei I.* Ed. H. Cazelles et al. Communio 10. Rome: L. A. S., 1969. 177–200. **Clark, W.** "Law." In *Old Testament Form Criticism.* Ed. J. Hayes. San Antonio: Trinity UP, 1974. 99–139. **Daube, D.** *Studies in Biblical Law.* Cambridge: Cambridge UP, 1947; New York: KTAV, 1969. **Dion, P.-E.** "Une inscription araméenne en style *awīlum ša* et quelques textes bibliques datant de l'exil." *Bib* 55 (1974) 399–403. **Ercole, G.** "The Juridical Structure of Israel from the Time of Her Origin to the Period of Hadrian." In *Populus Dei I.* Ed. H. Cazelles et al. Communio 10. Rome: L. A. S., 1969. 389–461. **Falk, Z. W.** *Hebrew Law in Biblical Times.* Jerusalem: Wahrmann Books, 1974. **Feldman, E.** *Biblical & Post-Biblical Defilement: Law as Theology.* New York: KTAV, 1977. **Fensham, F. C.** "The Possibility of the Presence of Casuistic Legal Material at the Making of the Covenant at Sinai." *PEQ* 93 (1961) 143–46. **Finkelstein, J. J.** "The Goring Ox: Some Historical Perspectives on Deodards, Forfeitures, Wrongful Death and Western Notion of Sovereignty." *Temple Law Quarterly* 46 (1973) 169–290. **Fohrer, G.** "Das sogenannte apodiktisch formulierte Recht und der Dekalog." *KD* 11 (1965) 49–74 (= *Studien zur alttestamentlichen Theologie und Geschichte [1949–1966].* BZAW 115. Berlin: de Gruyter, 1969. 120–48). **Frymer-Kensky, T.** "Law and Philosophy: The Case of Sex in the Bible." In *Thinking Biblical Law.* Ed. D. Patrick. *Semeia* 45 (1989) 89–102. **Gemser, B.** "The Importance of the Motive Clause in Old Testament Law."

VTSup 1 (1953) 50–66 (= *Adhuc Loquitur.* POS 7. Leiden: Brill, 1958. 96–115). **Gerstenberger, E. S.** *Wesen und Herkunft des »apodiktischen Rechts«.* WMANT 20. Neukirchen-Vluyn: Neukirchener, 1965. **Gese, H.** "Beobachtungen zum Stil alttestamentliche Rechtsatze." *TLZ* 85 (1960) 147–50. **Gilmer, H. W.** *The If-You Form in Israelite Law.* SBLDS 15. Missoula, MT: Scholars Press, 1975. **Gnuse, R.** *You Shall Not Steal: Community and Property in the Biblical Tradition.* Maryknoll, NY: Orbis, 1985. **Good, E. M.** "Capital Punishment and Its Alternatives in Ancient Near Eastern Law." *Stanford Law Review* 19 (1967) 947–77. **Gowen, D. E.** "Reflections on the Motive Clauses in Old Testament Law." In *Intergerini Parietis Septum (Eph. 2:14).* FS M. Barth. Ed. D. Hadidian. Pittsburgh Theological Monograph Series 33. Pittsburgh: Pickwick, 1981. 111–28. **Greenberg, M.** "Some Postulates of Biblical Criminal Law." In *Y. Kaufmann Jubilee Volume.* Ed. M. Haran. Jerusalem: Magnes, 1960. 5–28. ———. *The Jewish Experience.* Ed. J. Goldin. Repr. New York: Bantam Books, 1970. 18–37. ———. "More Reflections on Biblical Criminal Law." In *Scripta Hierosolymitana 31: Studies in Bible.* Ed. S. Japhet. Jerusalem: Magnes, 1986. 1–17. **Haas, P.** "'Die He Shall Surely Die': The Structure of Homicide in Biblical Law." In *Thinking Biblical Law.* Ed. D. Patrick. *Semeia* 45 (1989) 67–87. **Haran, M.** "Seething a Kid in its Mother's Milk." *JJS* 30 (1979) 23–35. **Hayes, J. H.** "Restitution, Forgiveness, and the Victim in Old Testament Law." *Trinity University Studies in Religion* 11 (1982) 1–23. **Hentschke, R.** *Satzung und Setzender: Ein Beitrag zur israelitischen Rechtssterminologie.* BWANT 83. Stuttgart: W. Kohlhammer, 1963. **Hermann, S.** "Das apodiktische Recht." *MIO* 15 (1969) 249–61. **Hoebel, E. A.** *The Law of Primitive Man: A Study in Comparative Legal Dynamics.* New York: Atheneum, 1983. **Horton, F. L., Jr.** "A Reassessment of the Legal Forms in the Pentateuch and Their Functions." SBLASP 2 (1979) 347–96. **Jackson, B. S.** *Theft in Early Jewish Law.* Oxford: Clarendon, 1972. ———. *Essays in Jewish and Comparative Legal History.* Leiden: Brill, 1975. **Japhet, S.** "The Relationship between the Legal Corpora in the Pentateuch in Light of Manumission Laws." *Scripta Hierosolymitana* 31 (1986) 63–89. **Jirku, A.** *Das weltliche Recht im Alten Testament.* Gütersloh: Bortelsmann, 1927. **Kilian, R.** "Apodiktisches und kasuistisches Recht im Licht ägyptischer Analogien." *BZ* 7 (1963) 185–202. **Knierim, R. P.** "The Problem of Ancient Israel's Prescriptive Legal Traditions." In *Thinking Biblical Law.* Ed. D. Patrick. *Semeia* 45 (1989) 7–25. **Köhler, L.** "Justice in the Gate." In *Hebrew Man.* Nashville: Abingdon, 1956. **Liedke, G.** *Gestalt und Bezeichnung alttestamentlicher Rechtssätze.* WMANT 39. Neukirchen-Vluyn: Neukirchener, 1971. **Martin-Achard, R.** "Brèves remarques sur la signification théologique de la loi selon L'Ancien Testament." *ETR* 57 (1982) 343–59. **Mendenhall, G.** *Law and Covenant in Israel and the Ancient Near East.* Pittsburgh: Biblical Colloquium, 1955. ———. "Ancient Oriental and Biblical Law." *BA* 17 (1954) 26–46. ———. "Covenant Forms in Israelite Tradition." *BA* 17 (1954) 50–76 (= *The Biblical Archaeologist Reader* 3. Ed. E. Campbell and D. Freedman. Garden City: Doubleday, 1970. 3–53). **Milgrom, J.** "The Legal Terms *šlm* and *brʾšw* in the Bible." *JNES* 35 (1976) 271–73. **Nielsen, E.** "Moses and the Law." *VT* 32 (1982) 87–98. **Noth, M.** "The Laws in the Pentateuch: Their Assumptions and Meaning." In *Laws in the Pentateuch and Other Studies.* Tr. D. R. Ap-Thomas. Edinburgh: Oliver & Boyd, 1966. 1–107. **Patrick, D.** *Old Testament Law: An Introduction.* Atlanta: John Knox, 1985. ———. "Studying Biblical Law as Humanities." In *Thinking Biblical Law.* Ed. D. Patrick. *Semeia* 45 (1989) 27–47. **Paul, S.** *Studies in the Book of the Covenant in the Light of Cuneiform and Biblical Law.* VTSup 18. Leiden: Brill, 1970. **Phillips, A.** *Ancient Israel's Criminal Law: A New Approach to the Decalogue.* New York: Schocken, 1970. ———. "Types of Formulation in Biblical and Mesopotamian Law" (Heb.). *Leshonenu* 34 (1970) 257–66. **Ploeg, J. van der.** "Studies in Hebrew Law: I. The Terms." *CBQ* 12 (1950) 248–59; "II. The Style of the Laws." *CBQ* 12 (1950) 416–27; "III. Systematic Analysis of the Contents of the Collections of Laws in the Pentateuch." *CBQ* 13 (1951) 28–43; "IV. The Religious Character of the Legislation." *CBQ* 13 (1951) 164–71; "V. Varia: Conclusions." *CBQ* 13 (1951) 296–307. **Rabast, K.** *Das apodiktische Recht im Deuteronomium und im Heiligkeitsgesetz.* Berlin: Heimatdienstverlag, 1949. **Rapaport, I.** "The Origins of Hebrew Law." *PEQ* 73 (1941) 158–67. **Rendtorff, R.** *Die Gesetze in der Preisterschrift.* FRLANT 62 Göttingen: Vandenhoeck &

Ruprecht, 1963. **Schottroff, W.** *Der altisraelitische Fluchspruch.* WMANT 30. Neukirchen-Vluyn: Neukirchener, 1969. **Schultz, H.** *Das Todesrecht im Alten Testament: Studien zur Rechtsform der Mot-Jumat-Sätze.* BZAW 114. Berlin: Töpelmann, 1969. **Wagner, V.** *Rechtssätze in gebundener Sprache und Rechtsatzreihen im israelitischen Recht.* BZAW 127. Berlin: de Gruyter, 1972. **Welch, J. W.** *A Biblical Law Bibliography: Sorted by Subjects and by Authors.* Provo, UT: J. Reuben Clark Law School, Brigham Young University, 1989. **Westbrook, R.** *Property and the Family in Biblical Law.* JSOTSup 113. Sheffield: JSOT, 1991.

THEOLOGICAL STUDIES

Brichto, H. C. "On Slaughter and Sacrifice, Blood and Atonement." *HUCA* 47 (1976) 19–55. **Brueggemann, W.** "The Kerygma of the Priestly Writers." *ZAW* 84 (1972) 397–414. **Childs, B. S.** *Old Testament Theology in a Canonical Context.* Philadelphia: Fortress, 1986. **Clements, R. E.** *Old Testament Theology: A Fresh Approach.* Marshalls Theological Library. London: Marshall, Morgan & Scott, 1978. **Crawford, R. G.** "Is the Penal Theory of the Atonement Scriptural?" *SJT* 23 (1970) 257–72. **Davidson, A. B.** *The Theology of the Old Testament.* Ed. S. Salmond. International Theological Library. Edinburgh: T. & T. Clark, 1961. **Eichrodt, W.** *Theology of the Old Testament.* Tr. J. Baker. 2 vols. Philadelphia: Westminster, 1961. **Feldman, E.** *Biblical and Post-Biblical Defilement and Mourning: Law as Theology.* New York: KTAV, 1977. **Firmage, E.** "The Biblical Dietary Laws and the Concept of Holiness." In *Studies in the Pentateuch.* Ed. J. Emerton. VTSup 41. Leiden: Brill, 1990. 177–208. **Fuhs, H. F.** "Heiliges Volk Gottes." In *Unterwegs zur Kirche: Alttesstamentliche Konzeptionen.* Ed. J. Schreiner. Quaestiones Disputatae 110. Freiburg: Herder, 1987. 143–67. **Gammie, J.** *Holiness in Israel.* OBT. Minneapolis: Fortress, 1989. **Gese, H.** *Essays on Biblical Theology.* Tr. K. Crim. Minneapolis: Augsburg, 1981. **Henrix, H. H.** "Von der Nachahmung Gottes: Heiligkeit und Heiligsein im biblischen und jüdischen Denken." *ErbAuf* 65 (1989) 177–87. **Henry, M.-L.** *Jahwist und Priesterschrift: Zwei Glaubenszeugnisse des Alten Testaments.* Arbeiten zur Theologie 3. Stuttgart: Calwer, 1960. **Hodgson, R.** "1 Thess 4:1–12 and the Holiness Tradition (HT)." SBLASP 21 (1982) 199–215. **Imschoot, P. van.** *Theology of the Old Testament. I. God.* Tr. K. Sullivan and F. Buck. New York: Desclée , 1954. **Jacob, E.** *Theology of the Old Testament.* Tr. A. Heathcote and P. Allcock. New York: Harper & Row, 1958. **Keller, J.** "Theological Linguistics: A Suggestion." *JRelS* 12 (1985) 46–55. **Klein, R. W.** "The Message of P." *Die Botschaft und die Boten.* FS H. W. Wolff. Ed. J. Jeremias and L. Perlitt. Neukirchen-Vluyn: Neukirchener, 1981. 57–66. **Knierim, R. P.** *Die Hauptbegriffe für Sünde im Alten Testament.* Gütersloh: Mohn, 1965. ———. "The Problem of an Old Testament Hamartiology." Review of Š. Porúbčan's *Sin in the Old Testament. VT* 16 (1966) 366–85. **Lyonnet, S.** *Sin, Redemption, and Sacrifice: A Biblical and Patristic Study.* AnBib 48. Rome: Biblical Institute Press, 1970. **McCarthy, D. J.** *Treaty and Covenant.* Rome: Pontifical Biblical Institute, 1963. **Milgrom, J.** "Ethics and Ritual: The Foundations of the Biblical Dietary Laws." In *Religion and Law: Biblical-Judaic and Islamic Perspectives.* Ed. E. Firmage, B. Weiss, and J. Welch. Winona Lake, IN: Eisenbrauns, 1990. 159–98. **Monty, V.** "La nature du peché d'après le vocabulaire hébreu." *ScEc* 1 (1948) 95–108. **Otto, R.** *The Idea of the Holy: An Inquiry into the Non-rational Factor in the Idea of the Divine and Its Relation to the Rational.* Tr. J. Harvey. London: Oxford UP, 1967. **Paul, S. M.** *Studies in the Book of the Covenant in the Light of Cuneiform and Biblical Law.* VTSup 18. Leiden: Brill, 1970. **Perlitt, L.** *Bundestheologie im Alten Testament.* WMANT 36. Neukirchen-Vluyn: Neukirchener, 1969. **Porúbčan, Š.** *Sin in the Old Testament: A Soteriological Study.* Aloisiana 3. Rome: Herder, 1963. **Rad, G. von.** "Die Theologie der Priesterschrift." In *Die Priesterschrift in Hexateuch.* BWANT 65. Stuttgart: W. Kohlhammer, 1934. 166–89 (= *Gesammelte Studien zum Alten Testament II.* Ed. R. Smend. TBü 48. Munich: Chr. Kaiser, 1973. 165–88). ———. "The Promised Land and Yahweh's Land in the Hexateuch." In *The Problem of the Hexateuch and Other Essays.* Tr. E. Dicken. New York: McGraw-Hill, 1966. 77–93. ———. *Old Testament Theology.* Tr. D. M. G. Stalker. Vol. 1. New York: Harper & Row, 1962. **Roach, C. C.** "Book of Leviticus." *Int* 4 (1950) 458–69. **Sabourin,**

L. *Redemption Sacrificielle: Une Enquête Exégétique.* Montreal: Desclée de Brower, 1961. **Schenker, A.** *Versöhnung und Sühne: Wege gewaltfreier Konfliktlösung im Alten Testament: Mit einem Ausblick auf Neue Testament.* BibB 15. Freiburg: Schweizerisches Katholisches Bibelwerk, 1981. **Terrien, S.** *The Elusive Presence: Toward a New Biblical Theology.* Religious Perspectives 26. San Francisco: Harper & Row, 1978. **Toorn, K. van der.** *Sin and Sanction in Israel and Mesopotamia: A Comparative Study.* Assen/Maastricht: Van Gorcum, 1985. **Vriezen, Th. C.** *An Outline of Old Testament Theology.* Newton Centre, MA: Branford, 1966. **Wyatt, N.** "Atonement Theology in Ugarit and Israel." *UF* 8 (1976) 415–30. **Zimmerli, W.** "Ich bin Yahweh." In *Geschichte und Altes Testament.* BHT 16. FS A. Alt. Tübingen: Mohr (Siebech), 1953. 179–209. ———. "I Am Yahweh." In *I Am Yahweh.* Tr. D. Stott. Atlanta: John Knox, 1982. 1–28. ———. *Old Testament Theology in Outline.* Tr. D. Green. Atlanta: John Knox, 1978. ———. "'Heiligkeit' nach dem sogenannten Heiligkeitsgesetz." *VT* 30 (1980) 493–512. **Zink, J. K.** "Uncleanness and Sin." *VT* 17 (1967) 354–61.

Introduction

The Hebrew Text of Leviticus

The Masoretic Text of Leviticus is a highly reliable text. As a part of the Pentateuch, the first part of the Hebrew Scriptures to be accepted as authoritative, it has been carefully copied from an early period.

The longest and oldest Hebrew text of Leviticus is 11QpaleoLev, which contains portions of Lev 22–27. It is a leather ms of Leviticus written in paleo-Hebrew script. It is dated to around 100 B.C. Mathews (*BA* 50 [1987] 50) points out that its use of the paleo-Hebrew script along with some other features indicates that it was produced by a scribe who shared the interests of the Essenes. The best preserved portion is seven continuous columns, one being blank, that contain portions. Because in 11QpaleoLev there are fifteen unique readings that are inferior to MT, Mathews concludes that 11QpaleoLev is not a superior witness to Leviticus (*CBQ* 48 [1986] 196–97). Other mss of Leviticus among the Dead Sea Scrolls, including nine in Hebrew, a couple in Greek, and one Targum, have survived only in small fragments.

The versions for the most part support the MT. The most important are the Samaritan Pentateuch and the LXX. Wevers has produced both a fine critical edition of the Greek text of Leviticus and a thorough analysis of that text. In *Text History* (72) he points out that establishing the best Greek text for Leviticus is complicated by two factors: (1) There are only a few tiny fragments of pre-Vaticanus Greek texts; this scarcity is compounded because A and B often represent a tradition that has limited support against "an overwhelming popular tradition" and that is demonstratively secondary. (2) The other complicating factor is that the LXX translator did not follow a consistent pattern of translation. In Wever's judgment he varied the translation for variation's sake. For example, "two" is rendered δύο, "two," in 3:4, ἀμφοτέρους, "both," in 3:10, and ζεῦγος, "pair," in 5:11. MT, however, has escaped much of the editorial activity that Sam and LXX experienced, implying that its textual tradition reaches behind theirs (Wenham, 15).

Numbered among the other versions are the Peshitta in Syriac, the Targums in Aramaic, and the Vulgate in Latin. Lane (*VT* 39 [1989] 468–79) apportions the Syriac mss into three groups: "Nestorian" or "Mosul," consisting of thirty-four mss; Takrit, named after a city on the Tigris, consisting of six mss from Wadi Natrun in Egypt; the Western group, which comes from a ms that is identified with the Jacobite monastic territory named Ṭûr ʿabdîn (470–71). He also claims that the translator(s) of the Syriac text have rendered the Hebrew very skillfully both in the terms chosen and in the word order. E.g., גר, "sojourner," is translated by a phrase, "those who turn themselves to me and dwell among you." Lane (477) conjectures that the translator(s) used a phrase to exclude a connotation carried by גור in Syr. Furthermore, this translation gives evidence that it was familiar with the discussions of the meanings of terms current in the rabbinic traditions of that day (478). As a result, this version has a more precise and systematic text than does the MT text.

There is not much diversity then among the texts of Leviticus. Both the few significant variations and many minor ones are cited in the *Notes.* Mathews (*CBQ* 48 [1986] 198–99) contends that the legal nature of the texts accounts for their consistency; their use in the community required that they be standardized.

The Structure of Leviticus

The Hebrew name for the third book of the Pentateuch comes from an ancient custom of calling a book by its first word ויקרא *wayyiqrāʾ*, "and he called." Its name in the LXX is Λευιτικον or Λευειτικον, a substantive for "The Levitical Book." The Vulgate rendered this Greek name into Latin as *Liber Leviticus.* Obviously the English name for this book comes via the Vulgate. The name used by the versions intimates that the material concerns the Levitical priesthood. Amazingly the term "Levite" appears only in 25:32–34, and in that reference solely in regard to the ownership of land and houses. The concern of this book, however, is pure worship and holy living led by the priests, the sons of Aaron. The central position of this book in the Pentateuch attests to the significance of this subject for Israel's *raison d'être.*

The material contained in Leviticus has its setting in a larger block of material on priestly matters that runs from Exod 25:1 to Num 10:10. Nevertheless, a heading and two summary statements (26:46; 27:34) demarcate Leviticus as a book in itself. The book opens with a complex introduction at 1:1–2. This heading does double duty: it introduces both the first speech (1:3–3:17) and the book as a whole. It makes a direct tie with the last chapter of Exodus, which reports that Moses finished setting up the tabernacle and that Yahweh's glory descended upon it. Now from this Tent of Meeting Yahweh addresses Moses with the regulations, instructions, and laws for worship at the new sanctuary. A summary statement at 26:46 likewise does double duty, concluding both the laws on holy living and the entire book. With the addition of chap. 27, another summary statement at v 34, though less detailed than that at 26:46, now marks the end of the book.

Leviticus is made up mostly of Yahweh speeches that Moses delivers to the congregation. These are usually headed by the statement that Yahweh spoke to Moses and commanded him to speak to another group. The introductory formula usually is expressed וידבר יהוה אל־משה לאמר: דבר אל . . . ואמרת (לאמר), "Yahweh spoke to Moses: Speak to . . . and say . . ." (4:1–2a*α*; 5:20[6:1]; 6:17–18a*α*[24–25a*α*]; 7:22–23a; 12:1–2a*α*; 17:1–2a; 18:1–2a; 19:1–2a*α*; 20:1–2a*α*; 21:1a–b*α* [ויאמר, "and he said"], 16–17a; 22:1–2a*α*, 17–18a; 23:1–2a, 9–10a*α*, 23–24a, 33–34a; 24:1–2a*α*; 25:1–2a*α*; 27:1–2a*α*). There are now and then slight variations to this formula; e.g., two commission formulae use צו, "command," in place of דבר, "speak" (6:2a*α*[9a*α*]; 24:2a*α*), and the introductory formula at 25:1 adds בהר סיני, "at Mount Sinai." Sometimes the introductory formula occurs without the commission formula—וידבר יהוה אל־משה לאמר, "Yahweh spoke to Moses" (5:14; 6:12[19]; 8:1; 14:1; 16:1; 22:26; 23:26; 24:13). One introduction is formulated "Yahweh spoke to Aaron" (10:8). A significant shift takes place in the section on ritual purity in that Yahweh addresses both Moses and Aaron (11:1; 13:1; 14:33; 15:1–2a). The coupling of Aaron with Moses underscores the importance of the priests' role in instructing the people in the matters of ritual purity. The audience to whom Moses is commissioned to deliver these Yahweh speeches is usually ישׂראל בני, "the Israelites" (4:2a*α*; 7:23a, 29a; 11:2a; 12:2a*α*; 15:2a; 18:2a; 19:2a*α* [עדת, "congregation of," is included]; 20:2a*α*; 23:2a*α*, 10a*α*, 24a, 34a; 25:2a*α*). Sometimes Aaron and/or his sons are identified as the audience of the commissioned speech: Aaron (6:2a*α*[9a*α*]; 21:17a; cf. 6:12–13a[19–20a]), Aaron and his sons (6:2a*α*[9a*α*], 18a*α* [25a*α*]; 22:2a*α*), the priests as sons of Aaron (21:1a), and Aaron, his sons, and the Israelites (17:2a; 22:18a).

The commission-to-speak formulae that direct Moses to speak to Aaron and the priests have their present setting among sermons that, by their canonical setting, were to be delivered to the whole congregation; this means that these sermons for Aaron and/or his sons were from time to time delivered to the whole congregation. The threefold audience of Aaron, his sons, and the Israelites in 17:2a and 22:18a supports this position. To say it another way, the high priest, Aaron's successor, and the priests sometimes heard these words as members of the congregation, not as a private professional message. The congregation likewise heard these instructions to the priests and became knowledgeable about special requirements laid on them for their service to the holy God at the sanctuary. By having this knowledge, the congregation was given some responsibility in encouraging the priests to live in harmony with these laws. This cooperation between the priests and the laity was a liberating dynamic for the nation Israel. An informed laity could not be easily dominated or oppressed by a priesthood that kept knowledge about the cult a closely guarded secret. In Israel God spoke to all Israelites, not to a select few. Thus the instruction of the congregation about this professional knowledge guarded against the growth of a rich priestly class that could dominate and exploit the people. Rather, in Israel the priests were Yahweh's servants to lead and assist the people in worship and in keeping the law.

The ends of several speeches and sections are marked by either summary statements (7:35–36, 37–38; 11:46–47; 13:59; 14:32, 54–57; 15:32–33; 23:37–38; 26:46; 27:34) or compliance reports (8:36; 10:7b; 16:34b; 21:24; 23:44; 24:23b). These structural signals serve as the framework for unfolding the structure of the Levitical material in the commentary.

Leviticus, furthermore, continues the pattern of instruction-compliance initiated in Exod 25–40. In that pattern Yahweh gave instructions to Moses, and then it is reported that Moses faithfully fulfilled them. One of these patterns ties Exod 25–40 to Leviticus. In Exod 29, Yahweh instructed Moses on the ordination of Aaron (Exod 29), and Lev 8 recounts the fulfillment of that instruction. The ordination service is placed here, for it could be conducted only after the regulations for the sacrifices had been given. Furthermore, the account of offering of the first sacrifices on the sanctified altar may be viewed as a fulfillment of the regulations pertaining to the various sacrifices just given in chaps. 1–7.

Another stylistic feature of the priestly material is important to note: history and laws are intertwined throughout Exodus-Numbers. The giving of the law is anchored to events in Israel's encounter with Yahweh. While the bulk of Leviticus consists of regulations, instructions, and laws, historical material can be found in 8:1–10:20 and the incident of blasphemy recounted in 24:10–23. That the preferred style is laws attached to narrative is confirmed by the attaching of laws to the report of the two tragic incidents in 10:1–20 and 24:10–23. An episode thus functions as the opportune framework for providing instructions. In chaps. 8, 9, and 16, there is a mixture of narrative and regulations. In chaps. 8 and 9 narrative dominates; nevertheless, these reports have a secondary function to serve as the regulations for ordaining Aaron's successors and other priests and for inaugurating any new sanctuary. The converse is possibly the case with the regulation for the Day of Atonement (chap. 16). This speech clearly presents the regulation for that solemn day, yet it may have been constructed on a report of the first observance of the Day of Atonement.

The introductory formulae, furthermore, have an important theological function. The words here are authoritative because they go back to what Yahweh had spoken to Moses. This double formulation of an introductory formula plus a commission-to-speak formula means that not only had Moses received a word from Yahweh, but he had also been commissioned to deliver it. The purpose of Leviticus then is to preserve divine sermons for the instruction of the congregation in cultic and ethical matters. The cultic laws appear mostly in chaps. 1–17 and the moral laws in chaps. 18–27. The ancients, however, did not make a clear distinction between these subjects as do contemporary people. As a result, exalted moral laws are set among cultic laws.

These sermons have been constructed and preserved for the oral instruction of the congregation. One setting in which they were delivered was the pilgrim festivals. Which sermons, which festivals, and how often is unknown, though Deut 31:10–11 instructs that its laws be read every seven years at the Feast of Booths. One proposed setting for the delivery of the sermons in Leviticus is a covenant renewal ceremony, though scholars have debated this issue (cf. Reventlow, *Das Heiligkeitsgesetz formgeschichtlich untersucht,* WMANT 6 [Neukirchen: Neukirchener, 1961] 163–66; von Rad, *The Form-Critical Problem of the Hexateuch and Other Essays,* tr. T. Dicken [New York: McGraw-Hill, 1966] 33–40; Weiser, *The Psalms,* tr. H. Hartwell, OTL [Philadelphia: Westminster, 1976] 35–52). If they were delivered at that setting, it was most likely not the only one for their delivery. It is easy to imagine that appropriate portions were delivered to guide a clan or group that had gathered at a local sanctuary for either a private or a public occasion. For example, the sermon on the whole offering or an appropriate section (chap. 1) might have been delivered at an occasion when a clan offered a whole offering, or it could have been delivered at an important public gathering before the community made a whole offering. The material contained in Leviticus then was for the oral instruction of members of the community whenever the priests or the tradition judged that to be the proper protocol.

As for the structure of the present book, it has primarily been viewed as consisting of either six divisions (Bertholet, v–viii; Baentsch, 306; Elliger, 7–10; Noth, 5–6) or two divisions (M. Segal, *The Pentateuch,* 45–57; cf. H. T. C. Sun, "An Investigation into the Compositional Integrity of the So-called Holiness Code (Leviticus 17–26)" [Diss., Claremont, 1990] 487–96). A few commentators have suggested other divisions: e.g., Wenham (3–6) finds four—chaps. 1–7; 8–10; 11–16; 17–27; Noordtzij (2–4) discovers nine—chaps. 1–7; 8–10; 11–15; 16; 17; 18–20; 21–25; 26; 27.

Sun ("Investigation," 487–96) sets forth a strong case for apportioning Leviticus into two divisions: chaps. 1–10 and chaps. 11–26 + 27. Several indicators show that chaps. 1–10 belong together. The subscription at 7:37–38 joins together chaps. 1–7 and chaps. 8–10, for it gives a list of the sacrifices covered in the preceding chapters and, with the mention of the ordination offering, it points toward the ordination of the priests in the coming subunit. Furthermore, chaps. 8–10 are linked to chaps. 1–7, for they recount offering for the first time at the new cult the sacrifices prescribed in the preceding chapters. Chaps. 6–7 also connect in both directions; they provide additional information about the sacrifices regulated in chaps. 1–5 and, being addressed primarily to the priests, they prepare for chaps. 8–10, where the priests stand at the center of the action. Thus chaps. 1–10 are a division with a lesser break at 7:38.

The second division (chaps. 11–26 + 27) is delimited by the subscription at 26:46, which lists three terms used in different portions of the section. The subscription encompasses chaps. 16–27 by including משפטים, "laws," a term occurring in chaps. 18–26 (e.g., 18:4, 5, 26; 19:15, 35, 37; 20:22; etc.), and חקים, "decrees," forms of which occur frequently in chaps. 16–27 (e.g., 16:29, 31, 34; 17:7; 18:3, 4, 5, 26, 30; 19:19, 37; etc.). Neither of these two terms occurs in chaps. 11–15. However, the subscription also uses התורת, "the laws," a term appearing in chaps. 11–15 (11:46; 12:7; 13:59; 14:2, 32, 54, 57; 15:32) but not in chaps. 16–26. By the inclusion of all three terms, 26:46 joins chaps. 11–15 with chaps. 16–26. Another tie between these two sections is the interplay between 11:43–45 and 20:25. A significant connector is also found in 10:10–11, which delineates the duty of the priests to distinguish between clean and unclean and the holy and the common. The first pair of terms, clean/unclean, ties into chaps. 11–15, and the second, holy/common, with chaps. 16–27. Sun adds the evidence that lexemes of the roots טמא, "unclean," and טהר, "clean," occur frequently in both chaps. 11–15 and 16–27. He notes that a series of subscriptions group chaps. 11–15 together and that there is a compliance report at 16:34b, but he does not judge these signals to be "of the highest structural level" (492). In this light he holds that chaps. 11–27 consist of two subunits, chaps. 11–15 and chaps. 16–26. As for chap. 27, it is a supplement that has been worked into the second division by its subscription; that subscription was designed to replace the one at 26:46 (492). Since Sun's study concentrated on chaps. 17–26, there is value in reporting that he finds the following sections in chaps. 16–27: chaps. 16; 17–22; 23; 24:1–9; 24:10–23; 25:1–26:45; 27:1–33.

While the analysis espoused by Segal and Sun has much to commend it, there are some factors that favor dividing this book into six divisions. First, the expanded narrative introduction to the Day of Atonement plus the paragraph with calendrical material (16:29–34a) sets this speech apart as an independent division. Second, the narrative genre of chaps. 8–10 explicitly distinguishes these chapters from the preceding and the following sermons; thus they constitute a division. Third, the distinctive introductory formulae found only in chaps. 11–15, in which Yahweh addressed both Moses and Aaron, as well as the homogeneity of the laws on ritual purity, group these chapters into a division. Fourth, the use of התורת, "the laws," in the subscription at 26:46 makes it serve not only chaps. 11–15 but also chaps. 6–7 (6:2[9], 7[14], 18[25]; 7:1, 11, 37). This is confirmed by the use of החקים, "decrees," in that subscription, for chaps. 1–10 prefer the masculine form of this term, while chaps. 16–26 prefer the feminine form (see *Comment* on 26:46). Sun acknowledges these facts but unfortunately suppresses their importance. He concludes that this summary statement does not serve to unite chaps. 11–26 into a division, but to close the whole book. Fifth, chaps. 1–7 and chap. 27 each have a clear heading or introduction and a subscription (7:37–38 and 27:34). Thus they constitute two divisions. This leaves chaps. 17–26. While this division lacks the structural signals that mark off the other divisions, it should be considered a unit, for the material is tied together by the theme of the holy and the use of formulae of Yahweh's self-introduction (see *Introduction* to chaps. 17–26). These factors support grouping Leviticus into six divisions. The divisions are logically ordered. Each one must necessarily follow the preceding one, for material in a preceding division is critical for a proper understanding of the section at hand.

These six divisions are outlined as follows:

- I. Regulations for Sacrifices 1:1–7:38
    - A. Heading to the Sacrificial Legislation and the Book 1:1–2
    - B. Regulations for Three Common Sacrifices 1:3–3:17
        - 1. Regulation for the Whole Offering 1:3–17
        - 2. Regulation for the Grain Offering 2:1–16
        - 3. Regulation for the Offering of Well-Being 3:1–17
    - C. Regulation for the Purification Offering 4:1–5:13
    - D. Regulation for the Reparation Offering 5:14–26(6:7)
    - E. Further Instructions about the Various Sacrifices 6:1(8)–7:38
- II. Ordination of the Priests and the First Sacrifices at the Tent of Meeting 8:1–10:20
    - A. Ordination of Aaron as High Priest and His Sons as Priests 8:1–36
    - B. The First Public Sacrifices at the Tent of Meeting 9:1–24
    - C. The Death of Two Priests and Attendant Regulations 10:1–20
- III. Laws on Ritual Purity 11:1–15:32
    - A. Instructions on the Classification of Animals as Clean and Unclean 11:1–47
    - B. Regulations on Ritual Purity of a Woman Who Has Given Birth 12:1–8
    - C. Instructions on Grievous Growths 13:1–14:57
    - D. Instructions on Uncleanness from Bodily Emissions 15:1–32
- IV. Regulation for the Day of Atonement 16:1–34
- V. Laws on Holy Living 17:1–26:46
    - A. Laws about Sacrificing Domestic Animals and regarding Blood 17:1–16
    - B. Laws Governing the Extended Family 18:1–30
    - C. Laws and Exhortations to Holy Living 19:1–37
    - D. Laws with Penalties for Sacrifice to Molek, Sorcery, and Sexual Offenses 20:1–27
    - E. Specific Regulations for the Priests 21:1–24
    - F. Regulations regarding the Priests Eating Sacred Food 22:1–16
    - G. Regulations about Animals Acceptable for Sacrifices 22:17–33
    - H. The Calendar of Festivals 23:1–44
    - I. Regulations regarding Oil for the Lampstand and Bread for the Table of the Presence 24:1–9
    - J. A Case of Blasphemy and Laws on Personal Injury 24:10–23
    - K. The Calendar for Seven-Year Cycles and Blessings and Curses 25:1–26:46
        - 1. Seven-Year Cycles: The Sabbatical Year and the Year of Jubilee 25:1–55
        - 2. Some General Commandments on Faithful Worship 26:1–2
        - 3. Blessings and Curses 26:3–46
- VI. Laws on Tithes and Offerings 27:1–34

The first division presents the regulations for the various sacrifices (chaps. 1–7). In the second division (chaps. 8–10), the cult is made fully operational with the ordination of Aaron and his sons (chap. 8) and the inauguration of the cult (chap. 9), despite the death of Aaron's two sons (chap. 10). This last incident interrupts the series of regulations and fulfillment accounts, for presumably this incident happened some time soon after the first sacrifices were offered. In 10:10–11 there is a description of the instructional duties of the priest to teach the people about the holy and the common, the clean and the unclean. The introduction of this priestly responsibility serves as a signpost to the next two large blocks of material, the third division (chaps. 11–15), which gives the instruction on ritual purity, and the fifth division (chaps. 17–26), which presents laws and instructions on matters of holy living. Between these last two blocks is the fourth division, the regulation for the Day of Atonement (chap. 16). This regulation likewise comes at the earliest possible point, for it assumes an operational cult (chap. 9) and an ordained priesthood (chap. 8), and it comes after the laws on ritual purity (chaps. 11–15), for a major purpose of this day is to cleanse the sanctuary from the impurities released by the various incidents of becoming unclean. The fifth division (chaps. 17–26) has material on many subjects. Thus it is the least homogeneous division, though ironically it has been named "the Holiness Code" and intently studied as a distinct corpus (see *Introduction* to chaps. 17–26). The sixth division, on vows, voluntary gifts, and tithes (chap. 27), is an appendix. Since such gifts are voluntary, it is appropriate that the regulation for them come at the end of the book, for all that precedes is mandatory. From the theological perspective, a holy life moves a person to be generous.

The keystone of the structure is chap. 16, the Day of Atonement. While the numbering of the outline does not locate it at the center, the logical arrangement of the material does. The instructions on sacrifices and ritual purity plus the reports of Aaron's ordination as high priest and the setting of the cult into operation find their culmination in the Day of Atonement. Then the laws on holy living come after chap. 16 because a forgiven and cleansed priesthood and congregation are spiritually prepared to heed the exhortation "be holy, for I, Yahweh, your God, am holy" (19:2). To say it another way, the priests and the congregation contritely and solemnly have sought Yahweh's favor in order that they may be spiritually empowered to live according to God's will as he has revealed it in the laws on holy living.

This discussion on structure shows that Leviticus has been very carefully constructed as the central book of the Pentateuch.

Authorship and Origin

Views about the authorship and the origin of the Book of Leviticus vary widely. This is clearly attested in works recently published by leading scholars, which investigate either a portion of Leviticus or themes central to it. Of the forces that contribute to this diversity two major ones are (1) the sparsity of materials available for reconstructing a history of Israelite worship and the priesthood and (2) the development of divergent methodologies for interpreting ancient texts.

Speech formulae stating that Yahweh spoke to Moses run throughout the book in order to underscore the authority of these words. Otherwise the method by which these materials were composed and joined together is not addressed. Given the paucity of direct evidence it is little wonder that efforts to reconstruct the composition and development of Leviticus have produced such vastly differing results.

This survey begins with the conservative view, which holds to the Mosaic authorship of Leviticus. Among its advocates are evangelical scholars, including G. Archer, W. H. Gispen, and R. K. Harrison, and Jewish scholars, including D. Hoffmann and M. Segal. This position is grounded on a high view of the inspiration of the Scriptures backed with rational arguments. Wenham (8–9) summarizes this position with four primary arguments. First, the text frequently says that Yahweh spoke these words to Moses (1:1–2; 7:37–38; 26:46; 27:34; as well as the numerous introductory formulae). These statements are backed by material that assumes a wilderness setting: e.g., sacrifices are to be made before the Tent of Meeting, not the Temple; the instructions for the examination of a person with a grievous skin disease assume that the congregation camped close together; and remains of sacrificed animals are to be disposed of outside the camp (e.g., 16:26–28). Second, the elaborate rituals in Leviticus are not anachronistic for the wilderness era as is demonstrable by comparison with the cultic practices of Israel's neighbors. Third, the laws herein do not adequately address the setting of the post-exilic community. The sexual laws of chaps. 18 and 20, for example, do not cover the issue of intermarriage, a crucial issue for Ezra and Nehemiah. Fourth, Ezekiel knew and quoted Leviticus, meaning that he accepted Leviticus as canonical.

Some conservative scholars concede that the work done by Moses has been modified and reshaped. Segal writes:

> Like the orations of the later prophets these legislative orations of Moses may have continued for some time to have been preserved orally until they were committed to writing by the prophet himself and by his disciples. The scrolls in which the orations were written may have contained single orations or collections of orations which were eventually gathered together and arranged according to plan in the narrative of the Pentateuch. It may be that not all the teaching of Moses was written down. Some of it may have continued to be handed down orally as Mosaic laws, as maintained by ancient Jewish tradition. To this remnant of genuine Mosaic tradition was added from time to time new legislative material developed orally later, but also attributed to Moses which served to explain or amplify or supplement the old written Mosaic orations. Some of this new material may have found its way into writing and was then inserted into the Pentateuch as Mosaic teaching (*Pentateuch,* 47).

For Segal, Leviticus is then primarily an anthology of the words Moses received from Yahweh. He posits that some of this material may have circulated orally and may have been augmented before it was put into its final shape in writing.

Opposite the conservative position stands the classical documentary hypothesis that the Pentateuch consists of four major sources. This theory was skillfully articulated by Wellhausen. He interpreted Israel's thought and experience along Hegelian lines. For him the early years of Israel were an era of spontaneous, charismatic worship. The Book of Samuel, for example, pictures people sacrificing wherever they so desired (cf. 1 Sam 16:2). Through the years customs and practices became formalized. In the post-exilic era the high priest took the place of a son of David as leader of the community. This rise of the priesthood was supported by the composition of the priestly document, the last of the four major documents that made up the Pentateuch. In the production of the Pentateuch the priestly material was woven into that of the Yahwist and the Elohist. Three examples in Leviticus may be cited as explicable in light of this reconstruction. (1) In this book, great importance is placed on the high priest, the type of role that he had in the post-exilic community; he is even called the anointed priest, taking on a Davidic title 4:3–12 (e.g., chap. 8; 16:3, 32; 21:16–23). (2) Some laws increase the priests' share of the offerings (e.g., 7:28–36). (3) In the era before the monarchy the dates of the festivals floated to coincide with the actual end of each harvest, but later they became fixed dates by the calendar in chap. 23 in order to make sure that all Israelites observed these times together. These changes, according to critical scholars, all have the earmarks of the post-exilic community.

A key question in this theory has been whether P ever stood on its own. Noth holds that it existed independently as a historical narrative (*Pentateuchal Traditions,* 8–19, 228–51) and that the law codes and cultic regulations were added later (Clements, 103). Cross, however, is persuaded that the priestly strata never existed as "an independent narrative document" (*Canaanite Myth,* 324). He bases this position on three types of evidence: the lack of basic Pentateuchal traditions (especially the crucial covenant ceremony), the use of framing devices, and the presence of archaizing language (Knight, 285). For him, "The Priestly tradent framed and systematized JE with Priestly lore, and, especially at points of special interest, greatly supplemented JE" (*Canaanite Myth,* 325). To produce this redactional work this school drew on both written and oral documents (*Canaanite Myth,* 324).

The majority of critical scholars argue that most of Leviticus arose independently from P. It consists of large blocks of material that had their own origin, growth, and circulation before being preserved in their present location: regulation of sacrifices (chaps. 1–7), laws on ritual purity (chaps. 11–15), and the Holiness Code (chaps. [16/17] 18–26; cf. E. Sellin and G. Fohrer, *Introduction to the Old Testament,* tr. D. Green [Nashville: Abingdon Press, 1968] 137–43). Noth judges these portions as so different from P that they cannot even be viewed as a planned expansion of P (14). Moreover, he assigns solely Lev 8–10 to P, but, more precisely, in his judgment, only chap. 9 belonged to the original P narrative (12–13).

Critical scholars have also debated the date of P. Cross (*Canaanite Myth,* 325), for example, dates it in the sixth century near the end of the exile. Other scholars like Vink (*OTS* 15 [1969] 1–44) argue for the time of Ezra's reform (early fourth century B.C.).

A few scholars have vigorously challenged the tenet of the documentary hypothesis that P was the last layer in the construction of the Pentateuch. One of the most comprehensive challenges has come from the Jewish scholar Y. Kaufmann. He published his studies in eight volumes in modern Hebrew from 1937 to 1956. Some of his work has been abridged and translated into English by M. Greenberg under the title *The Religion of Israel.* Kaufmann sought to turn the documentary theory around by proving that P pre-dated Deuteronomy. According to him, "In every detail, P betrays its antiquity" (206).

Wenham (12) has succinctly summarized Kaufmann's position into three principle arguments. First, the terms, laws, and rituals of P point to an era earlier than the post-exilic community. Since Leviticus includes words whose meaning had been lost by the time of the post-exilic community, how could it be so late? Second, Kaufmann points out that Deuteronomy and Joshua quote Leviticus, but not vice versa. This argument is hard to substantiate or refute because of lack of independent sources to function as a control point. The recent work of Knohl (cf. *HUCA* 58 [1987] 65–117) vividly demonstrates this difficulty. He takes a direction counter to most scholars by claiming that the Holiness Code is far more extensive than Lev 17–26 and that it is very late. His work is clear evidence that scholars have had a difficult time establishing conclusively which tradition influenced another tradition. Third, Kaufmann holds that the sacrificial laws, especially 17:2–4 and the laws on consuming blood, correlate best with the era of the judges. Unfortunately there is not enough material on either side of the scales of this argument for it to carry any weight. Brichto demonstrates the tendentiousness of many of Kaufmann's arguments (*HUCA* 47 [1976] 36–55). Although Kaufmann has not won many adherents to his reconstruction, he has significantly influenced the discussion and done much to show the antiquity of the laws, customs, and regulations found in P.

Other scholars have attempted to date P through an analysis of its literary character. Polzin has studied thoroughly the linguistic characteristics of the P writer by analyzing non-technical data, syntactical style, and other internal distinctions (Haran, "The Priestly Source," 89). He has concluded that this source reflects the stage after classical Hebrew and definitely before the Chronicler's language (*Late Biblical Hebrew,* 159). Hurvitz has concluded from several studies on the idioms and terminology of P that this material predates Ezekiel. He writes, "What there is in P is early (=pre-exilic) and what is missing is distinctively late (=exilic and post-exilic). The evidence of language thus demonstrates that P does not reflect nor anticipate the situations and conditions which characterize the exilic and post-exilic period. P's 'historical horizon' (Kaufmann) and its *Sitz im Leben* (Gunkel) are definitely indicative of the pre-exilic period" (*RB* 81 [1974] 55 = "The Priestly Source," 88). Hurvitz has been challenged in a few articles by Levine. At present the examples and scope of Hurvitz's work commend it above Levine's.

The claim of Hurvitz that P predates Ezekiel has received support from the comparative studies of Israelite cult and customs with other cults of the ancient Middle East by Haran and Weinfeld. Haran has demonstrated that the legal, cultic, and historical presuppositions of P are not in accord with the practices of the post-exilic period and must go back to an earlier era. He, furthermore, argues that P is too comprehensive and distinctive to have come about gradually over a long span of time (*JBL* 100 [1981] 330–31). Therefore, he postulates that it grew out of a crucial moment in history, namely the era of Ahaz-Hezekiah (late eighth century B.C.; *JBL* 100 [1981] 331–33). Zevit has entered this discussion by proposing the value of establishing the *terminus ad quem* for the composition of P. Analyzing socio-cultic, linguistic, and literary data, as well as the results of Kaufmann, Polzin, Hurvitz, and Milgrom, he concludes that P was essentially composed prior to the exile (*ZAW* 94 [1982] 510). Therefore, he sets 586 B.C. as the *terminus ad quem* for its composition.

Another set of scholars trained in source critical theory have applied the methods of form criticism and tradition history to P. They likewise have discovered that ancient material underlies P, including Leviticus. Gunkel took the lead in the study of the origin and growth of small literary units. Others, like Noth and von Rad, have applied this approach to larger blocks of material. Von Rad assigned the growth of the Pentateuch to traditions that circulated independently (primal history, patriarchal history, exodus tradition, Sinai tradition, settlement tradition; Rendtorff, *Introduction,* 160). Even though these scholars have based their work upon an acceptance of the Wellhausen position, Rendtorff judges that the results of their methods are no longer compatible with the documentary hypothesis (*Introduction,* 160). He also has undertaken a study of the traditions in the Pentateuch. In his *Introduction* (161) he summarizes his position:

> The individual units have been collected and shaped from very different perspectives and leading ideas. . . . The first basic feature of the Sinai pericope is the reciprocal relationship between narrative and communication of the law; this brings out on the one hand the special position of Moses and on the other the breaking of the covenant and its restoration. In addition, different collections of cult laws have been added which have been similarly combined under the overall leading ideas.

As Rendtorff has pointed out in this quotation, P consists of laws attached to a running narrative. That is why Leviticus is set in the narrative of Israel's stay at Sinai. Furthermore, the emerging of that narrative in chaps. 8–10 is not disjunctive, but integral to the context of the laws on sacrifices and ritual purity. As far as it is known, this style is distinctively Israelite. Its importance, then, needs to be integrated more fully into critical studies on P (cf. Amsler, "Les documents," 241–44). Therefore, the results of form criticism and traditio-historical criticism find that the Pentateuch is made up of blocks of material that had distinctive origins and transmission histories. While some scholars still postulate that these blocks were first united in distinctive sources that became woven together, others like Rendtorff and Winnett reason that the Pentateuch resulted from "a series of successive supplements of the previous written tradition" (Knight, 280–81, 274–75). Since the methodological approaches to ancient literature have advanced dramatically since Wellhausen, some scholars like Whybray (*The Making of the Pentateuch* [JSOTSup 53]) have concluded that the documentary hypothesis no longer has any validity as the basis for Pentateuchal studies.

At this point it may be helpful to summarize the results of an extensive traditio-historical study of Exod 25–Lev 16 done by Koch as illustrative of this methodology. The results of Koch's work testify both to the antiquity of the ground form of this material and to its amplification and standardization through the centuries. From an extensive analysis of this passage, Koch recognizes that an archaic text lies under the received text. It is characterized by short sentences, usually consisting of three or four words headed by a *waw* perfect. The monotonous, stereotyped style bears witness that these regulations were transmitted orally. The P writer took them over in this form and then systematized them into a programmatic document to serve the official cult (cf. Koch, *Priesterschrift,* 99). The extensive description of cultic practices of this old document points to its origin at a large cult center, scarcely before the establishment of the kingdom (97).

In Koch's judgment the priestly writer (Pg) drew on a wide variety of cultic traditions along with a collection of the regulations to put together this program for the continual interaction of God and humans as found in Exod 25–Lev 16 (Koch, *Priesterschrift*, 97–102). These materials included legends of the priests (Lev 10:1–5), basic sayings (Exod 31:1ff), statements of recognition (Exod 29:46; 31:13), multiple declaratory formulae (e.g., 1:9, 13, 17), and laws from the priestly *torah* (e.g., 2:11–13; 6:20b [27b]; 7:23f, 26; 11:8). Included also are apodictic laws that arose out of some conflict within the cultic community (6:6, 10a, [11], 16, 20a; 7:7, 7–10, 14, 15f, 19; 11:24f, 32–34; 14:46f; 15:5–13, 19–22, 28; 16:26a, 28). The short sentences were expanded to break up the monotony and to include additional information. As a result the apodictic laws became cast into casuistic style as a part of the systematization of the material. The Priestly writers also edited the material to achieve greater precision regarding exactly where and when and how something was to take place (Koch, *Priesterschrift*, 100–102). Koch speculates that the P writer comes from the Jerusalem sanctuary, for the text has been edited toward practices of this cult center.

The ground form of this program went through additional stages of editing. A single redactor, whom Koch labels Pe, added the material that recounts the execution of God's command. In Leviticus this hand is seen in chap. 8; 9:1–21; 10:12–14[15] (Koch, *Priesterschrift*, 102–3). To this redactor the holiness of the sanctuary preceded the holiness of the priests (8:10–12). He also raised the importance of the priests; they, like their father, were anointed (8:30; cf. 7:28–36; 16:6–7). To them were assigned additional portions of the sacrifices (6:11[18], 22[29]; 7:6, 34; 10:15). Another redactor (Ps) is responsible for a layer that ties social concerns into the laws, e.g., permitting the poor to present a lesser sacrifice (4:32–35; 5:7–13; 12:8; 14:21–32; Koch, 103). Also to this editor belong the subscripts (11:46–47; 13:59; 14:54–55, 57a; 15:32) as well as the material found in 6:12–16(19–23); 11:44–45; 16:1, 33. From a later editor (Pss), who had a similar outlook, come 5:1–6, 20–26(6:1–7); (7:8f); 10:16–20. Even more recent is 5:17–19. By demonstrating the antiquity of this corpus and pointing out many of the ways it has been changed, Koch (103–4) has pointed out the dynamic adjustment made to the text in order to explain each ritual procedure and to breathe new life into archaic forms and practices. (For an extensive discussion on the various approaches to the Holiness Code [chaps. 17–26], see the discussion at the head of the Laws on Holy Living in section V.)

These studies have raised many questions for which solid, conclusive answers are hard to obtain. How were the words Moses received from Yahweh preserved? Were they kept orally or in written form? Many scholars work on the assumption that the old regulations existed for centuries in oral form. This assumption is supported by the discovery that the legends and traditions of various peoples were preserved in oral tradition for long periods of time before being recorded. On the other hand, many ancient Near Eastern societies that predate Israel preserved their laws and stories in writing. Many scholars thus hold that both oral and written material were brought together to form the Pentateuch (cf. Knierim, "Criticism of Literary Features," 146). If this material was written down at the start, its use of numerous rhetorical devices such as key words, assonance, and the clustering of laws in groups makes it clear that the material was composed for memorization and oral delivery. Moreover, do Leviticus and other books in the

Pentateuch contain all or only part of the ancient material? For instance, were there more "sermons" than those that have been preserved? How was this material copied and passed on? Did multiple copies exist, leading to differing versions? It is very likely that many copies existed, given the many sanctuaries throughout ancient Israel and the likelihood that each sanctuary had an official copy. These copies would have taken on local characteristics, leading over time to differing versions. How did these texts and versions survive the many social traumas Israel experienced: wars, particularly the destruction of Shiloh, the many dramatic changes in the cult like the building of the first Temple and Josiah's reform, the dark apostasy of the late Kingdom period, or the great disruption caused by the exile? When the Israelite scribes decided to make a standard authoritative text of the rituals and laws of the cult, how did they go about producing it from the texts, versions, and traditions available to them?

In light of the multiplicity and complexity of these questions it is little wonder that scholars have arrived at many different judgments on the extent, origin, and composition history of P. Because of the lack of hard data on the development of the priests and the Levites and the paucity of information on the operation of the cult, especially the connection between outlying sanctuaries, such as the one at Arad, and the Temple in Jerusalem, there is little likelihood of any scholarly consensus developing (cf. Levine, "Priestly Writers," 684). Certainly, then, the Pentateuch and P remain a fertile ground for continued research, regardless of one's operating assumptions.

A few observations about the perspective of this commentator may be in order. In accord with conservative scholars, the formula "Yahweh spoke to Moses" is taken seriously. This means that this material originated with the revelation of Yahweh to Moses. This position influences the interpretation in a variety of ways. Two examples may be mentioned. (1) Laws and regulations (e.g., the program for the year of Jubilee) are considered to have emanated from this ancient era. (2) While certainly many cultic practices preceded Israel's origin, it is believed that Yahweh instructed Moses regarding the regulations for sacrifices offered at the new tabernacle in order to bring its operation into alignment with his holy character. In fact, it is inconceivable that the distinctive faith of Israel could have originated without a formative leader like Moses, for innovative social change usually requires a charismatic leader. Moses had such a formative role because of the special way Yahweh, the transcendant, holy God, communicated with him. Thus the testimony of Scripture that the revealed word preceded and directed the establishment of the Israelite cult is in accord with the nature of social process (cf. von Rad, *The Problem of the Hexateuch*, 22).

In recognition of the results of the careful work done by critical scholars, this commentary takes seriously the seams (e.g., between 8:6 and 7), breaks (e.g., 7:8–10), fissures (location of chap. 24), conflicting statements (compare 17:15–16 with Deut 14:21a and Lev 7:24), and the filling out found in the text. These difficulties in the structure of the units are dealt with in the *Form/Structure/Setting* sections of the commentary. Three of the many dynamics that contributed to these rough places may be mentioned: (1) The text bears the scars of a long history of transmission. (2) Some highly valued laws that circulated orally became attached at different locations, drawn by key terms and themes; e.g., laws on eating fat have been attached, but not worked into their contexts, at 3:17 and

7:22–27. (3) With the conviction that the tradition originated in Yahweh's revelation to Moses, the Israelite community through the centuries augmented, amplified, and adjusted the ancient material to make it applicable to changing social situations. The evidence for these adaptations to the text are visible in terms, procedures, and laws that reflect a culture vastly different from that of Israel's sojourn in the wilderness; e.g., the references to the sanctuary shekel in 5:15 and 27:3, 25 imply a highly developed cult that established its own weights, rather than the primitive cult of the wilderness. Noordtzij (12) correctly observes, " after Israel had settled in Canaan, the need arose more than once to adapt some of the regulations from the Mosaic period to the new circumstances that had then arisen."

While ancient Israelite society changed at a much slower pace than does a contemporary society, change took place, nonetheless. Some of these changes were caused by traumatic events in her history, e.g., the shift from a tribal league to a monarchy, the split of the nation into two kingdoms, the centralization of worship in Jerusalem, the demise of the Davidic house, and the ascendancy of the leadership of the high priest in the post-exilic community. The fact that variation in prescribed practices was tolerated under certain conditions is illustrated in some OT texts. For example, Aaron and his sons did not eat their portion of the purification offering after the death of Nadab and Abihu (10:16–20). Also the Passover held during the height of the reform led by King Hezekiah was observed in the second month rather than the first (2 Chr 30). It is postulated that some social changes were so major that the priests felt compelled to make additions and modifications to the text in order that the law could be kept. These enhancements of the text were done in the spirit of applying the revelation to Moses to a changing society.

Whenever additions were incorporated in the text, material as a rule was not deleted, as the fullness of some texts indicate. Lev 17:3–7, a very complex text from a literary point of view, is an example of the addition of interpretive words and phrases in order that a law might be applied to a changing society. Another example is the legislation concerning redemption (chap. 25). It seems to have undergone growth after the settlement in Canaan, for it provides laws on issues faced by a growing urban population, e.g., the laws on buying and selling of houses in walled cities (25:29–34). An example of the subtle filling out and adjusting of the text during its transmission is seen in the textual tradition to which the Septuagint belongs. In places pronouns have been replaced with nouns and the number, i.e., pl/sg, of several verbs has been changed to eliminate any uncertainty as to their antecedent. In chaps. 1–5, e.g., these changes reassign responsibilities at the altar from the laity to the priests in accord with later practice.

Most additions took place before the text was canonized, obviously. However, these additions and adjustments do not discount the statement "Yahweh spoke to Moses," for these changes were done with the conviction that Yahweh was active among his people, giving them insight into the ways they were to fulfill the laws he had given Moses in their daily lives. Before canonization, elements of the interaction between the text and the community became part of the written text. After canonization, this interpretive process continued even more energetically; it has been preserved in volumes that became the Mishnah and the Talmud.

The trauma of the exile was most likely the force that spurred the priests and the scribes to undertake the production of a standard edition of the ancient traditions and laws that has become known as the Pentateuch. It is possible that these leaders were encouraged in their efforts by officials of the Persian Empire who promoted ethnic and religious diversity throughout the empire by directing these multiple groups to search out and preserve the materials of their respective traditions. Unfortunately the number, variety, and quality of the texts available to the ancient scribes is unknown, and it is unknown how they collated the texts and handled variant readings. It is clear that whenever the Israelite scribes found two or more traditions or laws about a matter, they preserved all of them because of their reverence for the ancient traditions. They assembled the material they found into books, as the present form of Leviticus witnesses.

This commentary, then, holds to the full authority of the Word of God without neglecting the work of critical scholars. One of the great benefits of their work is that it brings to life the role that the text had in forming the ancient Israelite community. While their arguments and hypothetical reconstructions are debatable by their very nature and in some cases their proposals are implausible and fantastic, nevertheless, their works shed light on the interplay between the word and the community and how each affected the other. Thus their works alert students to the significant role that the community had in shaping and interpreting the text, and thereby it leads them into discovering ways that contemporary communities of faith may be shaped and empowered by the received Word of God. It must be remembered that the Pentateuch was a major force in forming the character and culture of Israel, not something received in the wilderness and placed in the controlled environment of a museum, and that the received text has resulted from the interplay of God's speaking and human response. Careful interpreters must consider both of these factors, not one to the exclusion of the other.

The History of the Exposition of Leviticus

(Prepared by William Yarchin, M.A.)

In the history of biblical interpretation, exposition focused on Leviticus has not been as frequent or as intense as in the case of Genesis or Isaiah or the Psalms. Nonetheless, references to and quotations from the book of Leviticus are scattered far and wide throughout the broad range of the Jewish and Christian exegetical traditions. Within that range, the interpreting of Leviticus has run a course between two poles. On the one hand, the Jewish commentators felt the need to explain the meaning of animal sacrifice and other cultic prescriptions to generations that could not observe them; Jewish exposition also had to respond to Christian interpretations of Levitical imperatives. On the other hand, Christian exegetes, following the lead of the Epistle to the Hebrews, needed to account for the prescriptions of the Levitical law in the light of the sacrifice of Christ, especially in the face of Jewish interpretations of Leviticus that had the advantage of historical priority. Leviticus, then, was for the Christian commentators part of the larger problem of the role and authority of the entire OT in Christian theology and liturgy. For centuries these two interpretive camps were to go on to differ methodologically in their treatment of the OT in general and of Leviticus in particular. With certain exceptions, the Jewish exegetes made little use of allegorical methods, while allegory and typology abounded in the Christian commentaries. Surprisingly, it is in pre-Christian documents of Jewish antiquity that the first allegorizations of Levitical prescriptions appeared.

The pseudepigraphic *Letter of Aristeas*, dating from about the second century B.C., includes a tropological allegorization of the dietary laws from Leviticus: e.g., the birds which are proscribed from the Levitical diet (Lev 11:11–19) are those birds whose behavior is tyrannical over other birds. The allegory serves to teach the avoidance of tyrannical human behavior (145–48). The aim of this allegorizing in the *Letter of Aristeas* is to demonstrate that the laws of Leviticus are in accord with reason (161).

Philo of Alexandria, who produced a great amount of commentary on the LXX Pentateuch at the turn of the millenium, did not write an exposition of Leviticus per se. Much of Philo's comments on the cultic prescriptions of Leviticus appear in those places in his literary corpus where he discusses subjects related to the Ten Commandments, treating the Levitical instructions as specifications of the general decalogical principle in question. Philo was addressing a philosophical audience of his day that was critical of ritual piety, and the sacrificial laws of Leviticus were a potential target for such critique. His response was to spiritualize the Levitical priesthood, the tabernacle, and the sacrifices in his interpretation of Torah. Philo's exposition equates the priest with the wise man who offers the sacrifice of the soul via philosophical reflection. The sacrifice in turn purges the soul of that which would hinder the soul's perfection. Such allegorizing of the cultic prescriptions from Leviticus into a moral and philosophical system for the development of the worshiper's inner integrity would become the standard approach in the patristic and medieval Christian exegesis of Leviticus.

Origen's expositions of Scripture from the third century A.D. are among the earliest examples in the Christian church of commentary on particular biblical books. His *Homilies on Leviticus* (PG, 406–574) exhibits the preference for the allegorical sense of Scripture characteristic of Philo and many interpreters from late antiquity. Origen's comments on Leviticus are given the form of sixteen essays, each of which is rooted in a short passage from the biblical text. These essays were probably generated for a preaching or liturgical context, focusing on the exposition of the spiritual sense of the text, rather than on the literal or historical meaning.

Homilies on Leviticus for the most part articulates Origen's Christological interpretation of the Aaronite priesthood, as part of an effort to define the Christian understanding of Scripture as distinct from Jewish interpretation. Origen's starting point was the literal (or carnal) sense of the text as opposed to the allegorical and typological (or spiritual) sense; Christians are able to discern the veiled, deeper truths of Leviticus, while Jews can perceive only the more literal meaning. Hence the Jews fail to see the full, Christian meaning in the laws of Leviticus. (Origen considered Moses himself to have had a special knowledge of this deeper sense of Levitical prescriptions.) For example, when commenting on Lev 7:15, which requires the meat from the offering of well-being to be eaten on the day of its offering, Origen maintains

> that the divine Word does not allow us to feed on yesterday's meat, but always on what is fresh and new. . . . This flesh, which is allotted to the priests for the sacrifices, is the

> word of God which they teach in the Church. Thus they are warned in this passage, by forms which have mystic meaning, not to set forth stale doctrines according to the letter, but by God's grace ever to bring forth new truth, ever to discover the spiritual lessons. If you produce today in the church what you learned yesterday from the Jews, this is just eating yesterday's flesh in the sacrifice (*Lev. Hom.* 5:8).

Following from Origen's exegesis, the allegorical approach to Leviticus (as well as to most Scripture) became the dominant approach, particularly among African and European patristic interpreters of Leviticus. Augustine, for example, whose program for theological study wielded enormous influence in Christendom from the fifth to the twelfth century, produced two brief exegetical treatments of Leviticus (*Locutionum in Heptateuchum liber tertius,* PL, 34, 515–22; *Quaestionum in Heptateuchum liber tertius,* PL, 34, 673–716) that favored the spiritual sense over the literal. Yet Augustine was usually careful to root the allegorical meaning in the letter of the text, to show how the latter indicated the former. These works on Leviticus took the form of brief notes on isolated passages, following their canonical sequence, to explain particular problems in their meaning. This was an expositional form used by Philo before Augustine and widely followed in medieval commentaries.

The first classically rabbinic exegesis of the book of Leviticus appeared in *Sipra* (Jerusalem: Makor, 1971), a running midrashic commentary to virtually the entire book of Leviticus dating from perhaps the third or fourth century, traditionally attributed to the rabbinic school of Akiba. The exegetical concern in *Sipra* is very much with the details of the Hebrew text, so that often an extraordinary amount of halachic discussion is generated by a single word or phrase from the text of Leviticus. In typically midrashic fashion, a given theme pointed out in a Leviticus verse will be illuminated by extended references to that theme from elsewhere in the OT.

The comments found in *Sipra* do not normally feature allegorical interpretations. Rather, the exegetical intention seems to be a clarification of the literal sense of the text, along with explanations as to why the verse in question would be written as it is. For example, in Lev 19:10 the text required Israel to leave the gleanings of the vineyard for the poor to gather. *Sipra* adds the inference that the Israelites are not to do the gathering for the poor, but that the poor do their own gathering. Again, at Lev 19:4, "Turn ye not unto idols nor make to yourselves molten gods; I am the Lord your God." We find in *Sipra*:

> 'Turn ye not unto idols'—Do not turn to them to worship them. R. Judah said, Do not turn to gaze at them. . . . At the beginning they are idols but if you turn after [to] them you make them a godhead.

In *Sipra* it is assumed that every single word in Leviticus and its arrangement is important. However, it is not always the text of Leviticus that is under discussion. Rather, much of *Sipra* presents rabbinic discussions of a whole range of political, theological, and legal issues, all framed according to a structure dictated by the contents of the book of Leviticus. This is characteristic of much of midrashic literature, including another early Jewish treatment of Leviticus, known as *Leviticus Rabbah* (Jerusalem: Mosad Harav Kook, 1976; ET, London: Soncino Press, 1939).

Palestinian Jewish scholars of the fifth century compiled the thirty-seven chapters of *Leviticus Rabbah.* This Hebrew document does not present a verse-by-verse commentary on Leviticus, nor does it focus on problem passages. Instead, each chapter of *Leviticus Rabbah* presents a topical essay rooted to a base text comprising one or two verses from a chapter of Leviticus. For example, the twentieth chapter of *Leviticus Rabbah* begins by citing the phrase from Lev 16:1 that mentions the death of Aaron's sons Nadab and Abihu. Then, through an extended series of midrashic observations on the meanings of various words in this phrase and in many other verses from the OT, this chapter develops almost tangentially into an essay on the meaning of the death of Aaron's sons. Their death is ultimately seen as an atoning death, a conclusion befitting the subject of Lev 16, which is the Day of Atonement. *Leviticus Rabbah,* then, is not a systematic treatment of the book of Leviticus but a compilation of rabbinic discussions on various topics, the springboard for which is provided by a verse selected from each of the sequential chapters of Leviticus. Although allegory does not dominate the exegesis found in *Leviticus Rabbah,* the unnamed rabbis who produced this volume did treat Leviticus so that virtually any word or phrase in the text could refer to almost any other phrase or theme from elsewhere in the OT. This use of midrashic exegesis allowed the interpretation of Leviticus to follow a structure of concerns developed outside of Leviticus itself, such as messianic or eschatological issues. It is likely that the book of Leviticus was chosen for this particular exegesis because it is the one-fifth of the Torah that presents the core mechanisms for the preservation of Israel's holiness in the wilderness. *Leviticus Rabbah* used Leviticus to address the protracted need for the Jewish communities of late antiquity to understand the maintenance of their status as holy unto the Lord within the wilderness of the long-established dominance of the gentile nations.

During the fifth century the Alexandrian Father Cyril wrote comments *(Glaphyra)* on certain Pentateuchal passages; a book of such "Elegant Comments" was devoted to Leviticus: *Glaphyrorum in Leviticum liber* (PG, 69, 539–90). Cyril's exegesis of OT legal and historical passages allowed much more freely for the literal sense of the text than had the exegesis of his Alexandrian predecessors, but overall the literal was regarded as less important than the spiritual significance. At Lev 2:14, concerning the grain offerings, Cyril maintains that the literal sense of the text is quite clear, requiring no spiritual interpretation. Yet at Lev 11:1–8, 13–19, on the distinction between what animals may and may not be eaten by the Israelites, Cyril moralizes that this teaches the sorts of persons to avoid in our association and asserts that the law must be understood spiritually. Thus Cyril presents patristic exegesis of Leviticus that, *pace* Origen, does not insist that all the details found in the OT yield a spiritual meaning or reference.

Around A.D. 450 the Christian priest of Jerusalem, Hesychius, wrote his lengthy verse-by-verse *Commentarius in Leviticum* (PG, 93, 787–1180), which has been preserved only in a sixth-century Latin version. His exegesis of Leviticus is strongly influenced by Origen, although it is less homiletical. Also during the fifth century Theodoret of Cyrus, one of the leading theologians of the Antioch school, produced his *Quaestiones in Leviticus* (PG, 80, 297–350), a relatively small portion of his larger work on the Octateuch. This work on Leviticus consists simply of comments on certain difficult passages in a question-and-answer format.

Procopius of Gaza, during the sixth century, produced a compilation of exegetical citations on passages in the Octateuch selected from earlier commentators of the Alexandrian tradition. His own comments on Leviticus (*Commentarii in Leviticum,* PG, 87, 689–794) are sparse and reflect the heavily allegorizing bent of his sources.

Although there is no critical edition of it available, the commentary on the Heptateuch by Raban Mauer of Mainz proved to be a major source for later Christian exegetes of Leviticus. Raban made available to these later writers an extensive commentary on Leviticus (*Expositiones in Leviticum,* PL, 108, 247–586), largely a compilation of expositions from earlier exegetes such as Augustine and Hesychius. Similarly the Spanish Christian encyclopedist Isidore of Seville, working without knowledge of biblical languages, in the seventh century wrote his *Quaestiones in Vetus Testamentum,* two books devoted to Leviticus (PL, 83, 321–40), which for the most part offered only a selection of earlier patristic opinions on problematic passages.

The great Jewish exegete Rashi produced his highly influential verse-by-verse commentaries on OT books late in the eleventh century. His treatment of Leviticus is greatly influenced by rabbinic traditions as preserved in *Sipra, Leviticus Rabbah,* the Talmud, and other midrashic sources, as well as the exegetical implications of *Targum Onqelos,* which he frequently consults. Rashi's commentary on Leviticus thus made available to Jewish communities and to subsequent exegetes an expert compilation of rabbinic opinion on the meaning of almost every passage from Leviticus and is currently available in numerous popular editions of the Hebrew Pentateuch (ET: *The Pentateuch with Rashi's Commentary,* tr. M. Rosenbaum & A. Silbermann [Jerusalem, 1973]). In keeping with his halachic sources, Rashi favored the literal meaning of Levitical passages with certain interpretive expansions, yet not so far as to allegorize. For example, at Lev 19:3, Rashi comments on the words, "Ye shall fear every man his father and mother," by noting that this text's literal sense, פשט *(pešat),* is self-evident. But he adds that the derived sense, מדרש *(midraš),* incorporates the behavior of the woman into the reference to the man ("every man") because the woman's behavior is under the control of the man. Thus, even though the text literally requires only the man of a household ("every man") to fear parents, the woman is also included in this prescription. This midrash comes from *Sipra.* To this Rashi adds that the verb "fear" is cast in the plural, and so both the man and the woman are included in that formulation.

Rashbam's exegesis of Leviticus, in *Perush Hattorah Lerashbam* (Jerusalem, 1965), was greatly influenced by his grandfather Rashi, although Rashbam stressed even more the literal, plain sense *(pešat)* of the text. Another distinction between the two is Rashbam's presentation of only one explanation of a text, rather than Rashi's multiple explanations.

Bekhor Shor (Joseph B. Isaac), writing in the twelfth century, would often use the literal sense of the Hebrew text of Leviticus to counter Christian allegorical interpretations from the Vulgate and attempted to provide a rational basis for his literal interpretations. Similarly, Rikam (Joseph Kimchi) later in that century wrote a commentary on the Pentateuch which stressed the *pešat* rather than halachic or homiletic interpretations of Leviticus.

Ibn Ezra, of the twelfth century, wrote a commentary on Leviticus as a part of his larger work on the Pentateuch (*The Commentary of Abraham Ibn Ezra on the*

Pentateuch: Vol 3: *Leviticus*, tr. J. Schachter [Hoboken, NJ: KTAV, 1986]). Ibn Ezra's commentary contains occasional detailed grammatical notes which support his often original interpretations of the Hebrew text. For example, at Lev 19:3, where Rashi had claimed that the plural form "fear ye" was used to include both the man and the woman of the household in this prescription, Ibn Ezra contends that the plural implies that witnesses to the infraction of this law must confront the transgressor (see also at Lev 10:19). There is only rarely any type of exegesis in his treatment of Leviticus other than the literal.

Rupert of Deutz in the twelfth century devoted two volumes to expounding Leviticus (*In Leviticum Commentariorum*, PL, 167, 743–836). These were books written in a monastery for other monks, and so they feature the characteristically monastic penchant for emphasizing the moral sense of Scripture (allegorically derived), to assist in the monk's incessant battle against carnal vices. Rupert overwhelmingly preferred the allegorical approach to Leviticus.

Thus, in Jewish-Christian polemics of the early Middle Ages, the book of Leviticus in particular became difficult for most monks to comprehend in a Christian sense particularly in face of Jewish claims about the plain meaning. A thirteenth-century monk known as Ralph of Plaix produced, over the course of six years, a twenty-book commentary on the Latin text of Leviticus (*Maxima Bibliotheca veterum Patrum* XVII [Lyons, 1677]), which was intended to provide the monks of his time with an interpretation of Levitical scripture to counter the Jewish understanding of the texts. This work proved to be a great influence on scholastic lectures on Leviticus for several generations.

Making extensive use of Augustine's *Locutiones* and *Quaestiones*, Ralph argued that the legal precepts of Leviticus were couched in a secret (allegorical) sign language so that the letter of the text was divinely intended not to clarify but to hide the spirit of the text. His argument maintained that the literal meaning of the text made no sense and so must be understood as a mystery with a deeper meaning that has eluded the Jewish exegetes (e.g., the apparent discrepancy when leavened bread is excluded as an offering in Lev 2:11, yet commanded as an offering in 7:13; a spiritual interpretation of "leaven" dissolves the problem). With this spiritualizing emphasis, Ralph's commentary on Leviticus then falls quite in line with the expositional trajectories set by patristic exegetes.

Ralph's interpretive approach contrasts with that of his contemporary, Hugh of St. Victor, whose *Adnotationes elucidatoriae in Leviticum* (PL, 175, 74–84) focused more on the literal sense of the Hebrew text and reflected consultation with the Jewish exegetical authorities. Hugh's work on Leviticus is not a full commentary on the book, however, but as a part of his larger work on the Pentateuch, forms a treatise on sacrifices and related Levitical cultic matters. His exegesis on Leviticus treats themes and chapters rather than individual verses or words.

The great Jewish scholar Maimonides did not produce a commentary specifically on Leviticus. The most direct comments of Maimonides on Levitical passages are found in his widely influential *Seper Hamizvot* (usually published as an introduction to his larger work *Mishneh Torah* [Israel: Pardes, 1955]), which was his own enumeration of the 248 positive and 365 negative prescriptions in the Torah. This work was first published in 1170 and reflects a vast knowledge of the whole range of rabbinic opinion on understanding Leviticus. After offering a brief explication of the plain sense of a given law, Maimonides typically refers the reader to the appropriate tractate of the Talmud for further explanation.

In the mid-thirteenth century Ramban, or Naḥmanides, wrote his commentary on the Pentateuch (*Perush Haramban Al Hattorah* [Jerusalem: Mosad Harav Kook, 1970]). His comments on Leviticus frequently utilize opinions from Rashi and Ibn Ezra as well as the early rabbinic opinions, but usually in a critical manner. For example, in Lev 10:3 Moses states, "This is that which the Lord spoke, saying, 'In those that approach me I will be sanctified, and before all the people I will be glorified.'" Ramban takes Rashi (following *Sipra*) to assert that God here tells Aaron that Nadab and Abihu are holier than Aaron; Ibn Ezra infers a prior, unrecorded conversation in which God told Moses that he would manifest his sanctity in those near to him (in this manner). But Ramban rejects these views, asserting that the plain meaning of "This is that which the Lord spoke" does not require that God communicated this speech to Moses or Aaron, but simply that God spoke these words to himself, foreseeing this incident. Ramban explained some of the dietary laws of Leviticus as health regulations, while he interpreted other prescriptions of the *kašrut* as keeping Israel from eating foods that negatively affect spiritual sensitivity.

Hezekiah B. Menoaḥ in the thirteenth century produced a commentary on the Pentateuch (*Al Ḥamishah Ḥumshei Torah* [Jerusalem: Mosad Harav Kook, 1981]), which in Leviticus restricts itself mainly to opinions from Rashi and Bekhor Shor and to certain midrashic interpretations. Later in the thirteenth century Baḥya B. Asher wrote an extensive commentary on the Pentateuch (Bomberg ed. [Warsaw, 1852]), which would stress sometimes a literal sense and sometimes a more mystical or symbolic sense of a passage. For example, where Lev 10:1 states that Nadab and Abihu placed incense upon the fire in their censers, Baḥya offers several different interpretations simply juxtaposed one after the other: first the *pešat* (they used fire not from the altar), then the *midraš* (they were drunk), then the *qabbalah* (they placed incense on the fire rather than on their censers, as they should have). During this same time Gregorius Barhebraeus produced his *Scholia in Leviticum syriace* (ed. G. Kerber [Leipzig: Drugulin, 1895]).

Among Christian biblical exegetes from the fourteenth century, the *Postilla litteralis super totam Bibliam* (Lyons: Vincent, 1545) of Nicholas Lyranus is of particular interest because of his copious use of rabbinic textual interpretations as transmitted by Rashi and Maimonides. Accordingly, the comments of Nicholas on Leviticus are frequently concerned with the plain meaning of the Hebrew text more than those of the Christian exegetes of preceding centuries had been.

Jacob B. Asher of fourteenth-century Spain produced a commentary on the Pentateuch (*Rezmai Baal Hatturim* [Constantinople, 1500]) with particular attention to Rashi and Ramban in the Leviticus passages.

Isaac B. Moses (Arama) was a fifteenth-century Spanish rabbi who wrote his commentary on the Pentateuch (*Aqedat Yitzḥaq* [Pressburg, 1849]) in the form of philosophical and allegorical homilies. Included in his sermons from Leviticus is a treatise (prompted by a *midraš* from *Leviticus Rabbah*) on the necessity for sacrifices, in which Arama maintains that Torah sacrifices, unlike pagan cultic systems, are of no advantage or necessity to God but are rather for the benefit of humans for their moral improvement.

Alonzo Tostado's *Commentaria in Leviticum* (Venice: Paulinum Berti Lucensem, 1615) is a lengthy volume.

A small portion of Dionysius de Ryckel's *Enarrationes piae ac eruditae in quinque Mosaicae legis libros* (Cologne: Quental, 1534) is devoted to expounding the book of Leviticus, as is a section of *Commentarii ilustres in quinque mosaicos libros* (Paris: Boulle, 1539) by Tomas de Vio Cajetan, and Franciscus Vatablus' *Annotationes in Vetus Testamentum* (Paris, 1729) from the following century. In these sixteenth-century commentaries is reflected an increasing use of the Hebrew text in Christian exposition of Leviticus.

The great Protestant theologian Jean Calvin was a prodigious exegete who expounded the whole Old and New Testament Bible. Addressing the OT, Calvin worked largely from the Hebrew text of his day and often acknowledged the exegetical contributions of the Jewish tradition, sometimes agreeing with the rabbis, sometimes differing with them. His treatment of Leviticus appears as a part of his harmony of the life and teachings of Moses (ET: J. Haroutunian & L. P. Smith [Philadelphia: Westminster, 1958]). For example, Calvin first treats a Leviticus passage (19:36–37 and also 20:8 and 22:31) along with various passages selected from Deuteronomy as a follow-up to his exposition of Exod 20:1–2. The Eighth Commandment ("Thou shalt not steal") provides the occasion to comment upon these Leviticus texts in this order: 19:11, 13, 35, 36 (on stealing and fraud); 25:35–38 (prohibiting usury); 19:15 (concerning equitable judgment in the courts); 24:18, 21 (on restitution); 19:9–10; 23:22 (gleanings to be left for the poor); and 25:39–55; 23–34 (on Jubilee). All these texts and their comments are woven among comments on various passages from Exodus, Numbers, and Deuteronomy.

Calvin's exegesis pursues the literal meaning of the text within certain hermeneutical preunderstandings: the law was given historically to ancient Israel, but provides instruction in a holy life especially for the Church. When the literal meaning apart from any symbolic elaboration can be easily fitted to the instruction to the Church, Calvin restricts himself to plain exposition, as in his treatment of Lev 19:12, concerning false swearing. But at those points where it is more difficult to expound with relevance for his European Christian readership, Calvin will, almost grudgingly, resort to allegorizing, as in Lev 11:2 (treated as a supplement to the first commandment): the "parted hoof" feature of kosher food speaks of "prudence in distinguishing the mysteries of Scripture," and "chewing of the cud" refers to "serious meditation on its heavenly doctrines."

Another commentary from the sixteenth century that emphasizes the literal meaning with only discreet use of allegorizing is that of Cornelius Jansen's *Pentateuchus sive commentarius in quinque libros Moysis* (Lyons: Beaujollin, 1677). This posthumous work, though usually working from the Hebrew text, made extensive use of patristic opinions on the Latin Leviticus. Note also the work of Pedro Serrano (*In Levitici librum commentaria* [Antwerp: Plantin, 1572]).

Ephraim Lunshitz in the early seventeenth century wrote a commentary to the Pentateuch (*Keli Yakar* [Lublin, 1602]) that showed a rich knowledge of a wide range of Jewish commentators. Certain portions of his exposition of Leviticus serve to counter Christian polemics against Judaism.

Note also the lengthy work by John Lorinus, *Commentarii in Leviticum* (Lyons: Cardon, 1619), and *Pentateuchus Moysis commentario illustratus* (Antwerp: Plantin, 1625) by the Jesuit hebraist Jacques Bonfrere, as well as the multi-volume

Commentaria in Scripturam Sacram by Cornelius Lapide (ed. A. Crampon [Paris: Vives, 1868]). The last of these three seventeenth-century works expounds the Hebrew text of Leviticus according to the fourfold senses of Scripture (literal, allegorical, tropological, anagogical) that were more in vogue in the older medieval commentaries, and often quotes from the Fathers.

The trend toward fuller attention to the literal sense of the Hebrew text among Christian exegetes of Leviticus continues in the works of Jean Le Clerc (*Mosis prophetae libri quinque* [Amsterdam: Wetstein-Smith, 1696]), Augustin Calmet (*Commentarius literalis in omnes libros Veteris Testamenti,* Latin tr. J. D. Mansi [Wurzburg: Reinner, 1789]), and E. F. K. Rosenmuller (*Scholia in Vetus Testamentum* [Leipzig: Barth, 1788]).

A more mystical Jewish approach to the exegesis of Leviticus appeared in the mid–eighteenth century with the publication of *'Or Haḥayyim* (Venice, 1742), a commentary on the Pentateuch by Ḥayyim ibn Attar. Ibn Attar's exposition of Leviticus is obscure to those not familiar with the indirect way of expression typical of qabbalistic interpretation. The Hasidic tradition of Judaism has favored Ibn Attar's exposition of Leviticus.

About 1770 Moses Mendelssohn, a very influential figure in the history of Jewish biblical exegesis, began to publish his German translation of the Hebrew Bible and its commentary. The commentary portion of this project was carried out by others commissioned by Mendelssohn. The exegesis of Leviticus fell to Naphtali Hirz Wessely, whose exposition (edited by Mendelssohn) reflects the state of the more critical biblical reading of the late eighteenth century (St. Petersburg: Buchdruckerei der kaiserlichen Akademie der Wissenshaften, 1852). Accordingly, Wessely pays close attention to historical and philological matters, citing where relevant the opinions of the traditional Jewish commentators.

Another Jewish treatment of Leviticus showing a more critical approach is that of Shadal, or Samuel David Luzzatto (*Hattorah,* vol. 3, *Vayyiqra* [Padua: Francisco Sacchetto, 1874]). This brief volume consists mostly of the Hebrew text of Leviticus with an Italian translation and brief comments on selected passages.

One of the most popular Jewish expositions of Leviticus comes from the hand of the eighteenth-century Russian Jew Meir Laib B. Yeḥiel Michael (Malbim), who commented on the whole OT. Although Malbim displays a thorough knowledge of the Jewish exegetical tradition of Leviticus, as do most Jewish commentators, he was also well acquainted with the works from the leading non-Jewish thinkers of the modern age. His discussion of the Love Commandment (Lev 19:18), for example, reflects an acquaintance with Kant's concept of the Categorical Imperative and points out that midrashic interpretations of Leviticus (Akiba in the *Sipra*) had anticipated Kant. In this way Malbim sought to fortify exegetically a traditional Jewish understanding of Leviticus in the face of a growing Reform school in Judaism. To this end Malbim rigidly employed the literal approach to exegesis, departing from the homiletical expositions that had characterized much of traditional Jewish biblical interpretation.

Andrew A. Bonar's lengthy *Commentary on the Book of Leviticus* (5th ed. [London: Nisbet, 1875]) has proved popular among conservative Protestant interpreters. Bonar accepts Mosaic authorship of Leviticus and argues for typological interpretation of Levitical legislation. Even more widely influential has been the work of C. F. Keil on Leviticus in the *Biblical Commentary on the Old Testament* with F. Delitzsch (tr. J. Martin [Edinburgh: Clark, 1872]). Keil's exegesis of Leviticus shows detailed interest in the Hebrew text and culls from the best of eighteenth- and nineteenth-century philological research from the Continent. Typology plays a much lesser role in Keil's exposition, although in his general remarks on Lev 1–5 he certainly allows for Christological interpretation of the Levitical sacrificial system. Leviticus is taken by Keil to be from the hand of Moses.

Similarly the contribution from F. Gardiner to the multi-volume *Lang's Commentary on the Holy Scriptures* (vol. 2 Anglo ed. [New York: Scribner, Armstrong, & Co., 1876]) accepts Mosaic authorship. This work draws heavily from the Church Fathers as well as from eighteenth- and nineteenth-century commentators on matters doctrinal, practical, and critical, including numerous text-critical observations. Another erudite conservative Protestant exposition of Leviticus was produced by George Bush (*Notes, Critical and Practical on the Book of Leviticus* [Chicago: H. A. Sumner & Co., 1881]). In this extensive verse-by-verse commentary, Bush considers the sacrificial laws to be no more than "a burdensome round of unmeaning ceremonies" apart from a measured NT typological interpretation. Along the same lines note S. H. Kellogg's large volume *The Book of Leviticus* (London: Hodder & Stoughton, 1891).

Research into modern Pentateuchal criticism as presented in several monographs during the eighteenth and nineteenth centuries began to show its influence in the Leviticus commentaries from about the mid-nineteenth century to the present. By 1869 Th. Nöldeke had identified the priestly narrative, which included all of Leviticus, woven throughout the Pentateuch alongside the other ancient sources J and E (*Untersuchungen zur Kritik des Alten Testament* [Kiel: Schwers'sche Buchhandlung, 1869]). The dating of P was formidably argued by J. Wellhausen to be post-monarchic, and thus Mosaic authorship of Leviticus was considered by many to be out of the question (*Die Composition des Hexateuchs und der historischen Bücher des Alten Testaments,* 2d ed. [Berlin: G. Reimer]). Critical analysis of P has further isolated certain literary components within Leviticus. In 1877 A. Klostermann identified Lev 17–26 as a section of the book unto itself, which he labeled the Holiness Code ("Beiträge zur Entstehungsgeschichte des Pentateuchs," *ZTK* 38 [1877] 401–5), derived from the formula "You are to be holy for I, Yahweh, your God, am holy," which occurs with some frequency in these chapters. The view of H and P in Leviticus as non-Mosaic literary products has grown to be a favored position in many commentaries, especially in the twentieth century.

In 1880 A. Dillmann produced for the Kurzgefasstes exegetisches Handbuch zum Alten Testament series his revision of A. W. Krobel's 1857 commentary on Exodus and Leviticus. Dillmann later updated this work further with V. Ryssel (*Die Bücher Exodus und Leviticus* [Leipzig: Hirzel, 1897]), yielding a careful and detailed work which was to have considerable influence on critical exegesis of Leviticus in Europe for several decades into the twentieth century.

Note also the exegesis from Hermann L. Strack's *Die Bücher Exodus-Leviticus-Numberi* (Kurzgefasster Kommentar [Munich: Beck, 1894]), Franz von Hummelauer's *Commentrius in Exodum et Leviticum* (Paris: Lethielleux, 1897), Alfred Bertholet's *Leviticus* (Tübingen: Mohr, 1941), Bruno Baentsch's *Exodus, Leviticus, Numeri* (Göttingen: Vandenhoeck & Ruprecht, 1903), and David Hoffmann's two-volume *Das Buch Leviticus übersetzt und erklart* (Berlin: Poppelauer,

1905 & 1906). Hoffmann's work, along with that of A. B. Erlich (*Randglossen zur hebräischen Bibel,* vol. 2 [Leipzig: Hinrichs, 1909]), represents the best full-length, modern Jewish treatment of Leviticus, which regularly utilizes traditional rabbinic opinions along with acute original and informed exegesis. Erlich often suggests emendations of the Hebrew text.

A brief treatment of Leviticus came forth from S. R. Driver and H. A. White, as a volume of P. Haupt's *Hebrew Polychrome Bible* (ET: London: Clark, 1898), displaying Driver's English translation in a color code to indicate the various literary sources (H, P, later additions). The book includes historical and philological notes on each chapter of Leviticus. Along similar source-critical lines A. R. S. Kennedy wrote his commentary for the New Century Bible in 1910 (*Leviticus-Numbers* [New York: Oxford, 1910]), offering only brief notes on the Hebrew text, as did A. T. Chapman and A. W. Streane in their 1914 Leviticus volume for The Cambridge Bible.

C. R. North's contribution on Leviticus in *The Abingdon Bible Commentary* (New York: Abingdon, 1920) 278–97, provides a concise commentary on larger portions of Leviticus, reflecting what has come to be the standard critical view of P and H in Leviticus as late, non-Mosaic literary products. So also does the work of W. F. Lofthouse, in his chapter on Leviticus in *Peake's Commentary on the Bible* (London: Thomas Nelson & Sons, 1937) 196–212. Lofthouse includes brief comparative anthropological observations on cultic purity with reference to Lev 11–14. Note also F. L. Ceuppens, *Het boek Leviticus,* for Beelen's Het Oude Testament (Brugge: Beyaert, 1934), and Paul Heinisch, *Das Buch Leviticus* in the Bonner Bible (Bonn: Hanstein, 1935).

The 1940 commentary by A. Noordtzij, *Het boek Leviticus* (Kampen: Kok, 1940), is a particularly noteworthy conservative Protestant work on Leviticus that has recently been made available in English (*Leviticus* translated for The Bible Student's Commentary by R. Togtman [Grand Rapids, MI: Zondervan, 1982]). Noordtzij traces much of the contents of Leviticus to the wilderness era but acknowledges that Israel would likely have added to the basic Mosaic body of legislation throughout the OT period. This Dutch scholar also notes the particular Jewish social structure during the post-exilic period, in the absence of the monarchic institutions. His commentary offers lucid observations on the consciousness of ancient peoples as it related to religion and worship and to the purpose for the cultic laws of Leviticus.

Other international expositions include Alberto Vaccari, *Levitico tradatto con note* in La Sacra Biblia del Pontificio Instituto Biblico (Florence: Salani, 1943) 275–340; Martin Thilo's *Das alte Testament ausgelegt für Bibelleser,* vol. 1 (Gutersloh: Bertelsmann, 1947) 281–350; A. Clamer, *Levitique, Nombres, Deuteronome,* vol. 2 of L. Pirot's Saints Bible (Paris: Letouzey et Ane, 1946) 1–207; W. H. Gispen, *Het boek Leviticus verklaard for the Commentar op het Oude Testament,* ed. G. Aalders, W. Gispen, and J. Ridderbos (Kampen: Kok, 1950); and Heinrich Schneider, *Das 2–5 Buch Moses: Leviticus,* for F. Notscher's Das Alte Testament (Wurzburg: Echter-Verlag, 1952).

Nathaniel Micklem authored the exegetical and homiletical sections to the book of Leviticus in *The Interpreter's Bible,* vol. 2 (Nashville: Abingdon-Cokesbury, 1953) 1–134; P. P. Saydon produced the Leviticus portion of *A Catholic Commentary on Holy Scripture* (ed. B. Orchard, E. F. Sutcliffe, R. C. Fuller, R. Russell [London: Thomas Nelson, 1953]) 229–44.

In 1962 Martin Noth published his *Das dritte Buch Mose, Leviticus* in the Alte Testament Deutsch series (Göttingen: Vandenhoeck & Ruprecht, 1962), which became available in English three years later (*Leviticus: A Commentary,* tr. J. E. Anderson, OTL [Philadelphia: Westminster, 1965]). In HAT Karl Elliger produced his extensive commentary *Leviticus* (Tübingen: Mohr [Siebeck], 1966). Elliger's volume offers the most thorough analyses of the literary sources within Leviticus to date. Twentieth-century critical studies of the Pentateuch have generally maintained the distinction in the priestly source between the basic narrative and the ritual prescriptions. In Leviticus, the primary narrative (often tagged "Pg") begins at chapters 8–10, reporting the consecration of Aaron and his sons according to the divine instructions in the preceding priestly narrative section found in Exod 39. Lev 16 is also regarded by many to belong to Pg. The ritual prescriptions of Lev 1–7 and the purity laws of Lev 11–14 are said to have been inserted later into the narrative by exilic or post-exilic redactors. The commentary by Elliger provides identification of two main literary hands at work (Po^1 and Po^2) in the additions within Lev 1–7. Elliger does not see the same literary process behind the purity-law chapters but rather an accumulation of disparate priestly purity rulings more or less thematically arranged. To the Holiness Code of Lev 17–26 Elliger assigns four literary strata (Ph^1—Ph^4). Many scholars consider H to have been a compilation independent of Lev 1–16. Elliger regards H as having incorporated much from older, pre-exilic priestly traditions but having taken literary form after the exile for the purpose of supplementing P. Most scholars regard Lev 27 as an even later addition.

Whether from a traditio-historical approach, as in Noth's work, or a literary-critical angle, as in Elliger, the critical commentaries in the twentieth century generally share the view that the book of Leviticus is the result of an involved process of tradition in the history of post-monarchic Israel.

Superb, concise treatments of Leviticus within one-volume commentaries on the whole Bible are found in *The Jerome Biblical Commentary* ([Englewood Cliffs, NJ: Prentice Hall, 1968] 67–85) by R. J. Faley, and in *The Interpreter's One Volume Commentary on the Bible* ([Nashville: Abingdon, 1971] 68–84) by Jacob Milgrom. These articles reflect the current state of research on the book of Leviticus, which understands much of the ritual material to date from early times in ancient Israel, though cast in a literary arrangement by the P school during post-exilic centuries.

Modern shorter commentaries include J. L. Mays, *The Book of Leviticus,* vol. 4 of The Layman's Bible Commentary (Richmond: John Knox Press, 1963); N. H. Snaith's *Leviticus and Numbers* (CBC [London: Nelson, 1967]); Rita J. Burns, *Exodus, Leviticus, Numbers* in the Old Testament Message series (Wilmington, DE: Michael Glazier, 1983).

Recently there have appeared exegetical commentaries by Protestant scholars with a fresh interest in expounding the Hebrew text historically yet with a relevance for modern Christian readers of Leviticus. Gordon J. Wenham has written a commentary for the NICOT series (*The Book of Leviticus* [Grand Rapids: Eerdmans, 1979]), offering full exegesis with an eye toward a Christian understanding of the regulations without rampant typology. Wenham does not insist on Mosaic authorship but cannot accept a post-exilic date for Leviticus. R. K. Harrison (*Leviticus: An Introduction and Commentary* for the Tyndale Old Testament Commentary series [Downers Grove, IL: Inter-Varsity Press, 1980]) argues for Mosaic authorship. Both Wenham and Harrison have made use of recent anthropological studies on ritual in ancient societies. Sharing the concern for a specifically Christian theological exposition of Leviticus is G. A. F. Knight's *Leviticus* in The Daily Bible Study Series (Philadelphia: Westminster Press, 1981), which allows for Mosaic origins of some Leviticus material.

The most recent commentary on Leviticus is the BKAT volume by Rolf Rendtorff, which to date has appeared only in two initial fascicles (Neukirchen-Vluyn: Neukirchener, 1985) covering Lev 1:1–5:26 (6:7) and providing an introduction to chaps. 1–7.

The history of the interpretation of Leviticus has its point of departure in the plain meaning of the text, or what the Jewish scholars have called the *pešat.* At some point during the biblical period, the cultic and social prescriptions of Leviticus had virtually no other meaning than the *pešat.* But as we have seen, as early as 100 B.C. the plain meaning posed problems for many Jews, and so alongside the *pešat* allegorical renderings grew. Spiritualized or allegorical interpretation went on to become the favored method in Christian exposition of Leviticus, particularly when Christian exegetes sought to apply texts from Leviticus to ethical and social issues of their respective ages. The Jews, however, soon discarded allegory and learned to augment the *pešat* of Leviticus through *midraš,* as first seen in *Sipra,* and this remained up until recent times their primary approach to expounding Leviticus for Jewish existence.

The Christian exegetes received from their canonical NT documents, such as the Epistle to the Hebrews, yet a third way to interpret the laws of Leviticus, in typology. This became the preferred method for Christian exposition of theology and doctrine from Leviticus, while allegory (to varying degrees) provided more practical interpretations from Leviticus for Christian life. So much attention was paid to allegory and typology that, from about the third century, Christian exegesis characteristically had little to say about the *pešat* of Leviticus.

Midrash, allegory, and typology began to lose their value for significant interpretation of Leviticus before the growing dominance of historical critical consciousness in biblical interpretation since the eighteenth and nineteenth centuries. The questions have been adjusted. To learn the meaning of Leviticus for existence before God (for which these methods sufficed since antiquity), exegetes have increasingly had to return to the *pešat* critically considered. For modern exegesis this has involved asking questions about authorship, literary sources, setting in life, anthropological and *religionsgeschichtliche* issues, etc. Thus most modern commentaries on Leviticus, Jewish or Christian, scarcely ever attempt to allegorize or do midrash, and only occasionally do we find recent exegesis that enthusiastically offers typological interpretations.

Currently, then, the exegesis of Leviticus continues to revolve around the *pešat,* and modern commentaries normally fall into one of two categories. There are those whose primary concern is the clearest presentation of the *pešat* that modern critical methodologies (source-, form-, tradition-criticism, etc.) can produce (Noth, Elliger, Rendtorff). Then there are those works, normally by Christian commentators, that aim to expound the theological and moral relevance of the *pešat* for modern believers (Knight, Wenham, Harrison).

Postscript: Two works on Leviticus have recently appeared. B. Levine has contributed *Leviticus* ויקרא to The JPS Torah Commentary published by The Jewish

Publication Society (1989). This is a delightfully crisp and lucid commentary. The volume has the Hebrew text of the Leningrad Codex B 19A in one column with the NJPS translation in an adjoining column. Levine provides insight into the text by drawing on comparative material from the ancient Middle East and the rich rabbinic traditions. The volume is enhanced by eleven excursuses on vital topics. R. L. Harris has just authored "Leviticus" in *The Expositor's Bible Commentary with the New International Version of the Holy Bible* published by Zondervan Publishing House (1990). This fine work, written from a conservative and evangelical perspective, offers an extensive introduction.

The Message of Leviticus

The message of Leviticus is important to biblical theology, for it addresses the fundamental issue of how the people of God may maintain their relationship with the holy God. Throughout this commentary in the sections entitled *Comment* and *Explanation,* the theology of the text is pursued. In order to provide some unity to that material and to encourage readers to turn to the detailed comments and explanations, a brief essay on some key theological themes is presented here: holiness, God's presence, the covenant, sacrifice, and Leviticus and the NT.

1. HOLINESS

In Leviticus Yahweh makes himself known to Israel as their holy God. Holiness is not one attribute of Yahweh's among others; rather it is the quintessential nature of Yahweh as God. This is supported by the declaration that his name is holy (20:3; 22:32), for as Eichrodt says, "[God's] nature and operation are summed up in the divine Name" (*Theology of the OT,* 1:274). Holiness thus distinguishes Yahweh from all other creatures (1 Sam 2:2). When Yahweh manifests himself, his holiness is visible as glory. Vriezen defines כבוד, "glory," as "the radiant power of His Being" (*An Outline,* 150). In the words of van Imshoot (*Theology of the OT,* 47), "Glory is not identical with holiness; it stresses power which is included in holiness; furthermore glory is often the exterior manifestation of power and holiness or of Yahweh Himself, while holiness always denotes Yahweh's intimate nature and has often a moral aspect which is not formally included in the concept of glory." "Holiness" thus refers to Yahweh's inner nature and "glory" to his outward appearing. Because his holiness "implies his absolute power over the world" (Vriezen, 151), mighty upheavals in nature attend God's appearing:

> For behold, Yahweh is coming forth out of his place,
> and will come down and tread on the high places of the earth.
> And the mountains will melt under him
> and the valleys will burst apart,
> like wax before the fire,
> like waters poured down a steep place (Mic 1:3–4; cf. Judg 5:4–5).

In such a manifestation Yahweh is truly "majestic in holiness, glorious in mighty deeds" (Exod 15:11; cf. Henrix, *ErbAuf* 65 [1989] 178–79). It is little wonder that the vision of the holy God is both awe-inspiring and frighteningly terrible (9:23–24). Humans either retreat in dread or bow in contrite worship. Because his glory is so consuming, God must wrap himself in clouds and deep darkness in order to protect those who serve and worship him (Ps 97:2–3).

Yahweh, being holy, is a קנא, "zealous," God (Deut 4:24). His zeal motivates him to create and to redeem (Isa 48:9–11). Conversely, when he is spurned, he corrects and punishes (26:14–39). קנא also connotes "jealousy." It is "an emotion springing from the very depths of personality: as the zealous one Jahweh is a person to the highest possible degree" (von Rad, *OT Theology,* 1:207). Because Yahweh is jealous for the integrity of his being God, he demands exclusive worship. Thus the first commandment of the Decalogue orders Israel to have no other gods (Exod 20:3). On this matter von Rad says, "Jahweh's zeal consists in the fact that he wills to be the only God for Israel, and that he is not disposed to share his claim for worship and love with any other divine power" (1:207–8). That is, his holy nature will not allow him to tolerate his people worshiping any other deity or object (19:4; 26:1). Blasphemy falls within this same perspective. To swear against God is the height of hubris, and to use his name vainly is an insult to his holy character. Blasphemy is thus such a brazen affront to the sovereign Lord that it carries the death penalty (24:10–23).

Because only Yahweh is intrinsically holy, any person or thing is holy only as it stands in relationship to him. Thus there are degrees of holiness depending on the proximity of an item or person to Yahweh. The degrees of holiness are clearly witnessed in the description of the Tent of Meeting and the pattern of OT worship. The closer a person or thing gets to God the more holy it becomes, and the holier it must be lest it be consumed by his holiness. The degrees of holiness are seen in the description of the wilderness encampment:

Holy of Holies	high priest
Holy Place	priests
altar of whole offering	Levites
court	congregation for worship
camp	congregation and resident aliens
outside the camp	those temporarily unclean
area away from camp	those with enduring uncleanness
wilderness	Azazel, demons, very unclean animals and birds

(Cf. E. Leach, *Culture and Communication,* 84–88.)

At the center of the camp was the sanctuary; its precincts were holy. Within the sanctuary stood the Tent of Meeting. It had two compartments. The forecourt was very holy. The innermost part of the sanctuary, the adytum, where Yahweh was present, was "the holy of holies," i.e., the holiest place. The camp itself was common, while the wilderness, the area most distant from the camp, was a frightful place, the abode of evil spirits.

The gradation in holiness was reflected in the order of the congregation. The people were holy (Exod 19:4–6). Therefore, they had to live by higher standards than their neighbors (18:2–5, 24–30). They lived in the camp and could enter the court of the sanctuary as long as they were in a state of ritual purity. The priests were holier, enabling them to serve at the altar and to enter the holy compartment of the Tent when duty required. They, thus, had to live by stricter standards than the congregation, particularly in regard to whom they could marry and for whom they might become defiled by a death (21:1–7). The high priest, being the holiest member of the community, had to live by an even higher standard. He had to marry a virgin, and he could not defile himself by the death of anyone save perhaps in the case of his wife's death (21:10–15). Only he was permitted to enter the adytum and then only on specific occasions (16:1–2). Yahweh affirmed the holy standing of the priests, for he said that he made the high priest (21:15) and all the priests holy (22:9, 16). Conversely, those who had an enduring uncleanness had to live outside the camp. That which was defiled, such as the goat for Azazel, was banished to the wilderness where it died.

Moreover, the classification of land animals parallels the stratification of the congregation: only large and small cattle free from defect could be offered on the altar (1:2; 22:18–29); Israelites were permitted to eat of a slightly larger group of ruminants (11:2–8); the animals that could serve them, like the camel and the horse, were a larger group (cf. Milgrom, "Ethics and Ritual," in *Religion and Law* [Winona Lake, IN: Eisenbrauns, 1990] 179–80). Certain animals, especially those that were carnivorous or eaters of carrion, were considered detestable for the Israelites.

Laws based on the polarity of holy/common afford further insight into the meaning of the holy. A place or item was holy either because it was in Yahweh's presence or had been dedicated to him. The common was the area of normal human activity without eternal significance. It was regulated by the laws regarding clean/unclean. That which was clean could inhabit the common area. Whatever was unclean had to be made ritually pure within a prescribed time or be removed outside the camp.

A person might enter the sanctuary to worship Yahweh only in a state of ritual purity. This is a vital issue since in the normal course of daily life a person inevitably became unclean. At this point it is important to note that there were degrees of uncleanness, usually measured in the length of time something made one unclean. A person might become unclean for a day, a week, a span of some weeks, or an indefinite period, depending upon the intensity of the uncleanness. Contact with an unclean animal's carcass and normal sexual bodily emissions, for example, made a person unclean until evening (e.g., 11:27–28, 31; 15:16–18). The longest defined periods of uncleanness occurred when a woman gave birth; she became unclean for forty days for bearing a boy and eighty days for bearing a girl (12:2–5). Indefinite and continuous impurity was caused by an abnormal discharge from the genitals or by a grievous skin disease (e.g., 13:46; 15:3, 25). Things that were unclean were either imperfect in some way or touched by the shadow of death. The closer one approached death the darker or the more intense uncleanness became.

Ritual impurity could happen in any number of ways. It might result from a decision such as to eat meat from an animal that had died naturally (11:39–40; 17:15), or it could happen accidentally, such as, in ignorance, touching an object that had been made unclean in a certain way (e.g., 15:4–11). It could also result from doing necessary chores such as disposing of a deceased animal (11:24–28). A few natural processes, including an emission of semen and menstruation, rendered a person unclean (15:16–23). No one, therefore, escaped becoming unclean from time to time. It is important to stress that there was no danger or stigma in becoming temporarily unclean. Such a condition was predominantly an encumbrance on daily living. The primary concern of these purity laws was to make sure that anyone who was unclean did not enter the courtyard of the sanctuary. The power and the danger lay not with the unclean, but with the holy. The holy would consume anything unclean that came into its presence.

Whenever a person became unclean in the course of daily routine, that person had to pursue the prescribed rituals for becoming clean in order to continue to live in the camp. In cases of mild uncleanness, a person had only to wait until evening (e.g., 11:24, 31), i.e., the beginning of a new day. In cases of more intense uncleanness, a person had to bathe and wait until evening (11:25; 15:5–8). These purification rituals continually reminded the congregation that all who wished to come up to the sanctuary had to prepare themselves to enter holy ground. They might never presume to enter God's presence casually. By preparing themselves ritually, they were in a position to approach God's presence with confidence, expecting his acceptance of their worship.

A serious consequence could result from becoming unclean only if one failed to take the steps to become ritually pure. After a time, such failure was considered volitional. That person was declaring that he had no desire ever again to enter God's presence (cf. 17:16). The penalty thus was the cut-off penalty.

The laws of ritual purity regulated the need for separating the holy from the common in the ancient Israelite community. In fact, separation is a major dimension of holiness. Whatever is holy has to be removed from its usual sphere and set apart unto God. This process is called sanctification (cf. 27:14–27). To be a holy nation, Israel had to separate herself from the other nations, especially all the forms of idolatry and immorality pursued by her neighbors (18:2–5, 24–25; 20:23–26). Milgrom ("Ethics and Ritual," 188) clearly points to the reason for this requirement: "the quintessence of immorality, not to speak of impurity, is imputed to the cult of idolators." Cultic laws, such as not eating blood, and the dietary laws served to separate Israel from her neighbors, especially from participating in their cultic practices (20:24–25). Differing calendars made it virtually impossible for her to syncretize her feasts with those of her neighbors. This separation was for the achievement of a higher purpose, namely that Israel might become a holy nation.

Israel was earnestly commanded to avoid all forms of divination, sorcery, and wizardry (19:3, 26; 20:6, 27). Most repugnant to God was the practice of burning children as sacrifices to a deity named Molek. Those sacrifices both defiled the sanctuary and profaned God's name (20:3). Activities involving sorcery often involved space devoid of any sacred quality (20:2–5; Isa 65:2–3, 7). Wizardry denied Yahweh's exclusive lordship over life given up in death, over the future, and over the unseen world. Such practices were founded on the premise that there was a material force that was superior to the gods, a force that was impersonal and could be manipulated by impersonal means (Y. Kaufmann, *The Religion of Israel,* 23–24). But Yahweh, the personal God, is to be approached in word, not through magical means.

At this point an aside may be helpful. Most contemporary readers find the laws and regulations of Leviticus dry and tedious. An insightful quotation from von Rad points out that these laws were far from lifeless for the ancient Israelites:

> The line of contact between the two opposed spheres of the clean and the unclean was by no means fixed—it was a battle-line, running irregularly through daily life, particularly the life of the laity. Haggai has preserved a very informative case arising in an individual's everyday home life (Hag. ii.10–13). Was ordinary food that had come into contact with consecrated flesh made *ipso facto* holy? The priests' answer is that it is not. A second question follows. Will it be unclean if it is touched by someone who is himself unclean through contact with a dead body? The answer is, yes. We can see that behind the two answers there is a problem. Human life is lived in two spheres. There are cases in which the potency of the unclean is greater than that of the holy; but in others, as for example in all processes of expiation, the holy is stronger. These were not questions of captious scrupulosity. On the contrary, there constantly arose in the life of the individual *status confessionis*, where in the decisions given the one way or the other the whole of Jahwism and of the individual's cultic existence before God was implicitly at stake (*OT Theology*, 1:273).

By regulating a myriad of daily matters, these laws on ritual purity sought to ingrain the concept of the holy into the social consciousness of the people. The clean, i.e., the pure, the whole, the just, coincided with the holy while that which was unclean corresponded to that which was imperfect, confused, and false. By the daily observance of the ritual laws, a person sanctifies himself, developing a noble character that is in accord with the moral law (Milgrom, "Ethics and Ritual," 188). Milgrom stresses that the ethical and the cultic are intricately bound together; "in the biblical view the Decalogue would fail were it not rooted in a regularly observed ritual, central to the home and table, and impinging on both senses and intellect, thus conditioning the reflexes into patterns of ethical behavior" (191).

Another polarity inherent to the holy is that of whole/defective. That which is whole, perfect, free from blemish witnesses to the holy. The defective is imperfect, marred, or corrupt. It is that which is no longer completely congruent with its design or purpose. Therefore, only animals free from defect could be offered on the altar (22:20–24). Similarly only priests free from bodily defects might serve at the altar (21:17–21). A priest who had a bodily defect, such as a broken or shriveled limb, could not officiate at the altar. These standards were not intended to create an inferior group in Israel or to make those with a handicap second-class citizens, for the regulations made it clear that a physically disqualified priest was to receive income from the altar (21:22–23), but they were given to communicate to the people of God the nature of holiness and its uncompromising purity.

Another way to express this polarity is life/death. The holy enriches life, the corrupt robs life. Death, the opposite of the holy, was most defiling. Several laws address the issue of corpses and carcasses. Anyone who touched an animal carcass became temporarily unclean (cf. 11:24–28, 39–40), and anyone who contacted a human corpse had to go through a special purification ceremony, lasting seven days (Num 19:11–19). Priests had to shun mourning rituals and avoid contact with the dead except for their closest relatives (21:1–4). The high priest had to avoid being made unclean by the dead body of any close relative (21:10–12). Death is totally incompatible with the holiness of Yahweh.

To underscore that unclean and/or illegal behavior participates in the realm of death, some laws contain a declaratory statement classifying certain behavior as most reprehensible. Several terms are used in these statements. The instructions classify animals as clean/unclean with several unclean creatures declared שקץ, "detestable, abhorrent" (11:11, 12, 13, 20, 23, 41, 42). By eating of these animals the people made themselves detestable (11:45; 20–25). In the laws regulating sexual relations, תועבה, "abomination," depicts fertility practices, illicit sexual practices, and sorcery (18:26–30; also 18:22; 20:14). תועבה communicates that involvement in these practices degraded the people of God. זמה, "wicked, obscene, lewd," characterizes sexual relations with both a mother and daughter (18:17; 20:14). Furthermore, it describes the effect on the land, making it full of זמה, "lewdness," when fathers make their daughters prostitutes (19:29). תבל, "a confusion," classifies unnatural behavior, i.e., behavior that crosses set boundaries, such as bestiality, a confusion both of species and of social roles (18:23; 20:15–16; Deut 27:21). חסד, "disgrace, something shameful" (cf. Prov 14:34), depicts a man's sexual intercourse with his sister or half-sister, and נדה, "odious, putrid," categorizes sexual relations with a brother's wife (20:21). This group of terms reveals the destructive force immorality unleashes against the community's spiritual vitality and the its solidarity by transgressions of these laws. These practices are so antithetical to holiness that doing them profanes God's holy name (18:21; 19:12; 20:3, 21; 21:6; 22:2, 32). Parenthetically, society today is more tolerant of the types of behavior condemned by these laws than was ancient Israel. Nevertheless, society still recognizes that certain types of behavior, such as heavy drug abuse, slowly and steadily destroy a person's health and hasten death. Neighborhoods populated by heavy drug users become putrid cesspools. In ancient Israel, Yahweh sought to protect the moral and spiritual decay of the Israelite nation by bringing a series of disciplines on his people when they rebelled against him (cf. 26:14–39).

No wonder some of these laws carry severe penalties. Those penalties are being put to death (20:2, 10–16), being cut off from the community (17:4, 9, 14; 19:8; 20:3, 5, 6, 17, 18; cf. 7:20 for a discussion), and dying childless (20:20–21). The formulation of the cut-off penalty indicates that God himself was considered to be the one who executed it. Whether or not the community aided him is hard to determine. By its nature the "childless" penalty was executed by God. Holiness required God to punish sin and wickedness (10:1–2; 24:10–12, 23).

On the positive side, holiness draws a person to God and the noble. The usual way that people experience Yahweh's holiness is as love. It was his holy zeal that moved him to create his own people by delivering the Israelites from Egyptian bondage. In this great event Yahweh demonstrated that his holiness is merciful and liberating (11:45; 19:36; 22:33; 23:43; 25:38, 42, 55; 26:13, 45). Moreover, Yahweh yearned to have fellowship with the people he created. Therefore, he exhorted them: "Be holy, like Yahweh, your God, is holy" (19:2; 11:44–45; 20:7, 26a; cf. Deut 7:6; 14:2; Matt 5:48). When they are holy, Yahweh may be present among them, blessing them.

The call to be holy like Yahweh means that the people are to develop in themselves characteristics similar to his own. The process of developing these qualities is sanctification. That process is reciprocal: Yahweh sanctifies (20:8; 21:8, 15, 23; 22:9, 16, 32) and the people are to sanctify themselves (11:44; 20:7). By keeping the law and by worship, the people sanctify themselves and revere Yahweh as holy in the congregation (22:32). Yahweh himself also sanctifies them through his holy power working in their lives, affirming the noble and purging out the corrupt.

Von Rad says, "Jahweh's holiness wants to penetrate the whole of man, and is not satisfied merely with his soul" (*OT Theology,* 1:207). Obedience promotes vital devotion and purity of heart.

Yahweh has revealed the character of his holiness in the laws. This fact is underscored with the frequent occurrence of the formulae of Yahweh's self-introduction, either "I am Yahweh" or "I am Yahweh, your God," with the laws in chaps. 18–22 (see *Excursus* at 18:4). These laws described for Israel the behavior that is congruent with Yahweh's holy nature. A study of these laws then produces insight into the nature of holiness.

According to the laws in chaps. 17–26, two qualities are the girding pillars of a holy life, i.e., justice and love. Justice means equity. This is stated fundamentally in the principle of *lex talionis,* an eye for an eye, a tooth for a tooth, a life for a life (24:20). This principle does not imply that punishment was carried out by inflicting bodily injury in kind, but that punishment for harm to a person is to be commensurate with the harm done, not greater, as revenge dictates, nor less, as indulgence desires. This principle was a great advancement in law codes, for it raised personal injury from a civil tort to criminal law, increasing the social worth of a citizen (cf. *Comment* on 24:19–20). Throughout these laws the worth of each person is affirmed.

For Israel, justice meant deciding matters according to the word of Yahweh. Several specific laws set the parameters of justice. In buying and selling there are to be just weights and measures and just balances (19:35–36). A merchant is not to take advantage of the customer by diminishing the goods purchased or increasing the cost by faulty measures, let alone doing both at the same time (cf. Amos 8:5). Justice leads an employer to pay a hired worker promptly. In the OT economy, that standard meant the worker was to be paid at the end of the day, not sometime later, for he needed the wage to buy food for his family's supper. In being true to justice one does not speak ill against another, either to harm that person's reputation or to win a judgment against that neighbor from the court (19:16). In rendering judgment, the courts in Israel were to judge impartially. Neither the great nor the poor were to be favored (19:15). Moreover, it is forbidden to take advantage of another's weakness or handicap; one law says "do not curse the deaf" (19:14).

The law calls for doing justice in love. The great commandment in 19:18 says, "Love your companion, who is a person like you." In 19:33–34 that law is expanded to include the resident alien who likewise is a person like oneself. The love ordered here is primarily expressed in deeds of kindness. The emphasis falls on helping another, not on one's feelings toward another. Israel was also to rise above the natural tendency of taking advantage of foreigners. This law has a supporting pillar in Israel's redemptive history (19:34). Because Yahweh showed mercy on Israel when they were slaves in Egypt, they were to show mercy to those who were disadvantaged in some way. Thus there are prohibitions against carrying a grudge or seeking vengeance (19:18). Other laws stipulate specific, practical ways to express love toward others. A farmer, for example, was not to reap a field to the very border or gather all the gleanings. Nor was he to strip all the produce of his orchards and vineyards. The gleanings were to be left so that the poor and resident aliens might go through the fields, gathering some food in dignity (19:9–10).

Certainly antithetical to love is hating a member of one's clan or of the nation. Justice and love within the clan required integrity in sexual relationships among its members (18:6–17; 20:11–14, 17, 19–21). That bond was not to be threatened by a male having sexual relations with a family member's wife, daughter, mother, or sister. Furthermore, because certain sexual practices, such as intercourse with a woman and her mother (18:17; 20:14) and bestiality (18:23; 20:15–16), were beyond the ordinary and thus unwholesome, they were banned as wickedness.

Since reverential fear is the proper human response to the manifestation of the holy God, "fear of God," a Hebraic expression somewhat similar to the NT term "faith," is the inner attitude of one living a holy life. Fear is a mixture of love, respect, and honor. By practicing the laws of justice and mercy, the people show their fear of God (19:14). In showing respect to elders and all worthy of respect, the people fear God (19:32). One is to fear (ירא) one's mother and father (19:3). Reverence for parents is to be similar to one's reverence for God (19:30). Moreover, the fear of God guards one from harming another (25:17), and it motivates one to let a neighbor live in peace. Such fear was to prevent a master from treating a slave with cruelty (25:43). Fear of God, then, is the inner disposition essential for developing a holy character.

As revealed in Leviticus, the holy is not an abstract, metaphysical concept hanging in thin air. Rather it is the essential quality that gives eternal meaning to serving Yahweh. The call to become holy like God affects every dimension of life. This call captivates the imagination and like a gyroscope directs one's longing for purpose toward life in Yahweh's presence. While the demands of holy living are overwhelming, the promise of God's presence empowering his people encourages pursuit of the call. A holy life is a blessed life, a life of personal growth, and a life of meaning and joy. It is a life lived in communion with the Holy God.

2. Presence

The presence of the holy God is central to the legislation in Leviticus. Koch (*Priesterschrift,* 101) boldly says that on every page of the priestly material there is a trace of the happiness and the wonders of Yahweh's presence as well as a deep fear aroused by the nearness of God.

Yahweh ordered the building of the tabernacle (Exod 26). Regarding the sanctuary, he said, "I have set my tabernacle in your midst" (26:11a; cf. Exod 29:46). From there he spoke directly to Moses (1:1), and there he met with his people. At times he manifested his presence in a spectacular way; his glory descended on the tabernacle in order that the whole congregation might see that he had come near (Exod 40:34–36; Lev 9:23; 16:2). Yahweh was also present among his people as the term התהלך, "he walked about," in their midst reveals (26:12a*α*). All of life, therefore, had to be lived in consciousness of Yahweh's immanent presence. Wenham (17) writes these differing ways of speaking about Yahweh's presence show that Israel distinguished between Yahweh's general presence among them and his localized presence in the Holy of Holies. Israel also distinguished the special manifestations of the glory from these two expressions of God's presence.

The descent of the glory of the Lord was an exhilarating experience. Nevertheless, the glory would devour anyone who approached the holy unclean or unworthily. This was vividly portrayed in the incident of Nadab and Abihu, Aaron's two sons, who were struck dead by fire for violating the holiness of the sanctuary (10:1–7). On the Day of Atonement when the high priest entered the Holy of Holies, he was to be aware that he entered the inner chamber where Yahweh was mightily present (16:2). Just before entering the Holy of Holies, he put incense on hot coals in a censer in order that the cloud of smoke rising from the censer would protect him in Yahweh's presence (16:12–13).

All activity at the tabernacle took place in Yahweh's presence. The phrase "before Yahweh," which runs throughout the sacrificial regulations, not only specifies the area in front of of the Tent of Meeting, but also recognizes that the various ceremonies were done in the presence of Yahweh. Sacrifices were not made for their own sake but in order that Yahweh might accept them (cf. 1:4). Yahweh's acceptance of the sacrifices, meaning that the sacrifice was empowered to achieve its spiritual goal, was symbolized in a variety of ways. The smoke ascending from the altar was ריח ניחח, "a pleasing aroma," to Yahweh. The priests ate meat from many of the offerings, symbolizing Yahweh's acceptance of the sacrifice. Since that meat was holy, they had to eat it in a holy place, i.e., close to the presence of Yahweh.

Special times and seasons in the calendar were declared holy. They were times to rest from one's labors and worship Yahweh. Israel was to keep the Sabbath by worshiping Yahweh (19:3, 30; 26:2). Sabbath observance was a great liberating force. It freed all inhabitants of Israel, masters and servants, from the mundane chores of earthly life to worship Yahweh, to enjoy the products of their labors and to have fellowship with their neighbors. At three annual pilgrim festivals, the tribes assembled together as one congregation before Yahweh at the central sanctuary (chap. 23). These festivals were times for rejoicing in the produce of the new harvest and praising Yahweh for his blessing on the harvest. At these feasts the people remembered what Yahweh had done in calling his people into existence. They not only recited what God had done; remembering actualized in their present experience the benefits achieved by those past events. These festivals were indeed joyful occasions lived out in Yahweh's presence.

Another way the presence of Yahweh was brought near was through the hearing of his word. Yahweh had spoken his will to Israel through Moses. Thereafter, at various assemblies before the sanctuary, succeeding generations heard this word from Yahweh when these sermons were delivered. Yahweh's presence in the delivery of the word was underscored by the frequently occurring statement of self-introduction, "I am Yahweh" or "I am Yahweh, your God" (these statements are concentrated in chaps. 18–20 and scattered in chaps. 11, 21–26). They underscore that Yahweh was revealing himself in these laws and regulations.

3. COVENANT

The covenant formalized the relationship between Yahweh and Israel (cf. Exod 19–24). It was based on Yahweh's saving Israel from Egyptian bondage. Therefore, the covenant was founded on what Yahweh had done, not on the natural process (Vriezen, *An Outline,* 141). This covenant was similar to a suzerainty covenant, for Yahweh, the superior party, initiated it in order that he might have a people who worshiped him. The slogan, "I shall be your God and you are my people" (26:12), speaks to the aim of the covenant.

While the term ברית, "covenant," occurs in Leviticus only eight times (2:13; 24:8; 26:9, 15, 25, 42 [3x], 44, 45; cf. Wenham, 29), the entire book has its literary setting in the framework of the Sinaitic covenant (Exod 19:1–Num 10:10). The covenant context of Leviticus is highlighted by chap. 26, which specifies the blessings for obeying God and the curses for disobedience. This text may even be that essential component of the Sinaitic covenant (Cross, *Canaanite Myth,* 318–19). The covenant then is the legal framework for interpreting Leviticus and the entire set of regulations and laws pertaining to the cult.

The primary reason two parties enter into a covenant is for continuing communion. In Israel's case, she was "admitted into God's sphere of life" (Vriezen, *An Outline,* 141). Since God was holy, Israel had to be sanctified in order to approach this sphere. To make this possible Yahweh mercifully revealed his will in the law and provided the cult as the means for a people prone to sin to maintain the covenantal relationship. Sacrifices offered at the tabernacle were essential for Israel to find expiation from her sins and thus to continue to be acceptable to Yahweh. Also at the tabernacle the tribes gathered to worship and praise God for his blessings, especially at the great pilgrim festival. The ceremonies of these feasts bonded the tribes together into Israel, the people of God. The distinctive nature of Israel's cult is clearly articulated by Vriezen: *"Israel's God does not demand a cult from which He could reap benefit, but on the contrary He gives His people a cult that enables them to maintain communion with Him by means of atonement"* (*An Outline,* 281). The cult was not only the place where the people approached Yahweh, but it was also the place were Yahweh came to Israel (Vriezen, 286). Rapprochement was a goal of God's entering into covenant with Israel. The cult thus had its authority and full significance within the structure of the covenant.

A major provision of the covenant was Yahweh's gift of the land to Israel. The land offered Israel the opportunity to become a nation. There all members of the nation could live as brothers and sisters caring for each other as full participants in the promises of the covenant. Ideologically Yahweh continued to be the owner of the land (25:23), and he allowed his people to live there as long as they kept the laws. The land was divided up to the tribes and then to the families. Each plot became a family's inalienable patrimony. The laws guarded against its being sold or lost through indebtedness.

The gift of the land, nevertheless, carried a danger. As Brueggemann writes, "Land is an opportunity to pervert justice. Land tends to diminish the value and even the presence of the brother or sister" (*The Land,* OBT [Philadelphia: Fortress, 1977] 66; Deut 24:17–18; cf. Amos 5:10–12). And "landed people are tempted to create a sabbathless society in which land is never rested, debts are never cancelled, slaves are never released, nothing is changed from the way it now is and has always been" (Brueggemann, *The Land,* 65). In Leviticus the laws of the sabbatical year and the year of Jubilee addressed this bent to greed and to enslavement that attends settlement. They regulated the use of the land in order that Yahweh's goals for Israel might be fostered, not frustrated. Every seventh year the land was to lie fallow. This practice allowed the people to be refreshed from the previous six years of hard labor. During this seventh year they could gather what grew of itself for their personal use, but the produce of that year could not be harvested, stored, and sold. The poor, widows, orphans, resident aliens, animals, and owners, nevertheless, could take for their daily need what grew by itself. The sabbatical year was thus a deterrent to the concentration of the nation's wealth in a few families. Observance of these sabbatical years required the congregation to trust Yahweh explicitly, believing that he would bless the harvest of the sixth year so that they could store up sufficient food for the fallow year and the planting time of the next year (25:18–22). It also taught them that there was much more to life than the accumulation of goods.

Tied into the year of Jubilee, every seventh sabbatical, were the laws of redemption that provided ways for Israelites beset by debt to reclaim their land or freedom. If an Israelite sold either himself or a patrimony to offset a debt, that person or his patrimony might be redeemed by one who acted as his next of kin. Usually that person was a brother, but there was an order of relations who bore this responsibility (25:48–49). A person could also redeem himself (25:26–27). But if the debtor or the patrimony was not redeemed, that person gained his own freedom in the year of Jubilee, and his patrimony was returned free from debt in the year of Jubilee. This year of proclamation of liberty was designed to help maintain an egalitarian society in Israel. Thus every family had a right to a parcel of land that could not be lost no matter how bad their misfortunes. Moreover, the laws of release were designed to prevent a group of Israelite slaves from developing and to prevent a deep social rift between the poor and the rich from developing in Israel through the centuries.

Furthermore, Leviticus teaches there was a connection between the land and morality. When Israel obeyed Yahweh, he blessed the land, and it yielded abundantly to support its occupants (26:3–13). On the other hand, when Israel disobeyed the laws or when she followed the ways of her neighbors, her sin released impurity that was not only drawn to the tabernacle but also polluted the land (18:24–28; 20:22–24). Brueggemann insightfully expresses this concept: "Israel's disobedience and carelessness not only offends Yahweh who may respond in anger, but it also affects the land. The land has its own life and its own meaning, and the trouble disobedient Israel may bring goes beyond its own borders. It is the land that is finally abused" (*The Land,* 119). Other texts say that idolatry, lewd conduct, and wizardry were powerful polluting forces (18:17, 21–23; 20:3, 17, 21). A polluted land loses its fertility. No longer able to support its inhabitants, the land becomes so deathly sick that it vomits out its inhabitants (18:24–28; 20:22). This warning corresponds to the ultimate curse under the covenant; the land would become desolate, and Israel would be dispersed throughout the earth before her enemies (26:27–33).

The blessings and curses detailed in Lev 26 fit the pattern of most ancient covenants from the Middle East. The superior party is committed to bless the obedience of the covenant party and threatens to curse that one's disobedience. Here Yahweh promised to bless them. But if Israel disobeyed him, he asserted that he would hold them accountable and punish them. In his gracious mercy Yahweh forewarned his people that he would chastise them in stages, ever hopeful that they would repent. But if they did not repent, Yahweh would increase his punishments until he had executed the ultimate penalty, expulsion from the land. But when Israel would be in exile, Yahweh would never forget his people. In captivity Israel might repent of her waywardness, seek Yahweh, and find forgiveness with the possibility of his leading them back to the promised land.

Leviticus thus makes it explicitly clear that Israel's right to continue to occupy the land Yahweh had given her resided in her morality. That is, Israel's title to the promised land was guaranteed by the covenant, but not her occupancy of it.

4. SACRIFICE

In the centuries before the kingship, the cult was the centripetal force that held the tribes together as Israel, the people of God. It was here that the identity and character of Israel were formed. "Cult" refers to every dimension of organized service to a deity. In Israel it included the Tent of Meeting, furniture, artifacts, and priests as well as the rituals, sacrifices, and sacred seasons. Yahweh gave Moses the plans for making the Tent and its furnishings, as well as the regulations for the sacrifices, and he established the Sabbath, the high days, and the feasts in order that Israel might have a cult that in every way was in harmony with his holy nature (Exod 25–Lev 16). The Tent was the place where Yahweh promised to manifest his presence and to bless his people (cf. 9:22–24). The rituals observed at the sanctuary were the formal side of worship designed to promote spiritual communion between God and the community. That this worship was formal does not mean that it was irrelevant or dead. In the words of Eichrodt, the cult was the "genuine expression of a living religion" (*Theology of the OT,* 1:98). Furthermore, the ceremonies promoted "the glorification of Yahweh, the maintaining of communion with him, and the cleansing from sin" (Vriezen, *An Outline,* 286).

An elaborate sacrificial system was a major component of the cult. The regulations and instructions for the various sacrifices are found mostly in Leviticus. These regulations establish the types of sacrifice, the materials appropriate for each sacrifice, and the various ritual procedures. They do not articulate the ideology underlying the sacrificial system. This lack has led to the formulation of multiple theories as to the meaning of sacrifice. All theorizing, however, comes up against the barrier recognized by von Rad: "There is a realm of silence and secrecy in respect to what God works in sacrifice" (*OT Theology,* 1:260). Without entering into debate with these theories at this point, some of the major theological themes related to making sacrifices as found in Leviticus may be presented.

Insight into ancient Israel's view of sacrifice is discernible from key terms in these regulations and from the structures in which they are given. Based on the structure of 1:1–5:26(6:7), the sacrifices consisted of two categories. To the first category belong sacrifices that can be presented as one so desires, the whole offering, the grain offering, and the offering of well-being (chaps. 1–3). The whole offering was the main sacrifice offered by the community. There was a daily morning whole offering, and Num 28:3, 8 speaks of a daily evening whole offering. On high days like the Sabbath (Num 28:9–10), the Day of Atonement (16:3, 5), and the days of the pilgrim festivals (Num 28:16–29:38), many additional whole offerings were made by the entire community. During times of crisis when the community made urgent petitions to Yahweh, additional whole offerings were made (Jer 14:12; Ps 20:2–5[1–4]). Little is said in the OT about occasions for an individual to present a whole offering, even though the regulations in chap. 1 are for whole offerings presented by individuals. The text in 22:18 speaks of presenting a whole offering in payment of a vow or as a freewill offering. When this kind of sacrifice was chosen for either of these purposes, it was much more expensive than fulfilling either of them with an offering of well-being, for in contrast to that offering nothing of an animal sacrificed as a whole offering was returned to the presenter.

While a grain offering could be made on its own (cf. 6:7–11[14–18], 12–16 [19–23]; Num 5:11–31), it usually accompanied an animal sacrifice making a meal of bread and meat (e.g., 7:12, 13; Num 15:2–5; 28:19–20, 27–29). At the Feast of Weeks people presented a new grain offering (מנחה חדשה), i.e., the firstfruits from the new harvest. It consisted of two loaves baked out of fine flour with yeast (23:16–17, 20; Num 28:26). The permission of yeast witnesses to the exuberant joy the community felt at harvest time. Many texts prescribe both a libation (נסך) and a grain offering (e.g., 23:13, 18, 37; Num 6:15, 17), but no regulation for a libation is found in the OT.

Usually an individual presented an offering of well-being as an expression of that person's reverence for Yahweh. Lev 23:19, which prescribes this offering in the liturgy for the Feast of Weeks, is the only text that prescribes a public offering of well-being. On special occasions such as the coronation of a king (1 Sam 11:15) or the dedication of the Temple (1 Kgs 8:64), sacrifices of this kind were freely made. Two reasons explain this: (1) the joyful nature of this sacrifice coincided with the festivities, and (2) the sacrifice itself provided meat for feasting. (It needs to be remembered that meat was a rarity for most ancient peoples.) There were three kinds of offerings of well-being: a praise offering, a votive offering, and a freewill offering (7:11–18; 22:21). A praise offering was presented to extol Yahweh for a special blessing. A votive offering was made in fulfillment of a vow that had been made imploring Yahweh to redeem or to bless in a certain way. A freewill offering was presented out of a grateful heart, overflowing with joy.

These three general offerings are also grouped by the phrase ריח ניחח, "a soothing aroma," i.e., the smoke rising from the burning of the fat and other parts (1:9, 13, 17, etc.; but for a purification offering in 4:31 [but cf. *Comment*]). The phrase ריח ניחח means that the aroma arising from the sacrifice moved Yahweh to be favorably disposed to its presenters. Should Yahweh be angry, the aroma placated his anger. More importantly it stimulated his memory. There is an intimate tie between smell and memory. Memory was a key catalyst in the dynamic interplay between Yahweh and his people. When the people of Israel sought to stir Yahweh's memory, they sought to have him act toward them in light of his past commitments, beginning with his promises to Abraham (Gen 12:1–3; cf. 26:42). Memory aroused Yahweh to act graciously toward the offerer(s). Whom Yahweh remembered, he blessed. This picture further communicates that a sacrifice was offered directly to Yahweh. Or to say it another way, making of sacrifice was not to be viewed as a routine done with little regard to God's response.

In the second category are sacrifices to expiate a sin: the purification offering (חטאת; 4:1–5:13) and the reparation offering (אשם; 5:14–19, 20–26[6:1–7]). These two types of sacrifices were made by individuals or the congregation because of a specific sin. A purification offering was presented to make expiation for a sin committed accidentally or out of human frailty. A reparation offering was for expiation from an offense for which restitution was possible or for violation of anything sacred.

These two sacrifices belong together as those that achieve expiation (כפר; 4:20, 24, 31, 35; 5:16, 18). "Expiate" means to purge the impurity released by a sin, to remove the sinner's guilt with the granting of forgiveness, and to restore the relationship between the sinner and God (cf. *Excursus* at 4:20–21). Whoever sinned presented the prescribed sacrifice(s), and the priest manipulated the blood. The tradition teaches that the presenter must approach the altar in a contrite, repentant spirit. The handling of the blood was the most crucial part of the ritual. Blood had this power because Yahweh had so endowed it, because it carried the animal's life force, and because it represented a life surrendered to the holy on behalf of the life of the offerer (cf. 17:11–12). If one of these sacrifices was offered according to its regulation and Yahweh accepted it (1:4), expiation was achieved. On this basis Yahweh granted the sinner forgiveness. Forgiveness did not automatically attend the presentation of a sacrifice; it resided in Yahweh's sovereign will.

According to 1:4 the whole offering also made expiation. Nothing is said about what type of sin it expiated. Interestingly, the phrase נסלח לו, "he is forgiven," is not used with a whole offering. Furthermore, there is a significant difference in the blood rites between a whole offering and a purification offering. The blood of a whole offering was dashed against the altar (e.g., 1:5b), but the blood of a purification offering, depending on its level, was sprinkled either before the curtain in front of the Holy of Holies and smeared on the horns of the altar of incense inside the Holy Place (e.g., 4:5–7a) or else smeared on the horns of the main altar (e.g., 4:25a) in order to cleanse these respective pieces of cultic furniture from the miasma released by the sin, which had become attached to the respective furniture, and to remove guilt. The rest of the blood was poured out at the base of the altar, not dashed against the altar (e.g., 4:7b, 25b). Another major difference between these two offerings was that all of a whole offering save for the hide was burned on the altar, but only the fat and entrails of a purification offering were burned on the altar (e.g., 4:8–10). The rest of the animal of this type of sacrifice was burned outside the camp (e.g., 4:11–12). These differences indicate that there was a vast difference in the effect of a whole offering from that of a purification or a reparation offering. There is no indication in the regulations that a whole offering was offered for specific sins. Since it had expiating force, it must then have expiated the offerer or the community from their basic sinfulness as humans.

Sacrifices served many purposes, but the primary purpose was to maintain communion between God and the supplicant(s). The variety of purposes addressed by a sacrifice may be discussed under three headings: sacrifice as a gift to God, sacrifice as a means of expiation, and sacrifice as a means of communion between Yahweh and members of the community.

a. *Sacrifice as a Gift to God*

Sacrifice was the presentation of a gift to Yahweh. The regulatory terminology communicates this clearly. A generic term for the various sacrifices is קרבן, "gift, oblation." The first rite in a sacrificial ritual is הקריב, "present," which, of course, comes from the same root as קרבן, "gift." The term אשה ליהוה means either "a fire offering for Yahweh" or "a gift to Yahweh" (cf. n. 1:9.g.). Based on the latter meaning, this phrase adds more weight to viewing sacrifices as gifts.

A sacrifice was a gift to Yahweh in recognition of his sovereign lordship. A citizen would not presume to enter the presence of a king without a gift; neither would a worshiper approach Yahweh, the King of Israel, without a gift. The term מנחה, which specifically means "a grain offering" in cultic texts, may witness to this perspective on a sacrifice, for in other passages it is used for "a present" offered to a superior (Gen 43:11) and for "tribute" (1 Kgs 5:1[4:21]) as well as any type of offering (1 Sam 2:29). The cost of sacrificing an animal, which for an ancient family was the basis of its livelihood, certainly bears witness to that family's recognition of Yahweh's lordship. Animals permitted as a sacrifice were even more valuable in that they normally had to be males without defect. Thus whenever an Israelite presented an offering, the family felt the cost.

The various sacrifices represented different kinds of gifts. It may be suggested that the presentation of a whole offering was an act of homage and devotion (de Vaux, *Studies*, 370; Kraus, *Worship in Israel*, 113–14). A purification offering or a reparation offering was a present of contrition and supplication. An offering of well-being was a gift of joyful praise or gratitude, and on occasion it was a gift of appreciative obligation.

b. Sacrifice as a Means of Expiation

Sacrifices were the primary means by which a person or the community as a whole overcame the wrong produced by a sin. To understand this role of sacrifice, it is helpful to consider the nature of sin. Although Leviticus does not address that issue directly, many ideas about sin may be gleaned from the texts. The texts assume gradations of sins. In Num 15:27–31, e.g., a distinction is made between acts done with a high hand, i.e., deliberate transgressions, and accidental and inadvertent sins (שׁגגה). According to Num 15:30, a high-handed act carries the "cut-off" penalty (cf. 7:21), which means, among other things, that it is beyond the power of the sacrificial system to remedy. The kinds of sin that could be expiated, however, included inadvertent sins and sins of deception (5:1–4 and 5:21–22[6:2–3]). Included in the list of expiable sins in 5:21–22(6:2–3) are clandestine practices to secure another's property, going even so far as to conceal such actions by swearing falsely, and the failure of a witness to heed a public oath requiring anyone who had been a witness to testify about a pressing community matter. Although, from a present-day perspective, these sins are considered willful and serious, expiation could be made for them under the ancient sacrificial system. The distinction between purification offerings, which were for sins of error, and reparation offerings, which were for accidental violations of the sacred and for restitutable offenses, further witnesses to a gradation in the kinds of sins. Another evidence of gradation is visible in the phrase מפשׁעיהם לכל־חטאתם, "from their acts of rebellion to all their sins," used twice in the regulation for the Day of Atonement (16:16, 21). פשׁע, "revolt," has its setting in the political sphere, but it can also apply to an individual's wrongdoing, pointing out the willful, hostile nature of an act against Yahweh. חטא, "sin," on the other hand, includes any kind of deviant behavior from a minor incident to a major transgression (cf. *Excursus* on חטא at the beginning of *Comment* to chap. 4). Thus the law recognizes lesser and greater sins. While specific sacrifices expiated the lesser sins, the Day of Atonement provided general expiation from all sins for the entire congregation. A significant insight is made by Milgrom (*Cult*, 104–27), who has discovered the way in which a willful sin might be expiated. He reasons that according to the law a person had the option of reducing a flagrant sin to an expiable sin by contrite repentance and the presentation of a reparation offering (cf. *Excursus* on אשׁם in *Comment* to 5:14–26[6:7]).

In light of the preceding, committing a sin produces a complex pattern of consequences. Because it is disobedience of a law given by God, a sin places a person's relationship with Yahweh in jeopardy. If a sin is committed against another, it, of course, damages the relationship between the parties involved. Any sin is thus detrimental to the community's welfare and solidarity. Another factor is that every sin carries its own penalty. This idea is twofold. On the one hand, a defined penalty attends a specific violation of a law (e.g., the laws in chap. 20). On the other hand, there is the principle of retribution, i.e., every sin is pregnant with its own consequences (e.g., Job 20:12–18). From either perspective, a sinful deed causes an obligation to hang over the head of the sinner. The doer is responsible for his act. The idiom נשׂא עון, (lit.) "one carries an iniquity" (cf. 5:1, 17), bears witness to the burden that accompanies every sin. That burden is either the penalty or the retributive punishment that attends a sinful act. The person experiences that burden as guilt. After a person has sinned, that person does not have any inner power to escape the harm due (cf. von Rad, *OT Theology*, 1:268). A sinful act, in addition, unleashes impurity, which is attracted to the sanctuary (cf. J. Milgrom, "Israel's Sanctuary: The Priestly 'Picture of Dorian Gray,'" *RB* 83 [1976] 390–99 and in *SCTT*, 75–84). Thus a sin committed produces a web of complications, personal, social, and spiritual.

The offering of the appropriate sacrifice was the way Israelites addressed these multiple consequences resulting from a sin. When the person who had sinned presented the animal at the altar, that one laid a hand on the animal's head, identifying the animal as his and making sure that the achievement of the sacrifice accrued to his favor. In making an offering, no surrogates were possible. It is assumed that at this step the offerer made a confession of sin or a word of praise or a statement of intent concerning the offering. The prophets, selected psalms, and the rabbinic tradition forcefully teach that personal remorse and contrition were essential for an expiating sacrifice to be effectual. Whenever the sin was against property, in addition to offering a sacrifice the guilty person had to restore that property or make compensation for it and pay a penalty of 20 percent. Restitution particularly aided the restoration of strained relationships on the human level. Furthermore, the achievement of expiation mended the relationships between the sinner and God and between the sinner and the community. That is why כפר is often translated "atonement." God forgave that sinner, restoring the relationship between the two of them. Forgiveness also meant that the person became free from the guilt attending the sin. Indeed expiation broke "the nexus of sin and calamity" (von Rad, *OT Theology*, 1:271). No longer did the guilty person have to fear retribution on any level, for all the harm released by a sin was addressed by making the appropriate sacrifice.

Another aspect of sin involves the status of the one who sins. The higher the spiritual leadership of the one who sinned, the greater the damaging force of that sin. A high priest and the entire congregation had to offer a high purification offering because their sins were more polluting (4:1–21). The political leader and a citizen offered a lesser purification offering, for their sins had less impact on the community's relationship with God (4:22–35). Because of the greater pollution released by a sin committed by those in the first group, blood rites from the sacrifice had to be done within the sanctuary (4:5–7a, 16–18a), and none of the animal's meat could be eaten (4:11–12, 21). In the case of a sin committed by a prince or an individual, the blood rites were done at the main altar, since miasma from a sin committed by one of them did not penetrate into the sanctuary (4:25a, 30a, 34a), and the meat became the priests' (6:19, 22[26, 29]). In eating this meat, the priests expressed God's acceptance of the sacrifice on behalf of the offerer.

c. *Sacrifice as a Means of Communion between Yahweh and Members of the Community*

Sacrifices were also a meal; that is why along with an animal one presented a grain offering, salt, oil, and wine (e.g., 7:12–13). Von Rad says, "The participants knew Yahweh to be invisibly present as the guest of honour" (*OT Theology*, 1:257). That communion was the intent of a sacrifice is seen in the phrase לחם אלהים, "the food of God" (21:6, 8, 17, 21; cf. 3:11; Num 28:2; Ezek 44:7). The use of this metaphor in the OT is amazing, for in contrast to the cults of Israel's neighbors in which the gods were sustained by the people's sacrifices, Yahweh was never thought to depend on sacrificial food for nourishment (Ps 50:12–13). The only connection between him and a sacrifice was the sweet savor of the smoke ascending from the altar. While this was true, it was also believed that Yahweh was a personal God who sought the fellowship of his people. The primary sacrifice for a shared meal between Yahweh and a family was an offering of well-being, for the majority of the meat was returned to the offerer. The meal from that sacrifice strengthened the spiritual bond between Yahweh and that family. In the words of Eichrodt, "the act of eating together signifies participation in a common source of life, and common contact with the power of a particular object creates an intimate association and fellowship which cannot be broken without the most serious consequences" (Eichrodt, *Theology of the OT,* 1:155). Moreover, because an animal was slaughtered according to a set ritual, such an occasion was a sacrament (1:154).

5. LEVITICUS AND THE NEW TESTAMENT

Leviticus makes some significant contributions to understanding the NT. Throughout the sections entitled *Explanation,* themes from Leviticus are traced into the NT.

Four of these contributions may be highlighted here. First, the information on the sacrificial system is vital to understanding Jesus' sacrificial death. Its perception of sin and atonement provides essential insight into both the need of and the benefits available through Jesus' sacrifice. Through his sacrifices all who believe on him have forgiveness of sins and eternal life (Rom 3:21–28; John 6:47).

Second, according to the NT, Jesus is the ultimate high priest. Leviticus offers insight into what this role meant for Jesus and what special requirements were laid on him in order to fulfill this role, both in his earthly ministry and in his session at the right hand of the Father (Heb 3–5, 7–10). The NT, furthermore, teaches that all believers in Jesus are priests (1 Pet 2:9; Rev 2:6; 20:6). Leviticus offers great insight into what that role for believers constitutes, and it lays before them the special requirements placed on priests to live a holy life in order that they might have the spiritual standing to perform their role effectively.

Third, the tabernacle and its operation were a gift under the covenant in order that the congregation might continue to have access to the Holy God. In the New Covenant, Jesus himself becomes the sanctuary for all who believe on him. Because the regulations and laws taught Israel how to approach God, they provide insight into how believers may approach God and worship him. Whereas one who sinned might find forgiveness through the proper sacrifice under the old covenant, believers who sin now have access to God for forgiveness through Jesus, their sanctuary. Jesus serves as their Advocate, their High Priest, in order that they might live a blessed life, free from bondage to sin, and with the hope of an eternal inheritance. The great spiritual benefits available through Jesus may be better appreciated through the study of Leviticus.

Fourth, the call to be holy like Yahweh is clearly restated in the NT. Jesus taught, "Be you perfect as your heavenly Father is perfect" (Matt 5:48). Peter heard this well, for he makes this call the keystone of his first epistle (1:15–16). Holiness is the goal of all believers in Jesus, who are called *οἱ ἅγιοι*, "the holy ones, saints" (Acts 9:13, 32; Rom 8:27; 12:13; Eph 2:19; etc.). Since all the laws in Leviticus offer insight into the nature of the holy, the study of these laws is profitable for Christians. Although Jesus did away with the laws of ritual purity (e.g., Matt 15:10–20//Mark 7:14–23), he strengthened the call to holy living. The laws of personal relationship continue to address Christians, though they have to be translated from one era to another and one culture to another, for they reveal the principles essential to holy living. In addition, through the study of the ancient law we discover how these principles were applied to concrete situations. Then we have paradigms for applying those principles to concrete situations in contemporary society.

I. Regulations for Sacrifices (1:1–7:38)

Bibliography

Abba, R. "The Origin and Significance of Hebrew Sacrifice." *BTB* 7 (1977) 123–38. **Albright, W. F.** *Penitence and Sacrifice in Early Israel.* Leiden: Brill, 1963. **Anderson, G. A.** *Sacrifices and Offerings in Ancient Israel: Studies in Their Social and Political Importance.* HSM 41. Atlanta: Scholars Press, 1987. **Baker, D. W.** "Division Markers and the Structure of Leviticus 1–7." *Studia Biblica 1978. I. Papers on Old Testament and Related Themes.* Ed. E. Livingstone. Sixth International Congress on Biblical Studies, Oxford, 3–7 April 1978. JSOTSup 11. Sheffield: JSOT Press, 1979. 9–15. ———. "Leviticus 1–7 and the Punic Tariffs: A Form Critical Comparison." *ZAW* 97 (1987) 188–97. **Bertholet, A.** "Zum Verstandnis des alttestamentlichen Opfergedankens." *JBL* 49 (1930) 70–78. **Blome, F.** *The Opfermaterie in Babylon und Israel.* Vol. 1. BibOr 4. Rome: Apud. Pont. Institutum Biblicum, 1934. **Boer, P. A. H. de.** "An Aspect of Sacrifice: II. God's Fragrance." In *Studies in the Religion of Ancient Israel.* VTSup 23. Leiden: Brill, 1972. 37–47. **Branden, A. van den.** "Lévitique 1–7 et le Tarif de Marseille, CIS I, 165." *Rivista degli Studi Orientali* 40 (1965) 107–30. **Büchler, A.** *Studies in Sin and Atonement in the Rabbinic Literature of the First Century.* London: Oxford UP, 1928. **Caquot, A.** "Un sacrifice expiatoire à Ras Shama." *RHPR* 42 (1962) 201–11. **Coleman, J. E.** "Origins of Old Testament Sacrifice." *CBQ* 2 (1940) 130–44. **Couturier, G.** "Le sacrifice d'«action de Gràces»." *Eglise et théologie* 13 (1982) 5–34. **Davidson, A. B.** *The Theology of the Old Testament.* Edinburgh: T. & T. Clark, 1961. **Davies, D. J.** "An Interpretation of Sacrifice in Leviticus." *ZAW* 89 (1977) 387–99 (= *Anthropological Approaches to the Old Testament.* Ed. B. Lang. Philadelphia: Fortress; London: SPCK, 1985. 151–62). **DeGuglielmo, A.** "Sacrifice in the Ugaritic Texts." *CBQ* 17 (1955) 76–96 (196–216). **Dion, P. E.** "Early Evidence for the Ritual Significance of the 'Base of the Altar': *around Deut 12:27 LXX.*" *JBL* 106 (1987) 487–90. **Donohue, J. J.** "Sin and Sacrifice: Reflections on Leviticus." *AER* 141 (1959) 6–11. **Durand, X.** "Du rituel sacrificiel au sacrifice biblique." In *L'Ancien Testament Approches et Lectures.* Ed. A. Vanel. Le point théologique 24. Paris: Editions Beauchesne, 1977. 31–61. **Dussaud, R.** *Les Origines cananéennes du sacrifice israelite.* 3rd ed. Paris: Presses Universitaires de France, 1941. **Fevrier, J. G.** "Les rites sacrificiels chez les Hebreux et a Carthage." *REJ* 3 (1964) 7–18. **Fransen, I.** "La loi du sacrilège (Lévitique 1,1–10,20)." *BVC* 30 (1959) 21–30. **Gayford, S. C.** *Sacrifice and Priesthood.* London, 1924. **Goodsir, R.** "Animal Sacrifice—Delusion or Deliverance?" In *Studia Biblica 1978. I. Papers on Old Testament and Related Themes.* Ed. E. Livingstone. Sixth International Congress on Biblical Studies, Oxford, 3–7 April 1978. JSOTSup 11. Sheffield: JSOT Press, 1979. 157–60. **Gray, G. B.** *Sacrifice in the Old Testament: Its Theory and Practice.* Oxford: Clarendon, 1925. Reprint, ed. H. M. Orlinsky with a prologomenon by B. Levine. New York: KTAV Publishing House, 1971. **Gray, J.** "Cultic Affinities between Israel and Ras Shamra." *ZAW* 52 (1949/50) 207–20. **Haldeman, I. M.** *The Tabernacle, Priesthood and Offerings.* New York: Revell, 1925. **Hamilton, V. P.** "Recent Studies in Leviticus and Their Contribution to Further Understanding of Wesleyan Theology." In *A Spectrum of Thought.* Ed. M. Peterson. Nashville: Parthenon Press, 1982. 146–56. **Haran, M.** "The Ark and the Cherubim." *IEJ* 9 (1959) 30–94. ———. "The Nature of the 'ʾŌhel Môʿēdh' in Pentateuchal Sources." *JSS* 5 (1960) 50–65. ———. "The Complex of Ritual Acts Performed inside the Tabernacle." *Scripta Hierosolymitana* 8 (1961) 272–301. ———. "The Symbolic Significance of the Complex of Ritual Acts Performed inside the Israelite Shrine" (Heb.). In *Y. Kaufmann Jubilee Volume.* Ed. M. Haran. Jerusalem: Magnes, 1960. 20–41. **Hendel, R. S.** "Sacrifice as a Cultural System: The Ritual Symbolism of Exodus 24,3–8." *ZAW* 101 (1989) 366–90. **James, E. O.** *Sacrifice and Sacrament.*

New York: Barnes & Noble, Inc., 1962. ———. *The Origins of Sacrifice.* Port Washington, NY: Kennikat Press, 1971. **Janowski, B.** *Sühne als Heilsgeschehen.* WMANT 55. Neukirchen-Vluyn: Neukirchener, 1982. **Kidner, F. D.** *Sacrifice in the Old Testament.* London: Tyndale, 1952. ———. "Sacrifice—Metaphors and Meaning." *TynBul* 33 (1982) 119–36. **Knierim, R.** *Die Hauptbegriffe für Sünde im Alten Testament.* 2nd ed. Gütersloh: Mohn, 1967. **Koch, K.** *Die Priesterschrift von Exodus 25 bis Leviticus 16: Eine überlieferungsgeschichtliche und literarkritische Untersuchung.* FRLANT 71. Göttingen: Vandenhoeck & Ruprecht, 1959. **Kraus, H.-J.** *Worship in Israel: A Cultic History of the Old Testament.* Tr. G. Buswell. Richmond, VA: John Knox Press, 1965. **Kurtz, J. H.** *Sacrificial Worship of the Old Testament.* Tr. J. Martin. Grand Rapids: Baker Book House, 1980. **Leach, E.** "The Logic of Sacrifice." In *Culture and Communication: The Logic by which Symbols Are Connected; An Introduction to the Use of Structuralist Analysis in Social Anthropology.* Cambridge: Cambridge UP, 1976. 81–93 (= *Anthropological Approaches to the Old Testament.* Ed. B. Lang. Philadelphia: Fortress; London: SPCK, 1985. 136–50). **Levine, B. A.** "Ugaritic Descriptive Rituals." *JCS* 17 (1963) 105–11. ———. "The Descriptive Tabernacle Texts of the Pentateuch." *JAOS* 85 (1965) 309–18. ———. *In the Presence of the Lord.* Leiden: Brill, 1974. **Lods, A.** "Israelitische Opfervorstellungen und -bräuche." *TRu* 3 (1931) 347–66. **Löhr, M.** *Das Raucheropfer im Alten Testament: Eine Archäeologische Untersuchung.* Schriften der Königsberger Gelehrten Gesellschaft. Geisteswissenschaftliche Klasse 4/4. Halle: Max Niemeyer, 1927. **Lyonnet, S.**, and **Sabourin, L.** *Sin, Redemption and Sacrifice: A Biblical and Patristic Study.* AnBib 48. Rome: Pontifical Biblical Institute, 1970. **McCarthy, D. J.** "The Symbolism of Blood and Sacrifice." *JBL* 88 (1969) 166–76. **Médebielle, A.** "Le symbolisme du sacrifice expiatoire en Israel." *Bib* 2 (1921) 146–69, 273–302. **Merx, A.** "Kritische Untersuchung über die Opfergesetze Lev. I–VII." *Zeitschrift für wissenschaftliche Theologie* 6 (1863) 41–84, 164–81. **Milgrom, J.** "Sacrifices and Offerings, OT." *IDBSup* 763–71. **Motyer, J. A.** "Priestly Sacrifices in the Old Testament." In *Eucharistic Sacrifice.* Ed. J. Packer. London: Church Book Room Press, 1962. **Oesterley, W. O. E.** *Sacrifices in Ancient Israel.* London: Hodder & Stoughton, 1937. **Ottosson, M.** "Sacrifice and Sacred Meals in Ancient Israel." In *Gifts to the Gods: Proceedings of the Uppsala Symposium 1985.* Ed. T. Linders and G. Nordquist. Acta Universitatis Upsaliensis. Boreas. Uppsala Studies in Ancient Mediterranean and Near Eastern Civilizations 15. Uppsala: Academiae Ubsaliensis, 1987. 133–36. **Rainey, A. F.** "The Order of Sacrifices in Old Testament Ritual Texts." *Bib* 51 (1970) 485–98. ____. "Sacrifice and Offerings." In *The Zondervan Pictorial Encyclopedia of the Bible.* Ed. M. C. Tenney. Grand Rapids: Zondervan, 1975. 194–211. **Rendtorff, R.** *Die Gesetze in der Priesterschrift.* FRLANT 62. 2nd ed. Göttingen: Vandenhoeck & Ruprecht, 1963. ———. *Studien zur Geschicte des Opfers im Alten Israel.* WMANT 24. Neukirchen-Vluyn: Neukirchener, 1967. **Rigby, P.** "A Structural Analysis of Israelite Sacrifice and Its Other Institutions." *Eglise et théologie* 11 (1980) 299–351. **Ringgren, H.** *Sacrifice in the Bible.* New York: Association Press, 1963. **Rodriguez, A. M.** *Substitution in the Hebrew Cultus.* Andrews University Doctoral Dissertation Series 3. Berrien Springs, MI: Andrews UP, 1979. 75–232. **Rost, L.** *Studien zum Opfer im Alten Israel.* BWANT 113. Stuttgart: W. Kohlhammer, 1981. **Rowley, H. H.** *Worship in Ancient Israel: Its Forms and Meanings.* London: SPCK, 1967. ———. "The Meaning of Sacrifice in the Old Testament." *BJRL* 33 (1950) 74–110. **Sirard, L.** "Sacrifices et rites sanglants dans L'Ancien Testament." *ScEc* 15 (1963) 173–97. **Snaith, N. H.** "Sacrifices in the Old Testament." *VT* 7 (1957) 308–17. ———. "The sin offering and the guilt offering." *VT* 15 (1965) 73–80. ———. "The Sprinkling of Blood." *ExpTim* 82 (1970/71) 23–24. **Steinmueller, J. E.** "Sacrificial Blood in the Bible." *Bib* 40 (1959) 556–67. **Stevenson, W. B.** "Hebrew ʿOlah and Zebach Sacrifices." FS A. Bertholet. Ed. W. Baumgartner. Tübingen: Mohr, 1950. 488–97. **Thompson, R. J.** *Penitence and Sacrifice in Early Israel outside the Levitical Law.* Leiden: Brill, 1963. **Urie, D. M. L.** "Sacrifice among the West Semites." *PEQ* 81 (1949) 67–82. **Vaux, R. de.** *Studies in Old Testament Sacrifice.* Cardiff: University of Wales, 1964. **Wyatt, N.** "Atonement Theology in Ugarit and Israel." *UF* 8 (1976) 415–30. **Yerkes, R. K.** *Sacrifice in Greek and Roman Religion and Early Judaism.* New York: Scribner, 1952.

Form/Structure/Setting

Lev 1–7 contains regulations for presenting various kinds of sacrifices and for offering different kinds of animals within each sacrificial category. Special attention is paid to the role of the priests in the rituals and to the portions that become the priests' as their source of income. However, there is no extensive treatment of the theological significance of the various sacrifices or of sacrifice in general. Emphasis is on the kinds and forms of sacrificial materials and the rituals for each kind of sacrifice.

This section is bounded by an introduction (1:1–2) and a conclusion (7:[35–36]37–38). The introduction ties this section to Exod 40, which recounts Moses' setting up of the Tent of Meeting in the wilderness and the divine glory filling it. It carries forward the theme that the directions God had given Moses on the mountain for making the cultic furnishings and setting the cult into operation were carried out exactly according to God's instructions.

This section consists of two units, chaps. 1–5 and chaps. 6–7. Both are concerned with the same sacrifices, but the sacrifices are listed in a different order and treated from a different perspective. The sacrifices in chaps. 1–5 appear in this order:

Whole offering (chap. 1)
Grain offering (chap. 2)
Offering of well-being (chap. 3)
Purification offering (4:1–5:13)
Reparation offering (5:14–26[6:1–7])

The order found in chaps. 6–7 is as follows:

Whole offering (6:1–6[8–13])
Grain offering (6:7–11[14–18])
Grain offering at ordination (6:12–16[19–23])
Purification offering (6:17–23[24–30])
Reparation offering (7:1–10)
Offering of well-being (7:11–21, 28–34)

The primary differences between these two lists are the location of the offering of well-being and the inclusion of the ordination offering in the second list. Rendtorff (*Lev,* 8) suggests that the order arises from the importance placed on the various sacrifices in different eras. The offering of well-being may, however, appear last in the second list, for in practice it was usually offered after the other sacrifices so that a clan or family might eat a festive meal after the various sacrificial rituals of the day. Moreover, Rainey (*Bib* 51 [1970] 486–88) differentiates these two lists according to the intent of the units: chaps. 1–5 are didactic and chaps. 6–7 are descriptions of administrative details.

Chaps. 1–5 fall into two parts: chaps. 1–3 and chaps. 4–5. The offerings in chaps. 1–3 concern sacrifices that are offered as a ריח־ניחוח ליהוה, "soothing aroma to Yahweh"—the whole offering (עלה), the grain offering (מנחה), and the offering of well-being (זבח שלמים). The rituals for the two offerings involving animals are ordered according to the kind of animal presented. Since these sacrifices may be offered freely by the laity, no occasion is defined for their being offered. The offerings described in chaps. 4–5 concern sacrifices that כפר, "expiate," specific sins: the purification offering (חטאת) and the reparation offering (אשם). The former offering is regulated according to the status of the person required to make the sacrifice, and the latter offering is regulated according to the nature of the offense. This latter regulation differs from the others in that it lacks a ritual prescription. With the offerings in chaps. 4–5 there are two pericopes that describe typical cases requiring these sacrifices (5:1–7; 5:20–26[6:1–7]). For anyone who had sinned, the presentation of one of these offerings was not optional. That person had to make such an offering to continue as a member of the covenant community.

The formula in 1:2a*β*+b encompasses the material in chaps. 1–5, but it serves as a specific heading to chaps. 1 and 3. The regulations for the whole offering and the offering of well-being (3:1–7) are dependent on the case statement אדם כי־יקריב מכם קרבן ליהוה, "anyone of you who presents an offering to Yahweh." The case is introduced by כי, "that" (1:2), and the regulations by אם, "if" (1:3; 3:1). This pattern suggests that at one stage these two offerings followed each other. The regulations for grain offerings (chap. 2) now separate these two sets of regulations; that the regulations for grain offerings are independent from the regulations for the whole offering and the offering of well-being is evidenced by their being headed by a case formula and by the wording of that formula, נפש כי, "a person that." The present location of chap. 2 results from the customary practice of presenting a grain offering with a whole offering.

The authoritative formula וידבר יהוה אל־משה, "Yahweh spoke to Moses," sets off chap. 4 from chaps. 1–3 and 5:14–26(6:7) from 4:1–5:13. Nevertheless, the formula of chap. 2 accords with that of the purification offering in 4:2. The similar style of נפש כי, "if a person," links together chaps. 2 and 4 along with 5:14–26(6:7). In the present order of the book, then, chaps. 1–5 are tied together by the alternating pattern of the formula for the cases a:b::a:b (chaps. 1:2::3:4–5).

The material found in chaps. 6–7 is a composite of instructions (תורות) concerning other details about the sacrifices. It is especially concerned with the holiness of the sacrifices and the proper handling of the remains after the sacrificial ritual has been performed. There is, furthermore, special interest in the parts that the priests receive. A major insertion deals with the daily grain offering presented by a priest at his ordination. At the core of this section are five instructions pertaining to the various sacrifices: the whole offering (6:1–6[8–13]), the grain offering (6:7–11[14–18]), the purification offering (6:17–23[24–30]), the reparation offering (7:1–10), and the offering of well-being (7:11–21). The instruction for the offering of well-being also has attracted two extended portions from the large corpus for instruction of the laity; the first pericope contains regulations about the eating of fat and blood (7:22–27), and the second gives more details about the various kinds of offerings of well-being (7:28–34). In the present setting this material, which is addressed to the priests, is included to increase the laity's knowledge about procedures at a cultic center. This position is supported by the broader heading about speaking to the Israelites at 1:2a*α*, which applies to all of chaps. 1–7 in the final form of Leviticus. The merit of this position is confirmed by the directions to "speak to the Israelites" in 7:23a*α* and 28a*α*, which supplement the restrictive headings to speak to Aaron and his sons found in 6:2a*α*

(9aα) and 18aα (25aα). The inclusion of these later pericopes in the corpus of chaps. 6–7 makes sense only if the final editor perceived that the audience of these chapters was the whole community. In this light chaps. 6–7 are composed from material taken from the priestly corpus and set here for the further instruction of the laity in the procedures of the cult. The two headings addressed to the priests have been preserved in order to communicate to the laity that they are learning professional information that may not be modified by them. The laity learn why the priests do certain things and what portions of an offering are the priests' rightful income. Moreover, this teaching equips the laity to make sure that the priests are doing their task properly. This leads to greater involvement of the laity in the ritual worship of Yahweh, rather than their dependence on the priests and passivity in the rituals at the sanctuary.

At the end of this section is a complex summary statement (7:35–38). Vv 35–36 are the conclusion to chaps. 6–7, but vv 37–38 serve to conclude chaps. 1–7. They make a tie back to 1:1. But they differ from 1:1, for in them Moses receives the laws on Mount Sinai rather than from the Tent of Meeting. Hoffmann (1:20–24) posits that the corpus found in chaps. 6–7 was given on Mount Sinai along with the material in Exod 25–31. In making mention of Mount Sinai, it establishes a connection with the report of Moses' ascension of Mount Sinai in Exod 24:15–18. Moreover, the presence of only one mention of the consecration sacrifice in chaps. 1–7, at 6:12–16[19–23], and its position in the list after the reparation offering rather than after the grain offering as its location in 6:12 are additional evidences that this list is not the exclusive summary to chaps. 6–7. Rather this summary ties chaps. 1–7 into Exod 29–40, and it points forward to Lev 9. The design of this concluding formula is not to contradict 1:1, in which Moses receives the revelation from the Tent of Meeting, but to tie chaps. 1–7 into the larger corpus of Exod 25–Num 10.

What is the historical setting for these regulations of sacrifices? They go back to the origin of Israel as a nation at Mount Sinai. As soon as Israel became the people of God under the covenant, their sacrificial practices, which had roots reaching far back into the patriarchal era, had to be regulated to conform to the worship of the one true God. Pure worship was essential in order to fulfill the commandment "you shall have no other gods before me" (Exod 20:3). Given the human proneness to sinning, maintaining fellowship with the holy God, the very purpose of the covenant, would be possible only if the people had ready access to means of atonement. The sacrificial system was inaugurated to provide that access. In other words, from its very inception a community or nation that worshiped Yahweh had to have cultic and sacrificial standards that were regulated to correspond to the exclusive demands of Yahweh, their holy God. The tradition recognizes this necessity, for it regularly underlines the authority of these regulations with the formula "Yahweh spoke to Moses."

These sacrificial instructions were composed for the instruction of the laity about the regulations for the presentation of sacrifices, particularly those presented by an individual. They may have had a place in the cultic ritual. The priest may have recited a specific regulation for the sacrifice being presented before beginning the ritual, or a priest may have delivered them each day when he began to receive public sacrifices. The fact that the basic ritual consists of short, simple sentences, as Koch (*Priesterschrift*, 45–61) has demonstrated, indicates that these rituals were originally composed for oral instruction. During the pre-exilic era these instructions would have been housed at the central shrine and at other altars throughout the land. Thus the laity scattered throughout the promised land would have access to them. When Jerusalem became the cultic center, a copy, becoming the standard copy, would have been kept at the Temple.

It is very likely that these regulations fell out of use during the various eras of apostasy in the history of ancient Israel. And it can be supposed that in various eras the regulations were used differently than suggested above. Thus they had a long and complex history of transmission before they came into their present form. Additions were incorporated to give authority to local practices. Other changes were made to bring the regulations into line with changing social and cultic practices. During seasons of conflict with the encroachment of specific pagan practices into the true worship of Yahweh, statutes and exhortations were incorporated to warn the people of the danger of such practices. Furthermore, words and phrases were added to the corpus to clarify details, to explain archaic terms, and to regulate more precisely various practices.

Such editorial activity took place throughout the time of the Judges and the Kingdom. There were, furthermore, periods of major changes in the cult, times that would have inspired such editorial work on the cultic corpus. Some of those times may be mentioned. David made Jerusalem the cultic center by bringing the ark to Jerusalem (2 Sam 6; 1 Chr 15–16). He did much to organize the orders of the priests and Levites to serve at the new cult center and to establish the choral music of the cult (1 Chr 15:10–24; 16:37–42; 23:1–24:3). Solomon followed David's ordinances at the new Temple (2 Chr 8:14–15). Nevertheless, he did not have as great an impact on the ordering of the priests and matters of worship as did David, his father. Later, during the various reform movements, various changes were made at the Temple, especially under Hezekiah (2 Chr 29–31) and Josiah (2 Chr 34:1–35:19). Certain practices would have been stressed and new procedures introduced both to correct improper practices and to set up barriers against syncretistic or pagan abuses. The fact that Hezekiah had to pulverize Nehushtan, the bronze serpent that Moses had lifted up in the wilderness for the people to be healed from the bite of fiery serpents (2 Kgs 18:4; Num 21:4–9), bears witness to how a sacred relic could be turned into an object of idolatry and the radical changes that these reforming kings undertook to establish pure worship of Yahweh. Under the reform of Hezekiah and even more so under that of Josiah, especially with their making Jerusalem the single cultic center, the ancient regulations had to be edited in order to standardize the variant, permissible practices from outlying shrines and in order to prohibit variant practices judged to be syncretistic. That is, the regulations that went back to Moses were treated as an ongoing tradition until they became canonized in the Pentateuch around the time of the exile. The term "ongoing" means that these regulations were adjusted to incorporate changing practices. The basic regulations had their authority from the revelation of the covenant at Mount Sinai. Nevertheless, God continued to speak to Israel. Therefore, all changes and adjustments were considered fully authoritative, and thus they were preserved under the authoritative heading "Yahweh spoke to Moses."

With the trauma of the exile, which threatened the existence of Israel as the people of God, the priests realized that the various cultic traditions and standards needed to be collected, arranged, and preserved. Their work preserved the traditions of their ancestors in the document that is called the Pentateuch.

Regarding the genre of this section of Leviticus, these regulations may be classified as rituals (Rendtorff, *Lev,* 18–20). Another possible category for them is instructions (תורות). But who is being instructed? Rainey (*Bib* 51 [1970] 486) says that this corpus is "a pedagogical classification for the training of sacerdotal specialists." While this classification is possible, the material is addressed to the laity, as the terms אדם, "one" (1:2; 3:1), and נפש, "person" (2:1; 4:2), indicate. Furthermore, the content of this corpus is directive, not detailed and exhaustive. This is confirmed by the use of תורה, "instruction," in the section addressed to the priests in chaps. 6–7 but not in chaps. 1–5 or those parts of chap. 7 addressed to the people. Specific details, such as directions about where the layman is to stand in relation to the priest and the animal, the type of knife to be used in the slaughter, the precise manner of slaughter, and what the laity and the priest are to say are missing. Priests had to know all of these details. Thus it is hard to see how these texts were the manual of instructions for priests. Rather they are a basic outline of the procedure for sacrifice with emphasis on the ritual acts to be performed by the laity and the priest. As Noth (20) states, the laity learned about their responsibilities for presenting sacrifices and those acts that they must let the priest perform. Thus, as Rainey says, these regulations in chaps. 1–5 are didactic and those in chaps. 6–7 are descriptions of administrative details.

The literary setting of these sacrificial regulations is between the erection of the Tent of Meeting (Exod 40) and the ordination of the priests (chaps. 8, 9). According to Koch (*Priesterschrift*), this location is necessary in order that the first sacrifices to be offered on the altar (chap. 9) might be performed according to the proper standards. In this light it is inappropriate to judge the sacrificial ritual as an intrusion interrupting the narrative of Exod 25–40 from its continuance in Lev 8–10.

A. Heading to the Sacrificial Legislation and the Book (1:1–2)

Bibliography

See *Bibliography* for Lev 1:1–7:38.

Translation

[1] *Yahweh*[a] *called to Moses and spoke to him from the Tent of Meeting,* [2] *"Speak to the people of Israel and say to them: When anyone*[a] *among you presents an offering to Yahweh, you are to present as your offering*[b] *an animal from either the herd or the flock."*

Notes

1.a. Syr places the subj Yahweh after ויקרא, "and he called."

2.a. The formula אדם כי, "if anyone," is rare in the OT, occurring elsewhere only in 13:2 and Num 19:14; usually the formula is נפש כי, "if any person" (e.g., 2:1: 4:2), or איש איש אשר, "if a man, one" (e.g., 17:3, 8, 10, 13).

2.b. Sam, LXX, and Syr read a pl noun קרבניכם, "your offerings."

Form/Structure/Setting

This heading serves specifically to introduce the first subsection (1:3–3:17). But in the final edition of Leviticus it serves as the heading to the entire book.

The occurrence of both וידבר, "speak," and ויקרא, "call" in v 1 indicates the composite nature of the opening formula. Both verbs are found in introductory formulae throughout the cultic legislation. The most frequent heading is וידבר יהוה אל־משה לאמר, "and Yahweh spoke to Moses saying" (e.g., 4:1; 5:14, 20[6:1]; 6:1[8], 12[19], 17[24]; 7:22, 28; etc.). However, the expression ויקרא אליו יהוה מן, "and Yahweh called to him from . . ." is found only three times in Exod (3:4 [אלהים, "God"]; 19:3; 24:16 [MT does not specify the subject while LXX reads יהוה, "Yahweh"]). Thus this latter formula is reserved for special situations. It is instructive to compare Lev 1:1–2a*α* with Exod 19:3b*α*:

מן־ההר לאמר	יהוה	ויקרא אליו
מאהל מועד לאמר	וידבר יהוה אליו	ויקרא אל־משה

This comparison reveals that the usual formula of Yahweh's speaking to Moses is combined with the rare, special revelatory formula. In place of the phrase "from the Mount," which appears in the special formula, here stands the phrase "from the Tent of Meeting," for Moses has just erected the Tent at the foot of Mount Sinai (Exod 40:34–37). The formula is saying that Moses, no longer needing to ascend Mount Sinai to have an audience with Yahweh, received these regulations in direct communication with Yahweh at the Tent of Meeting. In fact, these regulations were the first instructions given by Yahweh from the new sanctuary.

V 2 is a general statement about presenting sacrifices. All animal sacrifices are classified as קרבן, "an oblation, an offering, or a gift." This classification may have arisen in an era of standardizing cultic procedures, as at the establishment of the first temple in Jerusalem or at the reform under Ezra.

The heading also functions as the literary tie between Exod 25–40 and Lev 1–16.

Comment

1 The introduction is bulky because the editor combines the formula for a special revelation from Yahweh with the usual commission-to-speak formula that heads various cultic regulations to underscore the authority of the cultic regulations found in Leviticus. יהוה, "Yahweh," the Israelite proper name for God, is used because God is addressing his servant Moses directly from the Tent of Meeting.

In Exod 25–31 Yahweh gives Moses the plans for אהל מועד, "the Tent of Meeting." Exod 40 records that Moses carried out those plans as he set up the Tent and all of its furniture. There the Tent of Meeting is also called משכן, "the tabernacle"; this term occurs only four times in Lev (8:10; 15:31; 17:4; 26:11). In the cultic corpus both terms refer to the same building, but they convey a different emphasis. משכן, "tabernacle," denotes the place where God שכן, "dwells," while the אהל מועד, "Tent of Meeting," is the sacred tent where Yahweh יעד, "meets," with the leader or the people on special occasions of his own choosing (cf. Exod 29:42). Cross (*Canaanite Myth,* 300) points out that its meaning, "the tent of the council or assembly," is understood by the priestly writer as "the tent of the divine-human meeting," i.e., "the tent of revelation." The picture of the Tent of Meeting in these chapters coincides very closely to that of the first Temple built by Solomon (see Figure 1).

The Tent of Meeting was a small rectangular building covered with embroidered curtains. It was divided into two rooms. At the western end was a small square room called the Holy of Holies, which housed ארן העדות, "the Ark of the Covenant." In the outer rectangular room were השלחן, "the table," for the shewbread (cf. 24:5–9), מזבח הזהב, "the golden altar," and מנרה, "the candelabra or menorah" (24:2–4). In the courtyard outside the entrance, which faced toward the east, stood מזבח העלה, "the altar of the whole offering," and הכיור, "the laver." When Moses had finished putting everything in its place, הענן, "the cloud," bearing God's presence, covered the Tent, and כבוד יהוה, "the glory of Yahweh," filled the tabernacle. (Cf. F. Cross, "The Priestly Tabernacle," in *Old Testament Issues,* ed. S. Sandmel [London: SCM Press, 1969] 39–67; M. Görg, *Das Zelt Begegnung: Untersuchungen zur Gestalt der sakralen zelttraditionen Altisraels,* BBB 27 [Bonn: Peter Hanstein Verlag G.m.b.H., 1967]; M. Haran, *Temples and Temple-Service in Ancient Israel* [Oxford: Clarendon Press, 1978] 260–75; idem, *JSS* 5 [1960] 50–65; J. Morgenstern, "The Ark, the Ephod and the 'Tent of Meeting,'" *HUCA* 17 [1942/43] 153–266; 18 [1944] 1–52; G. von Rad, "The Tent and the Ark," in *The Problem of the Hexateuch and Other Essays* [Edinburg: Oliver & Boyd, 1966] 103–24.)

2 בני ישראל, "the people of Israel," is frequently rendered "the children of Israel." But, as Levine (4) points out, that translation does not communicate that Israel is a people joined together by a covenant. The conditional clause uses אדם, "man, one," as its subject. This term is rarely used in conditional clauses in the cultic legislation. Its use establishes a tie with Gen 1:26–27, which says that God created אדם in his own image, male and female he created them (cf. Gen 5:2). The use of אדם calls attention to the exalted worth humans have (F. Maass, "אָדָם *ʾādhām,*" *TDOT* 1:84–85). It is because humans bear the image of God that they may worship him and may be forgiven and blessed by him. Moreover, אדם includes both males and females. While males are dominant in the cult, for ancient Israel was a patriarchal society, females are not excluded. After giving birth (12:6–8) or after recovering from a chronic discharge (15:28–30), a woman had to present a sacrifice. Num 5:5–7 explicitly includes a woman in the instructions on how to make expiation for a breach of faith. Num 30 regulates vows made by women; it is possible that these vows included presenting an offering of well-being as a votive offering (7:16–17). Attention needs to be given to the place that the cult and the priestly writer do give to females (cf. M. I. Gruber, "Women in the Cult," in *Judaic Perspectives on Ancient Israel,* ed. J. Neusner, B. Levine, and E. Frerichs

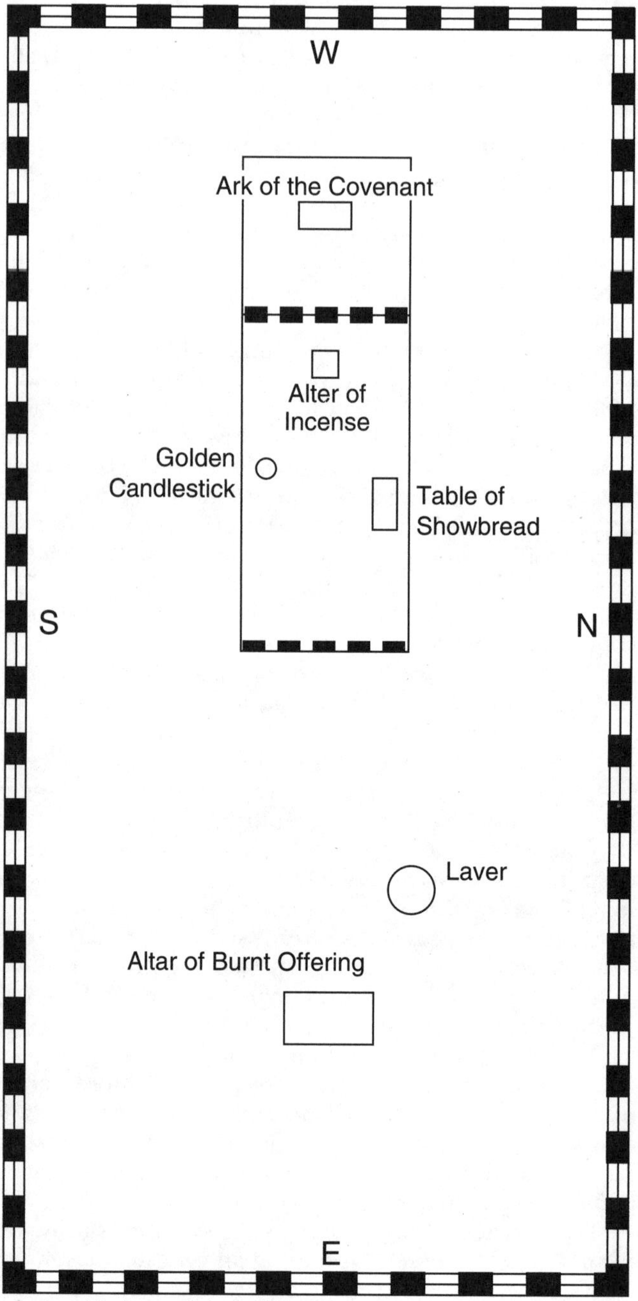

Courtesy of the American Schools of Oriental Research

Figure 1. Plan of the tabernacle and its courts.

[Philadelphia: Fortress, 1987] 36–40). In choosing to use אדם and נפש, "person," the law giver was choosing nonsexist, inclusive language. Furthermore, אדם is a racially inclusive term. It does not specifically mean "Israelites" in most of its usages; rather it is a universal term, especially in Gen 1–11 (Maass, *TDOT* 1:83–84). Therefore, this term makes it possible for Gentiles who conform to all the standards of the covenant to offer sacrifices to Yahweh.

The term for presenting an animal, קרב, "bring near," is a technical term in sacrificial regulations meaning "to present" an offering (cf. J. Kühlewein, "קרב *qrb* sich nähern," *THAT* 2:679; Rendtorff, *Studien*, 90–92, 113). Here it is specifically stated that an offering is given to Yahweh (ליהוה). This statement excludes any idea of presenting a sacrifice before the Tent of Meeting to any other deity or subordinate heavenly creature. This and similar phrases throughout the cultic law underscore the absolute monotheistic outlook of the cultic legislation. Worship is conducted directly with the supreme God; no heavenly intermediaries are ever considered to benefit from the offerings. Related to the verb הקריב, "present," is the technical term קרבן, "oblation, offering," that classifies all sacrificial offerings, including animals (1:2), vegetables and grains (2:1, 5), and articles of precious metals (Num 7:13; 31:50). It is used only for offerings or presents made to God (Dillmann, 428). This word occurs solely in Leviticus and Numbers, save for two occurrences in Ezekiel (20:28; 40:43). Transliterated into Greek, this term occurs in Mark 7:11; many English translations transliterate it as "korban" (cf. Matt 15:5–6; 27:6). In that passage it means goods or property dedicated to the Temple by a vow. Sons or daughters would make such a vow so that their parents could not presume on them for support. They used the law to deprive their parents of any assistance (cf. V. Taylor, *The Gospel according to St. Mark* [London: MacMillan, 1972] 340–42).

Explanation

The heading establishes the highest authority for the cultic legislation: Yahweh spoke directly with Moses from the Tent of Meeting. This legislation was given to Moses in order that he and the priests, his successors, might teach all the Israelites the correct procedures for presenting their sacrifices to God. Blood sacrifices were limited to animals from the herd or flock. The reason may be that an Israelite had to present an offering that came from his livelihood. Each offering was to cost him significantly; it was not to consist of an animal that he happened to kill by chance, as in hunting.

This legislation indicates that there was to be a close tie between the laity and the priests. The priests were to instruct the laity in the basic knowledge and procedures of the cult. Thus knowledge was not to be guarded by the priests in order that they might exploit it to dominate the people. Rather the laity participated with priests in making sacrifices, at least in the oldest era. The priests served to assist the laity in making the sacrifice correctly, in performing the rites at the altar, and in leading the laity to God. Their primary role was to make expiation for the party presenting the sacrifice so that that party might find forgiveness and reconciliation with Yahweh. For their labor they received specified portions of the various sacrifices. This cultic legislation is given in a way that seeks to build a bond between the priests and the laity under the covenant.

B. *Regulations for Three Common Sacrifices (1:3–3:17)*

1. *Regulation for the Whole Offering (1:3–17)*

Bibliography

Boer, P. A., de. "An Aspect of Sacrifice." VTSup 23 (1972) 37–47. **Hultgård, A.** "The Burnt-Offering in Early Jewish Religion: Sources, Practice and Purpose." In *Gifts to the Gods: Proceedings of the Uppsala Symposium 1985.* Ed. T. Linders and G. Nordquist. Acta Universitatis Upsaliensis. Boreas. Uppsala Studies in Ancient Mediterranean and Near Eastern Civilizations 15. Uppsala: Academiae Ubsaliensis, 1987. 133–36. **Loss, N. M.** "La partecipazione dei laici al rite dell' olocausto secondo Lv 1,3–13." *Sal* 23 (1961) 353–62. **Rendtorff, R.** *Leviticus.* BKAT 3/1. Neukirchen-Vluyn: Neukirchener, 1985. **Rüger, H. P.** "'Dann entfernt er seinen Kropf samt dessen Federn': Zur Auslegungsgeschichte von Lev 1,16." In *Wort und Geschichte.* FS K. Elliger. AOAT 18 (1973) 163–72.

Translation

3 *"If his offering is a whole offering,[a] he is to present a male from the herd without defect. He is to present it at the entrance to the Tent of Meeting that it may be acceptable[b] before Yahweh.* 4 *He is to lay his hand on the head of the whole offering[a] so that it may be acceptable on his behalf to make atonement[b] for him.* 5 *He is to slaughter[a] the bull[b] before Yahweh, and Aaron's sons,[c] the priests, will present the blood[d] and will dash the blood against the altar all around, which is at the entrance to the Tent of Meeting.* 6 *He is to skin[a] the whole offering and cut[a] it into pieces.* 7 *Aaron's sons,[a] the priests,[b] are to put fire on the altar and arrange wood on the fire.* 8 *Aaron's sons, the priests, will then arrange the pieces, the head,[a] and the suet[b] on the wood which is on the altar-fire.* 9 *He is to wash[a] its entrails and legs[b] with water, and the priest[c] will burn[d] all of it on the altar.[e] It is a whole offering,[f] a gift for a soothing aroma to Yahweh.[g]*

10 *"If his offering[a] for a whole offering[b] is from the flock, a lamb or a goat offered as a whole offering[c] from either the rams or the goats, he is to present a male without defect.[d]* 11 *He is to slaughter[a] it before Yahweh at the north side of the altar, and Aaron's sons, the priests, will dash its blood against the altar on all sides.* 12 *He is to cut[a] it into pieces, and the priest will arrange[b] them, including its head and its suet, on the wood which is on the altar-fire.* 13 *He is to wash[a] the entrails and the legs with water; then the priest will present all of it by burning it on the altar. It is a whole offering, a gift for a soothing aroma to Yahweh.*

14 *"If his offering to Yahweh is a whole offering of birds, he is to present[a] for his offering either doves[b] or young pigeons.[c]* 15 *The priest will present it at the altar, wring off its head, burn it on the altar, and drain[a] its blood against[b] the side of the altar.* 16 *He will remove its crop and its contents[a] and cast[b] them[c] to the east side of the altar where the fat ashes are placed.* 17 *He will tear it open by its wings, without severing[a] it completely. Then the priest will burn it on the wood of the altar-fire. It is a whole offering, a gift for a soothing aroma to Yahweh."*

Notes

3.a. The predicate nominative is placed first for emphasis; cf. n. 3:1.a.

3.b. Is the pronominal suffix objective or subjective? This is open to interpretation since its antecedent may be either the offering or the offerer. The next verse says it will be accepted for him, נרצה לו, suggesting that the offering is the antecedent in this verse.

4.a. Syr reads קרבנו, "his offering," in place of MT, העלה, "the whole offering." Interestingly this gesture of laying on of hands is not mentioned in the other rituals for a whole offering. Rendtorff (48) observes that the text says that the one presenting the animal "lays his hand on the head of the whole offering," not on the head of the bull. This language generalizes the gesture for all three rituals.

4.b. The inf constr states the purpose. The subj is not expressed. Most assume that the subj is the sacrifice (cf. 17:11). Dillmann (432) proposes that it is an abbreviated expression for לכפר (הכהן) עליו בו, "that the priest make atonement for him with it."

5.a. LXX reads שחטו, "they are to slaughter," assuming that the subj is "the priests," not the presenter.

5.b. בן, "son," may be used to express things that belong to a class or species (H. Haag, "בֵּן *bēn*," *TDOT* 2:152–53). An older view took it to mean the offspring of an animal, i.e., "the young bull."

5.c. Mss from Cairo Geniza omit בני אהרן, "Aaron's sons." This is possibly a witness to an older textual tradition.

5.d. Mss from Cairo Geniza omit את־הדם, "the blood." This may simply be an error of homoioteleuton.

6.a. Sam and LXX read pl verbs, taking the priests as the subj; cf. n. 5.a.

7.a. Syr reads הכהנים בני אהרן, "the priests, the sons of Aaron," which is an error of metathesis and which makes the subj הכהנים pl to conform to the verb and the appositional phrase.

7.b. A few Heb. mss, Sam, LXX, Syr, and Tg[mss] read a pl noun as in vv 5, 8 and as demanded by the subject בני אהרן, "the sons of Aaron." Generally the phrase is בני אהרון הכהנים, "sons of Aaron, the priests" (vv 5, 8, 11), or simply בני אהרון, "sons of Aaron" (3:5, 8, 13), or הכהן, "the priest" (vv 9, 12, 13, 15, 17). But here the reading is בני אהרן הכהן, "Aaron's sons, the priest." There is an error in the text that probably rose from a conflated reading (cf. S. Talmon, "Conflate Readings (OT)," *IDBSup* 170–73). In comparison with 6:1–6 it appears to Rendtorff (37) that הכהן, "the priest," was original and attracted the phrase בני אהרן, "sons of Aaron," from the context.

8.a. A few Heb. mss, Sam, LXX, Syr, and Tg[mss], read a *waw* before את; cf. n. 12.a. This may be a later change to incorporate the addition of these words into the text. The oldest text may have simply stated that the pieces were to be arranged; then the phrase את־הראש ואת הפדר, "the head and the fat," was added to make sure that these pieces were always placed on the altar in the right order.

8.b. פדר, "suet," occurs in the OT only with the whole offering (here, v 12; 8:20).

9.a. Cf. n. 6.a. In place of the sequence of sentences beginning with a *waw* pf, the verb of this sentence is impf because the dir obj precedes it. The grammar may be intended to convey the fact that this act is an accompanying act and not the next rite in the sequence.

9.b. The dir objs stand before the verb for emphasis. Even though these nouns are definite, they lack the sign of the dir obj, indicative of an archaic style. כרעים is the lower leg from the knee to the foot (Dillmann, 436). This term appears only in connection with cattle, members of the flock, and locusts (11:21).

9.c. LXX* reads a pl form: והקטירו הכהנים, "the priests will burn"; this is a witness to standardization of the rites so that they are performed by the priests.

9.d. Akk *qaṭāru* means "to smoke, make to smoke," and the Heb. cognates קטרת, "incense," and קיטור, "thick smoke," confirm that הקטיר means "to make something smoke."

9.e. The locative ה here indicates the place of the action (GKC §90d).

9.f. A few Heb. mss, Sam, LXX, Syr, and *Tg. Ps.-J.* add הוא as a copula; cf. 13:17.

9.g. The phrase ריח־ניחוח, "soothing aroma," frequently stands with אשה, "gift," in various combinations: אשה ריח־ניחוח ליהוה (fourteen times), ריח ניחוח אשה ליהוה (two times; Exod 29:18, 41, plus in inverted order in Lev 23:13), אשה לריח ניחח (two times; Lev 3:16; Num 18:17). The phrase ריח ניחוח occurs without אשה twenty-four times. As for the meaning of this phrase, ריח means "scent, odor, fragrance," such as the smell of a field (Gen 27:27), the fragrance of perfume (Cant 4:10), and the fragrance of nature such as the cedars of Lebanon (Hos 14:7 [6]). ניחוח, which occurs only after ריח, is taken to mean "soothing, quieting" (BDB, 629); de Boer (VTSup 23 [1972] 45–46) identifies it as an inf poʿlel of נוח. In this phrase it functions as a substantive. The phrase thus means "a soothing odor or aroma."

אשה was associated from early times with sacrifices, as its appearances in Deut 18:1; 1 Sam 2:28; 1 Kgs 9:25 attest. It has usually been taken from the root אש, "fire," to mean "an offering made by fire."

While the Tg renders it "a presentation," Jewish exegetes of the Middle Ages like Rashi and Ibn Ezra identify it as a fire oblation. Another possibility is to relate it to a root אנשׁ, which means "to establish friendly relations" (G. B. Gray, *Sacrifice*). Recently it has been rendered as "a food-offering" (NEB); this is gained by relating it to an Akk word *eššešu,* "offerings (made at *eššešu* festival)" (*CAD* 5:371–73)). This is supported by the fact that in a few passages לחם, "bread, food," is found in apposition to אשׁה, e.g., את־אשׁי יהוה לחם אלהיהם הם מקריבם, "they are presenting the gifts of Yahweh, the food of their God" (21:6; cf. 3:11, 16; Num 28:2, 24). If לחם is an insertion to define the unusual term אשׁה, this view has additional support. But if the two terms refer to distinct offerings and לחם is a food offering, אשׁה then has another meaning. Given the fact that אשׁה occurs both with the entire whole offering, which is entirely burnt on the altar, and with the grain offering, which is eaten by the priests (2:3, 10), אשׁה is thus not limited to a food offering. J. Hoftijzer ("Das sogenannte Feueropfer," VTSup 16 [1967] 114–34) relates אשׁה to Ugar *i͟tt* (*UT* 431), a word of uncertain meaning, which G. R. Driver (*Ugaritica* 6 [1969] 181–84) renders "generous, rich gifts." Rendtorff, therefore, concludes that אשׁה means that which is given to Yahweh from the sacrifice and which then belongs to him. Therefore, אשׁה is taken to mean "a gift."

10.a. Sam adds עלה, "a whole offering"; cf. n. 10.c., v 14.

10.b. Sam and LXX add ליהוה, "to Yahweh," as in v 14. This change, along with that of n. 10.a., is an effort to standardize the text to conform with v 14, but cf. v 3.

10.c. Sam omits this לעלה, "for a whole offering," because it reads עלה earlier in the sentence (cf. n. 10.a.).

10.d. Sam adds אל־פתח אהל מועד יקריב אתו, "at the entrance of the Tent of Meeting he is to present it"; cf. n. 3.b. LXX, on its part, adds *καὶ ἐπιθήσει τὴν χεῖρα ἐπὶ τὴν κεφαλὴν αὐτοῦ,* "and he will place his hand on its head," making this verse conform to v 4.

11.a. Cf. n. 5.a.

12.a. Cf. n. 6.a.

12.b. Sam reads an impf יערך, "he is to arrange," but this is simply the frequent error of confusing a *waw* for a *yod.* LXX and Vg read וערכו הכהנים, "the priests will arrange"; cf. n. 5.a.

13.a. Cf. n. 9.a.

14.a. The pf consecutive והקריב, "and he is to present," indicates the apodosis after the conditional clause (GKC §112ff).

14.b. Syr adds ליהוה, "for Yahweh."

14.c. MT בני היונה most likely includes various species of pigeons. בן, lit., "son," means here "class of." בן has been traditionally taken to mean "young" (e.g., Talmud, Rashi), but there is no linguistic evidence that requires that meaning (cf. v 5:6). Rendtorff also suggests that בני יונה refers to individual birds rather than to the species.

15.a. Sam spells this infrequently used Heb. word with an א instead of a ה. LXX and Vg have an active verb; whether this is the translators' preference due to the difficulty of the niph (so this translation) or their Heb. text read ומצה, "and he will drain," is difficult to tell; cf. 5:9.

15.b. For the difficult MT על, "on," Sam reads אל, "to," which also may be behind LXX's *πρός*, "toward."

16.a. For MT בנצתה, Sam, Syr, Tg, and *Tg. Ps.-J.* read בנצתו. The meaning of בנצתה is uncertain. From ancient times נוצה has been taken to mean "feathers" (as in Ezek 17:3, 7; Job 39:13; cf. Rendtorff, 76–78) or something loathsome (*b. Zebah.* 63b), such as the gizzard or its contents. H. Rüger (*Wort und Geschichte,* 163–72) cautions against finding a meaning for נצתה other than "feathers," since that is the clear meaning of this word in its other occurrences in the OT. While this caution is well argued, it does not exclude the possibility that the word in Leviticus is a homonym. Since it seems most improbable that a priest would pluck each bird and since the entrails and legs of a domesticated animal had to be washed of all filth, the rendering "content" is adopted to refer to the food in the digestive tract, from partly digested to feces; possibly then it is from the root יצא, "go out" (cf. Snaith, 32).

16.b. The verb השׁליך, "cast," is unusual as a cultic term (cf. Exod 22:30[31]). It appears to mean a demonstrative discarding of the crop and the feces or the feathers (Rendtorff, 76).

16.c. Sam, Syr, Tg, and *Tg. Ps.-J.* read the masculine pronoun אתו, "him," for MT אתה, "her," taking one of the birds instead of מראתו, "its crop," as the antecedent. The Eng translation requires a pl pronoun because of the compound obj.

17.a. Some Heb. mss and the versions read ולא, "and not," for MT לא, "not." While MT is the harder reading, the copula could easily have been omitted as an error of haplography. This phrase לא יבדיל, "without severing," is an example of a circumstantial clause headed by לא, "not," but not introduced by a *waw* (Joüon §159c; GKC §156f).

Form/Structure/Setting

The structure of the regulation for a whole offering is as follows:

Regulation for the whole offering (1:3–17)

I. Presentation of cattle (vv 3–9)
   A. Basic case (v 3a*α*)
   B. Ritual procedure (vv 3a*β*–9b*α*)
      1. Presentation, laying on of hands, and slaughter by the laity (vv 3a*β*–5a)
      2. Handling of the blood by the priest (v 5b)
      3. Skinning and cutting up of the animal by the laity (v 6)
      4. Preparation of the fire by the priest (vv 7–8)
      5. Washing of specified parts by the laity (v 9a)
      6. Burning of the animal by the priest (v 9b*α*)
   C. Statement of the purpose of the offering (v 9b*β*)
II. Presentation of a member of the flock (vv 10–13)
   A. Basic case (v 10a)
   B. Ritual procedure (vv 10b–13)
      1. Presentation and slaughter of the animal by the laity (vv 10b–11a)
      2. Handling of the blood by the priest (v 11b)
      3. Cutting up of the animal by the laity (v 12a)
      4. Arrangement of the animal and preparation of the fire by the priest (v 12b)
      5. Washing of specified parts by the laity (v 13a)
      6. Burning of the animal by the priest (v 13b*α*)
   C. Statements of sacrifice as a whole offering and of its purpose (v 13b*β*)
III. Presentation of birds (exception for the poor) (vv 14–17)
   A. Basic case (v 14a)
   B. Ritual procedure (vv 14b–17)
      1. Presentation of the birds by the laity (v 14b)
      2. Performance of the sacrificial rites by the priest (vv 15–17a)
   C. Statements of the sacrifice as a whole offering and of its purpose (v 17b)

(This outline is based on a protocol from R. Knierim's seminar.)

This regulation is divided into three sections, according to the animal presented:

1. From the herd (vv 3–9)
2. From the flock (vv 10–13)
3. From small birds (vv 14–17)

The first ritual is fuller than the other two. There are two reasons for this. First, details from the first ritual are assumed to be carried over to the ritual for a member of the flock. Second, some information, such as that for preparing the fire, is mentioned only here because it is assumed that a whole offering is to be the first sacrifice offered at the newly established Tent of Meeting.

The basic ritual consists of seven steps:

1. Presentation, הקריב (vv 3, 10, 14)
2. Laying a hand on the animal's head, סמך (v 4a)
3. Slaughter, שׁחט (vv 5a, 11a*β*)
4. Manipulation of blood, זרק (vv 5b, 11b)

5. Cutting of the animal, נתח (vv 6, 12a)
6. Washing of the innards and legs, רחץ (vv 9a, 13a)
7. Burning of the fat, הקטיר (vv 9b, 13b, 17aβ)

[Cf. Rendtorff, *Studien*, 89–111; idem, *Gesetze*, 5–7, 11–12]. A characteristic style of the rituals for large animals is the alternation of the action between the offerer and the priest. At an early period the offerer was an active participant in making a sacrifice. But as the cult became more formalized, the priests took over the duties after the presenter had laid hands on the animal's head (cf. 2 Chr 29:34; Ezek 44:11).

The ritual for offering "birds" differs so significantly from the preceding two rituals that it gives the appearance of being an appendix. In this ritual the priest performs all of the rites, and there is no mention of the offerer's laying hands on the bird's head. The differences may be explained by the postulate that this ritual arose at a much later date than the preceding ones, e.g., during the Second Temple era when the priests had assumed full responsibility for all sacrificial procedures (Elliger, 37; Porter, 23). This exception also fits the social character of the post-exilic Jerusalem, a small, poor community. However, the difference in ritual procedures may simply be accounted for by the fact that the birds are much smaller animals than cattle or sheep. As for the need of providing an alternative whole offering for the poor, this could have arisen during any era. At various times a significant portion of the population faced poverty, as Amos testifies for the eighth century B.C. and the book of Judges for the twelfth-eleventh century B.C. Thus this appendix may come from an early era.

As to the date of this regulation, the basic ritual is quite ancient, as evidenced by the short, simple sentences and the fact that many ritual acts are to be carried out by the laity (cf. Koch, *Priesterschrift*, 46–48; cf. Rendtorff, 6–9). It may be claimed that the core goes back to the formulation of the covenant at Mount Sinai.

Through the centuries this regulation underwent modifications and changes to align it with current practices. A major modification was the insertion of the phrase "the sons of Aaron" to identify specifically the priests who were to perform these rites (vv 5, 7, 8). When this happened, the original term "the priest" was pluralized along with the verb. In v 7 the term "the priest" and the singular subject with no phrase in apposition witness to an older text. The LXX has carried out the modifications even further. In several places it understands that the antecedent of the various verbs is the priests, not the laity: v 6 "they are to flay," "they are to cut"; v 9, "they are to wash"; v 12 "they are to cut"; v 13, "they are to wash." LXX witnesses to the time when the priests took over all the rites after the presenter had laid his hands on the animal's head.

Another insertion is the specification of the place to slaughter a member of the flock על ירך המזבח צפנה, "at the north side of the altar" (v 11a). This addition may have been made at a time when the area around the altar needed to be more carefully regulated because of an increase in the volume of offerings, such as at the establishment of the first temple.

Koch (*Priesterschrift*, 48) theorizes that three rites may have been transferred to the whole offering from other sacrificial rituals in an effort to standardize the rites: the laying on of hands, the dashing of the blood against the altar, and the cutting up of the animal. In *Studien* (92–93, 214–16) Rendtorff argues extensively that the act of laying a hand on the animal's head originally belonged to the ritual for a purification offering. But in his commentary (39–40) he admits that there is no solid evidence to support this theory. Elliger (34), however, claims that this act belonged originally to the whole offering. As for the blood rite, Rendtorff (*Studien*, 97–99) finds that this rite defined by the verb זרק, "dash, fling," is an essential act of an offering of well-being (e.g., 17:6). He, however, fails to discover any significance for this rite with the offering of well-being. Certainly there would have been as great a concern for the proper handling of the blood of a whole offering. Therefore, it seems just as likely that specific instructions were given for the handling of the blood for a whole offering when that offering was incorporated into the cult under the Sinaitic covenant. As for the cutting up of the animal, this regulation may also go back to the original standardization of sacrifices. Its antiquity is attested in the description of Elijah's preparation of his great sacrifice on Mount Carmel (1 Kgs 18:23, 33; cf. *Studien*, 105). But the specific mention of two parts, the head and fat (vv 8a, 12a), appears to be an insertion to insure that these two parts are placed properly on the altar.

The basic regulation underwent a systematizing and theologizing effort when the sacrificial corpus was collected and put in its present location. The whole offering became classified as an offering or oblation (קרבן; vv 2, 3, 10, 14). It was assigned expiating force (כפר; v 4b) because of the handling of the blood. Also the ascending smoke, being a soothing aroma (ריח ניחוח; vv 9b, 13b, 17b), won Yahweh's favor for the offerer. Emphasis on making the offering correctly was highlighted in order to insure that the offering was rendered acceptable (נרצה; vv 3b, 4b). Only an acceptable offering gained merit for the one who presented it.

Comment

Excursus: עלה, *"the whole offering"*

עלה, "the whole offering," comes from a root meaning (lit.) "to offer up, go up." This accords with the entire animal being consumed by fire. עלה is often rendered "holocaust," but today that word has assumed a specific historical meaning, i.e., the atrocities suffered by the Jews under Hitler's regime, so that "holocaust" is no longer a good translation for עלה. The translation "whole offering" is chosen since the whole animal is consumed on the altar.

The whole offering is the main sacrifice of the Israelite cult. At the cultic center a whole offering was offered up each morning. Some texts speak of a whole offering being offered each morning and a grain offering each evening (Ezek 45:13–15; 2 Kgs 16:15; 1 Chr 16:40; 2 Chr 2:3[4]; 13:11), but in a few texts a whole offering was offered up both in the morning and evening (Num 28:3–8; 1 Chr 16:40). The practice of the evening whole offering may have varied from era to era.

The festivals and special days of fasting called for the presentation of whole offerings. The standard for the New Moon and each day of the Feast of Passover and the Feast of Weeks was two bulls, one ram, and seven male lambs (Num 28). For the Feast of Booths there were numerous whole offerings: on the first day thirteen bulls, two rams, and fourteen male lambs (Num 29:12–16). The same number of whole offerings was offered each succeeding day save one fewer bull each day so that on the seventh day seven bulls were sacrificed (Num 29:17–35). On the final day of the feast one bull, one ram, and seven lambs were offered (Num 29:35–38). On the Day of Atonement the high priest offered up two whole offerings, one for himself and one for the people, after he had presented their respective חטאת, "purification offerings" (Lev 16:5). In addition to these primary whole offerings, other whole offerings consisting of one bull, one ram, and seven male lambs were sacrificed on this day (Num 29:7–11).

Whenever the king offered special sacrifices, the usual pattern was for him to offer whole offerings followed by offerings of well-being (שלמים; 2 Sam 6:17–18). 1 Kgs 9:25 says that Solomon presented whole offerings and offerings of well-being three times each year. Whether Solomon followed the festival calendar or a royal calendar is not recorded. A unique occasion on which whole offerings were freely and generously presented was a festival proclaimed by Hezekiah to commemorate the removal of pagan practices from Judah and the cleansing of the Temple (2 Chr 29:20–28). The whole offering was also offered freely on festive occasions as an expression of joy and enthusiastic devotion to Yahweh. When the ark that the Philistines had released reached Beth Shemesh, the citizens of that town offered up whole offerings joyfully to Yahweh (1 Sam 6:14).

Beside these presentations of whole offerings for the entire covenant community, each individual had the privilege of presenting whole offerings. In the ritual instructions of Lev 1, no occasion is mentioned for the individual's presentation of a whole offering. Thus he could present a whole offering freely in praise or petition. From other passages it is learned that one presented a whole offering for various purposes, as the fulfillment of a vow (22:18) or adherence to the stipulations of other laws; e.g., a new mother presented a whole offering as part of her purification ritual after childbirth (12:6–8), and one who had recovered from a skin disease presented a whole offering as part of the purification ritual (14:19, 20, 22, 31; 15:14, 15, 29, 30). Moreover, on taking the Nazirite vow the candidate presented a whole offering, a purification offering, and an offering of well-being (Num 6:14, 16). Should a Nazirite become defiled by being in the presence of a dead person, to purify himself he had to present several offerings, including a pigeon or a dove as a whole offering (Num 6:9–12).

The importance of a whole offering is also seen in the close tie that existed between it and the altar (Rendtorff, *Studien*, 86–88). After an altar was constructed, it was consecrated by the offering up of a whole offering on it (e.g., Gen 8:20; Judg 6:26; 21:4; 2 Sam 24:25; 1 Kgs 18:30–38). It is expressly said that whole offerings are to be offered on an altar (Deut 12:27).

The origin of the whole offerings reaches far back into antiquity, long before the cult was established in Israel. God permitted the continued use of this offering in the Israelite cult. Its ritual, though, was carefully regulated to accord with her monotheistic belief. In particular, the blood rite was carefully regulated and was assigned expiating merit (1:4). As an atoning sacrifice the whole offering was offered not so much for specific sins but for the basic sinfulness of each person and the society as a whole. Since individuals must often seek expiation for specific sins, a purification offering (חטאת) frequently preceded the presentation of a whole offering (9:7–14, 15–16; 2 Chr 29:20–36). In conclusion, the frequent presentation of whole offerings enabled the covenant community, despite the human proneness to sin, to maintain fellowship with the holy God.

3 A member of the herd (בקר), a male without defect (תמים), may be offered as a whole offering. Cattle, being the most valuable possession, are given prominence as sacrificial animals. They served as work animals and were valued for milk, meat, and hides (cf. B. Beck, "בָּקָר *bāqār*," *TDOT* 2:209–16). A male is required because of the higher value ancient society placed on the male. The animal is to be תמים, "complete, entire," i.e., free from any blemish or defect, either from birth, by accident, or by reason of illness. In Lev 22:22–24 the typical defects included are blindness, injury, maimed condition, irregular members, warts or festering sores, and damaged testicles. This standard prevented the offering of weak, deformed, or crippled animals, animals that had lost much of their value. More importantly, the animal's freedom from any defect accords with the pure, holy character of God.

The bull is to be slaughtered at the entrance of the Tent of Meeting (אל־פתח אהל מועד; cf. 17:3–9). This phrase refers to the court area between the gate and the altar. The laity may enter this area. But the area between the altar and the Tent possessed a higher degree of holiness. Only the priests are permitted to enter this area (cf. M. Haran, *Temples and Temple-Service in Ancient Israel*, 184–87). This area is also referred to by the phrase "before Yahweh." This latter phrase not only refers to a specific locality, but other passages indicate that it also means that something is done in the presence of Yahweh. This phrase thus specifies both a location and the reason why the sacrifice is performed in that location.

The sacrifice is to be offered according to the prescribed ritual so that it may be רצון, "acceptable," before Yahweh. רצון functions as a technical, cultic term to identify a sacrifice as having efficacious merit. Everything had to be done properly to insure that the sacrifice accomplished its purpose. At this point two elements are essential for a whole offering to be efficacious: the animal has to be free from defect, and the offerer himself has to lay his hands on the animal's head (cf. 22:17–30). The additional phrase כפרו עליו, "to make atonement for him," stands here to explicate further the clause "it may be acceptable on his behalf," נרצה לו. On the meaning of כפר, see the *Excursus* in chap. 4. In the cultic legislation כפר occurs with a whole offering only in this reference (elsewhere only in Ezek 45:15). Thus the inclusion of this term constitutes a theological interpretation of this sacrifice. Since there is no reference to a specific sin, it is assumed that expiation is made for the general sinful disposition of the presenter. Humans continually need to be cleansed from the impurity of sin in order to worship in Yahweh's presence.

The whole offering appeals to God's favor by sending up a ריח ניחוח, "soothing aroma" (vv 9b, 13b, 17b). Since this appeal to God for mercy is also a plea for fellowship with God, it is appropriate to use כפר, "make atonement, expiate," with this sacrifice, for it promotes reconciliation between the layman and God.

4 After bringing the sacrifice to the Tent of Meeting, the offerer lays his hand (סמך ידו) on the bull's head. סמך means "to lean on, rest on" (Judg 16:29; Amos 5:19; cf. F. Stolz, "סמך *smk* stützen," *THAT* 2:160–62). The worshiper pressed hard on the animal's head with a leaning motion.

Excursus: Laying on of Hand(s)

Bibliography

Merwe, B. J., van der. "The Laying on of Hands in the O.T." In *New Light on Some Old Testament Problems: Papers Read at 5th Meeting of Die O.T. Werkgemeenkap in Suid-Afrika.* Pretoria, South Africa, 1962. 34–43. **Péter, R.** "L'imposition des mains dans l'Ancien Testament." *VT* 27 (1972) 48–55. **Sansom, M. C.** "Laying on of Hands in the Old Testament." *ExpTim* 94

(1982/3) 323–36. **Volz, P.** "Handauflegung beim Opfer." *ZAW* 21 (1901) 93–100. **Wright, D. P.** "The Gesture of Hand Placement in the Hebrew Bible and in Hittite Literature." *JAOS* 106 (1986) 433–46. **Zeitlin, S.** "The Semikhah Controversy between the School of Shammai and Hillel." *JQR* 56 (1965) 240–44.

The meaning of this rite has received diverse explanations. Laying on of hands is a rite attested with various sacrifices: the whole offering, the offering of well-being (3:2, 8, 13), and the purification offering (4:4, 15, 24, 29, 33). Even though no ritual is given for making a reparation offering, it may be assumed that this rite was also a part of the ritual for that sacrifice. It is debated whether the person laid one or two hands on the animal. In a few places it is expressly stated that a person is to lay both hands on the object being presented (16:21; cf. Num 27:23; Deut 34:9). The usual term ידו, "his hand," is taken to mean that the presenter lays a single hand on the animal. Tg translates ידו, "his hand," in Lev 1–4 regularly with "his right hand." The Mishnah, however, requires the laying on of both hands (*m. Menaḥ.* 9.8).

Many proposals have been made to account for this rite. One position is that the person who is making the sacrifice transfers his sins to the animal (Noordtzij, 22–33). While this is the case with the goat for Azazel on the Day of Atonement (16:21), there are serious obstacles to transferring the meaning of that rite to other sacrifices. In regards to Azazel the high priest lays both his hands, not one, on the goat, and the goat, bearing the congregation's sin, becomes defiled. Therefore, it is released into the desert, not sacrificed on the altar. But the whole offering is burnt on the altar, suggesting that the animal has not been defiled. Rodriguez (*Substitution,* 217–19) and Kiuchi (*Purification Offerings,* 115) take exception to this claim, positing on the basis of 10:17 that the flesh of a purification offering could at the same time bear guilt and be classified as most holy. Their position is hard to accept since there is no conclusive evidence that the flesh of a purification offering had become polluted with guilt, for although that flesh is not burnt on the altar, it is either eaten by the priests or burned in a clean place outside the camp (4:12). Furthermore, the rite of laying on of a hand is part of the ritual of the offering of well-being, a sacrifice which has little concern with expiating sin (3:2).

Noth (22), however, thinks that a lay person transfers his own person to the animal. Another variation of this position is that with this gesture a person is claiming for himself the spiritual force or holiness that is gained through the offering (J. Pederson, *Israel,* 3–4:366). But it is still difficult to press these two interpretations to the offering of well-being.

Another theory claims that an identification is made between the offerer and the sacrifice (W. R. Smith, *Religion of the Semites,* 325; R. K. Yerkes, *Sacrifices in Greek and Roman Religions and Early Judaism,* 134). R. Péter (*VT* 27 [1972] 48–55) argues that laying a single hand on an offering is a gesture by which the offerer identifies the animal as his own, while the act of laying both hands on something (e.g., Lev 16:21; 24:14) signifies the transference of something from one party to the other, e.g., endowing another person with the special divine power that one has (Deut 34:9; H. H. Rowley, *Worship in Ancient Israel,* 133; cf. Hoffmann, 1:122). The extent of identification varies among those who hold this view. Rowley suggests that the offerer identifies himself with the animal in a way that its death removes whatever barrier stands between that person and God, and also with this rite the offerer symbolizes the surrender of the self to God in gratitude and loyalty (133). H. Gese (*Essays on Biblical Theology,* tr. K. Crim [Minneapolis: Augsburg, 1981] 104–8) believes that with this gesture the person who brings the sacrifice identifies himself with the animal so that the animal serves in that person's place. In the surrender of the animal's life on the altar to that which is holy, so too is the offerer's life symbolically surrendered. B. Janowski (*Sühne,* 220–21) takes a similar interpretation. He says that by this gesture the offerer participates in the death of the animal, which dies in place of him, a sinner. The death of the animal in that one's place symbolically represents the surrender of that person's life to God. In contrast to the rite of transference of sins to the goat for Azazel on the Day of Atonement, this rite represents a subjective transference; i.e., the animal's נפש, "life-force," takes the place of the presenter's נפש, "life-force" (cf. Lev 17:11). Kiuchi (*Purification Offering*, 116–19) likewise interprets the rite to symbolize substitution. He grounds this on the meaning of רצון as "acceptance" (cf. 7:18), but he points out that the text does not provide any clear evidence on the nature of the substitution. These positions may accord with a purification offering (4:1–5:13), although this rite is used with an offering of well-being (3:2), but nothing indicates that that offering was in any way considered a substitutionary offering (de Vaux, *AI*, 416, 448–49; Bertholet, 2–3). Whether the concept of substitution was behind the original gesture is impossible to determine from the OT texts.

While in the regulations in chaps. 3 and 4 the act of laying on of a hand is followed by the slaughter of the animal, Rendtorff (35–40) notices that in this passage the words following in v 4 are "so that it may be acceptable on his behalf to make atonement for him." He interprets this clause to be an explanation of this rite; i.e., the rite is necessary for a sacrifice to be spiritually efficacious for the individual who presents the animal. In other words, this gesture insures that the merits of the sacrifice accrue to the offerer. Furthermore, this rite distinctly eliminates a surrogate from making an offering on behalf of another, as the Jewish tradition stresses (cf. *b. Menaḥ.* 93b).

It is highly probable that while the offerer lays his hand on the head of a whole offering, he makes a confession of his unworthiness and his sinfulness as a frail human being and states his trust in God, either by reciting a prayer or by quoting from a psalm. Possible psalms for such occasions that have survived are Pss 40, 51, and 66. The priest may also have given a reply using a psalm such as Ps 20 or 50 (Wenham, 53). The offerer certainly recognizes that the animal's death is necessary, because the penalty for sin is death.

5 The offerer himself slaughters (שחט) the animal by cutting its throat. שחט is especially used for killing an animal for sacrifice. In post-biblical Heb. it came to mean to slay an animal by cutting its throat in accordance with the ritual laws (Jastrow, 1546; Milgrom, "Ethics and Ritual," 172–74).

The priest, here specifically identified as a בן אהרן, "son of Aaron," i.e., a priest who has the status that permits him to officiate at the altar of the central shrine, manipulates the דם, "blood." The blood, the means of atonement (cf. 17:11), is the most sacred element of the sacrifice and can be handled only by the priest. The priest catches the blood in a מזרק, "bowl" (cf. Exod 27:3; 38:3), stirring it to keep it from coagulating. Then he throws it or dashes it (זרק) against the large altar standing in the courtyard. In the Second Temple the blood was carried off to the base of the altar by a trough carved into the side of the altar. According to tradition (*m. Tamid* 4.11; *b. Zebaḥ.* 5.3b), the priest went to the northeast corner of the altar and threw the blood so that it fell on two sides of the altar. Then he went around to the southwest corner and threw the blood against the other two sides of the altar. In this way he covered the altar all around (על־המזבח סביב). According to *m. Tamid* 4.1, he poured out the rest of the blood at the base of the altar. The blood rite signifies that the animal's life is poured out to Yahweh.

6 The offerer skins (הפשיט) the animal for the whole offering. The skin is not to be burned on the altar. This act of skinning the animal is mentioned only in regard to offering a whole offering; its mention coincides with the instructions in 7:8 that the hide becomes the property of the officiating priest. In later times the priests, generally aided by the Levites, skinned the offerings (2 Chr 29:34; cf. 35:11); this change may simply have resulted from the desire to insure correct cultic procedure when the volume of sacrifices had greatly increased. Then the offerer cuts the animal into pieces (נתח אתה לנתחיה). נתח stands for the cutting up of living animals (Levine, 7). It is doubtful that the animal was randomly cut up; it was probably dressed according to set traditions (cf. *m. Tamid* 4.2, 3). It may be assumed that the animal was disemboweled.

7 The priest prepares a fire on the altar. This action of preparing a fire is mentioned only here in the sacrificial rituals, since this is written to address the very first offering. From then on the fire on the altar is never to go out (cf. 6:1–6[8–13]). The priest stacks the wood in a prescribed order. Then he takes some low-burning coals lying on the altar and puts them in the center of the piled wood. The altar was large, and there were probably many fires on its surface. From 1 Kgs 8:64 it is discovered that another fire could be made in the courtyard when the altar-hearth was not able to handle the volume of sacrifices.

8 The priest carefully arranges (ערך) the pieces on the wood pile. Special mention is made of placing the head (ראשׁ) and the suet (פדר) on the altar. These parts (specifically mentioned only here and in v 12 and 8:20) belong exclusively to God. The head would have been detached in skinning the animal. פדר refers to the fat net that envelopes the animal's entrails. According to *m. Tamid* 4.2f, this suet is laid on the altar in such a manner as to cover the wound of the head.

9 Since dirt and excrement defile the altar, the entrails (קרב) and the legs (כרעים) are to be washed to make sure that they are completely clean. The entrails must be emptied of fluids and partially digested food in order for them to burn and so as not to defile the altar. The legs, which would be soiled by dirt and other filth, must also be cleansed. כרע means (lit.) "to bend" and most likely refers to "the lower hind legs." The person who does the washing is not specified. The alternation of subject between laity and priest in this ritual along with the specific mention of priest with the next verb suggest that the offerer is the subject of this verb.

The priest now burns (הקטיר) the entire animal on the altar. Since this is a whole offering, the text specifically says that the priest burns את־הכל, "all." The term הקטיר is literally "turn to smoke." The whole offering is identified as אשׁה ריח־ניחוח ליהוה, "a gift for a soothing aroma to Yahweh." אשׁה refers to those parts of a sacrifice that are given to God, either willingly or in response to a duty. Closely joined to אשׁה, "a gift," is the phrase ריח ניחוח, "a soothing aroma," or "sweet smelling fragrance" (de Boer, VTSup 23 [1972] 40), for the latter phrase expresses the intent of this gift. The pleasant, soothing odor of the sacrifice that ascends toward heaven pleases God. While this metaphor is anthropomorphic, it is no more so than numerous other phrases in the OT, such as "the hand of God." Contemporary Western culture tends to overlook the powerful role the sense of smell plays in human life. Smell arouses one's memory and reaches very deeply into a person's emotions (B. Gibbons, "The Intimate Sense of Smell," *National Geographic* 170 [1986] 324–28, 337). It is an especially strong contributing factor to a pleasant experience, or it may stir up strong disgust. This metaphor of "a soothing aroma" is very appropriate, for the sacrifice is offered in order to move God to remember with mercy the one who makes the sacrifice. Usually a whole offering was presented not to cool God's wrath but to seek his goodwill before his wrath might be kindled. Furthermore, this metaphor serves well to say that God himself must accept each offering in order for it to be efficacious without in any way indicating that God is dependent on these offerings for sustenance. De Boer (VTSup 23 [1972] 47) thinks that ריח ניחוח is a technical term indicating "that the divinity accepts the sacrifice."

10–13 The second ritual in this regulation is for presenting a member of the flock, either a sheep or goat, as a whole offering. The details of this ritual are very similar to those of the above ritual. While some of the ritual acts are not mentioned, i.e., laying on of hands, bringing the blood near, skinning the animal, and building up the fire, they are implied.

10 A whole offering (עלה) may also be a member of the flock (מן־הצאן), either a lamb (מן־הכשבים) or a goat (מן־העזים). Sheep are the most frequently named sacrificial animals in the OT. The animal also must be a male, free from defect (תמים). Sometimes it is said that the lamb is a yearling (Lev 12:6; 23:12; Num 6:14; 28:3). While a goat is permitted, there are few references to its being offered as a whole offering. A goat is used most often for a purification offering (4:23, 28).

11 This time it is stated that the offerer is to slaughter the animal על ירך המזבח צפנה, "at the north side of the altar." The Tent opened to the east, the wash basin was on the west, and the ascent to the altar was to the south. Thus the north was the logical place for this activity. Noth (24) suggests that the north side of the altar may have been the place for the smaller animals; the larger ones would have been prepared in front of the altar. The identification of the specific place accords with 4:24, 29, 33, which say that the purification offering (חטאת)is to be slaughtered where the whole offering is slaughtered. The remainder of the ritual is essentially the same as for the offering of cattle.

14 Provision is made for those who are too poor to afford a member of the herd or flock for a whole offering. They may bring either מן התרים, "doves," or מן־בני היונה, "pigeons." Jewish tradition requires the doves to be full grown and the pigeons to be young. Such birds, being in abundance, were readily accessible to even the poorest citizens. It is thought that these were the only birds permitted for sacrifice in the cultic rituals, for they were the only birds the Hebrews had domesticated (cf. 2 Kgs 6:25; Cant 2:12; Noordtzij, 40–41). Nothing is said about the birds' being free from blemishes nor about their being male. This may be to give the poor more latitude in finding a whole offering (G. Dalman, *AuS,* 7:256–58).

15 In offering up one of these birds, the priest is to perform all of the sacrificial acts. He kills the bird by wringing or pinching off (מלק) its head. Then he presses (נמצה) the bird against the altar to squeeze out the small amount of blood.

16 The priest removes its מראתו, "crop, or alimentary canal," and its נצתה, "excrement." Usually נצתה is rendered "feathers" from נוצה. But it seems unlikely that the priest would pluck the feathers of such a small bird. Another possibility is to take this word from the Heb. root צאה, "excrement," as does Tg. Levine (8) believes it to be the content of the crop. This meaning coincides with מראה, "crop," the pouchlike part of the gullet that holds food during digestion. The priest casts (השליך) these elements on a refuse pile at the east side of the altar, the side away from the entrance to the Tent of Meeting, the place of דשן, "fat ashes" (cf. 4:12), i.e., ashes thickly mixed with fat from the burning sacrifices (also 6:3[10]; cf. A. Negoita-H. Ringgren, "דָּשֶׁן *dāshan*," *TDOT* 3:310–12). Ashes were piled up here until they were carried outside the camp for disposal in a clean place. During the era of the Temple these ashes were disposed of in the Kidron Valley.

17 After the priest tears open (שׁסע) the bird by its wings without severing or dividing it (לא יבדיל), he places it on the fire so that all of it is completely burned (הקטיר).

The sacrificing of these lesser animals possesses the same efficacious merit as with a bull or a member of the flock, as the phrase "a gift for a soothing aroma to Yahweh" indicates. Thus the poor worshiper has the same opportunity as the well-to-do both to express his full allegiance to Yahweh and to fulfill all obligations that require a whole offering.

Explanation

The whole offering was the offering presented most regularly at the central sanctuary. This regulation, though, focused on an individual's presentation of a whole offering. The greatest concern was that the sacrifice be made in a way that God would accept it. Thus the worshiper had to present at the entrance to the sanctuary a male animal free from any defects and then follow the prescribed ritual carefully. An acceptable sacrifice meant that Yahweh received the animal as expiation for the offerer's sinful disposition. Finding atonement through his offering, a person might approach the presence of the Holy God with confidence. He was free to present other offerings. Usually after making a whole offering one presented an offering of well-being (chap. 3), which served as a festive meal for his family or clan.

Since the presentation of whole offerings was a critical part of a person's worship of Yahweh, provision was made for those too poor to afford a bull, a sheep, or a goat. That person could present a dove or a pigeon. These birds, being very common, would have been readily accessible. Given the smallness of the bird, the ritual procedure varied markedly, but the effects were the same.

In presenting a whole offering an Israelite recognized both his complete sinfulness and God's total claim on his life, for the whole offering was completely given to God; nothing was returned to either the priest or the offerer. It was a costly gift taken from the foundation of a shepherd's or a farmer's wealth. In making this offering, the offerer acted in faith, trusting Yahweh to meet his daily need for food.

This offering granted a person forgiveness for human sinfulness in general. Such forgiveness was needed periodically. Since fallen man lives in a world under God's curse, daily one errs, failing to fulfill the whole law of God. The tensions that exist in human relationships on all levels bear witness to man's basic sinfulness. Since everyone succumbs to this sinfulness, a person must make expiation for his sinfulness on a regular basis to maintain fellowship with God. How often an ancient Israelite offered such an offering probably varied widely depending on a given person's consciousness of sin and his zeal for Yahweh. A minimum standard would likely have been an annual sacrifice presented at a festive occasion.

An understanding of the whole offering sheds light on many NT passages. While much of the language of the NT about the sacrificial death of Christ is general, making it hard to make connection with the specific sacrifices of the OT cultic legislation, the death of Christ may be compared to a whole offering. Like the animal required for this offering, he was a male, without defect (1 Pet 1:18–19). Having lived in complete obedience to God, he was blameless. For this reason his sacrifice was far superior to any of the offerings presented under the old covenant (Heb 9:23–26). On the altar of the cross Jesus gave himself up entirely to God his Father (Rom 8:32). Like a whole offering Christ's death was "a soothing aroma" to God (Eph 5:2). In contrast to the frequent presentation of whole offerings, Christ offered himself up once for all time (Heb 10:12). The finality of Christ's death put an end to the offering of animals as a part of faithful worship of God.

Thanks to Christ's sacrificial death, the believer no longer has to worship at a sanctuary made by hands where whole offerings are presented daily (Heb 7:27). Rather Jesus has secured an eternal salvation for his followers by taking his own blood into the heavenly Holy of Holies (Heb 9:11–14). The believer, like his OT counterpart, however, still needs daily atonement. Christ's death is sufficient. As John writes, "the blood of Jesus, God's son, continually cleanses us from all sin" (1 John 1:7).

Although the NT believer no longer brings animals to sacrifice at the Temple, the worship of God through Christ requires complete devotion as did the worship of Yahweh. The OT believer expressed his devotion and trust by making sacrifices from his herd. The NT believer, himself a priest, must also spontaneously express his love and trust in God. In place of animals he presents spiritual sacrifices (1 Pet 2:5). According to Heb 13:15–16, the believer offers the sacrifices of praise and of doing good and sharing his possessions with others. When one performs these sacrifices wholeheartedly, his offerings are acceptable to God. The concern that God accept an offering is common to both testaments.

Paul extends the metaphor of sacrifice for the believer further. He speaks of the believer's presentation of his body as a living sacrifice (Rom 12:1, 2). The offering he has in mind is the whole offering, for the believer is to present himself entirely just as the whole offering was entirely consumed on the altar. So too the believer is to be holy as the animal had to be free from defect. For this personal offering to be efficacious, it, like the whole offering, has to be acceptable to God. As a living whole offering, a believer's life is continually pleasing to God.

2. *Regulation for the Grain Offering (2:1–16)*

Bibliography

See *Bibliography* for Lev 1:1–7:38.

Translation

1 “When anyone presents an offering of grain to Yahweh, his offering is to be of fine flour. He is to pour oil on it and put incense[ab] *on it. 2 Then he is to bring it to Aaron’s sons, the priests.*[a] *From it*[b] *he is to take a handful of fine flour and oil with*[c] *all of its incense, and the priest will burn it for a memorial on the altar, a gift*[d] *for a soothing aroma to Yahweh. 3 The rest of the grain offering belongs to Aaron and his sons; it is a most holy portion*[a] *from the gifts for Yahweh.*

4 “When you present an offering of dough baked in an oven,[a] *it is to be of fine flour, unleavened bread mixed with oil, or unleavened wafers spread with oil. 5 If your offering is a grain offering cooked on a griddle, it is to be from fine flour, mixed with oil, without yeast. 6 You are to crumble*[a] *it and pour oil on it. It is a grain offering. 7 If your offering is a grain offering cooked in a pan, it is to be made from fine flour with oil. 8 You are to bring*[a] *the grain offering which is made*[b] *out of these ingredients to Yahweh. Present it*[c] *to the priest, and he will bring it to the altar. 9 The priest will offer up a memorial from the grain offering and burn it on the altar as a gift for a soothing aroma to Yahweh. 10 The rest of the grain offering belongs to Aaron and his sons; it is a most holy portion from the gifts for Yahweh.*

11 “You are not to prepare[a] *any grain offering which you present to Yahweh with leaven, because you must never burn*[b] *any yeast or any honey as a gift for Yahweh. 12 As an offering of firstfruits you may present them to Yahweh, but they are not to be offered up on the altar as a soothing aroma*[a] *13 You are to season*[a] *every offering of your grain offering*[b] *with salt. Do not let the salt of the covenant with your God*[c] *be lacking from your*[d] *grain offerings; you*[d] *are to present all your*[d] *offerings with salt.*[e]

14 “If you present a grain offering of first ripe grain to Yahweh, you are to present new ears roasted in fire or a paste of the rich yield[ab] *as your grain offering*[c] *of first ripe grain. 15 You are to add oil to it and put incense on it. It is a grain offering. 16 The priest will burn as a memorial some of the paste and some of the oil on all the incense as a gift to Yahweh.”*

Notes

1.a. Sam and LXX add a statement of identification: מנחה הי״א, “it is a grain offering.”

1.b. לבנה, “incense,” probably comes from the root לבן, meaning “white.” Many assume that incense has this name because of its white color, but Snaith (33) points out that the Greeks used an incense they called *libanotos*, for it came from the *libanos*-tree. Harrison (50) identifies the incense as balsamic resin from shrubs of the genus *Boswellia*.

2.a. Syr reads a sg, “the priest, Aaron’s son”; cf. n. 1:7.b.

2.b. Instead of משׁם, “from there,” Sam and LXX have ממנה, “from it.” MT is the harder reading unless a scribe made an unconscious error influenced by the series of *mems* in the vicinity; cf. the nearby ומשמנה, “and from its oil.”

2.c. על, “on,” here carries the meaning “in addition to, together with” (*IBHS* §11.2.13c).

2.d. On אשׁה, cf. n. 1:9.g.

3.a. This phrase is an example of the sg constr of a word followed by the pl abs of the same word to denote the superlative (GKC §133i).

4.a. LXX adds *δῶρον κυρίῳ ἐκ*, “a gift to the Lord out of . . .”

6.a. LXX translates the inf abs פתות, “crumble,” as a pf, *καὶ διαθρύψεις*, “and you are to crumble”; it may have read ופתות, or it may be an exegetical translation. While MT is the harder reading, the variant is solely a matter of pointing. The *waw* pfs in v 8 suggest that LXX is the better reading. Moreover, it is hard to imagine that the inf abs is used as the so-called emphatic impv in this position (GKC §113dd), for there is nothing necessarily emphatic here, and an inf abs does not occur elsewhere with this sense in the sacrificial legislation.

8.a. Instead of the second person sg והבאת, "and you are to bring," LXX has the third person sg, *καὶ προσοίσει*, "and he is to bring near." The context prefers the second person form.

8.b. Instead of the niph יֵעָשֶׂה, "it is to be made," LXX *ἂν ποιῇ* translates a qal יַעֲשֶׂה, "it is to make." LXX, though, may be a matter of translation rather than of a different Heb. text. It is possible to explain the niph as a pass used impersonally (GKC §121a; Baentsch, 316).

8.c. *BHS* proposes to repoint the pf form וְהִקְרִיבָהּ, "and he will present it," to an impv וְהַקְרִיבָהּ to agree in person with the initial verb והבאת. The proposal is a viable emendation and is adopted.

11.a. Instead of a niph third person fem sg תֵּעָשֶׂה, "you are to prepare," LXX apparently read a qal second person masc, *ποιήσετε* = תַּעֲשׂוּ, "prepare."

11.b. Instead of MT תקטירו, "you will burn," a few Heb. mss, Sam, LXX, and *Tg. Ps.-J.* read תקריבו, "you will present." This variant has good textual support, which suggests that it arose quite early in the textual tradition. MT is preferable, for the variant may be an error influenced by the preceding תקריבו. Elliger (39) views the variant as a dogmatic correction.

12.a. LXX adds *κυρίῳ*, "to the Lord," leveling the text to the more common expression in this corpus of sacrificial regulations.

13.a. LXX reads תמלח as a niph third person fem, *ἁλισθήσεται*, "one is to salt," while MT points the consonantal text as a qal second person sg. The MT form agrees with the following verbs.

13.b. LXX reads the second person pl suffix rather than MT's second person sg.

13.c. LXX reads *κυρίου* = יהוה, "of the Lord," for MT's אלהיך, "of your God." MT is preferred as the least expected reading.

13.d. LXX reads a second person pl form instead of MT's second person sg form.

13.e. LXX adds *κυρίῳ τῷ θεῷ ὑμῶν*, "to the Lord your God."

14.a. The string אביב קלוי באשׁ גרשׂ כרמל is difficult to translate. Syntactically it is a *casus pendens* in apposition to the dir obj מנחת בכוריך, "a grain offering of your first ripe grain." Perhaps גרשׂ and כרמל are synonyms for the precious kernels of husked grain, with כרמל being a more precise term than גרשׂ (Hoffmann, 1:160). This string may name a series of offerings: "new ears roasted in fire, groats, fresh grain." Or it may be translated as a chain: "crushed heads of new grain roasted in fire" (NIV). In the latter sense it probably refers to a paste made from grinding any of the produce of the garden.

14.b. LXX adds *τῷ κυρίῳ* = ליהוה, "to the Lord"; cf. n. 12.a.

14.c. LXX does not have a second person possessive pronoun with the noun "grain offerings," apparently reading הבכורים for MT בכוריך, "your grain offerings." LXX may have leveled the text so that both occurrences of this term were identical in this verse.

Form/Structure/Setting

The structure of the regulations for grain offerings is as follows:

Regulation for grain offerings (2:1–16)

I. Basic regulation for a grain offering (vv 1–3)
   - A. The case (v 1a)
   - B. The ritual procedure (vv 1b–2)
   - C. The disposition of the leftover grain (v 3)

II. Expanded regulation concerning baked grain offerings (vv 4–10)
   - A. Three kinds of baked grain offerings (vv 4–7)
     - 1. Baked in an oven (v 4)
     - 2. Prepared on a griddle (vv 5–6)
     - 3. Cooked in a pan (v 7)
   - B. Ritual procedure (vv 8–10)
     - 1. Ritual procedure proper (vv 8–9)
     - 2. Regarding the leftover grain (v 10)

III. Supplemental regulations (vv 11–16)
   - A. Prohibition about the use of yeast and honey (v 11)
   - B. Prohibition about firstfruits (v 12)
   - C. Stipulation concerning salt (v 13)
   - D. Regulations about firstfruits (vv 14–16)

In the ritual for a grain offering Rendtorff (*Studien,* 182; cf. *Gesetze,* 19) has uncovered four steps:

1. Preparation, יצק (vv 1, 6)
2. Presentation, הביא (vv 2a*α*, 8a)
3. Offering up of a memorial, קמץ, "pinch off," or הרים, "offer up" (v 9a*α*)
4. Burning, הקטיר (vv 2b, 9a*β*)

The basic regulation for the grain offering stated in vv 1–2 and 8–9 comes from the earliest era of Israel's cult. According to Koch (*Priesterschrift,* 49–50), the short sentences, impersonal third person forms, and unusual words like קמץ, "pinch," indicate that this regulation is quite ancient. Nevertheless, the full nature of vv 1–2 indicates that material has been added to define the offering more closely. An original הכהן, "the priest," as in vv 2b, 9, and 16, has been pluralized with the insertion of the phrase בני אהרן, "sons of Aaron," as in chap. 1 (e.g., v 5). This phrase may have been a marginal notation that found its way into the text. Also like the whole offering (עלה; chap. 1), it is classified as an offering or oblation (קרבן). Many, including Noth (27), take the instruction to put incense on a grain offering as a later adaptation. Koch dates this change to the time of the Kingdom.

Most critical scholars, such as Noth (27) and Elliger (44), take the statements of giving the leftover grain to the priest (vv 3 and 10) as a later addition. They think that in the earliest period the grain was returned to the offerer to be eaten at a festive meal. But it is possible that this statement is earlier than these scholars allow. Since only a portion of the grain was offered, some direction as to the disposal of the rest of the grain would have been needed in the earliest regulation.

While Koch argues that the ancient regulation treated only the presentation of raw grain, the possibility of presenting a baked grain offering may have existed from the earliest times given the simplicity of the offering and the baking process. Nevertheless, the stipulations for baked dough were expanded to include various kinds of bread in order to give official status to variant local practices (vv 5–7). This inclusion may have been completed during the early days of the Temple in Jerusalem, when it would have been deemed necessary to standardize various local practices. Rendtorff (*Gesetze,* 20) classifies vv 4–6 as *torah* style, but Koch (*Priesterschrift,* 51) judges these lines to coincide with the systematizing style of 1:2; 2:1, 14. Working from Ezek 46:20, Koch (51) posits that this is a Jerusalemite practice. Like the whole offering (עלה; cf. 1:9), a baked grain offering is classified as אשה ריח ניחח ליהוה, "a gift for a soothing aroma to Yahweh" (v 9b).

At the end there is an extended appendix, a series of stipulations that govern the presentation of a grain offering (vv 11–16): a prohibition against the use of yeast or honey with a grain offering (v 11); a prohibition against offering up firstfruits on the altar (v 12); a stipulation requiring the use of salt with every grain offering (v 13); and further regulations about the presentation of firstfruits such as a grain offering (vv 14–16). The second-person style of these stipulations indicates that they were injunctions spoken by the priests to the congregation. According to Rendtorff (*Gesetze,* 20), they belong to the priestly instruction (תורה). Koch agrees with this classification. The second person plural forms in vv 11–12 separate them from vv 13–15, which have second person singular forms. This variation indicates that vv 11–12 had a different origin from the rest of the regulation. No doubt the mention of ראשית, "firstfruits," in v 12 attracted the insertion of the longer regulations about firstfruits of grain (בכורים). These stipulations drawn from other cultic material would have been included at a time when there was the need to regulate widely divergent practices. The occasion for their inclusion then could have been any of the reforms sponsored by the various Judean kings in which they sought to establish pure worship of Yahweh throughout the realm.

Comment

Excursus: מנחה

מנחה has a wide range of uses in the OT. In non-cultic texts it may mean "gift(s)" presented to another person, especially those given by one obligated to another or by one who wants to win another's favor (e.g., 1 Sam 10:27; Gen 32:14[13]; 43:11). It also stands for "tribute" paid by a nation to its overlord (1 Kgs 5:1[4:21]). In a worship setting, מנחה is used for an offering without specifying the material presented; e.g., in Gen 4:3–5 it is used both for an offering from the fruit of the ground and for one from a member of the flock. But in cultic texts מנחה normally has a restrictive meaning, "a grain offering." The choice of מנחה for this offering adds a note that a grain offering is a gift for Yahweh in recognition of his lordship and his total claim on the presenter's life.

In Ps 20:4(3), מנחה parallels עלה, "a whole offering." מנחה may refer to any kind of meal offering presented to Yahweh and עלה to offerings that are consumed on the altar (cf. H.-J. Kraus, *Psalmen 1–59,* BKAT 15/1 [Neukirchen-Vluyn: Neukirchener, 1978] 311). Together these two terms encompass the variety of offerings presented at the sanctuary. More often, though, מנחה is paired with זבח to include the whole range of offerings (1 Sam 2:29; 3:14; Isa 19:21; Amos 5:25; Ps 40:7[6]). While it is possible that these two terms occurring together mean "grain" and "animal" offerings respectively, it is more likely that מנחה stands in place of עלה, "a whole offering" (cf. Rendtorff, *Studien,* 191–92). Then מנחה refers to sacrifices presented wholly to God, and זבח stands for those offerings that become a festive meal. In the late prophetic work of Malachi, מנחה is used for sacrifices in general (1:10, 11, 13; 2:12, 13; 3:3, 4). מנחה thus has a wide semantic range. As a result there are several passages in which the precise meaning of מנחה is in doubt (e.g., Zeph 3:10). This is the case in another usage of מנחה. It is sometimes used in a phrase for a time of the day as a reference to an offering presented at a set daily time. Generally עלה, "a whole offering," is used in this way, but in a few places there is mention of an evening מנחה (1 Kgs 18:29; Ezra 9:4, 5; Dan 9:21) and once to a morning מנחה (2 Kgs 3:20). Given the wide semantic range of מנחה, the precise nature of this daily מנחה is uncertain. It might refer to an animal sacrifice, particularly one that is not wholly consumed on the altar, or possibly to a grain offering.

In the cultic legislation, מנחה ordinarily stands for an offering of grain. A small portion is burnt on the altar and the rest becomes the priests'. It almost always accompanies עלה, "a whole offering" (Judg 13:15–16, 19; 2 Kgs 16:13, 15; Jer 14:12; 1 Chr 21:23), and frequently זבח שלמים, "an offering of well-being" (Lev 7:12–13; Num 6:17). Often נסך, "a libation," is offered with a grain offering (Num 15:1–21; 28–29).

A few texts speak about an independent מנחה. A priestly grain offering is described in 6:12–16(19–23). This passage seems to indicate that it is offered on the day of the priests' ordination and every day thereafter. In Num 5:11–15 there is a reference to a grain offering of jealousy (מנחת קנאת), which a husband who is apprehensive that his wife has been unfaithful must bring to the priest when he requests that his wife's fidelity be tested by an ordeal. At the Feast of Weeks the congregation is to present an offering of new grain (מנחה חדשה; 23:16–17; Num 28:26). On this occasion whole offerings are also presented with their accompanying grain offerings and libations (23:18).

1 נפש, "a person," prepares a grain offering from סלת, "fine flour." נפש is an inclusive term, covering both men and women (cf. *Comment* on 1:2). The grain offering is prepared from wheat that is ground and sifted; thus NEB translates סלת as "wheaten flour." Levine (9) holds that סלת is semolina, i.e., flour taken from the inner kernels. סלת, a luxury item in ancient society (cf. Ezek 16:13), is thus distinguished from קמח, "meal," a coarse mixture of whole grain and bran. שמן, "olive oil," is poured over the flour, and לבנה, "incense or frankincense," is to be spread on it.

2 The priest, בן אהרן, "a son of Aaron," is to קמץ, "pinch off," a handful and הקטיר, "burn it," as אזכרה, "a memorial," on the altar. אזכרה, "memorial," also appears with מנחה (vv 9, 16; 5:12; 6:8[15]; Num 5:26) and with shewbread (24:7). The root of אזכרה has not been agreed on by scholars. The versions, taking it from the root זכר, "to remember," understand it in the sense of "memorial." G. R. Driver (*JSS* 1 [1956] 99–100), however, renders it "token." But if it means "token," that would be a very weak term for anything that הקטיר, "was burned or smoked," on the altar. Strictly "memorial" refers to that portion which is burned on the altar, not the entire grain offering. The term "memorial" conveys the idea that the person who makes this offering is remembering God's grace in giving him his daily food. The offerer praises God as the giver of good things (Hoffmann, 1:147). H. Eising, however, proposes that אזכרה may indicate that Yahweh's name was pronounced as a portion of the grain offering was being consumed on the altar ("זָכַר *zākhar,*" *TDOT* 5:80). At this moment Yahweh is warmly remembered by the supplicant. W. Schottroff notes that אזכרה applies only to that portion of the grain offering that is burned on the altar (*"Gedenken" im Alten Orient und im Alten Testamentum: Die Wurzel zākar im semitischen Sprachkreis,* WMANT 15 [Neukirchen-Vluyn: Neukirchener, 1964] 337). For him the oldest meaning of אזכרה is "invocation (by name)," i.e., Yahweh's name was pronounced over the grain offering that was burned (335–37). He goes on to suggest that a psalm, e.g., Ps 38 or 70, may have been sung at this rite, for the titles to these two psalms employ להזכיר, "to extol, confess" (337). On the other hand, the offering stirs God's memory so that he will act graciously toward the one whom he remembers in light of his past commitments (cf. B. Childs, *Memory and Tradition in Israel,* SBT series 1, 37 [1962] 31–34). Schottroff agrees that this is a meaning of אזכרה, but he argues that this meaning became attached to this word over time. אזכרה is a critical term in the description of a grain offering, for it carries the spiritual value of this type of offering just as the terms כפר, "expiation," and רצה, "rendering acceptable," denote the spiritual merit of עלה, "a whole offering" (1:4).

3 הנותרת, "the rest of the grain offering," belongs to the Aaronite priests, contributing to their income (cf. v 10; 7:6–9). Because it belongs to the priests, it is defined as קדש קדשים, "a most holy portion." This classification for an offering means that it could be eaten only in a restricted area of the temple precinct by priests, who are ritually clean, but not by their wives or children or by the temple servants (cf. Ezek 42:13).

4 Besides raw grain, loaves or cakes may be baked and then presented as מנחה, "a grain offering." The first kind of baked grain offering mentioned is dough baked in an oven (תנור), i.e., a large ceramic pot. Such a pot was portable; in a house it was placed in a hole dug in the ground. The fuel was usually dried grass or stubble. The dough was baked against the inner cylinder that had been heated by the fire (Noth, 25).

The term for bread, חלה, refers to a twisted or round loaf. Tg translates it with גריצה, "bread," made of slices twisted together. It is to be prepared with שמן, "oil," but no leaven may be used. Harrison (54) observes that in antiquity leaven was a small piece of dough taken from a previous baking that had been left to spoil. While the reason that leaven is excluded is not mentioned, it is most likely because of its fermenting nature and its proneness to spoil.

One may also present רקיק, "wafers," made from dough that has been beaten thin. Oil is spread on them. It is not clear whether a little oil was put on top of the wafer or whether the entire log of oil was used.

5 Another type of baked grain offering is מחבת, "a flat cake or a pancake, grilled on a metal plate. In his model of Jerusalem under siege, Ezekiel represented the city's fortified wall with such a plate made of iron (Ezek 4:3). The cake is then to be broken or crumbled, and oil is to be poured on it before it is offered as a grain offering.

7 A third type of baked grain offering consists of dough deep fried in a deep pan with a lid (מרחשת; cf. 7:9). The dough was probably placed in boiling oil and cooked until crisp.

11 Yeast (שאר) and honey (דבש) may never be added to a grain offering from which any portion will be burned on the altar. In the OT the kind of honey is not specified save in Judg 14:8–9, where the context defines the substance as "honey from bees," clearly meaning wild honey. Whether beekeeping was practiced in Israel during the biblical period is uncertain, but doubtful. The majority of OT references to דבש mean nectar of fruit, particularly from dates and possibly from other fruits. Since honey was the basic sweetener in ancient times, "a sweet substance" may be a better translation for דבש (cf. A. Caquot, "דְּבַשׁ *d*^{e}*bhash*," *TDOT* 3:128–31). Of course, דבש did exclude the use of honey from bees in offerings that were to be burned on the altar. While the leftover portions may not be prepared with leaven (6:9–10[16–17]), honey may be spread on them.

Loaves of firstfruits baked with yeast, however, may be presented as תנופה, "an elevated or wave offering"; none of these loaves, of course, is to be burned on the altar (cf. 23:17). Moreover, honey is included among the firstfruits presented to God in 2 Chr 31:5. This regulation stands in marked contrast to the common use of honey in the cultic rituals of Israel's neighbors.

12 ראשית, "the firstfruits," belong exclusively to Yahweh (cf. Exod 34:26). This word for firstfruits comes from the root ראש, "head, top, first." It means the first produce and the choicest. The firstfruits include leaven and honey. These fruits are to be given to God, but they are not burned on the altar. They were usually presented at the Feast of Weeks (23:15–22; Exod 34:22). As a worshiper presented the firstfruits, he recited the account of God's saving deeds (Deut 26:1–11). Thereby he recognized that the bounty of the new crop resulted from God's blessing, not from some fertility rite.

13 All grain offerings are to be offered with מלח, "salt," the primary preservative in the ancient world. The use of salt renders the offering fit. Because of the restrictions about the use of leaven and honey with grain, the use of salt is specifically mentioned in order that no one would suppose that it is to be excluded. It was customary among the Arabs and the Greeks to commemorate the indissoluble bond of a covenant by eating salt together. Twice the term ברית מלח, "covenant of salt," occurs in the OT to emphasize the eternal, abiding nature of the covenant between God and his people or servant (Num 18:19; 2 Chr 13:5).

14–16 This stipulation regulates the offering of first ripe grain (בכורים). The Heb. comes from the root בכר, "to bear early or first." While בכרים may include the first produce of the ground and of trees (cf. Neh 10:36[35]; Snaith, 34), it specifically stands for grain. The term אביב, "fresh, young ears," refers to the just ripening grain. It is usually used in reference to barley, but it may include other grains as it does in this passage. Before being offered, the fresh ears are to be קלוי באש, roasted. Then they are ground, as the term גרשׂ, "crushed grain," or "grits," indicates. כרמל is translated "rich yield"; it means rich garden land and as a metonymy "abundant yield." כרמל is also a toponym for the low mountain range that stretches from the plain of Dothan to the Mediterranean Sea just south of Haifa. Some think that this range is called Carmel because of its great fertility. KB (475), however, lists a כרמל IV, "fresh grain." Some oil and incense are put on the crushed, roasted grain. This prepared מנחה is then made to smoke (הקטיר) on the altar as a memorial (אזכרה; cf. v 2). This offering is classified as אשה ליהוה, "a gift to Yahweh."

Explanation

A grain offering consisted of raw grain or of baked dough. While no leaven might be used, olive oil might be added to the flour. Incense was added to a raw grain offering. The officiating priest then picked up a handful of all the elements and burned them on the altar. The burning sacrifice became a memorial for the one making the offering. That is, it caused God to remember this person in covenant faithfulness. Whom God remembered he blessed.

While a grain offering could be presented at any time, it almost always accompanied a whole offering and frequently an offering of well-being. In both types, raw and baked, the leftover grain was classified as most holy. That means it became the exclusive property of the Aaronites and had to be eaten in a prescribed area of the Temple. It was mandatory that the firstfruits be presented to Yahweh. All the firstfruits were to be brought to the holy place and left. With this act the offerer dedicated his entire harvest to God, recognizing God's lordship over his entire yield. God accepted the firstfruits and released the rest of the harvest back to the farmer for his free use. The firstfruits were not, however, to be offered up on the altar as a soothing aroma, except for a grain offering from the first ripe grain. There was a special regulation for this kind of offering. The new ears were to be roasted and then ground up into a paste. Next the offerer spread olive oil on it and added incense, like with a regular grain offering. The priest burned a portion of the paste with some of the oil on top of all the incense as a gift to Yahweh.

In this passage there are specific regulations for all of Israel to observe. Nothing containing leaven could ever be placed on the altar. Honey, i.e., any sweet substance, was also forbidden. Since no reason for the restriction against leaven and honey is given, all suggestions are speculative. The most widely posited reason is that these elements, by reason of their fermenting qualities, altered the basic nature of the grain. By contrast, the use of leaven and honey was frequent in the different Near Eastern cults. There are references to sacrificing honey in texts from Egypt, Babylon, and Ugarit. Ritual texts from Babylon mention the blending of honey with grain and butter (cf. Caquot, *TDOT* 3:130). Therefore, a secondary motivation for this prohibition may have been to prevent the use of pagan rites at Israelite altars.

Salt, furthermore, was to be added to all grain offerings. Besides adding flavor, salt acted as a preservative, staying decay. In this stipulation appears the significant, though infrequent, phrase "salt of the covenant" (v 13; cf. Num 18:19; 2 Chr 13:5). Salt symbolizes the binding power of the covenant, a solidarity that prevents any animosity from breaking the bond of fellowship between the parties of the covenant. The parties in the Ancient Near East often expressed their bond of fellowship by sharing a meal that included bread and salt. Jesus' powerful aphorism "you are the salt of the earth" (Matt 5:13) may allude to the imagery of the salt of the covenant. There may also be a connection between the grain offering and Jesus' claim "I am the bread of life" (John 6:35, 48–51). Therefore, Jesus encourages all who believe on him to partake of sacrificial food freely when he invites them to eat his flesh and drink his blood so that they may have eternal life (John 6:47–58).

3. Regulation for the Offering of Well-Being (3:1–17)

Bibliography

Charbel, A. "La portata religiosa degli *š^{e}lāmîm.*" *RBibIt* 18 (1970) 185–94. ———. זבח שלמים: *Il sacrificio pacifico nei suoi riti e nel suo significato religioso e figurativo.* Bethlehem, Jerusalem, 1967. ———. "Posizione degli *š^{e}lāmîm* nella scrittura." *Sal* 36 (1974) 431–41. **Janowski, B.** "Erwägungen zur Vorgeschichte des israelitischen š^{e}lamîm-Opfers." *UF* 12 (1980) 231–59. **Médebielle, A.** "Le symbolisme du sacrifice expiatoire en Israel." *Bib* 2 (1921) 141–69, 273–302. **Moor, J. C. de.** "The Peace Offering in Ugarit and Israel." In *Schrift en Uitleg.* FS W. Gispen. Kampen: Kok, 1970. 112–17. **Moraldi, L.** *Espiazione sacrificale e riti espiatori nell'ambiente biblico e nell'Antico Testamento.* AnBib 5. Rome: Pontificio Istituto Biblico, 1956. **Schmid, R.** *Das Bundsesopfer in Israel: Wesen, Ursprung und Bedeutung der alttestamentlichen Schelamim.* SANT 9. Munich: Kösel-Verlag, 1964.

Translation

1 *"If a person's offering*[a] *is an offering of well-being and if he presents an animal from the herd, whether it is male or female,*[b] *he is to present an animal without defect before Yahweh.* 2 *He is to lay his hand on the head of his offering and slaughter it*[a] *at the*

entrance to the Tent of Meeting, and Aaron's sons, the priests, will dash the blood against the altar[b] on all sides. 3*And from the offering of well-being he[a] is to present a gift to Yahweh: the fat which covers the entrails and all the fat which is on the entrails,* 4*the two kidneys and the fat which is around them on the sinews[a] and the long lobe of the liver he is to remove[b] with the kidneys.* 5*Then Aaron's sons[a] will burn it[b] on the altar on[c] the whole offering, which is on the wood on the fire.[d] It is a gift for a soothing aroma to Yahweh.*

6*"If his offering is from the flock for an offering of well-being to Yahweh, he is to present a male or female without defect.[a]* 7*If he presents a lamb[a] as his offering, he is to present it before Yahweh.* 8*He is to lay his hand on the head of his offering and slaughter it before[a] the Tent of Meeting. Then Aaron's sons[b] will dash its blood[c] against the altar on all sides.* 9*From the offering of well-being he is to present a gift to Yahweh;[a] he is to remove[b] its fat[c] and the entire[d] fat tail cut off close to the backbone, also[e] the fat which covers the entrails and all the fat which is on the entrails,[f]* 10*the two kidneys and the fat which is around them on the sinews and the long lobe of liver, which he is to remove[a] with the kidneys.* 11*The priest will burn it[a] at the altar. The food sacrifice[b] is a gift to Yahweh.*

12*"If his offering is a goat, he is to present it before Yahweh.* 13*He is to lay his hand on its head and slaughter[a] it before[b] the Tent of Meeting. Then Aaron's sons[c] will dash its blood against the altar on all sides.* 14*He is also to present[a] a part of his offering as a gift to Yahweh; the fat which covers the entrails and all the fat which is on the entrails,* 15*the two kidneys and the fat which is around them on the sinews and the long lobe of the liver, he is to remove[a] with the kidneys.* 16*The priest will burn them on the altar; the food sacrifice[a] is a gift for a soothing aroma.[b] All the fat belongs to Yahweh.*

17*"This is a perpetual decree for your generations in all your settlements: never eat any fat or any blood."[a]*

Notes

1.a. LXX adds τῷ κυρίῳ, "to the Lord," as in 2:12.

1.b. There is a dual heading here. The first אם clause introduces the entire regulation and ties back to 1:2. The second אם clause heads the first segment of this regulation.

2.a. LXX[B] adds ἐναντίον κυρίου, "before the Lord," after ושחטו, "and he is to slaughter it."

2.b. LXX defines the altar as θυσιαστήριον τῶν ὁλοκαυτωμάτων, "the altar of the whole offerings."

3.a. LXX and Vg read a pl form, taking Aaron's sons, the priests, as the verb's antecedent.

4.a. Levine holds that כסלים is more accurately rendered "sinews, tendons" (16).

4.b. The pronominal suffix on the verb picks up the compound dir obj which precedes the verb for emphasis.

5.a. Vg omits "Aaron's sons," while LXX adds οἱ ἱερεῖς, "the priests," after "Aaron's sons" as in v 2; cf. n. 8.b. LXX is leveling the text to the other passages. On the inclusion of this phrase see n. 1:7.b.

5.b. The pronoun is sg, for all of these pieces of fat together are called חלב, "fat" (cf. n. 9.c.).

5.c. Levine provides an alternative reading by taking the prep על to mean "with," a meaning that it often has in this cultic legislation. The more literal rendering, "on," suggests not that this offering is burned on top of a whole offering but that a whole offering needs to have been offered that day before an offering of well-being is offered and that the parts of an offering of well-being are placed on that which remains of the smoldering whole offering.

5.d. Sam and LXX add אשר על־המזבח, "(which is) on the altar," as in 1:8, 12; but LXX may not read אשר, the relative pronoun.

6.a. תמים, "whole, without defect," stands before the verb for emphasis; it is resumed by the pronominal suffix on the verb.

7.a. Some Heb. mss read כבש for כשב, a variant Heb. spelling for "sheep."

8.a. LXX adds τὰς θύρας, "the doors," before "the Tent of Meeting" as in v 2. Frequently the MT reads פתח, "door," before the phrase "the Tent of Meeting," but three times (also v 13 and 4:14) it simply reads לפני אהל מועד, "before the Tent of Meeting." Each time, the LXX has a variant reading that includes "door." Again this appears to be a leveling activity by the LXX translators. Syr reads "before Yahweh (at) the entrance to . . ." (cf. LXX v 13), and one Heb. ms simply reads לפני יהוה, "before Yahweh."

8.b. LXX adds "the priests"; cf. n. 5.a.

8.c. For MT דמו, "its blood," Sam reads הדם, "the blood"; possibly LXX does so too, but LXX may be preferable Gk. rather than evidence of a different Heb. text.

9.a. Instead of ליהוה, "to Yahweh," LXX reads τῷ θεῷ, "to God."

9.b. Cf. n. 4.b.

9.c. The word חלב, "fat," stands for all the pieces to be burned, which are then enumerated (Hoffmann, 1:168).

9.d. In other parts of this regulation תמים means "without defect" (vv 1, 6); here it means "entire, whole."

9.e. Some Heb. mss, Sam, and *Tg. Ps.-J.* omit the conj "and" on את, the indicator of the dir obj; cf. v 4.

9.f. LXX has a much shorter text, reading καὶ τὸ στέαρ τῆς κοιλίας, "and the fat of the entrails," for MT ואת־החלב המכסה את־הקרב ואת כל־החלב אשר על־הקרב, "and the fat which covers the entrails and all the fat which is on the entrails." LXX may have resulted from an error of homoioteleuton, or it may have had a Vorlage that had suffered an omission by homoioteleuton, since some Heb. mss also omit portions of this passage.

10.a. Cf. n. 4.b.

11.a. Cf. n. 5.b.

11.b. Instead of MT לחם, "food (sacrifice)," LXX reads ὀσμὴ εὐωδίας, "a soothing aroma" (cf. v 5). This may be the result of a desire to avoid any idea of God's eating an offering. Certainly MT is the harder reading.

13.a. LXX reads the pl; cf. n. 3.a.

13.b. LXX reads ἔναντι κυρίου παρὰ τὰς θύρας, "before Yahweh at the doors to"; cf. n. 8.a. One Heb. ms reads לפני יהוה אהל מועד, "before Yahweh, the Tent of Meeting."

13.c. Sam and LXX add "the priests"; cf. n. 5.a.

14.a. With καὶ ἀνοίσει, "and he will offer up," LXX seems to have mistakenly read והקטיר, "and he will burn," for MT והקריב, "and he will present."

15.a. Cf. n. 4.b.

16.a. LXX omits לחם, "food"; cf. n. 11.a.

16.b. A couple of Heb. mss read אשה ליהוה, "a gift to Yahweh," as in n. 11.b. But Sam and LXX read the standard formula ריח ניחח ליהוה, "a soothing aroma to Yahweh," for MT לריח ניחח, "for a soothing aroma" (elsewhere only Num 18:17). MT is the harder reading and may have been composed in this way to avoid the use of ליהוה, "to Yahweh," twice in close proximity.

17.a. The compound dir obj precedes the verb for emphasis.

Form/Structure/Setting

The structure of the regulation for the offering of well-being is as follows:

Regulation for the offering of well-being (3:1–17)

I. Presentation of cattle (vv 1–5)
  A. The basic case (v 1a)
  B. Regulations (vv 1b–5)
    1. Qualifications of the animal (v 1b)
    2. Ritual procedure (vv 2–5a)
      a. Laying on of hands and slaughter by the laity (v 2a)
      b. Handling of blood by the priests (v 2b)
      c. Removal of fat by the laity (vv 3–4)
      d. Burning of fat by the priests (v 5a)
    3. Statement of classification (v 5b)
II. Presentation of animals from the flock (vv 6–16b*a*)
  A. Basic statement (v 6)
  B. Twofold division (vv 7–16b*a*)
    1. Presentation of sheep (vv 7–11)
      a. Basic case (v 7)

b. Ritual procedure (vv 8–11a)
   1) Laying on of hands and slaughter by the laity (v 8a)
   2) Handling of blood by the priests (v 8b)
   3) Removal of fat by the laity (vv 9–10)
   4) Burning of fat by the priests (v 11a)
c. Statement of classification (v 11b)
2. Presentation of goats (vv 12–16bα)
   a. Basic case (v 12)
   b. Ritual procedure (vv 13–16a)
      1) Laying on of hands and slaughter by the laity (v 13a)
      2) Handling of blood by the priests (v 13b)
      3) Removal of fat by the laity (vv 14–15)
      4) Burning of fat by the priests (v 16a)
   c. Statement of classification (v 16bα)

III. General prohibition against eating fat and blood (vv 16bβ–17)
   A. Statement about fat (v 16bβ)
   B. Prohibition proper (v 17)

This regulation is divided into two sections according to the kind of animal offered. The first section concerns the offering of cattle (vv 1–5) and the second a member from the flock (vv 6–16). The second section is subdivided into two rituals, one for presenting a sheep (vv 7–11) and one for presenting a goat (vv 12–16). Each section is organized similarly: a basic statement (vv 1a, 6, 7, 12), the prescription of the sacrificial ritual (vv 2–5a, 8–11a, 13–16a), and a definition statement (vv 5b, 11b, 16bα). Appended to the regulation is a prohibition against eating fat and blood (v 17).

The ritual has six steps:

1. Presentation, הקריב (vv 1b, 6b, 7, 12b)
2. Laying a hand on the animal's head, סמך (vv 2aα, 8aα, 13aα)
3. Slaughter, שׁחט (vv 2aβ, 8aβ, 13aβ)
4. Manipulation of blood, זרק (vv 2b, 8b, 13b)
5. Removal of the fat, הסיר (vv 3–4, 9–10, 14–15)
6. Burning of the fat, הקטיר (vv 5b, 11b, 16b)

(Cf. Rendtorff, *Studien,* 153–61.) As in the ritual for the whole offering, the lay person performs steps 1–3 and 5, and the priest does steps 4 and 6. The details of the sacrificial ritual concentrate on the slaughter of the animal and the offering up of its entrails and fatty parts.

In his analysis Koch (*Priesterschrift,* 51–52) agrees with this structure of the regulation for the offering of well-being. He suspects, however, that the step of the offerer's laying his hand on the animal results from an effort to make this ritual conform to that of the whole offering. This position is based on two primary observations. First, the text reads that the hand is laid on the head of the oblation (קרבן), a word loved by the priestly writers, instead of on a specific animal as in 1:4 and 4:4, 15. Second, this gesture as an act of transference has no significance with an offering of well-being. But as pointed out in chap. 1, it is next to impossible to uncover the original setting of this rite, and it is inaccurate to interpret it as a symbol of transference.

The editing found in chaps. 1 and 2 is also present here. The older reading הכהן, "the priest," has been altered to בני אהרן הכהנים, "Aaron's sons, the priests," in v 2b. Perhaps an original "the priest" was altered to "Aaron's sons" in vv 5a, 8b, 13b. Similar to the whole offering and the grain offering, this offering is classified as קרבן, "an oblation" (vv 1, 2, 6, 7, 8, 12a). Moreover, Noth (30) observes that the term "Tent of Meeting" (vv 2aβ, 8aβ, 13aβ) occurs here, whereas the term "before Yahweh" is used in chap. 1 (vv 5a, 11a). This has resulted from a later substitution.

The definition statement at the end of each ritual varies somewhat. The first (v 5b) states that the offering is simply אשה ריח ניחח ליהוה, "a gift for a soothing aroma to Yahweh." The second (v 11b) is quite different: לחם אשה ליהוה, "food as a gift to Yahweh." The use of "Yahweh" directly with the term "gift" is infrequent, perhaps suggesting a textual error. The third identifies the sacrifice as לחם אשה לריח ניחח, "a food-offering as a gift for a soothing aroma" (v 16bα). The use of the term לחם, "food," to define this offering seems more primitive, indicating that it has survived from an ancient regulation.

In the first ritual there is a notation about burning the designated parts of this offering on top of the whole offering (v 5a). Since this specification is absent from the other rituals (vv 11a, 16a), it may have been a marginal note that found its way into the text. Whenever this standard became adopted, it most likely applied to every offering of well-being regardless of the kind of animal presented.

At the end of the regulation there are two additions. The sentence כל־חלב ליהוה, "all the fat belongs to Yahweh," in v 16bβ emphasizes the portions that are to be burned on the altar (cf. Elliger, 49–50). Since this sentence seems to come from nowhere, possibly this is a case of a marginal notation that found its way into the final text. Its purpose may have been to settle a dispute about whether a particular fatty part was covered by the descriptions of the removal of the fat or whether it fell outside the regulation and could be returned to the offerer. The second addition, which may have been attracted to this place by the inclusion of the above phrase, is a decree that categorically forbids the eating of fat or blood (v 17). Elliger (51) assigns this verse and 7:22–27 to the same source. The decree here has a strong universalizing tone communicated by the buildup of all-inclusive terms: עולם, "perpetual," לדרתיכם, "for your generations," and בכל מושבתיכם, "wherever you live." This full style and the categorical nature of the decree vary markedly from the rest of this regulation, indicating that this decree originally had a different setting. It was included here to counter the practice at some shrines of returning some of the animal's unburnt fat to the offerer to be eaten with the meat (cf. 1 Sam 2:12–15). The date and the setting of this statement are hard to determine. Most scholars assign it to the post-exilic era, but such additions could have been added at any time of standardizing the cultic practices, such as during the reforms of Hezekiah (705 B.C.) or Josiah (622 B.C.).

Comment

Excursus: The Offering of Well-Being

The Hebrew phrase זבח שלמים is variously translated: "a sacrifice of peace offering" (AV; RSV), "a fellowship offering" (NIV), "a shared-offering" (NEB), "a communion sacrifice" (JB), "a sacrifice of well-being" (Harrison, 56). While זבח means "the killing" of an animal for a sacrifice, the word שלמים is harder to identify. If it comes from the root

שלם, "be complete, sound, whole, healthy," the plural form may mean "prosperity, well-being." Often Heb. uses a noun in the plural to capture an abstract idea carried by that word, to carry the variety of qualities inherent in the idea of the root, or to strengthen the idea of the root; e.g., קברים, "graves," in Job 17:1 probably means "graveyard," and in 1 Sam 2:3, דעות, (lit.) "knowledges," means "thorough knowledge" (cf. GKC §124b–f; *IBHS* §7.4.2). Therefore, the translation "an offering of well-being" is adopted. Another rendering that has strong merit is "a shared offering" or "a communion sacrifice." This position focuses on the fact that this sacrifice is shared by the presenter's family, the officiating priest, and God. There is שלם, "peace" or "harmony," between that family and God. Levine (15) defines שלמים as "tribute, gift of greeting" in light of Ugar *šalamūma,* which was offered by King Keret to the officer of forces attacking him, and in light of Akk *šulmānu,* "a gift of greeting." He thus prefers to translate זבח שלמים "a sacred gift of greeting."

According to Lev 7:12–16, an offering of well-being may be subclassified into three types: a praise offering, a vow offering, and a freewill offering. While the occasion for presenting an offering of well-being differs, the ritual varies only slightly for the different types, as will be noted in chap. 7. A primary aim of this sacrifice is for the offerer and his family or class, including invited guests, to eat the meat returned to them in a festive meal. All who partake of the meal are to be ritually pure (Lev 7:20). The meat is to be eaten the same day it is slaughtered if it be a praise offering, but for the other classes the meat has to be consumed by the second day (Lev 7:15–16). This festive meal is an expression of covenant renewal as the members fellowship together before God.

Since it was proper to offer up an offering of well-being at any time, it was the most frequently offered sacrifice, at least in the oldest times. It was offered on highest occasions in Israel's life. Some of those included: sealing the covenant at Mount Sinai (Exod 24:5), the installation of Saul as King of Israel (1 Sam 11:15), David's bringing of the Ark of the Covenant to Jerusalem (2 Sam 6:17–18), and the dedication of Solomon's Temple (1 Kgs 8:64).

The offering of well-being may be referred to by the full term זבח שלמים, or with either of these two words standing alone: שלמים (e.g., Lev 6:5[12]; 7:14, 33; Num 6:14; 15:8) or זבח (e.g., Lev 17:5, 7, 8; 19:6; 23:37; Num 15:3, 5, 8; Josh 22:26, 27). The cultic material prefers the full term, while a single term is usually found in other parts of the OT. Possibly זבח, "sacrifice," is the oldest term. Although this is a general term for sacrifice, it refers primarily to this offering by reason of its being the most common sacrifice. The full term came into use when the offerings were codified. Afterward the term שלמים, "well-being, peace," by itself could be used for this sacrifice. Nevertheless, each term may have had its own nuance; e.g., in Lev 17:5, 7, זבח, "sacrifice," is used for slaughtering of animals in the open field, but זבח שלמים, "an offering of well-being," stands for a sacrifice offered at the entrance to the Tent of Meeting.

Rendtorff (*Studien,* 119–68) pursues the historical development of this sacrifice. He argues that originally there were three distinct sacrifices: שלמים, "the concluding sacrifice," זבח, "the sacrifice," and זבח שלמים, "the sacrifice of well-being." For Rendtorff the oldest sacrifice is the שלמים offering. He observes that it is always named in conjunction with a whole offering (עלה). It is especially a royal sacrifice and an altar sacrifice, i.e., for the consecration of an altar. And it is always a public sacrifice offered at the conclusion of a festive occasion. Its name then coincides with its position in a series of offerings; thus its meaning comes from the meaning of שלם as "completion, finish." The ritual for this sacrifice stresses the manipulation of blood; the blood is dashed against the altar.

It is too difficult to get behind the various texts with enough certainty to sustain Rendtorff's position that the שלמים offering is primarily a "concluding" sacrifice. At best there would be only a few references to the sacrifice that concluded a great public gathering. While Rendtorff stresses that in lists of sacrifices שלמים always occurs last, this may be accounted for on other grounds, namely that the order of the sacrifices in the lists of sacrifices was composed according to the purpose of each sacrifice. A sacrifice that atoned for human sinfulness, either the whole offering or the sin offering, was offered first. Only after the head of the family had made expiation for his own sins and for those of his family, rendering himself and his family acceptable to God, were they in a position to enjoy a festive meal before God. Therefore, the theology of the sacrificial system tends to account for an offering of well-being almost always occurring last in the order of sacrifices.

זבח, the oldest term for "sacrifice," has the character of a private and occasional sacrifice, e.g., for a family (cf. 1 Sam 1:21) or a clan (1 Sam 20:6), according to Rendtorff. Never is it a public offering. This sacrifice may be presented to fulfill a vow (e.g., Ps 116:17–18) or to seal a parity covenant (e.g., Gen 31:54). In this sacrifice the blood is simply poured out, i.e., withdrawn from profane use. There is no special rite of manipulating the blood. Rendtorff concludes from these significant differences that there were two independent sacrifices.

Rendtorff argues next that the זבח שלמים arose from the union of "the concluding sacrifice" and "the sacrifice." He posits that this new sacrifice is basically a זבח sacrifice to which the blood rite of the שלמים offering has been added. The most prominent step in the ritual, carried over from the שלמים sacrifice, is the priest's burning of the fat. The priest always performed this function because the שלמים was a public offering. So in the newly combined sacrifice the lay person prepared the sacrifice, and the priest performed the rest of the ritual. It can be said that in the new sacrifice זבח lost its private character and the שלמים offering was no longer reserved for an occasional sacrifice offered at the conclusion of a festive occasion. After the development of the official זבח שלמים, it was proper to refer to an offering of well-being by either the single term שלמים or the phrase זבח שלמים.

While much is learned from Rendtorff's reconstruction, it is doubtful that the sacrificial terms are used with such ritualistic precision throughout the OT. For example, at the dedication of Solomon's Temple this sacrifice is referred to in three ways, זבח, זבח שלמים, and חלבי שלמים (1 Kgs 8:62–66). To account for the appearance of these different terms in the same context, Rendtorff has to postulate that a later redactor has added to this text. To resort to such a conjecture points out the weakness in his reconstruction of the history of these supposed three distinct sacrifices.

There may be a simpler way than Rendtorff's to account for the use of these three terms. It seems that זבח is a term that applies to sacrifice in general; primarily it is used for a sacrifice that permits the offerer to enjoy a festive meal. While it frequently refers to a private sacrifice, especially in non-ritualistic texts, it may be used for a public offering (e.g., 2 Kgs 10:19; Neh 12:43). The term שלמים is the oldest name for the official offering of well-being. In codification of the sacrificial rituals, the two terms were combined in order to have a precise term for the sacrifice designed to be a festive meal for the laity.

1 For an offering of well-being a person may present from cattle either a male or female. The general requirements for sacrifice under this category are more lax since this is a praise offering that was often offered spontaneously. Dillmann (450) notes that in the texts that make mention of the animal's gender in this type of offering it is always a male (e.g., Exod 24:5; 29:19; Num 6:14; 7:88; Mal 1:14). Nothing is said here about the animal's age.

2 The animal is killed at "the entrance of the Tent of Meeting." Since the bulk of the meat remains in control of the laity, the animal itself is not brought into the holy area. Whatever offering enters the holy place becomes consecrated to God and may not be taken outside again except to dispose of its remains (cf. 4:12).

3 Special consideration is given to the parts that are to be burned on the altar. חלב, "the fat," in particular, belongs to Yahweh. The phraseology החלב המכסה את הקרב, "the fat which covers the entrails," and כל־החלב אשר על הקרב, "all the fat which is on the entrails," is inclusive of all the fat. This language refers to the omentum, the membrane that encloses the intestines and to which the fat clings. All of these portions may be referred to solely by the term "fat." The plural of חלבים, "fat," may stand for the offering of well-being itself, i.e., as a metonymy; e.g., in 2 Chr 7:7 there is the list: העלות, "whole offerings," המנחות, "grain offerings," and החלבים, "the fat," i.e., offerings of well-being (cf. 2 Chr 35:14; Isa 1:11; 43:24). Another way of referring to this offering is the phrase חלבי שלמים "the fat [of the offering] of well-being" (1 Kgs 8:64 // 2 Chr 7:7; cf. G. Münderlein, "חֵלֶב *chēlebh*," *TDOT* 4:391–97).

4 The two kidneys and the fat which is beside them on the sinews (שתי הכליות ואת החלב אשר עלהם אשר על הכסלים) plus the lobe of the liver (היתרת על הכבד) are to be removed as a whole. כבד, "the liver," is literally the heavy organ; being full of blood, it weighs about three and a half pounds. The Talmud renders the phrase היתרת על הכבד as "the finger of the liver." This part is usually identified as the *lobus caudatus*, the caudate lobe (L. Rost, *ZAW* 79 [1967] 35–41). The ancients prized the liver and the kidneys both as centers of emotional life and as delicacies. The Hebrews viewed the liver as a vital organ; e.g., if an arrow pierced it, death followed (Prov 7:23). In the OT כליות, "the kidneys," are frequently associated with a person's feelings, his deep thoughts, and his conscience (Pss 16:7; 73:21; Jer 11:20; 17:10), so too in Mesopotamian literature. That is why "kidneys" often parallels לב, "heart," in the OT (Jer 17:10; cf. 20:12; Pss 7:10[9]; 26:2; *CAD* 8:11–14). Also the Hebrews associated the deep emotions of sorrow and joy with the liver (Lam 2:11; cf. Ps 16:9). People of the Ancient Near East believed that the gods wrote messages about portending events on the entrails, particularly the liver, of special animals. On various occasions the priests read the entrails of these animals to discern the gods' will (Ezek 21:21; cf. H. Wolff, *Anthropology of the Old Testament*, 64–66). The lobe of the liver was particularly critical for the right interpretation. Such divination, however, was strictly forbidden in Israel (cf. Deut 18:9–13). Instead of setting aside the lobe for divination, the innards of an offering of well-being were burned on the altar as a valuable gift to Yahweh. This sacrificial standard erected a barrier to the practice of such divination in ancient Israel.

5 The parts of the offering of well-being specified for burning are to be placed on top of the whole offering that is already being consumed. They are classified as אשה ריח ניחח ליהוה, "a gift for a soothing aroma to Yahweh." This phrase means that God is pleased to accept the sacrifice on behalf of the offerer.

9 אליה, "the fat tail," is specifically mentioned in regard to sheep, for it includes a peculiar feature of a species of broad-tailed sheep bred in Palestine, which had a tail weighing fifteen pounds or more. Thus it is essential that this fat of the tail be offered on the altar so that it would not be eaten.

11 לחם, which specifically means "bread," is often used for "food" in general. Originally it meant "meat"; this fact suggests that its use with sacrifices is archaic

(Noordtzij, 51). In a few passages לחם stands for offerings in general, often being in apposition to or in close association with אשה "gifts" (e.g., 21:6, 8, 17, 21, 22; 22:25; Num 28:2; Ezek 44:7). Given the fact that there are no OT texts indicating that Yahweh is dependent on the sacrifices for food as were the gods of the other ancient Near Eastern pantheons (cf. Ps 50:7–15), the use of this term is at first reading startling. Its use may be to emphasize that Yahweh himself shares with the sacrificer and his clan in the meal made out of the offering of well-being. This interpretation may explain why in the legislation of sacrifices (chaps. 1–7) לחם, "bread," is used only with the offering of well-being, since this is the only sacrifice that belongs essentially to the layman to be used for a festive meal.

12–16 A separate regulation is given for the presentation of עז, "a goat," because it is distinguished from the fat-tailed sheep. Since this term for goat refers predominantly to the female and since the terms "male" and "female" are absent from this section (cf. vv 1, 6), it is possible that only a female goat is permitted. The procedure in this regulation agrees with that for a sheep found in vv 7–11.

17 This verse is a general decree that prohibits the eating of "fat" and "blood" under all circumstances, as is conveyed by the building up of generalized phrases: חקת עולם, "a perpetual decree," לדרתיכם, "by your generations," and בכל מושבתיכם, "in all your habitations." No exceptions to this stipulation are to be made because of the circumstances of a particular time or a special location, such as distance from the central sanctuary. Some commentators assume that this phraseology arose during a time when the Israelites were living outside Palestine, i.e., during the exile. Porter (31), however, points out that it may simply mean "inside or outside" the camp, as expressly stated in 17:3, i.e., any place in Palestine (cf. Ezek 6:6, 14). Statements against eating blood are also found in 7:26–27; 17:10; 19:26 (cf. Gen 9:4; Deut 12:16, 23; 15:23).

No specific reason is given for the prohibition against eating any of the fat. The reason may be that the ancient Israelites located an animal's strength in its fat, as the expression the חלב גבורים, "fat of mighty men," indicates (2 Sam 1:22; cf. J. Heller, "Die Symbolik des Fettes im AT," *VT* 20 [1970] 106–8). As the source of strength, the fat was the sole prerogative of Yahweh, the Giver of strength. Deut 32:14, however, indicates that God gave the people fat as a tasty delicacy. This would be the fat that was not designated for the altar. Furthermore, the detailed description of the fat to be offered on the altar may indicate that at the earliest stages of the sacrificial laws the other portions of fat were returned to either the offerer or the priests for eating. This later addition then prohibited the eating of any fat (cf. 7:23–25).

Explanation

The offering of well-being was offered in praise to God. Such an offering could be presented to praise God for good fortune or success, in the fulfillment of a vow, or as a spontaneous expression of love for God. In fact, the Heb. word for "well-being" stands for the multiple benefits of life, health, and prosperity that attend God's blessing. Guests could be invited to join in such a festive occasion (1 Sam 9:12–13; 16:2–5; Deut 12:18; cf. Zeph 1:7). There are, however, a few references in the OT in which an offering of well-being was presented at a time of distress to entreat God's help (e.g., Judg 20:26; 21:4; 1 Sam 13:9; 2 Sam 24:25).

The bulk of the meat from the offering was returned to the presenter to become a festive meal. This meal expressed the deep and abiding relationship between this clan and Yahweh. According to Noordtzij (48), it also served as a reminder of the covenant. Only the fat, the two kidneys, the caul, and the lobe of the liver were burned on the altar. These prized portions, the animal's life center, were God's prerogative. Because the fat and the blood belonged to God, the partaking of these parts by Israelites was strictly forbidden. The odor of the burning fat ascended as a soothing aroma, which entreated Yahweh's continued favor. Hendel (*ZAW* 101 [1989] 384) finds that the burning of Yahweh's special portions in contrast to the presenter's meat being boiled symbolized the distance between Yahweh, the holy God, and the presenter. Thus the ritual procedure of this offering communicated both the bond and the distance between Yahweh and humans. The officiating priest also received a small portion of the animal (7:31–34).

The oblation portions of an offering of well-being were burned on top of the whole offering. This may indicate, though certainly not in all cases, that whoever presented an offering of well-being first presented a whole offering. It also meant that the offering of well-being was prepared after the morning whole offering. Theologically this procedure indicates that the whole offering with its atoning merits was foundational to an offering that emphasized fellowship. The whole offering rendered the offerer acceptable to God. Afterwards he was free to fellowship with his family or clan before God in a festive meal featuring portions of the offering of well-being.

In partaking of the meal, the participants released God's blessing on themselves, a blessing that would prosper their labors and protect the family members from harm. When this sacrifice was offered during a time of distress, the intention was to recapture God's presence, for God's nearness would drive away the cause of the agony.

No concessions are made in this regulation for anyone who did not have the means to bring a large animal. Since this sacrifice was not demanded but offered freely, there was no need to provide an exception for the poor. Moreover, small birds like pigeons or doves would be inadequate to provide a fellowship meal, which was an essential intention of this offering.

The term "offering of well-being" does not appear in the NT. Nevertheless there are a few references that have this offering in mind, e.g., Matt 9:13; 12:7; Acts 21:23b–26; possibly Rom 12:1 and Heb 13:15–16. Moreover, parallels may be made between this offering and the fellowship meals of the early believers.

In the NT the community of believers frequently broke bread together at their homes (Acts 2:46). Acts 2:45–47a says that they "ate together with glad and sincere hearts, praising God and enjoying the favor of all the people." In so doing they were fulfilling the design of the offering of well-being. From 1 Cor 11:17–34 it is learned that the Eucharist was celebrated when believers joined together for fellowship at a meal. The partaking of the bread and the wine was the practice of Christ's presence, similar to God's presence with those eating a festive meal from an offering of well-being. The highest purpose of both ceremonies is the praise of God (cf. 1 Cor 10:16). Whereas blood was strictly forbidden to the OT worshipers, the cup, representing Christ's blood, is freely made available to all who partake of the Eucharist. The design of the offering of well-being has been continued in the new covenant, and it has been changed to appropriate the full blessings and privileges gained for all believers by Christ's death.

C. *Regulation for the Purification Offering (4:1–5:13)*

Bibliography

Anderson, M., and **Culbertson, P.** "The Inadequacy of the Christian Doctrine of Atonement in Light of Levitical Sin Offering." *ATR* 68 (1986) 303–78. **Bailey, J. W.** "The Usage in the Post Restoration Period of Terms Descriptive of the Priest and High Priest." *JBL* 70 (1951) 217–25. **Elliger, K.** "Zur Analyse des Sündopfergesetzes." In *Verbannung und Heimkehr: Beiträge zur Geschichte und Theologie Israels im 6. und 5. Jahrhundert v. Chr.* FS W. Rudolph. Ed. A. Kuschke. Tübingen: Mohr (Paul Siebeck), 1961. 39–50. **Geller, M.** "The Šurpu Incantations and Lev. V.1–6." *JSS* 25 (1980) 181–92. **Hamilton, V. P.** "Recent Studies in Leviticus and Their Contribution to Further Understanding of Wesleyan Theology." In *A Spectrum of Thought.* Ed. M. Peterson. Nashville: Parthenon Press, 1982. 146–56. **Kiuchi, N.** *The Purification Offering in the Priestly Literature.* JSOTSup 56. Sheffield: JSOT Press, 1987. **Knierim, R.** "חטא *ḥṭ*ʾ sich verfehlen." *THAT* 1:541–49. ———. "שׁגג *šgg* sich versehen." *THAT* 2:869–72. **Koch, K.** "חָטָא *chāṭāʾ*." *TDOT* 4:309–19. **Loss, N. M.** "La terminologia e il tema del peccato in Lv 4–5." *Sal* 30 (1968) 437–61. **Marx, A.** "Sacrifice pour les péchés ou rite de passage? Quelques réflections que la fonction du *ḥaṭṭāʾt*." *RB* 96 (1989) 27–48. **Matthes, J. C.** "Der Sühnegedanke bei den Sündopfer." *ZAW* 23 (1903) 97–119. **Milgrom, J.** "The Cultic שׁגגה and Its Influence in Psalms and Job." *JQR* 58 (1967) 115–25 and in *SCTT* 122–32. ———. "The Function of the *Ḥaṭṭāʾt* Sacrifice" (Heb.). *Tarbiz* 40 (1970) 1–8. ———. "Sin-offering or purification-offering?" *VT* 21 (1971) 237–39 and in *SCTT,* 67–69 ———. "Two kinds of *Ḥaṭṭāʾt*." *VT* 26 (1976) 333–37 and in *SCTT,* 70–74. ———. "Israel's Sanctuary: The Priestly 'Picture of Dorian Gray.'" *RB* 83 (1976) 390–99 and in *SCTT,* 75–84. ———. "The Graduated Sin Offering of Lev 5:1–13" (Heb.). *Beth Mikra* 29 (1983/84) 139–48. ———. "The Graduated *Ḥaṭṭāʾt* of Leviticus 5:1–13." *JAOS* 103 (1983) 249–54. ———. "The Two Pericopes on the Purification Offering." In *The Word of the Lord Shall Go Forth.* FS D. N. Freedman. Ed. C. Meyers and M. O'Connor. Winona Lake, IN: Eisenbrauns, 1983. 211–15. ———. "The *Modus Operandi* of the *Ḥaṭṭāʾt*: A Rejoinder." *SBL* 109 (1990) 111–13. **Saydon, P. P.** "Sin-offering and Trespass-offering." *CBQ* 8 (1946) 393–98. **Schenker, A.** "Das Zeichen des Blutes und die Gewissheit der Vergebung im Alten Testament." *MTZ* 34 (1983) 195–213. **Schötz, P. D.** *Schuld- und Sündopfer im Alten Testament.* Breslauer Studien zur historischen Theologie 18. Breslau: Müller & Seiffert, 1930. **Spiro, A.** "A Law on the Sharing of Information." *PAAJR* 28 (1959) 95–101. **Vriezen, Th. C.** "The Term *Hizza*: Lustration and Consecration." *OTS* 7 (1950) 201–35. **Weinberg, Z.** "חטאת ואשם." *Beth Mikra* 55 (1973) 524–30. **Zohar, N.** "Repentance and Purification: The Significance and Semantics of חטאת in the Pentateuch." *JBL* 107 (1988) 609–18.

Translation

[1] *Yahweh spoke to Moses,* [2] *"Speak to the Israelites: When anyone sins*[a] *inadvertently against any of Yahweh's commandments which may not be broken*[b] *and breaks*[b] *any*[c] *of them:*

3 "If the anointed priest sins, bringing guilt[a] on the people, he is to bring a young bull[b] without defect to Yahweh as a purification offering[c] for his sin which he has committed. 4 He is to bring the bull to the entrance of the Tent of Meeting before Yahweh. He is to lay his hand on the bull's head[a] and then slaughter the bull before Yahweh. 5 The anointed[a] priest will take some of the bull's blood and bring it into the Tent of Meeting. 6 The priest will dip his finger in the blood and sprinkle some[a] of the blood seven times[b] before Yahweh, before the curtain of the sanctuary. 7 The priest will put some of the blood on the horns of the altar of fragrant incense[a] before Yahweh which is in the Tent of Meeting. The rest[b] of the bull's blood he will pour out at the base[c] of the altar of the whole offering which is at the entrance to the Tent of Meeting. 8 He will remove all the fat from the bull of the purification offering; the fat which covers[a] the entrails and all the fat which is on the entrails, 9 the two kidneys and the fat around them by the loins, and the long lobe of the liver he will remove with the kidneys 10 just as it is removed from a member of the herd[a] for the offering of well-being. Then the priest will burn them[bc] on the altar of the whole offering.[d] 11 But[a] the bull's hide and all its meat together with[b] its head and its legs, and its entrails and its offal[cd]—12 the rest[a] of the bull he will bring[b] outside the camp to a clean place where the fat ashes are poured out[c] and burn it on a wood fire;[d] it is to be burned on the place of the fat ashes.[c]

13 "If the whole congregation[a] of Israel sins in error[b] and the matter be hidden from the assembly's eyes, for they break[c] any of Yahweh's commandments which are not to be broken,[c] they realize guilt, 14 and when the sin which they have committed becomes known, the assembly is to present[a] a young bull[b] for a purification offering and bring it[c] before[d] the Tent of Meeting. 15 The elders of the congregation are to lay their hands on the bull's head before Yahweh, and one of them is to slaughter[a] the bull before Yahweh. 16 The anointed priest will bring some of the bull's blood into the Tent of Meeting. 17 The priest will dip his finger into the blood and sprinkle some of the blood[a] seven times before Yahweh, before the curtain.[b] 18 Some of the blood[a] he[b] will put on the horns of the altar[c] which is before Yahweh, which is in the Tent of Meeting. The rest of the blood[d] he will pour out at the base of the altar of the whole offering which is at the entrance to the Tent of Meeting. 19 He will remove all its fat and burn it on the altar.[a] 20 Then he is to do with this bull just as he did with the bull for the purification offering. Thus he will do with it. And the priest will make expiation for them, and they will be forgiven. 21 Then he is to bring[a] the bull outside the camp and burn[a] it just as he burned[a] the first bull. It[b] is a purification offering for the community.

22 "Whenever[a] a leader sins and breaks[b] any[c] of the commandments of Yahweh his God which may not inadvertently be broken,[b] he realizes guilt, 23 or when he is made aware[a] of his sin which he has committed, he is to bring as his offering a male goat without defect. 24 He is to lay his hand on the goat's head and slaughter it in the place where the whole offering is slaughtered[a] before Yahweh. It is a purification offering.[b] 25 Then the priest will take some of the blood of the purification offering with his finger and put it on the horns of the altar of the whole offering, and he will pour out the rest of[a] the blood at the base of the altar of the whole offering. 26 He will burn all its fat on the altar,[a] like the fat of the offering of well-being. So the priest will make expiation for him because of[b] his sin, and he will be forgiven.

27 "If any member of the community[a] sins inadvertently by breaking[b] any of the commandments[c] which are not to be broken,[b] he realizes guilt, 28 and when he is made aware[a] of his sin which he has committed,[b] he is to bring as his offering[c] a female goat without defect for his sin which he has committed. 29 He is to lay his hand on the head of the purification offering and slaughter[a] the purification offering[b] in the place[c] of the whole offering. 30 Then the priest will take some of its blood with his finger and put it on the horns of the altar of the whole offering, and he will pour out the rest of the blood at the base of the altar.[a] 31 He will remove all its fat, just as the fat of the offering of well-being is removed,[a] and the priest will burn it on the altar[b] (for a soothing aroma to Yahweh).[c] The priest will make expiation for him, and he will be forgiven.

32 "If he brings a lamb as his offering for his purification offering, he is to bring a female without defect. 33 He is to lay his hand on the head of the purification offering[a] and slaughter[b] it in the place where one slaughters[b] the whole offering. 34 Then the priest will take some of the blood of the purification offering with his finger and put it on the horns of the altar of the whole offering and pour out the rest of the blood at the base of the altar.[a] 35 He will remove all its fat, just as the fat of the lamb from an offering of well-being is removed,[a] and the priest will burn it[b] on the altar[c] on top of the gifts to Yahweh. The priest will make expiation for him for the sin which he has committed, and he will be forgiven.

5:1 "If a person sins in that he hears[a] a public oath and he has been a witness[a] or has seen or has come to know the matter, yet he does not make it known,[a] he will be held responsible.[b] 2 Or if[a] a person touches anything unclean, such as the corpse of an unclean animal, wild or domestic, or the corpse of an unclean creature that moves on the ground, and it is hidden from him, he has become unclean,[b] and he realizes guilt.[c] 3 Or if he touches any human uncleanness, any[a] uncleanness by which one becomes unclean, and it is hidden from him, when he comes to know it, he realizes guilt. 4 Or if a person swears rashly[a] to do evil or to do good, any sort of rash oath that a human swears, and it is hidden from him, when he is made aware of it, he realizes guilt for any of these oaths. 5 Whenever one realizes guilt[ab] in any of these cases, he must confess[c] how he has sinned, 6 and he must bring as his penalty[a] to Yahweh for his sin which he has sinned a female lamb[b] from the flock or a goat for a purification offering, and the priest will make expiation for him because of his sin.[c]

7 "If one cannot afford[a] a lamb, he is to bring to Yahweh[b] as his penalty[c] for the sin which he has committed two doves or two young pigeons, one for a purification offering and one for a whole offering. 8 He is to bring them to the priest, and the priest[a] is to offer first the one for the purification offering. He[b] will wring its head from its neck without severing it. 9 He will sprinkle some of the blood of the purification offering on the side of the altar, and the rest of the blood will be drained out[a] at the base of the altar. It is a purification offering.[b] 10 He will then make a whole offering of the second according to the regulation,[a] and the priest will make expiation for him because of the sin which he has committed, and he will be forgiven.

11 "If one cannot afford[a] two turtledoves or two young pigeons, he is to bring as his offering for his sin a tenth of an ephah of fine flour[b] for a purification offering. He may not put[c] oil on it, nor may he put incense on it, because it is a purification offering. 12 He is to bring it to the priest, and the priest[a] will pinch off a handful as a memorial. He will burn it on the altar with the gifts of Yahweh.[b] It is a purification offering. 13 The priest will make expiation for him for any[a] of these sins that he has committed, and he will be forgiven. The rest[b] is for the priest as is the grain offering."[c]

Notes

2.a. LXX adds ἔναντι κυρίου, "before the Lord."

2.b. Heb. uses the general term עשׂה, "do." Failing "to do" a commandment in cultic legislation is not a failure "to keep it," but a decision "to break it."

2.c. The prep מן, "from," used with partitive force with אחת, "one," means "any" (GKC §119w, n. 2).
3.a. אשמת, "bringing guilt on," is a fem inf constr of אשם (KB, 92; GKC §45d).
3.b. פר בן־בקר is "a calf," lit. "a young bull of the species ox." This phrase is used in lieu of the term עגל, "calf." Beck ("בָּקָר *bāqār*," *TDOT* 2:216) speculates that the author of this legislation wished to avoid a term associated with pagan cultic shrines such as those set up at Dan and Bethel by Jeroboam I (1 Kgs 12:28–33).
3.c. חטאת in this verse is used in two ways. It stands for transgressing a statute, and it refers to the offering presented to expiate a sin committed.
4.a. LXX adds ἔναντι κυρίου, "before the Lord," as in n. 2.a.
5.a. Sam and LXX add אשר מלא את־ידו, "who is consecrated," which is explicative of משיח, "anointed" (cf. 8:33). This addition witnesses to the tendency to fill out the text during its transmission.
6.a. The prep מן, "from," is used with partitive force.
6.b. Sam and LXX[BA] add באצבעו, "by his finger."
7.a. הסמים may be a loan word that stands for incense, medicine, or poison. Here it refers to the special incense made out of equal amounts of gum, resin, onycha, and galbanum mixed with frankincense (Exod 30:34–36 NIV; cf. M. Haran, *Temples*, 242–45).
7.b. כל, lit. "all," refers to the bulk of the animal's blood, for only a little was used in the blood rites.
7.c. P. Dion (*JBL* 106 [1987] 489–90) shows that in the Second Temple the base protruded out from the altar, rising a foot and a half, where it was not intercepted by the ramp, and projecting out a foot and a half (cf. *m. Zebaḥ*. 2.1; 3.2). This was constructed to make sure that no blood might be lost.
8.a. Instead of על, "on," many Heb. mss, Sam, Tg[mss], and *Tg. Ps.-J.* read את, the particle that indicates the dir obj, for it stands as obj of the ptcp (cf. 3:3, 9). The error may have arisen from the frequent use of על in the lists of the fat to be removed.
10.a. שור, "ox, bull, cow," usually stands for a single head of cattle of either sex, though it can be used collectively. Here it is distinguished from פר, "bull," which is the sacrificial animal required in this ritual.
10.b. LXX may have read והקטיר, "and he will burn," instead of MT והקטירם, "and he will burn them" (cf. vv 19, 35).
10.c. The antecedent of the pronoun is the various pieces of fat and the entrails just enumerated in vv 8–9.
10.d. In light of vv 20, 26, 31, 35, one expects the statement וכפר עליו הכהן ונסלח לו, "the priest will make expiation for him, and he will be forgiven." Its absence is very puzzling. Noth (41) thinks that it once stood here and has been omitted by a scribal error. The principle of the harder reading does not support his explanation. Furthermore, Kiuchi (*Purification Offering*, 126–28) has a complex explanation for this line's omission that is hard to evaluate. He builds his position on the premise arrived at in his study that "bearing guilt" is an essential component of כפר, "expiation." Since the high priest cannot bear his own guilt, this ritual for a high priest effectively cleanses the sanctuary, but it fails to remove his guilt. That removal is achieved on the Day of Atonement by the ritual with the goat for Azazel, which carries away his guilt and that of the congregation. Meanwhile, this ritual for a high priest's purification offering is efficacious, in Kiuchi's judgment (129–30), for the rite of sprinkling the blood has power in that it foreshadows the sprinkling rites on the Day of Atonement. Because it is impossible to imagine that the high priest would have to wait until the Day of Atonement to receive full expiation and forgiveness for an inadvertent sin, especially in light of his continuing to lead the cult, Kiuchi's theory appears to be wanting.
11.a. The *waw* has mild adversative force.
11.b. The prep על, "on," expresses addition (BDB, "על 4.c.," 755).
11.c. The distinction between קרב and פרש is unclear. Elliger (70) suggests that קרב refers to the honorable innards, e.g., heart and lungs, and פרש to the base parts, the intestines and their contents.
11.d. This entire verse is an extended *casus pendens* that functions as the obj of the verb הוציא, "he will bring out," in v 12. This unusual grammatical style suggests that v 11 is a later addition to define in detail what is included in the phrase "the rest of the bull."
12.a. Cf. n. 7.b.
12.b. LXX reads a pl verb.
12.c. This phrase שפך דשן, (lit.) "the pouring out of fat ashes" (cf. 6:4[11]), is the same in both occurrences though it is translated differently for sake of Eng meaning. It occurs only here in the OT. In its second occurrence the prep על, "on," is used instead of אל, "to," in order to permit the burning of these parts of a purification offering should there be no fat ashes at that time in the clean place outside the camp.

12.d. ושרף אתו על־עצים באש is lit. "he will burn it by fire on pieces of wood."

13.a. Milgrom sets the *terminus ad quem* for the use of עדה for the Israelites as the assembly of God's people with the establishment of a strong nation-state ("Priestly Terminology and the Political and Social Structure of Pre-monarchic Israel," *JQR* 69 [1978] 72–76 = *SCTT* 8–12). He goes on to conjecture that the post-exilic redactors substituted קהל for the archaic עדה in selected places in order to make the meaning of the ancient term clear. Incidentally, LXX renders עדה with *συναγωγή*, "synagogue," and קהל with *ἐκκλησία*, "religious community." In the late post-exilic era, Jewish writers distinguished these two Gk. terms thus: *συναγωγή*, "synagogue," stood for the present Israel as a "religious community," and *ἐκκλησία* for the ideal Israel.

13.b. The verb ישׁגו, "sin in error," comes from the root שׁגה. Hoffmann (1:183) distinguishes between שׁגה as a theoretical sin, a sin of thinking, and שׁגג as a sinful act.

13.c. Cf. n. 2.b.

14.a. The verb with the sg subj הקהל, "the assembly," is pl, suggesting that the various leaders each took part in slaughtering the animal. The *waw* on the verb is a *waw* of succession (Joüon §117d).

14.b. Sam and LXX add תמים, "without defect," making this verse agree with v 3. It is highly probable that this adjective has been lost as a result of a scribal error.

14.c. Cf. the first part of n. 14.a.

14.d. Instead of MT לפני, "before," LXX reads *παρὰ τὰς θύρας*, "at the doors," leveling the text to agree with v 4.

15.a. LXX reads a pl verb. The sg is used in place of a pl verb (cf. n. 14.a.) because only one of the elders may have sacrificed the bull (cf. Hoffmann, 1:185). PIR (163), however, understands it as an impersonal sg.

17.a. A few Heb. mss and Sam add מן־הדם, "some of the blood." This reading agrees with v 6. The MT reading מן־הדם after the verb טבל, "dip," is awkward compared to בדם, "in the blood," in v 6. Therefore, this verse probably should be reconstructed to read like v 6: בדם והזה מן־הדם. A compound error of haplography and metathesis could have led to the omission of one occurrence of דם, "blood."

17.b. Instead of פני הפרכת, "before the curtain," Sam and LXX read פני הקדשׁ, "before the holy place."

18.a. The phrase מן־הדם, "some of the blood," stands before the verb for emphasis.

18.b. Sam and LXX add הכהן, "the priest."

18.c. Instead of המזבח, "the altar," Sam and LXX read מזבח קטרת הסמים, "the altar of incense"; cf. v 7.

18.d. This phrase stands before the verb for emphasis (cf. n. 18.a.; also cf. n. 7.b.).

19.a. The term המזבחה, "on the altar," has a locative ה to indicate the place where something happens (GKC §90d).

21.a. LXX reads a pl verb as in v 12.

21.b. Sam reads היא for MT הוא because חטאת, "purification offering," is a fem noun.

22.a. This case differs from the other three cases by being introduced by אשׁר with the meaning "whenever."

22.b. Cf. n. 2.b.

22.c. Cf. n. 2.c.

23.a. GKC §69w takes the ו in הודע as an example where וֹ stands instead of וּ in the hoph. LXX reads *καὶ γνωσθῇ* = אם נודע, "if it is known," for MT או־הודע, so too Syr. The particle או, "or," is difficult in Heb. grammar, but this phrase should not be quickly emended, for it occurs again in v 28.

24.a. LXX reads a pl verb. LXX may have the preferred reading, for often in Heb. the pl verb functions as a virtual passive.

24.b. Sam and Tg read היא for MT הוא; cf. n. 21.b.

25.a. Many Heb. mss and LXX add כל, "all," as in vv 7, 18, 30, 34. To make sense, this Eng trans. reads like the variant, but MT represents the better text, for it is the more difficult text.

26.a. Cf. n. 19.a.

26.b. מן carries the meaning "on account of, because of" (GKC §119z). It might mean "from," i.e., the expiation removes the sin, but that is an awkward way to express that idea. Kiuchi (*Purification Offering*, 88; cf. Janowski, *Sühne*, 187, especially n. 12) points out that the prep על or מן after על, "for," introduces the motive or the reason for the atonement. Another strong possibility that this is an elliptical expression for יכפר על־לטהר את־מן, "he will make expiation for . . . to cleanse . . . from . . . ," as in 16:30.

27.a. MT is lit. "the people of the land" (עם הארץ).

27.b. Cf. n. 2.b.

27.c. Instead of ממצות, "from the commandments," some Heb. mss, Sam, and LXX read מכל מצות, "from all the commandments."

28.a. Cf. n. 23.a.

28.b. Sam and LXX add the prep phrase עליה, "on it"; cf. v 23, where the prep phrase בה, "in it," follows this same verb.

28.c. LXX omits קרבנו, "his offering."

29.a. LXX reads a pl verb; cf. n. 24.a.

29.b. LXX adds *τὴν χίμαιραν* = שׂעירה, "the goat."

29.c. Sam and LXX read אשר ישחטו את־העלה, "where the whole offering is slaughtered," as MT has in vv 24, 33.

30.a. Two Heb. mss, Sam, and Syr read מזבח העלה, "the altar of the whole offering," as in vv 7, 18, 25.

31.a. Sam reads יסיר, "he will remove," for MT הוסר, "it is to be removed."

31.b. Cf. n. 19.a.

31.c. The phrase ריח ניחח ליהוה, "a soothing aroma to Yahweh," which occurs frequently in chaps. 1–3 for the whole offering, the grain offering, and the offering of well-being, occurs only here in chaps. 4–5 in the regulations of the purification offering and the reparation offering. Noordtzij (63) suspects, probably correctly, that it may have been transposed into this regulation from the offering of well-being. Therefore, it is best to put this phrase in parentheses.

33.a. LXX omits לחטאת, "for a purification offering."

33.b. LXX reads a pl verb; cf. n. 24.a.

34.a. Sam and LXX read מזבח העלה, "the altar of the whole offering"; cf. n. 30.a.

35.a. Cf. n. 31.a.

35.b. Sam omits the acc אתם, "them," and LXX seems to have read a singular *αὐτό* = אתה, "it." MT "them" refers to all the fatty parts, while LXX "it" refers to the fat collectively.

35.c. Cf. n. 19.a.

5:1.a. When the noun נפשׁ, "soul, person," stands as the antecedent of a pronoun, there is a fluctuation of genders, for though it is fem, it usually stands for a masc subj.

1.b. נשׂא עונו means (lit.) "he must carry his iniquity." The concept is that a sin creates a debt on multiple levels—with the person himself, with the community, and with God—so whoever sins is held responsible to pay in full the debt caused by his sinning. In some contexts this phrase may mean "take away iniquity" = "forgive," but not in Leviticus or Ezekiel.

2.a. For MT אשׁר, "who," Heb. mss and Sam read כי, "that." The variant agrees with vv 1 and 4. It is preferred for parallel expression.

2.b. Instead of טמא, "he has become unclean," codices from the Cairo Geniza read ידע, "he comes to know," as in vv 3, 4. Elliger (56) suggests this alternative reading. It has much to commend it; the MT is followed as the harder reading.

2.c. LXX* accidentally omits ונעלם ממנו והוא טמא ואשׁם, "and it is hidden from him; he has become unclean and is guilty."

3.a. The ל serves to introduce this appositional phrase.

4.a. "Rashly" renders the phrase לבטא בשׂפתים. בטא means "to speak rashly or thoughtlessly" (BDB, 104). The joining of בשׂפתים, "with his lips," underscores the rashness of the oath; the words come solely from the lips (cf. Ps 106:33), not from the heart, i.e. the mind (cf. Prov 15:28).

5.a. Codices from the Cairo Geniza, LXX*, and Vg omit והוה . . . מאלה as a result of an error of homoioteleuton.

5.b. For יאשׁם, "he realizes guilt," Sam reads יחטא, "he sins." Milgrom (*Cult*, 10) argues that here אשׁם carries the emphasis "feel guilty."

5.c. After התודה, "he must confess," *Tg. Ps.-J.* and LXX add חטאתו, "his sin." This illustrates the tendency for the text to become full.

6.a. אשׁם, "guilt," may refer both to the transgression and to its consequences. Here it means the penalty for the sin (Milgrom, *Cult*, 6). The occurrence of אשׁם, "guilt, reparation offering," with חטאת, "sin, purification offering," is difficult and leads to the confusion of the precise meaning of these two terms in this passage.

6.b. כשׂבה, "female lamb," with this spelling occurs only here in the OT, no doubt influenced by the frequent occurrence in these regulations of "male lamb" spelled כשׂב (3:7; 4:35, etc.). The usual spelling is כבשׂה.

6.c. Instead of מחטאתו, "from his sin," Sam and LXX read על חטאתו אשר חטא ונסלח לו, "his sin which he sinned and he will be forgiven," as in 4:35. MT is preferred as the shorter reading. On meaning of מן, cf. n. 4:26.b.

7.a. Sam reads תשׂיג, as in v 11, for MT תגיע. Both words are virtually synonymous in this expression, which means lit. "his hand cannot reach enough for a lamb," i.e., he cannot furnish or afford a lamb.

7.b. Syr omits ליהוה, "to Yahweh."

7.c. Instead of את־אשמו, "his reparation or penalty," LXX reads *περὶ τῆς ἁμαρτίας αὐτοῦ* = את־חטאתו, "for his sin." MT is followed as the harder reading, but the variant is rooted in the confusion caused by the wide semantic range of אשם, "reparation, guilt," attested in this context. It is possible that the MT is elliptical for את־אשמו על חטאתו אשר חטא, "his reparation for his sin which he has committed," as in n. 6.a. (Elliger, 56).

8.a. LXX adds *ὁ ἱερεύς*, "the priest." The MT lacks הכהן and is preferred, though the Eng trans. requires naming the subj for clarity.

8.b. LXX again adds *ὁ ἱερεύς*, "the priest."

9.a. LXX reads *καταστραγγιεῖ* = יִמְצֶה, "he will drain out," a qal, instead of MT's niph יִמָּצֵה, "it will be drained out." There is also a spelling variant ימצא in some Heb. mss and Sam.

9.b. Sam and LXX read היא from MT חוא; cf. n. 4:21.b.

10.a. השיג usually governs the acc, but here the obj is introduced by ל. Hoffmann (1:204) states that the verb with the prep means that a person does not have the means to purchase two pigeons, whereas if this verb were followed by the acc it would mean that he did not possess as much as the value of two pigeons.

11.a. Cf. n. 7.a.

11.b. This phrase stands in apposition to קרבנו, "his offering," defining its specific nature.

11.c. Instead of ישים, "he will put" (cf. 2:15), Sam, LXX, and Syr read יצק, "he will pour," as in 2:1, 6. MT is preferred as the more difficult reading.

12.a. Sam omits הכהן, "the priest."

12.b. For את־אזכרתה והקטיר המזבחה על אשי יהוה, "as a memorial. And he will burn (it) on the altar with the gifts of Yahweh," LXX mistakenly reads *τὸ μνημόσυνον αὐτῆς ἐπιθήσει ἐπὶ τὸ θυσιαστήριον τῶν ὁλοκαυτωμάτων κυρίῳ*, "he will place its memorial on the altar of the whole offerings to the Lord," perhaps influenced by the frequent appearance of מזבח העלה, "the altar of the whole offering," in chap. 4 (vv 18, 25, 30, 34).

13.a. Cf. n. 4:2.c.

13.b. LXX reads *τὸ δὲ καταλειφθὲν ἔσται* = והיה הנותר, "and that which is left will be." LXX, like this Eng trans., felt it necessary to define the subj more specifically.

13.c. In lieu of כמנחה, "like the grain offering," LXX reads *ὡς ἡ θυσία τῆς σεμιδάλεως*, "as the sacrifice of the fine flour."

Form/Structure/Setting

The structure of the regulation for a purification offering (חטאת) is as follows:

I. Introductory formula (4:1–2aα)
II. Speech (4:2–5:13)
  A. Commission to speak (4:2aα)
  B. Speech proper (4:2aβ–5:13)
    1. Regulations for the usual purification offering (vv 2aβ–35)
      a. Basic case (v 2aβ+b)
      b. Four classifications of this offering by reason of offender's status (vv 3–35)
        1) Case of the anointed priest (vv 3–12)
          a) Basic instruction (v 3)
            (1) Case (v 3a)
            (2) Regulation (v 3b)
          b) Ritual procedure (vv 4–12)
            (1) Presentation of a bull (v 4a)
            (2) Laying on of hands (v 4bα)
            (3) Slaughter (v 4bβ)
            (4) Handling of the blood (vv 5–7)
            (5) Burning of the fat (vv 8–10)
            (6) Disposal of the remainder (vv 11–12)
        2) Case of the congregation (vv 13–21)
          a) Basic instruction (vv 13–14a)
          b) Ritual procedure (vv 14b–21a)

(1) Action of the assembly (vv 14b–15b)
(a) Presentation of a bull (v 14b)
(b) Laying on of hands (v 15a)
(c) Slaughter (v 15b)
(2) Action of the priest (vv 16–21a)
(a) Procedural instruction (vv 16–20a)
(i) Handling of the blood (vv 16–18)
(ii) Burning of the fat (v 19)
(iii) Treatment similar to first bull (v 20a)
(b) Statement of expiation and forgiveness (v 20b)
(c) Disposal of the rest (v 21a)
c) Statement of identification of sacrifice (v 21b)
3) Case of a prince (vv 22–26)
a) Basic instruction (vv 22–23a)
b) Ritual procedure (similar to above case) (vv 23b–26)
4) Case of an individual (vv 27–35)
a) Basic statement (vv 27–28a)
b) Ritual procedure (vv 28b–35)
(1) Basic procedure for a goat (similar to above case) (vv 28b–31)
(2) Alternate offering of a lamb (similar to presentation of a goat) (vv 32–35)
2. Regulations for the graduated purification offering (5:1–13)
a. Four cases requiring a graduated purification offering (vv 1–6)
1) Four cases (vv 1–4)
a) First case concerning a witness who fails to testify (v 1)
b) Second case concerning touching something unclean (v 2)
c) Third case concerning touching human uncleanness (v 3)
d) Fourth case concerning a rash oath (v 4)
2) Resolution of these cases (vv 5–6)
a) Confession of sin (v 5)
b) Presentation of offering (v 6)
(1) Sacrificial animal required (v 6a)
(2) Action of priest (v 6b)
b. Alternative materials for this kind of offering (vv 7–13)
1) First alternative (vv 7–10)
a) Identification of the sacrificial animals (v 7)
(1) Qualifying condition (v 7a*α*)
(2) Nature of animals (v 7a*β*–b)
(a) Two turtledoves or two young pigeons (v 7a*β*)
(b) Types of sacrifices (v 7b)
(i) One for a purification offering (v 7b*α*)
(ii) One for a whole offering (v 7b*β*)
b) Ritual procedure (vv 8–10)
(1) For a purification offering (vv 8–9)
(2) For a whole offering (v 10)
2) Second alternative (vv 11–13)
a) Identification of the materials (v 11)
(1) Qualifying condition (v 11a*α*)
(2) Definition of sacrificial material (v 11a*β*)
(3) Restrictions against using oil and incense with the flour (v 11b)
b) Ritual procedure (vv 12–13a)
c) Instruction for the leftover grain (v 13)

(This outline is based on a protocol from R. Knierim's seminar.)

The structural analysis discovers that there are two basic types of purification offering: the regular purification offering in 4:2a*β*–35 and the graduated purification offering in 5:1–13. The regular purification offering is further divided into two major categories: the greater one for the people as a covenant community and the lesser one for an individual. The high priest, the spiritual head of the community, is placed in the greater category while נשׂיא, "a prince," a tribal leader, is placed in the lesser category. The purification offering for the anointed priest and the congregation is classified as greater because it cleanses the more potent pollution that penetrates into the Tent of Meeting, because it is more elaborate, and because the animal may not be eaten at all. The lesser purification offering cleanses the main altar from the pollution caused by the less potent sins of either a leader or any individual.

The first part of this regulation prescribes five rituals for the presentation of a purification offering. These rituals are distinguished according to four classes of people: the anointed priest (הכהן המשׁיח; vv 3–12), the entire congregation of Israel (כל־עדת ישׂראל; vv 13–21), a prince (נשׂיא; vv 22–26), and any member of the community (נפשׁ אחת; vv 27–35). The last ritual is subdivided into two parts based on the kind of animals presented, a female goat (vv 27–30) or a female lamb (vv 31–35).

Each of these rituals has essentially the same formulation. Each begins with a reference to the occasion requiring the making of a purification offering, i.e., one's having sinned inadvertently against one of Yahweh's commandments. It is also stated that the person who has sinned is guilty, save in the case of the anointed priest, who brings guilt on the people (v 3a). Then come the detailed steps of the ritual, which may be enumerated:

1. Presentation, הקריב + הביא (vv 3–4, 14; vv 23, 28b, 32 [only הביא])
2. Laying of a hand on the animal's head, סמך (vv 4b*α*, 15a, 24a*α*, 29a, 33a)
3. Slaughter, שׁחט (vv 4b*β*, 15b, 24a*β*, 29b, 33b)
4. Manipulation of the blood:
   a. The greater purification offering:
      1) Taking some blood inside the Tent of Meeting, הביא + לקח + לקח (vv 5, 16 [only הביא])
      2) Sprinkling it seven times before the curtain, הזה (vv 6, 17)
      3) Putting some on the horns of the altar of incense, נתן (vv 7, 18)
      4) Pouring out the rest at the base of the altar, שׁפך (vv 7b, 18b)
   b. The lesser purification offering:
      1) Putting some blood on the horns of the altar of the whole offering, נתן + לקח (vv 25a, 30a, 34a)
      2) Pouring out the rest at the base of the altar of the whole offering, שׁפך (vv 25b, 30b, 34b)
5. Removal of the fat, הסיר + הרים (vv 8–10a, 19a [only הרים], 31a*αβ* [only הסיר], 35a*αβ* [only הסיר])
6. Burning of the fat, הקטיר (vv 10b, 19b, 26a, 31a*γδ*, 35a*γδ*)
7. Disposal of the remaining parts of the animal (only with the greater purification offering):
   a. Bringing the parts outside the camp, הוציא (vv 11–12a, 21a*α*)
   b. Burning these parts, שׂרף (vv 12b, 21a*β*)

At the conclusion of each ritual except the one for the anointed priest, there is the statement that the priest makes expiation for the guilty party and that party is forgiven (vv 20b, 26b, 31b, 35b). Regarding the exception, it may not have been considered appropriate for the anointed priest to proclaim his own forgiveness.

During its transmission this regulation has been filled out to produce a full, smooth text (cf. Koch, *Priesterschrift*, 53). The basic ritual is to be found in either the ritual for a prince or for an individual to present a goat (vv 22–31). The ritual for an individual was expanded to permit the offering of a female sheep (vv 32–35). The early date of this addition is attested by the avoidance of the technical term הקריב, "present," and the short sentences of the first line (v 32).

As for the greater purification offering, it is more difficult to detect the underlying ancient ritual. Koch (*Priesterschrift*, 55) and Elliger (60–62, 67) accept the one for the congregation as the older one. Nevertheless, in both rituals there are a number of short sentences headed by *waw* perfects. It seems that both rituals go back to the earliest period. However, they have been filled out during the long course of textual transmission. The most prominent additions are worthy of mention. In v 14 the sentence והקריבו הקהל פר בן־בקר לחטאת, "the assembly is to present a bull for a purification offering," merely repeats the following sentence, which is identifiable as older by the use of הביא, "he will bring." The editor of these words wished to be specific and desired the inclusion of the technical term הקריב, "present." In the ritual for the congregation, the phrase זקני העדה, "the elders of the congregation," has been inserted to identify the ones who were to lay their hands on the bull (v 15). The small altar on which the blood was put is more precisely identified as אשר לפני יהוה אשר באהל מועד, "the one which is before Yahweh, which is in the Tent of Meeting" (v 18a; cf. v 7a). Elsewhere the main altar, מזבח העלה, "the altar of the whole offering" (vv 15, 18, 25 [2x], 30, 34), throughout has been identified as אשר־פתח אהל מועד, "the one which is at the entrance of the Tent of Meeting" (vv 7b, 18b).

Koch (*Priesterschrift*, 54–55) believes, furthermore, that the rites for the disposal of the rest of the blood (vv 7b, 18b) and for the burning of the fat (vv 9b–10, 19), which are at home in the ritual for the offering of well-being, are later additions to the ritual of the purification offering. A clue to his interpretation is that the former rite is absent from the ritual for a purification offering in the regulations for the Day of Atonement (16:18–19). He may be correct that these rites were later additions to the ritual of the purification offering, but it is possible that their inclusion is earlier than he allows. The great concern for the proper disposal of blood would have been true of the earliest era. The handling of the fat for any sacrifice that was not wholly burned on the altar was critical since fat was never to be eaten (3:17). Some statement about these vital elements would have been essential in the oldest ritual. That they may have been taken over from an offering of well-being does not militate against their being integrated quite early into this ritual. Moreover, Koch builds part of his argument on the verbs for these rites being imperfect, rather than perfect. But because the direct object here is placed before the verb for emphasis, the verb properly stands as an imperfect.

The text has also been filled out to specify more exactly the location of various rites. The oldest layer identified the place for the ritual as לפני יהוה, "before Yahweh." But with the establishment of the cult, this general term was specified as אל־פתח אהל מועד, "at the entrance of the Tent of Meeting" (v 4a), or אשר באהל מועד, "which is in the Tent of Meeting" (vv 7a, 18a), or את־פני פרכת הקדש, "the face of the holy curtain" (vv 6b, 17b [without הקדש]). The former phrase is more general and applicable for sacrifice offered at any altar dedicated to Yahweh while the additions restrict the presenting of sacrifices to the central shrine.

Noteworthy in the ritual for the congregation (v 20b) is the position of the declarations about atonement being achieved and one being forgiven before the instruction about the disposal of the remainder of the bull (v 21a). According to Koch (*Priesterschrift,* 57), the location reflects a shift in the understanding of atonement. In the oldest tradition atonement was accomplished only after the sin-laden animal had been completely disposed. Later, it was considered to be achieved primarily through the manipulation of the blood. Thus, the rite of disposing of the animal lost its importance. The present order certainly indicates that the handling of blood was the means of atonement, not the disposal of the animal. But this fact does not require the postulate that there was a shift in theology, for the rituals for a lesser purification offering fail to mention that priests eat the meat (cf. 6:19[26], 22[29]).

The reference to the altar of incense (מזבח קטרת הסמים; vv 7a, 18a) has raised much discussion. Since there is no mention of this altar in the ritual for a purification offering on the Day of Atonement (chap. 16), it is the scholarly consensus that it was not a part of the archaic Holy Place. The earliest time for its introduction was the Solomonic temple (cf. Haran, *Temples,* 226, 228–29, 235–37). Its mention in Exod 30:1–10 is considered to be an adaptation of the wilderness tabernacle to the Solomonic temple (Haran, *Temples,* 191–92). The infrequent references to this altar make its history hard to trace. Since to argue from silence is precarious, the antiquity of this altar should not be too quickly dismissed (cf. Exod 30:1–10; 40:5, 26–27). Koch (*Priesterschrift,* 56) reasons further that since blood has been sprinkled in the Most Holy Place, it would be superfluous to spread blood on this altar, which was in an area of lesser holiness. Nevertheless, if impurity from a sin polluted the holiest place, it would also pollute the Holy Place. Thus it would be necessary to cleanse the horns of this altar in the Holy Place. The two blood rites then cleansed the entire Tent of Meeting.

Next is the question of the origin of a distinct ritual for the purification offering presented by the high priest. Most critical scholars assign it to the final stage of the composition of this regulation, sometime in the post-exilic era. In that era the high priest assumed leadership of the small, struggling religious community around Jerusalem. He assumed limited political power over that community, taking to himself many of the prerogatives of the house of David. The unusual title הכהן המשיח, "anointed priest," favors this interpretation, for the verbal adjective משיח, "anointed," may refer specifically to the Davidic monarch. This title is a key to dating the ritual. It is doubtful that it would have been used for the priest during the Kingdom period. This fact pushes the date of the composition to either the era before the Davidic kingdom or after its fall. While most scholars take the latter position, it is possible that the earliest high priests were anointed (cf. chap. 8). If so, this ritual might have existed quite early. The frequent occurrence of short sentences headed by *waw* perfects (vv 4, 5, 6, 7a*a*) supports the position that an ancient Vorlage underlies the present ritual. The choice of the term "anointed" for the high priest ties this regulation to the context of Exod 25–Lev 16, in which emphasis is given to the consecration and anointing of the high priest (Exod 28:41; 29; 30:30; 40:14–15; Lev 8).

Furthermore, this ritual points toward the ordination ceremony of the high priest coming in chap. 8. Thus the use of the term "anointed priest" is appropriate to the literary context of Lev 4 and does not necessarily date this ritual as late.

The specification about the disposal of the rest of the animal outside the camp in vv 11–12 and v 21 (cf. 16:27) is also considered a later addition by Elliger, since it is missing from the lesser purification offerings. But Koch (*Priesterschrift*, 57), observing that the underlying short sentences are headed by *waw* perfects, takes it as part of the basic ritual. Nevertheless, the older formulation has been expanded by the definition of the place outside the camp as "a clean place where the fat ashes are poured out" (v 12aβ) and the instruction "it is to be burned on the place of the fat ashes" (v 12b) in order to define its location precisely. The absence of this rite from the lesser ritual is not critical, for the meat of the lesser offering was disposed of by being eaten by the priests. Moreover, the detailed nature of v 11 and its grammatical function as a *casus pendens* witnesses that it is a detailed expansion enumerating specifically the parts to be disposed of outside the camp. In v 21a the definition of place is made by a statement of cross-reference. This same intention gave rise to the statement of cross-reference about the removal of fat to the regulation for an offering of well-being (vv 10a, 26a, 31a, 35a).

Appended to the basic regulation are three paragraphs (5:1–13) that give further specifications about another purification, which is known in the tradition as the graduated purification offering (Milgrom, *JAOS* 103 [1983] 249–54). Milgrom enumerates several evidences that this section had its own origin (249): (1) The lead into the opening law ונפש כי, "and if a person," builds off of the introduction at 4:2aβ + b, rather than being a continuation of 4:27–35. (2) This regulation specifies that confession is necessary, but such is not stated in chap. 4. (3) The phrase "any of these" (v 5) refers back to vv 1–4, not to anything in chap 4. (4) The classification of sins by שגגה, "inadvertent," is not continued; rather the term נעלם, "is hidden," is used. In fact, the sin in v 1 is deliberate while the sins in vv 2–4 are not defined by whether they are deliberate. Thus this is a regulation that had its own existence apart from its final literary setting.

The first paragraph enumerates four specific offenses that require the presentation of a purification offering (5:1–6). These cases are especially instructive for the laity, who must know which sacrifice to present for a given circumstance. The next two paragraphs permit the presentation of alternative materials for a purification offering by those who cannot afford a member of the flock: either two doves or two pigeons (5:7–10) or a tenth of an ephah of fine flour (5:11–13). These concessions would be necessary from the earliest era since they make it possible for the poorest members of the covenant to fulfill the requirements of a purification offering. The possibility of making a purification offering out of grain comes from an earlier period, for it is doubtful that an entrenched priesthood preoccupied with cultic standards would have permitted an expiating offering without the shedding of blood. This material may have been preserved in another source and placed here at the compilation of Lev 1–7.

The present regulation for a purification offering then consists of two different instructions that go back to an early era of Israel's origin and that have had some growth for specificity.

Comment

Excursus: The Purification Offering

The term for a "purification offering" (חטאת) comes from the root חטא, "fail, sin." This root is widely attested in the Semitic languages: Akk *ḫaṭū*, *ḫaṭṭū*, *ḫīṭu*, "fault, damage, sin"; Ugar *ḫṭʾ*, "sin"; Arab *ḫaṭiʾa*, "make a mistake" (K. Koch, "חָטָא *chāṭāʾ*," *TDOT* 4:310). It describes behavior that violates the community's standards. Because God set these standards, חטא is primarily a religious judgment on deviant behavior. It encompasses a wide range of wrongful behavior, from unintentional offenses to the gravest, most blatant acts (Exod 32:30–32; Deut 20:18; 2 Chr 33:19). Since in some OT contexts חטא means to "miss a mark" (e.g., Judg 20:16; Prov 8:35–36; 19:2), many scholars take this as the literal meaning of this root, but Koch (*TDOT* 4:311) challenges this view, pointing out that this word has a long history in Semitic language of describing religious disqualification.

In many cultic passages, especially in Lev 4, the term בשגגה, "inadvertently," is joined to חטא, "sin," in order to restrict it to offenses committed out of ignorance or human frailty (4:27; 5:25[6:6]). In Num 15:22–31 a sin committed inadvertently is contrasted to one done with ביד רמה, "a high hand," i.e., a deliberate, defiant action. An inadvertent sin may be committed in total ignorance, such as unknowingly eating food that has become unclean (cf. Ps 19:13[12]). It also includes offenses that one commits accidentally or out of negligence or because of a weak will. Thus חטא בשגגה, "to sin inadvertently," includes transgressions other than those done in ignorance. If pursued by a blood avenger, that person could flee to a city of refuge (Num 35:11, 15).

Traditionally חטאת has been rendered "a sin offering." But on the basis that חַטָּאת is built on the piel of חטא, which carries the opposite meaning of the qal, namely "de-sin, expunge, decontaminate, purify," Milgrom has challenged that rendering and proposed that a more accurate translation is "a purification offering" (*VT* 21 [1971] 237 = *SCTT* 67–69). This position is supported by the use of חִטֵּא, "cleanse," in a description of the action of presenting a חטאת, "purification offering." For example, in Ezek 43:20–23 (cf. Lev 8:14–15) חטא (4x) depicts the "de-sinning" of the altar by the act of כפר, "expiation," so that after seven days of these rites it is טהר, "cleansed," and מלא יד, "consecrated" (43:26). Ezek 45:18 has מקדש, "the sanctuary," as the object of חטא, "cleanse," with the presentation of חטאת, "a purification offering"; afterward in v 20 it states that כפר, "expiation," has been made for it (cf. Lev 14:49, 52). According to Num 19:17–19, one who has become unclean by contact with a corpse becomes חטא, "purged," and טהר, "clean," after being sprinkled twice, on the third and seventh days, with a solution that includes dust from the ashes of חטאת, "a purification offering." Further, the hithpael of חטא carries the meaning "purify oneself." In Num 19:12, 13, 20, a person who touches a corpse must take steps to purify himself in order that he might be clean (cf. Num 31:19, 20, 23; 8:21). Milgrom's proposal to translate חטאת, "a purification offering," is a much better rendering for this term in Eng, which unfortunately does not have a word that is closer to its literal meaning "de-sin." This name identifies the specific function of this sacrifice without blurring it with other sacrifices offered to expiate certain kinds of sins, particularly the reparation offering (אשם).

Purification offerings are prescribed for a variety of occasions and situations. Marx (*RB* 96 [1989] 29–38) organizes these into four categories. In the first category חטאת, "a purification offering," is offered for either sins of inadvertence (4:1–35) or a sin that becomes hidden in some way (5:1–7). In the second category a purification offering is prescribed as part of the rite of aggregation for one who has contacted something that makes that person unclean for an extended period: e.g., cleansing from contact with a corpse (Num 19:11–22), recovery from certain enduring sexual discharges (15:13–15, 28–30) or from a grievous skin disease (14:2–32), and cleansing after parturition (chap. 12). Third, a purification offering has a key place in rituals of consecration. These rituals were held only on very special occasions. Marx (*RB* 96 [1989] 33–34) lists three such occasions: (1) the investiture of the Levites (Num 8:1–36, 5–22), (2) the ordination of Aaron (8:1–36//Exod 29:1–37), and (3) the consecration of the altar (8:11, 15; Exod 29:36–37; cf. Ezek 43:18–27). It is for this purpose that purification offerings were offered at the dedication of the Second Temple (Ezra 6:16–17). A converse case required a Nazirite to make a purification offering at the termination of his vow (Num 6:13–20). Some scholars interpret this ceremony as desanctification, while Marx views it as a rite of passage. Kiuchi (*Purification Offering*, 55–56), however, interprets this ceremony in light of the ordination of the priests in Lev 8–9, especially with the ceremony at the end of their period of separation at the sanctuary in chap. 9, for, in his judgment, the status of the Nazirite parallels that of the high priest. Therefore, he concludes that a Nazirite must make a purification offering on this occasion to receive expiation or purification because he, like the high priest, approaches God (Num 6:13). In the fourth category one or more purification offerings are prescribed to be among the offerings presented on certain high days and during major festivals (e.g., Num 28–29), days or seasons that mark the transition of time. Significantly two of these pilgrim festivals occur at the fall and spring equinoxes denoting the transition in seasons.

Marx judges that the four different situations for which one or more purification offerings are prescribed have in common a transition from a former state or condition to a new state or condition. For him, the rituals of purification, consecration, and desacralization place the emphasis on separation (*RB* 96 [1989] 46). As additional evidence he (34) observes that the verbs that describe the effects produced by a purification offering depict a double movement: separation (טהר, "cleanse"; חטא, "de-sin") and aggregation (קדש, "sanctify"; מלא יד, "ordain"). He concludes that a חטאת, "purification offering," is offered as a "rite of passage" and that the best rendering of חטאת is "a sacrifice of separation."

Let us consider Marx's proposal in reference to each of the four categories. Under the first category, the offering of a חטאת separates one who has sinned from both the responsibility for and the impurity released by a sin, but the focus is on כפר, "expiation" and סלח, "forgiveness," i.e., cultic change more than change in social standing. In the middle two categories, i.e., the transition from an unclean state to a clean one and the consecration of a person to serve at the sanctuary, the ceremony of aggregation is complex and elaborate, as Marx notes (*RB* 96 [1989] 41–43). Recovery from either a chronic sexual discharge (15:14–15, 29–30) or parturition (12:6, 8) requires a person to present two animals, one for a whole offering and one for a purification offering, as part of the restoration to ritual purity. In the case of a person recovering from a grievous skin disease, there are an elaborate ceremony of aggregation (14:2–32) requiring a variety of offerings and a ritual washing that must be performed at the beginning and at the end of the week. At the ordination of Aaron as high priest there were several rituals, the presentation of חטאת, "a purification offering," being but one of them (chap. 8). In addition, Aaron and his sons remained at the sanctuary for an entire week as part of their rite of passage. Besides the required sacrifices, a specified passage of time is a crucial element in these rites of passage. Surely the prescription of an elaborate ritual plus a period of time would be superfluous if the חטאת, "purification offering," is primarily "a sacrifice of separation." Marx counters this objection with the position that the purification offering is at the heart of the rite of passage. On the contrary, the required period of separation gives evidence that the offering of a חטאת is not sufficient to produce the rite of passage. As for the prescriptions of חטאת in calendrical texts, it is hard to discover any prominence given to it, for usually only one is prescribed compared to the prescription of many whole offerings and grain offerings (cf. Num 28–29). Marx claims that the חטאת has a special place in these festivals (*RB* 96 [1989] 43). He bases this claim on the fact that it is the only sacrifice required to be offered in all these feasts (43). His point is strengthened by the absence of any prescription for a חטאת or "purification offering" on the Sabbath or the New Moon (Num 28:9–15). The focus of these high days and festivals, however, centers on the worship of Yahweh for which these sacrifices are essential, rather than on marking the transition in time and seasons.

If this evaluation of the middle two categories is correct, a חטאת, "purification offering," has a part in a rite of passage, though only as one element of a complex ritual. That is, in itself it does not achieve the rite of passage. But in the first and last categories the חטאת has little to do with a rite of separation. The significance of a חטאת on these various occasions resides more in the essence of a חטאת as a means of purifying from sin and impurity rather than in its marking a separation from a former state or situation. The cultic texts bear witness to the continual need for humans to have offerings that purge impurity and expiate sins in order that they might be in the presence of the Holy God with enthusiastic joy. Finally, the name Marx proposes for חטאת, "a sacrifice of separation," besides, at best, focusing on a restricted purpose for this sacrifice, possesses little meaning to most people untrained in sociology. Given these various considerations, the name "a purification offering," as proposed by Milgrom, is adopted for חטאת in this volume.

Unfortunately outside of Lev 4–5 there are virtually no references that say much about the extent and nature of a חטאת.

1 At the beginning of this regulation for a purification offering some overarching comments about it will be helpful. In the first part of this legislation (4:2–35) there are two basic regulations for a purification offering: the greater purification offered for the priest or the congregation (vv 2–21), in which blood from the sacrifice is brought inside the sanctuary and sprinkled in front of the curtain and placed on the horns of the altar in the Holy Place with the animal's flesh burned in a clean place outside the camp, and the lesser purification offering for a prince or an individual (vv 22–35), in which blood from the sacrifice is smeared on the horns of the altar in the courtyard and the flesh is eaten by the priests.

Kaufmann locates the distinction between these two types in the rite of burning (cited by Milgrom *VT* 26 [1976] 334 = *SCTT* 71). He claims that the animal of the greater purification becomes contaminated with the sin of the offerer, but the animal of the lesser one does not. But it is doubtful that the animal in either case becomes contaminated, for its blood is brought into the Holy Place and most of it is disposed of in a *clean* place outside the camp. A clean place would not be permitted to receive anything that had become defiled (but for a different position see Rodriguez, *Substitution*, 216–19). Levine distinguishes the two purification offerings on the basis of their effects: the greater one purifies the sanctuary, safeguarding it and the officiating priesthood from the polluting power of sin, and the lesser one expiates sins committed by the people or their leaders (*In the Presence of the Lord*, 103–8). But as Milgrom (*VT* 336 = *SCTT* 73) demonstrates, both types of this sacrifice have a purification function; the lesser purifies the outer court while the greater purges the inner sanctuary. Milgrom argues that the higher the cultic standing of the person who sins, the deeper the impurity unleashed by that sin penetrates into the sanctuary. Since the greater offering must purge a higher degree of impurity that is more contagious, Milgrom posits that this impurity infects the carcass of this purification offering, requiring it to be burned. This last point, unfortunately, is not fully developed by Milgrom, but it becomes the basis for another explanation set forth by Zohar.

In Zohar's interpretation (*JBL* 107 [1988] 613–15), the sinner removes the impurity from his sin, which primarily resides in the נפשׁ, the "locus of will and desire," by transferring it to the sacrificial animal when he lays a hand on its head. This is a process of dissociation; the sinner penitently regrets his sin and casts it away onto the animal. The impurity attaches itself primarily to that animal's blood and somewhat to its flesh. Through the blood rites, the sinner presents to God "the concretely disowned sin invested in blood." Zohar goes on to propose that the impurity is removed from the altar in one of two ways: (1) either God, by his power, wipes it out, or (2) "the residues of contamination" made less potent by being disowned are contained by God and finally removed on the Day of Atonement by the goat for Azazel. In light of this explanation he takes חטא, "purge," to mean basically "transfer, replace, displace" (*JBL* 107 [1988] 616). While it is true that impurity is contagious, there is little in the ritual of the purification offering that indicates that the impurity contaminates the sacrificial animal let alone the blood, for the animal's blood is sprinkled before the curtain and daubed on the horns of an altar and its choice entrails are burned on the altar. These various rites with blood do not accord with the position that the animal and its blood had become infiltrated with the impurity of the sin being expiated as Zohar argues. It is accurate, however, to think that the animal of a purification offering is closely identified with the sin of the offerer, for its blood is not dashed against the altar of the whole offering but only poured out at the base, and its flesh is not burned on the altar. Unfortunately the text does not give further explanation on these variances in this ritual. That the presenter's sin is removed is stressed by the formula that the priest makes כפר, "expiation," for the one making the offering so that he will סלח, "be forgiven" (4:20, 26, 31, 35; cf. Koch, *TDOT* 4:317, for a different interpretation). Given these various explanations, Milgrom's position that the manipulation of the blood removes the impurity emitted by the sinful deed and drawn to the sanctuary coincides with the various aspects of the ritual.

In addition, Milgrom (*VT* 26 [1976] 337 = *SCTT* 74) insightfully argues that the practice of allowing the priests to eat of the lesser purification offering struck a major blow against magical practices associated with the cult, since other religions diligently sought to destroy anything that possessed purifying power. The reason that the meat of the greater purification offering must be disposed of rather than eaten is that cultic laws prevent the priests from benefiting from either their own sins or the sins of the covenant community (cf. 6:23[30]). Since burning the animal on the main altar is not a rite in the ritual for a purification offering, the flesh of the greater purification offering, having been consecrated, has to be disposed of in a proper way by being burned in a clean place outside the camp.

In the cultic legislation the purification offering has a prominent role, for the priests are vitally concerned with removal of the pollution caused by sin. References to the purification offering outside the cultic legislation, however, are few, especially compared to those concerning the whole offering and the offering of well-being. This may be because this offering is primarily a private one presented for specific sins and for purification from ritual uncleanness, matters that do not frequently surface in the types of ancient Heb. literature that have been preserved.

בשׁגגה, "in error, inadvertently," is joined to חטא, "sin," in order to restrict this offering for the purpose of making amends for a sin committed out of either ignorance or human frailty (4:27; 5:25[6:6]; cf. Milgrom, *JQR* 58 [1967] 118 = *SCTT* 125). In Num 15:22–31 a sin committed inadvertently is contrasted to an action done with "a high hand," i.e., a deliberate, defiant action. Still today a clenched fist symbolizes determined, brazen defiance. Levine (19) points out that the rabbis understood inadvertent sin to have two aspects: (1) a mistake concerning the facts of the law and (2) unawareness that an act violated a law. Eating food without knowing that it had become unclean is an example of an inadvertent sin (cf. Ps 19:13[12]). Such inadvertent sins also encompass offenses committed accidentally or out of negligence or because of a weak will. A person may do something unwittingly but at the same time know what he has done; e.g., Deut 19:4–5 presents the case of one whose axe head flies off while he is chopping wood and kills a companion unintentionally. That worker is aware that he has killed someone, yet there is no premeditated design to his act. Thus he is not guilty of murder. In this light Milgrom (*JQR* 58 [1967] 117–18 = *SCTT* 124–25) holds that the notion of consciousness is present in the term שׁגגה, "error." But Milgrom has focused on only one side of שׁגגה. שׁגגה clearly is used for accidents and for sins committed unconsciously. Kiuchi (*Purification Offering*, 26), nevertheless, correctly holds that the latter meaning is primary for שׁגגה in chap. 4.

3 In this regulation there are four rituals, differentiated according to the status of the group or the person who has sinned. The first concerns the הכהן המשׁיח, "anointed priest." This is another term for the high priest. Outside of this passage and Lev 6:15(22), the high priest is never called the anointed priest in the OT. Elsewhere he is called הכהן הגדול, "the high priest" (21:10; Num 35:25, 28; Josh 20:6) or הכהן הראשׁ, "the chief priest" (2 Kgs 25:18; 2 Chr 19:11; 24:11; 26:20; 31:10; Ezra 7:5).

This case treats an inadvertent sin committed by the high priest. Although the text does not say that he sinned inadvertently, this qualifying phrase is implied because of its use throughout the various cases of this ritual and above all by the preceding general case (v 2), which applies to all of the categories. Whenever the high priest sins, he brings guilt on the people (לאשׁמת העם). This expression of guilt differs from the following cases in which the one who sins incurs guilt. Since the anointed priest represents the whole community before God, any sin he commits implicates the entire congregation. If he becomes defiled by sin, the entire congregation is placed in jeopardy of defilement. As long as the anointed priest is in a state of uncleanness, the people have no one to lead them to God. Such a situation for a community in covenant with God is grave. Thus it is urgent that the high priest make expiation for his sin.

A perplexing question comes to mind: how was it suspected that the anointed priest had sinned inadvertently? A possible conjecture is that the people became apprehensive about their standing before God, possibly because of poor fortune, e.g., a drought or a plague. Greatly troubled, the people would entreat the high priest to seek God for relief. While he searched for God's help, it might have been revealed to the high priest, possibly through the Urim and Thummim (Exod 28:30), that he had sinned inadvertently. Once he became aware of his fault, he had to make expiation for his inadvertent sin in order to remove the guilt from the people.

The higher the position of the person who has sinned, the more costly the animal required for sacrifice. The anointed priest has to present פר בן בקר, "a young bull," without defect (תמים). The threefold repetition of the term פר, "bull," in v 4 underscores that this is the only animal permitted for the anointed priest's purification offering. He brings the bull to the entrance of the Tent of Meeting. There he presses his hand on the bull's head to identify the animal as his offering (cf. 1:4). While making this gesture, it may be assumed, he confesses his sin, expresses his sorrow, and acknowledges God's Lordship, possibly by reciting a psalm of penitence.

5–7 The high priest (הכהן המשיח) himself manipulates the blood because there is no one higher to represent him before God. The manipulation of blood is quite different for this offering than for the other offerings. The priest gathers the blood into a vessel. Instead of dashing (זרק) the blood against the sides of the altar as with the whole offering (עלה; 1:5) and the offering of well-being (זבח שלמים; 3:2), the priest takes (לקח) it into the Holy Place. There he sprinkles (הזה) some of it seven times before the holy curtain (את פני פרכת הקדש). The difference between הזה, "sprinkling," the blood and נתן, "putting" or "smearing," it is not explained in the text. Vriezen (*OTS* 7 [1950] 231–33) interprets הזה as a rite for "hallowing the blood" by presenting it to Yahweh. Janowski (*Sühne*, 226–27) has discounted Vriezen's arguments. The curtain, which divided the two rooms of the sanctuary, the Holy Place from the Holy of Holies, had patterns of cherubim on it, establishing a connection between the curtain and the Atonement Slate (כפרת). According to Haran (*Temples*, 161), the curtain functioned as "a kind of projection and 'shadow' of the" כפרת. When the high priest sprinkled the blood toward the curtain, he indirectly sprinkled the Atonement Slate (Kurtz, *Sacrificial Worship*, 216–17). That the connection is intended in regard to this rite is clear from the use of הקדש, "the sanctuary," with veil, for הקדש occurs with "curtain" elsewhere only in 16:2 (Kiuchi, *Purification Offering*, 125). That the object of הזה, "sprinkle," is introduced by את פני, the sign of the direct object plus "face of," rather than by a preposition, is further evidence to Kiuchi (125) that the sprinkling is to be done in the direction of the Holy of Holies. הזה, "sprinkle," occurs with the cleansing of the Tent (v 17; 16:14–16; Num 19:4) and with an altar in 16:15b and 19; this fact leads Kiuchi (130) to conclude that this rite is more potent than נתן, "put or smear." The sprinkling is done seven times, connoting completeness.

Next the high priest puts (נתן) some of the blood on the horns of the altar of incense (על קרנות מזבח קטרת הסמים). This altar stood in the Holy Place before the curtain (פרכת). According to Exod 30:1–10, it was made out of acacia wood and overlaid with gold (cf. Exod 30:27; 31:8; 35:15; 37:25–28; 40:5, 26; 1 Chr 6:34[49]; 28:18; 2 Chr 26:16, 19). Its top was square, eighteen inches by eighteen inches, and it stood thirty-six inches high. At the corners were upward protrusions called horns. There is, however, another tradition that this altar stood just inside the Holy of Holies (cf. Heb 9:3–4). This tradition appears to be secondary, and its origin is unknown. Incense was burned daily on the altar; the ascending smoke represented the prayers of the community (cf. Ps 141:2). Daubing the extremities of the altar with blood cleansed the entire altar (cf. 8:23). The reason for this blood rite inside the Holy Place is that pollution from a sin committed by such a high official penetrates into the Holy Place itself. Also the degrees of holiness of the tabernacle correspond to the hierarchy of the community, meaning that the high priest's standing corresponds to the holiest place in the tabernacle; thus it is appropriate that his sin be expiated by sprinkling blood in the inner sanctum at the curtains leading to the Holy of Holies.

The high priest then takes the rest of the blood outside the Holy Place and שפך, "pours it out," at the base of the main altar. This term for "pouring out" is a general one, indicating that the priest is disposing of the bulk of the animal's blood, not performing a rite.

8–10 As in the ritual offering of well-being (cf. 3:3–5), the priest removes כל חלב, "all the fat," שתי הכליות, "the two kidneys," and היתרת על הכבד, "the lobe of the liver," and then burns (הקטיר) them on the altar. On the absence of the statement "the priest will make expiation for him, and he will be forgiven" (vv 20, 26, 31, 35), see note 10.d.

11–12 The rest of the animal, specifically עור, "the hide," בשׂר, "the flesh," ראשׁ, "the head," and כרעים, "the legs," along with the קרב, "entrails," and the פרשׁ, "offal," are brought מחוץ למחנה, "outside the camp," and שׂרף, "burned," on על־עצים באשׁ, "a wood-fire." The inclusion of עור, "the hide," which was not burned in the case of עלה, "a whole offering," indicates that nothing from this offering is to benefit humans (cf. Levine, 21). These parts are enumerated to make sure that the portions of the animal not burned on the altar are disposed of properly. This instruction is essential to prevent anyone from misusing any of the parts of this animal which are most holy. Furthermore, this standard prevents the priests from profiting in any way from their own sins.

שׂרף, "burn," a general term, is used instead of הקטיר, (lit.) "to turn into smoke." This burning then is not a ritual act but the proper disposal of the animal's remains since it is most holy and cannot be defiled. This regulation indicates that there was a place outside the camp for the disposal of ashes mixed with fat (דשן) from the sacrifices (cf. 1:16). That place was ceremonially clean (טהור), meaning that it was clearly marked and carefully regulated. In the greater purification offering, since the high priest is implicated, neither he nor his house may profit in any way from his sinning. But since the priests are not directly involved in the sin of a lesser purification offering, they are permitted and required to eat its meat (cf. 6:19[26]).

Milgrom suspects that the flesh of a purification offering is never burned on the altar because it becomes contaminated with the offerer's sin (*VT* 26 [1976] 334 = *SCTT* 71; cf. Noordtzij, 59). But the instruction to burn it in a clean place does not favor this view. Further, the priests are also instructed to eat the flesh of a lesser purification offering (6:19[26], 22[29]); it is impossible that they would be commanded to eat something defiled. Certainly the flesh of a lesser purification offering is not polluted. Milgrom addresses this distinction by arguing that a lesser purification offering is not contaminated because the sin is less potent (*VT* 26 [1976] 336 = *SCTT* 73). But if sin releases impurity, that impurity, though lesser, would affect this offering in the same way that it affected the greater offering. It is not necessary then to posit that the animal for a purification offering of either class becomes defiled by the offerer's sin. Possibly the flesh of a purification offering is not burned on the main altar in order to eliminate any idea that God "feeds on," i.e., benefits from, the sins of the people. Its consumption is an additional symbol of the removal of the presenter's guilt (Kiuchi, *Purification Offering*, 135).

13 In the second case the כל עדת ישׂראל, "entire congregation of Israel," has שׁגה, "erred." That the sin has been committed inadvertently is stressed by an additional sentence stating that something (דבר) is hidden (נעלם דבר) from their eyes. The kind of sin is not specified; neither is the dimension of the act identified by an indeterminative דבר, "thing." By following some faulty counsel, the community sins and becomes guilty (אשׁם). אשׁם has both a formal, legal meaning, "become culpable" for an act, and an emotional, dynamic meaning, "feel or realize guilt" (cf. *Comment* on 5:17–18; Kiuchi, *Purification Offering*, 31–34). The legal dimension is stressed here; i.e., the sinners are culpable for their act. Yet the text also assumes the dynamic nature of guilt; their guilt will eventually lead to their becoming aware that they have committed a wrong. This is stated in the next verse; the congregation becomes aware of (נודעה) their sin. Kiuchi (33–34) understands that נודעה, "become aware of," explicates אשׁם, "realize guilt," rather than being a consecutive action. The advantage of this explanation is that the text does not enter into how the sin becomes known, implying that it does so by the nature of guilt (אשׁם; cf. vv 23 and 28).

As to the nature of the sin, Wenham (99) thinks that it is probably one committed by the leaders as a group, e.g., the making of a covenant with elders of Gibeon without consulting Yahweh. Rashi, on the other hand, speculates that the people (Judg 9), violated some ceremonial regulation because of the leaders' failure to instruct them. Hoffmann (1:183–84) defines the sin as faulty behavior resulting from poor counsel given by the priests about a matter not explicitly stated in the law. In any case, whenever the community becomes aware that they have committed a sin, they must present a purification offering to make expiation for their sin.

In this case two terms for the community are used, עדה, "congregation" (vv 13, 15) and קהל, "assembly" (vv 13, 14). While the term עדה sometimes refers to the nation acting as a whole (e.g., Exod 12:3, 6; Num 20:1, 2), in other references it means a special assembly endowed with judicial authority (cf. Num 15:33–35; 27:2). קהל, "assembly," is a more general term for a group of people that has gathered together regardless of the reason; e.g., in Gen 28:3 it stands for a large assembling of people and in Ezek 23:24; 26:7 for soldiers arrayed for battle. Often this term represents the Israelites assembled for worship (Deut 5:22; 9:10; 1 Kgs 8:22, 65). Here it stands for the general assembly.

14 As in the case of the anointed priest, פר בן־בקר, "a bull," the most valuable sacrificial animal, is required of the congregation.

15 זקני העדה, "the elders of the congregation," representing the community, lay their hands on the animal. In the wilderness period a body of seventy elders, six from each tribe (there has always been a debate whether the group was composed of seventy or seventy-two members), helped Moses with administrative matters (Exod 24:1, 9; Num 11:16–17). This group is also called זקני העם, "the elders of the people" (Num 11:16).

16–18 Because the congregation has sinned, the anointed priest is required to carry out the blood rites. Pollution from the sin of the congregation also penetrates into the sanctuary. Furthermore, since the congregation is close to God in stature by reason of the covenant (cf. Exod 19:5–6), the blood rites must be done in the Holy Place like in the ritual for the anointed priest (cf. vv 5–7).

20–21 The priest makes כפר, "expiation," for the congregation, and they are granted נסלח, "forgiveness." In that נסלח is a passive, the implied subject is God. The inclusion of this term stresses that God himself accepts the merits of the sacrifice (cf. 1:4) and grants the offender(s) forgiveness. Because the priests participate in this sin as members of the covenant community, they may not receive any of the animal's parts. All the remains of the animal must be burned in a clean place outside the camp as with the purification offering of the anointed priest (vv 11–12).

Excursus: כפר, *"make expiation, atone"*

Bibliography

Dodd, C. H. *The Bible and the Greeks.* London: Hodder & Stoughton, 1935. 82–95. **Garnet, P.** "Atonement Constructions in the Old Testament and the Qumran Scrolls." *EvQ* 46 (1974) 131–63. **Gerleman, G.** "Die Wurzel *kpr* im Hebräischen." In *Studien zur alttestamentlichen Theologie.* Heidelberg: Lambert Schneider, 1980. 11–23. **Hartley, J.** "Expiation." *ISBE* rev. 3:246–48. **Herrmann, J.** *Die Idee der Sühne im Alten Testament: Eine Untersuchung über Gebrauch und Bedeutung des Wortes kipper.* Leipzig: Hinrichs, 1905. ———. "ἱλάσκομαι." *TDNT* 3:301–10. **Koch, K.** *Die israelitsche Sühneanschauung und ihre historischen Wandlungen.* Erlangen: Theologische Fakultät der Universität, 1956. ———. "Sühne und Sündenvergebung um die Wende von der exilischen zur nachexilischen Zeit." *EvT* 26 (1966) 217–39. **Lang, B.** "כִּפֶּר *kippær.*" *TWAT* 4:303–18. **Levine, B.** "Kippurim." *Eretz-Israel* 9 (1969) 88–95, 136. **Maass, F.** "כפר *kpr* pi. sühnen." *THAT* 1:842–57. **Médebielle, A.** *L'expiation dans l'A et le N.T.* Rome: Institut Biblique Pontificial, 1923. ———. "Expiation." *DBSup.* 3:1–262. **Milgrom, J.** "כפר על/בעד." *Leshonenu* 35 (1970) 16–17. ———. "Atonement in the OT." *IDBSup* 78–82. **Morris, L.** *Apostolic Preaching of the Cross.* London: Tyndale Press, 1956. 144–213. **Schenker, A.** "*kōper* et expiation." *Bib* 63 (1982) 32–46. **Sesboüé, B.** "L'expiation dans la révélation judéochrétienne." *Rencontre chrétriens et juifs* 3 (1969) 233–44. **Stamm, J. J.** *Erlösen und Vergeben im Alten Testament.* Bern: A. Francke, 1940. 59–84.

The etymology of Heb. כפר is debated. One approach is to identify it with Arab *kafara,* "to cover." Cited in support of this identification is the quotation of Jer 18:23 in Neh 3:37 (4:5); Nehemiah substitutes כסה, "cover," for Jeremiah's use of כפר. Another approach is to relate כפר to Akk *kuppuru,* "wipe off, smear." According to *CAD* (8:179–80) *kuppuru* means "to wipe off, clean, purify." Various things, such as people, buildings, including a temple, and other objects, may be purified by magical rites. The cultic usage of *kuppuru* indicates that there is a close connection between the Akk and Heb. terms. Returning to Jer 18:23, support for this position is found in the fact that מחה, "wipe out, blot out," stands parallel to כפר. Another explanation for כפר is that it is a denominative from the noun כֹּפֶר, "a ransom" (Exod 21:30; 30:20; Job 33:24; 36:18; Prov 13:8; cf. W. Eichrodt, *Theology of the OT,* 2:444–47).

That the action of כפר may be achieved by gifts or some type of payment is attested in Jacob's hoping to appease (כפר) his offended brother Esau במנחה, "with a present" (Gen 32:21[20]). But the use of מנחה, "gift," in that text, rather than כֹּפֶר, "bribe, ransom," calls into question the relationship of כֹּפֶר to כפר. If a tie exists between these two terms, it does not appear to be in the foreground in most uses of כפר in cultic texts. In fact, no sacrifice is referred to by כֹּפֶר. B. Levine (*In the Presence of the Lord,* 67–68), recognizing this difficulty, posits two verbs: כפר I, primary, and כפר II, a secondary denominative from the noun כֹּפֶר, which usually appears in the phrase כפר על נפשׁ, "serve or give a ransom for a life" (e.g., Exod 30:15–16). This proposal seems to be forcing the language to fit a theory.

Another complicating factor in gaining an understanding of כפר is that it occurs in a variety of syntactical relationships. Seldom does it take the direct object. When it has a direct object, it is either the sanctuary or the cultic furniture (16:20, 33; Ezek 43:20,

26; 45:20). It is also possible for the sanctuary or the furniture to stand after כפר על (8:15; 14:53; 16:16, 18; Exod 29:36, 37; 30:10 [2x]). Kiuchi (*Purification Offering*, 92–93) finds no distinction between these two uses of כפר with a cultic term as its object. כפר sometimes stands alone with the preposition ב, used either instrumentally (5:16; 7:7; 17:11b; 19:22; Exod 29:33; Num 5:8) or spatially (6:23[30]; 16:17a, 27). If the recipient of the action is a person, that person is preceded by either the preposition על, "on behalf of" (1:4; 4:20, 26, 31, 35; 5:6, 10, 13, 16, 18, 26[6:7]; 8:34; 10:17; 12:7, 8; 14:18, 19, 20, 21, 29, 31; 15:15, 30; 16:30, 33, 34; 17:11; 19:22; 23:28; Exod 30:15, 16; Num 5:8; 6:11; 8:12, 19, 21; 15:25, 28 [2x]; 28:22, 30; 29:5; 31:50; Ezek 45:15), or בעד, "for, on behalf of" (9:7 [2x]; 16:6, 11, 17b, 24; Ezek 45:17). In distinction from כפר על, כפר בעד occurs when the priest is making atonement for himself, as Milgrom notes (*Leshonenu* 35 [1970] 17; Kiuchi, 88–89). The careful avoidance of saying that a person is directly affected by the act of כפר may be a determined effort to avoid any implication that the purification resides automatically in the atoning ritual (Levine, *In the Presence of the Lord*, 66). Two passages contain the phrase כפר ל (Deut 21:8; Ezek 16:63), in which God stands as subject and his people as the recipients of his granting expiation.

Sometimes another verb in the context emphasizes an aspect accomplished by כפר or an attending result: טהר, "be clean" (qal 12:7, 8; 14:20, 53; cf. Num 8:21) or "cleanse" (piel 16:30), נסלח לו, "be forgiven" (4:20, 26, 31, 35; 5:10, 13, 16, 18, 26[6:7]; 19:22), קִדֵּשׁ (piel) "sanctify, consecrate" (8:15; 16:18–19; Exod 29:33, 36, 37; Num 6:11), and חִטֵּא (piel) "purge, de-sin" (8:15; 16:18–19; Exod 29:36). Kiuchi (*Purification Offering*, 96) concludes that חִטֵּא, "purge," overlaps with כפר, while קִדֵּשׁ, "sanctify, consecrate," is more distant. The phrase נשׂא עון, (lit.) "bear guilt," in the sense of "forgive" occurs with כפר in 10:17 (cf. 5:17–18) and Num 18:23aβ//8:19aβ (Kiuchi, 98). From this evidence Kiuchi (99) identifies כפר as the superordinate among these four terms, which may be arranged in the following pattern:

כפר

קִדֵּשׁ חִטֵּא טִהַר   נשׂא עון

Thus כפר has a twofold effect; it removes pollution and it counteracts sin. Few scholars advocate this twofold direction of כפר, but it has the advantage of clarifying why this word is clearly preferred over the many words for cleansing in sacrificial texts and also how it differs in its denotation from them.

Determining the best translation for כפר in Eng is complicated by the theological debate regarding whether כפר means "expiate" or "propitiate." Is the sacrificial system designed primarily to appease God or to remove sin?

In a few passages it is clear that כפר means "appease" anger, either one person's anger at another (Gen 32:21[20]; Prov 16:14; cf. Schenker, *Bib* 63 [1982] 34–37) or God's anger at humans (Num 25:13). However, when God stands as subject of this verb and sin is either the direct object or object of the preposition על, "on," or ל, "for," the idiom means "forgive," i.e., the idea being that God has purged or removed the sin so that the person finds forgiveness (e.g., Pss 65:4[3]; 78:38; 79:9; Ezek 16:63). The contexts of Pss 78:38 and 79:9 make it clear that the כפר action cools God's boiling anger.

Most frequently, however, כפר occurs in cultic texts; there it has a technical meaning for the achievement of certain sacrifices, namely a purification offering (חטאת), a reparation offering (אשׁם), or a whole offering (עלה). At the end of some rituals it is stated that the officiating priest has made expiation for (כפר על) the presenter of the sacrifice; sometimes included in the formula is the phrase "from [מן or על] his sin" (e.g., Lev 4:26, 35). In some texts כפר is closely tied to the manipulation of blood (e.g., 16:18; 17:11), indicating that this rite with blood is essential for achieving כפר. The frequency of the terms טהר, "be clean," and נסלח לו, "be forgiven," after the officiating priest has done the work of כפר indicates that כפר removes both the polluting force from one's sin and the guilt or blame that person bears. In cultic texts, then, the best rendering for כפר is "expiate," focusing on the removal of sin and its effects.

In these sacrificial regulations there is no explicit mention of God's wrath. While it is true that God sometimes pours out his fierce anger on his people because of their sinning, these occasions are rare (cf. Isa 54:7–8). In contrast to these rare occurrences of God's display of his anger, the cult is concerned with the usual, daily means of approaching God. Thus not God's kindled wrath but his potential wrath is the direct focus of the expiating sacrifices. To express it another way, a person who has sinned is aware that one who does not seek expiation stands in danger of facing God's anger. But if one takes the appropriate steps to expiate a sin and to win God's favor, that one will escape God's wrath before it is ignited. This interpretation, therefore, supports rendering כפר in cultic texts as "expiate," not "propitiate."

That כפר means technically "expiate, remove" is further substantiated by the fact that the altar and the various cultic objects benefit from the action of כפר. As Milgrom has shown (*RB* 83 [1967] 390–99 = *SCTT* 75–84), sin releases a miasma that is drawn to the sanctuary. In order for the cultic objects there to continue to function effectively, they must be purged. This is achieved by the various purifying sacrifices presented as occasions warrant and by the annual sacrifices made on the Day of Atonement. Moreover, the framework of this theology may be drawn on to understand how a house that has recovered from a grievous mildew (צרעת) is cleansed or expiated (כפר) by an elaborate ritual (14:49–53).

How expiation is achieved is not expressly addressed in these regulations. Certainly it is necessary that the entire ritual for the expiating sacrifice be performed appropriately before expiation may be achieved. At the heart of the expiating ritual, though, are the rites with the blood (cf. 16:18). The most definitive statement is found in Lev 17:11: "For the life of an animal resides in the blood; I have assigned it to you to make atonement for your lives on the altar, because it is the blood that makes atonement by the life." D. J. McCarthy (*JBL* 88 [1969] 166–76) has shown that attaching such significance to blood is unique to Israel among the cults of the Middle East, indicating that handling of the blood was assigned special significance because of Israel's unique theological outlook. This accords with the blood rites of the purification offering. The blood is sprinkled or spread on those cultic objects polluted by sin. The pouring out of the animal's blood is also important. The blood represents the animal's נפש, "life." The offerer has already identified himself (נפש) with the animal by laying his hands on the animal's head; with this gesture the offerer recognizes that the death of the animal will commute the penalty for his sin. It needs to be underscored that the sacrificial system loudly proclaims that the penalty of sin is death. Thus the giving of a life (נפש) on the altar for the life (נפש) of the offerer upholds justice. The blood rites then have a twofold function: to cleanse the sanctuary from the pollution of sin and to release the offerer from the penalty for his sinning. כפר, "make expiation," is the achievement of both of these goals.

Outside the cultic legislation there are a few passages that speak of atonement or expiation being achieved by means other than a sacrifice. Isaiah was cleansed from his sin when his lips were touched by a burning coal taken from the heavenly altar (6:7). David sought a means to turn away Yahweh's anger, which was being expressed in a prolonged famine because of Saul's breaking the covenant with the Gibeonites by hanging some of them: The Gibeonites said that expiation could be made by David's turning over to them seven members of Saul's house (2 Sam 21:1–9). According to one proverb, iniquity is כפר, "undone," בחסד ואמת, "by loyal love and truth" (Prov 16:6). Moreover, Isaiah says that when Jacob crushes the stones of the pagan altars and shrines scattered throughout the land, his guilt will be expiated (Isa 27:9). Deut 32:43 says that God avenges the blood of his servants by taking vengeance on their enemies in order that the land might be cleansed or expiated. In the most dramatic case Moses sought to make expiation for the people's grave sin by intercessory prayer, even pleading for God to remove his own name from the book of life in order that the people might be forgiven (נשׂא חטאתם; Exod 32:30–34). Intercession then is a means of atonement.

Three passages proclaim the harsh words that a specific sin cannot be expiated: the iniquity of Eli's house (1 Sam 3:14), blatant iniquity (Isa 22:14), and the הוה, "disaster," that will befall Babylon (Isa 47:11). In the same vein Jeremiah pleads with God that the iniquity of his opponents who persecute him relentlessly may not be expiated (18:23).

22 The third ritual is for an unintentional transgression committed by נשׂיא, "a prince." D. J. Wisemen suggests that נשׂיא could refer to a deputy or leader of secondary rank (*BS* [1977] 228; cf. E. A. Speiser, "Background and Function of the Biblical *Naśi*," in *Oriental and Biblical Studies*, 113–22). The lack of the definite article with נשׂיא may indicate that the term is to be used generally and not specifically (Harrison, 66); that is, it stands for tribal leaders in general (cf. Num 2:3, 5, 7 etc.), not a single leader like the king. For example, in Num 7 each tribal prince presents a goat for a purification offering. Ezekiel, however, uses this term with an elevated meaning for the Davidic leader of the new, ideal Israel (34:24; 37:25; 45:7, 16–17; 46:2, 4, 8, 10, 17; cf. 1 Kgs 11:34 for its only use in the historical books for the Davidic ruler). In Ezekiel this prince is to present a bull for a purification offering on the first day of Passover instead of a goat as here (45:22), further attesting to his higher status in Ezekiel than in this legislation. On the other days of the Passover he is to offer elaborate whole offerings and a male goat (שׂעיר עזים) for a purification offering (45:23). Incidentally Ezekiel also uses "prince" for foreign rulers (26:16; 27:21; 32:29; but cf. 37:25).

Because a prince is a secular leader of a tribe, not a cultic leader, his sin is not as potent as that of the anointed priest or the congregation, nor is the animal required, שׂעיר עזים, "a male goat," תמים, "without defect," as costly. Presumably the pollution released by his sin reaches only the main altar before the Tent of Meeting.

25–26 הכהן, "the priest," manipulates the blood. Since "the priest" occurs here without the term משׁיח, "anointed," it stands for any officiating priest. Again this fact points to the antiquity of this ritual and a broader use of the term "prince" as in Num 1:16, 44, for if the prince were the Davidic head of Israel, surely his stature would demand that the officiating priest be the high priest. The manipulation of the blood with this offering is simpler. Instead of taking blood into the holy place and smearing it on the horns of the altar of incense (v 5), the priest puts (נתן) some blood על קרנת מזבח העלה, "on the horns of the altar of the whole offering." The rest of the blood is poured out (שׁפך) at the base of this altar. No instructions are given about the disposal of the remains of the animal, for the meat belongs to the priests. Therefore, the blood rite takes place only at this altar. Because the priest is not a participant in this prince's sin, he has a right and an obligation to eat the animal's flesh (6:19[26], 22[29]).

27 The last ritual is for an inadvertent sin committed by any person (נפשׁ אחד). That person is a member of the people of the land (עם הארץ). This last term carried different sociological meanings in different periods of Israel's history. In early literature, as here, it refers to any member of the community. But in the period before the exile it stands for the landed aristocracy (e.g., Jer 1:18); then in the post-exilic community it refers to the populace, the mass (e.g., Hag 2:4; Zech 7:5). Later it came to mean the uneducated, common people (e.g., Acts 4:13).

28 Any covenant member who has sinned inadvertently is required to offer שְׂעִירַת עִזִּים, "a female goat," תְּמִימָה, "free from defect." An alternative offering of a female sheep (כֶּבֶשׂ . . . נְקֵבָה) is detailed in vv 32–35.

30 Cf. v 25.

5:1–4 At this place are the instructions for a graduated purification offering. Four cases requiring this offering are enumerated first. Most commentators consider these four cases to be parallel to each other, while a few, such as Noth (44) and Spiro (*PAAJR* 28 [1959] 95–101), claim that vv 2–4 are subordinate to v 1. According to the latter position, a witness to one of the errors described in vv 2–4 who fails to make known that knowledge, either to the person who erred or to the community, is liable before God. For, having withheld testimony, that person fails to protect the one who has erred and the community from the consequences that may result from not speaking, e.g., the danger faced by one who might enter the area of the sanctuary while being unclean. Spiro (100) holds that the phrase והוא ידע ואשם, "and he knows and is guilty" (vv 3, 4), applies to the witness. To maintain his position he recommends emendations for or elimination of v 2b. Kiuchi (*Purification Offering*, 23) rejects this alternative reading, pointing out that v 2 begins with או, "or," not אם, "if, whenever," used to introduce subordinate cases. The clauses are also formulated similarly enough to indicate that they are parallel. Thus these verses address four different situations.

Crucial to understanding the nature of these four cases is the phraseology ונעלם ממנו והוא ידע, "and it is hidden from him and he comes to know it" (vv 3–4). This sequence has received various interpretations (cf. Kiuchi, *Purification Offering*, 28). One position is that an act was done consciously, forgotten, and later remembered. A second position is that the act was done unwittingly and later the doer became aware of it. A third position holds that the act was done deliberately, forgotten, and then remembered. The verbs in these two sentences are to be interpreted sequentially, not simultaneously. נעלם means "it is hidden," i.e., it has escaped one's mind. This reading favors the first and third positions. The description of one who utters a rash oath in the fourth case indicates an act done consciously, but without premeditation. Thus the first position is preferable.

A person who errs in one of these matters becomes טמא, "unclean," and incurs אשׁם, "guilt." אשׁם is critical to the interpretation of chap. 5 (cf. the *Excursus* on the reparation offering). As a noun it means both "reparation" and "reparation offering." As a verb it means both "be guilty, be culpable" and "feel guilty" (cf. J. Milgrom, *Cult*, 6–12; also R. R. Hutton, "Declaratory Formulae" [Diss., Claremont, 1983] 107–11). A puzzling issue is how the person who has forgotten that he has become unclean becomes aware of his condition so that he can present a purification offering. An obvious way would be for someone who saw what took place to inform him, but in most cases there would be no eyewitness. The primary way that one learns about his unintentional sin then is through the dynamic of guilt. Even though a person sins unintentionally, he incurs guilt (אשׁם). This guilt eventually works its way into his conscience so that "he feels guilty" (אשׁם). The belief here is that psychological guilt awakens one to an inadvertent sin. Such guilt is not a mere figment of a person's imagination, however. As soon as one becomes conscious of his error, he must rid himself of his guilt by presenting a purification offering.

5:1 The meaning of the first case is debated. According to Noth (44), one who hears a person utter a curse but fails to report the violation thus incriminates himself, but in this law nothing defines the oath or curse as being itself unlawful (Kiuchi, *Purification Offering,* 30). In a second view J. Scharbert says, "The 'audible curse' is the conditional imprecation which the person who has been wronged pronounces on the thief, the thief's partner, or the dishonest person who finds what he has lost" (cf. Prov 29:24; "אָלָה *ʾālāh,*" *TDOT* 1:262). For such a curse to be effective it must be pronounced publicly. A third view takes it to mean that a person (נפש) sins (חטא) by failing to respond to a public oath (קול אלה), calling for any witness to the event in question to come forth and testify in order that the accused party might be properly judged. The oath (אלה) is against any witness who fails to come forth in defense of the community.

There are various ways in which a person may become a witness to an activity. One may see the wrongful act taking place. Or if one has not seen the act, one may come to know about it (ידע). It is not said how that one comes to know about it. Hoffmann (1:197) suggests that one learns about it from the guilty party. Another possibility is that the guilty party implicates the witness in the act; e.g., a thief shares some of the stolen loot with another, and that person thereby eventually comes to realize who has committed the robbery.

The interpretation that a person fails to testify when called upon by a general oath coincides best with the wording that he sins. The issue in this case is the well-being of the community. In ancient Israel, a close-knit society without a police force, the security of the community depended on each citizen's informing the leaders of any wrongdoing or clandestine activity. Failure to report any aberrant activity would endanger the community's safety and solidarity. Whoever sins in this way must bear the responsibility of his iniquity, נשׂא עונו, (lit.) "bear his iniquity." This phrase means that the guilty party is liable for such a failure, and that one's failure places him under the curse contained in the public oath.

5:2–3 The second case describes a person who touches something that makes one unclean, especially the carcass (נבלה) of an unclean beast (חיה), unclean livestock (בהמה), or an unclean crawling creature (שרץ; cf. 11:24–28, 32–40). The third case concerns touching any human uncleanness; this would particularly refer to contact with bodily fluids (cf. chap. 15) or objects contaminated by any kind of human uncleanness. In both cases the person becomes unclean but the incident is forgotten. When that one comes to remember it, guilt is incurred. In these two cases, it is difficult to pinpoint the aspect of the act that requires a purification offering, for becoming unclean is an ordinary occurrence that carries no guilt. The only dangers are either in entering a sacred area while unclean or in not taking the steps to become ritually clean. Milgrom claims that the prolonged period of uncleanness because of one's forgetfulness or negligence is what needs to be expiated (*JAOS* 103 [1983] 251–54). Kiuchi adds that such forgetfulness is "tantamount to disregarding the cultic and judicial order" (*Purification Offering,* 30).

4 The fourth case concerns the swearing of any oath rashly or impulsively. The opposites "to do evil," להרע, and "to do good," להיטיב, are juxtaposed to include all kinds of oaths. A person hastily, without meditation, puts himself under obligation by uttering an oath. Because one has sworn hastily, one is conscious of his action, but he is not fully aware of its implications. Such occasions arise from time to time, as in the heat of argumentation or when a surge of emotion prompts one to swear that he will take a specific course, either for ill or for good. Because such oaths flow out of strong emotional agitation, not out of careful thought, they are condemned, even if they are for doing good. The reason may be that a person pledges himself to undertake something from the wrong motive or that a person promises to do something beyond his ability. Since one will not be able to fulfill the oath, that one will frustrate both himself and those who are depending on him, bringing discord among community members. Therefore, his hasty oath, though intended for good, produces harm.

The fourth case reveals that God desires that his people make commitments or promises or take oaths only after careful reflection. This perspective is also found in the instructions in Deut 23:22–23(21–22) cited below (cf. Num 30:2):

> If you make a vow to Yahweh your God, do not be slow to pay it, for Yahweh your God will certainly demand it of you, and you will be guilty of sin. But if you refrain from making a vow, you will not be guilty.

Similarly Kohelet says, "It is better not to vow than to make a vow and not fulfill it" (Eccl 5:4[5]).

5 When a person who has sinned in any of these matters becomes aware of his אשׁם, "guilt," that one must confess (התודה) the wrong committed. It is to be a public confession, and it may accompany his sacrificial offering. Noordtzij (66) thinks that the confession took the form of the recitation of a liturgical formula.

6 To purge a sin one is to bring חטאת, "a purification offering." It is to be כשׂבה, "a female lamb," or שׂעירת עזים, "a goat." In this context אשׁמו appears; should it be translated as "his reparation offering" or as "his penalty"? Certainly the appearance of this word creates confusion between the offering required here and the reparation offering described below (vv 17–19). Snaith (41–42) interprets this use of אשׁם as nontechnical. Thus it does not refer to a special kind of offering but to the penalty.

7–10 Since a purification offering is mandatory for anybody who sins and since every person sins, it is an offering that every Israelite would have had to present from time to time. Therefore, the law makes concessions so that the poor may fulfill their obligation for presenting a purification offering.

The first alternative animals for this offering are two doves or two young pigeons. The phrase לא תגיע ידו די, "he does not have enough," to pay for a sacrificial animal may indicate that ordinarily the person who had sinned came to the sanctuary and purchased a lamb or a goat for his offering. The use of אשׁם, "penalty," in this verse is similar to its use in v 6. Of the two birds, one is offered as a חטאת, "purification offering," and the other as a עלה, "whole offering." No explanation is given for the fact that one bird becomes a whole offering in a regulation for a purification offering. Perhaps, given the size of the birds, the two together provided the two essential elements of a purification offering, manipulation of the blood and burning portions on the altar. Whereas blood from the first bird is sprinkled (הזה) against the wall of the altar, a powerful rite (cf. 4:5–7), the blood that is left is disposed of at the base of the altar as with a member of the flock, not completely drained against the altar as with a bird for a whole offering (1:15b). What is to be done with the rest is not stated. The Mishnah (*m. Zebaḥ.* 4:4) assigns it to the priest, as is the case with both other animals and with grain (5:13) offered as a purification offering. The second bird is sacrificed as a whole offering, according to the proper regulation (משפט), i.e., the ritual found in 1:14–17; its blood is drained against the side of the altar, its crop and its contents are removed, and then it is burned on the altar. This burning is done as a whole offering (עלה), perhaps because the flesh of a purification offering could not be burned on the altar. Yet since the vital entrails of a large animal for a purification offering have to be burned on the altar, this requirement is met in offering the two birds by offering one as a whole offering.

11 If a person cannot afford two small birds, it is possible for him to offer a tenth of an ephah of fine flour, an amount exceeding four pints. This is the smallest grain offering prescribed (cf. 6:20; Num 28:5). Elliger (75) is not convinced that this amount of grain would be cheaper than two doves, however. That, of course, would depend on the economic conditions of a given season. It is possible, though, to imagine that a poor person might have some flour on hand, but not enough money to purchase two doves. In contrast to the regular grain offering, no oil or incense is to be added to the grain in this case (cf. 2:1–2). The purification purpose of this offering requires austerity in its preparation.

12 Cf. 2:2. This offering is identified as a gift to Yahweh (אשׁי יהוה), but it is not stated that it is a soothing aroma to Yahweh (ריח ניחח ליהוה). This may be because oil and incense are not added to the offering. But then this later formula does not normally occur with a purification offering (except 4:31). Because this offering of grain serves as a purification offering, there is a statement of identification at the end of this prescription: חטאת הוא, "it is a purification offering."

13 That which is left over becomes the priest's, being part of his wages.

Explanation

The purification offering achieved expiation for sins committed inadvertently, out of negligence or failure. Although these sins were not blatant transgressions of God's law, they still were sins and caused defilement. The power of the defilement corresponded to the prominence of the sinner. The sins of the priest or the cultic community defiled the inner sanctuary, while those of the prince or an individual defiled the main altar. Everyone, from high priest to the ordinary person, had to present a purification offering for any inadvertent sin or sin committed and forgotten before its defilement had been removed. The most crucial rite of this ritual was the blood rite, for it purged the sanctuary and the altar from the uncleanness released by the sin. The burning of the fat on the altar entreated God's favor. As a result, the sins of the guilty person were expiated, and that one found forgiveness from God.

The situations that required the presentation of a purification offering teach Christians that all sin is harmful, disruptive of their relationship with God. This includes sins committed unintentionally, ignorantly, or in error (cf. Matt 12:36). Sin is sin regardless of intentionality or human frailty. This is not to deny that the greater the involvement of one's will in committing a sin the more serious the offense becomes. Nevertheless, so-called little sins must be expiated in order for one to maintain fellowship with God.

Under the old covenant sin defiled the Temple. In the new covenant the believer is pictured as the temple in which God dwells through the Holy Spirit. Any wayward behavior or wrong attitude expressed by a believer defiles the temple and grieves the Holy Spirit (Eph 4:30; 1 Thess 5:19). This includes the error of making rash promises (Lev 5:4). This fault needs to be underscored, for in today's evangelical churches emotional appeals are often made to move members of the congregation to make promises or commitments that are not thought out. Such appeals are fraught with the danger of leading people to make pledges that are beyond their ability to fulfill. Each believer needs to remember the counsel that it is better not to pledge than to pledge and not pay (Deut 23:22–23[21–22]; Eccl 5:4[5]). In place of making a multitude of promises, it is far better to follow the general exhortation to live a pure life, undefiled by harmful thoughts, improper attitudes, and immoral behavior (e.g., Eph 4:22–32; 5:3–4, 11; Col 3:5–10). Should anyone defile one's own life, that one may turn to Christ's perfect sacrifice for cleansing.

The regulation for the purification offering increases our understanding of Jesus' atoning death. The blood of Christ was central to the atoning power of his death. Similar to that of a purification offering, it was not cast against the sides of the altar; rather it was poured out. Only a very small portion of the animal's blood was sprinkled on the curtain or spread on the horns of the altar. The writer of Hebrews depicts Christ taking his own blood into the eternal Holy Place in the heavenly sanctuary (9:11–14). Moreover, just as the flesh of this offering was burned outside the camp, Jesus died outside the walls of Jerusalem. Jesus' sacrifice was efficacious. It achieved full atoning merit for all who believe on him without limitations of time, place, or nationality.

The standard to seek expiation for every sin, no matter how little, need not leave the believer in despair, for the NT teaches that Christ's blood continually cleanses from all sin (1 John 1:7) and that Christ continually makes intercession for his followers at God's right hand (Rom 8:34; Heb 7:25). When any believer sins inadvertently, he needs to remember that he has a faithful, compassionate advocate before God in Jesus Christ (1 John 2:1–2). Furthermore, the NT pictures the cleansing power of the blood of Christ as far greater than the purifying power of the purification offering. The latter expiated inadvertent sins, while the blood of Christ cleanses from all sin, including cold, premeditated sin (cf. 1 John 1:7). Hebrews proclaims that the blood of Christ cleanses a person's conscience from transgression that brings eternal death (9:14). So whenever a believer is troubled by real guilt for a conscious or unconscious sin, he needs to confess his sins, confident that Jesus will both forgive and purify him (1 John 1:9). All believers then need to avail themselves of the means of grace in order to keep themselves pure in a sinful world. Above all they need to partake of the bread and the wine of the Lord's table as a means of receiving the atoning merits of Christ's death. In this way they gain confidence and boldness before God, mindful that all believers, because they are purged by Christ's blood, have confidence to enter the presence of God in worship and to make their petitions known (Heb 10:19–20). Or, as it says in Rev 7:14, the followers of Jesus have their robes washed spotlessly white by the blood of the Lamb (cf. 1 Pet 1:2).

The standards for a purification offering also reveal that responsibility increases with one's role in the covenant community. The greater the role, the more extensive are the effects of that one's sinning. This principle continues under the new covenant. Jesus says that much is required from the one to whom much is entrusted (Luke 12:48). In the same spirit James warns that teachers, or leaders, will be judged more strictly (3:1).

D. Regulation for the Reparation Offering (5:14–26[6:7])

Bibliography

Déaut, R. le. "A propos d'une leçon du codex *Neofiti 1* (Lev. V 21)." *VT* 17 (1967) 362–63. **Hayes, J. H.** "Restitution, Forgiveness, and the Victim in Old Testament Law." *Trinity University Studies in Religion* 11 (1982) 1–23. **Joüon, P.** "Notes de lexicographie hébraïque XV. Racine אשם." *Bib* 19 (1938) 454–59. **Kellermann, P.** "ʾāšām in Ugarit?" *ZAW* 76 (1964) 319–22. ———. "אָשָׁם *ʾāšām.*" *TDOT* 1:429–37 **Knierim, R.** "אָשָׁם *ʾāšām* Schuldverpflichtung." *THAT* 1:251–57. **Loss, N. M.** "A propositio di Lv 5,15 (e 2,3.10). «Santo» e «Santissimo»: abozzo di uno studio lessicale sul nome «qodes»." *Sal* 30 (1968) 388–94. **Marx, A.** "Sacrifice de Réparation et Rites de Levée de Sanction." *ZAW* 100 (1988) 183–98. **Milgrom, J.** "The Compass of Biblical Sancta." *JQR* 65 (1974) 205–16. ———. "Priestly Doctrine of Repentance (Lev 5:20–26; 6:1–7)." *RB* 82 (1975) 186–205. ———. "The Legal Terms *šlm* and *brʾšw* in the Bible." *JNES* 35 (1976) 271–73. ———. "The Concept of *Maʿal* in the Bible and the Ancient Near East." *JAOS* 96 (1976) 236–47. ———. *Cult and Conscience.* Leiden: Brill, 1976. **Morris, L.** "ʾAsham." *EvQ* 30 (1958) 196–210. **Phillips, A.** "The Undetectable Offender and the Priestly Legislators." *JTS* 36 (1985) 146–50. **Saydon, P. P.** "Sin-Offering and Trespass-Offering." *CBQ* 8 (1966) 393–98. **Schötz, D.** *Schuld- und Sündopfer im Alten Testament.* Breslauer Studien zur historischen Theologie 18. Breslau: Müller & Seiffert, 1930. **Snaith, N.** "The Sin-Offering and the Guilt-Offering." *VT* 15 (1965) 73–80. **Thomson, H. C.** "The Significance of the Term *ʾasham* in the Old Testament." *TGUOS* 14 (1953) 20–26.

Translation

[14]*Yahweh spoke to Moses,* [15]*"When anyone commits a breach of faith and sins inadvertently in any of the holy things of Yahweh, he is to bring as his penalty*[a] *to Yahweh a ram without defect from the flock valued*[b] *in silver shekels by sanctuary weight*[c] *for a reparation offering.*[a] [16]*He is also to make restitution*[a] *for the sin he has committed against any holy thing; he will add 20 percent to it and give it to the priest. The priest will then make expiation for him with the ram of the reparation offering, and he will be forgiven.*

[17]*"If anyone*[a] *sins, breaking*[b] *any of all the commandments of Yahweh which is not to be broken,*[b] *without being aware of it, then he realizes guilt,*[c] *and he is held responsible.*[d]
[18]*He is to bring to the priest a ram without defect from the flock according to the value set*[a] *for a reparation offering, and the priest will make expiation for him concerning his error which he has inadvertently done so that he may be forgiven.* [19]*It is a reparation offering;*[a] *he has indeed*[b] *made reparation*[c] *to Yahweh."*

[20(6:1)] *Yahweh spoke to Moses,* [21(6:2)] *"If anyone sins and commits a breach of faith*[a] *against Yahweh in that he deceives his associate*[b] *in a matter of deposit or security*[c] *or something stolen, or he has extorted*[d] *his associate,* [22(6:3)] *or he has found something lost and denies it, or in that*[a] *he has sworn falsely about*[b] *anything that a person might do to sin thereby*[c]*—*23(6:4) *when one sins and realizes guilt, he must return what he has stolen, or what he has gotten by extortion, or the deposit which was entrusted to him, or the lost thing which he found,* 24(6:5) *or*[a] *anything*[b] *about which he has sworn falsely, he will restore*[c] *the principle*[d] *and will add to it (each time) 20 percent.*[e] *And he will give it to the victimized person*[f] *on the day of his reparation offering.* 25(6:6) *He is to bring to Yahweh as his reparation offering a ram without defect from the flock according to the value set*[a] *for a reparation offering.*[b] 26(6:7) *The priest will make expiation for him before Yahweh, and he will be forgiven for any of the things which one may do to incur guilt."*[a]

Notes

15.a. The first use of אשׁם after the verb הביא, "bring," is rendered "penalty" as in 5:6, 7. That is, אשׁם does not carry the technical meaning "reparation offering." The second אשׁם, however, defines the nature of the offering just as לחטאת, "for a purification offering," does in v 6a; thus it has the technical meaning.

15.b. The term בערכך, "according to your evaluation," is a technical term in which the pronominal suffix has lost any significance. It means "according to the value thereof" or "equivalent" (E. A. Speiser, "Leviticus and the Critics," 33). Milgrom (*Cult*, 13, n. 42) conjectures that the term with the prep ב means "payment" only. Earlier Zorell ("Zur Vokalisation des Wortes עֶרְכְּךָ in Lev. 27 und anderwärts," *Bib* 26 [1945] 112–14) proposed that this was a qitlal form, i.e., the third radical being reduplicated, but his proposal has not found acceptance.

15.c. This appositional phrase introduced by ב, "in, according to, in capacity of" restricts the value of the shekel (cf. GKC §119i).

16.a. שִׁלַּם, "pay, make good, make restitution," comes from the root שׁלם, "be complete, sound." When one pays what is owed, one has fulfilled his obligations and is at שׁלום, "peace," with his creditor.

17.a. MT ואם־נפשׁ כי is impossible Heb. The context prefers reading ונפשׁ כי, "and if anyone," as in 5:1, 4, 15, 21(6:2).

17.b. Cf. 4:2.b.

17.c. אשׁם here means "realize guilt" (cf. n. 15.a.); this meaning includes both the formal, legal obligation and the personal sense of apprehension and unsettledness resulting from a misdeed (cf. Milgrom, *Cult*, 9). It is this dynamic sense of guilt that makes a person aware that he has done something wrong.

17.d. Cf. n. 5:1.b.

18.a. Cf. n. 15.b.

19.a. LXX omits אשׁם הוא, "it is a reparation offering." This is an error of homoioarchton.

19.b. The inf abs standing before the verb emphasizes the certainty of the action.

19.c. Milgrom (*Cult*, 6) assigns to the phrase אשׁם ל an inchoative function and renders the phrase "he has become liable for reparation." But the phrase appears to define what has taken place.

21.a. In the phrase מעלה מעל, "commits a breach of faith," the noun following the verb from the same root is used for emphasis on the idea carried by this root.

21.b. BDB defines עמית as "associate, fellow, relation." It occurs ten times in Leviticus (18:20; 19:11, 15, 17; 24:19; 25:14 [2x], 15, 17) and elsewhere only in Zech 13:7.

21.c. The phrase תשׂומת יד means "security" or "pledge." In Aram this phrase means "trust, loan" (Jastrow, 1708). Snaith (43) points out that in the Talmud it refers to money entrusted to a partner in a business deal.

21.d. The next two finite verbs, או עשׁק, "or extort," and או מצא, "or he finds" (v 22), are interpreted as a continuation of the series headed by כחשׁ, "he deceives."

22.a. This sentence introduced by ונשׁבע, "and he has sworn," stands parallel to the series headed by כחשׁ, "he deceives," and is subordinate to מעל מעל, "he commits a breach of faith"; that is why the *waw* copula is translated "or in that."

22.b. *IBHS* (§11.2.13e) understands the prep על to introduce a norm, i.e., "the basis on which an act is performed."

22.c. *IBHS* (§11.2.5e) explains the ב on בהנה, "these," as the *beth* of specification, which qualifies the area that the verb effects: "with regard to."

24.a. LXX omits אוֹ, "or."

24.b. Sam, LXX, *Tg. Ps.-J.*, and Syr add דבר, "a thing," as in 5:2. This variant is preferred as a superior reading; MT could easily have arisen from an error of omission.

24.c. Cf. n. 16.a.

24.d. ראשׁ, (lit.) "head," means "sum or principle" in an economic setting (Milgrom, *JNES* 35 [1976] 273).

24.e. Instead of MT וחמשׁתיו, "(its) fifth or/and (each time) its fifth," Heb. mss, Sam, and LXX[BA] read וחמשׁית, "and a fifth," while Tg[mss] and *Tg. Ps.-J.* read וחמשׁתו, "and its fifth" as in v 16. PIR (168) prefers MT, reasoning that the variant arose to make intelligible an obscure reading.

24.f. The phrase לאשׁר הוא לו is a relative clause identifying the person who receives the 20 percent (cf. GKC §138e). The antecedent of לו, "to him," עמיתו, "his friend" (v 21), is identified in the Eng trans. for clarity.

25.a. Cf. n. 15.b.

25.b. Sam and LXX omit אל־הכהן, "to the priest." This variant is followed, for MT offers little sense as it stands (cf. PIR, 168). Possibly אל־הכהן was added in the margin to explain how it was to be brought ליהוה, "to Yahweh," and then inadvertently found its way into the text.

26.a. Milgrom (*Cult*, 6) renders לאשׁמה בה "to feel guilt thereby."

Form/Structure/Setting

The structure of this regulation is as follows:

I. Basic regulations for a reparation offering (5:14–19)
  A. Introductory formula (v 14)
  B. Speech proper (vv 15–19)
    1. First regulation (vv 15–16)
      a. Case (v 15a)
      b. Regulation proper (vv 15b–16)
        1) Prescription of animal required (v 15b)
        2) Restitution requirement (v 16a)
        3) Statement of expiation and forgiveness (v 16b)
    2. Second regulation (vv 17–19)
      a. Case (v 17a)
      b. Regulation proper (vv 17b–19)
        1) Declaration of guilt and responsibility (v 17b)
        2) Prescription of animal required (v 18a)
        3) Statement of expiation and forgiveness (v 18b)
        4) Declaratory formulae identifying the offering and the guilt of the offender (v 19)
II. Regulation of reparation offering for cases of getting something by deception (5:20–26[6:1–7])
  A. Introductory formula (v 20[6:1])
  B. Speech (vv 21–26[6:2–7])
    1. Case (vv 21–22[6:2–3])
      a. Basic case (v 21a[6:2a])
      b. Series of subcases (vv 21b–22[6:2b–3])
    2. Regulation (vv 23–26[6:4–7])
      a. Case of being guilty (v 23aα[6:4aα])
      b. Regulation proper (vv 23aβ–26[6:4aβ–7])
        1) Restoration of misappropriated goods (vv 23aβ–24aα[6:4aβ–5aα])
        2) Penalty of 20 percent (v 24aβ+b[6:5aβ+b])
        3) Prescription of a ram as a reparation offering (v 25[6:6])
        4) Expanded statement of expiation and forgiveness (v 26[6:7])

At this point in the cultic legislation come regulations for another sacrifice (5:14–19). The authoritative introduction (v 14) clearly marks this speech as the regulation for a reparation offering (אשׁם) distinct from the regulation for a purification offering (חטאת). The basic regulation consists of two parts (vv 15–16 and 17–19). Attached to it is another speech that enumerates the requirement of a reparation offering to expiate any of several ways of defrauding another person (5:20–26[6:1–7]).

Both speeches thus prescribe a reparation offering for situations in which a person commits מעל, "a breach of faith," against Yahweh. The first speech has two regulations. The first regulation concerns dealing faithlessly in matters of the sanctuary (vv 14–16). The second regulation treats an unintentional and unknown violation of any of God's commandments (vv 17–19). A declarative statement defining the sacrifice as a reparation offering concludes the second regulation (v 19). Any person guilty of a breach of faith in either of these ways is to present a ram with a set value as a reparation offering, and he is to make restitution by repaying what he has misappropriated plus pay a penalty of 20 percent. In contrast to the preceding regulations, the ritual for this offering is not given here. These two facts together mean that either the guilty party has to pay a penalty equivalent to the value of the specified ram instead of making a sacrifice, or, if a sacrifice is made, the prescribed ritual is either recorded elsewhere or assumed to be the same as for a purification offering. The agreement with the regulation for a purification offering is found in that in both of these regulations it states that the priest makes expiation for the guilty person, and he is forgiven (vv 16a, 18a).

The second speech (vv 20–26[6:1–7]) treats various kinds of deception used to acquire another's property that are also classified as breaches of faith (מעל) against Yahweh. The cases include deceiving an associate about a matter of a deposit or security or robbery (v 21bα[6:2bα]) or extorting a close associate (v 21bβ[6:2bβ]) or denying having found a lost item (v 22aα[6:3aα]). The usual procedure in ancient society for uncovering a suspected act of deception was for the suspected party to swear an oath of innocence (vv 23–26[6:4–7]). Such a procedure explains why such a case is classified as a breach of faith against Yahweh; the guilty party has sworn falsely about his involvement in the missing property, thereby profaning Yahweh's name (vv 22, 24[6:3, 5]). The fact that this person swore falsely in Yahweh's name raises his sin to a breach of faith (מעל) against Yahweh. To rectify matters the guilty person must take several steps. He must restore to the victim whatever he has taken (vv 23–24aα[6:4–5aα]) plus pay a fine of 20 percent (v 24aβ–b[6:5aβ–b]). Then he is to present a reparation offering, consisting of a ram without defect and having a set value (v 25[6:6]). Thereby the priest expiates his sin, and God forgives him (v 26[6:7]).

These two speeches for a reparation offering have many anomalies. Compared to the other regulations they are brief; they focus on the nature of the sin; they do not give the ritual procedure; and stress is placed on the value of the ram that is acceptable for this offering. These major variations have led to many different constructions as to the separate standing of אשׁם, "the reparation offering." Some consider the reparation offering to be basically a special kind of purification offering (cf. Elliger, 65–67), but others argue that it is a distinct sacrifice in its own right (cf. Milgrom, *Cult*). Certainly the editor who put 5:14–19 in its present place treated the reparation offering as a self-standing sacrifice, for he presents it in its own speech. In addition, it is included as a separate sacrifice in the supplemental material about the various sacrifices in 6:1(8)–7:38. In 7:1–6 the basic ritual procedure for a reparation offering is given to compensate for its absence in chap. 5. The editor who juxtaposed the speeches on the reparation offering to those on the purification offering implied that the ritual for the reparation offering was the same as that for a purification offering. The single difference for them was that the sacrificial animal had to be a ram without defect, possessing a minimal value.

Critical commentators, furthermore, disagree on how the three pericopes concerning the reparation offering came together, i.e., vv 14–16, 17–19, 20–26(6:1–7). Many (e.g., Koch, *Priesterschrift,* 6 and Noth, 47–48) judge vv 17–19 to be later than vv 14–16. Noth postulates that at an earlier stage vv 20–26(6:1–7) joined vv 14–16, for both are concerned with misdoings; later vv 17–19 were inserted, being the last addition to 4:1–5:26(6:7). But the style of vv 17–19 is similar to the other sacrificial laws in chaps. 4 and 5, as both Noth and Elliger observe. Furthermore, its scrupulous tone agrees with the widespread ancient obsession about having inadvertently violated sacred property (Milgrom, *Cult,* 76–83). Thus vv 17–19 look very much like an ancient prescription. In this light they are judged to continue to treat the violation of sacred property and thus are a proper continuation of vv 14–16. The first unit of the first speech deals with a known, though inadvertent, violation of sancta and the second with a suspected trespass of sancta (Milgrom, *Cult,* 82). Based on this connection, it is assumed that vv 17–19 were coupled with vv 14–16 from the time that this material was placed in written form. When Lev 1–7 was collected, both speeches on the reparation offering were placed back to back.

Comment

Excursus: אשם, *"guilt, reparation offering"*

The verb אשם ordinarily appears in the qal; once it occurs as a hiph (Ps 5:11[10]) and possibly once as a niph (Joel 1:18, though there is a textual variant נשמו, "be dismayed," which is considered better by Kellermann [*TDOT* 1:435]). Usually its basic meaning is "commit an offense, do a wrong" (BDB 79; Num 5:7b; 2 Chr 19:10 [2x—"sin," NIV; but "incur guilt," JB]). Its uses in the OT, however, do not support this definition as the basic meaning of אשם (Knierim, *THAT* 1:253). Rather its basic meaning is the "guilt, responsibility, or culpability" that a person must bear for having done something wrong. For example, in Hosea (4:15; 5:15; 10:2; 13:1; 14:1[13:16]) those who rebel against God and worship other gods such as Baal are culpable (אשם) before God (Kellermann, *TDOT* 1:435–36). Thus אשם describes the legal/moral standing of a person who has done wrong but has not yet been punished. In the world view of the OT, any person who does something wrong becomes obligated both to God and to society (cf. 2 Chr 19:10; Num 5:6; cf. Jer 51:5). Furthermore, it is possible for the nation as a whole to become guilty by collectively violating the covenant or acting unfaithfully against God (Isa 24:5–6; Hos 14:1[13:16]).

The best way to render the verb אשם in English is debated; e.g., RSV and NIV often translate it "be guilty," while NEB frequently uses "incur guilt." Milgrom (*Cult,* 7–12) argues that אשם means "feel guilty." He points out that in those verses where this term occurs with the additional phrase נשא עונו, "he must bear his responsibility," a tautology exists if אשם means "incur guilt." It also may have a consequential meaning, i.e., the suffering as qualms, pangs, or remorse produced by the guilt (Milgrom, *Cult,* 8–9). While Milgrom has made an excellent point, nevertheless, אשם has an objective usage for a person's ethical/legal culpability, rather than for a person's existential feelings. In that Hebraic thought tends not to make strict categorical distinctions, it is possible that both of these meanings are present in some occurrences of the verb; a person who is guilty and accountable before God would also experience the stirring of guilt in his conscience, awaking him to his need to take the steps to expiate his wrongdoing. That is, this dynamic understanding of guilt engendered the belief that a person who had sinned in ignorance would become aware of his wrongdoing and then take the steps necessary to amend his wrongdoing. Thus Kiuchi (*Purification Offering,* 34) proposes the translation "realize guilt." The formal meaning of אשם, however, dominates in cultic texts. This is attested in Lev 4:3, which says that the anointed priest sins (יחטא) and brings guilt on the people (לאשמת העם). If the primary meaning of אשם is "to feel guilt," the anointed priest, not the people, would have the troubled conscience.

Because of the close tie between guilt and punishment in ancient Hebraic thought, i.e., guilt is the forerunner of punishment (cf. Jer 2:3; Isa 24:6) or even the guarantee of punishment, in a few texts אשם means "condemn, punish" (e.g., Ps 34:22[21], "be condemned," RSV; "will have to pay," JB, where it stands parallel to מות, "put to death"; cf. v 23[22]). The use of אשם in Prov 30:10, rendered "be held guilty" in RSV and "suffer for it" in JB, connotes that a person who violates human relationships will pay a heavy price, possibly even death (cf. Kellermann, *TDOT,* 1:436).

The noun אשם means "guilt, culpability, compensation, reparation offering." It is the obligation that one must bear for wrongdoing (Knierim, *THAT* 1:254). Such obligation is normally experienced by the person as guilt (cf. Gen 26:10). Moreover, אשם stands for a guilty person's effort(s) to absolve his wrongdoing by making restitution. Usually the person has to restore that which has been damaged or misappropriated plus a penalty, which in Num 5:6–8 and Lev 5:16, 24(6:5) is set at 20 percent. The noun אשם may then have a secondary meaning of "restitution (of damages usually accompanied by a penalty)" (cf. Lev 5:6). While in the cultic laws restitution is primarily monetary, the text in Gen 42:21 indicates that suffering hardship in kind is incurred as fulfillment for a wrongful act committed against another.

In the sacrificial system, אשם became a technical term for a particular sacrifice offered to expiate sins classified as מעל, "a breach of faith," against Yahweh (5:15). Other kinds of wrongdoing like the cases enumerated in 5:21–22(6:2–3), which primarily concern the mishandling of another's property, could also be expiated by this type of sacrifice. It can be conjectured that these sins were included with this offering because the person guilty of such crimes elevated his offense to a breach of faith against Yahweh by swearing an oath of innocence in Yahweh's name before the court in an effort to clear himself of suspected wrongdoing. Since he has sworn an oath of innocence falsely, he has used Yahweh's name in vain; i.e., he has committed a breach of faith against Yahweh. Furthermore, an אשם could be presented by a person whose conscience was severely troubled, fearful that he had transgressed one of God's commandments even though he was unsure of the nature of his transgression (5:17–19). In this case the reparation offering is prescribed because of the interrelationship between the strong guilt, אשם, which the person felt and the name of the reparation offering itself, אשם. Milgrom (*Cult,* 104–27) goes much further in interpreting the role of the reparation offering in ancient Israel. In a very careful study he argues persuasively that a person who had committed a flagrant offense that was beyond the means of expiation provided in the cultic legislation could reduce his intentional sin to a lesser offense, i.e., an inadvertent transgression, for which there were the means of expiation by genuine repentance. He says, "Confession is the legal device fashioned by the priestly legislators to convert deliberate sins into inadvertencies, thereby qualifying them for sacrificial expiation" (*Cult,* 119). That is, in his view, the priests interpreted the cultic legislation to permit the forgiveness of flagrant violations of the law by the presentation of a reparation offering as long as there was genuine repentance. The theological dynamic evident in Ps 51 is well illuminated by Milgrom's reconstruction.

Since the reparation offering is accepted as a self-standing offering, the question of its distinction from חטאת, "a purification offering," arises. Many proposals as to the distinction have been put forth throughout the ages. Philo distinguishes the purification offerings as being made for unintentional sins, while the reparation offerings were presented for deliberate sins committed without a witness (Kellermann, *TDOT* 1:431). The confusion may be illustrated by contrasting the opposite positions of Saydon (*CBQ* 8 [1966] 397–98), who holds that a purification offering is required for intentional sins committed out of human frailty and a reparation offering is for inadvertent sins, with that of Thompson (*TGUOS* 14 [1953] 24), who reasons that a reparation offering makes atonement for intentional sins. Snaith (*VT* 15 [1975] 79–80) emphasizes that this offering alone requires restitution, but this position becomes hard to accept by reason of the lack of reference to restitution in the section 5:17–19. Levine (*In the Presence of the Lord,* 91–101) argues that the reparation offering was only presented by individuals for personal needs. Thus it never became part of public worship at the cult center. As for the purification offering, while there was one for private needs, the majority of references to it are for the people as a whole, e.g., the presentation of purification offerings at the major festivals. Milgrom (*Cult,* 127–28) goes on to point out that a reparation offering is presented for desecration of sancta and a purification offering is offered to remove the contamination of sacred cultic objects from the pollution arising from inadvertent sins. These insights given by Levine and Milgrom account best for the difference between these two offerings and clearly support the position that they are two distinct offerings.

The history of the reparation offering is variously reconstructed. Many scholars do not consider that this passage prescribes a distinct sacrifice, but rather that it presents the provision for making a "compensating" payment (אשם) in money in place of sacrificing an animal (Noth, 47; cf. Elliger, 75–78). Noth (47) interprets this provision to be a "progressive simplification and secularization of the cult material" that took place over a long period of time. Rendtorff (*Studien,* 207–11), however, takes a very different stance. He argues that the reparation offering was the oldest expiating sacrifice for an individual, while in the early period the purification offering was primarily for community trespasses. Then with the expansion of the purification offering to make expiation for an individual's sin, the reparation offering became relegated to a limited place in the cult over time. That a reparation offering was required as part of the aggregation ceremony for a healed leper and for a Nazirite who had been contaminated by a corpse (Num 6:9–12) supports the view that it was an ancient sacrifice. The editor who placed its regulation at this location, though, viewed it as an offering very similar to the purification offering. He, nevertheless, saw it as a distinct offering, for he put it into two speeches. Because of its closeness to the purification offering, he recorded only the ancient material that focused on the distinctiveness of the reparation offering.

In reference to dating this offering, Milgrom (*Cult,* 119–24) has uncovered another clue in its emphasis on repentance. The exilic prophets, particularly Jeremiah and Ezekiel, spoke much about repentance. Their favorite word for this concept was שׁוב, (lit.) "turn, return." But the term employed here for repentance is אשׁם. If this material were later than these exilic prophets, one would expect to find the term שׁוב. Thus this cultic material must be earlier than the exile. Furthermore, the difficulty that both the Greek and the Syriac translators had in rendering the terms חטאת, "purification offering," and אשׁם "guilt, feel guilty, reparation offering," in Lev 4–5 suggests that the distinction between these two sacrifices was no longer clear to them. This fact is hard to explain if the reparation offering was a development of the post-exilic community.

Therefore, the Leviticus text for the reparation offering is taken to reflect an early stage in Israel's cultic history.

The basic regulation for presenting a reparation offering, which is absent from Lev 5:14–26(6:7), is found in Lev 7:1–6: (1) It is to be slaughtered in the same place as עלה, "the whole offering." (2) Its blood is to be thrown (זרק) against all sides of the altar. (3) Its fat and prized entrails are to be removed (הסיר) and burned (הקטיר) on the altar. Since this is the only detailed sacrificial ritual in 6:1(8)–7:38, it is clear that it has been included to compensate for its absence in 5:14–19. The editor who juxtaposed the reparation offering to the purification offering at 5:14 assumed that the ritual for the reparation offering was the same as for the person who presented a sin offering. The single difference at that time was that the sacrificial animal for a reparation offering had to be a ram without blemish that possessed a minimal value.

A look at the few references to a reparation offering in the OT is instructive. In Num 6:7–21 a Nazirite, who swears to live a life of separation to Yahweh, must make a series of offerings should his vow be broken by someone's dying in his presence (vv 9–12). He first presents two small birds, one as a purification offering and the other as a whole offering. Next he reconsecrates his head and swears anew his vow of separation; then he makes a reparation offering by presenting a yearling male lamb. The reconsecration and the oath precede the reparation offering and function as the equivalent of financial restitution, which, of course, is impossible in this case. As Milgrom observes (*Cult,* 69–70), the Nazirite must replace the desecrated sacred objects, i.e., his hair and time of service, by consecrating his new hair and renewing his vows before his reparation offering can be made acceptable.

One with a grievous disease (צרעת) who has been healed must offer a male lamb as a reparation offering as part of the elaborate ceremony of aggregation (Lev 14:12, 21). The reason that this sacrifice is required is not immediately visible. It may be traced back to the intersecting of two general beliefs about one so afflicted. One is that illness is frequently a punishment for sin, and the second is that a grievous disease is the worst curse a person can experience. Therefore, it was thought possible that whoever came down with such an affliction may have violated something sacred, as Miriam (Num 12) and Uzziah (2 Chr 26:16–19) did. In light of 5:17–19 a reparation offering was made to cover any possibility that the leprosy might have come on that person because he had unknowingly violated sancta (cf. Milgrom, *Cult,* 80–82).

Furthermore, a man who mates with a betrothed slave must present a ram as a reparation offering (19:20–22). The best justification for the requirement of a reparation sacrifice lies in the explanation that not only has the girl been violated, but also the oath of betrothal taken before God has been broken (Milgrom, *Cult,* 133–37).

In post-exilic Jerusalem, Ezra required those who were guilty of mixed marriages to divorce their foreign wives and offer a reparation offering consisting of a ram (Ezra 10:29). He had convinced the people that they had committed a sacrilege (מעל) because they mixed the purity of the holy seed (זרע הקדש) with foreigners (Milgrom, *Cult,* 71–73; cf. Jer 2:3). Since each had individually committed a breach of faith against Yahweh by marrying a foreign woman, each was required to present a reparation offering.

In another example, the Philistines, wishing to free themselves from the plagues that had befallen them since taking the Ark of the Covenant, were instructed to return the Ark to Israel with a guilt offering (1 Sam 6:3, 4, 8, 17). Obviously the Philistines had violated sacred property in taking the Ark of the Covenant and above all in placing it before Dagon, their god. Thus a reparation offering was mandated. In their case the reparation offering consisted of five gold tumors and five gold mice, each for the five Philistine rulers. This offering then consisted of dedicated property rather than a blood sacrifice. Yahweh accepted these objects as reparation and healed (רפא) the Philistines from the plagues that he had put on them.

The most intriguing reference to the reparation offering occurs in Isa 53:10, in which the servant's death is described as a reparation offering. Unfortunately this reference occurs in an obscure phrase: "though he puts himself as a reparation offering [אם־תשׂים אשׁם נפשׁו], Yahweh's purpose will succeed in his power." While interpretations of Isa 53 vary widely, the traditional Christian interpretation holds that the servant suffers and dies vicariously for mankind's sin. His death is an atoning sacrifice. The choice of אשׁם to describe his sacrificial death may be twofold. First, it communicates that the servant's death compensates God fully for the damages he has incurred by mankind's sinning. Second, the servant's sacrifice provides expiation for every kind of sin, inadvertent and intentional. That is, the servant's sacrifice provides expiation for any person who appropriates its merits to himself, no matter how grave his sin.

15–16 A person is required to present אשׁם, "a reparation offering," if he commits מעל מעל, "a breach of faith," against Yahweh in respect to any of the holy things of Yahweh. The term קדשׁי יהוה, "holy things," includes that which is "most holy," קדשׁ קדשׁים. Whatever is most holy becomes the exclusive property of the Temple and/or the priests, including portions of the various sacrifices except from an offering of well-being. Other things, including the bread of the Presence (24:9), the temple incense (Exod 30:36), the Tent of Meeting (Exod 30:29), especially the adytum (Exod 26:33–34), and the furniture and furnishings of the Tent, are classified most holy. But does קדשׁי יהוה, "the holy things of Yahweh," here include קדשׁ, "that which is holy," e.g., things that belong to the priests, such as portions of the offering of well-being (7:31–34), tithes (27:30–33), firstfruits (Num 18:12–13), firstborn of domestic animals (Num 18:15), or anything dedicated (חרם) to Yahweh (Num 18:14)? The rabbinic tradition considers these to be "minor sancta" and thus not subject to this law (Milgrom, *JQR* 65 [1974] 208–10). But Milgrom demonstrates that the biblical writer includes "minor sancta" in this term, for in Lev 19:5–8 meat from an offering of well-being, which is "minor sancta," is classified as קדשׁי יהוה, "the holy things of Yahweh" (209). Comparative evidence from Hittite texts also supports taking קדשׁי יהוה in a wide sense (Milgrom, *JQR* 65 [1974] 211–15). A thing becomes "holy" at the time of its dedication, for many things like the tithe (27:30–33) and various offerings (6:18[25]; 7:1–2) are to be presented outside the sanctuary, not at the time it enters the sanctuary (Milgrom, *JQR* 65 [1974] 210). Holy things remain holy until they are properly disposed. The law does make provision for the redemption of a variety of things that are holy (27:9–25).

If a layman took for himself anything that was holy, he committed a breach of faith against Yahweh, since that item was dedicated to Yahweh himself. The phrase מעל מעל, "breach of faith," is normally followed by the prepositional phrase ביהוה, "against Yahweh." This phraseology is used especially for an act of faithlessness against a covenant partner. In Num 5:12, 27, מעל describes the unfaithful behavior of a wife who שׂטה, "strays," from her husband. Such an act of infidelity in marriage is also defined as a breach of faith against God (Num 5:6).

In the cultic sphere, מעל is a trespass against anything that is consecrated or holy. King Uzziah violated the priestly prerogative of offering incense in the Temple (2 Chr 26:16–18), and King Ahaz committed treachery (מעל) by altering the true worship of Yahweh at the Jerusalem Temple and by encouraging the worship of idols throughout the land (2 Chr 28:19–25; 29:19). In the attempt to take Ai, Achan committed treachery against Yahweh by violating the rules of objects devoted to God (חרם; Josh 7:1; cf. 27:16–21). His unfaithfulness became symbolic of such loathsome behavior (Josh 22:20; 1 Chr 2:7). A violation of an oath is also defined as מעל (Ezek 17:19–20). That is why God accuses Israel of unfaithfulness and sends her into captivity—she has been untrue to her God by breaking the oath of the covenant (Ezek 15:8; 2 Chr 36:14; Neh 1:8; Dan 9:7). Thus מעל is a trespass that is a direct affront against God himself (cf. R. Knierim, "מעל *mʿl* treulos sein," *THAT* 1:920–22).

The breach of faith covered in this first regulation is חטא בשגגה, "a sin committed inadvertently" (cf. 4:2). In other words, a person in some way unwittingly violates that which is holy; e.g., he eats some meat that is holy, not knowing at the time that it has been consecrated. Harrison (71) proposes two other ways that sanctuary property might have been misappropriated, either by presenting inferior animals or by failing to present a required offering because of forgetfulness.

Whoever commits such a sin has to offer a ram without defect (איל תמים) and make restitution by restoring that which he has misappropriated plus pay a penalty of 20 percent. This ram must possess a certain value measured in silver shekels of the sanctuary. This means that the guilty person may not offer any ram available to him. Surprisingly, the number of shekels that the animal should be worth is not given. Because the term shekels stands in the plural, the rabbis understood the minimum fine to be two shekels. The number of shekels was probably set by the officiating priest and varied from time to time. Keil proposes that the value of the ram was assessed "to fix upon it symbolically the value of the trespass for which compensation was required" (317). Snaith (43) identifies the shekel of the sanctuary as an ancient shekel of 224 grains; fifteen of these silver shekels equaled a gold shekel weighing 253 grains. This shekel is a "heavy" shekel. When the merchants adopted a lighter shekel, the Temple continued to accept only the heavy shekel. This practice led to the necessity of money changers at the entrance to the Temple area (cf. Mark 11:15; John 2:14; Porter, 45).

Rather than presenting a ram, Noth (47) understands the text to require the guilty person to pay to the Temple a certain sum, i.e., the set value of a ram. He gains support for this position from the reference to כסף אשם, "the money of the reparation offering," in 2 Kgs 12:17(16). This passage also speaks of כסף חטאות, "money of a purification offering." Some interpret this phraseology to mean that these sacrifices could be made by the payment of a set sum of money. Another interpretation believes this reference in 2 Kgs speaks about the payment of a tax, a fee, or a donation to the officiating priest at the time of the offering. E. A. Speiser ("Leviticus and the Critics," 33), however, evaluates the phrase בערכך כסף־שקלים (v 15b) to be a technical language for "convertible into silver shekels." This means that the guilty person presented a sum of money set by the priest; the priest then purchased the appropriate ram for that person's reparation offering (cf. Levine, *In the Presence*, 98). Levine argues that behind this language stands a development in the practice of the reparation offering. He postulates that in the earliest period the אשם was not an altar sacrifice but the payment of silver or an object of comparable value, such as the golden figurines of tumors and mice presented by the Philistines (1 Sam 6:1–18), as a means of expiation, which was devoted to the Temple to be used in its repair or for securing of cultic vessels (*In the Presence,* 99). Later, in this final form of this regulation, the money paid for such an offering had to be used to purchase the appropriate ram for sacrifice (*In the Presence,*

100). While these views that in the early period a reparation offering could be made by the payment of a set sum are well argued and such may have been the practice in a given period, it is hard to believe that the ancient sacramental theology would have permitted expiation for such serious offenses as the violation of sancta without an altar sacrifice with the appropriate manipulation of blood (cf. Noordtzij, 71). In fact, the declaratory formulae stating that expiation and forgiveness have been achieved for the presenter of a reparation offering in 5:16b, 18b, 26(6:7) are in accord with similar statements for a purification offering, which definitely required a slaughtered sacrifice and the careful manipulation of the blood (4:20b, 26b, 31b, 35b; 5:6b, 10b). The wording הכהן יכפר עליו באיל האשם, "the priest will make expiation for him with the ram of the reparation offering" (v 16), compensates for the absence of a regulation for the sacrificial ritual. It definitely implies that expiation is achieved by sacrificing the ram.

17–18 Another case requiring a reparation offering is stated. This time the transgression is not described more than that a person עשתה אחת מכל־מצות יהוה, "breaks one of Yahweh's commandments," without knowing it (לא־ידע). This latter phrase may mean either that the person does not know whether or not he has sinned, though he suspects he may have, as several rabbis teach, or that the person does not realize at the time of doing something that it was a violation of a law, as Kiuchi reasons (*Purification Offering,* 27). In this latter interpretation לא־ידע, "he does not know," does not imply "unconsciousness" of the act. The context indicates that the sin is against sacred property (cf. Milgrom, *Cult,* 74–83). Even though a person committed the sin in ignorance, he is אשם, "guilty." Milgrom argues that אשם means "feel guilty." But Kiuchi (*Purification Offering,* 34) claims that the formal meaning of אשם is primary; thus he renders it "realize guilt." That is, אשם connotes both a legal status and the idea that "guilt" works itself into the conscience of the one who has sinned so that a sinner becomes aware of his sin (cf. Milgrom, *Cult,* 3–12; Kiuchi, *Purification Offering,* 33–38). On becoming aware, the guilty party bears the responsibility for that iniquity (נשא עונו). This means he will be punished unless he presents a reparation offering to make expiation for the wrongdoing. Since the exact offense remains unknown, the required reparation offering consists solely of איל תמים, "a ram without blemish," according to the value of the sanctuary. This case thus does not require the making of restitution or the payment of a penalty. A person could, therefore, clear a guilty conscience troubled by fear of having violated sancta even though the precise error never becomes known. Milgrom (*Cult,* 76–80) provides many examples from the ancient Middle East that demonstrate that one of the greatest fears of ancient peoples was that of having inadvertently violated sancta.

The unintentionality of this sin is stressed by the use of the phrase שגגתו אשר שגג, "his error which he erred" (cf. Num 15:28). This phrase is an intentional substitute for the more frequent חטא בשגגה, "one sinned inadvertently," and it is built on the pattern of the frequent phrase, חטאתו אשר חטא, "the sin which one committed." To underscore the person's lack of understanding that his act was a transgression, הוא לא־ידע, "one did not know," is repeated with the personal pronoun for emphasis. With the reparation offering (אשם), the priest makes expiation for him and God forgives him (cf. 4:20).

19 This brief pericope closes with two declaratory statements. The first identifies the offering: אשם הוא, "it is a reparation offering." The second affirms that the goal of the offering is achieved: אשׁם אשׁם ליהוה, "one has surely made reparation to Yahweh." This time the term אשׁם refers to the achievements of the offering, not to making the offering. The accomplishment of reparation is stressed so strongly because God wishes to provide a party greatly troubled with guilt full assurance that the responsibility for any breach of faith has been fully met, even though that person remains in ignorance regarding the details of his transgression.

21–22(6:2–3) Here is a list of cases classified as מעל, "a breach of faith," against Yahweh, thus requiring a reparation offering. All these cases involve getting control of something that belongs to another person through cunning schemes or deception rather than outright force. As will be seen, these transgressions are elevated to a breach of faith because the wrongdoer denies, through an oath taken in Yahweh's name, having sinned. The list identifies three major ways of committing such transgressions. Each way is expressed by a perfect verb, and the verbs are connected by או, "or." This list is made complex in that the first case is subdivided into three subcases; the confusion is further increased by the difficulty of rendering these terms in this grammatical structure into English.

In the first category, a person gains possession of another's property by the use of כחשׁ, "deceit." Three different situations in which deceit is used are given; each situation is introduced by the preposition ב, "in." The first concerns holding back a deposit (פקדון) entrusted to one for safekeeping. Since there were no banks in ancient society, a person who wanted to secure something of value for a period of time, e.g., while away on a journey, turned it over to another for safekeeping. That person was a trusted close associate or friend (עמית). On return, the depositor expected his friend to return his valuable(s), but in this case that party fails to do so, denying that they are any longer under his control. The second subcase involves a matter of security or a pledge or a loan (תשׂומת יד) made to someone who later will not return it. An example of a wrong in this category is a creditor's holding back a security deposited (חבל) with him for a loan after the debtor has regained the right to reclaim the deposit, either because he has paid back the loan or because the law permits him to reclaim it under certain conditions of insolvency (Exod 22:25–26[26–27]; Deut 24:6, 17). The creditor uses deceit to keep the deposit for himself. The third subcase involves some type of robbery (גזל). Milgrom adduces the reason that גזל, "robbery," occurs here and not גנב, "theft," is that the person who has suffered loss is unable to identify the thief by definition and thus he is not able to take an oath against such an offender (Milgrom, *Cult,* 100–102). Another has confiscated his goods by deception.

In the second major case a person commits עשׁק, "extortion." Extortion classifies the getting of another's goods or money legally, but immorally. One way this is done is by withholding what a person has a right to receive, such as wages for a task done (19:13; Deut 24:14–15; Levine, 33). Another kind of extortion is twisting the law to squeeze another out of his property. The third major case concerns a situation in which a person finds something another has lost and then denies having done so with lies (כחשׁ).

None of these cases can be tried in court, for it is one person's word against another. That is, the victim has little recourse since he has no way of proving that the party whom he suspects actually has his property. To resolve such a situation the ancients usually required the suspected party to take a solemn oath of innocence as proof of his innocence. It was believed that if that person lied under oath, God would activate the curse implied by the oath. Nevertheless, this guilty party dares נשבע על־שקר, "to swear falsely," covering the immoral acquisition of another's property with a brazen lie. In so doing the guilty party compounds his wrongdoing, for he has committed מעלה מעל, "a breach of faith," against God by swearing falsely in God's name. Such an abuse of God's name surely violates the third commandment and comes under divine punishment (Exod 20:7). The hope for the victim to recover his property rests only with the wrongdoer's having a change of heart and making confession. This law recognizes that limitation and provides the means for the sinner to find expiation and at the same time for the victim to recover his loss. Thus a person who has the moral courage to confess his deceitful practice may take the prescribed steps to win forgiveness.

24(6:5) To gain forgiveness the guilty person must restore that which he has deceitfully confiscated to the rightful owner and pay a penalty equivalent to 20 percent of that property's value. It is debated whether one makes restoration in kind, preferably the confiscated item (D. Daube, *Studies in Biblical Law,* 141–43), or with a monetary equivalent (Milgrom, *JNES* 35 [1976] 272–73). From the term בראשׁ, "principle," Milgrom concludes that the restitution was to be made in money. Given that the tradition preserves both interpretations, it is possible that the wording of this text permitted restoration to be made either in kind or in monetary equivalence. The guilty party makes restitution on the day that he offers his reparation offering. Thus he seeks reconciliation both with God and with man. Num 5:5–10 extends this law to cover the eventuality that the victim has died. In that eventuality, the goods plus the penalty belong to the nearest גאל, "relation." In case there is no near relative, the goods are to go to the priest.

The 20 percent penalty prescribed here is considerably less than the restitution required elsewhere in the Pentateuch. According to Exod 21:37(22:1), a person who stole an ox or a sheep and slaughtered it or sold it must return 300 percent or 400 percent. But if the animal is alive, he must supply two animals (Exod 22:3[4]). The reduction of penalty is significant in order to encourage confession of wrongdoing. Milgrom (*Cult,* 115) finds a parallel practice among the Hittites. If a party confesses to being a thief, it is no crime; but if he is caught, the penalty is death.

25–26(6:6–7) In addition to making restitution and paying the penalty, the wrongdoer presents to the priest a ram having predetermined value for his reparation offering (cf. 5:15–16). The priest makes expiation for him, and God forgives him of his wrongdoing.

Explanation

The reparation offering was offered for a violation against sacred property and for any breach of faith against Yahweh. The violation against sacred property is defined as a sin committed unintentionally or inadvertently. Any person severely troubled by a guilty conscience, fearful that he may have violated some sancta but totally unaware of having committed any specific wrongdoing, could present this offering to clear his conscience. In both of these cases the ram had to possess a certain value set by the priest. This prescription of value and the requirement that the animal be a ram indicate the weightiness of the offense.

Another type of offense that required a reparation offering was getting control of another's goods by deception or other cunning means, such as extortion. When a person denied that he had falsely gotten another's property under oath, that behavior became classified as a breach of faith against Yahweh. Swearing falsely in Yahweh's name was a way of falling into a more serious sin, because a false oath profaned Yahweh's name. This is another text that witnesses to the principle that a sin against a fellow human being is at the same time a sin against God, for every human bears the image of God (cf. 1 John 4:20). Furthermore, such treachery reveals the corrupt nature of man. A guilty party uses religious ceremonies and practices to cover his offense against an associate.

Milgrom interprets this regulation further. He argues that any intentional sin could be reduced to a sin of ignorance by genuine repentance. Whenever a guilty person took this path, he lowered his sin to the level of an unintentional sin and gained the possibility of expiating his wrongdoing through presenting a reparation sacrifice. This interpretation certainly agrees with the theology of Ps 51. Having blatantly violated God's law, that repentant psalmist earnestly pleads for God's mercy (vv 4, 16a[2, 14a]):

> Wash me thoroughly from my iniquity,
> and cleanse me from my sin.
> Deliver me from bloodguiltiness, O God.

Besides contritely admitting his wrong, he earnestly cries out for a radical change in his inner being (v 12[10]):

> Create in me a clean heart, O God,
> and put a new and right spirit within me.

Whenever possible, restitution had to accompany the presentation of a reparation offering. That sacred property which a person had polluted or the property he had taken from his neighbor had to be restored in full plus an additional 20 percent added to its value. Restitution is a critical step in genuine repentance. It lays a solid foundation for the restoration of the relationship ruptured by an offense, and it reconstructs the offender's character on eternal values. The victim not only sees that the guilty person's repentance is genuine; he is also compensated for his losses. In ancient Israel, on the occasion of making restitution, the guilty person offered a ram without defect, which possessed a prescribed value. The priest made expiation for his sin, and the guilty person was forgiven, being fully reconciled to Yahweh, his God. His guilt for that trespass was removed forever.

In fulfillment of Isa 53, Christ offered himself as a reparation offering. His death thus made full compensation to God for the damages done by mankind's sins. Thus the death of Christ has won the possibility of atonement for all. There are no limitations to the types of sins that may be forgiven except for the sin against the Holy Spirit (Matt 12:31; Mark 3:29). Any sinner may find genuine forgiveness by faith in the atoning death of Christ.

To achieve forgiveness, a person needs to seek reconciliation with those he has wronged. Making restitution often provides the platform for genuine reconciliation. In the Sermon on the Mount Jesus teaches: "If you are offering your gift at the altar, and there remember that your brother has something against you, leave your gift before the altar and go; first be reconciled to your brother, and then come and offer your gift" (Matt 5:23–24). This teaching stresses the need of reconciliation between parties in order for God to accept one's gift. In making reconciliation a person experiences forgiveness. Freely forgiven by Christ, that one rejoices in forgiving those who have wronged him. As Jesus exhorts, "If you forgive men their trespasses, your heavenly father will also forgive you" (Matt 6:14). The NT does not teach cheap forgiveness. Genuine repentance precedes forgiveness. And restitution is an integral part of the standard of repentance (Luke 19:5). Through restitution a person expresses in a tangible form that he is accepting the full responsibility for his wrongdoing and is seeking both the welfare of a wronged associate and restoration of the relationship.

E. Further Instructions about the Various Sacrifices (6:1[8]–7:38)

Bibliography

Bach, D. "Rite et parole dans l'Ancien Testament: Nouveaux éléments apportés par l'étude de Tôdâh." *VT* 28 (1978) 10–193. **Charbel, A.** "La portata religiosa degli *šᵉlāmîm.*" *RBibIt* 18 (1970) 185–94. ———. "Nota a Lev. 7,34: *tᵉnûfāh* e *tᵉrûmāh* degli *šᵉlāmîm.*" *RBibIt* 21 (1973) 353–59. **Leeuwen, J. H. van.** "The Meaning of תֻּפִּין in Lev. 6, 14." *ZAW* 100 (1988) 268–69. **Loss, N.** "«Oblazione quotidiana» oppure «oblazione stabile»?" *RBibIt* 16 (1968) 409–30. **Milgrom, J.** "The Alleged Wave-offering in Israel and the Ancient Near East." *IEJ* 22 (1972) 33–38 (*SCTT,* 133–38). ———. "Hattĕnûpâ" (Heb.). In *Zer Li' gevurot* (Z. Shazar Vol.). Ed. B. Z. Luria. Jerusalem: Kiryat Sepher, 1972. 93–110 (*SCTT,* 139–58, Eng.). ———. "The *šôq hattĕrûmâ:* A Chapter in Cultic History" (Heb.). *Tarbiz* 42 (1972/73) 1–14 (*SCTT,* 159–70). ———. "Akkadian Confirmation of the Meaning of the Term *tĕrûmâ*" (Heb.). *Tarbiz* 44 (1974/75) 189 (*SCTT,* 171–72, Eng.). **Snaith, N.** "The Wave Offering." *ExpTim* 74 (1962/63) 127.

Translation

1(8) *Yahweh spoke to Moses:* 2(9) *"Command Aaron and his sons: This is the instruc-*
tion for the whole offering. The whole offering will remain on the altar-hearth[a] *all night*
until morning. The fire on the altar must be kept burning.[b] 3(10) *The priest is to put on*
his linen clothes,[a] *and he is to put*[b] *on linen breeches next to his body*[c] *in order that he*
may remove the fat ashes[d] *from the whole offering which the fire has consumed on*[e] *the*
altar and place them beside the altar. 4(11) *He is then to take off his clothes and put on*
other clothes in order that he may take the fat ashes outside the camp to a clean place.
5(12) *The fire on the altar must be kept burning; it must not go out. Every morning*[a] *the*
priest is to rebuild it with wood. Then he is to arrange the whole offering on it, and on

top of it he is to burn the fat[b] *of the offerings of well-being.* 6(13) *A continuous fire must be kept burning on the altar; it must not go out.*

7(14) *"This*[a] *is the instruction for the grain offering. The sons of Aaron are to present*[b] *it before Yahweh in front of the altar.* 8(15) *One of them*[a] *is to take a handful of*[b] *fine flour of the grain offering and its oil and all*[c] *the incense on the grain offering and burn it on the altar*[d] *as a soothing aroma, a memorial*[c] *to Yahweh.* 9(16) *Aaron and his sons are to eat*[a] *the rest of it. Being unleavened bread,*[b] *it is to be eaten in a holy place; they are to eat it in the court of the Tent of Meeting.*[c] 10(17) *It may not be baked with yeast.*[a] *I have allotted it*[b] *as their share of the gifts presented to me.*[c] *It is most holy, like the purification offering and the reparation offering.* 11(18) *Any male descendant among Aaron's sons*[a] *may eat it. It is a perpetual decree*[b] *for your generations for Yahweh's gifts. Anyone who touches these must be holy."*

12(19) *Yahweh spoke to Moses:* 13(20) *"This is the offering which Aaron and his sons are to present to Yahweh on the day when he*[a] *is anointed: a tenth of an ephah of fine flour as the regular grain offering,*[b] *half of it in the morning and half in the evening.*[c] 14(21) *It is to be prepared*[a] *with oil*[b] *on a griddle. You are to bring*[c] *it well-mixed,*[d] *and you are to present*[e] *pieces of a folded*[f] *grain offering as a soothing aroma to Yahweh.* 15(22) *The anointed priest who is his successor*[a] *will continue to prepare it. It is a perpetual decree to Yahweh.*[b] *All of it is to be burned.* 16(23) *Every grain offering from a priest is a total sacrifice; it may not be eaten."*

17(24) *Yahweh spoke to Moses:* 18(25) *"Say to Aaron and his sons: This is the instruction for the purification offering: The purification offering is to be slaughtered*[a] *in the place where*[b] *the whole offering is slaughtered;*[c] *it is most holy.* 19(26) *The priest who officiates*[a] *is to eat it. It must be eaten in a holy place, in the court of the Tent of Meeting.* 20(27) *Anyone who touches any of the meat must be holy. Whenever any of its blood is splattered on a garment, you must wash*[a] *that on which it has been spattered in a holy place.* 21(28) *Any clay pot in which it is cooked is to be broken, but if it is cooked in a bronze vessel, that vessel is to be scoured*[a] *and rinsed with water.*[b] 22(29) *Any male among the priests may eat it; it is most holy.*[a] 23(30) *But any purification offering which had some of its blood brought*[a] *into the Tent of Meeting to make expiation in the Holy Place must not be eaten. It must be burned with fire.*

7:1 *"This is the instruction for a reparation offering.*[a] *It is most holy.* 2 *The reparation offering is to be slaughtered*[ab] *in the place where*[c] *the whole offering is slaughtered,*[a] *and he is to dash*[d] *its blood against all sides*[e] *of the altar.* 3 *All its fat is to be offered: the fat tail,*[a] *the fat that covers the entrails,*[b] 4 *the two kidneys and the fat around them by the loins; and the long lobe of the liver he is to remove with the kidneys.* 5 *The priest is to burn them on the altar as a gift to Yahweh. It is a reparation offering.* 6 *Any male among the priests may eat it. It must be eaten in a holy place; it is most holy.*

7 *"The reparation offering is like the purification offering.*[a] *There is one standard for both of them; it belongs to the priest who makes expiation with it.* 8 *The priest who presents a whole offering for any person*[a] *receives the hide of the whole offering which he has presented*[b] *to him.*[c] 9 *Every grain offering which is baked in an oven and any that is prepared*[a] *either in a pan or on a griddle*[b] *belongs to the priest who presents it; it is his.*[c] 10 *Every grain offering, whether mixed with oil or dry, belongs equally*[a] *to all the sons of Aaron.*

11 *"This*[a] *is the instruction for an offering of well-being which is presented*[b] *to Yahweh.* 12 *If he presents it for a praise offering, then along with*[a] *the praise offering he is to present unleavened loaves mixed with oil, unleavened wafers spread with oil, and fine flour*

well-mixed,[b] i.e., loaves mixed with oil.[c] 13 In addition[a] to his praise offering as an offer-
ing of well-being, he is to present an offering with loaves of leavened bread. 14 One from
each offering he is to present as a contribution to Yahweh. It belongs to the priest who
dashes the blood of the offering of well-being. 15 The meat of his offering of well-being for
praise[a] is to be eaten on the day of his offering; none of it may be left[b] until the morning.
16 "If his sacrifice[a] is a votive offering or a freewill offering, it may be eaten on the day
he presents[b] his sacrifice; also whatever is leftover on the next day may be eaten.[c]
17 Whatever meat of the sacrifice is left until the third day is to be burned with fire. 18 If any
of the meat of his offering of well-being is indeed[a] eaten on the third day, the person who
has presented it will not be accepted. It will not be accounted to his credit; it has become
defiled meat. Whoever eats of it must bear the responsibility of his iniquity. 19 Meat which
touches anything unclean may not be eaten; it is to be burned with fire. As for other
meat,[a] anyone who is clean may eat such meat. 20 But if any person eats meat from an
offering of well-being for Yahweh while he is unclean, that person will be cut off from his
people. 21 If any person touches anything unclean—whether human uncleanness or an
unclean animal or an unclean, putrid object[a]—and eats from the meat of an offering of
well-being for Yahweh, that person will be cut off from his people."
22 Yahweh spoke to Moses: 23 "Speak to the children of Israel: Do not eat any fat of
cattle, sheep, or goats.[a] 24 The fat of any animal that has died naturally or has been torn
by wild animals may be put to any use, but you must never eat[a] of it. 25 Because[a] anyone
who eats fat of an animal from which a gift has been presented[b] to Yahweh, that person
who eats it will be cut off from his people. 26 You may not eat any blood,[a] either of birds or
animals, in any of your settlements. 27 Any person who eats blood, that person will be cut
off from his people."
28 Yahweh spoke to Moses: 29 "Speak to the children of Israel:[a] Anyone who presents an
offering of well-being is to bring some of his offering of well-being as an offering[b] to
Yahweh. 30 His own hands[a] are to bring a gift for Yahweh. He is to bring[b] the fat[c] with [d]
the breast to lift up[e] the breast[f] as an elevated offering[e] before Yahweh. 31 The priest will
burn the fat on the altar; the breast becomes Aaron's and his sons'. 32 You are to give the
right thigh from your offerings of well-being as a contribution[a] to the priest.[b] 33 A portion
of the right thigh belongs to the Aaronite who presents the blood and the fat of the offering
of well-being. 34 The breast of the elevated offering and the thigh of the contribution I
have taken from the offerings of well-being[a] of the children of Israel and given them to
Aaron, the priest, and to his sons as a perpetual portion from the people of Israel."
35 This is the perquisite of Aaron and the perquisite of his sons from the gifts to Yahweh
from[a] the day when they are presented[b] to serve as priests to Yahweh. 36 This[a] is what
Yahweh commanded the children of Israel to give the priests from[b] the day of their
anointing.[c] It is a perpetual decree for your generations.
37 This is the instruction for the whole offering, the grain offering,[a] the purification
offering, the reparation offering, the ordination offering, and the offering of well-being,
38 which Yahweh commanded Moses at Mount Sinai on the day when he commanded the
children of Israel to present their offerings to Yahweh in the wilderness of Sinai.

Notes

2.a. For MT מוקדה, "altar-hearth," other Heb. mss have מקדה, "burning," Sam has המקדה, "that which is burning," and LXX [ἐπὶ] τῆς καύσεως αὐτῆς = מוקדה, "[on] its burning." Elliger (81) postulates that the preceding prep על, "on," is an error of dittography or an insertion that arose from a misreading of היקדה, "which is burning," as מוקדה, "hearth." This alternative has merit, for Syr and

Tg support reading a ptcp. RSV takes this word to mean "a place of burning," while AV understands it as "burning mass."

2.b. LXX* adds *οὐ σβεσθήσεται*,"it must not go out," as in vv 5, 6(12, 13).

3.a. MT מדו, "his garment," presents an example of difficult Heb. grammar if this noun is in construct with בד, "linen." Possibly בד is in apposition to מדו (GKC §§128d; 131d; *IBHS* §16.4e). Kimchi posits that the *waw* is the connecting vowel of the constr. An easy error in many periods is the interchange of ו and י; therefore, Sam, Syr, Tg and *Tg. Ps.-J.* witness to the preferred reading מדי, "garments of."

3.b. A few Heb. mss read יהיו, "they are to be," for ילבשׁ, "he is to put on"; cf. 16:4.

3.c. בשׂר, "flesh," means here "skin," i.e., "body."

3.d. Cf. 4:12.

3.e. LXX's reading *ἀπό* suggests מעל, "from on," instead of MT על, "on." Syr probably read אשׁר־על,"which is on." This relative clause in MT is very rough.

5.a. The repetition of the phrase בבקר, "in the morning," means each and every morning. A couple of Heb. mss and LXX omit the second בבקר, "in the morning." This may result from an error of haplography.

5.b. חלבים, "fat parts," refers to the offerings of well-being, for these choice innards are the portion of the animal that are burned on the altar in this sacrifice (cf. chap. 3 *Excursus*).

7.a. Some Heb. mss, LXX, and Vg do not read the *waw* copula.

7.b. For MT הקרב, "bring near," an inf abs, Sam reads הקריבו, "they are to bring near"; but LXX has *ἣν προσάξουσιν* = אשׁר יקריבו, "which they are to bring near"; this variant is followed by Tg, *Tg. Ps.-J.* and Vg. It seems best to read הקריב a hiph pf instead of MT inf abs, for a sentence composed with the inf abs is very unusual (cf. GKC §113gg). Joüon (§123v) takes it as an injunction. The sg forms of the verb in v 8 indicate that the sg form is preferable and may have been changed to the pl with the insertion of בני אהרן, "Aaron's sons"; cf. n. 1:7.b.

8.a. For MT ממנו, "from it (masc)," mss from Cairo Geniza, Sam, and Tg^{mss} read ממנה, "from it (fem)," for the antecedent is מנחה, "the grain offering," a fem noun.

8.b. The prep ב is taken to mean "as consisting of" (GKC §119i; cf. Joüon §146e).

8.c. LXX omits כל, "all."

8.d. Instead of המזבח, "the altar," Sam reads המזבחה, "on the altar," as in 1:9. This latter variant is preferable. Also some Heb. mss, Sam, and LXX add אשׁה, "a gift," as in 2:2; the shorter reading is preferable.

8.e. אזכרתה, "its memorial," stands in apposition to ריח ניחח, "a soothing aroma." The term אזכרתה is particularly used with a grain offering, while ריח ניחח stands with various offerings (cf. 2:2, 9, 16).

9.a. Sam and LXX have a sg verb, possibly as witnesses to an earlier text that agreed with the sg verbs in v 8(15); cf. n. 7.b.

9.b. The acc מצות, "unleavened," occurs with the pass verb תאכל, "it must be eaten," to describe more precisely the nature of the sacrifice (GKC §118q). Standing first in this sentence, מצות receives some emphasis.

9.c. The pattern of v 9b is a:b:c::c:b. The reduplication underscores this decree. Also the fullness of the verse hints that the last clause has been added.

10.a. Cf. n. 9.b.

10.b. Instead of אתה, "it," LXX has *αὐτοῖς*, "to them," stressing that the priests receive the grain offering, again identifying the priests as Aaronites.

10.c. For MT אשׁי,"my gifts," i.e., "the gifts presented to me," an objective gen, a few Heb. mss, Sam, LXX, and Vg read אשׁי יהוה, "the gifts of Yahweh"; this variant reads the same as in v 11(18), thereby indicating that MT is preferred as an unusual reading.

11.a. Instead of בבני אהרן, "among Aaron's sons," LXX reads *τῶν ἱερέων*, "of the priests." This variant has much to commend it, for it runs counter to the direction of identifying the priests as Aaron's sons.

11.b. חק means "statute, decree," and according to Levine (37), by extension it means "due," one's rightful share. H. Ringgren ("חָקַק *ḥāqaq*," *TDOT* 5:144) considers חק a technical term for various offerings being the priests' legal portion. There is much to commend this position, but given the fact that חק עולם, "perpetual decree," is used a few times in Leviticus (e.g., 3:17; 7:36; 17:7) to underscore the enduring quality of various laws, there does not seem to be a valid reason to depart from that translation here. This is supported by the fact that לדרתיכם, "for your generations," occurs with the phrase here as in many places in Leviticus.

13 a. The dir obj occurs with a virtual pass verb and functions as the subj of the verb (cf. Joüon §128b).

13.b. Sam and LXX read למנחה, "for a grain offering," rather than מנחה, "grain offering"; the MT is followed as the harder reading. מנחה appears to be in apposition to סלת, "fine flour."

13.c. Sam reads בין הערבים, "at twilight," for MT בערב, "in the evening."

14.a. Elliger suggests pointing the pass תֵּעָשֶׂה, "it is to be made," as an active תַּעֲשֶׂה, "you are to make it." This has merit, for Heb. tends to avoid the pass, but in these instructions it is frequent.

14.b. Hoffmann (1:233) interprets the inclusion of the phrase בשמן, "with oil," to mean that this grain offering is to be prepared with more oil than a regular grain offering.

14.c. LXX and Vg read a sg verb.

14.d. רבך means "mix." In Mishnaic Heb., רביכה means "a soft mass of flour mixed with hot water and oil" (Jastrow, 1442). So Hoffmann (1:233) renders מרבכת, "well saturated."

14.e. LXX reads *θυσίαν*, "a sacrifice," for MT תקריב, "you are to present."

14.f. MT תפיני is an anomaly. *BHS* suggests תפתנה, "you are to break it," from the root פתת. Others try to construct the MT as a variant spelling from the root אפה, "bake." Hoffmann (1:234) suggests that it may be a component of תופי + ניא = "partially baked." That is, this grain offering is to be baked only lightly. Van Leeuwen suggests that the roots פין/פנן have the basic meaning "be bent." In that light this word may mean bread that is folded.

15.a. תחתיו is lit. "in his stead."

15.b. LXX omits ליהוה, "to Yahweh." The phrase חק־עולם, "a perpetual decree," appears throughout the cultic corpus; sometimes it occurs with a prep phrase ל + a human group. Its use with Yahweh is strange and may have arisen from a textual error.

18.a. Instead of the pass, LXX reads a third person pl *σφάζουσιν*, "they are to slaughter."

18.b. The noun מקום in constr stands before the relative pronoun אשר, "where" (Joüon §129q); cf. 4:24.

18.c. As in n. 18.a., LXX reads *σφάξουσιν*, "they are to slaughter," a future third person pl.

19.a. It is interesting to observe that the term המחטא, translated here "the one who officiates," lit. "the one who removes the sin," is translated in the Tg by דמכפר בדמה, "the one who expiates with blood."

20.a. For MT תְּכַבֵּס, "you must wash" (Sam), LXX, Syr, *Tg. Ps.-J.*, and Vg read יְכֻבַּס, "it must be washed." Since the active is normally preferred over the pass in Heb., MT is followed, but PIR (169) slightly favors the variant, taking the position that MT may be assimilation to a parallel passage.

21.a. *IBHS* (§22.6b, n. 30) considers מֹרַק, "is to be scoured," to be a qal pass pf.

21.b. *IBHS* (§22.6b, n. 31) considers שֻׁטַּף, "is to be rinsed," a qal pass pf though it is pointed as a pual.

22.a. LXX adds *κυρίου*, "Yahweh's."

23.a. Sam reads יביא, "he brings," for MT יובא, "it is brought." The variant is a matter of transposition of the *matres lexionis*. Sam may have wished to avoid a pass.

7:1.a. For האשם, "the reparation offering," LXX reads *τοῦ κριοῦ τοῦ περὶ τῆς πλημμελείας*, "the ram which is for the offense" (cf. 5:16 LXX)

2.a. The third person pl is indefinite and functions as a virtual pass.

2.b. LXX adds, *ἔναντι κυρίου*, "before the Lord."

2.c. Cf. n. 6:18.b.

2.d. While it is possible that the third person sg is indefinite and functions as a pass, cf. n. 2.a., it is more likely that this sentence is taken from a ritual and that the antecedent of the pronoun is the priest.

2.e. LXX reads *ἐπὶ τὴν βάσιν τοῦ θυσιαστηρίου*, "at the base of the altar."

3.a. Cf. *Comment* on 3:9.

3.b. Sam and LXX have a fuller text as in 3:3, 9, 14; 4:8: ואת כל החלב אשר על־הקרב, "and all the fat which is on the innards."

7.a. The particle is used with two nouns to convey that one of them is being compared to the other; in this case the subj occurs second and the obj of comparison first (*IBHS* §38.6a).

8.a. The particle את here stands before an indefinite noun (GKC §117d; Joüon §125h), but Bertholet (20) takes the phrase עלת איש as a technical term for "a private whole offering." If this is correct, it explains the use of את.

8.b. Sam reads a pl verb יקריבו, "they will present."

8.c. LXX omits לכהן, "to the priest." Since the MT לכהן לו, "to the priest, to him," is redundant, LXX is followed. The term לכהן appears to be added to define the antecedent of the phrase לו, "to him." Syr, however, reads לכהן, omitting לו.

9.a. The verb stands after the construct כל, "all," to form a relative clause.

9.b. In Sam המחבת, "the griddle," is definite as in 6:14(21).

9.c. Syr omits לו, "his."
10.a. The idiom איש כאחיו, lit. "a man like his brother," stands for equality.
11.a. LXX, Syr, and Vg do not read the *waw* conj.
11.b. Sam and LXX have a pl verb. In Heb. the indefinite pl may be used as a pass. In this case the indefinite sg is used as a pass.
12.a. The prep על expresses "in addition to" (cf. BDB, "על II.4.b.," 755).
12.b. Cf. n. 6:14.d.
12.c. LXX omits חלות בלולת בשמן, "loaves mixed with oil." This phrase is a gloss to explain סלת מרבכת, "fine flour well-mixed," since the term מרבכת is not widely used.
13.a. Cf. n. 7:12.a.
15.a. LXX adds αὐτῷ ἔσται, "(which) is his."
15.b. LXX reads a pl verb, which is preferable. It functions as a virtual pass.
16.a. זבח means "sacrifice" in general and an offering of well-being in particular (cf. *Excursus* on an offering of well-being [chap. 3]).
16.b. The inf constr stands after a noun in constr to form a clause with its pronominal suffix functioning as the subj of the clause.
16.c. LXX omits והנותר ממנו יאכל, "also whatever is leftover may be eaten." PIR (169) judges LXX to have resulted from an accidental omission.
18.a. The inf abs before the verb stresses the definiteness of the action; it may imply that whoever ate any of the meat on the third day did so defiantly.
19.a. Sam omits the *waw* on והבשׂר, "and the meat." LXX, Syr, and Vg seem to omit the word also; but the translators may simply have chosen not to translate it. Levine (44) interprets this to be an example of anacoluthon: a sentence begins in one direction and jumps to another idea.
21.a. For MT שׁקץ, "detestable, putrid thing," Sam, Syr, and Tg^{mss} read שׁרץ, "swarming thing," as in 5:2; 22:5. MT is followed as the harder reading. Since this list has only one of the three terms found in 5:22, בהמה טמאה, "unclean animal," there is no need to make the lists agree. PIR (170), however, leans toward the variant, judging MT to be a scribal error.
23.a. In MT this compound dir obj comes first for emphasis.
24.a. The inf abs standing before the verb underscores the action of eating.
25.a. LXX omits כי, "because."
25.b. Some Heb. mss, Sam^{mss}, and Tg read a pl verb. This is another example where Heb. uses an indefinite verb to function as a virtual pass.
26.a. Cf. n. 7:23.a.
29.a. Sam and LXX place the indir obj first for emphasis: אל בני ישראל תדבר, "to the children of Israel you are to speak."
29.b. The Heb. is קרבן, "offering, oblation," as in 1:2.
30.a. The grammatical subj ידיו, "his hands," uncharacteristically stands before the verb for emphasis.
30.b. The pronominal suffix on the verb repeats the dir obj, which precedes the verb for emphasis.
30.c. "Fat," חלב, stands for the fat net, the kidneys, and the liver, which are burned on the altar (cf. 4:8–9; 7:3–4).
30.d. Cf. n. 7:12.a.
30.e. In this context the terms להניף and תנופה are critical. The traditional rendering has been "wave" and "wave-offering," respectively. But J. Milgrom (*IEJ* 22 [1972] 33–38) has demonstrated that the meaning of הניף is "to elevate," not "to wave." In Lev 8:25–26 (cf. Exod 29:22–23), ten items are to be placed on the hands of Aaron and his sons so that they may present them as a תנופה. It is inconceivable that they could wave such a large mass before Yahweh. Nevertheless, it would be possible for them to raise these items in an act of dedication. Support for this interpretation comes from practices in other ancient Near Eastern cults. A relief from Karnak shows a person kneeling before a god as he lifts up a tray containing a sample of various foods—meat, bread, fruits, and vegetables (Milgrom, *IEJ* 22 [1972] 35–37 and "Hattěnûpâ," 157–58). By this act they dedicate these gifts to God. The gifts are removed from common use and transferred to God's realm. As far as תנופה is concerned, Milgrom ("Hattěnûpâ," 156) finds that this ritual act is required under two circumstances: (1) the gifts for presentation are still in the laity's control when they are brought to the altar, and (2) there is something distinct about presenting a portion of a sacrifice so that it requires a special additional act of sanctification. In this ritual the portions of the offering of well-being to be given to God are raised as a תנופה to dedicate them and remove them from profane use. Other proposals for תנופה may be mentioned. G. R. Driver ("Three Technical Terms in the Pentateuch," *JSS* 1 [1956] 100–105) assigns

to תנופה the meaning "additional payment," claiming that it is a cognate of Akk *nūptu.* G. Anderson (*Sacrifices and Offerings in Ancient Israel,* 134–35) favors this connection with Akk, for the verb *nāpu* is often used with *nūptu,* suggesting a parallel to תנופה/הניף. In an article in support of the meaning "wave offering," D. Hillers ("Ugaritic *šnpt* 'Wave-offering,'" *BASOR* 198 [1970] 142; *BASOR* 200 [1970] 18) argues that תנופה is cognate of Ugar *šnp,* "to wave." Anderson (135) finds many difficulties with this supposed cognate relationship.

30.f. Many Heb. mss, Syr, *Tg. Ps.-J.,* and Vg read a *waw* on the particle את. And instead of החזה, "the breast," LXX reads τὸν λοβὸν τοῦ ἥπατος, which may represent יתרת הכבד, "the lobe of the liver."

32.a. The right thigh of an offering of well-being is classified as a תרומה. In v 34, the unusual phrase שוק התרומה occurs. Traditionally תרומה has been translated "a heave offering," an offering presented with the ritual action of raising and lowering. This action is viewed as the counter ritual of the so-called "wave offering" (תנופה; cf. 7:30); the rite for that offering was understood to be back and forth movement of the offering. The first difficulty is that the תרומה is never done before Yahweh; thus it has no connection with the sanctuary (Milgrom, *SCTT,* 160). The second difficulty is that the verb behind this noun is הרים, "remove, set aside." In cultic texts הרים means "remove from (מן), donate" (22:15; Num 15:19–21; 18:19; Milgrom, *SCTT,* 160–61). From this analysis Milgrom assigns to תרומה the meaning "dedication" of things to Yahweh or "gift, present" (*SCTT,* 161–62). In the case of the right thigh, it is given directly to the priest; that is, it not being brought into the sanctuary and done with a special rite. Thus תרומה is not a ritual act. It is done outside the sanctuary. As for those parts that undergo a תנופה, "a raised offering," תרומה precedes the action of תנופה. Anderson (*Sacrifices and Offerings in Ancient Israel,* 137–44) provides an extended appendix on this term. While the data are perplexing, he favors the possibility that תרומה comes from an Old Amorite root *r-y-m,* "to give" (cf. W. von Soden, "Mirjam—Maria '(Gottes—) Geschenk,'" *UF* 2 [1970] 269–72). Anderson (134) likewise finds no basis for Driver's relating תרומה to a supposed Akk verb *tarāmu,* "to levy" (*JSS* 1 [1956] 100–105).

32.b. For MT לכהן, "to the priest," Syr reads ליהוה, "to Yahweh."

34.a. A few Heb. mss, LXX, and *Tg. Ps.-J.* have a second person pl pronominal suffix -יכם, "your," instead of the third person pl -יהם, "their," as in MT.

35.a. Here the prep ב has the force "from" as in Ugar.

35.b. The verb form after a prep is usually the inf constr (cf. GKC §114q-s). But here a pf stands after a noun in constr to form a relative sentence (cf. GKC §§130d; 155l). GKC §53l, however, explains הִקְרִיב as a variant spelling of the inf constr.

36.a. With καθά LXX seems to have read כאשר, "just as."

36.b. Cf. n. 7:35.a.

36.c. MT ביום משחו אתם is lit. "on the day when he anoints them."

37.a. Many Heb. mss, Sam, LXX, Syr, and Tg^{mss} read a *waw* on this word as with the rest of the nouns in the series. This variant is the preferred text.

Form/Structure/Setting

The structure for chaps. 6–7 is outlined as follows:

- I. Instructions presented in a series of speeches (6:1[8]–7:21)
  - A. First speech concerning the whole offering and the grain offering (6:1–11[8–18])
    - 1. Introductory formula (6:1[8])
    - 2. Speech proper (6:2–11[9–18])
      - a. Order to address Aaronites (6:2a*α*[9a*α*])
      - b. Instructions (6:2a*β*–11[9a*β*–11])
        - 1) Instruction concerning the whole offering (6:2–6[9–13])
        - 2) Instruction concerning the grain offering (6:7–11[14–18])
  - B. Second speech concerning the grain offering presented by the Aaronites (6:12–16[19–23])
    - 1. Introductory formula (6:12[19])
    - 2. Speech containing regulations (6:13–16[20–23])
  - C. Third speech concerning the purification offering, the reparation offering, and the offering of well-being (6:17[24]–7:21)

1. Introductory formula (6:17[24])
2. Speech proper (6:18[25]–7:21)
   a. Commission to speak (6:18aα[25aα])
   b. Three instructions (6:18aβ[25aβ]–7:21)
      1) Instruction concerning the purification offering (6:18–23[25–30])
      2) Instruction concerning the reparation offering (7:1–10)
         a) Regulation (7:1–7)
            (1) Introduction of instruction and declaratory formula of its being most holy (7:1)
            (2) Instruction concerning slaughter, blood, fat, and entrails (7:2–5)
            (3) Instruction on priests' right to eat from this meat (7:6–7)
         b) Insertion: identifying parts of various offerings that belong to the priests (7:8–10)
      3) Instruction concerning the offering of well-being (7:11–21)
         a) Introduction (7:11)
         b) Instructions proper (7:12–21)
            (1) Regulations regarding a praise offering and bread presented with it (7:12–15)
            (2) Regulations regarding eating meat from a votive or a freewill offering (7:16–18)
            (3) Laws on eating meat in connection with ritual impurity (7:19–21)

II. Appendix of two speeches (7:22–34)
   A. First speech concerning the eating of fat and blood (7:22–27)
      1. Introductory formula (7:22)
      2. Speech (7:23–27)
         a. Commission to speak (7:23a)
         b. Laws (7:23b–27)
            1) Prohibitions against eating fat, a command, and a law (7:23b–25)
            2) Prohibition against eating blood and law on eating blood (7:26–27)
   B. Second speech concerning the priests' portions of the offering of well-being (7:28–34)
      1. Introductory formula (7:28)
      2. Commission to speak (7:29a)
      3. Regulations (7:29b–34)
         a. Responsibility of laity to present the fat and the breast of an offering of well-being to Yahweh (7:29b–31a)
         b. Identification of the priestly portions of an offering of well-being (7:31b–34)

III. Summary statements (7:35–38)
   A. First summary statement concerning priestly portion (7:35–36)
   B. Second summary statement concerning authority of sacrificial regulations (7:37–38)

The material found in 6:1(8)–7:35 comes from a different corpus from that of the sacrificial regulations found in chaps. 1–5. It assumes the content of chaps. 1–5, for it complements the five regulations found there. It is initially marked off by the authoritative statement "Yahweh spoke to Moses" (6:1[8]) combined with the instruction to צו את אהרן ואת בניו, "command Aaron and his sons." Five sections are introduced by the formula "Yahweh spoke to Moses" (6:1[8], 12[19], 17[24]; 7:22, 28), and five sections are headed by the phrase זאת תורת, "this is the instruction of" (6:2[9], 7[14], 18[25]; 7:1, 11). The secondary commission-to-speak formula occurs four times: twice this commission is addressed to Aaron and his sons 6:2[9], 18[25]) and twice to the Israelites (7:23, 29). These varying formulae witness to the composite nature of this supplemental section and indicate that the material found in it was taken from different bodies of cultic instructions.

The primary interest of these additional instructions is the distribution of the parts of the animal not consumed on the altar, most of which are assigned to the priests. Also incorporated into the supplement is the ritual for cleaning the altar (6:3–4[10–11]), the standard for maintaining a continual fire on the altar (6:5–6[12–13]), and the handling of fat and blood (7:23–27). The primary orientation to the priests indicates that this material was taken from the corpus of priestly instructions (תורות). That this material is supplementary to chaps. 1–5 is confirmed by the pericope on the reparation offering (7:1–6), for it gives details about the sacrificial procedure for this offering, the very details missing from 5:14–26(6:7). The genre for this section then is instruction (of the laity by the priest). While Begrich ("Die priestliche Tora," BZAW 66 [1936] 63–66 = in *Gesammelte Studien zum Alten Testament* [Munich: Chr. Kaiser, 1964] 232–36) has shown that priestly instruction deals with clean and unclean, holy and profane, Koch (*Priesterschrift,* 61) claims that priestly instruction (תורה) also includes the description of cultic procedures.

This corpus begins with the whole offering (6:1–6[8–13]) as does the cultic legislation (chap. 1). The language indicates that there was a whole offering burning on the altar continually (Koch, *Priesterschrift,* 62). Because the altar is known as the altar of the whole offering, instructions about cleansing the altar and about the altar fire are included at this point. This instruction for removing the fat ashes from the altar is also concerned with the proper handling of the remains of the whole offerings.

Just as in the sacrificial corpus (chaps. 1–2), the instruction concerning the grain offering (6:7–11[14–18]) is treated after that for the whole offering. The center of interest here falls on the priests' eating from this offering. This instruction is mainly an explication of 2:3, 10.

The next section concerning the priests' grain offering (6:12–16[19–23]) appears to be a later insertion, for it interrupts the series of instructions. It is marked off by an introductory formula (6:12[19]). There is mention of a grain offering to be made by the priests on the day of the anointing of the high priest. The compiler places this material here to connect it with the general grain offering and to prepare for the anointing of Aaron, which will be recounted in chap. 8. Also the term תמיד, "continual," in v 13(20) connects this material with the mention of the continual fire on the altar (אש תמיד) in v 6(13).

With a new heading to the speech, the series of instructions continues (6:17[24]). This heading is required because of the above insertion, but Koch (*Priesterschrift,* 63) thinks that it is included because chap. 4, which treats this same subject, is set off from chaps. 1–3 by an authoritative heading. This instruction focuses on who has the right to eat from a purification offering and on laws about handling its flesh and blood.

In this supplement only the regulation concerning the reparation offering speaks about the sacrificial procedure regarding an animal (7:1–7). It is included simply because no regulation is given in the earlier treatment of this offering in

5:14–26(6:7). It might not have been included earlier because the editor of that portion assumed that the regulation for a reparation offering was very similar to that for an individual's purification offering. As time passed, the ritual for the reparation offering took on its own character. Therefore, the editor of this appendix wished to include that ritual in order to avoid any improper variations in the presentation of a reparation offering. Koch (*Priesterschrift*, 60–67), however, thinks that this ritual was composed for this context. But given the nature of the material in this cultic legislation, the editor most likely took it from the cultic instructions for the priests. He also included laws pertaining to priests' right to eat this sacrifice (7:6) and to the officiating priest's right to the meat (7:7). It is not necessary to take v 6 as a gloss as does Koch (*Priesterschrift*, 64), because the whole verse addresses the primary concern of chaps. 6–7 and the declaratory formula קדשׁ קדשׁים הוא, "it is most holy," forms an inclusion with 7:1.

The material in 7:8–10 appears to be clearly out of context, for the subject returns to identifying those parts of a whole offering and of a grain offering that belong to the priests. It then must be classified as a secondary piece that has been misplaced sometime in the history of transmission of the text.

The treatment of the offering of well-being comes last (7:11–21), for this sacrifice possesses a lesser degree of holiness than do the other sacrifices and in the sacrificial procedure this offering usually is offered last. Moreover, this sacrifice serves primarily as a meal for the clan of its presenter. Here it is classified into three kinds: a praise offering (תודה), a votive offering (נדר), and a freewill offering (נדבה). This material concerns the various standards for eating the meat of these different kinds of offerings of well-being in order that the offering may not lose its spiritual merit for the one who presents it. That is why the distinctions about this offering appear here rather than in the basic regulation found in chap. 3.

The instruction for the offering of well-being attracted two appendices, each one presented in its own speech. The first speech contains two prohibitions against eating fat or blood, a command concerning fat of carcasses, and two laws with the cut-off penalty (7:22–27). Rendtorff (*Gesetze*, 31) thinks that this material is taken from a priestly instruction (תורה) because of the second person plural form. These prohibitions are placed here because the laity only had access to meat from this type of sacrifice. The second speech concerns the priestly portions of an offering of well-being (7:28–34). The fact that these instructions appear in an appendix suggests that they address a change in sacrificial procedure. In an early era all of the meat of an offering of well-being may have belonged to its presenter, but with the establishment of the official cult, some of this offering became assigned to the priests.

These additional regulations conclude with a double summary statement (7:35–38), which belongs primarily to 6:1(8)–7:34, for the order of sacrifices in the summary corresponds to the list in chaps. 6–7, not chaps. 1–5. Nevertheless, in the setting of the book the second summary statement concludes the entire sacrificial corpus (chaps. 1–7; cf. Elliger, 91–93). The mention of the ordination sacrifice in the list points forward to the coming section about the anointing of Aaron and his sons (chaps. 8–10).

In its present form this supplemental corpus contains instructions for the laity regarding additional details about the various sacrifices, particularly about those portions of them that are assigned to the priests. The laity need to understand what portions of their sacrifices rightly belong to the priests in order to prevent any suspicion on their part that the priests are misappropriating any parts of the sacrifices. Teaching on these subjects also establishes a bond between the laity and the priests as the laity come to understand how the priests assist them in approaching God and how God shares portions of their sacrifices with the priests.

That the entire section is recorded for the laity is further attested by the fact that the material in 7:22–34 is specifically addressed to the Israelites (vv 23a, 29a). Furthermore, the instruction about the offering of well-being (7:11–21) assumes that the subject of the series of sentences is a layperson, indicating that this material was also composed as instruction for the laity. The compiler of this supplementary material thus felt no tension in joining these later pericopes to the instructions taken from the priestly corpus since he intended the entire corpus as instructions for the laity. That there is no major break at 6:1(8) indicates that chaps. 1–5 are intended to serve as the literary setting for this supplement; this is another witness to the view that this supplementary material in this setting is intended for the hearing of the laity. Moreover, if this material were primarily for the priests, it would be found wanting, being too abbreviated and too sketchy. While Elliger (93) posits that a redactor composed this material for this setting, its condensed, cultic legal style indicates that the majority of the material was taken from the corpus of priestly instruction. It may be concluded that an editor has sought to preserve particular instructions and regulations regarding the various sacrifices lacking in chaps. 1–5 and that he drew upon a wide variety of priestly professional knowledge.

Comment

2(9) This instruction requires the priests to make sure that the altar fire never goes out. The fire is on מוקדה, "the hearth." While no reason is given for this standard, a continual fire was desired in order that a soothing aroma might ascend to Yahweh without interruption. This regulation seems to presuppose an evening whole offering (cf. Exod 29:38–42; Num 28:2–8; and the *Excursus* on whole offering in chap. 1).

3–4(10–11) A priest is periodically to remove from the altar דשן, "the fat ashes," a mixture of wood ashes and fat produced by the burning sacrifices. Because his work starts at the altar, the priest must be properly clothed (cf. Exod 20:26). The word for breeches (מכנסים) means lit. "gather together"; the issue is that the legs of the pants were tightly drawn so that there would be no possibility of any exposure of the priest's genitals, lit. בשׂר, "flesh," to the altar. This standard contrasts with some of the ancient Near Eastern cultic practices in which the priest performed certain cultic ceremonies in the nude. The purpose of this standard is to eliminate the possibility of any use of human sexual powers as a way of approaching God or as a means of influencing the divine realm magically. The priest puts the ashes removed from the altar beside it. The Talmud (*b. Yoma* 22a) requires that the priest lay aside a small amount of ashes for the next day to insure continuity in the sacrifices. Then the priest takes off his special garments and puts on other garments of less sanctity in order to take the ashes outside the camp to a place that is ritually clean (cf. 4:12). This change of clothes is necessary so that he does not defile his official garments.

5–6(12–13) The fire on the altar is never to go out. תמיד means regularly or continuing something without interruption. The daily whole offering became known as the *tamid* (cf. מנחת תמיד, "the continual grain offering," in Num 4:16; Neh 10:34[33]). This word is also used for personal acts of devotion. One is to wait or hope continually on God (Hos 12:7[6]), to praise him continually (Pss 34:2[1]; 71:6), and to keep his law continually (Ps 119:44; cf. *TWOT* 1:493).

Each morning the priest is to arrange a new supply of wood on the altar and then stir up the fire. Snaith (44–45) comments that wood was brought into the Temple nine times a year. Five of the occasions were in the month of Ab (around August), for that was the best time of year to cut wood. The wood was sorted to eliminate any rot and worms; then it was stored in a room on the south side of the Temple Mound. There was a Feast of Wood-offering on the fifteenth of Ab.

The first sacrifice to be offered each morning is a whole offering. Afterwards other sacrifices are to be offered, especially offerings of well-being.

7(14) On the grain offering cf. chap. 2. The regulation here concerns the daily or *tamid* (תמיד) grain offering.

9-10(16-17) Since the grain offering is given to Yahweh, it is classified as קדש קדשים, "most holy" (2:3). That which is not burned on the altar becomes the priests', and they are to eat it in מקום קדש, "a holy place," i.e., a place set aside in חצר אהל־מועד, "the court of the Tent of Meeting." In the Second Temple this area was called the Court of the Priests (Snaith, 45). Because this grain is most holy, it may never be prepared with yeast. The grain offering carries the highest holiness, not the lesser holiness of the breast and thigh, which the priest receives from an offering of well-being (Hoffmann, 1:229). The word קדש, "holy," is used in its basic meaning of that which is separated to God; it carries no ethical overtones here.

11(18) The grain offering is available to any of the sons of Aaron, i.e., the priests who officiate at the altar. This statement means that the portion of a grain offering does not become the exclusive property of the priest who has offered that particular grain offering. Since the grain offering is dedicated for the altar, it is holy. Whoever (כל אשר) touches that which is holy must be holy. Many English translations render this line as the RSV does: "Whoever touches them shall become holy." Levine (37), however, correctly points out that whatever is unclean is contagious, but that which is holy is not. An object is made holy by being consecrated; therefore, Levine offers a more correct rendering of this line. The right of the priests to these offerings is an enduring right throughout the generations.

13–14(20–21) On the day of his anointing, the high priest is to present a grain offering consisting of a tenth of an ephah, approximately four pints, of סלת, "fine flour," on behalf of himself and his fellow priests. Half (מחצית) is to be presented in the morning and half in the evening. A problem arises because it is stated here that Aaron is to present this offering on the day of his anointing, which would take place but once, yet it is described as a continual (תמיד) offering. Many delete one term or the other depending on whether they read the passage as a specific regulation for a single day or as a general regulation. Tradition recounts that the high priest presented a daily grain offering (Sir 45:14; *m. Menaḥ.* 4.5; 6.2; Jos., *Ant* 4.10.7; Levine, 38). Tradition also understands this passage to mean that on the day of his anointing, the high priest presents two grain offerings, the daily grain offering and a special one for that high day (*b. Menaḥ.*

78a). Levine (39) notes that Ibn Ezra attempted to solve the problem by interpreting the preposition ב on ביום, (lit.) "in the day of," as "from," i.e., "from the day when he is anointed." Similarly Porter (50–51) suggests that this wording means "as soon as he is anointed," i.e., from the time he is installed in office. Another problem is that the grain offering presented at the ordination of Aaron (8:26–28) differs significantly from this prescription. Nevertheless, the decree in v 15(22) requires the successors of Aaron to present this prescribed grain offering. The best solution comes from Levine (39); he proposes that this passage and 8:26–28 come from two different traditions. The tradition here became the basis for the high priest's daily presentation of a grain offering, while the account in 8:26–28 gives the prescription for the grain offering to be presented at the ordination of the high priest.

15–16(22–23) Each successor to Aaron is to present such a grain offering. Furthermore, any grain offering presented by a priest must be כליל הקטיר, "entirely burned," for a priest may not profit from his own offerings. כליל concerns that which is whole or complete; e.g., in Isa 2:18 it stands for God's total destruction of idols. In sacrificial usage it means the total consumption of a sacrifice, and it is usually used with or in place of the term עלה, "whole offering." The description here indicates that the grain offering was a daily offering in its own right, but later it may have become part of the daily whole offering.

17–23(24–30) On the purification offering, cf. 4:1–5:13.

19(26) The officiating priest is described in an unusual way as המחטא, "he who offers the purification offering." The meat from the purification offering that is not burned belongs first to the priest who officiated at the altar. Because it is קדש קדשים, "most holy" (v 18[25]), he must eat it in מקום קדש, "a holy place" (cf. v 9[16]). In light of v 22(29) this verse is not saying that only the officiating priest may eat from a purification offering. Perhaps it is saying that the officiating priest needs to eat a portion of each purification offering he has offered up on the altar. The reason that the priest eats this offering is not stated. For various explanations on their eating from it, see *Comment* on 10:16–20. A simple, but possible explanation is put forth by Kidner (*Sacrifice*, 21). He postulates that when the priest, God's representative, eats from this offering, he symbolizes God's acceptance of the offering.

20–21(27–28) Whoever or whatever touches (נגע) the meat of חטאת, "a purification offering," יקדש, "must be holy" (cf. *Comment* on v 11[18]). נגע means to contact so as to leave an impression (cf. Hoffmann, 1:240). Any garment on which any of the blood from the purification offering is splattered (הזה) must be washed (כבס) in a holy place. Any vessel used for cooking the meat must be specially treated since it has been in contact with an offering. If the vessel is made of clay (חרשׂ), it is to be broken (שׁבר). But if the vessel is made of bronze (נחשת), it may be cleansed by a rigorous process that involves boiling (בשל), scouring (מרק), and then rinsing (שׁטף) in a steady stream of water. No reason is given in the OT for treating these vessels differently. Possibly it was thought that portions from a sacred offering penetrated more deeply into a clay vessel and could not be washed away whereas it did not remain in a bronze vessel so that vessel could be cleansed by washing. Any leftovers of an offering could not be eaten (7:15–17; Levine, 40).

23(30) Any purification offering from which blood is brought into the Tent of Meeting in order to make expiation—as was the case in a purification offering for a high priest or for the community (4:3–21)—may not be eaten. Whatever is left over must be consumed by fire (באשׁ תשׂרף).

7:1–7 On the reparation offering, cf. 5:14–26(6:7). This instruction supports the position that there was a reparation offering distinct from the purification offering. Also this description of the ritual is virtually identical to that of the ritual for a purification offering. The major difference is in handling the blood. With this offering as with a whole offering, it is זרק, "dashed," against all sides of the altar, while the blood of a purification offering is either הזה, "sprinkled," against the curtain of the holy place or נתן, "smeared," on the horns of the altar of incense or the main altar; cf. chap. 4.

7:6 As in the ritual of the purification offering, the majority of the meat of this offering, which is not burned on the altar, is קדשׁ קדשׁים, "most holy." Therefore, it becomes the priests'; they must eat it in מקום קדושׁ, "a holy place" (cf. 6:9, 19[16, 26]).

7:7–10 This section specifies who among the priests receive the holiest portions of each sacrifice. The officiating priest at each sacrifice has first rights to these portions. Here it is stated that the hide from a whole offering, the only part not consumed by fire, belongs to the officiating priest. Baked grain offerings belong to the officiating priest (2:4–8), while other grain offerings, dry and mixed with oil (2:1–3, 14–16), go to all the priests. These portions are to be distributed equally among the Aaronites. Hoffmann (1:247) takes this phraseology to mean those priests on duty for those sacrifices. The usual explanation for this distinction is that the baked offerings were very limited (Keil and Delitzsch, 323). But Hoffmann (1:245–47) cautions against such a neat distinction among grain offerings. He takes v 9 as detailing what should be done with the cooked grain offerings. In any case, the officiating priest had first claim to the appropriate parts of the sacrifices he presented, and the other priests also received some of the food. The matter of distribution was a problem. So in time the priests were divided into orders, with divisions alternating weekly and the families in a division serving for a day (cf. 1 Chr 24; Luke 1:8–9; *b. Taʿan.* 27a).

7:11–20 In this section there are three types of offerings of well-being: a praise offering (תודה), a votive offering (נדר), and a freewill offering (נדבה; cf. 22:21; Num 15:3; Deut 12:17). A praise offering is made to glorify God and to express one's love and appreciation for God's presence in the offerer's life. A votive offering is made in response to promises made at the taking of a vow. The faithful worshiper is also expressing his enthusiastic joy to God for fulfilling his vow. A freewill offering is offered spontaneously, joyfully, in order that a family or clan may celebrate a feast before God. For more on זבח שׁלמים, "the offering of well-being," see chap. 3.

7:12–13 With a praise offering, the standard is to present a grain offering of wafers or loaves. Three types of bread or wafers are described: חלות מצות בלולת בשׁמן, "unleavened bread mixed with oil," רקיקי מצות משׁחים בשׁמן, "unleavened wafers prepared with oil," and סלת מרבכת חלת בלולת בשׁמן, "bread of fine flour well-mixed with oil." In addition, the offerer is also to bring loaves of bread made with leaven (חלת לחם חמץ). The Mishnah (*m. Menah.* 7.1) prescribed that the offerer present the same amount of flour for the leavened bread as for the unleavened bread.

7:14 The priest is to take one of these cakes or loaves and offer it as תרומה, "a present or gift." Cf. vv 28–36.

7:15–18 The lay person who brings the offering of well-being receives the majority of the meat for a meal with his family or clan. If his offering is a praise offering, the meat has to be completely eaten the day on which the offering is made. But if the offering is a votive or a freewill offering, the meat may be eaten on the first or second day, but not the third. Any meat remaining beyond the set time becomes classified as פגול, "potently unclean, detestable, defiled" (cf. Ezek 4:14; Isa 65:4). Literally this word may refer to meat that has turned soft and is spoiling. It is rancid. If anybody eats such meat, the person who offered the sacrifice loses the benefits of his sacrifice. And the person who has eaten this meat has to bear the responsibility of his iniquity (עונו תשׂא; cf. 5:1). This formula is used for an offense that is both legal and sacred (W. Zimmerli, *Ezekiel 1*, tr. R. Clements, Hermeneia [Philadelphia: Fortress, 1979] 305). The exact penalty is not specified. Ordinarily with this formula the punishment comes from God, not the community (Zimmerli, 305). At the minimum a person who committed such a breach would become unclean and need to pursue the rite of cleansing.

7:19–21 Any person who wishes to eat from an offering of well-being must make sure that he is ritually clean before eating. Whoever eats meat while ritually unclean commits a serious breach against the cultic laws; thus the penalty is very severe. He is to be cut off from his people (נכרתה הנפש ההוא מעמיה). The precise nature of the punishment prescribed by this language is no longer known. Good (*The Sheep of His Pasture: A Study of the Hebrew Noun ʿAm(m) and Its Semitic Cognates*, HSM 29 [Chico, CA: Scholars Press, 1983] 85–90) holds that in priestly circles this phraseology means execution. The laws in Lev 20:2–5 suggest that it is the people's responsibility to carry out the penalty, but if someone commits a transgression that carries this penalty and the people fail to punish that person, Yahweh himself will carry out this penalty. Hutton (*Declaratory Formulae: Form of Authoritative Pronouncement in Ancient Israel* [diss., Claremont University, 1983] 138–42; cf. Zimmerli, 303–6) points out that execution is usually expressed by the term יומת, "be put to death." According to Num 19:13, one cut off becomes unclean; this description would be insignificant if the person had been put to death. Also there would be little concern over the purity status of one banished. R. Hutton gains a clue to the meaning of this technical phrase from Ps 37:22. In that passage "to be cut off" means to lose one's property or one's standing as a free citizen. Such a person loses his inheritance rights and the privilege of worshiping at the cultic center. The passive formulation indicates that the ultimate agent of the action is God (cf. 20:5, 6); this is confirmed by the many references in which God is the expressed subject of the verb כרת, "cut off" (e.g., Ezek 14:8, 13, 17, 19, 21, etc.). Thus this phraseology depicts one of the worst fates for a person who has been a member of the covenant community. Good also thinks that this language means that the guilty person will suffer misfortunes beyond death, though the text never specifies what those misfortunes are. This formula occurs frequently; e.g., Exod 12:15, 19; 30:33, 38; 31:14; Lev 17:4, 9, 14; 18:29; 19:8; 20:18; 23:29; Num 9:13; 15:30–31; 19:13, 20.

7:22–27 Included here are additional prohibitions against eating חלב, "fat," or דם, "blood" (cf. 3:16b–17). The penalty here is the same as that for eating meat in a state of ritual impurity; the person is cut off from his people (cf. vv 19–21).

7:28–36 An offering of well-being is presented for a family celebration. Therefore, the portions that are to be given to Yahweh and to the priests are underscored. In this pericope the portions of an offering of well-being that go to the priest are more specifically defined. The fat parts are אשׁי יהוה, "a gift to Yahweh"; they belong exclusively on the altar as described in chap. 3. This regulation adds that two portions, חזה, "the breast," and שׁוק הימין, "the right thigh," become the property of the priests. The breast is presented as תנופה, "an elevated offering" (cf. 7:14); therefore, it belongs to the priests in general (cf. Snaith, *ExpTim* 74 [1962/63] 127). The right thigh is תרומה, "a present," which then belongs to the priest who officiates at the sacrifice. It is given outside the sanctuary without a rite (Milgrom, *SCTT,* 162). Milgrom discerns three benefits in classifying the breast as "an elevated offering," belonging to all the priests, and the right thigh as "a present," belonging to the officiating priest: (1) it cut down on quarreling about food supply among the priests since all had access to the breast; (2) it discouraged the laity from waiting for a favorite priest to come on duty; and (3) the action of raising (להניף) the breast added pomp to the ritual for this offering (Milgrom, *SCTT,* 168). A תרומה, "contribution," is prescribed in a few texts: the thigh of the ordination offering (Exod 29:27), a bread offering (Num 15:19–20; cf. Lev 2:9; 6:8[15]), tithes (Num 18:24–28), holy gifts (Num 18:19), and booty from battle (Num 31:28, 52; cf. Dillmann, 496). No one is to dispute the portions that the priests receive, for Yahweh himself has established this regulation as חק־עולם, "a perpetual decree."

7:35 The phrase משׁחת אהרן, "the perquisite of Aaron," is difficult, for the Heb. term משׁחה usually means "anoint." The difficulty is compounded by the use of משׁח in 7:36 with the meaning anoint. Noordtzij (90–91) states that the Heb. term can mean both "anoint" and "portion"—"the portion of anointing." Another way of treating this word is to derive it from משׁח II, related to Akk *mišiḫtu,* "measurement" (KB), to mean "portion, share, perquisite, allotment." "Perquisite" is chosen as the English rendering since חק was translated "portion" in the preceding verse. As God's anointed servants, the priests have a right to the prescribed portions of the various offerings presented at the altar as a primary means of support. This income for their livelihood is guaranteed in order that they might give themselves fully and completely to the ministry at the Tent of Meeting.

37–38 Cf. *Form/Structure/Setting* at the beginning of chaps. 1–7. The inclusion of במדבר סיני, "in the wilderness of Sinai," after בהר סיני, "at Mount Sinai," is to stress that the Israelites began to present these sacrifices to Yahweh during their sojourn in Sinai (cf. Dillmann, 497).

Explanation

These instructions give special attention to the portions of the various sacrifices that become the priests'. These portions were most holy and could be eaten only in a holy place. Every priest who served at the altar was entitled to parts of the sacrifice he burned on the altar as his wage. This information was given to the laity so they might rejoice that the priests who served God on their behalf shared in their offerings.

The priests were worthy of these benefits for their faithful service at the altar. This idea is taken up by the NT to support the position that those who spent their time in proclaiming the gospel were worthy of support from their fellow believers (1 Cor 9:7–14; 1 Tim 5:18; Matt 10:10). He who gives his life to the ministry may accept the gifts of God's people gratefully and honorably.

Any of the meat belonging to the priests that was remaining had to be burned. The priests were not allowed to accumulate any portions. Rather they had to trust God to supply their daily food. They were to be sustained from the sacrifices, but they were not to become rich through these gifts. Their trust was always to be in God, not in the dues received from their priestly labors. This posture becomes a petition in the Lord's prayer: "Give us this day our daily bread" (Matt 6:11). In the same spirit the NT contains many exhortations to believers that they are not to absorb themselves in storing up material gain (Matt 6:19–21; Phil 4:19; Heb 13:5; 1 Tim 6:10). Rather they are to seek God first, and he will supply their daily needs (Matt 6:33).

The priests were responsible to clean the altar periodically and to dispose of the fat ashes outside the camp. Also they were to keep a fire burning continually on the altar so that the people might be in continual fellowship with God. Similarly, from the day of their anointing the priests were to offer a morning and an evening grain offering. These requirements emphasize that the priests themselves had to maintain continual fellowship with God. So too under the new covenant, each believer, who is a priest himself, must maintain daily fellowship with God. This demand requires effort, including the daily preparation to approach God.

Another key theme of this appendix is that the holiness of the offerings had to be preserved in their handling and their disposal. While worship in the NT appears to be less formal and more spontaneous than in the OT, the NT is concerned that worship be carried out in light of the truth that our God is a holy God, a consuming fire (Heb 12:29). While Christian worship is to be dynamic, led by the Spirit of God, it is also to be done with careful preparation so that there is a dignity to the service in order that God may be honored (cf. Heb 12:28). Paul exhorts that there be order, not confusion, in public worship (1 Cor 14:26–40). The highest moment of Christian worship is the Eucharist. Paul, motivated by the same beliefs that undergird this portion of Leviticus, is very concerned that the bread be eaten and the cup drunk in a worthy manner, i.e., a manner that recognizes its high sanctity (1 Cor 11:27–34).

II. Ordination of the Priests and the First Sacrifices at the Tent of Meeting (8:1–10:20)

Bibliography

Childs, B. "The Theological Role of the Priesthood." In *Old Testament Theology in a Canonical Context.* Philadelphia: Fortress, 1986. 145–54. **Cody, A.** *A History of Old Testament Priesthood.* AnBib 35. Rome: Pontifical Institute, 1969. **Cross, F. M.** "The Tabernacle: A Study from an Archaeological and Historical Approach." *BA* 10 (1947) 56–68. ———. "The Priestly Tabernacle." In *The Biblical Archaeologist Reader 1.* Ed. D. Freedman and G. Wright. Garden City, NY: Anchor Books, Doubleday, 1961. 201–28. ———. *Canaanite Myth and Hebrew Epic.* Cambridge: Harvard, 1973. 195–215. ———. "The Priestly Tabernacle in the Light of Recent Research." In *Temples and High Places in Biblical Times.* Jerusalem: The Nelson Glueck School of Biblical Archaeology of Hebrew Union College-Jewish Institute of Religion, 1981. 169–80. **Ferguson, E.** "Laying on of Hands: Its Significance in Ordination." *JTS* 26 (1975) 1–12. **Görg, M.** *Das Zelt Begegnung: Untersuchungen zur Gestaltder sakralen zelttraditionen Altisraels.* BBB 27. Bonn: Hanstein Verlag, 1967. **Greenberg, M.** "A New Approach to the History of the Israelite Priesthood." *JAOS* 70 (1950) 41–47. **Gunneweg, A. H. J.** *Leviten und Priester: Hauptlinien der Traditionsbildung und Geschichte des israelitisch-jüdischen Kultpersonals.* FRLANT 89. Göttingen: Vandenhoeck & Ruprecht, 1965. **Haran, M.** "The Priestly Image of the Tabernacle." *HUCA* 36 (1965) 191–226. **Kiuchi, N.** *The Purification Offering in the Priestly Literature.* JSOTSup 56. Sheffield: JSOT Press, 1987. 39–52, 67–85. **Möhlenbrink, K.** "Die levitischen Überlieferungen des Alten Testaments." *ZAW* 52 (1934) 184–231. **Rabe, V. W.** "The Identity of the Priestly Tabernacle." *JNES* 25 (1966) 132–34. **Robinson, R. B.** "The Levites in the Pre-Monarchic Period." *StBib* 7 (1978) 3–24. **Utzschneider, H.** *Das Heiligtum und das Gesetz: Studien zur Bedeutung der sinaitischen Heiligtumsltexts (Ex 25–40; Lev 8–9).* OBO 77. Freiburg: Universitätsverlag; Göttingen: Vandenhoeck & Ruprecht, 1988.

Form/Structure/Setting

This section continues the narrative form found woven through Exod 25–40. Chap. 8 recounts the fulfillment of the instructions Moses had received from Yahweh at Mount Sinai for the ordination of Aaron and his sons as priests (Exod 29), and chap. 9 relates the account of the glorious ceremony for the first public sacrifices on the new altar, inaugurating the sacrifices regulated in chaps. 1–7. That chap. 8 does not stand before Exod 40 has troubled many interpreters. Koch (*Priesterschrift,* 69) astutely responds to this issue by noting that it would not have been appropriate for Moses to begin the sacrificial process for the ordination of the priests before he had received the regulations for the various sacrifices. Chap. 10 reports two incidents: the death of Nadab and Abihu, Aaron's two eldest sons, for offering up illicit fire (10:1–7) and the confrontation between Moses and Aaron over Aaron's failure to eat the meat of the sacrifice that belonged to him after this tragic event (10:16–20).

A common thread running through these chapters is the phrase "[he did] as Yahweh commanded" (8:4, 5, 9, 13, 17, 21, 29, 34, 36; 9:6, 7, 10, 21; 10:7, 13, 15).

This recurring phrase makes conspicuous the strict obedience of Aaron and the people to Yahweh's instructions. The motif of obedience stands in high relief against the background of the people's idolatrous worship of the golden calf led by Aaron (Exod 32–33). It also contrasts with the motif of the people's murmurings recorded in Exod 15:22–17:16. In this setting the motif of obedience communicates to the coming generations who will hear these words that the congregation, whenever it so desires, can follow God's regulations and decrees. This motif also endorses the Aaronites as the only authentic priests.

There are many indications that chaps. 8–10 stand apart from chaps. 1–7. The liturgical vocabulary of chaps. 8 and 9 varies from that found in chaps. 1–7: נגש, "bring near" (8:14), for הקריב, "present, bring near" (e.g., 1:2–3); the use of the general term שפך, "pour out," (8:15; 9:9), instead of the liturgical term יצק, "pour out," as in 4:7; and the absence of the phrases לפני יהוה, "before Yahweh," except with the elevated offering (8:26, 27, 29), and אהל מועד, "the Tent of Meeting," in the sacrificial descriptions. Furthermore, there are variations in ritual procedure. In chaps. 8 and 9, the burning of the whole offering takes place in two stages (8:18–25; 9:12–14), whereas in the basic regulation it is done in a single step (1:9). The חטאת, "purification offering," presented on the first day of public sacrifices is a general purification offering, not the one presented for a specific sin committed by the high priest, as described in 4:3–12. That there is a significant difference between these two kinds of purification offerings is evident in the way the blood is handled. In the general ritual, blood is put on the horns of the main altar (v 15), not taken into the Holy Place to be sprinkled on the curtain and then put on the horns of the altar of incense as with a purification offering for a specific sin (4:6, 7). Moreover, in the list of the parts of the bull to be burned outside the camp, there is no mention of the bull's head (9:17) as there is in 4:11. The distinction between תנופה, "the elevated offering," and תרומה, "the contribution," has disappeared (9:21; 10:14–15; cf. 7:30–34). Furthermore, the description of the grain offering in 8:26–28 differs significantly from the regulation for grain offerings to be offered on the day of Aaron's anointing found in 6:13–14(20–21).

The agreement between chaps. 8 and 9 in such detail indicates that they come from the same source (cf. Koch, *Priesterschrift*, 69). Noth, however, evaluates these two chapters differently. In his judgment chap. 9 existed independent of its present context; for him the divergence in cultic terminology from chaps. 1–7 shows that this account does not presuppose these sacrificial regulations (75). He takes chap. 9 to be the continuation of the original priestly narrative found in Exod 39:32, 42, 43; 40:17 (76). As for chap. 8, he believes that it originally stood after Exod 39, and in his judgment it has gone through the same redactionary process as Exod 35–39 (68–69). Noth's position overlooks the number of similarities between chaps. 8 and 9. On the basis that chap. 9 is an account of the fulfillment of the instructions contained in chaps. 1–7 and that these two chapters come from the same hand, it is concluded that their author had this location in mind.

If this interpretation is accurate, how can one account for the divergences in chaps. 8 and 9 from chaps. 1–7? The author must have taken over older accounts of the ordination of the Aaronites and the inauguration of sacrifices at the central shrine. Respecting his ancient source, he did not level the liturgical language to conform to chaps. 1–7. Yet he assumed knowledge of the instructions found in those regulations, for he gives only brief descriptions of the various sacrifices.

The framework of chap. 10 is narrative and thus is in harmony with chaps. 8–9. This framework serves to highlight two cultic instructions: the procedure for burying priests who die in the sanctuary area (vv 3–7) and the proper handling of the portions of sacrifices that are to be eaten by the priests (vv 12–15). At the center of this chapter stands a prohibition attached to a description of the primary pedagogical duties of the priests (vv 8–11). The teaching role of the priests complements their liturgical role before the altar as inaugurated in chap. 9.

Chap. 10 underscores the perils of working at the sanctuary. It tones down the exaltation of the priests in the preceding two chapters by stressing the responsibilities that they bear. This chapter thus balances chap. 8, the ordination of Aaron and his sons, and it places chap. 9, the first public offerings at the Tent of Meeting, at the center of this unit. Without detracting from the honor belonging to the priests, the focal point falls not on the pomp and splendor of their ordination but on the inauguration of sacrificial worship at the divinely instituted sanctuary, the place for the people to find expiation and to commune with God. The priests are portrayed as honored servants of God who must obey his decrees and who bear the twofold responsibility of instructing the people and leading them in worship.

A. *Ordination of Aaron as High Priest and His Sons as Priests (8:1–36)*

Bibliography

See *Bibliography* for Lev 8:1–10:20.

Translation

1 *Yahweh spoke to Moses:* 2 *"Take Aaron and his sons, their vestments,*[a] *the oil for anointing, the bull for the reparation offering, the two rams, and the basket of unleavened bread.* 3 *Assemble all the congregation at the entrance to the Tent of Meeting."* 4 *Moses did just as Yahweh commanded him, and the congregation assembled*[a] *at the entrance to the Tent of Meeting.*

5 *Moses spoke to the congregation: "This is what Yahweh has commanded to be done."*
6 *Moses brought near Aaron and his sons and washed them with water.* 7 *He put on Aaron the tunic and bound it with a sash. He next clothed him with the robe and put the ephod on him. He fastened it with a woven band in order to secure the ephod tightly.*[a] 8 *Then he put the breastpiece on*[a] *him and put the Urim and Thummim in the breastpiece.* 9 *Next he set the turban on his head, and he put*[a] *on the front the golden plate,*[b] *the holy diadem, just as Yahweh had commanded Moses.*

10 *Then Moses took the anointing oil*[a] *and anointed the tabernacle and all that was in it and sanctified them.* 11 *He sprinkled some of it*[a] *on the altar seven times and anointed the altar,*[b] *all its vessels, the basin and its stand, to sanctify them.* 12 *He poured out some*[a] *of the anointing oil on Aaron's hand and anointed him to sanctify him.*

[13]*Moses then brought near Aaron's sons and clothed them with tunics, and he girded them with sashes*[a] *and put caps on them, just as Yahweh had commanded Moses.*

[14]*Moses*[a] *next brought near the bull for the purification offering. Aaron and his sons laid*[b] *their hands on its head.* [15]*He slaughtered the bull,*[a] *and Moses took the blood*[b] *and put it with his finger on the horns round*[c] *the altar to purify the altar. He poured out the rest of the blood at the base of the altar. So he sanctified it by performing the rite of atonement for it.* [16]*Moses*[a] *also took all the fat*[b] *which was on the innards and the lobe of the liver and the two kidneys and their fat, and he burned them on the altar.* [17]*But the bull with its hide and its flesh and its offal he burned with fire outside the camp just as Yahweh commanded Moses.*

[18]*Then Moses presented*[a] *the ram of the whole offering. Aaron and his sons laid their hands*[b] *on the head of the ram.* [19]*Moses slaughtered*[a] *it and dashed the blood against the altar all around.* [20]*The ram he cut*[a] *into pieces, and Moses burned the head, the pieces, and the suet.*[b] [21]*He washed*[a] *the entrails and the legs with water, and Moses burned the whole ram on the altar. It was a whole offering, a soothing aroma; it was a gift to Yahweh just as Yahweh had commanded Moses.*

[22]*Moses*[a] *then presented the second ram, the ram of ordination. Aaron and his sons laid*[b] *their hands on the ram's head.* [23]*He slaughtered it, and Moses took some of its blood and put it on the lobe of Aaron's right ear and on the thumb of his right hand and on the big toe of his right foot.* [24]*Then one*[a] *brought near Aaron's sons, and Moses put some of the blood on the lobes of their right ears and on the thumbs of their right hands and on the big toes of their right feet. Then Moses dashed the blood against the altar all around.* [25]*Next he took the fat, the fat tail,*[a] *all the fat which was on the entrails, the lobe of the liver, the two kidneys with their fat,*[b] *and the right thigh.* [26]*From the basket of unleavened bread*[a] *which was before Yahweh he took a loaf of unleavened bread, a loaf made with oil, and one wafer, and he put these on the fat portions*[b] *and the right thigh.*[c] [27]*He put all in the hands of Aaron and his sons and raised them before Yahweh as an elevated offering.* [28]*Then Moses took them from their hands and burned*[a] *them on the altar on top of the whole offering. They were ordination offerings; as a soothing aroma it was a gift to Yahweh.* [29]*Moses took the breast and raised it as an elevated offering before Yahweh; it was Moses' portion from the ram of the ordination just as Yahweh had commanded Moses.*

[30]*Moses then took some of the anointing oil and some of the blood from the altar and sprinkled Aaron and*[a] *his vestments and his sons and their vestments. So he sanctified Aaron, his vestments,*[b] *his sons, and their vestments.*[c]

[31]*Moses spoke to Aaron and his sons: "Boil the meat at the entrance*[a] *to the Tent of Meeting*[b] *and eat it there with the bread which is in the basket of ordination just as I commanded*[c] *saying, 'Aaron and his sons are to eat it.'* [32]*You are to burn the remainder of the meat and the bread with fire.* [33]*Do not go out from the entrance to the Tent of Meeting seven days until the days of your ordination are fulfilled, for your ordination*[a] *will last seven days.* [34]*What has been done*[a] *on this day Yahweh commanded in order to make expiation for you.* [35]*You are to stay at the entrance*[a] *of the Tent of Meeting day and night for seven days. You are to do what Yahweh requires, lest you die,*[b] *because thus I have been commanded."*[c] [36]*So Aaron and his sons did all the things which Yahweh had commanded by Moses.*

Notes

2.a. The article on בגדים specifies the garments which had been described to Moses in Exod 28.

4.a. Instead of MT niph, LXX reads *καὶ ἐξεκκλησίασεν* = וַיַּקְהֵל, "and he assembled," to agree with the form in v 3. MT is preferred as the harder reading.

7.a. MT יאפד is a denominative of אפד, "ephod, robe," to mean "secure, fasten on (an ephod) tightly."

8.a. For MT אל, "to," Sam, LXX, and Syr read על, "on."

9.a. Sam reads ויתן, "and he put," for MT וישם, "and he set." Sam has some weight since its wording differs from the opening וישם.

9.b. ציץ, which is related to the root נצץ, "shine, sparkle," means "plate, bloom, flower." In this context it is taken to mean "a plate of gold," a crown made for the forehead (U. Cassuto, *A Commentary on the Book of Exodus,* tr. I. Abrahams [Jerusalem: Magnes, 1967] 383–84). It is also possible that it was cast into the shape of a flower. On this cf. KB; H.-J. Kraus, "hôj als profetische Leachenklage über das eigine Volk," *ZAW* 85 (1973) 32, n. 67; Elliger, 112.

10.a. LXX reads *ἀπὸ τοῦ ἐλαίου* = משמן, "from the oil," for MT את־שמן. LXX is in accord with vv 12 and 30, while MT agrees with v 2. LXX appears to arise from a scribal error caused by the influence of the alternative expression.

11.a. The phrase ממנו, "from it," means "some of it."

11.b. LXX adds *καὶ ἡγίασεν αὐτό* = ויקדשהו, "and he sanctified it." In v 15 this phrase occurs after the noun המזבח, "the altar"; perhaps LXX was influenced by the wording there.

12.a. This is the partitive use of מן to mean "some"; cf. n. 11.a.

13.a. Sam, LXX, Syr, and Tg read the pl form as demanded by the context, but the sg stands in Exod 29:9.

14.a. LXX adds *Μωυσῆς*, "Moses," here and in vv 16, 18, 19, 22, 24, and 28. This addition makes the subj clear.

14.b. The verb is sg although the subj is compound because often the verb agrees with the first person of a compound subj (GKC §146f). The prominence of Aaron in this account may explain the use of the sg here.

15.a. This Eng trans. supplies an obj for וישחט, "and he slaughtered." Dillmann (507) interprets וישחט as a shortened way of referring to this step in the ritual that is described in the prescriptive account (cf. Exod 29:11).

15.b. Instead of את, LXX may have had a Heb. text with מן, "from, some of," as in v 23; but cf. n. 10.a.

15.c. סביב is an adverbial acc; it means that the priest goes around the altar to put blood on each of the altar's four horns.

16.a. Cf. n. 14.a.

16.b. Sam reads חלביהן, "their fat," a pl form. Sometimes the connecting vowel with the suffix הן is omitted after a consonant, but it is better to point MT חֶלְבְּהֶן (Joüon §94b; cf. GKC §91c).

18.a. Sam reads ויגש, "and he brought near" (as in v 14), instead of MT ויקרב, "and he presented." Since ויקרב is the usual form in these rituals, a scribe could have unthinkingly substituted it for the more unusual ויגש; therefore, Sam is accepted as the harder reading.

18.b. Sam and LXX read the sg ויסמך, "and he laid on," instead of the pl ויסמכו as in vv 14, 22. The variant is preferred, for it is easier to account for the pl arising from the sg rather than the other way.

19.a. Cf. n. 14.a. Syr seems to have read וישחטהו משה, "and Moses slaughtered it." The antecedent is not obvious. Since Moses is defined as the subj of the next verb as in v 15, it may be that Aaron and his sons are the subjs of this verb. This assumption agrees with 1:11–13, where the offerer is instructed to perform the slaughter, the cutting, and the washing, but according to Exod 29:17 Moses was to do these rites on this day.

20.a. Cf. n. 19.a.

20.b. Cf. n. 1:8.b.

21.a. Cf. n. 19.a.

22.a. Cf. n. 14.a. and Exod 29:19.

22.b. Cf. n. 18.b.

24.a. Cf. n. 14.a. The identity of the subj is left in question in MT; it was most likely Moses.

25.a. Cf. *Comment* on 3:9.

25.b. Cf. n. 16.b.

26.a. Instead of MT המצות, "the unleavened *bread*," LXX reads *τῆς τελειώσεως* = המלאים, "the ordination."

26.b. The pl חלבים, "fat pieces," refers to all the parts of fat enumerated in vv 25–26. Hoffmann (1:281) notes that the pl may denote the "best" pieces.

26.c. שוק הימין, "the right thigh," is mentioned specifically because it was part of the priests' income (Hoffmann, 1:281).

28.a. Cf. n. 14.a.

30.a. Heb.[mss], LXX, Syr, and *Tg. Ps.-J.* read ועל, "and on," for MT על, "on" (cf. Exod 29:21); the *waw* could have easily been omitted by a scribal error, but PIR (170–71) believes that the variant was made in order that this passage would conform to the instructions found in Exod 29:21.

30.b. Heb.[mss], Sam, LXX, Syr, and *Tg. Ps.-J.* read ואת; cf. n. 30.a.

30.c. LXX[B*A] omits ויקדש, "and he sanctified," in error.

31.a. LXX reads ἐν τῇ αὐλῇ, which may stand for בחצר, "in the court," instead of MT פתח, "entrance."

31.b. LXX adds ἐν τόπῳ ἁγίῳ = מקום קדש, "in a holy place"; cf. Exod 29:31.

31.c. LXX, Syr, and Tg read a pual pass to agree with v 35, also 10:13 (so Dillmann, 510), but cf. 10:18. MT is preferred as the harder reading.

33.a. Heb.[mss], LXX, and Syr correctly put the term יד, "hand," in the pl.

34.a. The impersonal עשה, "he did," functions as a virtual pass.

35.a. Cf. n. 31.b.

35.b. The final clause is introduced by ולא, "and not" (GKC §109g).

35.c. LXX reads ἐνετείλατό μοι κύριος ὁ θεός, "the Lord God commanded me," instead of MT צויתי, "I have been commanded."

Form/Structure/Setting

This is a straightforward, detailed narrative of the ordination of Aaron as high priest. There is no plot or intrigue. The author's interest resides in recounting that the ordination of Aaron and his sons as priests took place exactly as God had commanded. The structure of the account is as follows:

I. Introduction and instructions (vv 1–4)
  A. Narrative and introductory formula (v 1)
  B. Speech—instructions on bringing all materials and assembling the congregation for the ordination ceremony (vv 2–3)
  C. Compliance report (v 4)
II. The order of the ceremony for ordination of the high priest and the Aaronite priests (vv 5–35)
  A. Moses reports the divine authority for his ordaining the priests (v 5)
  B. The ordination ceremony (vv 6–30)
    1. The washing of the candidates and the robing of the high priests (vv 6–9)
    2. The anointing of the tabernacle, the altar, and the laver (vv 10–11)
    3. The anointing of the high priest (v 12)
    4. The robing of the Aaronite priests (v 13)
    5. The offering of sacrifices (vv 14–29)
      a. A purification offering (vv 14–17)
      b. A whole offering (vv 18–21)
      c. The ordination offering (vv 22–24)
      d. An elevated offering (vv 25–29)
    6. The concluding ritual of ordination (v 30)
  C. Special instructions to priests (vv 31–35)
    1. Introductory formula (v 31a*α*)
    2. Instructions proper (vv 31a*β*–35)
      a. Regarding eating of the sacrifices (vv 31a*β*–32)
      b. Regarding a seven-day period of separation at the sanctuary (vv 33–35)
III. Compliance report (v 36)

Lev 8 recounts Moses' compliance with the instructions Yahweh had given him regarding the ordination of Aaron as high priest and his sons as priests (Exod

29). For the most part the wording of these two accounts is so similar that one passage is dependent on the other or both adhered closely to a common source.

There are, however, some divergences in wording: e.g., Lev 8 uses *waw* imperfects while Exod 29 has *waw* perfects; Lev 8 has ויגש, "bring near, approach," in contrast to the use of the liturgical הקריב, "present, bring near," in Exod 29; Lev 8:16 reads אשר על, "which is on," whereas Exod 29:13 has the more usual המכסה את, "which covers." Besides these divergences there are some major variations in the order of the ceremony. The account of Moses' anointing the tabernacle and its furnishings (vv 10–11) is not mentioned in Exod 29. The instruction for that action is recorded in Exod 30:22–29. The inclusion of this rite in the account without any adjustments creates an apparent difficulty in the order of service, for a literal reading of the passage indicates that Aaron's sons remain unclothed during these initial anointing rites (v 6), for they are not clothed ceremoniously until after the cultic furniture and Aaron have been anointed (vv 7–13). Another divergence regards the purification of the altar. In Lev 8 the altar is first חטא, "purified," by having blood from Aaron's purification offering (חטאת) put on its horns (v 15). But in Exod 29 the cleansing of the altar is mentioned at the end of the regulation in reference to the seven-day period of the priests' separation (v 36). In Leviticus it is assumed that offerings may be presented only on an altar that has been dedicated and purified, while in Exod 29 the process of making offerings dedicates and cleanses the altar (cf. Koch, *Priesterschrift,* 68). Another variation surfaces in the inversion of two rites. According to Lev 8 Moses sprinkles a mixture of blood and oil on Aaron and his sons after they have presented the elevated offering (v 30), but in Exod 29 this sprinkling is to take place before they present the elevated offering (v 21). The manner of burning the whole offering deviates from the standard regulation. Lev 8:19–21 reads as though there are two stages in the rite of burning the whole offering: the first burning includes the pieces of the animal along with the head and some fat (פדר, "suet"), and the second burning includes the entrails and legs, but in Exod 29:15–18 all the parts of the whole offering are burned in a single step as described in the regulation of the whole offering in Lev 1. Finally there is also a minor variation regarding the person who prepares the meat of the ordination ram. In Exod 29:31 Yahweh orders Moses to cook the meat of the ordination ram for Aaron and his sons to eat, but according to the account in Leviticus Moses instructs Aaron and his sons to cook the meat (v 31).

To account for these divergences, Noth (20) and Elliger (107, 113–15) posit different authors for these two chapters. The fact that Lev 8 conforms less in terms and procedure to Lev 1–7 than to Exod 29 leads them to place Lev 8 prior to Exod 29. If that is the case, the author of Exod 29 borrowed heavily from Lev 8. It seems better, however, to postulate that both accounts were dependent on an ancient Vorlage containing the ritual for ordaining the high priest. The respective authors then adapted their source to fit their respective contexts. The verbs of Exod 29 are perfect consecutive, for the description looks forward to an event, while Lev 8 uses *waw* imperfects to describe that event. Other variations arose during the transmission of the text from typical scribal errors and from the scribal tendency to conform these accounts to standard cultic language. In addition, Lev 8 probably underwent minor editorial changes that reflected the changing practice of ordination during the various eras.

Lev 8 experienced a different editorial history than Exod 29. Some linguistic variations between these passages support this conclusion. One variation is the use of נגשׁ, "bring" (vv 14, 18 [Sam]; elsewhere only 2:8), instead of the technical cultic term הקריב, "present" (Exod 29:10). Incidentally, in this verse Exod 29 adds לפני אהל מועד, "before the Tent of Meeting," a phrase found in the sacrificial regulations (e.g., Lev 3:8, 13). In place of the simple וישׁחט, "and he slaughtered" (cf. Lev 8:15a), Exod 29:11 reads ושׁחטת את הפר לפני יהוה פתח אהל מועד, "and you are to slaughter the bull before Yahweh at the entrance to the Tent of Meeting." סביב, "all around," which appears in Lev 8:15, is missing in Exod 29:12. In Lev 8:16, 25 the lobe of the liver is described by יתרת הכבד rather than by the more precise phrase, היתרת על־הכבד found in Exod 29:13 (cf. Lev 3:4, 10, 15; 4:9; but יתרת הכבד in Exod 29:22).

Identification of the eras in which the high priest was anointed has become a critical issue in the interpretation of this passage. Wellhausen held that the high priest was only anointed in the era of the Second Temple. But there is no evidence that the rite of "anointing" in the pre-exilic community was limited only to the Davidic king. Certainly during the monarchy the anointing of the Davidic king grew in importance. And it is true that in the post-exilic community with the absence of any Davidic king the anointing of the high priest took on special importance, but these facts do not exclude the likelihood that the high priest was anointed in the earliest days of Israel's existence. Prior to the monarchy, Israel was a loosely bound group of tribes held together primarily by their worship of Yahweh at the central shrine. Thus the functioning of the cult was crucial to Israel's national identity. The leader at the cult center was the high priest. The installation of a high priest would have been a momentous occasion. Thus it is not unreasonable to assume that the high priest took office in a high ceremony in which he was anointed to show that God's favor and power were on him, enabling him for his teaching and intercessory role. A ceremony of anointing as described here certainly fits that social requirement.

Another issue is whether Aaron's sons were anointed. Some passages indicate that they were (Lev 10:7; Num 3:3), while others do not (Exod 29; Lev 4:2–12; cf. Koch, *Priesterschrift,* 69). A close reading of Lev 8, however, finds that while Aaron and his sons were both consecrated (קדשׁ) by being sprinkled with the oil and the blood (v 30; cf. v 24) and ordained (ימלא את־ידכם; v 33), only Aaron had the anointing oil poured over his head (v 12; however, cf. Exod 30:30). Thus it appears that strictly speaking Aaron's anointing was of a higher order than that of his sons. Therefore, the term "the anointed priest," as in Lev 4:2–12 specifically refers to the high priest (cf. 21:10).

This account eventually found its home in the Jerusalem Temple. It reached its greatest national influence in the Second Temple period, when the high priest replaced the king as leader of the covenant community.

Comment

2 Moses is to prepare for the ordination of Aaron and his sons by gathering everything necessary for the ceremony as he had been instructed (Exod 29:1–7). שׁמן המשׁחה, "the anointing oil," was a specially prepared compound (Exod 30:22–25). The ingredients included myrrh, cassia, cinnamon, cane, and olive oil. The contents of the basket (סל), an open basket woven from reeds, included three different kinds of bread: חלת מצה, "unleavened bread," חלת לחם שמן, "bread made with oil," and רקיק אחד, "a wafer" (cf. v 26; Exod 29:2–3). On this occasion Moses acts as high priest on behalf of Aaron and his sons, who are still laity.

3 The entire assembly is gathered together before the entrance to the Tent of Meeting. This description suggests that the elders of the various tribes assembled immediately before the Tent of Meeting and others gathered behind them. The ordination of Aaron and his sons was a major event in the history of Israelite faith. Given the open, participatory nature of Israel's cult, it was critical that the ordination be a public ceremony with all the tribes in attendance. Thereby the entire community acknowledged that God had chosen Aaron's house to serve them as priests.

4 It is stated that Moses did just as Yahweh had commanded. This affirmation occurs throughout this account of the priests' ordination (vv 5, 9, 13, 17, 21, 29, 34, 36; 9:6, 7, 10; 10:15). It stresses that obedience to Yahweh's instructions is essential for the ordination rite to be effective.

6 Moses הקריב, "presents," Aaron and his sons (Exod 29:4; 40:12). הקריב is the standard word for presenting an offering. Its use here indicates that Aaron and his sons are "presented" to Yahweh in order that they might be totally sanctified for service at the altar. Moses then washes (רחץ) them in order that they might be ritually clean for the ordination ceremony (Exod 29:4; 40:12). Ibn Ezra holds that he washed only their hands and feet (cf. Exod 30:19–20), while Rashi understands that he washed the entire body. On other occasions the priests washed only their hands and feet on entering the sanctuary to minister (Exod 30:19–21; 40:30–31), but for the ritual of the Day of Atonement the high priest had to bathe himself entirely. Since this is a high ceremony, the position that they were entirely washed is favored. Furthermore, the act of washing has its counterpart in washing parts of an animal presented for a sacrifice (1:9, 13; 8:21; 9:14; Exod 29:17). How and where the washing was done is not stated. Perhaps some type of a pool or a bath for immersion was set up in the courtyard of the tabernacle and screened off with a curtain.

7–8 After the washing, Moses clothes Aaron with the special priestly garments as he had been commanded in Exod 29:5–8. First he puts on him a tunic (כתנת), a loose, embroidered linen garment with short sleeves worn next to the body. He fastens it to his waist with a sash (אבנט). According to the Talmud the sash was an embroidered band, forty-eight feet long. Next Moses puts on him a robe (מעיל), a shirt-like garment woven in one piece that reached well below the knees. The hem of the robe was embroidered with pomegranates and golden bells. Then he puts on Aaron the ephod (אפד). אפד, which means literally "that which fits closely," refers in the OT to various types of garments. In the case of the high priest, it was a type of trousers with a bib. The ephod was made of gold, of rich violet, purple, and scarlet wool, and of fine linen (Exod 28:6). It was fastened with a band or a belt (בחשב האפד). Since there is no reference to sandals, Levine (50) thinks that the priests officiated barefoot (cf. Exod 3:5; Josh 5:15).

Next Moses puts on Aaron the breastpiece (חשן), worn across the chest and made out of the same material as the ephod (Exod 28:15). It was fastened to the ephod by rings on four corners and chains of gold. On the breastpiece were twelve stones set in rows of three, each engraved with a tribe's name. It also had pockets in which the sacred lots were placed. These lots are called האורים, "Urim," and התמים, "Thummim." The meaning of these Hebrew words is debated. One possibility is to derive אורים from the root ארר, "curse," so that the terms mean "curse" and "perfect." LXX and Vg, however, translate them "teaching and truth." But the best suggestion is "lights" and "perfection," respectively (*b. Yoma* 73b). The manner of handling them in order to receive an oracle is not described. The limited references to making inquiry through them indicate that the priest received a yes or no answer. Of course, a third alternative was not to receive any answer at all (1 Sam 28:6). Snaith (52) speculates that the surfaces of each lot had different colors, such as yellow and black. In that way they could be cast and yield three combinations: two yellow, two black, or one of each color.

Moses places a turban or tiara (מצנפת) on Aaron's head. This word indicates that the cloth was wound around the head several times. It is possible that the turban was wound around an inner cap and merely placed on the head. On the front of the turban was placed a golden plate (ציץ הזהב) bearing the inscription "holy to Yahweh." This was also known as "the sacred crown" or the holy diadem (נזר הקדש).

The high priest's wearing of these magnificent clothes contributed to the splendor and majesty of the worship of Yahweh at the Tent of Meeting. They also bore witness to his endowment with authority to minister on behalf of the people before the great and holy God. The symbolic importance of clothing throughout Scripture is attested in the metaphors that relate moral virtues to clothing; e.g., "let your priests be clothed with righteousness" (Ps 132:9) and the phrase "the garments of salvation" (Isa 61:10; cf. Job 29:14; Col 3:12; 1 Thess 5:8).

10–11 Moses next anoints המשכן, "the tabernacle," and all its furnishings with the special oil. He then sprinkles the anointing oil on the large altar (המזבח) seven times in addition to anointing all its utensils, the basin (הכיר), and its stand (כן). On the surface this ritual of anointing the cultic furniture appears out of place, for it is not mentioned in Exod 29 (cf. Exod 29:36). But it is prescribed in Exod 30:22–29 and 40:9–11 in conjunction with the anointing of Aaron and his sons (vv 12–15). There is no account, though, that Moses had already fulfilled the instruction to anoint this furniture. Therefore, he performed this rite at the beginning of the ordination ceremony. The anointing consecrated or sanctified (קדש) these objects. That which is sanctified is set apart to God and becomes holy. It is forever removed from secular use and is available for God's Spirit to use as a means of mediating God's grace to his people. In reference to the furniture, this act meant that the furniture was from now on fit to receive the offerings consecrated to God.

12 Next Moses יצק, "pours," some of the anointing oil on Aaron's head in order to sanctify him. It is debated whether Moses anointed Aaron's sons. Exod 29:7–9, Lev 6:13(20), and this passage do not mention their anointing, but it is referred to in Exod 28:41; 30:30; 40:15; Lev 7:36; 10:7; and Num 3:3 (Hoffmann, 1:276–77). Rashi explains the tension by saying that oil was poured on Aaron's head, while only the clothes of his sons were sprinkled with oil (v 30). In any case Aaron's anointing is elevated by being far more elaborate than that of his sons.

13 Moses brings Aaron's sons near to present (הקריב) them as priests (cf. v 6). He clothes them with coats or tunics (כתנת) bound by sashes (אבנט; cf. Exod 29:7–

9). Then he places caps (מגבעות) on their heads. These were skullcaps without a brim and made of fine linen (Exod 39:28). The priests' garments were much simpler than those of the high priest.

14–15 Moses brings near (הגיש) the bull of the purification offering (חטאת). Aaron and his sons lay their hands on its head (cf. 1:4). The sacrificial animal is a young bull, called here פר החטאת, "the bull of the purification offering." This is the same kind of animal prescribed as the offering for the anointed priest who has sinned inadvertently (4:3–12). Aaron slaughters the bull, possibly with help from his sons. Acting as the high priest, Moses takes some of the blood and smears it on the horns of the altar. This action purifies (חטא) the altar (מזבח) by removing any sin or uncleanness that has attached itself to the altar. חטא, which means "to sin" in the qal, means "to de-sin, purify" in the piel. This blood rite is not mentioned in 4:3–12; thus it must be a special rite for the ordination ceremony. It is further stated that this act of כפר, "making expiation," for the altar sanctifies (קדש) it. There are different views regarding what is atoned. One view (e.g., Noth, 70) thinks that any inadvertent sin committed by any of the priests to be ordained is expiated. But nothing in this regulation points in that direction (Kiuchi, *Purification Offering,* 42). It is more likely that this ritual removes any uncleanness that is present from either the altar or the priests before they are consecrated as holy (Kiuchi, 42–43), indicating that this purification offering has a slightly different function than the purification offerings prescribed in Lev 4:1–5:13. This rite, along with the fact that both the priests and the tabernacle and its furniture are anointed, underscores the close bond between the sanctuary and the priests. Both must be consecrated, anointed, and cleansed for the sacrificial system to function effectively.

17 Moses disposes of the remains of the bull outside the camp as with the greater reparation offering (4:11, 12, 21). The entire animal must be consumed. The priests may not eat from it since it is offered on their behalf. Moses may have taken these parts outside the camp himself since no other priests had yet been ordained.

18–21 Cf. Lev 1:10–13.

22 איל המלאים, "the ram of ordination," is sacrificed next. Aaron and his sons lay their hands on the ram's head, indicating that this is their sacrifice. The word for מלאים, "ordination," is a technical term. It is derived from the idiom מלא יד, "to fill the hand," and is formed into an abstract plural. Behind the word is the act of placing in the priest's hands portions from the sacrifices which he presents as תנופה, "an elevated offering" (cf. 7:28–34). The ritual of this sacrifice and the meal from portions of the ram indicate that this offering was presented according to the basic ritual for an offering of well-being (chap. 3).

23–24 Moses slaughters the ram and takes some of the blood and puts it on Aaron's right earlobe (תנוך אזן־אהרן הימנית), on his right thumb (בהן ידו הימנית), and on the big toe of his right foot (בהן רגלו הימנית). A similar action takes place in the ritual for the cleansing of the leper (14:14, 17, 25, 28). By covering Aaron's extremities with blood, Moses consecrates him totally to Yahweh. His ear is dedicated to receive Yahweh's instructions while his hands and feet are committed to carrying them out. The right side is chosen as the side of honor. Furthermore, Noth comments that "the application of the blood was intended to make a specially close connection between the priests and the altar against which the rest of the blood was thrown, and so with God" (72). Next Aaron's sons are brought near, and Moses puts some blood on the same extremities to consecrate them as priests. The rest of the blood is זרק, "dashed," ceremonially on all sides of the altar (cf. 1:5).

25–29 Moses takes the fat tail, the various fat parts, and the right thigh (שׁוק הימין) and adds to them three types of bread—חלת מצה, "unleavened bread," חלת לחם שׁמן, "bread mixed with oil," and רקיק, "a wafer"—the portions that are explicitly given to the priests for their service. He puts all of these elements in the hands of Aaron and his sons in order that they might raise them (הניף) as an elevated offering (תנופה). The connection between this ritual of "filling Aaron's hands" and the technical term for ordination, מלאים, lit. "the filling," is quite visible. By this rite of elevation Aaron and his sons offer to God those portions of the sacrifices that God has assigned to them (cf. 7:30–31). Then Moses takes these parts from their hands and burns (הקטיר) them on the altar on top of the whole offering (העלה). This rite diverges from an offering of well-being, in which the right thigh is considered to be תרומה, "a special gift," belonging to the officiating priest (7:32–34). In the ordination offering, however, it receives special sanctification by being elevated and then burned on the altar (cf. Milgrom, *SCTT,* 163). Since it is offered by the priests for their own ordination, they may not eat from it. This ordination offering is fully acceptable, for it is described as ריח ניחח אשׁה הוא ליהוה, "a soothing aroma, it is a gift to Yahweh" (cf. 1:9). Then Moses, as the officiating priest, presents the breast as an elevated offering (cf. 7:30–31, 34), and it becomes his portion. Wenham interprets the breast's going to Moses and the right thigh's being offered on the altar as symbolic of the fact that God and Moses were acting jointly as priest in the ordination of Aaron (142).

30 With a definitive act to conclude the ritual of ordination, Moses takes some of the anointing oil plus some of the blood and sprinkles it on Aaron, his garments, his sons, and their garments. This rite raises several questions. Why does this sprinkling come at the end of the ritual whereas the instructions in Exod 29:21 locate the sprinkling as part of the earlier rite with the blood? Noordtzij (100) suggests that the order in Exodus is logical, while that in Leviticus is historical. Another problem with this ritual is that this is the second sprinkling of Aaron with blood. But there is no requirement that there be only a single sprinkling of the high priest in the ordination ceremony. This second rite may have been a final, climactic gesture, emphasizing the bond between the priests who serve at the altar and God. Another question is whether the oil and blood were mixed together or sprinkled in succession. The latter view appears to be more likely given the separation of these two elements throughout the ritual description. Elliger (114–20) postulates that this was a pre-exilic practice that did not continue in the Second Temple period.

31–32 The priests are to cook the meat and eat it at the entrance to the Tent of Meeting. The meal, an occasion of fellowship between Yahweh and the newly ordained priests, seals the office of priesthood between Yahweh and Aaron's house. The meal is eaten at the entrance to the Tent of Meeting, for these newly ordained Aaronites have not begun to function as priests and yet they are no longer laymen who may eat the meat outside the sanctuary. Whatever is leftover of meat and bread must be burned with fire. Since this food is from an ordination offering, not a regular offering of well-being, it possesses a higher degree of holiness and may not be left until morning (cf. Noordtzij, 101–2).

33–35 To authenticate their ordination, the priests have to abide in the temple area for seven days. Ancients believed that a span of time was an essential part of a high ceremony that achieved a rite of passage. The greater the social change, the longer time span given to the ceremony; e.g., weddings took place over several days, and many days were given to mourning the dead. Here Aaron and his sons are undergoing a profound change of status, from laymen to priests. Thus they are to spend seven days before God at the Tent of Meeting. During this time they must be careful to observe all that Yahweh has commanded them. This is expressed by the injunction, "Do what Yahweh requires," שמרתם את־משמרת יהוה, lit. "Keep the charge of Yahweh" (cf. Ezek 44:8; 48:11; 1 Chr 23:32; Neh 12:45). This injunction is underlined with a death warning: ולא תמותו, "lest you die." This line fits the context of chaps. 8–10 well, for it sets the mind of the reader on the danger inherent in any violation of the holy.

Each day Aaron and his sons are to offer sacrifices. The kind and number of these sacrifices are not specified. Some have understood the text to mean that the sacrifices of the day of ordination were repeated daily. This seems unlikely, for the first day would be set off from the other days by more elaborate sacrifices. Another possibility is that each day they offered a bull as a purification offering (חטאת) along with the morning whole offering (עלה; Exod 29:35–42). These sacrifices daily cleansed the priests from the pollution of human sinfulness. This period of separation brought to completion the consecration of these men to the priestly task.

36 The concluding line affirms that Aaron and his sons were completely obedient to Yahweh's words. The ritual of their ordination was thus efficacious.

Explanation

In obedience to Yahweh's instructions, Moses ordained Aaron as high priest and his sons as priests before the community assembled in front of the Tent of Meeting. This occasion was a very high day in Israel's history.

At the beginning of the ceremony, Moses bathed Aaron and his sons completely in water. Washing was a vital rite in the OT cult. Nothing unclean was to be used or to function in the holy place. Furthermore, this ritual washing symbolized that these men set apart for the priesthood were morally pure.

Next Aaron was clothed in the magnificent garments of the high priest. Their majesty enhanced the splendor of the service at the Tent of Meeting. It corresponded to the awesome glory that attended the holy God's appearing in the cloud over the tabernacle. There was also a royal quality to these garments, indicating that the high priest ministered at the altar for a people who were God's kingdom on earth.

After anointing the tabernacle and all its furnishings, Moses poured some of the oil on Aaron's head. The oil symbolized that God would be graciously present with him, giving him the strength and the qualities of character to function effectively as high priest. Then Moses brought near and presented Aaron and his sons to Yahweh (vv 6, 13). The same verb (הקריב) is used for both this act (v 6) and the presenting of sacrificial animals (vv 18, 22). Thus Aaron and his sons were completely given over to Yahweh as were the sacrificial animals.

During the ceremony, blood from the ram slaughtered for an ordination offering was placed on the right extremities of Aaron's body: his earlobe, his thumb, and his big toe. The same rite was done to his sons. The placement of blood on the extremities of the side of honor sanctified their entire being for service at the altar. With their ears the priests hear God's word and then do it with their hands and feet. Later Moses sprinkled Aaron and his sons and their garments with a mixture of oil and blood from the altar as a further act of consecration. The use of blood in these rites symbolized the close bond between the priests and the altar, for their work at the altar secured expiation for the people's sins and prepared the way for them to commune with God.

Moses next removed the fat parts of the ram's entrails along with the right thigh, and he took from the basket samples of the various kinds of bread. He put all of these in the hands of Aaron and his sons as an elevated offering. This act of filling the priests' hands is captured in the Heb. term for ordination, מלאים־ידים, "fill one's hand." Since this was an ordination offering, made on behalf of the priests, it is Moses who burned all these portions on the altar. Then because he was acting as priest, Moses presented the breast as an elevated offering, which became his portion.

Having been consecrated, Aaron and his sons were instructed to boil designated portions of the meat at the entrance to the Tent of Meeting for a meal. They ate it along with bread from the basket. This act demonstrated Yahweh's acceptance of the new priests and the fact that they were in fellowship with him. Since this offering was part of the ordination, all leftovers had to be burned with fire.

To complete their ordination, Aaron and his sons remained at the entrance of the Tent of Meeting for seven days. Since their appointment as priests was a radical change in the tribal structure, time was an essential element to mark such a change, just as marriage ceremonies in ancient times lasted for days, allowing the community to integrate a new family unit into its structure. During this period the priests offered sacrifices for themselves daily in order to keep themselves pure and render praise to God.

The high priest of the Church is Jesus Christ. His high priestly role is portrayed most vividly in the Epistle to the Hebrews. His priesthood differs from Aaron's: it is done in the heavenly sanctuary (Heb 9:11–12), it is continuous (Heb 7:23–25; cf. 10:19–22), and it is of the order of Melchizedek (Heb 5; 7). As the ever-living high priest, Christ continually makes intercession before God for all who believe on him and always provides access to God for those who come to him. He is our advocate, pleading for our forgiveness and sanctification (cf. 1 John 2:1, 2).

As Christ is the great high priest of the kingdom of God, all who follow him become priests. Indeed the church is a kingdom of priests, a royal priesthood (1 Pet 2:9). To function effectively as priests, all believers must sanctify themselves by the work of the Spirit of Christ in their lives (Heb 9:14; 13:12; 1 Thess 5:23; 2 Tim 2:21; Titus 2:14). Then they can assist others in approaching God. Their role as priests takes many forms; e.g., rendering praise to God (1 Pet 2:9) and making intercessory prayer (cf. Eph 3:14–21), which includes pleading for the forgiveness of a person's sins (Jas 5:19, 20; 1 John 5:16) and praying for healing (Jas 5:14, 15). For their priestly service, Christ has given his church vast spiritual authority (Matt 16:19; 18:18–20). The primary function of the church is to serve a deeply troubled world as priests, mediators of God's grace and instructors of the way to God.

B. *The First Public Sacrifices at the Tent of Meeting (9:1–24)*

Bibliography

See *Bibliography* for Lev 8:1–10:20

Translation

1 *On the eighth day Moses summoned*[a] *Aaron, his sons and the elders of Israel.*[b] 2 *He said to Aaron, "Take a bull-calf for a purification offering and a ram for a whole offering, both without defect, and present them before Yahweh.* 3 *Then speak to the Israelites:*[a] *Take a male goat for a purification offering and a calf and a lamb, both yearlings without defect, for a whole offering,* 4 *and a bull and a ram for offerings of well-being*[a] *to be sacrificed before Yahweh with a grain offering mixed with oil, for today Yahweh will appear*[b] *to you."*

5 *They brought the things Moses had commanded to the front of the Tent of Meeting. All the congregation came near and stood before Yahweh.* 6 *Moses said, "This is what Yahweh has commanded you to do*[a] *in order that the glory of Yahweh may appear*[b] *to you."* 7 *Moses said to Aaron, "Approach the altar and perform the ritual*[a] *for your purification offering and your whole offering; make expiation for yourself and for your house.*[b] *Then perform the ritual*[a] *for the offerings*[c] *of the people, make expiation for them just as Yahweh has commanded."*

8 *Aaron approached the altar and slaughtered the calf as a purification offering for himself.*[a] 9 *Aaron's sons brought the blood to him. He dipped his finger in the blood and put some of it on the horns of the altar. Then he poured out the rest of the blood at the base of the altar.* 10 *On the altar he burned the fat, the kidneys, and the lobe of the liver from the purification offering,*[a] *just as Yahweh had commanded Moses.* 11 *Afterwards he burned the meat and the skin*[a] *with fire outside the camp.* 12 *Then he sacrificed the whole offering. Aaron's sons handed*[a] *to him the blood, and he dashed it against the altar all around.* 13 *They handed him the whole offering by its pieces and the head,*[a] *and he burned these*[b] *on the altar.* 14 *He washed the entrails and the legs and burned them*[a] *on top of the whole offering on the altar.*

15 *Then Aaron*[a] *presented the people's offerings.*[b] *He took the male goat, the purification offering for the people. He slaughtered it and offered it for a purification offering*[c] *as he did with the first offering.* 16 *He then presented the whole offering and performed the ritual according to the regulation.*[a] 17 *Next he presented the grain offering. He took a handful*[a] *of it and burned it on the altar in addition to the morning whole offering.* 18 *Then he slaughtered the bull and the ram, the people's offerings of well-being. Aaron's sons handed*[a] *him the blood, and he dashed it against the altar all around.* 19 *But the fat*

pieces from the bull and the ram—the fat tail, the layer of fat,[a] *the kidneys,*[b] *the lobe of the*
liver—[c] 20*they laid*[ab] *on the breasts; and he burned*[c] *the fat pieces on the altar.* 21*Aaron*
elevated the breasts[a] *and the right thigh*[b] *as an elevated offering before Yahweh just as*
Moses had commanded it.[c]
22*Then Aaron lifted up his hands toward*[a] *the people and blessed them. Having*
performed[b] *the rites for the purification offering, the whole offering, and the offering of*
well-being, he came down. 23*Moses and Aaron entered*[a] *the Tent of Meeting. When they*
came out, they blessed the people,[b] *and the glory of Yahweh appeared to all the people.*
24*Fire came out from before Yahweh and devoured the whole offering and the fat pieces*
on the altar. When all the people saw it,[a] *they shouted joyfully and bowed down on their*
faces.

Notes

1.a. This is the only occurrence of . . . ויהי in Leviticus (cf. Exod 40:17). The construction ויהי . . . קרא is similar to Exod 12:41, 51; 16:22, 27 (Baentsch, 347).

1.b. The presence of the term ולזקני ישׂראל, "and the elders of Israel," is suspicious, for Aaron is instructed to speak to the elders in v 3, an act that would be unnecessary if Moses had already addressed them. Also the priestly material prefers עדה, "congregation," with זקני, "elders." This phrase then is best considered a later insertion (cf. Bertholet, 27).

3.a. Instead of MT בני, "sons of," Sam and LXX read זקני, "elders of," to conform with v 1.

4.a. Here offerings of well-being are referred to solely by the term שׁלמים, "well-being," a more archaic way of specifying this kind of sacrifice (cf. *Excursus* in chap. 3).

4.b. LXX reads *ὀφθήσεται* = נראָה, niph pf, for MT נראֶה, a niph ptcp.

6.a. The verb is impf, for it is subordinate to the main verb, expressing the content of the command (GKC §120c). It is an asyndeton (GKC §107q).

6.b. The jussive is employed after a pf in order to express a wish (Joüon §116c; cf. GKC §120c).

7.a. The basic verb עשׂה, "do, make," here has the technical meaning "perform a ritual."

7.b. LXX reads *τοῦ οἴκου σου* = ביתך, "your house," instead of MT העם, "the people." LXX agrees with 16:6, 11. MT is very difficult, for it is unusual to expect the high priest's sacrifice to have benefits for the people. Also if MT is the correct text, it renders the second part of the verse superfluous. LXX is, therefore, followed. But PIR (172) takes the variant as simplification of a difficult text.

7.c. קרבן, "offering, oblation," is functioning as a collective since the people present four or five offerings.

8.a. LXX* does not read אשׁר לו, "which is his."

10.a. This long predicate comes first in the sentence for emphasis.

11.a. Cf. n. 10.a.

12.a. המציא, "cause to attain," here has the meaning "present, hand over" (Rashi, 36; cf. Zech 11:6). It may be functioning as a technical cultic term.

13.a. The head is specifically mentioned to make sure it did not become misplaced since it was separated from the animal before it was butchered. It is interesting that only the head is mentioned, for in 1:8 both the head and the fat (הפדר) are specified.

13.b. Eng requires a dir obj.

14.a. Cf. n. 13.b.

15.a. Aaron is supplied as subj for clarity in the Eng trans.

15.b. Cf. n. 7.c.

15.c. חִטֵּא, "de-sin," here means "offer a purification offering" (also 6:19[26]; 2 Chr 29:24). Koch ("חָטָא *chāṭāʾ*," *TDOT* 4:316) renders it "perform a ritual of purification."

16.a. משׁפט, "judgment, sentence, ordinance," here means the prescribed regulation; cf. 5:10.

17.a. Sam and LXX read the more infrequent כפיו, "his hands," for MT's כפו, "his hand."

18.a. Cf. n. 12.a.

19.a. Keil and Delitzsch (347) take המכסה, lit. "the covering," to include the entrails and the fat that surrounds them (3:3).

19.b. LXX has a fuller text with *καὶ τὸ στέαρ τὸ κατακαλύπτον ἐπὶ τῆς κοιλίας καὶ τοὺς δύο νεφροὺς καὶ τὸ στέαρ τὸ ἐπ᾽ αὐτῶν*, "the fat which covers the entrails, the two kidneys, and the fat which is on them," for it makes this passage conform to 4:9.

19.c. This entire verse is a *casus pendens* as predicate for the verb וישׂימו, "and they laid," found in v 20; this *casus pendens* is picked up in that verse by the dir obj את־החלבים, "the fat pieces."

20.a. Sam, LXX, and Syr read a sg verb, limiting this action to the high priest himself. Whether or not other priests could help the officiating priest arrange the sacrifice on the altar is an interesting question. MT is kept as the harder reading.

20.b. The dir obj "the fat pieces" is omitted from this translation, for it serves solely to pick up the long predicate placed before the verb; cf. n. 19.c.

20.c. LXX reads a pl verb, which is surprising in light of n. 20.a.

21.a. Since in v 20 the breasts were laid on the altar, it must be assumed that they were removed before the fat was burned. Baentsch (348) suggests that the breasts were laid on the altar to symbolize their being a sacrificial gift.

21.b. Cf. n. 10.a. The reference to the right thigh as part of תפונה, "the elevated offering," sets up a tension between this description and the regulation found in 7:30–34, in which the breast is to be presented as an elevated offering and the thigh as תרומה, "a contribution," given to the officiating priest. Another problem is that the term שׁוק, "thigh," is sg, yet two offerings of well-being have been presented (v 18). Milgrom ("The *šôq hattĕrûmâ*," *SCTT*, 164) resolves this conflict by judging the words שׁוק הימין, "the right thigh," to be an editorial insertion. The editor is assumed to be the same one who altered 10:15 (cf. n. 10:15.a.). If Milgrom is correct, the older account follows the regulations of 7:30–32.

21.c. Several Heb. mss, Sam, and LXX add יהוה את, "Yahweh (commanded Moses)"; cf. v 10 and 8:4, 13, 17, 21. MT simply reads צוה משׁה, "Moses had commanded." The Eng trans. must supply a dir obj as here or resort to putting the verb in the pass.

22.a. Sam, LXX, and Syr read על, "on," for MT אל, "to." This is a common variant.

22.b. The inf constr after the prep מן, "from," functions to make a clause (cf. GKC §119y, n. 3).

23.a. The sg verb ויבא, "and he entered," with the compound subj "Moses and Aaron" corresponds to the rule of Heb. grammar that a verb preceding a compound subj often agrees in gender and number with the nearest subj (GKC §146f). Also in this case it may suggest that Moses led Aaron into the Tent of Meeting.

23.b. LXX adds πάντα = כל, "all."

24.a. Sam and *Tg. Ps.-J.* read a pl verb. Since Eng "see" requires a dir obj, though ראה, "see," does not, one is supplied.

Form/Structure/Setting

The structure of chap. 9 is as follows:

I. Instructions to Aaron and congregation regarding offering the first public sacrifices (vv 1–5)
  A. Instructions given in commissioned speech (vv 1–4)
  B. Compliance report (v 5)
II. The promise of God's appearing (v 6)
III. The offering of the sacrifices (vv 7–21)
  A. Basic instructions to Aaron (v 7)
  B. The priest's personal offerings (vv 8–14)
    1. The purification offering (vv 8–11)
    2. The whole offering (vv 12–14)
  C. The people's offerings (vv 15–21)
    1. The purification offering (v 15)
    2. The whole offering (v 16)
    3. The grain offering (v 17)
    4. The offering of well-being (vv 18–21)
IV. The priestly blessing and the theophany (vv 22–24)
  A. The priestly blessing (v 22)
  B. Moses' and Aaron's entrance into the Tent of Meeting and their blessing the people again (v 23)
  C. The theophany (v 24)

After the newly ordained priests have spent seven days at the entrance to the Tent of Meeting, Aaron, assisted by his sons, offers up the first public sacrifices at the new sanctuary. He performs these rituals according to Moses' instructions. The directions for the day are backed up with the promise of God's appearing (v 4b). After detailing what the people are to bring, Moses repeats this promise (v 6). V 6 is the fulcrum point in this chapter, for it stands between Moses' preliminary instructions to Aaron (vv 1–5) and the account of presenting the sacrifices (vv 7–24). Furthermore, this account is lined with the recurring phrases "as Moses commanded" (vv 5, 21) and "as Yahweh commanded" (vv 7, 10) to communicate Aaron's careful obedience in carrying out the instructions he had received.

The body of the passage recounts the offering up of the sacrifices (vv 7–21). The lead sentence (v 7) sketches out the basic order of the service and underscores that the sacrifices are to make expiation. Aaron begins the ceremony by offering up sacrifices for himself (vv 8–14). It is noted that his sons assist him with the manipulation of the blood. Then Aaron sacrifices the offerings of the people (vv 15–21). Beside a purification offering (חטאת) and a whole offering (עלה) for cleansing from sin, the people present two offerings of well-being (זבח שלמים) to praise God.

Koch (*Priesterschrift,* 69–70) argues that chap. 9 is later than chaps. 1–5. His reasons include: (1) Moses addresses the people through Aaron (v 2) rather than directly (1:2; 4:2); (2) the priest performs all the ritual acts after the laying on of hands for the people's sacrifice (vv 15–18), while in chap. 1 the laity are involved in performing various rites of the sacrificial ritual; and (3) the purification offering is sacrificed first, while in the order found in chaps. 1–5 it is the third type of animal sacrifice. But these arguments may be countered. The uniqueness of this inaugural event may account for points 1 and 2. Further, in regard to point 2 the regulation in chap. 1 prescribes the procedure for a whole offering presented by an individual, not by the entire congregation as is the case here. Point 3 may be resolved by noting that the order of sacrifices in chaps. 1–5 corresponds to the pedagogical design of the material, while the order in chap. 9 is based on the liturgical order. The similar order of sacrifices for the Day of Atonement (16:11, 16) supports this view. Thus the disparity between chap. 9 and chaps. 1–5 is minimal. In fact, the abbreviated description of the rituals assumes knowledge of the detailed ritual accounts found in chaps. 1–5. Nevertheless, there are some differences in the sacrificial terminology used here and in chap. 8 from that in the preceding regulations (Koch, *Priesterschrift,* 69). The term for pouring out blood at the base of the altar is יצק (v 9) in place of שפך (4:7; Exod 29:12); the phrase לפני יהוה, "before Yahweh," loved in the regulations, is missing here as is אהל מועד, "the Tent of Meeting"; and there is a twofold burning for the whole offering—first the unwashed parts are burned; then the other parts are washed and burned (vv 13–14; 8:20–21)—in contrast to a single burning in the regulation (cf. Lev 1:9). These variations indicate that this account had an origin different from that of the regulations for the sacrifices. Nevertheless, the editor has taken an ancient account of the first public sacrifices and employed it as a report of the fulfillment of the regulations for the various categories of public sacrifices prescribed in chaps. 1–5 (7). The only sacrifice not offered on this high day was אשם, "a reparation offering," for it was a sacrifice prescribed for specific kinds of transgression.

The location of vv 22–24, which recount Aaron's blessing of the people, the appearance of Yahweh, and the consumption of the sacrifices by heavenly fire, is puzzling. On the surface it seems that the heavenly fire arrives too late, for sacrifices have been offered up on the altar for the last eight days (Noth, 82). Since the sacrifices were already burning, this statement, in his judgment, gives too small a place to the divine fire. Moreover, v 22 does not connect well with v 21. Koch (*Priesterschrift,* 70–71) forcefully argues that these verses originally belonged in a different context. He judges them to be a fitting conclusion to the unit found in Exod 25–Lev 7. At the close of that section there originally was a narrative about Aaron's performing the rituals found in chaps. 1–7 at Moses' bidding. In that narrative, while Aaron was preparing to burn the pieces of the sacrificed animals laid on the altar, the glory of Yahweh appeared unexpectedly; fire darted from the glory and consumed these sacrifices as a sign of Yahweh's pleasure. While it is quite possible that vv 22–24 originally had a different literary setting, such a reconstruction is too hypothetical to be of much value in interpreting the present text. In fact, these verses fit well in their present setting, for they reveal Yahweh's seal of approval on the newly inaugurated cult. That the divine fire consumed the sacrifices already burning is characteristic of the synergistic nature of biblical faith, i.e., God and man working together. God accepts and enhances what people have begun in obedience to his instructions. It needs to be noted that it is the people's sacrifices rather than the priests' sacrifices that the divine fire consumed. Therefore, appearance of the divine fire is to be interpreted as proof of God's complete acceptance of the new sanctuary as the main avenue for the people to approach him rather than the lighting of the first fire on the main altar.

Another problem in vv 22–24 is the twofold account of the priestly blessing of the congregation. Aaron blessed the people before Moses and he entered the Tent (v 22); upon leaving the Tent Moses and Aaron blessed the people again. Some commentators, such as Noth (81), find no reason for the presence of this second report of blessing the congregation. But Porter (75) observes that Solomon pronounced two different blessings at the dedication of the Temple (1 Kgs 8:14–21; 54–61). In so doing the king most likely followed precedent. Here the first act of blessing followed standard procedure, while the second one took place spontaneously, inspired by these leaders' encounter with Yahweh. The second act of blessing thus bears special witness to the joy and splendor of this high day.

Comment

1 At the end of the seven-day separation to complete the priests' ordination, a special day is proclaimed for the inauguration of the regular use of the new sanctuary. On this occasion the newly ordained priests are to offer up the first public sacrifices. Moses summons Aaron, the priests, and the elders of the congregation to assemble again before the Tent of Meeting. Even though there is no reference in chap. 8 to the assembly's being dismissed, that action may be assumed. Moses, as God's representative, directs Aaron regarding the order of the day.

2 Aaron is to present for himself and his house עגל בן־בקר, "a young bull," for a purification offering (חטאת) and איל, "a ram," for a whole offering (עלה). Rashi takes the phrase עגל בן־בקר to specify a two-year-old bull, while עגל alone refers to a yearling. *Targum Yerušalmi* connects Aaron's offering of a bull on this occasion with the incident of the golden calf (Exod 32–33) in order to claim that with this offering he removes the last stains of that grave sin. Even though Aaron has been in the sanctuary area for seven consecutive days and has presented offerings daily, he must again present a purification offering for himself. It is puzzling that Aaron, who after the ordination service in which a purification offering was offered for him has been residing at the sanctuary, must now offer another purification offering. Since he and his sons have spent all this time at the sanctuary, they are both clean and holy. Nevertheless, given the austere, terrifying holiness of Yahweh, who will appear this day at the Tent, it is absolutely necessary that Aaron make sure that he and the congregation have made atonement for themselves. Otherwise, they are in danger of being consumed by the divine fire. Kiuchi astutely remarks that the חטאת "in Lev 9 deals with not particular sins but rather sinfulness or uncleanness, assumed in the encounter of man—whether he is a priest or not—with God on any special occasion" (*Purification Offering,* 46). This requirement, therefore, witnesses to the ingrained sinfulness of human nature in this life.

3–4 Moses instructs Aaron, and Aaron instructs the people. This pattern is important throughout Israel's existence, for the priests are entrusted with teaching the people the word of God revealed to Moses at Sinai. This practice began on the very first day of public offerings at the newly erected altar. Aaron tells the people to bring a goat (שְׂעִיר־עִזִּים) for a purification offering and a calf (עגל) and a lamb (כבשׂ), both a year old, for whole offerings. The regulation for a purification offering requires the congregation to present a young bull (פר בן־בקר), but here and on the Day of Atonement they present a male goat (16:15). An explanation for this variation is not given. It may be that the rituals come from different eras or different cult centers. Or it may be that this is the standard for a purification presented by the people on a high day, while a bull is required when they seek expiation for a specific sin. They are also to bring a bull (שׁור) and a ram (איל) for offerings of well-being along with מנחה בלולה בשמן, "a grain offering mixed with oil." With the purification offering and the whole offering the people find atonement, and they make a festive meal from the offerings of well-being and the grain offerings. Thus on this first day of public offerings at the Tent of Meeting, the entire series of public sacrifices regulated in Lev 1–7 is presented. The reparation offering is excluded, for it served only to expiate specific sins (cf. 5:14–26[6:7]).

These instructions are undergirded with the great promise that Yahweh will appear to those assembled. That promise is so central to the importance of this day that it is repeated in v 6b. In the latter reference it is כבוד יהוה, "the glory of Yahweh," that will appear. כבד, lit. "weighty, heavy," stands for the splendor and glory of that which is majestic. In regard to a person, it stands for "the visible appearance of wealth and splendor which indicated" his importance (Porter, 72). In reference to Yahweh, it frequently refers to the cloud that both conveys and hides his divine splendor in order that those who behold it may not be consumed (Exod 13:21–22; 24:15–17). This cloud descended from time to time on the Tent of Meeting (Exod 33:9; 40:34–35; Num 16:42; cf. T. E. Fretheim, *The Suffering of God,* OBT 14 [Philadelphia: Fortress, 1984] 67–70, 79–84). This special appearance of

Yahweh will be an exhilarating moment. More importantly it will mean that Yahweh is making himself accessible to the people at the Tent of Meeting. Worship is more than the faithful carrying out of prescribed rituals; its goal is an encounter with God. This goal will be realized dramatically on this high day.

5 The entire congregation both willingly and immediately carries out the instructions Moses has given them. Their obedience contrasts markedly with the various episodes of their murmuring and rebellions recorded in Exod 15:22–17:16; 32–33, and Numbers. The people's obedience provides the moral foundation that renders their sacrifices effectual.

6 Moses underscores that they are doing הדבר, "the word," that Yahweh has commanded. The first part of this verse is similar to 8:5. To an obedient, responsive people Yahweh will appear; cf. vv 3, 4.

7 Moses instructs Aaron to approach the altar in order to begin functioning as high priest by performing the rituals for the various sacrifices. The expiating nature of the sacrifices is stressed. Through the offering of his own sacrifices, Aaron will כפר, "expiate," his own sins and those of his house. Then he is in position to offer up the people's offerings (קרבן) and make expiation for them. The people will be forgiven so that they may worship Yahweh in the fullest joy.

8–9 Aaron offers a purification offering for himself, which includes his sons. His sons help him by catching the blood in a basin and bringing it to him for the next rite. Aaron then spreads some of the blood on the horns of the large altar. This practice differs from that prescribed for a high priestly purification offering in 4:5–7. There are many ways to account for this variation. Possibly the practice in 4:5–7 was a later development. Wenham (149), however, suggests that the altar of incense at this time did not need atonement, for Aaron had not yet entered the Tent of Meeting. It is more likely, though, that this purification offering differs from the one prescribed in chap. 4, for it is being offered on a high day, rather than to expiate a specific sin committed by Aaron. Since the altar of incense and the sanctuary have not been polluted by a specific sin, they do not need to be cleansed by a blood rite performed inside the holy place.

17 The phrase מלא כפו, lit. "fill his hand(s)," stands in place of the older phrase קמץ מלא קמצו, "take a handful" (2:2). This phraseology underscores the high priest's recent ordination, given that this phrase also means "ordain." Furthermore, the phrase מלבד עלת הבקר, "beside the morning whole offering," indicates that the continual morning offering, the Tamid, has already begun, even though it has not been mentioned in this account. Possibly this offering is one of the sacrifices that Aaron and his sons offered each morning during their period of ordination. But Elliger (130) and Noordtzij (106) take the reference to the morning whole offering as a later addition, believing that the Tamid did not begin before this day. Levine (57) agrees with this assessment. He cites the explanation given in the Sipra; this whole offering is identified with the sacrifice just presented by the people.

22–24 When Aaron has finished offering the sacrifices, he raises his hands and blesses the people. The pronouncing of the divine blessing on the people was one of the great prerogatives of the priests (Deut 10:8). The primary priestly blessing is found in Num 6:24–26. This account locates the blessing as the concluding rite of public worship in ancient Israel (C. Westermann, *Blessing in the Bible and the Life of the Church*, tr. K. Crim [Philadelphia: Fortress, 1978] 44–45). But the blessing is far more than the conclusion of the service; it is the goal of the service. Westermann quotes from S. Mowinckel (*Religion und Kultus* [Göttingen: Vandenhoeck & Ruprecht, 1953] 64–66), "It was in order to receive blessing and make it secure in all its forms, that Israel, as a community and also as individuals, went to the sanctuary and took part in the worship offered there" (Westermann, 20). Aaron and Moses are invoking God to be present among the people, forgiving them and working for their well-being by bringing about the covenant promises (e.g., 26:3–13). When God blesses, he activates the vital powers in the created order for the good of the people blessed. The primary expression of his blessing is fertility, but for man it also includes success, sense of accomplishment, happiness, and victory over enemies (cf. J. Pedersen, *Israel, Its Life and Culture* [London: Oxford UP, 1964] 1–2:182–212; F. Horst, "Segen und Segenshandlungen in der Bibel," *EvT* 7 [1947/48] 23–37; J. Scharbert, "'Fluchen' und 'Segnen' im Alten Testament," *Bib* 39 [1958] 1–26; idem, "ברך *brk*; בְּרָכָה *bᵉrākhāh*," *TDOT* 2:284–95, 302–8; A. Murtonen, "The Use and Meaning of the Words *lᵉbårek* and *bᵉråkåh* in the Old Testament," *VT* 9 [1959] 158–77; C. Keller and G. Wehmeier, "ברך *brk* pi. segnen," *THAT* 1:353–76).

Then Moses and Aaron enter the Tent of Meeting to commune with Yahweh. Their entrance may be compared to the account of Moses and Aaron, along with Nadab, Abihu, and the seventy elders, going up Mount Sinai to fellowship in the presence of God after the sacrificial ceremony to seal the covenant. Up to this time only Moses had direct access to Yahweh by being able to enter the Tent of Meeting. From now on Aaron has access to Yahweh on behalf of the people in specially defined situations. Also Aaron's entering the Tent of Meeting with Moses symbolizes that he takes on the intercessory role as the nation's high priest.

It is striking that on leaving the Tent of Meeting Moses and Aaron bless the people again. Having been in the presence of God, they themselves have been blessed. Overflowing with the joy of this blessing, they share their abundance by again blessing the people who have been anxiously awaiting their coming out of the Tent of Meeting. Then the glory of Yahweh appears to all the people. While the nature of Yahweh's manifestation of his presence is not stated, it was most likely in the cloud as on other occasions in the wilderness journey (Exod 24:16). It was this glory that filled the tabernacle after Moses had erected it (Exod 40:34). Fire comes from the glory and consumes all the sacrifices. Earlier Aaron had begun to burn these sacrifices; now the divine fire quickly consumes the pieces of meat and fat slowly smoldering on the altar. Snaith (57), however, reconstructs the scene differently. In his view Aaron had burned his own offering and then prepared the people's sacrifices, but had not yet burned them. The divine fire comes and devours these first public offerings. With this manifestation Yahweh dramatically accepts the sacrifices offered at the new sanctuary. This appearance of Yahweh also corresponds to his appearance at the dedication of the Temple by Solomon (2 Chr 7:1; cf. 1 Chr 21:26; 1 Kgs 18:38).

Overcome by awe, the people נפל, "bow down," with their faces toward the ground in the presence of Yahweh. This is a spontaneous, purposeful act of contrition, for נפל, besides meaning "fall," may depict a quick change of posture that is not accidental or forced; e.g., Rebekah "alighted" (נפל) from her camel when she saw Isaac for the first time (Gen 24:64). Filled with ecstatic joy, the people lift their voices in רנן, "joyful shouts," praising God. רנן, an onomatopoeic word (BDB,

943), means "to let out shouts of joy" or "to sing jubilantly." It is the spontaneous response called forth by a glimpse of God's majesty (Isa 12:6) or by the wonders of his work (Ps 92:5[4]). The majority of the occurrences of this word in the OT are in relationship to the worship of Yahweh. This word expresses the joyful quality of Israelite worship (Cf. R. Ficker, "רנן "*rnn* jubeln," *THAT* 2:781–86).

Explanation

After Aaron and his sons had completed the seven days of separation in the court of the Tent of Meeting, the newly ordained priests began to function as priests on the eighth day by offering up sacrifices on behalf of the people. The people brought animals for a purification offering, whole offerings, and offerings of well-being. This order of sacrifices indicates that the congregation first sought expiation for their sins and then celebrated the occasion with a festive meal from the offerings of well-being. Yahweh himself had promised to appear to them on this great day. The promise of Yahweh's appearing is conditioned on the people's obedience to the instructions, not on their performing the sacrificial ritual perfectly.

After the people assembled, Aaron, acting according to Moses' instructions, presented his own purification offering first. The high priest had to make expiation for himself before he could offer the sacrifices of the people (cf. 16:11–14). Even though he was high priest, he was still human and, therefore, had to be continually cleansed from sin.

When Aaron had finished sacrificing the people's offerings, he lifted his hands toward God and blessed the people. His action was to let the power of God for prosperity and well-being rest on the people. His blessing was to activate the covenant promises, as the priestly blessing recorded in Num 6:24–26 indicates.

Afterwards Moses took Aaron into the Tent of Meeting. This was a most unusual step. It marked the climax of Aaron's ordination; now he had access to God and might enter the Tent of Meeting whenever his duties required it. In the Tent Moses and Aaron worshiped Yahweh and communed with him. When they came out, they blessed the people. At that moment the glory of Yahweh appeared over the Tent in a way that was visible to all the people. From the glory, fire came forth and burned up the sacrifices smoldering on the altar. The highest goal of worship, entrance into the presence of God himself, has been achieved. Similarly in the NT the new approach to God through faith in his son Jesus was inaugurated by a marvelous manifestation of God (Acts 2:1–4). On that great day tongues of fire rested on each person in the assembly. In both instances fire was closely associated with a mighty manifestation of God's presence.

Overcome by awe and wonder at Yahweh's holiness, the people prostrated themselves in humble worship. Then they raised their voices in ringing shouts of joy. The Israelites acknowledged Yahweh as their God and were grateful that he had instituted this system of worship. Because God is holy, men fear before him. Reverent fear is a positive force, because it checks the human proclivity to pride. This emotion moves a person to worship God in purity of heart. As one focuses on God, joy floods his whole being. Possibly the congregation broke out in spontaneous singing. Joy characterizes worship of both testaments. Isa 12:3, 6 says:

With joy you will draw water from
the wells of salvation;
Shout aloud and sing for joy, people of Zion,
for great is the Holy One of Israel among you.

And Jesus says, "These things I have spoken to you, that my joy may be in you, and that your joy may be full" (John 15:11; cf. Acts 8:5–8; 1 Pet 1:8).

Humans may approach God only by the way of atonement. That is, sinful people must receive expiation before they can enter the presence of God. In the NT all believers have access to God because Jesus' death has made expiation for their sins (Heb 9:11–14). This conviction encourages them to approach God's throne with reverent confidence (Heb 10:19–22). The goal of worship then in both testaments is to enter into God's presence. Whereas in ancient Israel God manifested his presence in the cloud and fire, Jesus promises to be present any time two or three gather in his name (Matt 18:20). His presence is made real by his Spirit, who communicates the glory of God to those assembled in Jesus' name.

C. *The Death of Two Priests and Attendant Regulations (10:1–20)*

Bibliography

Budd, P. J. "Priestly Instruction in Pre-exilic Israel." *VT* 23 (1973) 1–14. **Gradwohl, R.** "Das 'fremde Feuer' von Nadab und Abihu." *ZAW* 75 (1963) 288–96. **Haran, M.** "The Uses of Incense in the Ancient Israelite Ritual." *VT* 10 (1960) 113–29. **Kiuchi, N.** *The Purification Offering in the Priestly Literature.* JSOTSup 56. Sheffield: JSOT Press, 1987. 67–85. **Laughlin, J.** "'The Strange Fire' of Nadab and Abihu." *JBL* 95 (1976) 559–65. **Segal, P.** "The Divine Verdict of Leviticus x 3." *VT* 39 (1989) 91–95. **Zuurmond, R.** "Der Tod von Nadab und Abihu." *Texte und Kontexte* 24 (1984) 23–27.

Translation

1 *Aaron's sons, Nadab and Abihu,*[a] *each*[b] *took his firepan, put coals*[c] *in it and laid incense on it,*[d] *and presented illicit fire before*[e] *Yahweh which he*[f] *had not commanded.* 2 *Then fire darted out from Yahweh's presence and consumed*[a] *them; thus they died in Yahweh's presence.*[b] 3 *Moses said to Aaron, "This is what Yahweh meant when he said:*

Among those who are close to me[a] *I will show myself as holy;*
Before all the people I will show my glory.

Aaron remained silent.

4 *Moses summoned Mishael and Elzaphan, sons of Uzziel, Aaron's uncle, and said to them, "Come and carry your cousins outside the camp away from the sanctuary."* 5 *They came and carried them, still in their tunics, outside the camp just as Moses had spoken.*

6 *Moses then said to Aaron and to*[a] *Eleazar and Ithamar, his sons,*[b] *"Do not*[c] *let your hair be unkempt*[d] *or tear*[e] *your clothes, or you will die and Yahweh will be angry against all the congregation. But your relatives, all the house of Israel, will weep*[f] *for the destruction by fire which Yahweh has kindled.*[g] 7 *Do not leave the entrance to the Tent of Meeting*[a] *lest you die, because Yahweh's anointing oil is on you." They did according to Moses' instructions.*

8 *Yahweh spoke to Aaron,* 9 *"When you are to enter the Tent of Meeting*[a] *do not drink wine or strong drink, you and your sons, lest you die. This is a perpetual decree for all your generations:* 10 *distinguishing*[a] *between the holy and the common,*[b] *between the unclean and the clean,*[c] 11 *and teaching*[a] *the Israelites all the decrees which Yahweh has spoken to them through Moses."*

12 *Moses spoke to Aaron and Eleazar and Ithamar, his surviving sons, "Take that which is leftover of the grain offering from the gifts for Yahweh and eat that which is prepared without yeast beside the altar because it is most holy.*[a] 13 *Eat*[a] *it in a holy place because it is your portion*[b] *and the portion of your sons of the gifts for Yahweh, for thus I have been commanded.* 14 *And you, your sons, and your daughters*[a] *are to eat the breast of the elevated offering and the thigh of the special offering in a clean*[b] *place because they are given as your portion and the portion of your sons from the offerings of well-being presented by the Israelites.*[c] 15 *They must bring the thigh of the contribution*[a] *and the breast of the elevated offering*[b] *along with the fat pieces of the gifts in order to raise them as an elevated offering before Yahweh. This will be an enduring right*[c] *for you and your sons*[d] *just as Yahweh has commanded."*[e]

16 *When Moses inquired diligently*[a] *about the goat of the purification offering, behold, it had been burned.*[b] *Then he became angry at Eleazar and Ithamar, Aaron's surviving sons, and said,* 17 *"Why did you not eat the purification offering in the holy*[a] *place because it is most holy? It*[b] *has been given to you*[c] *to bear*[d] *the iniquity of the congregation by making expiation for them before Yahweh?* 18 *Since*[a] *its blood*[b] *was not brought into the inner part of the Holy Place, you should have indeed eaten it in the sanctuary*[c] *just as I have been commanded."*[d] 19 *Aaron replied to Moses, "Behold,*[a] *today they have presented their purification offering and their whole offering before Yahweh, yet such things as these have happened*[b] *to me. If I had eaten the purification offering today, would it have been considered right by Yahweh?"* 20 *When Moses heard this, he accepted it as right.*[a]

Notes

1.a. LXX reads *καὶ Αβιουδ*, "and Abioud."

1.b. אִישׁ, "man, one," in the phrase אִישׁ מחתתו has distributive force (cf. GKC §139b).

1.c. אֵשׁ, "fire," refers to the glowing embers that are put in the firepan.

1.d. Syr and Tg[mss] read עליהן, "on them," which agrees with the compound subj, instead of MT עליה, "on it," agreeing with the distributive use of אִישׁ (cf. n. 1.b.).

1.e. The prep לפני, "before," connotes "in the presence of."

1.f. LXX adds *κύριος*, "the Lord," as subj of the verb; but Vg reads a pass verb.

2.a. אכל, "eat, consume," here means more "slay," for their bodies were buried.

2.b. Cf. n. 1.e.

3.a. This is a substantive use of the adj קָרֹב; it means specifically the priests who serve in the presence of God by presenting (הקריב) sacrifices on the altar. Segal (92) suggests that the adj should be repointed with a *sere,* making it a verb, "those who approach." While this emendation offers a good reading, the fact that Ezek 42:13 and 43:19 employ the adj in the same general way that it is used here should make us very cautious of emending the text to support an interpretation. It seems that a gnomic saying is being quoted here; therefore, the form used is one that fits the saying rather than one that fits the immediate context. How the saying is being applied in this context is open to interpretation. *IBHS* (§9.5.2f) interprets the pronominal suffix as a gen of location.

6.a. Instead of ל, "to," before both names of Aaron's sons, Sam reads אל, "to," as does MT, before Aaron.

6.b. LXX adds τοὺς καταλελειμμένους, "those who survived," as in vv 12 and 16.

6.c. Sam reads לא, "not," which is the negative before the two subsequent verbs. MT's על, a negative particle, is certainly the harder reading and is followed (cf. GKC §109g).

6.d. The phrase פרע ראש, lit. "unloose the head," means to unloose the headband so that one's hair may fall freely.

6.e. פרם, "tear, rip (clothes) in pieces," is a word that appears only in Leviticus (also 13:45; 21:10).

6.f. בכה, "weep," governs the acc here as in Gen 23:2; Num 26:26; but it is used with על, "for," in Judg 11:37–38 (Baentsch, 350).

6.g. The Heb. emphasizes the destructive force of the fire by using a noun and a verb from the same root את־השרפה אשר שרף יהוה, "the destruction by fire which Yahweh burned."

7.a. The prep phrase ומפתח לאהל מועד, "and the entrance to the Tent of Meeting," occurs first for emphasis.

9.a. LXX adds ἢ προσπορευομένων ὑμῶν πρὸς τὸ θυσιαστήριον, "your approaching the altar."

10.a. LXX and Syr omit the copula, but that may be primarily to produce a smoother translation rather than because they had a different Heb. Vorlage. GKC §114p comments that the inf constr is not a redactor's insertion but could be an explanatory note on the injunction in v 9 not to drink wine or strong drink.

10.b. The pair קדש/חל, "holy/common," is infrequent in the OT; it is found in Ezek 22:26; 42:20; 44:23.

10.c. The pair טמא/טהר, "unclean/clean," is found several times in the Pentateuch (Lev 11:47; 14:57; 20:25 [2x]; Deut 12:15, 22; 15:22) and a few times in other places such as Ezek 22:26; 44:23.

11.a. הורה, "teach," has a double acc here; cf. Exod 4:15 (Baentsch, 351).

12.a. Cf. 2:3.

13.a. The *waw* pf functions to explain the injunction in v 12 (Joüon §119l).

13.b. חק, usually rendered "decree, statute," here has the special meaning of "due, rightful portion" (cf. Ringgren, *TDOT* 5:144).

14.a. For MT בנתיך, "your daughters," LXX reads καὶ ὁ οἶκός σου = וביתך, "and your house." MT is by far the harder reading, for one would not expect a reference to daughters in this kind of legislation.

14.b. For טהור, "clean," LXX reads ἁγίῳ, "holy," as in vv 13 and 17.

14.c. This gen is taken as a subjective gen.

15.a. According to the regulations found in chaps. 6–7, the right thigh of an offering of well-being was תרומה, "a contribution," assigned without ceremony to the officiating priest (7:32–33); it was not presented as תנופה, "an elevated offering." Therefore, v 15 appears to be in conflict with standard cultic practice. Milgrom ("The *šôq hattĕrûmâ*," *SCTT*, 164–70) analyzes the text and uncovers a historical development. He speculates that v 15 has been inserted into this context in order to require the joining of the right thigh with the breast as an elevated offering. He posits that the editor who made this change also inserted the term "right thigh" in 9:21. Milgrom goes on to reconstruct the historical setting for this change in practice. In his judgment it took place during Josiah's reform. When Josiah closed the outlying shrines, numerous priests migrated to the Jerusalem Temple. In order to feed this large influx, the right thigh was added to the elevated offering, thus making it available to all the priests, not just the officiating priest. By increasing the food supply, this change eliminated quarreling among the priests and added needed food to meet the growing demand. Finally in the Second Temple, the gestures for presenting the elevated offering and the contribution were united into one ritual.

15.b. Cf. n. 7:30.d.

15.c. Or חק עולם, "a perpetual decree"; cf. n. 13.b. and n. 6:11.b.

15.d. Sam and LXX add ולבנתיך, "and to your daughters," levelling the text to agree with v 14.

15.e. LXX adds τῷ Μωυσῇ, "to Moses."

16.a. The inf abs before the verb carries the note of diligence.

16.b. שרף is pointed as a pual perf, but *IBHS* (§22.6c, n. 31) takes it as a qal pass.

17.a. A gen qualifies the noun in constr (Joüon §167b).

17.b. MT reads אתה נתן לכם, "it he gave to you"; the implied subj is God, and אתה, "it," i.e., the purification offering, is placed first for some emphasis.

17.c. LXX adds φαγεῖν = לאכל, "to eat."

17.d. נשׂא, (lit.) "carry, lift," with עון, "iniquity, guilt," means "bear, accept" the penalty and/or the burden or guilt of a sin; i.e., one is liable for punishment. Conversely in non-cultic texts it means "forgive," being free from the liability for a sin. Here the idea of this idiom is that the priest accepts the burden of bearing the guilt of the congregation's sin in order to remove it.

18.a. The particle הן may function as an interjection or as a conditional particle.

18.b. The term את־הדמה, "its blood," is constructed with a pass verb. Because the verb is used impersonally, the obj is still subordinate to it (GKC §121ab).

18.c. LXX reads ἐν τόπῳ ἁγίῳ, "in a holy place," as in vv 13, 17 for MT בקדש, "in the sanctuary."

18.d. Cf. 8:31.

19.a. The pointing of the interrogative ה like an article is very unusual (GKC §100k). But the term היום, "today," indicates that it is functioning as an interjection; cf. n. 18.a.

19.b. The root of תקראנה is קרה, "happen, befall," and it functions on the analogy of a ל״א verb (GKC §75rr).

20.a. The idiom וייטב בעיניו, "it was good in his sight or view," means "he was satisfied" with Aaron's explanation.

Form/Structure/Setting

Chap. 10 consists of numerous units woven together in a chiastic structure:

I. The incident of Nadab and Abihu with instructions about burial of the dead (vv 1–7) — A
- A. The illicit offering of Nadab and Abihu (vv 1–3) — *α*
- B. Instructions for the burial of the two deceased priests (vv 4–7) — *β*
  1. Introductory formula (v 4a+bα^1)
  2. Twofold speech (vv 4bα^2–7a)
  3. Compliance report (v 7b)

II. Prohibition and description of the priests' role (vv 8–11) — B
- A. Introductory formula (v 8)
- B. Speech (vv 9–11)
  1. Prohibition against priests' use of liquor while on duty (v 9)
  2. Priests' instructional role (vv 10–11)

III. Instructions on eating from the sacrifices for the priests and the Aaronites' failure to eat (vv 12–20) — A'
- A. Instructions about eating sacrificial meat (vv 12–15) — *β'*
- B. Dispute about the Aaronites' not eating their assigned portions (vv 16–20) — *α'*
  1. Moses' search and angry response (vv 16–18)
  2. Aaron's reply (v 19)
  3. Moses' satisfaction (v 20)

Two contrasting incidents set the boundaries for this chiasm. At the head is the incident of Aaron's two oldest sons' offering of אש זרה, "illicit fire," before Yahweh (vv 1–3). Yahweh becomes angry and immediately strikes down these two priests. At the base is an incident which shadows the first. Aaron and his sons deviate from the cultic decrees by failing to eat the priestly portions of the purification offering. Moses becomes very angry at Aaron. Throughout the Pentateuch Moses is seldom pictured as angry save when God's glory has been dishonored, as by the people's worship of the golden calf (Exod 32:19). Moses' anger then reveals the seriousness of the Aaronites' failure, but the fact that Moses, not Yahweh, becomes angry communicates that the error of the surviving priests is less serious than that of Nadab and Abihu. Instructions are joined to both of these incidents. This is a common trait of the priestly writer (Koch, *Priesterschrift,* 72). Attached to the first account are instructions on how to bury the dead priests.

Preceding the second account are instructions about various offerings that the priests are to eat. The locations of the instructions are inverted for stylistic symmetry. At the center of this chiasm stands an injunction against the priests' drinking liquor while on duty (vv 8–9) along with a statement of the priests' key tasks of making proper cultic distinctions and teaching the people (vv 10–11).

The choppy reporting of the first incident, which is confined to the briefest language in vv 1–2, indicates that only a curtailed report of that account has been preserved. The editor used this incident to warn all, especially the priests, about the dangers of transgressing the holy. Moses interprets the incident by quoting an ancient, cryptic saying about God's absolute holiness (v 3). Next, much attention is given to the burial of the offenders and the rites of mourning (vv 4–7). For a modern audience this material on burial and mourning seems out of proportion to the reporting of the incident. But for the ancients such instruction was critical on many fronts. The community needed guidance on the appropriate ways to respond to such a catastrophe in order to prevent God's wrath from spreading to the congregation. Furthermore, the handling of the deceased was an issue foundational to the priestly purity regulations. These instructions address a specific event; nevertheless, they also serve as the standard for handling the corpse of any priest who dies in the sanctuary area. Also, the personal nature of these instructions draws attention to the responsiveness of the surviving priests to divine instructions. Their being addressed and their responsiveness above all meant that the newly established priesthood was still intact and thus able to function in a way that was acceptable to God. That is, the transgression of Nadab and Abihu did not taint the rest of Aaron's household. This last fact indicates that their transgression was highly personal in nature.

The incident of Nadab and Abihu explains why the priesthood descended through Aaron's youngest sons, Eleazar and Ithamar. It may also reflect, however, a deep-seated conflict among priestly families at a critical time in the history of the Israelite priesthood (cf. Noth, 84). There have been many attempts to identify the historical setting for this tragedy. Snaith (246), for example, postulates that this incident reflects the conflict between the Zadokite priests of the central sanctuary at Jerusalem and the non-Zadokite priests scattered throughout the land, which was caused by Josiah's unifying all cultic worship at Jerusalem. The recording of this incident then is designed to exclude all non-Zadokite priests from serving at the altar in Jerusalem. Unfortunately Snaith's reconstruction does not address the specific nature of Nadab and Abihu's transgression. In fact, nothing in the account indicates that they were prohibited or restricted in any way from serving at the altar. Laughlin (*JBL* 95 [1976] 563–65) looks to the post-exilic period as the setting for this conflict. According to his reconstruction, these sons of Aaron attempted to perform a Zoroastrian ritual known as the enthronement of fire. Their effort brought them into conflict with the priestly ideology of the perpetual flame (6:1–6 [8–13]). Unfortunately Laughlin is unable to identify the priestly order condemned by the incident. Thus he fails to explain why it is Aaron's two eldest sons who committed the transgression.

Given the diversity of positions and the lack of any consensus, it is better to accept the text as reporting a deep conflict in the newly installed priesthood at the Tent of Meeting. This incident has to do with the exclusion of alien rituals from the new cult and the exclusion of certain families from serving as priests.

Under the enthusiasm of the moment, Nadab and Abihu performed some rite with their censers that involved fire not taken from the altar of the whole offering; that is why the fire they used is called אשׁ זרה, "illicit fire." At the minimum they were trying to incorporate some pagan ritual dear to them into the cult of Yahweh. That the family of Aaron was knowledgeable about the rituals of pagan cults has some support in the Egyptian names that occur in the Levitical genealogies and in Aaron's leadership in setting up the golden calf as an object of idolatrous worship (Exod 32). Also they were attempting to promote themselves and their families over the newly designated high priest, Aaron, by demonstrating to the people that they had special access to Yahweh. Their actions thus threatened both the integrity of the new cult and the identity of the legitimate priesthood.

The position that this incident has an early origin is supported by several details. It employs the "loved patriarchal" motif that the younger is chosen over the older: Jacob over Esau, Joseph over his brothers, Manasseh over Ephraim. Also the cryptic style, which conceals the precise nature of the transgression, accords with the early epic style, not with the fuller, prosaic style of the late period. In addition, the names of Nadab and Abihu are woven into the fabric of the priestly material of the Pentateuch (e.g., Exod 6:23; 24:9; 28:1), and this incident is firmly rooted in the priestly tradition (Num 3:2–4; 26:60–61; 1 Chr 24:1–2). Finally this account fits its context tightly; the devouring fire is the same fire that consumed the sacrifices at the conclusion of the first public sacrifices (9:24). These facts support placing the setting for this incident at the first public sacrifices.

At the center of Lev 10 stand vv 8–11. They are marked off by an authoritative heading (v 8). It is distinctive in that Yahweh speaks directly to Aaron. This unusual style highlights the center. It contains a prohibition against the priests' drinking intoxicating beverages while on duty at the sanctuary (v 9) coupled with a statement on the priests' duties of distinguishing between the clean and unclean, the holy and profane, and of teaching the people (vv 10–11). That this material appears to be foreign to the context and that vv 10–11 are complex clauses with no apparent context lead many scholars, such as Bertholet, von Rad, Noth, and Koch, to judge this material as a later insertion. This unit, however, bridges the account of the two incidents. Any priest whose mind would become foggy from too much alcohol could put himself in jeopardy of God's wrath by accidentally violating the holiness of the sanctuary as did Nadab and Abihu. Their deaths underscore the urgency of a priest's having a clear mind to make right decisions in cultic matters. Thus the prohibition is given. Then the reference to the priests' duty to make distinctions is well illustrated by Aaron's prudent action in the second incident. Moreover, this statement about the priests' responsibilities bridges chaps. 1–7 and chaps. 11–15. The issue of distinguishing the holy from the common is central to the sacrificial legislation (chaps. 1–7), while distinguishing the clean from the unclean is the theme of the coming chaps. 11–15.

The third section begins with instructions about the parts of various offerings that belong to the priests (vv 12–15). Koch (*Priesterschrift,* 73) observes that this material continues the theme of fulfillment reports found in chaps. 8 and 9 (cf. 2:3, 10; 6:9[16]; 7:29–34; Exod 29:26–28). That Moses, not Yahweh, speaks to Aaron and his sons about known decrees supports this position. It corresponds to 8:31–35, where Moses repeats instructions found in Exod 29. Thus this passage treats details about the first public offerings that did not get included in chap. 9. This point also favors viewing the account of the first public sacrifices as the setting for this incident.

The final pericope (vv 16–20) reports a heated dialogue between Moses and Aaron about the failure of the priests to eat their portion of the purification offering as prescribed in 6:22–23(29–30). Aaron acknowledges their failure and gives Moses a solid reason. Moses accepts his explanation. This incident reveals that the priests have some freedom in interpreting the regulations as they apply to daily situations as long as the interpretation does not tarnish God's holiness. This incident also illustrates how the priests are to resolve disputes about the law. Two prominent priests debate the issue, with the one convincing the other as to the proper response on the basis of a sound argument. The remarkable quality of this account is that the lesser figure, Aaron, persuades the greater figure, Moses. This report bears witness to the authenticity of this narrative and teaches that a dispute about the law is to be resolved by sound judgment, not by vaunting one's authority.

Comment

1 Nadab and Abihu, Aaron's two eldest sons, violated the sanctity of the cult. The exact nature of their transgression is veiled by the cryptic description. That they attempted to perform an illicit cultic act in the worship of Yahweh is clear from the accumulation of words that have a technical cultic meaning and have occurred frequently in chaps. 8–9. These words are לקח, "take," נתן, "put," שׂים, "put," הקריב, "present," and קטרת, "incense."

מחתה, "censer," from the root חתה, "to take, catch," refers to a utensil for catching ashes from the grate or for carrying live coals, such as a firepan (Exod 27:3) or censer or snuff dish (Exod 25:38). Such a utensil was used to settle the contest between Korah with his company and the Aaronite priesthood (Num 16:1; 17:11[16:46]). On their censers Nadab and Abihu presented before Yahweh אשׁ זרה, "unauthorized or illicit fire." Is it possible that the root זור, which frequently stands for aliens, suggests the presentation of fire according to the ritual of a foreign cult (cf. Num 3:4; 26:61)? In any case the adjective זרה, "alien, strange, deviating, unauthorized, illicit," means that their fire was other than that specifically prescribed for use in the cult (L. A. Snijders, "זוּר/זָר *zûr/zār*," *TDOT* 4:55–56).

Because the nature of their transgression is obscure, there have been numerous suggestions. Snaith (58–59), taking זרה to mean "laity," posits that their sin was that of laymen trying to act as priests. But these men are listed as priests elsewhere, as in Exod 28:1 and Num 3:1–3. Another view is that they offered an unauthorized incense offering (Keil and Delitzsch, 351). Levine (59) points out that if there is a connection between this phrase and קטרת זרה, "strange incense," as forbidden in Exod 30:9, these men broke that decree. But their transgression concerns illicit fire, not illicit incense. The use of the phrase אשׁ זרה strongly indicates that a key element of their transgression is the source of their fire. They must have taken it from some place other than the altar of the whole offering (Laughlin, *JBL* 95 [1976] 560–61). Their transgression, though, may have been more involved. They may have been trying to introduce a pagan ritualistic practice into the worship of Yahweh, possibly connecting that ritual with the appearance of Yahweh. Furthermore, it is possible that these priests attempted to enter the

Holy of Holies, which they were not allowed to enter, or, if they were allowed, they did not take the proper precautions (cf. 16:12–13; Gradwohl, *ZAW* 75 [1963] 288–96). By taking such a step they might have been seeking to usurp the high priest's privilege of offering incense in the Holy Place (Exod 30:7–9; cf. Noordtzij, 108). Kiuchi (*Purification Offering,* 78–81) argues from the reference to this incident in 16:1–2, which gives the background for the instructions to Aaron about entering the Holy of Holies to make atonement for himself and his house on the Day of Atonement, that the restrictions placed on Aaron in those verses confirm that the sin of Nadab and Abihu involved an untimely attempt to enter the Holy of Holies and that in their attempt they usurped the privilege of Aaron. If these two priests had succeeded in exalting themselves over their father and brothers, they would have created a deep rift in the priesthood that would have tarnished the true worship of Yahweh at its very inception.

2 Their offering of illicit fire was met by the divine fire. אשׁ, "fire," proceeded from the theophanic presence of Yahweh and אכל, "consumed," Nadab and Abihu. This language means that these two men died immediately. It does not mean, however, that their bodies were incinerated, for their clothed corpses were left for burial (v 5).

For moderns this incident is strange and enigmatic. At first blush it appears that Yahweh is a capricious, vengeful deity, unworthy of human devotion, but it must be remembered that Yahweh is a holy and jealous God, consuming all who profane his glory (cf. Deut 4:24). The manner of the death of these two men accords with the epithet of Yahweh: "Yahweh your God is a devouring fire, a jealous God" (Deut 4:24). Yahweh, the true God, is holy. His holiness is powerful, affecting all that comes into his presence. It cleanses, consumes, or transforms. Its power might be compared to electricity. Electricity is a useful, wonderful source of energy, but in order to work with it safely one must be very careful and astute. Whoever touches uninsulated, hot wires is severely shocked, burned, or, depending on the voltage, instantly killed. When a person approaches God properly, his holiness imparts life (cf. Isa 57:15) and inspires wonder (cf. Exod 3:3–4). But should anything that is profane or unclean enter God's presence, it is consumed.

3 Moses offered Aaron a word from Yahweh as an interpretation of this tragic event. That word states an essential principle about the way in which Yahweh relates to the priests and the people. Yahweh asserted that he will reveal his holy character among those who are near him. That is, he will act in ways that bear witness to his holy character. Parallel to אקדשׁ, "I will show myself as holy," is אכבד, "I will show my glory, or I will be honored." In certain contexts כבד with Yahweh as its subject means that he definitively and dramatically punishes those who resist his will. E.g., in Exod 14:4, 17, and 18, Yahweh promised that he was about to show his glory against Pharaoh and his army by defeating them (cf. Ezek 28:22; Isa 26:15; Hag 1:8). To account for the parallel between "those who are close to me," i.e., the priests, and "the people," Segal (*VT* 39 [1989] 93) points out that according to Num 18:1–7, if any priest violates the sanctity of the sanctuary, the whole community comes under God's wrath until those who are in the wrong are removed. For this reason כבד is used with all the people; i.e., whenever Yahweh reveals his holiness among the priests, he is also showing his glory to the people. On the one hand, this saying has a general meaning: Yahweh's holiness requires reverence from his priests, identified by the term קרבי, "those who are close to me." In Ezek 43:19, the priests are identified as הקרבים אלי . . . לשרתני, "those who are close to me . . . to serve me," and in 42:13 as קרובים ליהוה, "those who are close to Yahweh," i.e., who serve at the altar in presenting the various offerings to Yahweh (cf. Exod 19:22 which uses נגש for קרב). The closer one gets to God, the more he must sanctify himself and the greater caution he must exercise in all matters. By sanctifying themselves and by mediating between Yahweh and the people in the way that Yahweh has instructed, the priests honor (כבד) him before the people. On the other hand, this saying declares that Yahweh has revealed his holiness in putting to death Nadab and Abihu. Furthermore, his swift action has spared the people from his wrath. One reason this tragic incident has been recorded is that the congregation might have a heightened awareness of Yahweh's holiness and be moved to honor him (cf. Segal, *VT* 39 [1989] 92).

On hearing these words Aaron דמם, "remained silent" (cf. A. Baumann, "דָּמָה *dāmāh* II," *TDOT* 3:263–64). Whether he was silent because he had been struck dumb with grief before the stunning event or because Moses' words provided essential solace is not clear from the context. Elliger (137) takes דמם to mean that Aaron was struck lifeless by the dread of the holy. Because of the events surrounding the golden calf (Exod 32–33), Aaron had a profound appreciation of Yahweh's holiness and thus could grasp the gravity of his sons' error. Aaron clearly accepted what had taken place without lashing out at Yahweh. In turn Yahweh accepted Aaron's attitude and accounted it to his merit, as will be seen later in this chapter.

4–5 Since the officiating priests were forbidden to handle the dead (cf. 21:1–4, 11–12), Moses קרא, "summoned," Mishael and Elzaphan, sons of Uzziel, Aaron's uncle (cf. Exod 6:22), to carry the corpses away from the sanctuary. Nothing more is known of Mishael. Elzaphan was the head of the Kohathites (Num 3:30), and a father's house came from him (1 Chr 15:8; 2 Chr 29:13). Presumably they buried the deceased outside the camp.

6–7 Special instructions are given to Eleazar and Ithamar, Aaron's surviving sons. They must not mourn the dead by letting their hair פרע, "hang loose." This means that they must not allow their hair to grow freely and be unkempt (cf. 21:10). According to the Talmud (*b. Sanh.* 22b), this term refers to hair that is uncut after thirty days. Also they are not to פרם, "tear" or "rend," their garments as a sign of mourning. These restrictions, which are standard for the high priest (21:10), are applied to the sons of Aaron in this case because they are on duty at the sanctuary. Death, the punishment for sin, is antithetical to the worship of the holy God and thus may not be allowed to defile that which is holy. In this case it means that the priests may not leave the sanctuary area during the high time of presenting the first public sacrifices. If the priests fail to follow these instructions, they will die, and God's wrath will be turned against the whole congregation (עדה). In this language it is evident that the priests represent the entire community before God. Nevertheless, God is not insensitive to the human sorrow that Aaron and his family feel. Therefore, Moses says to him that all the people, identified as Aaron's kinsmen (אחים), will mourn the deceased on behalf of Aaron and his sons. The priests obeyed Moses' instructions.

8 This heading is the only one in Leviticus in which Yahweh addresses Aaron alone (also in Num 18:1, 8, 20). Elsewhere in Leviticus where Yahweh addresses

Aaron, the text always reads "Moses and Aaron" (11:1; 13:1; 14:33; 15:1). This means that the following words have tremendous importance for the priests. It also means that Yahweh continues to recognize Aaron as high priest despite the transgression of his two eldest sons.

9 While ministering before Yahweh, the priests must be clear headed in order that they might be able to follow all the decrees precisely. They have to be especially alert lest they place their lives in danger by violating the sacred. They also have to have good judgment in order to instruct the people properly about the meaning and application of the law. Therefore, the prohibition is given that requires them to avoid all intoxicating drinks, specifically wine (יין) and other liquors (שׁכר), while on duty in the sanctuary. שׁכר is a general term that can include wine, but when present along with the word *wine,* it refers to any intoxicating drink made from grains or dates or other kinds of fruits. Distilling was not practiced in ancient Israel.

The inclusion of this prohibition at this location has spawned much speculation. It is possible that wine and other liquors were freely used to comfort those mourning the loss of loved ones (Hoffmann, 1:296). Another possibility, favored by the rabbis, is that alcohol was a contributing factor in the sin of Nadab and Abihu. While there is nothing in the text that supports this interpretation, the final editor who placed this decree here probably assumed that there was some connection between alcohol and this tragic incident. In any case, the priests on duty have to be alert in order not to profane the holy in any way. Drunkenness is condemned in many scriptures (e.g., Prov 20:1; 23:29–35; Hos 4:11; Isa 5:11–12).

10–11 In contrast to this strict prohibition in v 9, comes the statement expressing the fundamental duty of the priests. Two highly important duties of the priests are להבדיל, "to make the proper distinctions," that the law requires and להורת, "to teach," the people the decrees that Yahweh has given (cf. Ezek 44:23). The priests interpret the law in response to specific situations put to them by members of the congregation. Their judgments are to rest on proper distinctions between הקדש, "the holy," and החל, "the common," between הטהור, "that which is ritually clean," and הטמא, "that which is ritually unclean" (cf. Ezek 22:26). The "holy" is anything set apart for sacred use, such as all the objects in the area of the Tent of Meeting. Once an object becomes holy, it is separated forever from common use. The "common" refers to that which is used in the normal, daily course of life. It is the ordinary. The distinction between the "clean" and the "unclean" refers to matters of ritual purity. The unclean is something that has become ritually contaminated and may not be brought into the area of the sanctuary. The common, by contrast, is neutral. It is not by nature unclean. Rather it is simply that which is outside the area of the sanctuary. But whatever becomes unclean must be disposed of or else go through a process of purification in order to be pronounced clean. The unclean must never enter an area that is holy, lest it be consumed. Thus a person who is in a state of ritual impurity must be careful not to approach the sanctuary, but outside of that he suffers no harm. The dominant requirement placed on him is that he purify himself ritually so that he can worship at the sanctuary. A person who is ritually clean is free to worship Yahweh.

12–15 Moses addressed Aaron and his surviving sons, Eleazar and Ithamar. This style indicates that Aaron continued as high priest and that his two sons were the official successors of Nadab and Abihu. The last step in the sacrificial ritual is the eating of the portions permitted for the priests. The priests have the right to the leftovers of the grain offerings (cf. 2:3, 10; 6:9–11[16–18]). Also they are to eat the parts of the breast (חזה) and the thigh (שׁוק) of an offering of well-being (7:30–34). The priests are to eat these in a holy place just as Yahweh has commanded.

16–20 Moses investigated and found that the meat from the people's purification offering had not been eaten. According to the regulations (6:17–23 [24–30]), the priests were to receive a portion of those purification offerings from which the blood had not been taken into the inner sanctuary. Because these offerings were most holy, they had to be eaten in a holy place. Their eating the meat was part of the total consumption of the sacrificed animal and took the place of burning of the animal's flesh outside the camp (cf. 4:11–12, 21).

The meaning of v 17b is not obvious (cf. *Comment* on 6:19[26]). One interpretation is that by their eating from the purification offering, the priests removed the people's sin; this interpretation requires the position that that flesh had absorbed the iniquity or uncleanness of the sin (cf. Rendtorff, *Studien,* 215–16; Rodriguez, *Substitution,* 130–36). As was pointed out in chap. 4, it is inconceivable that flesh which has absorbed uncleanness can be eaten in a holy place (6:17[24]) or burned in a clean place (4:12; 6:23[30]). Milgrom (*SCTT,* 70) also discounts this view by interpreting v 17b to mean that the priests received this offering because they had the obligation of bearing the congregation's responsibility (נשׂא עון) by performing the rites of cleansing before the Lord. That is, the priests received the flesh of the purification offering as a gift for their duties, which were hazardous. Moreover, Milgrom (*SCTT,* 71) argues that there is no evidence from the Ancient Middle East that impurity could be removed by eating. But it needs to be pointed out that עון is stronger than "responsibility"; it means "iniquity, guilty," i.e., the transgression and/or the culpability for transgressing (Kiuchi, *Purification Offering,* 50–51). Janowski (*Sühne,* 238–39, n. 272) reasons that לשׂאת, "to bear," is explicated by לכפר, "to make expiation"; i.e., the priests bore the guilt of the congregation by performing the expiating blood rites for them, not by eating the flesh of the offering (so Kiuchi, 47).

Therefore, on this day when Moses discovered that the surviving priests had not eaten the purification offering, which was both their privilege and their obligation, he became angry at Eleazar and Ithamar. Milgrom (*SCTT,* 74) claims that the priests' eating the purification offering was a bold step against magical and demonic practices; Moses was so angry because it appeared that the newly ordained priests were afraid to eat this kind of meat, in a way thereby renouncing the distinction of Israel's worship. Rashi (41) comments that Moses showed his anger toward Aaron's two sons out of deference to Aaron. Nevertheless, Aaron, acting as a responsible father, took up the defense of his sons and himself, offering Moses a reasonable response. He explained that his eating of that offering in light of the terrible events of that day would not be pleasing to Yahweh. Rashi (42a) points out further that Eleazar and Ithamar showed constraint and respect both for family authority and for Moses by letting their father reply. That Eleazar had the ability to speak eloquently is seen in the incident in Num 31:21–24. Moses accepted Aaron's reasoning.

Kiuchi takes another course to explain Aaron's position (*Purification Offering,* 77–85). He reasons that Aaron refused to eat this meat because of the guilt that he bore on account of his sons' sin (cf. Num 18:1). He cites as support for this position the contrast between the congregation's mourning after this incident (v 6b) and their great joy when the divine fire fell and consumed the first sacrifices, indicating their being in a situation opposite to that described in 9:24. But here, according to Kiuchi, Aaron was aware that he, the high priest, stood in need of atonement to remove this guilt. He was also perplexed as to what steps to take in order to remove this guilt from himself and his house, for no rituals like those prescribed for the Day of Atonement (chap. 16) had yet been given. Kiuchi then goes on to argue that the ritual to remove the high priest's guilt is found in the ancient layer of the ritual of the Day of Atonement.

Kiuchi is correct that ancient Israelites had a corporate understanding of guilt. A patriarch bore responsibility for the failures of members of his family. Corporate guilt, nevertheless, varied in relationship to the nature of the sin committed by a member of the family. In this case Aaron's sons had acted so blatantly on their own that Aaron's responsibility was minimal. While Aaron bore some responsibility as head of his house, that responsibility manifested itself in his abstaining from some of his privileges as high priest and his mourning the death of sons rather than in his sensing the need for a new ritual to expiate his and his house's sin as Kiuchi proposes. That is, there is no causal connection between Aaron's anguish in chap. 10 and the regulation given in chap. 16 for making expiation for the sins of Aaron and his house.

This incident stands in marked contrast to the tragedy at the beginning of this chapter. It is recorded to illustrate that the priests have some freedom in applying the regulations to daily situations as long as their interpretation does not tarnish God's holiness. Furthermore, it illustrates how the priests are to resolve disputes about the law. Two prominent priests debated the issue, with the one convincing the other as to the proper response on the basis of a sound argument. The remarkable feature of this account is that the lesser figure, Aaron, persuaded the greater figure, Moses. Thus a dispute about the law is to be resolved by sound judgment presented in open discussion rather than by one person's vaunting of authority. This incident also reveals that Aaron, though he could not formally mourn the death of his sons, felt the pain of their loss deeply and expressed his mourning in a quiet, but definitive manner. The concession made to Aaron shows that Yahweh is not unsympathetic to human sorrow caused by his judgment against wickedness.

Explanation

God is a holy God. In all matters the people must act responsibly toward that holiness. Worship must be done reverently according to the decrees and according to correct procedures. And God is to be honored and praised in the pattern of one's daily living. That which is true for the laity is truer for the priests. The priests must never violate the sanctity of the holy place. Any such violation results in death. On this occasion Nadab and Abihu, Aaron's oldest sons, lost their lives in offering alien or illicit fire. As a result of their disobedience, their families also lost their position as priests in Israel.

The incident of Nadab and Abihu has some parallel to the death of Ananias and Sapphira (Acts 5:1–11). Both parties instantly died in the presence of God for violating his holiness. Both incidents are recounted at the inception of a covenant between God and his people. These accounts serve as a warning that all who are members of the covenant community serve the Holy God. They cannot lie to him or worship him in a way that is improper. There can be no deception or manipulation in serving God.

Furthermore, the account of Nadab and Abihu underscores the principle that whoever wishes to be close to God must not let enthusiasm overcome discipline and discretion in worship. Those who serve God must be ever mindful that judgment begins with those who minister at his house (1 Pet 4:17). Each one will be held accountable according to the standard he holds and for the skills he has been given (Matt 7:2; Luke 6:37–38).

The law forbids the priests from drinking wine or strong drink while on duty. They were not to dull their alertness in any way lest they violate the sacred even accidentally. Nor were they permitted to induce a state of ecstasy with the help of strong drink. A similar standard is set forth in the NT. Believers are to be alert, faithful, and attentive to prayers (Eph 6:18; 1 Pet 1:13; 4:7; 1 Tim 2:8). Paul exhorts, "Do not get drunk with wine, for that is debauchery; but be filled with the Spirit" in order to minister to one another with songs of praise (Eph 5:18–20; cf. 1 Thess 5:7–8). Likewise the leaders of the church, such as bishops and deacons, must be temperate (1 Tim 3:3, 8).

The priests had the responsibility of distinguishing between the holy and the common, between that which was ritually clean and that which was ritually unclean. They also had the great responsibility of both teaching the people the decrees contained in the law and interpreting the multiple decrees in relation to specific issues put to them by the laity. That is, they guided the people in the application of the law to daily living. The laity thus were dependent on the priests' keen insight in order to guide them in the way that would be most pleasing to God. To be effective teachers and judges on cultic matters, the priests had to be alert, not having their minds dulled by strong drink.

At the close of this day, Moses remembered that portions of the purification offering were to be eaten by the priests. But to his consternation he discovered that the goat of the purification offering had been burned. He became angry at Aaron and his surviving sons. Aaron responded by pointing out that the events of the day had greatly saddened him. Therefore, he believed that God would not be pleased if he and his sons ate from the purification offering. Aaron's explanation reveals that he had acted responsibly in this matter. He had not resisted God's commands but had acted out of an inner sense that his behavior honored God, even though it was a technical violation of the ritual decrees. Moses accepted Aaron's reasoning and left the matter alone.

The tension between Aaron's deviation from the regulations with God's approval and the deviation of his sons, resulting in God's immediate and final judgment, sets forth the teaching that there are proper and improper ways to deviate from a given regulation. The regulations are standards set to honor God and to promote his holiness. Any alteration of a standard that dishonors God will be confronted by God's consuming holiness. The priests then are to guard themselves from blatantly violating the sacred. However, any variation based on sound reason backed by the motivation to give glory to God is tolerable and acceptable.

III. Laws on Ritual Purity (11:1–15:33)

Form/Structure/Setting

Lev 11–15 is a series of instructions governing ritual purity. The order of their arrangement is based on two principles. The first is an ascending order in the length of time of uncleanness, from a few hours for eating unclean food (chap. 11) to several weeks for parturition (chap. 12) to a possible lifetime for one stricken with a grievous skin disease (chaps. 13–14). The second principle is an inclusio. In chaps. 11–14 the length of time that something makes a person unclean ascends; then chap. 15 presents types of uncleanness caused by a discharge from the genitals that correspond to each of the varying lengths of uncleanness:

A.	Dietary instructions	chap. 11	hours
B.	Parturition	chap. 12	months
C.	Defiling growths on skin, garments, and walls of houses	chaps. 13–14	years
D.	Discharges from genitals	chap. 15	hours/a week/years

The instructions of ritual purity come after the sacrificial regulations (chaps. 1–7), for this corpus gives directions for the presentation of specific kinds of sacrifices on three occasions: the cleansing of a new mother (12:6, 8), the ritual of aggregation for one who had recovered from a grievous skin disease (14:1–32), and the sacrificial requirements for a man or a woman who had recovered from an abnormal discharge (15:14–15, 29–30). These instructions for making specific sacrifices assume the sacrificial legislation found in chaps. 1–7.

Furthermore, the role of the priests presented in 10:10–11 foreshadows the link between chaps. 11–15 and chaps. (17) 18–26. The priests were to distinguish between הקדש, "the holy," and החל, "the common," and between הטמא, "the unclean," and הטהור, "the clean." The material in chaps. (17) 18–26 addresses the distinction between the holy and the common, while the material in chaps. 11–15 treats the distinction between the clean and the unclean. Thus the decrees, instructions, and exhortations found in chaps. 11–15, (17) 18–26 may all be identified as priestly instructions for the people to live in a way that was pleasing to the Holy God. As for the regulations on ritual purity, the people had to be informed about God's standards lest they enter the area of the sanctuary while unclean and be consumed by the divine holiness as were Nadab and Abihu (10:1–3).

The close tie between these instructions about uncleanness and the laws on holy living found in chaps. (17) 18–25 surfaces in the dietary instructions (chap. 11). At the end of that section there is an exhortation for the people to follow the dietary laws as a means to sanctify themselves so that they might be holy (11:44–45). This exhortation is grounded in the divine self-proclamation אני יהוה, "I am Yahweh," which is found often throughout chaps. 18–25. Perhaps at one time these dietary laws were a part of the laws on holy living; this possibility is supported by the reference to distinguishing clean/unclean animals in 20:25–

26. Moreover, the parallel passage on dietary instructions in Deut 14:3–20(21) is preceded and concluded by the stated purpose that Israel is to be a holy people (vv 2, 21a*α*). Thus these instructions about ritual purity are closely connected with the laws for holy living found in chaps. (17) 18–26.

These two sets of instructions, on cleanness and holy living, surround the key chapter of Leviticus, which regulates the Day of Atonement (chap. 16). In fact, the instructions on ritual purity interrupt the narrative frame of the priestly material, as is evidenced by the opening verses of chap. 16, which mention the tragic death of Nadab and Abihu, recounted in chap. 10. These instructions about ritual purity, however, necessarily precede the ritual for the Day of Atonement, for they make intelligible a key purpose of that ritual, the purification of the whole cultic center from the people's uncleanness (16:16, 19, 33). That is, the uncleanness resulting from the failures of the people and their routine activities that made them unclean not only rendered each party involved unclean for a time, but that uncleanness was drawn to the tabernacle and the altar, threatening to make them unclean (cf. Milgrom, "Israel's Sanctuary: The Priestly Picture of Dorian Gray," *SCTT,* 75–89). The sacrifices of the Day of Atonement removed all such threatening uncleanness from the people and from the tabernacle in order that the cult might be empowered to function effectively.

These instructions then are for the priest to teach the people in matters of ritual purity and holy living. Positively expressed, the priests had the duty to teach the people how to conduct their lives and how to make themselves clean for worship at the tabernacle. But one may ask why did the people need to know all these details? It was because families had to govern themselves in their observance of these regulations on ritual purity. It was the responsibility of the head of the family to make certain that the members of his family were ritually clean so that they might confidently approach the altar. Similarly, family members had to know the regulations about skin diseases in order to know when a growth on a family member's skin obligated the family to take that person to a priest for an examination. Since the priests did not function as police, compliance with these standards was the responsibility of the elders of each tribe. Therefore, these regulations had to be general knowledge for widespread adherence to be a reality among each generation of the people of God and to guarantee God's continual presence among the people.

Excursus: Ritual Purity

Bibliography

André, G., and **Ringgren, H.** "טָמֵא *ṭāmēʾ*." *TDOT* 5:330–42. **Booth, R. P.** *Jesus and the Laws of Purity: Tradition History and Legal History in Mark 7.* JSNTSup 13. Sheffield: JSOT Press, 1986. **Carroll, M. P.** "One More Time: Leviticus Revisited." *Archives européennes de sociologie* 19 (1978) 339–46 (=*Anthropological Approaches to the Old Testament.* Ed. B. Lang. Philadelphia: Fortress, 1985. 117–26). **Childs, B.** "The Role of the Ritual and Purity Laws." In *Old Testament Theology in a Canonical Context.* Philadelphia: Fortress, 1985. 84–91. **Döller, J.** *Die Reinheits—und Speisegesetze des Alten Testaments in religionsgeschichtlicher Beleuchtung.* ATA 7/2–3. Münster: Verlag der aschendorffschen Verlagsbuchhandlung, 1917. **Douglas, M.** *Purity and Danger.* London: Routledge & Kegan Paul, 1966. **Eilberg-Schwartz, H.** "Creation and Classification in Judaism: From Priestly to Rabbinic Conceptions." *HR* 26

(1987) 357–81. **Ellen, R. F.,** and **Reason, D.** *Classifications in Their Social Context.* London: Academic Press, 1979. **Feldman, E.** *Biblical and Post-Biblical Defilement and Mourning: Law as Theology.* The Library of Jewish Law and Ethics. New York: Yeshiva UP; KTAV, 1977. 3–76. **Frymer-Kensky, T.** "Pollution, Purification, and Purgation in Biblical Israel." In *The Word of the Lord Shall Go Forth.* Ed. C. Meyers and M. O'Connor. FS D. N. Freedman. Winona Lake, IN: Eisenbrauns, 1983. 399–414. **Gispen, W. H.** "The Distinction between Clean and Unclean." *OTS* 5 (1948) 190–96. **Grunfeld, D. I.** *The Jewish Dietary Laws.* London: Soncino, 1972. **Hartley, J. E.** "Clean and Unclean." *ISBE* rev. 1:718–23. **Hauck, F.,** and **Meyer, R.** "*καθαρός.*" *TDNT* 3:414–31. **Hübner, U.** "Schweine, Schweineknochen und ein Speiseverbot im Alten Israel." *VT* 39 (1989) 225–36. **Kaufmann, Y.** *The Religion of Israel.* Chicago: The University of Chicago Press, 1960. 55–58, 103–8. **Milgrom, J.** "The Biblical Dietary Laws as an Ethical System." *Int* 17 (1963) 288–301 (=*SCTT,* 104–18). ———. "The Graduated *ḥaṭṭāʾt* of Leviticus 5:1–13." *JAOS* 103 (1983) 249–54. **Moyer, J.** *Concept of Ritual Purity among the Hittites.* Ann Arbor: University of Michigan Microfilms, 1969. **Paschen, W.** *Rein und Unrein: Untersuchung zur biblischen Wortgeschicte.* SANT 24. Munich: Kösel-Verlag, 1970. **Ringgren, H.** "טָהֵר *ṭāhar.*" *TDOT* 5:287–96. **Schapiro, D.** *L'Hygiene alimentaire des Juifs devant la science moderne.* Paris: Erelji, 1930. **Stein, S.** "The Dietary Laws in Rabbinic & Patristic Literature." *Studia Patristica.* Texte und Untersuchungen zur Geschicte der altchristliche Literatur 64. 2 (1957) 141–54. **Toombs, L. E.** "Clean and Unclean." *IDB* 1:641–48. **Vaux, R. de.** "Les sacrifices de porcs en Palestine et dans l'Ancient Orient." BZAW 77 (1958) 250–65. **Wright, D. P.** *The Disposal of Impurity in the Priestly Writings of the Bible with Reference to Similar Phenomena in Hittite and Mesopotamian Cultures.* Ann Arbor: University of Michigan Microfilms, 1984.

Also see *Bibliography* to chap. 11.

The Concept of Clean and Unclean

Ritual purity was a vital dimension of daily life in ancient Israel. Decrees regarding ritual purity are found throughout the priestly legislation of the Pentateuch, but the core legislation comes in Lev 11–15. In these chapters cleanness and uncleanness are regulated in regard to meats (chap. 11), births (chap. 12), skin diseases and growths in garments and on walls of a house (chap. 13–14), and bodily emissions (chap. 15). It is the duty of the priests to instruct the people in these rules of ritual purity, interpret specific rules as they apply to complex situations, and inspire compliance.

The standard of ritual purity in the OT is built on the view of God's holiness and of human earthly existence being under the curse of death (cf. Paschen, *Rein und Unrein,* 63–64, 195; André and Ringgren, *TDOT* 5:331). Observance of ritual purity promotes a life blessed by God, while impurity points to death. Indeed the severest impurity results from contact with a corpse and from grievous skin diseases that foreshadow death. The laws of ritual purity teach the people how to govern their living in such a world so that they may approach the holy God at the sanctuary.

The key verse in the cultic legislation regarding ritual purity tells the priests, "You are to distinguish between the holy and the common, and between the unclean and the clean" (Lev 10:10). The poles are holy/common (קדש/חל) and clean/unclean (טהר/טמא). These two sets of terms, while overlapping, are not identical. Being clean does not make something holy, but what is holy is always clean. The one who is clean may encounter the holy without danger. While cleanness is noncommunicable, uncleanness is readily transmitted (cf. Hag 2:12–14). Nevertheless, there is no harm in becoming unclean inadvertently or from normal behavior. Becoming unclean is not a threatening situation. Parenthetically, uncleanness in the normal course of life is used metaphorically for sin, but the ordinary ways of becoming ritually unclean are not from sinful acts. While some sinful acts, particularly sexual sins and idolatry, are considered to be polluting, there is no unified teaching in the OT that breaking other decrees simultaneously makes the offender ritually unclean. In fact, in the prophets it is apparent that many who had sinned grievously in matters of injustice were still ritually pure and thus able to participate fully in the ceremonies at the sanctuary (cf. Isa 58:1–9a). In any case the primary danger with becoming unclean exists in approaching an area that is holy while unclean. The holy is dynamic, consuming whatever in its presence is unclean. Moreover, becoming unclean is not a matter to be taken casually, for if a person does not properly cleanse himself, that failure becomes an intentional act of disobedience against God.

Some types of uncleanness, such as eating from an unclean animal, can be avoided, while other types, such as from menses, cannot. In matters of choice a devout ancient Israelite sought to follow these laws. Nevertheless, unavoidable causes of uncleanness frequently made a devout person unclean.

A person becomes clean again by a ritual process, which varies according to the nature of the uncleanness. In the mildest cases, a person washes himself and waits until sunset, the beginning of a new day for the Israelites, while in the worst case, recovery from a grievous skin disease, that person has to wash several times and offer a series of sacrifices over a period of days before becoming clean (Lev 14:1–32). These different ways of becoming clean attest that there are degrees of uncleanness.

A primary purpose of the laws of ritual purity then is for each person to prepare himself, making himself clean, before he goes to the sanctuary to worship Yahweh. Morally frail humans could not enter the sanctuary presumptuously, lest the consuming holiness of God destroy them. That is, each person and each family have to be conscious of their daily living so that they might take the necessary steps to be clean in order to enter the sanctuary. The laws of ritual purity keep the people mindful of the wide gulf that separates a sinful people from the holy God, and yet they speak of God's grace in providing a way for sinful, frail humans to prepare themselves to bridge that gulf and enter into his presence. In the same direction, these regulations guard against either bringing anything that belongs basically to earthly existence or the common into the holy area or incorporating such earthly practices into the worship of Yahweh. They also produce in the people a deeper comprehension of the confession that Yahweh is the Holy One of Israel.

EXPLANATIONS OF RITUAL PURITY

Various proposals

Numerous proposals have been put forth to account for these standards of clean and unclean. Most of these explanations address themselves to one dimension of ritual purity such as the dietary laws, rather than to the overall pattern. Six of these explanations will be mentioned:

(1) A frequent explanation for the dietary laws is that they promote good health through a proper diet; e.g., pork often carries trichinosis and rabbits tularemia. R. Harrison has skillfully defended this view in his commentary on Leviticus (121–26). Even though it has widespread support, it is difficult to accept. Knowledge about the connections of a particular disease with a specific meat is the result of modern science. It is doubtful that ancient Israelites had discovered the relationship between certain symptoms of illness and the eating of pork. Moreover, wild boars seldom have trichinosis, and proper cooking of pork makes the disease rare. The evidence that Israel's neighbors ate pork indicates that they knew ways to prepare and cook this meat to decrease any ill effects. Conversely, some ruminants also are a host for parasite organisms (Harrison, 126). The greatest obstacle to the health interpretation is that the NT removes all distinctions between edible and inedible animals. This change is based on the teachings of Jesus and the apostles (Mark 7:14–20; Acts 10:9–16). It

is inconceivable that God would do away with rules he had given to promote good health.

Nevertheless, close adherence to all the laws of ritual purity certainly promoted the community's health, especially in antiquity. Frequent washings, separation from dead bodies of every kind, and the disposal of all that was unclean in an unclean place outside the area of habitation struck a mighty blow against a host of diseases and plagues. The health benefits, however, were a by-product of the purity laws save for their testimony to the belief that Yahweh is the Giver of life, not death.

(2) Another way to view these laws is that they carry symbolic significance. Stein ("Dietary Laws," 144–46) traces this type of interpretation back to Pseudo-Aristeas, the High Priest Eleazar, and Philo, who all wrote before Christ. Philo, for example, writes, "For just as a cud-chewing animal after biting through the food keeps it at rest in the gullet, again after a bit draws it up and masticates it and then passes it on to the belly, so the pupil after receiving from the teacher through his ears the principles and lore of wisdom prolongs the process of learning, as he cannot at once apprehend and grasp them securely, till by using memory to call up each thing that he has heard by constant exercises which act as the cement of conceptions, he stamps a firm impression of them on his soul. But the firm apprehension of conceptions is clearly useless unless we discriminate and distinguish them so that we can choose what we should choose and avoid the contrary, and this distinguishing is symbolized by the parted hoof. For the way of life is twofold, one branch leading to vice, the other to virtue and we must turn away from the one and never forsake the other" ("The Special Laws," 4:107-9 in *Philo*, tr. F. Colson, Loeb Classical Library [Cambridge, MA: Harvard UP, 1960] 8:73, 75). Although the NT did not take this approach to the issues of clean and unclean, it was taken up by the early church fathers, as the *Letter to Barnabas* attests. This method of allegorical interpretation has continued until modern times. Bonar (208) says, for example, that the association of pigs with mire reminds one of the filth of iniquity. While clean and unclean symbolize moral purity and sin respectively, there is no textual support to find typological figures in the specific habits of the various animals.

(3) Abandoning any attempt to discover a rationale for the purity laws, several interpreters hold the position that they are solely arbitrary decrees (e.g., Maimonides, *Mishnah Torah, The Book of Cleanness* viii. *Immersion Pools* 11:12. *The Code of Maimonides, Book Ten. The Book of Cleanness*, tr. H. Danby [New Haven: Yale UP 1954] 535 as cited by Neusner, *The Idea of Purity*, 7).

(4) An intriguing view has been recently put forth by J. Milgrom (*SCTT*, 104–18). He argues that the system of dietary laws was instituted to prevent humans from degenerating into random killers. These laws ingrained in the covenant people a deep reverence for life by reducing the number of edible animals to a few, requiring humane manner of slaughter, and prohibiting the partaking of blood (*SCTT*, 110). While ancient Israelites were permitted to hunt for food, they were discouraged from hunting for the glory of killing game indiscriminately, as has been the sport of many gentile peoples. Thus the dietary laws teach reverence for life (*SCTT*, 113, 115–18).

(5) B. Levine has taken another approach (*In the Presence of the Lord*, 55–91). He believes that impurity is an active demonic force endangering both the community and the deity at the sanctuary. The blood rites performed at the sanctuary then are apotropaic rites necessary both to cleanse the cultic objects and personnel and to protect Yahweh from these evil forces. To support this interpretation Levine has to interpret the biblical material in light of evidence drawn from the cultic systems of Israel's neighbors. The major difficulty with his position is that the scriptures never portray impurity as a demonic force.

(6) Social anthropologists look for a comprehensive, unifying view to account for the laws of ritual purity. The most complete view that has found acclaim has been put forth by M. Douglas in *Purity and Danger*. This view will be discussed below.

A possible explanation

While interpreters enjoy speculating about the reason for the purity laws, the biblical text gives few reasons for the particular standards. Nevertheless it states that the main reason for the purity instructions was to keep Israel separate from the neighboring nations in order to promote God's call for Israel to be a holy nation (20:24, 26; 18:3). Close adherence to these regulations thus guarded the Israelites from following the immoral customs of their neighbors and from incorporating pagan rites into their worship of Yahweh. The dietary laws in particular made it difficult for Israelites to fellowship at the same table with their neighbors and blocked their participation in festivals to foreign gods (cf. 11:44–45; Deut 14:2, 21).

Indeed, the laws of ritual purity distinguished that which was holy and appropriate for use in the worship of God from that which was common and thus relegated solely to the realm of earthly existence. Among matters classified as common are included some of the most essential aspects of human existence, such as sexual intercourse, parturition, and burial. Participation in any of these activities rendered a person unclean. That does not mean that the purity laws demeaned these practices in any way. Rather they prevented any of them from taking place in the area of the sanctuary; that is, nothing associated with these vital areas of life could ever be used as an approach to worship. Specifically fertility rites were never to be a means of worshiping Yahweh, and sex could not be deified as it was in polytheism. The potent uncleanness caused by a corpse plus the strict standards for the priests about touching a corpse and mourning the deceased struck a fatal blow against ancestral worship and any veneration of the dead that bordered on worship. Thus the laws of ritual purity guided Israel in taking the correct approach in seeking Yahweh.

These ideas move us to consider Douglas's analysis. Her work presents the most comprehensive system to account for the vast variety of laws on ritual purity. She works from the premise that the laws of purity/impurity are broad categories by which a society gives structure to its world. In Israel the standards of purity bear witness "to the Holy as wholeness and completeness" (*Purity,* 51). They provide a host of symbols ingraining in the people's minds the wholeness, purity, and unity of God (57). Since "holiness is unity, integrity, perfection," only animals that are complete, without defect, may be sacrificed. Similarly only priests who are whole may serve at the altar. For a pastoral people cud-chewing animals with a split hoof are proper for food (*Purity,* 54–55). But those animals that have only one of these characteristics or neither of them are imperfect and hence unclean. Among fish, fowl, and insects, the clean are those that use a means of propulsion appropriate to the sphere in which they live (*Purity,* 55). Fish must have scales and fins. Fowl hop on two legs and fly with wings. She proposes that the reason for the birds enumerated as unclean resides in their nature to dive and swim, in addition to their flying, making them "not fully birdlike" (*Purity,* 56–57). Regarding four-footed flying creatures, they are unclean because they mix the spheres in which they live (*Purity,* 55–56). Animals that swarm, regardless of the sphere in which they live, are unclean because such movement is contrary to holiness (*Purity,* 56). "Swarming things are neither fish, flesh nor fowl. Eels and worms inhabit water, though not as fish; reptiles go on dry land, though not as quadrupeds; some insects fly, though not as birds" (*Purity,* 56). Of all explanations put forth, this system is the most comprehensive and most appealing.

Carroll accepts that the premise by which Douglas accounts for ritual purity is insightfully valid, but he finds wanting her position that the animals classified as unclean are those that do not employ the means of locomotion distinctive to their classification. Nevertheless, he concedes that her accounting for the distinction of clean/unclean among the "water animals" is consistent with the textual description (Carroll, "One More Time," 118–19). Conversely, her explanation for categorizing various "flying animals," "land animals," and "swarming things" as unclean lacks precision. Setting forth another hypothesis, Carroll (120–25) points out that the nexus is nature (animals)/culture (humans). Animals that invade culture are thus taboo. Since, in his judgment, only humans are permitted to eat meat (Gen 9:3), those animals and birds that eat meat are classified as unclean. To account for the list of flying insects, he expands this explanation to include those insects that bite, such as gnats, or sting, such as bees, or harm culture, such as moths, since they eat garments and destroy objects made by humans.

Based on the manner in which Carroll and Douglas account for the function of ritual purity within a society, the nexus may be between life (order)/death (disorder) (cf. Feldman, *Defilement and Mourning,* 31–76). The majority of animals forbidden as food are scavengers, carnivores, or eaters of carrion. Another class of forbidden animals is those associated with the barren wilderness and ruins, like the wild boar and the birds of prey, the very places the ancients considered to be the abode of demons. Also unclean are animals that live in the ground and are thereby associated with the realm of the dead (cf. W. Kornfeld, *Kairos* 7 [1965] 146–47). For example, Isa 65:2–7 (cf. 66:17) recounts that Israelites held seances at night among the tombs, eating pork and broth made from unclean animals. While Douglas correctly notes that the text does not state that these animals are unclean because of their role in the occult (*Purity,* 55), this explanation, nevertheless, accords with her position that things classified as unclean symbolize that which is imperfect, incomplete, chaotic. Furthermore, sorcery, witchcraft, and necromancy belong to that same arena and thus are an anathema. They delve into the fearful and chaotic dimensions of existence (*Purity,* 102). This explains why every kind of sorcery is categorically condemned in the laws for holy living (19:26, 31; 20:6). It is not going astray then to claim that the regulations governing ritual purity are designed to prevent the practice of sorcery by declaring unclean those animals that symbolize a confusion of classes, ugliness, and desolation, the very symbols loved by wizards and sorcerers. In the same vein grievous skin diseases make one unclean for they foreshadow death; they signal that life is being eaten out of a person. Similarly, grievous growths in garments and buildings eventually destroy those objects. Bodily discharges are not repulsive enough to be categorized with death, but, if they are not dealt with properly, they spawn the forces of death. So also the loss of blood at menses makes one unclean, both because blood is taboo (cf. 17:11) and because loss of blood robs one of strength or life's power. Contact with carcasses makes one unclean until evening (11:24–28), while contact with a corpse makes one unclean for seven days (Num 19:11–13). There is a special ritual that requires being sprinkled with a special solution on the third and seventh days after contacting a corpse in order to become clean (Num 19:14–19). Thus death or any of its foreshadowings is the basis of the concept of uncleanness.

Feldman *(Defilement and Mourning)* writes clearly on this point:

> Death represents the *absence* of God and the absence of *qedusha*: it is *tum᾽ah.* And *tum᾽ah* and *qedusha* can have no relationship with one another (59).
>
> Once life is removed and death enters, holiness is removed and *tum᾽ah* enters. The void left by the departure of *qedushah* is now filled by the forces of *tum᾽ah.* These new forces of death and *tum᾽ah* are now, in their own realm, as powerful as life and *qedushah* once were in their own realm. *Qedushah* and *tum᾽ah,* then, are two sides of a coin. On one side, man combined with God (life) is holy; on the obverse, man without God (death) is *tamé* (65).

Therefore, that which is clean accords with life, health, and holiness, while that which is unclean accords with death, illness, and the profane. The sociological approach to these laws on ritual purity renders them more comprehensible to contemporary people.

Daily observance of the purity rituals was a tremendous force in the social and the spiritual development of Israel. They promoted the solidarity of the Israelites. Moreover, faithful observance encouraged the spiritual development of the people by ingraining obedience to God deep in the consciousness of every devout Israelite (cf. Milgrom, "Ethics and Ritual," 186–91). As Douglas says, "By rules of avoidance holiness was given a physical expression in every encounter with the animal kingdom and at every meal" (*Purity,* 57). Faithfulness in the small matters of the law fostered an attitude of loyal love to God that equipped a person to withstand strong temptation to wrongdoing. Thus observance of ritual purity sensitized each person's moral and spiritual awareness. It set their course to pursue spiritual values over personal ease and material gain.

SYMBOLIC USE OF CLEAN/UNCLEAN IN THE OT

Often in the OT clean and unclean symbolize morality (cf. Eccl 9:2). The phrase "clean hands" parallels "a pure heart" in Ps 24:4 (cf. Job 17:9). Clean hands mean that one is both ceremonially clean and has faithfully done God's commands. Conversely, defiled hands mean that one has aggressively broken the law (Isa 59:3). Isaiah speaks of doing good as making oneself clean (1:16). Conversely, hypocritical righteousness is compared to a person's being unclean and to a polluted garment (Isa 64:5[6]). According to Neusner (*The Idea of Purity,* 15), the metaphorical uses of clean/unclean or pure/impure make no attempt to tie into the specific laws of ritual purity. Rather these terms serve as powerful symbols of the moral dimension of human action, which is rooted in motivation. He identifies several ways in which terms of clean/unclean are employed for moral behavior (13–15). First, God loathes impurity. In Ezek 14:11 those who stray from God defile themselves with their transgressions, and in Ezek 20:26 God himself defiles or rejects Israel for her untrue worship (cf. Hag 2:11–14). Second, idolatry is an especially pungent pollutant (Jer 2:23; 19:13; Ezek 23:30; 36:18, 25; Ps 106:38–39). Therefore, whenever God renews Israel, he removes their idols and cleanses the people (Ezek 37:23). To be cleansed from iniquity is to be forgiven (Jer 33:8; Ezek 36:33; cf. Ps 51:4[2]; Ringgren, *TDOT* 5:295). Third, illicit sexual relations are very defiling (Lev 18; 20; Jer 13:27; Ezek 23:17; 33:26; 43:7; Ps 106:39). Fourth, both witchcraft and the shedding of innocent blood are terribly defiling (Lev 18:21; 20:2–6, 27; Ps 106:37–39; Jer 19:4–5; Ezek 16:17–22; 24:8–11; cf. Deut 19:10; Isa 65:2–7).

Pollution from immorality has devastating effects on Israel's covenant relationship with Yahweh. Many texts in the OT depict Israel's woeful indulgence in immorality and idolatry as polluting the land (e.g., Lev 18:24–30; 20:22–23; Deut 21:23; Jer 2:7; Ezek 22:24; Mic 2:10), her inheritance under the covenant (e.g., Gen 15:17–21). This pollution makes the land infertile (Hos 4:3; Isa 24:4–8). When the land becomes too polluted, it can no longer support its inhabitants. It vomits them out. Then for Israel to return to her homeland, both she and her land must be cleansed or purified (Isa 4:4). In the ideal age nothing unclean will enter the holy city (Isa 35:8; 52:1; cf. Rev 21:27); therefore, Israel will never again be under the threat of judgment.

RITUAL PURITY AND THE NT

The NT abolishes the laws of ritual purity. Paul says, "I know and am persuaded in the Lord Jesus that nothing is unclean in itself; but it is unclean for anyone who thinks it unclean" (Rom 14:14; cf. Titus 1:15). Jesus condemned the Pharisees for having forgotten the weightier matters of the law while they scrupulously practiced ritual purity (Matt 23:23–28; cf. Luke 11:37–41). He compared them to whitewashed tombs, full of deadmen's bones and all uncleanness (Matt 23:27). In light of OT standards, his criticism could scarcely be any more scathing. There is a threefold reason for doing away with ritual purity. First, Jesus inaugurated a new order which touches every aspect of life, leading to a totally redeemed life for all of nature as his resurrection promises (Rom 8:19–23). Second, Jesus broke down the barrier of separation between the Jew and the Gentile. Doing away with the laws of ritual purity symbolized his great liberating accomplishment (Eph 2:11–21). Since God purifies the heart by faith, all believers, both Jew and Gentile, are clean before him (Acts 15:8–9; cf. 10:9–16, 34–35). Only the sacrament of baptism is kept by the church as an expression of this inward transformation (Rom 6:3–11; Eph 5:26). Third, the NT church has no central sanctuary that must be guarded from the impurities of this world, for the old sanctuary has been replaced by spiritual worship (John 2:19–20; 4:20–24; Mark 14:58) centered in the heavenly Temple (Heb 9:11–12; cf. R. Brown, *The Gospel according to John I–XII*, AB 29 [Garden City, NY: Doubleday, 1979] 124–25).

The NT continues to employ the terms "clean/unclean" and "defilement" to describe moral behavior. Defilement symbolizes sin, especially the corrupt nature of the heart. Jesus taught that what comes out of the heart, i.e., evil thoughts, distorted passions, and pride, defiles a person, not what enters his mouth (Mark 7:14–23; Matt 15:17–20). Paul uses *ἀκαθαρσία*, "uncleanness," for the immorality practiced by the Gentiles (Rom 6:19; 2 Cor 12:21; Eph 4:19; 5:3, 5; 1 Thess 4:7; Hauck, *TDNT* 3:428–29). This uncleanness alienates the Gentiles from God (Rom 1:24–25; Eph 4:17–19). Therefore, Paul exhorts all believers, "Cleanse ourselves from every defilement of body and spirit," for then we "make holiness perfect in the fear of God" (2 Cor 7:1). The one who walks in the light of Jesus is cleansed from all sin (1 John 1:7, 9; cf. Heb 1:3). The word of God is the instrument of this inner cleansing (John 15:3; cf. Eph 5:26). A pure heart and a clear conscience are the goal of each believer (Matt 5:8; 1 Tim 1:5; 3:9; 2 Tim 1:3; 2:22). This purity is expressed in sincere, energetic love of one another, not in adherence to a list of rules (1 Pet 1:22; cf. Titus 2:14; Heb 9:14).

A. *Instructions on the Classification of Animals as Clean and Unclean (11:1–47)*

Bibliography

Bare, G. *Plants and Animals of the Bible.* London: United Bible Societies, 1969. **Cansdale, G.** *Animals of Bible Lands.* England: Paternoster, 1970. **Douglas, M.** "Deciphering a Meal." *Daedalus* 101 (1972) 61–81 (=*Implicit Meanings.* London: Routledge & Kegan Paul, 1975. 249–75). ————. *Purity and Danger.* London: Routledge & Kegan Paul, 1966. **Driver, G. R.** "Birds in the OT: I. Birds in Law." *PEQ* 87 (1955) 5–20. ————. "Birds in OT: II. Birds in Life." *PEQ* 87 (1955) 129–40. **Fink, E.** "Essai d'explication d'un passage du Lévitique." *REJ* 63 (1912) 121–23. **Jirku, A.** "Leviticus 11:29–33 im Lichte der Ugarit-Forschung." *ZAW* 84 (1972) 348. **Khalifé, L.** "Étude sur l'histoire rédactionelle des deux textes parallèles: Lv 11 et Dt 14, 1–21. *Melto* 2 (1966) 57–72. **Kornfeld, W.** "Reine und unreinen Tiere im Alten Testament." *Kairos* 7 (1965) 134–47. **Łach, S.** "Le sacrifice *zebaḥ šᵉlāmîm.*" *Folia Orientalia* 11 (1969) 187–94. **Milgrom, J.** "Ethics and Ritual: The Foundations of the Biblical Dietary Laws." In *Religion and Law: Biblical-Judaic and Islamic Perspectives.* Ed. E. Firmage, B. Weiss, and J. Welch. Winona Lake, IN: Eisenbrauns, 1990. 159–91. **Moran, W. L.** "The Literary Connection between Lv 11,13–19 and Dt 14,18." *CBQ* 28 (1966) 271–77. **Parmelee, A.** *All the Birds of the Bible.* New York: Harper and Brothers, 1959. **Pinney, R.** *The Animals in the Bible.*

Philadelphia: Chilton Books, 1964. **Schulz, A.** “Der Hase als Wiederkräuer.” *BZ* 9 (1911) 12–17. **Simoons, J.** *Eat Not This Flesh: Food Advances in the Old World.* Madison, WI: The University of Wisconsin Press, 1961. **Trublet, J.** “Alimentation et sainteté; Lévitique 11 Deutéronome 14.” *Christus* 29 (1982) 209–17. **Vaux, R. de.** “Les sacrifices de porcs en Palestine et dans l’Ancient Orient.” BZAW 77 (1958) 250–65. **Wenham, G.** “The Theology of Unclean Foods.” *EvQ* 53 (1981) 6–15. **Wigand, K.** “Die altisraelitsche Vorstellung von unreinen Tieren.” *ARW* 17 (1914) 413–36. **Wright, D. P.** “Observations on the Ethical Foundations of the Biblical Dietary Laws: A Response to Jacob Milgrom.” In *Religion and Law: Biblical-Judaic and Islamic Perspectives.* Ed. E. Firmage, B. Weiss, and J. Welch. Winona Lake, IN: Eisenbrauns, 1990. 193–98. **Yerkes, R. K.** “The Unclean Animals of Leviticus 11 and Deuteronomy.” *JQR* n.s. 14 (1923/24) 1–29.

Translation

1 *Yahweh spoke to Moses and Aaron,*[a] 2 *“Speak to the Israelites: These are the creatures that*
you may eat from all the animals.[a] 3 *You may eat any animal that has a split hoof, divided*
into two[a] *parts,*[b] *and*[c] *chews the cud.*[d] 4 *However, you may not eat from those that only*
chew the cud or have a split hoof. The camel,[a] *although it chews the cud, does not have a*
split hoof;[b] *you are to consider it unclean.* 5 *The hyrax,*[a] *although it chews the cud, does not*
have a split hoof; you are to consider it unclean. 6 *The hare,*[a] *although it chews the cud,*
does not have a split hoof; you are to consider it unclean. 7 *The pig,*[a] *although it has a split*
hoof, completely divided, does not chew[b] *the cud; you are to consider it unclean.* 8 *You are not*[a]
to eat their meat nor come into contact with their carcasses; you are to consider them unclean.
9 *“From*[a] *all these creatures which live in water you may eat; anything that has fins*
and scales, whether in the seas[b] *or in the streams,*[c] *you may eat.* 10 *But anything that does*
not have fins and scales,[a] *whether in the seas or the streams, including any*[b] *small*
creatures in shoals or any large creatures in water,[c] *you*[d] *are to detest them.* 11 *You are to*
detest them; you are not to eat[a] *any*[b] *of their meat; you are to detest their carcasses.* 12 *You*
are to detest anything[a] *living in water that does not have fins and scales.*[b]
13 *“These*[a] *among the birds*[b] *you are to detest. They are not to be eaten;*[c] *they are detestable:*
the griffon vulture, the bearded vulture, the black vulture, 14 *the kite, every kind of buzzard,*
15 *every*[a] *kind of crow,*[b] 16 *the eagle owl, the short-eared owl, the long-eared owl,*[a] *every kind*
of hawk, 17 *the little owl, the cormorant, the long-eared screech owl,* 18 *the barn owl, the*
scops owl, the Egyptian vulture, 19 *the stork,*[a] *every kind of heron, the hoopoe,*[b] *and the bat.*
20 *“You are to detest every*[a] *flying insect that darts about.* 21 *However,*[ab] *you may eat*
some[c] *of the flying insects*[d] *that dart about: those that have jointed legs*[e] *for hopping*[f] *on*
the ground. 22 *From these*[a] *you may eat: every kind of locust, katydid, desert locust, or*
grasshopper. 23 *But*[a] *you are to detest every other flying insect that has four pair of legs.*[bc]
24 *“By these*[a] *you will make yourself unclean; whoever comes in contact with one of*
their carcasses will be unclean until the evening. 25 *Whoever picks up one of their carcasses*[a]
is to wash his clothes,[b] *and he will be unclean until the evening.*
26 *“Every*[a] *animal that has*[b] *a split hoof, but is not*[c] *divided into two parts, or does*
not chew the cud, you are to consider unclean. Whoever comes into contact with one of
them[d] *will be unclean.* 27 *You are to consider unclean every four-footed animal that goes*
on its paws; whoever comes into contact with one of their carcasses becomes unclean
until the evening. 28 *Whoever picks up their carcasses*[a] *is to wash his clothes, and he will*
be unclean until the evening. You are to consider them unclean.
29 *“The following*[a] *are very unclean*[b] *for you among the creatures crawling on the*
ground: the mole-rat, the mouse, every kind[c] *of dabb lizard;* 30 *the gecko,*[a] *the monitor*

lizard, the lizard, the skink[a] *and the chameleon.* 31*Among all*[a] *the crawling creatures these are unclean for you; whoever comes into contact with one of them after it is dead*[b] *will be unclean until evening.* 32*And anything on which one of them falls after it is dead*[a] *will be unclean: any wood vessel, clothing, leather article, sackcloth, any utensil used for work. It is to be put*[b] *in water; it will be unclean until evening; then it will be clean.* 33*Any clay vessel into which one of these falls,*[a] *everything in it will be unclean, and you are to break it.* 34*Any food*[a] *which may be eaten that has water on it will be unclean, and any drink in any vessel that may be drunk will be unclean.* 35*Whatever one of their carcasses*[a] *falls on becomes unclean. An oven or stove is to be smashed;*[b] *they are unclean. You are to consider them unclean.* 36*However, a spring*[a] *or a cistern for collecting water*[b] *remains clean. But whatever comes in contact with one of their carcasses becomes unclean.* 37*If*[a] *one of their carcasses falls on any seed for sowing, it remains clean.* 38*But if*[a] *water has been put on seed*[b] *and one of their carcasses falls on it, you are to consider it unclean.*

39 *"When*[a] *any animal*[b] *which is permissible for eating dies, whoever touches its carcass will be unclean until evening.* 40*Whoever eats from its carcass*[a] *is to wash his clothes,*[b] *and he will be unclean until the evening. Whoever picks up its carcass is to wash his clothes, and he will be unclean until the evening.*

41 *"Any creature that crawls on the ground is*[a] *detestable;*[b] *it is not to be eaten.* 42*You*[a] *may not eat any of the creatures that crawl on the ground,*[b] *whether it goes on its belly or darts about on four legs or*[c] *has many legs, for they are detestable.*[d] 43*Do*[a] *not make yourselves detestable with any of the creatures that crawl. Do not make yourselves unclean*[b] *with them or become unclean*[c] *by them* 44*because I am Yahweh your God. Sanctify yourselves*[a] *and be holy because I am holy.*[b] *Do not make yourselves unclean*[c] *by any creature that scurries on the ground* 45*because I am Yahweh,*[a] *who brought you up from the land of Egypt to be your God. You will be holy because I*[b] *am holy.*

46 *"This is the instruction concerning animals, birds, every living creature that scurries about in the water, and every creature that crawls on the earth.* 47*Its purpose is to distinguish between the unclean and the clean, and between living creatures that may be eaten*[a] *and those which may not be eaten."*[a]

Notes

1.a. LXX and Vg omit אלהם, "to them." Rarely does an indir obj stand after לאמר, "saying" (but see Gen 23:5, 14). The versions, like this Eng trans., may have simply chosen not to translate it in order to produce a better reading.

2.a. בהמה means "large land animals" and often "domesticated animals" as in 1:2.

3.a. A few Heb. mss, LXX, and Syr add שתי, "two," as in Deut 14:6. MT may have resulted from an error of omission.

3.b. These descriptions of animal characteristics use cognate accusatives: מפרסת פרסה ושסעת שסע, lit. "dividing a hoof and cleaving a cleft," and גרה לא יגר, "it does not chew its cud," in v 7.

3.c. LXX, Syr, and Vg read a copula; that may be a translator's prerogative rather than a variant Heb. text. Hoffmann (1:326) states that the phrase מעלת גרה, "chew the cud," is asyndetic in order to stress that both characteristics are necessary for an animal to be considered clean.

3.d. The dir obj in MT is a long *casus pendens* preceding the verb; it is picked up by the sign of the dir obj with a pronominal suffix.

4.a. The definite article is used to mark out a class of animals (*IBHS* §9.5.2f).

4.b. LXX adds καὶ ὀνυχιζόντων ὀνυχιστῆρας, "and having cloven hooves," as in v 3 and Deut 14:7.

5.a. Cf. n. 4.a.

6.a. Cf. n. 4.a.

7.a. Cf. n. 4.a.

7.b. For MT יגר, "it chews," a reciprocal use of the niph, Sam reads יגור, a qal impf as though from an ע"ו root, as in Deut 14:8.

8.a. The use of the negative לא with an impf has emphatic force, expecting full compliance (GKC §107o).

9.a. Some Heb. mss and the versions read a *waw* on the opening particle (את) as in vv 5–7; its absence may occur because this verse opens another section.

9.b. LXX reads a *waw* on בימים, "in the seas."

9.c. Cf. n. 3.d.

10.a. Sam and LXX add במים, "in the water." While this term could have been lost by haplography, it may have been included from the influence of its later occurrence in the verse and the nature of the following words.

10.b. This is a partitive use of the prep מן, "from" (GKC §119w, n. 2). This use of מן is frequent in this instruction.

10.c. This long phrase is a *casus pendens* to the pronominal subj of the noun clause.

10.d. LXX does not have לכם, "for you."

11.a. Cf. n. 8.a.

11.b. Cf. n. 10.b.

12.a. Many Heb. mss and the versions begin the verse with a *waw.* MT is accepted as the more unusual text.

12.b. Cf. n. 10.a.

13.a. The demonstrative pronoun after the sign of the dir obj, את־אלה, "these," anticipates the coming list of birds.

13.b. Cf. n. 10.b.

13.c. Instead of MT יֵאָכְלוּ, "it is to be eaten," Sam reads תאכלו, "you are to eat." MT is followed as the harder reading. Also cf. n. 8.a.

15.a. Many Heb. mss and the versions read a *waw* on the opening particle. The style of vv 15–20 indicates that this variant is preferable, but PIR (174) does not agree.

15.b. LXX[B*A] does not have this verse; it is also missing in Deut 14:14.

16.a. Sam and LXX add למינו, "after its kind." This phrase is used at various places throughout this list of unclean birds. It could easily have been added by influence from one of the places where it is present.

19.a. LXX reads *καὶ γλαῦκα*, "and an owl," which may stand for והתחמס, "and the short-eared owl," as in v 16 and Deut 14:15.

19.b. For MT הדוכיפת, "hoopoe," Sam reads הדגיפת.

20.a. A few Heb. mss and the versions begin the verse with a *waw.* MT is preferred, for this verse starts a new section (cf. PIR, 175).

21.a. Some mss of LXX do not have the opening אך, "surely, only, however."

21.b. The untranslated demonstrative pronoun זה, "this," anticipates the following description; cf. n. 13.a.

21.c. Cf. n. 10.b.

21.d. שרץ העוף is lit. "swarmer of the wing." This is an indefinite noun even though the gen is definite (GKC §127a, e).

21.e. This term for legs is a dual.

21.f. Many Heb. mss and Sam read בהם, "with them" (masc), in place of MT's בהן, "with them" (fem).

22.a. Cf. n. 13.a.

23.a. A few Heb. mss and LXX* do not read the beginning *waw.*

23.b. The dual indicates that the legs were considered to be in pairs (GKC §88f).

23.c. Cf. n. 10.c.

24.a. The phrase לאלה, "by these," points toward the לכל־הבהמה, "(by) every animal," in v 26 (Baentsch, 360). This phrase signals a new section.

25.a. A few Heb. mss and Syr read את־נבלתם, "their carcass(es)," as in vv 28 and 40 instead of MT's מנבלתם, "from their carcass(es)" (cf. n. 10.b.).

25.b. Sam adds ורחץ במים, "and wash with water"; cf. n. 40.b.

26.a. A few Heb. mss, LXX*, and Syr read a *waw* on the first word, לכל, "every."

26.b. The third person pronoun הוא resumes and stresses the subj (GKC §141h).

26.c. LXX does not read איננה, "there is not."

26.d. In place of בהם, "them," a few Heb. mss and LXX read בנבלתם, "their carcass(es)." MT is the harder reading. The variant makes clearer what is to be assumed from the context.

28.a. Instead of MT את־נבלתם, "their carcass(es)," Sam and LXX read מנבלתם, "one of their carcass(es)," as in n. 25.a.

29.a. The demonstrative pronoun זה, "this," anticipates the following list; cf. n. 21.c.

29.b. Baentsch (360) interprets the use of a definite adj with an indefinite noun as having superlative force (GKC §133g). To capture the force of the article, this Eng trans. uses "very."

29.c. LXX* does not have למינהו, "after its kind."

30.a. LXX does not read the *waw.*

31.a. Instead of MT בכל, "among all," Sam and LXX read מכל, "from all, some."

31.b. The inf constr after a prep forms a temporal clause with the pronominal suffix functioning as the subj.

32.a. Cf. n. 31.b.

32.b. Instead of the hoph יובא, "it was brought," Sam has יבוא, "it comes," and LXX reads βαφήσεται, "it is to be dipped."

33.a. This long phrase is a *casus pendens* for the dir obj of the verb תשברו, "break"; it is picked up by the pronominal suffix on the sign of the acc.

34.a. LXX reads a *waw* at the beginning of the verse.

35.a. Cf. n. 10.b.

35.b. The versions read a pl verb for MT יתץ, "it is to be broken," because the subj is compound. While this may fit the demands of translation, the variant is preferable since the compound subj precedes the verb (cf. GKC §146d, e). GKC (§53u) and *IBHS* (§22.6c, n. 32) take יתץ as a qal pass.

36.a. In place of MT מעין, Sam and LXX read מעין מים, "from a spring of water."

36.b. LXX reads a *waw* so that this term becomes a third type of reservoir for water.

37.a. The conj כי introduces a conditional sentence; according to BDB 7.b. (473), it heads a case that is more likely to occur than a condition introduced by אם.

38.a. Cf. n. 37.a.

38.b. Sam reads a definite noun, הזרע, "the seed." MT is preferred, for the noun has a collective meaning, "any seed." LXX reads πᾶν, "all," as v 37, but that may not reflect a variant Heb. text, for it may be translating the idea of the Heb. text.

39.a. Cf. n. 37.a. The trans. of כי here is "when," for this kind of a case is a common occurrence.

39.b. Cf. n. 10.b.

40.a. In place of MT את־נבלתה, "its corpse," LXX reads מנבלתם, "from their corpse," as in n. 25.a.

40.b. LXX* adds καὶ λούσεται ὕδατι, "and he is to wash with water," as does the variant in n. 25.b.

41.a. Cf. *IBHS* §8.4.2b.

41.b. LXX has ὑμῖν, "to you," as is frequently the case in the declaratory formula of this chap. MT is followed as the more unusual reading.

42.a. A few Heb. mss and the versions begin the verse with a *waw.*

42.b. The *ḥolem waw* is a large letter in Heb. mss, for it is the central letter of the Pentateuch (GKC §5n; *b. Qidd.* 30a).

42.c. Some Heb. mss omit עד, "until"; this word is hard to account for.

42.d. Cf. n. 41.a.

43.a. Cf. n. 34.a.

43.b. Cf. n. 8.a.

43.c. The quiescent א is omitted in MT's spelling of נטמתם, "you become unclean."

44.a. There is a *hireq* in the final syllable before a שׁ instead of the usual *pataḥ* (GKC §§44d, 54k).

44.b. LXX adds κύριος ὁ θεὸς ὑμῶν, "the Lord your God"; cf. 18:2.

44.c. Cf. n. 8.a.

45.a. Sam and Syr add אלהיכם, "your God"; cf. 18:2.

45.b. LXX* adds κύριος, "the Lord."

47.a. *IBHS* (§23.3d) understands the niph to have ingressive-stative force, describing a state that is necessary or preferred (cf. *IBHS* §37.4d; GKC §116e).

Form/Structure/Setting

The structure of this passage is as follows:

I. Introductory formula (v 1)
II. Speech (vv 2–47)
   A. Commission to speak (v 2a)

- B. Speech proper (vv 2b–47)
  - 1. Classification of animals as clean and unclean (vv 2b–23)
    - a. Concerning land animals (vv 2b–8)
      - 1) Classification of edible land animals (vv 2b–3)
      - 2) Classification of inedible land animals (vv 4–8)
    - b. Concerning fish (vv 9–12)
      - 1) Classification of edible fish (v 9)
      - 2) Classification of inedible fish (vv 10–12)
    - c. Concerning birds (vv 13–19)
      - 1) Command to detest certain birds (v 13a)
      - 2) List of twenty detestable birds (vv 13b–19)
    - d. Concerning flying insects (vv 20–23)
      - 1) Command to detest flying insects (v 20)
      - 2) Exception to command (vv 21–22)
        - a) Classification of edible flying insects (v 21)
        - b) List of edible locusts (v 22)
      - 3) Declaratory statement of their being detestable (v 23)
  - 2. Instructions concerning impurity (vv 24–40)
    - a. Uncleanness communicated by a carcass of a flying insect (vv 24–25)
    - b. Uncleanness communicated by a carcass of an unclean land animal (vv 26–28)
      - 1) Classification of unclean land animals and uncleanness communicated by them (vv 26–27)
      - 2) Instructions for cleansing from contact with one of their carcasses (v 28)
    - c. Uncleanness communicated by creatures that crawl (vv 29–38)
      - 1) Identification of creatures that crawl (vv 29–30)
        - a) General statement of uncleanness (v 29a)
        - b) List of crawling creatures (vv 29b–30)
      - 2) Uncleanness communicated by their carcasses (vv 31–38)
        - a) Law for persons made unclean (v 31)
        - b) Laws for objects made unclean (vv 32–38)
          - (1) General law for an article made unclean (v 32)
          - (2) Laws regarding various articles contacted by a carcass (vv 33–38)
    - d. Uncleanness communicated by carcasses of large edible land animals (vv 39–40)
  - 3. Laws on eating crawling animals and parenesis (vv 41–45)
    - a. Concerning inedible crawling animals (vv 41–43)
    - b. Parenesis to be holy with formulae of Yahweh's self-introduction (vv 44–45)
  - 4. Summary statement (vv 46–47)

These instructions about clean and unclean animals open in the standard fashion with an introductory formula. The formula, however, is different from the numerous preceding ones in that for the first time Yahweh speaks to both Moses and Aaron, though in 10:8 Yahweh speaks directly to Aaron. The inclusion of Aaron in the formula here and in 13:1; 14:33; 15:1 accords with the focus of chaps. 11–15 on the priests' important duty of making a distinction between the clean and the unclean (10:10–11). In addition, the inclusion of Aaron here reinforces the significance of his entry with Moses into the Tent of Meeting following the first public offerings (9:23). These details intertwine chaps. 11–15 with chaps. 8–10.

This chapter addresses two major subjects: classification of animals as clean and unclean (vv 2b–23, 41–45) and regulation of uncleanness from contact with an animal's carcass (vv 24–40). A summary statement (vv 46–47) binds these two sections together.

The first section consists of four units arranged according to the sphere in which the animals live:

1. Animals (land)	(vv 2b–8)
2. Fish (water)	(vv 9–12)
3. Birds (air)	(vv 13–19)
4. Insects (land and air)	(vv 20–23)

The author expanded the threefold sphere from his source, as witnessed to in Deut 14, to a fourfold sphere. The number four means that these laws encompass all animals on the earth, for a fourfold description of space was considered to encompass all earthly creatures or things, e.g., Job 23:8, 9.

Each unit of this section has its distinctive structure. After a statement permitting the eating of land animals, there is a twofold principle defining the characteristics of those land animals that may be eaten (vv 2b–3). Next those land animals not permitted for food are identified by principle (v 4a), followed by a list of four forbidden animals to illustrate how the principles are to be applied (vv 4b–7). This unit ends with two prohibitions: not to eat any of these unclean animals or to touch their carcasses (v 8a); they are supported by a declaratory formula (v 8b).

The second unit (vv 9–12) is composed of a series of general statements without any examples. The opening verse identifies which fish may be eaten (v 9). Following are general instructions governing unclean fish (vv 10–12). In place of the term טמא, "unclean," as in Deut 14:10b, inedible fish are declared to be detestable (שקץ; vv 10, 11, 12), a strengthening of the feeling of repulsion toward unclean creatures. This term is also used for inedible birds, insects, and swarming things in vv 13, 20, 23, 41, 42. Koch (*Priesterschrift,* 76) notes that this kind of systematization is characteristic of the priestly writer. Uncharacteristic of the author of Leviticus, however, is the absence of examples of either edible or inedible fish.

The third unit enumerates birds that may not be eaten. After an introduction prohibiting the eating of detestable birds, underscored by a declaratory formula (v 13a), there is a list of twenty birds forbidden as food (vv 13b–19). No principles for classifying these birds as inedible are given, nor are there any examples of edible birds. Also in distinction from the other units there is no repetitive statement that functions as an inclusio. While it is possible to take v 20 as the last member of this unit (Koch, *Priesterschrift,* 76), it is better to place it at the head of the next unit, for this statement is categorical, in contrast to the naming of birds in the preceding verses, and with v 23 it forms an inclusio for the fourth unit.

The fourth unit, about flying insects (vv 20–23), is closely tied to the last unit by the catch words עוף, "bird, wing" (vv 13, 20, 21, 23) and שקץ, "detestable" (vv 13, 20, 23). After the initial statement rules out all winged insects as food (v 20), an exception introduced by אך, "surely," identifies by principle some winged insects as edible (v 21). Then comes a list of four kinds of edible locusts (v 22). Concluding this unit is a statement about flying insects being detestable (v 23). In comparison with Deut 14:19, which clearly places flying insects with unclean fowl, the author of Lev 11 developed the statement on flying insects into its own unit in order to make it clear that various kinds of locust are edible and in order to place animals into four categories because of the importance of the number four as stated earlier.

The second section, consisting of four units (vv 24–40), concerns uncleanness communicated by coming into contact with a carcass. Vv 24–25 function as a general heading to this second section. V 24 describes the fact and the nature of uncleanness from contact with a carcass, and v 25 describes the procedure for becoming clean again. That a shift in subject has taken place at v 24 is also evidenced by the change in style. Instead of direct address in the second person, the typical sentence has an imperfect verb with a participial clause as its subject. The style throughout this section then is more impersonal than that of the first section.

The author first treats uncleanness from large land animals to establish a parallel with the first section (vv 26–28//vv 2–8). It may be noted that the characteristic of having paws (lit. "walking on its hands," v 27) has been added here to the two basic characteristics classifying land animals as inedible. This unit closes with a description of the procedure for ritual cleansing plus a declaratory formula (v 28).

The next unit considers rodents and lizards as unclean (vv 29–38). A general statement about their uncleanness (v 29a) introduces a list of eight swarmers (vv 29b, 30). This unit is developed by defining the uncleanness that contact with one of their carcasses causes either a person (v 31) or various objects used in daily life (vv 32–35). Directions for handling things that have become unclean are also given. Then objects not made unclean by one of these carcasses are identified, with an exception that seed with water on it is unclean (vv 36–38).

Next come laws about uncleanness from touching or eating the carcass of a clean animal that has died a natural death (vv 39–40). This piece treats issues central both to this section and to the preceding one, namely touching a carcass and eating, respectively. These laws about eating from the carcass of a clean animal circulated independently; otherwise they would have been attached to the first pericope on clean/unclean animals. This view is supported by the location of a parallel law in Deut 14:21a coming at the end of the entire legislation on clean/unclean animals, fish, and birds. In its present location this brief pericope both ends the instructions on uncleanness from touching a carcass and turns the subject back to the issue of edible/inedible creatures, which is continued in the next unit. Nevertheless, because the issue of touching a carcass is congruent with the preceding material, this pericope is placed with the second section.

The third section (vv 41–45), which concerns "edible swarmers," joins with the opening section to frame the material on uncleanness from contact with carcasses. Such structure means that this chapter in its present form is a whole, not a composite of two distinct sets of cultic instructions about two distinct subjects (as Elliger, 145–49). Integrated into this last unit is an exhortation to be holy to provide strong spiritual motivation for the Israelites to observe these instructions (vv 44–45). This parenetic piece patterns the style found often in the section on holy living (chaps. 17–26). Within this exhortation there are ties to its immediate context, e.g., the terms שׁרץ, "a creature that crawls, swarms" (v 44b to vv 41–43 plus vv 10, 20, 21, 23, 29, 31), and טמא, "unclean" (vv 44b to vv 39, 40, 43b and frequently in this chapter) and the contrast of קדש, "holy" (vv 44, 45) with שקץ, "detestable" (vv 41, 42, 43, and often in the chapter). The repetitive style of this exhortation serves the rhetorical purpose of the author.

A summary statement (vv 46–47) concludes this instruction. V 47, chiastically styled, ties the chapter together as a whole. Distinguishing the unclean (הטמא) from the clean (הטהר) is the primary concern of vv 24–40 while distinguishing החיה הנאכלת, "edible creatures," from those החיה אשר לא תאכל, "which are inedible," is the interest of vv 2b–23, 41–45. Also this list is itself chiastically arranged, with the unclean on the circumference and the clean in the center:

הטמא "the unclean"	החיה הנאכלת "living things which may be eaten"
הטהר "the clean"	החיה אשר לא תאכל "living things which you shall not eat"

A parallel account on edible/inedible creatures is found in Deut 14:3–20(21). The closeness of these two accounts raises the question of their interconnectedness.

The instruction in Deuteronomy opens with a prohibition against eating anything that is an abomination (v 3); it is followed by a list of ten edible land animals, both domestic and wild (vv 4–5). The number ten in conjunction with the list of twenty fowl indicates that the use of lists with multiples of ten names goes back to the original source. This list of ten edible land animals is missing in Leviticus. In Deuteronomy it is followed by the characteristics of edible animals (vv 6–7a//Lev 11:3–4a). While the statement of these characteristics is basically the same in both books, their position is different; in Leviticus they come after a statement of permission to eat certain land animals (v 3) and before any animals are named. Then Leviticus gives four examples of animals that may not be eaten because they lack one of these two characteristics. The same four animals are named in Deuteronomy, but Leviticus applies the principles to each example rather than to each of two groups as does Deuteronomy. Both texts conclude with a double prohibition against eating the meat of unclean animals and touching their carcasses (v 8b//Lev 11:8a); Leviticus adds a declaratory formula (11:8b).

The classification of fish in Deut 14:9–10 is straightforward and comprehensive; permission to eat those with fins and scales is followed by prohibition against eating those that lack fins and scales. Leviticus has the same order, but it stresses that unclean fish are inedible by stating four times in three verses (vv 10–12) that those lacking fins and scales are detestable. Moreover, the author of Leviticus defines the term במים, "in water," to include both בימים, "the seas," and בנחלים, "the streams," i.e., saltwater and freshwater fish. Also he enhances the repulsion of these inedible fish by using the term שקץ, "detestable," whereas Deuteronomy uses the standard term טמא, "unclean."

The next unit in both books presents a list of some twenty fowl prohibited as food (vv 12–18//Lev 11:13–19). The account in Deuteronomy, however, is framed by a general principle declaring all clean fowl edible (vv 11, 20). The absence of this principle from Leviticus is striking. There are some variations in the order of the two lists found in Deuteronomy, and the MT of Deut 14 has twenty-one instead of twenty birds (but LXX^{B} has nineteen and LXX^{L} has twenty). These facts indicate that there has been some textual disturbance in the transmission of this list in Deuteronomy. At the end of the list of inedible birds in Deuteronomy, flying insects are classified as unclean and inedible (v 19). In that context this statement is part of the instruction concerning fowl, for a statement permitting the eating of clean fowl follows it (v 20). However, in Leviticus the statement on the detestable nature of flying insects is expanded into an independent unit (vv 20–23). Characteristics defining flying insects are given, and much effort is expended to permit the eating of certain flying insects, both by a categorical statement (v 21) and by a list of four edible locusts (v 22). This unit concludes by classifying flying insects as detestable (v 23). Thus the author of Leviticus takes a different path than the threefold structure employed by the author of Deuteronomy in that he expands the statement about flying insects into a fourth unit.

Following these instructions about clean/unclean animals, the two passages go different ways. Deuteronomy has two prohibitions (v 21); one forbids the eating of an animal that dies a natural death, and the other forbids the boiling of a kid in its mother's milk. Leviticus, on the other hand, provides extensive material on the uncleanness communicated via the carcasses of unclean animals (vv 24–38).

The close resemblances between these two passages, especially the almost identical long list of unclean birds, means either that one of the authors relied on the material found in the other or that both authors used texts that went back to a common source. All of these possibilities have been advocated; e.g., Noth (91) thinks that Deuteronomy is more original (cf. Moran, *Bib* 28 [1966] 271–77), but Noordtzij (119–20) takes Leviticus as the more ancient text. Elliger (148), however, comments that it is not easily discernible which passage is earlier.

Khalifé discovers from a careful analysis of both passages that both authors have adapted the material to fit their theological outlook and the programmatic intent of their work. Furthermore, the results of his study favor the view that these two passages eventually go back to a common source, but the sources available to the respective authors were not identical. This fact is made evident by the existence of material characteristic of author A not being present in his material, though it stands in author B's. For example, though the author of Leviticus likes categorical, definitive statements, a general permission to eat clean fowl opens and closes the unit on birds in Deut 14:11–20. Such a statement is missing from Leviticus. On top of that the long list of inedible fowl in Deuteronomy is headed by the phrase "these are the ones which you may not eat" (v 12a); this statement is also missing in Leviticus. Khalifé's analysis of the language of this unit (61), furthermore, points out that some key terms that are not common to the book of Deuteronomy and that are typical of the phraseology in Leviticus occur in Deuteronomy. He concludes that the author of Deuteronomy did not compose this material but took it over from his source. And since this material that is typical of Leviticus is not in Leviticus, this author's source was other than the one used by the author of Deuteronomy. Moreover, the author of Leviticus did not have a copy of Deuteronomy at hand, for if he had, he would certainly have included this material.

The comparative work brings out the distinctive characteristics of the author of Leviticus. He adapts the material from his source to reinforce the principles for classifying animals as clean or unclean, and he likes to show how to apply the principles to specific cases in order to teach the congregation the ways of applying these principles to animals not mentioned. Three examples of his style may be given: the application of the characteristics for identifying large land animals as edible to four specific, borderline cases (vv 4–7), the threefold reiteration of the characteristics classifying fish as unclean (vv 9, 10, 12), and the verbatim repetition of the statement classifying most flying insects as detestable (v 20a=v 21aβ). His purpose is pedagogical. He uses repetition to drill his audience in the correct application of the principles and to drive home the point. Furthermore, he has a keen interest in making the identification of unclean animals more precise, as is seen in his defining the phrase "in the waters" to include both seas and rivers (v 9). He does not want anyone to assume that fish in rivers are not covered by this instruction. In the unit on flying insects he adds the phrase ההלך על ארבע, "goes on all fours," to classify edible insects more definitively, a classification that unfortunately escapes us. In addition, the author of Leviticus seeks to strengthen the community's concern about inedible animals by replacing the usual word טמא, "unclean," with the stronger term שׁקץ, "detestable" (vv 10, 11, 12, 13, 20, 23, 41, 42; plus the verbal form of this root in vv 11, 13, 43). Also he increases the use of declaratory formulae to add greater authority to this material.

Whereas Noth (91–92) identifies the classification of animals as priestly instruction for the laity and the technical material, such as in vv 24b, 25, as priestly professional knowledge, this analysis finds that all of the material is priestly instruction for the laity in matters of ritual purity. The rhetorical nature of this text is evident in the author's use of repetition, emphasis on general principles, use of categorical terms, and use of strong words. This style is designed to implant these laws in the people's minds. The people needed to know these instructions to order a multitude of daily matters so that they might be a holy people before Yahweh.

Comment

2–7 בהמה, "land animals," that may be eaten by the Israelites are identified. While חיה is often used for wild animals and בהמה for domesticated animals, as in 1:2, here בהמה has a wider range of meaning and is synonymous with חיה (cf. Deut 14:4–5). To be edible, an animal has to have a hoof completely divided into two parts, and it must chew the cud. The language describing these characteristics uses assonance with cognate accusatives in order to underscore the distinctive features of clean animals. "Chewing the cud" stands for the practice of some animals to swallow lightly chewed food, regurgitate it, and chew it thoroughly at leisure before swallowing it again. As the identification of the clean animals shows, this is not the precise meaning of the מעלה גרה. Rather it means an animal's chewing its food thoroughly. Domesticated animals with these two characteristics are cattle, sheep, and goats. Among wild animals the deer (איל), the gazelle (צבי), the roebuck (יחמור), the wild goat (אקו), the ibex (דישׁן), the antelope (תאו), and the mountain sheep (זמר) are included (Deut 14:5).

Animals that chew the cud but do not have a split hoof are excluded as food: e.g., the camel (גמל), the hyrax or rock-badger (שׁפן), the hare (ארנבת), and the pig (חזיר). Although the camel has a split hoof, its sole is thick and cushiony so that the split does not appear (Baentsch, 35). Incidentally, the Arabs offered the camel as a sacrifice, and the camel was eaten throughout the Middle East; but because it was such a valuable animal, its meat was considered a luxury (Simoons, *Eat Not This Flesh,* 88). Some venerated parts of the camel are still employed as medicine and in magic. Other groups like the Israelites avoided eating the camel. The hyrax is mentioned here, for while it does not technically chew the cud, its manner of continuous chewing is quite similar to that of a ruminant. שָׁפָן is often taken to be the rabbit or the hare, but Bare (*Plants and Animals,* 98) identifies it with the rock-badger or hyrax. It may reach a weight of six to eight pounds (Cansdale, *Animals,* 130). It likes to eat leaves, roots, and locusts. ארנבת is the hare, which is larger than a rabbit and lives above ground. Cansdale (131) identifies the hare's chewing the cud with its habit of "reflection," i.e., at certain times of the day it eats its moist droppings. The hare was considered by some as a holy animal; parts from its body were made into amulets. The pig (חזיר) is also excluded for, even though it has a split hoof, it does not ruminate. A solid hoof excludes animals like the horse and the donkey. Other animals forbidden are the dog, the cat, and the bear (v 22).

7 Archaeological evidence has proven that pigs were eaten throughout the Middle East (Simoons, *Eat Not This Flesh,* 13–19); thus the ancients knew how to prepare and cook pork properly. In Egypt during the Third Dynasty (twenty-seventh century B.C.), domestic pigs were kept. For centuries there was no negative attitude toward the pig in Egypt, but much later (fifth century B.C.) the pig was considered a source of uncleanness. Nevertheless, in the late period Egyptians continued to sacrifice the pig at certain cycles of the moon (Simoons, 15–16). Attitudes toward the pig in other parts of the Middle East varied. Some groups associated them with demons because the wild boar inhabited desolate places and ate carrion. Isa 65:4 and 66:3, 17 witness to the sacrifice of pigs by Israelites in the worship of the dead.

8 A person becomes ritually unclean only by eating animals classified as unclean, not by touching them or raising them. Thus animals like the donkey and the camel could be domesticated and used as work animals without communicating uncleanness. However, contact with one of their carcasses makes one unclean.

9–12 Fish, those "in the seas" (בימים), i.e., in large bodies of water, and those "in the rivers" (בנחלים), which have fins and scales are clean. Douglas (*Purity,* 55) holds that animals that are equipped for the kind of locomotion appropriate to their sphere are clean. "In the water scaly fish swim with fins" (*Purity,* 55). Those creatures living in water without fins and scales were especially repulsive to the ancient Israelites, for in vv 10–12 the stronger term שקץ, "detestable, abhorrent," is used four times to describe them. This root replaces the usual word טמא, "unclean," used in the first unit and in the parallel passage in Deuteronomy. It is used for inedible animals in the following units (vv 13, 20, 23, 41, 42). The utter contempt that this word conveys is visible in Isa 66:17 and Ezek 8:10. שקוץ, another form of this root, stands for filth (Nah 3:6), unclean food (Zech 9:7), and frequently for idols or idolatrous practices (e.g., Deut 29:16[17]; 2 Kgs 23:13, 24; Jer 4:1; 7:30; Ezek 5:11; 7:20; 11:18, 21; 20:7, 8, 30; 37:23). It is also used for the people of Israel corrupted by worship of idols (Hos 9:10). The verb occurs in v 43; 7:21; 20:25; also in Deut 7:26 and Ps 22:25(24).

10 שרץ המים, "swarming creatures of the waters," describes those creatures that go about in shoals (Snaith, 63). This term is also applied to insects (vv 20–

21, 23), rodents and reptiles (vv 29, 31), and creatures that move about on their bellies like snakes and caterpillars (vv 41–43). U. Cassuto (*A Commentary on the Book of Genesis,* tr. I. Abrahams [Jerusalem: Magnes, 1961] 49) states that שׁרץ "is 'movement,' with specific reference to the abundant, swift movement of many creatures who jostle one another as they proceed criss-cross in all possible directions." The term נפשׁ החיה, "living creature," refers to larger animals. This verse declares unclean any small or large animal living in shallow or deep, fresh or salt water that does not have fins and scales. There are no exceptions for water creatures.

13–19 Unclean birds are enumerated in a list giving twenty names. Apparently the ancient Hebrews found no characteristic for classifying these unclean birds together. The list is primarily composed of birds of prey and those that feed on carrion. The majority of these birds live in desert places and ruins. These kinds of animals were associated with demonic spirits. This list consists of fifteen land birds, three water birds, and two others (Driver, 19). The recurring term למינו, "according to its kind," includes many varieties of a species and possibly similar species, thus greatly expanding the number of unclean birds. Driver (*PEQ* 87 [1955] 19–20) discerns that the birds are listed according to size: large birds of prey, crow-type birds, larger owls, smaller birds of prey, and smaller owls.

13 נשׁר, the "eagle," or the "griffon-vulture," occurs some twenty-eight times in the OT. Since it is described as feeding on carcasses and carrion, it stands for a species of vulture (Bare, *Plants and Animals,* 74). Many passages refer to its great size and strength. The griffon-vulture is three to four feet in length and has a wing span up to eight feet (Cansdale, *Animals,* 144). Because this bird dominates the sky, several tribes and nations have adopted it as their symbol. In Palestine the rugged terrain of the desert and the rocky cliffs of the wadis provide abundant homes for griffon-vultures. פרס is the lammergeier or bearded vulture (Pinney, *Animals,* 150). It feeds on remains left by griffon-vultures. עזניה is the short-toed, bearded vulture (cf. Cansdale, 145–46) or the black vulture (Bare, 78). Others have rendered this term "osprey," but Cansdale (145–46) judges this identification to be very doubtful.

14 דאה is a kite; this Heb. root means "to dart about." The red kite and the black kite live in Palestine (Cansdale, *Animals,* 146). Kites feed after vultures. איה, which is onomatopoeic for a bird's call, may stand for the buzzard. These birds are excellent hunters, preying on various small animals like rodents, frogs, and snakes.

15 Every kind of "crow," ערב, lit. "the black one," is prohibited for food. While this Heb. term is usually rendered raven, Cansdale (*Animals,* 181–83) identifies the rook, the jackdaw, the jay, the fantailed raven, the hooded crow, and the raven as members of the crow family known to Palestine. The diet of this species ranges from small or weak living creatures to carrion and refuse.

16 בת היענה, lit. "daughter of greed," or "the daughter of the wilderness," (Driver, *PEQ* 87 [1955] 12), is traditionally taken as the ostrich. But, as Driver (13) points out, the list in vv 16–18 consists of different kinds of owls. Owls are known for their weird howling, nocturnal habits, and keen eyesight. It may be more appropriate to identify this bird as "the eagle-owl." It haunts caves and ruins (Isa 13:21; Jer 50:39). תחמס is unidentified. Tg renders it the nighthawk, Driver "the short-eared owl" (13), and others "falcon" or "kestrel" (Bare, *Plants* *and Animals,* 104). The term שחף has not been clearly identified. Driver (13) suggests the "long-eared owl," but Bare (98) says it is generic for "sea gull." Other suggestions include a cuckoo or a kind of owl. נץ is a bird of prey, most likely a hawk. Palestine, however, is not rich in hawks. Cansdale (*Animals,* 146–47) reasons that this term probably included falcons, for there are many kinds of falcons in Palestine. But Bare (74–76) identifies it as a specific term for "the sparrow hawk."

17 Most render כוס "the little owl," which is eight and one-half inches long (Cansdale, *Animals,* 149), but Driver suggests "the tawny owl" (*PEQ* 87 [1955] 14). Driver takes שלך, from a root meaning "dart," and identifies the bird as one that fishes, "the fish owl" (14–15). But Cansdale (175) prefers to take this term for the cormorant, found in large numbers in Palestine near bodies of water. ינשוף may be related to either a root meaning "evening" or one meaning "hissing" (cf. Isa 34:11). If the latter alternative is correct, Driver's (15) translation "screech owl" is excellent. Bare (*Plants and Animals,* 120) suggests either "the long-eared owl" or "the short-eared owl."

18 תנשמת is some kind of night bird. Driver renders it "the little owl" (*PEQ* 87 [1955] 15). Older sources identify it as "the water hen," but recently it has been taken as "the barn owl" or "the white owl" (Bare, *Plants and Animals,* 108). קאת, if related to the root קיא, is lit. "vomiter." LXX and Vg read "pelican," but there is no indication here that the bird in question has to do with the sea. In fact, in Isa 34:11 this creature loves to inhabit devastated lands. It is more likely a small owl like the scops owl, which is smaller than a robin and eats insects (Parmelee, *All the Birds,* 111; Driver, 16). רחם is a type of vulture; Cansdale (*Animals,* 145) identifies it as the Egyptian vulture. Driver (16–17), however, prefers the osprey, which dwells near large bodies of water.

19 חסידה is usually identified as the stork. Cansdale (*Animals,* 157–58) mentions that the white stork and the black stork pass through Palestine. Their diet is mainly small animals supplemented with some plants. According to Bare (*Plants and Animals,* 28), אנפה has not been clearly identified. It is generic for herons, bitterns, and egrets. On their long legs herons walk in shallow water, poking into the silt for food; thus the heron is not strictly speaking a bird of prey. Driver (*PEQ* 87 [1955] 17–18) renders it the cormorant, for he makes a connection between this term and the Heb. word "nose." דוכיפת may be "the hoopoe," which has a prominent crest. The bat (עטלף), a flying mammal, is a mixture of classes. Most bats of Palestine feed on insects (Cansdale, 136). They inhabit caves, abandoned buildings, and hollow trees.

20–23 Almost all small land animals are classified as unclean. The phrase ההלך על־ארבע, "go on all fours," is an expression for darting about. E. Fink (*REJ* 63 [1912] 122–23) takes feet (רגלים) in v 23 as a dual, meaning four pairs of legs. He accounts for the four pairs by including the antennae every insect has as numbered with the feet. Unfortunately Fink's explanation does not help very much with the phrase "go on all four" in v 20. For clarity in the English translation this phrase is rendered "dart about." Four locusts are named as exceptions to flying insects' being unclean. They are clean because they have a pair of larger, jointed legs for hopping. According to Douglas (*Purity,* 66), their hopping action along with their ability to fly makes them comparable to birds; thus their movement is appropriate to the sphere in which they live.

Milgrom ("Ethics and Ritual," 189), however, finds her explanation wanting since locusts may "walk" as well as hop; he proposes that their classification as edible is an exception in deference to the ancient pastorals' fondness for this food. Incidentally, John the Baptist is famous for eating locusts (Matt 3:4; Mark 1:6). Four names are given, but precise identification has not been achieved. The first, named ארבה, is "the locust," the most common term in the OT for this species. This kind of locust was responsible for the eighth plague against Egypt (Exod 10:12–19). Next is סלעם, lit. "the swallower" or "the destroyer," which occurs only here in the OT; it may be "the katydid" or "the bald locust" (so versions). Bare (*Plants and Animals,* 102) suggests "a large cricket." Others postulate that it may be a stage in the development of the desert locust (Bare, 102). חרגל, only here in the OT, may describe a fast-moving creature if it is related to an Arab root meaning "run swiftly." It is often taken as "cricket," "cicada," or "katydid," but Cansdale (*Animals,* 239) doubts that a cricket would be suitable for food. This term also may refer to a stage in the growth of a locust. חגב is the "grasshopper" (Isa 40:22; Num 13:33). The last term has been identified with an Arab root meaning "hide," for it is assumed that a swarm of them blots out the sun. Cansdale (238), however, observes that texts like Num 13:33 indicate that it is a small creature. He thus identifies it as a nongregarious grasshopper. While it is accurate that locusts are identified with plagues, as in Exod 10:12–19 and Joel 1, Cansdale (240–41) notes that only three kinds of locusts, the migratory locust (the most common), the desert locust, and the Moroccan locust, do extensive damage to crops. Whether this list makes it possible to eat all kinds of locusts or only the four named is debated among the rabbis (*b. Ḥul.* 65). The dominant view is that eating other kinds of locusts is prohibited.

24–25 Whoever comes into contact with a flying insect's carcass becomes unclean. If one accidentally נגע, "touches," one of their carcasses, he is unclean until evening, the beginning of a new day. But if he נשׂא, "picks up," a carcass, he is more contaminated. In addition to waiting until evening, he must wash his clothes. However, carcasses of animals that have been ritually slaughtered do not make one unclean.

26 This verse says that touching an unclean land animal makes one unclean. The context would indicate that it is contact with one of their carcasses that makes a person unclean, not touching a live unclean animal. Perhaps a word has fallen out of this verse, as the variant suggests. It is also possible that this is stated elliptically; the fact that the uncleanness is conveyed by the carcass of an unclean animal is to be understood from the context.

27 An animal that הולך על־כפיו, "walks on its paws" (lit. "palms"), is one that walks on the middle part of its foot, e.g., dogs, cats, and bears. Their forefeet are hand-like. According to Douglas (*Purity,* 56), since they use their "hands" for walking, a perversion of the normal order, they are unclean. But Carroll ("One More Time," 123) takes a different approach. He understands the כפים, "palms," to refer to pads on the feet. This then includes lions, bears, wolves, etc. Carroll notices that all of these are carnivores and are unclean because they eat meat.

29 Small animals that are close to the ground and שׁרץ, "swarm," or "teem about" (cf. v 10) are unclean. Many of these animals are carnivorous or eat carrion. Contemporary zoologists identify חלד as "the mole-rat"; others render it "the rat" or "the weasel" (cf. Bare, *Plants and Animals,* 50; Cansdale, *Animals,* 127–28).

עכבר, generic for "small rodents," includes various species of mice, including mice, dormice, jerboas, and some rats (Cansdale, 132). In Isa 66:17 there is a reference to eating mice and swine. צב is some type of large lizard. Bare (110) suggests "the desert monitor," while Cansdale (199) prefers "the spiny-tailed lizard" or "the dabb lizard," which grows to be nearly two feet long and has a powerful, spiny tail used in defense.

30 These five names appear to be for various kinds of lizards. אנקה, lit. "groaner," likely refers to the gecko, which makes a low, moaning sound. כח is often identified with the monitor lizard, the largest of the lizards, reaching up to four feet. They are carnivorous. Some people hunt them for food (Cansdale, *Animals,* 200). Others identify it with the chameleon, known for its ability to change color and the strength in its claws (Cansdale, 200–201). Others, however, take the last word in the list, תנשמת, as the chameleon; another possibility for that last Heb. term is "mole," but Cansdale discounts this suggestion (201–2). Since this is a list of lizards and since the identity of תנשמת is unknown, it is rendered chameleon in the English translation. Bare (*Plants and Animals,* 66) takes לטאה as a generic term for true lizards. חמט stands for lizards adapted to living in sand, like skinks (Cansdale, 201). Members of this family have short legs or none at all and are shiny in appearance (Bare, 50).

32 Any article on which the carcass of an unclean animal falls becomes unclean. That which is made out of wood, cloth, hide, or sackcloth has to be washed and remains unclean until evening. If the article is made out of clay, it has to be שבר, "smashed" (v 33). No reason is put forth for this distinction in treatment based on the kind of material. It is possible that the ancients considered clay more porous than these other materials, but the practice of glazing pottery makes this conjecture unlikely. Another possibility is that clay vessels, more than other kinds, were associated with food ready for eating. In any case, clay vessels, being cheap and plentiful, were much more easily replaced than those made out of other materials.

33–34 This decree declares unclean any food or drink in a vessel contaminated by contact with an animal's carcass.

35 Anything on which a carcass falls becomes unclean. If it is a תנור, "portable oven" (cf. 2:4), or a כירים, "stove" (only here in the OT), a cooking stove with two burners set in the ground (Noordtzij, 128), it is to be broken. These stoves, being made out of clay, could be replaced without great expense.

36 If a carcass falls into a well or a cistern, the water does not become unclean. The reason is that in these sources water, a purifying agent, is continually renewed. But whoever removes the carcass becomes unclean.

37–38 If a portion of a carcass falls on seed for sowing, the seed, being dry, remains clean. But if there is water on the seed when the carcass falls on it, it becomes unclean. Standing water was thought to conduct uncleanness. Wenham (180), however, thinks that the wet grain is being soaked so that it can be used as food.

39–40 The carcass of any clean animal that dies of itself, that has not been ritually slaughtered, carries uncleanness to any person who touches it. Any who eat of it or carry it have to wash their clothes and be unclean until the evening. The key factor in rendering this carcass unclean is that the blood is still in it. The possibility for an Israelite to eat such meat is striking; this instruction may address the community's need for food under trying conditions, like a time of famine, or the need to provide food for the poor (cf. 17:15–16; but cf. Exod 22:30[31]; Deut 14:21).

41–43 A primary instruction is reiterated here for emphasis and as background to the exhortation found in vv 44–45. שׁרץ, "swarm, teem" (cf. v 10), includes numerous small creatures like snakes and insects (cf. vv 9–12). Some render מרבה רגלים, lit. "one having many legs," as centipedes (Bare, *Plants and Animals,* 68). According to Douglas, "swarming" is not a type of propulsion adapted to any sphere. Since swarming cuts across classifications, these creatures are unclean. The term for "belly" (גחון) appears only here and in Gen 3:14, in which the serpent in the garden is cursed to crawl on its belly.

44–45 To this instruction about small, scurrying (רמשׂ) creatures is attached an exhortation for the Israelites to sanctify themselves (cf. 20:25, 26; Deut 14:2, 21a). This call grows out of the central purpose of God for Israel, namely that they be his people, a holy nation (Exod 19:5, 6). They must sanctify themselves because Yahweh their God is holy. This theological principle is the cornerstone of the decrees and instructions found in chaps. 17–26. Its appearance here indicates that it is also the undergirding principle for observing the standards of ritual purity. Also it is found in Exod 19:6; Num 15:40; Deut 23:15(14). Specifically, the people are to observe the dietary laws and to monitor uncleanness communicated by contact with carcasses so that they may be clean when they enter God's presence for worship.

46–47 This instruction concludes with a summary statement giving the purpose of this instruction. It is designed to make a clear distinction between the clean and unclean among animals and between those that may be eaten and those that may not be eaten. Thus it guides the priests in carrying out their responsibility of distinguishing between the clean and the unclean for the people (10:10).

Explanation

In this passage God identifies the animals that may or may not be eaten by his people. These animals are treated according to the sphere in which they live: land, water, air, and land-air.

In following these dietary laws, the Israelites obeyed God's instructions several times each day, developing deep in their consciousness an attitude of obedience to God. That all the people observed these laws at every meal was a mighty force of solidarity, uniting the people as God's special treasure (Exod 19:5). It separated the Israelites from their polytheistic neighbors and became a distinguishing mark of their national identity. The importance of these dietary laws increased when the Jews became dispersed among the nations. They have become a significant force in preserving Jewish identity. They erect a high barrier against assimilation and amalgamation of the Jewish people, which would lead to the loss of their racial identity. Today, keeping kosher is a distinguishing mark of a very devout Jew and communicates the understanding that that person belongs to the chosen people of God.

Clean and unclean also have symbolic force. Unclean animals symbolize disorder, mixture, untruth. Clean animals symbolize order, wholeness, integrity; these symbols point to God's holiness. Observance of the ritual purity laws internalizes these values deep in the national consciousness. It especially develops the people's awareness of the holiness of God.

The instructions about the uncleanness carried by a carcass build on the belief that death is a curse for disobeying God. Death is the most contagious uncleanness. Anything a carcass touches must be destroyed or cleansed. These purity rules demythologized and desacralized death. Because contact with a dead body made one unclean, ancestral worship was prevented from taking hold in Israel. Death was robbed of its power to tyrannize the living.

In the NT the great council of Jerusalem decided not to shackle converted Gentiles with keeping the dietary laws. Whereas the dietary laws distinguished the Jew from the Gentile, their abolishment means that the wall of separation has been broken down (Eph 2:11–21). Now all, Jew and Gentile, free and slave, male and female, are one in Christ (Acts 15:13–21; Gal 3:28). This abolishment is also grounded on Jesus' teaching that what defiles a person is not the food that enters his body, but the passions that flow out of a defiled heart (Mark 7:14–23). Jesus freed his followers from observing endless rules. Nevertheless, with freedom goes responsibility. A believer is free to eat any food, but one is not free to unsettle another's faith by insensitive behavior (Rom 14:15). In genuine concern for a fellow believer, a believer is to avoid any offending food. Freedom is to be governed by considerate love. Abused freedom leads to libertine living and moral ineptitude, but freedom exercised in love leads to zealous service of God in the giving of oneself to hurting people (1 Pet 1:22). There are no barriers preventing a believer from reaching through natural filth and moral defilement to any person crying out for help. The followers of Jesus are to look outwardly, expressing compassion to the needy (Acts 20:35; Rom 15:1), and they are to look inwardly, purifying the heart (Matt 5:8; Acts 15:9; 1 Tim 1:5).

B. Instructions on Ritual Purity of a Woman Who Has Given Birth (12:1–8)

Bibliography

Macht, D. I. "A Scientific Appreciation of Lev. 12:1–5." *JBL* 52 (1933) 253–60. **Zeitlin, S.** "The Semikhah Controversy between the School of Shammai and Hillel." *JQR* 56 (1965) 240–44.

Translation

1 *Yahweh spoke to Moses,* 2 *"Speak to the Israelites:*[a] *Whenever a woman conceives*[b] *and gives birth to a male, she will become unclean for seven days, as she becomes unclean in the days of her menstruation.*[c] 3 *On the eighth day his foreskin*[a] *is to be circumcised.* 4 *She has to stay at home thirty-three days more for purification*[ab] *from her bleeding.*[cd] *She is not*

to touch anything consecrated nor enter the sanctuary[e] *until the days of her purification are fulfilled.*[f] [5]*If she gives birth to a female, she will become unclean for fourteen days*[a] *as in her menstruation. She has to stay at home sixty-six days for purification*[b] *from her bleeding.*

[6]*"When the days of her purification for either a son or a daughter are fulfilled,*[a] *she is to bring a year-old lamb*[b] *for a whole offering and a young pigeon or a dove for a purification offering to the priest at the entrance to the Tent of Meeting.* [7]*He is to present it*[a] *before Yahweh and make expiation*[b] *for her, and she will be clean*[c] *from her flow of blood. This is the instruction for a woman who gives birth for*[d] *either a male or a female.*

[8]*"If she cannot afford*[a] *a lamb, she is to take two doves or two young pigeons, one for a whole offering and one for a purification offering. The priest is to make expiation for her, and she will be clean."*

Notes

2.a. Instead of לאמר, "saying," LXX has ἐρεῖς πρὸς αὐτούς, "say to them"; cf. 15:2.

2.b. The hiph הזריע is used to emphasize the process, "conceive a child" (H. D. Preuss, "זָרַע *zāraʿ*," *TDOT* 4:144). Sam and LXX have a niph תזרע, "she is pregnant," but the MT is followed as the harder reading.

2.c. נדת דותה, lit. "the impurity of her being unwell," means "her menstruation" (15:19, 20, 24, 25, 33). נדה means "impurity, stain, pollution" (KB, 635–36) and carries a sense of disgust. But Levine (97) takes it from a root נדד, "to cast, hurl"; thus it describes the flow of blood. דוה means "be faint, weak, unwell." A woman would be viewed as weak during her period, for she loses the life force believed to reside in the blood (17:11). Menstruation, because of the blood, rendered a woman unclean; thus, if Levine is correct, נדה means "impurity, odious, indecent" secondarily.

3.a. Sam has את, the sign of the definite dir obj. LXX also takes בשר ערלתו, "his foreskin," as the dir obj. In the MT reading the niph ימול, "he is to be circumcised," has an acc, which in an active sentence would be a secondary acc, defining the nearer obj of the action (cf. GKC §117ll).

4.a. Elliger notes the distinction in the use of טהרה and טהר (158, n.). טהרה may mean the process of purification as in Neh 12:45; 1 Chr 23:28; 2 Chr 30:19. Otherwise it usually means the onset of purity as in 13:7, 35; 14:2, 23, 32; 15:13; Num 6:9. In these verses טהר, "purification," is used without distinction from טהרה. But at one time they were distinguished: טהר, "purification," and טהרה, "determination or declaration of purity."

4.b. LXX understands טהרה to be "her purification," not "purification."

4.c. On דמי, "blood of," see 20:9.

4.d. The understanding of the phrase דמי טהרה led to a dispute between the Pharisees and the Sadducees. The former rendered it "pure blood," the latter, with the Samaritans, "blood of her purification" (Bertholet, 41).

4.e. In Lev מקדש, "sanctuary," occurs most often in the material on holy living (19:30; 20:3; 21:12 [2x], 23; 26:2, 31; also 16:33; Exod 25:8; Num 3:38; 10:21; 18:1; 19:20). This fact gives further support to the position that the material on ritual purity (chaps. 11–15) is closely tied to the material on holy living (chaps. [17] 18–26).

4.f. The inf constr after a prep forms a temporal clause with the dir obj functioning as the subj.

5.a. שבעים, "fourteen," is a dual.

5.b. Cf. nn. 4.a.b.c.d.

6.a. Cf. n. 4.f.

6.b. Age is expressed with the word בן, "son of," in construct followed by the year (cf. 1:5). The term בן־שנה means "a year old" (Exod 12:5; cf. Lev 9:3; 14:10; 23:18, 19). The pronominal suffix on שנה may indicate that the animal could be less than a year old (Joüon §129j, n.), but Keil and Delitzsch (376) argue that the two terms are interchangeable.

7.a. LXX does not have a dir obj; it may have sought to avoid the problem that the sg pronoun causes because the preceding verse requires the offering of two animals. Koch (*Priesterschrift,* 79) notes that Schötz posited that the sg pronoun indicates that originally only a lamb for a whole offering was required. Later two offerings were required because of the influence of two offerings being required for the poor (usually two small birds are substituted for an animal offering as in 5:7). In support of this interpretation is the smallness of the purification offering in comparison to the whole offering.

7.b. Heb. mss, Sam, LXX, Syr, and *Tg. Ps.-J.* add הכהן, "the priest."

7.c. LXX has καὶ καθαριεῖ αὐτήν, "and it cleanses her."

7.d. The ל functions as a prep "for" and not as a sign of the dir obj.

8.a. Cf. n. 5:7.a.

Form/Structure/Setting

This regulation treats ritual purity in regards to the birth of a child. The structure is outlined:

I. Introductory formula (v 1)
II. Speech (vv 2–8)
  A. Commission to speak (v 2aα)
  B. Speech proper (vv 2aβ–8)
    1. About giving birth (vv 2aβ–5)
      a. Concerning birth of a male child (vv 2aβ–4)
        1) Time of impurity (v 2aβ+b)
        2) Instruction about circumcision (v 3)
        3) Additional time of separation for purification (v 4)
          a) Time of separation (v 4a)
          b) Restrictions regarding contact with the holy (v 4b)
      b. Concerning birth of a female child (v 5)
        1) Time of impurity (v 5a)
        2) Time of separation (v 5b)
    2. Sacrifices for purification (vv 6–7)
      a. Specification of animals (v 6)
      b. Sacrifices (v 7a)
        1) Presentation (v 7aα^1)
        2) Results (v 7aα^2+aβ)
          a) Expiation (v 7aα^2)
          b) Cleanness (v 7aβ)
    3. Summary statement (v 7b)
    4. Appendix: alternative sacrifices for the poor (v 8)
      a. Reason (v 8aα)
      b. Directions (v 8aβ+b)
        1) Specification of animals (v 8aβ)
        2) Results (v 8b)
          a) Expiation (v 8bα)
          b) Cleanness (v 8bβ)

This speech regulates the time of uncleanness for a mother in giving birth (vv 2aβ–6, 5a), her time of separation (vv 4, 5b), circumcision of a male child (v 3), and the sacrifices required (vv 6–8). There is a summary statement at v 7b analogous to 11:46–47; 14:54–57; 15:32–33. An appendix (v 8) prescribes alternative sacrifices for the poor.

The basic regulation is quite ancient. Elliger (156–57) correctly notes that the regulations of purity about birth had a long and complex origin. This material has been adapted to its context, for it assumes both the sacrificial legislation (chap. 15) and the theme of ritual purity initiated in chap. 11. The absence of

Aaron's name in the introductory formula is striking for this section on ritual purity (cf. 11:1). This omission may occur because of the vital role that sacrifices have in this regulation, for Aaron's name is also missing at 14:1, the introduction to the ritual of restoration for one who has recovered from a grievous skin disease. The exception clause (v 8) for the poor was appended quite early, no later than the time of the judges, as reasoned for the inclusion of 1:14–16, though most scholars assign it to the post-exilic period (e.g., Elliger, 157).

This regulation assumes the sacrificial regulations found in chaps. 1–5. The עלה, "whole offering," is mentioned before the חטאת, "purification offering," as is the case in the sacrificial legislation (chaps. 1–5). In addition, the offering requiring the more valuable animal is mentioned first. The order is then descriptive, not prescriptive. Thus it may be assumed that the purification offering was presented first, then the whole offering, as on other occasions (e.g., 9:7; 16:11, 15, 24; *b. Zebaḥ.* 90a). The smallness of the purification offering suggests that the requirement of this offering for one who could afford a lamb developed out of the double offering prescribed for the poor.

While Noth classifies this regulation as priestly professional knowledge (97), the material is too general for that genre. This regulation is for the instruction of the family head on how to handle the birth of a child.

As far as the location of this chapter, some, as Dillmann (550) and Elliger (157), reason that at one time it was a part of chap. 15, since both chapters deal with uncleanness in regard to bodily discharges from the genitals. But chap. 12 is concerned with giving birth, an unusual occurrence and a high moment in family life, with several days of uncleanness followed by the offering of sacrifices. Chap. 15, on the other hand, for the most part, treats normal bodily discharges, which cause uncleanness for a day or a week; reference to sacrifices comes only for abnormal situations (vv 14–15, 29–30). The reason, however, that chap. 12 is located between the dietary laws and the regulations for grievous infections is that it stands in the continuum of increasing degrees of impurity and decreasing commonness of grievous growths (chaps. 13–14) as reasoned in *Form/Structure/Setting* for chaps. 11–15.

Comment

2 The laws of ritual purity regulate the birth of a child, both because of its essential role in human existence and because of uncleanness from bodily secretions; e.g., menstruation renders a woman unclean for seven days (15:19). The afterbirth, the continued discharge of blood, and the mother's physical weakness are ominous aspects of parturition. A mother of a son is unclean for seven days, while a mother of a daughter is unclean for fourteen days. Seven is a prominent number, symbolizing perfection (cf. 4:6). The reason for the greater length of uncleanness for bearing a girl is not stated. Some suppose that the ancients thought that giving birth to a girl was fraught with greater danger (Noordtzij, 131). Others hold that they believed women to be subject to stronger attacks by demons (Elliger, 168; Noordtzij, 131). This position, however, has no support in the OT. Others argue that the ancients thought that the discharges following the birth of a girl lasted longer. Macht, a physician, sought to prove that this belief was grounded in fact (*JBL* 52 [1922] 253–60). The evidence he gathered indicates that the discharges after bearing a girl are a little longer than for a boy, but not enough longer to account for the doubling of the time of separation. Nevertheless, if the ancients believed that such was the case, their belief itself would be sufficient to require a longer time of purification for giving birth to a girl. Possibly these laws take into account that a girl was a future mother who would have her monthly periods of uncleanness (Harrison, 135). It is difficult to know what weight to give this suggestion. The difference may reside primarily in the lower social standing of women in ancient Israel. Although women had more rights in Israel than in many of the surrounding nations, their social position was a long way from being equal with that of men; e.g., the price for redeeming a woman was significantly less than that for a man (27:2–7).

Whatever weight can be assigned to any of these interpretations, the text makes it clear that it was the discharge of blood that rendered a new mother unclean, as the three references to the discharge of blood (lochia) in these eight verses indicate (vv 4, 5, 7). Bodily secretions in general made a person unclean, but the flow of blood was especially ominous. Douglas (*Purity and Danger,* 51) observes that a bleeding body is not whole. What is not complete is unclean. The giving off of blood is also threatening and can lead to death. Moreover, because the afterbirth was classified as unclean, none of it nor any of the continuing discharge of blood could be used for any magical purpose (cf. Bertholet, 41; Noordtzij, 131). Being unclean means solely that the mother is to be separated from the holy until this abnormal situation is corrected, until her body is whole again.

3 A male child is to be circumcised on the eighth day as Yahweh directed Abraham (Gen 17:10–14). It is appropriate that the sign of the covenant is on the organ of reproduction, for God promised to Abraham a great nation (Gen 12:2), even numerous descendants (Gen 17:6; 22:17). No longer was this a puberty rite done at age thirteen as some peoples such as the Arabs practiced. This rite consecrates the child to Yahweh and identifies him as a member of the covenant community. Yahweh's claim on a person's life is from infancy.

4–5 After seven or fourteen days of uncleanness, the mother is no longer technically unclean, yet she is required to stay at home (ישׁב; cf. Deut 21:13; Baentsch, 362) and to avoid all contact with that which is holy. If she bears a boy, her separation lasts thirty-three days; for a girl it is sixty-six days. The total number of days for the purification of a mother is forty and eighty, respectively. Forty, a multiple of the key number four, which symbolizes totality by reason of the four cardinal directions, marks a major social transition or a complete period of endurance such as in fasting or punishment. For example, during the judgment of the great flood it rained forty days and nights (Gen 7:9, 12; for other kinds of examples see Deut 9:9, 10; 1 Sam 17:16; 1 Kgs 19:8; Matt 4:2), and Israel stayed in the wilderness forty years (Deut 2:7; 8:2; 24:4[5]; Josh 5:6; Ps 95:10; cf. Ezek 29:11–13; Acts 1:3; M. Pope, "Number, Numbering, Numbers," *IDB* 3:664–66). The forty-day or eighty-day period of purification marks the significant change in a family that the birth of a child causes.

6–7 At the end of the days of her purification, the mother has to present sacrificial offerings. She is to bring a year-old כבשׂ, "lamb," for עלה, "a whole offering" (cf. chap. 1), and a pigeon or dove for a חטאת, "purification offering" (cf. chaps. 4–5). In this case the whole offering is greater than the offering for an abnormal discharge (15:14–15, 29–30). Dillmann (552) proposes that a greater offering is required because the offering also benefits the infant. In any case the whole offering is made in grateful praise to Yahweh for the gift of a child; Noordtzij (133) considers it an expression of "a renewed dedication of life." But why does the mother need expiation? There is no indication, such as the need for making a confession, that either the act of conception or the process of birth was considered an act of sin. That the focus is not on some specific act of sin is evident in that a purification offering, not a reparation offering, is required and that the animal for this offering is the least expensive possible. Hoffmann (363) identifies the impurity to be expiated as that which prevents the mother from entering the sanctuary. These sacrifices then cleanse the new mother from her basic sinfulness and provide forgiveness so that she might enter the presence of the holy God with confidence. Throughout the sacrificial regulations it has been seen that mankind by the very nature of being human needs expiation from basic sinfulness; even the newly anointed priests had to offer daily sacrifices for expiation while they remained in the area of the sanctuary for a week (8:33–35).

Two very interesting facts are uncovered in this verse. First, a woman as well as a man had the privilege and the obligation to present sacrifices at the sanctuary. While a woman's role at the sanctuary was less involved than a man's, she was not excluded from presenting sacrifices there, and on occasion she was required to do so. Second, the offerings were the same whether the mother bore a son or a daughter. This fact undercuts any interpretation that the different lengths of impurity indicated that a baby boy had more intrinsic value than a baby girl.

8 Cf. 1:14–17; 5:7–10; 14:21–22, 30–31; 15:14–15, 29–30; Num 6:10–11.

Explanation

The birth of a child is a great, momentous event, even more so in ancient Israel where the population was very small and people lived shorter lives. Birth is fraught with mystery, wonder, and danger. As a mother approaches the door of death, she brings new life into the world. That the mother became ritually unclean on giving birth strikes moderns, however, as strange and unrealistic. Again the law does not give any rationale for this standard. From the Pentateuch and other parts of the OT it can be affirmed that sexual intercourse in marriage was not considered sinful (e.g., Prov 5:15–19; Canticles). High value was placed on children. They were considered a special blessing from God (Lev 26:9; Deut 28:11; Pss 113:9; 127:3–5; 128:3–4; 144:12–13). Therefore, the cause of the mother's uncleanness must not be sought in the process of bringing forth a new life. The text makes it clear that it was the discharges of blood following birth that rendered a new mother unclean. The mother had to be separated from the holy until this abnormal situation was corrected, until her body was whole again.

Another place to seek an explanation for the impurity after giving birth is in the theology. In giving birth the woman challenges the penalty of death on mankind for sinning against God in the Garden of Eden (Gen 2:16–17), for each birth insures the continuation of the race. Symbolically each birth strikes a blow on the head of the paradisiacal serpent, the champion of death (Gen 3:15). Giving birth was a momentous act of victory. But the regulations of ritual purity did not allow a new mother to exalt herself as divine in her great accomplishment.

These regulations relegated her triumph to the sphere of this earth without diminishing her great joy in bringing forth new life. The only negative in her time of separation was that she might not go into the precinct of the tabernacle nor touch anything holy. Furthermore, the time of separation had many practical benefits. It gave the new mother time to recover fully from her labor before returning to her normal chores. It also kept her from immediately becoming pregnant again.

It is very perplexing that giving birth to a girl made a mother unclean twice as long as a boy. Lest the focus be too heavy on this difference, there are some affirmative aspects of this regulation. The sacrifices a mother was to offer were the same for either a girl or a boy; this fact indicates that both genders were considered equal before God. Since the difference in the length of impurity was a transitory matter, this differentiation solely concerned the earthly status of the genders. That means it was a difference that could be changed, and gratefully it has been changed in the work of Christ. For in him there is neither male nor female (Gal 3:28).

The mother had to present a whole offering and a purification offering as part of the purification process. This instruction has an encouraging note, for it is one of the few texts informing us that women could make sacrifices at the sanctuary. The whole offering might have been a praise offering for God's blessing expressed in the gift of a child. In any case the offerings expiated her from any defilement of human sinfulness and gave her freedom to worship at the sanctuary and touch that which was holy. Since these offerings were required of all, an alternate type of animal was permitted for the poor.

Mary the mother of Jesus followed this regulation after the birth of Jesus. She offered up two birds, the offering of the poor, for her purification (Luke 2:22–24). Joseph and Mary's observance of this standard bears witness to their desire to keep the whole law and to their piety.

C. Instructions on Grievous Growths (13:1–14:57)

Bibliography

Browne, S. G. *Leprosy in the Bible.* London: Christian Medical Fellowship, 1970. ———. "'Leprosy' in the New English Bible." *BT* 22 (1971) 45–46. **Cochrane, R. G.** *Biblical Leprosy: A Suggested Interpretation.* Glasgow: Pickering & Inglis, 1963. **Crocker, P. T.** "Archaeology, Mildew, and Leviticus 14." *Buried History* 26 (1990) 3–11. **Davies, M. L.** "Levitical Leprosy: Uncleanness and the Psyche." *ExpTim* 99 (1988) 136–39. **Einsler, A.** "Beobachtungen über den Aussatz im heiligen Lande." *ZDPV* 16 (1911) 247–55. **Görg, M.** "'Ausschlag' an Häusern: Zu einem problematischen Lexem in Lev 14,37." *BN* 14 (1981) 20–25. **Gramberg, K.** "'Leprosy' and the Bible." *BT* 11 (1960) 10–23. **Harrison, R. K.** "Leprosy." *IDB* 3:111–13. ———. "Leper; Leprosy." *ISBE* rev. 3:103–6. **Hulse, E. V.** "The Nature of Biblical 'Leprosy' and the Use of Alternative Medical Terms in Modern Translations of the Bible." *PEQ* 107 (1975) 87–105. **Köhler, L.** "Aussatz." *ZAW* 67 (1955) 290–91. **Lie, H. P.** "On Leprosy in the Bible." *Leprosy Review* 9 (1938) 25–31, 55–67 (=*Acta Dermato-Venereologia* 18 [1937]

624ff.). **Masterman, E.** "Hygiene and Disease in Palestine in Modern and in Biblical Times." *PEQ* 50 (1918) 13–20, 56–71, 112–19, 156–71; 51 (1919) 27–36. **Meier, S.** "House Fungus: Mesopotamia and Israel (Lev 14:33–53)." *RB* 96 (1989) 184–92. **Möller-Christensen, U.** *Bone Changes in Leprosy.* Bristol: John Wright, 1961. **Muir, E.** "Editorial." *Leprosy Review* 9 (1938) 48–49. **Nida, E.** "The Translation of 'Leprosy.'" *BT* 11 (1960) 80–81. **Pilch, J. J.** "Biblical Leprosy and Body Symbolism." *BTB* 11 (1981) 108–13. **Sawyer, J. F.** "A Note on the Etymology of *ṣāraʿat.*" *VT* 26 (1976) 241–45. **Seidl, T.** *Tora für den >>Aussatz<<-Fall: Literarische Schichten und symtaktische Strukturen in Levitikus 13 und 14.* ATSAT 18. St. Ottilien: EOS-Verlag, 1982. **Snaith, N. H.** "Spirit of Righteousness (Lev 14:22)." *Today* 11 (1955) 508–11. **Swellengrebel, J.** "The Translation of 'Tsaracath' and 'Lepra.'" *BT* 11 (1960) 69–80. **Wallington, D.** "'Leprosy' and the Bible. Conclusion." *BT* 12 (1961) 75–79. **Wilkinson, J.** "Leprosy and Leviticus: The Problem of Description and Identification." *SJT* 30 (1977) 153–69. ————. "Leprosy and Leviticus: A Problem of Semantics and Translation." *SJT* 31 (1978) 153–66.

Translation

1 *Yahweh spoke to Moses and Aaron:* 2 *"When anyone has a swelling or an eruption or a shiny patch on his skin, it might be a lesion of a serious skin disease on the surface of his flesh; he is to be brought to Aaron the priest or to one of his sons who is a priest.*
3 *The priest is to examine the lesion on the surface of his flesh. If the hair in the sore has turned white and the appearance of the lesion lies beneath the skin, it is a lesion of a serious skin disease. After the priest has examined it,*[a] *he is to pronounce him unclean.*[b]
4 *If the shiny patch on the surface of his skin is white but there is no appearance of involvement under the skin*[a] *and the hair*[b] *has not turned white,*[c] *the priest is to confine the infected person seven days.* 5 *On the seventh day the priest is to examine it;*[a] *and if,*[b] *in his observation,*[c] *the lesion has stayed and the lesion has not spread in the skin, the priest is to confine him for another seven days.* 6 *The priest is to examine it on the seventh day, a second time; and if the lesion has faded and has not spread in the skin, the priest is to declare him clean.*[a] *It is an eruption. That person is to wash his clothes, and he is clean.* 7 *But if the eruption has truly spread*[a] *over the skin after he has shown himself to the priest and been declared clean, he is to appear another time before the priest.* 8 *The priest is to make an examination.*[a] *If the eruption has spread, the priest is to pronounce him unclean. It is a grievous skin disease.*

9 *"Whenever*[a] *anyone has*[b] *a grievous skin disease, he is to be brought to the priest.*
10 *The priest is to make an examination; and if there is a white swelling in the skin, turning*[a] *the hair white, and there is ulcerating tissue in the swelling,* 11 *it is a chronic disease on the surface of his skin. The priest is to pronounce him unclean. He need not*[a] *confine him, for he is unclean.* 12 *If a grievous disease*[a] *suddenly*[b] *breaks out all over one's skin and the disease*[a] *covers all the skin of the affected person*[c] *from head to foot wherever the priest looks,* 13 *the priest is to make an examination; and if the disease has covered his entire body, he is to pronounce the person with a lesion*[a] *clean. Since it has turned all white, he is clean.* 14 *Whenever ulcerated tissue appears in it, he becomes unclean.* 15 *The priest is to examine the ulcerated tissue and pronounce him unclean. The ulcerated tissue is unclean, for it*[a] *is a grievous skin disease.* 16 *If the ulcerated tissue recedes*[a] *and turns white, he is to come to the priest.* 17 *The priest is to examine it;*[a] *and if the lesion has turned white, the priest is to pronounce the person with the lesion clean. He is clean.*

18 “Whenever someone has a boil in his skin[a] and it heals 19 and on the site of the boil
a white swelling or a reddish-white shiny spot[a] appears, the person is to show himself to
the priest. 20 The priest is to make an examination. If its appearance[a] goes lower than the
skin and the hair in it has turned white, the priest is to pronounce him unclean. It is a
sore of a grievous skin disease that has broken out in the boil. 21 If, when the priest examines it,[a] there is no white hair in it and there is no involvement lower than the skin[b]
and it has faded, the priest is to confine him for seven days. 22 If it truly spreads[a] over the
skin, the priest is to pronounce him unclean. It is a lesion.[bc] 23 But if at that moment[a]
the shiny spot is unchanged and has not spread, it is a scar from the boil, and the priest
is to pronounce him clean.
24 “Or whenever someone has a burn on his skin and the raw tissue turns[a] into a
reddish-white or white shiny spot, 25 the priest is to examine it; and if the hair has turned[a]
white in the shiny spot and its appearance shows involvement beneath the skin, it is a
grievous skin disease which has broken out in the area of the burn. The priest is to
pronounce him unclean; it is a lesion of a grievous skin disease. 26 But if, when the priest
examines it,[a] there is no white hair in the shiny spot and there is no involvement lower
than the skin but it has faded, the priest is to confine him for seven days. 27 On the seventh day the priest is to examine him.[a] If it truly has spread over the skin, the priest is to
pronounce him unclean; it is a lesion of a grievous skin disease.[b] 28 If at that moment the
shiny spot, however, has stayed, has not spread in the skin, and has faded, it is a swelling from the burn. The priest is to pronounce him clean, for it is a scar from the burn.
29 “If a man or a woman has[a] a lesion[b] on the head or on the chin, 30 the priest is to
examine the lesion; and if its appearance lies beneath the skin and the hair in it is yellow
and thin, the priest is to pronounce him unclean. It is a scurfy patch; it[a] is a grievous skin
disease of the head or the chin. 31 But if, when the priest examines the scurfy patch, there
is no appearance beneath the skin and there is no black[a] hair in it, the priest is to confine
the person with the scurfy patch seven days. 32 On the seventh day the priest is to examine
the lesion;[a] and if the scurfy patch has not spread, there is no yellow hair in it, and the
appearance of the scurfy patch does not lie beneath the skin, 33 he is to shave himself,[a]
except for the scurfy patch, and the priest is to confine him for another seven days. 34 On
the seventh day the priest is to examine the scurfy patch; and if the scurfy patch has not
spread and its appearance does not lie beneath the skin, the priest is to pronounce him
clean. He is to wash his clothes, and he is clean. 35 But if the scurfy patch truly spreads
over the skin after he has been pronounced clean, 36 the priest is to re-examine it;[a] and if
the scurfy patch has spread in the skin, the priest does not have to look for yellow hair;
that person is unclean. 37 But if in his observation[a] the scurfy patch[b] is unchanged and
black hair has begun to grow in it, the scurfy patch is healed. That person is clean, and
the priest is to pronounce him clean.
38 “Whenever a man or a woman has shiny spots or white shiny spots on the surface of
the skin,[a] 39 the priest is to make an examination; and if the shiny spots on the surface of the
skin[a] are dull white, it is a rash[b] that has broken out on the skin.[c] That person is clean.
40 “Whenever a man loses[a] his hair, he is bald[b] and he is clean. 41 If he loses[a] his hair
from his forehead, he is bald[b] and he is clean. 42 But if he has a reddish-white lesion on
the scalp[a] or the forehead,[a] it is a grievous skin disease breaking out on his scalp or his
forehead. 43 The priest is to examine it;[a] and if the swollen lesion on his scalp or his forehead is reddish-white like the appearance of a lesion of a grievous skin disease on the
surface of the skin,[b] 44 he is a man with a grievous skin disease and he is unclean. The
priest must pronounce him unclean,[a] for the lesion is on his head.

[45]*"Any person with a grievous skin disease must wear torn clothes, let his hair be unkempt, cover the upper lip, and cry, 'Unclean! Unclean!'* [46]*As long as*[a] *he has the lesion, he continues to be unclean. He is unclean; he must live alone; his dwelling must be outside the camp.*

[47]*"If any clothing has a spot of a grievous mildew—any woolen or linen clothing,* [48]*any woven or knitted*[a] *cloth of linen or wool, any leather or leatherwork—*[49]*if the spot in the clothing or the leather*[a] *or the woven or the knitted material or anything made of leather is greenish*[b] *or reddish,*[b] *it is a spot of a grievous mildew and is to be shown*[c] *to the priest.* [50]*The priest is to examine the spot, and he*[a] *is to confine the infected material for seven days.* [51]*On the seventh day he*[a] *is to examine the spot. If the spot has spread in the garment, the woven or the knitted material, or the leather for whatever purpose the leather has been worked, it is the spot of a persistent*[b] *grievous mildew, and the material is unclean.* [52]*He is to burn the garment, the woven or the knitted material of wool or linen, or any article of leather having such a spot. Because it is a persistent*[a] *grievous mildew, the material is to be burned.* [53]*But if, when the priest examines it, the spot*[a] *has not spread in the garment, the woven or the knitted material, or the article of leather,* [54]*the priest is to order that they wash the material having the spot, and he*[a] *is to confine it*[b] *for a second seven days.* [55]*The priest is to make an examination after it has been washed*[a] *of the spot; and if the spot has not changed its appearance,*[b] *even if the spot has not spread, it is unclean. You are to burn it with fire,*[c] *whether the fungus*[d] *has affected the back or the front.*[e] [56]*If, when the priest makes an examination, the spot has faded after it has been washed,*[a] *he is to tear*[b] *the spot*[c] *from the garment, the leather, or the woven or the knitted material.* [57]*But if it reappears in the garment, or the woven or the knitted material, or any article of leather, it*[a] *is breaking out afresh; you are to burn*[b] *with fire whatever has the spot.*[c] [58]*The garment, the woven or the knitted material, or any article of leather which is washed and the spot goes away, it is to be washed a second time; then it is clean.* [59]*This is the instruction concerning a spot of a grievous mildew*[a] *in clothing of wool or linen, woven or knitted material, or any article of leather,*[b] *to pronounce it clean or unclean."*

[14:1]*Yahweh spoke to Moses,* [2]*"This is the regulation for the person with a grievous skin disease at the time of his cleansing. He is to be brought to the priest.* [3]*The priest is to go outside the camp, and the priest is to make an examination; and if the afflicted person has been healed of the grievous skin disease,* [4]*the priest is to order that one is to take*[a] *for the one being cleansed*[b] *two living, clean birds,*[c] *some cedar wood, scarlet thread*[d] *and hyssop.* [5]*Then the priest is to order that he slay*[a] *one of the birds over fresh water in a clay pot.* [6]*He then*[a] *is to take the living bird*[b] *with the cedar wood, the scarlet thread, and hyssop, and he is to dip it with the living bird in the blood of the bird slain over fresh water.*[c] [7]*He is to sprinkle the person being cleansed from a grievous skin disease seven times and pronounce him clean.*[a] *Then he is to release the living bird in the open field.* [8]*The one being cleansed is to wash his clothes, shave all his hair, bathe with water, and he will be clean. Afterwards he may come into the camp, but he is to dwell outside his tent seven days.* [9]*When the seventh day comes,*[a] *he is to shave off all his hair; i.e., he is to shave his head, his beard, his eyebrows, and all the rest of his hair.*[b] *He is to wash his clothes and bathe his skin with water. Then he will be clean.*

[10]*"On the eighth day he is to take two lambs without defect*[a] *and a year-old ewe without defect, along with three-tenths of an ephah of fine flour and one log of oil.*[b] [11]*The priest who pronounces him clean is to station the one being cleansed and the materials for his offerings*[a] *before Yahweh at the entrance to the Tent of Meeting.* [12]*The priest is to take one*

of those lambs[a] *and present it for a reparation offering with the log of oil,*[b] *and he is to*
lift them up as an elevated offering before Yahweh. 13 *He is to slaughter*[a] *the lamb in the*
place where he slaughters[b] *the purification offering and the whole offering,*[c] *in the holy*
place,[d] *because like the purification offering the reparation offering*[e] *belongs to the priest;*
it is most holy.[f] 14 *The priest is to take some of the blood*[a] *of the reparation offering, and*
the priest[b] *is to put it on the right earlobe of the one being cleansed, on the thumb of his*
right hand, and on the big toe of his right foot. 15 *The priest is to take some oil*[a] *and pour*
it in the palm of the priest's left hand, 16 *and the priest*[a] *is to dip his right finger into some*
oil[b] *which is in his left hand and sprinkle some oil*[b] *with his finger*[c] *seven times before*
Yahweh. 17 *The priest is to put some of the oil*[a] *remaining in his palm on the right earlobe*
of the one being cleansed, on the thumb of his right hand, and on the big toe of his right
foot—on the place of[b] *the blood of the reparation offering.* 18 *The rest of the oil*[a] *that is left*
in the priest's hand he[b] *is to put on the head of the one being cleansed; and the priest will*
make expiation for him before Yahweh. 19 *The priest is to perform*[a] *the ritual of a purifi-*
cation offering and make expiation[b] *for the one being cleansed because of*[c] *his*
uncleanness.[d] *Afterwards*[e] *the priest is to slaughter*[b] *the whole offering.* 20 *The priest is to*
offer up the whole offering and the grain offering on the altar.[a] *Thus the priest will make*
expiation for him, and he will be clean.

21 *"If he is poor and cannot afford these,*[a] *he is to take one male lamb as a reparation*
offering for elevation to make expiation for him and a tenth of an ephah of fine flour
mixed with oil for a grain offering, a log[b] *of oil,* 22 *and two doves or two young pigeons,*
which he can afford; one[a] *is to be for a purification offering and one*[b] *for a whole offer-*
ing. 23 *On the eighth day he is to bring them to the priest for his cleansing at the entrance*
of the Tent of Meeting before Yahweh. 24 *The priest is to take the lamb for a reparation*
offering[a] *and the log of oil, and the priest*[b] *is to lift them up as an elevated offering be-*
fore Yahweh. 25 *He is to slaughter the lamb for a reparation offering.*[a] *The priest is to take*
some[b] *of the blood of the reparation offering and put it on the right earlobe of the one*
being cleansed, on the thumb of his right hand, and on the big toe of his right foot. 26 *The*
priest is to pour some[a] *of the oil into the priest's left palm.* 27 *With his right finger the priest*
is to sprinkle some[a] *of the oil in his left palm seven times before Yahweh.* 28 *The priest is to*
put some of the oil which is in his palm on the right earlobe of the one being cleansed, on
the thumb of his right hand, on the big toe of his right foot—on the place of the blood
of the reparation offering. 29 *The priest*[a] *is to put the rest of the oil*[b] *which is in his palm*
on the head of the one being cleansed to make expiation[c] *for him before Yahweh.* 30 *From*
the doves or the young pigeons which he can afford, he is to make[a] 31 *one*[a] *a purification*
offering and one a whole offering with the grain offering, and the priest[b] *will make*
expiation before Yahweh for the one being cleansed. 32 *This is the instruction for anyone*
who has a grievous skin disease and who cannot afford (the regular offerings) for his
cleansing."

33 *Yahweh spoke to Moses and Aaron,* 34 *"When you enter the land of Canaan, which*
I am about to give you as a possession, and I put a grievous growth in a house[a] *in the*
land of your possession, 35 *the owner of the house is to go and inform the priest, 'I have*
seen some kind of growth in my house.' 36 *The priest is to order that the house be emptied*[a]
before the priest comes to examine the growth, so that nothing in the house is pronounced
unclean. Afterwards[b] *the priest is to come to examine the house.* 37 *The priest*[a] *is to ex-*
amine the growth; and if the growth[b] *in the walls of the house is a greenish or reddish*
eruption[c] *and its appearance is deeper than the surface of the wall,* 38 *the priest is to exit*
the house by the entrance and close the house up for seven days. 39 *On the seventh day the*

priest is to return and make an examination;[a] *and if the growth has spread*[b] *in the walls of the house,* 40 *the priest is to order that the stones affected by the growth be torn out*[a] *and discarded*[a] *in an unclean place outside the city.* 41 *He is to have all the inside of the house scraped,*[a] *and they must dispose of the plaster which was taken off*[bc] *in an unclean place outside the city.* 42 *Then they are to take other*[a] *stones*[b] *and replace those stones, and they are to take*[c] *other mud and plaster*[c] *the house.*

43 *"If the growth breaks out again*[a] *in the house after*[b] *the stones have been torn*[c] *out and the house has been gouged*[d] *and plastered,* 44 *the priest is to come and make an examination; and if the growth has spread*[a] *in the house, it*[b] *is a persistent*[c] *fungus in the house. It is unclean.* 45 *The house is to be demolished;*[a] *its stones, its wood,*[b] *and all of the house's*[c] *plaster are to be taken*[d] *outside the city to an unclean place.* 46 *Whoever enters the house while it is closed up*[a] *will be unclean until the evening.* 47 *Whoever sleeps in the house is to wash his clothes,*[a] *and whoever eats in the house is to wash his clothes.*[a]

48 *"However, when the priest comes and makes an examination, if the growth has not spread*[a] *in the house after the house has been plastered, the priest is to pronounce the house clean, for the growth is cured.* 49 *To purify the house he is to take*[a] *two birds,*[b] *some cedar wood, scarlet thread, and hyssop.* 50 *He is to slaughter one bird over fresh water in a clay vessel.* 51 *Then he is to take the cedar wood, the hyssop, the scarlet thread,*[a] *and the living bird, dip them*[b] *in the blood of the slain bird and*[c] *the fresh water, and sprinkle*[d] *the house seven times.* 52 *He is to cleanse*[a] *the house with the blood of the bird, the fresh water, the living bird, the cedar wood, the hyssop, and the scarlet thread.*[b] 53 *Then he is to send the living bird outside the city in the open field. So he will make expiation for the house, and it will be clean.*

54 *"This is the instruction for every kind of grievous disease and for a scurfy patch,* 55 *for a grievous growth in clothing or in a house,* 56 *for a swelling, an eruption, or a shiny patch,* 57 *and for one to declare*[ab] *when it is unclean or when it is clean. This is the instruction for grievous growths."*

Notes

3.a. Sam and LXX read וראה, "and he has examined or made an examination," for MT and 11QpaleoLev וראהו, "and he has examined it." Most Eng trans., such as RSV and NIV, render the pronominal suffix "him." But in the first part of this verse the object is named, and it is "the lesion," הנגע, not the person. In other verses like 13:25, 26, the gender of the pronoun indicates that its antecedent is the disease, not the person.

3.b. Many interpret the piel to have a declarative use: טמא, "declare unclean" (13:8, 11, 15, 20, 22, 25, 27, 30, 44, 59), and טהר, "declare clean" (13:6, 13, 17, 23, 28, 34, 37, 59; 14:7, 48; cf. *IBHS* §24.2g). But Koch (*Priesterschrift*, 82) points out that the person's status did not change until the priest's pronunciation; thus the piel means "to alter definitively one's position as clean or unclean." Both ideas are present: the priest declares and his declaration determines the person's actual social status.

4.a. LXX* adds *αὐτῆς*, "its." This may simply be a translator's preference to use the possessive pronoun with a part of a person's body.

4.b. Tg and *Tg. Ps.-J.* read וּשְׂעָרָהּ, "and its/his hair." Also LXX adds *αὐτοῦ*, "his"; cf. n. 13:4.a.

4.c. LXX adds *αὐτὴ δέ ἐστιν ἀμαυρά*, "but it is dull."

5.a. Cf. n. 13:3.a.

5.b. The conditional nature of the statement is borne by the context, not by והנה, "and behold," which occurs after verbs of seeing and discovery to introduce what is seen or discovered (Joüon §167l, n. 177i; e.g., 13:6, 8, 10, 13, etc.; Gen 8:13; Deut 13:15[14]; 17:4; cf. *IBHS* §40.2.1e). Kogut (*Scripta Hierosolymitana*, 31 [1984] 148) says that והנה "introduces an object content clause which complements the verb of seeing."

5.c. For MT בעיניו, "in his eyes (observation)," LXX ἐναντίον αὐτοῦ, "before him," could equal בעיניו, "in its appearance," with נגע as the antecedent as in 13:55; Bertholet (44) follows LXX; also BDB, "עין 4.b.," 744–45).

6.a. Cf. n. 13:3.b.

7.a. The inf abs before the verb strengthens the verbal idea, and, being in a conditional sentence, the actual presence of this condition is emphasized (GKC §113n, o).

8.a. LXX reads וראהו, "and he is to examine it"; cf. n. 13:3.a.

9.a. Sam, LXX, and Syr read an initial *waw*. The frequency of the initial *waw* in this regulation makes its absence questionable.

9.b. The verbal inflection agrees with the fem *nomen rectum* צרעת, "a grievous skin disease" (GKC §145a).

10.a. הפך, "it turned," is intransitive (Elliger, 163).

11.a. LXX does not have a negative.

12.a. צרעת, "grievous disease," has the definite article because it is an abstract term (*IBHS* §13.5.1g).

12.b. The inf abs before the verb strengthens the verbal idea; here it adds a note of suddenness (cf. GKC §133m, o; cf. n. 13:7.a.).

12.c. Levine points out that הנגע, "the lesion," is a metonymy for the person affected with lesions.

13.a. Cf. n. 13:12.b.

15.a. Sam and Tg read היא for MT הוא, "it," since its antecedent, צרעת, "a grievous skin disease," is fem; cf. 13:8, 11.

16.a. Levine (79) points out that ישוב can mean recede; cf. 2 Kgs 20:9.

17.a. Cf. n. 13:3.a.

18.a. A few Heb. mss, LXX, Syr, and Vg read בערו, "in his skin," for MT בו־בערו, "in it, in his skin," as in 13:24, but MT is more like an Aram construction. The versions may simply not have translated בו, rather than having had a different Heb. text.

19.a. In the phrase בהרת לבנה אדמדמת, "a shiny, reddish-white spot," the second adj is in apposition to the first, restricting it further (GKC §131i). אדמדמת is a *qataltalah* form, a reduplication of the last two letters; this form has diminutive force (Joüon §87b).

20.a. Sam and a LXX ms read a masc pronominal suffix מַרְאֵהוּ, "its appearance," for MT fem pronominal suffix מַרְאֶהָ.

21.a. Sam, LXX*, and Syr read יראה, "he is to examine," for MT יראנה, "he is to examine it."

21.b. For MT מן־העור, "than the skin," LXX has ἀπὸ τοῦ δέρματος τοῦ χρωτός, "than the skin's surface"; cf. n. 13:3.a.

22.a. Cf. n. 13:7.a.

22.b. LXX has ἁφὴ λέπρας = נגע צרעת, "a lesion of a grievous skin disease"; this text may have come about from influence of other verses, such as v 2, with the full phrase.

22.c. LXX adds ἐν τῷ ἕλκει ἐξήνθησεν, "it has broken out in the boil."

23.a. תחתיה means "on the spot, here and now" (Judg 7:4; Bertholot, 44), but BDB ("תחת 2.a.," 1065) takes it to mean "in its place."

24.a. LXX adds ἐν τῷ δέρματι, "in the skin."

25.a. For MT נהפך, "it has turned itself," Sam reads הפך, "it has turned," as MT in 13:3, 10, 13, 20.

26.a. Cf. n. 13:21.a.

27.a. This time the antecedent is the person, for the disease is fem. Cf. n. 13:3.a.

27.b. Cf. n. 13:22.b.

29.a. The verb stands in the masc, even though it has a compound subj that is both masc and fem, because of the dominance of the masc in ancient Israelite society (*IBHS* §6.5.3a).

29.b. Cf. n. 13:22.b.

30.a. Sam reads היא for MT הוא; cf. n. 13:15.a.

31.a. Instead of MT שׁחר, "black," LXX has ξανθίζουσα, "yellow," as in 13:30, 32, 36, but cf. 13:37. LXX seems to be an error caused by the surrounding readings.

32.a. For MT הנגע, "the lesion," Sam reads הנתק, "the scurfy patch"; cf. n. 13:53.a.

33.a. Many mss have a large ג, for this is the middle letter of the Pentateuch (*b. Qidd.* 30a).

36.a. Cf. n. 13:3.a.

37.a. *BHS* conjectures that בעינו, "in its appearance," should be read for MT בעיניו, "in his eyes (observation)"; cf. n. 13:5.c.

37.b. LXX adds ἐπὶ χώρας, "on the spot, at that moment"; cf. 13:23, 28.

38.a. For MT בשׂרם, "their flesh," LXX has τῆς σακρὸς αὐτοῦ, "his flesh."

39.a. Cf. n. 13:38.a.

39.b. LXX adds καθαρός ἐστιν, "he is clean."

39.c. For MT בעור, "on the skin," LXX reads ἐν τῷ δέρματι τῆς σαρκὸς αὐτοῦ, "on the surface of his skin."

40.a. *IBHS* (§22.6b, n. 31) takes יִמָּרֵט, "lose," as an old qal pass pointed as a niph.

40.b. קרח and גבח (v 41) are built on the *qittel* form, which designates bodily defects.

41.a. Cf. n. 13:40.a.

41.b. Cf. n. 13:40.b.

42.a. Sam, LXX, Syr, and Tg^mss read the pronominal suffix on בקרחת, "on the scalp" (also 11QpaleoLev), and בגבחת, "on the forehead."

43.a. For MT אתו, "it" Sam reads אתה, possibly taking as the antecedent צרעת, "a grievous skin disease," instead of נגע, "a lesion."

43.b. LXX reads the possessive pronoun αὐτοῦ, "his"; cf. n. 13:4.a.

44.a. The inf abs preceding the verb of the same root stresses the certainty of the verbal idea (GKC §113n).

46.a. This is an example of a noun clause introduced by אשׁר, "who, which," coming after a noun in the construct (*IBHS* §38.8c).

48.a. The terms בשׁתי או בערב have been traditionally translated "warp or woof." But it seems impossible that a spot could be in one without being in the other. Snaith (72) suggests that these words mean "yarn" or "piece" respectively. He arrives at this by taking שׁתי as standing for the bulk of threads that hang down in a loom and ערב as the resultant product of the weaving. Harrison (146) takes the phrase as a term referring to the whole garment. NIV renders it "woven or knitted material"; JB uses "fabric or covering."

49.a. LXX's reading ἐν τῷ δέρματι ἢ ἐν τῷ ἱματίῳ, "in the leather or in the clothing," inverts the order of MT.

49.b. Cf. n. 13:19.a.

49.c. This is an example of the hoph having a dir obj (cf. GKC §121a, b).

50.a. A couple of Heb. mss and LXX read הכהן, "the priest."

51.a. LXX reads ὁ ἱερεύς, "the priest"; cf. 13:50.a.

51.b. The meaning of ממארת is uncertain. KB (513) defines it as "virulent, malignant," a fem hiph ptcp of מאר, "pain, prick." LXX and Vg render it "persistent or incurable." Sam reads ממראת, "from appearance."

52.a. Cf. n. 13:51.b.

53.a. Fragments from Cairo Genizah read הנתק, "the scurfy patch" (cf. 13:30), for MT הנגע, "the spot," a variant as in n. 13:32.a.

54.a. Some Heb. mss, LXX, Sam, and Tg add הכהן, "the priest," as does the variant in n. 13:50.a.

54.b. LXX reads τὴν ἁφήν, "the spot," instead of the pronominal suffix on the verb.

55.a. This hothpael, a rare verbal form, takes a dir obj (cf. n. 13:49.c. and GKC §§54h, 121b; *IBHS* §26.3b). The ת of the preformative has assimilated into כ, the first root radical.

55.b. For MT עינו, "its appearance," Sam reads עיניו, "his eyes (observation)," in agreement with nn. 13:5.c. and 13:37.a.

55.c. For MT תשׂרפנו, "you are to burn it," LXX reads κατακαυθήσεται, "it will be burned."

55.d. MT פחתת is a *hapax legomenon.* It may refer to a type of fungus (KB, 873). Snaith (72) assigns to it the meaning "rot" by taking the lit. meaning of the root to be "eat out, perforate."

55.e. בקרחתו או בגבחתו, "on the back or on the front," is composed of two words for baldness, (lit.) "on the bald head or the bald forehead."

56.a. Sam reads הכבסו, "they are to wash," for MT הֻכַּבֵּס, "it has been washed"; cf. n. 13:55.a.

56.b. Sam reads a pl verb קרעו, "they are to tear," to agree with the preceding pl form הכבסו, "they are to wash" (cf. n. 13:56.a.).

56.c. MT reads אתו, "it," referring to the spot; a full obj is supplied in the Eng trans. for clarity.

57.a. LXX supplies the subj λέπρα = צרעת, "a grievous mildew," for the pronoun.

57.b. Cf. n. 13:55.c.

57.c. The acc pronominal suffix is followed by a nominal phrase in apposition to it. This is a rare construction in biblical Heb. (Joüon §146e; *IBHS* §12.4a).

59.a. Sam reads הצרעת, "the grievous mildew."

59.b. Sam reads העור, "the skin, leather," for MT עור, "skin, leather." The absence of the article is the normative style throughout this regulation, but MT has the article on this phrase in 13:52.

14:4.a. Sam, LXX, and Syr read ולקחו, "and they will take." This agrees with 13:4; 14:36, 40. The versions may have rendered MT as an impersonal pl. MT is followed as the more unusual reading; PIR (179) takes it as an impersonal sg.

4.b. מטהר, "who is being cleansed," is a hith ptcp in which the ת of the preformative is assimilated into the first radical, a ט (GKC §54c).

4.c. צפור, "bird," is onomatopoeic for chirping.

4.d. שני stands for "scarlet (cloth)." תולעת specifically means the worm *Coccus ilicis,* which is used in making purple dye. The female worm is dried to get a scarlet-crimson dye.

5.a. Cf. n. 14:4.a.

6.a. Heb.[mss], LXX, Syr, and Vg all begin the sentence with a *waw.* Since the verses in the context begin with a *waw,* this variant is followed.

6.b. The dir obj stands first for emphasis; being a *casus pendens,* it is picked up after the verb by the pronoun אתה, "it."

6.c. Sam reading is anarthrous מים חיים, "fresh water."

7.a. LXX reads καὶ καθαρὸς ἔσται, "and he will be clean" = טהר as in 14:8, 9.

9.a. The temporal clause is introduced by והיה, but the verb of the main clause (יגלח, "he is to shave") does not begin with a *waw* (Joüon §176f).

9.b. There is a chiasm with the phrase "shaving of the hair": "shave":object::expanded object:"shave." The reiteration of the verb and the specification of the kinds of hair are to emphasize that the shaving is to take place everywhere hair grows on the body.

10.a. Sam and LXX add בני שנה, "a year old," to agree with other texts such as 9:3.

10.b. For MT ולג אחד שמן, "one log of oil," Sam and LXX invert the order, ולג שמן אחד.

11.a. MT is simply אתם, "them"; a noun is supplied for clarity in the Eng trans.

12.a. After the definite noun הכבש, "the lamb," the number האחד, "the one," has determinative effect (Joüon §142m).

12.b. This construct phrase is an example of a gen of measure (*IBHS* §9.5.3f).

13.a. LXX reads a pl verb (cf. n. 14:4.a.).

13.b. Sam and LXX both have a pl verb ושחטו, "they slaughter" (cf. n. 14:13.a.), in order to convey more forcefully the indefiniteness of the subj.

13.c. LXX names these two sacrifices in inverted order.

13.d. This phrase is in apposition to the longer phrase defining the place for slaughter; it is added to stress that the place is holy.

13.e. A few Heb. mss and Sam read כאשם, "like the reparation offering" (cf. 7:7). Elliger accepts this reading as a better alternative (163). LXX also has this variant, but it does not have the prep כ, "like," with the purification offering.

13.f. Cf. n. 2:3.a.

14.a. The prep מן, "from," may be used with a noun with the sense of "some," that is, separation from the whole (GKC §119w, n. 2).

14.b. A few Heb. mss, Sam, and LXX omit הכהן, "the priest"; cf. n. 14:24.b.

15.a. Cf. n. 14:14.a.

16.a. LXX does not have הכהן, "the priest."

16.b. Cf. n. 14:14.a.

16.c. 11QpaleoLev and Sam do not have באצבעו, "with his finger."

17.a. Cf. n. 14:14.a.

17.b. A few Heb. mss, LXX, Syr, and *Tg. Ps.-J.* add τὸν τόπον = מקום, "the place of," as in 14:28. MT, which is supported by 11QpaleoLev, results from a scribal error.

18.a. The prep ב has the sense "consisting of" (GKC §119i).

18.b. LXX adds ὁ ἱερεύς, "the priest."

19.a. עשה, "do, make," is a general term that sometimes is used in the sacrificial legislation to mean "perform" the appropriate ceremony; cf. 9:16, 22.

19.b. LXX adds ὁ ἱερεύς, "the priest." In the second position this Eng trans. adds this subj for clarity.

19.c. On the use of מן with כפר + על, "make expiation for," cf. n. 4:26.b.

19.d. In place of MT על־המטהר מטמאתו, "for the one being cleansed from his uncleanness," LXX has a different text, περὶ τοῦ ἀκαθάρτου τοῦ καθαριζομένου ἀπὸ τῆς ἁμαρτίας αὐτοῦ, "for the uncleanness of the one being cleansed from his sin."

19.e. Tg reads אחרי כן, "afterwards," for MT's אחר, "after."

20.a. Sam and LXX add לפני יהוה, "before Yahweh."

21.a. Cf. n. 5:7.a.

21.b. A Heb. mss and LXX have in addition אחד, "one," as in 14:10.

22.a. LXX reads ἡ μία = האחד, "one," as in the next phrase and 14:31. This reading is preferred; MT is a case of haplography.

22.b. Sam and LXX^{min} read ואחד, "and one."
24.a. This gen defines the purpose for the sheep (GKC §128q).
24.b. A few Heb. mss, Sam, LXX, and *Tg. Ps.-J.* omit הכהן, "the priest." MT appears to be a later addition for clarification.
25.a. Cf. n. 14:24.a.
25.b. Cf. n. 14:14.a.
26.a. Cf. n. 14:14.a. Also this phrase comes first for emphasis.
27.a. Cf. n. 14:14.a.
29.a. MT lacks a definite subj, but the term "the priest" occurs as the gen with כף, "palm." In the Eng trans., "the priest" is supplied as the subj and a possessive pronoun takes the place of "the priest's" with the word "palm."
29.b. Sam reads בשמן, "with (from) the oil," for MT מן־השמן, "from the oil."
29.c. In place of MT לכפר עליו, "to make expiation for him," LXX has *καὶ ἐξιλάσεται περὶ αὐτοῦ ὁ ἱερεύς*, "and the priest is to make expiation for him." LXX reading agrees with the formula found frequently in Leviticus, as in 14:31 and in chaps. 4–5 (e.g., 4:20, 26, 31).
30.a. Cf. n. 14:19.a.
31.a. MT has את אשר־תשיג ידו, "which he can afford," but it is missing in LXX and Syr. Since MT is a case of dittography, the variant is accepted.
31.b. Sam omits הכהן, "the priest."
34.a. Even though the pronominal suffix makes the *nomen rectum* definite, the construct chain as it is here may be indefinite (GKC §127c; Joüon §140a).
36.a. The third person pl masc functions as a virtual pass (GKC §144f).
36.b. For MT ואחר, "and after" (cf. 14:8, 19), Sam has the most frequent spelling of this word, ואחרי; cf. 14:43 for the same variant.
37.a. Sam, LXX^{Mmin}, and *Tg. Ps.-J.* add הכהן, "the priest," for clarification. This word has been added to the Eng trans. for clarity.
37.b. A few Heb. mss and LXX omit והנה הנגע, "and behold the growth."
37.c. MT שקערורת has received many explanations. One position is to take it from a root קער, "be or make deep," with a שׁ preformative to mean "depression, hollow" (BDB, 891). Another view takes it from שקע, "sink," to gain a similar meaning. J. Kraemer (*Š^{e}qaʿ^{a}rurot:* A Proposed Solution for an Unexplained Hapax," *JNES* 25 [1966] 125–27) explains this word by relating it to *iqšaʿarra,* an Arab IV stem, "to be rough; to be dry scabby; to be affected by tremor," leading to a noun meaning "coarse, crusty, scaly spots, scaly." This position, however, has some hard phonological barriers: the metathesis of *q* and *š* and the correspondence of Arab *š* to Heb. *š* (Görg, *BN* 14 [1981] 21). Görg (22–25) argues that the Heb. comes from an Egyptian expression *sqr r rwtj,* "blow or damage to the outside = eruption." The Heb. pointing has mistakenly taken this term as a pl
39.a. LXX adds *τὴν οἰκίαν*, "the house," as dir obj in order to produce a better Gk. trans.
39.b. LXX reads a negative, *οὐ*, before the verb.
40.a. The indefinite third person pl functions as a virtual pass.
41.a. A Heb. ms, Sam, LXX, Syr, Tg, and *Tg. Ps.-J.* read a third person pl form as in n. 14:40.a.
41.b. LXX* omits אשר הקצו, "which they took out."
41.c. Sam reads הקיצו, "they took out." *BHS* proposes הקצעו, "they scraped," with support of Syr, Tg, and *Tg. Ps.-J.*; this verb occurs earlier in the sentence. While this proposal is appealing, there is support for MT since another form of this verb occurs in 14:43; cf. n. 14:43.d.
42.a. LXX^{BA} reads *στερεούς*, "solid," for MT אחרות, "other."
42.b. LXX adds *ἀπεξυσμένους*, "scraped."
42.c. Sam and LXX read pl forms to agree with the preceding verbal forms.
43.a. The verb ישוב, "it returns," is used with another verb to denote repetition (GKC §120d; BDB, "שׁוב qal 8.," 998).
43.b. Cf. n. 14:36.a.
43.c. LXX reads an inf constr *τὸ ἐξελεῖν*, "to take away," while Sam reads a pl pf verb חלצו, "they tore"; the series of inf constrs favors rendering this verb as an inf constr, which requires repointing MT as חַלֵּץ, "pulling, tearing out."
43.d. For MT הקצות, "cutting, taking out, gouging," which GKC §53l takes as a rare variant spelling of the inf constr, LXX reads *τὸ ἀποξυσθῆναι*, "to scrape." *BHS* suggests reading הקציע, "to scrape," with support of Tg. MT is followed because this same word occurs in 14:41 (cf. n. 41.c.). It is hard to imagine a similar spelling error for different forms of this root in two different verses.
44.a. For MT פשה, "it has spread," Sam reads פרח, "it has sprouted."
44.b. Sam omits הוא, "it."

44.c. Cf. n. 13:51.b.

45.a. Sam, LXX, and Syr read ונתצו, "it is to be demolished," a virtual pass, for MT's sg form; cf. n. 14:40.a. This Eng trans. follows the variant.

45.b. LXX's reading καὶ τὰ ξύλα αὐτῆς καὶ τοὺς λίθους αὐτῆς, "and its wood and its stones," inverts the order of MT.

45:c. LXX does not have הבית, "the house."

45.d. Sam, LXX, and Syr have a pl form, functioning as a virtual pass. This Eng trans. follows this variant.

46.a. MT הַסְגִּיר, "to shut up," is a rare variant spelling of the inf constr (GKC §53l), but Bertholet (48) takes the form as a pf and the sentence as a relative sentence.

47.a. LXX twice adds καὶ ἀκάθαρτος ἔσται ἕως ἑσπέρας, "and he will be unclean until evening."

48.a. Cf. n. 14:44.a. LXX reads an inf abs of the same root before the verb as in 13:27.

49.a. Sam reads a pl, ולקחו, "they will take," or "they are to be taken" (a virtual pass), for the sg in MT; cf. n. 14:40.a.

49.b. LXX* adds ζῶντα καθαρά, "living, clean," as in 14:4.

51.a. Sam and LXX invert the order, reading ואת שני התולעת ואת האזב, "the scarlet thread and the hyssop," in agreement with 14:6 and the order in 14:49. This appears to be a leveling of the text.

51.b. LXX^BA reads αὐτό = אתה, "it," for MT אתם, "them."

51.c. LXX does not have ובו, "and in," but ἐφ, "on."

51.d. LXX reads in addition ἐν αὐτοῖς, "with them."

52.a. The piel of חטא, "sin," means "de-sin, cleanse, purify"; cf. n. 8:15.c.

52.b. Sam inverts the order of MT to read ובשני התולעת ובאזב, "with the scarlet thread and with the hyssop"; cf. n. 14:51.a.

57.a. Some Heb. mss, LXX, and Syr correctly read the conjunctive *waw:* ולהורת, "and to declare, instruct."

57.b. The inf constr is without a definite time and a definite subj (cf. Joüon §124s). The subj is indefinite, for the sentence is general.

Form/Structure/Setting

This section treats impurity caused by certain skin diseases and by growths on garments and in houses. The basic structure of the passage is outlined:

I. First speech: Identification of grievous skin diseases and growths in clothing (13:1–59)
A. Introductory formula (v 1)
B. Speech proper (vv 2–59)
1. Concerning skin diseases (vv 2–46)
a. Series of cases (vv 2–44)
1) First case—lesion of the skin (vv 2–8)
a) Basic case (vv 2–3)
(1) The symptoms (v 2a)
(2) Presentation to a priest (vv 2b–3)
(a) Presentation required (v 2b)
(b) Examination by the priest (v 3)
(i) Examination proper and symptoms (v 3a)
(ii) Pronouncement—unclean (v 3b)
b) Variation of basic case (vv 4–8)
(1) Symptoms found at initial examination (v 4)
(2) Second examination prescribed (vv 5–8)
(a) First alternative—disease stayed (vv 5–6)
(b) Second alternative—disease spreading (vv 7–8)
2) Second case—ulcerating tissue (vv 9–17)
a) Basic case (vv 9–11)
(1) Requirement to be brought to a priest (v 9)

- (2) Examination by the priest (vv 10–11)
  - (a) Symptoms (v 10)
  - (b) Judgment by the priest (v 11)
- b) Variations to above case (vv 12–17)
  - (1) First variation—turning white all over (vv 12–13)
  - (2) Second variation—raw flesh (vv 14–15)
  - (3) Third variation—raw flesh that turns white (vv 16–17)
- 3) Third case—change in a healed boil (vv 18–23)
  - a) Basic case (vv 18–19)
  - b) Alternative symptoms to basic case (vv 21–23)
    - (1) Symptoms requiring seven-day confinement (v 21)
    - (2) Two possible situations on examination after confinement (vv 22–23)
- 4) Fourth case—an infected burn (vv 24–28)
  - a) Basic case (vv 24–25)
    - (1) Symptoms (v 24)
    - (2) Examination and judgment (v 25)
  - b) Alternatives to basic case (vv 26–28)
    - (1) Symptoms requiring seven-day confinement (v 26)
    - (2) Two possible situations at second examination (vv 27–28)
- 5) Fifth case—a lesion in beard or hair (vv 29–37)
  - a) Basic case (vv 29–30)
  - b) Variations to above case (vv 31–37)
    - (1) An alternative situation (vv 31–34)
      - (a) Symptoms of scurf that require a seven-day confinement (v 31)
      - (b) Examination, second confinement, and judgment (vv 32–34)
    - (2) Recurrence of symptoms after one has been declared clean (vv 35–37)
      - (a) Symptoms (v 35)
      - (b) Two possible situations (vv 36–37)
- 6) Sixth case—white spots all over body (vv 38–39)
  - a) Symptoms (v 38)
  - b) Examination and judgment (v 39)
- 7) Seventh case—baldness (vv 40–44)
  - a) Cases that are clean (vv 40–41)
  - b) Case that is unclean (vv 42–44)
    - (1) Symptoms (v 42)
    - (2) Examination and judgment (vv 43–44)

b. Exclusion from community of a person with a grievous skin disease (vv 45–46)
  - 1) Bearing of that person (v 45)
  - 2) Exclusion from camp (v 46)

2. Concerning a grievous mildew in clothing (vv 47–59)
  - a. The case (vv 47–58)
    - 1) Types of material and symptoms (vv 47–49)
    - 2) Examination (vv 50–58)
      - a) Examination and seven-day confinement (v 50)
      - b) Two possible situations (vv 51–58)
        - (1) First possible situation—a persistent mildew (vv 51–52)
        - (2) Second possible situation requiring a second confinement with two alternatives (vv 53–58)

(a) Examination (vv 53–54)
(b) Results (vv 55–58)
(i) Garment to be burned (v 55)
(ii) Garment to be washed and confined again; two possible outcomes—to be burned or clean (vv 56–58)
b. Concluding formula (v 59)
II. Second speech: Restoration of a person healed from a grievous skin disease (14:1–32)
A. Introductory formula (v 1)
B. Speech proper (vv 2–32)
1. Heading (v 2a)
2. Ritual of restoration (vv 2b–32)
a. Ceremony for readmission to the community (vv 2b–8)
1) Examination by priest (vv 2b–3b*α*)
2) Ritual of cleansing (vv 3b*β*–8a)
a) Preparation for ritual (vv 3b*β*–4)
b) Ritual with the two birds (vv 5–7)
c) Ritual of washing and shaving (v 8a)
3) Reentry into camp (v 8b)
b. Ceremony of full reinstatement (vv 9–32)
1) Primary ritual (vv 9–20)
a) Preparation by shaving and washing (v 9)
b) Ritual of full reinstatement (vv 10–20)
(1) Prescription of animals and materials for offerings (v 10)
(2) Ritual of sacrifices (vv 11–20)
(a) Presentation of person healed and materials (v 11)
(b) Series of sacrifices (vv 12–20)
(i) Reparation offering (vv 12–18)
(1) Reparation offering proper (vv 12–13)
(2) Consecration of person healed (vv 14–18a)
(*α*) Blood rite (v 14)
(*β*) Oil rite (vv 15–18a)
(3) Results—expiation (v 18b)
(ii) Purification offering (v 19a)
(iii) Whole offering with grain offering (vv 19b–20)
2) Alternative sacrifices for the poor (vv 21–32)
a) Alternative ritual (vv 21–31)
(1) Prescription of animals and materials for offerings (vv 21–22)
(2) Ritual of sacrifices (vv 23–31)
(a) Presentation of materials (v 23)
(b) Series of sacrifices (vv 24–31)
(i) Reparation offering (vv 24–29)
(1) Reparation offering proper (vv 24–25a)
(2) Consecration of person healed (vv 25b–29a)
(*α*) Blood rite (v 25b)
(*β*) Oil rite (vv 26–29a)
(3) Results—expiation (v 29b)
(ii) Purification and whole offerings (vv 30–31)
b) Summary statement (v 32)
III. Third speech: Treatment for a house with a grievous growth (vv 33–53)
A. Introductory formula (v 33)
B. Speech proper (vv 34–53)
1. Basic case (vv 34–42)
a. A grievous growth in a house (v 34)

b. Response of the house's owner (vv 35–42)
  1) Report to priest (v 35)
  2) Initial examination of house and first quarantine (vv 36–38)
  3) Second examination of house (vv 39–42)
    a) Examination proper (v 39)
    b) Procedure for removing infected area (vv 40–41)
    c) Repair of area removed (v 42)

2. First alternative—recurrence of mildew (vv 43–45)
  a. Statement of case (v 43)
  b. Response (vv 44–45)
    1) Examination (v 44)
    2) Demolition of house (v 45)
3. Uncleanness for those who enter a quarantined house (vv 46–47)
4. Second alternative—cessation of growth (vv 48–53)
  a. Examination by priest and pronouncement—clean (v 48)
  b. Ritual of restoration of the house (vv 49–53)
    1) Prescription of materials for sacrifices (v 49)
    2) Ritual of sacrifices (vv 50–53)
      a) Sacrifices proper (vv 50–53a)
        (1) Slaughter of one bird (v 50)
        (2) Ritual with living bird (vv 51–53a)
      b) Results—expiation and cleanness (v 53b)

IV. Summary statement (vv 54–57)
  A. List of grievous growths (vv 54–57a)
  B. Identification as instruction (v 57b)

In this division there are three speeches. Each speech is headed by an introductory formula. In the first and the third formulae, Yahweh addresses both Moses and Aaron. Aaron is included because these laws about ritual purity are a central concern of the priests (cf. 10:10–11; 11:1). But in the second formula Yahweh addresses only Moses. The fact that this unit treats sacrificial procedure may account for Aaron's absence, that is, this formula is constructed like those found in chaps. 1–7 with Yahweh speaking to Moses. Other indicators of the sections are three summary statements: at 13:59 for the section 13:47–59, 14:32 for 14:21–32, and 14:54–57 for all of 13:1–14:53. Comparing the introductory formulae with the summary statements reveals four sections: 13:1–46; 13:47–59; 14:1–32; 14:33–53. In the final form of Leviticus these four sections make one unit.

The initial section about grievous skin diseases consists of seven cases (13:2–44) plus the prescription for the behavior of a person with a serious skin disease (13:45–46). The cases are organized first by diseases of the skin (13:2–28) and then by inflammations of the scalp (13:29–46; Elliger, 178). The sixth case (13:38–39) is distinct from the rest in its simplicity and brevity; it treats only a disturbance of the skin that does not render a person unclean. Each case begins with a casuistic formulation, with the subject followed by a conditional כי, indicative of impersonal case law (Noth, 104). In the apodosis, symptoms are given followed by the steps that a priest is to take in order to determine whether a lesion is to be classified as צרעת, "a grievous skin disease." The protasis and variations to the basic case are presented in a series of sentences headed by *waw* perfects. If the symptoms are clear and decisive, the priest immediately pronounces a person clean or unclean. But if the priest is unable to judge the symptoms conclusively, he orders a seven-day quarantine followed by a re-examination. If the second examination is inconclusive, another seven-day quarantine is ordered. As soon as the priest has conclusive evidence, he makes a definitive pronouncement. A declaratory statement of identification often accompanies a pronouncement. But toward the end of the list a declaratory formula of clean/unclean tends to stand alone without a priestly pronouncement (vv 36, 39, 40, 41; both forms occur in vv 37, 44). Within a case there are instructions to cover a variety of conditions. The variety of possible situations makes the structure of most cases quite complex.

In this regulation, as well as those for garments and houses, the priest has a critical role. He must examine a person or object with a suspicious growth to determine whether it renders the person or the object unclean. The priest, however, is not acting as a physician. He offers no cure, nor does he prescribe any remedy. His purpose is to regulate those who have access to the sanctuary in order to keep it and the congregation from defilement by entrance into the area of the sanctuary by one who is unclean. The priest determines the status of a person with a suspicious growth on their skin by pronouncing that person either clean or unclean. It is his pronouncement that changes or affirms a person's status.

The second section of the first speech (13:47–59) concerns the handling of articles of clothing stricken by a grievous mildew. This section opens in casuistic formulation. The basic case specifies the kinds of materials and the types of suspicious symptoms that require a priestly examination (13:47–49). The regulation then covers a variety of situations, some of which require periods of confinement for an infected garment. The structure here is similar to that for cases of a grievous skin disease. A summary statement (13:59) concludes this section.

The second speech prescribes an elaborate ritual for restoration to the community of one who has recovered from a grievous skin disease (14:1–32). In style, vocabulary, and outlook it agrees with the regulations about grievous skin diseases in 13:2–46 (Elliger, 174). The rites of sprinkling the healed person with blood and oil and the staging of the ritual over a span of several days correspond to the anointing of the high priest (chap. 8), for this kind of ritual drastically changes the status of the parties involved. This elaborate ritual assumes the sacrificial regulations found in chaps. 1–5, for it expands only on rites peculiar to this ritual, such as the ritual with the living bird and the rites with the blood and oil. For the poor, alternative offerings are permitted except for the lamb of the reparation offering (14:21–32). There is an appendix permitting alternative offerings for the poor. That it is an appendix is attested by its own summary statement (14:32). Also special stress is placed on the priest's role. This stress corresponds to the critical role the priest has in determining whether a person is unclean. In that judgment he has a condemning role; by contrast in this ritual he has a redeeming role, preparing a person to be able to enter God's presence again.

The third speech concerns the handling of a grievous growth in a house (14:33–53). That this regulation comes from a different corpus is attested by its different structure: the case begins with כי, a relative clause expands the basic case, and God states in the first person that he is the one who strikes a house with a grievous growth. It also differs by giving special instructions for procedures to be done before the priest makes his initial examination (14:36). This instruction is included to cut down on the financial loss that a grievous growth would inflict on the house's owner. Then various steps are given for the identification of the growth and for the attempt to remove that growth from the house (14:37–42). If the growth persists, the house must be demolished (14:43–47). However, if it desists, there is a ritual for the cleansing and continued occupation of that house (14:48–53). This ritual echoes that for a person healed of a grievous skin disease.

The summary statements attest to the composite nature of this speech. They give clues to the composition clusters of this unit (cf. Fishbane, *Biblical Interpretation*). These four sections are grouped under the rubric זאת תורה לכל־נגע הצרעת, "instruction about every kind of a mark from a grievous growth" (v 54a). That the summary statement for the basic regulation about grievous skin diseases comes at the end indicates that the other regulations on grievous growths became attached to this regulation. At one stage the ritual for the restoration of one recovered from a grievous skin disease followed the regulation. That ritual was expanded with a unit on alternate offerings for the poor, as the limited summary statement at 14:32 attests. Then the inclusion of the regulation about a grievous mildew on an article of clothing (13:47–59), which has its own summary statement, separated the regulation on skin diseases from the ritual of restoration. Since this section and the preceding one both concern grievous growths (צרעת), this section did not need an introductory formula. The fourth section, about a grievous growth in the walls of a house (14:33–53), was the last to be placed in this division. It was composed to extend the issue of uncleanness from repulsive growths to buildings, a different situation produced by the settlement of Canaan (cf. Wenham, 211–12; Noth, 110). This section does not have its own summary statement because the final summary statement follows it. A question arises: Why was it not placed after the regulation about garments, especially since garments and houses are coupled in the summary statement at 14:55? The reason for its location resides in its having a ritual of restoration. Given the elaborate nature of the ritual of restoration for a person healed of a grievous skin disease, the less elaborate ritual for a recovered house needed to follow the more elaborate one in order not to diminish the former's importance. And this ritual of restoration for a house is far more intelligible to the audience in light of the greater ritual.

In the final form, the four sections yield a modified A:B::A':B' pattern: A—dealing with diseases of the skin; B—dealing with growths or blotches in objects. The first half is concerned only with the identification of spots on the surface of the skin or clothing; the second half is concerned with both the identification of such spots and the restoration of what had been affected.

As for the arrangement of the material within each section, the works of N. Lund ("The Presence of Chiasmus in the OT," *AJSL* 46 [1929] 115–19) and M. Fishbane (*Biblical Interpretation,* 442–43) uncover chiastic structures within this regulation. According to Lund, the structures of the three units, 14:10–20, 21–32 and 49–53, use chiasmus. Fishbane goes on to show an internal chiastic arrangement within the several cases of skin diseases. The chiasm is based on the three critical symptoms mentioned in 13:2: (1) שׂאת, "swelling"; (2) ספחת, "eruption," or פשׂה תפשׂה, "truly spread"; (3) בהרת, "shiny patch." In the first section they occur in the following chiastic pattern: 1, 2, 3 in v 2; in vv 3–17 3, 2, 1 (vv 4, 6, 10, respectively); in vv 18–23 1, 2, 3 (vv 19, 22, 23, respectively); in vv 24–28 3, 2, 1 (vv 24, 27, 28, respectively); in vv 29–44, 1 is ruled out by nature of the disease, 2, 3 (vv 35, 38, respectively). This fine artistic style served as a mnemonic device to aid the priests' memorization of these regulations for oral instruction.

Noth (103–4) assigns this series of regulations to the priestly professional knowledge. The detail in these cases and the critical role that the priest plays favor this classification. However, if this material were for the training of priests to make an accurate diagnosis for pronouncing a person, a garment, or a house clean or unclean and for carrying out all the requirements necessitated by these regulations, a host of specifics are missing. Two examples serve to illustrate the point. There are no specifications regarding the size of a skin infection that would require an examination by a priest. Furthermore, no directions are given about the confinement of a person infected, i.e., the location of the place of confinement and regulations about the manner of care for such a person, such as eating and general hygiene. The priestly professional knowledge would have addressed these subjects and have had many more specifics about handling a wide variety of skin diseases and defiling growths. This material was adapted from priestly professional knowledge for the instruction of the laity (cf. Elliger, 178). The people needed to be taught the basic symptoms of skin irritations, growths in garments, and eruptions on the wall of a house that required an examination by a priest, for they had the responsibility of initiating the process for the priest to make such an examination. This law also informed them of the basic procedure that the priest was to take before making a definitive pronouncement. In this way the people could comply with the law in obedience to God, rather than in becoming subject to a priestly class who controlled them by keeping them in ignorance about these regulations governing the identification and handling of grievous growths in order to have power over the people as well as their garments and houses.

The origin of these regulations regarding grievous growths, then, goes back to the earliest day of the sanctuary, for the first devotees of Yahweh would have been zealous for cultic purity. In portions of this long speech Koch (*Priesterschrift,* 79–88) has been able to uncover simple statements headed by *waw* perfects. This points to the antiquity of the original regulations concerning impurity from grievous infection. However, for the most part, the simple sentences have been expanded into bulky, complex sentences. This indicates that through the centuries these regulations have been embellished with details to make more precise the identification of grievous infections. That is, the final text has resulted from a long, continuous editorial process. Since this editorial process has not been uniform, it is impossible to uncover layers of editorial activity. The final form may be assigned to the time when Leviticus was canonized.

Comment

13:1 In the laws of ritual purity Yahweh characteristically addresses both Moses and Aaron; cf. 11:1.

13:2 The basic case covers anyone (אדם); this word is chosen to include all, young and old, male and female (cf. 1:2). The dominant word in these chapters is צרעת, "a grievous skin disease." In LXX it is translated by *λέπρα*, "leprosy," and in Latin by *lepra.* Wilkinson (*SJT* 31 [1978] 154–56) notes that it is a generic, not a technical term, for it is used as a descriptive, not an etiological purpose, and it is used in a ritual, not a medical, context.

Excursus: צרעת *and Leprosy*

צרעת, the crucial term in this regulation, is a generic term for repulsive changes in the surface condition of human skin, clothing of wool or of linen, articles of leather, and the walls of a building. Among diseases of the skin it encompasses swellings, a crusty or scabby rash, inflamed areas, and scurf of the scalp or beard (Browne, *Leprosy*, 10). Working with the material in Leviticus, Hulse takes צרעת to include "psoriasis, seborrhoeic dermatitis, fungus infections of the skin particularly favus, patchy eczema, and pityriasis rosea" (*PEQ* 107 [1975] 96). It is sometimes compared to snow (כשלג; Exod 4:6; Num 12:10; 2 Kgs 5:27). Formerly interpreters considered the point of comparison to be the color white and translated the phrase "as white as snow." But Hulse (*PEQ* 107 [1975] 93–95) persuasively reasons that the comparison is with the flaking of snow, not its color. A skin disease classified as צרעת lasted for months or for years. Therefore, a person with a suspicious sore on his skin was quarantined once or twice for seven days in order to exclude skin diseases of short duration, like scarlet fever, from being classified as צרעת. The term צרעת also conveyed strong feelings of dread and repulsion, somewhat like cancer and AIDS do today, for one struck by צרעת was excluded from the community with little hope of recovery.

The understanding of Lev 13–14 has been hampered by the translation of צרעת as leprosy in standard Eng versions. This rendering has its roots in the history of biblical translation. LXX rendered צרעת by λέπρα. Most Latin translators followed the LXX and transliterated this word into Latin as *lepra*. Eng translators adopted the same practice and rendered it "leprosy." LXX, however, is an accurate translation, for Gk. λέπρα is a general term for a variety of skin diseases like psoriasis and fungal infections. Hippocratic writings use this term for "an itchy or powdery thickening of the skin most prevalent in the spring" (Hulse, *PEQ* 107 [1975] 88). The difficulty of understanding comes about because the Eng term "leprosy" has become a technical medical term for an infectious disease caused by the bacillus *Mycobacterium leprae*. This disease, also known as Hansen's disease after G. Hansen, the physician who identified this bacillus in 1868, attacks the skin, disturbs the nasal membrane, and affects the lymph nodes and peripheral nodes. The bacillus invades the nerve fibers, producing loss of sensation and leading to mutation of bodily parts. It distorts one's appearance and slowly debilitates its victims. It is infectious, but not nearly as infectious as popular opinion believes. In ancient times the Greeks observed the difference between skin diseases and true leprosy. For the latter infection, Greek authors such as Celsus and Pliny the Elder employed the terms ἐλέφας, "elephant," or ἐλεφαντίασις, the disease "elephantiasis," so-called because the victim's skin becomes rough and thick like an elephant's. For centuries these two terms, ἐλέφας and ἐλεφαντίασις, were restricted to true leprosy. But in medieval times some Arabic authors began to employ the term *lepra* for Hansen's disease, and unfortunately they were followed by later European authors (Hulse, *PEQ* 107 [1975] 88–89). Only in the nineteenth century did the Eng term become restricted to Hansen's disease, but by then it had become the standard practice to render צרעת and Gk. λέπρα in Eng as "leprosy." This has led to and has promoted the popular belief that Lev 13–14 concerns Hansen's disease. Unfortunately this identification has increased the dread that this disease still arouses. Affirmatively, Jesus' attitude to those with "leprosy" has motivated several to spend their lives in working to improve the well-being of those with Hansen's disease.

In the following discussion, the term "Hansen's disease" will be used for modern-day leprosy to avoid confusion, although it is not the best practice to call a disease after a person.

It is clear that צרעת is a broad term. Did it include Hansen's disease? That is doubtful for two reasons: the symptoms of צרעת do not coincide with those of Hansen's disease, and this dreaded disease probably had not reached Palestine during OT times (but for the opposite opinion cf. R. Harrison, "Leprosy," *ISBE* rev 3:105).

The studies of contemporary leprologists reveal several differences between the description of צרעת and Hansen's disease. Browne (*Leprosy*, 14) states, "medically speaking, none of the references to *ṣāraʿat* includes any of the specific signs and symptoms of leprosy. The signs mentioned witness against, rather than for, leprosy. Furthermore, none of the characteristic features of leprosy are so much as hinted at; these are, anaesthetic areas of skin, progressive ulceration of the extremities, depressed nose, and facial nodules. These are obvious departures from the normal that would be noticed by observant laymen, and were in fact noted in other lands when true leprosy occurred." This last note is important, for it is reasonable to expect that lay observers in ancient Israel would have noted the major symptoms of Hansen's disease, distinguishing it from other forms of צרעת. Furthermore, the regulations give the impression that צרעת changes fairly rapidly, but in Hansen's disease the skin undergoes minor changes over years except in rare, acute cases. Again, צרעת involves a person's hair and scalp far more than is usual in the case of Hansen's disease (Lie, *Leprosy Review* 9 [1938] 27–28; Cochrane, *Biblical Leprosy*, 13).

A second major argument against the position that צרעת included Hansen's disease is that current research casts doubt on the presence of this disease in ancient Palestine. Hansen's disease was known in the ancient world, particularly in India and in China, by 600 B.C. (cf. Cochrane, *Biblical Leprosy*, 3–7). The first conclusive reference to leprosy in Europe is dated in the third century B.C. In that reference it is considered a new disease, and it is called *ἐλεφαντίασις* not *λέπρα*. But whether it was known in ancient Palestine is disputed. With increased scientific knowledge of the effects of this disease on the skull, Möller-Christensen has examined numerous skeletons from Egypt, and only two cases of Hansen's disease have been found, both from Nubia and both from the early Christian era (cited in Browne, *Leprosy*, 17). Furthermore, he examined remains of some six hundred people from Lachish without finding any evidence of Hansen's disease (Browne, *Leprosy*, 17). These facts cast doubt on the Hebrews' having been acquainted with this dreadful disease. By the time of Christ it is highly probable that it had reached Palestine, leaving open the possibility that some NT cases could have included this disease (Hulse, *PEQ* 107 [1975] 88). Unfortunately, the NT accounts of people with *λέπρα* provide no detailed description of any of the symptoms to lead toward an identification of the disease involved (Browne, *Leprosy*, 22–24).

The cases of צרעת reported in the OT are few, but very dramatic; usually God, out of great displeasure, struck a person with צרעת. The first case, however, was a startling sign given to Moses at the burning bush. God instructed him to place his hand in his bosom. When God ordered him to take it out, it was scaly like snow (Exod 4:6). Then he placed his hand in his bosom again, and when he took it out it had been restored whole. During a contest over leadership, God became very angry with Miriam and smote her with צרעת (Num 12:10). She was put outside the camp for seven days until God caused her to recover from the disease. Naaman, a Syrian commander with צרעת, found healing by dipping seven times in the Jordan (2 Kgs 5:9–14). When Gehazi, Elisha's servant, became greedy for the rewards Naaman had offered to Elisha but which Elisha had turned down, he was striken with the disease Naaman had had (2 Kgs 5:27). The most remarkable case in the OT is the time when King Uzziah was struck with צרעת while raging at the priests who were trying to correct him after he had unlawfully entered the Temple to burn incense on the altar of incense (2 Chr 26:16–21). Another incident, reported in 2 Kgs 7:3–8, informs us that in the Kingdom period those with צרעת lived outside a village, surviving as scavengers. None of these accounts, however, gives enough clinical details to diagnose the specific malady involved (Browne, *Leprosy*, 12–14). But they do testify to the sense of horror and dread that attended being afflicted with צרעת.

In the NT, the term *λέπρα*, which corresponds to צרעת, occurs some thirteen times, all in the Synoptic Gospels. Jesus healed several afflicted with "leprosy"; usually the word used for the healing is "cleansed" in order to communicate that the afflicted were both healed and ritually pure. When a Samaritan recovered from "leprosy" by obeying Jesus' instructions, the text uses "healed," for ritual purity at the Temple was not an issue for him (Luke 17:12–19). In one case Jesus instructed the person healed to fulfill the ceremonial law (Matt 8:2–4; Mark 1:40–45; Luke 5:12–15). "Leprosy" symbolized one of the most loathsome barriers against being a part of the people of God. Therefore, Jesus' cleansing of those with grievous skin diseases symbolized his messianic mission to overcome all barriers that separated selected segments of the population from God (cf. Matt 11:5; Luke 7:22). Jesus not only healed these "lepers"; his work cleansed them so that they could again participate in the community and have access to God at the Temple. It is clear, though, that the NT writers used *λέπρα*, the term occurring in the LXX translation of Lev 13–14 because they wanted to present Jesus' response to these laws.

Given the wide-ranging usage of צרעת in the OT, there is no single Eng word that may be used for rendering this Heb. word. Fortunately some modern Eng translations have moved away from use of the term "leprosy." NEB sometimes renders it "a malignant skin-disease" (Lev 13:2, 3, 8, etc.), or "a chronic skin disease" (13:11); NIV uses "an infectious skin disease" (13:2, 3, 9, etc.) and "infectious disease" (13:8, 15). Unfortunately these two versions revert to the translation "leprosy" in many narrative texts like 2 Kgs 5:1–27; 7:3; 15:5, though happily they include a qualifying footnote. The problem with the term "malignant" is that it means cancer and conveys the idea of an uncontrollable growth (Hulse, *PEQ* 107 [1975] 101). This commentary has chosen "a grievous skin disease," for "skin disease" is an accurate description of the ailment, and the term "grievous" conveys the emotional dimension of צרעת without suggesting any of its clinical properties. In regard to clothing, NEB has "a stain of mold" (13:47) and NIV "mildew." In this work it is rendered "grievous mildew" to keep before the reader the fact that the same term is being used with emotional connotations. For a growth in a house, NEB has "a fungus infection" and NIV "a spreading mildew" (14:34); this translation uses "a grievous growth." For these three conditions Hulse (*PEQ* 107 [1975] 103) suggests the translations "a repulsive scaly skin disease," "an objectionable powdery condition," and "an objectionable scaling condition."

In the first case something abnormal breaks out on one's skin. The phrase בעור־בשרו, (lit.) "in the skin of one's flesh," means the surface or outer layer of the skin. When a breaking out takes place on the skin, it becomes an issue whether the lesion is צרעת, a grievous, repulsive skin disease. If it is, a priest must make a pronouncement of that fact. The primary issue of this regulation then is what kind of disturbance in a person's skin requires a priestly examination to determine whether that disturbance is a grievous skin disease (צרעת). Three basic symptoms that require a priest to make an examination are given. The first symptom is שׂאת, "a swelling." This meaning is gained by taking this word from the root נשׂא, "lift up, raise" (Wilkinson, *SJT* 30 [1977] 155–57). LXX, however, renders it *οὐλή*, "scar." Snaith (70) goes with LXX by taking שׂאת as cognate to Arab *šiʾatu*, "color, mark." Levine says more precisely that it means "local inflammation, boil, mole" (76). The next symptom is ספחת, taken by KB (72) to be "scurf," and by BDB (705) to be "an eruption" or "a scab" (cf. Wilkinson, 157). LXX renders it *σημασία*, "the decisive appearance (of a disease)" (Liddell & Scott, 1593). Because the precise meaning of this term is unknown, this translation simply uses "eruption." The third symptom is בהרת, "a shiny patch" from בהר, "shine, be bright." Any of these changes in the skin might be נגע־צרעת. The term נגע, which is from a root meaning "touch, reach, arrive, inflict," means "mark, spot, stroke, sore, lesion, disease." Incidentally this term is the name of the tractate in the Mishnah concerning skin diseases. In the phrase נגע צרעת, נגע is the broader, more general term for a lesion or a disease, and צרעת is usually the more restricted term for a repulsive, defiling skin disease. Only some sores (נגע) are classified as צרעת.

The phraseology covers numerous growths on the skin, like pimples, blisters, boils, tumors, scabs, dandruff, and sores. The Mishnah confirms this fact by stating that different rabbis identified sixteen, thirty-six or seventy-two types of grievous skin disease (*m. Neg.* 1.4). These sores break out and spread across the skin. Because they drain, show the blood, and are foul smelling, they render a person unclean. The issue here is ritual contamination, not the identification of a contagious disease. The stricken party must be brought (הובא) to a priest, either Aaron, i.e., the high priest, or an Aaronite priest. The passive הובא, "must be brought," suggests that members of the victim's family or clan, concerned for both their fulfilling of the law and the ritual purity of the family, took it as their duty to take their afflicted kinsman to the priest. This manner of phrasing the law addresses the natural tendency of a person to hide any blemish or affliction as long as possible, particularly when such a skin disease might lead to that person's being separated from the community.

3 After the afflicted person arrives at the sanctuary, a priest makes an examination to decide whether the sore is spreading or is an irritation that will heal quickly. First he is to observe whether any hairs (שׂער) within the sore have turned white. According to Snaith (70), שׂער, masc sg, means "hairs," and שׂערה, fem sg, means "hair." Second, he is to observe whether the sore has penetrated into underlying areas of skin. Since עמק means "deeper," it may be asked how a disease of the skin might be depressed, for most infected areas cause a rise above the skin's surface. The answer is that the disease involves the deeper layers of the skin, damaging the hair follicles (cf. Wilkinson, *SJT* [1977] 160–62). The presence of these two symptoms qualifies this condition as צרעת, "a grievous skin disease." The lesion is active and spreading, not static.

When the priest determines that נגע, "a lesion," is נגע צרעת, "a grievous skin disease," he pronounces the afflicted person unclean (טמא אתו). The pronouncement is critical, for it changes a person's status from "clean" to "unclean," excluding that person from further participation in the cult. Thus the use of the piel טמא in this case is not strictly declarative, for the pronouncement alters a person's status (Koch, *Priesterschrift,* 82, n.). In this role the priest functions as an official of the covenant community before God, not as a physican. His sole task is to identify a sore as being a grievous skin disease or not in order to determine the status of a person for cultic participation. There is no indication that the priest prescribes any medicine or performs any ritual for the healing of the afflicted person. His primary concern is the protection of the sanctuary from defilement caused by an unclean person's entering its precinct. His goal is not to stop a contagious disease from spreading in the community. Nevertheless, this practice of isolating those with serious skin diseases contributed to the community's health. A high standard of ritual purity promotes the general state of a community's health by making it harder for many diseases to spread. This benefit, though, was a byproduct of the regulations of ritual purity, not their primary intent.

4–6 If the symptoms are not so conclusive, the priest confines a person with such a suspicious lesion for a period of seven days, probably in a specific area outside the camp. The seven-day period coincides with the seven-day week in

Israel and, with the significance of the number seven, is symbolic of completeness. On the seventh day, the priest re-examines the afflicted person. If there is no evidence that the sore has spread, the priest confines the afflicted person for another seven days.

On the second seventh day the priest again examines the person. If the disease shows no sign of being inflamed, having faded כהה, i.e., "grown faint or dull" (Isa 42:4), the priest pronounces that person טהר, "clean." כהה describes eyesight that has dimmed (Gen 27:1), a wick that is smoldering (Isa 42:3), and a person who is faint or weak (Isa 42:4; Gen 27:1). The priest's pronouncement removes any cloud of suspicion about that person's having a dreaded skin disease. The suspicious patch is only מספחת, "an eruption." The affected person is to wash his clothes as a physical demonstration that he is truly clean. Being clean, he continues to have full access to the sanctuary.

7–8 If, however, on the second examination the priest discovers that the eruption פשׂה תפשׂה, "has truly spread," the priest pronounces that person unclean, for it is צרעת, "a grievous skin disease." The use of the infinite absolute before the verb stresses that infection or eruption has spread significantly, not just a little. The lesion is active and thus defiling.

10–11 This case involves that which has already been identified as a grievous skin disease (צרעת); the hair in a swelling (שׂאת; cf. v 2) has turned white and the flesh is living, raw flesh (מחית בשׂר חי), i.e., ulcerated tissue. Such a sore is unclean because at times it bleeds and has a discharge that may be purulent or serious (cf. Wilkinson, *SJT* [1977] 162). Hulse (*PEQ* 107 [1975] 98) identifies this condition as thin areas of bleeders from scratching off the scales from psoriasis. This type of sore so obviously makes a person unclean that the priest is instructed not to confine the afflicted person for a period of time. Rather he is to pronounce that person unclean immediately.

12–13 If a person has צרעת, "a skin disease," that suddenly breaks out and covers his entire body so that his skin turns white from head to foot, that person is not unclean. The priest makes clear his status in the cultic community by pronouncing him clean. The reason a person with such a condition remains clean is that there are no open, i.e., raw, sores, nor is there any involvement beneath the skin's surface. This disease is not considered terrifying or dangerous. It is most likely vitiligo or leukoderma, a loss of skin pigmentation in patches of the skin (Harrison, 142). Even though vitiligo makes a person unsightly, it does not have any seeping sores or pus that would render its victim unclean. This disease is also noncontagious. Gehazi's illness may fall under this classification (2 Kgs 5:27). G. R. Driver (*DB* 570a), however, interprets the phrase "white skin all over" to refer to desquamation, i.e., the crust from an illness that covers the body, peels off, and leaves new white skin.

14–17 When one is afflicted with בשׂר חי, "raw flesh," i.e., a sore that festers and oozes (cf. vv 10–11), the priest, after examination, is to pronounce that person unclean. This condition is classified as צרעת, "a grievous skin disease." On the other hand, whenever the ulcerated skin recedes and turns white, new skin has replaced the sore. This is a sign of healing. Therefore, the victim is to come to the priest. This last phrase is conventional language, for in actuality he would have to ask the priest to come to him for, being unclean, he resides outside the camp. After the priest confirms that the skin has healed, he pronounces him clean.

18–23 This regulation concerns a localized inflammation in a boil or ulcer (שְׁחִין) that had healed. When שְׂאֵת לְבָנָה, "a white swelling," or בַּהֶרֶת לְבָנָה אֲדַמְדֶּמֶת, "a reddish-white shiny spot," appears in the area of the former lesion, the person must show himself to the priest. If the lesion's appearance goes lower (שָׁפָל) than the skin, i.e., in subcutaneous tissue, and the hair in it has turned white, the priest is to pronounce him unclean. However, if the color of the lesion has faded and none of these symptoms is present, the afflicted person is to be confined for another seven days. When the priest re-examines him, if the shiny sore has spread (פָּשָׂה), he is to be pronounced unclean. But if it has not spread, he is to be declared clean. It is only inflamed old scar tissue (Harrison, 143). It is identified as צָרֶבֶת הַשְּׁחִין, "a scar from a boil"; Snaith (71) renders it "puckered scar," based on the meaning of the root צרב, "blaze, burn, scorch." Then the phrase stands for the flesh that has been consumed by the inflammation (Keil and Delitzsch, 380). Hulse (*PEQ* 107 [1975] 98) thinks this condition could be what is known as "pustular" psoriasis in which sterile pus collects in the outer layer of the skin just below the masses of scales.

24–28 This section treats a burn (מִכְוַת אֵשׁ) which fails to heal. Harrison (143) says that the burn has become infected and has produced a pustular. The symptoms for declaring a burn unclean are white hair, subcutaneous activity, and a spreading effect. Hulse (*PEQ* 107 [1975] 98) identifies this condition as psoriasis. But if there is no spreading of the sore, the priest is to confine the afflicted person for another seven days. If at the end of this second span of seven days the priest discovers that the sore has spread, he pronounces the person unclean. But if the sore has stayed in place and its color כֵּהָה, "has faded" (cf. v 6), the priest pronounces that person clean.

29–37 This regulation specifically names men and women, underscoring that women are included in it, but that does not mean that the preceding regulations do not apply to women. Possibly the concern with facial hair might lead some to doubt that this regulation applied to women, so it was formulated to counter this possibility. Hulse (*PEQ* 107 [1975] 98–99) identifies the symptoms as psoriasis or seborrhoeic dermatitis, while the yellow hair points to favus. The term נֶתֶק is taken from the root meaning "pluck, tear off." One position takes it to refer to "an itch," because a person with a harsh itch continually scratches the infected area, tearing the scab. Another position put forth by Wilkinson (*SJT* 30 [1977] 158) is that this term refers to scales pulled or torn off the skin's surface. Then נֶתֶק is scall, a scaly condition of the scalp or beard. Snaith (71) notes that dry scall could be psoriasis and moist scall could be eczema. He suggests that "scurfy patch" is a fine translation, for it describes the initial stage of these afflictions. This condition is hard to identify with any certainty. According to Harrison (144), in addition to psoriasis, it could be a ringworm type of infection such as *tinea tonsurans* or *tinea favosus* (favus). This organism invades the skin and forms yellow "crusts around the hair follicles."

A person is unclean if he has a scurfy patch that has involvement beneath the skin and in which the hair is yellow and thin. The yellow hair favors an identification with favus. That the hair is thin means that it has been stunted (cf. *m. Neg.* 10.1). But if there is no subcutaneous involvement and there is no black hair in it, the priest is to confine the person for another seven days. Then the priest re-examines that person. If the scurfy patch has not spread and the hair is not affected, the person must shave his body except for the infected area and be confined for a second period of seven days. On the seventh day the person must shave his hair in order to remove all scaling and make the area better accessible for examination. If the scurfy patch has not spread and there is no activity beneath the skin, the priest pronounces him clean. That person has to wash his clothes; then he is clean, i.e., he is permitted full access to the Temple. But if the scurfy patch has spread, that is reason enough for the priest to pronounce him unclean.

38–39 This section treats irritations of the skin that have the appearance of a grievous skin disease but are not. A person has white shiny spots (בהרת לבנת) that break out over the skin, but these spots are dull in color. At first small white spots appear. Eventually they spread over the whole body. There was no cure for this disease. While Snaith (71) and Hulse (*PEQ* 107 [1975] 95) identify this ailment as vitiligo leukoderma—but cf. vv 12–17—Harrison (145) thinks that the condition described here may involve papules or herpes simplex.

40–44 The next ailment concerns baldness, particularly a case that starts at the forehead and moves backward. Baldness does not place a person in danger of being declared unclean. If, however, a reddish-white mark appears in the bald area, the priest is to pronounce that person unclean. Only if there is a swollen sore on the area of baldness is the person considered to have a grievous skin disease.

45–46 Anyone who is declared unclean by reason of a grievous skin disease must clothe himself like one in mourning. The breath of death is on him. He is to wear old, torn clothing and to let his hair go unkempt. Also he is to cover his lower face שׂפם (lit. "moustache," but the lower face in Ezek 24:17, 22; Mic 3:7). In these later references this practice is a sign of mourning for the dead. The afflicted party cries out "unclean, unclean" (cf. Lam 4:15) to warn anyone who approaches his way of the dangers of becoming unclean by coming into contact with him. The law is concerned with spreading ritual uncleanness and not with whether the disease is contagious. Added to the apprehension of becoming ritually unclean from contact with this affected person there may have been the dread of catching that person's disease. The afflicted person has to dwell outside the city the rest of his life or until he becomes clean.

47–58 The legislation here covers unsightly, repulsive growths like mold, mildew, or other fungus in a garment made out of wool (בגד צמר), linen (בגד פשׁתים), or leather (עור). Since such growths are abnormal and produce flaking, the Hebrews used the same term (צרעת) for these conditions as for a grievous skin disease. While the common categorization of a growth on human skin and on the surface of cloth is strange to moderns, the conditions are similar in that a foreign growth mars the surface of prized material, destroying its original wholeness. The legislation prefers the less critical term נגע, (lit.) "mark, blow," for the abnormal growth over צרעת, "a grievous skin disease or mildew," in order not to prejudice the judgment of a growth in a garment. The same is true in the legislation about a growth on the walls of a house (14:33–44). This variation may also occur because of the lack of definitive words for various kinds of growths in garments and walls. In the case of cloth, a repulsive growth is greenish or reddish in color. In a warm and damp place it is easy for such a growth to take place in a garment that has not been recently washed. The handling of an infected garment is similar to that of a person with a grievous skin disorder. The infected garment is shown to the priest. He confines it for seven days; then he re-examines it. If the growth has spread, it is identified as צרעת, "a grievous mildew." The garment is declared unclean (הוא טמא); it must be burned. But if there has been no significant change in the garment, it is to be washed and then confined for seven more days. If on the second examination the spot has not changed its appearance, i.e., the mildew has not faded, the garment is unclean and must be burned. But if the spot has כהה, "faded," the area infected is to be cut out of the garment. Should the mildew or the growth return, it is classified as פרחת, "spreading," and the garment must be burned. Any garment that appears normal after the first washing must be washed again. If it appears normal after the second washing, it is pronounced clean.

59 This is a summary statement, but only for the section on grievous mildew in cloth or leather.

14:1 This section opens with a typical introductory formula found in Leviticus, but here Aaron is not mentioned as he often is in the laws of ritual purity (chaps. 11–15, but cf. 12:1). The reason may be that this regulation is concerned with sacrificial procedures, not strictly with ritual purity, and thus this formula conforms to the introductory formula found frequently in chaps. 1–7.

2–3 When a person has recovered from a grievous skin disease, he is to appear before the priest. For this purpose, the priest must travel outside the camp to the afflicted person, for that person, being unclean, cannot enter the camp to meet the priest. The priest is to examine him and determine whether he has recovered from his defiling affliction. Since a priest has pronounced him unclean, the recovered person must be pronounced clean by a priest in order to be allowed to return to normal life in the community. The priest may declare him clean only after that person has gone through an elaborate ritual of restoration, involving several stages over a span of time. The readmission of a person who has been banned from the community is a radical social change. Anthropologists label this procedure "rites of aggregation" (Wenham, 208). There are many similarities between the ritual here and the one for the cleansing of a person who becomes unclean from contact with a corpse; cf. Num 19:12. This similarity underscores the fact that a person with a grievous skin disease has been considered essentially dead by the community.

This elaborate ritual draws on elements from a variety of other rituals. It lasts eight days as does the consecration of the priests (chaps. 8–9). The rite of consecrating the person by anointing his right extremities with blood and oil coincides with a similar rite in the ritual for anointing the high priest and his sons (8:23–24). These points of contact are further indications of the radicalness of the change of status from unclean to clean in this case. In this ritual of aggregation all four basic sacrifices are offered, signifying that the recovered person once again has full access to the altar.

4 For the cleansing ritual the priest takes two birds, cedar wood, two scarlet threads, and hyssop. The living birds are to be clean. Hoffmann (1:396) states that חיות, "living," means that they are to be healthy and whole. The species of bird is not specified. Cedar, a highly prized wood, which Solomon used extensively in his building projects, may have been chosen because it gives off a strong, pleasant scent and, being very resistant to decay, symbolizes endurance. Scarlet thread, by reason of its bright red color, is used to mark things of great significance (e.g., Gen 38:28, 30; Josh 2:18, 21). The color red symbolizes blood and expiation, the victory of life over death (Isa 1:18). Though unexpressed, the thread probably bound the hyssop to the cedar. Hyssop, most likely several varieties of marjoram thymus, including *Origanum maru* L., grows freely in Palestine, protruding from a city's walls (Num 19:6; Ps 51:9[7]; cf. R. K. Harrison, "The Biblical Problem of Hyssop," *EvQ* 26 [1954] 218–24). It has a tight cluster of leaves with good absorbing quality and can be used to transfer a little liquid (Num 19:18; Matt 27:48). These three objects were also used in the preparation of the ashes to be used in the cleansing rite for one defiled through contact with a corpse (Num 19:6).

5–7 Each bird is treated in a distinct way. The priest kills one bird in an earthen vessel over running (lit. "living," חיים) water. "Living" refers to water from a stream or a well (v 50; 15:13; Gen 26:19; Num 19:17), water that has not been standing at all. Living water represents its life-giving power; it is not the source of death as is stagnant water. According to the Talmud *(b. Soṭa)* a fourth of a pint was sufficient. Some of the blood is drained into the water. The water is essential since the slaughtered bird yields only a little blood. Then the priest dips the hyssop, serving a little like a sponge, into the blood and sprinkles the healed person seven times. This action for purification is not an expiating rite, for there is no evidence that the bird is killed according to the standards for a specific sacrifice. Rather its fate symbolizes the fearful destiny of one suffering from a grievous skin disease. The second bird is released into the open country (על פני השדה). This last phrase could refer to the cultivated land outside a city, but more often it refers to the open countryside. This rite is similar to the release of the scapegoat on the Day of Atonement (16:21–22); a significant difference is that the recovered person does not touch the bird nor make any confession over it. If the parallel is valid, then this bird carries off the impurity of this person, removing it from the center of population and the location of the sanctuary (cf. D. J. Davies, "An Interpretation of Sacrifice in Leviticus," *ZAW* 89 [1977] 397). Keil and Delitzsch (385–86), however, take the position that the release of the bird symbolizes the healed person being released from the chains of death and being allowed to live in liberty among his countrymen.

8 Next the healed person must wash his clothes, shave his hair, and bathe himself (cf. Num 6:18; 8:7; Deut 21:12–13). Shaving for the ancient Israelites was drastic since they were not permitted to shave their sideburns or the corners of their beards (19:27). This thorough washing and shaving removes all surface impurity and symbolizes the complete removal of the contamination of impurity from the person. Afterwards the healed person may enter the camp. But he must dwell (ישׁב) outside his tent for seven days, for the passage from a state of uncleanness to a state of cleanness is not yet complete. He must not risk bringing any contamination on his family or the objects in his tent.

9 On the seventh day the healed person must shave again. Shaving again so soon appears a little strange, but the priestly standards were meticulous in making sure that a person was ritually pure. Here it is specified that he must shave his hair (שׂער), his beard (זקן), his eyebrows (גבת עיניו), and all his other hair. Unfortunately, the reason for either the initial shaving or this second shaving is not stated. But since the disease had been a skin disease, shaving all the hair removed any suspected uncleanness and enabled a thorough examination of the person's entire body to make sure that there were no sores of concern anywhere. Harrison (150–57) observes that the shaving renders the person like a newborn, one who is entering a new phase of existence. Then the healed person must wash his clothes and his skin. The shaving and the washing would carry away any remaining scales from the skin disease lodged in his hair. Uncleanness from the skin disease was very contagious, and the removal of all scales was highly desired. After taking these steps, the formerly afflicted person becomes clean enough to be allowed to reenter the community again, but he has not yet achieved full status of being clean. The steps in returning one who has been isolated back to society should not seem strange, for even today a critically ill person often goes through various levels of care within the hospital itself and then in a nursing home before being allowed to return home.

10 On the eighth day, the healed person is required to present a series of sacrifices. He is to take two male lambs without defect and a year-old female lamb without defect. In addition, the person is to bring three-tenths of an ephah of flour, about a third of a bushel. This large amount of flour is unusual, especially since the grain was offered only with the whole offering (v 31). Also he is to bring a log of oil, i.e., a short pint. This amount of oil exceeds the usual amount by three times. These large quantities are peculiar to the offerings for this occasion.

11 The priest העמיד, "presents," or "stations," the recovered person and his offerings at the entrance to the Tent of Meeting, before Yahweh. The term "present" here is not the usual term הקריב in the sacrificial regulations as in 1:2. Rather the term here is used in 16:7, 10 for the two goats presented on the Day of Atonement, primarily the goat for Azazel, and in Num 5:16, 18, 30 for a woman suspected of adultery who is brought near to stand before Yahweh. This verb then is used for someone or something made to stand at the entrance to the Tent of Meeting in order that a significant decision may be made about that one's status. This moment of the ritual of aggregation would be filled with overpowering emotion for the one who had been exiled. Now he knows for certain that he again has access to Yahweh at the sanctuary and that he has good standing in the community. What a moment of ecstasy!

12 One male lamb is presented as אשׁם, "a reparation offering," along with a log of oil. These are also offered as תנופה, "an elevated offering" (cf. 7:29–30). The oil for this offering is presented as an elevated offering (cf. 7:30), for it must be sanctified, i.e., given over to Yahweh, before it can be used for anointing (cf. Milgrom, *SCTT,* 147). Also, the priests were anointed with oil, though that oil was a special compound and already sacred (Exod 30:23–25). As for the reparation offering, it needs to be raised because it is offered in a different way from the usual reparation offering. Since the blood of this offering is essential for the ritual for the purification of a person who has become unclean by a grievous skin disease, that person cannot commute this sacrifice into money, contrary to Milgrom's position (*SCTT,* 148–59). Furthermore, the usual order of presenting the purification offering before a reparation offering is reversed in this case because of the priority of the use of the blood from this sacrifice. All of these variations point to the special quality of the ritual of the reparation offering for one who has recovered from a serious skin disease. Moreover, the fact that a lamb (כבשׂ), not a ram (איל; 5:15–18; 5:25[6:6]), is the sacrificial animal is another distinction of this reparation offering. Similarly, a Nazirite who has been defiled by a corpse (Num 6:12) is required to present a lamb for a reparation offering. Given the importance of this sacrifice in this ritual, it is classified as קדשׁ קדשׁים, "most holy" (cf. 2:3, 10). It is difficult to know why a reparation offering is required. Snaith (75) speculates that it is required because the community lost the benefits of this person's labor during the time of his exclusion, but that the loss could not be assessed. Wenham (210) posits that this offering may be to compensate God for the loss of sacrifices and tithes that were not presented while the person was excluded from the community. Milgrom takes another approach (*Cult,* 80–82). Working from the accounts in which God afflicted a person who had committed a flagrant violation of the holy with a grievous skin disease (e.g., Num 12:10; 2 Chr 26:19–20), Milgrom holds that this offering was required to address the contingency that this afflicted person might have unwittingly transgressed against the holy. Perhaps an alternative explanation is possible. Since a reparation offering is prescribed for transgression against holy property, this kind of offering is required because the disease marred a person who bears the very image of God (Gen 1:27; Ps 8:6[5]) and separated him from free access to God at the central sanctuary. Therefore, the offering that expiates a violation of that which is holy (cf. 5:15–16) is required for full restoration of a person who has recovered from a grievous skin disease. In any case, these rites with the blood and the oil sanctify the restored person so that one may again live among the covenant people.

14 The priest puts blood on the person's extremities, on the right earlobe, on the right thumb, and on the right large toe. This rite is similar to that for the anointing of the high priest and the other priests (8:24). It indicates that a radical change has taken place in the person's status before God. Now that this person is being restored to the community, it is imperative that his whole being be consecrated to God, his ears to hear God's word and his hands and feet to do God's will. Since the blood of this offering is also splashed against the altar, the use of the same blood on the healed person binds him to the altar, giving him access to it again.

15–18 The priest sprinkles some of the oil seven times before Yahweh. He thereby enhances the consecration of the oil. Then he puts some of the oil on the same extremities of the healed person that have been smeared with blood. Then he pours out the rest of the oil on his head. A strong bond is made between the person anointed with oil and Yahweh, symbolizing that Yahweh will richly bless this person. According to Keil and Delitzsch (388), this rite represents the spirit of life that this person has received from God. It expresses the restoration of the joy of a blessed daily life to the recovered person, for it was the daily custom for a well person to put oil on one's head (Eccl 9:8; cf. Pss 23:5; 104:15). The anointing with oil takes place before the standard offerings, for it means that these offerings are made on behalf of one who is alive again. The person is fully reconciled to the community.

V 18b says that the priest makes expiation for him. Is it the rite with the oil that produces expiation or is it the reparation offering with the anointing with the blood and the oil? Since expiation is associated with blood far more than with oil (cf.17:11) and since the oil is placed over the blood, vv 12–18 present the various rites done in conjunction with the reparation offering. Then v 18b is the conclusion to the unit, meaning that the reparation offering along with the rites of consecration result in expiation.

19–20 Next the priest offers up the healed person's purification offering (חטאת; cf. chaps. 4–5), whole offering (עלה; cf. chap. 1), and grain offering (מנחה; cf. chap. 2). These offerings also have expiating (כפר) force (cf. 4:20, 21) in order to cleanse thoroughly the recovered person from all defilement caused by his former uncleanness. This cleanses any inadvertent sins, known or unknown, as well as the basic sinfulness of being human. The repetition of "expiate" stresses that this person is thoroughly forgiven and fully cleansed. From now on he may enter God's presence with confidence.

21–32 There are special concessions for the sacrifices in the rite of aggregation of a poor person. These alternative sacrifices evidence the compassion for the poor built into the cultic law. In fact, a person's isolation from the community would quickly reduce him to poverty. However, it may be assumed that members of his family provided the materials for these offerings. But one's family might be very poor, having faced the burden of caring for the exiled person's household. The recovered person may substitute two doves or two young pigeons for the purification and the whole offering (cf. 1:14–17), but no substitution is permitted for the reparation offering. Thereby it is seen that the reparation offering is essential for the full restoration of the person healed from a grievous skin disease. The ritual for these alternative offerings is similar to the one described above.

33–36 This regulation considers the treatment of נגע צרעת, "a grievous growth," or "fungus," on the walls of a house. The term "growth" is chosen to render נגע, (lit.) "mark, growth, plague," in order to include a variety of virulent growths. צרעת is the same term used in 13:2–46 for grievous skin diseases and in 13:47–59 for grievous mildew on a garment. With a house it is most likely some type of fungus like mildew or mold. The term "grievous" is used in the translation of צרעת to communicate the disgust such a growth causes and to show that the same Heb. term covers repulsive growths on the three different types of surfaces. Throughout this part of the regulation the more general term נגע, rendered in these verses "growth," is the term occurring frequently rather than צרעת, "grievous growth," which occurs only twice in this speech (vv 34, 44). The text clearly states that if such a grievous growth appears in a house, God is the one who has caused it. Throughout the OT God is the source of all that happens (e.g., Isa 45:7), for the ancient Israelites tended not to make fine distinctions in levels of causation. These statements build the strongly monotheistic outlook of the OT. Here Canaan is called "the land of your possessions" (cf. 25:10, 24; Josh 22:19); it is Israel's inheritance guaranteed by her covenant with Yahweh.

Whenever נגע, "a growth," appears anywhere in a house, the owner is to inform the priest. Before coming to inspect the house, the priest orders that all its contents be removed lest they along with the house be proclaimed unclean. This step forcefully indicates that a growth did not make something unclean until a priest had officially pronounced it unclean. Also it is another indication of the compassion in the laws; efforts are made to cut the owner's losses while preserving the integrity of the sanctuary. Rashi (64) notes that this step particularly applies to earthenware since other types of vessels could be cleansed.

37–42 The color of the growth and the extent of its involvement determine whether it is defiling. If a greenish or a reddish שקערורת, "eruption," appears in a house's walls, a priest must be summoned to inspect such a house. The growth might be a fungus, a mold, or dry rot; or it might be the piling up of calcium nitrate, which results from the gases of decaying material on the lime of the plaster (Snaith, 75). Another possibility could be the activity of some insects within the walls. The term for wall (קיר) refers to a flat surface; it could be an outer or inner wall (Snaith, 76). Israelite houses typically were made of mud bricks laid on a foundation of stones piled up in two or three layers. The inside walls were plastered with limestone sometimes mixed with sand (Harrison, 156). Such a coating sealed the house against water. Görg (*BN* 14 [1981] 25) reasons that the regulation is seeking to identify a destructive process that works from inside the walls to the outside and is recognizable by sinking and discoloration of a wall. The priest first orders that the house be הסגיר, "closed up," for seven days. Levine comments that הסגיר is used here to establish a parallel between the handling of a house and a person with צרעת, "a grievous disease" (cf. 13:5). If the growth expands, a section of stones in the infected area is to be removed to an unclean place outside the camp. Then the walls are to be scraped and the scrapings taken outside the camp to an unclean place. According to Jewish tradition, only the area in which the growth was found had to be scraped. The hole made in the wall is to be filled with new stones and then plastered. It is clear that every effort is taken to preserve the house for occupancy.

43–45 If the growth reappears, the priest is to come and inspect the infected wall again. If he finds that it is a spreading growth (נגע), a destructive fungus (צרעת ממארת), the house must be torn down (נתץ). נתץ, "tear down," is used for the complete destruction of something. All the rubbish is to be disposed of in an unclean place outside the camp. Proper disposal removes the cause of the uncleanness from the community.

46–47 Whoever enters a house under quarantine becomes unclean till evening. Then he is to wash himself. But if someone sleeps or eats in such a house, he becomes unclean and has to wash both his clothes and himself. This verse is another witness to the fact that there are degrees of impurity.

48–53 If the growth does not spread in a house, the priest pronounces the house clean. Then offerings are to be made for it similar to those for a person who has recovered from a grievous skin disease (vv 4–7). The offerings חטא, "purify," the house from any defilement caused by the suspected growth. It is stated that כפר, "expiation," is made for the house. The house has to be purged from the curse of such a growth that has its origin in humankind's disobedience against God.

54–57 This summary statement functions as a conclusion to both chaps. 13 and 14. It states that this is the regulation or the instruction (תורה) concerning grievous growths on a person or object.

Explanation

The laws regarding ritual purity treat the appearance of a repulsive, distorting growth on a person, a garment, or the walls of a house. Since wholeness symbolized holiness, such distortions represented the curse of sin, death, and alienation from God. Such grievous diseases or growths rendered their victim unclean as long as they were present. The severity of such uncleanness required that a person be exiled from the community, a garment burned, and a house torn down.

Because the penalties were so severe, the law took great pains to make sure that a suspected grievous affliction was accurately diagnosed.

A person who became an outcast because of a grievous skin disease was cut off from access to the sanctuary and worship of God. Did the fact that one was stricken mean that that one had sinned? No doubt popular belief held that such a person was a sinner. But it is important to observe that the law itself did not make such an accusation. That such a position is not central to these regulations is seen in their prescribing the ritual for a person who had recovered from a grievous skin disease to be readmitted to the community. This possibility offered hope to anyone afflicted with such a loathsome disease—not only the hope that he might recover, but also that he could return to a normal life. Furthermore, in the ritual of aggregation there was no emphasis on the recovered person's making a confession of sin. It is true that the sacrifices expiate sin (14:18–19), but since there was no direction to confess a specific sin, as in the regulations found in chaps. 4–5, the expiation was for human sinfulness in general and for the purification of the recovered person. The absence of such an emphasis on confession indicates that the law did not make a quick, automatic equation between a person afflicted with a grievous skin disease and that person's having sinned. Nevertheless, there are specific cases in the OT in which God struck one with a grievous skin disease for some flagrant sin, e.g., Miriam (Num 12:1–15), Gehazi (2 Kgs 5:26–27), and Uzziah (2 Chr 26:16–21). From these remarkable accounts grew the belief that a grievous skin disease was divine punishment for some flagrant sin. Eventually it became the popular attitude to think that a person who broke out with a grievous skin disease was being judged by God for some grave sin. Because of such a belief, the people were prejudiced against anyone who was so afflicted. The Book of Job was written to challenge the faulty assumptions of such prejudice and to reverse the terrible, condemning attitude expressed toward any righteous person who was afflicted with a grievous disease. While in the OT God sometimes used such an affliction as punishment for a brazen sin, that did not mean that everyone with such a disease was being punished by God for specific wrongdoing.

The inclusion of garments and houses in this general regulation is instructive. An individual or the community does not have an inherent right to use anything regardless of its condition. Rather, each one is to take care of his possessions so that they do not threaten their users. If a possession became contaminated, its owner had to try to remove the contamination. If his efforts failed, he had to destroy the object. In today's complex, technological world this means that a person or a corporation is responsible to see that products produced by either not only perform their designed tasks, but also do not harm their users. To prevent a product or a process from harming a person and polluting the environment is an ethical responsibility. All of us have that responsibility in regard to taking care of what we own.

In the NT, there are several reports of Jesus' healing people with serious skin diseases. These healings bore witness to the inauguration of a new era; the Kingdom of God was at hand. In bringing healing to those afflicted with a grievous skin disease, Jesus was doing away with the levitical regulations and breaking down the barriers that isolated the afflicted from the fellowship of God's people. Jesus' visit to Simon the "leper's" house, where Mary anointed him (Matt 26:6; Mark 14:3), is further evidence that he treated those cleansed from a grievous skin disease as full members of his kingdom. He reached out to those afflicted as a witness that the gospel was proclaimed to all, including the most despised outcasts (cf. Matt 11:6; Luke 7:22). He opened the way of salvation for all to travel. None are excluded by race, wealth, appearance, or health from entering the narrow gate to the Way. The ministry of Jesus thus put an end to the observance of these laws, but not to the ethical principles undergirding them.

Whenever a community faces a threatening illness, it is clear from the OT that steps need to be taken to protect the community as a whole. The NT reveals that these steps need to be taken with compassion and concern toward the afflicted. People are not to be isolated indiscriminately. Furthermore, the church is to help those afflicted, compassionately caring and interceding for them. The church can work hard to dampen any hysterical responses. As for those afflicted, they have the responsibility to take all reasonable precautions to prevent the spread of their disease. They can take comfort in knowing that in Christ those afflicted with a grave ailment are not removed from the means of grace—though these means may have to be brought to them when they cannot attend public services because of either weakness or danger to the public.

D. Instructions on Uncleanness from Bodily Emissions (15:1–33)

Bibliography

Selvidge, M. "Mark 5:25–34 and Leviticus 15:19–20: A Reaction to Restrictive Purity Regulations." *JBL* 103 (1984) 619–23. **Wenham, G. J.** "Why Does Sexual Intercourse Defile (Lev 15 18)?" *ZAW* 95 (1983) 432–34. **Wilcox, R. R.** "Venereal Disease in the Bible." *British Journal of Venereal Diseases* 25 (1949) 28–33. **Whitekettle, R.** "Leviticus 15.18 Reconsidered: Chiasm, Spatial Structure and the Body." *JSOT* 49 (1991) 31–45.

Translation

1*Yahweh spoke to Moses and Aaron:* 2*"Speak*[a] *to the Israelites and say*[b] *to them: Any man*[c] *who has a discharge from his genitals,*[d] *his discharge*[e] *is unclean.* 3*This is*[a] *his uncleanness by means of his discharge: whether his genitals have a seepage because of his discharge or his genitals are obstructed*[b] *by his discharge,*[c] *it is his uncleanness.* 4*Every*[ab] *bed on which*[c] *he who has a discharge lies*[d] *becomes unclean, and every*[b] *piece of furniture on which*[c] *he*[e] *sits*[d] *becomes unclean.* 5*If one touches his bed, he is to wash his clothes, bathe in water, and be unclean until evening.* 6*Whoever sits on anything on which*[a] *he who has a discharge has sat is to wash his clothes, bathe in water, and be unclean until evening.* 7*Whoever touches the body of him who has a discharge is to wash his clothes, bathe with water, and be unclean until evening.* 8*If he who has a discharge spits on one who is clean, that person is to wash*[a] *his clothes, bathe in water, and be unclean until evening.* 9*Every saddle on which*[a] *he who has a discharge rides becomes unclean.*[b] 10*Whoever touches anything that has been under him becomes unclean until* *evening. He who carries such an object is to wash his clothes, bathe with water, and be unclean until evening.* 11*As for anyone whom one with a discharge touches without rinsing*[a] *his hands*[bc] *with water, he is to wash*[de] *his clothes, bathe with water, and be unclean until evening.* 12*Any earthenware vessel which he who has a discharge touches is to be broken, and any wooden article*[ab] *is to be rinsed*[c] *with water.*[d]

13*"When he who has a discharge is cleansed from his discharge, he is to count seven days for his cleansing, wash his clothes, and bathe his body in running*[a] *water; then he becomes clean.* 14*On the eighth day he is to take for himself two doves or two young pigeons*[a] *and come*[b] *before Yahweh at the entrance to the Tent of Meeting and give them to the priest.* 15*The priest is to offer*[a] *them, one for a purification offering and one*[b] *for a whole offering. The priest is to make expiation for him before Yahweh because of*[c] *his discharge.*

16*"Whenever a man has an emission of semen,*[a] *he is to bathe*[b] *his entire body in water and be unclean until evening.* 17*Every garment and everything made of leather which gets semen on it is to be washed in water, and it becomes unclean until evening.* 18*Whenever a man*[a] *lies with*[b] *a woman*[c] *and has an emission of semen, both are to wash in water, and they become unclean until evening.*

19*"Whenever a woman has a discharge, that is, her discharge is blood from*[a] *her genitals,*[bc] *she is to be in her menstrual period*[d] *for seven days. Whoever*[e] *touches her becomes unclean until evening.* 20*Everything on which she lies during her period becomes unclean; everything on which she sits becomes unclean.* 21*Whoever touches her bed is to wash his clothes, bathe*[a] *with water, and be unclean until evening.* 22*Whoever touches any article*[a] *on which she sits is to wash his clothes, bathe with water, and be unclean until evening.* 23*If there*[a] *is anything on the bed*[b] *or on the furniture on which she sits, when anyone touches it,*[c] *one becomes unclean until evening.* 24*If a man*[a] *does lie*[b] *with her and her menstrual blood gets on him,*[c] *he becomes unclean*[d] *indeed for seven days, and every bed on which he lies becomes unclean.*

25*"If a woman has a discharge*[a] *of blood for many days,*[b] *but not*[c] *at the time of her menstrual period, or*[d] *if she has a discharge beyond her menstrual period, all the days that the discharge makes her unclean*[e] *will be like the days of her period; she is unclean.* 26*Every*[ab] *bed on which she lies during all the time of her discharge becomes like a bed during her period;*[c] *and every*[b] *piece of furniture on which she sits will become unclean like the uncleanness of her period.*[d] 27*Whoever*[a] *touches these things*[b] *becomes unclean; that one is to wash his clothes, bathe*[c] *in water, and be unclean until evening.*

28*"If she has become cleansed*[a] *from her discharge, she is to count seven days, and after that she becomes clean.* 29*On the eighth day she is to take two doves or two young pigeons and bring them to the priest at the entrance to the Tent of Meeting.* 30*The priest is to offer*[a] *one for a purification offering and one for a whole offering. The priest is to make expiation for her before Yahweh because of the discharge that made her unclean.*[b]

31*"So you are to keep the Israelites separate*[a] *from that which makes them unclean, lest they die in their uncleanness by defiling my tabernacle which is among them."*

32*This is the regulation for a man with a discharge and for him who has an emission of semen, becoming unclean*[a] *thereby,* 33*and for a woman who is unwell with her menstrual period, that is, for any male or any female who has a discharge and for a man who lies with an unclean woman.*[a]

Notes

2.a. LXX reads a sg verb; MT is followed because a similar passage in 11:1–2 has a pl verb. 11QpaleoLev supports MT.

2.b. LXX has a sg verb here to agree with its reading of a sg verb at the opening.

2.c. The repetition of the noun אִישׁ אִישׁ, "man, man," yields a distributive sense (GKC §123c); cf. 18:6; 20:1. A few (e.g., Elliger 193) think that the repetition includes both men and women, but the definitive sexual nature of these laws does not favor that position.

2.d. בשׂר, "flesh," is euphemistic for both male and female genitals, here and v 19.

2.e. זובו, "his discharge," is a *casus pendens*, and the remainder of the clause is structured as pred-subj (*IBHS* §16.3.3d.15).

3.a. In place of MT תהיה, "it is, becomes," LXX reads ὁ νόμος, "the law," as in v 32; 11QpaleoLev supports MT.

3.b. This is the only occurrence of the root חתם, "seal," in the hiph; thus it may have a technical sense.

3.c. Sam and LXX add טמא הוא כל־ימי־זב בשׂרו או החתים בשׂרו מזובו, "he is unclean all the days of the discharge from his genitals or his genitals are blocked by his discharge." 11QpaleoLev supports LXX. From 11QpaleoLev and LXX, K. A. Mathews (*BA* 50 [1987] 52–53) reconstructs the first three words as טמאתו היא ב, "it is his uncleanness in him," joining them to the preceding sentence. MT resulted from an error of haplography.

4.a. A few Heb. mss and Syr begin the sentence with a *waw* as is found in the various surrounding verses. LXX supports MT.

4.b. On כל meaning "every" before a definite noun, cf. GKC §127c, e.

4.c. The indeclinable אשׁר, "which," is resumed by the prep phrase עליו, "on it." This style is frequent in this speech.

4.d. The use of the impf connotes that the action is the usual or habitual action (Rashi, 69).

4.e. LXX reads ὁ γονορρυής = הזב, "he who has a discharge," as in stich a. This is an example of levelling the text.

6.a. Cf. n. 4.c.

8.a. In place of MT וכבס, "and he is to wash," a Heb. ms, Sam, LXX, Syr, and Tg[mss] read יכבס, "he is to wash." This is a frequent spelling error that arises from confusing a *yod* for a *waw* or vice versa. In light of vv 5, 6, and 7, the variant is the superior text.

9.a. Cf. n. 4.c.

9.b. LXX adds ἕως ἑσπέρας, "until evening," possibly from the influence of the frequent occurrence of this phrase in this speech.

11.a. On שׁטף cf. 6:21.

11.b. A few Heb. mss and Sam read ידו, "his hand."

11.c. A subordinate clause is introduced by a *waw* on the acc. The acc בדיו, "his hands," stands first for emphasis.

11.d. Cf. n. 8.a, but without the support of Tg[mss].

11.e. The apodosis is introduced with a pf consecutive; this adds some emphasis to the main clause (GKC §112ff, mm); also vv 16, 17, and 18.

12.a. Heb. mss, LXX, and Vg read וכלי, "and a vessel of," for MT וכל־כלי, "and every vessel of." The variant may have risen by haplography.

12.b. In the phrase כלי־עץ, "a wooden vessel," the gen is a gen of substance (cf. *IBHS* §9.5.3d).

12.c. *IBHS* (§22.4n31) suggests that ישׁטף is a qal pass pointed as a niph.

12.d. LXX adds καὶ καθαρὸν ἔσται, "and it is clean."

13.a. LXX[BA] does not have חיים, "living." These translators may have had a Heb. text with an error of haplography.

14.a. Cf. n. 1:14.c.

14.b. LXX's καὶ οἴσει αὐτά = והביאם, "and he is to bring them," in place of MT ובא, "and he is to come." MT has a reading similar to LXX in v 29. The use of the following נתנם, "he is to give them," supports MT; this additional wording is absent in v 29, being implied in והביאה, "and she is to bring."

15.a. Cf. n. 14:19.a.

15.b. A couple of Heb. mss and the versions do not have the article on האחד, "one." Elliger (192), furthermore, suggests that probably the article is to be read on both occurrences of אחד, "one," as in v 30 and 14:31.

15.c. On this use of the prep מן with כפר + על, "make expiation for," cf. n. 4:26.b.

16.a. שׁכבת־זרע is an interesting construct chain; it is a euphemism. שׁכבת, "lying," is a verbal noun, and זרע, "seed," is the goal of a man's "lying" with a woman. This is an adverbial gen, or it could be the gen of effect (cf. *IBHS* §9.5.2c). Orlinsky ("The Hebrew Root ŠKB," *JBL* 63 [1944] 19–44) proposes that it comes from a root שׁכב meaning "pour, pour out," rather than שׁכב, "lie down," but KB does not recognize his proposal.

16.b. Cf. n. 11.e.

18.a. For MT איש, "a man," Sam reads אישה, "her husband."

18.b. Baentsch (378) observes that the acc אתה, "her," should be the prep אתה, "with her," for שׁכב, "lie," does not take an acc (Num 5:13, 19; cf. BDB, "שׁכב 3," 1012).

18.c. In MT ואשה, "and a woman," stands first for emphasis.

19.a. This use of the prep ב has the force "from" as in Ugar (cf. *UT* 10.5).

19.b. Cf. n. 2.d.

19.c. The phrase דם יהיה זבה בבשׂרה, "her discharge is blood from her genitals," stands in apposition to זבה, "her discharge." Baentsch (378) suggests that it is better to take דם, "her blood," as acc after זבה and read והיה, "and it became." While the emendation is fine, it should be avoided, especially lacking any textual support. In Elliger's judgment (192, 197) this is a circumstantial clause defining further the nature of the discharge (GKC §156d).

19.d. On נדה, "impurity," see n. 12:2.c.; though it is a euphemism, it is rendered here "menstrual period, period."

19.e. Many Heb. mss and LXX do not read the *waw*.

21.a. LXX adds *τὸ σῶμα αὐτοῦ*, "his body."

22.a. Sam and Tg read the article on כלי, "vessel, article."

23.a. Levine (97) states that הוא, "it, there," refers not to a specific antecedent, but to a situation.

23.b. LXX adds the pronoun *αὐτῆς*, "her."

23.c. The prep + inf const yields a clause in which the pronominal suffix functions as the subj of the clause.

24.a. Cf. n. 18.a.

24.b. The inf abs before an impf intensifies the verbal idea, emphasizing the importance of the condition (GKC §113n).

24.c. The protasis is a double condition in which the second condition introduced by ותהי, "and it happens," is subordinate to the initial condition (Joüon §167e). Joüon prefers the impf תהיה to the jussive, while Elliger (192) recommends a pf, והיתה.

24.d. Sam reads יטמא, "he becomes unclean," for MT וטמא, "and he becomes unclean"; this is a variant based on the frequent confusion of *waw* and *yod* at various stages of the Heb. script; cf. n. 8.a.

25.a. זוב, "discharge, flow," is a cognate acc for emphasis.

25.b. This is an example of acc of time, referring to the duration of an action (*IBHS* §10.2.2c; GKC §118k).

25.c. בלא, a combination of prep ב, "in, with," and לא, "not," means "without," and before a word for time it means "outside of, before" (BDB, "לא, 4.a.(*b*)," 520; KB, "לא, 15.a").

25.d. LXX reads *καί*, "and," in place of MT או, "or."

25.e. This is an example of a gen of effect; i.e., the relationship between the constr and the gen is causal (*IBHS* §9.5.2c).

26.a. A few Heb. mss, LXX*, Syr, and *Tg. Ps.-J.* read a *waw* at the beginning of the verse; cf. n. 4.a.

26.b. Cf. n. 4.b.

26.c. The constr chain משׁכב נדתה, (lit.) "the bed of her period," is extraordinary. It may be an attributive gen because the gen qualifies the nature of the bed, but only for the length of time the condition described by the gen lasts.

26.d. This is a gen of quality; i.e., the quality of this uncleanness is the same as uncleanness caused by a menstrual period (cf. *IBHS* §9.5.1j).

27.a. A couple of Heb. mss and LXX omit the *waw*.

27.b. A few mss and LXX read בה, "her," for MT בם, "them."

27.c. Cf. n. 21.a., but without *αὐτοῦ*, "his."

28.a. *IBHS* (§30.2.1b.3) exegetes the pf as having ingressive force: "she has become cleansed."

30.a. Cf. n. 15.a.

30.b. Cf. n. 25.e.

31.a. For MT והזרתם, some Heb. mss, Sam, and Syr read הזהרתם, "you will warn." LXX reads *καὶ εὐλαβεῖς ποιήσετε*, "and you will show discretion." Although נזר, "separate," has an unusual use here, MT is to be followed as the harder reading. Snaith (77) understands נזר to be used here as in 22:2 with the meaning "observe strict rules in respect of ritual uncleanness."

32.a. This is inf constr in fem form, mostly from intransitive verbs (GKC §45d).

33.a. This adj is used as a substantive.

Form/Structure/Setting

The structure of this chapter may be outlined as follows.

I. Introductory formula (v 1)
II. Speech (vv 2–31)
  A. Commission to speak (v 2a)
  B. Speech proper (vv 2b–31)
    1. Uncleanness of a male from discharges (vv 2b–17)
      a. Regarding abnormal discharges (vv 2b–15)
        1) Laws concerning abnormal discharges (vv 2b–12)
          a) Primary law (vv 2b–3)
            (1) Basic statement (v 2b)
            (2) Definition of qualifying discharges (v 3)
          b) A series of laws regarding secondary uncleanness (vv 4–12)
            (1) Regarding a bed or a seat (vv 4–7)
            (2) Regarding spitting (v 8)
            (3) Regarding a saddle and things underneath a male with a discharge (vv 9–10)
            (4) Regarding a person touched by a male with a discharge (v 11)
            (5) Regarding vessels used by a male with a discharge (v 12)
        2) The procedure for restoration to a state of cleanness (vv 13–15)
          a) Basic procedure (v 13)
          b) Prescription for sacrifices (vv 14–15)
            (1) The action of the cleansed person (v 14)
            (2) The action of the priest (v 15)
      b. Regarding normal discharges (vv 16–17)
        1) The basic case (v 16)
        2) Extension of uncleanness (v 17)
    2. Uncleanness for both male and female from intercourse (v 18)
    3. Uncleanness of a woman from discharges (vv 19–30)
      a. Regarding normal discharges (vv 19–24)
        1) Primary law (v 19a+bα)
        2) Laws regarding secondary uncleanness (vv 19bβ–23)
          a) Regarding touching her (v 19bβ)
          b) Regarding things lain on or sat on (vv 20–23)
        3) Regarding sexual relations at the time of a female's discharge (v 24)
      b. Regarding abnormal discharges (vv 25–30)
        1) Laws regarding abnormal discharges (vv 25–27)
          a) Primary law (v 25)
          b) Secondary uncleanness for beds and chairs (vv 26–27)
        2) The procedure for restoration to a state of cleanness (vv 28–30)
          a) Basic procedure (v 28)
          b) Prescription for sacrifices (vv 29–30)
            (1) The action of the cleansed person (v 29)
            (2) The action of the priest (v 30)
    4. General exhortation (v 31)
III. Summary statement (vv 32–33)

This speech treats ritual impurity that results from a flow or discharge (זוב), either normal or abnormal, from a person's genitals. This regulation, which is made up of a series of conditional laws in a variety of formulations (Noth, 113), is cast in a chiastic pattern:

A Introduction (vv 1–2a)
 B Abnormal discharges from a male's genitals (vv 2–15)
  C Normal discharges from a male's genitals (vv 16–17)
   D Sexual intercourse (v 18)
  C' Normal discharges from a female's genitals (vv 19–24)
 B' Abnormal discharges from a female's genitals (vv 25–30)
A' Concluding exhortation and summary statement (vv 31–33)

This pattern indicates that the regulation was composed essentially as it is found.

In the four subsections of these laws on uncleanness from a discharge (vv 2b–12, 16–17, 19–24, 25–30), there is a primary law followed by a series of laws treating secondary cases of uncleanness of both persons and objects that result from contact directly or indirectly with a person with a discharge. The main law for a male with an abnormal discharge is in v 2b, including the case and the consequence. Attached to this law is a series of nine laws that define a variety of secondary cases of uncleanness resulting from contact, directly or indirectly, with a person with a discharge. Between the main law and the secondary laws is a statement of definition introduced by וזאת תהיה, "and this is how it will be . . . ," that defines a discharge as applying to two kinds, i.e., either a discharge that flows or a discharge that is stopped (v 3). This is the longest series of secondary laws of uncleanness in this speech. Since these cases come in the first section, these details on specific situations of secondary uncleanness may be applied where appropriate in the other sections, especially the section of secondary kinds of uncleanness from a female with an abnormal discharge. Laws on secondary cases of uncleanness are formed either with the relative אשׁר, "who, which" (vv 4, 5, 9, 11, 12), or with a participle (vv 6, 7, 10 [2x]). The use of either of these two forms depends primarily on the form that fits the terms needed to describe the situation rather than on any distinct legal nuance or rhetorical force. In place of the consequence, these secondary laws have directions for the restoration of one who has become unclean to a state of ritual purity.

In the primary law for the section on uncleanness for a woman with a normal period (v 19), the case is stated in v 19a, and in place of the consequence there is a statement that defines the length of her uncleanness (v 19bα). Then secondary laws of uncleanness are attached. These laws occur in three forms: the participial form (vv 19bβ, 21, 22), the relative form (v 20 [2x]), and the conditional form (אם, "and if"; vv 23, 24). These secondary laws occur in the section on uncleanness from a normal discharge, for a woman's uncleanness, because it is occasioned by blood and lasts longer, is more polluting than a man's.

The section on uncleanness for a woman with an abnormal discharge opens with the basic law (v 25). In this case there is a statement of definition for two situations, either a period lasting beyond its normal cycle or a discharge at an unexpected time (v 25a$\beta\gamma$). The consequence that she is unclean is a twofold statement (v 25b), one stating that she is unclean (v 25bα) and the other giving the length of her uncleanness by comparison to that of a normal discharge (v 25bβ). Appended to this primary law are laws on secondary uncleanness resulting from the basic case, formulated as a relative clause (v 26 [2x]) or as a participial clause (v 27). The sparsity of detail about secondary types of uncleanness from contact with a female with either a normal or an abnormal discharge implies that all the other types of situations detailed above would also apply.

Two brief sections (vv 16–17, 18) treat a normal emission of semen, either accidentally or during intercourse. The case (v 16a) is followed by prescription for restoration to ritual purity (v 16b). An additional law in the relative form treats secondary uncleanness of clothing that comes into contact with the semen (v 17). At the center of this speech is the law in the relative form on temporary impurity of both a male and a female from semen emitted during intercourse (v 18).

The section treating abnormal discharges of a male (vv 2b–15) and also the one on abnormal discharges of a female (vv 25–30) conclude with a brief prescription for restoration to ritual purity for a man who has recovered from an abnormal discharge. These regulations for restoration have been composed for this speech, as their brevity clearly indicates. In the priestly professional knowledge these laws would have contained far more information on the rituals for the person who had recovered and on making the sacrifices to guide the priest in each step of the ritual.

Overall these laws consider four ways uncleanness is communicated by a person with a discharge from the genitals. (1) Such a person who has a discharge becomes unclean himself; (2) any person or (3) anything that comes into contact with the unclean person, particularly in close contact to the source of the uncleanness, becomes unclean; (4) a person who touches any object made unclean by a person with a discharge becomes unclean. The sequence of uncleanness may be schematized:

person with a discharge	>	self		
person with a discharge	>	another person		
person with a discharge	>	an object	>	a person who touches that object

This speech is welded together by several recurring terms and phrases. The most frequently used root in this regulation is, of course, טמא, "unclean" (טמא: vv 2, 4 [2x], 5, 6, 7, 8, 9, 10 [2x], 11, 16, 17, 18, 19, 20 [2x], 21, 22, 23, 24 [2x], 25, 26, 27 [2x], 31, 32, 33; טמאה: vv 3 [2x], 25, 26, 30, 31 [2x], 33). The key root uniting these cases of impurity for a male and a female is זוב, "flow, discharge." Another important word is בשר, "flesh." It is used both for the entire body (vv 7, 13, 16) and as a euphemism for "genitals" (vv 2, 3 [2x], 19). In the secondary laws the key terms for both a male and a female include: נגע ב, "touching" (vv 5, 7, 10, 11, 12, 19b, 21, 22, 23, 27); ישב, "sitting" (vv 6, 20, 23); שכב, "lying" (vv 4, 20, 24, 26); רכב, "riding" (v 9); נשא, "lifting" (v 10). The directions for becoming clean in cases of secondary defilement are usually formulated יכבס בגדיו ורחץ במים וטמא עד־הערב, "he is to wash his clothes, bathe in water, and be unclean until evening" (vv 5, 6, 7, 8, 10, 11, 21, 22, 27; and with a part missing, vv 16, 17, 18; cf. v 13), while this full sequence does not occur in chaps. 11–14. These three sets of phrases are also frequent in this block: יכבס בגדיו, "he is to wash his clothes" (11:25, 28, 40 [2x], 13:6, 34; 14:8 [with את], 9, 47 [2x]), ורחץ במים, "he is to bathe in water" (14:8, 9), and וטמא עד־הערב, "he is to be unclean till evening" (11:25, 28, 32, 40 [2x]; with יטמא, 11:24, 27, 31, 39; 14:46).

This information indicates that the speaker has composed a well-ordered speech of a series of conditional laws about uncleanness from sexual discharges.

Whether he composed the material or drew on existing laws is difficult to determine. The distinct nature of the laws in vv 16–18, however, suggests that they had an origin different from that of the other laws. The strange formulation of v 18 does indicate that the speaker adapted it to be the center of the speech. In contrast to the basic laws for a male in v 2b and v 16, which begin with איש כי (איש), "if a man," this law begins with ואשה אשר as though it meant "if a woman," almost like the beginning of the basic laws for a woman in vv 19 and 25 (ואשה כי, "and if a woman"). This style is used to point forward to these two sections. Yet in alignment with the preceding two laws, the subject of the verb is איש, "a man," so that ואשה, "a woman," is actually a *casus pendens* resumed as object of the verb by the accusative אתה, "her," or the prepositional phrase אתה, "with her." This law, therefore, which falls at the center of the chiasm, has been adapted for this location.

Otherwise, the number of additions to the speech is minimal. A couple of them are very evident. Elliger (193) states that the last segment of the summary statement (v 33b) has the earmarks of an addition, for the lead word ולאיש, "and for a man," is no longer governed by the construct תורת, "instruction of." Since these words tie the law in v 24 directly into the speech, he judges the law in v 24 to be a later addition. While this prepositional phrase appears to be an addition, the statement in v 33b begins with לאיש, "for a man," in order to be parallel with the preceding לזכר ולנקבה, "for a male and for a female." Furthermore, the other long relative sentence in the summary statement (v 32b) is suspicious, for it interrupts the sequence of parallel nouns governed by the construct. Since these words function to incorporate vv 16–18 into the speech, this fact adds more evidence to the suspicion that vv 16–18 had their origin in another setting. The variations in the formulation of restoration to ritual purity as noted above contribute to this interpretation. On the other hand, the chiastic structure and the fact that there are two sections on a female favor the position that the regulations dealing with normal discharges (vv 16–17 [18]) belonged to the earliest composition of the speech. The law in v 23 has signs that it had an origin in a different setting. The conditional ואם, "and if," plus the internal conditional clause בנגעו־בו, "when anyone touches it," along with a statement of a consequence rather than a prescription for restoration, are all signs that this law has been added into the speech. In its former setting it may had been coupled with the law of v 24 in another setting and included here when v 24 was inserted.

Finally it is clear that the exhortation to Moses and Aaron in v 31 to warn the Israelites against all impurity has been added into the speech for its present setting, for it stands aloof from the context. Elliger (196) interprets this warning to be an insertion to tie the laws on ritual purity to the sections surrounding them. This finds support in the use of the phrase ולא ימתו, "lest they die," for this phrase occurs in the following 16:2, 13 as well as the preceding 8:35 and 10:6, 7, 9. This language specifically ties into the account of the death of Aaron's two sons. This warning then was added as a bridge from this section of laws regarding ritual purity to chap. 16.

The audience of this speech is clearly the people, for they have to regulate themselves in regard to these matters. Since these matters are very private, there would have been virtually no way to monitor compliance. Only in reference to the sacrifices that a person who has recovered from an abnormal discharge has to make is there any involvement of the priests. This information is formulated for the knowledge of the laity, not the priests, given the sparsity of details. The inclusion of these laws provides additional evidence that in Israel the laity needed to be informed in order for the cult to function effectively.

Because these laws on defilement caused by discharges from the genitals are foundational to life and to the issue of ritual purity, they go back to the earliest days of Israel's origin.

Comment

1 Cf. 11:1.

2 Any man who has זוב, "a discharge" or "a flow," from his בשׂר, "flesh" or "body," becomes unclean. בשׂר is used here euphemistically for the penis.

3 Uncleanness is divided into two categories. The first is a seepage from his genitals (רר בשׂרו). ריר, "flow," describes the discharge of a thick, sticky, slimy fluid (cf. Job 6:6; 1 Sam 21:14[13]). Some have reasoned that the flow could be an abnormal discharge from the intestines or blood from hemorrhoids. These possibilities, however, face two major obstacles: (1) the entire chapter is concerned with discharges from the genitals and (2) there is no mention of blood in these cases with a male, which would certainly be expected in a priestly document if blood were the determining factor of uncleanness. The precise identification of the discharge is uncertain, suggesting that a wide variety of ailments are included in this regulation. These ailments cause "a discharge of mucus resulting from a catarrhal inflammation of the urinous tract" according to Noordtzij (150). A diagnosis that is certainly covered by this language is gonorrhea (Harrison, 160), even though Levine thinks not (92). This infection results in a purulent secretion. A person may naturally recover from gonorrhea after some months up to a year. Any abnormal discharge, no matter what the cause, makes a person unclean. The second category is that one's בשׂר, "genitals," are החתים, "obstructed," by זוב, "a discharge." The verb החתים, (lit.) "stop," probably describes an obstruction of the urethra that makes urination painful and difficult. Several ailments can produce such a condition.

4–11 Uncleanness is contagious. Anything that the source of the discharge comes into close contact with becomes unclean. Thus anything a man with a discharge touches, sits on, or lies on becomes unclean. Anyone who touches any of these objects that have thus become unclean becomes unclean until the evening. One who becomes unclean secondarily becomes clean again by washing his clothes, bathing (רחץ) in water, and waiting until evening. Usually the term רחץ, "bathe, wash," is understood to mean the immersion of the entire body (e.g., 2 Kgs 5:14). This is not a heavy obligation. The same requirement is made of anyone who touches the skin of an unclean man. Apparently a person with a discharge may touch another person in the course of daily life without making that person unclean as long as the one with the discharge has rinsed (שׁטף) his hands. A person who becomes unclean by being touched by one with an abnormal discharge becomes clean by following the same procedure as mentioned above.

8 If a man with a discharge spits on another, a gesture of extreme contempt (Num 12:14; Deut 25:9), that person becomes unclean. It is clear that the spit is viewed as carrying the properties of the unclean person from whom it came (cf.

Num 12:14; Deut 25:9). A person spat upon must follow the same procedure mentioned above to become clean.

9 The term מרכב encompasses anything on which a man sits while riding, including a saddle, a cloth, or a seat in a chariot (Snaith, 76).

12 The dishes that a person with a discharge uses have to be specially treated. A ceramic dish is to be broken, while a wooden vessel is to be rinsed (שטף) with water (cf. 11:32–33). This regulation sought to prevent a person's uncleanness from spreading to others by means of vessels used for eating.

13–15 When a person with a discharge is cleansed or healed, he may be readmitted to worship at the sanctuary. It is interesting to observe that the word for recovery here is טהר, "becomes clean." Health and cleanness are coupled as the aim of these regulations on ritual purity. The one who has recovered must wait seven days after his recovery, no doubt to make sure that the recovery is genuine (cf. 14:10; 15:28). On the eighth day that person is to wash his clothing and bathe his body in running water. On the use of fresh, running (חיים) water, see *Comment* on 14:5–7. Afterwards he is to present a sacrifice. The animals for the sacrifice are the least costly, two doves or two young pigeons (cf. 1:14–17). He presents them to the priest, and the priest offers one as חטאת, "a purification offering" (chap. 4), and the other as עלה, "a whole offering" (chap. 1). Thereby, the priest כפר, "makes expiation," for the person as a frail human, for any kind of sin that may have been connected with his disorder, and for his absence from the worship of Yahweh.

16–17 An emission of semen renders a man unclean, either an accidental emission like a nocturnal one (cf. Deut 23:11–12[10–11]) or a normal emission during intercourse. All clothes and garments of leather that the semen touches become unclean. They are to be washed with water; at evening they become clean again.

18 An emission of semen during sexual intercourse renders both the man and the woman unclean. Uncleanness resulting from normal sexual relations is of the mildest type. Both parties remain unclean only until the evening. Purification is accomplished by washing in water. No sacrifice is required. Uncleanness from an emission of semen excluded a man even from an army camp, but after washing he could return at evening, according to Deut 23:11–12(10–11) (cf. 1 Sam 21:5–6[4–5]).

A couple's becoming unclean in this way is not a serious issue; the major limitation is that it prevents them from entering the area of the sanctuary. Otherwise they continue their normal duties. This law does require couples to abstain from coitus whenever they plan to go to the sanctuary for their own sacrifices, a festival, or a special revelation (e.g., Exod 19:15; Lev 16:29). This regulation, furthermore, excludes any sexual intercourse from taking place in the sanctuary area, a practice promulgated at various pagan shrines, especially those based on fertility. In Israel, fertility was the result of God's blessing, not of some fertility rites designed to magically manipulate the natural forces (cf. Ps 127:3–5). This standard thus keeps sexual intercourse out of the area of the holy (קדש) and relegates it to the common realm (חל). On the other hand, there is no hint at all that the uncleanness from legitimate sexual intercourse carried any stigma or in any way was viewed as a sin of any degree.

Since sexual intercourse, above all in the context of marriage, is essential to carry out God's command given to humans at creation, "Be fruitful and multiply" (Gen

1:28), and his great promise of numerous descendants to Abraham (Gen 15:5), it is baffling that legitimate sexual intercourse renders the participants unclean. One explanation posits that generally any loss of bodily fluids makes one unclean (cf. J. Moyer, *Concept of Ritual Purity among the Hittites.*). This explanation is applicable to this situation, and it has the advantage of being basic and uncomplicated. Recently two new proposals have been set forth. Working from the premise that the cultic laws are constructed on a life-death polarity, Wenham (*ZAW* 95 [1983] 433–34) proposes that the loss of "life fluids" from either male or female sexual organs renders one unclean because such loss may make one ill, and, should it continue unchecked, leads to death. Certainly the flow of blood during menstruation is the loss of a life fluid (cf. 17:11), but it is hard to imagine that the loss of semen may be placed in the same category. Whitekettle (*JSOT* 49 [1991] 33) is certainly correct in discounting Wenham's argument by pointing out that during legitimate sexual intercourse semen is transferred from husband to wife "within a uniting whole" (cf. Gen 2:24). Working from the general polarity tabernacle (purity)/wilderness (impurity), Whitekettle (39–44) reasons that the cause for uncleanness in this case resides in the fact that the penis fails to function exclusively as an instrument of insemination, for it is also the organ for the elimination of urine, which, being a non-life/waste product, belongs to the spatial sphere identified as wilderness. Because of it dual function, the penis crosses "anatomical functional boundaries" (44). In fact, the confusion of its life-producing role with its role in disposing waste causes it to be classified as "unholy." For Whitekettle, it is this confusing, ambiguous function of the penis, which becomes evident during sexual intercourse, that causes an emission of semen to make a couple unclean for a brief time. This suggestion is insightful. Nevertheless, these dual functions of the penis, being quite distinct, are not confused during sexual intercourse. In this light, the first explanation remains the best tangible explanation. The theological reason, as stated earlier, is that Yahwistic faith wished to relegate sexual intercourse to the realm of the ordinary, common side of human life (cf. *Excursus* on ritual purity at *Form/Structure/Setting* on chaps. 11–15). Without degrading sexual intercourse, this law prevented it either from being practiced at the sanctuary or from being incorporated into any ritual performed at the sanctuary.

19–24 A woman's monthly menstrual flow (זוב) renders her unclean for seven days. A woman becomes unclean, because there is a flow from her body, the flow is blood, and this phenomena was mysterious to ancient peoples. The time of her ritual impurity is seven days because of the importance of the number seven and because this length of time covers any woman who had a period that lasted longer than that of most women. Anyone who touches a woman during her period becomes unclean until evening. The instructions for that person to bathe as a part of becoming clean are missing. Whether this resulted from an error in the transmission of the text is difficult to tell. The cases in the context suggest that a person who became unclean in this matter would assume that bathing was necessary. Whoever touches anything on which she has lain or sat becomes unclean until evening. That person must wash her clothes and bathe in water. This standard must mean that a woman would have her own bed and chair for this time of the month.

These laws do not discriminate unduly against women. Both men and women are made unclean by discharges from their genitals. A woman becomes unclean from her menses longer than a man from an emission of semen solely because of the difference in nature; i.e., the flow of menstrual blood lasts longer than an emission of semen. In support of this position it is important to note that neither a woman nor a man has to make any sacrifice in order to become clean, for their flows are natural. Furthermore, these restrictions during the time of menses help a woman regain her strength. They are particularly beneficial to those women who experience great discomfort during this cycle, such as cramps, excessive bleeding, low backaches, headaches, and/or irritability (Harrison, 164).

24 If a man lies with a woman during her period, he becomes unclean for seven days. Whatever he lies on becomes unclean. While the length of his uncleanness is longer than in other cases cited above, there is no grave stigma attached to his deed or any sense that he has sinned, for he does not have to offer up an offering as part of his becoming clean. In fact, the intensity of his uncleanness is down played, for no instructions are given for his recovery. This last regulation, however, stands in contrast to the strong penalty of being "cut off" from the people for lying with a woman during her period in 20:18 (cf. 18:19; Ezek 18:6; 22:10). The best way to account for this apparent discrepancy in severity of the consequences is to hold that these texts address different situations. In this text it is assumed that a man surprisingly and unwittingly discovers that he has come into contact with menses, probably from intercourse at the inception of the woman's menstrual period, while in the other law a man brazenly breaks the decree by knowingly lying with a woman during her period (cf. Keil and Delitzsch, 394; Wenham, 220). Lying with a woman is much closer contact than that of touching something on which she has sat, yet the penalty here is not any severer. This points in the direction of understanding that the coming into contact with her menses happens inadvertently. Baentsch (378) takes another approach; he does not think this passage involves intercourse, but rather that a man who is sleeping beside a woman comes into contact with menses. Another solution reasons that this passage is later and seeks to lighten a harsh law (cf. Porter, 122).

25–27 A woman who has a discharge of blood beyond the time of her menses is considered unclean as long as she has this discharge. One such condition is menostaxis, a type of prolonged menstrual bleeding (Harrison, 164). This is an abnormal and distressing disorder. As with a woman in menses, her bed and anything on which she sits becomes unclean. Anyone who touches these objects that have become unclean becomes unclean until evening. A person who has become unclean in this way must wash their clothes, bathe in water, and wait until evening to become clean.

28–30 When a woman is cured טהרה, (lit.) "becomes clean" (cf. vv 13–15), from an abnormal flow of blood, she is to wait seven days, again to make sure that the cure is genuine. On the eighth day she brings to the priest two doves or two young pigeons for a sacrifice, one for חטאת, "a purification offering," and one for עלה, "a whole offering." These are, of course, inexpensive sacrifices. With these offerings the priest makes expiation for her before Yahweh. Since this is an abnormal flow of blood, this woman must offer sacrifices as part of her ritual cleansing. It is also instructive that the law requires a woman to make a sacrifice and that in cases of recovery from uncleanness caused by an abnormal discharge the sacrificial requirements for her full restoration to the community are the same as those for a man (vv 14–15). This reveals that a woman had significant standing in Israel's cult and that she had access to the area around the altar for making an offering. While it does not say that she is to wash her clothes and bathe in water, these requirements may be assumed.

31 The reason for these laws is that Israel is to be separate (הזיר) to God. נזר communicates a clearly defined separation between the common and the holy. Thus this root is chosen for the Nazirite, who separates himself to God by special vows (Num 6:1–21). Israel is to keep that which is profane or common out of the area of the tabernacle. Whenever an Israelite contacts uncleanness, that person is to remove his uncleanness before entering the sanctuary. If the people follow these standards, they will not risk being consumed by the Holy nor will they defile the tabernacle. It is important to notice that the sanctuary is called "my tabernacle [משכני] which is among them." God emphasizes that at the tabernacle he is present among the people. The major reason then for the laws dealing with clean and unclean is to prevent the Israelites from defiling the tabernacle by not taking care to follow the laws of ritual purity. Of course, if the tabernacle becomes unclean, they will have no effective place to meet God and find expiation from sin.

Explanation

These laws teach that people, both male and female, have responsibility for governing themselves in regard to any discharge from their genitals. Since a discharge made a person unclean, both the male and the female, each one had to be careful not to approach the sanctuary while unclean, and each one had to take the steps necessary to return to ritual purity. While it is true that a female became unclean longer, this fact does not cast greater shame on a female, for the length of her uncleanness was grounded solely in the way of nature; i.e., a menstrual discharge lasts longer than an emission of semen. Furthermore, both males and females in their uncleanness communicated this uncleanness to other persons and to articles on which they sat and slept. Any object they made unclean made unclean any person who sat or slept on it. Since this regulation does not prescribe any inspection of persons who had a discharge by a priest, as in cases of grievous skin diseases (chaps. 13–14), these persons had to monitor themselves in this matter.

Both normal and abnormal discharges from a person's genitals rendered a person unclean. Normal discharges, though, made a person unclean for a brief period of time. A male who had an emission of semen became unclean until evening. During her monthly menses a female became unclean for seven days. It needs to be remembered that becoming unclean for a brief span of time was not that complicated or negative or even that unusual. The major problem occurred in bringing the unclean into the vicinity of the holy. An abnormal discharge in either a male or a female, however, made that person unclean until the discharge ceased.

These laws were not designed to deny sexual passion within a marriage, nor were they intended to give either gender dominance over the other. They teach that discharges from the genitals had to be properly handled in order that the sanctuary not be defiled and that a person not be placed in jeopardy by entering the sanctuary in a state of impurity. In following these laws of ritual purity a person learned to control sexual passion. In addition, disciplined, moral expression of passion coupled with cleanliness in regard to discharges from the genitals had the by-product of curtailing venereal diseases and other kinds of illness that are sexually transmitted. In fact, the requirement of bathing for anyone who had become unclean by contact with any discharge, either directly or indirectly, promoted the general health of the ancient community. Good sexual hygiene increased the fertility of both males and females and fostered the birth of healthy offspring. Thus these laws encouraged natural increase in the people of God. They offered very practical ways to promote the fulfillment of God's promise to Abraham of numerous offspring, so numerous that their number would be greater than that of the stars in heaven (Gen 15:5; 22:17).

The primary purpose of these laws on ritual purity in regard to sexual discharges was to separate from the holy any activity that belonged to the sphere of the common, the sphere of earthly existence. These laws relegated sexual activity to the common area. There sexual intercourse was to be fully enjoyed as long as couples displayed moral responsibility in relating to each other (cf. chaps. 18 and 20). But sexual intercourse was never to take place in the area of the sanctuary. Sexuality was not a way to achieve spiritual enhancement, nor was it a way to commune with God. There was to be no confusion on this issue among the covenant people. The belief that sexual congress could manipulate the productivity of the natural order, as was believed in the various fertility cults of Israel's neighbors, was despicable in the sight of OT law revealed by God. All practices based on such a belief, therefore, were to be banished from Israel.

While these regulations are not specifically cited in the NT, they are assumed. The most noteworthy case is the report of the woman who had an issue of blood for twelve years (Mark 5:25–34; Matt 9:20–22; Luke 8:43–48). She had spent her wealth on seeking a cure, but to no avail. In desperation and concealed within the crowd for anonymity, she touched Jesus' garment in faith hoping for healing. To her surprise Jesus asked, "Who touched me?" Fear welled up in her, for she knew that her touch communicated uncleanness. Trembling she admitted that she had touched Jesus. Jesus responded, "Daughter, your faith has made you well; go in peace, and be healed of your disease." One can imagine her relief, joy, and happiness. This incident reveals that Jesus is Lord over all defiling discharges. As Lord he brings those who are unclean to wholeness and purity. It also teaches that Jesus did not let either the laws of uncleanness nor the conventional attitude toward women stop him from reaching out to anyone in need. He healed those with grievous skin diseases. He touched the dead. He let the lady act, answer, and display her faith unhindered; in fact, he commended her bravery and outgoing action. Thereby Jesus showed that under the new covenant he was doing away with the old regulations that separated the holy from the common and male from female. That does not mean he did away with that distinction totally, but it does mean that he would not let such a line prevent people from receiving God's forgiving grace. His actions reveal that God has come to humans and calls them to himself in whatever condition they happen to be. Jesus has thrown wide open the access to God for every person.

Further evidence of the newness of the new covenant is found in Jesus' response to the question about his disciples not washing their hands before eating. This was a very frequent ritual for devout Jews to insure ritual purity before eating bread, but it was based on tradition, not on the OT purity laws (Matt 15:2; Mark 7:2–5). Jesus informed his critics that it is not what enters the mouth that defiles a person, but what comes out of the mouth (Matt 15:11). As typical of his teaching, Jesus elevated the moral issue over the ceremonial law.

The exhortation in Heb 13:4, "let marriage be held in honor among all, and let the marriage bed be undefiled," uses a metaphor from the laws of ritual purity as it calls for personal integrity in marriage relationships. This exhortation highlights the ethical premise underneath the laws of ritual purity. This example illustrates how the study of these laws on ritual purity has value for believers in Jesus by informing them of the principles that lie behind them. From another perspective, the study of these laws produces in the believer a great appreciation for the glorious freedom that Jesus' redemptive work has won for all who believe on him.

IV. Regulations and Calendar for the Day of Atonement (16:1–34)

Bibliography

Aartun, K. "Studien zum Gesetz über den grossen Versöhungstag Lv 16 mit Varianten: Ein ritualgeschichtlicher Beitrag." *ST* 34 (1980) 73–109. **Adler, S.** "Der Versöhnungstag in der Bibel, sein Ursprung und seine Bedeutung." *ZAW* 3 (1883) 178–85. **Aḥituv, S.** "Azazel." *EncJud* 3:999–1002. **Ashbel, D.** "The Goat Sent to Azazel" (Heb.). *Beth Mikra* 11 (1965/66) 89–101. **Athidiajah, M.** "The Goat for Azazel" (Heb.). *Beth Mikra* 6 (1960/61) 80. **Ben-Mordecai, C. A.** "The Iniquity of the Sanctuary." *JBL* 60 (1941) 311–14. **Benzinger, I.** "Das Gesetz über den grossen Versöhnungstag Lev. XVI." *ZAW* 9 (1889) 65–89. **Brawer, A. J.** "השׂעיר לעזאזל וצפור המצורע." *Beth Mikra* 12 (1967) 32–33. **Büchsel, F.**, and **Herrmann, S.** "*ἱλαστήριον*." *TDNT* 3:318–23. **Davis, D.** "An Interpretation of Sacrifice in Leviticus." *ZAW* 89 (1977) 387–99. **Derrett, J. D. M.** "'Love thy neighbour as a man like thyself'?" *ExpTim* 83 (1971/72) 55–56. **Driver, G. R.** "Three Technical Terms in the Pentateuch." *JSS* 1 (1956) 92–105. **Feinberg, E. L.** "The Scapegoat of Lev. sixteen." *BSac* 115 (1958) 320–33. **Fryer, N. W. L.** "The Meaning and Translation of *Hilastērion* in Romans 3:25." *EvQ* 59 (1987) 99–116. **Görg, M.** "Beobactungen zum sogenannten Azazel-Ritus." *BN* 33 (1986) 10–16. **Grabbe, L. L.** "The Scapegoat Tradition: A Study of Early Jewish Interpretation." *JSJ* 18 (1987) 152–67. **Haran, M.** "The Complex of Ritual Acts Performed inside the Tabernacle." *Scripto Hierosolymitana* 8 (1961) 272–302. **Hruby, K.** "Le *yom ha-kippurim* on jour de l'expiation." *Orient syrien* 10 (1965) 41–74, 161–92, 413–42. **Janowski, B.** *Sühne als Heilsgeschehen.* WMANT 55. Neukirchen-Vluyn: Neukirchener, 1982. **Kiuchi, N.** *The Purification Offering in the Priestly Literature.* JSOTSup 56. Sheffield: JSOT Press, 1987. 77–85, 143–59. **Kümmel, H.** "Ersatzkönig und Sündenbock." *ZAW* 80 (1968) 289–318. **Landersdorfer, S.** *Studien zum biblischen Versöhnungstag.* Münster: Aschendorffschen Verlagsbuchhandlung, 1923. **Langdon, S. H.** "The Scape-Goat in Babylonian Religion." *ExpTim* 24 (1912/13) 9–13. **Löhr, M.** *Das Ritual von Lev. 16 (Untersuchungen zum Hexateuchproblem III).* Schriften der Königsberger Gelehrten Gesellschaft 2/1. Berlin: Deutsche Verlagsgesellschaft für Politik und Geschichte, 1925. **Manson, T. W.** "'*ΙΛΑΣΤΗΡΙΟΝ*.'" *JTS* 46 (1945) 1–10. **Messel, N.** "Die Komposition von Lev. 16." *ZAW* 27 (1907) 1–15. **Milgrom, J.** "Atonement, Day of." *IDBSup* 82–83. ———. "Day of Atonement." *EncJud* 5:1384–87. **Möller, W.**, and **Payne, J. B.** "Atonement, Day of." *ISBE* rev. 1:360–62. **Morris, L. L.** "The Meaning of *ἱλαστήριον* in Romans iii. 25." *NTS* 2 (1955/56) 33–43. ———. "The Day of Atonement and the Work of Christ." *Reformed Theological Review* 14 (1955) 9–19. **Rylaarsdam, J. C.** "Atonement, Day of." *IDB* 1:313–16. **Sabourin, L.** "Le bouc émissaire, figure du Christ?" *ScEc* 11 (1959) 45–79. **Schur, I.** *Versöhnungstag und Sündopfer im Alten Testament.* Commentationes humanarum litterarum 6/3. Breslau, 1930. **Strand, K. A.** "An Overlooked Old Testament Background to Revelation 11:1." *AUSS* 22 (1984) 317–25. **Strobel, A.** "Das jerusalemische Sündenbock-Ritual: Topographische und landeskundliche Erwägungen zur überlieferungsgeschichte von Lev. 16,10.21f." *ZDPV* 103 (1987) 141–68. **Stuhlmacker, P.** "Recent Exegesis on Romans 3:24–26." In *Reconciliation, Law, & Righteousness: Essays in Biblical Theology.* Philadelphia: Fortress, 1986. 94–109. **Tarragon, J.-M. de.** "La *Kapporet* est-elle une fiction ou un élément du cult tardif?" *RB* 88 (1981) 5–12. **Tawil, H.** "ʾAzazel The Prince of the Steppe: A Comparative Study." *ZAW* 92 (1980) 43–59. **Vriezen, Th. C.** "The Term *Hizza*: Lustration and Consecration: The Day of Atonement Lev xvi." *OTS* 7 (1950) 219–33. **Wyatt, N.** "Atonement Theology in Ugarit and Israel." *UF* 8 (1976) 415–30. **Young, N. H.** "The Gospel according to Hebrews 9." *NTS* 27 (1981) 198–210. ———. "'Hilaskesthai' and Related

Words in the New Testament." *EvQ* 55 (1983) 169–76. **Zani, A.** "Tracce di un'interessante, ma sconosciuta esegesi midrašica giudeo-cristiana di Lev 16 in un frammento di Ippolito." *BO* 24 (1982) 157–66.

Introduction

The regulation for the Day of Atonement is a division unto itself, for it begins with a historical reference in the introductory formula (v 1) and concludes with a compliance report (v 34b). It stands at the center of the Book of Leviticus, and, of course, the Book of Leviticus is the center of the Pentateuch. Its literary position highlights the importance of this solemn day for the Israelite community, especially in the era when the Pentateuch received its final shape.

This regulation stands at the earliest possible location in the priestly legislation. In order for it to be fully intelligible, it requires the preceding material, specifically the pattern for the tabernacle and its furniture (Exod 25–40), the regulations for the purification offering (4:1–5:13) and the whole offering (chap. 1), the ordination of the priesthood (chap. 8), and the inauguration of the new cult (chap. 9). Since the rituals of this day remove the impurities resulting from the people's uncleannesses, it requires the presentation of the laws on ritual purity (chaps. 11–15). But what about the laws in chaps. 17–26? While all information is beneficial to understanding the work of the Day of Atonement, those laws, which treat, for the most part, irreparable deeds, do not need to come before this regulation for recharging the cult and for guaranteeing the congregation's standing before Yahweh. Rather this regulation prepares for the coming material on holy living. It may be said that the moral and spiritual energy for the people to fulfill the laws in chaps. 17–26 comes out of their finding complete expiation on the Day of Atonement. The ritual for the Day of Atonement thus appropriately stands before the laws on holy living.

It is very difficult to date the origin of this high day, for there are no references to it in either the former or the latter prophets. Elsewhere in the Pentateuch there are only three references: (1) There is a very brief regulation concerning it in the calendar of Lev 23 (vv 29–32)—from the brevity of that section it is clear that that text assumes the regulations found in chap. 16, especially vv 29–34a. (2) A brief liturgical agenda for this day is found in the calendar of Num 28–29 (29:7–11), even though this day is not specifically named. (3) In Lev 25:9 the year of Jubilee is scheduled to begin on the Day of Atonement. There is, in addition, a similar ritual in Ezek 45:18–20. That text prescribes an offering to cleanse the sanctuary on the first day of the first month that is to be repeated on the seventh day of that month; an alternative reading is the seventh month, but that reading is considered inferior by Zimmerli (*Ezekiel 2*, tr. J. D. Martin, Hermeneia [Philadelphia: Fortress, 1983] 483). A close look at that ritual finds, however, that it is quite different from that for the Day of Atonement. The lack of reference to this day in Ezekiel, then, is extraordinary given Ezekiel's great interest in matters of the Temple. This has led many scholars to conclude that this day must have originated after Ezekiel's time. Milgrom (*EncJud* 5:1387) discounts this argument by noting that the cleansing ceremony for the Temple is a part of Ezekiel's whole program, which is novel to Ezekiel, and thus his work does not provide any information on the origin of the Day of Atonement.

The puzzle of this day's origin is compounded by the reference in Neh 9:1 to the twenty-fourth of the seventh month being a day of fasting. If the Day of Atonement was observed in the seventh month, why was another fast day held, especially coming after the joyful Feast of Tabernacles? W. Möller and J. B. Payne (*ISBE* rev. 1:362) speculate that Ezra reinstated the Day of Atonement, but, for some unknown reason, he had to postpone it for two weeks until after the conclusion of the Feast of Tabernacles. A reading of Neh 9:1–3 finds, however, that on this twenty-fourth day there were fasting, confession of sins, and reading of the law, but nothing is said about the sacrificial rituals required on the Day of Atonement. Thus the design of this fast day was different from that of the Day of Atonement. Milgrom (*IDBSup* 83), furthermore, points out that the Day of Atonement would not have been an appropriate day for writing a covenant and confirming it as was done on that day (Neh 10:1[9:38]). He goes on to speculate that the Day of Atonement was not mentioned by Nehemiah because the priests, rather than the people, bore the responsibility for this solemn day.

The lack of historical reference to this day and the prominence given to Aaron in this regulation led the Wellhausen school to place the origin of the Day of Atonement well into the post-exilic era. There is, nevertheless, much evidence that points to the antiquity of the observance of this day. First, according to Koch's study (*Priesterschrift,* 92–96), an ancient ritual underlies the present text. Second, the rite of riddance with the goat for Azazel has the earmarks of an ancient ritual, for early rites of riddance are attested at Ugarit and among the Hittites that parallel the ritual of releasing this goat into the wilderness (Aartun, *ST* 34 [1980] 91–94). It is hard to imagine that such a rite of riddance arose during the stringent monotheistic outlook of the post-exilic community, especially since the goat is sent to the desert, the abode of demons. Third, the loss of the meaning of the term עזאזל, "Azazel," also points to an early origin (cf. Noth, 119, 123–24). A fourth clue to its antiquity is the vital function of the blood rites at כפרת, "the Atonement Slate." These blood rites must have come from an earlier time, for this piece of cultic furniture disappeared during the exile. It is not mentioned in Ezekiel's reconstructed Temple, and Jeremiah says that the Ark of the Covenant, also presumably the Atonement Slate and the cherubim, will never be built again (3:16; cf. W. Möller and J. B. Payne, *ISBE* rev. 1:362).

Drawing historical conclusions from the lack of references to a matter, moreover, is dangerous. This can be seen by the sparsity of references to this day in post-exilic literature, even though the Day of Atonement had grown significantly in importance in the post-exilic community. These references include Sir 50:5–7; 3 Macc 1:11; Philo, *De specialibus legibus* 2.193–223; Josephus, *Ant.* 14.4.3; Acts 27:9; Heb 6:19; 9:7, 11–14 (W. Möller and J. B. Payne, *ISBE* rev. 1:362). This lack of references to an important custom is also attested in the infrequent mention of the three pilgrim festivals in the pre-exilic books. The sparsity of those references is amazing in that leaders would have chosen those occasions for special events; e.g., Josiah celebrated the completion of the restoration of the Temple at the Feast of Passover (2 Kgs 23:21–23). Since a leader would have chosen a time of feasting, not a day of fasting, for a special occasion, it is understandable why there are more references to these feasts than to the Day of Atonement. Unless a disaster or a threat such as war came at the beginning of the seventh month, there would have been no special occasion to refer to the

Day of Atonement in the OT material that has come down to us. Moreover, the lack of references may be because of the fast lasting only a single day and because of its mournful nature. This deficiency then should carry little weight in arguing against the antiquity of the observance of this day. Nevertheless, the silence in the pre-exilic era is disturbing.

Some other considerations may help account for the silence about the Day of Atonement. Remarkably this day does not have a name in chap. 16, and, if the calendric portion in this regulation (vv 29–34a) is a late addition, this day might not have received a fixed date until the post-exilic era (cf. Aartun, *ST* 34 [1980] 98–99). If these facts are correct, reference to this day in pre-exilic texts would be much more unlikely. Furthermore, it is very possible that this day did not receive much national importance in the Kingdom period. Since the tribes settled throughout Canaan would have waited until after this fast day to make their pilgrimage to the Feast of Tabernacles in the seventh month, the primary responsibility for the observance of this day would have fallen to the priesthood and possibly to the community in the immediate environs of the central shrine. Furthermore, it is quite possible that this day fell into disuse under the reigns of wicked kings like Ahaz and was not revived until the time of the Second Temple. In this light it can be confidently assumed that its observance did not receive the attention in the Kingdom period that it came to have in the post-exilic era.

Given these considerations, contemporary scholars have come to a more complex understanding of the origin and development of this day than espoused by earlier critical scholars. The conclusions of two scholars will illustrate this point. In an extensive study of the traditions witnessed to in this text, Aartun (*ST* 34 [1980] 103) recognizes the antiquity of the two main rituals, the expiating ritual and the ritual for the removal of sin by an animal released into the wilderness. From the language used in this text and tradition history of Israelite cultic customs, he concludes that the Day of Atonement arose from the combination and reworking of these two rituals at the end of the exile or the beginning of the post-exilic period. Milgrom, on the other hand, holds that the observance of this day reaches back into the Kingdom period (*EncJud* 5:1387). He places its origin sometime after Solomon's Temple, considering it unlikely that Solomon would have suspended this day had it fallen during the extended celebration of his Temple's completion, which lasted seven or eight days in the seventh month, ending on the twenty-second day (1 Kgs 8:65–66; 2 Chr 7:8–10). But given the possibility that the date for this day had not been fixed by Solomon's time, Solomon had no need to suspend it. Thus its origin could be earlier than Solomon's time.

The composite of evidence, therefore, favors assigning an early origin to the basic rites of this day of expiation. The rough state of the text, as will be discussed below, witnesses to a long, complex development of the traditions regarding this day.

This day greatly increased in importance in the late Second Temple period, for its observance gave Israel, who had gone through the exile because of her sins, confidence that her sins were expiated and that she was acceptable to God. It was so important that it could be referred to by numerous terms such as "the great fast" (Acts 27:9), "the feast of the fast" (Philo), and "the day" or "the great day" (the Mishnah; Rylaarsdam, *IDB* 1:313). In fact, a whole tractate in the Mishnah named *Yoma* was given over to the rites and regulations of this day.

Amazingly, with the destruction of the Second Temple and the ending of sacrifices, this day grew even more in importance in Judaism. Today its observance unites Jews around the globe in a multitude of communities with very diverse theologies and traditions. For the early Christians, the Day of Atonement played a significant role in their interpretation of Jesus' death. Good Friday, became the Christians' Day of Atonement, so to speak, a day of self-denial, penance, expiation, and reconciliation.

Translation

1 *Yahweh spoke to Moses after the death*[a] *of Aaron's two sons who died when they drew*
near[b] *before Yahweh.* 2 *Yahweh said to Moses: "Speak to Aaron, your brother, not to enter*[a] *at*
any time[b] *into the Holiest Place*[c] *within*[d] *the curtain in front of the Atonement Slate,*[e]
which is on the Ark,[f] *lest he die, for I will appear in the cloud*[g] *over the Atonement Slate.*
3 *"In this way*[a] *Aaron is to enter the holy place: with a young bull*[b] *for a purification*
offering and a ram[c] *for a whole offering.* 4 *He*[a] *is to wear the holy linen tunic, and he is*
to have on his body[b] *the linen trousers, and he is to tie on the linen sash, and he is to*
wear[c] *the linen turban. These are sacred garments. He must bathe himself*[d] *in water*
before putting them on. 5 *From the Israelite community*[a] *he is to take two male goats for a*
purification offering[b] *and a ram for a whole offering.*
6 *"Aaron is to bring near*[a] *the bull for his own purification offering in order to make*
expiation for himself and for his household. 7 *Then he is to take the two goats and set*
them before Yahweh at the entrance to the Tent of Meeting. 8 *Aaron is to cast lots over the*
two goats, one lot for Yahweh and one lot for Azazel.[a] 9 *Aaron is to present the goat on*
which the lot to Yahweh fell and make[a] *a purification offering.* 10 *And the goat on which*
the lot for Azazel[a] *fell is to be stationed*[b] *alive before Yahweh to make expiation with it by*
sending it to Azazel,[c] *into the wilderness.*
11 *"Aaron is to present his*[a] *bull for a purification offering to make expiation for him-*
self and his house. He is to slaughter his bull for the purification offering. 12 *He is to take*
a firepan[a] *full of burning coals from the altar before Yahweh and two handfuls of finely*
ground fragrant[b] *incense and bring them within*[c] *the curtain.* 13 *He is to put the incense*
on the fire before Yahweh, and the smoke of the incense will cover the Atonement Slate
which is over the testimony in order that he does not die. 14 *He is to take some of*[a] *the bull's*
blood and sprinkle it with his finger over the surface of the Atonement Slate eastward,
and he is to sprinkle some of[a] *the blood with his finger seven times*[b] *before the Atonement*
Slate.[c]
15 *"He is then to slaughter the people's goat for a purification offering*[a] *and bring its*
blood[b] *within the curtain and do with*[c] *its blood just as he did with the bull's blood. He*
is to sprinkle it on the Atonement Slate and before the Atonement Slate. 16 *In this way he*
will make expiation for the Holiest Place because of[a] *the uncleannesses of the Israelites*
and their acts of rebellion and for all their sins. Thus he is to do for the Tent of Meeting,
which dwells among them in the midst of their uncleannesses. 17 *No one may ever be*[a]
inside the Tent of Meeting when he enters to make expiation in the Holiest Place until
he exits, having made expiation for himself, for his house, and for all the assembly[b] *of*
Israel.
18 *"He then is to go out to the altar which is before Yahweh and make expiation for it.*
He is to take some of[a] *the bull's blood and some of*[a] *the goat's blood and put it on the*
horns roundabout the altar. 19 *He is to sprinkle some of*[a] *the blood on it seven times*[b] *with*

his finger. Thus he will cleanse it and sanctify it from the uncleannesses of the Israelites.

20 *"When Aaron has finished making expiation for the Holiest Place, the Tent of Meeting, and the altar,*[a] *he is to bring near the living goat.* 21 *Aaron is to lay both*[a] *his hands on the living goat's head and confess over it all the iniquities of the Israelites, all their acts of rebellion, and all their sins;*[b] *he is to put them on the goat's*[c] *head and send it away into the wilderness by the hand of one waiting in readiness.*[d] 22 *The goat is to carry on it all*[a] *their iniquities to a desolate place, and he is to release the goat in the wilderness.*

23 *"Aaron is to come to the Tent of Meeting and take off the linen garments he had put on before he entered the Holiest Place and leave them there.* 24 *He is to bathe himself in water in a holy place and put on his (priestly) clothes. Then he is to go out and perform the ritual*[a] *for his own whole offering and the people's whole offering, making expiation for himself*[b] *and for the people.*[c] 25 *He is to burn the fat of the purification offering on the altar.*[a]

26 *"The man who releases the goat for Azazel*[a] *is to wash his clothes and bathe himself in water; afterwards he may enter the camp.* 27 *The bull for the purification offering and the goat for the purification offering, whose blood*[ab] *has been brought into the Holiest Place*[c] *to make expiation, are to be taken*[d] *outside the camp and burned*[e] *with fire along with their hides, their flesh, and their offal.* 28 *He who burns them is to wash his clothes and bathe himself in water. Afterwards he may enter the camp.*

29 *"This*[a] *is to be*[b] *a perpetual ordinance for you. On the tenth day of the seventh month you are to afflict yourselves*[c] *by not doing any work—the citizen and the alien who lives among you—*30 *because on this day he is to make expiation for you to make you clean; and you will be clean from all your sins before Yahweh.* 31 *It*[a] *is a sabbath of solemn rest*[b] *for you, and you must afflict yourselves. It is a perpetual ordinance.* 32 *The priest who is anointed*[a] *and ordained*[b] *to be priest in his father's place is to make expiation.*[c] *He is to put on the sacred linen garments.* 33 *He is to make expiation*[a] *for the Most Holy Place*[b] *and he is to make expiation*[a] *for the Tent of Meeting and the altar, and he is to make expiation*[a] *for*[c] *the priests and all the congregation.*[d] 34 *This is to be a perpetual ordinance for you in order to make expiation for the Israelites because of*[a] *all their sins once*[b] *a year."*

And he did[c] *just as Yahweh had commanded Moses.*

Notes

1.a. The inf constr after the prep forms a temporal clause; the main clause is introduced by a *waw* consec.

1.b. LXX adds *ἐν τῷ προσάγειν αὐτοὺς πῦρ ἀλλότριον* = בהקריבם אש זרה, "when they entered with strange fire" (also Tg, Syr, and Vg; cf. Num 3:4). PIR (183) takes MT as the preferable text, postulating that the variant arose from the influence of another text.

2.a. The jussive with the negative אל conveys a warning (GKC §109c).

2.b. The use of כל, "all," is ambiguous (Joüon §160k). The meaning is that he may not enter any time at his own discretion, but only at those times permitted by God.

2.c. הקדש means any place around the area of the Tent where a priest officiates, including the main altar (Haran, *Temples*, 172, n. 50). Here it means "the Holiest Place," which is sometimes called קדש הקדשים, "the Holy of Holies" (e.g., 21:22). In this speech it is used frequently for the most sacred place of the Tent of Meeting with which it is often mentioned (vv 2, 3 [this could be for the area of the Tent], 16, 17, 20, 23, 27; cf. v 33.b.). It is used in this way in 4:6; 10:4 and Ezek 41:21, 23.

2.d. Two prep have joined with בית, "house," to form a compound prep מבית לי, "within" (BDB, "בית, 8.b.," 110; GKC §130a[3]).

2.e. Another position for consideration is put forth by M. Görg in "Eine neue Deutung für *kăpport*," *ZAW* 89 (1977) 115–18; he traces this term back to an Egyptian word and renders it "footplate."

2.f. LXX reads ἐπὶ τῆς κιβωτοῦ τοῦ μαρτυρίου, "on the ark of the testimony."

2.g. In this clause the prep phrase בענן, "in the cloud," stands first for emphasis.

3.a. The demonstrative pronoun בזאת, (lit.) "with this," anticipates the object, i.e., a bull and a ram, which occurs at the end of the sentence. It comes first to stress that Aaron cannot enter the Holy of Holies unprepared. It is possible that "this" also includes the garments (v 5) and the correct ritual order (cf. Dillmann, 575). If the latter items are included in this term, the pronoun has been chosen to begin the sentence, for the predicate would be far too long to be put in its place.

3.b. On פר בן־בקר, "a young bull," see *Comment* on 4:3.

3.c. איל, "a ram," for עלה, "a whole offering," is prescribed also in 8:18, 9:2, and Num 15:24.

4.a. Sam, LXX, and Syr read a *waw* at the beginning of the verse.

4.b. בשרו, (lit.) "his body, flesh," is euphemistic for his pudenda; cf. n. 15:2.d. In the Israelite cult a priest was to be careful to avoid any possible exposure of himself (cf. Exod 20:26; 28:42–43).

4.c. צנף means "wrap, wind"; it is the verb for putting on a מצנפת, "turban" (Exod 28:4, 37, 39). In this verse Rashi understands צנף to mean "put on" (73a); but Exod 29:6 and Lev 8:9 use שים, "put." The note in Rashi, however, prefers to render צנף, "wrap," since the prep ב, "in, with," stands before מצנפת, "turban."

4.d. Sam and LXX add כל, "all," before בשרו, "his body."

5.a. Cf. n. 4:13.a.

5.b. According to Bertholet (54), לחטאת, "for a purification offering," stands not merely for the purification offering, but for the entire rite of purification. This interpretation extends the word to cover both goats, but it faces the difficulty that it interrupts the parallel between לחטאת and לעלה, "for a whole offering." The speaker at this point only wanted to refer to the official offerings and did not wish to distinguish the differing rituals with the two goats.

6.a. Dillmann (576) notes that הקריב here has the meaning "bring near" as in vv 1 and 3, not its technical meaning "present" as in v 11.

8.a. LXX reads τῷ ἀποπομπαίῳ, "to the one carrying away (evil)" (Liddell-Scott, 213). The meaning of עזאזל has been lost. Some suggestions of its meaning are instructive. The versions understand עזאזל to be a compound of עז, "goat," and אזל, "turn off" = "the goat that departs" or "the goat has gone away" (Snaith, 79). This rendering led to the Eng trans. "escape-goat" > "scapegoat." Levine (102) suggests that this term may have developed from עז־אל, "a mighty goat," with the duplication of ז, עזזאל > עזאזל. Keil and Delitzsch (398) understand it as an intense form of עזל > עזלזל > עזאזל (with the liquid softening to a vowel; cf. GKC §30n). In *b. Yoma* 67b or 39a, עזאזל is rendered "a fierce, difficult land," since עזז is taken to mean "strong, fierce" (Levine, 102). Hoffmann (1:444), however, identifies it as a Heb. term meaning "complete destruction."

Working with the idea that this may be the name of another deity, Wyatt (429) proposes, on the basis that the original form was עזזאל, that this term is a title of ʿAṯtar, a deity known from Ugarit who was the morning star and the son of Asherah. He makes this connection on the basis of the two goats required for sacrifice on this day as being identified with the twin hypostases of ʿAṯtar. This speculative suggestion has not found much support.

9.a. MT ועשהו, "and he made it," is elliptical for "he performed the ritual of . . ."; cf. 9:16 and Exod 29:38.

10.a. Cf. n. 8.a.

10.b. For MT יעמד, "it is to be stood, presented," LXX has στήσει αὐτόν = יעמיד אתו, "he is to set it."

10.c. LXX adds ἀφήσει αὔτον, "he will release it."

11.a. For MT אשר לו, "which is his," LXX[BA] reads τὸν αὐτοῦ καὶ τοῦ οἴκου αὐτοῦ μόνον, "which is his and his house's alone." LXX stresses that the high priest makes the first sacrifice for not only himself, but also for his house, i.e., the active priests.

12.a. On המחתה, cf. 10:1

12.b. On סמים, cf. n. 4:7.a.

12.c. Cf. n. 2.c.

14.a. This is a partitive use of the prep מן to designate an indefinite portion of something (BDB, "מן, 3.b.," 580).

14.b. This is an acc of manner, describing the way an action is to be done (GKC §118m; *IBHS* §10.2.2e).

14.c. ולפני הכפרת, "and before the Atonement Slate," stands before the verb for emphasis; in order to stress that there are two blood rites that take place in reference to the Atonement Slate, the speaker puts the references to this slate back to back with only "eastward" between them. In fact, the words מדם . . . הזה . . . על־פני הכפרת . . . לפני הכפרת יזה . . . מן־הדם, "from the blood . . . he is to sprinkle . . . before the Atonement Slate . . . before the Atonement Slate he is to sprinkle . . . some of the blood," stand in a chiastic relationship: a:b:c::c:b:a.

15.a. LXX adds *ἔναντι κυρίου*, "before the Lord."

15.b. In place of MT's את־דמו, "its blood," LXX[B*A] reads *ἀπὸ τοῦ αἵματος αὐτοῦ*, "some of its blood," as in v 14; cf. n. 8:15.a.

15.c. After עשׂה, "do, make," את is a prep, not the sign of the dir obj (Bertholet, 55).

16.a. On this use of מן, cf. n. 4:26.b.

17.a. לא־יהיה, "it will not be," is a strong negative (Baentsch, 385).

17.b. LXX adds *υἱῶν*, "children of," before Israel.

18.a. Cf. n. 14.a.

19.a. Cf. n. 14.a.

19.b. Cf. n. 14.b.

20.a. LXX adds *καὶ περὶ τῶν ἱερέων καθαριεῖ*, "and he makes purification for the priests."

21.a. LXX does not read שׁתי, "two."

21.b. הטאתם in *BHS* is a spelling error for חטאתם.

21.c. LXX has *τοῦ ζῶντος*, "living," as is used with "goat" earlier in this verse; this is an example of the leveling of the text.

21.d. עתי, "timely, ready" (BDB, 774), only here in OT.

22.a. LXX does not read כל, "all."

24.a. Cf. n. 9.a.

24.b. LXX adds *καὶ περὶ τοῦ οἴκου αὐτοῦ* = ובעד ביתו, "and for his house."

24.c. LXX adds *ὡς περὶ τῶν ἱερέων*, "as for the priests."

25.a. On המזבחה, cf. n. 4:19.a.

26.a. LXX reads *τὸν διεσταλμένον εἰς ἄφεσιν*, "the one set apart for forgiveness."

27.a. In a pass construction the dir obj becomes the subj, but in Heb. this is an example where the obj of the action is still kept in the acc with a pass verb (GKC §121b).

27.b. LXX does not translate the pronominal suffix on דם, "blood."

27.c. The long dir obj stands before the verb for emphasis as is frequently the case in chaps. 1–7; cf. n. 27.d.

27.d. LXX and Syr read a pl verb; so Baentsch (386). The pl is preferable, since this verb and the one following function as virtual pass (cf. GKC §144f).

27.e. Sam reads a sg verb (also Elliger, 201); cf. n. 27.c.

29.a. LXX adds *τοῦτο*, "this"; for the sake of sense this Eng trans. follows the LXX, which may mean the LXX is the translator's desire to provide an intelligible Gk. reading rather than evidence for a different Heb. Vorlage.

29.b. The opening, והיתה, "and it is to be," designates what is to come; it does not point back to the preceding procedure (Hoffmann, 1:462).

29.c. עָנָה means "humble, afflict, weaken." A person is to humble himself or constrain himself by denying himself food and other daily joys. Such self-denial accords with the solemn, mournful attitude of repentance. ענה נפשׁ occurs in Isa 58:3, where it stand parallel to צום, "to fast." This passage indicates that ענה נפשׁ is a strict fast, i.e., no food or water and the wearing of sackcloth and ashes (cf. Ps 35:13).

31.a. Sam and *Tg. Ps.-J.* read הוא in place of MT היא; also 23:32.

31.b. Also 23:32; this phrase is used for the Sabbath in 23:3; Exod 31:15; 35:2 (cf. 16:23) and for the sabbatical year in 25:4.

32.a. For MT ימשׁח, "he anoints," LXX reads a pl verb, while Syr and Vg have the verb in the pass; for sense in Eng, the rendering of the versions is followed.

32.b. LXX reads a pl verb; cf. n. 32.a.

32.c. For MT וכפר, "and he is to make expiation" (cf. v 33), Sam and LXX read יכפר, "he is to make expiation." This is an example of the common error of the interchange of a *waw* and a *yod*. The series of sentences beginning with *waw* pfs favors MT.

33.a. This verse begins with וכפר, "and he makes expiation"; both the first stich and the verse end with יכפר in order to emphasize the action of "expiation"; the threefold use of this root also underscores this action.

33.b. This is the only occurrence of the constr chain מקדשׁ הקדשׁ, "the holy sanctuary." Hoffmann (1:463) takes מִקְדַּשׁ as a construct of מִקְדָּשׁ, "the holy place," not מקדשׁ, "sanctuary" (cf. Num 18:29). Hoffmann is followed and the phrase is taken to mean the most important part of the sanctuary.

33.c. A few Heb. mss and Sam do not have a *waw* on the prep על, "on, for."

33.d. The phrase עם קהל occurs only here in MT; the phrase קהל־העם, "the assembly of the people," occurs in Judg 20:2; Jer 26:17; Ps 109:32.

34.a. Cf. n. 16.a.

34.b. The cardinal number is used adverbially (Joüon §102f).

34.c. LXX renders the verb as a pass; Syr has a pl verb, suggesting a virtual pass. But if this sentence is part of a historical report of the first observance of the Day of Atonement, the antecedent for the pronoun is Aaron. MT is followed as the harder reading.

Form/Structure/Setting

The position of this speech as the keystone of the Pentateuch highlights the climax of the sacrificial system on this high, solemn day. The goal of the Day of Atonement is to expiate the priests' and the people's sins and to cleanse the sanctuary so that the people may be in fellowship with God and continue to have access to him at the altar, which has been cleansed to keep it operational.

The structure of this chapter is as follows:

- I. Introduction (vv 1–2a*α*)
  - A. First introductory formula with reference to death of Aaron's sons (v 1)
  - B. Second introductory formula (v 2a*α*)
- II. Speech (vv 2a*β*–34a)
  - A. Commission to speak (v 2a*β*)
  - B. Speech proper (vv 2a*γ*–34a)
    - 1. Warning (v 2a*γ*–b)
    - 2. Regulations for the Day of Atonement (vv 3–28)
      - a. Instructions of preparation and liturgical agenda (vv 3–10)
        - 1) Instructions of preparation (vv 3–5)
          - a) Preparation required of the high priest (vv 3–4)
            - (1) Offerings required of the high priest (v 3)
            - (2) Clothing for the high priest and his ritual bathing (v 4)
          - b) Offerings required of the congregation (v 5)
        - 2) Liturgical agenda (vv 6–10)
          - a) High priest's purification offering (v 6)
          - b) The two goats from the congregation (vv 7–10)
            - (1) Determining the destiny of the two goats (vv 7–8)
            - (2) Liturgy with each goat (vv 9–10)
              - (a) A purification offering (v 9)
              - (b) Liturgy with the goat for Azazel (v 10)
      - b. Ritual of the Day of Atonement (vv 11–28)
        - 1) Rituals with the purification offerings (vv 11–19)
          - a) Presentation of the high priest's purification offering (vv 11–14)
            - (1) Presentation and slaughter of the bull (v 11)
            - (2) Rituals in the Holy of Holies (vv 12–14)
              - (a) Ritual with the incense (vv 12–13)
              - (b) Ritual of sprinkling blood on the Atonement Slate (v 14)
          - b) Presentation of the congregation's purification offering (vv 15–16)
          - c) A prohibition against anyone's being present in the Holy Place and a summary statement (v 17)
          - d) Rites at the altar with blood from both purification offerings (vv 18–19)
        - 2) Ritual with the goat for Azazel (vv 20–22)
          - a) Confession of all sins over the goat (vv 20–21b*α*)
          - b) Release of the goat to the wilderness (vv 21b*β*–22)

3) Ritual with the whole offerings (vv 23–25)
   a) Instructions for the high priest to change his garments (vv 23–24a)
   b) Sacrifice of the whole offerings (vv 24b–25)
4) Instructions in relationship to matters that take place outside the camp (vv 26–28)
   a) Procedure for readmittance of the one who releases the goat for Azazel (v 26)
   b) The disposal of the residue of the purification offering and procedure for readmittance of the one who makes the disposal (vv 27–28)

3. Calendrical instructions (vv 29–34a)
   a. Decrees (vv 29–33)
      1) Definition of this day as a solemn day of self-affliction (vv 29–31)
      2) The extent of expiation achieved (vv 32–33)
   b. Summary statement (v 34a)

III. Compliance Report (v 34b)

At the outset of this discussion it needs to be noted that this speech is for the instruction of the congregation; it is not the liturgical regulation from the priestly professional knowledge. While it is headed by the commission of Moses to speak to Aaron (v 2aβ), this heading does not necessarily mean that the speech contains the full text of the high priest's liturgical directions for the ritual of the Day of Atonement. Rather this heading gives an authoritative basis to this regulation, and it initiates the high priest's central role in this liturgy. The major reason for judging this speech to be for the instruction of the laity is the skeleton nature of the information provided. Details essential for the high priest to carry out the various rituals are missing. The details contained herein are sufficient to inform the laity of the various rites performed on this day, but they are far from sufficient for the high priest to follow. For example, Aaron was to enter into the Holy Place carrying a censer, incense, and blood from his own sacrifice (vv 12–14). How one person would have been able to carry all of these items is not described; whether the high priest had to go in and out of the Holy Place twice at this time to fulfill these directions is not stated. It is, furthermore, forcefully debated whether the altar in vv 18–19 was the altar of the whole offering or the incense altar in the Holy Place (4:7, 18); this would have been an intolerable uncertainty for the high priest. A third example comes in vv 23–24. They prescribe that Aaron bathe himself and then change his clothes, yet no directions are given regarding where and how this bathing was to take place; in fact, a literal reading of these verses gives an impossible progression, as will be discussed in the *Comment.* Such ambiguity would have been insufferable if this were the text for this day from the priestly professional knowledge. The intent of this speech then was to instruct the laity in order that they might understand the liturgical procedures of this day and their purposes, because the achievements of this day were essential to their continued well-being as the forgiven people of God. These instructions also encouraged the people's resolve to adhere to the ordinances requiring them to afflict themselves by a total fast and to cease from all work (vv 29, 31).

Another important characteristic of this speech to be set out at the beginning of the discussion on its structure is that it has several peculiar linguistic features. Several words are used distinctly in this speech. טמאת, "uncleannesses," in the plural, is rare in the OT. Of its five occurrences three are here (vv 16 [2x], 19) and the other two are in Ezek 36 (vv 25, 29; the occurrences in Ezekiel could be a result of a literary connection with this speech [so H. Haag, *Was lehrt die literarische Untersuchung des Ezechiel-Texts?* (Freiburg in der Schweiz: Paulusdrucherei, 1953) 38]). The use of הקדש for the Holy of Holies (vv 2, 16, 17, 20, 23, 27, but in v 3 for the area of the Tent) is unusual. It is used unquestionably this way and elsewhere only in Ezek 41:23 (cf. 41:21; for taking הקדש throughout Lev 16 to mean "the sanctuary" see Messel [*ZAW* 27 (1907) 10–11]). The more usual phrase is קדש הקדשים, "the Holy of Holies" (e.g., Exod 26:33). It is, furthermore, curious that ענן, "cloud," in its two occurrences is used differently (cf. Aartun, *ST* 34 [1980] 77). In v 2 it refers to the visible manifestation of Yahweh's glory; but in v 13 it is for a cloud of incense. This latter use is found again only in Ezek 8:11. The inexplicable word "Azazel" occurs only in this text (vv 8, 10 [2x], 26). The use of אחיך, "your brother," with Aaron, which occurs with Aaron in Exod 4:14; 7:1, 2; 28:1, 2, 4, 41; Num 20:8; 27:13; Deut 32:50, comes only here in Leviticus. There is also a curious and not readily explicable fluctuation in terms for the audience: עם, "people" (vv 15, 24 [2x]), עדה, "congregation" (v 5), and קהל, "assembly" (v 17); the tautological phrase עם הקהל, "the people of the assembly," occurs in the OT only in v 33. Unexpectedly the key term כפר, "expiate," is used in three configurations: כפר בעד, כפר את, and כפר על. כפר על is the usual expression with people, and it occurs this way in the last section of this speech (vv 30, 33 [2x], 34; cf. 1:4; 8:34). But in other places in this speech כפר על has a different force. In v 10 it has as its object the goat that will carry away the people's sins, and in v 16 the sanctuary is its object. In place of the usual כפר על stands כפר בעד (vv 6, 11, 17, and 24). This preposition with כפר occurs elsewhere only in 9:7 and Ezek 9:7; 45:17 (cf. Exod 32:30 with חטאתכם, "your sins," as object of בעד; cf. 2 Chr 30:18). The form כפר את has the tent or the altar or the sanctuary as its direct object (vv 20, 32, 33 [2x]). This last configuration occurs elsewhere only in Ezek 45:20 with הבית, "the sanctuary," as the direct object. But in a few other places כפר has a direct object; it stands before the noun "iniquity" in Ps 78:38 and Dan 9:24, and in two texts it has a pronominal suffix (in Ps 65:4[3] פשעינו, "our iniquities," is the antecedent, and in Ezek 43:20 "the altar" is the antecedent). Quite remarkable is the omission of the phrase נסלח, "he/she is forgiven," in conjunction with כפר as it is used in the regulation for the lesser purification offering in 4:20, 26, 31. These facts indicate that there has been a shift in the usage of כפר. The goal of atonement on this day, then, is different from that for the purification offerings (chap. 4). In contrast to the expiation of a certain sin as the purification offering achieves, these rituals expiate the aggregate of the sinful deeds committed by members of the congregation or the congregation as a whole during the last year, and certain of the blood rites cleanse the cultic furniture from the pollution drawn to the sanctuary from the priests' and the people's sins and incidents of their becoming unclean. This cleansing is the distinct achievement of expiation on this day, as is clearly expressed in the wording of v 30a, יכפר עליכם לטהר אתכם, "he is to make expiation for you to make you clean." In addition to these unusual linguistic features, there are several syntactical peculiarities (cf. Aartun, *ST* 34 [1980] 78–80). A conclusion drawn from the composite of these linguistic anomalies is that this regulation went through a long, complex editorial process before it reached its present form.

In an analysis of the structure of this speech, the first striking fact is that there are two introductions. V 1 is a narrative introduction that recalls the incident of Nadab and Abihu (10:1–7). Whereas some (e.g., Noth, 117) assume that the historical reference indicates that this chapter once followed chap. 10, Koch (*Priesterschrift,* 92–93) holds that its inclusion is to call to mind the event of chap. 10 without indicating its position in relationship to chap. 10. Koch comes to this position by observing the wide gap between vv 1 and 2 (cf. Messel, *ZAW* 27 [1907] 2–6). In his judgment v 2 has no connection with the incident of Nadab and Abihu, for the restriction in v 2 is general in nature, i.e., against entering the Holy of Holies at any time, not against a specific action such as bringing strange fire into the sanctuary as Nadab and Abihu did. V 2, furthermore, is closely tied to the following material, while v 1 may be separated from the speech proper without any loss. Therefore, v 1 belongs to the historical narrative that runs throughout the priestly material in Exodus-Numbers. This opening verse, nevertheless, captures the solemn tone of this high day and brings attention to the awesome holiness of God by recalling what happened to Aaron's two sons. Another possible fact may be communicated by vv 1 and 34b. They frame this speech in such a way that this is not only the regulation for this solemn fast; it is at the same time the report of the first observance of the Day of Atonement. V 1 then comes from the editor who assembled the priestly legislation.

The speech proper has three portions. After the initial warning (v 2aβ–b), the second one gives the regulation for the Day of Atonement as Yahweh spoke to Moses and Moses addressed Aaron (vv 3–28). It is in the impersonal third person and is dominated by *waw* perfects. The third portion is a calendrical text, which locates this solemn day in the liturgical calendar (vv 29–34a). It is marked off by the personal address in vv 29–31, showing that this part of the speech is addressed directly to the congregation.

The first portion opens with a warning (v 2aβ–b) against entering the Holy of Holies at any time. Many scholars assume that specific time(s) and occasion(s) when the high priest might enter the sanctuary followed this warning (Messel, *ZAW* 27 [1907] 5–6; cf. Noth, 119; Elliger, 203). That specific time is now stated in v 29. Messel (6) thinks that with the inclusion of vv 29–34 the older time specifications became displaced (cf. Koch, *Priesterschrift,* 93). If, however, v 2 is a warning and not an instruction, then the identification of specific time(s) is not missing.

The second portion has two sections. The section in vv 3–10 has two parts. The first part (vv 3–5) sets out preparatory requirements: the animals required for the high priest (v 3) and those for the people (v 5) and the clothing required of the high priest (v 4). Most critical scholars regard v 4 as an intrusion, but the clothing worn by the high priest while serving on this high day was a very important detail, especially since that clothing was much simpler than his usual regal vestments. The importance of this detail is confirmed by a reference to the high priest's clothing in two other sections (vv 23–24 and 32b). This reference, furthermore, establishes a thematic tie with other texts in the priestly material, namely Exod 28; 39:1–31; Lev 8:7–9; 10:6. The second part of this section (vv 6–10) gives the liturgical order of this day, concentrating on the determination of the destiny of the people's two goats (vv 7–10). Vriezen identifies the genre of this second part as "a liturgical festival agenda" (*OTS* 7 [1950] 229).

The next section (vv 11–28) presents the ritual order of this day in skeleton form. There is some obvious overlapping between this section and vv 6–10. In fact, v 11a has the same wording as v 6. A scribe may have chosen the same sentence as a way of communicating that the following regulation is to be understood as returning to the same point in the progression of the ritual as at v 6. The shift in contexts produces, however, a shift in the meaning of the important word הקריב. In v 6 it has the broad meaning "complete the sacrificial ritual," while in v 11 it has the narrow meaning "present," since the next rite is שחט, "slaughter," a specific rite. This rite is specifically mentioned, for this regulation gives special consideration to the unique blood rites done inside the Holy of Holies (vv 14–15). Inserted parenthetically between the slaughtering and the sprinkling of the blood are special instructions on making smoke from incense (vv 12–13) in order that the high priest might create a cloud to protect himself from Yahweh's glory in the Holy of Holies. Usually these verses are treated as an insertion, but an ancient author did not have the ability to use footnotes to present essential, though parenthetical, information.

The next ritual is the slaughter of the people's purification offering and the manipulation of its blood (v 15). The purpose of this blood rite receives an expanded, though parenthetical, explanation in vv 16–17. Surprisingly, this explanation makes a major shift in the direction of the work of כפר, "expiate" (cf. Vriezen, *OTS* 7 [1950] 226). Instead of the expected statement that expiation is made for the people, as is the case with the high priest (v 11a), it states that the Holiest Place is atoned (כפר) from the uncleanliness of the Israelites. That cleansing is the issue in v 16 is confirmed by the next rite, the daubing of some blood on the horns of the altar to make expiation for (כפר על) it and then the sprinkling of blood on it seven times in order to cleanse (טהר) it and sanctify (קדש) it (vv 18–19). There is a shift then from expiating the people's sins to cleansing the sanctuary from the impurities released by the people's and priests' sins and the occasions of their being unclean (chaps. 11–15). A possible reason for this shift may have been to distinguish between the achievements of the ritual with the living goat and those of the ritual with the goat offered to Yahweh. Since the living goat clearly carried away the congregation's sins (vv 21–22), the blood rite with the goat for Yahweh must have another purpose, i.e., to purge the sanctuary. This is the way the summary statement in v 20 reads. This refinement in the achievements of the blood rites of the people's purification offering did not affect the purpose of the high priest's purification offering since he did not make any offering comparable to the living goat. But another tradition did not accept this division in the purposes of the people's two goats, for v 17b, which is awkwardly phrased and placed (cf. Landersdorfer, *Studien,* 87), states that the blood rites in the Holiest Place make expiation for both the priests and the assembly of Israel. This summary statement was included, probably from another tradition, to state that the blood rites from the people's purification offering made expiation for the people just as the high priest's purification offering made for himself and his household. This position was reinforced by the use of the inclusive phrase in v 16, ומפשׁעיהם לכל־חטאתם, "and from their acts of rebellion to all their sins." That this phrase overburdens v 16a suggests that it is an addition. The last portion (vv 29–34a) also witnesses to the effort to hold together two traditions by stressing that expiation is made for both the priests and the people as well as for the cultic furniture (vv 30–34). Interestingly, it states in v 30 that the people are "expiated" in order "to be cleansed" (יכפר . . . לטהר).

Next comes the ritual in which the people's sins were transferred to the living goat (vv 20–22). The goat here is called השעיר החי, "the goat that lives," instead of the goat for Azazel. This descriptive name corresponds to the name of the bird, i.e., הצפר החיה, "the living bird," released at the ceremony to reinstate a person who had recovered from a serious skin disease (14:6–7). This name for the goat suggests that this ritual had a different tradition history than the liturgical instructions about the two goats in vv 7–10. The details here about the high priest laying his hands on the goat's head and the man in readiness to lead the goat into the wilderness are a further witness to this portion's being a more rustic account than that found in vv 7–10.

The next ritual is the sacrifice of the high priest's ram and the people's ram as whole offerings (vv 23–25). This section ends with parenthetical instructions concerning those who have obligations outside the camp, because of the particular rites of this day (vv 26–28). This parenthetical material is to inform the congregation about two vital procedures on this day so that they will understand how certain activities are carried out in order to be in compliance with the laws on ritual purity that were such a vital part of the ordering of their everyday lives.

The third portion (vv 29–34) is a calendrical prescription for the inclusion of this solemn day in the national calendar. The distinct style and language of this portion reveal that it is in accord with the material concerning this day in the calendrical text (23:26–32). This material is immediately distinguished from the preceding by the use of direct address, the second person plural and the divine first person. Nevertheless, vv 32–33 stand in the third person impersonal style, but they are held in this section by v 34a, according to Elliger (207). In his judgment the return to the impersonal style was to make the laws in these verses categorical. The ties with the calendrical text are clear: ענה את־נפשתיכם, "afflict yourselves," in vv 29, 31 and 23:27, (29), 32; כפר עליכם, "make expiation for you," in vv 30, 33b, 34; 23:28 and as is the usual expression in the preceding sacrificial legislation; חקת עולם, "perpetual ordinance," in vv 29, 31, 34 and 23:31 along with 17:7; 23:14, 21, 41; 24:3, 9 (this phrase occurs earlier in 3:17; 7:36; 10:9 and with the alternate spelling חק־עולם in 6:11[18], 15[22]; 7:34; 10:15); שבת שבתון, "sabbath of solemn rest," in v 31 and 23:32; כל־מלאכה לא תעשו, "do not do any work," in vv 29 and 23:28, (30), 31; היום הזה, "this day," in v 30 and 23:28, 29, 30 (the last two verses have בעצם, "on this very," in front of this day). There are other linguistic ties between this portion and the Holiness Code, and sometimes there are ties with what precedes. The use of אזרח, "citizen," in v 29 finds a connection with what follows (17:15; 18:26; 19:34; 23:42; 24:16, 22), but none with the speeches that precede. Nevertheless, אזרח stands in some disjunction with chap. 17, for that speech uses the phrase איש איש מבית ישראל, "an Israelite," in the first three laws (vv 3, 8, 10), but אזרח occurs in 17:15. To אזרח, "citizen," is joined the phrase הגר הגר בתוככם, "the alien who lives among you." This phrase occurs frequently in chap. 17 (vv 8 [יגור], 10, 12, 13) and several times in the Holiness Code (18:26; 19:33 [יגור], 34; 20:2; גר, "alien," also occurs in 23:22; 24:16, 22; 25:23, 35, 47 [2x]), but not in the preceding material in Leviticus.

These characteristics unique to vv 29–34a in chap. 16, along with the brevity of the calendrical material for this day in 23:26–32 in comparison with the material on the other festivals in chap. 23, suggest that some of the material in vv 29–34a may have been taken from that or a similar festival calendar. It is also conceivable that the author who composed that portion of chap. 23 composed this section. In either case the calendrical material was added to this regulation for an unnamed day of expiation in order to make sure that there would be no debate as to which day in the calendar was being regulated by this speech. Certainly these two texts were not composed independently. For example, as stated above, this editor sought to preserve both perspectives on the achievements of expiation by the special blood rites, for v 30 speaks of both כפר, "making expiation," and טהר, "cleansing," and in v 33 the cult is expiated as well as the priests and the people. Another example of a tie to vv 3–28 is v 32, wherein Aaron is given prominence and yet is to wear the simpler sacred linen garments as prescribed in v 4. Another change is that the editor of this last portion stressed the role of Aaron's successor (v 32). That is why he established a tie with the account of the ordination of Aaron in chap. 8 by using the terms משח, "anoint" (8:12; 21:10; cf. 4:3, 5, 16; 6:13[20], 15[22]; 7:35–36), and מלא יד־, "fill the hand" (8:33; also 21:10). As far as genre is concerned, this portion belongs to the same general genre as the second section of the first portion, liturgical directions in a calendrical text. It is also evident that this last portion became attached to this regulation at a later date.

From this analysis the character of this entire speech may be addressed. Noth says that there is "a strange lack of continuity and unity about the whole" (117). Or in the words of Vriezen (*OTS* 7 [1950] 225), there is a "lack of coherence." The speech is beset with repetitions, unique usage of words, overlappings in the ritual order, gaps in details, parenthetical statements, and theological tensions. There have been several attempts to interpret the origin and development of this speech by analyzing these rough places. But given the paucity of data, these attempts have produced a wide variety of conjectures with virtually no consensus. Another proposal without some new evidence will not prove to be very helpful. Nevertheless, some observations may have value in the interpretation of this speech.

How can the literary unevenness and the theological tensions in this speech be accounted for? As stated above, the literary features indicate that it circulated as a self-contained document. Each of the various central sanctuaries in Israel's history would have had its own copy of the ritual, and each local sanctuary may have had its own copy. It is very likely that the wording of a text at a given sanctuary became adapted to the particular manner in which the rites were done at that sanctuary. E.g., one sanctuary may have placed more emphasis on the rite of riddance, while another emphasized the sprinkling of the blood in the Holy of Holies. Another example is that in one tradition the goat was known as the living goat and in another as the goat of Azazel. How many of these texts survived is, of course, unknown. Their transmission and survival were complicated by the strong possibility that this austere day fell out of observance during seasons of apostasy in the Kingdom era. When the post-exilic scribes came to establish the canonical text for this day, they apparently had to work with differing texts, most likely fragmented texts, containing different emphases. How the post-exilic scribes collected them and worked on them to provide a single authoritative text is unfortunately unknown. It is reasonable to assume that they found the texts on the Day of Atonement in two genres: a liturgical text for a calendar and a regulation for the ritual of this day. There may have been fragments from a third genre, a report of the first observance of this solemn day. The goal of the scribes was to produce the best text that preserved the variety of traditions they had received. As typical of the Jewish community, the scribes strove to keep the variety of traditions intact, even those in tension, so that all these traditions might enrich the observance of the day. The scribes were more concerned with preserving what they had received than with making a smooth literary piece. For them the received tradition was far more important than a consistent text free from any theological tensions. Such a scenario, furthermore, means that it is virtually impossible to uncover and date the various developments leading to the present text. It is held, therefore, that the literary complexity of this chapter is evidence that the scribes collected and edited well-worn texts in order to preserve the traditions of this day in the Pentateuch. The word Yahweh spoke to Moses was not frozen and hidden in some vault, but it was heard, copied, and made contemporary until it was canonized. In other words, it went through a long, complex transmission history before it received its final form.

It is instructive to observe how the scribes assembled the various texts that had come to them. They employed the literary principle of interchange to tie the speech together. With this technique they molded together the different rites from the different texts. The result is a remarkable tapestry. The most distinctive threads are the offerings required of the high priest and the congregation (A = high priest [1 = bull; 2 = ram]; B = people [1α = goat for Yahweh; 1β = goat for Azazel; 2 = ram]):

high priest's bull and ram (v 3b)	$A^1 + A^2$
people's goats and ram (v 5)	$B^{1\alpha} + {}^{1\beta} + B^2$
high priest's bull (v 6)	A^1
people's goats (vv 7–10)	$B^{1\alpha} + {}^{1\beta}$
sacrifice of high priest's bull (vv 11–14)	A^1
sacrifice of people's goat (vv 15–17a)	$B^{1\alpha}$
ritual at the altar with blood of bull and of goat (vv 18–19)	$A^1 + B^{1\alpha}$
people's goat for Azazel (vv 20b–22)	$B^{1\beta}$
rams for whole offerings (v 24b)	$A^2 + B^2$
further ritual with the purification offering (v 25)	$A^1 + B^{1\alpha}$
regarding person who released goat to Azazel (v 26)	$B^{1\beta}$
regarding disposal of remains of purification offerings (vv 27–28)	$A^1 + B^{1\alpha}$

The pattern of this interchange is quite variegated because of the interplay of handling five animals: two animals offered early for the high priest and two offered for the congregation plus the people's goat for Azazel.

Another theme interchanged in a variegated pattern is the object of expiation, priests (A), people (B), or parts of the sanctuary (C):

priests (v 6b)	A
people (v 10b)	B
priests (v 11a)	A
holy place (v 16)	C^1
priests and people (v 17b)	A + B
altar (v 18)	C^2
holy place and altar (v 20a)	$C^1 + C^2$

priests and people (v 24a)	A + B
people (v 30)	B
holy place, Tent, and altar (v 33a)	$C^1 + C^3 + C^2$
priests and people (v 33b)	A + B
people (v 34a)	B

Another thread in the tapestry is the reference to Yahweh's appearing in the cloud. This is said expressly in v 2b, and there are directions for using incense to form a cloud to conceal Aaron from Yahweh's presence in vv 12–13. Another thread is the danger inherent in entering the Holy of Holies. The chapter opens with a warning about the penalty of death for approaching the Holy of Holies unworthily or at an unassigned time (v 2). This penalty is mentioned again in v 13b, and in the same vein there is the parenthetical instruction, which assumes this warning, that no person may be present in the Tent when the high priest enters to make expiation in the Holy of Holies (v 17a). The importance of כפרת, "the Atonement Slate," for the blood rites of this day is another colorful thread. It is mentioned twice in v 2 in anticipation of its vital role in the blood rites performed inside the Holy of Holies (vv 14, 15).

A curious thread that ties to the concerns of ritual purity in chaps. 11–15 is the instruction for the high priest's washing and changing his clothing (v 4). Additional instructions about his bathing and changing his garments come in vv 23–24a, to return again in v 32b. Connected with this theme is the reference to the bathing and changing of clothes of the two people who had obligations outside the camp (vv 26, 28). While the two whole offerings are not emphasized, they are kept before the audience by being mentioned three times (vv 3, 5, and 24). They are given a little more attention by the rite of the high priest's bathing himself and putting on his regal clothes before making them (vv 23–24a). The principle of interchange has, therefore, been chosen to hold together the diverse, complex material in this speech. The end product may be judged to be a rough text or a beautifully variegated text, depending on one's viewpoint.

Another clue as to how this speech was assembled is the possible presence of a chiastic pattern:

A narrative and introduction (vv 1–2)
  B calendrical agenda (vv 3–10)
    C liturgical regulations (vv 11–28)
  B' calendrical instructions (vv 29–34a)
A' compliance report (v 34b)

The center of the chiasm appropriately receives the emphasis. In fact, v 11 is considered by virtually all analysts to mark a major transition. This layer comes from the old regulation for this day. The layers on both sides of the center treat the day as a part of the calendar. This is clear in vv 29–34a as seen above. Vv 3–10 appear to be older than vv 29–34a. It is possible that the scribe who located vv 29–34a may have been responsible for the chiastic arrangement of this speech, especially the balancing of this calendrical text with the liturgical festival agenda in vv 3–10. The difference in the use of כפר, "expiation," nevertheless, indicates that these two paragraphs came from different sources. The speech is finally enveloped with a narrative introduction (v 1) and a compliance report (v 34a); this material came from the editors who put the priestly material together.

In the *Form/Structure/Setting* section of chap. 9, it was argued that that speech, which reported the ordination of Aaron and his sons as an event, also served as the regulation for the ordination of future high priests. These dual purposes may govern this speech too, but with emphasis in reverse order. As it stands, this speech presents the regulation for the observance of the annual Day of Atonement. Yet there are some indicators that at the same time it reports the first observance of this fast day. The clearest proof of this position is the final compliance statement (v 34b), which states that Aaron did as Yahweh had commanded Moses. This may be taken to mean that Aaron celebrated the first Day of Atonement at Mount Sinai. That possibility finds greater significance in the historical tie in v 1. Here then is reported another event that took place in Israel's wilderness experience (Exod 16–Num 36) after the death of Aaron's sons. A major difficulty with this proposal is that Moses set up the Tent of Meeting on the first day of the first month (Exod 40:2), and he took the census reported in Numbers on the first day of the second month (Num 1:1). In this scheme the Day of Atonement would have been observed in the first month. That would have been a very full month indeed. It would have had to occur after the eighth day of the month (9:1). This may account for its coming on the tenth day of the month. In addition, there may be further connections between the events of chap. 10 and this day. The first observance of this day may have been to purge the sanctuary from the pollution of the transgression of Nadab and Abihu. That this day has neither a name nor a date in the primary text (vv 2–28) may mean that in the First Temple the date of this day floated. It was not until the inclusion of the calendrical material in vv 29–34 that the date for this day was set as the tenth of the seventh month. Whether there ever was a narrative account of the first observance of this day separate from the regulations for it is impossible to know.

Among critical scholars, Elliger observes these two different purposes in this speech (208; cf. Porter, 125). To begin, Elliger believes that the priestly narrative of the festive high day for the first public worship of the new cult followed by the transgression of the two priests (8:1–10:9) needed a counterpart in the inauguration of the Day of Atonement (208). The old historical report is found in vv 1–2bα, 3a(?), 4, 11, 14–15, 17, 20b, 22b–24, 34b. How much of this report has been lost is unknown. In this account the theological center was the sprinkling of the blood for atonement of the priests and the people. Then, in Elliger's judgment, this Vorlage was consciously reworked without altering the received text in order to address more fully the process of expiation. To this second stage belong vv 3 (outside of a), 5–10, 16 (less aγ), 18–20a, 21 (less aϵ), 22a, and 25–28. This editor elevated the importance of the release of the sin-laden goat. In fact, the importance of this goat was placed on the same level as that of the goat to Yahweh (vv 7–10). This editor adjusted the theology to include the rites with both the goats. The rites with the blood from the goat for Yahweh cleansed the sanctuary and the altar of impurity (vv 16, 18–20a), and the rite with the living goat removed all moral guilt to Azazel in the wilderness (vv 21, 22a). The combined material was the report of the installation and the first observance of the Day of Atonement. In the third stage this report was turned into the ceremony for the annual observance of this day. The editor preferred the divine first person form.

He inserted vv 2b$\beta\gamma$, 12f, and especially vv 29–34a. He moved so far away from the historical base that he expressly made Aaron's successor answerable for the continued observance of this regulation (v 32). Theologically he did not distinguish so sharply between טמאת, "uncleannesses," and עונות, "iniquities"; these two concepts were united under the general term חטאת, "sins." The achievements of the rites with the people's two goats were placed under a single rubric (vv 16aγ and 21aϵ). This editor laid special emphasis on the character of this day as a day of penance by stressing self-denial and cessation of all work. To this layer Elliger (209), in opposition to von Rad *(The Problem of the Hexateuch)* and Rendtorff, assigns the cloud produced by the incense (vv 2$\beta\gamma$ and 12–13). This final stage may have taken place with the inclusion of the Holiness Code or at the latest in the time of Ezra. This reconstruction, which is very different from the approach suggested here, agrees in the claim that this speech served significantly different purposes and contains a variety of theological emphases.

In summary, this speech is the regulation for the oral instruction of the congregation on the liturgical order and distinct rituals of the Day of Atonement. This speech was delivered to the Israelites on those occasions when all of Leviticus was delivered. It may also have been delivered as part of the observance of this day.

Comment

1–2 In the first heading to this speech there is reference to the tragic deaths of Aaron's two sons, Nadab and Abihu, reported in chap. 10. Since no further information about the incident is found in this chapter, why does this reference stand at the head of the regulation for the Day of Atonement? The reason is to sternly warn the high priest to conduct himself properly when he enters the Holy of Holies on the Day of Atonement so that he does not lose his life as they did (cf. 22:2). The high priest may not enter הקדש, "the Holiest Place," any time he wishes. He may enter only on specified occasions like the Day of Atonement. Some hold that this instruction accords with later practices, as reflected in Heb 9:6–7, which limited his access to the Holy of Holies to this one day of the year. On this high day Yahweh himself promises to appear in a cloud over כפרת, "the Atonement Slate." That is, Yahweh will manifest his presence in ענן, "the cloud," which both reveals and conceals his presence (cf. Exod 25:22). Rashi (73), however, takes the wording to mean that God constantly manifests himself here in the cloud.

Within the Holy of Holies, set apart from the Holy Place by an elegant פרכת, "curtain" (Exod 26:31), was the Ark of the Covenant. The Ark was a rectangular chest made out of acacia wood and overlaid with gold (Exod 25:10–20). Gold rings on the sides of the Ark permitted poles of acacia wood overlaid with gold to be inserted so that the Ark could be transported by appointed Levites. On top of it was a table or sheet of gold called כפרת, which traditionally has been translated "mercy-seat," for here God displayed his mercy in providing his people a place for finding atonement. The כפרת, forty-four inches by twenty-six, was identical to the top of the Ark of the Covenant. It was made of pure gold, being one piece with the two golden cherubim over which Yahweh was enthroned (Exod 25:17–22; cf. 1 Sam 4:4; Ps 99:1). From between the cherubim and over the כפרת, Yahweh met with Moses (Exod 25:22). The fact that the כפרת was made of pure gold accounts for its height not being given; it probably was quite thin. Since the כפרת

sat atop the Ark and since there is no mention of a lid or door for the Ark, some have postulated that the כפרת functioned as the lid for the Ark (Rashi, 227, and Kimchi, and modern interpreters like Dillmann, 313, Elliger, 211, and Cassuto, *A Commentary on the Book of Exodus,* tr. I. Abrahams [Jerusalem: Magnes, 1967] 332–36). A few derive the meaning "lid" for כפרת by claiming that the etymology of the verb כפר is "cover," like the Arab root *kfr.* This position faces some difficulties. First, as mentioned in the *Excursus* on כפר (at 4:20–21), this etymology merits little weight. Second, the term ארון, "ark, chest," implies an enclosed box that would not need a separate lid (Janowski, *Sühne,* 274–75). Third, כפרת is much more closely connected with the cherubim than with the Ark (Janowski, 275, 339–46; Exod 25:18–19). In Haran's judgment, the Ark and the Atonement Slate "constitute fundamentally separate objects" (*Temples,* 248). Fourth, in 1 Chr 28:11 the Holy of Holies is called בית הכפרת, "the house of the Atonement Slate." This name for this part of the Tent of Meeting seems impossible if כפרת simply meant "lid" (Keil and Delitzsch, 168). In this light כפרת was not viewed as being primarily a lid for the Ark. The reason that this piece of furniture received the name כפרת then lies with its cultic function. It is at the כפרת that the most critical blood rites for achieving expiation were performed on the Day of Atonement, for the כפרת was the cultic line of demarcation between Yahweh and his people, the place where God's people might find forgiveness from the transcendent God, who manifested his presence in the cloud (Janowski, *Sühne,* 347). Working from a similar perspective and taking כפר to mean "propitiate," some render כפרות "a place of propitiation," "propitiatory covering," or "a propitiatory" (cf. B. Childs, *The Book of Exodus* [Philadelphia: Westminster Press, 1974] 524; Fryer, *EvQ* 59 [1987] 113). This receives support from both the LXX translation, *ἱλαστήριον,* and the Vg, *propitiatorium.* But on the basis of the *Excursus* on כפר at 4:20–21, כפר predominantly means "expiate," and, because the blood rites performed here cleansed the Holiest Place (v 33), a name with "expiation" or "atonement" is preferable for this piece of furniture. Working with the very limited vocabulary for atonement in modern English, we use the name Atonement Slate. Slate makes clear that כפרת is a thin object, and atonement describes its function as the place where the people of the covenant maintained fellowship with their God by means of the expiating blood rites performed here on the Day of Atonement.

In the Ark were the tablets of the Ten Commandments, which symbolize the covenant between Yahweh and Israel. To maintain this relationship between Yahweh, the holy God, and Israel, a sinful people, atonement is necessary. The Atonement Slate plays a critical role in securing that atonement. Since it stands as the boundary between the enthroned God and the tablets of the covenant, figuratively speaking, Yahweh looks down on the covenant through the blood dabbed on the Atonement Slate, leading him to govern his people out of mercy and forgiveness.

3–4 The high priest is to bring for himself and his house two animals, a young bull for a purification offering (חטאת; cf. 4:3) and a ram for a whole offering (עלה; 1:10–13; 8:18–21). For the ceremony the high priest is to put on linen garments, i.e., pants, robe, sash, and turban. These are not the stately garments of majesty and dignity that the high priest normally wears (cf. 8:13), neither does he put on the gold and jewels (Exod 28:5–39). Rather he wears simpler garments like the other priests usually wear while on duty at the altar (Exod 28:40–42). On this solemn day he approaches God dressed humbly and contritely. "White" stands for simplicity, purity, and holiness; this symbolism is especially appropriate for his entering into Yahweh's presence. The garments, nevertheless, are sacred (קדשׁ) like the more ornate garments, for they have been made for this purpose and are housed at the sanctuary. They cover the high priest totally, in modesty and respect before God. The high priest puts on a turban; this distinguishes him from the other priests. Before putting on these clothes, the high priest is to wash himself in water, insuring his ritual purity before he begins to function as the high priest on this high day (Exod 28:2, 4; 31:10; 35:19; 39:1).

5 The congregation (עדה; cf. 4:13), represented by tribal leaders, is to present two goats for a purification offering (חטאת) and a ram for a whole offering (עלה; cf. 8:18). It is interesting to note the statement that both goats are for a purification offering, even though only one is offered on the altar (vv 9, 15). It is possible that only the purification offering is mentioned to keep the verse short and uncomplicated, or it is possible, as Kiuchi (*Purification Offering,* 147–56; also Feinberg, *BSac* 115 [1958] 332–33) holds, that the rituals with the two goats combine to make a single purification offering. According to him, the rite with Azazel is a special adaptation of the burning of the flesh of the ordinary חטאת, "purification offering," outside the camp. While both goats are necessary to take away the people's sin, there is no indication in the wording of v 9 or vv 15 + 20b–22 that the ritual with the goat sent to the wilderness was considered a purification offering.

6 The high priest is to present (הקריב) his own bull for a purification offering first (cf. v 11a). הקריב here has a comprehensive meaning, i.e., to follow the entire ritual for making this kind of offering (Levine, 104). He thereby makes expiation (כפר) both בעדו, "for himself," and בעד ביתו, "for his own house," i.e., all the other priests. The use of בעד, "in behalf of," with כפר, "expiate," instead of the usual על, "for," may carry a different nuance as Garnet ("Atonement Constructions . . . ," *EvQ* 46 [1974] 144) suggests; namely בעד conveys "a note of extra solemnity." Or it may have arisen in this speech to keep distinct the use of כפר, "expiate," when dealing with persons and when dealing with objects (cf. *Form/Structure/Setting*). The high priest must make expiation for himself and his house before he is able to act as high priest on behalf of the people.

7–10 The high priest is next to have the two goats presented by the congregation stationed at the entrance to the Tent of Meeting. There he is to cast lots over them to decide which one is to be sacrificed on the altar to Yahweh and which one is to be released into the wilderness to Azazel. Some, as Baentsch (383) and Porter (127), suggest that the Urim and the Thummim (cf. Exod 28:30) may have been used to make this determination. Noth (121) describes a process by which two stones, one marked for Yahweh and the other for Azazel, either in writing or by a symbol, were placed in a container, shaken up, and then drawn out. Whatever process was used, Aaron is to take the goat for Yahweh and sacrifice it as a purification offering (חטאת) by performing the appropriate ritual. The other goat is to be stationed (העמיד) live before Yahweh. Then comes the phrase כפר על, which usually means "make expiation for it," i.e., the goat. The final phrase of this verse, "by sending it to Azazel into the wilderness," is in apposition to "to make expiation by it" in order to define how expiation will be accomplished with this particular goat. The precise meaning of כפר על is debated. One view interprets it to mean that atonement is made for Azazel (Keil and Delitzsch, 348); this interpretation only leads to a truism. That leads others to view this phrase to be the result of a scribal error (e.g., Noth, 121; Elliger, 201). Others render it "to atone over" the goat for Azazel (e.g., Kurtz, *Sacrificial Worship,* 410). Kiuchi (*Purification Offering,* 150–51) identifies the agent of the infinitive as the goat for Azazel and the object of the preposition to be Aaron. He finds v 22 to support his reading, for in that verse it is clear that this goat bears the iniquity. Clearly this phrase is included to underscore the fact that the rite with the goat for Azazel has expiating force, but the object of the expiation is hard to identify. It is possible that the congregation is the object, even though that noun is feminine. V 22 supports this position, for it states that Azazel carries their, i.e., the Israelites', iniquities to the wilderness. Kiuchi has an intriguing interpretation. According to him, Aaron "bears the guilt of the Israelites when he makes atonement for sancta (vv 14–19)" (*Purification Offering,* 152). He then devolves this guilt on Azazel, and that goat carries it into the wilderness. While this position is suggestive, another way to look at the various rites of this day is that the pollution and burden produced by human sin produce many trajectories requiring that the process of expiation address these different trajectories. The blood rites in the sanctuary and at the altar cleanse these holy instruments from the pollution reached by sin, while the goat bears the guilt and the burden produced by sin away from the congregation. In any case, the rites of this day indicate that both the sprinkling of the blood in the Holy of Holies and the release of the goat to Azazel are necessary for full expiation of the community from all the consequences of their sins.

The name עזאזל, "Azazel," occurs only four times in the OT, all in this chapter (vv 8, 10 [2x], 26). Its meaning has been disputed from ancient times. There are four major explanations. The first one takes it as a descriptive term for the goat itself. LXX and Vg understand it to be a composite of two words, עז, "goat," and אזל, "go away," i.e., "the goat which departs." This position was continued in early authors like Aquila, Theodotion, Ibn Ezra, and Hieronymus (cf. Landersdorfer, *Studien,* 19–20). A major difficulty with this widely held view is that the goat is "for Azazel" and is to be sent "to Azazel" (vv 8, 10, 26). It is hard to understand how the goat can be either for itself or sent to itself. A second possibility is articulated by Feinberg (*BSac* 115 [1958] 331–33). He takes Azazel to be an abstract term meaning "entire removal"; the phrase לעזאזל then means "for removal." An argument against this position is that there are few abstract terms in Leviticus; in fact, the entire ritual of the Day of Atonement, including the release of this goat, is a symbolic enactment of spiritual realities. Neither does this meaning establish a good parallel with ליהוה, "for Yahweh." A third view, which comes from the rabbinic tradition, takes this word as the place to which the goat departs. Rashi identifies the word as "a rocky precipice" (also *Tg. Ps.-J.* on v 10b, Sipra, Kimchi; Landersdorfer, *Studien,* 18). *B. Yoma* 63b renders it "hardest of the mountains" as though it were written עזז אל (Aḥituv 999). R. Saadia renders it Mount Azaz (Landersdorfer, *Studien,* 18), and Jastrow (1060) gives for it "a rough and rocky mountain." G. R. Driver (*JSS* 1 [1956] 98) supports this position; he takes it as a place name from the root עזז, which is cognate to Arab *ʿazâzu,* "rough ground." While there is much to commend this position, there are two difficulties. (1) לעזאזל, "for Azazel," is parallel to ליהוה, "for Yahweh" (vv 8–10), suggesting that

Azazel is some type of being rather than a place. (2) If לעזאזל meant "to a rocky precipice," why is the place to which the goat goes called ארץ גזרה, "a separate land," in v 22? A fourth position holds that עזאזל is the name of a demon or even the devil himself (Keil and Delitzsch, 398). In later intertestamental literature it was the name of a principal evil spirit (Enoch 8:1; 9:6; 10:4–8; 13:1–2; 54:5; 55:4; 69:2). In a similar vein M. Segal refers to a tradition in the Talmud that it is a compound of the names of two fallen angels ("The Religion of Israel before Sinai," *JQR* 53 [1962/63] 250). The position that this was the name or names of a demon has the advantage of the two names being truly parallel (so de Vaux, *AI*, 509). Many object to this identification, however, for they cannot conceive that the Scriptures would prescribe a sacrifice or a gift to a demon (cf. Harrison, 170–71). Nevertheless, there are no indications at all that this goat was offered as a sacrifice. It was not ritually slaughtered; nor were there any rites for manipulating its blood. In fact, because it carries the people's sins, this goat was unclean, thus disqualifying it as a sacrifice. While the OT is very careful not to personify evil in a figure such as Satan, it does recognize that there are cosmic forces hostile to Yahweh. These forces are represented as either sea monsters, such as Leviathan (e.g., Isa 27:1), or satyrs that inhabit the desert (e.g., Isa 13:21). The fact that these satyrs were thought to be goatlike favors the possibility that Azazel stands for one of these demons, especially given the fact that part of the name Azazel in Heb. means "goat." Whether Azazel was the head of the demons or the forerunner of Satan, there is no way of knowing, but it can be affirmed that such an identification is not the intent of the usage of this name in this passage. If Azazel was a demon, this rite means that the sins carried by the goat were returned to this demon for the purpose of removing them from the community and leaving them at their source in order that their power or effect in the community might be completely broken. The difference between the third and the fourth options is not that great, for a society frequently names a place after an identity and vice versa.

However the name Azazel is understood, the fact that such a rite of riddance was a part of the Day of Atonement is very significant. The use of שׁלח, "send away," in v 21 for the release of this goat into the wilderness carries the idea that it was released in order "to wander or roam freely, unhindered" (cf. Job 39:5; Landersdorfer, *Studien*, 27). In the rite of aggregation for one cured of a grievous skin disease, שׁלח is also used for the release of the bird (14:7). Furthermore, the fact that that bird is called הצפור החיה, "the living bird" (14:7), just as this goat is called השׂעיר החי, "the living goat," in v 20 attests that these two rites have the same basic intent. In the earliest time, the goat was most likely sent away from the camp to roam freely in the wilderness until its death. The initial meaning of this ritual was to provide a visual representation to the assembly of the reality that on this day their sins had been completely wiped out and the power of these sins was terminated forever (cf. Harrison, 171). This rite of riddance in Israel corresponds to the widely attested practice found among a variety of peoples, bearing witness to the deep social consciousness within communities that impurity or evil must be removed periodically from their midst. For such a ritual in Egypt, see Görg (*BN* 33 [1986] 12–13) and in Babylon see de Vaux, *AI* (508; also see Landersdorfer, *Studien*, 23–26; J. G. Frazer, *The Golden Bough* [New York: The MacMillan Company, 1925] 538–87).

11–13 The instruction for Aaron to bring near (הקריב; in contrast to v 6 here it has a restricted meaning) his own bull for a purification offering (חטאת) is repeated. This verse begins another protocol of the liturgy for the Day of Atonement. It contains emphases different from those of the preceding brief liturgy. It, in any case, begins the liturgy at the same point as v 6. The many elements of the ritual not specified here may be assumed to be the same as those in the regulation for a purification offering offered by the anointed priest (4:3–12). Only the primary difference, i.e., the manner of manipulating the blood, is addressed in this regulation. Before taking the blood into the Holy of Holies, the high priest is to fill a censer (מחתה) full of glowing coals taken from the altar and put on the coals two handfuls of finely ground incense (סמים דקה; Exod 25:6). The adjective דקה, "fine," communicates that the highest quality of incense is to be used on this day (Rashi, 75). The thick smoke ascending from the censer fills the Holy of Holies, protecting the high priest from the presence of Yahweh (cf. Porter, 130; Noordtzij, 165; Harrison, 172). Keil and Delitzsch (399) explain the purpose of the smoke differently. In their judgment the burning incense represents the prayers of the people entreating Yahweh to accept the blood of the offerings and to graciously forgive his people. The former explanation is supported by the phrase ולא ימות, "lest he die," in v 13bβ. This rite, furthermore, explains why the high priest was not so overcome by the glory of Yahweh that he, like Moses (Exod 34:29–35), would have to veil himself in order to continue officiating at the various rites of this day. The latter interpretation, on the other hand, accounts for the careful details of this ritual, i.e., taking live coals from the main altar, putting fine incense on them, and putting them in a censer. These two explanations are not mutually exclusive. As seen in the discussion of the phrase ריח ניחח, "a soothing aroma" (cf. 1:9), a pleasant aroma arouses Yahweh's favor (Ps 141:2; cf. Dillmann, 579). The effect of such an aroma on Yahweh is vividly attested in the incident recorded in Num 17:8–15 (16:43–50). Yahweh's wrath was kindled against Korah and his family and was about to consume the congregation. In haste Aaron took a censer and put into it fire from the altar and laid incense on top of the fire. Then he went quickly out into the assembly to make expiation for the people. In this way he stopped the plague, the instrument of Yahweh's wrath.

14 In the Holy of Holies the high priest is to sprinkle some blood on the surface of הכפרת, "the Atonement Slate," while facing eastward. Since Yahweh is viewed as enthroned over the cherubim, facing eastward, this blood is sprinkled directly in front of Yahweh's feet (cf. Vriezen, *OTS* 7 [1950] 232–33). Then the high priest is to sprinkle (הזה) some blood with his finger before the Atonement Slate seven times (cf. *Comment* on 4:5–7). The number seven indicates completeness. No explanation is given for the twofold rite of sprinkling the blood. Conversely, the consecration of the animal for sacrifice at the altar may be the point at which all parts of the animal, including its blood, are consecrated. Keil and Delitzsch (399) take the first rite to be for the expiation of the priests' and the people's sins and the second rite for the cleansing of the sanctuary. While there is no textual support to prove or disprove this position, it does accord with the aim of full expiation in the final form of the text.

15 Next the high priest is to slaughter the people's goat for a purification offering (חטאת). Presumably he leaves the Holiest Place and comes out to the court to perform all the rites for this kind of a sacrifice. He is to take some blood from this sacrifice inside the Holiest Place and sprinkle it over the Atonement Slate and then sprinkle some of it seven times against the Atonement Slate.

16 This rite of sprinkling the blood cleanses (כפר) the Holiest Place from the impurities (טמאת) of the Israelites' transgressions that have penetrated into the Holiest Place. All cases of uncleanness of the people (chaps. 11–15) pollute the sanctuary to some measure. For the sanctuary to function effectively and for it to continue to abide in the midst of the people, it must be cleansed annually. In addition, this rite cleanses the Holiest Place from the פשעים, "acts of rebellion," and from the חטאת, "sins," of the Israelites. The choice of these terms recognizes that the people sin not only accidentally and out of ignorance, but also willfully. The term פשע, "act of rebellion," stands for any acts that were intentional violations of God's law. This word covers the community's disposition to strive for its own good, placing itself above God, and it certainly encompasses any violation of the first four commandments of the Decalogue. Milgrom points out that this is the only occurrence of this term in the priestly code. Its usage certainly communicates that willful sins were expiated by this rite. The second term, חטאת, stands for sins in general, regardless of magnitude. The use of these two terms with the prepositions מן, "from," and ל, "to," means that every kind of wrongdoing, from an overt act to something done accidentally, is covered by this ritual. The expiation accomplished is for the people as a whole. Kiuchi (*Purification Offering,* 128) holds that the phrase in v 16b, "thus he is to do for the Tent of Meeting," means that the high priest is to perform rites of sprinkling in the Holy Place in reference to the altar of incense as he is instructed in vv 14–15 to do in the Holy of Holies. The difficulty with this proposal is that it lacks support in the tradition. As a result of the achievements of this high day, a forgiven people may continue to worship Yahweh, their God, at a cleansed sanctuary.

17 Given the holiness of the Tent of Meeting and the high priest's awesome task of manipulating the blood in the Holy of Holies, no one may be present in the Holiest Place while the high priest is performing these blood rites. That person would contaminate the Tent, rendering ineffectual the ritual performed by the high priest and giving cause for the consuming power of Yahweh's glory to come against everyone in the Tent.

18–19 The priest is to go out to the altar; he is to put (נתן) blood from both the bull, i.e., his own offering, and the goat, i.e., the offering of the people, on the horns of the altar roundabout (cf. 8:15). Next he is to sprinkle (הזה) blood on the altar seven times with his finger. This is the only time that any regulation prescribes "sprinkling" the main altar. Kiuchi (*Purification Offering,* 129) posits that this procedure is followed because "sprinkling" is more powerful than "putting" blood on the altar. With this rite the high priest cleanses (טהר) the altar and sanctifies (קדש) it from the impurities of the people. Only here and in 8:15 is the altar said to be קדש, "sanctified" (Kiuchi, 129). Hoffmann (1:450) comments that טהר removes past defilement and קדש sanctifies the altar for future use. The identification of this altar is uncertain. Is it the altar of incense in the Holy Place or is it the altar of burnt offerings before the Tent? Most gentile scholars like Dillmann (579–80) identify it as the altar of burnt offerings before the Tent (cf. 8:15). Rashi (24–25) and Hoffmann (1:450), like many Jewish interpreters, reason that this altar is the golden altar inside the Holy Place before the curtain. Since יצא, "go out," would suggest that the high priest leaves the sanctuary, Rashi explains that this verb means that the high priest must go outwards from the Holy of Holies to the east side of this altar in order to begin the sprinkling at the northeast corner of the altar. Harrison (173) agrees for two reasons. First, since the altar to be sprinkled is so closely associated with the Holiest Place and the Tent, it must be the one inside the Tent. Second, this altar of incense was smeared with blood in two of the regulations of the purification offering (4:7, 18). However, it is more natural to take יצא, "go out," to mean to leave the Tent of Meeting and to understand מזבח to be the altar of whole offerings. Since the altar is not more specifically defined, one expects it to be the object that would first come to mind when this term was heard. Furthermore, nothing is said about any of the three pieces of furniture in the Holy Place. If the sprinkling of the blood in the Holy of Holies cleanses all parts of the Tent, it seems logical that a blood rite is also necessary to cleanse the main altar, representative of the furniture in the court, especially since this altar is used so heavily in the operation of the sanctuary. That the rite of sprinkling the altar of the whole offering only took place on the Day of Atonement indicates that its efficacy is intricately tied to the preceding cleansing of the Holy of Holies (Kiuchi, *Purification Offering,* 129). Since blood has been put on both the Atonement Slate and on the altar of whole offering, the entirety of the sanctuary, both the inside and the outside, is cleansed.

20–22 When the high priest has finished performing the rituals of expiation, he is to bring forward the living goat. He is to place both of his hands on the goat's head (cf. 1:4) and התודה, "confess," over it all the sins of the people. Three terms are also used here for the people's sins: עונות, "iniquities," פשׁעים, "rebellions", and חטאת, "sins" (cf. v 16). These three terms together encompass all dimensions of humans' breaking of God's law. Furthermore, all these terms are in the plural, indicative of the frequency and the totality of humans' sinning. By confessing these sins with both hands placed on the goat's head, the high priest transfers the sins of the community to the goat. Rabbinic tradition stressed that the high priest's confession had to "be matched by the remorse of the people" (Milgrom, *EncJud* 5:1386) in order to be effectual. The goat is sent away into the wilderness (מדבר). It is sent out under the control of a person prepared for this task in order to make sure that it does not run about through the camp and that once it has reached the wilderness it does not turn back into any inhabited area, because being laden with the sins of the people this goat is a terrible polluting force. It is thought that in the early period the goat wandered around in the wilderness until it expired. Later the priests made sure that the goat did not wander back into civilization, for they had it led to a cliff and pushed over, plunging it to its death.

In this rite the sins are pictured as a burden or weight that is נשׂא, "carried away," by the goat. Interestingly נשׂא is often used metaphorically for "forgive" (cf. 5:1). This goat, which carries these sins away from the camp, is to leave them in an ארץ גזרה, "inaccessible area," believed by the ancients to be the abode of demons or evil spirits. Thus the goat takes these sins to the place of their origin and leaves them there, breaking the power that they had of binding and oppressing the people.

23–25 Aaron now is to remove his special linen robes and leave them at the sanctuary, for they have been infected by holiness (v 4). These directions are very elliptical. A casual reading of the text has Aaron disrobe in the Tent of

Meeting. Such a practice would have been repulsive to ancient Israel, for the priests were to avoid any exposure of their genitals at the sanctuary (Exod 20:26; Levine, 107). Levine (108) postulates that the high priest is to remove his garments in a screened area near the Tent. This interpretation takes בא אל, which usually means "enter," to mean here "approach." There the high priest is to wash himself and put on his usual priestly garments. He now may put on his elegant garments, for he has made expiation for himself and the Tent. By bathing, the high priest removes some of the holiness that has penetrated him from being in the Holy of Holies so that he may function at the altar of the whole offering without endangering the congregation standing in that area. Next he is to offer up the two whole offerings, first for himself and then for the people. These whole offerings make further expiation for himself and the people. At this time he is to burn the fat of the purification offering on the altar (cf. 4:8–10, 19).

26 The person who has sent (שׁלח) the goat to Azazel has become unclean in dealing with an animal laden with the congregation's sins. On returning to the camp he is to wash his clothes and bathe himself in water. The requirement that someone who has become impure is to bathe before being permitted back into the camp is standard procedure (e.g., Num 19:8). This restores this person to ritual purity in order that he may enter the camp to be a part of the congregation for the rest of the ceremonies of this high day.

27–28 The parts of the bull and the goat that are not burned on the altar for the purification offerings must be disposed of properly. These parts, i.e., ערת, "the hides," בשׂר, "the meat," and פרשׁ, "the offal," are to be brought outside the camp and burned with fire (cf. 4:11–12). The one who takes them outside must wash his clothes and bathe himself in water to become ritually clean. Why he must do this is not immediately clear since it is argued in chap. 4 that the flesh of the purification is most holy, not being defiled by the offerer's sin. Kiuchi (*Purification Offering,* 135–41) suggests that the cleansing is required because the remains of the purification offerings symbolize death and that the person who handles them contacts death and thus must go through ritual cleansing. Afterwards he may enter the camp and participate in the remaining observances of the day.

29–31 At this point decrees are given to place this solemn day in Israel's calendar (cf. chap. 23). The Day of Atonement is to be observed on the tenth day of the seventh month. The number seven, made up of the sacred numbers three plus four, is the number of completeness in ancient Israel. This day, being the most solemn day in the year, is placed in the seventh month. The tenth day is chosen because ten is the joining of the key numbers three and seven. Special restrictions are placed on this day. The people are to ענה את נפשׁ, "afflict themselves." ענה is used in place of צום, "fast," in order to communicate that more than not eating is required. Unfortunately, the full extent of the affliction is not stated. It certainly includes fasting, but probably includes wearing sackcloth, mourning, and prayer as well (cf. Ps 35:13). In the post-exilic era fasting increased as a sign of repentance and seeking God's mercy (e.g., Ezra 8:21–23), and certain days of the year became regular fast days (Neh 9:1; Zech 8:19). Nevertheless, the Day of Atonement continued to be the most solemn day of the year. The Mishnah (*m. Yoma* 8.1) specifies that "eating, drinking, anointing, putting on sandals, and marital intercourse are forbidden." The great holiness of this day led to its being called שׁבת שׁבתון, "a sabbath of solemn rest." שׁבתון is composed of שׁבת, "sabbath," plus the suffix ון, making it an abstract to designate a special kind of sabbath, one to be observed more stringently and more zealously (KB, 1312). Levine (109–10) points out that this phraseology has superlative force. The phrase is translated "a sabbath of solemn rest" to capture both the complete rest and the devout, festive worship observed on this day. These standards apply to both the אזרח, "citizen," and the גר, "alien," living within Israel. The ordinance for this day is to last as long as there is a people of Israel. חקת עולם, "a perpetual decree," is repeated three times in this section (vv 29a, 31b, 34a) to add the fullest weight to the continued observance of this day. This language underscores the centrality of this day for the covenant people. In Judaism, the Day of Atonement has grown in importance until today it is one of the key practices that bind together the diverse communities of Jews throughout the world. This standard is repeated in v 31 for emphasis.

30 The people are cleansed (טהר) from their sins (חטאת) by the act of expiation (כפר). The people are both forgiven and pure. Therefore, they may stand with humble boldness in God's presence.

32 It is explicitly stated that each successor to Aaron who has been anointed (משח; cf. 8:12) and consecrated (מלא את־ידו; cf. 8:22, 33) is to carry out the observance of the Day of Atonement.

33 It is reiterated for emphasis that on each successive Day of Atonement expiation is made for three areas of the cult—the Holy of Holies (מקדש הקדש), the Tent of Meeting (אהל מועד), and the altar (המזבח)—as well as for the priests and כל־עם הקהל, "all the people of the congregation."

34 והיתה־זאת, "this is to be," the opening part of v 34, is like the opening of v 29, forming an inclusio for this section. It reiterates that this is חקת עולם, "a perpetual statue" (cf. v 29), and it reiterates the purpose of this day, i.e., to make expiation for all the sins of the Israelites. The second half of the verse is a compliance report stating that one (from the context the antecedent is taken to be Aaron) did just as Yahweh had instructed him through Moses. This note of fulfillment accords with this being a report of the first observance of the Day of Atonement.

Explanation

The Day of Atonement is the highest day in the Jewish calendar. On this day Jews afflict themselves by abstaining from all earthly pleasures. They deny their bodies as they spur themselves to seek God solemnly for forgiveness of their sins.

In early Israel, the high priest officiated on this day. Clothed in regular priestly garb of linen garments that symbolized purity and humility, he first offered for himself a bull as a purification offering. The bull corresponded to his status as the spiritual head of the congregation. Carrying a censer with hot coals, he brought blood from his purification offering into the Holy of Holies. Once inside the veil, he put incense on the coals to create a cloud of smoke to protect himself from God's awesome presence over the cherubim. Inside the Holy of Holies he sprinkled some of the blood on the Atonement Slate, and before the Atonement Slate he sprinkled blood seven times. He left the Holy of Holies, came outside, and sacrificed one of the people's goats as a purification offering. He took some of the blood from that offering inside the Holy of Holies and did the same rites as with the blood from his own purification offering. When he came outside of the Tent of Meeting, he took some of the blood from both purification offerings, smeared some on the horns of the great altar, and sprinkled some on the altar seven times.

In this manner all the furnishings of the Tent of Meeting were cleansed from the pollution of Israel's sins. Given the reality that humans by nature sin continually, pollution of the sanctuary was unavoidable. Therefore, it had to be cleansed yearly by these blood rites on these key sacred objects in order that it might continue to function efficaciously as the place for the worship of Yahweh.

Next the high priest presented the living goat. He laid both his hands on the goat and confessed over it the sins of the people. Laden with these sins, the goat was sent away into the wilderness by one appointed for this task. That person's responsibility was to make sure that the goat went away from the camp and did not wander back into it. In later times the goat was cast over a precipice to make sure that it died. This goat died in the wilderness, the haunt of demons and evil spirits. The purpose of this ritual was to remove the sins from the area where the people lived, to return them to their source, and to leave them there in order that they would have no more ill effect within the community. This rite completely broke the power of these sins over the people of God.

The high priest then removed his linen garments, washed himself, and put on his regal priestly garments. He proceeded to offer his own whole offering and the people's whole offering. Afterwards the fat of the purification offering was burned on the altar, for it was to be burned on top of a whole offering. These whole offerings may be interpreted as offerings of homage and of praise to Yahweh for providing his people this way to remove all sin and impurity from their midst. Afterwards the remains of the two purification offerings were carried outside the camp and burned. Given the gravity of this day, none of the meat of these purification offerings might be eaten by the priests. The rich variety of rituals performed on the Day of Atonement had a twofold purpose: forgiveness for the covenant people of God from all their sins and freedom from the power of sin.

In Judaism the Day of Atonement continues to be the most important and solemn day of the year. Now that sacrifices are no longer offered, Jews observe it by fasting, abstinence, and prayers of penance as they seek God for forgiveness.

In the NT Jesus' death fulfilled the entire intent of the high Day of Atonement. In fact, because Jesus was both the perfect high priest and an offering free from blemish, his death consummated the entire OT sacrificial system. The variety of the OT sacrificial rituals, each in its own way, bears witness to the dimensions of Jesus' work on the cross. In addition, his death was like that of the paschal lamb, for none of his bones were broken and he died at Passover (Exod 12:46; John 19:14, 36; 1 Cor 5:7; cf. Ps 34:21[20]). It was, furthermore, like the sacrifice Moses made to seal the covenant between Yahweh and Israel at Sinai (Exod 24:3–8), for his death inaugurated a new covenant between God and all who believe on him (cf. 1 Cor 11:23–26; Matt 26:28; Heb 12:24; cf. Heb 7:22; 8:6). Jesus, therefore, is "the mediator of a new covenant" (Heb 9:15–22; cf. Jer 31:31–34).

In the Book of Hebrews Jesus is the perfect high priest who did not need to offer any sacrifice for himself. Whereas every year on the Day of Atonement the high priest had to offer up a purification offering for his own sins as the first ritual of this day, Jesus, being blameless, offered himself to God once for all as the perfect sacrifice for all humans (Heb 7:26–28). That is, in death Jesus, who knew no sin, became a purification offering like those sacrificed on the Day of Atonement, for the blood of his sacrifice was sprinkled in the heavenly Holy of Holies (Heb 9:11–12). His sacrifice never has to be repeated. Because his sacrifice was perfect, no more are the sacrifices of the Day of Atonement required. According to Hebrews, after his death and his ascension Jesus finalized the ritual of atonement in the heavenly sanctuary, one not made with hands (Heb 9:25–28). There he lives ever to make intercession for his people. The atonement that Jesus has secured, thus, is not temporal but eternal.

In Rom 3:25 Paul makes another dramatic comparison between Jesus' death and a key rite performed on the Day of Atonement. He states that "God set forth [Jesus] as the means of expiation through faith in his blood . . ." The key term here is "means of expiation" or "place of atonement." This term refers to the Atonement Slate, the slate of gold over the Ark of the Covenant located inside the Holy of Holies. Paul has in mind that on the Day of Atonement it was over this slate and before it that the high priest sprinkled the blood of the purification offerings in order to secure expiation both for himself and for all the people. Now God has put forth Jesus as this Atonement Slate. Whereas the Atonement Slate was hidden deep inside the Holy Place, Jesus died in full public view. This radical change in location of the Atonement Slate symbolizes that Jesus' death achieves expiation for everyone who has faith in him. To express it another way, God has made his crucified son the Atonement Slate, the boundary between the holy and the sinful, where humans may find forgiveness of all their sins and reconciliation with God. This new Atonement Slate is readily accessible to anyone who has faith. One may approach this place of atonement without preparation through ritual purity, fasting, and self-denial. This dramatic shift of the blood rite from inside the Holy of Holies on the Day of Atonement to the cross planted on a hill outside Jerusalem is foundational to the radical shift in the way to God under the new covenant. Jesus himself displaces the tabernacle and its entire sacrificial system, and he creates the new people of God without any barriers of race, social status, or gender. In making this radical change, God has revealed his righteousness both by expiating human sin in order that those who believe might have a just standing before him and by providing redemption to everyone who has faith in Jesus.

In what way does Jesus' death correlate with the ritual of the goat released to Azazel? First, Jesus himself bore the people's sins as that goat did. He, who knew no sin, became sin for all humans (2 Cor 5:21; cf. Gal 3:13; Heb 9:28; 1 Pet 2:24). Second, just as the goat laden with the people's sins had to be led outside the camp to die in the wilderness, Jesus had to die outside the camp because he had become sin (cf. Heb 13:12; John 19:17; Matt 21:39; Luke 20:15). Hebrews expresses this thought using a different ritual. Just as the carcasses of the purification offerings had to be burned outside the camp, so too Jesus suffered outside the city's gates (Heb 13:11–12). Third, Jesus' descent into hell as confessed in the Apostles' Creed is explicable in light of the ritual with the scapegoat. Just as the goat's departure to the wilderness was a rite of riddance, leaving the people's sins with Azazel, the prince of evil, so Jesus took all sin to hell, the center of sin, to leave it there in order to free humans from the bondage of their sins.

These comparisons to the ritual for Azazel are important, for they teach that Jesus' death broke the power of sin to enslave a human being.

Jesus' death has thus accomplished the full intent of both the Day of Atonement and the whole sacrificial system. The global community has gained a tremendous spiritual advantage, for all the spiritual merits achieved by following the rituals of the ancient Day of Atonement are readily available to anyone at any time and in any place through belief in Jesus (Heb 7:24–27; cf. 9:23–28; 10:19–25). To say it another way, all believers in Jesus have a perfect sacrifice and a blameless high priest as their advocate in the heart of the heavenly sanctuary ever ready to make intercession for them (1 John 2:1).

V. Laws on Holy Living (17:1–26:46)

Bibliography

Baentsch, B. *Das Heiligkeits-Gesetz Lev XVII-XXVI: Eine historisch-kritische Untersuchung.* Erfurt: Hugo Güther, 1893. **Bettenzoli, G.** "Deuteronomium und Heiligkeitsgesetz." *VT* 34 (1984) 385–98. **Cholewiński, A.** *Heiligkeitsgesetz und Deuteronomium: Einevergleichende Studie.* AnBib 66. Rome: Biblical Institute Press, 1976. **Cortese, E.** "L'esegesi di H (Lev 17–26)." *RBiblt* 29 (1981) 129–46. **Delitzsch, F.** "Pentateuch-kritische Studien 12: Das Heiligkeitsgesetz." *Zeitschrift fur kirchliche Wissenschaft und kirchliche Leben* 1 (1881) 617–26. **Eerdmans, B. D.** *Alttestamentliche Studien* 4: *Das Buch Leviticus.* Giescn: Töpelmann, 1912. **Elliot-Binns, L. E.** "Some Problems of the Holiness Code." *ZAW* 67 (1955) 26–40. **Feucht, C.** *Untersuchungen zum Heiligkeitsgesetz.* Theologische Arbeiten 20. Berlin: Evangelische Verlagsanstalt, 1964. **Graf, K.** *Die geschichtlichen Bucher des Alten Testaments: Zwei historische-kritische Untersuchungen.* Leipzig: T. O. Weigel, 1866. **Horst, L.** *Leviticus XVII-XXVI und Hezekiel: Ein Beitrag zur Pentateuchkritik.* Colmar: Eugen Barth, 1881. **Kayser, A.** *Das vorexilische Buch der Urgeschichte Israels und seine Erweiterungen: Ein Beitrag zur Pentateuch-kritik.* Strassburg: C. F. Schmidt's Universitäts-Buchhandlung, 1874. **Kilian, R.** *Literarkritische und Formgeschichtliche Untersuchung des Heiligkeitsgesetzes.* BBB 19. Bonn: Peter Hanstein, 1963. **Klostermann, A.** "Ezechiel und das Heiligkeitsgesetz." In *Der Pentateuch: Beiträge zu seinem Verständnis und seiner Entstehungsgeschichte.* Leipzig: U. Deichert'sche Verlagsbuchhandlung, 1893. 419–47. **Knohl, I.** "The Priestly Torah Versus the Holiness School: Sabbath and the Festivals." *HUCA* 58 (1987) 65–117. **Koch, R.** "Vers une morale de L'Alliance?" *StMor* 6 (1968) 7–58. **Küchler, S.** *Das Heiligkeitsgesetz Lev 17–26: Eine literarkritische Untersuchung.* Königsberg: Kümmel, 1929. **Morgenstern, J.** "The Decalogue of the Holiness Code." *HUCA* 26 (1955) 1–27. **Paton, L.** "The Relation of Lev XX to Lev. XVII–XIX." *Hebraica* 10 (1894) 111–21. ———. "The Holiness Code and Ezekiel." *The Presbyterian and Reformed Review* 26 (1896) 98–115. ———. "The Original Form of Leviticus xvii.-xix." *JBL* 16 (1897) 31–77. ———. "The Original Form of Leviticus xxi., xxii." *JBL* 17 (1898) 149–74. ———. "The Original Form of Leviticus xxiii., xxv." *JBL* 18 (1899) 35–60. **Rabast, K.** *Das apodiktische Recht im Deuteronomium und im Heiligkeitsgesetz.* Hermsdorf: Heimatsdienstverlag, 1948. **Rad, G. von.** *Studies in Deuteronomy.* Tr. D. Stalker. SBT 9. Chicago: Regnery, 1953. **Reventlow, H. G.** *Das Heiligkeitsgesetz: Formgeschichtlichuntersucht.* WMANT 6. Neukirchen: Neukirchener, 1961. **Sun, H. T. C.** "An Investigation into the Compositional Integrity of the So-called Holiness Code (Leviticus 17–26)." Diss., Claremont, 1990. **Thiel, W.** "Erwägungen zum Alter des Heiligkeitsgesetzes." *ZAW* 71 (1969) 40–73. **Wagner, V.** "Zur Existenz des sogenannten 'Heiligkeitsgesetzes.'" *ZAW* 86 (1974) 307–16. **Wellhausen, J.** *Die Composition des Hexateuchs und der historischen Bucher des Alten Testaments.* Vierte unveranderte Auflage. Berlin: de Gruyter, 1963. ———. *Prolegomena to the History of Ancient Israel.* (Repr. of Meridian Books Library Edition 1957.) Gloucester, MA: P. Smith, 1973. **Wurster, P.** "Zur Charakteristik und Geschichte des Priestercodex und Heiligkeitsgesetzes." *ZAW* 4 (1884) 112–33. **Zimmerli, W.** "'Heiligkeit' nach dem sogenannten Heiligkeitsgesetz." *VT* 30 (1980) 493–512.

Form/Structure/Setting

The Character of the Holiness Code

Since the late nineteenth century, chaps. (17) 18–26 have been considered to be a corpus separate from the rest of the priestly material. The ethical concerns of these chapters formulated in a vigorous style stand out against the preceding cultic regulations cast in a stilted, stereotyped style. Unlike the preceding regulations, these moral laws are motivated by strong exhortations to do what Yahweh has commanded. The key exhortation is "You shall be holy, for I, Yahweh your God, am holy" (see *Excursus* at 19:2). This exhortation expresses the goal of Yahweh's covenant with Israel; i.e., Israel is to be a holy people distinct from all other nations (Exod 19:5). The laws and instructions in this code lead Israel to express this holiness in personal relationships and through integrity in cultic matters.

Frequently the laws in this corpus are distinctively substantiated by Yahweh's self-introduction. The proclamation is usually formulated אני יהוה, "I am Yahweh" (18:5, 6, 21; 19:12, 14, 16, 18, 28, 30, 32, 37; 20:8, 24; 21:12, 15, 23; 22:2, 3, 8, 9, 16, 30, 31, 32, 33; 25:38; 26:2, 13, 45), or אני יהוה אלהיכם, "I am Yahweh, your God" (18:2, 4, 30; 19:3, 4, 10, 25, 31, 34, 36; 20:7; 23:22, 43; 24:22; 25:17, 55; 26:1, 44). Another marked feature of this code is that most of the laws are formulated categorically. Some label this formulation apodictic (cf. A. Alt, "The Origins of Israelite Law," in *Essays on Old Testament History and Religion,* tr. R. A. Wilson [Garden City: Doubleday, 1968] 101–71; G. Liedke, *Gestalt und Bezeichnung alttestamentlicher Rechtssätze: Eine formgeschichtlich-terminologische Studie,* WMANT 39 [Neukirchen-Vluyn: Neukirchener, 1971]). When a penalty is stated, it is usually the death penalty or the cut-off penalty (e.g., chap. 20). Because of these characteristics, in 1877 Klostermann named this corpus *Das Heiligkeitsgesetz,* "the Holiness Code." This name has continued to refer to these chapters in Leviticus.

Earlier scholars identified the material of this code by its distinct vocabulary:

כי קדש אני יהוה, "because I, Yahweh, am holy," 19:2; 20:26; 21:8; similar forms 11:44, 45; 20:8; 21:15, 23; 22:9, 16, 32;

איש איש, "everyone," 17:3, 8, 10, 13; 18:6; 20:2, 9; 22:4, 18; 24:15; also 15:2; Num 5:12; 9:10;

ונתתי אני, "I shall give," 17:10; 20:3, 5 (שמתי, "I shall put"), 6; 26:17;

הכרתי, "I shall cut off," 17:10; 20:3, 5, 6 (only first person form of הכרת);

הלך בחקות, "walk in statutes," 18:3; 20:23; 26:3 (Ezekiel, e.g., 5:6, 7; 11:20);

חקתי ומשפטי, "my statutes and my laws," 18:4 (reversed), 5, 26; 19:37; 20:22; 25:18; 26:15, 43 (reversed);

שמר . . . ועשה, "observe . . . and do," 18:4; 19:37; 20:8, 22; 22:31; 25:18; 26:3 (often in Deuteronomy, e.g., 4:6; 16:12; 26:16);

שאר, "flesh, close relative," 18:12, 13, 17 (fem); 20:19; 21:2;

שאר בשרו, "his close relative," (lit.) "flesh of his flesh," 18:6; 25:49;

זמה, "a lewd act," 18:17; 19:29; 20:14 (2x; often in Ezekiel, e.g., 16:27, 43, 58; 23:21, 27, 29, 35, 44, 48 [2x], 49);

עמית, "associate," 18:20; 19:11, 15, 17; 24:19; 25:14 (2x), 15, 17; also 5:21(6:2 [2x]) and Zech 13:7;

שבתי, "my Sabbaths," 19:3, 30; 26:2 (also Ezekiel, e.g., 20:12, 13, 16, 20, 21, 24; 22:8, 26);

אלילים, "idols," 19:4; 26:1 only here in Pentateuch and several times in Isaiah;

ויראת אלהיך, "and fear your God," 19:14, 32; 25:17, 36, 43;

דמיו בו (דמים בם), "his blood is on him," 20:9, 11, 12, 13, 16, 27 (also Ezek 18:13; 33:5).

(This list is adapted from the list found in S. R. Driver, *An Introduction to the Literature of the OT,* 7th ed. [Edinburgh: Clark, 1898] 49–50.)

Later scholars challenged the validity of identifying this code by its distinctive vocabulary, pointing out that many of these terms and phrases occur in other blocks of material in the OT, such as Deuteronomy's use of שמר . . . ועשה, "observe and do." As a result, contemporary scholars do not place much weight on vocabulary in their reconstruction of the growth and development of the Holiness Code; nevertheless, they continue to identify the formulae of Yahweh's self-introduction with the Holiness Code. In place of vocabulary, they employ form analysis and tradition history in determining the nature, development, and extent of the Holiness Code.

The Holiness Code is ordinarily taken to include chaps. 17–26. A survey of the content and arrangement of this material is helpful for understanding the history of scholarship in reference to these chapters. Although an introduction to a new corpus is lacking at 17:1, the following chapters stand off from the rest of Leviticus, primarily being framed by the summary statement and compliance report at 16:34 and the subscript at 26:46. Incidentally there is a secondary break at 21:24, since that verse is a compliance report. This material on holy living functions as a counterbalance to the laws on ritual purity (chaps. 11–15), with the liturgy for the Day of Atonement (chap. 16) functioning as a pivot. Chaps. 11–15 describe the types and causes of uncleanness that are removed from the entire nation on the Day of Atonement, and chaps. 17–26 set forth the ethical and cultic standards that a forgiven people must follow.

The material in chaps. 17–26 has been collected in blocks, but there is no definitively discoverable arrangement of these blocks (e.g., cf. Eissfeldt, *OT: An Introduction,* tr. P. R. Ackroyd [New York: Harper and Row, 1965] 234). This material has been assembled primarily by common themes, key words, and association of ideas. A brief look at the arrangement of the material in this section will be helpful.

Chaps. 18–20 form the core of this corpus. In fact, they are grouped in an ABA' pattern:

A Laws governing sexual relationships (chap. 18)
  B A variety of ethical and cultic laws (chap. 19)
A' Laws governing sexual relationship with penalty (chap. 20)

Chap. 19 is the center of this trilogy. The theme of this speech is the opening exhortation to be holy (v 2). The laws found in this speech are a mixture of moral commands and cultic regulations. This strongly indicates that while the author of this code stressed moral laws far more than are found in other portions of the priestly material, he did not consider that the observance of moral laws carried greater value than the observance of cultic laws in order for Israel to be a people holy to her God. The content of this speech, however, is very fragmented, being held together by the recurring use of the formula of Yahweh's self-introduction. Chaps. 18 and 20 govern sexual relationships and prohibit sorcery. These two speeches are impassioned by powerful parenetic material (18:2–6, 25–30; 20:7–8, 22–26).

Chaps. 21–22 provide special laws for the priests and for sacrifices. Chap. 21 sets forth the standard for the purity of the priesthood in essential matters such as marriage and bodily integrity. Chap. 22 adds material on the integrity of sacrificial material and the handling of sacrifices.

Surrounding chaps. 18–22 are instructions on worship. Chap. 17 legislates that all sacrifices be made at an official altar and that no blood be consumed. The central issue then for the laws of chap. 17 is integrity in handling an animal's blood. Chaps. 23 + 25 regulate the times for worship. Chap. 23, a calendrical text, opens with a law on observance of the sabbath and then regulates the three annual pilgrim festivals, namely the Feast of Passover and Unleavened Bread, the Feast of Weeks, and the Feast of Booths. It also makes the first day of the seventh month a day of rest, and it sets the date for the Day of Atonement. Chap. 25 regulates multiple-year cycles, i.e., the seven-year sabbatical cycle and the fifty-year cycle or the Year of Jubilee. Integrated into the observance of Jubilee are the laws on redemption of a patrimony and a debtor slave. These high festive days and special years are to be observed in order to exalt the worship of Yahweh over material concerns. Because Yahweh is a holy God, he demands that sacred times be proclaimed for community worship and celebration.

Chap. 24, which itself has two distinct sections, is wedged between these two speeches. The reason for its location is far from obvious. The first section regulates the quality of the oil for the menorah in the Holy Place (vv 1–4) and the bread of the Presence for the table (vv 5–9). These regulations have some tie with chaps. 23 and 25, for they are calendrical in nature in that they govern periodic rituals regarding worship at the Temple. The second section (vv 10–23) reports a case of blasphemy to which laws treating blasphemy and injury to persons and animals have been appended. The attaching of laws to an incident is a familiar pattern in the Pentateuch (cf. chap. 10). Why this particular incident was drawn to or set in this context remains an enigma.

This section concludes with the blessings and curses in chap. 26. This chapter is a fitting end both to this section and to this book. It places all of the material on cultic purity and ethical integrity within the context of the covenant. In other words, all of Leviticus is to be understood as having its authority and significance within the context of the covenant. Not only does this speech offer blessings and curses; it also offers instructions for the possibilities of restoration to the community should it ever enter exile (vv 40–45). It stands as an enduring word of hope to Israel.

The position of chap. 17 in relationship to the Holiness Code has been debated since the identification of the Holiness Code. Since this speech deals solely with sacrifices, it is more in accord with the preceding legislation than with the following material, which treats primarily ethical and purity issues. Thus the Holiness Code lacks a heading that identifies the following material as constituting a special corpus like that found at Deut 12:1. Because of its concern with sacrifices and its location, a few scholars group it with chap. 16. This location fails, for a compliance report at the end of chap. 16 definitively sets it off from the following. Most critical scholars, thus, have defended chap. 17 as a part of the Holiness Code. They note that language in this speech ties it to the Holiness Code: the use of the divine first person (vv 10–12, 14; cf. 26:3, 6, 17), the formula איש איש מבית ישראל, "any Israelite" (vv 3, 8, 10, 13), the "cut-off" penalty in the divine first person (v 10; cf. vv 4, 9, 14; 20:5), and the penalty נשא עונו, "he is held responsible" (v 16; cf. Bertholet, 58; Baentsch, 388). In accord with the Holiness Code is the desire to remove all forms of pagan practices (vv 5, 7; cf. 20:5, 6; Porter, 138). Nevertheless, it needs to be stated that several terms in this speech reflect the style of the priestly writer: אהל מועד, "the Tent of Meeting" (vv 4, 5, 6, 9), the concern about eating blood (vv 10–14), והקטיר החלב, "and he is to smoke the fat" (v 6), לריח ניחח ליהוה, "a soothing aroma to Yahweh" (v 6), and קרבן, "offering, oblation" (v 4). One way to account for this language is the position that chap. 17 was redacted by a priestly editor. Baentsch (388), e.g., judges it to be an old section of the law that has been thoroughly edited in the thought of the priestly writers. Conversely, the motivations for the law against eating blood in vv 11–12 and the phrase מזבח יהוה, "the altar of Yahweh" (v 6), are uncharacteristic of the priestly material.

Some who place chap. 17 as part of the Holiness Code explain its lead position by the practice of ancient codes, which put cultic laws at the beginning of legal material: Exod 20:24–26 for the book of the covenant, Deut 12 for Deut 12–28; Ezek 40–42 for Ezek 40–48; Exod 25–31 for the priestly material (Bertholet, 58; Eissfeldt, *OT: An Introduction,* 233). In this same vein Kilian (*Literarkritische,* 178–79) argued that chap. 17 was placed at the head of the Holiness Code by a priestly redactor who used the covenant code and Deuteronomy as a pattern. This redactor did not include a special heading for this block of material because he was incorporating it into the priestly material. The consensus of scholars, therefore, assigns chap. 17 to the Holiness Code.

History of Research on the Holiness Code

The identification of Lev 18–23, 25–26 as an independent corpus began in 1866 with Graf. He separated chaps. 18–26 from 1–16 on the basis of unique expressions and distinctive formulae (Graf, *Die geschichtlichen Bucher,* 75). Given the linguistic ties between this corpus and Ezekiel, Graf postulated that Ezekiel was its author. In 1874 Kayser accepted Graf's position and went on to provide a fuller linguistic characterization of the Holiness Code (Sun, "Investigation," 3). He assigned chap. 17 to the corpus (Sun, 3). Next Klostermann recognized the existence of this code and labeled it *Heiligkeitsgesetz,* "the holiness code." He also investigated its ties with Ezekiel, concluding that instead of being its author, Ezekiel had immersed himself in this material (cf. Sun, 4). Klostermann judged that the present corpus contains only fragments of an original legal collection, since material that originally belonged to it, like Exod 12:12b; 29:38–46; Lev 7:15ff; 11:43–45, appears elsewhere ("Ezechiel," 378).

In 1876, Wellhausen went on to claim the literary independence of the Holiness Code from the priestly material because of its distinctive characteristics. He held that older laws that existed independently were collected into an independent corpus H; then a priestly redaction incorporated the Holiness Code into the priestly narrative by merging texts from both sources and making additions to the Holiness Code from the viewpoint of the priestly school (Sun, "Investigation," 8). Sun points out that this construct would be followed for several decades by scholars who supported the existence of the Holiness Code.

In several articles published between 1894 and 1899, Paton sought to identify the various strata of this corpus. He identified three primary strata: the original holiness material, pre-priestly parenetic material that accepted the deuteronomistic programs of centralization, and the work of a priestly redactor who improved the meaning with glosses and the addition of cultic material to bring the Holiness Code into harmony with the position of the priestly school (Sun, "Investigation," 9).

Bertholet (1901) accepted the prevailing critical position and undertook the identification of the various redactions more closely (Sun, "Investigation," 9–10). He found twelve independent sections which the redactor of the Holiness Code brought together and filled out with a variety of other material. In 1903, Baentsch (*Leviticus,* 387–88), on the other hand, uncovered three independent strata, namely chaps. 18–20 + 23–25; 21–22; 17. These strata were assembled by the compilers of chap. 26 into the Holiness Code. At the time this corpus was inserted into the priestly material, some other fragments were added.

At this time an attack on the independent existence of the Holiness Code came from Eerdmans (1912); he founded his opposition on his inability to find any basic structure that held all the material together (Sun, "Investigation," 11). Furthermore, he observed that the call to holiness is not limited to this corpus, being found in several other OT texts, such as 11:44–45; Exod 19:6; 22:30(31); Deut 7:6; 14:2, 21; 26:19; 28:9. He pointed out, in addition, that the vocabulary distinct to this corpus also occurs in other places of the OT; therefore, the remaining terms and phrases that are distinctive to this corpus are far from sufficient to prove that this is an independent document (Sun, 12). Küchler supported Eerdmans' position with a historical evaluation of the material (Sun, 12–13). He dated most of this material to the early pre-exilic era. Scholars have, for the most part, remained unpersuaded by the arguments of Eerdmans and Küchler.

Sun ("Investigation," 15) points out that at this point in the history of research in the Holiness Code, the approach taken to understanding this corpus shifted dramatically as scholars began to apply to it the tools of form criticism and traditio-historical criticism. The initial effort was published by von Rad in his monograph *Studies on Deuteronomy* (1947 [German]; 1953 [Eng ed.]). He devoted a chapter to the study of the Holiness Code because, like Deuteronomy, it contains a series of pareneses in the context of sermons. In his analysis this corpus in Leviticus differs from Deuteronomy on two accounts (*Studies,* 25–26). First, the instructions are addressed now to the priests, now to the community, while in Deuteronomy the sermons are for the instruction of the community. Second, the sermons in the Holiness Code are addresses of God, not sermons from Moses. That is, impersonal laws have been set in divine sermons. This style is accomplished primarily by introductory formulae that identify Yahweh as the speaker and by the repeated use of various forms of the formula "I am Yahweh." The parenetic material had its home in these sermons. For a setting, von Rad suggested a community gathering of a popular nature for instruction (31). He concluded that the bulk of the Holiness Code is teaching based on a variety of old laws in parenetic form (35), while conceding that it is not easy to account for this material being put into Yahweh speeches. Sun (16) perceived that von Rad had shifted the approach to this corpus away from literary issues to an investigation into the growth and development of the various sections.

Kornfeld (1952) studied the Holiness Code by focusing on the sexual laws in chaps. 18 and 20. He accepted the established parameters of this code and argued that it had a unified and coherent structure (Sun, "Investigation," 17). He dated this document to the late monarchy at the time of the deuteronomist (Sun, 12).

In an article in *ZAW* 67 (1955) 26–40, L. E. Elliot-Binns cautiously set out the tentative conclusions of his work on the Holiness Code. He reasoned that the Holiness Code was a written document consisting of several sections assembled over many years. The material from this group reaches beyond Lev 17–26. In his judgment, its compilation took place earlier than that of Deuteronomy, with which there is no contact, and later than that of Ezekiel, with which there is a definite relationship. He speculated that the Holiness Code was assembled by members of the Jerusalem Temple.

In 1961 Reventlow published an extensive form-critical study of this code. His study is very helpful for understanding the interplay between this corpus and its setting. He views the sermons to be for the oral instruction and exhortation of the laity assembled at a covenant renewal ceremony. He identified the ground layer of this code to be the apodictic laws found in chaps. 17–20 and the nucleus of that layer to be the Decalogue, which can be recovered in chap. 19. These laws were drawn from a large reservoir of apodictic laws (*Heiligkeitsgesetz,* 162). Over time additional material from this reservoir became attached to the nucleus by thought and word associations and by the need of the moment. The blessings and curses of Lev 26 also belong to the ground layer. Next the rich instructional material, which lends support to the apodictic laws, was added (163). This step included chap. 17 and the cultic material in chaps. 21–25. The last stage in the growth process was the inclusion of homiletic material, which is identifiable by the use of direct address. This homiletic material took a variety of shapes, including parenesis and theologically reflective material.

For Reventlow, the setting in which this corpus came together was the covenant festival, which reached all the way back to Israel assembled at Mount Sinai. In this cultic setting, the material grew out of the dynamic interplay between the preacher and the audience. Older material, like the Decalogue in chap. 19 and the laws in chap. 17, which came from the wilderness tradition, was updated with supplements. But other material, like the laws of chaps. 23 and 25, had its home in Canaan among a settled population. The same is true for the content of the majority of the blessings and curses in chap. 26. As a result of this growth process, the older desert material now stands in creative tension with newer material applicable to a settled people. This tension belongs to the homiletic design of the sermons. When the congregation heard these sermons, contemporary Israel was led back to Sinai as grounds for heeding the call to obedience in the present. Reventlow postulated that the preacher who delivered these sermons had this role as an official cultic preacher and was viewed as Moses' successor. According to this reconstruction, this code was not the product of a literary process; rather it grew out of a repetitive cultic celebration. The final form of this code came together at the covenant festival, which in the Kingdom period had its final home at Jerusalem.

A significant contribution of Reventlow's study is its focus on the rhetorical design of this material. It takes seriously the assertion that this material consists of ancient speeches that were delivered for the instruction of the congregation. Sun ("Investigation," 20), however, perceived that Reventlow's study is limited because it treats the various subunits of the Holiness Code, not the code as a self-existing corpus.

Using literary criticism, Kilian (1963) undertook the difficult task of identifying the various literary layers making up the Holiness Code. He found that there were two major redactions. The first one produced the proto-Holiness Code. This redactor used a variety of source material, expanded it, and added comments. This earlier code consists of portions of 18–22, 25 (*Literarkritische*, 164):

Lev 18:6–23 (save for small additions in vv. 7, 9, 11)
Lev 19:5–8a, 11–18, 26–28, 30
Lev 20:2aβ*b, 3*, 7, 8, 9*, 10–21, 27
Lev 21:1bβ–8, 10*, 11, 12*, 13–15, 17b*, 18–20, 21*, 22*, 23aβb
Lev 22:2aβb, 3*, 4*, 5, 6b, 7–10, 11*, 12–16, 18b*, 19(*?), 20–25, 27–32
Lev 25:2b, 3, 4*, 5a, 6f, 14, 17 (only part), 25*, 35*, 36f, 39, 40a, 43, 44, 47, 53

This redactor was responsible for the form of the laws, the employment of the shorter formula of Yahweh's self-introduction, and ordinances with חלל, "profane" (Kilian, 164–65). The punishment stipulated in the laws falls in the realm of the cult, not in the realm of the civil courts (166). This redactor, however, did not do any historical reminiscing. The older material was organized into two parts: the moral (chaps. 18–20) and the cultic (chaps. 21–22, 25; *Literarkritische*, 167–68). As for the date of this material, it was compiled after Deuteronomy, since it assumes the centralization of the cult and evidences a familiarity with the deuteronomistic preaching, and before the fall of Jerusalem (169). Afterwards another redactor took over this work and added several pieces plus much of chaps. 23–24 and chap. 26 to make it a corpus:

Lev 18:2b–4, 24, 30
Lev 19:2aβ–4, 9f, 23–25, 31, 33–36
Lev 23:10aβ–11a, 12*, 14a(?), 15–17, 18aα, 19b, 20*, 22, 39aβ, 40, 42, 43
Lev 24:16aα, 16b, 17, 18a, 18b, 19, 20a, 20b, 21, 22
Lev 25:2aβ, 17 (part), 18–22, 38, 42, 46b*, 55
Lev 26:1f, 3–9, 11–13, 15, 16*, 17, 19f, 22*, 25*, 26, 29–33, 36, 37a, 39, 40aα, 42, 45

Part of this material was an expansion of the legal material. Drawing on old material, the redactor supplemented the old code with material such as the calendar and the principle of restitution (*Literarkitische*, 169–70). He also expanded the parenetic material (170). In addition, he preferred the longer formula of Yahweh's self-introduction and used history for motivation. Kilian dated this second redaction to the exilic period on the bases of Aramaisms, e.g., אזרח, "citizen," and its reliance on Ezekiel (171–72). This redactor had the great hope that the holy people of God would be recreated as in their initial creation in the deliverance from Egypt (173–74). Kilian concluded that Ezekiel was influenced by the earlier code and that, in turn, Ezekiel influenced the final redactions of the Holiness Code. Given the ties between this redaction and Ezekiel, he conjectured that this redactor belonged to Ezekiel's circle (185). Later this corpus received some additions and editorial changes by priestly writers in order that this material could be incorporated into the priestly code (174–76). One of these priestly redactors inserted chap. 17 into its position at the head of the corpus (176–79). His work accounted for the absence of an introduction to the Holiness Code, for he constructed chap. 17 in order to integrate this code into the priestly work. In Sun's judgment ("Investigation," 25), the way in which Kilian has reconstructed the origin and the development of the Holiness Code provides the grounds for accepting it as a self-standing corpus. The big question, as Sun points out, is whether these results can be substantiated.

In 1964 Feucht promoted the independent existence of the Holiness Code. It was composed, in his judgment, out of two collections (Sun, "Investigation," 25). The first is chaps. 18–22, 23:9–22 (with Num 15:37–41), which came into existence before the early stages of Deuteronomy in the early seventh century in Judah (O. Kaiser, *Introduction to the Old Testament,* tr. J. Sturdy [Minneapolis: Augsburg Publishing House, 1977] 114). The second collection is chaps. 25–26; it postdates Deuteronomy, for it shows deuteronomic influence.

In a massive commentary on Leviticus published in 1966, Elliger opened up a new dimension to the discussion of the origin of the Holiness Code by denying that it ever had an independent existence (16). He concluded that this material was grafted into the priestly material in two stages, each of which was supplemented independently. There are thus four identifiable layers in Lev 17–26. In the first stage a person collected material, some of which reached back before the monarchy. He did not edit any of that material; instead he placed his contribution at the beginning and the end of the blocks of material that he received. He loved the longer divine self-introductory formula, being very conscious that Israel lived by the kingly favor of Yahweh and his fatherly blessings (16). At the center of his theological outlook is the interaction between Yahweh and his people as expressed in the command "Be you holy because I, Yahweh your God, am holy" (19:2). This old collection began with much of chap. 25 and contained major portions of 17–19 + 26. Next the editor of this first layer relocated chap. 25 to the last position, added comments, and inserted material into what he received; he also added portions of 21:1–15 and chap. 20 (17–18). The reason that he added the laws with penalty (chap. 20) was to underscore the seriousness of the call to holiness. With the same intent he preferred the shorter formula of Yahweh's self-introduction. This editor was concerned that the law be observed not only by the community but by each individual as well. In Elliger's analysis, the third hand did major work in expanding the subjects addressed by this section of the legislation (18–19). He placed chap. 20 before chap. 21 in order to incorporate other material concerning the cult and the priests, e.g., 21:16–24; 22:17–22, 25b, and the ground form of chap. 23. He might have been responsible for placing chap. 17 at the head of this law code. The material he found he left intact, although he made some rearrangements. He added the compliance reports at 21:24 and 23:44. Elliger also assigned to him the addition of 21:9 and 20:27. Finally the work of this hand was supplemented by that of another redactor who worked heavily in chaps. 22–24. He was basically dependent on the preceding redactor for his theological outlook and literary style. Elliger (22) noted that some other pieces became attached to this legal corpus over time. In summary, all of these redactional efforts identified by Elliger were to supplement the priestly material; i.e., they were not undertaken to produce and augment an independent code (Sun, "Investigation," 28–29).

In 1969 Thiel entered the debate with a detailed article published in *ZAW* 71 (1969) 40–73. Starting with the assumption of the existence of the Holiness Code, he concluded that much of the material in the Holiness Code contains older elements of a variety of genres, but the literary form of that material is no longer discernible. Thiel postulated that this corpus went through a priestly revision in which it was stylized as Yahweh speeches. This revision was marked by the divine self-introduction formulae and parenetic material. Later it was redacted by the priestly school when it became incorporated into the priestly material. To this redaction belong the elements cast in priestly language and set at Mount Sinai. The Holiness Code reached its final form during the exile. In his judgment, the theology and terminology are so much like those of Deuteronomy that he located the origin of this code in the same circle, i.e., the preaching of the Levites. As far as its date, it came about later than Deuteronomy, as the priestly revisions attest.

Wondering about the independent existence of the Holiness Code because of the fragmented sources identified in earlier studies, Wagner (1974) investigated whether Lev 17–26 is part of a larger section. If it is, the existence of "a Holiness Code" fades away (*ZAW* 86 [1974] 308). From his study he concludes that Lev 11–22 is a unit, which treats impurity (312–13):

A. Impurity of people (chaps. 11–20)
   1. Reparable impurity (chaps. 11–15)
   2. Irreparable impurity (chaps. 17–20)
B. Impurity of persons and things taking part in the cult (chaps. 21–22)

He went on to argue that Lev (17) 18–26 is part of the larger unit of Exod 25–Lev 26. Therefore, this corpus, being part of the framework of a larger unit, had no independent life (*ZAW* 86 [1974] 315). Zimmerli (*VT* 30 [1980] 501) was unpersuaded by Wagner's structural argument since the formula of Yahweh's self-identification is absent from Lev 11–16. Sun, moreover, has correctly argued that Wagner's structural argument was inadequate to substantiate his conclusion ("Investigation," 34).

In 1976 Cholewiński published a detailed comparative study of the Holiness Code and Deut 12–26. Before doing the comparative work, he undertook a thorough investigation of the redactional history of the Holiness Code. From his study he determined that the core of the Holiness Code was the product of five redactional efforts. He assigned each of these a number preceded by the letter H. The core material for each redaction is as follows: H1: 17:3–9; H2: 18:6–23; 19:11–18, 26–28, 30, 32; H3: much of chaps. 20–22; H4: 23:4–8, 23–25, 33–38; H5: much of chap. 25 (*Heiligkeitsgesetz,* 132–35). Although these various sections came from groups who belonged to the same spiritual milieu, there is no literary unity among these pieces (135). Each of these efforts thus produced a certain body of material, rather than each one adding a strata that ran throughout the existing corpus. While H3 and H4 were composed for inclusion in the priestly work, H1 + H2 + H5 may have been collected and circulated as a pamphlet. According to Cholewiński's interpretation, this code came about more like the growth of a snowball than by additions and changes made to a basic core.

The redactional work of a group of priests, which Cholewiński identified with the label HG, arranged these documents into their present uniformity and gave them a characteristic imprint around a central theme (*Heiligkeitsgesetz,* 135, 337). These redactors were members of a priestly wing of the deuteronomistic reformers who had gone into exile and worked in Babylon (344). This identification allowed Cholewiński to account for the mixture of priestly and deuteronomistic terminology in the final corpus. The document compiled by HG received five small additions from various sources with the same essential theological and cultic outlook. Finally there was a late priestly redactor who made some touches in 17:1–9, 15–16; 18:26b; 19:2a, 20–22; 21:22 and added chap. 24 (140–41). According to Cholewiński, these various redactors belonged to the priestly circles, and they did their work after the groundwork of the priestly texts had been completed.

Cholewiński, therefore, obviously rejected the view that the Holiness Code went through a major priestly redaction. Rather he held that it was composed by members of the priesthood who were members of the deuteronomistic circle and who knew the priestly material. In his judgment (*Heiligkeitsgesetz,* 334–38), they joined their material to the priestly work in order to change various theological positions of the older priestly school. E.g., in chap. 25 this code challenged the priestly view that the land was the unconditional possession of Israel with the dogma that Yahweh was the owner of the land (334). This group, furthermore, attacked the priestly belief that the covenant was indissoluble and not dependent on human effort with the tenet that Israel's obedience is essential to the continuation of the covenant (26:9–12; *Heiligkeitsgesetz,* 335).

Because the HG redactors were members of the deuteronomistic circle, there are many characteristics of the deuteronomistic circle in this corpus. They took the deuteronomistic legal corpus as a model for assembling these documents into the Holiness Code. These redactors were in agreement with many of the tenets of the deuteronomistic movement; nevertheless, they sought to correct prescriptions considered too radical or inadequately grounded from a theological perspective. The primary example of disagreement with the deuteronomistic reform was their rejection of its permission of profane slaughter (Deut 12:13–15, 20–28; Lev 17:1–9). In addition, the Holiness Code reintroduced the Feast of Unleavened Bread as a self-standing feast and reinstated the sacral character of the seventh year. The holiness school sought to fill gaps in the deuteronomistic laws; e.g., they specified the punishment for certain offenses (chap. 20), included a list of forbidden sexual relationships (18:6–23), and gave additional laws regarding the priests (chaps. 21–22). Sometimes these redactors of the Holiness Code wished to address social problems differently than does Deuteronomy. This is clearly evident in the social problems addressed by chap. 25 in contrast to their treatment in Deut 15:1–18. So the Holiness Code both supplemented and modified the legislation of Deuteronomy. It is for these reasons that Cholewiński located the roots of the major redactional effort in the deuteronomistic reform. Cholewiński's results, therefore, agree with Elliger's that this corpus was compiled as an addendum to the basic priestly material and thus did not have a life of its own (*Heiligkeitsgesetz,* 138–39).

In a detailed article in *HUCA* 58 (1987) 65–117, Knohl published some of the results of his studies in the Holiness Code. His thesis is that Lev 17–26 is a late addition to the priestly material and that material from this source is found in more places of the Pentateuch than has been believed (65). In his judgment, it was the work of the "holiness school," which labored after both the priestly school and the deuteronomistic school. Both the theological outlook and the understanding of the liturgy of the holiness school differed markedly from those of the older priestly school. An example of the difference between these groups, in the judgment of Knohl, concerns the understanding of the festivals and the Sabbath (66). The priestly school taught that the festivals were occasions to offer sacrifices in obedience to the divine command, but the Sabbath was not accorded much significance. By contrast, the holiness school treated the festivals as joyful occasions celebrating the produce of the fields and as times of historical remembrance. This school raised the Sabbath to a central place by requiring that it be observed as a day of complete rest (19:3; 23:3; 26:2). An example of other material that Knohl assigned to the "holiness school" indicates the far-reaching dimensions of his theory. He finds the perspective of the holiness school in reference to the Sabbath in several other texts, such as Exod 31:12–17 and 35:1–3 (73–74). Knohl claimed that this school edited and arranged the material regarding the tabernacle and the golden calf in order to exalt the Sabbath by placing its sanctity on the same level as that of the sanctuary (74). Their point of view is clearly stated in Lev 19:30 and 26:2, where categorical commands on keeping the Sabbath and revering the sanctuary are coupled. Knohl, furthermore, considered the story of the giving of manna recounted in Exod 16 to be an older tradition expanded by the holiness school, not the priestly editors (74–76). In fact, Knohl assigned the final recension of the priestly material to this school; thus their hand is found in many more places than Lev 17–26 (66). These examples reveal how far-reaching and revolutionary Knohl's work is. As far as Lev 17–26 is concerned, his work has added to the evidence against considering this material as a self-contained document. Knohl's efforts, which are just coming to light, will surely stimulate much debate for some time to come.

In a doctoral dissertation (1989) under the direction of R. Knierim, Sun thoroughly analyzed the structure of each form-critical macro unit in this corpus as the point of departure for investigating the composition history of the traditionally accepted Holiness Code. He found that the different speeches in the Holiness Code came from a variety of times. He dated some of the material to the post-deuteronomic era. For example, Sun argued that the earliest recoverable layer of Lev 17, namely vv 1–4, appears to presuppose a knowledge of Deut 12. Furthermore, the calendar preserved in chap. 23 appears to be younger than its priestly parallel in Num 28–29, but older than the calendars in Exod 23 and Deut 16. The laws pertaining to the sabbatical year and the year of Jubilee (chap. 25) reflect the laws of the fallow year in Exod 23 and those regarding the release of slaves in Deut 15. Others, giving evidence of a long and complicated composition history, may be of ancient origin, such as the earliest recoverable layers in chaps. 18–20. Nevertheless, Sun did not find any evidence to corroborate the possibility of an early origin for any of these texts.

After analyzing the compositional history of each unit, Sun concluded that the traditional Holiness Code had no existence prior to its present location as an independent legal corpus. The basis for this conclusion was threefold: the texts contained in the corpus appear to be of widely varying ages; no evidence of a compositional layer that went through the entire corpus was found; and some texts appear to have been composed with the intention of supplementing other material in the corpus (e.g, 22:1–16 vis-à-vis 21:16–23[24] and 22:26–33 vis-à-vis 22:17–25). In place of this hypothesis, Sun proposed that the compositional process that resulted in this corpus was one of literary supplementation over a long period of time, the earliest core of the corpus being contained in the old material found in chaps. 18–20.

The work of contemporary scholars has, therefore, cast great doubts on the existence of "a Holiness Code" as an independent, self-contained document. While blocks within this corpus stand close together—18–20, 21–22, 23 + 25—there is no unity among these various blocks. In addition, if this corpus be viewed as homogeneous, no explanation has been able to account for the presence of chaps. 17, 24, and 26. Neither has anyone yet demonstrated that there is a redactional layer that goes through the whole corpus. Therefore, it can be concluded that in whatever way this collection of speeches came together, they were assembled for their present position in Leviticus. These speeches continue to address the issue of ritual purity that is the main concern of chaps. 11–15, and they move on to address ethical relationships. These laws are, furthermore, in harmony with the high purpose of the sacrificial system, namely the goal of purging the Israelites from the harm and guilt caused by their sins in order that they might have communion with the holy God and live a holy life as Yahweh prescribed. These laws are designed thus to offer specific content to the call for his people to be holy as he is holy. The magnet holding all of these statutes together is the self-revelation of Yahweh.

As has been pointed out, many linguistic signs indicate that this material belongs with the priestly teaching. This connection means that the priestly writers were interested in ethical holiness as well as cultic holiness. In fact, a primary goal of cultic purity is to promote ethical purity. The practice of discipline in cultic purity prepares the human spirit for the ingraining of ethical integrity, for by obeying God's law in outward form, a person or a community molds the inner spirit into conformity with the holy God.

This section of Leviticus is a series of divine sermons, as von Rad and Reventlow have stressed. They are formulated for delivery and to motivate the congregation to live up to Yahweh's laws. Thus this material is composed for hearing, not for private reading, study, and analysis. This fact accounts for some of the literary unevenness found in the material. Such disjunctive material would not necessarily have troubled an ancient audience. Other breaks, lacunae, dislocations, and difficulties have arisen out of a complex matrix: the origin of these speeches, their transmission, their collection, and their final assembly. For example, since these instructions were compiled for oral delivery, the succession of preachers who delivered them used the opportunity of the spontaneous nature of an oral presentation to add comments, anecdotes, extraneous material, and exhortation into the speech, compelled by a desire to communicate with the audience. A clear example is the placing of the case of the half-breed blasphemer in 24:10–23 as the scaffolding for the presentation of laws on personal injury. This reconstruction seeks to account for how the material reached its final shape. While the core material goes back to Sinai, it has been augmented and updated in the context of the cult in order to keep the Word of God vital and contemporary in Israel's changing social milieu.

Whether there was a particular school or circle in Israel that preserved and produced documents that taught and exhorted the people to live a holy life is an open question. When and where this group existed will be debated for some time to come. If such a school existed, it had characteristics in common with both the priests and the deuteronomists. It was concerned with high moral living and with cultic purity. In trying to identify this group there will need to be some consensus on which passages outside chaps. 17–26, such as Lev 11, belong to its outlook.

These studies on the Holiness Code are intriguing and suggestive. They are most helpful in that they take every part of the text seriously in search of clues to how the final product was put together. This has resulted in a clearer and more precise exegesis of the material. Unfortunately the conclusions of the bulk of these studies are built mostly on speculations, rather than on hard data, by the very nature of the documents that have survived from antiquity. This is evident in the wide diversity of these conclusions. Nevertheless, these studies are valuable as they probe the various stages in the development of Israelite culture and cultic practices. They add substance to the skeleton of Israel's history. They offer the student a fuller, though tentative, picture of Israel's religious practice, its growth and development. The findings of these insights and postulations must, nevertheless, be held cautiously subject to adjustment in the light of further studies.

A. Laws about Sacrificing Domestic Animals and regarding Blood (17:1–16)

Bibliography

Aloni, J. "The Place of Worship and the Place of Sacrifice according to Leviticus 17:3–9" (Heb.). *Shnaton la-Mikra* 7 (1983) 21–49. **Brichto, H. C.** "On Slaughter and Sacrifice, Blood and Atonement." *HUCA* 47 (1976) 19–55. **Dewar, L.** "The Biblical Use of the Term 'Blood'." *JTS* 4 (1953) 204–8. **Füglister, N.** "Sühne durch Blut—Zur Bedeutung von Leviticus 17, 11." In *Studien zum Pentateuch.* Ed. G. Bravlik. FS W. Kornfeld. Wien: Herder, 1977. 143–64. **Grintz, J. M.** "'Do not eat on the blood.'" *ASTI* 8 (1972) 78–105. **Kiuchi, N.** *The Purification Offering in the Priestly Literature.* JSOTSup 56. Sheffield: JSOT Press, 1987. 101–9. **McCarthy, D.** "The Symbolism of Blood and Sacrifice." *JBL* 88 (1969) 166–76. ———. "Further Notes on the Symbolism of Blood and Sacrifice." *JBL* 92 (73) 205–10. **Metzinger, A.** "Die Substitutionstheorie und das alttestamentliche Opfer mit besonderer Berücksichtigung von Lev 17, 11." *Bib* 21 (1940) 159–87, 247–72, 353–77. **Milgrom, J.** "A Prolegomenon to Leviticus 17:11." *JBL* 90 (1971) 149–56 (=*SCTT* 96–103). **Morris, L.** "The Biblical Use of the Term 'Blood'." *JTS* n.s. 3 (1952) 216–27; *JTS* n.s. 6 (1955) 77–82. **Rodriguez, A. M.** *Substitution in the Hebrew Cultus.* Andrews University University Doctoral Dissertation Series 3. Berrien Springs, MI: Andrews UP, 1979. 233–60. **Sabourin, L.** "Nefesh, sang et expiation (Lv 17, 11, 14)." *ScEc* 18 (1966) 25–45. **Schenker, A.** "Das Zeichen des Blutes und die Gewissheit der Vergebung im Alten Testament: Die sühnende Function des Blutes auf dem Altar nach Lev 17.10–12." *MTZ* 34 (1983) 195–213. **Schwartz, B. J.** "The Prohibitions concerning the 'Eating' of Blood in Leviticus 17." In *Priesthood and Cult in Ancient Israel.* Ed. G. Anderson and S. Olyan. JSOTSup 125. Sheffield: JSOT, 1991. 34–66. **Snaith, N.** "The Meaning of שְׂעִירִים." *VT* 25 (1975) 115–18. ———. "The Verbs *zābah* and *šāḥaṭ*." *VT* 25 (1975) 242–46. **Steinmueller, J. E.** "Sacrificial Blood in the Bible." *Bib* 40 (1959) 56–67. **Stibbs, A. M.** *The Meaning of the Word 'Blood' in Scripture.* London: Tyndale Press, 1959.

Translation

1 Yahweh spoke to Moses: 2 "Speak to Aaron, his sons,[a] and all the Israelites[b] and say to them: This is the word which Yahweh has commanded: 3 Any[a] Israelite[bc] who sacrifices a bull, a sheep, or a goat within the camp or outside 4 instead of bringing it to the entrance of the Tent of Meeting[ab] to present[c] an offering to Yahweh before the tabernacle of Yahweh—that man is to be considered guilty of bloodshed.[d] He has shed blood, and that man[e] will be cut off from his people. 5 This is so the Israelites will bring the sacrifices which they have been sacrificing in the open field,[a] that is, that they bring[b] them to Yahweh to the entrance of the Tent of Meeting, to the priest, and they are to sacrifice them[c] as offerings of well-being to Yahweh. 6 The priest is to dash the blood on the altar[a] of Yahweh[b] at the entrance to the Tent of Meeting and burn the fat as a soothing aroma to Yahweh. 7 They shall no longer offer their sacrifices to the goat demons with whom[a] they prostitute themselves. This is a perpetual decree for them and for their generations.

8 "Say to them:[a] Any[b] Israelite or resident alien[c] living among them[d] who offers up[e] a whole offering or an offering of well-being[f] 9 and does not bring it to the entrance of the Tent of Meeting[a] to perform the ritual[b] before Yahweh, that man will be cut off from his people.

10 "If any[a] Israelite[b] or resident alien living among them[c] eats any blood,[d] I will set my face against that person who has eaten blood and cut him off from his people, 11 for the life of an animal resides in the blood.[ab] I[c] have assigned[d] it to you to make atonement for your lives[e] on the altar, because it is the blood[f] that makes atonement by the life. 12 Therefore, I say to the Israelites, 'None of you shall eat blood; also the resident alien living among you shall not eat blood.'[a]

13 "If any Israelite[a] or resident alien living among them[b] captures[c] game or fowl that it is lawful to eat, he is to pour out its[d] blood and cover it with earth, 14 because the life of every animal is its blood [it is its life[a]] Thus I say to the Israelites: 'You shall not eat the blood of any animal,[b] because the life of every animal is its blood; whoever eats[c] it will be cut off.'

15 "If anyone, either a native or a resident alien,[a] eats from an animal found dead or mauled, he is to wash[b] his clothes and bathe[b] in water, and he becomes unclean until evening; then he becomes clean.[c] 16 But if he does not wash (his clothes)[a] and bathe his body, he will bear his iniquity."

Notes

2.a. 11QpaleoLev omits ואל־בניו, "and to his sons." This is attributed to an error of haplography.

2.b. The same threefold number of those addressed by Moses occurs also in 21:24 and 22:18.

3.a. The repetition of the noun איש איש, "man, man," yields a distributive sense (GKC §123c); cf. 15:2; 18:6.

3.b. For MT מבית, "from the house of," some Heb mss, LXX, and Syr read מבני, "from the sons of," as in v 13. The divergence from v 2 supports MT.

3.c. LXX* adds *ἢ τῶν προσηλύτων τῶν προσκειμένων ἐν ὑμῖν*, "or the resident aliens living among you," as in vv 8, 10, 13, and 16:29. Many believe that the LXX preserves the original text, for the laws in chap. 17 occur in the same form with little variation. If so, it is best to read בתוכם, "in their midst," with Elliger (219) instead of בתוככם, "in your midst," as in vv 8, 10, 13. MT, nevertheless, is preferred as the shorter text.

4.a. Sam and LXX add לעשות אתו עלה או שלמים ליהוה לרצונכם לריח ניחח וישחטהו בחוץ ואל־פתח אהל מועד לא הביאו, "to present it as a whole offering or one of well-being to Yahweh for your acceptance as a soothing aroma, and he slaughters it outside, and he does not bring it to the entrance of the Tent of Meeting." Sun ("Investigation," 66–67) gives weight to this variant. He argues that the Vorlage to LXX, however, contained a dittography in this variant; he reconstructs the original to read לעשות אתו לעלה או שלמים ליהוה לרצון לריח ניחח, "to perform with it the ritual for a whole offering or an offering of well-being to Yahweh for acceptance as a soothing aroma." This variant is a witness to how this speech has grown throughout the centuries.

4.b. The prep phrase ואל פתח אהל מועד, "and to the entrance to the Tent of Meeting," stands first for emphasis.

4.c. Sam, a few LXX mss, *Tg. Neof.*, and Syr read a pronominal suffix on the inf להקריב, "to present."

4.d. דם, "blood," is a key term in this chapter. Here it is used as a metonymy to mean "guilty of bloodshed," i.e., a brutal murder. Such a crime received the severest penalty.

4.e. For MT האיש ההוא, "that man," LXX has ἡ ψυχὴ ἐκείνη, "that person," as in 22:3. And it goes on to read τοῦ λαοῦ αὐτῆς, "his people," since ψυχή, "soul, person," is fem.

5.a. פני השדה, "face of the field," means "an open field" in distinction to an area enclosed by city walls or a court.

5.b. This *waw* is the *waw apodosis,* which takes up the same verb למען אשר יביאו . . . והביאם, "in order that they bring . . . and that they bring them." LXX does not read the pronominal suffix on the second הביא.

5.c. The acc אתם, "them," receives emphasis, for it is far removed from the verb and ends the verse.

6.a. For MT על־מזבח, "on the altar," LXX has τὸ θυσιαστήριον κύκλῳ ἀπέναντι, "round about the altar before . . . "

6.b. Sam has אשר, "which."

7.a. The relative pronoun is resumed by the pronominal suffix on the prep אחריהם, "after them."

8.a. The prep phrase stands first for emphasis; cf. 20:2; 17:2aβ.

8.b. Cf. n. 3.a.

8.c. The term גר, "resident alien," occurs several times in chaps. 17–26: e.g., 17:8, 10, 12, 13; 20:2; 22:18. Frequently the phrase אשר יגור בתוכם, "who sojourns among you," appears with it. It is sometimes joined with אזרח, "citizen" (e.g., v 15), or with תושב, "inhabitant" (e.g., 25:23, 35). LXX adds τῶν υἱῶν, "the sons of," before הגר, "the resident alien."

8.d. Instead of the 3rd person pronominal suffix Sam, LXX, Syr, Tg^{mss}, *Tg. Ps.-J.*, and Vg read בתוככם, "in your midst." This variant may have arisen as a case of dittography.

8.e. Instead of MT יעלה, "he will offer up," Sam and LXX read יעשה, "he will do [the ritual of]," the same verb as used in v 9.

8.f. MT זבח means "a sacrifice"; it is an older term for an offering of well-being. Tg renders it by נכסת קודשא, the phrase it uses for an offering of well-being. The Tg, like this Eng trans., may be seeking to make its trans. clearer rather than being a witness to a different Heb text.

9.a. Cf. n. 4.b.

9.b. The Heb is simply לעשות, "to do," but the context indicates that it is elliptical for performing the entire ritual prescribed; cf. 9:16, 22; 14:19, 30; 16:9, 24.

10.a. Cf. n. 3.a.

10.b. Cf. n. 3.b.

10.c. Cf. n. 8.d.

10.d. A couple of Heb mss, Syr, and Vg omit דם, "blood."

11.a. With αἷμα αὐτοῦ = בדמו, LXX reads a pronominal suffix on דם.

11.b. The nominal clause introduced by כי, "because," stands first for emphasis.

11.c. The personal pronoun אני, "I," is used with the verb to underscore God's resolve.

11.d. נתן, lit. "give, put," with God as subject means "appoint, assign" (e.g., Num 8:19; 18:8, 9; Milgrom, *SCTT* 97 [*JBL* 90 (1971) 150]).

11.e. The term נפשתיכם, "your souls or yourselves," is translated "your lives" in order to render each occurrence of נפש in this verse by the same term.

11.f. The pronoun הוא makes this a nominal sentence and highlights הדם, "the blood," as subject (cf. GKC §135c).

12.a. In vv 10–12 Schenker (*MTZ* 34 [1983] 197–98) finds several chiastic patterns:

v 10	Prohibition				A
		v 11a	Reason	*α*	
v 11	Reason	v 11b	Instituted by Yahweh	*β*	B
		v 11c	Reason	*α*	
v 10	Repetition of prohibition				A

V 11, the center of the larger chiasm, has its own chiasm. The center and the point of emphasis is v 11b. Schenker finds a chiasm in the meaning of נפש, "life, person":

v 10	person
v 11a	life
v 11b	persons
v 11c	life
v 12	person

Furthermore, vv 10–12 stand at the center of the laws in chap. 17; the preceding two laws treat the slaughter of domesticated animals (vv 2–9) and the following two laws concern eating from animals that may not be sacrificed (vv 13–16).

13.a. Sam and *Tg. Ps.-J.* read מבית, "from the house of," for MT's מבני, "from the sons of"; cf. n. 3.a.

13.b. Some Sam mss and the versions read בתוככם, "among you"; cf. n. 8.d.

13.c. The sg verb indicates that the pl subj is to be interpreted distributively; i.e., each violator is to be so punished (GKC §145e).

13.d. Many LXX mss do not read the pronoun "its"; this may be a matter of the translator's preference.

14.a. It is not surprising that a Heb mss, LXX, Syr, and Vg do not read בנפשו, "by its soul." This may be a choice of translation because of the redundancy in the verse. Neither JB nor NEB render this term. Bertholet (60) takes the evidence from the versions to argue that this phrase was added later to bring this verse into conformity with v 11. About the only way to translate the phrase בנפשו, "in its life," is to take the prep ב as *beth essentiae* (so Keil and Delitzsch, 410). This sentence then corresponds to Deut 12:23, הדם הוא הנפש, "the blood is the life" (cf. Milgrom, *SCTT* 96 [*JBL* 90 (1971) 149]). However, in the discussion on v 11 in the section comment it is questioned whether such a ב exists. PIR (186) explains בנפשו הוא as a relative clause with the preceding דמו, "his blood," being the subject; they translate it "<as long as> it (i.e., the blood) is in its body." Since this phrase is most likely an insertion, it is bracketed in the trans. Cf. C. Gordon, "'In' of Predications or Equivalence," *JBL* 100 (1981) 612–13.

14.b. This construct chain, which is the dir obj, stands before the verb for emphasis.

14.c. Sam, LXX, Syr, Tg, and *Tg. Ps.-J.* have a sg participial form אכלו, "whoever eats it"; cf. 19:8; GKC §145l. PIR (186) interprets the MT as a distributive pl.

15.a. The prep ב on both nouns in opposition is the estimative *beth*, which establishes the range of an issue (*IBHS* §11.2.5e).

15.b. Though נפש, "person," a fem, is the antecedent of the masc verbs וכבס . . . ורחץ, "he is to wash . . . and to bathe," the grammar follows the sense rather than precise grammatical form (GKC §145a).

15.c. Sam omits וטהר, "and he becomes clean."

16.a. A Heb ms reads בגדיו, "his garments," in place of MT ובשרו, "and his body." LXX adds τὰ ἱμάτια, "the garments," as is frequently the idiom, e.g., Lev. 15:5, 6, 7, 8, etc. This Eng trans. adds these words for clarity. While the MT may be an error of haplography, the shorter reading is preferable. In fact, in v 15 the object is used with כבס, "wash," but not with רחץ, "bathe"; the obverse is the case in v 16. Therefore, this variation in supplying the dir obj of these verbs may be a planned literary style so that the obj is implied where it is not stated.

Form/Structure/Setting

The structure of this speech is as follows:

- I. Introductory formula (v 1)
- II. Speech proper (vv 2–16)
  - A. First speech (vv 2–7)
    - 1. Commission to speak (v 2a)
    - 2. First speech proper (vv 2b–7)
      - a. Superscription (v 2b)
      - b. Law concerning slaughter of sacrificial animals (vv 3–7a)
        - 1) Law against sacrificing away from the Tent of Meeting (vv 3–4)
          - a) Case (vv 3–4a)
          - b) Consequence (v 4b)

- 2) Reasons (vv 5–7a)
  - a) Grounded in basic standard of handling blood of a sacrifice (vv 5–6)
  - b) Designed to prevent sacrificing to evil spirits (v 7a)
- c. Subscription (v 7b)

B. Second speech (vv 8–16)
- 1. Brief commission to speak (v 8a*α*)
- 2. Second speech proper (vv 8a*β*–16)
  - a. Series of three laws (vv 8a*β*–14)
    - 1) Law concerning illegitimate sacrifice (vv 8a*β*–9)
      - a) Case (vv 8a*β*–9a)
      - b) Consequence (v 9b)
    - 2) Law against eating of blood (vv 10–12)
      - a) Primary law (v 10)
        - (1) Case (v 10a)
        - (2) Consequence (v 10b)
      - b) Reasons (vv 11–12)
        - (1) Primary reason (v 11)
        - (2) Supporting reason with two prohibitions (v 12)
          - (a) Introductory formula (v 12a*α*)
          - (b) Twofold prohibition against eating blood (v 12a*β*+b)
    - 3) Law concerning handling blood of wild animals (vv 13–14)
      - a) Law proper (v 13)
        - (1) Case (v 13a)
        - (2) Instruction for proper handling of blood (v 13b)
      - b) Reasons with a prohibition and a general law against eating blood with "cut-off" penalty (v 14)
  - b. Laws concerning eating meat from a dead animal (vv 15–16)
    - 1) Basic law (v 15)
      - a) Case (v 15a)
      - b) Instruction about restoration to a state of cleanliness (v 15b)
    - 2) Subsequent law on failing to pursue ritual cleansing (v 16)
      - a) Case (v 16a)
      - b) Consequence (v 16b)

The speech consists of two sections (vv 2–7 and 8–16), each headed by its own introduction. The introduction to the second unit is the briefest possible: אלהם תאמר, "you will say to them." Standing in the midst of the speech, it serves as a rhetorical device to call attention to the authority of the coming words. The theme of the first section is the presentation of all sacrifices on the altar to Yahweh, and the central issue of the second section is that blood may not be eaten.

The structural signals divide the chapter into two sections as the above outline indicates. But, as Sun observes ("Investigation," 83–87), the content divides the chapter into three sections: (1) on illegitimate sacrifice (vv 2–9), (2) on handling blood (vv 10–14), and (3) on eating from an animal's carcass (vv 15–16). Some tension exists, therefore, between the content and the structure. Which of these two forces should be followed? The similar formulation of the protasis of the laws in vv 8–14 and the similar compound subject—איש איש מבית (מבני) ישׂראל ומן הגר אשר יגור בתוכם, "every Israelite and every resident alien in their midst"—in the three laws found in vv 8–14 are additional signals, lending support to placing vv 8–9 with the following laws, not the preceding one. Thus the structural signals are followed.

Five laws constitute the scaffolding for this speech, and three reasons have been attached to this scaffold (vv 5–7, 11–12, 14). The case of the first four laws is formulated similarly: איש איש מן . . . אשר, "if any person . . ." (vv 3, 8, 10, 13). This legal form is often labeled apodictic, but contemporary study in ancient law brings that classification into question. In any case, these laws are universal in scope, applying to everyone living in Israel at all times. The consequence for the first four laws is the "cut-off" penalty, though in the fourth law it comes in the motivation; נכרת האיש ההוא מקרב עמו (מעמיו), "that person will be cut off from the midst of his people(s)" (vv 4b, 9b, 10bβ [הכרתי אתה מקרב עמה, "I [Yhwh] will cut him off from his people"]; 14bβ [יכרת, "one will be cut off"]). In the third law the consequence is stated more forcefully by being put in the divine first person. How to account for this variation, however, is not clear. It must have taken place when the motivation, which also uses the divine first person, was attached to the law. Since the use of the first person form is not consistent in this speech, it is very possible that the speaker who put the speech together found the shift to the first person in the source from which he took this third law and its supporting motivation. That the first person form has remained tells us that the rhetorical force of the direct address won out over the traditional third person legal form.

The case of the fifth law, though still universal in scope, has a different formulation. The case is a relative clause: וכל־נפש אשר, "any person who" (v 15). The compound phrase qualifying the subject, באזרח ובגר, "either a citizen or a resident alien," is in accord with the scope of the preceding three laws but employs a distinct phraseology. In place of the "cut-off" penalty stand instructions regarding ritual purity (v 15b). These factors indicate that this law had its home in a different corpus. Another distinctive about this law is that it is supported not by a reason but by a subordinate law that specifies the penalty for anyone who fails to abide by the instructions of the primary law. The severity of the penalty, of course, provides strong motivation for the preceding law. These directions regarding ritual purity in regard to eating are in the same arena as the purity laws in chap. 11 (cf. vv 32, 40). This fact indicates that this last law had its home in a corpus on ritual purity in regard to food. The sequence of terse sentences in these two laws points to an ancient origin. This unit became attached to this speech, because of the thematic tie with the preceding law, which addresses the issue of eating meat from non-sacrificial animals.

A puzzling aspect of this speech is the inclusion of both the first and second laws (vv 4–5 and vv 8–9), for their goal is so similar that to the modern mind they appear redundant. The variations in their formulations, though, indicate that while these laws are overlapping, they are not duplicates. They regulate a common issue from a different viewpoint. The first law prohibits the ritual slaughter of an animal as an offering of well-being away from the altar. Every such sacrifice is to be presented as קרבן ליהוה, "an offering to Yahweh." The goal of this law is to stop all ritual slaughter in the open country in order that no sacrifices be presented to the field spirits. The second law, on the other hand, directs that every kind of sacrifice be presented on the central altar. The vocabulary of the second law indicates that it is older than the preceding one: the general phrase לעשות, "to do," i.e., "to perform a sacrifice," is used instead of the technical liturgical phrase להקריב קרבן, "to present an offering" (cf. 1:2), and the merism עלה וזבח, "whole offering and sacrifice," i.e., "all sacrifices," refers to an offering of well-being simply by זבח, an archaic way (cf. chap. 3 for *Excursus* at the beginning of *Comment*). The much simpler formulation of this law supports this judgment. By contrast the first law is filled with technical terms found throughout the priestly legislation: שׁור או כשׂב או עז, "bull or sheep or goat" (7:23; 22:27; Num 18:17), במחנה, "in the camp" (Exod 32:17; Lev 24:10; Num 11:26, 27), מחוץ למחנה, "outside the camp" (e.g., Exod 29:14; Lev 4:12, 21; 6:4[11]; 8:17; 9:11; 16:27; 24:14, 23; Num 5:3, 44; 12:14, 15), להקריב קרבן, "to present an offering" (1:3, 14; 3:7, 14; 7:14; Num 6:14; 9:13; 15:4), משׁכן יהוה, "tabernacle of Yahweh" (singular here to Leviticus, but in Num 16:9; 17:28[13]; 19:13; 31:30 and in Chronicles, e.g., 1 Chr 16:39; cf. Cholewiński, *Heiligkeitsgesetz*, 24, n.), דם שׁפך, "he has shed blood" (Gen 9:6; cf. Num 35:33). Most of these technical terms, however, could have entered this law through a growth proccss, rather than being a part of its original formulation. The final form of this law conforms to the priestly style. The declaratory formula דם שׁפך, "he has shed blood," which is a sentence pronounced by a court, does suggest, however, that this law may have had its setting in the legal corpus of an ancient priestly court instead of the priestly professional knowledge. This original setting for this law may account for the growth process; i.e., technical terms became attached to the law in order to enable the court to apply it definitively to specific situations. An illustration of how this law was adapted to changing cultic situations may account for the inclusion of both phrases פתח אהל מועד, "the entrance of the Tent of Meeting," and לפני משׁכן יהוה, "before the tabernacle of Yahweh." The latter phrase was included to have the law apply to the Temple in the Kingdom period. This law then had a different origin from that of the other laws.

The consequence of the third law (v 10), which prohibits eating blood, has been recast from the impersonal third person to direct divine address stated twice—ונתתי פני ב, "I shall set my face against," and והכרתי, "I shall cut off"—in order to give it greater rhetorical force. The clue that it has been reworked is that the case is still in the third person singular (v 10a). The use of the divine first person is in harmony with the style of the holiness material, as the similar wording in 20:6b confirms (Kilian, *Literarkritische,* 18). The two reasons (vv 11 and 12) in support of this law both employ the divine first person, נתתי, "I have given," and אמרתי, "I have said." As shown in note 12.a., Schenker shows the various chiasms within vv 10–12, which add to the rhetorical power of the central portion of this speech. The multiple chiasms also indicate that these verses as they stand come from the speaker. That is, though the material was taken from the priestly professional knowledge, it was formulated for its present setting.

The fourth law (v 13) regulates the handling of blood from edible game. The issue about eating the meat of permissible game is a concern of the food laws in chap. 11. Though the case has been expanded somewhat, its straightforward and basic formulation points toward its being an ancient law. The anomaly, though, is that in place of the consequence are instructions for handling the blood (v 13b). Kilian thinks that the "cut-off" penalty in v 14bβ was originally the consequence of this law, but Sun ("Investigation," 103) is not persuaded. That the next law has an instruction in the position of the consequence supports accepting this law as it stands. These facts indicate that this law was taken from a different legal setting than were the preceding laws, i.e., a legal corpus concerning ritual purity in regard to food such as is found in chap. 11.

When these laws were assembled in this speech, reasons were added to encourage compliance with them. These motivations enhance greatly the speech's rhetorical quality. An elaborate motivation (vv 5–7) supports the first law. Like laws in general it is cast in the impersonal style of the third person plural. The use of the older way of referring to an offering of well-being simply by זבח, "sacrifice," in both vv 5a and 7a, offers a hint that an older formulated reason has been expanded and made more definitive with the inclusion of technical priestly terms such as זבחי שלמים, "sacrifices of well-being," along with v 6, which was taken from a liturgical regulation (cf. 3:2b, 5). The repetition within this motivation supports this position. The occurrence of והבאם ליהוה, "that they may bring them to Yahweh," picks up the initial יביאו, "they bring," and moves it to completion; the verb has been repeated to bear the weight of the additions. The inclusion of אל הכהן, "to the priest," after אל פתח אהל מועד, "to the entrance of the Tent of Meeting," is redundant, but it has been included, possibly by a later hand, to underscore the need for a priest to be on duty to officiate at the making of a sacrifice. This inclusion drew the liturgical instruction in v 6 about the priest's זרק, "dashing," blood on the altar; then הקטיר החלב, "burning the fat," became attached (cf. Cholewiński, *Heiligkeitsgesetz*, 20–21). In v 6a פתח אהל מועד, "the entrance of the Tent of Meeting," has been inserted after מזבח יהוה, "the altar of Yahweh," even though the two phrases together overburden the line, in order to make a specific tie with the law (v 4a*α*) and to make sure that the main altar is meant by the phrase פתח אהל מועד, "at the entrance of the Tent of Meeting." (For a very interesting traditio-historical possibility on this phrase, see Cholewiński, *Heiligkeitsgesetz*, 24–26.) The fact that מזבח יהוה is a rare phrase in the sacrificial legislation is evidence that it is the original phrase. In v 7b לדרתם, "to their generations," has been added to reinforce the phrase חקת עולם, "a perpetual decree." In the employment of technical cultic terms and repetitions, this motivation is in accord with the preceding law. That is, the repetitions indicate that terms have been added to contemporize the motivation. But a different vocabulary from that law points to its having a different origin, i.e., בני ישראל, "Israelites," in place of בית ישראל, "the house of Israel," זבח, "sacrifice," in place of שחט, "slaughter," זבח, "a sacrifice," instead of קרבן, "offering," and על פני השדה, "on the open field," in place of מחוץ למחנה, "outside the camp" (Elliger, 222).

Vv 11 and 12 provide several reasons in support of the preceding law. V 11 opens with a nominal sentence, moves to a prohibition introduced with a divine speech formula אני נתתי לכם—"I have assigned it for you"—and concludes with a complex nominal sentence similar to the opening one. The use of the divine first person confronts the bearers with a word from Yahweh. The interplay of the terms נפש, "life" (3x), דם, "blood" (3x), and כפר, "expiate" (2x), creates great rhetorical force. V 12 gives additional motivation to observing the law in v 10 with two prohibitions against eating blood. These prohibitions are vigorously introduced by the divine speech formula על־כן אמרתי לבני ישראל, "therefore, I say to the Israelites." This rhetorical style carries the imprint of the ancient speaker.

The reason (v 14) in support of the law in v 13 is formulated similarly to the motivations in vv 11–12. It has two parts. In both parts there is a nominal statement about the essence of blood followed by a law; the first law is a prohibition, and the second is a universal (apodictic) command. The first reason is underscored with a divine first person introduction. The universal law carries the "cut-off" penalty, which is at home in this speech. The many parts of this complex motivation are connected by the interplay of three terms: נפש, "life" (3x), כל־בשר, "all flesh" (3x), and דם, "blood" (3x). Besides providing a motivation for the preceding law, this reason ties that law more tightly into this setting.

The lack of a reason being attached to the second law (vv 8–9) may be accounted for on the basis that the speaker considered this law to be virtually a restatement of the first law (vv 3–4). If that is correct, the reasons given in vv 5–7 then apply to that law also in its present setting.

From this description it is very clear that this speech is a complex mixture of materials. Its diverse nature has led to numerous reconstructions of how it came together. Kilian (*Literarkritische,* 8–16) and Feucht (*Untersuchungen,* 30–31) accept the first four laws as the kernel of this speech. Kilian (16–17) finds that the first expansion was the pre-priestly portion of vv 5–7, an interpretation of the preceding law. Then the speech went through two priestly redactions (17–20). In the first one the laws were expanded to cover the גר, "resident alien." In the second the editor included parenetic material (vv 10, 11, 12, 14) designed in the style of the holiness material. Elliger (224), however, assigns to the base layer the middle three laws; to them was added the law in vv 3–4 (similarly Cholewiński, *Heiligkeitsgesetz,* 17–18); for him vv 15–16 are an appendix. Sun ("Investigation," 95–106) argues that vv 1–4 were an original priestly composition to which the reasons in vv 5–7 were added. The speech continued to grow in stages over time. At each stage one of the following laws with its reason was added in the order in which they appear. The variety of these scholarly judgments indicates that there are not sufficient clues in the text to provide any certainty for a detailed reconstruction of the composition history of this speech.

A few conjectures, nevertheless, may be set forth. The speaker took the first law from the priestly court material and the next four from the priestly professional knowledge, the first two from the section on making sacrifices and the last two from the section on ritual purity in regards to food. To make up the speech, he composed reasons for some of the laws; he may have been led in this direction by finding one or more of the laws like the law in v 10 already supported by a motivation. For his reasons, he drew on the priestly tradition. Some later additions filled out the reasons. Whether the speaker was responsible for the divine first person is difficult to tell given its inconsistent usage. The fifth law was probably taken from the priestly professional knowledge and appended to this speech by another hand. In any case, it is evident that the thread uniting all these laws and their attendant reasons is the issue of eating blood; דם, "blood," occurs in vv 4 (2x), 6, 10 (2x), 11 (2x), 12 (2x), 13, 14 (3x). The central three laws and their reasons are further bound together by the term נפש, "life, soul," which also occurs in v 15.

While the present speech appears choppy to a modern reader, it needs to be remembered that this speech was composed for proclamation to the community assembled at the central sanctuary for instruction and for exhortation. An excellent speaker can overcome this unevenness as he delivers the speech to teach, warn, and exhort the people in their worship of Yahweh. The rhetorical force of this speech is enhanced by taking the audience back to the time of their origin at Sinai as a covenant people through the use of archaic wording, e.g., פתח אהל מועד, "the entrance to the Tent of Meeting," and יעלה עלה או־זבח, "one who is offering up a whole offering or a sacrifice" (cf. Reventlow, *Heiligkeitsgesetz,* 50–52). This style thus places in tension laws phrased for the desert setting, such as the first one (vv 3–4), and guidance for a settled community, such as the motivation in vv 5–7. The use of the divine first person and direct address, besides giving an immediacy to these words, recaptures the picture of Yahweh's speaking to his people through Moses. This tension witnesses to the dynamic character of Israel's faith. At the hearing of the ancient laws, contemporary Israel was called to obedience just as ancient Israel had been. Although the outward form of that obedience changed over time, as the inclusion of terms and phrases to contemporize the laws shows, the basic principles endured. The ancient word made contemporary carried the same authority as its original delivery, for the design of the inclusions was to have the law apply to current practice and understanding. That is, making the law contemporary did not seek to break with the past; rather it sought to promote obedience to the ancient laws in the present. The common bond between the past giving of the word and the present hearing of the word is the worship of Yahweh, who revealed himself at Sinai.

Despite many scholars who hold that for the most part the material is late, this speech contains a basic tradition that goes back to the time of the wilderness, as Reventlow (*Heiligkeitsgesetz,* 34, 40–41, 50) and Kilian (*Literarkritische,* 12–13) hold.

Comment

1–2 דבר . . . ואמרת, "speak . . . and say"; this full introductory formula with a double command signals a new section (cf. 15:1). The threefold indirect object of דבר, "speak," namely Aaron, his sons, and all the Israelites, means that this material applies to both priests and laity. Furthermore, it indicates that this is the opening of a major section of the book. The enumeration of those addressed is required since the preceding speech (chap. 16) is addressed primarily to Aaron. This threefold audience occurs elsewhere in 21:24 and 22:18. The primary audience of the laws found in chaps. 17–26, nevertheless, is the people, for these laws treat issues that Yahweh desires the people to know both for direction in their own living and for understanding the obligations placed on the priests in daily living. Aaron and his sons may have been included to stress their role in teaching the people these laws.

3 The opening regulation addresses the שׁחט, "slaughter," of domesticated animals, namely שׁור, "a bull," כשׂב, "a sheep," or עז, "a goat" (cf. 22:27), anywhere, either במחנה, "in the camp," or in the countryside, מחוץ למחנה, (lit.) "outside the camp," for only these animals are permissible as sacrifices (cf. 1:2). Observance of this law insures that the blood of all sacrificial animals is disposed of properly and guarantees that both God and the priests receive their proper portion of the slaughtered animal.

The interpretation of this law, nevertheless, is complicated because the word שׁחט, "slaughter," has both a popular meaning for ordinary slaughtering of an animal (e.g., as Gen 37:31) and a restricted cultic meaning for the ritual slaughter of an animal (cf. 1:5). The big question then is whether שׁחט is used broadly or restrictively. That is, does this law require that every domesticated animal be slaughtered at the altar of the central sanctuary, or does it only require that every ritual sacrifice be performed there?

This question has been widely debated. A broad understanding of שחט holds that this law prohibits all profane slaughter (e.g., Wellhausen School). This widely held interpretation understands that in Israel every slaughter of a domesticated animal was considered to be a sacrifice. If this view is accurate, this law requires that the slaughter of every domesticated animal be done at the altar before the Tent of Meeting. Such a stringent requirement would have been impractical for Israel save in two brief periods of her history, i.e., during the wilderness journey and immediately after the return from Babylon. Only in these two periods did the bulk of the population live in close enough proximity to the central altar to Yahweh to keep this standard.

Some conservatives, accepting the broad meaning of שחט, "slaughter," take the position that this law applied only to the wilderness period. In that setting the proximity of the people to the altar along with the infrequency of families' being able to make a sacrifice, given the poverty of the people at that time, enabled strict compliance with this law. Later when the people settled the promised land, this strict standard was abrogated by the laws of Deut 12:15–16, 20–27 (cf. Keil and Delitzsch, 409; Kaufmann, *The Religion of Israel,* 180ff; Segal, *The Pentateuch,* 52; Harrison, 179; Wenham, 241). This position, however, faces a major obstacle. The supporting reason in v 7 states that the law is חקת עלם, "a perpetual decree," לדרתם, "to coming generations" (v 7b). While it might be argued that this statement applies only to the prohibition against sacrificing goats to demons (v 7a; Keil and Delitzsch, 409), it is structurally defensible that v 7b applies to vv 3–7a (cf. *Form/Structure/Setting*). Thus there is no internal evidence that this law was designed only for the time of Israel's sojourn in the wilderness. A variation of this position is proposed by B. J. Bamberger (179). He speculates that this law arose in the early days of the post-exilic community in order to discourage pagan customs of the people who remained in the land during the exile. When the population grew and then spread out, the practice of Deuteronomy was restored. Unfortunately, there is not sufficient evidence to evaluate this creative proposal.

Most critical scholars find that the only setting in which such a decree could have been implemented was the small post-exilic community settled around Jerusalem just after the return from exile. This view also faces major difficulties. If this law arose at that time, it would have been applicable for only a short span of time in Israel's history, the few years after the return from exile. Even during the post-exilic period the implementation of this decree would have placed severe hardship on pockets of Israelites scattered throughout Palestine who looked to the Temple as their worship center, the very people the small struggling community at Jerusalem needed for moral and financial support in their adventure to rebuild the capital city. The Jewish population scattered throughout the land could hardly bring all their animals to Jerusalem for slaughter. Moreover, it is reasonable to suppose that the visionary hope of an Israel restored to full splendor as portrayed in various prophets around the time of the exile and afterwards would have militated against that small, hopeful community's formulating such a stringent standard. The early post-exilic era thus does not offer fertile soil for the origin of this decree.

Given these obstacles to the two dominant views, we need to look for another possible interpretation. It is possible that this law addresses only the slaughter of consecrated animals as offerings of well-being (Rashi, 78). While the tone of the context suggests that it covers all slaughter as sacrifice, the view that the verb שׁחט has a restricted sense, i.e., referring to ritual slaughter, has the support of many Jewish scholars like Rabbis Akiba and Sipra. Snaith (*VT* 25 [1975] 243–44) points out that שׁחט is normally used in priestly material for legitimate, sacred slaughter, and Levine (113) accepts the restricted meaning based on the argument that שׁחט has a narrower meaning in sacrificial texts. Milgrom argues that שׁחט technically means "cut the throat" ("Ethics and Ritual," 173). In this light, then, this law specifically requires that all sacrificial slaughtering be done at an official altar (Noordtzij, 174–75). This interpretation finds that this law is in accord with the law in Deut 12:15–16. Whereas the wording of Deut 12:15–16 permits profane slaughter away from the altar, this law and the following one state the obverse, stressing that an animal intended for an offering of well-being has to be slaughtered at the altar. This law, therefore, does not address the issue of the ordinary slaughtering of domesticated animals. In support of this position is the requirement that only animals without defect could be presented at the altar (1:3; 3:1, 6). If this law dealt with the slaughter of all edible domesticated animals, there would need to be further laws on what to do with edible animals having a defect, for such animals were a significant percentage of a herd. Such laws would be similar to the exceptions provided in the laws on the sacrifice of all firstlings in Deut 15:19–23. Any such qualifying regulations are glaringly absent. Furthermore, the wording in v 4 strongly favors the interpretation that this law concerns a consecrated animal, not any animal from the flock, for it specifically speaks about "an offering to Yahweh" (קרבן ליהוה; cf. 1:2) that is presented (הקריב), i.e., offered according to ritual standards. Such language does not apply to profane slaughter. The motivation supporting this law in v 5 has the same viewpoint, for it speaks of eliminating the sacrificing (זבחים) of animals in the open field. The use of זבח, "sacrifice," in this motivation refers to official sacrifices.

This law then addresses the presentation of offerings of well-being, stipulating that any such offering must be presented at an altar consecrated to Yahweh. The close tie between slaughter and sacrifice in the ancient mind made this regulation necessary. Yahweh wished to make sure that the profane slaughter of clean animals without defect in an open field was not turned into a sacrificial ritual, for such practice would be prone to becoming polluted with pagan customs, such as believing that these quasi sacrifices placated the spirits of the field. The tendency to follow syncretic practice would have been greater in the absence of any priest to officiate. Yahweh definitely wished to prevent the people from thinking that they were making a legitimate sacrifice any time they slaughtered an animal at any place other than a consecrated altar.

This interpretation receives some support from the law in vv 8–9. That law states that when the people עלה, "offer up," whole offerings or sacrifices, they must perform the sacrificial ritual at the entrance to the Tent of Meeting. Thus the most normative understanding of vv 3–4 is that the slaughter of any clean domesticated animal as an offering of well-being had to be done at a consecrated altar.

4 קרבן is a general term for the various offerings (cf. 1:2). The Tent of Meeting (אהל מועד) is identified with the tabernacle of Yahweh (משכן יהוה; cf. 1:1; 8:10). The latter phrase signals that Yahweh himself is present in the tabernacle as ruler of his people. The case concerns a person who slaughters a domesticated animal as a sacrifice away from the altar of the sanctuary. Because that animal has been slaughtered away from the altar, its blood, which effects expiation, has not been cast on the altar. The casual pouring out of blood is viewed as blood shed in vain. Such an act is declared דם שפך, "he has poured out blood." This declaratory formula elsewhere stands for killing a human; it suggests a verdict pronounced by a court. The use of the verb חשב, "consider, reckon," indicates that a court, perhaps a cultic judicial body, pronounces the sentence (Elliger, 226). This language conveys the seriousness of this cultic offense. The penalty for such a violation is that the person is נכרת, "cut off," from the people. In 7:20 this opaque phrase is taken to mean that the person either loses his inheritance rights and access to the sanctuary or he is banished. The passive form means that God himself executes the judgment. Misappropriation of the means of expiation receives such a grave penalty, for a person abuses the only means of finding forgiveness from the holy God.

5 A major purpose of this law is to stop the random sacrificing of animals without regard to place. It covers זבחים, "sacrifices," especially private ones. The use of זבח is an archaic way of referring to זבחי שלמים, "offerings of well-being" (cf. *Excursus* in chap. 3), which is used in the last sentence of this verse. In this type of sacrifice the blood is dashed against the altar, the fat and the entrails are burned on the altar, the breast and the right thigh become the priest's, and the rest of the meat is returned to the one who had brought the sacrifice for use in a festive meal (cf. chap. 3). This type of sacrifice was the one most frequently offered by a family or clan. Because it was a less formal type, people would more readily be inclined to offer it away from the altar before the Tent of Meeting.

6 The reason for slaughtering the animals at the Tent of Meeting is reiterated. It is so that the priest may זרק, "dash" or "throw" (cf. 1:5), the blood against the altar and הקטיר, "burn," the fat as ריח ניחח ליהוה, "a soothing aroma to Yahweh" (cf. 1:9). The altar is specifically identified as מזבח יהוה, "the altar of Yahweh." Only here in the sacrificial legislation is the altar specifically identified as Yahweh's in order to eliminate all private altars. Further, this phrase communicates that in his grace God has provided this piece of furniture as a place for his sinful people to serve him.

7 A major motivation for this legislation is to prevent the Israelites from sacrificing to demons. The demons are referred to by the term שעירם, "he-goats," i.e., demons who were thought to appear in the form of goats; Snaith (*VT* 25 [1975] 115–18), however, identifies שעירם as fertility deities, but his position is unconvincing. In Isa 13:21 and 34:14 these satyrs inhabit open fields, ruins, and desolate places. Possibly Jeroboam I even had במות, "high places," constructed for such demons (2 Chr 11:15). The practice of this kind of worship is also attested at the time of Josiah, for in his reform he had the high places to goat demons smashed (this position is based on reading השערים, "goats, demons," for MT השערים, "gates" [2 Kgs 23:8]). The worship of such spirits was a tyrannical force, binding the people in the chains of fear and superstitions. These laws were designed to guard the Israelites from becoming enslaved by such evil practices. The powerful lure of this illicit worship is expressed by the phrase זנים אחריהם, "prostituting themselves" or "playing the harlot," with these demons. זנה, "prostitute," conveys the nuance that following such practices tarnishes the people's love for Yahweh. Their worshiping other gods is an act of infidelity like that of an adulteress (cf. 20:5, 6; Exod 34:15, 16; Judg 2:17; 8:27, 33). This metaphor loudly proclaims the exclusive claims of Yahwistic faith. One reason this metaphor became associated with false worship is that many of the pagan shrines involved fertility worship. This language also communicates that the people have to bear shame for their wandering affection. Several prophets employed this vivid metaphor freely in their accusation against the covenant people for forsaking Yahweh, their God (e.g., Hos 1–4, 9; Jer 2, 3; Ezek 16, 23; cf. B. Wiklander, "זָנָה *zānāh*," *TDOT* 4:101–2).

This statute is enduring for the coming generations, as the two phrases חקת עולם, "a perpetual decree," and לדרתם, "to their generations," convey. Does the phrase "a perpetual decree" apply to the immediately preceding regulation or to the laws in this section (vv 3–7)? The structural analysis favors taking it as a subscript of this section; thus it applies to the entire section.

8–9 The brief introductory speech formula stresses that the following laws are for the people. The first law has the same general intent as the law in vv 3–4. It is included in this speech for emphasis and to extend the preceding law in two directions: to other sacrifices and to aliens. The two terms עלה, "whole offering," and זבח, "sacrifice," are a merism, i.e., two diverse terms employed to cover all sacrifices, for עלה is the principal official public sacrifice (cf. Num 28:3–8) and זבח is usually a private sacrifice (cf. *Excursus* on offering of well–being in chap. 3). The עלה, "whole offering," receives some emphasis in that the verb chosen for sacrificing is עלה, "to offer up." This emphasis is given because the preceding law focuses on offerings of well-being; this one includes all the other sacrifices. This law specifically states that it applies both to בני ישׂראל, "Israelites," and to הגר אשׁר־גור בתוכם, "the resident alien being among you." Since the resident alien is part of the community, he has to respect the basic laws pertaining to the cult. He is to observe the Sabbath (Exod 20:10) and the Day of Atonement (Lev 16:29). An alien is never to misspeak the name of Yahweh (Lev 24:16) or to offer a child to Molek (Lev 20:2). Moreover, this law hinders a resident alien from producing and spreading pagan worship in the land by his own sacrificial practices.

10 Throughout the ancient world it was a common practice to consume animal blood in a variety of forms. This practice is strictly forbidden in Israel, for both the Israelite and the resident alien (cf. 3:17; 7:26–27; 19:26; Gen 9:4; Deut 12:16, 23; 15:23; 1 Sam 14:32–34). כל, "all," before דם means any form in which the blood might be consumed, e.g., as a food itself or in the meat (cf. Elliger, 227). This law certainly excludes the eating of any meat that has not had the blood fully drained from it. The penalty for violating this law, being cut off from the community, is strongly underscored, for it is stated twice and in the divine first person (cf. v 4). For the first person usage see 20:6.

11 This verse sets forth both an essential reason and a theological reason for the severity of the penalty for eating blood (v 10). Because this is the only text in the OT that comes close to giving a reason why blood effects atonement, there is great interest in uncovering its meaning.

The theological reason is that God himself has bestowed this power on blood. The introductory words ואני נתתיו לכם, "I have assigned it to you," are forceful, introducing a definitive statement. Milgrom (*SCTT,* 97) demonstrates that נתן, (lit.) "give," with God as subject in the priestly legislation means "bestow, give, assign" (e.g., 6:10[17]; 7:34; 10:17; Num 8:19; 18:8, 19). That is, blood in itself does not effect expiation, only blood from an animal sacrificed before Yahweh according to certain prescribed rituals. Moreover, this verse does not say that there are no other ways for expiation to take place, for other texts assign expiating force to various sacrifices and procedures: a vegetable offering (5:11–12), the oil rite for a person who has recovered from a grievous skin disease (14:15–18), the payment of a coin (Exod 30:15–16), the intercession of Moses (Exod 32:30), and God himself (Pss 65:4[3]; 78:38; 79:9). Nevertheless, the handling of blood from a ritually sacrificed animal is the primary means of expiation given by God to his people. By making this connection Yahweh has graciously given his people a visible way to find forgiveness of their sins (cf. Schenker, *MTZ* 34 [1983] 201). The required manipulation of blood teaches that guilt is not automatically removed; it can be removed only by the participation of the guilty person in the way prescribed by Yahweh. In fact, in rabbinic thought blood came to be the only means of atonement (*b. Yoma* 5a; cf. *b. Zebaḥ.* 6a; *b. Menaḥ.* 93b). This position is stated in Heb 9:22.

The essential reason is found in the statement נפש כל־בשר דמו, "the blood is every animal's life force" (v 14a*α*; cf. Gese, *Essays on Biblical Theology,* 107). נפש has a wide range of usage in Heb., i.e., "throat, neck, desire, soul, person, self, life" (H. W. Wolff, *Anthropology of the OT,* 11–25). Here נפש means "life" as in some other texts; e.g., 24:17—"whoever kills the life [נפש] of a man shall be put to death"—and Prov 19:8a—"whoever gets wisdom loves his life [נפש]" (cf. Wolff, 18–20). Hebraic anthropology locates a person's life both in the breath (Gen 2:7) and in the blood. When a person ceases to breathe, he dies. Breath, being invisible and intangible, symbolizes the fleeting, mysterious aspect of human existence. Blood, on the other hand, is tangible. The ancients observed that as an animal loses its blood, its strength wanes, and with the continued loss of blood it dies. Therefore, blood serves as the tangible center of an animal's life force. In the words of von Rad, "It is not the blood in itself that effects expiation, but the blood in so far as the life is contained in it" (*Old Testament Theology,* 1:270). Blood also symbolizes a life given up in death. Both of these meanings of blood are present in this text. As for the phrase כל־בשר, (lit.) "all flesh," it includes every animal. בשר, "flesh," expresses the bond between humankind and animals (cf. Gen 6:12, 13, 17, 19; 7:15, 16, 21). In addition, the choice of בשר, which means "meat" as well as "flesh," keeps the passage focused on the issue of eating meat with the blood in it.

The crux for discerning the essential reason that blood effects expiation comes in the last sentence of this verse, which reads כי־הדם הוא בנפש יכפר, (lit.) "for it is the blood which makes expiation by the life" (cf. Deut 12:23; Gen 9:4). The phrase בנפש, (lit.) "in/by life or soul," has stimulated a variety of interpretations based on the use of the preposition ב. The ב may be the *beth essentiae* or the *beth* of equivalence. This sentence then is translated: "For it is the blood, i.e., as life force, that expiates" (Milgrom, *SCTT,* 96; NEB). In v 14b*α* it is expressly stated that כי נפש כל־בשר דמו בנפשו הוא, "the life of every animal is its blood." The use of the prepositional phrase בנפש in this sentence is, unfortunately, so obscure that it does not help the exegesis of the preposition ב in v 11. In fact, בנפש may have found its way into v 14b*α* from the influence of v 11.

Working with this meaning of the preposition ב, Milgrom proposes a creative interpretation for this verse. He holds that this reason gives additional support to the law in v 10 against eating meat with blood in it; this law, therefore, applies exclusively to offerings of well-being (זבח שלמים), since this was the only kind of offering from which an Israelite was permitted to eat meat. In support of this position, Milgrom points out that the first law of this speech condemns the improper handling of an animal's blood as "manslaughter" (vv 3–4). These facts lead Milgrom to conclude that the proper handling of the blood of an animal sacrificed as an offering of well-being at the altar expiated the lay presenter from the guilt of manslaughter for having slain that animal (*SCTT,* 101–3). The value of Milgrom's exegesis is that it carefully considers every phrase in this verse. He correctly notes that the intent of the biblical author is not to present a theory of expiation by blood. If such were the case, that author would have placed this verse close to the front of the sacrificial regulations. A significant problem with Milgrom's position, though, is that it attributes expiating force to an offering of well-being, which does not have that force in the regulation for it (chap. 3) nor in any other passage. Recognizing this difficulty, Milgrom counters by claiming that the blood of an offering of well-being does not expiate a specific sin, but only the responsibility incurred for slaughtering the animal. But in that vv 10–11 are concerned with eating blood of a legitimate sacrifice, no sin, above all not manslaughter, has been committed in the legitimate slaughter of an animal (Kiuchi, *Purification Offering,* 102–3). Milgrom's position has another major difficulty if the interpretation of v 11 as a general principle applicable to sacrifices in general is valid. This broader view finds support both in the general language of the law and in the context. The preceding law (vv 8–9) concerns all sacrifices because it uses the merism עלה, "whole offering," and זבח, "sacrifice (of well-being)," to include every kind of sacrifice (Schenker, *MTZ* 34 [1983] 209–10; cf. 7:26–27; Deut 12:25–27). In addition, the fact that the following laws go on to the issue of eating from non-sacrificial animals indicates that the handling of blood in vv 10–12 is a general concern, not just a concern with offerings of well-being (cf. Füglister, "Sühne," 147). Another difficulty with this position comes with exegeting the ב as the *beth essentiae* (cf. GKC §119i), for the existence of such a usage of the preposition ב is very questionable, as Brichto (*HUCA* 47 [1976] 26–27) points out. Finally, there is Schenker's argument (*MTZ* 34 [1983] 209) that since blood cannot be separated from the life, a sacrificed animal's blood cannot serve as payment for its own life which has been taken.

An interpretation similar to Milgrom's comes from Brichto (*HUCA* 47 [1976] 28). He bases his interpretation, however, on taking the meaning of כפר to be "serve as כֹּפֶר 'ransom.'" V 11 thus means that the blood of the slain animal serves as כפר, "compensatory payment," in exchange for that life that was taken. According to this interpretation, the taking of an animal's life is a right granted by God, the creator of life, and can only be done in acknowledgment of him. Schenker (*MTZ* 34 [1983] 207–9) rejects this interpretation with five reasons: (1) the preposition ב with כפר gives the instrument of, not the price of, expiation; (2) blood and life may not be separated according to v 11c as Brichto's position requires; (3) if God required a compensatory payment for slaughtering an animal, this demand would also be needed for wild animals, but vv 13–14 do not make this stipulation; (4) this position requires that the three uses of נפש have three distinct meanings: "life-essence," lives of Israelites, life of the slain animal, respectively, but the same word is used to note commonality; (5) as with Milgrom's interpretation, Brichto's explanation applies only to offerings of well-being, but the location of the verse, as argued above, requires that it apply to all sacrifices.

Another way of interpreting בנפש understands the ב to be the *beth pretii,* i.e., giving the cost of expiation; expiation then is achieved by the payment of דם,

"blood." The sacrificial animal's blood is the ransom required to free the life of the person who has presented the sacrifice. This position echoes the principle of *lex talionis*, נפש תחת נפש, "life for life" (24:20). In Deut 19:21 the preposition ב is used in this principle instead of the preposition תחת, "in place of." Working with this exegesis of ב, some have claimed that this verse offers a substitutionary theory of atonement. This theory normally requires that the sacrificial animal bear the presenter's sin, but the nature of the Levitical sacrificial rituals does not support this requirement. As argued in 1:4 a person's sin is not transferred to the sacrificial animal since it is inconceivable that the flesh of an animal made unclean by their sins would be burned on the altar (cf. Füglister, "Sühne," 146–47). That is, if the sacrificed animal took on the offerer's sins, no part of it could have been placed on the altar; rather it would have had to be destroyed outside the camp as was the case on the Day of Atonement with the sin-laden goat which, because it carried the congregation's sins, had to be sent into the wilderness (16:20–22). These points rule against resting an elaborate (penal) substitution theory of atonement on the pillar of this prepositional phrase.

In another position Füglister ("Sühne," 145–46) argues that ב is the *beth instrumenti*, i.e., stating the means or the basis by which expiation is achieved. The advantage of this exegesis is that it interprets the use of the preposition ב in line with the majority of other occurrences of כפר ב (Exod 29:33; Lev 5:16; 7:7; 19:22; Num 5:8; "Sühne," 147). Füglister (147) then argues that blood has expiating power because it is an animal's life-force, not because it symbolizes the animal's death. This position needs to be tempered with the realization that the blood manipulated at the altar is blood taken from an animal in its death; thus it also represents life surrendered in death (cf. L. Morris, *JTS* n.s. 6 [1955] 82; Kiuchi, *Purification Offering*, 108–9). In any case, blood has cleansing power (e.g., 16:16, 30) because it carries an animal's life-force. By purifying the altar or other cultic furniture polluted by uncleanness released by the presenter's sin, blood restores its efficacy and grants renewal to the one offering the sacrifice (cf. 20:3; 15:31; Füglister, "Sühne," 155–56).

There is yet another important element in how blood effects atonement. This understanding rests on interpreting the play on נפש, "soul, life, person," in this verse, not on the exegetical force of the prepositional phrase בנפש, "by a life" (cf. Kiuchi, *Purification Offering*, 106). נפש occurs three times: the first usage is general for all life, animal and human; the second refers to human lives; and the third refers to the slain animal's life. This play on נפש is central to the meaning of this verse both because a threefold repetition carries emphasis in Hebrew and because the grammar has been stretched to make this word play. Furthermore, this interchange in the meanings of נפש would have little significance unless the animal's life had some essential correspondence to the supplicant's life. When a person comes under the threat of being estranged from Yahweh on account of a sin, that person (נפש) presents to Yahweh a gift, an animal's life (נפש). Since the animal's life has a value analogous to that of the supplicant's own life, Yahweh accepts the sacrifice as the basis for maintaining the divine-human relationship. The words of Gese (*Essays on Biblical Theology*, 107–8) are insightful:

> The decisive factor for the cultic act of atonement is that this sacrifice of life is not a mere killing, a sending of life into nothingness, but it is a surrender of life to what is holy, and at the same time an incorporation into the holy, given expression throughout

> contact with blood. By means of the atoning rites in which blood is applied, the *nephesh* is dedicated to and 'incorporated into' the holy.

Yahweh accepts that surrendered life as a basis for offering forgiveness to the supplicant. Forgiveness frees one from the burden and shame of a transgression in order to live in confidence before God. In other words, the offering of a sacrificed animal according to the prescribed ritual establishes the judicial basis for Yahweh to grant the presenter forgiveness. Kiuchi (*Purification Offering,* 108) communicates this idea a little differently. For him, instead of the animal dying in place of its presenter as held by the usual explanation of substitutionary atonement, the sacrifice dissolves the sin-death nexus (see table from Kiuchi, 108, italics mine):

Sin/Uncleanness ⟶ *Sacrifice* Death

Substitution, therefore, is an element in the efficaciousness of the blood rites in a sacrificial ritual. This position supports the understanding of the power of blood as a life-force, and it is built on the exegesis of ב as the instrumental ב.

It needs to be remembered that the foremost issue addressed by this verse is the reason that the blood of an animal cannot be eaten. Since God has assigned blood as the tangible element in effecting expiation, blood carries the strongest taboo. It may not be eaten or misappropriated in any way. The number of laws against misappropriating sacred objects to the worship of demonic spirits in chaps. 17–20 indicates that a major reason for this prohibition against eating blood is to prevent any uses of that which is holy in the worship of field spirits and to prevent any attempt to ingest divine power into one's body by partaking of the sacred. Therefore, blood, the tangible center of human life, must never be put to common (חל) use (cf. 10:11). It must always be handled properly as the exclusive property of Yahweh, the Creator of that life.

12 For emphasis this verse gives two prohibitions against eating blood. These prohibitions are accentuated by the opening divine speech formula אמרתי, "I have said."

13–14 This law addresses the proper slaughter of edible wild animals (ציד חיה) or birds (עוף). The blood from the slaughter of clean game is to be שׁפך, "poured out," on the ground and then covered. Blood left uncovered is thought to cry out for revenge (cf. Gen 4:10). The penalty for eating the blood of any animal, including that of wild animals, is the "cut-off" penalty (נכרת; cf. v 4). When a person gives God the animal's life-blood in place of his own, that person's sins are expiated and he is forgiven.

15–16 This law regulates eating from any animal found dead. Two words are used for a carcass: נבלה, an animal that died of natural causes or accidentally, and טרפה, an animal that had been mauled by another wild animal (cf. 11:39–40). The reason eating from these animals makes one unclean is that the blood of such an animal has not been properly drained from the meat. Any casual violation of this standard, though, is not considered a serious breach of the cultic laws. A guilty party is to wash his clothes and bathe in water and be considered unclean (טמא) until evening. Then he becomes ritually clean (טהר). However, if one who has become unclean by eating from the meat of a dead animal fails to perform the ritual cleansing, his error becomes an act of deliberate transgression of the law about eating blood. As a consequence he has to bear the responsibility of his transgression (נשׂא עונו; cf. 5:1). Other laws in the Pentateuch also regulate the use of dead animals. A priest is expressly forbidden to eat such meat (22:8; Ezek 44:31). The law in Exod 22:30(31) expresses great contempt for the carcass of a mauled animal (טרפה), saying that meat from such an animal may not be eaten but is to be cast to the dogs. Deut 14:21, moreover, prohibits an Israelite's eating from an animal found dead (נבלה), but it permits such meat to be given to גר, "a resident alien," or sold to נכרי, "a foreigner." Deuteronomy thus strengthens the standard for an Israelite but eases it for a stranger or an alien, making available to them an inexpensive source of meat. These variations in the law on this matter illustrate how the law was living in ancient Israel; i.e., the application of standards was modified or augmented in different eras as the understanding of each era sought to fulfill the principle of law in its own specific ways.

Explanation

In this speech both the making of any sacrificial offering away from an official altar and the consumption of blood in any form were prohibited. An ancient popular practice of making sacrifices in an open field was fraught with the danger of mixing pagan practices with a sacrifice offered to Yahweh. For example, to increase the yield of the harvest some were tempted to make the sacrifice not only to Yahweh but also to spirits that they thought inhabited the fields. Any such syncretistic practices undercut genuine worship of Yahweh. Furthermore, casual sacrifice would present the temptation to misappropriate an animal's blood, primarily by not draining fully the blood from the slain animal with the result that blood might be eaten with the meat. To put it another way, these stringent regulations regarding blood sought to eliminate any superstitious practices with blood from arising in Israel, e.g., the practice of eating or drinking the blood of an offering in order that one might ingest either spiritual powers or divine life. Given the importance of handling an animal's blood properly, this legislation required that the blood of wild game be properly drained, and it regulated the eating of meat from animals that were found dead. This speech, therefore, required that all offerings be brought to the sanctuary where a priest could oversee the slaughter, manipulate the blood as prescribed, and burn the fatty portions on the altar as a soothing aroma to Yahweh.

Blood of an appropriate sacrificial animal possessed power, both cleansing and expiating, for it was both an animal's life-force and the representation of that animal's life. On the principle of *lex talionis,* the ritualistic manipulation of an animal's blood redeemed the life of the one who presented the offering. Since it was God himself who ordained that the pouring out of an animal's blood at the altar was the means of expiation, all blood became his exclusive property.

These laws about the consumption of blood are the cornerstone of keeping kosher in Judaism. It is not at all surprising that the practice of abstaining from any consumption of blood became an issue for the acceptance of Gentiles in the early church. The leaders of the church vigorously debated which OT laws the new gentile converts should keep. At the great council of Jerusalem reported in Acts 15, the council decided to place four abstinences on the Gentiles: idols, unchastity, meat of animals strangled, and blood (vv 28–29; 21:25). The last two of these standards, which meant that the Gentiles were not to eat meat from which the blood had not been properly drained and were not to eat blood itself in any of the variety of ways it was prepared, were grounded on these regulations in Lev 17. In imposing these laws on the Gentiles, the church leaders were not only being sensitive to Jewish Christians; they also wished to keep the importance of proper handling of blood before all converts, for Jesus' shed blood was central to his atoning work on the cross.

In the NT Jesus' death on the cross is often referred to by the phrase "the blood of Christ." This phrase communicates that Jesus' death was far different from an ordinary death; it was a sacrifice made to God. The death of Jesus is interpreted then in terms of the OT sacrificial system, for as the writer of Hebrews says, "without the shedding of blood there is no forgiveness of sins" (9:22). Because Jesus, the sinless Son of God, obediently submitted himself to a cruel death on the cross, his death has secured expiation for all who believe on him regardless of race, sex, or social status (cf. Phil 2:6–11; Heb 5:7–10; 9:14). Furthermore, since Jesus was the perfect and the ultimate sacrifice, the animal sacrifices prescribed in the OT are no longer required under the new covenant (cf. Heb 9:12).

The NT phrase "the blood of Jesus" thus symbolizes the redemptive power inherent in Jesus' work for all peoples (cf. 1 Pet 1:18–21; Rev 1:5; 5:9). Because of his death, all who believe on him find forgiveness of their sins (Eph 1:7–8; Col 1:14). Through Jesus all believers are reconciled to God and rescued from the wrath of God (Rom 5:9–10; Eph 2:13; Col 1:20). In addition, the effect of Jesus' death is expressed in the language that his blood cleanses the conscience from dead works in order that any person may serve God enthusiastically by showing love to others (Heb 9:14; 10:24; 13:12; 1 John 1:7; 1 Pet 1:2; 2:24; 2 Cor 7:1; Titus 2:14). The benefits of having a pure conscience are great; e.g., persons with a clear conscience may enter God's presence boldly to present their petitions (Heb 10:19–22). The merits of Jesus' death also enable believers to successfully withstand attacks from the forces of cosmic evil (Rev 12:11; cf. Heb 13:20–21). Using vivid imagery, the revelator says that those who have come through the tribulation are those who have their garments purified by the blood of the Lamb (7:14). From another perspective, just as the worship of Yahweh was to be pure and undefiled, so too is the worship of God through Christ (Jas 1:27). Just as Israel was not to give any place in her sacrificial system to placating demons, neither are believers to carry on worship in a way that might give any acknowledgment to demonic forces or make light of Jesus' sacrificial death (1 Cor 10:14–22).

A radical difference between the OT and the NT in the symbolic use of blood, nevertheless, arises in the celebration of the Eucharist. In the OT the partaking of blood in any form, even blood in meat, was strictly forbidden. This standard, as mentioned above, is still followed by devout Jews. However, in the Eucharist, the meal that commemorates the making of the new covenant, believers partake of the bread and the wine, elements that represent the body and the blood of the Lord Jesus (Matt 26:27–28; Mark 14:23–24). By eating these elements a believer shares in the benefits of Jesus' death (1 Cor 10:16; 11:25; Heb 9:15–22). The discourse in John 6:52–59 is amazingly radical in its vivid imagery. Jesus boldly speaks of eating his flesh and drinking his blood. These words are especially scandalous to devout Jews as they depict the definitive newness of the fellowship between God and humans in the new covenant. The intent of these words in John is not primarily to offend Jewish listeners, but to pronounce boldly that in partaking of these elements a believer commemorates Jesus' death and enters into the deepest communion with his Lord. In other words, a believer abides in Jesus, and Jesus abides in that believer (John 6:56). Partaking of the Eucharist, furthermore, carries the promise of eternal life and participation in the final resurrection (John 6:54, 57).

B. Laws Governing the Extended Family (18:1–30)

Bibliography

Alpert, R. T. "In God's Image: Coming to Terms with Leviticus." In *Twice Blessed: On Being Lesbian, Gay, and Jewish.* Ed. C. Balka. Boston: Beacon, 1989. **Bigger, S. F.** "The Family Laws of Leviticus 18 in Their Setting." *JBL* 98 (1979) 187–203. **Chamberlayne, J. H.** "Kinship Relationships among the Early Hebrews." *Numen* 10 (1963) 153–69. **Elliger, K.** "Das Gesetz Leviticus 18." *ZAW* 67 (1955) 1–24. ———. "Leviticus 18." *TLZ* 29 (1954) 303–6. **Epstein, L. M.** *Marriage Laws in the Bible and the Talmud.* HSS 12. Cambridge: Harvard UP, 1942; New York: Johnson Reprint Collection, 1968. **Fox, R.** *The Red Lamp of Incest.* New York: E. P. Dutton, 1980. **Frymer-Kensky, T.** "Law and Philosophy: The Case of Sex in the Bible." In *Thinking Biblical Law.* Ed. D. Patrick. *Semeia* 45 (1989) 89–102. **Haas, P.** "'Die He Shall Surely Die': The Structure of Homicide in Biblical Law." In *Thinking Biblical Law.* Ed. D. Patrick. *Semeia* 45 (1989) 67–87. **Halbe, J.** "Die Reihe der Inzestverbote Lev 18:7–18." *ZAW* 92 (1980) 60–88. **Hoffner, H. A., Jr.** "Incest, Sodomy and Bestiality in the Ancient Near East." In *Orient and Occident.* FS C. H. Gordon. Ed. H. Hoffner, Jr. AOAT 22. Kevelar: Butzon & Bercher; Neukirchen-Vluyn: Neukirchener, 1973. 81–90. **Horton, F. L., Jr.** "Form and Structure in Laws Relating to Women: Leviticus 18:6–18." In *Society of Biblical Literature 1973 Seminar Papers 1.* Ed. G. MacRae. Cambridge: SBL, 1973. 20–33. **Jasper, G.** "Polygamy in the Old Testament." *African Journal of Theology* 2 (1969) 27–57. **Jügen, E.,** and **Rüterswörden, U.** "Unterweltsbeschwörung im Alten Testament: Untersuchungen zur Begriffs- und Religionsgeschichte des *ʾōb.*" *UF* 9 (1977) 57–70. **Kaiser, W. C., Jr.** "Leviticus 18:5 and Paul: 'Do This and You Shall Live' (Eternity?)." *JTS* 14 (1971) 19–25. **Kennett, R. H.** *Ancient Hebrew Social Life and Custom as Indicated in Law Narrative and Metaphor.* The Schweich Lectures of the British Academy 1931. Repr. Munich: Kraus, 1980. **Knierim, R.** "The Role of the Sexes in the Old Testament." *LTQ* 10.4 (1975) 1–10. **Krebs, W.** "Zur kultischen Kohabitation mit Tieren im Alten Orient." *FF* 37 (1963) 19–21. **Luria, S.** "Tochterschänderung in der Bibel." *ArOr* 33 (1965) 207–8. **McKeating, H.** "Sanctions against Adultery in Ancient Israelite Society, with Some Reflections on Methodology in the Study of Old Testament Ethics." *JSOT* 11 (1979) 57–72. **Neufeld, E.** *Ancient Hebrew Marriage Laws: With Special References to General Semitic Laws and Customs.* London: Green and Col., 1944. **Phillips, A.** "Some Aspects of Family Law in Pre-exilic Israel." *VT* 23 (1973) 349–61. **Porter, J. R.** *The Extended Family in the Old Testament.* Occasional Papers in Social and Economic Administration 6. London: Edutext, 1967. **Rattray, S.** "Marriage Rules, Kinship Terms and Family Structure in the Bible." SBLASP 26. Ed. K. Richards. Atlanta: Scholars Press, 1987. 537–44. **Richter, H.-F.** *Geschlechtlichkeit, Ehe und Familie im Alten Testament und seiner Umwelt.* 2 vols. Beiträge zur biblischen Exegese und Theologie 10. Frankfurt am Main: Peter Lang, 1978. **Rodd, C. S.** "The Family in the Old Testament." *BT* 18 (1967) 19–26. **Schultz, H.** *Das Todesrecht im Alten Testament: Studien zur Rechtsform der Mot-Jumat-Sätze.* BZAW

114. Berlin: Alfred Töpelmann, 1969. 130–62. **Soltero, C.** "Nota crítica a Lv 18,30." *Bib* 49, (1968) 370–72. **Stager, L. E.** "The Archaeology of the Family in Ancient Israel." *BASOR* 260 (1985) 1–35. **Stegner, W. R.** "The Parable of the Good Samaritan and Leviticus 18:5." In *The Living Text: Essays in Honor of E. W. Saunders.* Ed. D. E. Groh and R. Jewett. Lanham, MD: UP of America, 1985. 27–38. **Stendebach, F. J.** "Überlegungen zum Ethos des Alten Testaments." *Kairos* 18 (1976) 273–81. **Tosato, A.** "The Law of Leviticus 18:18: A Reexamination." *CBQ* 46 (1984) 199–214. **Ukleja, P. M.** "Homosexuality and the Old Testament." *BS* 140 (1983) 259–66. **Vermes, G.** "Leviticus 18:21 in Ancient Jewish Bible Exegesis." In *Studies in Aggadah, Targum, & Jewish Liturgy.* Ed. J. Petuchowski. 1981. 108–24. **Wenham, G. J.** "The Restoration of Marriage Reconsidered." *JJS* 30 (1979) 36–40. **Wolf, C.** "Terminology of Israel's Tribal Organization." *JBL* 65 (1946) 45–49.

Translation

1 *Yahweh spoke to Moses:* 2 *"Speak to the Israelites and say to them: I am Yahweh your*
God. 3 *You shall not do according to the customs*[a] *of Egypt where*[b] *you dwelt nor do ac-*
cording to the customs[a] *of Canaan to where*[c] *I am bringing you, and you shall not walk*
by their decrees.[a] 4 *You shall do*[a] *my laws*[bc] *and keep*[a] *my decrees*[bc] *to walk by them. I am*
Yahweh your God. 5 *You shall keep my decrees*[a] *and laws*[ab] *which a human does and lives*[c]
by them. I am Yahweh.[d]

6 *"No one*[a] *of you shall approach*[b] *any close relative*[c] *to have sexual relations.*[d] *I am*
Yahweh. 7 *You shall not dishonor your father and your mother*[a] *by having sexual*
relations[b] *with your mother; she*[c] *is your mother.* 8 *You shall not have sexual relations with*
your father's wife; she is your father's closest relative. 9 *You shall not have sexual relations*[a]
with your sister, either your father's daughter or your mother's daughter, whether she was
born at home or elsewhere. 10 *You shall not have sexual relations*[a] *with your son's*
daughter or your daughter's daughter, because they are part of your family. 11 *You shall not*
have sexual relations with the daughter of your father's wife,[a] *born of your father; she is*
your sister. 12 *You shall not have sexual relations with your father's sister; she*[a] *is a close*
relative of your father. 13 *You shall not have sexual relations with your mother's sister,*
because she is a close relative[a] *of your mother.* 14 *You shall not dishonor your father's*
brother by approaching his wife;[a] *she*[b] *is your aunt.* 15 *You shall not have sexual relations*
with your daughter-in-law; she[a] *is your son's wife. You shall not have sexual relations with*
her. 16 *You shall not have sexual relations with your brother's wife; she is your brother's*
closest relative. 17 *You shall not have sexual relations with a woman and her daughter.*
You shall not marry and have sexual relations[a] *with either her son's daughter or her*
daughter's daughter; they are her close relatives.[b] *It is a lewd act.*[c] 18 *You*[a] *shall not*
marry your wife's sister as a rival wife[b] *and have sexual relations with her while the*
former is still living.

19 *"You shall not approach a woman to have sexual relations with her while she is*
unclean during her period. 20 *You shall not have intercourse*[a] *with your associate's wife*
to become defiled[b] *by her.* 21 *You shall not give any of*[a] *your children to pass*[b] *to Molek, for*
you must not profane the name of your God. I am Yahweh.[c] 22 *You shall not lie with a man*
as with a woman; it[a] *is a detestable act.*[b] 23 *You shall not have intercourse*[a] *with any*
animal to become defiled[b] *by it. A woman shall not stand*[c] *before a beast*[d] *for copulation;*[e]
it[fg] *is a confusion.*[h]

24 *"Do not defile yourselves*[a] *by any of these ways, because by all these the nations which*
I am going to drive out before you have become defiled. 25 *Because the land was unclean,*
I punished it for its iniquity; the land vomited out its inhabitants. 26 *You*[a] *shall keep my*

decrees and my laws. You shall not do any of[b] these detestable practices, neither the na-
tive nor the alien living among you, 27*for the people who lived in the land before you*
committed all these[a] detestable practices so that the land became unclean. 28*Will not[a] the*
land vomit you out if you defile it[b] just as it[c] vomited out the nation[d] which was before
you. 29*Because[a] anyone who does any of[b] these detestable practices[cd]—the persons who do*
them will be cut off from their people. 30*Keep my charge[a] so that you do not do any of[b]*
the detestable[c] decrees[d] which are being practiced before your coming. Do not defile your-
selves with them.[e] I[f] am Yahweh your God."

Notes

3.a. The terms used for customs and decrees stand before their respective verbs for emphasis.

3.b. בה, the prep with a fem pronominal suffix, is the retrospective pronoun for the indeclinable אשר, "which/where" (GKC §138).

3.c. שמה, "thereward," an adv of place, defines more specifically the indefinite relative אשר, "which," the two together = "where" in Eng (cf. GKC §138c).

4.a. Three verbs often occur with משפטים, "judgments," and חקות, "decrees": עשה, "do" (e.g., 18:4, 30; Ezek 5:7; 20:11); הלך, "walk in" (e.g., 18:3; 20:23; Ezek 5:6, 7; 37:24), and שמר, "keep" (e.g., 18:5, 26; 19:19; Ezek 20:18). Sometimes the verbs שמר and עשה occur together and sometimes they are joined (19:37; 20:8; Deut 7:12), such as שמר לעשות, "keep guard by doing" (20:22; Ezek 37:24; Deut 5:1; 11:32). The phrase שמר ללכת, "keep/guard by walking," occurs here (cf. Elliger, 237, n.). These combinations emphasize the diligent observation of the law.

4.b. Cf. n. 3.a.

4.c. משפטים, "laws, judgments," in the priestly legislation often occurs with חקות, "decrees," and it usually follows that term (e.g., 18:26; 19:37; 20:22; 25:18; 26:15; but reverse 18:4; 26:43). This combination occurs frequently in Ezekiel (5:7; 11:12, 20; 18:9; 20:11, 13, 19, 21, 25; 36:27; cf. 5:6; 18:17; 20:16, 24; 37:24). In Deuteronomy this combination appears, but often with the spelling חקים, "decrees" (Deut 4:1, 5, 8, 14; 5:1, 31; 11:32; 12:1; 26:16; with another word added in the list 4:45; 6:1, 10; 7:11; 26:17; also Ezek 20:18). When משפט, "laws, judgment," occurs alone, it is in the sg (e.g., 5:10; 9:16; 19:15, 35; cf. Num 15:16; 24:22; 35:12; etc.; Elliger, 237, n.).

5.a. LXX reads *πάντα*, "all," before both decrees and laws.

5.b. LXX adds *καὶ ποιήσετε αὐτά*, "and do them"; cf. n. 4.a.

5.c. For MT וחי, "and living" (cf. GKC §76i), Sam and Tg read וחיה, "and one lives." Tg adds בחיי עלמא, "by eternal life."

5.d. LXX adds *ὁ θεὸς ὑμῶν*, "your God," as is often found in chaps. 18–26. MT is preferred as the shorter reading.

6.a. Cf. n. 17:3.a.

6.b. Kornfeld (*ZAW* 87 [1975] 212) points out that an unpublished text reads תקריבו, "make to come near," a hiph in place of the MT qal to emphasize the aggressive action of the offender.

6.c. The prep phrase אל־כל־שאר בשרו, "to any close relative," is the controlling phrase for the coming series of laws. It stands between the subj and the verb for emphasis. The Eng trans. of these laws is less literal than in the other chapters because of the euphemistic language; as a result the redundant phraseology of the original is lost in this translation.

6.d. ערוה means "nakedness" and is a technical term for the genitals. It stands as acc of גלה, "uncover," to mean "to cohabit" (BDB, 788–89).

7.a. In the series of laws through v 17, the dir obj ערות, "nakedness of," stands first for emphasis. Even though it is definite, it does not have the sign of the acc; this may be because of the crisp archaic construction of these laws. Levine (120) notes that ו on וערות אמך, "nakedness of your mother," introduces a circumstantial clause that further defines the father's nakedness.

7.b. תְגַלֶּה, "you may uncover," instead of the expected תגלה here and in vv 12, 13, 14, 15, 16, 17; 20:29 is explained as a result of Aram influence (GKC §75hh; Joüon §79n).

7.c. LXX reads *γάρ*, "for" = כי; also it reads a *waw* on the second occurrence of תגלה, "you will reveal."

9.a. For MT ערותן, "their nakedness," several Heb. mss, Sam, LXX, and Syr read ערותה, "her nakedness." Sun ("Investigation," 116) thinks that the pl was attracted to the defining appositional phrase in v 9a.

10.a. Horton notes that in this prohibition the dir obj has been reintroduced even though it first stands as a *casus pendens* because "the verb-object relationship has become obscured to the native ear" ("Form and Structure," 25).

11.a. At this place LXX* adds οὐκ ἀποκαλύψεις, "do not uncover," making this law conform to the pattern of the twofold usage of לא תגלה, "you will not reveal," as found in v 7.

12.a. A few Heb. mss, LXX, Syr, and Vg add כי, "for."

13.a. A few Heb. mss and Sam do not have שאר, "flesh, close relative."

14.a. Several Heb. mss and the versions read a *waw* on the prep אל, "to."

14.b. Cf. n. 12.a.

15.a. LXX reads γάρ, "for"; cf. n 12.a.

17.a. LXX and Syr read the third person fem pl suffix; cf. n. 9.a.

17.b. LXX reads οἰκεῖαι γάρ σου εἰσιν, "for they are your close relative." *BHS* suggests pointing MT שַׁאֲרָה, "relative," as שְׁאֵרָהּ, "her relative"; this trans. follows *BHS*.

17.c. זמה always carries a bad sense except for Job 17:11. It describes violent, wanton deeds as heinous crimes. It occurs several times for sexual offenses such as adultery (Job 31:11), harlotry (Jer 13:27; Ezek 16:27; 22:9, 11; 23:21; etc.), and incest (Lev 20:14); cf. S. Steingrimsson, "זמם *zmm*," *TDOT* 4:89–90. Ezek uses זמה to describe the unfaithfulness of Israel and Judah in order to bring to the mind of his audience the sexual laws of Leviticus. The wording of Ezek 22:9 specifically recalls these sexual laws in Leviticus (Steingrimsson, *TDOT* 4:90). זמה may be translated "obscene, lewd, repulsive."

18.a. LXX does not read the initial *waw*.

18.b. צרר may be a denominative from צרה, "rival wife," meaning "take as a rival wife" (BDB, 865; KB, 991), but this is the only such use of צרר. LXX* seems to have read צרה, "for a rival wife" (Sun, "Investigation," 120). Sun interprets צרר as the verb "harass" and translates the line "to harass her by uncovering her nakedness as long as she is alive." This is an intriguing alternative, but the context demands a more technical usage for צרר.

20.a. Orlinsky (*JBL* 63 [1944] 40) proposes that שְׁכָבְת means "penis"; cf. n. 15:16.a. This proposal has merit.

20.b. MT לטמאה is a fem inf constr (GKC §45d). The prep ל indicates the results of the action (cf. GKC §114f).

21.a. This is a partitive use of the prep מן. It has the sense "even one" or "any" (GKC §119w, n.).

21.b. For MT להעביר, "to pass over," Sam reads להעביד, "to serve." At certain stages of Heb. script, ר and ד are hard to distinguish. LXX may support the variant, for it has λατρεύειν, "to worship."

21.c. In place of MT אלהיך, "your God," LXX reads τὸ ὄνομα τὸ ἅγιον, "the holy name," as in 20:3 and 22:2, 32. LXX seems to have risen from the influence of those texts.

22.a. LXX reads γάρ, "for" = כי.

22.b. תועבה depicts ritualistic and moral behavior that is repugnant. W. F. Albright (*From Stone Age to Christianity* [Baltimore: John Hopkins University Press, [2]1957] 423) takes it from Egyptian *wʿb*, "to be pure," with the opposite meaning in Heb. This term occurs six times in Lev (18:22, 26, 27, 29, 30; 20:13) for the immoral sexual practices of Israel's neighbors. It does not appear elsewhere in the priestly material, but it occurs often in Deut, Ezek, and Prov. In Deut several activities are abhorrent or detestable to God: idolatry (7:25; 27:15), eating unclean animals (14:3), sacrificing animals with defects (17:1), human sacrifice (12:31), practicing witchcraft (18:9–14). These activities are infringements against the exclusive claims of Yahweh (Paschen, *Rein*, 24). Proverbs has a numerical saying that presents seven things abhorrent to Yahweh (6:16–19). Ezekiel uses it for profane action or violation of the sacred order (Humbert, *ZAW* 72 [1960] 228–29): inordinate sexual acts (22:11; 33:26), idolatry (e.g., 6:9, 11; 7:20; 11:18, 21; 14:6), idolatry under the image of harlotry (16:36, 43, 57; 23:36), immorality (18:12, 13, 24), profaning the Temple (43:8), and violation of sacred ritual (44:6, 7). These perverted actions cause anxiety and disgust (Gerstenberger, *THAT* 2:1054). תועבה thus expresses the vile nature of actions and attitudes that are incompatible with the fear of Yahweh. Cf. P. Humbert, "Le substantif *toʿēbā* et le verbe *tʿb* dans l'Ancien Testament," *ZAW* 72 (1960) 217–37; E. Gerstenberger, "תעב *tʿb* pi verabscheuen," *THAT* 2:1051–55; *TWOT* 2:976–77.

23.a. Cf. n. 20.a.

23.b. Cf. n. 20.b.

23.c. Sun ("Investigation," 122) interprets תעמד, "she/you will stand," as a second person masc sg and repoints the verb as a hiph. This alternative has the advantage of continuing the series of second person forms, but the context does not indicate that these laws primarily regulate illicit sexual behavior that one is forced to perform by another party.

23.d. LXX reads πᾶν, "any," before "beast."

23.e. MT לרבעה is a fem form of inf constr, a form often found with the prep ל (GKC §45d). The pointing of MT, however, takes the ה as a pronominal suffix, but *BHS* prefers to read a fem form as in 20:16. רבע, "lie stretched out," is often used for unnatural cohabitation (BDB, 918; Jastrow, 1444). The inf constr with the prep ל defines the activity more exactly (GKC §114o).

23.f. Sam, some Heb. mss, Syr, Tg[mss], and *Tg. Ps.-J.* read היא, a fem pronoun, in lieu of MT הוא, a masc pronoun.

23.g. Cf. n. 22.a.

23.h. תבל only occurs here and in 20:12. BDB (117) takes it from the root בלל, "mix, confuse," to mean "confusion," i.e., "a violation of nature or the divine order." LXX renders it *μυσερόν*, "foul, loathsome."

24.a. This is an example of a hithpael with the ת of the preformative assimilated to the first radical ט (GKC §54c). *IBHS* (§23.6.4a) points out that in regard to a couple of verbs, including טמא, "be unclean," the niph pf and the hithpael impf are employed to supplement or complement one another.

26.a. A few Heb. mss, LXX, Syr, and Vg do not read the pronoun אתם, "you." This variant resulted from an error of haplography. The use of the personal pronoun underscores God's calling Israel to obedience.

26.b. Cf. n. 21.a.

27.a. This is a rare spelling of the fem pl demonstrative pronoun as האל (GKC §34b, n.). Sam and 11QpaleoLev have the usual spelling האלה.

28.a. Sun ("Investigation," 123) takes לא, "not," as an emphatic adv or particle in light of the phrase בטמאכם, "in your defiling." It is also possible to take לא as an asseverative לו, "surely." It is hard to decide between these alternatives; this Eng trans. casts the phrase as a question to maintain the meaning that the context demands.

28.b. This conditional clause is constructed by a prep; it governs the inf constr בטמאכם, "in your defiling" (cf. GKC §164g). The pronominal suffix then functions as subj of the clause.

28.c. This is an example of the omission of the personal pronoun היא as subj of a participial clause (GKC §116s), but *BHS* suggests placing the accent on the penult so that קאה, "vomit," is a third person fem sg pf instead of a fem ptcp.

28.d. LXX, Syr, and Tg read הגוים, "nations," as in v 24, instead of MT's הגוי, "the nation." MT is followed as the harder reading. PIR (188) exegetes הגוי as a collective noun.

29.a. Sun ("Investiation," 124) takes כי as an emphatic particle "indeed" (KB, 448). The grammar is difficult in any case; possibly this verse has the rhetorical device of aposiopesis.

29.b. Cf. n. 21.a.

29.c. This is a long *casus pendens* that is resumed by הנפשות, "the persons."

29.d. Cf. n. 22.b.

30.a. For MT משמרתי, "my charge," LXX reads *τὰ προστάγματά μου*, "my commandments."

30.b. Cf. n. 21.a.

30.c. Cf. n. 22.b.

30.d. In the constructive phrase חקות התועבת, "the detestable decrees," the genitive expresses an attribute of the *nomen regens* (GKC §128p).

30.e. Instead of בהם, "them," a masc pronominal suffix, Sam reads בהן, a fem pronominal suffix, to accord with its antecedent התועבת, "the detestable things."

30.f. 11QpaleoLev, LXX, and *Tg. Neof.* have כי, "because."

Form/Structure/Setting

The structure of this chapter is outlined as follows:

I. Introductory formula (v 1)
II. Speech (vv 2–30)
  A. Commission to speak (v 2a)
  B. Speech proper (vv 2b–30)
    1. First parenetic section (vv 2b–5)
      a. Formula of Yahweh's self-introduction (v 2b)
      b. Parenesis proper (vv 3–5)
        1) Two prohibitions against following foreign practices (v 3)

- 2) Two exhortations to keep God's laws, each supported by formulae of Yahweh's self-introduction (vv 4–5)
- 2. Laws regulating a variety of sexual unions (vv 6–23)
  - a. General law (v 6)
  - b. Two sets of laws (vv 7–17a)
    - 1) Prohibitions against incest (vv 7–18)
      - a) Primary relationships (vv 7–23)
        - (1) With a mother (v 7)
        - (2) With a father's wife (v 8)
        - (3) With a sister (v 9)
        - (4) With a granddaughter (v 10)
        - (5) With a stepsister (v 11)
        - (6) With a paternal aunt (v 12)
        - (7) With a maternal aunt (v 13)
        - (8) With an aunt, wife of father's brother (v 14)
        - (9) With a daughter–in-law (v 15)
        - (10) With a brother's wife (v 16)
        - (11) With a mother and a daughter (v 17a)
      - b) Additional prohibitions against certain kinds of marriages (vv 17b–18)
        - (1) Against marriage to a woman and her granddaughter (v 17b)
        - (2) Against marriage to a wife's sister (v 18)
    - 2) Prohibitions against certain sexual practices and sacrifice to Molek (vv 19–23)
      - a) Against sexual relations with a woman during menses (v 19)
      - b) Against relations with a neighbor's wife (v 20)
      - c) Against offering up children to Molek (v 21)
      - d) Against homosexuality (v 22)
      - e) Against bestiality, male and female (v 23)
- 3. Second parenetic section (vv 24–30)
  - a. Parenesis proper (vv 24–30a)
    - 1) Admonition with historical substantiation (vv 24–25)
    - 2) Parenesis supported by threat of expulsion from the land (vv 26–29)
    - 3) Exhortation to keep these laws (v 30a)
  - b. Formula of Yahweh's self-introduction (v 30b)

The core of this speech is a legislation of sexual laws (vv 6–23). It is framed by parenetic material warning Israel against following the practices of her neighbors and calling her to be a holy people (vv 2b–5; 24–30). The legislation consists of two sets of laws. The first set prohibits incest with a close relative (vv 7–17a + 17b–18), and the second set condemns a variety of sexual offenses (vv 19–20, 22–23) plus the offering of children to Molek (v 21). These laws are directed to the head of a father's house, whose responsibility it is to deter any infraction of them (cf. A. Phillips, "Family Laws," *VT* 23 [1973] 361). This position accounts for the lack of penalties with these sexual laws.

A brief description of the family structure in ancient Israel provides a look at the social setting addressed by these laws. The basic unit was a father's house (בית אב), which was composed of three to five generations living in close proximity (cf. Gottwald, *The Tribes of Israel* [Mary Knoll, NY: Orbis Books, 1979] 285–92). The eldest son was head of his own house, taking over when his father had begun to lose strength because of advancing age. When this son's house increased, his brother(s) could set up his/their own father's house. Brothers continued to live close by. In many families, especially smaller ones, an elder brother played a vital role. Gottwald (*Tribes of Yahweh,* 285) speculates that a father's house could have consisted of fifty to a hundred people. At the next level was the משפחה, "an association of families" (Gottwald, 257). When a father's house faced hardship, the larger משפחה came to its aid. Several associated families formed a tribe (שׁבט or מטה).

Do these laws prohibit marriage to next of kin, or do they regulate incest? Both positions have been advocated. The language לגלות ערוה, "to uncover nakedness of," which depicts a driven, passionate sexual encounter, favors interpreting these as decrees about incest (cf. Noordtzij, 183). The question may not be accurate, for this is not an either/or issue; as Gottwald (*Tribes of Yahweh,* 302) points out, prohibited incestuous unions are never legitimated by marriage.

Turning to look at the laws in detail, there is a general, categorical law (v 6) at the head of all the laws. It is formed with second person plural forms in order to establish a tie with the style of the preceding parenetic material. The use of איש איש addresses all the hearers (cf. Horton, "Form and Structure," 30–31; Halbe, *ZAW* 92 [1980] 68). The main verb, קרב "draw near," is more generic than the verbs of the incest decrees—גלה, "reveal," and שׁכב, "lie"—in order to encompass both that series of laws and the second series of laws, as the occurrence of this verb in v 19 proves. The phrase שׁאר בשׂר, "close relative," points to both the incest and the marriage laws. The key phrase of the incest laws, לגלות ערוה, "to uncover the nakedness," is used. This law is formulated for the heuristic purpose of providing a guideline for the courts in deciding cases of sexual relationships not explicitly covered in the following series of laws, according to Horton (30). Finally, its being supported by the self-introduction formula אני יהוה, "I am Yahweh," establishes another tie with the parenetic framework. Thus this law provides the ideological foundation for the following sexual laws and functions literarily as the head of the list.

As for the structure of the individual laws, those in vv 7–16 fall into two basic patterns, according to a study by Halbe (*ZAW* 92 [1980] 69). The first pattern, A:B::C::B':A', is illustrated by v 15:

A ערות כלתך, "nakedness of your daughter-in-law"
  B לא תגלה, "do not uncover"
    C אשׁת בנך הוא, "she is your son's wife"
  B' לא תגלה, "do not uncover"
A' ערותה, "her nakedness"

The prohibition is stated basically in A + B and then restated chiastically in B'+ A'. At C, the center and the point of emphasis, stands a declaratory formula, functioning as the substantiation for the law. The laws in vv 7, 11, 14, and 15 are composed in this pattern, but the laws in vv 11 and 14 have been modified (Halbe, *ZAW* 92 [1980] 80). In v 11 the identification of the sister as מולדת אביך, "begotten of your father," has been inserted in place of the usual B element in order to clarify the relationship addressed by the decree. The law in v 14, with the pattern A:B:B':C, is a variation of this pattern, possibly for variety or because of the inclusion of אל־אשׁתו לא תקרב, "you shall not approach his wife" (Halbe, 78–80). The law in v 9, which in its present form does not fit either pattern, has been extensively altered to extend the circle of those who qualify as one's sister (cf. Halbe, 77–78).

The second pattern, A:B:A', is illustrated by v 8:

A	ערות אשת־אביך,	"nakedness of your father's wife"
B	לא תלגה,	"do not uncover"
A'	ערות אביך הוא,	"it is your father's nakedness"

Part A identifies the relationship prohibited, while A', echoing the language of A, is a declaratory formula, serving to substantiate the prohibition. The prohibition, at the center, is the focal point. Examples of this type are the laws in vv 8, 10, 12, 13, 16. The law in v 10 has an expanded form; two relatives are identified, and this is carried through with the plural pronoun הנה in the declaratory formula.

The position that these laws are formulated from two basic patterns does not support Elliger's analysis (*ZAW* 67 [1955] 6–12) that an original decalogue, which included a law against the union of a father-daughter after v 9, was then expanded into a dodecalogue with the addition of vv 13 and 17a or Feucht's attempt (*Untersuchungen,* 31–32) to find a double decalogue, one in vv 6–16 and a second in vv 17–23.

The absence of laws prohibiting sexual relations between a father and a daughter and between a brother and a full sister is puzzling. Several exegetes (e.g., Elliger, *ZAW* 67 [1955] 2; Kilian, *Literarkritische,* 16) have argued that a law about a daughter has fallen out after v 9 as a result of an error of homoiarchton. Such an error could easily have resulted because of the similarity in the form of these laws. In support of this position is the fact that there is such a law in the Code of Hammurabi. The absence of a law against such a union in the two other sets of incest laws in Lev 20:11–21 and Deut 27:20–23, however, does not support inserting such a law here (cf. Luria, *ArOr* 33 [1965] 207–8). The reason for its absence may have been socio-economic; i.e., an Israelite father would not think of severely reducing the marriage price his daughter could command by having relations with her. While there may be some validity to this proposal for the absence of such a law, it does not account for the absence of a law against a brother-full sister union. The proposal that best accounts for the omissions of both is set forth by Rattray (SBLASP 26 [1987] 542; see Figure 2); she proposes that the phrase שאר בשרו, "his close relative," which is defined in 21:2–3 as father, mother, daughter, brother, unmarried sister, excludes a mother, a daughter, or a full sister from a man's sexual advances. If this is correct, why then is a mother specifically mentioned in v 7, particularly since incest with a mother is universally abhorred and not very likely to happen? Rattray's answer is that the list is headed by the most repugnant case. But that explanation is not the full reason for the presence of this law. This law not only excludes sexual relations between a son and his mother; it begins with the phrase ערות אביך, "the nakedness of your father," even though the inclusion of this phrase overburdens the structure of this law. This phrase has been placed before the phrase ערות אמך, "the nakedness of your mother," in order that this law may function to classify all the following incestuous unions as either a violation of one's father or of one's mother (cf. Horton, "Form and Structure," 29–31). This formulation then gives the law a heuristic function; i.e., it provides a basis for the courts to decide a wide variety of

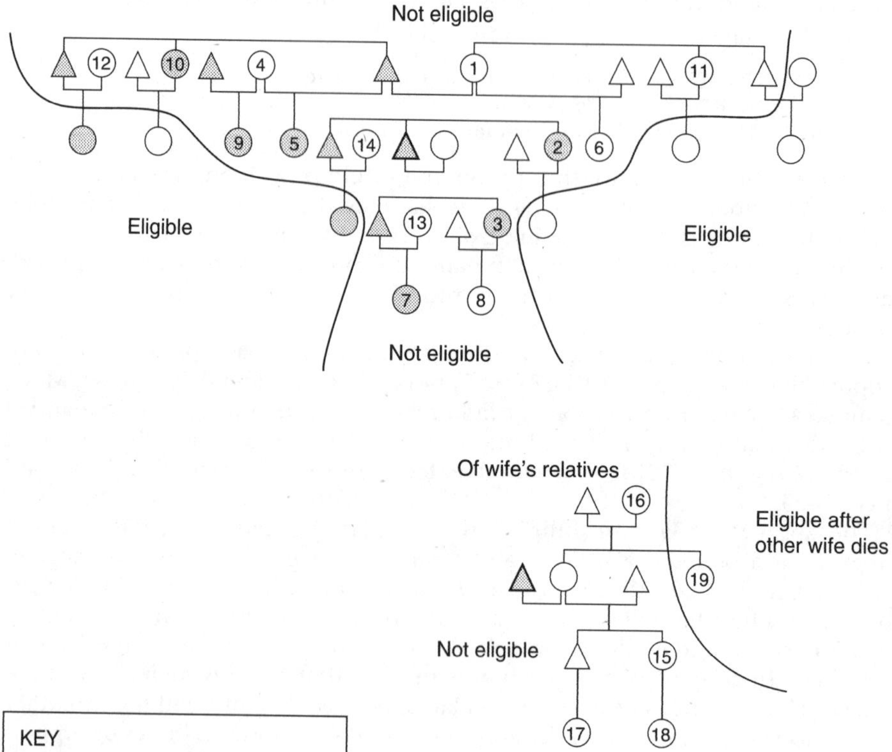

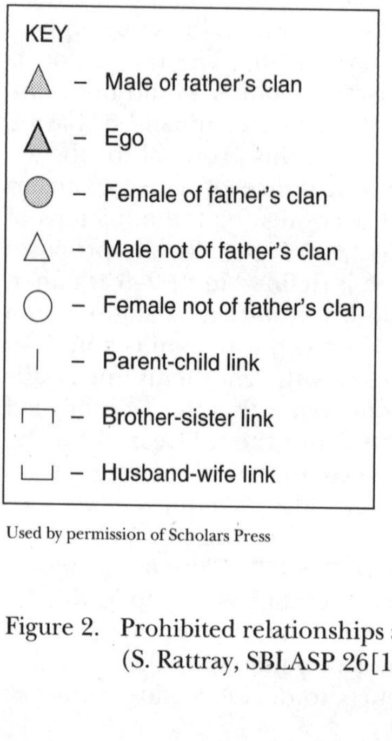

1. *ʾēm* (v 6, 7)
2. *ʾāḥôt* (v 6)
3. *bat* (v 6)
4. *ʾēšet ʾāb* (v 8)
5. *bat ʾāb* (v 9)
6. *bat ʾēm* (v 9)
7. *bat bēn* (v 10)
8. *bat bat* (v 10)
9. *bat ʾēšet ʾāb* (v 11)
10. *ʾăḥôt ʾāb* (v 12)
11. *ʾăḥôt ʾēm* (v 13)
12. *ʾēšet ʾăḥî ʾāb*(v 14)
13. *ʾēšet bēn* (v 15)
14. *ʾēšet ʾāḥ* (v 16)
15. *bat ʾiššâ* (v 17)
16. *ʾēm ʾiššâ*(v 17)
17. *bat ben ʾiššâ* (v 17)
18. *bat bat ʾiššâ* (v 17)
19. *ʾăḥôt ʾiššâ* (v 18)

Figure 2. Prohibited relationships according to Lev 18:6–18 (S. Rattray, SBLASP 26[1987] 544).

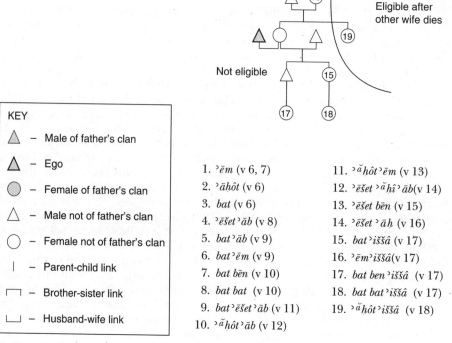

incest cases, in Horton's view (30–31). This understanding, in fact, supports Rattray's explanation that this law accounts for the absence of laws about other incestuous unions that were certainly prohibited in ancient Israel.

The laws in vv 17b and 18 have been added to the series of incest laws, for these two laws deviate from the preceding ones with the use of the technical term לקח, "take in marriage." Further evidence for this position is found in the change in the nature of the declaratory formula. The law in v 17b is supported by the declaratory formula זמה הוא, "it is a lewd act." Instead of identifying the offense as a violation of a close relative, as in the preceding laws, this formula defines such an act as an ethical violation, as do the declaratory formulae in vv 19–23. Thus these two laws address a different kind of relationship than do the incest laws. They have been attached here because they prohibit two types of marital alliances that were close to, but not precisely considered, incestuous.

The laws in the second set are prohibitions against defiling or perverted sexual acts. A variety of linguistic threads tie the laws in vv 19–20 + 22–23 together. Both laws in vv 19 and 20 begin with ואל אשה, "and to a wife." The laws in vv 20 and 23a have the phrase לטמאה בה, "for impurity by it," while the law in v 19 has טמאה, "impurity, uncleanness." טמאה signals that these prohibitions are against polluting sexual unions. This fact ties this set to the concern against moral and cultic defilement in the parenetic material. The use of the verb תקרב, "draw near" (vv 6, 14), and the phrase לגלות ערותה, "to reveal the nakedness of," in the law in v 19 forms a bond with the preceding laws. The root שכב, "lie," is a key thread of the second series. The verb תשכב, "lie," occurs in v 22, the noun שכבתך, "your seed," in vv 20 and 23, and משכב, "act of lying," in v 22. Furthermore, a progression can be detected in the arrangement of these laws, moving from activities that are a distortion of normal sexual practice to unnatural sexual practices: sexual intercourse with a wife during menses (v 19) or with a neighbor's wife (v 20), the sacrifice of children to Molek (v 21), unnatural sexual activities, homosexuality (v 22), and bestiality (v 23).

The declaratory formulae that substantiate the laws of the second series differ considerably from that of the first set of laws. The substantiation or motivation for the laws in the first set is one's social responsibility. The laws of the second set are motivated by declaratory formulae that express the defiling, immoral nature of these illicit practices: תועבה הוא, "it is a detestable act" (v 22), and תבל הוא, "it is a perversion" (v 23); זמה הוא, "it is a lewd act," occurs in v 17b. These formulae in the second series are very strong, for they speak of the destructive effect such offenses have on the relationship between the people and Yahweh their God.

To a modern reader the law in v 21 appears out of place in the second set of laws (cf. *Excursus* on Molek sacrifices at 20:2). There are several indicators, though, that it was formulated for this location. The opening phrase מזרעך, "any of your seed," ties directly to לזרע, "for seed," in v 20aβ. The prohibition לא תתן, "do not give," resounds the prohibitions found in vv 20a and 23. The strong wording, "profane the name of your God," expresses that this activity is even more polluting than the other offenses in this set and accords with the strong declaratory formulae of this set. Furthermore, the grounding of the law with the self-introduction formula "I am Yahweh" increases the weight of this prohibition as well as establishing a tie with the first series of laws (v 6) and the parenetic framework (cf. v 2). Thus the speaker composed this law carefully to fit this context. The close tie between sexual offenses and sacrifices to Molek is further attested by the placing of laws against offerings to Molek just prior to a series of laws against sexual offenses in chap. 20. Israel thus made an ideological connection between sexual offenses and certain pagan rites. On the one hand, this activity was destructive to family solidarity like other sexual offenses. On the other hand, that a culture could equate two subjects that appear so diverse to the modern way of thinking is attested by the evidence that the Chiricahua, an American Indian tribe of the Southwest, equated incest and witchcraft as the worst offenses of the social and the religious realms respectively (R. Fox, *The Red Lamp of Incest,* 32–34).

In the parenetic material that frames the legislation, the first section (vv 2b–5) warns the people not to follow the customs of the Egyptians and Canaanites (vv 2b–3) and exhorts them to obey Yahweh's laws and decrees (vv 4–5). Their observance is encouraged with the promise of life (v 5). In the third section (vv 24–30) the focus is on the bond that exists between the people and the land. There are three groups of parenetic statements. The second one leads into the threat that Israel will be driven from the land if she disobeys the laws God has given (v 28). This threat becomes the focal point of the parenesis. This is achieved both by position and by the repeated use of three roots that disclose the defilement that comes from following pagan customs and practices: טמא, "unclean" (vv 24 [2x], 25, 27, 28, 30), תועבה, "detestable things" (vv 26, 27, 29, 30), and קיא, "vomit" (vv 25, 28 [2x]). Furthermore, the frequent occurrence of the formula of Yahweh's self-introduction in the parenetic material (vv 2b, 4b, 5b, 30b) stresses that these exhortations have their authority in Yahweh's holy character.

The union of past tense and future tense in this parenetic material is intriguing. As it stands, this material addresses Israel both as she is about to enter the land (vv 2b–4, 24, 30) and as though she is already in the land (vv 5, 25–29; cf. Elliger, 233–34; idem, *ZAW* 67 [1955] 17–23). This tension between the past and the future is a rhetorical device to contemporize the ancient law for each audience hearing this speech (cf. Reventlow, *Heiligkeitgesetz,* 60–64). Israel is called to obey these laws in the present in light of her redemptive history. The opening parenesis leads the audience to inquire what laws God wants them to obey in order that she might not be like her neighbors. The legislation at the center answers that inquiry by giving those laws to Israel. The concluding parenesis motivates Israel to avoid the practices of her neighbors with the threat of expulsion for defiling the land by such activities. The solemnity of the threat is grounded in the remembrance of what happened to the Canaanites who had occupied the land because of their detestable practices. To vivify this threat, the bond between the people and the land is personified; i.e., indulgence in immoral acts will make the land so sick that it will vomit out its inhabitants. Thus the speech is so constructed that it addresses its present audience with the immediacy of obeying these laws given at Mount Sinai.

This speech then is for the priests' oral instruction of the laity. The style of the speech supports this position. A host of mnemonic and rhetorical devices both facilitate the priests' memorization of this speech and serve to imprint these decrees deeply in the minds of the hearers. First, as noted above, the laws are cast in similar patterns. Second, several roots are repeated in a variety of forms: עשה, "do" (12x), טמא, "defile" (8x), תועבה, "detestable" (5x), שמר, "keep" (5x), חקות, "decrees" (4x), משפטים, "laws" (3x), קיא, "vomit" (3x), הלך, "walk, go" (2x). Forms of the term ערוה, "nakedness," occur twenty-one times, and forms of the verb גלה, "uncover," occur sixteen times. Third, there is a fivefold repetition of the commandment not to behave like other nations (vv 3 [2x], 24, 27, 30). Fourth, the authority of these decrees is strengthened by the frequent use of declaratory formulae. Fifth, the formula "I am Yahweh" occurs three times (vv 5, 6, 21), and the formula "I am Yahweh your God" appears three times (vv 2, 4, 30).

The dates proposed for these incest laws vary widely. Elliger (*TLZ* 29 [1954] 304) locates the old kernel (vv 7–17a) in a nomadic era. Kilian (*Literarkritische,* 28) and Reventlow (*Heiligkeitsgesetz,* 54) assign the laws to the wilderness period. Bigger (*JBL* 98 [1979] 198), however, believes that the decrees govern a household, not an extended family, and thus come from a much later time when the people lived in smaller groups in an urban setting. These different proposals show that it is hard to date ancient material. The incest laws, however, fit in well with the wilderness period, for, on the one hand, they prohibit relationships that are mentioned without any disapproval in earlier times, such as that between Judah and Tamar, his daughter-in-law (Gen 38). On the other hand, the evidence from the rest of the OT, with only a few exceptions, reflects the family relationships desired herein. Therefore, these laws came into existence at the time of Israel's transition from a tribal community to a nation.

Comment

1–2 Yahweh continues to give Moses the words he is to address to Israel (cf. 1:1–2; 4:1–2, etc.). This speech opens with the formula of God's self-identification: "I am Yahweh your God." By calling himself "your God," God is identifying himself with his people just as he did with the patriarchs, Abraham, Isaac, and Jacob (e.g., Exod 3:6, 15). This formula brings to mind the preamble to the Decalogue (Exod 20:2; cf. Wenham, 250–51), reminding the audience that these laws have their setting in the covenant at Mount Sinai. Israel is made aware that she is obligated to observe these laws because of the holy character of the God she worships.

Excursus: The Phrase "I Am Yahweh (Your God)"

Bibliography

Elliger, K. "Ich bin der Herr—euer Gott." In *Theologie als Glaubenswägnis.* FS K. Heim. Evang.-Theol. Fakultät in Tübingen. Hamburg: Im Furche-Verlag, 1954. 9–34. **Zimmerli, W.** "I Am Yahweh." In *I Am Yahweh.* Tr. D. Stott. Atlanta: John Knox Press, 1982. 1–28.

Two formulae of Yahweh's self-introduction, אני יהוה, "I am Yahweh," and אני יהוה אלהיך, "I am Yahweh, your God," occur in clusters in Lev 18–26, Isa 40–55, and Ezekiel. They are scattered through other parts of the Pentateuch and the Prophets, but their occurrences in the poetic books are minimal (only in Pss 46:11[10]; 50:7; 81:11[10]; Elliger, "Ich bin der Herr," 9). In Leviticus these formulae usually come after a law or at the end of a group of laws. The long formula, however, has a lead position one time in the laws on holy living, namely at 18:2. There it functions strategically as a preamble to the laws on holy living, corresponding to its use at the head of the Decalogue (Exod 20:2; Zimmerli, "I Am Yahweh," 3). An example of the short formula having an introductory use occurs in two critical passages coming in succession:

in Exod 6:2–5, where God reveals his identity to Moses, and in Exod 6:6–8, which gives Moses' commission to tell the people the good news that God will deliver them (Zimmerli, 7–12).

Should the long formula אני יהוה אלהיך be translated "I am Yahweh, your God" or "I, Yahweh, am your God"? Zimmerli believes that the long formula is an expansion of the shorter one אני יהוה, "I am Yahweh," and thus should be translated "I am Yahweh, your God" (*I Am Yahweh,* 4, 24). The addition of אלהיך, "your God," emphasizes that Yahweh "stands" in a divine and lordly relationship to "his people Israel" (Zimmerli, 4). The long formula may be further expanded by a variety of relative clauses. In 19:36, a clause recounting the Exodus is attached to the long formula (cf. 25:38; 26:13), and in 20:24 it is expanded with a relative clause stating God's purpose in giving Israel the land. At times a participial clause is attached; e.g., מקדשכם, "the one sanctifying you" (20:8; 22:32; similarly 21:15, 23; 22:9, 16). Ordinarily the predicate follows the formula, but in some examples it stands at the head of the formula, throwing the divine name Yahweh into an attributive relationship to the subject, e.g., Lev 19:2: קדוש אני יהוה אלהיכם, "I, Yahweh, your God, am holy" (cf. 20:26; 21:8; Zimmerli, 4–6).

These self-introduction formulae function to locate the authority of a passage, law, or summons to obedience in the name of the giver of that word, namely Yahweh. That is, a formula raises the authority of a law or a series of laws above the socio-political sphere to the divine sphere. Consequently, in obeying these laws the people express their loyalty to Yahweh. This nuance is evident in the use of the long formula to strengthen decrees protecting the rights of the poor and the sojourner (23:22), for Israel is to relate to these unfortunate people just as her God has mercifully related to an enslaved people (cf. Deut 15:12–15; 16:12; 24:17–22). Furthermore, the use of one of these formulae keeps before the people Yahweh's holy character as revealed in the words that the formula underscores.

Elliger ("Ich bin der Herr," 10–25) finds a distinction in the use of these two formulae in Lev 18–26. In his analysis, he distinguishes the theological force of the two formulae. For him the long formula, "I am Yahweh, your God," is tied closely to Yahweh's saving deeds on behalf of his people (e.g., 18:2–4). It communicates the incomprehensible grace of Yahweh, the God who keeps his promises. The short formula, "I am Yahweh," calls to mind that Yahweh is the holy, jealous God, who punishes wrongdoing and rewards obedience (e.g., 18:5, 6, 21). It summons obedience to the decrees both by appealing to the worship of the holy God and by instilling fear of being consumed by that holiness. To state this another way, for Elliger the formula "I am Yahweh" communicates Yahweh's austere, exalted wholeness, which demands true devotion, while the addition of "your God" to the formula contributes the note that Yahweh, the Holy One, is working among his people and for his people so that they may worship him as their God. Elliger (10–16) goes on to identify layers in the text based on which formula is used. Zimmerli, however, finds that this careful distinction between the formulae falters before their indistinguishable uses in several texts; e.g., in Lev 22:33 and 26:45 the short formula, "I am Yahweh," is tied to affirmations about the Exodus as well as in Exod 6:6–8, a critical passage about the revelation of the name of Yahweh in relationship to his delivering Israel from Egyptian slavery. Zimmerli ("I Am Yahweh," 3) concludes that there is no distinct pattern for the employment of one formula in preference to the other.

As to the original life of the formula of divine self-introduction, Zimmerli ("I Am Yahweh," 7–13) traces it back to Yahweh's promise to deliver his people out of Egypt (Exod 6:6–8). In the related passage of Ezek 20:5–7, a historical recounting of this event, the formula is applied to both the Exodus and Yahweh's giving the law at Sinai. The position of the formula in these two texts, along with the frequent wording in Ezekiel "you will know that I am Yahweh" (e.g., 6:7), indicates that Yahweh's intent is for his people to come to know him in the fullness of his name. Thus "the self-introduction is a self-revelation" (Zimmerli, 10); it expresses Yahweh's committing himself to those to whom he has revealed himself (Zimmerli, 10–11). Applying these insights to Lev 18–26, Zimmerli says, "Each of these small groups of legal maxims thereby becomes a legal communication out of the heart of the Old Testament revelation of Yahweh" (12). In the speech-structure of Leviticus, Yahweh speaks directly to a mediator, usually Moses, and that person in turn delivers the word from Yahweh to the congregation in the authority of the formula of Yahweh's self-introduction; this means that both the mediator and the congregation hear the awesome אני יהוה, "I am Yahweh" (Zimmerli, 12–13). The role of this formula in Lev 18–26 then is to teach that Israel's distinctive existence as a people rests on Yahweh's self-revelation of his holy character.

3 Israel is not to follow the customs (מעשׂה) of the Egyptians nor of the Canaanites. When they settle in Canaan, they might be tempted to put into practice some Egyptian customs that had enamored them. Or they might envy some of the practices of the Canaanites so much that they would imitate them. The customs in view are cultic practices rooted in fertility rites and alternative patterns of family relationships. Nor is Israel to walk in the decrees (חקות) of the neighbor nations. "Walk" means to follow these decrees in everyday life by inclination (cf. 20:23; 26:3; Ezek 5:6, 7; 11:20; 18:9, 17; etc.).

4–5 משׁפטים refers to laws in general. Israel is to occupy herself with doing God's משׁפטים, "judgments," and keeping his חקות, "decrees." חקות, coming from the root חקק, "inscribe," refers to definitive decrees, particularly those prescribed by God. Though not limited to a single use, חק often stands for a general, categorical decree (*TWOT* 1:317; G. Liedke, "חקק *ḥqq* einritzen, festsetzen," *THAT* 1:631–32). Often משׁפטים appears with חקות (e.g., 19:37; 20:22); together the two terms mean the whole law given by Yahweh. This command is stated in v 4 and repeated in v 5 with the verbs עשׂה, "do, behave," and שׁמר, "keep," in order to underscore the call to obedience. The term עשׂה, "do," is a very general term, meaning to act according to these laws. שׁמר, "keep," communicates that the will must be exercised in order "to do" the commandments. This style of language is loved in Deuteronomy. In v 5 "keeping" is applied to both laws and decrees. These decrees are to be practiced continually so that they may be ingrained into a person's way of living, their walk. The keeping of God's commandments bears the promise of life (cf. 26:3–13; Deut 28:1–14; also see references to this verse in Ezek 20:11, 13, 21; Neh 9:29). Since humankind disobeyed God in the Garden of Eden (Gen 3), they have been denied access to the tree of life. God has opened a way to life through obedience to the law. What is meant by life here? The text is imprecise. Placed in the context of the parenesis (vv 24–30), it means that Israel will have a secure, healthy life with sufficient goods in the promised land as God's people. Later interpreters (as *Tg. Ps.-J.* and *Tg. Onq.* and early Jewish commentators like Ramban [245]) have taken "life" to mean eternal life. There is little support in the Pentateuch for such a reading of this text. But in the context of both Testaments, God's further revelation in Jesus informs us that God gives his people the gift of eternal life in the resurrection at the end of the age. This is an example of how the language of the OT, while in itself not expressing a specific belief, nevertheless prepares the hearer for the fuller revelation of God.

6 At the head of the series of sexual laws stands a general law prohibiting sexual intercourse with a close relative, one defined as שׁאר בשׂר, "inner flesh of his flesh." שׁאר denotes the flesh with its blood, while בשׂר refers to the outer flesh and can be a legal term for "a family member" (Wolff, *Anthropology*, 29). Lev 21:2–3 lists mother, father, son, daughter, brother, and unmarried sister as one's שְׁאֵר, "flesh." This phrase then expresses the tight bond among family members. ערוה refers to "the pudenda." There is a distinction between nudity and nakedness. Nudity is carried by ערום and עירם, while ערוה and עריה refer to nakedness (Horton, "Form and Structure," 20). From an ancient Israelite perspective, the ערוה is the most private part of the body. It may be properly גלה, "exposed," only in a marriage relationship. The improper or casual exposure of one's ערוה, "pudenda," causes shame (Isa 20:4; Mic 1:11). "To reveal, uncover" another's גלה ערוה, "nakedness," is to have sexual intercourse with that person. This then is a general law that prohibits sexual intercourse between persons of close kinship. Horton (30–31) points out that it functions as a heuristic rule, providing the courts with a basis for deciding cases that are not covered in the following specific laws. Rattray (SBLASP 26, [1987] 542) thus rightly observes that this law forbids sexual relations between a father and a daughter and between a brother and a full sister, even though these cases are not included in the following laws. Another foundational reason why a person is not to engage in illicit sexual relations is expressed by the use of the formula of Yahweh's self-introduction, "I am Yahweh" (cf. v 2). By committing incest a person dishonors Yahweh, who has set these boundaries.

7 A son may not have sexual relations with his mother, because she is his father's wife. This inclusion of the phrase ערות אביך, "the nakedness of your father," along with ערות אמך, "the nakedness of your mother," is striking. Besides overloading the stich, the father is not immediately involved in this specific act. This dual phrase, however, is very important, for it begins these incest laws. Both the father's nakedness and the mother's nakedness are the guiding principle for the incest laws, because it was their nakedness, either by blood line or by marriage, that excluded a son from sexual relationships with next of kin; in any such relationship he dishonors his father or his mother. As for this specific law, the reference to the nakedness of both parents expresses the unity of a married couple—that they are one flesh (Gen 2:24). The dishonoring of a wife by uncovering her nakedness is at the same time the dishonoring of her husband, i.e., the uncovering of his nakedness (Gen 49:4; Deut 23:1[22:30]). In this view a marriage bonds a husband and a wife more closely than does a blood relationship. This law also means that if a father dies, a son cannot take his mother as wife to promote her status and enhance her security (Deut 27:20).

8 A son may not have sexual relations with a wife of his father's other than his mother, for such an act would dishonor his father (Deut 23:1[22:30]; 27:20). Keil and Delitzsch (414) take "father's wife" to include both another wife in a polygamous marriage and a concubine. A primary motivation for a son to take over his father's concubines was the desire to usurp his father's position, for the taking of another's concubines symbolized that a usurper had indeed taken over his opponent's authority (e.g., 2 Sam 16:21–22; 1 Kgs 2:22). This custom indicates the gravity of Reuben's deed in sleeping with Bilhah, one of his father's concubines (Gen 35:22; 49:4). 1 Chr 2:24 reports an example of a son taking his father's wife, but see translation of this verse in R. Braun, *1 Chronicles* (WBC 14 [Waco, TX: Word Books Publisher, 1986] 36); in any case this marital alliance is the exception. Both Ezekiel (22:10) and Paul (1 Cor 5:1–4) denounce such a relationship. See 20:11 for the penalty.

9 A son may not have sexual relations with his sister, whether she is a full sister or a half sister by either his father or his mother, either born at home or elsewhere (cf. Kornfeld, 114–17). This standard contrasts with the practice of Egyptian royalty in marrying their own sisters. The sister is further identified as born at home or abroad, either to his father or to his mother. The precise meaning of חוץ, "abroad, elsewhere," is debated. Hoffmann (2:14), in accord with Jewish tradition (*b. Yebam.* 23a), takes this phrase to mean a blood sister born out of wedlock, while Neufeld (*Ancient Hebrew Marriage Laws,* 197) understands that the law is identifying a stepdaughter who is brought up outside this family as a half sister, i.e., she is raised by her mother's household. The dominant interpretation is that this is a daughter born to one's mother in a previous marriage (cf. Porter, *The Extended Family,* 3). If this is the case, some posit that the father is living with this wife's family, while others hold that the father took his new wife's children into his household, and they became a part of his family unit. Bigger (*JBL* 98 [1979] 190), however, doubts that a family would let any daughters leave with their widowed mother because of their economic value. Though such an occurrence might have been rare, it is conceivable given the complexity of some family situations. Ruth, a Moabitess, accompanied Naomi, her mother-in-law, back to Israel (Ruth 1:16–22). Another position, advocated by Wenham (256) and Porter (*Leviticus,* 146), understands "abroad" to include a half sister who is brought up outside the home. This last position is the most favorable, for it interprets each phrase as having legal application. This law thus applies to both full sisters and half sisters. For the penalty see 20:17.

10 A father may not have sexual relations with a granddaughter, the child of either his son or his daughter. The reason given is that the daughter and the granddaughter are his nakedness, i.e., they bear his very identity. To abuse them is to dishonor himself. It may seem strange that a granddaughter's nakedness is her grandfather's nakedness, not her father's. The reason is that in a father's house the grandfather is head of the family.

11 There have been many attempts to discover how this law identifies a different relationship from those included by the law in v 9. Porter (*The Extended Family,* 16) observes that this law is straightforward and specific, while that in v 9 is composed to cover a wide range of circumstances. The dominant interpretation of this law is that a son may not have sexual relations with a girl born to his father by a woman other than his mother, including a concubine or a maid (e.g., Rashi, 82b; Keil and Delitzsch, 414–15; Hoffmann, 2:16; Porter, *Leviticus,* 146; Snaith, 86). The critical issue for interpreting this law is a determination of the precise meaning of the phrase מולדת אביך, "one begotten of your father." Does it identify only a consanguineous relationship (Bigger, *JBL* 98 [1979] 197), or is it used legally to identify a daughter born to one's father's wife in a former marriage and adopted by one's father (Dillmann, 596; Neufeld, *Ancient Hebrw Marriage Laws,* 199; Kornfeld, 119)? The circuitous phrase בת־אשת אביך "daughter of your father's wife," in contrast to the direct phrase בת אביך, "your father's daughter," in the law in v 9, suggests that there is a significant difference in the sisters being identified. This phraseology favors the second alternative of the above question. If this interpretation is correct, the phrase מולדת אביך, "one begotten of your father," plus the declaratory formula אחותך הוא, "she is your sister," means that a daughter born to a father's wife in a previous marriage who accompanies her mother to one's father's house is both legally and socially one's sister and must be treated as a full or a half sister.

12–13 The circle of prohibited relationships extends to one's aunts, on both sides of the marriage, for they are close blood relations of one's parents. This law protecting a paternal aunt rests on the uncle's high status in the extended family. In extended families, the head's brother often had major responsibility. The incident of Saul's searching for donkeys that had run away sheds a little light on this family structure. His father sent him to look; yet Saul reported back to his uncle (1 Sam 10:14–16; cf. Porter, *The Extended Family*, 18). Secondarily this law addresses situations in which an uncle and a nephew are of similar age. It came into force after the marriage of Moses' parents (Exod 6:20). Cf. Lev 20:19.

14 Certain sexual relationships between people related to a family by marriage are prohibited. A man cannot have sexual relations with his father's brother's wife. By such an act he would dishonor his near relative whose wife she is. The scribes teach that this decree applies only to the wife of a brother on the father's side of the family. She must be treated like a blood-related aunt. Cf. 20:20 for the punishment.

15 A father may not dishonor his son by having sexual relations with his son's wife (כלה) and thus create strife with his closest descendant. At their wedding the father blessed his son's marriage; now in violating his son's wife he corrupts the very relationship he had blessed. In 20:12 this action carries the death penalty. Ezekiel sternly condemns such practices during his time (22:11).

16 One may not have sexual relations with a brother's wife because such activity would dishonor his brother. Cf. Lev 20:21 for the penalty. The practice of levirate marriage was an exception to this general decree, for it was instituted to perpetuate the deceased brother's name and inheritance in Israel (Deut 25:5–10; cf. Neufeld, *Ancient Hebrew Marriage Laws*, 43–44).

17 A man is not to have sexual relations with both a mother and her daughter. This prohibition is expanded to prohibit the marriage of a woman and one of her granddaughters, the child of either her son or her daughter. The reason is that both women are of the same שארה, "flesh" (cf. v 6). Given the natural relationship of the women, this new union would produce bitter tension among those who should love each other and be on equal footing as wives (Bigger, *JBL* 98 [1979] 201). On the one hand, Keil and Delitzsch (415) take this law to specifically exclude relations with a stepdaughter. Porter (*The Extended Family*, 20–21), on the other hand, applies this law to a situation in which a man takes a wife whose mother, being a widow, joins this man's family. For example, when Ruth married Boaz, Naomi probably went with her to Boaz's household, for the account says that Naomi was nurse to Ruth's child (Ruth 4:13–17). This law specifically forbids sexual relationships with a widowed mother-in-law. Hittite laws permit a free man to cohabit with free women, sisters and their mothers, in different lands without penalty, but not in the same place, for that is a capital crime; he may cohabit with sisters and their mother if they are slaves, without penalty (#191, #194; *ANET* 196). In Israel the violation of this law is labeled זמה, "a lewd act."

18 A man may not marry his wife's sister while his wife is living. Anthropologists have found that in some cultures this is a preferred marriage (Rattray,

SBLASP 26 [1987] 539). The reason given here is that he is not to make a sister צרר, "a rival wife." This language recognizes the continual strife between women of the same husband and their rivalry for their husband's affection. Such rivalry could easily rise beyond the point of reasonable tolerance when the wives were sisters, e.g., the contention between Leah and Rachel over their husband Jacob (Gen 29:28–35; 30:1–2, 14–24). This decree is in force only while the first wife is living (#194; *ANET* 196). Tosato (*CBQ* 46 [1984] 199–214) explains this law differently. Based on evidence from Qumran (11QTemple 57:17–19; 66:15–17), he interprets the phrase אשה אל־אחתה, (lit.) "a wife to her sister," as referring to any two women; therefore, this law is a prohibition against polygamy. Sun ("Investigation," 119) correctly finds Tosato's explanation wanting in light of the use of the terms for relationship in the context of this law.

19 See 15:20; also 12:7; 20:18.

20 Sexual relations with an associate's wife (עמית; cf. 5:21[6:2]) are forbidden (cf. Exod 20:14; Deut 22:22). Since such a relationship is not with a blood relative, the term ערוה, "nakedness," is not used. The penalty for such a violation is found in Lev 20:10. Adultery is strongly condemned in the OT. Proverbs 6:32 says, "He who commits adultery has no sense; he who does it destroys himself."

21 Parents are not to העביר, "devote" or "offer," any of their זרע, "offspring," to Molek (cf. 20:2–5; 1 Kgs 11:7; 2 Kgs 23:10; Jer 32:35). העביר means literally "to transfer through." Its use with this repulsive type of sacrifice avoids those terms that describe legitimate sacrifices. The children are sacrificed to Molek. The exact form of the sacrifice is debated (see *Excursus* on Molek at 20:2). Such false sacrifice directly profanes God's holy name. חלל, "to profane," is to debase that which is holy. Since God placed his name among his people, their practice of false worship tarnishes God's reputation among the nations (Ezek 36:20–21).

22 Homosexuality is forbidden (20:13; cf. Rom 1:27; 1 Cor 6:9), being classified as detestable (תועבה; cf. vv 26, 27, 29; 20:13). Something detestable is an activity that God abhors. One dimension of the horrendous incident reported in Judg 19 involved the homosexual drive of some of the men of Gibeah in Benjamin against a stranger. Their wanton behavior led to their being proscribed by all the other tribes.

23 Bestiality is forbidden for both a man and a woman. A man is not to lie with an animal, and a woman is not to flaunt herself seeking to seduce a beast. The use of רבע, "lie down (to copulate)," which occurs in 19:19 for breeding of animals, underscores the animalistic nature of such an act. Krebs (*FF* 39 [1963] 19) argues that this law is designed to counter rites between humans and animals practiced in certain pagan cults of the Ancient Middle East, such as the Egyptian cult at Mendes (Egyptian Dedet). He gathers some evidence to prove that such rites took place more often than has been supposed. These ritualistic uses of bestiality show that this law was designed to fulfill the exhortation against following the practices of the Egyptians and the Canaanites (vv 3, 24). Bestiality would not be that uncommon in an agrarian society. In fact, Hittite law assigns the death penalty to lying with some animals, cattle, sheep, and pigs, but lying with a horse or a mule carries no penalty (#187, #188, #199, #200[A]; *ANET* 196–97). The myths from Ugarit report sexual relations between gods and animals; e.g., the mighty storm god Baal had sexual relations with a cow in an attempt to magically escape the tentacles of Mot, the god of death and the underworld (cf. U. Cassuto,

A Commentary on the Book of Exodus, tr. I. Abrahams [Jerusalem: Magnes, 1967] 290). The cosmology of the OT places barriers between the divine realm and the human realm and between the human realm and the animal realm; any mixing of these barriers is considered unnatural, a confusion (תבל; Exod 22:18[19]; Lev 20:15–16; Deut 27:21). The confusion is both of species and of social roles (Bigger, *JBL* 98 [1979] 203). Such mixing is contrary to wholeness and holiness; as M. Douglas states, "holiness requires that different classes of things shall not be confused" (*Purity*, 53).

24–25 These laws are given in order to prevent Israel from adopting the various sexual practices of the peoples who inhabited Canaan. These practices defile God's people. Israel's polytheistic neighbors energetically pursued fertility rites to insure the fertility of their fields, flocks, and households. But for Israel a close bond exists between human behavior and the fertility of the land. When the people obey God's laws, God blesses the land, and it bears abundantly. But if the people defile themselves by immoral, particularly sexual, practices such as the former inhabitants of the land practiced, they will defile the land. The land will become so nauseated by such behavior that it will vomit out its inhabitants. It is God himself who will administer the emetic causing the land to vomit out its inhabitants. Only by getting rid of that which is making it sick can the land recover. This language is picturesque to describe a time of drought or plague; it means that God will punish his people's immoral behavior by withholding rain and sending plagues. The crops will wither and vanish. Faced by death, the people will be forced to leave their land in search of food. Or war may be the emetic that God will use. Ironically the very fertility rites the people engage in to increase the fertility of their land will pollute the land. Israel must not be deceived by the beliefs behind the practices of her neighbors.

26 Israel can avoid the terrible fate described in the last two verses by following God's law. Everyone in her midst, both the citizen and the alien, is to keep God's laws in order to preserve the land undefiled.

27–28 This principle of defiling the land and being expelled from the land serves as an apologetic for Israel's occupying the land of others. The former inhabitants have defiled the land by their abominable practices; now the land is about to spew them out. But Israel too is accountable to God. She must guard herself from defiling the land and being spewed out also.

29–30 This principle regarding these detestable practices is applied to individuals. Those guilty of such behavior are to be cut off (נכרת) from the people (cf. 7:20). The doing of God's whole law is the best preventive against immorality and divine punishment.

Explanation

The decrees regarding incest and improper sexual relations promote the integrity of the extended family. Since the family was the core block of the covenant community, a solid family unit was crucial for Israel to be a vital nation under Yahweh. In antiquity, membership in a father's house was essential for survival. Only closely knit families could provide food for all members and protect themselves from enemies and natural forces. Family members had to be free to work together in close relationships without fear of sexual molestation, and each one had to respect the marital bonds of all other family members. Thus observance of these decrees formulated a basis for family stability and for the protection of the women of that family. In addition, these decrees guarded the purity of a family's lineage.

These laws state that no male may dishonor another close relative by sleeping with that relative's mate. Incest carries the possibility of spawning jealousy and hatred, leading to strife and violence among family members. The account of Tamar and Amnon (2 Sam 13:1–19) bears witness to the disruptive force of incest; strife and hatred reverberated for years in David's family (2 Sam 13:20–18:33). Thus the penalties for these transgressions are severe, including the death penalty, the penalty of being cut off by God from his covenant people, and the penalty of dying childless (20:10–21).

Even though women had less status than men in ancient Israelite society, this legislation has a high regard for women. Women are not to be the indiscriminate objects of men's sexual passion. No, they are human beings worthy of respect as persons. A woman's dignity, grounded on her role in the family, was not to be violated by the sexual aggression of males in that household. Her husband's honor was intimately bound to hers. This is visible in the justification given for prohibiting non-blood close relatives from having sexual unions: such a union dishonors the husband. The honor of the family resides in the integrity of the personal bond between husband and wife, not in the wife's being the husband's property. To dishonor one member of a couple is to dishonor the other. Thus laws of this nature pointed the way for the elevation of the position and the honor of women in society.

While not much is said about children, the laws about grandchildren indicate that children are not to be abused or molested. Moreover, the laws against offering children to Molek reveal that children are not to be treated as objects that may be used as the parents desire or as expendable in order to move the divine world to answer the anxieties and whims of their parents.

There are decrees against abnormal sexual relationships. Adultery, homosexuality, and bestiality are forbidden. Such activities fall outside the boundaries of acceptable sexual unions. Such sexual unions are confusing and repulsive. They destroy rather than enhance human dignity before God.

These laws also rule against participation in any sort of divination, spiritism, sorcery, or necromancy. Turning to these dark sources for insight into the future implies that a person does not trust God to meet his future needs. Furthermore, it implies that God himself is subject to external, impersonal forces. Necromancy is especially repulsive, for OT belief finds that death is the ultimate curse, the source of the greatest defilement. To seek spiritual experience by contacting the dead is to deny that God is the living God (Deut 5:26; Josh 3:10; Jer 10:10; Ps 18:47[45]), the sustainer of life (Ps 104:30). Conversely, the promise of life is the wonderful promise of obeying these laws (Lev 18:5).

The NT builds on and enhances the goal of these laws regulating family relations and prohibiting wizardry. The NT promotes the respect men have for women and women for men (1 Tim 5:1–2; Gal 3:28). Each believer is to put away lust and prejudice (Col 3:5; Matt 5:28; Gal 5:24; 1 Thess 4:5; 2 Tim 2:22). The NT teaches that the way one partner treats the other directly affects a person's spiritual life (1 Pet 3:7). Each believer is called to the highest standard of self-giving love. This standard dramatically affects interpersonal relationships, beginning in the home. Wives win their husbands to Christ by a holy, loving disposition (1 Pet 3:1–6). Children are to obey their parents (Eph 6:1–3; Col 3:20). Conversely, parents are not to abuse or exploit their children as the dark side of modern society does. Paul exhorts parents, "Do not provoke your children to wrath" (Eph 6:4), for provoking can twist a child's spirit, undermining the development of a good character (Col 3:21). Husbands are to love their wives even as Christ loved the church (Eph 5:25–27). This exhortation is grounded on the greatest expression of love ever seen in the world. The dynamic of love and respect between a husband and a wife builds a solid home even in today's turbulent society.

The church faces a very difficult task encouraging believers to build solid families, for the modern megalopolis with its highly mobile lifestyle undercuts the solidarity of a family. Nevertheless, the church needs to take up this challenging task with resolve, for a family provides the most favorable environment for the spiritual and moral development of believers. There is also another avenue of hope. Given the bonding that members in Christ experience, the church itself has the opportunity to become a body of families. By broadening the size of the nuclear family through the fellowship of believers, the church will help address some of the pressing social ills of modern urban society.

Since modern society looks at adultery and homosexuality far more permissively than does this legislation, where should the church stand on these issues? In the NT these kinds of sexual unions are still viewed as transgressions of God's law (Rom 1:24–27; 1 Cor 6:9–10). Nonetheless, the church needs to show compassion and concern to any who live by such open or alternative lifestyles (Jude 22–23). It needs to relate to these people just as Jesus treated adulteresses. With patient tenderness the church can lead those who live by these practices into a new, redeemed life, a life of holiness (2 Tim 2:24–26). Change in a redeemed person's lifestyle often takes place slowly; nevertheless, as a person is open to the work of the Holy Spirit, amazing changes take place (Rom 12:1–2).

Another foundational issue addressed in this speech is the bond between human behavior and the land's ability to support the human race. This speech teaches that immoral behavior pollutes the land. The land will become so polluted that it will not be able to support well all its inhabitants. As Leviticus says, the land will become so sick from this pollution that it will vomit out its inhabitants. In the OT this metaphor functions as a strong argument against the pursuit of pagan practices that promote fertility through sexual rites. Israel's neighbors believed that these rites guaranteed the productivity of their land and their flocks. But for Israel the land is fruitful solely because God blesses it. God blesses it in response to his people's obedience. But if Israel turns to follow the defiling fertility practices of her neighbors, instead of making her land more fruitful she will actually defile it. The land will become so defiled that it will no longer support Israel.

This understanding of the relationship between moral behavior and the land's ability to support a people seems very foreign to us. However, it is not as foreign as it appears on first reading. Modern people are learning the hard way that a close tie exists between human behavior and the purity of the land. Out of greed and disrespect people have abused the land, such as by overusing fertilizers and pesticides to produce a valuable crop in abundance or by stripping the land of its timber and leaving the hillsides desolate. The results of these procedures are grievous. The land loses its fertility. The water supply is endangered. The food chain is poisoned. Species become extinct. People become ill, seriously ill. Only with much effort can the ecosystem be made pure again. While this OT text does not speak of conservation as such, it does address the issue that there is a close tie between the land and people's moral behavior. These two issues touch when sinful attitudes lead to poor management of the earth's resources. The multiple hazards from the rampant pollution of the environment tell us that the earth's population is facing several major crises. At the heart of these crises lie the human attitudes of greed for wealth and lust for an easy, sensual life. To date we are not willing to have less and pay the price of revamping our means of production in order to ensure pure water, air, and land. The pollution all about us urgently calls us to repent and take a different course before the planet vomits out the human species.

In conclusion, the goal of this speech is life: a long life as a blessing for obedience to God's laws, a happy family life, and a life supported by a fertile land. This chapter calls on the people of God to be diligent in obeying the divine law. As the people of God we are to live by the revealed word of God. This revelation shows the way to life. That promise comes to its highest fulfillment in Jesus who says, "I am life" (John 14:6; cf. John 10:10). Today the church is called to live a distinct life, a holy life in obedience to God, just as Israel was (1 Pet 1:14–16; 2 Pet 3:11). This means that believers have to live by a higher standard than do their secular neighbors, a standard constructed on the confession that God is holy (Matt 5:13–16, 48).

C. Laws and Exhortations to Holy Living (19:1–37)

Bibliography

Albertz, R. "Hintergrund und Bedeutung des Elterngebots im Dekalog." *ZAW* 90 (1978) 348–74. **Amusin, J. D.** "Die Gerim in der sozialen Legislatur des Alten Testaments." *Klio* 63 (1981) 15–23. **Auerbach, E.** "Das Zehngebot—Allgemeine Gesetzes-Form in der Bibel." *VT* 16 (1966) 255–76. **Berger, K.** *Die Gesetzesaulegung Jesu: Ihr historischer Hintergrund im Judentum und im Alten Testament. Teil I: Markus und Parallelen.* Neukirchen-Vluyn: Neukirchener, 1972. 80–136. **Brongers, H. A.** "Fasting in Israel in Biblical and Post-Biblical Times." *OTS* 20 (1977) 1–21. **Carmichael, C. M.** "Forbidden Mixtures." *VT* 32 (1982) 394–415. **Davidson, R.** "Some Aspects of the Old Testament Contribution to the Pattern of Christian Ethics." *SJT* 12 (1959) 373–87. **Derrett, J. D. M.** "'Love thy neighbour as a man like thyself'?" *ExpTim* 83 (1971) 55–66. **Freedman, B.** "Leviticus and DNA: A Very Old Look at a New Problem." *JRE* 8 (1980) 105–13. **Gese, H.** "Der Dekalog als Ganzheit betrachtet." *ZTK* 64 (1967) 121–38 (=*Von Sinai zum Zion.* Beiträge zur evangelischen Theologie 64. Munich: Chr. Kaiser, 1974. 63–80). **Gewalt, D.** "Taube und Blinde nach Levitikus 19,14." *DBAT* 22 (1985) 119–39. **Grintz, J. M.** "'Do not eat on the blood.'" *ASTI* 8 (1972) 78–105. **Hockerman, Y.** "Rebuke of One's Fellow according to the Bible and Rabbinic Sources" (Heb.). *Beth Mikra* 28 (1982/83) 140–46. **Hogg, J. E.** "'Love thy Neighbor'." *AJSL* 41 (1924/25) 197–98. **Houtman, C.** "Another look at forbidden mixtures." *VT* 34 (1984) 226–28. **Jagersma, H.**

Leviticus 19: Identiteit-Bevrijding-Gemeenschap. Studia Semitica Neerlandica 14. Assen: Van Gorcum, 1972. **Johnson, L. T.** "The Use of Leviticus 19 in the Letter of James." *JBL* 101 (1982) 391–401. **Keller, J.** "Theological Linguistics: A Suggestion." *JRelS* 12 (1985) 46–55. **Koch, R.** "L'imitation de Dieu dans la morale de l'Ancien Testament." *StMor* 2 (1964) 73–88. **Kugel, J. L.** "On Hidden Hatred and Open Reproach: Early Exegesis of Leviticus 19:17." *HTR* 80 (1987) 43–61. **Loss, N. M.** "A proposito di Lev. 19,19b e di Deut. 22,10." *RBibIt* 6 (1958) 361–64. **Maass, F.** "Die Selbstliebe noch Leviticus 19, 18." *FS F. Baumgärtel.* Ed. J. Herrmann. Erlangen: Universitätsbund Erlanger, 1959. 109–13. **Magonet, J.** "The Structure and Meaning of Leviticus 19." *HAR* 7 (1983) 151–67. **Malamat, A.** "'Love Your Neighbor as Yourself': What It Really Means." *BAR* 16 (1990) 50–51. **Mathys, H-P.** *Liebe deinen Nächsten wie dich selbst: Untersuchung zum alttestamentlichen Gebot der Nächstenliebe (Lev 19, 18).* Orbis Biblicus et Orientalis 71. Göttingen: Vandenhoeck & Ruprecht, 1986. **Montefiore, H.** "Thou Shalt Love Thy Neighbor as Thyself." *NT* 5 (1962) 157–70. **Morgenstern, J.** "The Decalogue of the Holiness Code." *HUCA* 26 (1955) 1–27. **Mowinckel, S.** "Zur Geschichte der Dekalog." *ZAW* 55 (1937) 218–35. **Muraoka, T.** "A Syntactic Problem in Lev. xix. 18b." *JSS* 23 (1978) 291–97. **Piper, J.** *'Love your enemies': Jesus' love command in the synoptic gospels and in the early Christian paraenesis.* Cambridge: Cambridge UP, 1979. 30–32, 91–95. **Raitt, T. M.** "Holiness and Community in Leviticus 19:2ff." *Proceedings, Eastern Great Lakes and Midwest Biblical Societies* 6 (1986) 170–78. **Ratschow, C. H.** "Agape, Nächstenliebe und Bruderliebe." *ZST* 21 (1950) 160–82. **Sampley, J. P.** *"And the two shall become one flesh": A Study of Traditions in Ephesians 5:21–33.* Society for New Testament Studies. Monograph series 16. Cambridge: UP, 1971. 30–34, 139–41, 158–60. **Schwartz, B. J.** "A Literary Study of the Slave-girl Pericope—Leviticus 19:20–22." *Scripta Hierosolymitana* 31 (1986) 241–55. **Schwartz, G.** "Begünstige nicht . . . ?" *BZ* 19 (1975) 100. **Ullendorff, E.** "Thought Categories in the Hebrew Bible." In *Studies in Rationalism, Judaism & Universalism in Memory of L. Roth.* Ed. R. Loewe. London: Routledge and Kegan Paul; NY: The Humanities Press, 1966. 276–78. **Vriezen, T. C.** "Bubers Auslegung des Liebesgebots, Lev. 19, 18b." *TZ* 22 (1966) 1–11. **Zimmermann, F.** "An Examination of Some Biblical Passages." *JBL* 65 (1946) 312.

Translation

1 *Yahweh spoke to Moses:* 2 *"Speak to the congregation*[a] *of Israelites and say to them:*
You will be holy, because I, Yahweh your God, am holy.

3 *"Each*[a] *of you shall revere his mother and his father.*[b] *You shall keep my sabbaths;*[c] *I*
am Yahweh your God. 4 *Do not turn to idols,*[a] *and you shall not make molten images*[b] *for*
yourselves;[c] *I am Yahweh your God.*

5 *"Whenever you sacrifice an offering of well-being to Yahweh, you are to sacrifice it so*
that it will be acceptable on your behalf.[a] 6 *It is to be eaten on the day that you sacrifice it*
and the next day; whatever is left until the third day is to be burned with fire. 7 *If it is ever*[a]
eaten on the third day, it is defiled meat; it will not be accepted. 8 *Whoever eats*[a] *it will be*
held accountable, because he has profaned that which is holy to Yahweh. That person[b]
shall be cut off from his people.

9 *"When you reap*[a] *the harvest of your land, you shall not reap*[b] *right up to the edges*
of your field, and you shall not gather the gleanings of your harvest. 10 *You shall not strip*[a]
your vineyard bare nor gather the fallen[b] *grapes of your vineyard. You are to leave them*
for the poor and the resident alien;[c] *I am Yahweh your God.*

11 *"You shall not steal; you shall not lie; you shall not deceive an associate.*[a] 12 *You shall*
not swear falsely by my name and thus profane[a] *the name of your God. I am Yahweh.*[b]

13 *"You shall not exploit your friend, and you shall not rob him. You*[a] *shall not hold*
back the wages of a hired worker until the morning. 14 *You shall not curse the deaf; you*

shall not put a stumbling block before the blind, but you will fear[a] *your God; I am Yahweh.*[b]

15 *"You shall not do*[a] *injustice in judgment. You*[b] *shall not be partial to the poor nor favor the great.*[c] *You are to judge your associate in righteousness.* 16 *You shall not go about as a slanderer*[a] *among your relatives;*[b] *you*[c] *shall not jeopardize your friend's life;*[d] *I am Yahweh.*[e]

17 *"You shall not hate your brother in your heart, but you shall openly*[a] *dispute with your associate lest*[b] *you be held responsible for sin because of him.* 18 *You shall not seek revenge*[ab] *or bear a grudge*[c] *against any of your fellow countrymen. You shall love your companion*[d] *as yourself.*[e] *I am Yahweh.*

19 *"You shall keep my decrees.*[a] *You shall not mate*[b] *two different kinds of animals.*[ac] *You shall not sow your fields*[ad] *with two kinds of seeds. You shall not wear clothing*[a] *made of two kinds of yarn.*[e]

20 *"If a man has intercourse*[a] *with a woman who is a slave*[b] *betrothed*[c] *to another man but who has never*[d] *been ransomed or given her freedom,*[e] *there is to be an inquiry.*[fg] *They shall not be put to death,*[h] *because she has not been freed.*[i] 21 *He is to bring a reparation offering for Yahweh to the entrance to the Tent of Meeting; it is a ram of reparation.* 22 *The priest is to perform the rite of expiation for him before Yahweh with the ram of reparation for his sin which he has committed. He will be forgiven of the sin which he has committed.*

23 *"When you enter the land*[a] *and plant any kind of fruit tree, you are to regard its fruit*[b] *as unharvestable.*[c] *You will consider it unharvestable for three years; it shall not be eaten.* 24 *In the fourth year all its fruit is*[a] *to be regarded as a holy gift, an offering of praise*[b] *to Yahweh.* 25 *In the fifth year you may eat its fruit; thus its yield will be increased*[a] *for you. I am Yahweh, your God.*

26 *"You shall not eat anything with the blood*[a] *in it. You shall not*[b] *practice augury, and you shall not practice divination.*

27 *"You shall not cut the hair at the sides of your head, and you shall not*[a] *trim*[b] *the edge of your beard.*[b] 28 *You shall not make gashes*[a] *on your bodies for the dead.*[b] *You shall not tattoo yourselves. I am Yahweh.*[c]

29 *"Do not degrade your daughter by making her a prostitute so that the land may not be prostituted and become full of lewdness.*

30 *"You are to keep my Sabbaths and revere my sanctuary. I am Yahweh.*

31 *"Do not turn to ghosts*[a] *and do not seek departed spirits*[b] *to become unclean by them. I am Yahweh, your God.*

32 *"You are to stand in the presence of the aged, show respect for the elderly,*[a] *and fear your God. I am Yahweh.*[b]

33 *"When an alien lives among you*[a] *in your land, you shall not mistreat*[b] *him.* 34 *You are to treat the alien living among you as*[a] *a native. You shall love him*[b] *as a person like you, for you were aliens in Egypt. I am Yahweh, your God.*

35 *"You shall not do injustice in measures*[a] *of length, weight, or capacity.* 36 *You are to have an honest*[a] *scale, an honest*[a] *weight, an honest*[a] *ephah,*[bc] *and an honest*[a] *hin.*[d] *I am Yahweh, your God, who brought you out of Egypt.*[e]

37 *"You shall keep all my decrees and all my laws, and you shall do them. I am Yahweh."*[a]

Notes

2.a. A few Heb. mss omit כל־עדת, "all the congregation of," while LXX omits כל, "all"; 11QpaleoLev appears to support LXX, giving this reading greater weight (*PLS*, 36–37). This is the only place that עדה, the official assembly of Israel, occurs in a commission-to-speak formula in Leviticus. עדה occurs in Leviticus, though, a few times, e.g., 4:13, 15; 8:3–5; 9:5; 10:6 (cf. n. 4:13.a.). Sun ("Investigation," 172) judges MT to be an inferior text as a result of harmonization to a more common reading.

3.a. The subj איש, "man," standing at the head of a command in the pl, has individualizing force.

3.b. The placing of the dir obj between the subj and the verb is highly unusual. The order of "mother" preceding "father" in an ancient patriarchal society is also unusual (cf. 21:2; 20:19). LXX, Tg^mss, Syr, and Vg invert this order possibly to conform to the preferential order of listing a father first in their respective societies. MT is accepted as the harder reading.

3.c. In the Heb. text the dir obj comes first for emphasis.

4.a. This term for god, אליל, "little god, godling," "was created as a disparaging pun on and as a diminutive of *ʾel* ['the Strong One'] or *ʾelohim* ['god'] (Ps 97:7)," according to H. Preuss ("אֱלִיל *ʾelîl*," *TDOT* 1:285; cf. S. Schwertner, "אֱלִיל *ʾelîl* Nichtigkeit," *THAT* 1:167–69). This term is not used as an adj. In the prophets idols are scornfully ridiculed as the product of human hands (Isa 2:8, 20; Hab 2:18–19; cf. Ps 96:4–5; cf. Ps 97:7). In the day of judgment these worthless objects will not afford their worshipers any help and will be cast away by their enemies (Isa 2:20; 31:7). Idols are weak, and worshiping them is a vain exercise.

4.b. מסכה, "molten image," comes from the root נסך, "pour out." It refers to an idol made from molten metal either poured into a cast or over a frame made of wood or cheap metal (Isa 40:19–20). Such idols were cast of gold (Exod 32:4, 8), silver (Isa 30:22), bronze, or iron (cf. *TWOT* 2:1376).

4.c. In stich A there is a chiastic pattern—negated verb:object in form of prepositional phrase::object:negated verb.

5.a. This verse has a modified chiastic pattern; it begins and ends with the verb זבח, "sacrifice."

7.a. Sam reads a qal inf abs אכל instead of the niph האכל. The inf abs before the verb emphasizes the verbal idea.

8.a. As in 17:14, Sam and the versions read אכלו, "the one who eats"; MT is to be understood as a distributive pl (PIR, 188–89).

8.b. In place of MT הנפש ההוא, "that person," LXX reads *αἱ ψυχαὶ αἱ ἔσθουσαι*, "the persons who eat."

9.a. The inf constr has a double acc; the pronominal suffix functions as subj of a temporal clause since the inf constr stands after a prep; the other acc functions as dir obj.

9.b. The inf + ל standing as obj of the verb כלה identifies the direction of the action (GKC §114m).

10.a. עלל means "to glean" and may be related to Arab *ʿalla*, "to do a second time." It also means "to treat severely" (Lam 1:22; 3:51). Thus it means "to glean" with thoroughness (cf. Snaith, 90).

10.b. פרט occurs only here in OT; it refers to loose grapes, grapes not in a cluster, those growing singularly or those that have fallen off.

10.c. In the Heb. text this compound indir obj stands at the head of this sentence for emphasis.

11.a. Cf. n. 5:21.b.

12.a. Interpreting the grammar differently, Hoffmann (2:39) takes the negative particle of the preceding sentence to apply to חללת: "do not profane" (so GKC §152z). Nevertheless, it is possible to take the second sentence as a result clause. LXX reads a pl verb and a pl pronominal suffix on אלהי, "God," so that both stichs agree in number.

12.b. LXX adds *ὁ θεὸς ὑμῶν*, "your God," conforming this formula to the longer one found at the beginning of this chapter (vv 2, 3).

13.a. Several Heb. mss, Sam^mss, LXX, Tg^mss, and *Tg. Ps.-J.* read a *waw*.

14.a. LXX inserts *κύριον*, "Lord."

14.b. Cf. n. 12.b.

15.a. Sam has a sg verb form, bringing this verb into conformity with the rest of the verse.

15.b. A few Heb. mss and Syr read a *waw*.

15.c. Magonet (*HAR* 7 [1983] 158) has keenly observed that the combination דל, "poor," and גדול, "great," an unusual pair, has been chosen for assonance. Usually דל is paralleled with עָשִׁיר, "rich" (Exod 30:15; Prov 10:15; 22:16; 28:11), and גדול with קטן, "small" (1 Sam 5:9; Jer 6:13). This is a skilled rhetorical device.

16.a. The substantive רכיל, "slanderer," is an acc used to describe the bearing of the one who is הלך, "going about" (GKC §118q).

16.b. Many Heb. mss, Sam, and LXX read a sg noun בעמך, "with your people," but this pl occurs in 21:1, 4, 14, 15; 23:29 and Gen 49:29.

16.c. Many Heb. mss, Sam^mss, Syr, and Tg^mss have ולא, "and not."

16.d. Magonet (*HAR* 7 [1983] 158) points out that in two phrases of this verse consonants have been alternated in successive words for rhetorical effect. In the phrase לא־תלך רכיל, "you shall not go about as a slanderer," כ and ל are interchanged, and in the phrase לא תעמד על־דם, "you shall not jeopardize a life," מ and ד are interchanged.

16.e. Cf. n. 12.b.

17.a. The inf abs before the verb strengthens the idea conveyed by the verb; it adds weight to the antithesis between these two clauses (GKC §113n, p; cf. Joüon §125q).

17.b. A few Heb. mss do not read the *waw.*

18.a. Syr omits לא תקם, "you shall not seek revenge." LXX reads ולא, "and not," as in the majority of verses in this series.

18.b. LXX adds *σου ἡ χείρ*, "your hand," as subj.

18.c. נקם, "take vengeance," and נטר, "keep, bear a grudge," occur together in Nah 1:2. Keil and Delitzsch (421) understand נטר, lit. "watch for," to mean in this context "to cherish a design on a person, or to bear him malice" (cf. Ps 103:9; Jer 3:5, 12; Nah 1:2). נטר occurs only here with את.

18.d. אהב with ל only 19:34 and 2 Chr 19:2 (Bertholet, 68). The ל here introduces the dir obj of אהב (Joüon §125k; *IBHS* §11.2.10g; also 2 Chr 19:2). Mathys (*Liebe,* 4–5) shows how some authors like M. Buber (*Two Types of Faith,* tr. N. Goldhawk [London: Routledge & Kegan Paul, 1951] 68–75) and E. Ullendorff ("Thought Categories," 277) interpret אהב ל as having slightly less force than the usual אהב את; for them it means "to have love, to like someone, to treat kindly." Since some of these writers hold that this phraseology makes fulfillment of the command more possible, Mathys argues that these authors are motivated in their judgment more by theology than by linguistic principles. But some distinction needs to be made, even though slight, between these two expressions.

18.e. The precise meaning of כמוך, "like you," is debated. Does it have adverbial force and thus modify the verb, "love like yourself" (so LXX)? If this were the intended meaning, the expected term would be כנפשך, but Mathys (*Liebe,* 6–9) argues that there is no major distinction between these two phrases. Another way of taking this phrase, according to Muraoka (*JSS* 23 [1958] 294–96), is as a non-restrictive relative clause modifying רעך, "your companion"; NEB thus renders it "as a man like yourself." In a similar vein Ullendorff ("Thought Categories," 276–77) interprets כמוך as a brachylogy, the כי, "for," being omitted: "for he is as yourself." But Mathys (9) points out that כמוך does not function as a clause; rather it is in apposition to the preceding noun רעך, "your companion" (cf. Job 35:8; Neh 6:11; Deut 18:15). Ullendorff's reading has much to commend it, for it accounts for the presence of the phrase without attributing to the ancient text an advanced understanding of the relationship between self-love and love of a companion. Muraoka also suggests that Sir 28:1–7 may be an exposition on this commandment.

19.a. In this verse all four dir objs stand first for emphasis.

19.b. רבע means "to lie down" and by extension "to copulate, breed." When it appears in OT for "copulation," it is used for an abnormal sexual union (18:23; 20:16). R. L. Harris (2:606–7) proposes another way to read this line. He assigns to רבע its basic meaning of "lie down": "Do not make your animals fall down with an unequal yoke." This reading brings this verse into alignment with Deut 22:10.

19.c. בהמה is collective. Regarding such breeding, the OT does witness to mules being present in ancient Israel (2 Sam 13:29; 18:9; 1 Kgs 1:33; 18:5, etc); it is unlikely that all these mules came from foreign sources (1 Kgs 10:25; Ezek 27:14; Isa 66:20; cf. Bertholet, 68); nor were they looked on that disparagingly. This is one of the motivations for Harris to seek another reading of this line (cf. n. 19.b.).

19.d. In place of MT שדך, "your field," LXX reads *καὶ τὸν ἀμπελῶνά σου*, "and your vineyard," being influenced by the similar verse in Deut 22:9. שדה is taken as a collective.

19.e. שעטנז, "yarn," a unique form, suggests that it is a foreign word. Albright proposed that it is an Egyptian word; that word has not been attested, but in light of Coptic Lambdin reconstructs the Egyptian as *šaʿd-núbğ* (T. Lambdin, "Egyptian Loan words in OT," *JAOS* 73 [1953] 155). This word appears again only in the parallel passage of Deut 22:11. There it is a cloth made out of צמר, "wool" and פשתים, "linen." Thus it means cloth woven from two different materials.

20.a. Cf. n. 15:16.a.

20.b. Schwartz (*Scripta Hierosolymitana* 31 [1986] 244) points out that the usual term for a slave-girl is אמה; he reasons that שפחה is chosen here for assonance with חפשה, "free," a key term in this law.

20.c. This is the only occurrence in OT of חרף, "betrothed, assigned" (KB, 342), i.e., a contract of marriage has been set, but not yet executed.

20.d. MT הָפְדֵּה is a hoph inf abs; since it stands before a verb in the niph, it is best to repoint it as a niph inf abs הִפָּדֵה (so *BHS;* cf. GKC §113w; Joüon §123p). Schwartz (*Scripta Hierosolymitana* 31 [1986] 246) states that the inf abs is used to highlight the contract. He goes on to claim that the hoph communicates both that her owner is obligated to let her be redeemed and that her fiancé is obligated to pay the price of redemption.

20.e. חפשׁה, "freedom," only occurs here in OT. Schwartz (*Scripta Hierosolymitana* 31 [1986] 247) points out that the use of נתן, "give," with this noun conveys the possibility that her owner could free her *gratis*.

20.f. This is the only OT occurrence of בקרת. If it comes from the root בקר, it may mean "inquiry" (so Rashi), but KB takes it to mean "liable for damages" related to Akk *b/paqru* (from E. A. Speiser, "Leviticus and the Critics," *Y. Kaufmann Jubilee Volume* [1960] 33–36). Milgrom (*ZAW* 89 [1977] 43) discovers that the meaning "indemnity" for the Akk term does not exist. Therefore, "inquiry" is the best rendering. Schwartz (*Scripta Hierosolymitana* 31 [1986] 249–51) rejects Milgrom's position by the argument that the girl's ambiguous status is "a primary datum," hence not verifiable. He proposes בקרת is from the root בקר, "split, divide," and means "discrimination, distinction." If Milgrom's position can be maintained, it offers the best sense, for the facts of this type of case need to be established for this specific law to be applied.

20.g. Sam adds לו, "to him"; LXX adds αὐτοῖς, "to them."

20.h. Sam reads a sg form יומת; this variant levels the text to conform to the sg verbs preceding and following this verb.

20.i. *IBHS* (§22.6b) identifies חפשׁה, "freed," as a qal pass, though it is pointed as a pual.

23.a. LXX adds ἣν κύριος ὁ θεὸς δίδωσιν ὑμῖν, "which the Lord God gives to you." This is a frequent formula that has crept into the LXX text. Clearly the MT is preferred as the shorter reading.

23.b. LXX takes ὁ καρπὸς αὐτοῦ, "its fruit," as subj of the next clause.

23.c. וערלתם ערלתו את־פריו, lit. "and you will regard its fruit as truly uncircumcised." The cognate acc underscores the unacceptableness of its fruit for the covenant people, just as the uncircumcised stand outside the covenant.

24.a. Sam reads a pl verb.

24.b. Sam reads חלולים, "profane, common," for MT הלולים, "praise." This variant would mean that this offering renders future harvests profane, i.e., available for common use (PIR, 192).

25.a. Sam ms reads לאסיף, "to gather," in place of MT להוסיף, "to add." Elliger (261) prefers this variant, or he suggests that MT is a spelling variant for אסף. However, the promise of increase for observing laws that restrict access to food occurs elsewhere, as in 25:18–22.

26.a. For MT על־הדם, "on the blood," LXX reads ἐπὶ τῶν ὀρέων = על־הרם, "on the mountains" (cf. Ezek 18:6, 11, 15; 22:9). This variant is attractive, for the Israelites would go out to the mountain to worship other gods and spirits. MT may elliptically describe a cultic practice, but the meaning of the idiom has not been preserved.

26.b. Two Heb. mss, Sam, and LXX read ולא, "and not." This variant supports the alternate reading in n. 26.a., for it makes a series out of the verse rather than two distinct ideas.

27.a. A Heb. ms, Sam, a couple of LXX mss, Tg, and Vg read ולא, "and not." Cf. n. 18.a.

27.b. Sam, LXX, Syr, and Tg have a pl verb and a pl pronominal suffix on זקן, "beard." *Tg. Onq.* agrees with MT. This change agrees with the pls in the first stich.

28.a. Sam reads ושׂרטה; cf. 21:5. The dir obj comes first for emphasis.

28.b. In a few texts, נפשׁ means "a deceased person." Originally the phrase was נפשׁ מת, "a dead person" (Num 6:6), and then נפשׁ was used elliptically for this expression (21:1; 22:4; Num 5:2; 6:11; 9:10; Hag 2:13; BDB, "נפשׁ 4.c.15," 660).

28.c. A few Heb. mss, LXX, and Syr add אלהיכם, "your God," as in n. 12.b.

31.a. The identification of אוב has not been settled. Some identify it with אוב, "a bottle made out of skin" (e.g., Job 32:19). Working from this etymology, some postulate that ventriloquism was a technique employed in seances. Hoffner ("Second Millennium Antecedents to the Hebrew *ʾōb*," *JBL* 86 (1967) 385–401; "אוֹב *ʿôbh*," *TDOT* 1:130–34) puts forth the view that אוב is "a non-Semitic migratory word": *aptu* in Akk, *a-a-bi* in Hittite, *ʾēb* in Ugar mean "sacrificial pit." Hittite ritual texts offer insight into how such pits were used. At a site chosen by the gods, a pit was dug. Oblations of a variety of substances such as cheese, butter, a mixture of milk and honey, oil, wine, or blood from a sacrifice were poured into the pit along with gifts of jewelry, objects such as a silver model of an ear, and a replica of a ladder (*TDOT* 1:132). These oblations sought to entice and facilitate the coming up of ghosts. Such a ritual was performed at night. The preferred sacrifices were black animals, especially pigs and dogs. According to Hoffner (*TDOT* 1:133), אוב has three uses in the OT: (1) a pit by which the deceased are called up (1 Sam 28:7–8), (2) the deceased ghost itself (Isa 29:4), and (3) a person skilled in calling up the deceased for seances, i.e., a necromancer (here; 20:6, 27; Deut 18:11; 1 Sam 28:3, 9; 2 Kgs 21:6; 23:24; 2 Chr 33:6; Isa 8:19). J. Lust ("On Wizards and Prophets," VTSup 26 [1974] 133–42) accepts Hoffner's description of the practice of calling up departed spirits through sacred pits, but he disputes Hoffner's description of the etymology of אוב. He takes אוב from אב, "father," to mean "spirit of a deceased father" for that is what the people seek out in order to divine from a departed ancestor. Then אוב can mean "ghost" or "an image" representing the ghost (VTSup 26 [1974] 137). Lust's view has much to commend it. It is that the term refers both to the ghost and to the person skilled in bringing up the ghost, i.e., a necromancer (in 20:27 אוב clearly has the latter meaning, while in this verse it could be either one). With the verb פנה, "turn to," here and in 20:6 the focus of the passage is on communicating with ghosts and departed spirits, not the medium per se, so it is rendered "ghost" here. Of course, the distinction would not be that great for ancient people, for to communicate with the dead they would have to go through a medium.

31.b. ידעוני comes from the root ידע, "know." It is variously rendered: "magician" (JB), "spiritist" (NIV), "wizard" (KJV), "sorcerer" (JB in Isa 19:3), and "familiar spirit" (NEB in Isa 8:19). The fact that it always occurs with אוב, "medium, ghost," and that it stands in contexts of consulting the dead (e.g., Isa 8:19; 19:3) indicates that it is a technical term for one who practices necromancy. The construction of the name for a spiritist from the root ידע suggests that such a person was viewed as either having great skill to perform such an exercise or had a close acquaintance with a departed spirit. By extension this term may refer to the departed spirit itself.

32.a. The first stich is chiastically ordered: prep phrase:verb::verb:prep phrase.

32.b. Cf. n. 12.b. A couple of LXX mss add ὁ θεός σου, "your God."

33.a. A Heb. ms, Sam, and the versions read the pl pronoun אתכם, "you," as in the similar phrase in v 34; this variant makes this form parallel to the following בארצכם, "in your land."

33.b. ינה means "oppress, maltreat, take advantage of" (cf. Deut 23:17[16]). Most often the objects of this verb are the poor, the needy, orphans, widows, and aliens (25:14, 17; Exod 22:20[21]; Jer 22:3; Ezek 18:12, 16; 22:7, 29). Zephaniah calls Jerusalem "the oppressing city" (3:1).

34.a. The prep כ, "like," conveys that "the agreement between the things compared is complete" (*IBHS* §11.2.9b).

34.b. Cf. n. 18.d.

35.a. Cf. F. Zimmermann, "An Examination of Some Biblical Passages," *JBL* 65 (1946) 312.

36.a. In this series the gen expresses the character of the noun in constr and is translated as an adj (GKC §128p; Joüon §129f; *IBHS* §9.5.3b).

36.b. LXX omits איפת צדק, "a just ephah."

36.c. Ephah is equivalent to a bath (Ezek 45:11) and a tenth of a homer. This term occurs in the OT usually as a dry measure. Given a 22-liter bath, an ephah is 19.9 dry quarts or 23.2 liquid quarts (there is some evidence for the use of a bath twice that size in some times and places; E. M. Cook, "Weights and Measures," *ISBE* rev. 4:1049–51).

36.d. Hin comes from an Egyptian term for a liquid and dry measure. In OT it is normally used as a liquid measure. A hin is one-sixth of an ephah, 3.8 liquid or 3.3 dry quarts based on a 22–liter bath (E. M. Cook, *ISBE* rev. 4:1050–51).

36.e. On this form see W. Gross, "Die Herausführungsformel—Zum Verhältnis von Formel und Syntax," *ZAW* 86 (1974) 425–53.

37.a. Cf. n. 12.a.

Form/Structure/Setting

The structure of this speech is outlined as follows:

I. Introductory formula (v 1)
II. Speech (vv 2–37)
 A. Commission to speak (v 2a*α*)
 B. Speech proper (vv 2a*β*–37)
  1. Central thesis—call to holiness (v 2a*β*–b)
  2. Body of speech (vv 3–36)
   a. First set of laws (vv 3–18)
    1) On fearing parents, keeping the Sabbath, and avoiding idolatry (vv 3–4)
    2) Regarding the handling of an offering of well-being (vv 5–8)
    3) Five sets of prohibitions and commandments (vv 9–18)

a) Against gleaning fields and vineyards and for leaving leftovers for the poor (vv 9–10)
b) Against theft and deceit (vv 11–12)
c) Against oppression of others and abuse of the handicapped and for fear of God (vv 13–14)
d) Against injustice and slander and for just judgment (vv 15–16)
e) Against hate and taking vengeance and for loving one's neighbor (vv 17–18)

b. Second set of laws (vv 19–29)
1) Against mixture of diverse elements (v 19)
2) Regarding sexual relations between a man and a betrothed slave (vv 20–22)
3) Regarding fruit trees (vv 23–25)
4) Against eating blood and practicing divination (v 26)
5) Against cutting of hair and marking the body (vv 27–28)
6) Against selling a daughter into prostitution (v 29)

c. Third set of laws (vv 30–36)
1) Regarding keeping the Sabbath and revering the sanctuary (v 30)
2) Against necromancy (v 31)
3) For respect of elders (v 32)
4) For love of aliens (vv 33–34)
5) For just weights and measures (vv 35–36)

3. Concluding exhortation to keep these laws (v 37)

This speech presents numerous laws pertaining to the practice of holiness in all aspects of daily life. Given the diversity of these laws, it is hard to find a definitive structure to this speech. These laws, however, cluster around three topics: faithfulness in worship (vv 3aβ–8, 12, 21–22, 27–28, 30–31), expression of love and respect in interpersonal relationships (vv 11, 13–14, 17–18, 19–20, 29, 32–34), and practice of justice in business and at court (vv 15–16, 35–36). All these laws reveal God's desire that Israel bring every area of her life into conformity with his holy character.

The speech is headed by the thesis: Israel is to be holy because God is holy (v 2aβ+b). The recurrence of the verb שׁמר, "keep," signals the three divisions of this speech (cf. Magonet, *HAR* 7 [1983] 165–66). At the head of the first and the third divisions is the command את־שׁבתתי תשׁמרו, "keep my Sabbaths" (v 3aβ and v 30aα). Another command heads the second division: את־חקתי תשׁמרו, "keep my decrees" (v 19aα). The conclusion (v 37) uses שׁמר, "keep," in the exhortation ושׁמרתם את־כל־חקתי, "keep all my decrees." This concluding exhortation echoes the language of 18:4, 5, 26 and 20:8, 22a (identical), establishing a tie with both the preceding and the following speeches.

There are other literary ties between the first and the third divisions in addition to the command "keep." The first division has the great commandment to love one's neighbor (v 18aβ). A similar command to love the resident alien comes in the third division (v 34aα + b). One prohibition is stated in the first division and repeated in the third one: לא־תעשׂו עול במשׁפט, "you shall not do injustice in judgment" (vv 15aα, 35a). For chiastic effect it precedes the command "to love" in the first division, while in the third division it follows that command. The application of this prohibition differs between the divisions, however. In the first division the context is about showing favoritism to a party at court (vv 15–16), while in the third division the context regulates just weights and measures (vv 35–36). Another link between the first and the third divisions is the exhortation not to turn (אל פנה) to other objects of worship (vv 4, 31). The objects of false worship, however, are different: idols in the first division and ghosts in the third. Since these forms of false worship stand at opposite poles, the use of these two prohibitions in this manner condemns every kind of false worship.

There are a couple of other patterns in this speech. Both times the materials regarding sacrifices (vv 5–8, 21–22) are followed by laws regulating agricultural practices (vv 9–10, 23–25). Wenham (267) has uncovered a significant pattern in vv 11–18. Each of the four units, consisting of two verses each, ends with the self-introductory formula אני יהוה, "I am Yahweh." Within these units there is a climactic use of the terms for the people with whom one is to relate:

vv 11–12		associate (אמית)		
vv 13–14				friend (רע)
vv 15–16		associate (עמית)	people (עמים)	friend (רע)
vv 17–18	brother (אח)	associate (עמית)	countrymen (בני עם)	friend (רע)

Wenham (267) notes that this pattern of slowly filling out a list of synonyms alerts the hearer, leading one to listen for all four terms in the fourth couplet. These various patterns along with the three major, intertwining cords organize this speech with great rhetorical power.

The first one of these three intertwining cords is קדוש, "holiness." Holiness, the central theme of this speech, is first met in the call to holiness in v $2a\beta + b$. The phrase קדש יהוה, "the holiness of Yahweh," appears in v 8. V 24 speaks of fruit from young trees that is a holy gift (קדש) because it belongs to God. The term מקדש, "holy place, sanctuary," occurs in v 30. Other terms, phrases, and themes contribute to the theme of holiness. The use of שם, "name," for God in v 12 (2x) calls to the Israelite mind holiness, for God's name is holy (e.g., Isa 57:15). The concepts of "fear" and "holiness" are interwoven, for fear is a primary human response to the holy (R. Otto, *The Idea of the Holy* [Oxford: Oxford UP, 1967] 12–24). No wonder the term ירא, "fear," appears four times: fearing God twice (v 14b, 32b), fearing or revering his sanctuary (v 30a), and fearing one's parents (v $3a\alpha$). Underscoring further the theme of holiness are the recurring formulae of Yahweh's self-introduction: אני יהוה אלהיכם, "I am Yahweh, your God" (vv 2, 3, 4, 10, 25, 31, 34, 36), and אני יהוה, "I am Yahweh" (vv 12, 14, 16, 18, 28, 30, 32, 37; cf. *Excursus* at 18:5). These formulae proclaim the identity of Yahweh as the Holy One of Israel. Finally the theme of "holiness" attracts its counterpart, חלל, "profane, desecrate." This term is used twice, once against desecrating God's name by taking a false oath in his name (v 12) and once of shaming a daughter by making her a prostitute (v 29a).

The second major, intertwining cord is the interplay between this speech and the Decalogue of Exod 20 as the following chart shows:

	Decalogue	Lev 19
1.	No other gods (Exod 20:3)	
2.	No molten images (20:4–6)	v 4a
3.	No vain use of God's name (20:7)	v 12
4.	Remember the Sabbath (20:8–12)	vv 3a*β*, 30a*α*
5.	Honor father and mother (20:12)	v 3a*α*
6.	No murder (20:13)	v 16a*β*
7.	No adultery (20:14)	v 29 (20–22)
8.	No stealing (גנב; 20:15)	vv 11a, 13 (35–36)
9.	No false witness (20:16)	vv 11b, 16a*α*
10.	No coveting (20:17)	vv 17–18 (9–10)

While there is no direct reference to the first commandment, the entire tenor of the speech, being monotheistic, supports this commandment. The commandment against coveting is observed by not hating but loving one's neighbor (vv 17–18). Both the commandment not to hate a brother in v 17a and the commandment to love others as oneself (vv 18a*β*, 34) would eradicate all murder from the community. In this speech numerous specific laws are mixed in with the categorical laws in order to demonstrate how the general laws are to be carried out in daily life. For example, the categorical commandment לא תגזל, "do not rob," finds application in the prohibition not to keep a hired hand's wages overnight (v 13). In addition to treating ethical issues, the speaker also addresses issues of worship. After categorical commandments about keeping the Sabbath and not making images (vv 3a*β*–4), he gives specific instructions about handling food from an offering of well-being (זבח שלמים; cf. chap. 3). He includes laws dealing with both the ethical and the cultic dimensions of life, since these two areas are inexorably bound together in a holy life. In fact, B. Childs (*The Book of Exodus,* OTL [Philadelphia: Westminster, 1974] 396) points out that the ethical and the cultic are fused in OT law from the earliest level of the tradition.

Some linguistic similarities are observable between this speech and the Decalogue. The speaker uses the emphatic, categorical form of prohibition, i.e., לא plus the imperfect, as does the Decalogue. Whereas in the Decalogue the verbs are singular, there is a mixture of singular and plural verbs here. Why is there such a mixture? The preponderance of plural forms suggests that the speaker took these lines from a source without making any changes and that he used singular forms for his material. But this reconstruction is not supported by the command לא תגנבו, "you [pl] shall not steal," in v 11a. In the Decalogue it is לא תגנב, "you [sg] shall not steal" (Exod 20:15). The mixture of second person plural and singular forms is then a rhetorical device by which the speaker addresses both Israel as a community and each member of that community. This variation fails to serve as an indication of sources used by the speaker. This position finds support in the use of איש, "a man," with a plural imperfect verb in v 3a to apply this collective law to every member of the audience.

Another point of concurrence between this speech and the Decalogue is the preamble to both works. The opening exhortation, קדשים תהיו כי קדוש אני יהוה, "be holy because I Yahweh am holy," is the preamble to this speech (Morgenstern, *HUCA* 26 [1955] 10–12); it functions like the expanded self-introductory formula that is the preamble to the Decalogue (Exod 20:2//Deut 5:6). With the term "holy" Yahweh declares his distinct nature as the Holy One of Israel (e.g.,

Isa 41:20; 43:3;). Israel is to become "holy" like her God. This implies the covenant relationship and its obligations (Morgenstern, 11). In addition, the expanded self-introduction of Yahweh at the end of this speech, אני יהוה אלהיכם אשר־הוצאתי אתכם מארץ מצרים, "I am Yahweh your God who brought you out of the land of Egypt" (v 36b), is for the most part identical to the preamble to the Decalogue. These two statements frame the laws of this speech. Therefore, without entering into the complicated issues of traditio-historical study of the Decalogue and its relationship to this speech (cf. B. Childs, *The Book of Exodus,* 388–401; J. I. Durham, *Exodus,* WBC 3 [Waco, TX: Word Books, 1987] 278–83), it may be stated that in its canonical context this speech is an exposition of the Decalogue.

This is an appropriate place to mention the primary direction of literary studies on this speech. Critics have concentrated their efforts on finding one or two decalogues as the center of this speech. Morgenstern (*HUCA* 26 [1955] 39–66) initiated this approach. Several have followed his lead, putting forth a variety of proposals as to the original decalogue and its growth. Kilian and Elliger, e.g., have proposed that a double decalogue forms the core of this speech. According to Kilian (*Literarkritische,* 58–59), the first decalogue is a group of prohibitions expressed with singular verbs found in vv 13aα, 13aβ, 14aα, 14aβ, 15aβ+aγ, 16aα, 16aβ, 17a, 18aα, 18aβ. Elliger (254), however, argues that this is a dodecalogue, recognizable by the singular second person verbs (12b–14; 15aβ–18). Kilian (59) notes the strong social direction of this series as it addresses how one should relate to others. The second decalogue is made up of prohibitions formulated in the second person plural. Kilian (60–62) gains this decalogue by joining vv 11 (3), 12a (Elliger includes 15aα), 26 (3), 27a (Elliger includes all of v 27), 28a, 28aα, 28aβ recognizable by the second person plural forms. The issues in this decalogue are property rights and cultic issues (Elliger, 254). These studies demonstrate that this speech consists of groups of laws central to Israel's cult. Whether these laws were initially grouped by tens and twelves is unknown. The major obstacle to this literary analysis is that the text has to be rearranged in order to gain a pure decalogue. A close look at the text shows that some verses split by this method are well balanced in their present construction. V 13, of which Kilian accepts only stich A for the decalogue, e.g., is a whole, consisting of two prohibitions on one side of the *athnaḥ* and an expanded prohibition on the other side. This is good rhetorical style, for the prohibition in stich B is a specific application of the general prohibitions in stich A. As for v 15, Kilian (*Literarkritische,* 58) takes two parts of it for his first decalogue, while Elliger (254) assigns the first part to the second decalogue and the other three parts to the dodecalogue. But as this verse stands it has good balance, moving from general to specific and then from specific to general, being arranged chiastically:

general	specific	
לא־תעשׂו עול במשׁפט "you shall not do injustice in judgment"		A
	לא־תשׂא פני־דל "you shall not be partial to the poor"	B
	ולא תהדר פני גדול "you shall not honor the great"	B'
בצדק תשׁפט עמיתך "you shall judge your friend in righteousness"		A'

Furthermore, A and B employ synonymous and antithetical parallelism. In B and B' the verbs are synonymous, while the direct objects are antithetical; the prohibition is repeated with synonymous verbs for emphasis, and the antithesis of "poor-great" communicates that this prohibition applies to all people. In part A, the verbal idea is stated negatively and then positively. The terms qualifying the verbal idea are antithetical: עול, "injustice" (A), and בצדק, "in righteousness" (A'). As it now stands, this verse is intricately composed and should not be divided. Therefore, these attempts to reconstruct an original decalogue sometimes fail to notice the design of the laws in their final form.

The third major, intertwining cord holding this speech together is the principle of loving a person like oneself (v 18b), which is expanded by the parallel commandment to love the resident alien (v 34a). It functions as the basic principle for the numerous prohibitions regulating a person's relationship to another. This commandment undergirds the various commandments to extend mercy and show respect: i.e., to leave portions of the harvest for the poor and the sojourner (vv 9–10), not to hold back the wages of a worker (v 13b), and to honor the elderly (v 32).

While the structure of this speech is loose, it is still existent. In fact, the short, crisp prohibitions and commandments interspersed with longer, fuller legal material offer rhetorical variety and impact. The content of this speech, laws for the oral instruction of the community in the requirements of living a holy life, definitely fits the setting of a covenant renewal ceremony like other speeches in Lev 17–26.

Comment

2 Moses is directed to speak to the entire עדה, "congregation," of Israel. עדה signals that the people are assembled as a community under the covenant (cf. 4:13).

The theme for the laws on holy living found in chaps. 17–26 is stated at the head of this chapter. Israel is to be קדש, "holy," because Yahweh, her God, is קדש, "holy" (11:44–45; 20:7, 26; 21:8; Deut 7:6; 14:2; 26:19; 28:9). Holiness is the quintessential quality of Yahweh. In the entire universe, he alone is intrinsically holy. The nominal sentence, Yahweh is holy, points in this direction. That God is holy means that he is exalted, awesome in power, glorious in appearance, pure in character. God's holiness is contagious. Wherever his presence is, that place becomes holy. Since Israel's holiness is learned and is derived from Yahweh, the command for Israel to become holy is expressed in a verbal sentence; the use of the verb היה, "be, become," captures the maturing dimension of holiness on the human plane. Being Yahweh's representative on earth, Israel is to evidence in her community characteristics that are similar to God's. Whereas God's holiness is dynamic, outgoing, Israel makes herself holy by separating herself from sin and all that defiles in order to experience the sanctifying presence of God.

3 Two basic commandments head this speech. They reiterate the fifth and fourth commandments of the Decalogue (Exod 20:8–12; Deut 5:12–16). The first one, fearing one's parents, is the foundation of social morality, and the second, keeping the Sabbath, is essential for spiritual vitality. Children are enjoined to revere (ירא) both mother and father (cf. Exod 20:12; Deut 5:16; 27:16). The use of ירא, "fear," for parents is most unusual. In the Decalogue it says, "Honor [כבד] your father and your mother" (Exod 20:12; Deut 5:16). When ירא, "fear," is used to express respect and devotion, God is usually the object. In this commandment, "fear" means a child is to acknowledge his parents' authority. This command thus gives parents an exalted place in a child's life. Furthermore, the initial position of the mother in this command is striking (cf. 20:19; 21:2). Clearly the mother is being honored. While Baentsch (396) and Noordtzij (193) explain it as that which would be expected in a polygamous family (cf. 18:9), it may rather be from the prominent role a mother has in rearing children. From a comparison of the place of parents in other Middle Eastern documents, Albertz (*ZAW* 90 [1978] 356–74) conjectures that the setting for such a command might have been their transference of the estate to their son or children as they withdrew from active management of the land; the son or children then were to revere their parents by caring for them in their old age. For him (372–73), the front position of the mother is thus explicable in light of her husband's great concern that his wife be taken care of should she outlive him, as often was the case. While it is doubtful that this setting is the only one for this command, it is very likely that this command does address care of parents in their old age.

The next command is to keep the Sabbath (cf. 23:3), the seal of the covenant. The covenant committed Israel to an intimate relationship with God. To foster the vitality of that relationship, the Sabbath was instituted as a special day for every family in Israel to worship God (cf. v 30a; Exod 20:8; cf. Lev 23:3; 26:2a). In the Decalogue the command is "to remember" (זכר) the Sabbath so as to observe it as a holy day to worship Yahweh (cf. B. Childs, *Memory and Tradition* [London: SCM Press, 1962] 47–48, 52–56). Here the verb is שׁמר, "keep," meaning to observe the special customs and practices of that day. The Scriptures are amazingly silent on what those practices should include; this silence shows that God entrusts to human insight the specific ways to live up to his general instructions.

4 This prohibition against worshiping idols reiterates the first two commandments of the Decalogue (Exod 20:3, 4). Israel shall not worship any other אלילים, "gods" (also 26:1), nor shall she make any אלהי מסכה, "molten gods." Possibly the choice of the verb פנה, "turn," is to call to mind the phrase על־פני, "before me," in the first commandment. פנה אל means to change directions; in passages with worship it means to focus one's attention on serving another diety (cf. Deut 31:20; Hos 3:1; Ps 40:5[4]; Job 5:1). The second commandment prohibits the making of any פסל, "image," worked out of stone, wood, or metal (Exod 34:17). This prohibition comes after the incident of Aaron's making a עגל מסכה, "molten calf" (Exod 32:4, 8). Images are forbidden because they are inadequate, and thus false, representations of Yahweh's identity (Childs, *The Book of Exodus,* 409; idem, *Old Testament Theology in a Canonical Contest,* 66–68). Moreover, Yahweh has revealed himself to his people through the word, not in a specific form (Deut 4:12, 15–19). This dynamic of the God who speaks and whose words act cannot be confined to a static representation.

5–8 When Israel sacrifices offerings of well-being (cf. chap. 3) to worship God, they are to sacrifice them in such a manner that God will accept them (cf. 1:3; 22:29). The people are not to follow the ritual and assume that God automatically receives their sacrifices. Why is there a reference to presenting a sacrifice in this speech on holy living? The answer is that the call to holiness embraces every dimension of life, including the ethical and the cultic (Noordtzij, 191). Laws about זבח שׁלמים, "the sacrifice of well-being," may occur here because humans offer this type of sacrifice as a spontaneous or promised response to God's blessing (cf. chap. 3; 7:11–21; Hoffmann, 2:33). In addition, since sacrifices of this type are the only ones from which the laity may eat, there is special concern that the family or clan not relax the observance of the laws pertaining to how this meat is to be handled. This meat may be eaten for one or two days, but on the third day whatever is leftover has to be disposed of (7:16–18). Such leftover meat is called פגול, "defiled meat" (7:18). Anyone who eats from defiled meat violates the sacredness of the cult. Such an act destroys the benefits of the sacrificial offering by making it no longer רצה, "acceptable." Profaning (חלל) that which is holy by treating it as common bears the severest penalty. A person who commits such an offense is to be נכרת, "cut off," from the covenant עם, "people" (see 7:19–21).

9–10 A landowner shall not endeavor to gather as much as he possibly can from his fields, either by harvesting the corners of the field or by going back over his field to gather the grain that has fallen while reaping. The ancients harvested grain by gathering a bundle of stalks in one hand and cutting them with a sickle held in the other hand. This same standard applies to the owner of a vineyard. Vines shall not be stripped, nor shall the fallen grapes be picked up (cf. Deut 24:19–21). The fallen grain and the corners are to be left for the עני, "poor," and the גר, "resident alien," לקט, "to glean." These people have little income and, during hard times, little hope of earning a living. God wants the landlords to be thankful for their harvest and to express their acknowledgment that God has richly blessed them by sharing some of the harvest with the unfortunate (Ruth 2). These decrees undercut the strong human temptation to greed in the presence of plenty. This standard of generosity is prudently formulated. On the one hand, it does not place an added burden on the landlord, for he does not have to pay for the collection of these gleanings. On the other hand, the poor and the foreigner maintain their dignity, for in place of a handout they are given the privilege to labor for their own needs. They have to expend effort to benefit from God's grace manifested through the landlord's generosity. Observation of this practice reflects God's merciful concern for the unfortunate. A generous landlord might have his workers leave extra sheaves for the poor as Boaz did for Ruth (Ruth 2:15–16). The similar law found in Deut 24:19–22 is rooted in Israel's saving history. Since God showed his love for Israel in Egypt where they were both poor and aliens, he wishes that his people in turn will express kindness to the unfortunate. This law is expressed as a principle; later the rabbis established that a sixtieth part of a harvest was the minimum amount for compliance with this law (*m. Peʾa* 1.1–2).

11–12 A person shall not steal; this is the eighth commandment (cf. Exod 20:15; Deut 5:19). גנב is a theft done in secret (Milgrom, *Cult*). Following this prohibition there are three prohibitions against falsehood. כחש has a wide range of meanings such as "fail, belie, deceive, deny, deal falsely"; J. Oswalt (*TWOT* 1:437) suggests that "deception" is the primary meaning. שקר means "to act falsely towards, go back on one's word." Often one who is lying is forced into a situation in which he must back up his words by a formal oath taken in God's name. When a person lies under an oath taken in God's name, he חלל, "profanes," God's name. Since a name bears one's identity, a person denies the purity of God's character by using his name or reputation to substantiate a deceptive word (cf. 18:21). Why does a crime against property head this list? The answer is found in comparing this text with 5:21–23(6:2–4); there these verbs occur together to indicate that deception and swearing false oaths were used to secure control of an associate's (עמית; see 6:2[9]) property. Such practice is prohibited by the ninth commandment (Exod 20:16; Deut 5:20). From another perspective, stealing leads one into deception, and subsequently it can lead one to swear falsely under oath in order to cover up the initial crime. Dealing with a neighbor deceptively breaks the bonds of friendship based on trust and is the opposite of the command to love one's neighbor (v 18). Cf. Matt 5:34–37; Jas 5:12.

13 The first two of these three prohibitions are general statements, and the third provides a specific application of the general prohibitions. An Israelite shall not עשק, "oppress," a friend. One is not to make another's life harder by the use of force so that the oppressor can have more. An Israelite shall not גזל, "rob," another. The basic meaning of גזל is "to snatch something violently" (J. Schupphaus, "גָּזַל *gāzal*," *TDOT* 2:456). In Job 24:9 it is used for the grabbing of a child from his mother's breast. It also depicts the strong snatching from the weak what they want (Gen 31:31; Deut 28:31; Job 24:2), such as defrauding a person of his field or home (Mic 2:2). This term often occurs with the root עשק, "oppress" (Lev 5:21, 23[6:2, 4]; Deut 28:29; Jer 21:12; 22:3; Ezek 18:18; 22:29; Mic 2:2; Ps 62:11[10]; Eccl 5:7[8]). It thus describes the brazen taking of something from another either by physical force or by exercising one's power of position or influence. One example of oppression, the practice of holding back a hired day-laborer's wage, is mentioned. This practice deprives that laborer of the possibility of purchasing food for his family for the evening meal and for the following day (Deut 24:14–15; cf. Jer 22:13; Matt 20:8). An employer may not use for his own convenience and profit an accounting practice that works a hardship on his laborer's family. A laborer who has not been quickly paid cries out to God for relief, and God will hold the employer responsible for causing this undue hardship (Deut 24:14–15; cf. Jas 5:4). God judges severely those who mistreat their laborers for personal gain.

14 A person is not to take advantage of a handicapped person, particularly by playing on that person's handicap. In front of a deaf person one shall not swear an oath, an oath designed to harm or ridicule that person. In Deut 27:18 a curse is laid on one who leads a blind person astray. Similarly a person is prohibited from placing מכשל, "a stumbling block," in the path of a blind person. The oath and the stumbling block include anything that might harm the handicapped person either for one's own profit or out of spite. The person who fears God will never act so cruelly (cf. v 3). Everyone needs to keep in mind the fact that God looks after the disadvantaged and holds accountable any who take advantage of them. The arrangement of the decrees in this verse is two specific prohibitions followed by a general command. This pattern reveals that a pious life leads to a high regard for human life and encourages compassion for those who suffer from a serious handicap.

15 Never should injustice (עול) be done in rendering a legal judgment (משפט). The prohibitions not to favor the poor nor to honor the great guard against rendering unjust decisions. Judges and councils, being human, are open to influence from factors other than the merits of a case. But in rendering a judicial decision no favoritism is to be shown to anyone, regardless of status (cf. Jas 2:1, 9). The command not to favor the poor is surprising in light of the concern throughout the OT for the widow, the orphan, and the poor (e.g., Exod 22:20–26[21–27]; 23:6; Deut 24:17–18; 27:19). This prohibition seeks to prevent that concern from causing the elders to lean a judgment in favor of the unfortunate solely because that person is poor (cf. Exod 23:3). Justice may not be perverted even for the disadvantaged. Next it states that "the great" are not to be הדר, "honored" or "favored," by allowing their position to influence a judgment. The people are to judge a close associate (עמית; cf. v 11) righteously. דל, "poor," and גדול, "great," are used to include everyone. Since God is just, his people must establish justice in their courts as the foundation of their covenant relationship with him. The inner strength of a nation resides in the integrity of its judicial system.

16 A person shall not go about as a slanderer (רכיל). The basic meaning of the verb רכל is "go about from one place to another, traffic" (BDB, 940; Ezek 17:4; 27:3) and the noun רכיל means "slanderer." This term occurs in six references (Jer 6:28; 9:3[4]; Ezek 22:9; Prov 11:13a; 20:19a*a*) and depicts one who maliciously spreads untruth about another. It usually occurs with הלך, "go," to emphasize that this kind of person aggressively spreads a distorted tale. Since a person is known by his reputation, the spreading of malicious gossip about a person damages that one's influence and discredits his character (cf. Jer 6:28; 9:3[4]; 2 Cor 12:20; Eph 4:31; Jas 4:11; 5:9; 1 Pet 2:1). Neither may one תעמד על־דם, "act against the life," lit. "stand on the blood," of a friend. This idiom is variously interpreted. One view takes it to mean "to place in jeopardy" a person's life. Spreading a slanderous lie can put one's life at risk, especially in a society in which the death penalty is prevalent. *Targum Onqelos* and Ibn Ezra understand the idiom "not to stand over blood" to mean "to conspire against" (Levine, 127). Another view takes it to mean "to stand aside, neglect" another at a critical time, such as by failing to testify in a person's defense when one has evidence to clear the person in jeopardy. Wenham (268) notes that in an ancient village feuds and personal animosities could easily distort the decision of a court consisting of local elders. Another view assigns it the meaning "to survive, rely on" (cf. Gen 27:40; Ezek 33:26; Levine, 127). This has led to the NJPS translation "Do not profit by the blood of your fellow." All of these views agree that this line is saying that one person is not to place another person's life at risk.

17 No one shall hate his brother (אח) in his heart. Hatred festering in one's heart distorts the thinking and stimulates the imagination into pondering ways to seek that brother's harm. When one hates another without addressing the basic complaint, one easily succumbs to compromising his own integrity by speaking deceit (cf. Prov 10:18). That person may even fall to slandering that brother. If a person has a just complaint against an associate (עמית; cf. v 11), he is to הוכח, "dispute openly," with that person. הוכח means "reprove, rebuke," and it also has a forensic sense, i.e., "argue one's case" (Job 13:3, 15). Its basic meaning is "to establish what is right" (Amos 5:10; Isa 29:21; G. Liedke, "יכח *jkḥ* hi. feststellen, was recht ist," *THAT* 1:730). Proverbs uses הוכח frequently in the sense of "reprove, rebuke"; e.g., reproof benefits a wise person even though the giving of reproof is unpleasant (9:7–8b; 19:25; 25:12; 28:23). Does הוכח here mean "reprove" or "dispute in court"? Since the decrees in the immediate context are concerned with justice in the court, הוכח has to do with taking one's complaint against another to court. Thereby the contention is made public, and the court can render a just decision to resolve the conflict. The next sentence says לא תשא עליו חטא, (lit.) "you will not carry sin for/concerning him." The idiom נשׂא plus a word for sin usually means "to bear the responsibility for a sin" (20:20; 22:9; 24:15; Num 18:32 with חטא, "sin," as here; cf. 5:1 [cf. n. 5:1.b.], 17; 19:8 with עון, "iniquity"). But the exact meaning of this idiom as used here is not immediately obvious. One possible meaning is that by formally pursuing a complaint against a brother, one keeps hatred from growing and venting itself in unjust or oppressive behavior designed to harm the offending neighbor. Or this sentence could mean that if a neighbor has truly wronged one, that person does not come to share in the other's sin by keeping silent. Hoffmann (2:43) understands the language to mean that one is guilty of a sin for not reproving his neighbor.

In an extensive study, Kugel (*HTR* 80 [1987] 49–54, 57–58) shows that in the early tradition two basic ways of interpreting this sentence developed. *T. Gad* (6:3–4) in *The Testament of the Twelve Patriarchs* interpreted this passage to mean that an offended party is not to reproach the offending party so insistently and so persistently that he moves the offender to swear. Further such contentiousness itself becomes a sin. That is why it is said in the "Manual of Discipline" (1QS 5:24–6:1) from the Qumran community that one is to reproach another "in truth and humility and in loving consideration to a man." This is a moral interpretation of this text. The other interpretive tradition is witnessed by the "Damascus Document" (CD 9:2–8 and also in 1QS 5:24–6:1). The reproach is considered to be a necessary step in the judicial process. Before formalizing a complaint against another by taking that person to court, the offended party must have officially reproached the offender (cf. Matt 18:15–17). This is a formal, judicial interpretation of the passage. Otherwise, the offended party falls into the sin of using another's fault or misdeed as a pretext to humble and/or to harm that person. Kugel's study shows how two different interpretations of the same passage may grow in different portions of the community committed to following Scripture.

18 The next two prohibitions speak out against נקם, "seeking vengeance," and נטר, "bearing a grudge." נטר means "to keep, maintain," e.g., the keeping of a vineyard (Cant 1:6; 8:11–12). Applied to God or humans, it means to carry or store up anger toward another (Jer 3:5, 12). A person who stores up his anger against a fellow citizen plottingly waits for an opportune time to vent that anger with נקם, "vengeance." With בני עמך, "your countrymen" (lit. "sons of your people"), this laws speaks strongly about a fellow citizen. The desire for vengeance moves one to seek the harm of his enemy, even though it is a fellow countryman, in a mean and decisive way. His anger so distorts his thinking that he cannot act astutely and judiciously toward the one he hates, who likewise is a member of Israel, the people of God. Elsewhere, the Scriptures teach that when one is taken advantage of, he is to commit his loss to God and trust God for vindication of his honor. God says, "It is mine to avenge; I shall repay" (Deut 32:35a; cf. Ps 94:1). In his own time God will hold the guilty accountable. In the meantime, those who trust in him can be patient, confident that God will right the wrong they are bearing.

Following these prohibitions comes the great commandment to love one's companion or friend (רע) like oneself. This command is stated positively for force. In this speech on holy living, it means that a person sanctifies oneself in order to act in love toward an acquaintance. רע means "friend, companion, acquaintance";

it is used for a wide variety of relationships, from a close friend (Job 2:11) to a mere acquaintance (20:10; Exod 21:14; cf. J. Hogg, *AJSL* 41 [1924/25] 197–98). Here it refers to anyone in Israel with whom a person has contact; thus Mathys (*Liebe,* 38) renders it "fellow countryman."

There is an interesting point of grammar in this verse. The object of אהב, "love," is usually in the accusative, but in this case it is preceded by the preposition ל, "to." Mathys (5) holds that the latter construction is an Aramaism and that there is no significant difference in meaning between the two phraseologies, for in some texts את and ל appear to be used interchangeably (cf. 2 Chr 10:6 with 10:9). However, Malamat (*BAR* 16 [1990] 50–51) claims that אהב ל means "be of use to, be beneficial to, assist"; he points out that in 2 Chr 19:2 אהב ל parallels עזר, "help" (cf. 1 Kgs 5:15[1]). Since both expressions occur in Hebrew, there probably is a slight difference in nuance, with אהב ל centering on helpful action that is motivated by concern for another. Certainly in the parable of the good Samaritan the emphasis is on love that acts to benefit another (Luke 10:25–37).

The standard for loving or being beneficial to another person is that that person is like one's very own self, thus being worthy of one's love. The classic illustration of such love for another is the relationship between David and Jonathan; "Jonathan loved him like himself" (כנפשו; 1 Sam 18:1; cf. 18:3; 19:1; 20:17; 2 Sam 1:26). G. Wallis ("אָהַב *ʾāhabh,*" *TDOT* 1:111) states in regard to this verse that "even if the OT does not explicitly demand self-denial and altruism, it advocates the kind of behavior which equates concern for the well-being of one's neighbor with the assertion of one's own will. In no case should one allow his own selfish interests to prevail when this would be harmful to his neighbor." In v 34 the command to love an acquaintance is extended to the גר, "resident alien" (also Deut 10:19). Jesus took this commandment, elevated it as the second of the two great commandments, and expanded the circle of "an acquaintance" to include all fellow humans, particularly anyone in need (Matt 22:39–40; Mark 12:31; Luke 10:25–37; cf. Matt 5:43–47; 19:19; Luke 10:27; Rom 13:9–10; Gal 5:14; Jas 2:8).

In this last of four couplets four terms for people are used to convey inclusiveness—אח, "brother," עמית, "associate," בני עמך, "your countrymen," and רע, "friend" (see *Form/Structure/Setting*). This use of these terms in this series, which begins with the prohibition not to hate and concludes with the command to love, encompasses every member of the covenant community. The use of these terms adds motivation to these laws. That is, the call is for one to reflect: are you acting negatively or positively toward another who belongs to the same group as you do (cf. Mathys, *Liebe,* 39)?

19 The Israelites are not allowed to mate different kinds of animals (בהמה), nor are they allowed to sow a field with two kinds of seeds, nor are they to develop textiles of two different kinds of material (cf. Deut 22:9–11). In cultic legislation בהמה, "cattle," includes both large and small domesticated animals, especially those that move about in herds (cf. G. J. Botterweck, "בְּהֵמָה *b^ehēmāh,*" *TDOT* 2:9–10, 12). C. Houtman (*VT* 34 [1984] 227–28) says that this law seeks to prevent the blurring of the variety of species and kinds that God created; that is, it seeks to preserve the diversity in the created world. These חקות, "decrees," against the mixing of things also contribute to the social consciousness that the holy is pure and unadulterated (cf. Douglas, *Purity,* 53).

20–22 Sexual relations between men and women are carefully regulated by the law (e.g., chaps. 18 and 20). This case concerns the relations of a free man with a slave girl pledged to another man. While the slave in Israel had a higher status than has been found to be the case in other law codes of the Ancient Near East, the slave did not have the same rights as a full citizen. Laws in Deuteronomy help provide some background for understanding this passage better. The law in Deut 22:23–24 holds that if a man forces a betrothed free woman, both are to die. From law codes of the ancient Middle East it is learned that if a female slave is ravished by a free man, that man would compensate the slave owner, but he is not subject to the death penalty (Milgrom, *ZAW* 89 [1977] 46). Moreover, a master could allow a female slave to be redeemed; the redeemer could be a person who wished to marry her. In this case a female slave has been pledged to another man, but she has not yet been redeemed (הפדה) nor given her freedom (חפשה) by her master (cf. Exod 21:8). Since she has been betrothed, her owner has no right to receive further compensation because she has been violated; since she is still a slave, her assailant is not subject to the death penalty. An inquiry (בקרת) into the matter is to be undertaken to make sure that the facts are correct. Though this man who forced her is beyond the punishment of the law, he, nevertheless, is guilty before God for having violated this woman. In Milgrom's judgment (*ZAW* 89 [1977] 46, 48–49), that man has committed the "great sin" of adultery, which is a sin against God because as a member of Israel he has sworn to keep the covenant. Thus he has committed מעל, "a breach of faith" (cf. 5:4; Milgrom, *ZAW* 89 [1977] 47). That is why he must make amends or expiation for his sin by presenting a reparation offering (אשם; cf. 5:14–26[6:7]). The animal prescribed is a ram (איל; cf. 5:15–16). There is no mention of compensation with this sacrifice, as is sometimes the case with a reparation offering, since the lady has been betrothed but not redeemed. The reparation offering is efficacious, as the statements that the priest makes expiation (כפר) for him and he receives forgiveness (סלח) from God communicate (cf. 4:20).

23–25 This series of laws regards the first yield of newly planted fruit trees. The inclusion of a few agricultural laws is to communicate that every area of Israel's life is governed by the call to holy living. The Israelites may not eat any of the small amount of fruit from a newly planted tree in the first three years; it is to be considered ערלה, "uncircumcised." The fruit of the fourth year is to be regarded as קדש, "holy," meaning that all of it belongs totally to God so that none of it may be eaten or used for food. It is called הלולים ליהוה, "praises to Yahweh"; i.e., the fruit of this year is given in praise to Yahweh. It is treated like the firstfruits (2:14). From the fifth year on, the Israelites are free to harvest the fruit for themselves, giving to Yahweh the firstfruits of each harvest. This statute is motivated by the promise that God will increase the harvest of the orchards for those who are obedient. This kind of law reinforces the community's consciousness that Yahweh is the owner of the land.

26 The opening prohibition is literally against "eating on the blood" (לא תאכלו על־הדם; cf. 3:17; 7:27; 17:10–14; 1 Sam 14:32–34). This phraseology is elliptical, and its precise meaning eludes modern interpreters. If the preposition על means "with," the use of "eat" instead of "drink" indicates that "the blood" refers to either a pudding of blood or meat laden with blood. While על may have this meaning, the object of the preposition על is usually joined with a named substance that stands as the direct object of "eat" (e.g., Exod 12:8; Num 9:11; cf. Ezek 33:25). Another interpretation takes על to mean "over" (cf. Füglister, "Sühne," 151–52). In the worship of chthonic deities, the animal was sacrificed on the ground, rather than on an altar or stone, and the blood drained into a deep trench dug out near the place of sacrifice and allowed to soak in before the meat from that sacrificial animal was eaten (cf. 1 Sam 14:31–34; J. Grintz, *ASTI* 8 [1972] 85). This blood rite was to draw the spirits to the surface and to enhance their power of foretelling. Since the following prohibitions concern some type of divination involving the use of blood, this interpretation has great weight. Another possibility is to follow the alternative reading of אל הרם, "on the mountains," in place of "on the blood" found in LXX. This variant may refer to sacred meals taken on hills in an effort to commune with spirits of those who had died (cf. Deut 12:2–3; Isa 57:7; 65:7). However, it is best to stay with the more difficult reading in the MT.

There are two prohibitions against the practice of divination. נחש may be "augury," the discerning of the future by interpreting signs and premonitions such as the movement of animals, smoke rising from a censer, or the shape or movement of metals. Joseph used a goblet (גביע) for divination (נחש; Gen 44:2, 5, 15). One way such a goblet was used was to pour various liquids on water standing in the cup; its owner read the configurations formed on the water. Often occurring with נחש is ענן in the polel; it is another term for divination, but the precise activity to which it refers is unknown. Two suggestions have been made (*TWOT* 2:685). One is that this term is related to עָנָן, "cloud," a word with the same consonants. If this is correct, the future was determined by reading the movements of clouds. The other suggestion is that this is an onomatopoetic word for the sound that a necromancer makes while engaged in communicating with a spirit.

Divination is soundly denounced throughout the Scriptures because it is constructed on the conviction that there is an impersonal force, sometimes called necessity or fate, that determines the destiny of all things, including that of the gods (cf. Deut 18:9–12; Y. Kaufmann, *The Religion of Israel*, tr. M. Greenberg [Chicago: The University of Chicago Press, 1960] 21–24, 32–33). Such conviction denies that God is all powerful. Therefore, participation in these kinds of practices undercuts the foundation of the revelation that Yahweh is the supreme God, the sovereign Creator. Given the driving human thirst to know the future, however, practices of divination, which were common among the other nations, were hard to eliminate from Israel (cf. 2 Kgs 17:17; 21:6; Isa 2:6; 8:19; Ezek 22:9).

27 Hair is a sign of a person's vital force and beauty. The manner of dressing one's hair has strong cultural and religious overtones. Among some peoples, shaving or trimming the hair in a certain style may be a symbol of office; in other situations it is a sign of mourning (21:5; Deut 14:1; Jer 16:6; Ezek 44:20; Amos 8:10). Therefore, regulations regarding the cutting of one's hair are germane to the Holiness Code. The hair of the temples shall not be rounded off. The beard shall not be shaved close to the face. To this day men of very orthodox Jewish communities observe this statute by allowing long ringlets of hair to grow on the sides of their faces.

28 The body is a marvelous creation of God. Its wholeness represents the beauty and perfection of holiness. Thus the body is to be kept whole. It is not to be intentionally harmed or marred in any way. Specifically prohibited is the pagan custom of lacerating the body as a means of mourning (cf. Deut 14:1;

Jer 16:6; 41:5; 47:5; 48:37, which speak of Israelites gashing their bodies as part of their mourning rites). This practice was to increase one's sorrow. In Snaith's view (94), however, it was primarily done to offer blood to the departed spirit. A couple of texts from Ras Shamra speak about mourners lacerating themselves (*UT* 67 VI:5–26; 62:1–29). In mourning for Baal, El the Kind "cuts his skin with a razor; he cuts his cheeks and chin, he raked his arms with a reed, he plowed his chest like a garden, he raked his back like a valley" (tr. M. Coogan, *Stories from Ancient Canaan* [Philadelphia: Westminster, 1978] 109; H. Ringgren, *Israelite Religion,* tr. D. Green [Philadelphia: Fortress, 1966] 240–42). Laceration may have been included in the rites of Baalistic fertility worship, especially when Baal appeared to be deaf to the pleas of his followers (cf. 1 Kgs 18:28).

Marking the body is also prohibited. While the exact meaning of קעקע is unknown, it could refer either to making tattoos on the body or to painting the body. Painting the body was a pagan practice. Those preparing to attend a ritual painted their bodies (C. Gordon, *The Common Background of Greek and Hebrew Civilization* [New York: W. W. Norton, 1965] 136, 168). Elliger (263) thinks this was done to ward off spirits of the dead. Bodily markings also served as a sign of belonging to a certain cult (Noordtzij, 205).

29 A person in heavy debt might be tempted to sell his daughter into prostitution in order to raise a sum of money. But such a practice profanes (חלל) the honor of his daughter. This is prohibited, for the land itself would be prostituted (cf. 18:24–27) and become full of זמה, "lewdness" (cf. 18:17). Sin fosters sin; prostitution draws to itself a host of crimes (cf. Deut 23:18–19[17–18]; Amos 2:7; Hos 4:14; Ezek 33:37–39). Furthermore, in ancient thinking such activity defiled the very land that supported the wrongdoers. Here is a tie back to 18:24–30.

30 This verse recurs in 26:2. The people are to keep the Sabbath (v 30aβ) and to revere the sanctuary. Reverence for the sanctuary means to regard it as the place where God reveals himself in splendor and awe. It means that the people are careful to conduct themselves circumspectly whenever they are in its areas; e.g., anyone in a state of uncleanness may never enter its precincts. Reverence for the Temple also guards against the importation of pagan cultic practices into the precincts of the Temple (e.g., Ezek 8; Noordtzij, 206). This law is important, for the operation of the sanctuary is essential for the maintenance of the covenant and for approaching God with the offerings required by the law.

31 The Israelites are not to turn to אבת, "ghosts," and ידענים, "departed spirits," for conversation and divination. In many places in the Ancient Near East, communication with the dead was sought through mediums and spiritists. פנה, "turn," is sometimes used of turning to God but more often of turning to other gods in worship (v 4; Deut 31:18, 20; Hos 3:1). The second term, בקש, "seek," in its religious usage expresses making significant effort in the worship of God (2 Sam 21:1; Hos 5:6, 15; Zech 8:21–22; but in Isa 8:19; 19:3 with אבות and ידענים). Noordtzij (207) observes that this is its only use in reference to spirits of the dead. This language then intimates that these seekers are endeavoring to inquire of Yahweh through contact with departed spirits (cf. S. Wagner, "בקש *biqqēsh,*" *TDOT* 2:238). The practice of turning to departed spirits in order to find special knowledge is witnessed to in the account of Saul's seeking out a witch in order that he might speak with the deceased Samuel (1 Sam 28). Yahweh abhors such practices, for death is directly opposed to his very being as the living God.

32 Persons with שֵׂיבָה, "silvery white hair," are to be highly honored (Prov 16:31; 20:29). Elders have the wisdom of much experience. When such an elder enters the assembly, the people are to rise in honor (cf. Job 29:7–10). Showing proper honor to the elders is an expression of one's fear of God.

33–34 The people are not to הונה, "mistreat" or "oppress" (cf. 25:14, 17; Exod 22:20[21]; Deut 23:17[16]; Jer 22:3; Ezek 45:8; 46:18), foreigners residing in Israel. Since aliens are ignorant of local customs, standards, prices, etc., and since they have little recourse in a dispute except for the honor of the host people, they are subject to all kinds of schemes devised to take advantage of them. Israelites, however, are to have special regard for strangers. They are to love them as persons like themselves (cf. v 18), and they are to treat them like אזרח, "natives." אזרח means "one born at home, a nation." This command to love is motivated by Israel's remembering that they had been resident aliens in Egypt. This motivation underscores the common human bond between aliens and Israelites.

35–36 The general prohibition not to do injustice (also v 15a*α*) is applied here to the use of weights and measures. Everything used for determining amounts is to be exact or right (צדק) according to the determined standard, including scales, weights, and measures of capacity and quantity. An easy way to practice deception in commercial transactions is to use false measures (cf. Deut 25:13–16; Ezek 45:10–12). A corrupt merchant would have two sets of weights and measures, using a bigger measure for receiving and a smaller one for distribution (cf. Amos 8:5; Mic 6:10–11). Such a double standard increases profits greatly. Weak members of society are struck a double blow, getting fewer goods and paying more. Israel is to obey this law about just weights and measures and all these laws as she remembers her great God Yahweh, who brought her out of Egyptian bondage. The grace God has shown Israel in redeeming her from slavery calls Israel to express her gratitude by acting justly in all her activities. That is, the high standard to which Yahweh calls the people of Israel finds both its reasonableness and its greater authority in light of how much he has done for them.

37 This verse is a concluding exhortation to put into practice the חקים, "decrees," and משפטים, "laws," given here, for they are identified as Yahweh's expressed will.

Explanation

This speech is a loud, clear, bold call to holy living. Israel, the people of the covenant, must pursue a holy life in order to serve their holy God. Holiness is the quintessential nature of God. God alone is the Holy One, and his holiness is contagious. Whatever place he inhabits is holy (Isa 57:15). Thus, for him to dwell among his people they must make themselves holy. While their holiness derives from God himself, they are to prepare themselves so God will be present among them, sanctifying them. This call to holy living has four major foci: The covenant people are to worship God fervently with a single mind. They are to love others. They are to practice justice and remove injustice. They are to avoid all falsehood and idolatry.

A holy Israel worships Yahweh with a single mind. The people may not turn to other gods or make any graven images. They are to fear God alone. Fear of the holy God leads to trust. The devout trust God for protection and blessing. Since they commit their destiny to God, they must never turn to divination or witchcraft.

The practice of divination implies a lack of trust in the ability of God to guide and protect them in the face of future upheavals. Nor may the people of God seek to commune with departed spirits, for God is God of the living. Affirmatively the people must follow the prescribed regulations in order not to profane God's holy name in the least. Concern for holiness means that worship is conducted according to the regulations revealed by God.

The people are given daily patterns to follow in order to orient their thinking around the central theme: God is holy. That which is holy is pure. As a symbol of this purity, they are not to sow a field with two kinds of seed or make cloth out of two kinds of material. In the same manner they are not to mar themselves either by cutting their bodies or by tattooing them such as in times of deep mourning. The physical body, which sustains a person's life, is to be kept whole as witness to the holiness of its Creator.

Scripture reveals that love and holiness are intertwined. Holiness finds tangible expression in loving. Holiness purifies human love to be a dynamic interest in the well-being of another person. Each Israelite is enjoined to love one's neighbor, a person like oneself. This commandment is close to the golden rule: "Do unto others as you would that they do to you" (Matt 7:12; Luke 6:31). Love keeps one from oppressing another. The rich are to have concern for their laborers; they will not hold back the wages of a day-laborer. The people are to have compassion for the handicapped; thus they are never to harm or take advantage of a person's handicap. Holy love moves the people to show mercy to the poor. An attitude of concern expressed in giving overcomes greed and selfishness. Farmers are not to harvest the corners of their fields or pick up the gleanings. Nor are they to keep on harvesting their vines. Why? In order that the poor, the unfortunate, and foreigners might have the opportunity to come to the fields and gather grain or fruit for their needs. These decrees tell us that those whom God blesses have an obligation to be mindful of the difficult circumstances of the poor. The formulation of these decrees is amazing in the concern for the dignity of the poor. The poor are given access to a food supply, but not as a hand-out; they have to go out to a harvested field and pick up the gleanings. On their way home they can hold their heads high, for they have labored for that which they are bringing home. This practice teaches that we are to be mindful both of the needs of the poor and of their dignity as people for whom God cares.

Whereas hatred leads one to bear grudges and seek vengeance, love destroys hatred. Hatred eats one's character like a malignant cancer, but love builds human character. Love is outgoing, with a genuine thoughtfulness for others. Not only are Israelites to love their neighbors, but they are also to love the aliens. While there is natural inclination to be concerned for the welfare of a close companion or an acquaintance, love for an alien is far from automatic. People tend to despise foreigners, treat them with disrespect, and, whenever possible, take advantage of them. Israelites, conversely, are to show love for foreigners who live among them, treating them as citizens like themselves. A powerful motivation is joined to this command. Israel is to remember that she had been a slave in a foreign land when God reached down and delivered her. Memory is a key means for understanding God's demands on his people. Sometimes the standard to which God calls his people seems unrealistically high. But meditation on what God has done for them reminds the community of God's great, outreaching love, which has been expressed in his deliverance of Israel from Egyptian bondage and his supplying their needs in trying circumstances. Since God has done so much for his people, he is in a position to ask them to do as much for others. When Israel heeds this call, they are acting like God to others. That is, to those whom they show kindness they are both communicating God's love and making themselves holy as God.

The speech contains laws based on the key teaching that God is the owner of the land (cf. chap. 25). He grants Israel the right to be its long-term tenants as long as Israel follows the laws and precepts he has given. He has even given some laws that encourage the wise management of the land, laws that especially counter the human drive to exploit the land in order to amass wealth. One set of precepts regulates the planting of fruit trees. None of the fruit of newly planted trees may be eaten for three years. The produce from the fourth year must be given completely to Yahweh. Then the farmer is given full use of the harvest from the fifth year on. Observance of this standard carries the promise that the trees will yield a greater harvest.

Genuine love promotes justice, and justice is the firm foundation of holy love. The union of justice and holiness keeps love from being sentimental and justice from being cruel. Nevertheless, for love to be upbuilding it must be true to justice. Justice receives a key place in this speech. It is mentioned both in specific decrees and in principle. The courts are not to render unjust decisions, and Israel is to have just weights and measures. This last standard is so fundamental that modern countries have bureaus of weights and measures. It must be remembered that this standard was legislated in a society several thousand years ago. Although the prohibition "do not steal" is followed by the vast majority of people, the temptation to increase one's income by falsifying the nature, quality, or quantity of a small item is strong and easily given into. In the case of selling a product, a merchant can increase profits by wide margins by decreasing the measure for dispensing the product even slightly and increasing the weight for accepting payment. Amos soundly condemned those merchants who practiced this method in his day (8:5). The temptation to cut corners to one's own advantage and a neighbor's loss is strong in every era. But succumbing to this very human tendency leads one astray on the way of holiness. Should the deviation become habitual, that person leaves the holy way as surely as one who consciously breaks one of the Ten Commandments (cf. Jas 2:8-12).

A holy people must certainly practice justice at court. They may not use the legal system to cloak their greed for gain and lust for power. Here the lawgiver enjoins the people not to extend any favoritism to anyone, whether that person is poor or great. This exhortation does not condemn mixing mercy with justice based on principle and wisdom; rather, it is striving to make sure that no person receives any special favors because of name, position, wealth, or power of persuasion. While the OT continually calls for the poor to receive justice, this injunction demands that no favoritism be shown the poor in the legal system solely because they are poor. Judgments must be based on equal justice to every person before judgments may be honorably tempered with mercy.

For justice to be done, the truth must be told. Thus there are several prohibitions about deceiving and speaking falsely. These prohibitions, of course, must be followed in court proceedings. When a witness, either a plaintiff or a defendant, is questioned, that person's testimony is often backed up by an oath taken in God's name to confirm that person's truthfulness. Should one swear falsely, God's name is belittled. The swearer denies God's holy character just as surely as by worshiping an idol.

The principles underlying the precepts of this chapter are affirmed by the NT. Jesus identified love of God as the first commandment and love of neighbor as the second (Matt 22:37–40; Mark 12:20–31; Luke 20:27–28). This second commandment is found echoed in other NT texts like Rom 13:9; Gal 5:14; and Jas 2:8. In Judaism at the time of Jesus there was a great debate over who was one's companion or neighbor, some groups favoring a broader definition than others. Jesus entered that debate; in the parable of the Good Samaritan, he broadened the definition of neighbor to include anyone who stands in need of help. Furthermore, in the Sermon on the Mount, Jesus identifies one's enemies, i.e., those who curse, hate, patronize, and persecute a believer, as the object of love (Matt 5:43–48). Jesus was both challenging the interpretation of "acquaintance" by the scribes and rabbis and also bringing out the full intend of the Levitical law.

Peter identifies the central theme of this chapter as the keystone of his epistle: "As he who called you is holy, be holy yourselves in all your conduct; since it is written, 'You shall be holy, for I am holy'" (1 Pet 1:15–16). For Peter as well as the other writers of the NT, holiness is expressed in love. "Having purified your souls by your obedience to the truth for a sincere love of the brethren, love one another earnestly from the heart" (1 Pet 1:22). Genuine love among believers leads to unity of spirit (1 Pet 3:8). Such love finds a host of practical expressions such as the showing of hospitality to one another and to travelers (1 Pet 4:9).

Motivated by love for God, believers must conduct themselves uprightly in order to honor God in the community (1 Pet 2:12). They are to avoid all evil, including murder, theft, and causing mischief (1 Pet 4:15). Other NT texts emphasize that they are to be generous, abounding in deeds of mercy, seeking to lay up their treasures in heaven (Matt 6:19–21; 1 Tim 6:17–20). In giving, they emulate God's gift of his son for the redemption of the human race. Instead of advancing their own positions, they are willing to suffer in order to advance the kingdom of God (1 Pet 1:13–14, 17). Christ himself is their highest example, motivating them to endure hardship and suffering (1 Pet 2:21–24).

In developing the call to believers to fulfill the royal law revealed in Scripture, James is deeply influenced by Lev 19. L. Johnson has demonstrated that "James made conscious and sustained use of" vv 12–18 in his epistle (*JBL* 101 [1982] 399):

19:12	Jas 5:12
19:13	Jas 5:4
19:15	Jas 2:1, 9
19:16	Jas 4:11
19:17b	Jas 5:20
19:18a	Jas 5:9
19:18b	Jas 2:8

James's use of Leviticus, however, is filtered through the teachings of Jesus. The central ethical precept is to love one's neighbor as oneself (2:8). In so doing one avoids treating people with partiality (2:1, 9). Neither does one defraud another or hold back the wages of a hired hand (5:4). Because the tongue can cause so much havoc among humans, James teaches that believers need to bridle the tongue, avoiding oaths and letting one's "Yes" be "Yes" and one's "No" be "No" (5:12). All who follow this counsel neither slander (5:9) nor speak evil of others (4:11). From James's perspective, then, Lev 19 is a guide for becoming a person with a single mind toward the Lord (1:8, 27).

Paul, too, preaches that God has called his people in holiness (1 Thess 4:7). For him believers are to "abound in love to one another and to all men" (1 Thess 3:12). God's sanctifying presence at work in those who love him produces in them sound and blameless character (1 Thess 5:23). Both testaments, therefore, consider holy living to be the highest expression of a believer's love for God.

D. *Laws with Penalties for Sacrifice to Molek, Sorcery, and Sexual Offenses (20:1–27)*

Bibliography

See *Bibliography* for 18:1–30.

Translation

1 *Yahweh spoke to Moses:* 2 *"Say*[a] *to the people of Israel:*[b] *Any*[c] *Israelite*[d] *or any alien living in Israel who gives any of*[e] *his children to Molek*[f] *must be put to death.*[g] *The people of the land shall stone him.* 3 *I will set my face against that man. I will cut him off from his people, because he has given one of*[a] *his children to Molek,*[b] *thus*[c] *defiling my sanctuary and profaning*[d] *my holy*[e] *name.* 4 *If the people of the land indeed*[a] *close their eyes from that kind of man whenever he gives his child*[b] *to Molek*[c] *by not putting him to death,* 5 *I*[a] *will set my face against that man and his family and will cut them off from their people, both him and all those who follow him to prostitute themselves after Molek.*[b]
6 *If a person*[a] *turns to ghosts*[b] *and departed spirits*[c] *to prostitute himself after them, I will set my face against that person and will cut him*[d] *off from among his people.*[e]
7 *"Sanctify yourselves*[a] *and be holy, because I am Yahweh*[b] *your God.* 8 *Keep my decrees*[a] *and do them. I am Yahweh, your sanctifier.*
9 *"If*[a] *anyone*[b] *curses his father and his mother, he must be put to death. He has cursed his father and his mother; his blood*[c] *is on him.* 10 *If a man commits adultery with his friend's wife,*[a] *both the adulterer and the adulteress must be put to death.*[b] 11 *If a man lies with his father's wife, he dishonors his father.*[a] *Both of them must be put to death; their blood is on them.* 12 *If a man lies with his daughter-in-law, both of them must be put to death. They have done that which is a perversion; their blood is on them.* 13 *If a man lies with a man as one lies with a woman, both of them have done that which is detestable. They must be put to death;*[a] *their blood is on them.* 14 *If a man takes a woman and her mother, it is a lewd act. Both he and the two women must be burned with fire so that no lewdness will be among you.* 15 *If a man has intercourse*[a] *with an animal, he must be put to death, and you must kill the animal.*[b] 16 *If a woman approaches an animal to lie with*

it,[a] *you shall kill the woman and the beast. They must be put to death; their blood will be on them.* [17]*If a man marries his sister, his father's daughter or his mother's daughter, and they have sexual relations together, it is a disgrace. They shall be cut off before the children of their people, for he has dishonored his sister and will bear the responsibility.*[a] [18]*If a man lies with a woman during her period and has sexual relations with her, he has uncovered her fountain, and*[a] *she has revealed the fountain of her blood. Both of them shall be cut off from their people.* [19]*Do not have sexual relations either with your mother's sister or your father's sister,*[a] *for that would shame a near relative. They will be held responsible.* [20]*If a man lies with his aunt, he dishonors his uncle. They will be held responsible for their sin;*[a] *they will die*[b] *childless.*[c] [21]*If a man marries his brother's wife, it is odious.*[a] *He has shamed his brother; they will be*[b] *childless.*

[22]*"Keep all my decrees and laws and do them in order that the land*[a] *where*[b] *I am bringing you to dwell may not vomit you out.* [23]*You shall not follow the decrees of the nation*[a] *which I am casting out before you; because they did all these things,*[b] *I am disgusted*[c] *with them.* [24]*But I said to you, you*[a] *will inherit their land. I myself*[a] *will give it to you to possess, a land flowing with milk and honey. I am Yahweh your God, who has set you apart from the nations.*[b] [25]*You shall distinguish between clean and unclean animals, between unclean and clean birds. Do not make yourselves detestable by any animal, bird, or anything that crawls on the ground, which I have set apart as unclean*[a] *for you.* [26]*You will be holy to me, because I Yahweh*[a] *am holy,*[b] *and I have set you apart from the peoples*[c] *to be mine.*

[27]*"If*[a] *a man or a woman among you is a necromancer or medium, they*[b] *must be put to death. They shall be stoned;*[c] *their blood will be on them."*

Notes

2.a. In place of MT תאמר, "you will say," Sam reads תדבר, "you will speak"; one Heb. ms has תדבר לאמר, "you will speak saying."

2.b. In this instance בני ישראל, "the people of Israel," comes first for emphasis (by contrast, e.g., 18:2).

2.c. The repetition of איש has individualizing force; cf. n. 17:3.a.

2.d. In place of MT מבני, "from the sons of," Sam reads מבית, "from the house of."

2.e. The prep מן, "from," is used with partitive force (GKC §119w[2]).

2.f. LXX renders the term למלך, "to Molek," with ἄρχοντι, "to the ruler," taking it as a title in participial form.

2.g. Cf. 18:21b. This inf abs before an impf strengthens the idea carried by the verb (cf. Exod 19:12; 21:12; 31:14).

3.a. Cf. n. 2.d. This phrase precedes the verb for emphasis.

3.b. Cf. n. 2.f.

3.c. The compound prep למען gives the effect, not the aim, of the action (Joüon §169g; cf. *IBHS* §38.3b, n. 25).

3.d. For MT ולחלל, "and to profane," Sam reads וחלל, "and profane." This variant could be a scribal error resulting from the number of לs in this word.

3.e. According to GKC §128p, קדש, "holiness," often is used as a periphrasis for the adj קדוש, "holy."

4.a. The inf abs stands before the verb to stress the willful, deliberate action of the people.

4.b. Cf. n. 2.d.

4.c. Cf. n. 2.f.

5.a. The personal pronoun is used with the verb to underscore God's resolve.

5.b. In place of MT אחרי המלך, "after Molek," LXX reads εἰς τοὺς ἄρχοντας, "to the rulers."

6.a. This law is constructed similarly to the laws in 2:1 and 17:13 with the use of נפש, "person" (Baentsch, 402).

6.b. Cf. n. 19:31.a.

6.c. Cf. n. 19.31.b.

6.d. In place of MT אתו, "him," Sam and LXX read אתה, "her," for the antecedent. נפש, "person," is fem, but in support of MT see 2:1.

6.e. Sam and LXX read עמה, "her people," for MT עמו, "his people"; cf. n. 6.d.

7.a. Sam and LXX* omit והתקדשתם, "you are to sanctify yourselves." This may be an error of haplography.

7.b. A few Heb. mss and LXX add קדוש, "holy," as in v 26.

8.a. Sam adds כל, "all."

9.a. Sun ("Investigation," 229) offers the best explanation for the initial כי; he takes it to be an emphatic particle (cf. n. 18:29.a.).

9.b. Cf. n. 2.c.

9.c. Sam reads דמו, "his blood," a sg form for MT's pl דמיו. In other places in MT, דם is sg as Josh 2:19; Ezek 33:4. The use of דם, "blood," or דמים, the plural for murder, communicates that the aggressor has poured out the victim's life-force. That "blood" envelops the aggressor, clinging to his hands and his head (cf. 2 Sam 3:28–29; 1 Sam 25:33; cf. K. Koch, "Der Spruch 'Sein Blut bleibe auf seinem Haupt' und die Israelitische Auffassung vom vergossenen Blut," *VT* 12 (1962) 405–9; his position is in response to H. G. Reventlow, "'Sein Blut komme über sein Haupt,'" *VT* 10 (1960) 311–27). How may the community be freed from the power of shed blood? Only with the death of the murderer. Since his own blood rests on his head, it does not envelop another.

10.a. Some Heb. and LXX mss omit איש אשר ינאף את־אשת, "a man who commits adultery with the wife of." The variant is followed, for MT has resulted from an error of dittography (Bertholet, 71); but PIR (194) accepts MT, stating that the repetition is included for legal precision. Similarly, Fishbane (*Biblical Interpretation,* 169) holds that v 10ab legally restricts the first clause by identifying the woman as the wife of a neighbor, but, as Sun ("Investigation," 229–30) points out, אשת איש means a "married woman," making אשת רעהו, "wife of his friend," a tautology. Further, a few Heb. mss, Sam, and the versions read a *waw* on אשר, "who," in this variant.

10.b. In place of this verb in the sg, LXX*, Syr, and Vg read a pl verb as occurs in this phrase in vv 11–13 and preferred by the compound subj. But in Heb. grammar the verb that stands before a compound subj may be in the sg form. Perhaps the versions preferred the pl form for a smoother translation rather than because they had a different Heb. Vorlage.

11.a. The obj ערות אביו, "nakedness of his father," stands before the verb for emphasis.

13.a. LXX appears not to have read the inf abs מות, "dying."

15.a. Cf. n. 18:20.a.

15.b. The dir obj comes before the verb for emphasis and to cast the verb תהרגו, "you will kill," to the end of the verse for greater emphasis.

16.a. Read אִתָּהּ, "with it," for MT אתה, "it" (Bertholet, 71). On רבעה cf. n. 18:23.e.

17.a. LXX reads ἁμαρτίαν κομιοῦνται, "they will bear [their] sin."

18.a. Many Heb. mss, LXX, Tg^{mss}, and *Tg. Ps.-J.* add a conjunctive *waw* here. This is the preferred reading.

19.a. Sam and LXX invert the order to read אחות אביך ואחות אמך, "your father's sister and your mother's sister." This long obj stands before the verb for emphasis.

20.a. LXX omits חטאם ישאו, (lit.) "they will bear their sin."

20.b. Sam reads יומתו (hoph), "they must die."

20.c. ערירי has traditionally been rendered "childless" from the root ערר, "strip, expose, demolish." In two of the passages in which this word occurs, namely Gen 15:2 and Sir 16:3, this meaning fits well. But in the two other occurrences of this word, which are in curse formulae, there is some doubt as to "childless" being the precise meaning. The difficulty is clearly seen in Jer 22:30. Jehoiachin (Coniah) was put under the curse "to be written down childless," but he already had several children. 1 Chr 3:17–18 names seven sons, and a Babylonian tablet found near the Ishtar Gate in Babylon names five sons (S. Schultz, "Jehoiachin," *ISBE* rev 2:976). Given this difficulty, other meanings for this term have been suggested. J. Fitzmeyer (*The Genesis Apocryphon of Qumran Cave I, A Commentary,* BibOr 18 [Rome: Pontifical Biblical Institute, 1966] 163) proposes "stripped, despoiled." Maarsingh (*Leviticus,* 180–81) gives "debased *entwürdig.*" Most versions, however, continue to render this Heb. term "childless," but NEB translates this Leviticus passage as "they shall be proscribed" and Jer 22:30 as "stripped of all honor."

It is very possible that this term may have both a precise technical meaning, "childless," and a more general meaning such as "despoiled." The second, parallel curse in the Jeremiah text, "a man who will not have any success in his day," supports this position, especially if this curse is intended as an amplification of the preceding one. It is also possible that the curse means to die as though he were childless. This would still be a harsh curse against any person, for in those times children were looked on as a valuable basis of security, namely to care for their parents during old age and to attend their grave after death. To be cursed as "childless" would mean then that none of this person's children would bear these responsibilities for the person cursed, leaving him to suffer disgrace in his old age and unhonored in death. The Jeremiah passage supports this position, for the curse against Jehoiachin goes on to declare that he would not have a successor on the throne of David.

21.a. Cf. n. 12:2.c.

21.b. LXX reads *ἀποθανοῦνται*, "they will die," as in v 20. MT is preferred as the harder reading. It is possible to translate it "they will become childless."

22.a. Sam places the subj before the dir obj, but the subj stands in its present location because of the unusually long relative clause that follows it.

22.b. The indeclinable אשר is resumed by the adv שמה, "thereward."

23.a. Some Heb. mss, Sam, and versions have a pl noun; both the sg and pl appear in 18:24–30, esp. v 28.

23.b. The dir obj appears before the verb for emphasis.

23.c. MT ואקץ is impf qal of קוץ, "feel a loathing, sickening dread" (cf. Exod 1:12; Num 21:5; 22:3; 1 Kgs 11:25; BDB, 880–81).

24.a. The personal pronoun appears before the verb for emphasis and rhetorical effect. The pronoun אתה, "you," is set in opposition to אני, "I," with אתננה, "I will give it."

24.b. LXX adds *πάντων*, "all."

25.a. The inf with the prep, לטמא ל, functions as a gerund: "as (being) unclean" (GKC §114o). Sam, LXX, and Syr read לטמאה, "for uncleanness," though the versions may be rendering the Heb. into their respective languages rather than having a different Heb. text.

26.a. LXX adds *ὁ θεὸς ὑμῶν*, "your God."

26.b. קדוש, "holy," is missing in Sam and a couple of Gk. mss.

26.c. Cf. n. 24.b.

27.a. Sam, LXX, Syr, and Tg[mss] read אשר in place of MT כי.

27.b. LXX has *ἀμφότεροι*, "both," which renders שניהם, "two of them," in several verses, such as vv 11–13.

27.c. In place of MT באבן ירגמו אתם, Sam and LXX read באבנים תרגמום, "you will stone them with stones." Perhaps the variant is a better text, because it is more unusual. Generally the phrase באבן, "with stone," is in the sg (v 2; 24:23); the pronominal obj is sometimes attached to the verb and other times occurs with את.

Form/Structure/Setting

The structure of this speech may be outlined as follows:

- I. Introductory formula (v 1)
- II. Speech (vv 2–27)
  - A. Commission to speak (v 2aα)
  - B. Speech proper (v 2aβ–27)
    - 1. First set of laws (vv 2aβ–6)
      - a. Sacrifice to Molek (vv 2aβ–5)
      - b. Sorcery (v 6)
    - 2. First parenesis, call to holiness (vv 7–8)
    - 3. Second set of laws (vv 9–21)
      - a. Cursing parents (v 9)
      - b. Various sexual relationships (vv 10–21)
        - 1) Laws carrying death penalty (vv 10–16)
          - a) Adultery (v 10)
          - b) Incest (vv 11–12)
            - (1) Sexual relations with a father's wife (v 11)
            - (2) Sexual relations with a daughter-in-law (v 12)
          - c) Male homosexuality (v 13)
          - d) Marriage to a woman and her mother (v 14)
          - e) Bestiality (vv 15–16)
            - (1) By a male (v 15)
            - (2) By a female (v 16)

        2) Laws carrying cut-off penalty (vv 17–18)
            a) Marriage to a sister (v 17)
            b) Sexual relations during menses (v 18)
        3) Law carrying accountability—sexual relations with a paternal or a maternal aunt (v 19)
        4) Laws carrying penalty of dying childless (vv 20–21)
            a) Sexual relations with an uncle's wife (v 20)
            b) Sexual relations with a sister-in-law (v 21)
4. Second parenesis (vv 22–26)
    a. Exhortation to keep these laws (vv 22–23)
    b. Promise of taking possession of the land (v 24)
        1) Promise proper (v 24a)
        2) Expanded formula of Yahweh's self-introduction (v 24b)
    c. Command to distinguish between clean and unclean animals (v 25)
    d. Call to holiness (v 26)
5. Law against sorcery with death penalty (v 27)

This speech has the pattern A:B::A':B'::A (A = laws and B = parenesis). The first set of laws specifies the penalty for anyone who offers a child to Molek and for the community that fails to punish anyone who offers a child to Molek (vv 2aβ–5) and for sorcery (v 6). The second set of laws gives the penalties for cursing one's parents (v 9) and for various sexual offenses (vv 10–20). A comparison of the two sets of laws (A + A') finds a chiastic pattern between their structures: specific laws:a general law::a general law:specific laws. In A, laws about offerings to Molek (vv 2–5) are followed by a law against sorcery in general (v 6). A', by contrast, begins with a categorical law against cursing one's parents (v 9) followed by laws against specific sexual offenses (vv 11–20). The single law at the end against sorcery (v 27) forms an inclusio with the first set of laws.

The first set of laws (A) concerns sorcery, either by making sacrifices to Molek (cf. *Excursus* on Molek at v 2) or in communicating with departed spirits. Both kinds of offenses are called לזנות אחרי, "whoring after" (v 5 and in v 6). The penalty for sorcery is God's saying, ונתתי את־פני בנפש ההוא, "I will set my face against that person"; it is interpreted as והכרתי אתו מקרב עמו, "I will cut him off from among his people." This same double expression of a penalty occurs in v 3 and again in v 5 with slight modifications. These similarities indicate that the law in v 6 has been designed to be an integral member of the first set of laws.

The laws in the second series are composed out of four elements: I case; II penalty; III reason; IV declaratory formula. The pattern for each decree is as follows:

	(v 9)	I, II, III, IV
1.	(v 10)	I, II
2.	(v 11)	I, III, II, IV
3.	(v 12)	I, II, III, IV
4.	(v 13)	I, III, II, IV
5.	(v 14)	I, IV, II, III
6.	(v 15)	I, II (twofold)
7.	(v 16)	I, II, II, IV
8.	(v 17)	I (expanded), IV, II, III, IV
9.	(v 18)	I, III (threefold), II
10.	(v 19)	I, III, IV
11.	(v 20)	I, II, IV, II
12.	(v 21)	I, IV, III, II

Laws 1 and 6 only have two elements, the case and the penalty. The other laws are expanded with reasons and declaratory formulae. The sequence of I–IV occurs in the opening general law and in law 2 (vv 9, 12). Six other laws (vv 11, 13, 14, 17, 20, 21) have all four elements, but in a variety of patterns. In law 7 (v 16) the penalty is stated and then restated in lieu of the reason because of the nature of the offense. Law 8 (v 17) has been expanded far more than any other; the case is stated and then restated in greater detail, and two declaratory formulae are included. The very full form of this law indicates both that there was special concern to guard against the marriage of a man to his half sister and that the courts required a more precise definition to enforce this law; thus some of these elements entered the law through the centuries. In law 9 (v 18) the reason is repeated three times, driving the point home. Law 10 (v 19) has been adapted from a code of laws like the one in chap. 18 (cf. vv 12–13) with the addition of a reason and a penalty. These variations in the pattern of these laws is for rhetorical force.

Based on subject matter, these laws seem to be randomly ordered. They, however, are held together both by key words and by the nature of the penalties. The primary threads uniting them are two words and a phrase: שׁכב, "lie" (vv 11, 12, 13, 15 [נתן שׁכבתו], 18, 20), לקח, "marry" (vv 14, 17, 21), and גלה ערוה־, "reveal the nakedness of" (vv 11, 17, 18, 19, 20, 21; this is the key phrase in chap. 18). The webbing is made tighter by the way these terms are interchanged; e.g., ערוה, "nakedness," the dominant word in the latter portion of these laws, appears in v 11, and שׁכב, "lie," the key term at the beginning, is used in v 18 and v 20. For clarity the speaker uses קרב, "draw near," over שׁכב, "lie," in v 16 to highlight the abnormal character of bestiality. As far as the order is concerned, these laws are arranged by decreasing severity of penalty. The first seven laws (vv 9–16) carry the death penalty: מות יומת, "he will surely die." Several times the death penalty is qualified by the declaratory formula דמ־ ב־, "(their) blood is on (them)" (vv 9, 11, 12, 13, 16). This formula means both that the guilty are deserving of death and that those who execute the penalty are free from any obligation for shedding the blood of the guilty. Twice, the penalty is being "cut off" (נכרת; vv 17, 18). The penalty of the last two laws (vv 20, 21) is "childlessness" (עריריִ). In three laws (vv 17, 19, 20), the declaratory formula נשׂא עונ־, "one will be held guilty" (v 20, חטא־), occurs to underscore the certainty that the penalty will be executed.

The single law at the end of the speech (v 27) seems to hang free from any attachment to the immediate context. Why does this speech end with a single law? Perhaps this law became dislodged from the first set of laws by a scribal error, being preserved in the margin of some manuscripts. A scribe, not knowing where to insert it, placed it at the end of the speech. A closer look, however, shows that it forms an inclusio with the first section (vv 2–6), for the terms אוב, "ghost, necromancer" and ידעני, "departed spirit, medium," occur in v 6 and the death penalty by stoning accords with v 2. In addition, the position of this law as the final word of this speech accentuates the several prohibitions against sorcery found in chaps. 18–20 (18:21; 19:26, 31; 20:2–5, 6) by directing the hearers' minds back to these laws.

Among these sets of laws there are two parenetic portions. The first one (vv 7–8) has an exhortation to holiness (v 7, as in 19:2) and an exhortation to obedience (v 8; cf. 18:4–5, 26, 30; 19:37; 20:22). Both exhortations are grounded with the formula of Yahweh's self-introduction (cf. 18:2). The second exhortation leads into the second set of laws as the initial conjunction כי on v 9 signals (Feucht, *Untersuchungen,* 35; Elliger, 268). Because of the close tie between vv 8 and 9, some place v 7 as the conclusion of vv 2–7 and v 8 as the heading of vv 8–21 (Feucht, 35; Elliger, 269–70). The fact that vv 7 and 8 are not formulated as laws argues against this alternative analysis of the structure.

The second parenetic portion (vv 22–26) is held together by the dual themes of possessing the promised land and separation from the nations. This parenesis begins with an exhortation to keep all these laws, supported by a threat (v 22) and an injunction against following pagan practices (v 23). Next comes the promise that God is soundly committed to giving Israel the land where she can live הבדיל, "separate," from the other nations (v 24). Building on the key term הבדיל, "separate," the speaker exhorts the people to make the distinctions (הבדיל; v 25; 11:47) required by the dietary laws (chap. 11), for the dietary laws have been given to keep Israel apart from the defiling customs and laws of her neighbors (cf. chap. 11). This exhortation is composed out of several key terms found in those dietary laws; טהר, "clean," and טמא, "unclean," are used five times along with שׁקץ, "detestable," and רמשׂ, "creep" (cf. 11:10, 11, 12, 13, 20, 23, 41, 42, 43; and 11:44, 46 respectively for the last two words). The inclusion of this exhortation establishes an arc between the laws of holy living (chaps. 17–26) and the laws of ritual purity (chaps. 11–15). This arc demonstrates the close connection between these two major sections of Leviticus from the cultic perspective of ancient Israel. This parenesis concludes with a general call to holiness with the promise that God will הבדיל, "set apart," his people from other peoples (v 26).

The content of this speech, both the laws and the parenetic portions, is very close to that of chap. 18. The most obvious difference between these two speeches is that the laws in chap. 20 state the penalties for the various offenses. Moreover, the laws of chap. 20 cover a wider variety of sexual transgressions. The tone of the laws in chap. 20 is less passionate than that of chap. 18 as conveyed by less colorful vocabulary and by bulkier formulations. The laws are also arranged differently. The laws in chap. 18 begin with incest (vv 7–18) and turn to a variety of sexual offenses (vv 19–23), while the laws in chap. 20 are a mixture of decrees against sorcery, incest, certain types of marriages, and sexual offenses. These differences indicate that the focus of each speech is distinct. The speech in chap. 18 is addressed to a father's house, particularly to the head who has the responsibility of enforcing them. This speech, by contrast, is delivered to the community, especially the leaders who are obligated to carry out the prescribed penalties. The different orientation of this speech means that it is not merely a copy of the speech in chap. 18 with additions. Another reason that two speeches dealing with sexual offenses are included is that the lawgiver wished to address this issue from differing perspectives in order to promote family solidarity for the growth of Israel into a strong nation in covenant with God.

This speech is composed for the oral instruction of the congregation at the appropriate festivals. The penalties serve as a deterrent to such offenses. The reasons address the hearers' ethical consciousness and sets their minds against such activity. And the declaratory formulae appeal to the audience's emotions by poignantly defining such acts as polluting or as incurring great guilt. The speaker is earnestly seeking to persuade the people from committing any of these offensive activities.

Comment

2 This law against offering children to Molek applies to both citizens of Israel and aliens living among them (cf. 18:21). In vv 2–4 the verb for assigning one's offspring or children to Molek is נתן, "give, assign, surrender, yield, leave." This is a term with a wide range of meanings. Sometimes, though infrequently, נתן may be used with the presentation of something for the priests' use in the cult (e.g., 5:16; 22:14; Exod 30:15; Ezek 20:28). In regard to the presentation of children to Molek, the verb is usually נתן or העביר, "transfer" (cf. the *Excursus* on Molek below). The use of נתן here does not say much about the nature of the sacrifice, but it does communicate the resolve of the worshiper to turn over a child completely to the control of Molek. There is a play on נתן for it is not only used three times for "giving" a child to Molek; it is also used in the idiom in v 3 in which Yahweh says, "I will set [נתן] my face against that man." The choice of נתן in this idiom underscores God's response to such a detestable offering; i.e., just as a person "gives" a child to Molek so will God himself "give" his personal attention to punish that presenter.

Making such a valuable offering to a pagan deity carries the death penalty. The עם הארץ, "people of the land," the citizens of Israel (cf. 4:27), have the responsibility of stoning the transgressor to death. This method of execution dispersed the responsibility for carrying out the punishment throughout the community. According to tradition, this penalty was discharged by casting the guilty party from a high place; they stoned that person only if the fall was not fatal (Hoffmann, 2:63). OT references to punishment by stoning include: blasphemers (24:16; cf. 1 Kgs 21:9–14), breakers of the Sabbath (Num 15:35–36), idolaters (Deut 13:11[10]; 17:5), incorrigible children (Deut 21:21), a bride who was not a virgin (Deut 22:21), a man who lies with a betrothed virgin and the betrothed virgin he forced (Deut 22:24), and an ox that gores a man or a woman (Exod 21:28–29; Wenham, 277).

Excursus: Molek

Bibliography

Baudissin, W. W. *Jahve et Moloch: sive de ratione inter deum Israelitarum et Molochum intercedente.* Leipzig: Fr. Guil. Gruneow, 1874. **Bea, A.** "Kinderopfer für Moloch oder für Jahwe?" *Bib* 18 (1937) 95–101. ———. "Moloch in den Maritafeln." *Bib* 20 (1939) 415. **Cazelles, H.** "Molok." *DBSup* 5 (1957) 1337–46. **Cohen, S. J. D.** "From the Bible to the Talmud: The Prohibition of Intermarriage." *HAR* 7 (1983) 23–39. **Daumer, G. Fr.** *Der Feuer- und Molochdienst der alten Hebräer als urväterlicher, legaler, orthodoxer Kultus der Nation.* Braunschweig: Fr. Otto, 1842. **Day, J.** *Molech: A God of Human Sacrifice in the OT.* UCOP 41. Cambridge: University of Cambridge Press, 1989. **Dhorme, E.** "Le dieu Baal et le dieu Moloch dans la tradition biblique." *Anatolian Studies* 6 (1956) 57–61. **Dronkert, K.** *De Molochdienst in het Oude Testament.* Leiden: Brill, 1953. **Dussaud, R.** "Melqart." *Syria* 25 (1946–48) 205–30. ———. "Milk, Moloch, Melqart." *RHR* 49 (1904) 163–68. ———. "Précisions épigraphiques touchant les sacrifices d'enfants." *CRAIBL* (1946) 371–87. **Ebach, J. H.** "PGR = (Toten-) Opfer? Ein Vorschlag zum Verstandnis von Ez. 43,7.9." *UF* 3 (1971) 365–68. ——— and **Rüterswörden, U.** "ADRMLK, 'Moloch' und BA'AL ADR: Eine Notiz zum Problem der Moloch-Verehrung im alten Israel." *UF* 11 (1979) 219–26. **Eissfeldt, O.** *Molk als Opferbegriff* *im Punischen und Hebräischen und das Ende des Gottes Moloch.* Beiträge zur Religionsgeschichte des Altertums 3. Halle: Max Niemeyer, 1935. **Février, J. G.** "Essai de reconstruction du sacrifice Molek." *JA* 248 (1960) 167–87. ———. "Molchomor." *RHR* 143 (1953) 8–18. **Ghillany, F. W.** *Die Menschenopfer der alten Hebräer.* 1842. **Green, A. R. W.** *The Role of Human Sacrifice in the Ancient Near East.* ASOR Dissertation Series 1. Missoula, MT: Scholars Press, 1975. **Heider, G. C.** *The Cult of Molek: A Reassessment.* JSOTSup 43. Sheffield: University of Sheffield Press, 1985. **Hoftijzer, J.** "Eine Notiz zum Punischen Kinderopfer." *VT* 8 (1958) 288–92. **Jirku, A.** "Gab es im AT einen Gott Molek (Melek)?" *ARW* 35 (1938) 178–79. **Kaiser, O.** "Den Erstgeborenen deiner Söhne sollst du mir geben: Erwägungen zum Kinderopfer im Alten Testament." In *Denkender Glaube:* FS C. H. Ratschow. Ed. O. Kaiser. Berlin: de Gruyter, 1976. **Kornfeld, W.** "Der Moloch: Eine Untersuchung zur Theorie O. Eissfeldts." *WZKM* 51 (1952) 287–313. **Löwengard, M.** *Jehova, nicht Moloch, was der Gott der alten Hebräer.* 1843. **Moore, G. F.** "Biblical Notes: 3. The Image of Moloch." *JBL* 16 (1897) 161–65. ———. "Molech, Moloch." In *Encyclopaedia Biblica.* Ed. T. K. Cheyne and J. S. Black. NY: MacMillan, 1902. **Mosca, P. G.** "Child Sacrifice in Canaanite and Israelite Religion: A Study in *Mulk* and *mlk.*" Diss., Harvard University, 1975. **Plataroti, D.** "Zum Gebrauch des Wortes *MLK* im Alten Testament." *VT* 28 (1978) 286–300. **Pope, M.** "The Cult of the Dead at Ugarit." In *Ugarit in Retrospect.* Ed. G. D. Young. Winona Lake, IN: Eisenbrauns, 1981. **Ratosh, J.** "'*ʿēbr*' in Scripture or the Land of *hʿbrym*" (Heb.). *Beth Mikra* 47 (1970/71) 549–68. **Ribar, J. W.** "Death Cult Practices in Ancient Palestine." Diss., University of Michigan, 1973. **Schaeffer, C. F. A.** "Sacrifice à M-l-k, Molech ou Melek." In *Ug 4.* Ed. C. F. A. Schaeffer. MRS 15. Paris: Imprimerie Nationale, 1962. **Schlögl, N.** "Das Wort *molek* in Inscriften und Bibel." *WZKM* 45 (1938) 203–11. **Schmidtke, F.** "Träume, Orakel und Totengeister als Künder der Zukunft in Israel und Babylonien." *BZ* n.s. 11 (1967) 240–46. **Smith, M.** "A Note on Burning Babies." *JAOS* 95 (1975) 477–79. **Snaith, N. H.** "The Cult of Molech." *VT* 16 (1966) 123–24. **Soggin, J. A.** "Child Sacrifice and the Cult of the Dead in the Old Testament." In *Old Testament and Oriental Studies.* BibOr 29. Rome: Pontifical Biblical Institute, 1975. **Stager, L. E.** "Carthage: A View from the Tophet." In *Phönizier im Westen.* Ed. H. G. Niemeyer. Madrider Beiträge 8. Mainz am Rhein: Philipp von Zabern, 1982. ———. "The Rite of Child Sacrifice at Carthage." In *New Light on Ancient Carthage.* Ed. J. G. Pedley. Ann Arbor: University of Michigan, 1980. ——— and **Wolff, S. R.** "Child Sacrifice at Carthage—Religious Rite or Population Control?" *BAR* 10 (1984) 30–51. **Vermes, G.** "Leviticus 18:21 in Ancient Jewish Bible Exegesis." In *Studies in Aggadah, Targum and Jewish Liturgy in Memory of Joseph Heinmann.* Ed. J. Petuchowski. Jerusalem: Magnes, 1981. 108–24. **Weinfeld, M.** "Burning Babies in Ancient Israel: A Rejoinder to Morton Smith's Article in *JAOS* 95 (1975), pp. 477–79." *UF* 10 (1978) 411–13. ———. "The Molech Cult in Israel and Its Background." In *Proceedings of the Fifth World Congress of Jewish Studies.* Ed. P. Peli. Jerusalem: World Union of Jewish Studies, 1969. ———. "The Worship of Molech and of the Queen of Heaven and Its Background." *UF* 4 (1972) 133–54. ______. "Moloch, Cult of." *EncJud* 12:230–32. **Wilke, F.** "Kinderopfer und kultische Preisgabe im 'Heiligkeitsgesetz'." In *Festschrift zur 57. Versammulung deutscher Philologen und Schulmänner in Salzburg, 1929.* Vienna: Rudolf M. Rohrer, 1929.

The term מלך, "Molek," occurs five times in Leviticus plus three times in other OT texts—1 Kgs 11:7, 2 Kgs 23:10, and Jer 32:35; but the occurrence in 1 Kgs 11:7 is considered by most scholars to be the result of a textual error for מלכם, "Milcolm" *(BHS).* The understanding of this term has been debated for a long time. Many scholars have postulated that the spelling of this deity's name should be Melek or Malik, meaning "king"; this position began with A. Geiger (*Urshrift und Uebersetzungen der Bibel* [Breslau, 1985] 301 sited by Day, *Molech,* 56). According to these scholars, the pointing, מֹלֶךְ, came about as a result of the polemic against idolatry. They hold that the biblical writers' hatred for Baal and other pagan deities sometimes led them to substitute בשת *bōšet,* "shame," for Baal; e.g., the name Ishbaal (1 Chr 8:33; 9:39) is spelled Ish-bosheth in

2 Sam 2:10. In other texts these writers overwrote the name of a deity with the vowels of *bōšet;* e.g., the name Astarte < Astart is changed to Ashtoreth (Day). Several scholars have challenged this explanation (e.g., M. Tsevat, "Ishbosheth and Congeners: The Names and Their Study," *HUCA* 46 [1975] 71–87). Heider (*Cult of Molek,* 223–28) even claims that מֹלֵךְ, a participle, is the correct form of this deity's name. Day (56–58), however, has refuted the alternative positions and has returned to the explanation that the pointing in the MT is a caricature of this deity.

Interpretations of the worship practices to Molek have likewise varied widely. Even the early rabbinic tradition had differing interpretations. In a comment on Deut 18:10, R. Judah ben Elai (A.D. second century) understood that in this worship children were dedicated to a pagan god. Another rabbinic tradition interpreted Lev 18:21 as a prohibition against mixed marriages in order to curtail idolatry (cf. *m. Meg.* 4.9). A third view understood that Lev 18:21 prohibited sexual intercourse with a cult prostitute. The rabbinic tradition as a whole, thus, did not believe that children were put to death. But in 1686 John Spencer challenged this position by asserting that in this cult children were put to death by fire (in *De legibus Hebraeorum ritualibus et earum rationibus* [Hagae-Conitumi: Arnold Leers, 1686]). His position received support from accounts of child sacrifice at Carthage; cf. F. Münter, *Religion der Kathager* (2d ed. [Copenhagen: John Heinrich Schubothe, 1891]) and F. C. Movers, *Die Phönizien* (Bonn: Eduard Weber, 1841). W. W. Baudissin (1874) added to the discussion the claim that the Phoenicians transmitted the worship of Molek to Israel.

In 1935 O. Eissfeldt put forth a new explanation for מלך, "molek," postulating that it was a technical term for a particular kind of sacrifice, not the name of a deity. In his judgment, only as a result of Josiah's reform did Molek become worshiped as a deity. M. Weinfeld challenged Eissfeldt's position and revived the hypothesis that the cult of Molek did not involve child sacrifice (*EncJud* 12:230–32). He also challenged the claim that this cult and its practices came from Phoenicia or Carthage. For him the cult of Molek involved the dedication of children to Adadmilki, Ishtar, and the King and Queen of Heaven. Working from another direction, P. Mosca defended Eissfeldt's thesis of a molk type of sacrifice. He reconstructed a cult of child sacrifice, which had its roots in Phoenicia and Canaan and which was sanctioned by the official Yahwistic cult up until 722 B.C. in the North and until Josiah's reform in the South. G. C. Heider next theorized that the worship of Molek in Israel developed from a Syro-Palestinian deity Malik, later Milku/i or Molek, which was worshiped as a chthonic deity in Mesopotamia, Mari, Ugarit, and Israel. J. Day takes a similar position arguing strongly that Israel took this cult over from the Canaanites (*Molech,* 24–31).

These studies in Molek have raised several fundamental questions; among them, were children actually sacrificed and was Molek a deity or a type of sacrifice?

The laws in Lev 18:21 and Lev 20:2–5 against giving children to Molek are tersely constructed. The two key terms for the act of worship involving children are נתן, "give" (20:2, 3, 4), and העביר, "cause to pass through or over, transfer" (18:21). Because these terms have a wide range of usage in the OT, their precise meaning has to be determined in order to help define the nature of this worship. From other texts regarding Molek, some information on the usage of these terms is gained. In 2 Kgs 23:10, באשׁ, "with fire," is added to העביר, "cause to pass through, over, transfer," to make clear that the child-sacrifice was indeed burned (cf. 2 Kgs 16:3, 17:17; 2 Chr 33:6; Deut 18:10; Num 31:22–23). This passage testifies that a major center for such sacrifices was the Fire-Pit or Tophet (תפת) in the Valley of Hinnon.

More is learned about practices at the Fire-Pit from Jeremiah, who preached fervently against that worship. In 32:35 he condemns the transfer of children to Molek on במות בעל, "the high places of Baal" (cf. 26:29–33), in the Valley of Hinnon. In 7:31 he speaks against those who have built במת תפת, "the high places of the Fire-Pit," in the Valley of Hinnon to burn their children by fire (שׂרף . . . באשׁ). In 19:5 he categorizes the burning of children by fire on the high places of Baal as "whole offerings" to Baal (עלות לבעל). These references unequivocally testify that children were actually burned in offerings made to Molek and to Baal. The reference to offering children to Baal is corroborated by Punic texts that speak of human sacrifices to Baal-ḥammon (Day, *Molech,* 24–37). Unfortunately the relationship between Molek and Baal in the making of this type of sacrifice is not clear. J. Day argues convincingly that, though certain practices in the cult of Molek were similar to those in the cult of Baal, Molek was a distinct deity and was not confused with Baal (*Molech,* 34–36).

Texts from Ezekiel add further support to the position that children were actually burned. Ezek 16:21 speaks of שחט, "slaughtering," children and making them offerings (נתן בהעביר). שחט, "sacrifice," is the critical term, for it denotes ritual slaughter (cf. Ezek 20:25–26, 31). This text suggests that children were ritually killed before they were burned, and it adds to the evidence that in cultic contexts העביר is a technical term for the sacrifice of children. While Ezekiel does not name Molek, the terms describing the practice of offering children are so similar to the above references that Molek may be included among the idols mentioned in 20:31 and 23:37. Furthermore, Day (*Molech,* 16) points out that Isa 57:5–9, where Molek is mentioned, also uses שחט, "slaughter," for the killing of children.

Additional support may be gained from other passages that speak of offering up children even though Molek is not specifically named. Deut 12:31 witnesses to some practice of burning children by Israel's neighbors. This practice is portrayed as similar to the offering of children to Molek. In addition, 2 Kgs 16:3, 17:17, and 21:6 add significant data. They record that either a person or the people "caused [their sons and/or daughters] to be transferred by fire" (העביר . . . באש). To these texts Day adds Isa 30:33 as a witness to burning the sacrifice unto destruction (*Molech,* 17); the cultic language here implies a reference to Molek worship. These secondary witnesses add support to the position that the children were consumed by fire.

In light of these texts, העביר functions as a technical term in cultic texts, meaning "to transfer" a sacrifice to a deity by burning. When באש, "in fire," occurs with העביר, it is apparently for emphasis. The inclusion of that phrase is not required for העביר to mean that the sacrifice was actually killed. נתן, "give, make," is a general term focusing on the presentation of the sacrifice, both the will and the act of making the sacrifice.

As for the question of whether Molek stands for a type of sacrifice or the name of a deity, the phrase זנות אחרי, "to go whoring after," in Lev. 20:5 definitely suggests a deity, not a type of sacrifice, for this phrase is often used for Israel's pursuing other gods (e.g., Exod 34:15, 16; Deut 31:16; Ezek 6:9; 20:30). In addition, Weinfeld has clearly demonstrated that names such as מלכ אמר or מלכאדם, which Eissfeldt and de Vaux employ to support a molk type of sacrifice, are better understood as theophoric names, supporting the position that Molek was the name of a god (*EncJud* 12:231).

A puzzling issue is why these laws against sacrificing children to Molek in Leviticus occur among laws regulating incest, other illicit sexual relations, and practices of soothsaying. First, it may be postulated that just as violations of the standards of incest and sexual morality could threaten the solidarity of a clan or at least cause great discord among family members, as the incident of Amnon and Tamar did in David's family (2 Sam 15–19), so too could the offering of children to Molek threaten a clan's solidarity or cause great discord among family members.

Second, these laws on Molek come among laws on incest and illicit sexual practices because both were considered abhorrent and extremely defiling. See the commentary for the vocabulary pertaining to the various kinds of defilement identified with these violations in Lev 18 and 20. Specifically in regard to Molek worship, both 2 Kgs 23:10 and Jer 32:35 classify such sacrifices as תועבה, "a detestable act" (cf. Lev 18:22, 26, 27, 29, 30; 20:13). תועבה depicts the terribleness of the sacrifice of children also in 2 Kgs 16:3. In Lev 20:3 the giving of children to Molek is said to defile (טמא) the sanctuary and to profane (חלל) God's holy name. Thus this offense carried the death penalty (Lev 20:2) as well as God's personal judgment, not only against those worshipers but also against those Israelites who tolerated such worship (20:3, 5).

Third, these practices may occur together because the Israelite social consciousness connected them. A witness to such a connection in a society's outlook comes from a very distant land. According to R. Fox (*Red Lamp of Incest,* 32–34), the Chiricahua, an American Indian tribe who lived in the Southwest, treated both incest and witchcraft as the gravest violations of both the spiritual and the social orders. Given the position discussed in reason four, that Molek worship was a kind of witchcraft, the parallel between Israel and the Chiricahua may offer insight into the orientation of Israel's social consciousness.

Fourth, justification for the placement of these prohibitions may reside in the nature of Molek worship, namely its connection with ancestral worship. In several texts the sacrifice of children stands in conjunction with soothsaying and necromancy (Lev 20:2–6; Deut 18:10; 2 Kgs 17:17; 21:6; 2 Chr 33:6). Working with this evidence, Heider postulates that there was a cult of the dead practiced in Canaan and in Israel. Ps 106:28b, an interpretation of the event recorded in Num 25, speaks of the Israelite's joining in a Moabite festival and eating sacrifices offered to the dead. Heider (*Cult of Molek,* 388–89) interprets this ritual as a מרזח, "funeral feast" (cf. Amos 6:7; Jer 16:5). Isa 63:3–5a describes worship that took place at night in secret with a meal of pork and broth made from unclean things, heightening the occultic dimensions of this worship. This text provides another witness to the worship of the dead. From this evidence, Heider posits that Molek worship was related to these feasts for the dead. Therefore, Molek worship may be associated with ancestral worship, making it more understandable why these laws against Molek have been placed with other laws regarding intimate family matters. This interpretation of Molek worship makes intelligible the joining of a law against necromancy with the laws against Molek in 20:2–6, for a primary goal of necromancy was communication with deceased relatives. How much of Heider's reconstruction of the nature of Molek worship may be accepted is open to question since it is quite speculative. Nevertheless, it gains significant support from the evidence presented by Day (*Molech,* 46–55, 58–64) that Molek was an underworld deity intimately associated with the worship of the dead.

These reasons for the context of the laws on Molek worship are not mutually exclusive. In light of any one or more of them these laws fit their context.

(This has been prepared with extensive help from Timothy R. Dwyer, Ph.D., formerly a student of Prof. J. Milgrom, the University of California at Berkeley.)

3 God himself turns against any person who offers a child to Molek by cutting that person off (נכרת) from the people. The reason is that such a gross sin both defiles (טמא) the sanctuary (cf. 16:33) and profanes (חלל) God's holy name. The phrase שם קדשי, "my holy name," lit. "name of my holiness," communicates that the essential characteristic of God is "holiness"; cf. 19:2. The twofold description of the defiling nature of such an act is founded on the close connection between God and the Temple, where he is enthroned.

If the community puts the guilty party to death (v 2), what does this statement about God's punishing such a person add? Ibn Ezra offers the explanation that if the abominable practice of offering children to Molek is not punished, God himself will enter the picture and cut off that person from the midst of his people. But then, as Hoffmann notes (2:64), vv 4–5 lose their impact. A second and better explanation put forth by Ibn Ezra is that this additional punishment results in the rooting out of this person's descendants. But nothing in this context indicates that such a transgressor's offspring are to be punished. Rather this verse expresses God's extreme loathing of such a transgression. He personally excludes such a person from the covenant community, meaning that that person will have none of this community's benefits in the age to come.

The use of the term זרע, "seed, offspring, family," for the child offered to Molek is pregnant with meaning. God made the first promises of the covenant to Abraham and to his זרע, "seed" (Gen 12:7; 15:18; 24:7; cf. 13:15; 28:3, 13–14), and he established the covenant with Abraham and his seed after him (Gen 17:7; cf. vv 8–14). Abraham was then instructed to circumcise Isaac, his seed, as the seal of the covenant (cf. H. Preuss, "זָרַע *zāraʿ*; זֶרַע *zeraʿ*," *TDOT* 4:151–52). Preuss says, "Thus *zeraʿ* articulates more than mere blood relationship, a shared heritage and growth; it also indicates more than the intimate solidarity of the individual with the fathers and the people. It expresses an organic cohesion within history under the same God, under his guidance in judgment and salvation, the unfolding into the future of the gifts given and promised to the fathers by Yahweh, and the assurance of standing in this heritage and being able to apply it to oneself" (Preuss, *TDOT* 4:162). This means that the promise is never given to a patriarch alone, but it is for his descendants as well. His seed is God's blessing and is the continuation of the promise. Consequently, when an Israelite offers any of his seed to Molek, he thwarts God's purpose at the very source of its continuance. It is for this reason that God sets such stern penalties for engaging in Molek worship.

4–5 If the people of the land take the easy path and ignore anyone's offering a child to Molek by not putting the guilty person to death, God himself will punish the guilty party and the entire family (משפחה) who make such a disgusting sacrifice (cf. Exod 20:5). The intentionality of the people's looking the other way is underscored by the hiphil inf abs העלם, "closing [their eyes]," standing before the verb "close" (יעלימו). Those who make such an offering are said to זנה אחרי המלך, "prostitute themselves after Molek." They so zealously set their affections on the worship of Molek that they forsake their love for Yahweh.

6 God himself turns against any person who זנה אחרי, "prostitutes himself" (cf. v 5), by pursuing communication with אבת, "ghosts," and ידענים, "departed spirits" (cf. 19:31). The penalty for such action is to be cut off from the people (cf. 7:21).

7–8 Cf. 11:44; 19:2. Structurally this brief parenesis both concludes the laws against sorcery and heads the next section about sexual offenses. Instead of pursuing Molek worship and seances, the people must התקדש, "sanctify themselves." They sanctify themselves each time they obey the laws given by God. Sanctification involves affirmative action; it is exercising one's will to do God's will. Sanctification is also pursued by consciously avoiding any activity that defiles. Standing at the head of the family laws, this call to holiness also teaches that how one treats one's parents and how one conducts oneself in sexual relationships directly affect the development of one's character. Holiness is practiced at home as well as at the sanctuary. Thus every time the people obey God's word, they activate the sanctifying presence of God in their midst. Yahweh does the sanctifying; he is present among his people as the Holy God.

9 No person may curse his father or his mother, for such action flagrantly violates the commandment to honor one's father and mother (Exod 20:12; Lev 19:3). It is noteworthy that both parents are mentioned in this law, thus placing the parents on equal footing. Such formulation promotes the value of women both in ancient and in modern times. קלל, "to curse," means to pronounce an oath against another, imploring the forces of nature to bring on that person the harm defined in the curse. For example, a child may curse his parents' crops or their handicraft so that they fail and his parents go hungry. Or out of jealous anger he may curse something they are undertaking, such as a long journey, building a new house, or adopting a child, so that their plan might end in disaster. Such a curse is flagrant rebellion against parental authority (cf. Elliger, 275). Such cursing carried the death penalty (cf. Exod 21:17; Prov 20:20; Deut 21:18–21; Matt 15:4; Mark 7:10). That the one who curses is worthy of the death penalty is affirmed by the phrase דמיו בו, "his blood is on him." Often the formula is דמיו (יהוה) בראשו, "his blood be on his head." It means that this person has forfeited his right to life (Josh 2:19; Ezek 33:4). This phrase also communicates that whoever punishes the guilty person by taking his life does not come under the laws of blood revenge.

Given the position of this law at the head of the laws on sexual offenses, it is possible the speaker saw that violating a close relative's wife or committing a sexual offense is similar to cursing one's parents, for such offenses shame the parents and threaten the solidarity of that family.

10 Cf. 18:20; Deut 22:22.

11 A son is not to have intercourse with his father's wife, either his own mother or another wife of his father. The reason is that she bears his father's ערוה, "nakedness." Cf. 18:8; Deut 23:1(22:30); 27:20; Ezek 22:10. Both parties are subject to the death penalty. This penalty implies that the woman encouraged or at least consented to her husband's son's advances.

12 If a father lies with his daughter-in-law, he violates his son's honor. Such an act is labeled תבל, "a confusion"; bestiality is also so labeled in 18:23. Cf. 18:15; Ezek 22:11.

13 Male homosexuality is identified as תועבה, "something detestable, repugnant" (cf. 18:22). Such an act carries the death penalty.

14 The man who לקח, "takes," both a woman and her mother is to be burned (cf. 18:17). In this context Wenham (280) understands לקח to carry the meaning "to live with" instead of its technical meaning "marry," for he believes that no such union would have been given public sanction. The punishment prescribed is the burning of the man and the two women; this punishment, though, may not be in place of stoning but in addition to it, i.e., burning the corpse (cf. Josh 7:15, 25; Lev 21:9; Judg 14:15; 15:6; Gen 38:24). "Burning" deprived these offenders of a proper burial and thus increased significantly their punishment in the eyes of ancient man. It also cleansed the land from the defilement of such זמה, "a lewd act" (cf. 18:17; Hoffmann, 2:71–73). Burning as a form of punishment may go back to God's use of this means to put to death those who dared to enter the sanctuary with something foreign or those who brazenly challenged his purpose (e.g., 10:12; Num 16:35). The feminine plural accusative אתהן, "them," means that both women must die. The question of why both women should be put to death has greatly troubled the rabbis, because marriage to one of the women was legal; only marriage to the second one was illegal. Jewish tradition has various interpretations for this. R. Ishmael argues that only the last one married is subject to the death penalty; he interprets אתהן, "them" to mean "one or the other." But R. Akiba understood אתהן to mean "both women." Rashi (93, n.) reasons that both women were forbidden to the man, for he had been previously married. Another possible reason for both women coming under penalty is that since they are mother and daughter, some scheming among them for such a living arrangement to take place is assumed.

15–16 Cf. 18:23; Exod 22:18(19); Deut 27:21. Bestiality carries the death penalty for both the human and the beast. In some way guilt from this unnatural act attaches to the beast. The beast must be put to death to remove the impurity from the community.

17 A man who לקח, "takes," i.e., marries, a sister either by his father or his mother and consummates the marriage commits חסד, "a disgrace" (cf. 18:9, 11; Deut 27:22; Ezek 22:11). Usually חסד, a significant term in the OT, expresses "loyal, faithful love." The homonym חסד, possibly from another root, means "disgrace, something shameful." This second root occurs only twice, here and in Prov 14:34. Since a brother is to guard his sister's honor, he is held responsible; עונו נשׂא, "he must bear his iniquity" (cf. 7:18; 19:8). The wording of this law, that "he sees her nakedness and she sees his nakedness," means that both are passionately involved. Therefore, both are נכרת, "cut off" (cf. 7:21, 27; 19:8; Num 19:13, 20). The weight of this punishment is strengthened with the wording "in the sight of the children of their people." Nevertheless, a greater burden falls on the brother. He is held responsible because he has the greater responsibility of guarding his sister's honor.

18 Cf. 18:19; 12:2, 7; 15:19, 24; Ezek 22:10. When a man has sexual relations with a woman during menses, the man and the woman are held accountable. The reason given is that he has הערה, "laid bare," מקרה, "her fountain," and she has גלה, "revealed," מקור דמיה, "the source of her blood" (cf. 12:7). This reason is rooted in the mystery of sex and in the taboo against blood (cf. Elliger, 276).

19 Cf. 18:12–13. Sexual relations with either a mother's sister or a father's sister are forbidden. This is another example in the laws on holy living where the mother is mentioned before the father (cf. 19:3; 21:2). The initial position of a mother's sister stresses that a sister of either parent is excluded. Usually incest laws are stricter on the father's side; but aunts on both sides of the family are forbidden.

20 If a man has sexual relations with his uncle's wife, they both must bear the responsibility for their act (חטאם ישׂאו). This wording for responsibility is unusual in that חטא, "sin," has been substituted for עון, "iniquity." Their punishment is to die childless, ערירי, (lit.) "stripped." This is a heavy penalty, for it means the end of both of their families. This penalty is the direct opposite of the custom of marriage designed to insure the continuance of a family line. Snaith (97–98) restricts the meaning of this word to "stripped of posterity," i.e., no legitimate heir to maintain his father's remembrance (cf. 2 Sam 18:18). Of course, only God could guarantee the execution of this penalty. The harshness of this penalty is attested in Jeremiah's cursing Jehoiachin with this curse (22:30).

21 Cf. 18:16. Outside of the conditions that required a brother to marry his deceased brother's wife, i.e., levirate marriage (Deut 25:5–6), one may not marry a brother's widow. In this case one brother might be seeking to take over his deceased brother's estate and name inappropriately, folding his dead brother's estate into his own and removing the remembrance of his brother. Such a union is so repugnant that it is called נדה, "odious, foul, impure," a word for "menstruation" (cf. n. 12:2.c.). NJPS translates it "indecency." The penalty is being or becoming עריריי, "childless." The emphasis on this penalty is that they will have no offspring to carry on their line and to attend their memory after their death. If there were children already born to either of these parties, this penalty means that they will outlive their children.

22–23 Cf. 18:3–5, 24–30. God points out that he is the one who is going to expel the nations that are in the land, because he קוץ, "loathes," their defiling practices. קוץ communicates deep feelings of repulsion and contempt produced by continuous irritation (cf. Gen 27:46; Num 21:5; 22:3).

24–26 God will fulfill his promise, and Israel will ירש, "possess," the land. ירש means both "to take possession of" and "dispossess," for one people gains possession of a land by driving out another people. Israel will gain possession of a land flowing with milk and honey by driving out the other nations because God is with her. Canaan, the land of the promised inheritance, was first described as a land flowing with milk and honey when God called Moses to lead Israel out of Egypt (Exod 3:8, 17; cf. Deut 6:3). חלב, "milk," refers to goat's milk and דבש, "honey," to syrup from the date. In the promised land Israel is to live differently than the people whom she is going to drive out, because God has set her apart (הבדיל) to follow his decrees and laws. To promote Israel's separation from her neighbors, God has given her specific dietary laws (chap. 11). God requires his people to distinguish between clean and unclean animals in order that they do not make themselves שקץ "detestable" (cf. 11:9–12; 41–44), by eating any of these animals that are unclean.

27 Cf. v 6; 19:31. This law against necromancy specifically applies to either a man or a woman who practices this skill. The death penalty is prescribed for a necromancer and a spiritist; it is to be executed by stoning (cf. v 2).

Explanation

See *Explanation* for 18:1–30.

E. Special Laws for the Priests (21:1–24)

Bibliography

Bailey, J. W. "The Usage in the Post Restoration Period of Terms Descriptive of the Priest and High Priest." *JBL* 70 (1951) 217–25. **Zipor, M.** "Restrictions on Marriage for Priests (Lev 21,7.13–14)." *Bib* 68 (1987) 259–67.

Translation

1 *Yahweh said to Moses: "Say to the priests, the sons of Aaron, and say to them: No one may make himself unclean for a death* [a]*among his relatives*[b] 2 *except for his*[a] *closest relatives: his mother, his father,*[b] *his son,*[c] *his daughter, his brother.*[d] 3 *But he may make himself unclean for*[a] *his marriageable*[b] *sister, who is near to him and who does not have*

a husband.[c] 4*He may not make himself unclean for those related by marriage,*[a] *for he would defile himself.*[b]

5*"They shall not make bald*[a] *patches on their heads*[b] *or shave off the corner of their beards or make gashes*[c] *in their bodies.*[d] 6*They are to be holy to their God; they shall not profane the name of their God, because they present the gifts*[a] *of Yahweh, the food*[b] *of their God; they are to be holy.*[c]

7*"They shall not marry a harlot, a hierodule,*[a] *and they shall not marry*[b] *a divorced*[c] *woman, because each priest*[d] *is holy to his God.*[e] 8*You are to make sure he is holy,*[a] *because he presents the food*[b] *of your God.*[c] *You*[d] *are to regard him as holy, because I Yahweh, who sanctify you,*[e] *am holy.*

9*"If a priest's*[a] *daughter defiles*[b] *herself by harlotry, she defiles her father.*[c] *She is to be burned with fire.*

10*"The priest, who is pre-eminent among his brothers,*[a] *on whose head the anointing oil has been poured,*[b] *and who has been ordained to wear*[c] *the priestly garments,*[d] *is not to let his hair be unkempt nor to tear his clothes.* 11*He shall not enter any place of the dead.*[ab] *He shall not make himself unclean for his father or his mother.*[b] 12*He shall not leave the sanctuary in order that he not profane the sanctuary of his God, because the consecration*[a] *of the anointing oil of his God is on him. I am Yahweh.*

13*"He*[a] *is to marry a young virgin.*[bc] 14*He shall not marry a widow, a divorcee, a hierodule,*[a] *or a harlot,*[bc] *but he is only to marry a virgin from his own people.*[d] 15*He is not to profane his offspring among his relatives,*[a] *because*[b] *I am Yahweh who sanctifies him."*

16*Yahweh spoke to Moses:* 17*"Speak to Aaron:*[a] *No one from your seed, in any generation,*[b] *who has a blemish may come near to present*[c] *the food of his God.* 18*No*[a] *one who has a blemish*[b] *may come near: one who is blind, lame, disfigured,*[c] *or deformed,*[d] 19*one who has an impaired leg or impaired hand,*[a] 20*or who is a hunchback,*[a] *has a withered member,*[b] *a discoloration of the eye,*[c] *a festering rash,*[d] *lichen,*[e] *or damaged*[f] *testicles.* 21*None of the offspring of Aaron, the priest, who has a blemish*[a] *may come near to present*[b] *the gifts for Yahweh.*[c] *He who has a blemish shall not come near to present the food of his God.*[d] 22*He may eat the food of his God,*[a] *both that which is most holy and that which is holy.*[b] 23*But he shall not enter the curtain or approach the altar, because he has a blemish, and he may not defile my sanctuary,*[a] *because I am Yahweh who sanctifies them."*[b]

24*Thus Moses spoke to Aaron, to his sons, and to all the Israelites.*

Notes

1.a. Cf. 19:28.b.

1.b. In place of MT עמיו, "his relatives," Sam, Syr, Tg, and *Tg. Ps.-J.* read a sg noun עמו, "his people." LXX reads a pl pronoun "their."

2.a. LXX has a pl pronoun.

2.b. Sam, LXX, and Syr invert MT to read לאביו ולאמו, "for his father and his mother." Cf. n. 19:3.a.

2.c. Sam, LXX[mss], and Tg[mss] omit the *waw,* "and."

2.d. Sam and LXX[mss] omit the *waw,* "and."

3.a. LXX reads ἐπὶ τούτοις, "for these," in place of MT לה, "for her." Unless the antecedent of "her" is a result of attraction to the fem in the first part of this verse, it is inexplicable and thus an error of transmission (Sun, "Investigation," 267).

3.b. G. Wenham ("*Betûlāh* 'a girl of marriageable age,'" *VT* 22 [1972] 326–48) argues that בתולה means "a young lady of marriageable age." It is then not a technical term for "a virgin"; otherwise the clause "who does not have a husband" would not be needed. Through the centuries this term took on this technical meaning, but this did not clearly take place until the Christian era in Wenham's judgment.

3.c. This is a *casus pendens*, which is picked up by לה, “for her,” before the verb.

4.a. MT בעל בעמיו, “a husband among his people,” has troubled interpreters. Dillmann (619) emends בעל to באבל, “in mourning.” Bertholet (74) and Elliger (279) read לבעלת־בעל, “for one married” (cf. Deut 22:22). The expression is taken to mean those related to him through marriage. For different readings of MT עמיו, “his relatives,” see n. 1.a.

4.b. MT החלו, “defile oneself, be profaned,” is a niph inf constr (GKC §67t).

5.a. Sam supports the qere and adds a *waw* at the beginning, ולא יקרחו, “and they shall not shave.” The ketib לא יקרחה, “one shall not shave,” is a scribal error arising from the following cognate acc קרחה, “bald spot.” LXX puts this verb in the second person pl.

5.b. LXX adds ἐπὶ νεκρῷ, “for the dead”; cf. Deut 14:1.

5.c. For MT שׂרטת, “gash,” Sam has the spelling שׂרטה.

5.d. V 5 is arranged chiastically. V 5aα is inverted in both v 5aβ and v 5b: verb with cognate acc:location::location as a constr:verb::location:verb with cognate acc.

6.a. Cf. n. 1:9.g.

6.b. To avoid a too vivid anthropomorphism, LXX renders לחם, “bread,” with δῶρα, “gifts”; similarly Tg uses קורבן, “oblation”; cf. n. 3:11.b. These two versions continue this practice in vv 8, 17, 21, 22.

6.c. For MT קדש, “holiness,” Sam and the versions read a pl form קדשים, “holy ones,” as at the opening of the verse. The text of 11QpaleoLev appears to support Sam. The variant is preferred grammatically, but Sun (“Investigation,” 269) accepts MT as the harder reading.

7.a. The term חללה, coming after זנה, “a harlot, one who is free sexually,” is not readily definable (Zipor, *Bib* 68 [1987] 259–67). Four possibilities have been put forth. (1) It comes from חלל II, “pierce, hollow,” to mean “a girl deflowered,” but this meaning is redundant to זנה. (2) It is related to מחולות, “dancers,” to mean “one devoted” to sacred prostitution (cf. M. Z. Levin, “חללה,” *Beth Mikra* 29 [1984] 180–81). (3) Zipor (265) returns to the most commonly accepted root חלל I, “profane,” to mean “hierodule.” (4) Levine (143) offers another interpretation of זנה וחללה; he takes it as a hendiadys meaning “a woman degraded by harlotry.” The occurrence of חללה in v 14 favors the third explanation. On cultic prostitute see E. J. Fisher, “Cultic Prostitution in the Near East,” *BTB* 6 (1976) 225–36. Zipor observes that there is a chiasm between v 7 and v 14 in the listing of the ladies whom a priest may not marry (Heb. order):

v 7	גרושה	divorced	חללה	hierodule	זנה	harlot		
v 14	זנה	harlot	חללה	hierodule	גרושה	divorced	אלמנה	widow

Since אלמנה is added to the list for a high priest, it stands first for emphasis.

7.b. LXX does not read לא יקחו, “they shall not marry.” This omission may result from the translator’s preference for a better Gk. reading.

7.c. MT reads גרושה מאישה, (lit.) “cast out by her husband.” In this phrase the prep מן, “from,” marks the agent (*IBHS* §11.2.11d).

7.d. The subj “priest” is inserted in the Eng trans. to provide a clearer reading; this is also required by the shift from the pl in v 7a to the sg in v 7b.

7.e. LXX reads τῷ κυρίῳ, “to the Lord [Yahweh].”

8.a. LXX reads a third person sg verb in place of the second person sg in MT.

8.b. 11QpaleoLev does not have את, the sign of the dir obj. Cf. n. 21:6.b.

8.c. LXX reads κυρίου θεοῦ ὑμῶν, “the Lord your God,” in place of MT אלהיך, “your God.” LXX results from a fuller reading.

8.d. LXX does not read לך, “for you.”

8.e. In place of MT מקדשכם, “sanctifying you,” 11QpaleoLev, Sam, and LXX read מקדשם, “sanctifying them,” as in v 23; a similar variant is also found in 22:32.

9.a. In the phrase איש כהן, the specific noun is in apposition to the generic noun (Joüon §131b). This is the only occurrence of this phrase (Sun, “Investigation,” 271).

9.b. MT תחל is a niph impf of חלל with compensatory lengthening of the vowel in the first syllable (GKC §67t).

9.c. LXX and Vg insert τὸ ὄνομα, “the name.”

10.a. 11QpaleoLev reads a sg pronominal suffix מאחו, “from his brother.”

10.b. MT יוצק is a hoph impf; the impf is expressing continuous condition (Baentsch, 407).

10.c. The inf constr with the prep ל presents attendant circumstances (GKC §114o).

10.d. This is an expanded *casus pendens;* it is resumed by the pronominal subj, which is part of the verb.

11.a. LXX and Syr read a sg form; cf. Num 6:6. 11QpaleoLev supports MT. On this meaning of נפש, "soul," as "deceased," cf. n. 19:28.b.

11.b. The prep phrase stands before the verb for emphasis. Levine (144–45) gives an alternative way of rendering the prep "on," namely as "on account of": "he shall not enter any place on account of deceased persons."

12.a. נזר here means "consecration," not the holy diadem, נזר הקדש, which is on the high priest's turban (8:9; Exod 24:6; 39:30).

13.a. Both the use of and the position of the personal pronoun הוא, "he," is emphatic. It stresses that this law applies to the high priest.

13.b. Cf. n. 21:3.a. Wenham thinks that it is this context that gives בתולה the meaning "virgin," but the use of this term also conveys that the girl is to be "young, a teenager" (*VT* 22 [1972] 337–38); cf. n. 3.a.

13.c. LXX adds ἐκ τοῦ γένους αὐτοῦ, "out of his generation."

14.a. Cf. n. 7.b.

14.b. Sam, LXX, *Tg. Ps.-J.* and Vg read a *waw,* "or." Bertholet (75) comments that if זנה is not a gloss after v 7, the *waw* needs to be read.

14.c. This is a compound *casus pendens* for the dir obj; it is resumed by את־אלה, "these." This list stands before the verb for emphasis.

14.d. Cf. n. 1.b.; a Heb. ms reads this variant.

15.a. Cf. n. 1.b.

15.b. LXX does not read כי, "because."

17.a. LXX does not have any equivalent for לאמר, "saying."

17.b. In place of MT לדרתם, "in their generations," LXX reads εἰς τὰς γενεὰς ὑμῶν, "in your generations."

17.c. For MT להקריב, "to present," Sam reads להגיש, "to approach"; one Heb. ms omits this word.

18.a. Some Heb. mss and LXX omit כי, "that." Its initial position carries emphasis.

18.b. The expanded subj stands before the verb for emphasis.

18.c. חרום means "split" (e.g., Isa 11:15). Tradition has taken this to mean "a twisted, broken, or cleft nose" (cf. KB, 340); Jastrow (503) renders it "flat-nosed." Keil and Delitzsch (432) take this word to mean any mutilation, especially one of the face.

18.d. שׂרוע means "stretched out"; in regard to a member of the body it means one that is unusually long (cf. Jastrow, 1632). Giesen (*TDOT* 5:202) suggests that it may have to do with difficulty in hearing; interestingly in this light LXX reads ὠτότμητος, "with slit ears."

19.a. In LXX, these two illnesses occur in inverted order.

20.a. גבן is taken to mean "hunchback" (BDB, 148; KB, 167); this is how most Eng trans. render it. NEB, however, renders it "misshapen eyebrows" based on another Jewish tradition.

20.b. דק, "thin, skinny," is applied to gaunt cows (Gen 41:3–4) and to finely ground incense (Lev 16:12). For a human, one suggestion is "dwarf" (cf. KB, 220). Keil and Delitzsch (433) take this term to include an unnaturally thin or withered body or member of the body. Tg renders it with דוקא, which Jastrow (288) defines as "a veiled or withered spot," and he adds in parentheses "or *withered in growth, dwarf.*" Harrison (211) notes that a dwarf is only an undersized person, not a deformed person. Keil's position is accepted, for it is closer to the root meaning.

20.c. For MT בעינו, "in his eye," Syr, (LXX), Tg, and *Tg. Ps.-J.* read בעיניו, "in his eyes." תבלל means "confusion, obscurity" (BDB, 117); BDB suggests that in this setting it may mean "defective eyesight." Rashi (98) takes it to mean a white line across the eye reaching to the black iris. In the same spirit Snaith (101) proposes that it means any defect that keeps the white and black parts of the eye from being pure in their respective colors.

20.d. For גרב, BDB (173) gives "itch, scab" and KB (193) "festering rash." This term also occurs in 22:22 and Deut 28:27 for a skin ailment.

20.e. ילפת is rendered by BDB (410) "scab, scurf." Keil and Delitzsch (433) give "ringworm." Tg translates it with חזזן, "one afflicted with lichen, a cutaneous disease connected with desquamation and sometimes ulceration" (Jastrow, 442). JB renders it "running sore" and NEB "eruption."

20.f. For MT מרוח, BDB (598) gives two possibilities: one from the root מרח to mean "be rubbed away, damaged," the other from the root רוח to mean "enlarged." KB interprets this construct chain to be an epexegetical genitive; i.e., the genitive provides the more precise definition (GKC §128x). It describes abnormal testicles, which in the opinion of the ancients rendered that person sterile. Noordtzij (220) postulates that MT could be repointed מְרֻוַח, "hernia."

21.a. Cf. n. 18.b.

21.b. For MT יגש להקריב, "he comes near to present," Sam reads only יגיש, possibly to agree with its reading in v 17.

21.c. For MT את אשׁי יהוה, "the gifts for Yahweh," LXX reads *τὰς θυσίας τῷ θεῷ σου ὅτι*, "the sacrifices for your God, because."

21.d. Placing of the dir obj before the inf, an Aramaic style, occurs in a few places in the OT as here (GKC §142f, n.). But Sam places this dir obj after the verb. Cf. n. 6.b.

22.a. Sam does not read לחם אלהיו, "the food of his God." Cf. n. 6.b.

22.b. The compound dir obj stands before the verb for emphasis.

23.a. LXX reads *τὸ ἅγιον τοῦ θεοῦ αὐτοῦ*, "the holy place of his God." MT מקדשׁי is in the pl; the use of the pl designates all the various precincts inside and outside the Temple area.

23.b. The pl pronominal suffix refers back to the precincts of the Temple; cf. n. 23.a.

Form/Structure/Setting

The structure of this speech may be outlined as follows:

- I. Two speeches regarding the Aaronite priests (vv 1–23)
  - A. First speech about the purity of the priests (vv 1–15)
    - 1. Introductory formula (v 1aα)
    - 2. Speech (vv 1aβ–15)
      - a. Twofold commission to speak (v 1aβ–bα)
      - b. Speech proper (vv 1bβ–15)
        - 1) Concerning the Aaronite priests (vv 1bβ–9)
          - a) Prohibitions (vv 1bβ–5)
            - (1) Prohibitions in reference to relatives who die (vv 1bβ–4)
              - (a) Prohibition proper (v 1bβ)
              - (b) Exceptions enumerated (vv 2–3)
              - (c) Prohibition restated (v 4)
            - (2) Prohibition about mourning rites (v 5)
          - b) Laws in reference to the holiness of priests (vv 6–8)
            - (1) Two commandments and prohibition (v 6)
            - (2) Prohibition regarding marriageable women for a priest (v 7)
            - (3) Commandments to sanctify the priests (v 8)
              - (a) Two commandments and reason (v 8a–bβ)
              - (b) Expanded formula of Yahweh's self-introduction (v 8γ)
          - c) Law regarding a priest's daughter who becomes a harlot (v 9)
        - 2) Concerning the high priest (vv 10–15)
          - a) Identification of high priest (v 10a)
          - b) Laws in regard to high priest (vv 10b–15)
            - (1) Prohibitions in reference to deceased (vv 10b–12)
              - (a) Series of prohibitions (vv 10b–12bα)
                - (i) Prohibition regarding mourning practices and contact of a deceased relative (vv 10b–11)
                - (ii) Prohibitions to guard the sanctuary from being profaned (v 12a–bα)
              - (b) Formula of Yahweh's self-introduction (v 12bβ)
            - (2) Laws about marriageable women for the high priest (vv 13–14)
            - (3) Prohibition against defiling posterity (v 15)
              - (a) Prohibition proper (v 15a)
              - (b) Expanded formula of Yahweh's self-introduction (v 15b)
  - B. Second speech about blemishes that disqualify an Aaronite priest (vv 16–23)
    - 1. Introductory formula (v 16)
    - 2. Speech (vv 17–23)
      - a. Commission to speak (v 17a)
      - b. Speech proper (vv 17b–23)

1) Basic prohibition (v 17b)
2) Prohibition restated with catalogue of disqualifying characteristics (vv 18–20)
3) Prohibition and privilege of a disqualified priest (vv 21–22)
   a) Restatement of primary prohibition (v 21)
   b) Privilege of a disqualified priest to sacred food (v 22)
4) Prohibition against such a priest's activity at the sanctuary (v 23)
   a) Prohibition proper (v 23a–b*α*)
   b) Expanded formula of Yahweh's self-introduction (v 23b*β*)

II. Compliance report that Moses delivered the speeches (v 24)

Two speeches make up this portion. The first is addressed to the priests (v 1) and the second to Aaron (v 16). The content of the first speech concerns both the priests (vv 2b–9) and the high priest (vv 10–15). The second speech covers every priest, but it is addressed to Aaron, for the high priest bears the responsibility of barring a priest with a disfigurement from working at the altar. While the priests are the immediate audience of these speeches, this portion's setting in the book of Leviticus, as underscored by the statement at 21:24, means that these instructions to the priests have been preserved for the oral instruction of the whole community. The people are addressed not only to learn about the requirements laid on the priest, namely about uncleanness from contact with one who has died, women whom they may marry, and bodily defects that disqualify them. They are also to take responsibility to make sure that the priests sanctify themselves by living a holy life as God has commanded (v 8). Furthermore, this knowledge about the rules for a holy priesthood provides the congregation greater insight into the nature of holiness.

Each speech of this portion is headed by an introductory formula (vv 1, 16), and each one concludes with the self-introduction formula expanded by a participial clause, אני יהוה מקדש, "I am Yahweh who sanctifies" (vv 15, 23). This clause also occurs at 21:8 to strengthen that word of exhortation directed to the congregation.

The first speech has two parts. The first part (vv 1–9) contains regulations for the priest, and the second (vv 10–15) regulations for the high priest. In both, the issues of uncleanness from contact with a corpse and of marriageable women are treated in the same sequence. The first section has received two additions: an exhortation, possibly addressed to the congregation (v 8), and a regulation about a priest's daughter's acting as a harlot (v 9). The placement of an exhortation in a series of laws is typical of the style of the material on holy living (cf. chap. 18). The second addition took place at a time when the behavior of daughters of the priests had become questionable. It was taken from the priestly professional knowledge and included in the general instruction for the congregation, no doubt to solicit their support in putting an end to such practices. The second speech (vv 16–23) offers a catalogue of bodily defects and diseases that disqualify a priest from serving at the altar.

Several key roots, all associated with holiness, bind these speeches together: קדש, "holy" (vv 6 [2x], 7, 8 [4x], 12 [2x], 15, 22 [3x], 23 [2x]); טמא, "unclean" (v 11); חלל, "profane" (vv 6, 9, 12, 14, 15, 23). Sacrificial terms like קרב, "draw near, present" (vv 6, 8, 17 [2x], 18, 21 [2x]; cf. 6, 8), are also key by reason of the subject matter.

Most of the material is written in the third person impersonal style, fluctuating between the singular (vv 1b–4, 7b, 8, 10–15, 17b–23b*α*) and the plural (vv 5–7a,

23bβ). This shift in number does not require two different authors (e.g., Kilian, *Literarkritische,* 89–91), for the speaker simply has drawn from two different places in the priestly professional knowledge. This impersonal style indicates that the material was taken from that source (cf. Begrich, "Die priestliche Tora"). The speaker has added a little material in direct address. He has inserted v 8 as a parenesis calling the congregation to look after the sanctification of the priests. The formulae of Yahweh's self-introduction may be attributed to him (vv 15b, 23bβ). In v 23b he also gives the exhortation not to profane the sanctuary.

Regarding the origin of some of this material, Noth (163) assigns the rules about the holiness of the priests and about the exclusion from office for bodily blemishes to the time before Israel became a state. However, he observes that the cultic picture in vv 10–15 is that of "a united priesthood, with a hierarchical head" (154). He dates this to the time of the exile after the formation of Deuteronomy, but before the clearer definition of the high priest's role at the time of Haggai and Zechariah. Nevertheless, this picture of the high priest coincides with the ceremony of his anointing and the offering of the first sacrifices on the altar in chaps. 8–9. This material then has its origin at the time of the formation of Israel as a nation in the wilderness.

Comment

1a Moses is instructed to speak specifically to the priests, the Aaronites, i.e., the priests who offer the sacrifices and serve at the sanctuary. Special standards are placed on those who work in the holy area in order to preserve the holiness of the sanctuary.

1b–3 The opening law regulates the priests' contact with the dead. Death, a major trauma in human experience, is an issue central to every religious system. Each religion regulates the customs about burial and the honor given to the one who has died. In many ancient societies the dead were venerated. The early Egyptians were so preoccupied with death that the Pharaohs spent years preparing their final resting place, a pyramid, at great national expense. In Israel, however, a high barrier was erected between death and the sanctuary because death, the final curse for human sin, was most defiling (Num 19:11–22). Since veneration of the dead was not to become a part of the worship of Yahweh, the handling of the deceased was relegated to the sphere of the common. Yahweh is the God of the living, not the God of the dead (Luke 20:38). Thus the laws and the rites of Israel's cult curtailed any worship of the dead.

Israelite priests could not participate in or even attend funeral ceremonies for members of the congregation. In the case of a death of an immediate family member, a priest could become unclean for a parent, one of his children, a brother, or an unmarried sister. No permission is granted for a married sister, since she belongs to another family. The absence of any mention of a priest's wife is amazing. The reason may simply be that the case of a wife would be permissible because of her being his closest relative; then she is included in the term שׁאר, "relative" (see 18:6). The example of Ezekiel's not mourning his wife's death does not negate this position, for on that occasion Ezekiel, a priest, was given specific, personalized instructions by Yahweh (Ezek 24:15–18).

4 Since the wording of this verse is difficult, its interpretation is disputed. Wenham (290) suggests that this verse may anticipate v 7 by saying that a priest should not defile himself by marrying a woman of questionable character. It seems best, however, to interpret the verse within its immediate context. Then this decree is saying that a priest should not become unclean in matters of death even for his wife. Such a stringent obligation does not seem justified (cf. vv 1b–3). Rashi explains the decree as preventing a priest from burying a wife who has become unfit to be his wife, but nothing in the text says anything about a wife's being unfit. The best interpretation has been put forth by Cazelles and accepted by Kilian (*Literarkritische,* 85): a priest is not to become unclean by mourning for one of his wife's relatives. If this is the case, עם, "people," in v 4 carries a narrow meaning for a small group in contrast to its use for a tribe in v 1b.

5–6 When the priests mourn for their nearest relatives (cf. 19:27, 28; Deut 14:2), they are not to follow the mourning customs of the surrounding nations (cf. 1 Kgs 18:28). Any cutting of the flesh or shaving the hair would mar their bodies, which are to be whole and complete as a witness to holiness. The forbidden act of shaving means the making of a bald spot on the hair above the forehead (Deut 14:1). A twofold reason is stated: (1) they shall not profane (חלל) the name of their God, and (2) they must be holy since they offer the gifts of Yahweh (אשׁי יהוה). Holiness gives them power to act confidently and effectively as intermediaries between God and the people. If they practice these pagan customs of mourning, they dishonor the name of their God, the very name by which they minister at the sanctuary. Such defilement destroys their holy character, causing them to lose their effectiveness as priests.

7 A high standard is set for the person whom a priest may marry. He may not marry a lady who has been זנה, "a harlot." Since this restriction would be obvious, this strong term applies here to a woman who had lost her virginity without specifying the frequency (cf. Hoffmann, 2:87–88). If a priest married a woman who had been sexually loose, he could not be sure that the first offspring of his marriage was his. Another woman excluded is a hierodule, a woman who had participated in pagan cultic practices. Whereas a hierodule was called קדשׁה, "a holy woman" (cf. Hos 4:14), in pagan circles, in the law she is called חללה, "a profane woman." Whenever Israel came under strong pagan influence, it would be conceivable that the ideal woman for a priest, who was holy, should be such a holy woman. But the standard of holiness revealed in the law anathematizes such a belief. Furthermore, a priest could not marry גרושׁה, "a divorced woman," possibly since her pledge of faithfulness to another man had been violated. Marriage to any of these kinds of women would render the priest impure, meaning that he could not officiate at the altar.

8 The speech shifts from indirect to direct address in this verse. Who is directly addressed? In light of v 1 it could be the priests. Then the priests themselves would monitor their own observance of the law. Hoffmann (2:89) interprets the use of the singular as being directed to Moses, the representative of the covenant community; he bases this on the form אמרת, "you will say," in v 21b*a*. But in the broader context of chaps. 17–26, "you" refers to the congregation; this position is confirmed by the inclusion of v 24. The congregation then is exhorted to sanctify the priest; i.e., they are to take responsibility to make sure that a priest lives by these decrees in order that he may be able to present the sacrifices. Each priest is to live a holy life for the benefit of the congregation. It is then reiterated that Yahweh is the Holy One, the one who achieves the sanctification.

9 A priest's daughter who becomes a prostitute חלל, "defiles," her father. Since in ancient Israel the family was a solid unit, the activity or character of each member reflected on the other members. In this case it was necessary to remove the cause of the defilement from the priest's family and from the congregation. The penalty for a daughter of a priest who becomes a prostitute is burning, because fire cleanses away the defilement. Most interpreters understand the penalty to be stoning to death and then burning the corpse. There is no evidence that cremation was favored in Israel; thus, burning the corpse was part of the humiliating punishment, signifying that this daughter was totally removed from the face of the earth.

10 The high priest is head of all the priests. Here a full title for his office is used: הכהן הגדול מאחיו, "the priest who is greater than his brothers." He is the one on whose head שמן המשחה, "the oil of anointing," has been poured (chap. 8; 16:32; Num 35:25) and the one who has been ordained (lit. "he has filled hands"; cf. 8:22). After being ordained, he dons the majestic garments made for the office of high priest (8:6–9; Exod 28:1–29:9). The high priest must come directly from the family of Aaron (Num 25:10–12). Being the one person in Israel who serves closest to Yahweh in the Holy Place and the Holy of Holies (chap. 16), he has to live by a higher standard of holiness than do the other priests.

11–12 Because of the antithesis between holiness and death, the high priest may not be defiled by contact with a corpse even for a close family member (also Ezek 44:25). During the time of mourning for a family member, he may not even observe the outward signs of letting his hair be unkempt, of not using oil, or of tearing his clothes. For compliance with the decree not to let his hair grow, *b. Sanh.* 22b limits the time a high priest can go without cutting his hair to thirty days. Nothing is said about the death of the high priest's wife. What concessions may have been made in this regard are not mentioned.

During the time of mourning for a close relative, the high priest is not permitted to leave his dwelling place in the sanctuary. That is, he is to stay at his post so that he may be on duty for the benefit of the whole congregation. His obligation to God surpasses his family responsibilities (Wenham, 291).

13–15 The high priest is more restricted in whom he can marry than are the priests. He may not marry a widow, a divorced woman, a hierodule, or a woman who has had sexual intercourse (זנה; cf. v 7). The women are mentioned in order of increasing undesirability. The high priest may marry only a virgin. In that way he guarantees that his first offspring, potentially the next high priest, is of pure stock. This virgin is to come מעמיו, "from his people." This term has been taken narrowly to mean "a priest's daughter" (Philo) or more broadly "an Israelite" (Hoffmann, 2:93). From this the rabbis debate whether it is permissible for him to marry a proselyte. The purity and singleness of his devotion to God are to be reflected in the purity and singleness of his marriage relationship.

17–21 To serve at the altar, a priest has to be whole in body. His bodily perfection is an external expression of the idea of holiness (M. Douglas, *Purity,* 51–52). Any bodily defect renders a person imperfect, unfit to function as priest. The wholeness of the priest, just like the wholeness of an animal acceptable for sacrifice, corresponds to and bears witness to the holiness of the sanctuary and the holiness of God. Defects that exclude one from functioning as priest include: עור, "being blind"; פסח, "lame"; חרום, disfigured in any way, but Giesen ("חרם *ḥrm* II," *TDOT* 5:202) defines חרום more specifically as "a speech impediment caused by perforated or twisted nasal septum, and perhaps also a cleft palate, which lends the voice a nasal quality"; שׂרוע, "being deformed," i.e., having a member of the body malformed, too short or too long, or possibly having something extra like an extra finger or possibly having slit ears; שׁבר רגל, "a broken leg or foot"; שׁבר יד, "broken hand"; גבן, "hunchback"; דק, "a withered or very thin member"; תבלל בעינו, "a discolored spot or streak in the eye"; גרב, "a festering rash or sore"; ילפת, "lichen, scurf, or scabs"; or מרוח אשך, "a crushed testicle." This list of defects corresponds to that for animals in 22:22–24 (cf. Milgrom, "Ethics and Ritual," 180–81). The skin diseases mentioned here, גרב, "a festering rash," and ילפת, "scurf or lichen," are not included under the term צרעת, "a grievous skin disease," in chap. 13. This fact informs us that there were other skin diseases that did not isolate a person from the community. Yet they were considered serious enough to keep a priest from serving at the sanctuary. This is another indication of the higher standard placed on a priest.

22–23 A priest who has any such defect may, however, eat from the offerings classified as holy and most holy. Holy portions include the priestly portions of the offering of well-being (7:31–34), the firstfruits (Num 18:12–13), the first-born of clean animals (Num 18:15), tithes (Num 18:26), and other devoted things (Num 18:14; Noordtzij, 220). The most holy portions are the priestly portions of the purification, reparation, and grain offerings (6:22[29]; 7:1, 6; 2:3, 10; 6:9–11[16–18]) and the bread of the Presence (Lev 24:8–9). Though these blemishes exclude a priest from serving at the altar, he is not reduced to poverty or forced to earn his living by another profession.

24 This verse states that Moses has been faithful and has delivered the words he received from Yahweh to the Aaronites and the people of Israel in obedience to God's command. Coming at this place, it means that he spoke them to the congregation. The people are to be informed as to the special standards by which the priests have to live; they are not to be guarded as private professional knowledge. The people are given access to the basic information about the priests. This procedure helped guard against the development of a priestly caste that dominated the people's access to God. The congregation is to appreciate their special role and the stringent discipline placed on the priests.

This compliance report accords with similar reports at 8:21b, 36; 16:34b. Periodically in this cultic legislation it is recorded that Moses and/or the people did what Yahweh had instructed them to do. The material to which this compliance report is applied is difficult to determine. It could be just chap. 21. It then addresses the slight tension that the opening introductory formula causes, namely that these laws addressed specifically to the priests come in a setting of the oral instruction of the people. Another possibility is that it includes all the material from 17:1–21:23; that is, it goes back to the last compliance report. If that is the case, then why did it not come after chap. 22 since chaps. 21 and 22 are tied closely together by matter of both subject and style? It is then taken to redirect the introductory formulae to the two speech units in chap. 21 from being addressed not just to the priests, but to all the people.

Explanation

The priests had a vital leadership role in ancient Israel. They instructed the people in God's ways, they interceded on behalf of the people, and they kept the cult operational. Working closer to God than did the people, they had to sanctify themselves by living by higher standards. Since the high priest entered behind the veil, he had to live an even holier life.

The higher standard of holiness placed on the priests is regulated in this speech in three ways: avoidance of uncleanness from contact with the dead, limitation of marriageable partners, and restrictions caused by bodily defects. First, the priests were carefully regulated in regard to uncleanness from contact with a corpse. Death is most defiling, for it is the direct opposite of life, the curse of sin. Yahweh is the living God, i.e., the God who gives and sustains life. A priest was permitted to become defiled by a corpse only for a very close relative, but the high priest could not become defiled for anyone save possibly his wife. This standard taught the ultimate value of life. It also prevented fascination with the dead as expressed in undue honoring of the dead and any type of worship of the dead.

The second area of restriction regards the person whom a priest could marry. Since a man and a woman become one flesh in marriage, a priest could marry only a virgin or a widow. He could not be joined to a woman who had been a holy woman at a pagan shrine or one who had been divorced. The higher standard placed on the high priest says that he could marry only a virgin.

The third restriction is that a priest had to be physically whole. No person who had a deformity, was disfigured, or had a rash could act as priest. Physical wholeness corresponds to the holiness of his task. While such a person could not function as a priest, he maintained the prerogatives of a priest in regard to support and living quarters. Neither he nor his family was placed under financial hardship because of his physical handicap.

Christ, our high priest, measured up to the highest standards of holiness in his absolute moral purity (2 Cor 5:21; Heb 4:14–15; 7:25–28; 1 Pet 2:22; 1 John 3:5; cf. John 8:46; Acts 3:14). He carried out his high priestly role on earth in complete obedience to God (Heb 7–8; 10:19), and he continues to function in the heavenly sanctuary as high priest for all who believe on him (Heb 10:11–25). As the head of the Church, he is sanctifying her as his bride so that she may become holy and without defect (Eph 1:4; 5:25–27; Col 1:22). His sanctifying work will reach its fulfillment at the marriage supper of the Lamb, when he will marry a pure, spotless bride (Rev 19:7–8).

These responsibilities and prerogatives of the priests offer insight to the members of the new covenant, for all believers in Christ are priests (1 Pet 2:4–10; Rev 1:6; 5:10; 20:6). To function effectively as priests they must keep themselves holy and blameless before God (2 Pet 3:11–12, 14; Phil 1:10; 2:15; 1 Thess 5:12–23; Titus 2:11–14). In place of a keen concern for ritual purity, there is a diligent striving for moral purity. Leaders and overseers of the church are to conduct themselves with greater discipline than is required of the laity. This is seen in the higher standards demanded for leaders (1 Tim 3:1–13; Titus 1:5–9). The priests of the new covenant are not to be unduly preoccupied with affairs of this life, which have the kiss of death on them (Matt 6:25–34; Luke 12:33–34; cf.

Luke 9:60; 14:33). Instead their energy is to be spent in bringing the redemptive power of the kingdom of God to troubled people throughout the world.

F. *Laws regarding the Priests' Eating Sacred Food (22:1–16)*

Translation

1 *Yahweh spoke to Moses:* 2 *"Speak to Aaron and his sons: let them treat with due re-*
spect the holy offerings of the Israelites which they are consecrating to me in order that
they do not defile my holy name. I am Yahweh.
3 *"Say to them: If any of your descendants,*[a] *in any generation, in a state of unclean-*
ness, comes near the holy offerings which the Israelites consecrate to Yahweh, that person
will be cut off from my presence. I am Yahweh.[b]
4 *"If any descendant of Aaron*[a] *has a grievous skin disease*[b] *or a discharge, he may not*
eat any of[c] *the holy offerings until he is clean. Anyone who touches anything defiled by a*
corpse[d] *or anyone who has an emission of semen,*[e] 5 *or anyone who touches any crawling*
thing that makes one unclean, or any person by whom he is made unclean by whatever
kind of uncleanness[a]—6 *the person who touches any such thing will be unclean until*
evening, and he shall not eat any[a] *of the holy offerings unless he wash his body in water.*
7 *When the sun sets, he becomes clean. Afterwards he may eat of the holy offerings, for*
they are his food. 8 *He shall not eat*[a] *of any animal found dead or ripped by wild animals*[b]
to become unclean by it.[c] *I am Yahweh.*
9 *"The priests shall keep my instructions lest they become guilty*[a] *by them and die*
thereby because they defile it.[b] *I am Yahweh*[c] *who sanctifies them.*
10 *"No laity*[a] *may eat anything holy. Neither may a priest's guest nor his hired worker*
eat anything holy. 11 *But if a priest purchases a slave with money, he may eat of it,*[a] *and*
as for slaves born[b] *in his house, they*[c] *may eat of his food.* 12 *If a priest's daughter mar-*
ries a layman, she shall not eat any of the holy contributions.[a] 13 *But if a priest's daughter*
is widowed or divorced, without children, and she returns to her father's house as in[a] *her*
youth,[b] *she may eat of her father's food. No lay person,*[c] *though, may eat of it.*
14 *"If anyone eats of a holy offering inadvertently, he is to add 20 percent to it and*
give to the priest the holy offering. 15 *They shall not profane the holy offerings of the Isra-*
elites which they have elevated to Yahweh 16 *lest they bring on*[a] *themselves guilt requiring*
reparation[b] *when they eat of the holy offerings. I am Yahweh who sanctifies them."*

Notes

3.a. For MT מכל־זרעכם, "from all your seed," a few Heb. mss, LXX[mss], and Vg read מזרעכם, "from your seed."

3.b. LXX* adds ὁ θεὸς ὑμῶν, "your God."

4.a. A few Heb. mss and LXX add הכהן, "the priest"; cf. 1:7; 21:21.

4.b. Cf. chap. 13.

4.c. The prep ב has partitive force. GKC (§119m) says that this usage carries "the idea of an action extending *to* something with at the same time the secondary idea of participation *in* something."

4.d. טמא־נפש, is a gen of instrument: "unclean because of a corpse" (*IBHS* §9.5.1d; Joüon §129i). On this meaning of נפש, cf. n. 19:28.b.

4.e. Cf. n. 15:16.a.

5.a. This long series of nominal clauses beginning in v 4b functions as a long *casus pendens;* it is resumed by נפש, "person, one," in v 6.

6.a. This is a partitive use of the prep מן, to mean "some, any" (BDB, 580).

8.a. Sam and Vg read a pl verb.

8.b. The compound dir obj stands before the verb for emphasis.

8.c. LXX uses a pl pronoun for a better Gk. trans. since the antecedent is pl.

9.a. Cf. 19:17; 20:20; 24:25.

9.b. The antecedent of these third person sg pronouns is the comprehensive term קדש, "holiness" (Bertholet, 76). LXX, however, has pl pronouns to agree with verbs at nn. 9.a. and 9.b.

9.c. LXX* adds *ὁ θεός,* "God."

10.a. The subj stands before the prohibition for emphasis.

11.a. LXX makes the law more explicit by rendering the prep phrase בו, "of it," with *ἐκ τῶν ἄρτων αὐτοῦ,* "of his food."

11.b. Sam[mss], LXX, Syr, Tg, and *Tg. Ps.-J.* read a pl constr; MT may be an error rising from the presence of the preceding two *yods.* The following "they" indicates that this phrase, a *casus pendens,* was pl.

11.c. LXX reads a *waw* on הם, "they."

12.a. Cf. n. 7:32.a.

13.a. Some Heb. mss read the prep ב, "in," instead of כ, "like."

13.b. There is a difference of opinion about how much is included in the protasis. Some interpreters take ושבה, "and she returns," to be part of the conditional clause with the main clause beginning with מלחם, "from bread." But Rashi (100b) assigns ושבה to the main clause: "If she has no children, she may return." The note in Rashi points out that the accentuation on ושבה supports Rashi's interpretation.

13.c. In this context זר, "stranger, outsider," is used for one who does not belong to a priestly family (cf. Deut 25:5 for a similar usage of זר; Kilian, *Literarkritische,* 94).

16.a. In this idiom for "incur guilt," this is an unusual occurrence of the hiph of נשא, "lift up."

16.b. The phrase עון אשמה, lit. "iniquity of reparation," is difficult, for עון can mean either "iniquity" or the "guilt" from committing an iniquity and אשמה can mean either "guilt," "trespass," or "a reparation offering" (cf. 5:14–26[6:7]). It is not surprising that this phrase has been variously rendered: RSV, "inquity and guilt"; NIV, "guilt requiring payment"; NEB, "guilt and its penalty"; and JB, "a fault demanding a sacrifice of reparation." Since the transaction is specified in the following words, עון then means "guilt," making אשמה refer to either the penalty of or the compensation for the transgression. Since the focus of this legislation is the removal of wrongdoing, אשמה most likely refers to the reparation that will compensate for the offense.

Form/Structure/Setting

The structure of this speech is as follows:

- I. Introductory formula (v 1)
- II. Speech (vv 2–16)
  - A. Twofold commission to speak (vv 2–3aα)
    - 1. First commission to speak with command (v 2)
      - a. Commission to speak proper (v 2aα)
      - b. Basic command to guard the holy things (v 2aβ+b)
        - 1) Command proper (v 2aβ+bα)
        - 2) Formula of Yahweh's self-introduction (v 2bβ)
    - 2. Second commission to speak (v 3aα^1)
  - B. Speech proper (vv 3aα^2–16)
    - 1. Foundational, categorical law about approaching anything holy while unclean (v 3aα^2+b)
      - a. Law proper (v 3aα^2+bα)
      - b. Formula of Yahweh's self-introduction (v 3bβ)

2. Laws about eating/not eating sacred food (vv 4–16)
    a. In regard to priests (vv 4–9)
        1) Identification of types of uncleanness (vv 4–7)
            a) Law for enduring types of uncleanness (v 4a)
            b) Law for transitory types of uncleanness (vv 4b–6bα)
                (1) Basic case (vv 4b–6aα)
                (2) Consequence (v 6aβ+bα)
            c) Concessions and law about restoration (vv 6bβ–7)
        2) Prohibition against eating from animals found dead (v 8)
            a) Prohibition proper (v 8a)
            b) Formula of Yahweh's self-introduction (v 8b)
        3) Parenesis (v 9)
            a) Parenesis proper (v 9a)
            b) Formula of Yahweh's self-introduction (v 9b)
    b. In regard to persons close to a priest who may/may not eat sacred food (vv 10–14)
        1) Laws based on person's relationship to a priest (vv 10–13)
            a) Persons forbidden to eat (v 10)
            b) Servants of priests permitted to eat (v 11)
            c) A priest's daughter's right to eat (vv 12–13a)
            d) Repetition of law about a stranger's being forbidden to eat (v 13b)
        2) Law of restitution for eating sacred food inadvertently (v 14)
    c. Summarizing prohibition (vv 15–16)
        1) Prohibition proper (vv 15–16a)
        2) Formula of Yahweh's self-introduction (v 16b)

This brief speech has been appended to the two speeches of chap. 21. It is an expansion on the statement in 21:22, ומן־הקדשים יאכל, "and they may eat of the holy offerings" (Elliger, 285, 287); that is why this treatment about handling holy things and eating sacred food is included here. Like those speeches, it is addressed to the Aaronites; the commission-to-speak formula names both Aaron (= 21:17a) and his sons (= 21:2aβ). This speech is considered a separate unit, for the concluding formula at 21:24 sets off chap. 21 as a defined unit. It is distinct from chap. 21 in that it treats the issue of transitory uncleanness in contrast to the issues of inherent or enduring uncleanness treated in chap. 21. From another perspective, chap. 21 considers issues close to a priest's identity, namely death of a family member, marriageable women, and bodily defects, while this speech looks at handling of sacred food.

This speech has two commission-to-speak formulae. The first one (v 2) introduces an overarching command that the priests are to נזר, "consecrate," the holy offerings, protecting them from contact with anything that is unclean. The second formula heads the body of the speech. The body has four sections. The first one (v 3) regulates the priests' eating of sacred food. A series of impersonal case laws guards against any priest's eating from sacrificial gifts while in a state of uncleanness. It is concluded with a parenesis underlined by a grave penalty for failure (v 9); this parenesis is grounded with a self-introduction formula expanded by a participial clause: אני יהוה מקדשם, "I am Yahweh who sanctifies them." Typically, exhortations are found throughout this division on holy living. The brief self-introduction formula, אני יהוה, "I am Yahweh," strengthens the basic command (v 2), the first law (v 3), and the prohibition in v 8. The second section (vv 10–13) specifies members of a priest's house who have or do not have access to the sacred food. The third section (v 14) prescribes how one who has inadvertently (בשגגה) eaten that which is holy may rectify the error. The fourth section (vv 15–16) is a warning to the priests about profaning the holy things of the Israelites. An expanded self-introduction formula, "I am Yahweh who sanctifies them," underscores this warning and brings the speech to a conclusion.

Key terms unite this speech: forms of the root קדש, "holy" (vv 2 [3x], 3 [2x], 4, 7, 9, 10 [2x], 12, 14 [2x], 16 [2x]); חלל, "profane" (vv 2, 9, 15); forms of טמא, "uncleanness" (vv 3, 4, 5 [3x], 6, 8); טהר, "clean" (vv 4, 7); and forms of אכל, "eat" (vv 4, 6, 7, 8, 10 [2x], 11 [2x], 12, 13 [2x], 14, 16). The formula of Yahweh's self-introduction is another uniting thread (vv 2, 3, 8, 9, 16).

Comment

2 The priests are to be careful to נזר, "consecrate," the holy gifts which the Israelites give to Yahweh. If they fail in this regard, they profane Yahweh's holy name.

3 A priest, like a regular citizen, becomes unclean during the course of daily routine. Whenever he becomes unclean, he cannot contact anything that is holy. The holy must never be defiled. The holy things here are specifically the elevated offerings that have not gone to the altar (7:28–34). Perhaps there was a tendency not to consider them as holy since they had not been on the altar and thus to treat them more casually. Defilement of the holy carries the severe cut-off penalty (cf. 7:20–21). Never again could such an offender serve at the altar.

4–5 Those who are unclean for a long, indefinite period are specified. One צרוע, "afflicted with a grievous skin disease" (cf. chap. 13), or one with a זב, "discharge," such as gonorrhea (cf. 15:1–12), may not eat sacred food until becoming clean, i.e., recovering from the disease and going through the rite of aggregation (14:1–20; 15:13–15).

Next are mentioned four circumstances that render a person unclean, but only until evening: touching anything that has become unclean from contact with a carcass or a corpse (5:2; 11:8, 11, 24–28, 32–40; Num 19:11, 14–16), an emission of semen (15:16, 18), or touching either an unclean שרץ, "crawling animal" (11:29–30; 41–45), or a person who passes on uncleanness (e.g., 15:2–12). This series is presented in conditional clauses, but the main clause is not given. It is implied to be the same as the last law: "from the holy things he may not eat until he becomes clean" (v 4a$\gamma\delta$).

6–7 A priest who is unclean is to bathe his body, and he becomes clean at sunset. Then he may eat from these offerings.

8 This decree against eating from a clean animal that has died naturally (נבלה) or been torn by beasts (טרפה; 11:39–40; 17:15) is specifically applied to the priests because of their service at the sanctuary (cf. Ezek 44:31, which specifies any bird [מן־העוף] or any animal [מן־הבהמה]). This decree is formulated more stringently for the priests than for the laity (17:15–16).

9 The priests are exhorted to keep God's charge given in the law. If they do not keep the law, they bring sin on themselves and are liable to suffer death. The consequence is potentially so severe because they חלל, "profane," that which is holy. They must be mindful that these laws are given by Yahweh who sanctifies them.

10 Those who labor for the priests, even if they stay in quarters provided by the priests, may not eat any of the holy offerings. A זר, "stranger," here means any person, Israelite or foreigner, who lives among the priests but does not have membership in the lineage of Aaron, and תושב means a guest who stays with a priest for a brief time (Snaith, 102).

11 Slaves purchased by a priest and children born to them after they have come into the priest's household may eat of the sacred food, for they have become members of the family. This standard is in accord with the instruction to Abraham that he is to circumcise purchased slaves, making them part of the covenant people (Gen 17:12–13).

12–13 A priest's daughter, of course, has access to sacred food. But should she marry outside the tribe, she forfeits her right to the תרומת הקדשים, "holy contributions" (cf. v 3). The contribution is a portion of an offering that is "dedicated" to Yahweh but does not go to the altar (cf. 7:32). If this portion is excluded, then all portions from the sacrifice are excluded to her. However, if she returns home as a widow or a divorcee without any children, her right to this food is reestablished.

14 If a person (איש) eats inadvertently (בשגגה) of sacred food (cf. 4:2), he must restore the sacred food plus 20 percent. The errant party is not identified. Does it mean a priest (most interpreters) or a layman (Keil and Delitzsch, 435)? Since a layman who eats sacred food is subject to a greater penalty according to 5:14–16, this law must be dealing with a priest's inadvertency.

15–16 Because these two verses consist of verbs in the third person plural, the identification of the party who desecrates the holy offerings continues to be unclear. Keil and Delitzsch (435) take the subject to be the people; they then interpret v 16 to mean that the priests are to make those who are guilty submit to the consequences of their action by making compensation as defined in v 14. But if the subject of v 15 is the priests, as seems preferable in light of v 14, then v 16 means that their desecrating activity brings guilt on the people (cf. Noordtzij, 224; Elliger, 294). In either case this warning obligates the priests to be very alert while on duty at the sanctuary. They are to guard against any desecration of the holy gifts to the altar, for such an act would bring guilt requiring reparation (עון אשמה). This guilt is specifically incurred when the priests eat of sacred food that has been contaminated. Every rite in the sacrificial ritual, therefore, had to be done according to the regulation in order that an offering may be acceptable on behalf of its presenter(s).

Explanation

The priests had to be very careful to separate the holy from the common and to distinguish between the clean and the unclean. They could never bring the unclean into the area of the holy. They had to handle that which was holy so that it was not defiled, and they had to handle the food from the offerings that became theirs so that it did not become defiled. Should priests become lax in these standards, they profaned the holy name of God.

The priests had to watch out for themselves in order not to violate any of the rules of cultic purity. Their family members had certain rights to the offerings. These rights were extended to the household servants and slaves of the priests. A daughter, however, forfeited her privilege to this food if she married outside the priestly clan. Yet if she lost her husband by death or divorce and she had no children, she could return home and this right was restored to her.

If a priest misappropriated sacred food in error, he could amend his mistake. He had to restore that which was accidentally consumed and add 20 percent to it.

Just as the priests of old, the overseers, ministers, and elders of the church have a higher responsibility than the laity. They are to keep themselves pure by obedience to God's word (1 Tim 3:2; 5:22; Titus 1:6–9). They are to lead the congregation out of love and from a willing, encouraging spirit (1 Pet 5:2; Titus 2:7–8). They are not to be executives lusting for power, but models of God's redeeming grace (1 Pet 5:3). Indeed these leaders are worthy of respect and honor (1 Pet 5:5; 1 Tim 5:1, 17). With their responsibilities go privileges. Overseers and ministers are worthy of support from the congregation (1 Cor 9:9–14; 1 Tim 5:17–18; Matt 10:10; Luke 10:7). That support includes the needs of their families. Ministers, however, must be careful not to squander or misappropriate the gifts from God's people (cf. 1 Tim 6:7–11). Whenever they err, they need to correct the situation by confession and reasonable restoration of that which they have misused.

G. *Laws about Animals Acceptable for Sacrifice (22:17–33)*

Translation

17 *Yahweh spoke to Moses:* 18 *"Speak to Aaron and his sons and all the Israelites*[a] *and say to them: Whenever any one*[b] *from the house*[c] *of Israel or from the resident aliens*[d] *in Israel presents an offering, either for any of their vows or for any of their freewill gifts, which may be presented*[e] *to Yahweh*[f] *for a whole offering,* 19 *it is to be a male free from defect from*[a] *cattle, sheep, or goats for it to be accepted for you.* 20 *You shall not present*[a] *any animal which has a blemish, because it will not be accepted on your behalf.*
21 *Whenever anyone presents an offering of well-being to Yahweh to fulfill*[a] *a vow or for a freewill offering,*[bc] *from*[d] *cattle or from*[d] *sheep, it is to be perfect in order to be acceptable; it shall not have any blemish.* 22 *You shall not present to Yahweh any animal that is blind, has a broken limb, is mutilated,*[a] *has seeping sores,*[b] *a festering rash,*[c] *or a skin disease,*[de] *and you shall not make from them a gift to Yahweh on the altar.* 23 *But you may make*[a] *as a freewill offering a bull or a sheep that has any member that is too long or stunted,*[b] *but such will not be accepted for a vow.*[c] 24 *You shall not present*[a] *to Yahweh an animal with bruised,*[b] *crushed, torn, or cut-off testicles. You shall not do this in your own land.*
25 *You shall not get any such as these from foreigners and present them as food*[a] *for your God. Because of deformities*[b] *and blemishes in them, they will not be accepted on your behalf."*

26 *Yahweh spoke to Moses:* 27 *"Whenever a calf or a lamb or a goat is born, it is to remain with its mother seven days. From the eighth day on it will be acceptable for an offering, a gift to Yahweh.* 28 *You shall not slaughter on the same day a cow or a ewe*[a] *and its young.* 29 *When you sacrifice*[a] *a sacrifice of praise to Yahweh, you are to sacrifice it*[b] *in a manner that it will be accepted on your behalf.* 30 *It is to be eaten on that day; you*[a] *shall not leave any of it over until morning. I am Yahweh.*

31 *"Keep my commandments and do them. I am Yahweh.*[a] 32 *You shall not profane my holy name, for I will be proclaimed holy in the midst of the Israelites. I am Yahweh,*[a] *your sanctifier,*[b] 33 *who has brought you out of Egypt to be your God. I am Yahweh."*

Notes

18.a. In place of MT בני, "sons of," LXX reads συναγωγῇ, "congregation"; cf. n. 19:2.a.

18.b. On איש איש, cf. 17:3; 18:6.

18.c. Instead of MT מבית, "from the house of," LXX and Tg[mss] read מבני, "from the sons of."

18.d. Some Heb. mss, Sam, LXX, Syr, and Vg add הגר, "who sojourns." MT could easily have come about by haplography; on the other hand, the frequency of the phrase הגר הגר, "the alien who sojourns," could have led to a fuller text. MT is followed as the simpler text, but PIR sides with the variant, graded B. LXX reads in addition πρὸς αὐτούς, "among them."

18.e. The third person pl is a virtual pass (GKC §144f).

18.f. LXX* reads τῷ θεῷ, "to God," in place of MT ליהוה, "to Yahweh."

19.a. The prep ב carries the sense of "among" ("in the domain of"; GKC §119i).

20.a. LXX adds κυρίῳ, "to the Lord."

21.a. פלא means "to be wonderful, extraordinary" (BDB, 810). It appears only three times in the piel, and each time it has a sacrifice as dir obj (Num 15:3, 8). BDB renders it "make . . . special," while KB (876) gives "fulfill . . . special." It also occurs twice in hiph in relation to a sacrifice (27:2; Num 6:2); for that usage BDB gives "do a hard/difficult thing" and KB "perform . . . wonderful." R. Albertz ("פלא *pl*ʾ ni. wunderbar sein," *THAT* 2:416) comments that the context does not give any hint that the sacrifice is "special." He takes פלא to mean "fulfill, perform"; he thinks it is highly likely this comes from a second root פלא, which has been preserved as a technical sacrificial term.

21.b. A Heb. ms, Sam, and *Tg. Ps.-J.* omit ל, "to," on נדבה, "freewill offering."

21.c. LXX adds ἐν ταῖς ἑορταῖς ὑμῶν, "in your feasts."

21.d. Cf. n. 19.a.

22.a. MT חרוץ is a qal pass ptcp of חרץ, "cut, sharpen" (BDB, 358). It means an animal that has been mauled or torn by something sharp.

22.b. For יבלת, BDB (385) gives "a running sore or an ulcer." KB (367), however, relates it to Akk *ublu*, "warts." But Dillmann (627) takes it from יבל, "flow," to mean a sore that seeps; this explanation is preferable because of the etymology. In 11QpaleoLev, יבלת and ילפת have exchanged places.

22.c. Cf. n. 21:20.d.

22.d. Cf. n. 21:20.e.

22.e. This series of defects is a *casus pendens* that stands first for emphasis; it is resumed by the dir obj אלה, "these."

23.a. This verb is pl in Sam; this change was made to agree with the pl verbs in the context. עשה, "do, make," is a bland term for doing the sacrificial rite for this type of offering.

23.b. This compound *casus pendens* stands first for emphasis; it is resumed by אתו, "it," and it is also resumed by the afformative of the verb ירצה, "it will be accepted."

23.c. The dir obj stands before the verb for emphasis. LXX adds the possessive pronoun σου, "your," to define more precisely εὐχήν (נדר), "the vow." LXX may have had a different Heb. text, or it may have sought to clarify the Gk. trans.

24.a. LXX with προσάξεις αὐτά read MT לא תקריבו, "you shall not present [2nd person pl]" as "do not present [2nd person sg] it."

24.b. Sam, LXX, and Vg do not read the *waw* on מעוך.

25.a. Cf. n. 21:6.b.

25.b. משחת is a *muqtal* form from the root שחת, "spoil, ruin, mar"; BDB (1007–8) renders it "corrupt, be spoiled, marred" and KB (609) "injured, defect." 11QpaleoLev reads משחתים הם for MT משחתם בהם; this variant may be a hoph ptcp, "they are deformed." Sam and LXX have a conflate reading משחתם בהם, "their deformities in them."

28.a. Instead of MT או־שה, "or a ewe," Sam and LXX* read ושה, "and a ewe" as in v 23.

29.a. In this cultic legislation זבח means more than "slaughter," which is usually שחט; it means to perform the entire sacrificial ritual (Elliger, 301).

29.b. Some Heb. mss, Sam, LXX, and Syr read the pronominal suffix on the verb תזבחהו, "you are to sacrifice it." This reading is preferable.

30.a. A LXX ms and Syr read ולא, "and not."

31.a. Sam and LXX* fail to read אני יהוה, "I am Yahweh." The shorter reading is preferable. Since this phrase appears so frequently in these verses, it could easily have been added.

32.a. A couple of Heb. mss omit אני יהוה, "I am Yahweh."

32.b. In place of MT מקדשכם, "the one sanctifying you," Sam and Tg[mss] read מקדשם, "the one sanctifying them"; cf. n. 21:8.e.

Form/Structure/Setting

The structure of this unit is outlined as follows:

- I. First speech (vv 17–25)
  - A. Introductory formula (v 17)
  - B. Speech (vv 18–25)
    - 1. Commission to speak (v 18a)
    - 2. Speech proper (vv 18b–25)
      - a. Laws about animals for whole offerings (vv 18b–20)
      - b. Laws about animals for offerings of well-being (vv 21–24)
        - 1) Basic law (v 21)
        - 2) Characteristics disqualifying animals for sacrifice (vv 22–24)
      - c. Prohibition against offering animals gotten from a foreigner (v 25)
- II. Second speech (vv 26–33)
  - A. Introductory formula (v 26)
  - B. Speech proper (vv 27–33)
    - 1. Laws (vv 27–30)
      - a. Laws about sacrificing young animals (vv 27–28)
      - b. Law about eating a praise offering (vv 29–30)
    - 2. Parenesis (vv 31–33)

This portion is set apart from the preceding speech by being addressed to Aaron, his sons, and the people (cf. 17:2). The responsibility to make sure that only acceptable animals are brought to the altar falls on both the priesthood and the laity. The issue here is not official sacrifices but private sacrifices (Elliger, 296).

This portion has two short speeches: one on the traits that disqualify an animal as acceptable for an offering (vv 17–25) and one giving restrictions on the selection of an animal for sacrifice (vv 26–30). These two speeches are followed by a parenesis (vv 31–33).

The first speech is primarily concerned with נדרים, "vow offerings," and נדבות, "freewill offerings," presented as either עלות, "whole offerings" (chap. 1), or זבחי־שלמים, "offerings of well-being" (chap. 3). Since these offerings are voluntary and private, the people may have had a tendency to be less rigorous about presenting animals of the highest quality.

Since some minor defects are permitted in an animal for a freewill offering but not for a vow offering, the catalogue of disqualifying blemishes comes in the material on an offering of well-being. The catalogue of animal blemishes corresponds to that for priests (21:18–20; cf. Milgrom, "Ethics and Ritual," 180–81). The number of blemishes listed in both catalogues is twelve, and both lists begin with blindness (עור) and end with damaged testicles. Five terms are identical: blind, elongated limbs, broken bones, sores, and scabs (Milgrom, 180). The comparison of the grouping of defects in the two catalogues yields a chiastic structure: the defects enumerated in the pattern for a priest are four, two, six, while for an animal the pattern is six, two, four. This chiasm indicates that the unit was composed to tie this speech closely to the speech in chap. 21.

Some of the details in this speech do not seem to accord with the regulations of chaps. 1–7, which speak of one whole offering (chap. 1) and three kinds of offerings of well–being (7:11–18). The apparent contradiction with the whole offering may simply be that in the speech on the regulations for this offering in chap. 1 no coverage is given to the kinds of whole offerings a person could present just as the different kinds of offerings of well-being are not addressed in the regulation for this sacrifice in chap. 3, but later in 7:11–18. The absence of any reference to a תודה, "praise offering," as an offering of well-being in vv 18–25 is more perplexing. But the treatment of it in v 29 indicates that the speaker did not choose to talk about it in vv 18–25, especially since its mention is to underscore a distinction between it and the other two kinds of offerings of well-being, namely that meat from a praise offering could only be eaten on the day of the sacrifice (7:15) in contrast to the permission to eat of a vow and a freewill offering presented as an offering of well-being on the day of its sacrifice and the day after (7:16). Therefore, while this passage teaches that vow offerings and freewill offerings could be presented either as whole offerings or as offerings of well-being, such, however, may not have been the case for praise offerings.

A second brief speech has been drawn to the first. This speech provides laws about the slaughter of animals. A newborn animal could not be sacrificed until the eighth day, and it is forbidden to sacrifice an animal and her offspring on the same day. In this regard the law is showing both a concern for animal life and that animal life must be taken with respect and compassion.

This portion closes with an exhortation to keep God's commandments, corresponding to the exhortations at 18:2–5, 24–30; 19:37; 20:22–26. While this parenesis specifically applies to this portion on animals for sacrifice, it also applies to all of chaps. 21–22, bringing this larger section to a conclusion.

These speeches are attached here for two reasons. First, since the majority of offerings of well-being may be eaten by both the priests and the laity, it comes after the speech on regulations about the priests' prerogatives of eating the sacred food. Second, just as the priests have to be free from blemishes to serve at the altar (21:17–23), so too must the animals presented at the altar be free from all blemishes. Both the priests and the sacrificial animals are to be תמים, "whole," as a witness to the holiness of Yahweh.

These speeches are a mixture of laws in impersonal style and direct address in the second person plural save for the second person singular in v 23b. The speaker has taken material from the priestly professional knowledge and put it in direct address in order to speak to his audience directly.

A few key terms unite these two speeches: הקריב, "present" (vv 18 [2x], 20, 21, 22, 24, 25), קרבן, "offering, oblation" (vv 18, 27), the root רצה, "be acceptable, accept favorably" (vv 19, 20, 21, 23, 25, 27, 29), תמים, "perfect, complete, without defect" (vv 19, 21), and מום, "blemish" (vv 20, 21, 25). The central theme then is the presentation for sacrifice of animals that are acceptable to God for the benefit of the person presenting the offering.

Comment

18 This law is addressed to everyone (איש איש; cf. 17:3; 18:6; 22:4); no distinction is to be made between an Israelite (מבית ישראל) and a resident alien (מן־הגר בישראל). It is important to underscore that an alien who lived in Israel had the opportunity to worship Yahweh as his God. If he chose to worship Yahweh, he presented the same kinds of offerings as did an Israelite. He did not have to adhere to a higher standard nor were any concessions made for him. Anyone may present נדר, "a votive offering," or נדבה, "a freewill offering," as עלה, "a whole offering" (cf. chap. 1). This means that the entire offering was consumed on the altar (on votive and freewill offerings, cf. 7:16).

19–20 בקר, "cattle," כשבים, "sheep," and עזים, "goats," are the animals prescribed in the regulation for the whole offering (1:3–13). Since these two kinds of whole offerings are voluntary, no provisions for substitute animals for the poor are provided (cf. 1:14–17). The fundamental issue is to make sure an offering is accepted (רצה) by God so that it is efficacious for the one who presents it. For an offering to be accepted by God, the animal has to be a male, perfect or without defect (תמים), and without flaw (1:3) or blemish (מום). The first of these terms is positive and the second one is negative so that together they cover every kind of defect. One could never presume that God just might accept an animal with a defect, no matter how small. Malachi bears witness to lax standards regarding the quality of animals offered in the Second Temple of his day (1:14). The people presented animals that were blind, lame, and sick (1:8; cf. v 13). Yahweh curses any one who vows an animal from his flock and then sacrifices in place of that animal one that is damaged (משחת); such a person is a double-dealer (נוכל 1:14).

21–24 In regard to זבח־שלמים, "an offering of well-being" (cf. chap. 3), an animal may not have any defect, whether the offering be presented in fulfillment of נדר, "a vow," or as נדבה, "a freewill offering." This point is reiterated, for these kinds of offerings are presented not to meet the requirements God has set down, but purely from the motivation of the laity. It is reasonable to imagine that a worshiper might assume that God would be more lenient in regard to the animals permitted for this class of offering. His assumption is valid only in regard to a freewill offering, as seen in v 23.

Specific defects or blemishes are listed: עור, "being blind," שבור, "having any limb or part broken," חרוץ, "mutilated," יבלת, "seeping sores or ulcers," גרב, "a festering rash," or ילפת, "lichen, scurf, or scabs." No animal with any of these defects may be offered as אשה, "a gift" (cf. 1:9), on the altar to Yahweh. Elliger (300) interprets this last sentence to mean that the official sacrifice (אשה) stands as the norm for private sacrifices.

If an animal has a member that is longer (שרוע) than normal, or conversely, if a member is stunted (קלוט), it could not be offered. Dillmann (628) considers these adjectives to apply to the number as well as the size of a part of the body. This law covered an animal that was oversized or dwarfed. An exception is made here as to the perfection of an animal for נדבה, "a freewill offering," but not one for נדר, "a vow." This exception indicates that a vow is considered a most serious matter.

Any deformities of an animal's testicles rendered it unfit as an offering. These included testicles that were altered or damaged in any way: מעוך, "bruised," כתות, "crushed," נתוק, "torn," or כרות, "cut off." These terms may represent four different methods of castrating an animal. Since such an animal was no longer whole, it did not accord with the standard of holiness. It would always be tempting to take such an animal from the herd and give it as an offering to God.

Interpretation of the sentence "you shall not do [thus] in your land" is divided. Some (such as Wenham, 295, and Elliger, 300) take this prohibition to mean that no animal may be castrated in Israel. But, as Dillmann (628) comments, if that were the case, there would be no need to have this law against sacrificing castrated animals. Another view understands "in your land" to contrast with the land of foreigners; i.e., Israel is not to let happen in her land what her neighbors do. Dillmann (629) takes "in your land" to be in contrast to "in the wilderness." This means that this law is to continue to be enforced in the promised land.

25 This law prevents Israelites from buying inferior animals from foreigners and offering them on the altar.

27–29 Some basic compassionate concerns are set for the selection of animals to be offered. Newly born animals may not be taken from their mother until after the seventh day (Exod 22:29[30]). This time sequence parallels the time set for circumcising an infant on the eighth day. In addition, a mother and her offspring are not to be sacrificed on the same day. A similar standard restricting the taking of both a bird and her young for food appears in Deut 22:6. The reason for these regulations is not stated. Perhaps the decree against offering a mother and her offspring on the same day countered some pagan cultic practice that was rooted in magical practices to increase fertility (cf. Noth, 163). Another explanation may be that a person with a small herd might put his livelihood in danger should he offer both a bearer and her offspring out of religious enthusiasm. This law may be generated by what has become known as humanitarian concerns (Haran, "Seething a Kid in Its Mother's Milk," *JJS* 30 [1979] 23–35). Though God encourages generous giving, he does not encourage foolish giving.

Many times it is expressed that an animal for sacrifice should be a year old (e.g., 9:3; 12:6; 23:12), but no upward limit is put on the age of an animal for sacrifice. In Judg 6:25 there is reference to offering up a bull that was seven years old.

30 Food from an offering of well-being could not be left until morning (cf. 7:15–18; 19:5–8).

31–32 The people are exhorted to שׁמר, "observe," these מצות, "commandments," from God and to עשׂה, "do," them (cf. 18:4, 5, 26a*α*; 19:37; 20:22a). מצות is a term seldom used in the Holiness Code (26:3) and only a few times in the regulations on sacrifices, 4:2, 13, 22, 27; 5:17 (Elliger, 297). Conversely, the people are warned not to חלל, "profane," God's holy name by violating any of these decrees (cf. 18:21; 21:12a*γ*). God is to be treated as holy in the midst of his people by their enthusiastic, wholehearted observance of these decrees (19:12b). Faithful observance honors God. When the people honor God, he is in their midst sanctifying them (20:8; 21:8). Since he sets his name in the midst of his people, they must conduct themselves in a way that will not defile it. For whenever they transgress any of God's laws, they shame his name, i.e, tarnish his reputation. His reputation is intricately tied up with Israel, for Yahweh has identified himself as the God who delivered Israel from the land of Egypt, where they were in bondage to a powerful nation (cf. 19:36; 25:38; 26:13). This great act of salvation reveals his love for his people and his desire that they make him their God (cf. 11:45;

25:38; 26:45). Because of what Yahweh has done for them, they have every reason to keep his commandments.

Explanation

The holy God required that animals sacrificed on the altar be free from all defects. An imperfect gift indicates that its giver does not comprehend the absolute perfection of the God to whom that person is making the offering. To be perfect an animal had to be free from any defect and whole sexually. The sexual power of the created order has been created and blessed by God. A castrated animal has lost one of its vital powers and is no longer complete.

God, the Creator of all life, was concerned lest people have a calloused attitude toward animals that they were sacrificing on the holy altar. He gave laws, therefore, designed to ingrain in humans care for animals. Two such laws are found here: a newly born animal cannot be sacrificed until the eighth day, and a dam and her offspring cannot be sacrificed on the same day.

The standard of a perfect sacrifice is the cornerstone of NT Christology. Jesus is the final, ultimate sacrifice because he was completely free from any sin (Heb 9:14). Truly Jesus was the lamb of God without blemish or spot (1 Pet 1:19; John 1:29; Rev 5:6; 7:9; 12:11; 13:8; 15:3; 17:14; 19:9; 21:22).

H. The Calendar of Festivals (23:1–44)

Bibliography

Amadon, G. "Ancient Jewish Calendation." *JBL* 61 (1942) 227–80. **Amsler, S.** "Les documents de la loi et la formation du Pentateuque." In *Le Pentateuque en question.* Ed. A. Pury. La Monde de la Bible. Genève: Éditions Labor et Fides, 1989. 244–57. **Andreasen, N.-E.** *The Old Testament Sabbath: A Tradition-Historical Examination.* SBLDS 7. Missoula, MT: SBL, 1972. ———. "Recent Studies of the Old Testament Sabbath: Some Observations." *ZAW* 86 (1974) 453–69. ———. *Rest and Redemption: A Study of the Biblical Sabbath.* AUSMR 11. Berrien Springs, MI: Andrews UP, 1978. **Atkinson, C. W.** "The Ordinances of Passover-Unleavened Bread." *ATR* 44 (1962) 70–85. **Auerbach, E.** "Die Feste im Alten Israel." *VT* 8 (1958) 1–18. ———. "Neujahrs- und Versoehnungs-Fest in den biblischen Quellen." *VT* 8 (1958) 337–43. **Avishur, Y.** "*pĕrî ʿēs hādār* (Lev 23:40)—A Fruit Which Isn't a Fruit and a *hādār* Which Isn't a Citron" (Heb.). *Beth Mikra* 34 (1988/89) 135–39. **Ben Shachar, Z.** "The Day after the Šabbāt" (Heb.). *Beth Mikra* 24 (1979) 227–28. **Block, D.** "New Year." *ISBE* rev. 3:529–32. **Cazelles, H.** "The Bible and Liturgical Times: Eschatology and Anamnesis." *StLit* 14 (1981) 23–33. **Clines, D. J. A.** "The Evidence for an Autumnal New Year in Pre-Exilic Israel Reconsidered." *JBL* 93 (1974) 22–40. **Dressler, H. H. P.** "The Sabbath in the Old Testament." In *From Sabbath to Lord's Day; A Biblical, Historical, and Theological Investigation.* Ed. D. Carson. Grand Rapids: Zondervan, 1982. 21–41. **Engnell, I.** "Paesah-Massot, A Hebrew Annual Festival of the Ancient Near East Pattern." In *Proceedings of the Seventh Congress for the History of Religion.* Amsterdam: North Holland Publishing Company, 1951. ———. "New Year Festivals" and "The Passover." In *A Rigid Scrutiny: Critical Essays on the Old Testament by I. Engnell.* Tr. and ed. J. T. Willis. Nashville: Vanderbilt UP, 1969. 180–84, 185–96.

Füglister, N. *Die Heilsbedeutung des Pascha.* SANT 8. Munich: Kösel, 1963. **Gandz, S.** "The Calendar of Ancient Israel." In *Homenaje a Millás-Vallicrosa.* Barcelona: Consejo Superior de Investigaciones Cientificas, 1954. **Goldstein, B. R.**, and **Cooper, A.** "The Festivals of Israel and Judah and the Literary History of the Pentateuch." *JAOS* 110 (1990) 19–31. **Gölz, F.** "Vom biblischen Sinn des Sabbat." *Theologische Beiträge* 9 (1978) 243–56. **Görg, M.** "*Paesah* (Pascha): Fest des 'schlagenden' Gottes?" *BN* 43 (1988) 7–11. **Goudoever, J. van.** *Biblical Calendars.* Leiden: Brill, 1961. **Haag, H.** *Vom alten zum neuen Pascha: Geschichte und Theologie des Osterfestes.* SBS 49. Stuttgart: Katholische Bibelwerk, 1971. ———. "Das Mazzenfest des Hiskia." In *Wort und Geschichte: FS Kal Elliger.* Ed. H. Gese and H. P. Rüger. AOAT 18. Kevelaer: Butzon & Bercker; Neukirchen-Vluyn: Neukirchener, 1973. 87–94. **Hahn, F.** "Schabbat und Sonntag." *EvT* 46 (1986) 495–507. **Halbe, J.** "Passa-Massot im deuteronomischen Festkalendar: Komposition, Entstehung und Programm von Dtn 16 1–8." *ZAW* 87 (1975) 147–68. ———. "Erwägungen zu Ursprung und Wesen des Massotfestes." *ZAW* 87 (1975) 324–46. **Hallo, W. W.** "New Moons and Sabbaths: A Case Study in the Contrastive Approach." *HUCA* 48 (1977) 1–18. **Haran, M.** "The Passover Sacrifice." In *Studies in the Religion of Ancient Israel.* VTSup 23 (1972) 86–116. **Henninger, J.** *Les fêtes de printemps chez les Sémites et la Pâque israélite.* Études bibliques. Paris: J. Gabalda, 1975. **Hoenig, S.** "The Duration of the Festival of Matzot." *JQR* 49 (1958/59) 274–77. **Horn, P. H.** "Traditionsschichten in Ex 23,10–33 und Ex 34,10–26." *BZ* 15 (1971) 202–22. **Jastrow, M.** "On «ממחרת השבת» (the Day after the Sabbath)." *AJSL* 30 (1914) 97–110. **Katz, P.** "מִקְרָא in der griechischen und lateinischen Bibel." *ZAW* 66 (1953) 253–55. **Keel, O.** "Erwägungen zum Sitz im Leben des vormosaischen Pascha und zur Etymologie vom פֶּסַח." *ZAW* 84 (1972) 414–34. **Knohl, I.** "The Priestly Torah Versus the Holiness School: Sabbath and the Festivals." *HUCA* 58 (1987) 65–117. **Kraus, H.-J.** "Zur Geschichte des Passah-Massot-Festes im Alten Testament." *EvT* 18 (1958) 47–67. ———. *Worship in Israel: A Cultic History of the Old Testament.* Tr. G. Buswell. Oxford: Basil Blackwell, 1966. **Kutsch, E.** "Die Wurzel עצר im Hebräischen." *VT* 2 (1952) 57–69. ———. "מִקְרָא." *ZAW* 66 (1953) 247–53. ———. "Erwägungen zur Geschichte der Passafeier und des Massotfestes." *ZTK* 55 (1958) 1–35. ———. "Der Sabbat-ursprünglich Vollmondtag?" BZAW 168 (1986) 71–77. **Laff, P.** *Die Pascha-Feier Israels: Eine literarkritische und überlieferungsgeschichtliche Studie.* BBB 36. Bonn: Peter Hanstein, 1970. **Lewy, H.**, and **Lewy, J.** "The Origin of the Week and the Oldest West Asiatic Calendar." *HUCA* 17 (1942/43) 1–152. **MacRae, G. W.** "The Meaning and Evolution of the Feast of Tabernacles." *CBQ* 22 (1960) 251–76. **Manfred, G.** "Päsah: Fest des 'schlagenden' Gottes?" *BN* 43 (1988) 7–11. **Martin-Achard, R.** *Essai biblique sur les fetes d'Israel.* Paris: Librairie protestante, 1974. **May, H.** "The Relation of the Passover to the Feast of Unleavened Cakes." *JBL* 55 (1936) 65–82. **McKay, J. W.** "The Date of Passover and Its Significance." *ZAW* 84 (1972) 435–47. **Moore, J.** *New Year with Canaanites and Israelites.* Kampen Cahiers 21 and 22. Kampe: Kok, 1972. **Morgan, D.** "The So-called Cultic Calendars in the Pentateuch: A Morphological and Typological Study." Diss., Claremont University, 1974. **Morgenstern, J.** "The Origin of Maṣṣoth and the Maṣṣoth Festival." *AJT* 21 (1917) 275–93. ———. "The Three Calendars of Ancient Israel." *HUCA* 1 (1924) 13–78. ———. "Additional Notes on 'The Three Calendars of Ancient Israel.'" *HUCA* 3 (1926) 77–107. ———. "Supplementary Studies in the Calendars of Ancient Israel." *HUCA* 10 (1935) 1–148. **Oesterley, W.** "Early Hebrew Festival Rituals." In *Myth and Ritual.* Ed. S. H. Hooke. London: Oxford UP, 1933. **Otto, E.** *Das Mazzotfest in Gilgal.* BWANT 107. Stuttgart: W. Kohlhammer, 1975. ———. "Feste und Feiertage: II. Altes Testament." *TRE* 11 (1983) 96–106. **Pedersen, J.** "Passahfest und Passhlegende." *ZAW* 52 (1934) 161–75. **Robinson, G.** "The Idea of Rest in the Old Testament and the Search for the Basic Character of Sabbath." *ZAW* 92 (1980) 32–42. ———. *The Origin and Development of the Old Testament Sabbath: A Comprehensive Exegetical Approach.* Beiträge zur biblischen Exegese und Theologie 21. Frankfurt am Main: Peter Lang, 1988. **Rost, L.** "Weidewechsel und altisraelitischer Festkalendar." *ZDPV* 66 (1943) 205–16. **Rylaarsdam, J.** "Booths, Feast of." *IDB* 1:455–58.

———. "Feasts and Fasts." *IDB* 2:260–64. ———. "Passover and Feast of Unleavened Bread." *IDB* 3:663–66. ———. "Weeks, Feast of." *IDB* 4:827–28. **Sauer, G.** "Israels Feste und ihr Verhältnis zum Jahweglauben." In *Studien zum Pentateuch.* FS W. Kornfeld. Ed. G. Braulik. Wien: Herder, 1977. 135–41. **Schmitt, R.** *Exodus und Passa: Ihr Zussamenhang im Alten Testament.* 2 neubearbeitete Auflage. Orbis Biblicus et Orientalis 7. Freiburt: Universitätsverlag; Göttingen: Vandenhoeck & Ruprecht, 1981. **Segal, J. B.** *The Hebrew Passover: From the Earliest Times to A.D. 70.* London Oriental Series 12. London: Oxford UP, 1963. ———. "The Hebrew Festivals and the Calendar." *JSS* 6 (1961) 74–94. **Siker-Gieseler, J.** "The Theology of the Sabbath in the Old Testament: A Canonical Approach." *Studia Biblia et Theologica* 11 (1981) 5–20. **Snaith, N. H.** *The Jewish New Year Festival.* London: SPCK, 1947. **Stewart, R.** "The Jewish Festivals." *EvQ* 43 (1971) 149–61. **Tsevat, M.** "The Basic Meaning of the Biblical Sabbath." *ZAW* 84 (1972) 447–59. **Vaux, R. de.** *Ancient Israel: Its Life and Institutions.* Tr. John McHugh. London: Darton, Longman & Todd, 1961. **Wambacq, B. N.** "Les origines de la Pesah israelite." *Bib* 57 (1976) 206–24. ———. "Les origines de la Pesah israelite (suite et fin)." *Bib* 57 (1976) 301–26. ———. "Les Massot." *Bib* 61 (1980) 31–54. **Welch, A. C.** "On the Method of Celebrating Passover." *ZAW* 45 (1927) 24–29. **Wolff, H. W.** "The Day of Rest in the Old Testament." *CTM* 43 (1972) 498–506. **Zeitlin, S.** "Notes relatives au calendrier juif." *REJ* 89 (1930) 349–59. **Zerafa, P. O. P.** "Passover and Unleavened Bread." *Ang* 41 (1964) 235–50.

Translation

1 *Yahweh spoke to Moses:* 2 *"Speak to the Israelites and say to them: The appointed feasts*
of Yahweh which you will proclaim as sacred assemblies;[a] *these are*[b] *my appointed feasts.*
3 *For six days*[a] *work is to be done;*[b] *then on the seventh day is a Sabbath of solemn rest, a*
sacred assembly;[cd] *you will not do*[e] *any work. It is a Sabbath to Yahweh in all your*
settlements.

4 *"These*[a] *are the appointed feasts of Yahweh, the sacred assemblies*[b] *which you are to*
proclaim at the time appointed for them. 5 *In the first month on the fourteenth*[a] *day of the*
month between twilight and dark is Yahweh's Passover.[b] 6 *On the fifteenth day of this*
month is the Feast of Unleavened Bread to Yahweh. Seven days you are to eat unleavened
bread. 7 *On*[a] *the first day you are to have a sacred assembly; you are not to do any usual*
work. 8 *You are to present gifts*[a] *to Yahweh for seven days.*[b] *On*[c] *the seventh day is a sa-*
cred assembly;[d] *you are not to do any usual work."*

9 *Yahweh spoke to Moses:* 10 *"Speak to the Israelites and say to them: When you come to*
the land which I am giving you and you reap its harvest, you are to bring the sheaf[a] *of the*
firstfruits of your harvest to the priest. 11 *He is to raise up the sheaf before Yahweh for*
acceptance on your behalf. On the morning after the Sabbath the priest is to raise it up.
12 *On the day when you raise up the sheaf,*[a] *you are to offer a year-old male lamb without*
defect for a whole offering to Yahweh. 13 *The grain offering with it is to be two-tenths of*
an ephah of fine flour mixed with oil, a gift to Yahweh, a soothing aroma;[a] *and the drink*
offering[b] *with it is to be a fourth of a hin of wine.* 14 *You will not eat bread, roasted grain,*
or fresh grain[a] *until this very day, until you have brought*[b] *the offering*[c] *of your God. This*
is a perpetual decree for your generations in all your settlements.

15 *"You are to count*[a] *from the morning after the Sabbath, from the day when you*
brought the sheaf as an elevated offering;[b] *it is to be*[c] *seven full weeks;* 16 *you are to count*
fifty days unto the morning of the seventh Sabbath; then you are to present a new grain
offering to Yahweh. 17 *From your settlements you are to bring*[a] *two loaves of bread*[b] *for an*
elevated offering; it is to be made of two-tenths[c] *of an ephah of fine flour; they are to be*
baked with leaven as (an offering of) first ripe grain to Yahweh. 18 *In addition to*[a] *the*

bread you are to present seven[b] year-old lambs without defect, one young bull, and two
rams;[c] they are to be a whole offering to Yahweh with their grain offering and their drink
offerings, a gift for a soothing aroma to Yahweh. 19 You are to offer[a] one male goat for a
purification offering and two year-old lambs for an offering of well-being.[b] 20 The priest is
to raise them with the bread of the first ripe grain as an elevated offering before Yahweh,
with the two lambs;[a] they will be holy to Yahweh for the priest.[b] 21 You are to make a
proclamation on this very day;[a] you are to hold a sacred assembly. You are not to do any
usual work.[b] It is a perpetual decree in all your settlements for your generations. 22 When
you reap the harvest of your land,[a] you will not completely reap the corners of your fields,
nor will you gather the gleanings of your harvest.[b] You are to leave them for the poor and
the alien. I am Yahweh your God."

23 Yahweh spoke to Moses: 24 "Speak to the Israelites: In the seventh month on the first day
of the month you are to observe a solemn rest, a memorial proclaimed with trumpet blasts,
a sacred assembly.[a] 25 You will not do any usual work; you are to present gifts[a] to Yahweh."

26 Yahweh spoke to Moses:[a] 27 "Moreover,[a] on the tenth of this seventh month is the
Day of Atonement.[b] You are to have a sacred assembly. You are to practice self-denial
and present gifts[c] to Yahweh. 28 You[a] will not do any work on this very day, because it is
the Day of Atonement,[b] for making expiation for yourselves before Yahweh your God.
29 Indeed[a] any person who does not practice self-denial[b] on this very day is to be cut off[c]
from the people. 30 As for any[a] person who does any work on this very day,[b] I will make that
person perish[c] from among the people.[d] 31 You[a] will not do any work;[b] it is a perpetual
decree for your generations in all your settlements. 32 It is for you a Sabbath of solemn rest;
you are to practice self-denial. On the ninth day of this month in the evening,[a] from
evening to evening, you are to observe[b] your Sabbath."[c]

33 Yahweh spoke to Moses: 34 "Speak to the Israelites: On the fifteenth day of this seventh
month is the Feast of Booths for seven days to Yahweh.[a] 35 On[a] the first day is a sacred
assembly. You will not do any kind of work. 36 You are to present gifts[a] to Yahweh for
seven days.[b] On the eighth day[c] you are to observe a sacred assembly, and you are to
present gifts[a] to Yahweh. It is a solemn holiday. You will not do any kind of work.

37 "These are the appointed feasts of Yahweh which you will proclaim as sacred assemblies
to present gifts to Yahweh, whole offerings, grain offerings, sacrifices, and drink offerings[a] as
prescribed for each day 38 apart from the Sabbaths of Yahweh, apart from your gifts,[a] apart
from your vow offerings, apart from your freewill offerings, which you give to Yahweh.

39 "Moreover,[a] on the fifteenth day of the seventh month,[b] when you have gathered the
produce of your land,[c] you are to celebrate the Feast of Yahweh[d] for seven days;[e] the first
day is a solemn rest and the eighth day is a solemn rest. 40 On the first day you are to take
the fruit of magnificent trees,[a] fronds of palm trees, boughs[b] of leafy trees and of willows[c]
by the brook, and you are to rejoice before Yahweh your God for seven days.[d] 41 You are to
celebrate it as a festival to Yahweh for seven days[a] in the year. You are to celebrate it in
the seventh month as a perpetual decree for your generations. 42 You are to dwell in booths[a]
for seven days. All the citizens of Israel are to dwell[b] in booths[c] 43 in order that your descendants may know that I made the Israelites dwell in booths when I brought them out
of the land of Egypt.[a] I am Yahweh your God."

44 Moses declared to the Israelites the appointed feasts of Yahweh.

Notes

2.a. Tg has a sg form.
2.b. The pronoun הם, "they," functions as a copula.

3.a. This is an example of the acc of time, which specifies the duration of an activity (cf. GKC §118i). This use of the acc occurs frequently in this chapter.

3.b. For MT תעשה, "it will be done," a third person fem niph impf, Sam reads יעשה, "it will be done," a third person masc niph impf, while LXX has *ποιήσεις*, "you will do," interpreting the MT form as a second person sg qal impf. PIR (198) explains these variants as a simplification of a difficult reading.

3.c. These two constr chains are in apposition to ביום השביעי, "on the seventh day."

3.d. LXX adds *τῷ κυρίῳ*, "to the Lord."

3.e. LXX* reads a sg form.

4.a. Sam and some LXX mss read a *waw.*

4.b. Tg[mss] reads a sg form; cf. n. 2.a.

5.a. Sam, LXX, and Vg add יום, "day," as in v 6 and Num 28:16.

5.b. On the meaning of פסח, "passover," see J. Durham, *Exodus*, WBC 3, 155. Levine suggests in his commentary (156) that the root of this word may come from the qal, "straddle, hedge" (1 Kgs 18:21); this identification led to the NJPS translation, "a protective offering."

7.a. LXX reads a *waw;* cf. n. 8.a.

8.a. For MT אשה, "gifts" (a collective), LXX has *ὁλοκαύτωμα*, "a whole offering," which MT usually renders עלה as in v 12. However, in this verse mss from Cairo Genizah add עולה, "a whole offering."

8.b. Cf. n. 3.a.

8.c. A Heb. ms, Sam, LXX, and Syr read a *waw.*

8.d. LXX adds *ἔσται ὑμῖν*, "you will have" = יהו לכם; cf. vv 7, 21, 27, 36.

10.a. Sam and *Tg. Ps.-J.* read an article on this word.

12.a. The inf constr occurs after the temporal phrase ביום, (lit.) "on the day of," to form a temporal clause. Its occurrence after the main verb is very unusual (Sun, "Investigation," 367–68). Here, as often, the inf constr has a double acc; the pronominal suffix on the inf functions as the subj of the clause, and the second acc, introduced by the particle את, is the true acc.

13.a. LXX adds *τῷ κυρίῳ*, "to the Lord," as this formula is frequently phrased; cf. 1:9.

13.b. The ketib is נסכה, "the drink offering," and the qere נסכו, "the drink offering with it" (as written in Sam).

14.a. Cf. 2:14–16, *Comment.*

14.b. This is a concession clause introduced by עד, "until," plus inf constr. Cf. n. 43.a.

14.c. Cf. 1:2, *Comment.*

15.a. LXX, like this Eng trans., does not have anything for לכם, "for yourselves," for it overburdens the trans. in some languages.

15.b. This temporal clause is composed of the inf constr being introduced by the phrase "from the day of"; cf. n. 12.a.

15.c. LXX omits this word.

17.a. On the mappîq in the א, cf. GKC §14d.

17.b. Sam, LXX, Syr, and Tg add חלות, "loaves of bread." PIR (198) understands שתים, "two," to be in apposition; then MT is the preferred reading.

17.c. *BHS* suggests that LXX *ἐκ δύο* implies a Heb. text משני.

18.a. על is taken to have the meaning "in addition to" (BDB, "על" 4.b., 755).

18.b. In place of the constr שבעת, "seven," in MT, Sam and Tg read the abs שבעה.

18.c. Sam and LXX add תמימם, "without defect."

19.a. LXX has a third person pl form.

19.b. Sam reads the article on this word. LXX adds *μετὰ τῶν ἄρτων τοῦ πρωτογενήματος*, "with the bread of the firstfruits," filling out this line like v 20.

20.a. Sam and LXX read the article on this word.

20.b. LXX adds *τῷ προσφέροντι αὐτὰ αὐτῷ ἔσται*, "it is to be for him (the priest) who presents them."

21.a. LXX divides the Heb. differently than does the MT. For בעצם היום הזה, "on this very day," LXX reads *ταύτην τὴν ἡμέραν κλητήν*, "(you will call) this day chosen," and for מקרא־קדש יהיה לכם, "you will have a sacred assembly," LXX reads *ἁγία ἔσται ὑμῖν*, "it will be holy for you," placing מקרא with the preceding phrase.

21.b. LXX adds *ἐν αὐτῇ*, "in it."

22.a. The temporal clause is composed by the prep ב plus the inf constr; cf. n. 12.a.

22.b. In place of MT בקצרך, "in your harvest," Sam reads לקצר, "to harvest."

24.a. LXX fills out the elliptical Heb. with *ἔσται ὑμῖν*, "it will be for you."

25.a. Cf. nn. 3.a. and 8.b.

26.a. Syr adds דבר אל־בני ישראל לאמר להם, "speak to the Israelites and say to them."

27.a. LXX renders אך, an adverb that establishes a contrast with the preceding (BDB, 36), simply by *καί*, "and."

27.b. Sam and LXX do not read the article on this word.

27.c. Cf. n. 8.b.

28.a. LXX does not have an equivalent for the *waw*.

28.b. LXX adds *ὑμῖν*, "for you."

29.a. LXX does not render כי, "that." Sun ("Investigation," 372) exegetes כי as having emphatic force.

29.b. *IBHS* (§25.5) interprets this pual as having reflexive force.

29.c. LXX does not have an equivalent for the *waw*.

30.a. LXX does not read כל, "all, any."

30.b. This long clause is a *casus pendens* for the dir obj; it is resumed by את־הנפש ההוא, "that person."

30.c. In place of the bold first person verb האבדתי, "I shall make perish," with Yahweh as the antecedent of the pronoun, LXX uses a passive *ἀπολεῖται*, "(that soul) will perish"; the LXX translators are seeking to avoid a too vivid anthropomorphism. Sun ("Investigation," 372) notes that this is the only text where האביד, "to make perish," stands for the usual נכרת, "to be cut off," in a penalty (cf. *Comment* on 7:19–21).

30.d. For MT עמה, "her people," Sam has עמיה, "her peoples," as in v 29.

31.a. A few Heb. mss, Sam, and Syr read a *waw*.

31.b. The dir obj stands before the verb for emphasis.

32.a. Some Heb. mss, LXX, and Vg omit בערב, "in the evening."

32.b. For MT תשבתו, "you are to rest, observe rest," a qal, Sam reads a hiph תשביתו.

32.c. The use of the cognate acc שַׁבָּת, "rest, Sabbath," underscores keeping all the regulations of the Sabbath.

34.a. Cf. n. 3.a.

35.a. LXX begins the sentence with *καί*, "and."

36.a. Cf. n. 8.b.

36.b. This temporal phrase, being first, receives emphasis. It is used to highlight the beginning temporal phrase of the next sentence, i.e., ביום השמיני, "on the eighth day."

36.c. Sam reads a *waw* on this word; LXX reads *καὶ ἡ ἡμέρα ἡ ὀγδόν*, "and the eighth day."

37.a. In place of MT עלה ומנחה זבח ונסכים, "whole offering, and grain offering, sacrifice, and drink offerings," LXX reads *ὁλοκαυτώματα καὶ θυσίας αὐτῶν καὶ σπονδὰς αὐτῶν*, "whole offerings and their sacrifices and their drink offerings."

38.a. Sam adds כל, "all."

39.a. Cf. n. 27.a.

39.b. LXX adds *τούτου*, "this."

39.c. Cf. n. 22.a.

39.d. LXX renders MT תחגו את־חג־יהוה, "you are to celebrate the feast of Yahweh," by *ἑορτάσετε τῷ κυρίῳ*, "you are to hold a feast to Yahweh."

39.e. Cf. n. 3.a.

40.a. The phrase פרי עץ הדר could be "the choice fruit of trees" (NIV) or "the product of magnificent trees" (most Eng trans.). The grammar indicates that the latter is favored, for this phrase is generic and is specified by the following three phrases, standing in apposition to it (cf. Levine, 163).

40.b. Sam and LXX read a pl form; Heb. may have a collective sense.

40.c. Where MT has וערבי־נחל, "and (of) willows from the brook," LXX reads *καὶ ἰτέας καὶ ἄγνου κλάδους ἐκ χειμάρρου*, "and boughs of the willow and the 'chaste tree' out of the brook"; *A Lexicon Abridged from Liddel and Scott's Greek-English Lexicon* ([Oxford: Clarendon Press, 1958] 6) says that *agnus castus* is a tall tree like the willow. "Of" is added in this Eng trans. to gain the correct meaning.

40.d. Cf. n. 3.a.

41.a. LXX does not have the sentence "and you are to celebrate it as a feast to Yahweh for seven days"; this resulted from an error of haplography.

42.a. The Hebrew uses the definite article to note the special type of booths constructed for this feast (GKC §126q, r). בסכת, "in booths," stands first for emphasis (cf. n. 42.c.).

42.b. Although the subj is sg in Heb., the verb is pl, because the subj has a collective sense (GKC §145b).

42.c. The pattern of this verse is a:b:c::d:b:a. At the center are two different elements; element c specifies the length of the feast—שבעת ימים, "for seven days"—and element d identifies those who are required to participate in this feast—כל־האזרח בישראל, "every citizen of Israel." But in this verse the emphasis falls on element a, בסכת, "in booths," for it both encircles the decree and stands first, which is not its usual grammatical position.

43.a. Cf. n. 12.a.

Form/Structure/Setting

The structure of this speech may be outlined as follows:

I. Speech about the Sabbath, the Passover, and the Feast of Unleavened Bread (vv 1–8)
 A. Introductory formula (v 1)
 B. Speech (vv 2–8)
  1. Commission to speak formula (v 2aα)
  2. Speech proper (vv 2aβ–8)
   a. Superscription and the Sabbath (vv 2ab–3)
    1) Superscription concerning feasts (v 2aβ+b)
    2) Concerning the Sabbath (v 3)
   b. Calendar of Passover and the Feast of Unleavened Bread (vv 4–8)
    1) Superscription to the ancient calendar (v 4)
    2) Regulations concerning Passover and the Feast of Unleavened Bread proper (vv 5–8)
     a) Calendrical fixation for Passover (v 5)
     b) Calendrical fixation and regulations for the Feast of Unleavened Bread (vv 6–8)

II. Speech about sheaf offering and the Feast of Weeks (vv 9–22)
 A. Introductory formula (v 9)
 B. Speech (vv 10–22)
  1. Commission to speak formula (v 10aα)
  2. Speech proper (vv 10aβ–22)
   a. Concerning offering of sheaf of firstfruits and the Feast of Weeks (vv 10aβ–21)
    1) Regulations concerning the offering of the sheaf of firstfruits (vv 10aβ–14)
    2) Regulations concerning the Feast of Weeks (vv 15–21)
     a) Regulations proper (vv 15–21a)
      (1) Calendrical fixation (vv 15–16a)
      (2) Regulations proper (vv 16b–21a)
     b) Subscription (v 21b)
   b. Laws appended concerning the poor (v 22)
    1) Two prohibitions and a command (v 22a+bα)
    2) Formula of Yahweh's self-introduction (v 22bβ)

III. Speech about sounding the trumpet (vv 23–25)
 A. Introductory formula (v 23)
 B. Speech (vv 24–25)
  1. Commission to speak formula (v 24a)
  2. Speech proper (vv 24b–25)
   a. Calendrical fixation (v 24b)
   b. Regulations (v 25)

IV. Speech about the Day of Atonement (vv 26–32)
 A. Introductory formula (v 26)
 B. Speech proper (vv 27–32)
  1. Calendrical fixation (v 27aα)
  2. Regulations (vv 27aβ–32)
   a. First statement of regulations (vv 27aβ–31)

1) Regulations proper (vv 27aβ–31a)
a) Liturgical regulations (vv 27aβ–28)
b) Two universal laws with punishment (vv 29–30)
c) Prohibition (v 31a)
2) Subscription (v 31b)
b. Restatement of two regulations and calendrical fixation (v 32)
V. Speech about the Feast of Booths (vv 33–43)
A. Introductory formula (v 33)
B. Speech (vv 34–43)
1. Commission to speak formula (v 34a)
2. Speech proper (vv 34b–43)
a. First unit on the Feast of Booths (vv 34b–36)
1) Calendrical fixation (v 34b)
2) Regulations (vv 35–36)
b. Subscription to ancient calendar (vv 37–38)
c. Appendix on the Feast of Booths (vv 39–43)
1) Calendrical fixation (v 39aα)
2) Regulations (vv 39aβ–41)
a) Regulations proper (vv 39aβ–41a)
b) Subscription (v 41b)
3) Further commands and historical grounding (vv 42–43)
a) Regulations proper (vv 42–43a)
(1) Regarding dwelling in booths (v 42)
(2) Purpose: grounded in saving history (v 43a)
b) Formula of Yahweh's self-introduction (v 43b)
VI. Statement of compliance (v 44)

It is important to notice at the beginning of this discussion that the audience of this group of speeches and the ones following in chaps. 24–26 differ from those in chaps. 21–22, for here Moses is to address the congregation, while in chaps. 21–22 he was commanded to speak to the priests, Aaron and his sons. This change in audience signals a shift from regulations specifically for the priests (chaps. 21–22) to matters for the whole congregation (chaps. 23–26).

This speech presents Israel's festal calendar. It regulates five festivals—Passover and the Feast of Unleavened Bread (vv 4–8), the Feast of Weeks (vv 9–22), the day for sounding the trumpet (vv 23–25), the Day of Atonement (vv 26–32), and the Feast of Booths (vv 33-36). In contrast with the festal prescriptions found in Exod 23:14-17, 34:18–26, and Deut 16:1–17 this calendar along with the one in Num 28–29 includes two additional high days, i.e., the first and the tenth days of the seventh month. The primary purpose of this text is to set the dates for the celebration of these five feasts. Sometimes the duration of the feast is given (vv 5a, 34b, 39a). A secondary purpose is to provide some ritual prescriptions in order to expand and confirm the rituals of a given feast. Two genres are thus intertwined: calendrical fixations and ritual regulations (cf. Reventlow, *Das Heiligkeitsgesetz,* 103). This kind of mixture is commonplace in an ancient calendar as the calendars from Babylon, Ugarit, and Egypt attest (Morgan, "Cultic Calendars," 220–21).

The present text has two overlapping structures. The most obvious and dominating structure is the basic speech framework similar to many of the speeches in Leviticus. It opens with an introductory formula (v 1) followed by a commission-to-speak formula (v 2aα). This speech concludes with a compliance formula at v 44; such a formula occurs in a few other places in Leviticus (e.g., 8:36; 16:34b). This structure communicates that this chapter is a single speech, even though several introductory speech formulae occur throughout the speech. In fact, the inclusion of introductory speech formulae within a larger speech has previously been observed in chaps. 6–7 and chaps. 13–14, though not with the same frequency as here.

The inner structure is marked by five speech reports identified by the introductory formulae at vv 1, 9, 23, 26, 33. Each of these speeches presents the regulations for one of the festivals. A closer look reveals that these speech reports have been imposed on an ancient calendar, for beneath the framework of these speeches lies such a calendar. This calendar is marked off by the heading אלה מועדי יהוה, "these are the appointed feasts of Yahweh" (v 4), and the summary statement אלה מועדי יהוה אשר־תקראו אתם, "these are the appointed feasts of Yahweh which you are to proclaim" (v 37). This ancient calendar was divided into five speeches in order to place the regulations for each of the feasts into self-contained speech units. This sectioning of the calendar took place after it had been placed in the form of a speech, for the first feast (vv 4–8) does not have its own introductory formula. In fact, the person who subdivided the calendar into separate speeches requires the standard introduction to the entire speech (vv 1–2aα) to do double duty; i.e., it introduces the speech as a whole as well as the regulations on Passover and the Feast of Unleavened Bread (vv 5–8). The inclusion of two superscriptions identifying these feasts as מועדי יהוה מקראי קדש, "the appointed feasts of Yahweh the sacred assemblies" (vv 2b and 4a), supports this analysis. The final author placed the first superscription to head the speech as a whole (v 2aβ + b), and kept intact the other one from the ancient calendar (v 4).

Why were several introductory speech formulae employed within a single speech? The answer is functional. Each section has been provided with its own introductory formula in order that in itself it may serve as a word of instruction. That is, at the celebration of any one of these feasts the regulation pertaining to that feast may be read for the instruction of the people assembled at a shrine on the occasion of that particular feast. Each formula then functions both to mark the beginning of the regulations for a feast and to establish the authority of that specific regulation. The subdividing of the speech, though, did not prevent the whole from being delivered in its entirety as a single speech. On those occasions that called for the presentation of the entire speech, these formulae both marked off the various feasts and reinforced to the congregation that each feast or high day was specifically ordained by God.

In addition to the division of the calendar into five speeches, there are signs that the ancient calendar has undergone a variety of changes and expansions. The ancient calendar is characterized by short, crisp sentences in an impersonal, legalistic style. According to Reventlow (*Das Heiligkeitsgesetz,* 105), the three essential members of a lead sentence of that ancient calendar were the date, the feast's name, and the phrase ליהוה, "for Yahweh." He suggests that possibly a fourth and a fifth member were the phrases ביום מקרא־קדש, "on the day is a sacred convocation," and לא תעשה כל־מלאכת עבדה, "do not do any kind of work." Cholewiński (*Heiligkeitsgesetz,* 82–83) has a similar list and adds the general prescription about presenting sacrifices—והקריב אשה ליהוה, "and he is to present gifts to Yahweh." Morgan ("Cultic Calendars," 67) identifies the genre of a statement that gives the date and a phrase as to the identity of the feast as "calendrical fixation." Only a few verses remain completely in the archaic impersonal style (vv 5, 13, 20, 29, 34). The speaker redirected this impersonal style by incorporating material formulated in direct address. These changes have strengthened the rhetorical force of this speech. This more forceful style enables the speech to achieve another goal, namely to motivate the people to faithful observance of these five festivals in accordance with Yahweh's instruction. The expansions, though, are a centrifugal force on the speech. To counter this force, the speaker used a variety of phrases to pull it together. These uniting threads are the following key terms and phrases: מועד, "appointed feast" (vv 2 [2x], 4 [2x], 37), מקרא קדש, "a sacred assembly" (vv 2, 3, 4, 7, 8, 21, 24, 27, 35, 36, 37), שבת, "Sabbath" (vv 3, 11, 15 [2x], 16, 32 [2x]), שבתון, "a solemn rest" (vv 24, 32, 39 [2x]), קרא, "call" (vv 4, 37), מלאכה, "work" (vv 3, 7, 8, 21, 25, 27, 30, 31, 35, 36), ליהוה, "to Yahweh" (vv 3, 5, 6, 12, 13, 16, 17, 18 [2x], 20, 25, 27, 34, 36 [2x], 37, 38, 39 [חג־יהוה, "the Feast of Yahweh"], 41), לפני יהוה, "before Yahweh" (vv 28, 40), בכל מושבתיכם, "in all your settlements" (vv 3, 14, 17 [ממושבתיכם, "from your settlements"], 21, 31), and בעצם הים הזה, "on this very day" (vv 28, 30).

Four major supplements have been made to the ancient calendar. At the very beginning, instructions on observing the Sabbath have been added (cf. Elliger, 311; Noth, 168). From a modern perspective the law regarding the Sabbath, which comes every seven days, appears to be an intrusion into a festal calendar, for the repetitive regularity of this day's observance is distinct from the once-a-year occasion of a feast. The inclusion of a commandment on the Sabbath along with material on calendrical fixations of major festivals is not unique to this speech. In Exod 23, just prior to the brief festal prescriptions (vv 14–17), comes the command to keep the Sabbath (v 12). Amidst the festal prescriptions found in Exod 34:18–24 occurs the commandment to keep the Sabbath (v 21). This style of combining commands and prescriptions occurs often in the Pentateuch. Three additional reasons for the inclusion of the Sabbath can be given. First, the people's faithful observance of the Sabbath would establish the pattern for their faithful observance of the festivals. Second, the Sabbath plays a role in determining the time for the celebration of the Feasts of Weeks (vv 15–16). Third, the laws on Sabbath observance carry over to special solemn days during the feasts; i.e., certain days of a feast are to be observed like a Sabbath. The special vocabulary in this instruction on the Sabbath gives additional evidence that it has been formulated for this speech, specifically the terms מלאכה, "work," שבת שבתון, "a sabbath of solemn rest," מקרא־קדש, "a holy assembly," and בכל מושבתיכם, "in all your dwellings," because these terms are among the recurring terms in this speech (see list above). This commandment on the Sabbath then has been made to fit this festal calendar and is an integral part of the speech's final formulation.

A second addition occurs at the end of the speech (vv 39–43; Elliger, 305–6; Noth, 125). It presents special instructions for the Feast of Booths. This section has the earmarks of a later addition. First, it comes after the subscription to the ancient calendar (vv 37–38). Second, it begins with a detailed calendrical fixation (v 39) so similar to the one in v 35 that it might be considered redundant unless it had an independent existence. Nevertheless, these two instructions for this feast had different origins as is evidenced by the vast differences between the two units.

The name of the feast is חג הסכות, "the Feast of Booths" in v 34, but in v 39 it is called חג ליהוה, "the Feast of Yahweh." This latter title indicates the exalted position of this feast at the time the second calendrical fixation and liturgy for it were composed. In the first unit the first and eighth days of the feast are מקרא־קדש, "a sacred assembly" (vv 35, 36), while these days are שׁתבון, "a day of solemn rest" (v 39), in the second unit. The second unit, however, goes beyond the first in prescribing the use of branches from glorious trees. It also makes the major contribution of tying this feast to Israel's history. Finally, only the first unit defines the eighth day as עצרת, "a solemn holiday" (v 36). This second unit, therefore, most likely came from the calendar of a local sanctuary where the celebration of this feast had developed in a special way. A scribe, who had access to this alternate calendar on this feast, included it in this official calendar for two reasons. First, this calendar enriched the observance of this feast with the description of ritual practices not prescribed elsewhere. Second, it enlarges the spiritual meaning of this feast by tying it to Israel's saving history, namely the years of Yahweh's preserving his people in the wilderness. This historical connection, of course, adds much to the significance of the tradition of erecting booths at this festival. The scribe kept both pieces, for he viewed both calendars as coming from the tradition and thus of equal authority. The formula of Yahweh's self-introduction (v 43b) applies either to the commands in v 42 or is the conclusion to the festal regulation in vv 39–43a. The former is preferred, since many laws in the laws on holy living are supported by this formula, but none of the calendrical regulations employ this formula. In any case, this regulation on the Feast of Weeks was at home in the groups that produced the material in chaps. 18–20.

A third expansion of the old calendar is found in the extended treatment of the Feast of Weeks (vv 9–22; cf. Elliger, 307–9). The length of this expansion is visible by comparing these instructions with those for this feast found in Num 28:26–31. Since this feast is basically ignored in the other calendrical texts, the author has drawn on various sources of priestly professional knowledge in order to define more precisely the date for this feast and to offer prescriptions for its rituals. Knohl (*HUCA* 58 [1987] 81, 85) goes much further. He argues that the holiness school revised the old passage to change an old local custom to a public ceremony at the central sanctuary.

The first part of the speech for the Feast of Weeks opens with ritual instructions about the offering of the עמר, "sheaf," rather than with the date of the feast (vv 9–14). That is, it gives regulations for the offering of firstfruits, a key ritual of the covenant community associated with the grain harvests (cf. 2:14). To the prescription for presenting the sheaf of firstfruits (vv 10–11) is joined a prescription for presenting specific sacrifices (vv 12–13). This subunit closes with a prohibition (v 14). While the day for offering the firstfruits fell during the Feast of Unleavened Bread, these regulations on the offering of the firstfruits are included in the second speech, not the first, for the purpose of establishing the time reference for setting the date for the Feast of Weeks. Much detail on the offering of the sheaf however, has been included, because this ritual is not found elsewhere in the Torah. The Feast of Weeks falls fifty days after offering the sheaf of the first grain. A fifty-day period (seven times seven plus one) was very important to ancient Semitic peoples, for it marked a major block of time (cf. H. and J. Lewy, *HUCA* 17 [1942/43] 47–115). The Year of Jubilee attests to the importance of the number fifty in ancient Israel. The date for the Feast of Weeks, based on counting fifty days, heads a new paragraph in this second speech report. Strangely, the specific name of this feast is not given. However, regulations for offering sacrifices are given along with the regulation for offering bread baked with leaven (vv 17–20). These two days, the offering of the sheaf and the Feast of Weeks, framed the beginning and the end of the grain harvests.

The fourth supplement comes at the end of the speech on the Feast of Weeks (v 22); a law is included to regulate the gleaning of the fields for the benefit of the poor. This style is unique to this speech. This law is a repetition of the law in 19:9–10 save that any reference to vineyards is omitted. This omission is proof that this law has been intentionally adapted for this location, since the Feast of Weeks celebrates the harvest of grain, not the harvest of vineyards and orchards. Why is this law included when there are no other such laws in this calendar? Regulations on firstfruits plus this law frame the calendrical instruction regarding the Feast of Weeks. Both those regulations and this law are based on the theology that Yahweh is Lord of the land and its produce. Israel recognizes his lordship by giving the firstfruits to him. They further recognize that Yahweh, their Lord, is holy and merciful, by observing the law to leave the gleanings of the harvest to the poor and to resident aliens. Their obedience lets them celebrate the bountiful harvest with full joy. This recognition of Yahweh's lordship is certainly at home in the Holiness Code. This emphasis on Yahweh's lordship is affirmed by the inclusion of the longer formula of Yahweh's self-introduction (v 22bβ; cf. *Excursus* at 18:1–2). This formula occurs here because it has been attached to the preceding law as in chap. 19. Therefore, this law joins with the liturgical regulations regarding firstfruits to frame the instructions on the Feast of Weeks.

In summary, this speech consists of an ancient calendar that was portioned into several speech units. During Israel's history, additions were made to the calendar to reflect the increasing importance of the pilgrim festivals. Whenever this speech was given the basic form it now has, materials on the Sabbath and the Day of Atonement were included in the speech so that the speech would address the special times for the community's worship as determined both by the regular flow of time and by the special seasons of the calendar.

Sun ("Investigation," 400; cf. Elliger, 309–10) considers the calendrical fixation for the Day of Atonement (vv 26–32) to be a secondary insertion. Sun bases this on its "idiosyncratic linguistic formulation." As argued in the *Form/Structure/Setting* to chap. 16, this passage and 16:29–34a are closely tied together linguistically, indicating that they either come from the same hand or else one section has been adapted from the other. The brevity of both sections favors the former view. In this context, the initial part of the material has been formulated according to the ancient style (see above and Cholewiński, *Heiligkeitsgesetz,* 88–90). The rest of the material is distinct to this portion. This material on the Day of Atonement has, therefore, been tied into the ancient calendar in order to establish the relationship of this most solemn fast day with the other major festivals celebrated in Israel.

Morgan ("Cultic Calendar," 118–21) identifies the genre of this text and Num 28–29 as "a calendar." Morgan distinguishes the genre "calendar" from the genre he labels "festal prescriptions" as found in Exod 23:10–19; 34:18–24; and Deut 16:1–17. A "calendar" text identifies a festive occasion when all the people are to assemble for worship, determines its time and duration, and sets forth certain ritual regulations (Morgan, 219). This festal calendar has been put into a speech for the instruction of the congregation assembled during a festival. Portions of this calendar could be used at any cultic center on the occasion of a particular feast for the instruction of the people about that feast.

Comment

2 This legislation concerns מועדי יהוה, "the appointed feasts of Yahweh." מועד, which comes from the root יעד, "to appoint, set," means "appointed time, set time," i.e., a time holding special significance. This is the noun used in the phrase אהל מועד, "Tent of Meeting" (cf. 1:1). The term occurs here in the plural to communicate that there are several "appointed times/seasons" throughout the year. The genitive יהוה, "Yahweh," could be either objective—"feasts for Yahweh"—or subjective—"feasts set by Yahweh." Gen 1:14 supports the latter by affirming that the heavenly bodies, i.e., the sun, the moon, and the stars, have been created by God to fix the times for these high days. These are also feasts for Yahweh, because they are occasions to worship and praise him for abundantly blessing the fields and the flocks and for calling Israel into existence. Both meanings then are conveyed by this phrase. Closely related to this term is the phrase מקרא קדוש, which is variously translated: "sacred day of celebration" (Noordtzij, 227), "a sacred assembly, convocation" (NIV, NEB), "a sacred occasion" (NJPS), "the sacred assemblies" (JB), and "holy convention" (Wenham, 301). מקרא is more restrictive than מועד, being applied to special high days during a feast. The use of מקרא in this phrase may come from the practice of positioning official observers to look for the first sign of the new moon; on sighting the new moon they sent מקרא, "a call," throughout the land proclaiming the beginning of the high day. The term מקרא occurs in a few clusters in the OT: this chapter (11x), Num 28–29 (6x), and Exod 12:16 (2x). A day is called מקרא קדש, for it is a high time during the festival in which the community lays aside all usual work in order to assemble in worship of God and in celebration of the joys of life. These days are קדוש, "holy, sacred," for the worship of Yahweh is their singular focus.

3 The root שבת means "to stop work, rest." To stress that it is a day of total rest in honor of Yahweh, the phrase שבת שבתון, "a sabbath of solemn rest," is used (cf. vv 24, 32, 39; *Comment* on 16:29–30). There is a prohibition that no מלאכה, "work," may be done on the שבת, "Sabbath" (cf. Exod 16:23–30; Num 15:32–36). Since מלאכה, which connotes the skill for and benefits of work, is a more inclusive term than עבדה, "work, labor," the kinds of work excluded by this command are quite broad. It is amazing that nowhere does the priestly legislation have specific laws as to what kinds of work are forbidden or even any guidelines as to how much effort may be spent before it qualifies as work. This is more amazing in light of the numerous laws on the Sabbath in rabbinic writings. This fact teaches that God prefers to give his people principles to live by and let them fill in the details. This, of course, gives the law an enduring quality that allows it to be applicable to a variety of cultural contexts amidst the changing times. From the Pentateuch it is discovered that the kinds of work not permitted on the Sabbath included plowing and harvesting (Exod 34:21), preparing food by baking and boiling (Exod 16:23), making a fire (Exod 35:3), and gathering of wood

(Num 15:32–36). In Jer 17:21 carrying loads was forbidden, and according to Amos 8:5 and Neh 13:15–21, buying and selling were outlawed. The phrase בכל מושבתיכם, "in all your settlements," means in all your homes, not just at the sanctuary (cf. Exod 35:3; Porter, 180).

The Sabbath then is a day of total rest and a time for the community to focus its attention on the worship of Yahweh. The phrase שבת הוא ליהוה, "it is a Sabbath to Yahweh," communicates that it is to be observed in honor of Yahweh (cf. Isa 58:13–14). This day is so important to Israel that its observance is one of the Ten Commandments (Exod 20:8–11; Deut 5:12–15). The origin of the Sabbath, unfortunately, remains elusive. Other nations of the ancient Middle East observed holy days, usually tied to the cycle of the moon, but the pattern of a weekly Sabbath so far has proved to be unique to Israel.

The fourth commandment on observing the Sabbath is very liberating, for not only are the landowners given rest but also their servants and their animals. This is a tremendous step in the advancement of humanity, for long before the organization of labor unions it recognizes the right of all laborers, regardless of their status, to periodic times of rest. Even the animals are to rest. This law frees all workers from daily toil to enjoy the results of their labor and the world God has created. God is proclaiming that humans are not bound to endless toil. There is much more to life than work. People need time to enjoy the products of their labors. The Sabbath is to be a day of joy and praise (Exod 23:12; Deut 5:12–15; Isa 58:13; Hos 2:13[11]). Furthermore, the Sabbath is a sign of the covenant (Exod 31:13–17), a sign that distinguishes the covenant between Yahweh and Israel. Observing Sabbath keeps the covenant strong and vital. Siker-Gieseler (*Studia Biblica et Theologica* 11 [1981] 13) comments that "the extent to which Israel keeps the Sabbath is a sign to which Israel wishes to acknowledge God as sanctifier and creator." No wonder that in the priestly material there are frequent exhortations for the people to observe the Sabbath (19:3, 30; 26:3; Exod 23:12; 35:2; Num 15:32–36; 28:9, 10).

4 This superscription is the main heading to this ancient calendar. This is a reiteration of the latter part of v 2.

Excursus: Calendars in the OT and Israel's Pilgrimage Festivals

There are five festal calendars in the Pentateuch: Exod 23:14–17; 34:18–26; Deut 16:1–17; Lev 23; Num 28–29. The only other festal calendar is the brief one found in Ezek 45:18–25. In varying degrees of detail, these passages set the dates and durations and sometimes give liturgical directions for the annual celebrations in Ancient Israel. The calendars of Exod 23:14–17 and 34:18–26 are usually viewed as the oldest of the calendars. These two are similar, outlining the same three feasts—Unleavened Bread, Weeks, and Booths—in the same order. Since these calendars do not specify any precise dates, it is assumed that the date of each festival was set according to the time of the respective harvest for a given year.

The calendar of Deut 16:1–17 likewise prescribes three annual feasts. The ritual regulations are more developed and integrated in this calendar (e.g., vv 2–8) than are those in Exodus. There is also a more exact reckoning of the dates and durations of the feasts. Here Passover is given prominence. It is to be celebrated as a pilgrim festival in the month of Abib, which is a shift from its origin as a household celebration (Exod 12:1–13). The Feast of Unleavened Bread, however, is not mentioned by name. Nevertheless, the prohibition against the use of leaven (vv 3–4, 8; cf. Exod 23:15; 34:18, 25), the ritual prescriptions (vv 3–4, 8; cf. Exod 23:18), and the use of the same historical rationale (vv 1, 4, 6; cf. Exod 23:15; 34:18) indicate that this feast is assumed to be part of Passover. In v 9 the time for the Feast of Weeks is stated, and vv 13 and 15 specify seven days as the duration of the Feast of Booths. This calendar stresses that each feast is to be celebrated "in the place that he [YHWH] will choose" (16:2, 11, 15).

The calendars of Lev 23 and Num 28–29 set more precisely the time for the beginning of each festival and its duration. While the agricultural character of the three pilgrimage feasts is still evident (e.g., Lev 23:10, 22, 39–40; Num 28:26), the dates of the feasts are no longer connected with the harvests but with specifically numbered days in designated months. The characteristics of these calendars in regard to dates and liturgical regulations indicate that their setting was a central sanctuary. Passover and the Feast of Unleavened Bread are closely linked, but their distinctiveness is maintained because their temporal relationship is more precisely defined. These calendars, in addition, set the dates for two more high days: the blowing of trumpets on the first day of the seventh month Tishri (Num 29:1–6), and a ritual to remove the sins of the people on Tishri 10 (Num 29:7–11).

The calendar of Ezek 45:21–25 primarily sets the dates for two seven-day feasts, one in the first and another in the seventh month, and it prescribes the offerings required of the ruling prince. Passover is the only feast named. There is no mention of the Feast of Unleavened Bread, but it is assumed in the reference to unleavened bread and the seven-day (not eight days as in Lev 23 and Num 28) duration assigned to Passover. From the date and duration of the festival in the seventh month, it is certain that the Feast of Booths is intended. The sacrifices prescribed for the prince at this fall festival parallel those prescribed for him for Passover. In comparison with Num 29:17–38, the sacrifices for this feast are significantly reduced in number, perhaps because of special concern for the prince in Ezekiel. The Feast of Weeks and the New Year are ignored, perhaps because the prince would not have a prominent liturgical role on these high days. Attached to this calendar (vv 18–20) is the prescription of two days of atonement for the cleansing of the Temple: the first day of the first month and the seventh day of the same month (LXX has the first day of the seventh month, but Zimmerli [*Ezekiel 2*, 483] does not find that this variant outweighs the MT).

The differences in these festival calendars inform us that Israel's observance of the various feasts was not static, but dynamic. This understanding is confirmed by the continued expansion of the feasts in Israel's history with the addition of a Purim (Esther) and Hanukkah.

A significant issue in the development of the feasts in Ancient Israel was the setting of specific dates for these festivals. Most scholars believe that in the early eras there were no fixed dates for the feasts. Being celebrations of the harvest, each feast began whenever the people finished that particular harvest, a time that varied from season to season because of varying weather patterns. This position is substantiated by the variety of names for two of the feasts: Weeks (Exod 34:22; Deut 16:10; Num 28:26) is also called "harvest" (Exod 23:16a), and "firstfruits of wheat harvest" (Exod 34:22; cf. Num 28:26), and late in the post-exilic era it received the name "Pentecost" (2 Macc 12:31–32 and Tob 2:1), while Booths has the name "feast of ingathering" in Exod 34:22. Segal, however, takes another position, holding that the spring and the fall festivals were initially tied to the equinox. Thus the respective harvest celebrations were made to fit into the festivals (cf. Segal, *JSS* 6 [1961] 85). In either case, as Israel increased in size and political power, it became necessary to set dates and predetermined sanctuaries in order that people from all over Israel could assemble at the national festivals (Segal, *Passover*, 128). The calendars of Leviticus, Numbers, and Ezekiel attest that specific dates were set for the feasts (Lev 23:5, 6, 34; Num 28:16, 17; 29:12; Ezek 45:21, 25).

Then one must ask when these three feasts became observed as pilgrimages. The first evidence appears in the reference to Elkanah's making pilgrimages to the central sanctuary (1 Sam 1:3, 21; cf. Kutsch, *ZTK* 55 [1958] 32–33). The limited details intimate that the feast was the Feast of Booths. If this is correct, the celebration of this feast by a pilgrimage began prior to the establishment of the monarchy. Kutsch holds that the term "yearly" indicates that in that time pilgrimages to Shiloh and Bethel were made at the Feast of Booths. Later the other two agricultural feasts became observed by pilgrimages. Some argue that Deut 16:16 gave the direction for this change (cf. Auerbach, *VT* 8 [1958] 16–17). After the cult was centralized at Jerusalem, the role of these pilgrimages increased.

Next, in order to understand the calendar in Lev 23 better, the origin and the development of the three primary festivals are considered. Given the limitations of this excursus, only a few of the recent numerous studies on the various festivals are taken into account. The spring festival was the union of Passover and Unleavened Bread. The development of the connection between these two feasts is a very complex traditio-historical question. The first surprising fact is that Passover is not explicitly mentioned in the oldest calendars. In the later calendars, however, it is consistently combined with Unleavened Bread. In contrast to the other major feasts, Passover is referred to only once in the OT as חג, "a pilgrimage feast," and that in connection with the Feast of Unleavened Bread (Exod 12:14). Based on the rites associated with these two feasts, scholars have argued for the nomadic origin of Passover and the agricultural origin of the Feast of Unleavened Bread.

The major reason for claiming a nomadic origin for Passover is the central role of the sacrifice of a year-old lamb, a practice at home among semi-nomads (de Vaux, *AI,* 2:489; cf. Kraus, *Worship,* 46–48). A number of distinctive features of this sacrifice favor this position: the lamb was roasted over a fire, no utensils were used, unleavened bread and bitter herbs attended the meal, there was no altar or priest, and there was the unique rite of putting blood on the doorposts of the houses (de Vaux, *AI,* 2:489). Certainly the central role of making a sacrifice stands in marked contrast to the emphasis on the produce of the fields in the other feasts. It is conjectured by several scholars that the original goal of this feast was to promote the fertility of the herd and to win protection for the flock during the drive to new pasture (Ringgren, *Israelite Religion,* 187). Nevertheless, there are some scholars who dispute the nomadic origin of Passover (see Engnell, "The Passover," 192–93; Segal, *Passover,* 91–95). Wambacq (*Bib* 57 [1976] 301–26), for example, argues that the connections between Passover and an ancient nomadic festival are too general for carrying any weight as evidence that the one rose out of the other. Rather, in his judgment, the specific rites attached to Passover, such as eating unleavened bread, witness that this feast had its origin in the formative historical event of the Exodus from Egypt that gave birth to Israel as a nation.

As for the date of Passover, the importance placed on celebrating it at night indicates that this feast was originally set on or near the full moon, as noted in the calendars of Leviticus, Numbers, and Ezekiel (Martin-Achard, *Essai biblique,* 33; Kutsch, *ZTK* 55 [1958] 18–19; de Vaux, *AI,* 2:490). During Israel's history, the place for the celebration of Passover has alternated between the home and the sanctuary. It was originally celebrated at each home. Later it became a pilgrim festival celebrated at the Temple (Num 28:16–25; Deut 16:1–8; Ezra 6; Jub 49:16; John 11:55–57; cf. Matt 20:18). After the fall of Jerusalem in A.D. 70, its celebration returned to the home. Some attribute its change to a pilgrim festival as the result of the centralizing tendencies of the Deuteronomists. From a refined perspective based on Josh 5:10–12, which reports an early celebration of this feast at Gilgal, the celebration of Passover at a central sanctuary was not a deuteronomic innovation; rather the deuteronomic reform moved its celebration from a local sanctuary to Jerusalem (Noth, 169; cf. Kraus, *Worship,* 50–51). De Vaux (*AI,* 2:488), on the other hand, views the process to have taken place in reverse order. He argues that Passover moved from being observed at the central sanctuary of the tribal federation to the home with the weakening of tribal bonds and decentralization of cultic worship produced by the settlement in Canaan; only under Josiah's reform did it become a pilgrimage to the central sanctuary. The movement from the home to regional cultic centers and eventually to Jerusalem, however, seems to be the more logical progression.

As for the Feast of Unleavened Bread, its origin is obscure, being complicated by its relationship to Passover. Most scholars hold that the Feast of Unleavened Bread had its original setting in an agricultural community (Kraus, *Worship,* 47–48). It was a feast for the grateful celebration of the barley harvest and the dedication of the first sheaves to God. By the people's giving God the firstfruits of the new harvest, the rest of the harvest was released to their use. To symbolize this break in the annual cycle, fresh kernels of grain were roasted and baked into loaves, but nothing from the past, such as yeast, could be used (Porter, 182; Kraus, *Worship,* 48). Kraus (*Worship,* 48–49) claims that when Israel took over the Feast of Unleavened Bread from her Canaanite neighbors, she modified the feast in three ways: (1) She attributed the feast to Yahweh (Exod 23:15; Lev 23:6). This means that she did not recite any myths of fertility such as the victory of Baal over Mot. (2) The festival was for the entire nation assembled at a central shrine (Exod 23:17; 34:24). (3) This festival was tied to Israel's redemptive history. The oldest calendars in Exodus, however, connect this feast to the Exodus, and in Josh 5:11 eating the first ears of grain in Canaan took place on this day.

Wambacq and Halbe have investigated the origin of the Feast of Unleavened Bread anew and have concluded, independent of each other, that this feast does not have its origin in an agricultural setting. They marshal many reasons. The mention of unleavened bread does not automatically demand an agricultural setting, for such bread was the food of both bedouins and farmers in any situation when there was not time for dough to be leavened such as when they were in transit (Halbe, *ZAW* 87 [1975] 339; cf. Wambacq, *Bib* 61 [1980] 38). Only this feast of the three annual festivals in the oldest sources is dated in a month with a name, Abib, which is a pre-exilic name (Halbe, 334; cf. Wambacq, 35–36); this fact points to the antiquity of the observance of this feast. Wambacq (37–42) works through the various texts referring to the Feast of Unleavened Bread and does not find any connection made between unleavened bread and the harvest of grain. This tie, which has been made by critical scholars, thus lacks textual support. Halbe, furthermore, argues quite forcefully that the observance of a feast of unleavened bread was by its very nature not tied to an agricultural way of life as has been supposed by scholars (336–37), for a seven-day feast after the harvest had begun would place the ripened grain in jeopardy of being destroyed by a natural disaster like the sirocco. In other words, observing a festival at such a time would have been in such conflict with the sense of urgency farmers have at harvest that it could neither have arisen nor survived in an agrarian setting.

The arguments of these two scholars are so strong that the prevailing critical position on the origin of this feast must be set aside. Furthermore, not only does the earliest OT tradition connect eating of unleavened bread with the Exodus (Exod 23:15; 34:18; cf. Halbe, *Bib* 61 [1980] 339), but the union of Passover and the eating of unleavened bread is also attested in the first celebration of Passover in Canaan as reported in Josh 5:10–12 (cf. Exod 12:34, 39). As a result, unleavened bread served not only to symbolize the haste of leaving Egypt, but as the first food eaten in the promised land, it also served as a symbol of the fulfillment of the Exodus promise (Halbe, 341). This celebration took place while the new harvest was still in the process of ripening, and thus was not in tension with agricultural interests. This is the way it is regulated in the oldest festal calendars (Exod 23:15 and 34:18). In this light, then, the Festival of Unleavened Bread was indigenous to Israel.

In Wambacq's judgment (*Bib* 61 [1980] 51), however, the Feast of Unleavened Bread initially lasted only a day. The two earliest reports of this feast support his position. Obviously at the Exodus Israel did not stay around to celebrate this feast for seven days, and the account in Josh 5 reads as though the feast was held for only a day. Eventually this feast became extended to a week-long celebration (Wambacq, 51; Exod 13:6; Deut 16:8; 2 Chr 30:21; 35:17). With this change Wambacq considers it probable that the people spent only the first day at the sanctuary and observed the rest of the feast referring to the eating of unleavened bread at home (38). Later the entire week was spent at the sanctuary.

To answer the question of how and when these two feasts became joined, there have been many imaginative proposals. In de Vaux's judgment (*AI,* 2:491–92), they were combined during Josiah's reform. Since this reform made Passover a pilgrimage festival like the Feast of Unleavened Bread, the latter was celebrated immediately following Passover regardless of the day, for the date of Passover was already fixed at the full moon. De Vaux dates this change just before the exile, marshalling additional support from the fact that Ezekiel knew these dates (45:21). Nevertheless, the fact that the date of Passover was set by the full moon and Unleavened Bread by the Sabbath produced enduring disputes on the correct interpretation of these calendrical texts among various Jewish groups (cf. *Comment* on vv 15–16). Lev 23:3–8 witnesses to the merger of these two feasts.

Another issue is the relationship of the Feast of Unleavened Bread to Passover, i.e., one feast being given prominence in one era and then the other rising in prominence. When Israel became settled in the land, Passover faded into the background (2 Kgs 23:22; Halbe, *ZAW* 87 [1975] 341). The spring festival was then celebrated as the Feast of Unleavened Bread. This change accomplished the binding of an agricultural way of life into Israel's redemptive history. Halbe interprets Deut 16:1–7 as a later program to raise Passover to a pilgrim festival to be celebrated at the central shrine, thus taking the place of the Feast of Unleavened Bread in the oldest calendars. Morgenstern puts forth another reason for Passover's rise in importance; he attributes that change to the desire to reduce the danger of foreign practices linked with astrology penetrating Israelite worship because of the linkage of the Feast of Unleavened Bread with the spring equinox (*HUCA* 1 [1924] 46–49).

Although Passover rose in prominence, the use of unleavened bread was preserved, being eaten for seven days. Later the recognition of the long-standing practice of observing Unleavened Bread led to the compromise of considering the spring feast a double feast, Passover/Unleavened Bread (cf. Ezra 6:19–22; Halbe, *ZAW* 87 [1975] 342–43). In fact, Halbe sees two traditions in Deut 16:1–8. In one tradition only Passover was a pilgrim feast (vv 6–7); afterwards the people returned home and ate unleavened bread for seven days. But v 8 prescribes that Unleavened Bread be observed as a week-long feast at the sanctuary. The calendar of Lev 23 accepted the conjunction between Passover and Unleavened Bread and enhanced the solemnity of the first and last days of Unleavened Bread (cf. Num 28:16–25).

The second of the agricultural celebrations in the festival cycle, the Feast of Weeks, celebrated the completion of the wheat harvest. It is called חג הקציר, "feast of the harvest" (Exod 23:16), חג שׁבעת, "feast of weeks" (Exod 34:22; Deut 16:10, 16), and שׁבעתיכם, "your weeks" (Num 28:26). According to Lev 23:15, it was to be celebrated seven weeks after bringing the sheaf of the elevated offering. The fifty-day period gave to this feast the name *πεντηκόστη*, Pentecost, "fifty." Coming at the end of the wheat harvest, it was a joyous harvest occasion at which the firstfruits of the wheat harvest were offered (Exod 23:16; 34:22). While this feast was basically a harvest festival, Israel, nevertheless, observed it ליהוה, "to Yahweh" (Lev 23:16; Num 28:26; Deut 16:10; Kraus, *Worship,* 57). This means that it was grounded in the Lordship of Yahweh, not in the forces of nature.

The only unambiguous references to the Feast of Weeks in the OT occur in connection with the other annual feasts. 1 Kgs 9:25, e.g., states that there were three annual festivals. Amazingly it is omitted in the festival calendar of Ezek 45. Porter (184) reasons that the paucity of references to this feast in the OT occurs because it only lasts a single day. In Kraus' judgment, this feast was eventually extended to a week-long celebration (Num 28:24; *Worship,* 56). Others propose that the lack of references lies in its not being connected with the spring or fall equinoxes. The best explanation of the minor role played by the Feast of Weeks, though, is that it is not explicitly linked with Israel's salvation history (Martin-Achard, *Essai biblique,* 53), although late in the Second Temple it became connected with the giving of the covenant at Sinai (Jub 6:1–21; 14:1–20). This association, however, may be hinted at in 2 Chr 15:10–14, which refers to a feast to renew the covenant celebrated in the third month. The date in Exod 19:1 for Israel's gathering at Sinai to receive the law from God supports this connection. In the post-exilic community a covenant renewal ceremony was an important part of this feast (Kraus, *Worship,* 59).

The third major festival, which was celebrated in the fall, is חג הסכות, "the Feast of Booths" (Lev 23:34, 42; Deut 16:13; 31:10; 2 Chr 8:13; Ezra 3:4; Neh 8:14–15; Zech 14:16). Its names, חג האס(י)ף, "the feast of ingathering" (Exod 23:16; 34:22), חג יהוה, "the feast of YHWH" (Lev 23:39; Judg 21:19; Hos 9:5), חג ליהוה, "feast in honor of YHWH" (Lev 23:41; Num 29:12), or simply החג, "the feast" (1 Kgs 8:2, 65; 12:32; Ezek 45:25; Neh 8:14; 2 Chr 5:3; 8:7; John 7:2), are a strong indication of its importance for ancient Israel (Porter, 188). It was to take place after the produce of the orchards and vineyards had been brought in and the wine had been pressed (Deut 16:13). Snaith (25) believes it was the most important feast in pre-exilic times. This feast was known as the most joyous, characterized by singing and dancing. Deuteronomy and Leviticus say that the feast is to last seven days, but Lev 23:36 adds an eighth day, עצרת, a day of "solemn assembly," and no labor. In Lev 23:42–43 this feast is tied to Israel's redemptive history, the time of sojourning in "booths" in the wilderness. As a result, it was both a time of joyful celebration for the new produce and a time of remembering how Yahweh had guided and cared for his people.

A variety of texts seem to have their setting in an early form of this celebration (Judg 9:27; 21:19–21; 1 Sam 1:3, 21; cf. Hos 9:5; 1 Kgs 12:32; van Goudoever, *Biblical Calendars,* 30; Kutsch, *ZTK* 55 [1958] 32; Snaith, 24; MacRae, *CBQ* 22 [1960] 251–52). Why did this feast take on the name סכות, "booths"? What role did "booths" play in it? The first prescription to live in booths comes in Deut 16:13. Lev 23:40 implies that the branches to be gathered by the pilgrims were the materials for constructing the booths. Such materials, however, would not have been available in the desert. The shelters used in the wilderness were tents, not booths or huts. Some scholars, therefore, search for another setting that gave birth to this feast. They speculate that that setting was the practice of erecting temporary shelters in the fields during the fall harvest as a place for workers to eat, sleep, and watch the harvest (MacRae, 255; de Vaux, *AI,* 2:501). MacRae postulates that at the close of the harvest the people broke out into joyful celebration right in the fields where they were working. He says, "The huts might serve as a cultic symbol of the celebration itself" (255). This joyful celebration was eventually moved from the fields to the sanctuary, and as noted above it became tied into the wilderness traditions (Morgenstern, *HUCA* 1 [1924] 58; Martin-Achard, *Essai biblique,* 78; MacRae, 259; Cazelles, *StLit* 14 [1981] 30–31).

Several other reconstructions have been proposed to account for the origin and the historicizing of this feast. Kraus, e.g., searches for its origin in an ancient tent feast. He finds evidence of such a setting in the wilderness tradition, which pictures Israel's living in tents, with the priesthood and the Tent housing the Ark of the Covenant at the center (Num 2–3). After the settlement in Canaan, booths took the place of tents. During the Kingdom period the remembrance of the Davidic covenant became a central part of this feast. MacRae (*CBQ* 22 [1960] 259–61) reviews Kraus' proposal, judging that there is not enough evidence in the texts for this reconstruction. MacRae (260–63) sets forth another proposal, conjecturing, as several have, that during the era of the Judges the Israelites took over an ancient Canaanite pilgrim festival involving tents.

He grounds much of this proposal in the literal meaning of חג, "a pilgrimage." The roots of this Canaanite feast were in an ancient nomadic pilgrimage to a sanctuary, which involved tents and took place in the fall. While MacRae (263) admits that his proposal rests on nothing firm, his work, along with that of Kraus, supports the possibility of an early origin for this festival.

According to Deut 31:10–13, there was a covenant renewal ceremony at this feast every seven years. It is possible that during the monarchy the focus of the feast shifted from the Sinaitic covenant to the covenant between David and Yahweh, as Kraus has proposed (cf. 2 Sam 7:8–16; Ps 132). This may account for Solomon's choosing the time of this feast for the dedication of the magnificent Temple (1 Kgs 8:2). At the time of Ezra, the leaders of the post-exilic Jewish community revived the celebration of this feast (Neh 8:13–18). On this occasion the people enthusiastically erected booths everywhere, from the courts of the Temple and the squares of the city to the roofs of private homes. During this reform, Ezra read from the law of God on each day of this feast.

Two primary proposals have been made as to the character of the Israelite celebration at this feast. The first proposal locates the celebration of Yahweh's enthronement in this feast (cf. J. Gray, *The Biblical Doctrine of the Reign of God* [Edinburg: Clark, 1979] 10–32). Mowinckel and other Scandinavian scholars hold that it was the life-setting for the reenactment of the enthronement psalms, including Pss 47, 93, 96–99 (*The Psalm in Israel's Worship,* tr. D. R. Ap-Thomas [New York: Abingdon Press, 1967] 1:106–92). In their reconstruction, Yahweh's enthronement took place on New Year's Day, a day that originally was a key part of the Feast of Tabernacles. A major difficulty with this proposal is that Mowinckel has relied far too heavily on Babylonian practices without sufficient collaborating texts from ancient Israel for reconstructing an ancient Israelite enthronement festival in this feast. Taking a different path, Kraus has attempted to show that the central theme of this festival was the proclamation of the Kingdom of God (H.-J. Kraus, *Die Königsherrschaft Gottes im Alten Testament,* BHT 13 [Tübingen: Mohr (Siebeck), 1951]; also *Worship,* 203–8). Rather than seeing the festival as an enthronement of Yahweh, Kraus interprets it as a royal Zion festival. The emphasis was Yahweh's covenant with David and his election of Zion as the seat of his reign (Ps 132). After the fall of Jerusalem, this festival became the setting that spawned Israel's eschatological hope for the coming reign of God. A key passage for this hope is Isa 52:7–10, composed during the exile in Kraus' judgment. Deutero-Isaiah's vision of Yahweh's coming peaceful reign inspired the composition of the enthronement psalms, which Kraus interprets as eschatological. Kraus draws on several other eschatological texts that portray the universal reign of Yahweh in metaphors drawn from the Feast of Tabernacles in support of this position. Zech 14:16–19 specifically names this feast as the feast celebrating the earthly reign of Yahweh. In fact, this feast may be the setting for the whole apocalyptic message of Zech 12–14. Moreover, it is possible that Isa 24–27, often called "the Little Apocalypse," and Isa 60–62 have their setting in the Feast of Booths. These eschatological passages witness that this feast took on Messianic significance.

The second proposal posits that a covenant renewal was part of the Feast of Booths (cf. Deut 31:10–13; Josh 24). Von Rad (*The Form-Critical Problem of the Hexateuch,* 33–40) and Weiser (*The Psalms,* tr. H. Hartwell, OTL [Philadelphia: Westminster, 1976] 35–52) have championed this view. Central to this renewal are a number of elements: Yahweh's theophany (Ps 50:2–3); a recapitulation of Yahweh's acts in history, possibly in cultic drama; covenant renewal, the proclamation of judgments; and the pronouncing of blessings and curses (Ringgren, *Israelite Religion,* 194–95).

These proposals seek to recapture some of the rites and activities that filled this week of celebration. In any case, it is certain that the themes of covenant and the reign of Yahweh were especially tied to the Feast of Booths. The type of ceremonies used to portray these themes is open to hypothetical reconstructions because of the limited amount of surviving evidence. Nevertheless, these reconstructions are creative proposals that show the vital role these feasts had in the life of ancient Israel.

These reconstructions point to the tradition behind Jesus' powerful words proclaimed at the Feast of Tabernacles as recorded in John 7. According to that report, Jesus went up to Jerusalem secretly to attend the Feast of Tabernacles. On the last day of the feast, the highest day, most likely while the high priest was pouring out the water, a rite tied into the hope for abundant fall rains necessary for an abundant harvest in the spring, Jesus cried out, "If any one thirst, let him come to me and drink. He who believes in me, as the scripture has said, 'Out of his heart shall flow rivers of living water'" (John 7:37; cf. Zech 14:17; R. Brown, *The Gospel according to John I-XII,* 327). People within the crowd began to discuss among themselves the meaning of this saying and whether Jesus was the Messiah. Their discussion about the Messiah attests that the connection between this feast and Israel's messianic hope was alive in the NT era.

In addition to these three pilgrim festivals, Lev 23 prescribes two additional celebrations, the first day of the seventh month and the tenth day of the seventh month. The first day of the seventh month was the day for sounding the ram's horn (23:24; Num 29:1–6). Strict rest was to be observed, prescribed sacrifices were to be offered, and an assembly of the congregation was to be held. Some scholars, like Cazelles (*StLit* 14 [1981] 29) and Morgenstern (*HUCA* 10 [1935] 74–75, 80), interpret this joyful celebration as a New Year's festival. It has been postulated that this celebration was put into Israel's calendar in order that the Jews might have a festival that corresponded to the Babylonian New Year's festival, and yet to avoid mythological influences the Jews put their New Year's Day in the fall, a half year away from the Babylonian celebration (Auerbach, *VT* 8 [1958] 341). This speculation conflicts with the absence of any mention of a New Year's Day in the OT (Auerbach, 338–41). Even in the late reference of Ezra's reading the law on the first of Tishri (Neh 7:73b–8:12), there is no indication that that day was the New Year. In fact, neither Josephus nor Philo (*De specialibus legibus* 11.188) includes a festival of the New Year in his list of feasts. Rather this high day in the calendars of Lev 23 and Num 29 was set as preparation for the important feasts coming in this seventh month (Kraus, *Worship,* 67–68). Nevertheless, Tishri 1 did become the New Year's Day in Judaism, but the reasons for this development remain obscure (Clines, *JBL* 93 [1974] 628).

The phrase ראש השנה, "the head of the year," which has become the Heb. term for the "New Year," occurs only in Ezek 40:1, not, however, for Tishri 1, but for Tishri 10 (cf. Zimmerli, *Ezekiel 2,* 345–46), but, according to de Vaux, for Nisan 10 (*AI,* 2:502–3). Zimmerli shows that this date in Ezekiel is set in line with Lev 25:9, which has the year of Jubilee begin on Tishri 10. In two texts, Lev 23:27 and 25:9, Tishri 10 is called the Day of Atonement. The importance of this high day is demonstrated by the requirement of total rest (Lev 23:32) and the elaborate ritual prescribed in Lev 16. It was common in ancient times to begin the annual cycle with a day of atonement. That is why some scholars hold that Tishri 10 was initially Israel's New Year's Day. In Snaith's opinion it became the New Year's Day feast as a result of the change from a lunar calendar to a solar calendar, which is ten days longer. Thus, the first ten days of the month of Tishri were regarded as "outside the calendar" and became days of penitence (Snaith, 135). Snaith's position has not received a wide following. Nevertheless, in Judaism the Day of Atonement has become the most solemn day of the year and is very distinct from New Year's Day. See the material on chap. 16.

(Steven Wilkens, Ph.D., helped prepare this material.)

5 Dates were set in ancient Israel by the month, not the week. The months were numbered. In neighboring countries the months and the days had names, the names of various gods. By referring to days and months simply by numbers, Israel, however, sought to avoid this polytheistic practice of deifying the movement of time. Nevertheless, after their contact with the Babylonians they began to refer to the months by names. In this calendar the numbering of the months begins in the spring.

The first feast of the calendar is Passover. It commemorates the Exodus from Egyptian bondage. While many scholars hold that this feast had its roots in an early semi-nomadic, spring festival, the distinctive Israelite character of the Feast of Passover witnesses to its being intrinsically tied to her saving history.

This calendar gives little detail about the celebration of Passover; thus it assumes the knowledge of other regulations such as those found in the Book of Exodus (12:1–13, 21–27). This feast falls on the fourteenth day of the first month; this date is the first full moon after the spring equinox. It begins between the two evenings (בין הערבים). Since the center of this festival was each family's preparing a year-old lamb for a meal, the time is for the slaughter of the lambs. This imprecise phrase, however, has received a variety of interpretations. Frequently it is understood as the time between the sun's setting and full darkness. Rabbi Nathan (*Mekilta Bo* 5) says it begins after high noon when the sun starts to incline to the west (Levine, 156). According to *m. Pesaḥ.* 5.1, the paschal sacrifice started to be offered after 3:00 P.M. in the Second Temple.

6–8 Following on the heels of Passover is חג המצות, "the Feast of Unleavened Bread," lasting seven days. This feast received its name because no leaven may be used at all during this time. The term מצות became the term for small, round wafers made from the new grain and baked without leaven. This spring festival is referred to by either name in various passages; e.g., Passover is said to last seven days in Ezek 45:21, but in 2 Chr 30:13, 21 and Ezra 6:22 both feasts are called Unleavened Bread.

חג, "festival," means a festival with a religious purpose (Haran, *Temples,* 290). Only three celebrations are identified by this term in the OT: Unleavened Bread, Weeks, and Booths. The etymology of חג has not been settled. Hrbek takes it from the root חג, "(be) round, circular, crooked"; the meaning then developed into "form or describe a circle," then "dance" (reported by G. Botterweck, "חָג *chagh,*" *TDOT* 4:203). Haran (*Temples,* 289), however, argues that it is an overinterpretation to extend the meaning of this root to "dance." In any case חג in the OT stands for "a festal gathering." Such a festival ordinarily required a pilgrimage to a shrine (Haran, *Temples,* 290).

No usual labor (כל־מלאכת עבדה) may be done on the first day and the last day of this feast. These terms occur together as a hendiadys; they are rendered "daily labor" (NEB), "regular work" (NIV), and "heavy work" (JB). This phraseology intentionally brings to mind the fourth commandment just reiterated in v 3: "Six days you are to labor [עבד] and do all your work [כל־מלאכתך]" (Exod 20:9). While on the other days of this festival, there were special activities, nevertheless, people could work and do normal chores.

There is a brief general ritual prescription specifying that each day אשה, "gifts," a collective (cf. n. 1:9.g.), are to be made to Yahweh. The general language here for sacrifices assumes the detailed prescription of sacrifices for each day of this feast in another text; such a list is found in Num 28–29. On this feast, see Exod 12:14–20; 13:3–10; Num 28:17–25; Deut 16:3–9; Ezek 45:21–24.

9–14 The second speech opens with a ritual prescription. It regulates the offering of firstfruits. This is important in itself and also it is important because it starts the counting for the next festival (cf. Exod 23:19a; 34:26a). It stipulates the requirement of offering the first עמר, "sheaf," of the harvest; it was probably barley since it ripened first. עמר is often translated "sheaf," i.e., a bundle of stalks. But in Jewish tradition (Num 15:20; *b. Menah.* 66a, 68b), עמר is a cake made out of barley meal mixed with water (Noordtzij, 234). The ritual prescribed here is a community offering of firstfruits (Keil and Delitzsch, 460). This prescription then is different from that prescribed in Num 18:12–13 and Deut 26:1–11, for those texts address the presentation of firstfruits by an individual (Noordtzij, 233). Noth (170) takes an alternative understanding. He suggests that each landowner brought a bundle of the first ears. The priest received them over a period of time and offered them on the set day.

11 In the ritual prescribed here, the priest takes the עמר, "sheaf," and הניף, "elevates," it to Yahweh. This gesture symbolizes making a present to Yahweh (cf. 7:30). They are gifts of praise to Yahweh for his blessing on the fields. This ritual is performed in order that the offering may be rendered רצנכם, "acceptable on your behalf"; that means the offering achieves the purpose for which it is presented (cf. 1:3–4). After the ritual, they are given to the priests. This is to be done during the Feast of Unleavened Bread. In v 15 the possible meanings of ממחרת השבת are discussed.

12–13 Accompanying the offering of the cake of barley is the offering of עלה, "a whole offering," a year-old lamb תמים, "without defect." There is also a grain offering of two-tenths of an ephah, about 7 quarts or 7.28 liters, mixed with oil. This offering is twice the normal grain offering (Num 28:13). It is identified as אשה ליהוה, "a gift to Yahweh," and ריח ניחוח, "a soothing aroma" (cf. 1:9). In addition, there is to be נסכה, "a drink offering," consisting of a fourth of a hin of wine, about 2.5 pints or 1.5 liters (cf. Snaith, 106).

14 None of the new barley may be eaten until the firstfruits have been offered to Yahweh, the supreme God. This ritual expresses the people's affirmation that God is the owner of the land and the Lord of his people. Since God is Lord, the first yield of the crops, the best, must be given to him. After receiving the firstfruits, God, in turn, releases the rest of the harvest for his people's use. Cf. 2:14 for קלי, "roasted grain," and כרמל, "fresh grain."

15–22 This is the regulation for the second pilgrim festival, but it is not named here. Its name in other OT texts varies: חג השבעות, "the feast of weeks" (Exod 34:22; Deut 16:10), חג הקציר, "the feast of harvest" (Exod 23:16), and יום הבכורים, "the day of first ripe grain" (Num 28:26). It marked the end of the grain harvests. An offering of the new מנחה, "grain," is to be made in the form of two loaves of bread baked from meal of the new wheat, a tenth of an ephah for each loaf (3.64 liters; Noordtzij, 236). חמץ, "leaven," is to be used (Exod 34:22), symbolizing that this day is a joyous occasion. Noth (172) postulates that each landowner is to bring two loaves. These loaves are to be elevated to Yahweh (cf. v 11), but they may not be placed on the altar, for they contain leaven. After the ritual they are given to the priests. On בכרים, "firstfruits," see 2:12; Exod 22:29(30); 23:19; 34:26; Num 18:12–13.

The date for this festival is seven weeks after the firstfruits were offered on the day ממחרת שׁבת, "after the Sabbath." The identification of this day for offering the firstfruits has been debated. Van Goudoever (*Biblical Calendars*, 18–29) enumerates four interpretations of שׁבת for beginning the counting of fifty days. In the first, שׁבת, "sabbath," is for the first day of the Feast of Unleavened Bread, the fifteenth of Nisan. שׁבת, "sabbath," then is taken to mean a solemn day of rest, not the seventh day of the week. M. Fishbane notes that Josh 5:10–12, which reports the first Passover celebrated on entry into the promised land, describes the people's eating bread and קלי, "roasted grain," on the fifteenth of Nisan (*Biblical Interpretation,* 147–49). He demonstrates that Josh 5:10–12 is an exegesis of Lev 23:10–14. Fishbane (149–51) goes on to argue that שׁבת in these two passages has its old technical sense of "full moon." The LXX, *Sipra ʿEmor* 23:11, 15, *Targum Yerušalmi* and *Targum Onqelos,* Philo (*Special Laws* 2:162, 176), and Josephus (*Ant.* 3.10.5) support this position (van Goudoever, *Biblical Calendars,* 18–19). The second position is that שׁבת is the Sabbath falling during the Feast of Unleavened Bread. Three groups, the Boethusians, the Samaritans, and the Karaites, all who very likely had priestly origins, follow this tradition (van Goudoever, 23). Bertholet (80) holds that Deut 26:9 supports this position. A third position is that it is the day after the Feast of Unleavened Bread, the twenty-second of Nisan. A Jewish sect in Ethiopia follows this practice; van Goudoever (25) posits that the origin of this tradition can be traced back into the post-exilic era. The fourth position is that שׁבת is the Sabbath immediately following the Feast of Unleavened Bread. Van Goudoever (25) thinks that the Book of Jubilees supports this position, though indirectly. In any case he discovers that concern for counting the fifty days was more important to the sects than it was in mainstream Judaism (29). For Christians the Council of Nicaea set the counting of the fifty days from Sunday to Sunday for πεντηκοστή, Pentecost, thus following the priestly calendar (van Goudoever, 182).

The date in the heading at Exod 19:1 connects the giving of the law at Mount Sinai with the Feast of Weeks. After the destruction of the Second Temple in A.D. 70, this feast became a Feast of the Law.

18–21 In addition to the loaves of bread, seven lambs, one year old and without defect, a young bull, and two rams are to be offered as עלה, "a whole offering" (cf. chap. 1), to Yahweh with their מנחת, "grain offerings" (cf. chap. 2), and נסכים, "drink offerings." These are אשׁה ריח־ניחח ליהוה, "a gift for a soothing aroma to Yahweh" (cf. 1:9). In addition, a goat (שׂעיר־עזים) is to be offered as חטאת, "a purification offering" (cf. chap. 4) and two year-old lambs as זבח שׁלמים, "an offering of well-being" (cf. chap. 3). Levine (159) observes that this is the only law to prescribe offerings of well-being as a public sacrifice. Two lambs with bread made from the first ripe grain are also to be presented as תנופה, "an elevated offering," to Yahweh. It is an elevated offering since this offering of well-being is presented by the congregation, not by an individual (Noordtzij, 236). Being an elevated offering, it does not go to the altar and it becomes the property of the priests. This offering is called קדשׁ, "holy"; thus the appropriate parts are given to the priest. Later practice correlates this list of offerings with the list given in Num 28 by considering those in Num 28 as the official offerings and by taking this passage as directions for additional offerings (Noordtzij, 237). The day of these offerings is proclaimed as מקרא־קדשׁ, "a sacred assembly"; no usual work is to be done.

22 This law orders landowners to leave the corners of a field unharvested and reiterates the prohibition of the gleaning of fields after the harvest in order to leave some grain for the poor; cf. 19:9–10. It recurs here to teach the people that in addition to making gifts of the harvest to Yahweh they need to express compassion toward the poor. Giving generously is not only to be directed heavenward but also earthward, in order to fulfill the whole desire of God.

23–25 This speech sets the first day of the seventh month as a high day. The seventh month is the most sacred month of the calendar because of the great importance of the number seven to the Israelites. It is the most festive month of the year with three different occasions for celebrating. In this month is the most solemn day of the year, the Day of Atonement, and the most joyous festival, the Feast of Booths. Part of the reason this month is full of festivals is that it falls at a time when agricultural work is at a minimum, at the end of the harvests of grapes and olives and just before preparing the ground for the winter grains.

The first day of the month is a day of שׁבתון, "solemn rest" (cf. v 3), no usual work is to be done. It is מקרא קדשׁ, "a sacred assembly" (cf. v 2; Num 29:12). And it is זכרון, "a memorial," commemorated with a loud תרועה, "blast," of the ram's horn (Ps 81:4[3]); NEB renders תרועה "acclamation." The sounding of horns marked important occasions in ancient Israel, such as here to announce a high day. They were blown at certain times in the ritual of certain sacrifices. Most often the blasts of horns called the people into assembly and the troops into formation. Porter (188) contrasts the Babylonian New Year's festival, which was a time for setting the destinies for the coming year, to this day in Israel. Israel believed that her future was determined by God's acting toward his people in remembrance of his promises to them. Thus the term זכרון, "memorial," characterizes the significance of this day. Does Israel remember God and his deeds or does God remember Israel? The use of זכרון in the priestly texts favors the latter view (cf. Childs, *Memory and Tradition*, 67; H. Eising, "זָכַר *zākhar*," *TDOT* 4:78). God gave Israel signs and rituals to use in order to make him remember them. By arousing God's memory, the people move him to act toward them graciously in terms of his promises to the forefathers, especially the promises made to Abraham (Gen 12:1–3) and the terms of the covenant. Memory is a vital means for both parties of a covenant to keep the covenant relationship alive. The purpose of the memorial is then to promote the continuance of the covenant relationship on the part of both parties (Childs, 68).

On this day אשׁה, "gifts," i.e., a series of prescribed offerings, are to be made to Yahweh. These offerings are enumerated in Num 29:2–6 (cf. Ezek 45:18–19). Neither this text nor any of the other four passages with calendars in the Pentateuch give the significance of this day. In the post-exilic community, from the time of the Seleucids, this feast became the New Year's Day, Rosh Hashana (cf. Ezek 40:1; Dillmann, 646–47). The origin of the Jewish New Year's Day is much debated, partly because scholars cannot determine whether the calendar began in the spring or in the fall. Some suggest that there was more than one calendar, such as a cultic calendar beginning in the spring and a civil calendar beginning in the fall with New Year's Day. In this text, however, this day has not reached the status of a New Year's Day. The lack of details and rituals for the celebration of this day in ancient Israel may result from the prominence the New Year's festival had in the polytheistic religions of Israel's neighbors, being central to their mythological outlook.

26–32 The tenth day of the seventh month is the the Day of Atonement, which is treated at length in chap. 16. Here it is called יום־הכפרים, (lit.) "the day of atonements" (pl elsewhere only in 25:9). The plural is one of the ways Hebrew expresses the superlative; the wording thus means this is a day of full and complete expiation or atonement. The entire nation observes this day. It is a day of rest. This fact is stressed, for three times it is stated that no מלאכה, "work," may be done (vv 28, 30, 31) and in v 32 there are two statements instructing that this is a day of complete rest (שבת שבתיון; cf. v 3; 16:31). Because this is a most solemn day, a day of mourning for the nation's sins, the people are to afflict themselves (עניתם את־נפשתיכם; cf. 16:31). This language means that the people are to follow a total fast for the full day. Added to their spiritual afflictions are their prayers. Therefore, even though the high priest is the key figure in the solemn ceremonies at the Tent of Meeting according to the regulation in chap. 14, the entire community contributes significantly to the spiritual merit of this day by fasting and abstaining from all earthly pleasures. אשה, "gifts," are to be made to Yahweh.

The penalty for not observing this day is the "cut-off" penalty (נכרת; cf. 7:19–21). This penalty is explained by the additional sentence in v 30, האבדתי את־הנפש ההוא מקרב עמה, "I will make that person perish from the midst of the people." God himself is the one who takes responsibility for punishing any who violate these laws regarding the Day of Atonement.

This law says that the Day of Atonement is to be celebrated from evening to evening. This is the only place in this calendar where the precise time for a high day is set. This expression, being unique, bears emphasis. Whether other festivals began in the evening in ancient Israel is debated. Levine (161) cites Rashbam as a rabbi who argued that the Sabbath and other festivals began at dawn. Much later the rabbinic tradition established that all days begin in the evening.

33–36 This is the calendar for the most gala feast of the year, חג הסכות, "the Feast of Booths," or "Tabernacles" (cf. Deut 16:13–15; 31:9–13; Num 29:12–39, where the daily offerings for this feast are given). It lasts for seven days beginning on the fifteenth of the month at full moon. In Exod 23:16 and 34:22 it is called "the feast of ingathering." Of all the feasts this one can be simply referred to as "the feast" (1 Kgs 8:2, 65; 12:32; 2 Chr 7:8–9; Neh 8:14; John 7:37). It gets the name the Feast of Booths from the term סכה, "booths," i.e., temporary shelters made out of branches, which are erected by the pilgrims at this festival. A booth has a roof, but usually one side is left open. This joyous festival commemorates the harvest of the vine and the olive trees (cf. Judg 21:19–21; 1 Sam 1:3–5).

The first day of the feast is מקרא־קדש, "a sacred assembly" (cf. v 2); no work may be done. An eighth day is added to the feast. This day is also a sacred assembly, meaning no work could be done. This day is further called עצרת, a term that has received a variety of renderings since its precise meaning has not been preserved: "a solemn gathering" (NJPS), "a sacred assembly" (Wenham), "the closing assembly" (NIV), and "the closing ceremony" (NEB). The closing day, the eighth day, of the week-long festival for the dedication of Solomon's Temple was also called עצרת. Noth (175) postulates that it means "a taboo day," and he suggests the translation "special feast-day." The root meaning of עצר, "detain, restrain," accords with its use for a national day of fasting (Joel 1:14; 2:15). Its being used for the final day of a week-long festival brings to mind the special ceremonies performed on the last day of a festival. Later it came to be the day on which the reading of the Torah ended and a new cycle began. "A solemn holiday" may be the best rendering for עצרת. In that this term stands for the whole day, using "assembly or gathering" for it is too limiting. Furthermore, since "solemn" may refer to either a sublime or a somber occasion, it captures the feelings of jubilation at the great festivities of this day mixed with sadness that it is the last day of the feast.

37–38 This is a summary statement for the calendar text. The various feast days are times for making a variety of offerings, including the following kinds: עלה, "the whole offering," מנחה, "the grain offering," זבח, "the sacrifice," i.e., the offering of well-being, נסכים, "drink offerings." These are to be presented in addition to the offerings prescribed for the Sabbath and the gifts (מתנות) of the people, their נדרים, "vow offerings," and their נדבות, "freewill offerings." מתנות, "gifts," includes all the offerings presented that are not burnt on the altar, such as the gifts of the princes of the tribes (Num 7) and the tithes, firstfruits, and elevated offerings (Num 18:11, 29; Keil and Delitzsch, 447). This term has a wider meaning than קדשים, "holy things" (Elliger, 322). נדבות, "freewill offerings," includes the offerings of well-being and also whole offerings that are offered in fulfillment of vows and in spontaneous praise (Keil and Delitzsch, 447). This instruction particularly guards against any Israelite attempting to get double value from an offering, i.e., making a festive offering and claiming it as one of his other gifts or obligations.

39–43 Additional prescriptions for the Feast of Booths are given. On the first day of the feast, the people are to take פרי עץ הדר, "fruit of the glorious trees": כפת תמרים, "palm branches," ענף עץ־עבת, boughs of trees with thick, intertwined foliage (KB, 735), and ערבי־נחל, "willows of the river bed" (wadi). ערבי־נחל is the *Salix fragilis* and *Salix alba,* which are plentiful in Palestine (Snaith, 108), though some identify this tree as the poplar (*populus euphratica*). This interpretation understands that three kinds of glorious trees are listed (cf. Keil and Delitzsch, 448). Later Jewish tradition understood הדר to be הדור from the root דור, "enduring," i.e., a non-deciduous tree. They used the citron for the fruit of this tree (Levine, 163). Jewish tradition also understood that each worshiper was to have one of each of these branches. So branches from each of these trees were bound together by a gold thread to make a festive plume called לולב, "lulab." Pilgrims carried this *lulab* in procession during this feast, such as in the march from Gihon Spring to the Temple, with water for the ritual outpouring of water.

The people are to erect סכת, "booths," to dwell in during this week. While it is not explicitly stated, one could infer that these booths are to be made out of branches from the trees mentioned here. These booths are to be constructed like the temporary shelters that were erected in the fields to enable a person to live there during the harvest in order to protect the fields from robbers, both humans and animals (Neh 8:16). In the tradition as prescribed here, these booths came to symbolize the temporary shelters the people lived in during the wilderness journey. There is a little tension in that in the wilderness the people lived in אהלים, "tents," not booths. But there is a deeper play on the tradition, for the first resting place of the Israelites in their exit from Egypt was סכת, "Succoth" (Exod 12:37; Num 33:5). Levine (163) points out that סכות is a double entendre, a place name and a type of habitation. These shelters, however, are not to recall the hardship of the wilderness, but the grace of God in providing for his people in so many ways in such an austere environment (Keil and Delitzsch, 449–50). This interpretation is supported by the construction of the booths out of the glorious trees of the promised land, not from the shrubs of the wilderness (cf. Deut 8:7–8). These booths are a symbol of the people's gratefulness to their caring God during this joyful feast. In this way this feast became tied to Israel's saving history. It is specifically stated that during this feast כל־האזרח בישׂראל, "all citizens of Israel," are to live in booths.

44 This verse stresses that the distinctive features of these festivals, which reached back into Israel's past, have their authority in God's speaking to Moses at Mount Sinai.

Explanation

This calendar sets the dates and the duration of five annual festivals. It also provides some sacrificial regulations for these high days. The calendar opens with a commandment on the Sabbath. The Sabbath is a day of rest observed on the seventh day of every week. The establishment of this day has been a tremendous liberating force for humans. God frees all of his people, master and servant, mistress and maid, rich and poor, noble and peasant, from the bondage of daily work in order to enjoy the fruits of their labors and to worship Yahweh, their Creator and their Redeemer. In observing this day, the people submit their material goals to the sovereignty of God, the Creator (cf. Tsevat, *ZAW* 84 [1972] 455). By faithful observance of the Sabbath, the people proclaim the lordship of God over their daily lives.

Rest is an essential feature of the Sabbath. Every Sabbath morning when the Israelites arose and all work was forbidden, their thoughts gravitated to the way they might spend this day in worship of God. If any work were permitted, some would be drawn away from community worship to attend to some pressing need, but the absoluteness of this standard guards against the strong pull of such earthly demands. Knowing that any relaxation of this prohibition against work would erode full community participation in this day of rest and in the annual feasts, this calendar highlights the Sabbath.

Rest, like that of the Sabbath, is the goal of one's spiritual journey. It symbolizes the security and the blessings that a person has because of a relationship with God. Two NT texts employ rest as a metaphor for the messianic work of Jesus. Jesus himself invites all those who are bowed down under a heavy burden to find rest in him (Matt 11:28–30), and the Letter to the Hebrews exhorts all who follow Jesus to enter the blessed Sabbath-rest God has provided for them (4:1–11).

After the commandment on the Sabbath, the calendar sets the time for five annual festivals: Passover and the Feast of Unleavened Bread, the Feast of Weeks, the trumpet blast on the first day of the seventh month, the Day of Atonement, and the Feast of Booths. Among these festivals are the two major pilgrim festivals, the first and last feasts of this list. Each of these two feasts celebrates both the fresh yield of a new harvest and a special redemptive act of God in Israel's history. These two points of orientation are not at odds with each other, for just like the dual purpose of the Sabbath these harvest celebrations both praise God the Creator and the Sustainer for the harvest and recount the great saving deed of God in praise of him as their Lord and Guide. These two pictures of God are intertwined in the Scriptures, and they are juxtaposed in the worship of Yahweh. The picture of God the Creator promotes his power, wisdom, and majesty. The picture of God the Redeemer reveals his mercy, love, and immanence. The merciful God of redemption is neither opposed to himself nor to the universe he has created. That he is Creator means he has the power to accomplish his will; that he is Redeemer means that he has the will and the motive to act for the deliverance and the welfare of his people. Both images of God are essential to see clearly the God who exists and loves. From the human side both the delight with the produce of the new harvest and the saving acts of Yahweh contribute to the dynamic of their celebration. These elements are not in competition; rather they augment each other.

The spring festival is Passover and the Feast of Unleavened Bread. At the center of the Passover, the first day of the festival, is a special meal of a year-old lamb roasted over a fire. It is eaten with bitter herbs and unleavened bread. This meal commemorates Israel's last night in Egypt. On that night the angel of death went through Egypt, slaying all the first-born except for those in homes with blood sprinkled on the doorpost in accordance with Yahweh's instructions. Grief stricken, Pharaoh ordered the Hebrew slaves to leave. On that night Israel as the people of God was born.

Following right on the heels of Passover is the Feast of Unleavened Bread. This feast commemorates the beginning of the barley harvest. The fresh grain is eaten without leaven. This regulation forms a historical tie with the Exodus and the Passover in that the bread prepared on the night of the first Passover was unleavened, a symbol of the haste associated with the remarkable deliverance of that night.

The second feast of this calendar is the Feast of Weeks. This feast celebrates the end of the wheat harvest. In Israel's history this feast became associated with the giving of the law at Mount Sinai and the making of the covenant (cf. Exod 19:1). It takes place fifty days later. That is the reason it is often called the Feast of Pentecost. The number fifty is critical to this feast, for fifty days to the ancient outlook marked an inclusive span of time. This calendar specifies that the counting of the fifty is to start with the day of offering up the sheaf of the firstfruit of grain. The sheaf is offered during the Feast of Unleavened Bread, but the exact day is disputed.

The offering of the firstfruits is a ritual act by which the community acknowledges Yahweh's ownership of the land and his rightful claim to the current harvest. For the people themselves to eat of the firstfruits would be a direct affront to Yahweh's having blessed their land. Because Yahweh is Lord, he rightly demands the firstfruits. As soon as the people present the firstfruits, symbolized in this rite of raising up the sheaf as an elevated offering, Yahweh releases the rest of the harvest back to his people for their use. After this ritual the people may live off the harvest with deep gratitude for the harvest Yahweh has given them. By this ritual humans recognize their place in their community under God.

This ritual of firstfruits thus enabled the people to enjoy the produce of the land with a good conscience, and it seeks to undercut human greed and avarice such as led the rich man to say to himself, "Soul, you have ample goods laid up for many years; take your ease, eat, drink, be merry" (Luke 12:19). God gives material gifts to his people to use for their own sustenance, not that they turn themselves into tyrants of selfishness. The law to leave the gleanings of the harvest and the corners of the field standing in order that the poor and aliens may glean freely addresses this same issue. The laws about firstfruits and about gleanings erect a high barrier in Israel against greed. Having kept these laws of firstfruits and gleaning, the people come together to celebrate at the Feast of Weeks. At this time of thanksgiving they may eat bread prepared with leaven. This symbolizes that they are fully participating in the blessed benefits of obedient service to Yahweh.

The next three high times fall in the seventh month. Since seven is the most sacred number, the most solemn day and the most joyous feast fall in this month. This month is also pivotal from an agricultural perspective, for it comes at the end of the harvest of the olive trees and the vineyards and just before the heavy fall rains. The tasty fruits of this harvest are products that make life easier and happier, e.g., oil for anointing the body, for cooking, for light, and wine to gladden the human heart (Ps 104:15). Coming at the end of the long, dry summer, it is the time of awakening anticipation for the necessary heavy, fall rains.

The first day of the seventh month is a high day, a day of rest. The day is marked by blasts of the ram's horn. It is a memorial. That is, the sounding of the trumpet arouses Yahweh's remembrance of his past commitments to his people in order that he will act toward them in the present in light of his promises. Little else is said about this day in the OT. In Judaism it became New Year's Day, but this day does not have that status in this text.

On the tenth day of the month is the Day of Atonement (cf. chap. 16). This is the most solemn day of the year. Not only is no work to be done, but the people are to fast. The special rituals performed on this day by the high priest secured expiation for the entire community. Faithful observance of this day guarantees the effectiveness of the sanctuary and all its apparatus for seeking Yahweh in the coming year. It also guarantees that Yahweh has forgiven his people all their sins and guarantees his continued dwelling among his people in the Holy of Holies. Because this day was so solemn and so essential for the community to remain in harmony with Yahweh, the penalty of being cut off from the community for failure to observe the ordinances of this day is underscored.

The third high occasion of this month is the Feast of Booths. This feast begins on the fifteenth day of the month and lasts for seven days plus a closing eighth day. It is also called the feast of Yahweh. It is the most gala feast of the year. The people journey to the central sanctuary. There they construct booths, temporary shelters, to live in during the feast. These booths came to symbolize the long period of the forefathers' having to live in tents during the sojourn in the wilderness. While Yahweh wanted the people to remember that it was their forefathers' disobedience that extended the length of the wilderness sojourn, the booths are primarily to arouse the people's memory of his gracious ways of sustaining their forefathers during those years when they lived in tents. By comparing their present dwellings with these booths the people may realize again how much Yahweh has done for them in giving them the land of inheritance and homes in which to live.

Yahweh is jealous that his people celebrate each of the festivals. Participation unites the community around the great deeds Yahweh has done for his people. It stimulates the growth of the community's trust in God. The rituals of this feast tie the people directly into their saving heritage. At the same time the people are thankful to God for the produce of the new harvest, and together they remember what God has done. Celebration stimulates the corporate memory, keeping alive what God has done to give birth to and to form the nation Israel. It enables each generation to participate in the formative events of the nation. This participation through memory keeps alive the benefits initiated in those great saving deeds. An active memory endows the distinct customs and practices of each feast with meaning. Through observance of these feasts, the people keep in force the divine purposes initiated in the mighty acts of God.

These festivals have importance in the NT in a variety of ways. Several events in the ministry of Jesus take place in conjunction with one of the feasts. Sometimes a saying had its setting in a festival. On the last day of the Feast of Booths, e.g., Jesus said, "If any one thirst, let him come to me and drink. He who believes in me, as the scripture has said, 'Out of his heart shall flow rivers of living water'" (John 7:37–38). This saying is made fully intelligible in light of the customs and hopes of the Feast of Booths. At this feast the Jews remembered the sojourn in the wilderness, and they prayed that God would send the heavy rain necessary for a bountiful harvest. Jesus tied his saying into the incident of water flowing from the rock struck by Moses in the wilderness (Num 20:2–13) and into the people's hope for the coming rains. Furthermore, this feast had become associated with the Day of the Lord and the triumph of the Messiah over all of Israel's foes (Brown, *John,* 1:326–27). In addition, certain eschatological texts, such as Zech 14:8 and Ezek 47:1, pictured life-giving water flowing from the threshold of the Temple. Therefore, through this saying Jesus was telling the assembly that their prayers for water and for the Messiah were being answered in him in a marvelous and unexpected way. Clearly this saying of Jesus takes on rich meaning in light of its setting in the Feast of Booths.

More importantly, God continued to act in the NT in light of his promises and in accordance with what he had done for Israel. Thus he chose two of these feasts to accomplish new acts of redemption. Jesus died for our sins on the afternoon before Passover, while lambs for that special family meal were being slaughtered. Then God raised him from the dead on the first day of the week after Passover during the Feast of Unleavened Bread. Jesus' great saving deed corresponds to the Exodus from Egypt. Just as the Exodus is the formative saving deed for the covenant between Yahweh and Israel, so the death and resurrection of Jesus constitute the formative saving deed for the new covenant between God and all who believe in Jesus. The language and events of the Exodus serve as superb metaphors for interpreting God's full saving work in the death and resurrection of Jesus.

Fifty days after Jesus' resurrection, at the Feast of Weeks or Pentecost, the Holy Spirit was poured out on the disciples gathered in Jerusalem. Whereas under the old covenant the law was written on tablets of stone, under the new covenant the Spirit writes God's law of love on hearts of flesh. Furthermore, after the Holy Spirit descended on the disciples, Peter proclaimed to the multitude assembled at Jerusalem the meaning of these events. Every member of that multitude heard the message, each one in their own language. This miracle powerfully symbolized that the new covenant is for all who believe regardless of their nationality or their language.

Amazingly, the church has nothing that corresponds to the joyous Feast of Booths. In the OT, however, the reign of Yahweh is associated with this feast.

Several prophets use symbols from this feast in their oracles of the coming reign of God (e.g., Isa 52:7–13; Zech 12–14). They foresee an era when God himself will establish a peaceful reign over the entire world from his throne in Jerusalem (Isa 2:2–4; Mic 5:1–4). Yahweh will resolve all disputes. Peace will reign supreme. All nations will stream to Jerusalem both to be taught of Yahweh and to celebrate these great feasts, above all the Feast of Booths. Therefore, the Feast of Booths continues to hold a word of promise for all believers. It points to the return of Jesus and to his universal reign as King of Kings and Lord of Lords.

As the last point, let us briefly reflect on the role of the Sabbath in the NT. The Sabbath was a point of controversy between the Jews and Jesus. Jesus attacked the overscrupulous observance of the Sabbath by the orthodox religious groups of his day. He did this for many reasons. Their burdensome Sabbath laws had turned a joyous day of worship into a day bogged down with weights too heavy for any person to carry. These groups had placed the law above spontaneous love of God. In a way, the law had become their God. Their meticulous observance of their laws kept them from fellowship with God. There was an even greater reason that Jesus attacked the Pharisees' understanding of the Sabbath. He was showing that the Sabbath, the seal of the old covenant, was about to be broken with the inauguration of the new covenant. In attacking the hypocritical use of the Sabbath, which squeezed out acts of mercy and compassion, Jesus was revealing the newness of the wine of his ministry, which was going to burst asunder the wineskins of the old covenant. Jesus' ministry has given his followers freedom from keeping the Sabbath. However, living in such a materialistic era, we need to experience the freedom from bondage to toil and material goods that was the original goal of the commandment to keep the Sabbath. We need a day to worship God, the Father, and Jesus, our Lord. We need a regular time each week to partake of the means of grace. We need a day to exercise our corporate memory, a day to activate among us the redemptive power of the cross. We must seek to recapture the social formative power associated with the Sabbath without making a day of worship a heavy burden.

Just as the liturgical calendar was important to Israel, so too the liturgical calendar is important to the church. Observance of that calendar brings us into contact with the mighty redemptive acts of God on our behalf. Whenever we celebrate these redemptive acts we build the community's memory. More importantly we unleash in our communities of faith the sanctifying power of God's Spirit. A sanctified people is an empowered people, a redemptive force in contemporary society.

I. Regulations regarding Oil for the Lampstand and Bread for the Table of the Presence (24:1–9)

Bibliography

Beck, H. F. "Bread of the Presence." *IDB* 1:464. **Boer, P. A. H. de.** "An Aspect of Sacrifice: I. Divine Bread." In *Studies in the Religion of Ancient Israel.* VTSup 23. Leiden: Brill, 1972.

27–36. **Callaway, P. R.** "ʾRBYH in the Temple Scroll XXIV,8." *RevQ* 12 (1986) 269–70. **Forbes, R. J.** *Studies in Ancient Technology.* Vol. 3. 2nd ed. Leiden: Brill, 1965. **Levine, B. A.** "The Descriptive Tabernacle Texts of the Pentateuch." *JAOS* 85 (1965) 307–18. **Meyers, C. L.** *The Tabernacle Menorah: A Synthetic Study of a Symbol from the Biblical Cult.* AASOR 2. Missoula: Scholars Press, 1976. **Pelletier, A.** "Une particularité du rituel des 'pains d'oblation' conservée par la Septante (Lev. xxiv 8 & Ex. xxv 30)." *VT* 17 (1967) 364–67. **Ross, J. F.** "Oil." *IDB* 3:592–93. **Sperber, D.** "The History of the Menorah." *JJS* 16 (1965) 135–59. **Yarden, L.** *The Tree of Light: A Study of the Menorah, the Seven-Branched Lampstand.* Ithaca: Cornell UP, 1971.

Translation

1 *Yahweh spoke to Moses:* 2 *"Command the Israelites, Let them bring*[a] *you*[b] *pure, pounded olive oil for the light in order that the lamps may be kept burning continually.* 3 *Outside the curtain before the testimony*[a] *in the Tent of Meeting, let Aaron*[b] *attend*[c] *them from evening until morning before Yahweh continually. It is a perpetual decree for your generations.* 4 *He is to keep*[a] *the lamps in trim on the lampstand of pure gold*[b] *before Yahweh continually.*[c]

5 *"You are to take*[a] *fine flour and bake*[ab] *twelve loaves from it; two-tenths of an ephah is to be in each loaf.* 6 *You are to set*[a] *them in two*[b] *rows, six in a row, on the table of pure gold*[c] *before Yahweh.* 7 *In*[a] *each row*[b] *you are to place*[c] *pure frankincense*[d] *so that the bread may be a memorial; it is a gift*[e] *to Yahweh.* 8 *Every Sabbath*[a] *he is to set it*[b] *in order before Yahweh continually; it is from the Israelites as a perpetual covenant.* 9 *They become Aaron's and his sons; and they are to eat them*[ab] *in a holy place, because they are*[c] *most holy from the gifts to Yahweh. It is a perpetual decree."*

Notes

2.a. In this construction the jussive with a *waw* after the imperative expresses the content of the command (Joüon §177j).

2.b. In place of MT אליך, "to you," LXX* reads μοι, "to me."

3.a. עדות, "testimony," is used for the Decalogue both in the phrase לחת עדות, "tablets of the testimony" (Exod 31:18; 32:15) and standing by itself (Exod 25:16, 21). This "testimony" is placed in the Ark of the Covenant (Exod 25:16, 21); this Ark is sometimes called ארן העדות, "the ark of the testimony" (Exod 25:22; 26:33, 34). Only here does the phrase פרכת העדות, "the curtain or veil of the testimony," occur. In Exod 27:21, the parallel text, it is פרכת אשר על־העדות, "the curtain which is on the testimony" (cf. Exod 30:6; Elliger, 327).

3.b. Several Heb. mss, Sam, and LXX add ובניו, "and his sons," as in Exod 27:21 in order that these texts may be in harmony.

3.c. ערך means "arrange, order"; it is used for "setting" tables (Prov 9:2; Isa 21:5; 65:11) and "working in, with" dough (cf. Jastrow, 1118). Durham (*Exodus,* WBC 2, 379; n. 21.a.) interprets ערך in reference to lamps to mean setting them in order, fueling, trimming, and lighting them.

4.a. LXX reads a second person pl form; cf. nn. 5.a., 6.b., 7.c. The pl is consistent with the variant in n. 3.b.

4.b. The meaning of the adj טהרה, "clean, pure," is uncertain. It may describe the lampstand as "clean," ritually prepared for use in the sanctuary. Jewish tradition takes it as a substantive referring to the fact that this piece of furniture is made of pure gold. In v 6 there is a similar use of טהר with the table on which the bread of the Presence was placed. Meyers (*Tabernacle Menorah,* 167–68) suggests that the use of טהרה with מנרה, "lampstand," may describe the "brightness" of the lampstand, in a visual sense and perhaps also in a cosmic sense (cf. Exod 31:8; 39:37). She (195, n. 9) thinks that the association of טהר with table in v 6 has been influenced by the description of the lampstand. It is difficult to decide between these positions; given the occurrence of טהר in v 6, the traditional rendering has been followed.

4.c. In place of MT תמיד, "continually," Sam and LXX have עד בקר, "until morning." Sun ("Investigation," 410) views this as a harmonization with the reading of v 3.
5.a. Cf. n. 4.a.
5.b. אפה, "bake," may take a double acc: to bake something into something (GKC §117ii).
6.a. Cf. n. 4.a.
6.b. Instead of MT שתים, "two," an abs form, Sam reads שתי, "two," a constr.
6.c. Cf. n. 4.b.
7.a. Levine (166) interprets the prep על in this context to mean "near, together with."
7.b. Syr and *Tg. Ps.-J.* read a pl form. PIR (199) interprets the sg as a distributive sg.
7.c. Cf. n. 4.a.
7.d. LXX adds καὶ ἅλα, "and salt."
7.e. In place of MT אשה, "a gift," LXX has the pass ptcp προκείμενα, "laying." On אשה, cf. n. 1:9.g.
8.a. A few Heb. mss, LXX, and Syr omit the second occurrence of ביום השבת, "on the day of the Sabbath."
8.b. The Heb. uses the impf with a pronominal suffix as a virtual pass.
9.a. Instead of MT אכלהו, "they are to eat it [masc]," Sam and *Tg. Neof.* read אכלוה, "they are to eat it [fem]"; this is a case of metathesis of the *waw*. Although the pronoun refers to the loaves collectively, this Eng trans. prefers the pl form for clarity.
9.b. In v 9 there is a fem subj for the first verb and a masc object for the second verb. The subj and obj would seem to need to refer to לחם, "bread," which is masc. Possibly, though, the subj of the first verb is the fem חלה, "loaf of bread," in v 7 (de Boer, "Divine Bread," 31). Certainly this shift in gender is puzzling.
9.c. Sam reads fem היא for MT masc הוא; cf. n. 9.b.

Form/Structure/Setting

Within chaps. 17–26, chap. 24 has anomalous features. While there are reports of two Yahweh speeches to Moses, the focus is not on commissioning Moses to deliver a message to an audience. In the first report Moses is commissioned to command the Israelites to maintain two cultic practices within the sanctuary. In the second report there is an account of a judicial problem along with Yahweh's instructions to Moses specifying the punishment for this violator and the giving of a set of laws for the Israelites.

Another problematic issue is the lack of any connection between the two reports. The introductory formula for the Yahweh speech, v 1, introduces only the speech in vv 2–9. This is reinforced by the compliance report in v 23, which concerns vv 10–22 alone. Why these two short pieces have been placed together remains uncertain. Furthermore, it is difficult to account for the location of these instructions and laws within the context of the laws on holy living. They come between a ritual calendar (chap. 23) and the regulations for the sabbatical year and the year of Jubilee (chap. 25), but this chapter has little to do with calendric concerns save that the ritualistic practices were done on a regular basis. Thus this material seems to be arbitrarily dropped in between chaps. 23 and 25. To resist this conclusion, some scholars explain the location of vv 10–23 as an event that followed closely the revelation of the material in vv 1–9 (Keil and Delitzsch, 453; Harrison, 220). The advantage of this explanation is its recognition that Exodus-Numbers is a webbing of regulations within the context of a narrative. The narratives unfold the story of the wilderness sojourn and provide a life-setting for the regulations. Unfortunately there is no other evidence for evaluating this position. As for the location of the first unit, Dillmann (652) observes that it concerns rituals that use the produce of the harvest (קציר) and the vintage ingathering (אסיף) in the service of Yahweh. In that way these regulations are tied to the festivals regulated in chap. 23, which celebrate the harvesting of those products. From another direction, Bertholet (83) points out that there is a contrast between the focus of chap. 23 on special festivals to Yahweh and that of 24:1–9 on regular, continuous worship of Yahweh. Better explanations for the positions of this chapter elude us. Since the sections of this chapter constitute two distinct speeches, they are treated separately.

The structure of the speech in vv 1–9 may be outlined as follows:

I. Introductory formula (v 1)
II. Speech (vv 2–9)
  A. Concerning oil for the lamp (vv 2aα–4)
    1. Commission formula (v 2aα)
    2. Speech proper (vv 2aβ–4)
      a. Commandment to Israelites about supplying the oil (v 2aβ + b)
      b. Commandment about Aaron's tending the lamp(s) (v 3)
      c. General commandment about this ritual (v 4)
  B. Concerning the bread before Yahweh (vv 5–9)
    1. Instructions to Moses (vv 5–7)
      a. Regarding preparation of the bread (v 5)
      b. Regarding arrangement of the bread on the table in the holy place (vv 6–7)
    2. Instructions to the priests regarding weekly arrangement of the bread on the Sabbath (v 8)
    3. Laws assigning the bread to Aaronites and regulating their eating of it (v 9)

The introductory formula of this speech is typical, but the commission formula is not, for the term צו, "command," is found elsewhere only in 6:2(9). The phrase "command the children of Israel" is, however, found in Num 5:2; 28:2; 34:2; 35:2. Generally Moses is to deliver a message, but here he is to command the children of Israel to carry out the following instructions. It is noteworthy that in the parallel account in Exod 27:20–21, where vv 20–21 are nearly identical to vv 2–3 here, the forms of צוה differ: תצוה, "you are to command" (Exod 27:20), and צו, "command" (Lev 24:2). Haran (*Temples,* 209) suggests that in Exodus, Moses was "forewarned of his future duty" and in Leviticus he was actually ordered to do it.

In these instructions the children of Israel are to bring the pure oil, while the responsibilities within the Tent are given to Moses and Aaron. The precise identity of the antecedent of "you" in the various statements is obscure. In v 2 it seems to be Moses; in that case it may be assumed that he watches over the oil brought by the people for the lamp (v 2aβ+b). The identity of the "you" in vv 5–7, i.e., the one who is in charge of taking the flour, making the bread, and arranging it on the table, is difficult to determine. The immediate assumption is that it is Moses. The wording of vv 8–9, however, assigns to Aaron and his sons the responsibility of replacing the bread and arranging the new loaves on the table. In this light the antecedent of "you" in vv 5–7 may be Aaron. This position receives support in v 3 where Aaron is charged with taking care of the lamps. That other manuscripts and versions read a plural form of "you" in vv 5–7 and "to me" in place of "to you" in v 2 indicates that ancient interpreters also had difficulty in defining the antecedent of "you." If the antecedent of these pronouns is Moses, it may mean that the first time the oil was brought and the bread prepared and arranged, it was Moses' privilege to carry out these instructions. Thereafter, it became the responsibility of Aaron and his sons. This shift in responsibility finds some support in the wording of vv 8–9. In fact, to the hearers of this text, the social context of the rituals may have established the antecedent of "you" as Aaron. This interpretation accounts for each of these directions regarding who would be the one to take on Moses' role. Later 1 Chr 9:32 reports that the Kohathites have the charge of preparing the loaves.

As the outline shows, this regulation has two distinct parts: one concerning the oil for the lamp (vv 2aβ–4) and one concerning the bread before Yahweh (vv 5–9). These two matters, though not always linked together, are related in that both take place in the Holy Place and both are about rituals in handling the regular replenishment of perishable materials.

Beyond this conceptual relationship between the lights and the bread, the instructions concerning the oil and the bread have been linked semantically and structurally. Semantic links include the use of the following terms: (1) תמיד, "continually," is used four times (vv 2, 3, 4, 8) to express the regularity and the permanency of these rituals. (2) ערך, "arrange, set in order, trim" (vv 3, 4, 8), occurs along with מערכת, "row" (vv 6, 7). The primary meaning of ערך goes more naturally with bread than with lights, for one arranges bread on a table, but one does not ordinarily arrange lamps unless this term has the meaning "trim" as a technical meaning (see n. 3.c.). In any case the author employed this verb, though in two different ways, as one of the threads holding these two units together. (3) לקח, "take," occurs in vv 2 and 5, but with different nuances. (4) חק עלם, "a perpetual decree," occurs in vv 3, 9, and ברית עלם, "a perpetual covenant," in v 8. (5) לפני יהוה, "before Yahweh," occurs in vv 3, 4, 6, 8. Each item is placed לפני יהוה, "before Yahweh," i.e., before the most holy place of the sanctuary, and each item is made of the finest material. (6) זך, "pure," occurs with olive oil in v 2 and with frankincense in v 7. (7) טהר, "clean," occurs in vv 4 and 6. The adjective טהר, "clean," is associated with each of the utensils that holds these perishable items (cf. n. 4.b.). The intertwining of this terminology indicates beyond doubt that these two sets of instructions have been composed to occur together.

The structures of vv 2aβ–4 and 5–9 are also somewhat parallel. The instructions of each unit open with the verb לקח, "take" (vv 2, 5), and have the verb ערך, "arrange," at the end (vv 3, 4, 8). The second unit is a little longer and more involved than the first because of the great attention given to the preparation of the flour. If v 4 is an addition, both units then, at one time, ended with the formula חק עלם, "a perpetual decree" (vv 3, 9).

In the first unit three instructions are given. The first instruction is that the children of Israel take (לקח) the oil for the lamp to Moses. The second instruction is that Aaron is to maintain and tend the lamp. The third instruction is that he, assumedly Aaron, is to tend the lamps. In each of these instructions the word תמיד, "continually," emphasizes the regularity of these rituals. The following chart indicates subject, verb, and object of each instruction:

	Subject	Verb	Object
v 2b	children of Israel	לקח "take"	oil
v 3	Aaron	ערך "trim"	lamp
v 4	(Aaron)	ערך "trim"	lamps

The structure of these verses is not merely a list of three items, however. The first two instructions can be clearly distinguished from one another because the priest's duty of tending the lamp must sequentially follow the people's duty of supplying the oil. The relationship between the second and third instructions is less clear, for both pertain to tending (a) lamp(s) by Aaron. In v 4 the plural "lamps" replaces the singular "lamp" and the term מנרה, "lampstand," replaces the term מאור, "light." It is unclear whether the lamp to be tended in v 3 is the same as the lamps in v 4. How is the lamp to be distinguished from the lamps, or, if they are the same, why is v 4, which adds little to v 3, necessary at all? Noth (177) accounts for this variation by claiming that v 4 assimilates the instructions in vv 2–3 to the מנרה, "the lampstand," of Exod 25:31–37. In any case, v 4 has a different origin, for מנרה, "lampstand," is used in place of מאור, "light" (v 2; cf. Exod 39:37), and נרות, "lamps," is used in place of נר, "lamp(s)" (v 3).

The bread of the Presence is mentioned elsewhere in the Pentateuch in the instructions for building a table of acacia wood for the sanctuary (Exod 25:23–30). There is also a reference to this bread being on the table when Moses inspected the finished Tent of Meeting (Exod 39:36). Exod 40:22–23 recounts that Moses set up the table and put the bread on it. It is puzzling, then, that instructions about baking and arranging the bread of the Presence come so much later in Leviticus. One explanation might be that this account in Leviticus treats the ongoing replenishment of perishable materials used in the operation of the cult, whereas the account in Exod 25–40 was primarily concerned with the initial implementation of the cultic practices. In any case this passage provides additional, important details about the bread of the Presence, including the number of loaves, the quantity of flour in each loaf, the weekly replenishment with new bread, and the priests' responsibility of eating the old bread. As elsewhere in Leviticus, the text gives information about important practices at the Tent of Meeting, but the information is wanting because of the sparsity of specific information. In what sense, though, would these practices, which by their very nature would not be visible to the people, have any interest for them? Foremost, the people have the obligation of supplying the oil and the flour for these rituals. Through these instructions they learn about the rituals in which these elements are used. Furthermore, in carrying out these rituals the priests represent the people to God. That is, these rituals are for the benefit of the entire community, not just for the priests. These regulations have been formulated for the instruction of the whole congregation, even though they may have been adapted from the priestly professional knowledge. This speech like the others in Leviticus has been composed for delivery at a festival.

(This material has been prepared in conjunction with Stephen A. Reed, Ph.D.)

Comment

2–3 These verses pertain to the instructions for supplying the oil for the Menorah, the seven-branched מנרה, "lampstand," and for tending it. These instructions treat the oil for the lamp. They have already been given in virtually the same wording in Exod 27:20–21.

The prescription for making the Menorah is found in Exod 25:31–40; the report of its having been made comes in Exod 37:17–24; and the report of its being anointed and set up is found in Exod 40:9, 24–25. In Num 8:1–4, Aaron is directed to place the lamp in the Holy Place in order that it may light the table with the bread of the Presence (Budd, *Numbers,* WBC 5, 86–87). Directions for its transport are found in Num 3:31 and 4:9.

The people are to bring the oil, and Aaron is to trim the נר, "lamps." The olive oil for the lamp has to be of the highest quality; it is to be beaten by hand and strained to ensure its purity (Snaith, 109). Incidentally, it is also to be used with the continual whole offering (Exod 29:40; Num 28:5). This kind of oil burns brightly with little smoke (Durham, *Exodus,* WBC 3, 380). It was valued so highly that it could be used in payment of international debt; for example, in payment on his huge debts to Hiram, the King of Tyre, Solomon sent oil of this quality (1 Kgs 5:25[11]). The מאור, "light," is to burn תמיד, "continually," i.e., every night from evening to morning. מאור may be used in lieu of מנרה, "lampstand," as the phrase מנרת המאר, "the lampstand for the light" in Exod 35:14 attests (Durham, 380). The term תמיד refers to a permanent ritual, but as Haran suggests this does not mean necessarily " 'non–stopping, unceasing, continual,' but rather that the ritual acts in question are to be repeated at regular intervals and at fixed times" (*Temples,* 207). The lamps stayed lit during the night. They were tended twice a day, at dusk and dawn. Josephus refers to a later practice in which three lights of the lampstand were kept burning all the time (*Ant.* 3.8.3).

The use of the term נר, "lamp," needs to be considered, for it is נר, a singular form, in v 2 and נרות, a plural form, in v 4. This double usage occurs elsewhere. Exod 27:20 describes the lighting of a lamp (note also 1 Sam 3:3), but other texts, such as Exod 30:7–8 and Num 8:2–3 refer to the lamps in the plural. Noordtzij (243) claims that the singular נר, "light," of v 2 and the plural נרות, "lights," of v 4 speak of the unity and multiplicity of the seven-branched lampstand. Then it is possible that נר is used collectively as Haran suggests (*Temples,* 208, n. 4). Taking another approach, C. Meyers postulates that there was a single lamp tradition associated with the Tent of Meeting and a plural lamp tradition in connection with the tabernacle. In this passage they were merged together (*Tabernacle Menorah,* 26).

5 The second part of these speeches gives some regulations on the bread for the table of the Presence. This bread is called חלה, "bread" (cf. 2:4), and it is to be made out of סלת, "fine flour" (cf. 2:1). According to the Talmud (*b. Menaḥ.* 76b) the flour is to be sifted eleven times. The bread is often called לחם פנים, "the bread of the Presence" (Exod 25:30; 35:13; 39:36; 1 Sam 21:7[6]; 1 Kgs 7:48; 2 Chr 4:19; NEB, NIV). The precise translation and meaning of the expression "the bread of the Presence" has been debated. The early translations offer a variety of phrases for this bread. The Hebrew means literally "bread of the face" or "facial bread." NJPS uses "bread of display" (Levine, 165). JB has "the bread of the continual offering" (Exod 39:36), and KJV uses "shewbread." De Boer suggests that "*hapānîm* indicates Yhwh's face which might have been portrayed on the loaves by a bread stamp" ("Divine Bread," 35). This is Yahweh's bread, and it is at his disposal (de Boer). Therefore, "Yhwh himself is the host who presents himself to his believers, giving divine strength, divine life" (de Boer, 35). There is evidence that various ways of adorning bread were used in antiquity. G. Galavaris says that "in antiquity, bread and cakes that were to be used for religious purposes were given various forms or had designs pressed upon them relating the bread directly to the deity for whom it was destined or revealing the purpose for which the bread was offered" (*Bread and the Liturgy: The Symbolism of Early Christian and Byzantine*

Bread Stamps [Madison: The University of Wisconsin Press, 1970] 22). This suggestion, however, is doubtful given the second commandment against making any image or likeness of God (Exod 20:4 // Deut 5:8). Johnson, however, takes the position that פנים conveys the meaning that this is Yahweh's personal bread ("Aspects of the use of the term פָּנִים in the Old Testament," in *FS O. Eissfeldt,* ed. J. Fück [Halle und der Salle: Max Niemeyer, 1947] 159). In any case God views this bread, which is placed in his presence, and thus accepts it (Levine, 165). It may be added that this bread is referred to by a variety of terms in the OT. It is called מערכת, "layer-bread," in 1 Chr 9:32; 23:29; Neh 10:34(33); לחם התמיד, "the continual bread" (and the table is שׁלחן הפנים, "the table of the Presence"), in Num 4:7; and לחם קדשׁ, "holy bread," in 1 Sam 21:5(4).

Another issue concerns the size of these loaves. Each loaf is to have two-tenths (of an ephah) of "fine flour" (סלת; cf. 2:1). While the term "ephah" is not in the text, assumedly the "tenth" is a tenth of an ephah (de Vaux, *AI,* 1:200). Determination of the size of an ephah is uncertain. Wenham (310) figures that each loaf had about 3 liters or 3.5 pounds of flour. This amount of flour would have produced a very large loaf indeed.

6 The twelve loaves were placed on a small table (3 feet x 1.5 feet), which was low to the ground (Exod 25:23–30//37:10–16). The twelve loaves represent the twelve tribes, although the text does not explicitly make that affirmation (cf. Josephus, *Ant.* 3.6.6). Since the surface of the table is roughly 3 feet by 1.5 feet or 90 by 45 centimeters and since it also had to have room for other utensils (Exod 25:29), it is hard to imagine how all of the bread could have fit on the table. Were the loaves laid out in two rows, or were they stacked in two columns of six loaves each? Given the size of these loaves, some scholars have suggested that the bread may have been in two piles rather than two rows. That the way of handling these loaves varied is supported by the fact that later sources refer to more than one table. The Chronicler mentions tables for the bread of the Presence (1 Chr 28:16); the Solomonic Temple had ten tables according to 2 Chr 4:8, 19. Conversely, 1 Kgs 7:48 mentions only one table.

7 לבנה זכה, "pure incense," is to be placed with each row. But where is this incense to be placed? Noordtzij (243) thinks that originally the incense was sprinkled on the bread; but the fact that the priests ate the bread would argue against this position. Later tradition had the incense put into two golden cups next to the bread; then the incense was burned on the altar (Noordtzij, 243). Possibly the incense was placed on top of the piles of bread. When the incense burns, God smells the pleasant aroma and remembers the bread of the Presence. The burning incense makes this ritual אזכרה, "a memorial" (cf. 2:2); it stirs God's memory, leading him to participate in covenant fellowship with his people.

8–9 According to vv 8–9, fresh bread is to be placed on the table each Sabbath. Then the priests are to eat the old bread. This regulation is unusual, for bread is usually baked and eaten on the same day. Whether the loaves are to be made without leaven is not expressly stated. De Boer points out the obvious problem that "the bread would have been moulded and stone-hard" over a week later when the priests ate it ("Divine Bread," 27). Thus the fact that the priests are to eat these loaves seven days later certainly favors the cakes' being unleavened. In later sources it is explicitly stated that the bread was unleavened (*m. Menaḥ.* 5.1; Josephus, *Ant.* 3.6.6; 10.7).

Being most holy, this bread could only be eaten by the priests in a holy place (cf. 6:9[16]). The bread is first given to Yahweh, and he, in turn, gives it back to the priests. It is possible that the priests' partaking of this bread symbolized that all members of the twelve tribes are in table fellowship with Yahweh.

Explanation

The lampstand and the table of the bread of Presence along with the altar of incense were the only pieces of furniture inside the Holy Place of the tabernacle. The lamps on the stand and the bread on the table had to be tended on a regular basis. The lamps were trimmed and replenished with oil regularly in order that they might burn throughout the night, every night. The bread of the Presence was changed weekly.

Unfortunately more is not said about the nature and significance of these rituals. It can be imagined that these rites provided Israel with powerful symbols. The continually burning lamp reminded her that God is the God of light. He is to be worshiped in light and not in darkness (cf. Isa 45:18–19). The table with the twelve loaves of bread on it represented the twelve tribes in fellowship with God. That is, God served as the host, having a meal prepared for the twelve tribes at his place of residence. This meal was eaten weekly by the priests as representatives of the people inside the holy chamber in the presence of God.

While the instructions governing the maintenance and the use of the oil and the bread of the Presence are minimal, these laws were not to be observed so rigidly that they deny desperate human need. Once when David was an outlaw and closely pursued by King Saul, he and his men hungered greatly (1 Sam 21:2–7[1–6]). They stopped at the sanctuary of Nob, where Ahimelech was serving as priest. David expressed to the high priest their desperate need of food. Ahimelech responded by handing over to them the bread of the Presence. He required only that David and his men were not unclean from contact with women. This account has been raised in importance by Jesus' use of it to counter the Pharisees' complaint that his disciples broke the Sabbath by plucking some grain to eat while going through a field (Matt 12:1–8; Mark 2:23–28; Luke 6:1–5). Based on the tradition that categorized such activity as harvesting, the Pharisees interpreted the act of the disciples as work, meaning that the disciples had broken the fourth commandment of the Decalogue. In response Jesus justified the activity of his disciples by citing the bold action of Ahimelech on behalf of David. Ahimelech took that which was most holy and gave it to laity without divine condemnation. Jesus was arguing that common sense and compassion for human need far outweigh a stringent interpretation of the law.

These two symbols of light and bread were taken by Jesus and applied to himself. He said, "I am the light of the world" (John 8:12; 9:5). On another occasion he said, "I am the bread of life" (John 6:35, 48). By these sayings Jesus made the claim to fulfill the functions of the Holy Place of the Tent of Meeting for all who believe on him. The great benefits of the offerings and rituals done at this sanctuary are now provided to the Church through Jesus. Believers have the true light that lights the entire world, the light that shines in darkness and does not go out (John 1:5). And they partake of the body of Jesus in Holy Communion; in so doing they have table fellowship with the Triune God by reason of the atoning merits of Jesus' death. After taking the Eucharist, all the communicants have the confidence that their sins are forgiven and that they are accepted as members of God's family.

J. A Case of Blasphemy and Laws on Personal Injury (24:10–23)

Bibliography

Alt, A. "Zur Talionsformel." *ZAW* n.f. 11 (1934) 303–5 (= *Kleine Schriften zur Geschichte des Volkes Israel I.* Münich: C. H. Beck'sche Verlagsbuchhandlung, 1953. 341–44. = In *Um das Prinzip der Vergeltung in Religion und Recht des Alten Testaments.* Ed. K. Koch. Wege der Forschung 125. Darmstadt: Wissenschaftliche Buchgesellschaft, 1972. 407–11). **Brichto, H. C.** *The Problem of "Curse" in the Hebrew Bible.* SBLMS 13. Philadelphia: Society of Biblical Literature and Exegesis, 1963. **Crüsemann, F.** "'Auge um Auge . . .' (Ex 21,24f). Zum sozialgeschichtlichen Sinn des Talionsgesetzs im Bundesbuch." *EvT* 47 (1987) 411–26. **Daube, D.** *Studies in Biblical Law.* Cambridge: Cambridge UP, 1947; New York: KTAV, 1969. 102–53. **Diamond, A. S.** "An Eye for an Eye." *Iraq* 19 (1957) 151–55. **Doron, P.** "A New Look at an Old Lex." *JANESCU* 1 (1969) 21–27. **Finkelstein, J. J.** "Ammiṣaduqa's Edict and the Babylonian 'Law Codes.'" *JCS* 15 (1961) 91–104. **Fishbane, M.** *Biblical Interpretations in Ancient Israel.* Oxford: Clarendon Press, 1985. **Fisher, E. J.** "*Lex Talionis* in the Bible and Rabbinic Tradition." *Journal of Ecumenical Studies* 19 (1982) 582–87. **Frymer-Kensky, T.** "Tit for Tat: The Principle of Equal Retribution in Near Eastern and Biblical Law." *BA* 43 (1980) 230–34. **Gabel, J. B.**, and **Wheeler, C. B.** "The Redactor's Hand in the Blasphemy Pericope of Leviticus xxiv." *VT* 30 (1980) 227–29. **Hayes, J. H.** "Restitution, Forgiveness, and the Victim in Old Testament Law." *Trinity University Studies in Religion* 11 (1982) 1–23. **Levy, L.** *Treason against God: A History of the Offense of Blasphemy.* New York: Schocken Books, 1981. **Livingston, D. H.** "The Crime of Leviticus xxiv 11." *VT* 36 (1986) 352–54. **McCarthy, C.** *The Tiqqune Sopherim.* Göttingen: Vandenhoeck & Ruprecht, 1981. **Mikliszanski, J. K.** "The Law of Retaliation and the Pentateuch." *JBL* 66 (1947) 295–303. **Mittwoch, H.** "The Story of the Blasphemer Seen in a Wider Context." *VT* 15 (1965) 386–89. **Reed, S.** "Blasphemy in the Hebrew Bible." Paper presented at Annual Meeting of the Pacific Coast Region of SBL, March 17, 1989. **Scharbert, J.** "«Fluchen» und «Segnen» im Alten Testament." *Bib* 39 (1958) 1–26. **Schult, H. S.** "Lev 24:15b und 16a," *DBAT* 7 (1974) 31–32. **Thiselton, A.** "The Supposed Power of Words in the Biblical Writings." *JTS* n.s. 25 (1974) 283–99. **Weingreen, J.** "The Case of the Blasphemer (Leviticus xxiv 10ff.)." *VT* 22 (1972) 118–23. **Weismann, J.** "Talion und öffentliche Strafe im Mosaischen Rechte." In *Um das Prinzip der Vergeltung in Religion und Recht des Alten Testaments.* Ed. K. Koch. Wege der Forschung 125. Darmstadt: Wissenschaftliche Buchgesellschaft, 1972. 325–404.

Translation

10*Now an Israelite*[a] *woman's son, whose father was an Egyptian, came out of his dwelling*[b] *into the camp of*[b] *the Israelites. Then the Israelite woman's son and an Israelite*[c] *began to quarrel*[d] *in the camp.* 11*The Israelite woman's son then misspoke*[a] *the Name*[b] *and cursed.*[c] *They brought him to Moses. His mother's name was Shelomith,*

the daughter of Dibri, of the tribe of Dan. 12 *They put him*[a] *in custody waiting for the will*
of Yahweh to be revealed[b] *to them.*[c]
13 *Then Yahweh said to Moses:* 14 *"Lead the one who has cursed outside the camp. Let*
all who heard him lay their hands on his head, and let all the congregation[a] *stone him.*
15 *You are to speak*[a] *to the Israelites: Whoever*[b] *curses his God*[c] *will be held responsible for*
his sin.[d] 16 *One who misspeaks the Name of Yahweh will be put to death. The entire con-*
gregation must surely stone[a] *him. Whenever anyone, either the resident alien or the*
native,[b] *misspeaks the Name,*[c] *he will be put to death.* 17 *Whenever any person strikes and*
kills a human,[b] *he will be put to death.* 18 *Whoever*[a] *strikes and kills a beast*[b] *will make it*
good, life for life. 19 *When one causes a disfigurement in his associate, it will be done to*
him as he has done: 20 *fracture for fracture, eye for eye, tooth for tooth; just as he has*
disfigured a person, it will be done to him. 21 *Whoever strikes and kills a beast will make*
it good;[a] *whoever strikes and kills a human*[b] *will be put to death.*[c] 22 *You*[a] *are to have one*
standard[b] *for the resident alien and for the native, for I am Yahweh your God."*
23 *Then Moses spoke to the Israelites, and they brought the one who had cursed outside*
the camp and stoned him with stones.[a] *Thus the Israelites did just as Yahweh had com-*
manded Moses.

Notes

10.a. The gentilic of יִשְׂרָאֵל, "Israel," occurs infrequently: יִשְׂרְאֵלִית (fem) three times, here and v 11, and יִשְׂרְאֵלִי (masc) here and 2 Sam 17:25 (Joüon §88Mg).

10.b-b. This phrase has been added to the Eng trans. to clarify the situation.

10.c. Sam does not have the article on this word; this is the preferred reading (so Elliger, 330).

10.d. The rarely used נצה I means "struggle, fight with" (BDB, 663; KB, 675); it occurs in the niph in Exod 2:13; 21:22; Deut 25:11, and in the hiph in Num 26:9 (2x) and Ps 60:2 (title). These references indicate that the fighting was fierce. מַצָּה, "strife, contention," is a noun from this root (Isa 58:4; Prov 13:10; 17:19).

11.a. It is debated whether ויקב comes from the root נקב, "pierce, bore through," or from קבב, "curse" (BDB, 867; if from קבב, then the form here is an example of Aram impf doubling [GKC §67g]). The basic meaning of נקב is "bore, pierce through," e.g., boring a hole in the lid of a box (2 Kgs 12:10[9]) and carving a tunnel out of rock (so used in the Siloam inscription). In addition to these concrete meanings, this root means "name, designate." Those, such as Bertholet (85), who take ויקב from קבב, "curse," face the difficulty of the use of the ptcp form נקב in v 16 unless there is a play on the roots קבב and נקב between vv 11 and 16, as Bertholet thinks. Current understanding of the meaning of these terms, however, fails to uncover that wordplay. Another position suggests a form נקב II as a by-form of קבב (BDB, 867; *TWOT* 596).

11.b. LXX mss and Tg add יהוה, "lord"; cf. n. 16.b. Some (e.g., Baentsch, 420) postulate that the original text read either שֵׁם יהוה, "name of Yahweh," or יהוה, "Yahweh," and later sources either substituted the term השׁם or removed the name יהוה so that the personal name of God would not stand after a verb meaning "curse."

11.c. The two verbs for cursing ויקב . . . ויקלל may be taken together so that the latter modifies the former: "he spoke a curse blasphemously" (Levine, 166).

12.a. 11QpaleoLev reads the sign of the acc with pronominal suffix יניחו אתו, "they put him," instead of the pronoun attached to the verb as MT ויניחהו.

12.b. פרשׁ occurs only four times in the OT (qal only here; niph in Ezek 34:12; pual in Num 15:34 and Neh 8:8). It has the meaning "make distinct, clear, translate clearly" (BDB, 831; KB, 918). Fishbane (*Biblical Interpretation,* 100–102) renders it "to make a legal ruling." The noun פָּרָשָׁה, "precise statement, exact amount (of money)," appears in Esth 4:7, and "full account (of one's deeds)" is found (NIV) in Esth 10:2. In Prov 23:32, יַפְרִשׁ is taken by KB as from this root, but BDB assigns it to a different root, פרשׁ II.

12.c. Instead of MT לָהֶם, "them," LXX and Vg^{mss} read לוֹ, "him."

14.a. Cf. n. 4:13.a.

15.a. In place of MT תדבר לאמר, "you are to speak, saying," LXX has *λάλησον καὶ ἐρεῖς πρὸς αὐτούς,* "speak and say to them."

15.b. On the distributive use of איש איש, "a man, a man," see n. 20:2.b.
15.c. In place of MT אלהיו, "his God," LXX[BA] reads *θεόν*, "God."
15.d. Cf. n. 5:1.b.
16.a. The pl verb stresses that each member of the congregation is to participate in the stoning. The inf abs standing before the verb underscores the congregation's obligation to take such action (cf. GKC §113n).
16.b. The use of the prep כ . . . כ, "like . . . as well as," communicates that the parties are on the same level (*IBHS* §11.2.9b; cf. §38.5, n. 29). Other laws expressly addressed to foreign residents include Exod 12:19, 49; Lev 16:29; 17:15; 18:26; Num 9:14; 15:30 (Wenham, 311).
16.c. LXX adds *κυρίου*, "the Lord," so that this phrase conforms to its occurrence at the beginning of this verse; perhaps יהוה was accidentally omitted from MT; cf. n. 11.b.
17.a. The seeming tautological terms נפש אדם, "a person, a man or human," also occur together in Num 19:11, but with a different nuance—"any human corpse" (Baentsch, 421). Interestingly the law in v 18 uses נפש, "person," and the one in v 21 אדם, "man."
17.b. LXX adds *καὶ ἀποθάνῃ*, "and he dies."
18.a. Some Heb. mss, LXX, and Vg omit נפש, "person."
18.b. Cf. n. 17.b.
21.a. LXX omits "the one smiting a beast shall make restitution."
21.b. Cf. n. 17.b.
21.c. LXX reads מות יומת, "he will surely die," as in v 17.
22.a. LXX does not have anything for לכם, "for you."
22.b. *BHS* and GKC §134d propose to read an abs noun in place of a noun in constr, since אחד, "one," follows the noun; cf. Num 15:16. משפט, "judgment, sentence, ordinance," may also mean "norm, standard" (Levine, 168).
23.a. Syr adds וימת, "so that he dies."

Form/Structure/Setting

This section has three units: a report of an incident of blasphemy and the judicial consequences (vv 10–12), a report of a speech by Yahweh to Moses (vv 13–22), and a compliance report (v 23). The thread connecting these units is the case of the blasphemer. The structure of this section may be outlined as follows:

I. The case of the blasphemer (vv 10–12)
  A. Blasphemy spoken during a quarrel (vv 10–11aα)
  B. Confinement of blasphemer while awaiting direction from God (vv 11aβ–12)
II. Yahweh's announcement of a solution to the case of the blasphemer and other laws (vv 13–22)
  A. Introductory formula (v 13)
  B. Announcement proper and laws (vv 14–22)
    1. Instructions about the blasphemer's sentence (v 14)
    2. Commission to Moses to address people (vv 15–22)
      a. Commission formula (v 15a)
      b. Speech proper (vv 15b–22)
        1) Specific laws (vv 15b–21)
          a) Regarding cursing God (vv 15b–16) — *Law letter*
            (1) Concerning cursing God/gods (v 15b) — A
            (2) Concerning blasphemy of Yahweh's name (v 16) — B
              (a) Basic law (v 16a) — A
              (b) Legal principle that law of blasphemy applies alike to native and resident alien (v 16b)
          b) Regarding killing and personal injury (vv 17–21)
            1) Laws (vv 17–21)
              (a) Concerning killing a human (v 17) — C
              (b) Concerning killing a beast (v 18) — D

(c) Concerning injury to a human (vv 19–20) E
(i) Case (v 19a)
(ii) Regulation: *lex talionis* (vv 19b–20)
(d) Concerning killing a beast (v 21a) F
(e) Concerning killing a human (v 21b) G
2) Legal principle that laws apply alike to native and resident alien (v 22)
a) Legal principle (v 22a)
b) Formula of Yahweh's self-introduction (v 22b)

III. Compliance report of carrying out penalty against the blasphemer by Moses and people (v 23)
A. Report of Moses' delivery of Yahweh's message (v 23aα)
B. Report of people's compliance (v 23aβ–b)

An analysis of the narrative pattern of this pericope uncovers two basic parts: the problem and the solution. Based on C. Westermann's definition of a narrative, i.e., "a narrative gives literary form to a sequence of events leading from tension to its resolution" (C. Westermann, *The Promises to the Fathers: Studies on the Patriarchal Narratives*, tr. D. Green [Philadelphia: Fortress, 1980] 36), this passage qualifies as a narrative.

This section is distinct within Leviticus in that a Yahweh speech to Moses is headed by a narrative functioning as a framework for the following laws. The structure of chap. 10, nevertheless, has some similarity to this pattern. After the account of the death of Nadab and Abihu, Aaron's sons (10:1–7), Yahweh gives Aaron a specific law plus general instructions (10:8–11).

M. Fishbane (*Biblical Interpretations,* 98), furthermore, has shown that this case is structurally and substantively similar to three other cases in the Pentateuch, which are also "*ad hoc* legal situations set during the period of the desert wanderings" (Num 9:6–14; 15:32–36; 27:1–11). In all of these cases a situation arises that cannot be adjudicated on the basis of any legal precedents. Therefore, in order to resolve the problem the Israelites must seek more guidance. In the case at hand, the leaders took the case to the supreme authority, i.e., first to Moses and then to God. According to Fishbane, the pattern of these incidents is fourfold: (1) a difficult case is brought to Moses (v 11); (2) uncertainty about the specific law for adjudicating the case on hand leads to God being consulted (v 12); (3) Moses receives specific instructions from Yahweh (vv 13–14); (4) there is a report that the instructions received from Yahweh have been carried out (v 23; Fishbane, 102). This pattern may indicate the basic protocol that the community followed in resolving particularly perplexing legal cases.

In this passage, unfortunately, the precise reason for the difficulty in setting the punishment is not stated. The problem was not deciding whether a trial was needed, since the act of blasphemy had taken place in public, but the need to render a just sentence. Fishbane (*Biblical Interpretations,* 101) puts forth two fundamental questions that this case raised: is a half-Israelite subject to the law against blaspheming God or cursing a prince (Exod 22:27[28]), and what is the proper punishment for a half-Israelite who violates this law? The question in applying this law thus concerns the status of a half-breed. That accounts for the great attention the text gives to the offender's lineage. This issue became very important in exilic or post-exilic times (Noth, 179). But that fact does not dictate that this situation was composed for that era, because the issue of misusing God's name knows no time line.

Whether this case was initially a single incident, its canonical location as the first instance of blasphemy recorded raises this account to the paradigmatic case for blasphemy. This position carries over to laws in vv 15 and 16; they become the basis for all future legislation about blasphemy.

In the second part of the Yahweh speech (vv 15–22), Yahweh commissions Moses (v 15a) to deliver a message containing seven laws to the Israelites (vv 15b–22). Each of these laws may be divided into two essential parts (see the outline above): statement of the case and regulation of the case. Nevertheless, it is not a simple matter to account for the assembling of this series. There is no discernible common theme, and the formulations of the cases and regulations vary. The first case is expressed by איש איש, "anyone" (v 15b), and the following cases are alternated by participial formulations (vv 16, 18, 21) and by איש כי, "if a human" (vv 17, 19). This style is made more complex by the use of two participial clauses in v 21. As for the penalties, there are a variety of formulations: מות יומת, "he will surely die" (vv 16a, 17), יומת, "he will die" (vv 16b, 21), שלם, "restitution" (vv 18, 21), נשא חטאו, "be held responsible" (v 15), and *lex talionis* (vv 19–20). These facts display the dissimilarities in this series of laws.

A careful observation of this material, however, provides some interesting unifying points. First, the principle that there is one standard for both the alien as well as the citizen receives stress. This principle is attached to the law in v 16b, and it occurs again in v 22 as a general principle indicating that it applies to all the laws in this series. This principle is very important for the case at hand, although no clear statement in any of these laws is made as to the legal status of a half-breed. Second, the laws identified as A-D plus F-G occur in pairs. Both laws A and B regulate blasphemy/cursing. Both laws C and D pertain to killing—first a human and second a beast. Both laws F and G pertain to killing—first a beast and second a human. Law E presents the principle of *lex talionis*; it is stated first in principle (v 19b), and it is restated in detail (v 20). Third, there is a chiastic pattern among the laws in vv 16b–22 (B:C:D:E::F:G:v 22a). Law C is identical in subject matter, though not in structure, to law G, and law D is nearly identical to law F. Law B has a point in contact with the concluding principle in that both contain the phrase כגר כאזרח, "as is the resident alien, as the citizen." In this chiasm law E, which presents the principle of *lex talionis* as its regulation, stands at the center of the series of laws (cf. Wenham, 312); this general legal principle is, therefore, the point of emphasis. Fourth, there is a contrast between the first two laws and the rest of the laws; the first two laws concern an offense committed against the deity, and the next five laws pertain to offenses against humans or animals. These observations disclose that these laws have two foci. The chiastic structure focuses on the principle of *lex talionis* stated at the center, while the recounting of the incident of the half-breed's act of blasphemy focuses on the laws against cursing the name of God at vv 15–16. By employing both of these literary techniques, the speaker highlights both a specific law and the principle underlying the laws on personal injury. It is clear that these laws have been artfully compiled for their present setting in the report of this specific case of blasphemy.

As for the compliance report (v 23), it consists of two parts corresponding to the two main parts of vv 13–22. Moses first delivers a message (דבר) in v 23a; this corresponds to the message Yahweh delivers (דבר) in vv 15–22. Then the congregation is to הוציא, "bring out," the blasphemer for execution (v 23aβ–b); this step corresponds to the command found in v 14 to הוצא, "bring out," the blasphemer. It also establishes a link all the way back to the opening word of the narrative, ויצא, "and he went out" (v 10). By content this verse ties primarily to the second unit, but the use of this subtle chiastic pattern binds the compliance report to the whole section. Nevertheless, the pattern of this verse does not dictate the structure of this passage.

Elliger (330) defines the genre of this section as a legal aetiology. Whether or not one accepts this classification, the attaching of these laws to the account of blasphemy makes the legal instructions much more vivid and forceful (cf. Elliger, 330).

(This material has been prepared in conjunction with Stephen A. Reed, Ph.D.)

Comment

10–11 One day a man born to an Israelite mother and an Egyptian father יצא, "went out," into the midst of the Israelites. Keil and Delitzsch (453) understand this wording to mean that the man left his encampment, which was set apart from the main camp where the Israelites lived. The text makes it clear that this man was of mixed blood. The man's mother's name, her family's name, and her tribe are given to demonstrate her unquestionable Israelite lineage. Inside the main camp this man got into a quarrel with an Israelite. In the heat of the contest he pronounced (נקב) the name of God, Yahweh, in such a way that he קלל, "cursed" or "blasphemed." Regrettably the text does not state what the man said or did that earned the charge of blasphemy. This raises many questions. Was the blasphemy connected directly with the fighting? Did the half-breed curse the Israelite by uttering God's name or by invoking God? Or did he misspeak God's personal name, or did he direct his curse against Yahweh in the name of Yahweh?

The interpretation of this incident is hindered by our lack of knowledge about the precise meanings of the two terms used for cursing, נקב and קלל. In fact, trying to gain a precise understanding of the ancient view of blasphemy is itself very difficult, for the ancient Hebrews wished to avoid any hint of cursing God in speaking about cursing God (Reed, "Blasphemy"). This perspective, therefore, led them to employ all sorts of euphemisms when referring to blasphemy; e.g., Job's wife counsels Job to curse (ברך, [lit.] "bless") God and die (Job 2:9). The primary reason for the use of euphemisms in this regard was to escape the conundrum that writing or saying exactly what had been said in an act of blasphemy would itself be an act of blasphemy. Therefore, the words chosen here for "curse" are most likely mild words for this type of speech.

An added difficulty is that while there are several Hebrew words for cursing, there is no technical Hebrew term for blasphemy. A study of נקב and קלל indicates that both have a wide range of meanings. Since נקב has as its object השם, "the Name," in v 11 and its fuller form שׁם יהוה, "the name of Yahweh," in v 16, it appears that נקב is the lighter term. נקב means "bore through, stipulate, determine, name, designate" (by a name, either positively [Amos 6:1] or negatively) (Prov 11:26; KB, 678–79). With this range of meanings it is clear how נקב may serve as a euphemism for "belittle, defame, use disparagingly." In this light Gabel and Wheeler (*VT* 30 [1980] 229) hold that the half-breed merely spoke the special name of God. Others, however, take נקב to mean to "utter the name of God with impious and contemptuous words" (Weingreen, *VT* 22 [1972] 121; cf. J.

Scharbert, "נָקַב *nāqab*," *TWAT* 5:590–91). According to this second position, נקב conveyed to the ancient audience the aggravated and calumnious way the divine name was spoken, but this position seems to be reading too much into this word. As for קלל, it means "to be swift, slight, be lightly esteemed," "curse," i.e., treat with contempt (BDB, 886; C. A. Keller, "קלל *qll* leicht sein," *THAT* 2:641–43). In only two OT references does it have אלהים, "God," as its object, v 15 and Exod 22:27(28). 1 Sam 3:13 is considered by most to be a third such reference; there the MT reads להם, "to them," in place of אלהים, "God." The MT is considered to be one of the *tiqqune sopherim*, i.e., a text in which the scribes have changed an offensive or embarrassing reading, such as one that is too anthropomorphic, to an easier reading. Three other times in this passage (vv 11, 14, 23) קלל is used for "blasphemy," but without an object. The reluctance of the ancient Israelite authors to use a name of God with קלל is very evident. This indicates that קלל was moving away from its literal meaning "to esteem lightly" to "to curse." Nevertheless, Keller (*THAT* 2:644) states that the literal meaning stands behind its use as a word for "cursing," distinguishing it from harsher words for cursing like ארר and אלה.

In this passage the use of קלל, "curse," as a *waw* consecutive after נקב further defines נקב. The two terms together may be a hendiadys (Levine, 166). Certainly these two verbs are to be taken together, indicating that they describe a single act of wrongdoing, not two distinct acts (Livingston, *VT* 36 [1986] 353). It may be concluded that the use of נקב with השם, "the Name," means that this half-breed distinctly spoke the revealed name of God and that the addition of קלל means that he spoke it in a disparaging manner. Whether he cursed his Israelite opponent using God's name or cursed God himself is difficult to know. Based on a passage in the Mishnah (*Sanh.* 7.5), Livingston (353) concludes that the reason this case was treated so seriously was that the offender cursed Yahweh with the very name of Yahweh.

Those who heard this man's words perceived that he had directly violated the third commandment of the Decalogue (Exod 20:7//Deut 5:11; cf. Exod 22:27[28]). Because of the severity of this offense, they brought him immediately to Moses. Moses put him into custody until he could learn from God exactly what should be done with this offender. The question before the community was not the guilt of the half-breed, but what was the appropriate penalty by reason of his ambivalent social standing.

12 The use of prisons in the ancient Middle East was minimal. In a small country or among a tribal group they were virtually nonexistent. So the reference to detaining this guilty person in משמר, "a guard house," is a rare example of imprisonment in ancient Israel. A similar example of detainment is reported in Num 15:34.

13–14 Yahweh answered Moses by instructing him to take the blasphemer outside the camp; all who had heard the curse had to lay their hands on that person's head, and then all the congregation was to stone him. The death penalty attended this offense, for it was a sin against the very essence of God as borne by his Name. The execution was to be done outside the camp in order to avoid defiling the camp by taking a human life. But why did the hearers have to lay their hands on his head? One view is that all who heard the blasphemy had incurred guilt due to the gravity of that sin (Wenham, 311). Offering another view, Noordtzij describes the hearers as being "infected by the potent magical words"

(245). A third view holds that the hearers had to remove the guilt they had incurred by hearing the blasphemy (Porter, 194). But there is a fourth way to view the responsibility of the hearers. Their hearing the words of blasphemy made them witnesses to a transgression of one of the commandments in the Decalogue; thereby they became obligated to take the proper steps leading to the offender's conviction and punishment (cf. 5:1). Their burden as conveyed by the word נשׂא, "bear," was not in becoming guilty by hearing, but in having to take action against another person. Such action required them to overcome the natural human resistance toward accusing a fellow human. When they stoned the offender, they were to "lay their hands on his head" (cf. 1:4). This gesture meant that they acknowledged that this person was the guilty party and that his blood was on his own head; i.e., because this party was guilty, the hearers did not incur any guilt in the taking of his life (cf. 20:9).

15–16 Attached to the report on this incident of blasphemy is a series of laws. The first two laws state the penalty for blasphemy, distinguishing between cursing God or gods and misspeaking the name of Yahweh. The former act carries an indefinite penalty; i.e., a person who commits such a sin must be held responsible for his sin. The latter offense carries the death penalty. The distinction between these two laws rests on two issues. First, they use different terms for God. In v 15 it is אלהיו, which is either "his God," the Creator of heaven and earth, or "his gods," the deities of other nations and even evil spirits (so Schult, *DBAT* 7 [1974] 31). In v 16 the sin is against יהוה, "Yahweh," the specific name of the God who has revealed himself to Israel (cf. Exod 6:3). The second distinction is that the first law uses קלל, "curse," and the second law נקב, "misspeak a name" (see vv 11–12). The first law, therefore, is general; if a person, an Israelite or a foreigner, curses God or the gods, the god he has cursed will punish that person's brazen presumption.

Blasphemy against foreign gods was not considered a serious matter in ancient Israel. The incident of Gideon's pulling down the altar of Baal and cutting down the sacred grove lends support to this position (Judg 6:25–32). For desecrating a Baalistic shrine, the people demanded Gideon's death, but Gideon's father intervened on his son's behalf, arguing, "If [Baal] is a god, let him contend for himself, because his altar has been pulled down" (Judg 6:31). This argument moved the people to let Gideon go free.

The second law rules that no person, neither an Israelite nor a foreigner, may distinctly speak in a light or disparaging manner the name Yahweh, the revealed name of God. Whenever such a misuse of Yahweh's name should occur, the עדה, "congregation" (cf. 4:13), becomes obligated to punish the blasphemer by stoning that person to death, for the community found its existence to reside in its devotion to Yahweh. The death penalty is stressed by being expressed three times in v 15: twice with יומת, "he is to be put to death" (cf. 20:2, 9) and once by רגם, "to stone" (cf. 20:2, 27). Furthermore, this law expressly states that it applies both to an Israelite citizen (אזרח) and to a resident alien (גר). The inclusion of this detail on the extent of this law plus its repetition in v 22, forming a chiastic structure (see *Form/Structure/Setting*), indicate that a primary reason for choosing the above case to frame this group of laws was to underscore the standard that those of mixed blood and foreigners living in Israel are subject to the laws of blasphemy, whether or not they worship Yahweh as their God.

Later Jewish tradition interpreted vv 15 and 16 in an expanded manner, claiming that one should not curse using any name of God. They held that whoever uses the Name will be stoned, but if a person uses a name other than the tetragrammaton, that one will be either scourged or banished (*m. Sanh.* 7.5; *b. Sanh.* 56). Furthermore, these laws along with other passages inspired the Jews of the Second Temple period to discontinue pronouncing YHWH, the tetragrammaton. As a result of this position, when contemporary Jews come across this name for God while reading the Scriptures, they usually say either אדני, "my Lord," or השם, "the Name."

17 The penalty for murder is death. The law makes a distinction between manslaughter and murder (Exod 21:12–14).

18 In the case of killing an animal, the person who causes the death of an animal is responsible for making restitution for the loss. Why is such a situation even considered? The phrase מכה נפש, "one who smites a 'soul'," is common to both this law and the preceding one on the murder of a human. Since the shedding of an animal's blood is held so highly in the OT laws of Leviticus (esp. chap. 17), it might have been possible for some to set forth the position that anyone who kills an animal is worthy of the death penalty. This law countered that possibility. It requires that just compensation be made (שלם) for the slain animal, as the brief statement of *lex talionis*—נפש תחת נפש, "life for life"—communicates. This principle will be expanded in the next set of laws.

19–20 This set of laws opens with a specific law (v 19), moves to a generalized list of injuries (v 20a), and returns to a specific law (v 20b). The issue in v 19 concerns causing a מום, "disfigurement," any type of an enduring bodily mutilation, in an associate or neighbor (עמית; cf. 5:21[6:2]). In 21:17 and 22:20–21 מום stands for various physical deformities (Levine, 168). The principle of punishing an offender with the same injury that he has inflicted is called *lex talionis. Lex talionis* is the standard of justice, one for one, not two or more for one or one for two or more. It sets a measurable, precise, equivalent penalty for each offense. It stands as the basic principle in several ancient judicial systems; e.g., it is found in the Code of Hammurabi (§190) and before that in the laws of Lipit-Ishtar (§25). There is a major difference between the Hebraic law and the Code of Hammurabi, though, for in the latter code this standard is applied only in the case of freemen.

The occurrence of *lex talionis* in the OT used to be quite embarrassing to interpreters who viewed it as a remnant of a barbaric society. Recent study, however, has turned this opinion on its head. Scholars have discovered that the laws of Eshnunna (§§42–48) and the laws of Ur-Nammu (§§15–19), which predate the Code of Hammurabi by a few centuries, set fines for personal injury. Only injuries against the gods and the king were treated seriously. Later the laws of Lipit-Ishtar and the Code of Hammurabi introduced the principle of *lex talionis.* Thereby these law codes elevated injuries against persons from purely civil torts to criminal law, according to J. J. Finkelstein (*JCS* 15 [1961] 98; A. Diamond, *Iraq* 19 [1957] 154; T. Frymer-Kensky, *BA* 43 [1980] 233). These lawgivers had come to realize that inflicting personal injury damages both the welfare of society and the moral order in the community (Finkelstein, 98). This does not mean, however, that "tit for tat" was practiced literally, either in Babylon or in ancient Israel. In fact, in some texts where this principle is stated, it cannot be meant literally. In Deut

19:20–21, e.g., this principle comes after laws against acting as a malicious witness in order to provide a legal principle for determining the just retribution deserved by one who is guilty of being a false witness (T. Frymer-Kensky, 232).

Additional support for the position that *lex talionis* was not practiced literally in ancient Israel is provided by the fact that only two texts report the penalty of mutilation. According to Deut 25:12, a woman who tries to help her husband during a fight by seizing his opponent's genitals is to have her hand cut off. In Num 16:14 there is a reference to plucking out an eye as punishment, though this reference is in a taunt. Therefore, *lex talionis* primarily serves as the basis for establishing equivalence of loss in a given case. For example, a slave who lost an eye was given his freedom in return for his loss (Exod 21:26). Of course, one of the difficulties in determining equivalencies for the loss of a bodily member is that it is possible that the courts will require too high a compensation of the offender. Thus in stating *lex talionis* the law is providing a principle both for the court to determine a just award in cases of personal injury and for the court to correct any abuses of unjust compensation that might arise by exacting either too much or too little from offenders. *Lex talionis,* nevertheless, was applied literally in cases of premeditated murder (Num 35:16–21). Since a person has intrinsic value, being made in the image of God (Gen 9:5–6), no compensation is sufficient for the taking of a human life (cf. Ps 49:8–9[7–8]). Punishment in kind in case of murder is, however, not equivalent to blood vengeance (Noordtzij, 248–49).

21 Cf. vv 17–18.

22 Cf. vv 15–16.

23 This report underscores the fact that Moses and the people carried out Yahweh's instructions. This type of report is found often in Exodus and Leviticus to underscore the obedience of the people to the word of Yahweh their God.

Explanation

This section prescribes the death penalty for all who blaspheme the name of Yahweh, and it states the principle of *lex talionis.* The intentional misuse of God's name is a very serious offense. The third commandment states that a person may not take the name of Yahweh, his God, in vain (Exod 20:7//Deut 5:11). That is, among other things, a person may not swear falsely by an oath taken in the name of God. It also means that a person may not lightly use the name of Yahweh under any circumstance.

The NT continues to regard blasphemy as a blatant sin against God (Jas 3:9–12; 1 Tim 1:20). Jesus, therefore, calls for his followers to use simple, straightforward language. He exhorts them to let their "yes" be yes and their "no" no (Matt 5:37; cf. Jas 5:12). When a person's words are straightforward and true, that person has no need to back up his words with an oath. The apostles build on this principle, exhorting believers to use sound speech that is beyond condemnation (Titus 2:8). Paul wants the people to season their speech with salt in order that they may offer answers to others in a manner that will be uplifting (Col 4:6). By controlling the tongue, believers subject their whole being to the graces of the Spirit (Jas 3:2, 13). Thereby one promotes peace in the fellowship and bears the fruits of righteousness (Jas 3:18).

In ancient Israel an act of blasphemy carried the death penalty. The Scriptures attest that the community held to this standard. A person charged with this crime, even if charged falsely, stood in mortal danger. Queen Jezebel, knowing this, had a trumped-up charge of blasphemy brought against Naboth in order to have him put to death so that Ahab, her husband, could occupy the vineyard that Naboth refused to sell to the king on grounds of ancient Israelite law that a tribal inheritance was inalienable (1 Kgs 21:1–14). In the NT, Jesus was brought before the high priest because of his threat to the stability of the Jewish community (Matt 26:57–68). The high priest sought cause against Jesus but found nothing until he was able to interpret a statement of Jesus as blasphemy (Matt 26:65). On that grounds the high priest led the crowd to cry out that Jesus deserved to be put to death. Later, in the first days of the church, the Jewish authorities were troubled by the aggressive, powerful preaching and teaching of the apostles, for their witnessing produced many converts. The preaching of Stephen was especially troubling. In order to stop Stephen's effective work, they accused him of blasphemy. At Stephen's trial they became so angered by his defense that some Jewish leaders proceeded to stone him to death (Acts 6:8–15; 7:54–60).

The second major theme of the section, the principle of *lex talionis,* establishes a just basis for deciding the penalty for specific cases. This principle is found not only in the OT, but also in the law codes of other peoples of the Ancient Middle East. Thus it was a basic statement of the principle of justice common to many peoples. It is a heritage from the Ancient Middle East that judges harm done to others to be a criminal act, an act detrimental to the welfare of society as a whole. In Israel the application of this principle does not mandate physical injury for someone who physically harms another save in the case of murder. Rather it sets the basis for determining just compensation. The laws attached to the principle eliminate any distinction between alien and native, between rich and poor, in the application of the laws given by God to Israel. Only in a few other laws does the OT make a distinction between a slave and a free person. Thus consideration of status in the Israelite community normally was not to enter into the determination of a sentence against someone who had broken the law. *Lex talionis,* however, was to be applied literally in cases of murder, for no compensation is adequate for the loss of a human life.

In Matt 5:38, Jesus quotes the principle of *lex talionis* and then calls his disciples to follow a higher law, the law of non-resistance against one who is evil. He teaches that anger against another is very serious and, in some cases, is as serious as murder (Matt 5:21–26). Jesus is thus undermining the confidence of those who wrongly think that they are righteous because they live by the letter of the law as expressed in the standard "an eye for an eye and a tooth for a tooth." Commitment to this principle has the potential of promoting retaliation under the guise of righteous indignation. It may even move a person to vaunt one's self at a neighbor's expense. In contrast, Jesus calls his followers to suffer loss without calling for retaliation. This principle is stated in Jesus' famous saying, "If one smites you on the right cheek, turn to him the other" (Matt 5:39). While this adage is frequently mocked as unattainable, those who follow Jesus closely know that in the daily course of life many situations arise in which they have a just basis to assert their own rights, but they do not do so because such assertion would produce strife and discord. Whenever believers accept loss or suffer harm without seeking redress and whenever they return kindness for abuse, they promote peace among people (cf. Jas 3:18), and they bear witness to the remarkable transforming grace of Jesus. In this way believers become the salt of the earth (Matt 5:13). By such redemptive actions believers are mindful of the saying, "Never avenge yourselves, but leave it to the wrath of God; for it is written, 'Vengeance is mine, I will repay, says the Lord'" (Rom 12:19; Heb 10:30; cf. Lev 19:18; Deut 32:35).

In other places the NT leaves the carrying out of justice to the civil authorities (Acts 25:11; Rom 13:4; 1 Pet 2:14, 20). Believers are thus asked to bear abuse and wrongdoing gladly as they participate in the sufferings of Jesus (1 Pet 4:13). This means that justice in society is promoted by the civil government, but peace among members of a community is promoted by believers practicing forgiveness and the endurance of wrongs done to them.

K. The Calendar for Seven-Year Cycles and Blessings and Curses (25:1–26:46)

Form/Structure

The final section of the laws on holy living (chaps 17–26) consists of chaps. 25 and 26. It is marked off by an introductory formula (25:1) followed by a commission-to-speak formula (25:2a*α*) and a summary statement (26:46). Both of these formulae have בהר סיני, "at Mount Sinai," forming an inclusio. The significance of this point is elevated by recognizing that only this introductory formula in Leviticus portrays Yahweh speaking to Moses on Mount Sinai.

The last verse is a concluding formula. Does it stand as the conclusion to the laws on holy living (chaps. 17–26) or to the material of chaps. 8–26, since there was a similar concluding formula at 7:37–38, or to the entire book of Leviticus? The use of the terms חקים, "decrees," and משפטים, "laws," establishes a connection with 18:4, 5, 26, 30; 19:37; 20:22; 25:18; 26:43. In conjunction with 18:4 it forms an outer frame for the laws on holy living. The use of חקים, "decrees," here is masculine, but in the references just listed it is feminine; however, in a few other places in Leviticus it is masculine, namely, 6:11(18), 15(22), 7:34; 10:11, 13, 14, 15; 24:9. The use of the masculine is evidence that the summary statement has a larger function than to frame chaps. (17) 18–26. This judgment is confirmed by the inclusion of the term תורת, "laws," which occurs fifteen times in 6:2(9)–15:32, but not once in chaps. 17–26. The summary statement then is for the entire book.

Three sections make up this long speech: calendrical fixation of the sabbatical year and the year of Jubilee and attending laws (25:2a*β*–55), some general laws (26:1–2), and blessings, curses, and restoration (26:3–45). As these titles indicate, the two largest blocks of material treat separate topics. Why then are these two major units grouped into a single speech, especially when other texts are placed into small speech units (e.g., chaps. 22 and 23)? Unfortunately there is no ready answer. A significant clue to the answer is that the severest curse, i.e., exile, is a consequence of not keeping the sabbatical year (26:33–35). Israel's being taken into exile will allow the land to enjoy its sabbaths. Should Israel not obey God and fail to keep the sabbatical years, God will drive her out in order that the land may lie fallow to make up for the years it should have lain fallow. The reasoning behind this condition assumes that if Israel does not keep the laws God has given her, she most certainly will not keep the sabbatical year.

Since this work has usually followed the structural analysis in setting up divisions of the material, although some short speeches on the same or a related topic were grouped together for discussion (e.g., 5:14–26[6:7]; 22:17–33), the structure will be followed, even though this becomes a very long section. Given the great length of this speech, the discussion will be divided into three sections based on the major division of the structure.

The basic structure of this speech is as follows:

I. Introductory formula (25:1)
II. Speech (25:2–26:45)
  A. Commission to speak (25:2aα)
  B. Speech proper (25:2aβ–26:45)
    1. Legislation concerning seven-year cycles (25:2aβ–55)
    2. Some general commandments (26:1–2)
    3. Blessings, curses, and restoration (26:3–45)
III. Summary statement (26:46)

1. *Seven-Year Cycles: The Sabbatical Year and the Year of Jubilee (25:1–55)*

Bibliography

Aḥuvia, A. "What is *Hona'ah?*" (Heb.). *Beth Mikra* 18 (1972/73) 51–57. **Alexander. J. B.** "A Babylonian Year of Jubilee?" *JBL* 57 (1938) 75–79. **Auerbach, E.** "Das Zehngebot—Allgemeine Gesetzes-Form in der Bibel." *VT* 16 (1966) 255–76. **Bacchiocchi, S.** "Sabbatical Typologies of Messianic Redemption." *Journal for the Study of Judaism* 17 (1986) 153–76. **Cardellini, I.** *Die biblischen "Sklaven"-Gesetze im Lichte des keilschriftlichen Sklavenrechts: Ein Beitrag zur Tradition, Überlieferung und Redaktion der alttestamentlichen Rechtstexte.* BBB 55. Königstein/Ts; Bonn: Peter Hanstein, 1981. 280–311. **Cortese, E.** "L'anno giubilare: profezia della restaurazione?" *RBiblt* 18 (1970) 395–409. **Daube, D.** *Studies in Biblical Law.* Cambridge: Cambridge UP, 1947; NY: KTAV, 1969. **David, M.** "The Manumission of Slaves under Zedekiah." *OTS* 5 (1948) 63–79. **Ellison, H. L.** "The Hebrew Slave: A Study in Early Israelite Society." *EvQ* 45 (1975) 30–35. **Finkelstein, J. J.** "Some New Mishnarum Material and Its Implication." In *Studies in Honor of Benno Landsberger on His Seventieth Birthday, April 21, 1965.* The Oriental Institute of the University of Chicago Assyriological Studies 16. Chicago: University of Chicago Press, 1965. **Freeley-Harnik, G.** "Is Historical Anthropology Possible? The Case of the Runaway Slave." In *Humanizing America's Ironic Book.* Ed. G. Tucker and D. Knight. SBL Biblical Scholarship in North America 6. Chico, CA: Scholars Press, 1982. 95–126.

Gamoran, H. "The Biblical Law against Loans on Interest." *JNES* 30 (1971) 127–34. **Ginzberg, E.** "Studies in the Economics of the Bible." *JQR* 22 (1931/32) 343–408. **Gnuse, R.** "Jubilee Legislation in Leviticus: Israel's Vision of Social Reform." *BTB* 15 (1985) 43–48. ———. *You Shall Not Steal: Community Property in the Biblical Tradition.* Maryknoll, NY: Orbis Books, 1985. 10–47. **Gordon, C. H.** "Parallèles nouziens aux lois et coutimes de l'A. T." *RB* 44 (1935) 38–41. ———. "Sabbatical Cycle or Seasonal Pattern?" *Or* n.s. 22 (1953) 79–81. **Gressmann, H.** "Jobeljaar." In *Religion in Geschichte und Gegenwart.* Ed. H. Gunkel and O. Scheel. Tübingen: Mohr, 1912. 580–81. **Hoenig, S.** "Sabbatical Years and the Year of Jubilee." *JQR* 59 (1969) 222–36. **Hogg, J. E.** "The Meaning of לצמתת in Lev. 25:23–30." *AJSL* 42 (1925/26) 208–10. **Horst, F.** "Das Eigentum nach dem AT." In *Kirche im Volk, Heft 2: Das Eigentum als Problem evangelischer Sozialethik.* Essen: Essener Druckerei Gemeinwohl, 1949. 87–102 (= In *Gottes Recht: Gesammelte Studien zum Recht im AT.* ThB 12. Munich: Chr. Kaiser, 1961. 203–21). ———. *Das Privilegrecht Jahwes: Rechtsgeschichteliche untersuchungen zum Deuteronomium.* FRLANT 45. Göttingen: Vandenhoeck & Ruprecht, 1930 (= *Gottes Recht.* ThB 12. Munich: Chr. Kaiser, 1961. 17–154). ———. "Zwei Begriffe für Eigentum (Besitz): נַחֲלָה und אֲחֻזָּה." In *Verbannung und Heimkehr: Beiträge zur Geschichte und Theologie Israels im 6. und 5. Jahrhundert v. Chr.* FS W. Rudolph. Ed. A. Kuschke. Tübingen: Mohr (Siebeck), 1961. 135–56. **Hubbard, R., Jr.** "The Go'el in Ancient Israel: Theological Reflections on an Israelite Institution." *Bulletin for Biblical Research* 1 (1991) 3–19. **Japhet, S.** "The Relationship between the Legal Corpora in the Pentateuch in Light of Manumission Laws." *Scripta Hierosolymitana* 31 (1986) 63–89. **Jirku, A.** "Das israelitische Jobeljahr." In *FS R. Seeberg.* 2. *Zur Praxis des Christentums.* Leipzig: Scholl, 1929. 169–79 (= In *Von Jerusalem nach Ugarit.* Gesammelte Schriften. Graz, Austria: Akademische Druck- u. Verlaganstalt, 1966. 319–29). **Johnson, A. R.** "The Primary Meaning of √גאל." VTSup 1 (1953) 67–77. **Kapelrud, A. S.** "The Number Seven in Ugaritic Texts." *VT* 18 (1968) 191–99. **Kaufman, S. A.** "A Reconstruction of the Social Welfare Systems of Ancient Israel." In *In the Shelter of Elyon: Essays on Ancient Palestinian Life and Literature.* FS G. W. Ahlström. Ed. W. Barrick and J. Spencer. JSOTSup 31. Sheffield: JSOT Press, 1984. 277–86. **Kilpatrick, G. D.** "Luke 2,4–5 and Leviticus 25,10." *ZNW* 80 (1989) 264–65. **Kline, R. W.** "A Liberated Lifestyle: Slaves and Servants in Biblical Perspective." *Currents in Theology and Mission* 9 (1982) 212–221. **Klostermann, A.** "Über die kalendarische Bedeutung des Jobeljahres." In *Der Pentateuch: Beiträge zu seinem Verständnis und seiner Entstehungsgeschichte.* Leipzig: U. Deichert'sche, 1893. 419–47. **Lambert, G.** "Jubilé hébreu et jubilé chrétien." *NRT* 72 (1950) 234–51. **Lang, H.** "The Jubilee Principle: Is It Relevant for Today?" *The Ecumenical Review* 38 (1986) 437–43. **Leggett, D. A.** *The Levirate and Goel Institutions in the Old Testament with Special Attention to the Book of Ruth.* Cherry Hill, NJ: Mack, 1974. **Lemche, N. P.** "The 'Hebrew slave.'" *VT* 25 (1975) 129–44. ———. "The manumission of slaves—the fallow year—the sabbatical year—the jobel year." *VT* 26 (1976) 38–59. ———. "*Andurārum* and *Mīšarum:* Comments on the Problem of Social Edicts and Their Application in the Ancient Near East." *JNES* 38 (1979) 11–22. **Lemoine, F.-M.** "Le jubilé dans la bible." *Vie Spirituelle* 81 (1949) 262–88. **Lewy, J.** "The Biblical Institution of *Deror* in the Light of Akkadian Documents." *Eretz Israel* 5 (1958) 21–31. **Lieber, D. L., Greenburg, M., Safrai, S.,** and **Rothkoff, A.** "Sabbatical Year and Jubilee." *EncJud* 14 (1971) 574–86. **Loretz, O.** "Ugaritisches ṣamātu und hebräisches ṣm(y)tt." *BZ* n.f. 6 (1962) 269–79. **Maloney, R. P.** "Usury and Restrictions on Interest-taking in the Ancient Near East." *CBQ* 36 (1974) 1–20. **Meinhold, A.** "Zur Bezeihung Gott, Vol, Land, im Jobel-Ausammenhang." *BZ* 29 (1985) 245–61. **Mendelsohn, I.** *Slavery in the Ancient Near East.* New York: Oxford UP, 1949. **Miller, P. D., Jr.** "Luke 4:16–21." *Int* 29 (1975) 417–21. **Moore, M. S.** "Haggo'el: The Cultural Gyroscope of Ancient Hebrew Society." *Restoration Quarterly* 23 (1980) 27–35. **Morgenstern, J.** "Jubilee, Year of." *IDB* 2:1001–2. **Neufeld, E.** "The Socio-economic Background of *Yōbēl* and *Šemiṭṭā.*" *Rivista degli Studi Orientali* 33 (1958) 53–124. ———. "*Ius redemptionis* in Ancient Hebrew Law." *RIDA* 8 (1961) 29–40. **North, R.** "The Redeemer God." *Int* 2 (1948) 3–16. ———. "Biblical Echoes in the Holy Year." *AER* 123 (1950) 416–36. ———. "The Biblical Jubilee and Social Reform." *Scripture* 3 (1951) 323–

35. ———. *Sociology of the Biblical Jubilee.* AnBib 4. Rome: Pontifical Biblical Institute, 1954. **Offord, J.** "Archaeological Notes on Jewish Antiquities: XLI. Land Ownership in Ancient Palestine and Egypt and the Jubilee Year." *PEQ* 50 (1918) 37–39. **Ploeg, J. van der.** "Studies in Hebrew Law: IV. The Religious Character of the Legislation." *CBQ* 13 (1951) 169–71. **Rabinowitz, J. J.** "A Biblical Parallel to a Legal Formula from Ugarit." *VT* 8 (1958) 95. **Ringe, S. H.** *Jesus, Liberation and the Biblical Jubilee.* Philadelphia: Fortress, 1985. **Sarna, N.** "Zedekiah's Emancipation of Slaves and the Sabbatical Year." In *Orient and Occident.* Ed. H. Hoffner, Jr. AOAT 22. Kevelaer: Butzon & Becker, 1973. 143–49. **Schaeffer, H. D.** *Hebrew Tribal Economy and the Jubilee as Illustrated in Semitic and Indo-European Village Communities.* Leipzig: Hinrichs, 1923. **Seeligmann, I. L.** "Lending, Pledge, and Interest in Biblical Law and Biblical Thought" (Heb.). In *Studies in Bible and the Ancient Near East.* FS S. E. Loewenstamm. Ed. Y. Avishur and J. Blau. Jerusalem: E. Rubinstein's, 1978. 183–205. **Selms, A. van.** "Jubilee, Year of." *IDBSup* 496–98. **Snaith, N.** "The Hebrew Root G'L (1)." *ALUOS* 34 (1972) 60–67. **Stamm, J. J.** *Erlösen und Vergeben im Alten Testament: Eine Begriffsgeschliche Untersuchung.* Bern: A. Francke , 1940. ———. "גאל *g'l* erlösen." *THAT* 1:388–92. **Stein, S.** "The Laws on Interest in the Old Testament." *JTS* n.s. 4 (1953) 161–70. **Stone, E.** *Die hebräische Jobelperiode.* Hamburg: 1912. ———. "The Hebrew Jubilee Period." *Westminster Review* 175 (1911) 684–96. **Strobel, A.** "Die Ausrufung des Jobeljahres in der Nazarethpredigt Jesu: Zur apokalyptischen Tradition Lc 4:16–30." In *Jesus in Nazareth.* Ed. W. Eltester. BZNW 40 (1972) 38–50. **Sutherland, J. R.** "Usury: God's Forgotten Doctrine." *Crux* 18 (1982) 9–14. **Szlechter, E.** "Le prêt dans l'Ancien Testament et dans les Codes mésopotamiens d'avant Hammourabi." *RHPR* 35 (1955) 16–25. **Uffenheimer, B.** "Sabbath, Sabbatical Year, and Jubilee" (Heb.). *Beth Mikra* 30 (1984/85) 28–40. **Vischer, L.** "Ein heiliges Jahr?" In *Ökumene: Möglichkeiten und Grenzen heute.* Ed. K. Froehlich. Tübingen: Mohr (Siebeck), 1982. 151–70. **Wacholder, B. Z.** "The Calendar of Sabbatical Cycles during the Second Temple and the Early Rabbinic Period." *HUCA* 44 (1973/74) 153–96. **Wallis, G.** "Das Jobeljahr-Gesetz, eine Novelle zum Sabbathjahr-Gesetz." *MIO* 15 (1969) 337–45. **Westbrook, R.** "Jubilee Laws." *ILR* 6 (1971) 209–26. ———. "Redemption of Land." *ILR* 6 (1971) 367–75. ———. "The Price Factor in the Redemption of Land." *RIDA* 32 (1985) 97–127. ———. *Property and the Family in Biblical Law.* JSOTSup 113. Sheffield: JSOT, 1991. **Westphal, M.** "Sing Jubilee." *The Other Side* 150 (March 1984) 22–24. **Wright, C. J. H.** "What Happened Every Seven Years in Israel? Old Testament Sabbatical Institutions for Land, Debts and Slaves; Part I." *EvQ* 56 (1984) 129–38. ———. "What Happened Every Seven Years in Israel? Old Testament Sabbatical Institutions for Land, Debts and Slaves; Part II." *EvQ* 56 (1984) 193–201. ———. *An Eye for an Eye: The Place of Old Testament Ethics Today.* Downers Grove, IL: InterVarsity Press, 1983. 57–59, 60–61, 78–79, 82–84, 101–2, 156–57. ———. *God's People in God's Land: Family, Land, and Property in the Old Testament.* Grand Rapids: Eerdmans; Exeter: Paternoster, 1990. **Yaron, R.** "Redemption of Persons in the Ancient Near East." *RIDA* 6 (1959) 155–76. ———. "A Document of Redemption from Ugarit." *VT* 10 (1960) 83–90. **Zimmerli, W.** "Das 'Gnadenjahr des Herrn.'" In *Archäologie und AT.* FS K. Galling. Tübingen: Mohr (Siebeck), 1970. 321–32. (= In *Studien zur alttestamentlichen Theologie und Prophetie.* Gesammelte Aufsätze 2. TBü 51. Münich: Kaiser, 1974. 222–34). **Ziskind, J. R.** "Petrus Cunaeus on Theocracy, Jubilee and the Latifundia." *JQR* 68 (1978) 235–54. **Zuchkermann, B.** "Über Sabbatjahrcyclus und Jobelperiode: ein Beitrag zur Archäologie und Chronologie . . . mit einer angehängten Sabbatjahrstafel." In *Jahresberichte des jüisch-theologischen Seminars.* Breslau: Korn, 1857.

Translation

1 *Yahweh spoke to Moses at Mount Sinai:* 2 *"Speak to the Israelites and say to them: When you enter the land which I am going to give you, the land*[a] *will observe a sabbath to Yahweh.* 3 *Six years*[a] *you will sow your fields, and six years you will prune your vineyards and gather the produce.* 4 *Then in the seventh year the land will have a sabbath*

*of solemn rest,[a] a sabbath to Yahweh. You shall not sow your fields nor prune your vine-
yards. 5 You shall not reap that which grows of itself[ab] nor harvest the grapes[c] of your
untrimmed[d] vines. The land is to have a year of solemn rest. 6 Whatever the land yields
for you[a] in the sabbath year will be food for you, your male servant,[b] your female servant, your hired worker, and the guest[b] who is living with you, 7 and for your cattle and
the animals which are on your land. All its produce will be for food.*

*8 "You will count seven sabbaths of years—seven times seven years—so that the seven
sabbaths of years amount to forty-nine years. 9 Then you will sound[a] the trumpet[b] on the
tenth day of the seventh month; on the Day of Atonement you will sound the trumpet
throughout your land. 10 You will declare the fiftieth year[a] to be holy, and you will proclaim emancipation[b] in your land to all its inhabitants. It will be the Jubilee for you.
Everyone will return to his family's property,[c] and everyone will return to his extended
family. 11 It will be the Jubilee, i.e., the fiftieth year, for you; you shall not sow, nor reap
what grows of itself, nor harvest its untrimmed vines. 12 For it is the Jubilee, and it is to
be holy for you. You may eat the produce of your fields.*

*13 "In the year of Jubilee everyone is to return to his family's property. 14 If you sell[a]
property to a fellow countryman[b] or you purchase[c] from a fellow countryman, do not take
advantage[d] of each other. 15 According to the number of years since the Jubilee you are to
buy from your fellow countryman, and he is to sell it to you on the basis of the number of
productive years. 16 In proportion to[a] a great number of years its price will be greater, and
in proportion to[a] a few number of years its price will be less, because he is selling you a
certain number of its harvests. 17 You are not to take advantage of each other, but you are
to fear your God,[a] because[b] I am Yahweh your God.[c]*

*18 "You will keep my decrees[a] and observe my laws[b] and do them in order that you may
dwell in the land securely. 19 The land will yield its fruit; you will eat to satisfaction and
dwell there securely. 20 Whenever you ask, 'What shall we eat in the seventh year if[a] we do
not sow or gather our produce?'[b] 21 I shall order my blessing to you in the sixth year so
that the land will yield[a] produce[b] for three years. 22 When you sow in the eighth year,[a]
you will eat from the old harvest, and you will continue to eat the old produce[b] until the
ninth year when its produce arrives.*

*23 "The land[a] shall not be sold in perpetuity[b] because the land is mine and you are
resident aliens and tenants with me. 24 In all the land of your possession you must provide for the right of redemption of the land.*

*25 "If[a] one of your brothers[b] becomes poor[c] and sells any of[d] his property, his nearest[e]
relative is to come and redeem what his brother has sold. 26 If a man has no one to redeem
it but he prospers and gains enough for its redemption, 27 he is to calculate the value for
the years since its sale and return the balance[a] to the person to whom he has sold it. Then
he may return to his own property. 28 But if he does not gain enough to get it back, the
property sold remains with the buyer until the year of Jubilee. It will revert back in the
Jubilee, and he will return to his own property.*

*29 "If one sells a house in a walled city, he retains the right of redemption until the end
of the year of its sale.[a] Its right of redemption will be during that time. 30 If it is not redeemed before a full year has passed, the house in the walled[a] city will become the buyer's
and his descendants' in perpetuity. It will not revert back at the Jubilee. 31 However,
houses in villages without surrounding walls are to be treated[a] as fields. They have a right
of redemption,[b] and[c] they revert back[d] at the Jubilee.*

*32 "Regarding Levitical cities, houses in the cities of their possession[ab] carry an en-
during right of redemption for the Levites 33 which any of the Levites may exercise;[a] and*

a house sold in a city[b] *of their possession*[c] *will revert back at the Jubilee because houses in the Levitical cities are*[d] *their possession among the Israelites.* [34]*But the pasture lands*[a] *belonging to their cities shall not be sold because such*[b] *is their*[c] *inalienable possession.*[d]

[35] *"If one of your brothers becomes poor and cannot support himself among you, you are to help*[a] *him as you would a resident alien*[b] *or a temporary resident so that he*[c] *can continue to live among you.* [36]*Do not take from him interest on money or food,*[a] *but you will fear your God*[b] *so that your countryman may continue to live*[c] *among you.* [37]*You shall not lend him money at interest or charge interest*[a] *on credit for your food.* [38]*I am Yahweh your God, who brought you out of Egypt to give you the land of Canaan and to be your God.*

[39] *"If one of your brothers among you becomes poor and sells himself to you, you shall not make him do the work*[a] *of a slave.* [40]*He is to be treated like a wage earner or a temporary resident among you; he is to work for you until the year of Jubilee.* [41]*Then he and his children will be released from you,*[a] *and he will return to his clan and his ancestral possession.* [42]*Because they are my servants whom I brought out of Egypt, they are not to be sold according to the price of slaves.* [43]*You are not to rule over them ruthlessly,*[a] *but you will fear your God.*[b]

[44] *"The male and female slaves*[a] *which you have are to come from the surrounding nations; from them you may buy male and female slaves.*[a] [45]*You may also buy children*[a] *of temporary residents living among you*[bc] *and from their clans which are among you and have been born in your land. They become your property.* [46]*You may will them to your children as property, and you may make them serve*[a] *forever. But regarding your brothers, the Israelites, you shall not rule over a brother ruthlessly.*

[47] *"If an alien or a temporary resident among you becomes rich and one of your brothers beside him becomes poor and sells himself to an alien, a temporary resident*[a] *among you, or to a member of*[b] *the alien's clan,* [48]*he still has the right of redemption after*[a] *he has sold himself; one of his brothers may redeem him.* [49]*Or an uncle*[a] *or a cousin may redeem him; or any close relative of his extended family may redeem him; or*[b] *if he prospers, he may redeem himself.* [50]*He and his owner are to calculate from the year he sold himself until the year of Jubilee; the price of his sale is to be set according to the wages of a hired worker for that number of years.* [51]*If there are many years left, in proportion to*[a] *their number, he is to pay as the price of his redemption some of the money from his purchase.* [52]*If there are few years left until the year of Jubilee, he is to calculate and pay the price of his redemption in proportion to*[a] *the number of years.* [53]*He is to be treated as a worker hired from year to year, and you are to see that he is not ruled over*[a] *ruthlessly.* [54]*But if he is not redeemed in any of these ways, he is to go free in the year of Jubilee, both he and his children,* [55]*because the Israelites are my servants; they are my servants, whom I brought out of Egypt. I am Yahweh your God."*

Notes

2.a. LXX repeats here the clause ἣν ἐγὼ δίδωμι ὑμῖν, "which I am giving to you."

3.a. The designation of time stands first for emphasis. This is an example of the acc of time (GKC §118i).

4.a. Cf. *Comments* on 6:29–31 and 23:3.

5.a. Instead of MT את, Sam, LXX, and Syr read ואת, "and." Either reading is possible; MT is kept since it is the more unusual reading.

5.b. ספיח is growth from the fallen grain of the last harvest; it may also include the secondary growth of what has been left in the field. Sam and Tg read a pl from ספחי, "growths," as in v 11 for MT ספיח, "growth."

5.c. The *dageš forte* strengthens a consonant with a *šewa* (GKC §20b).

5.d. נזיר is growth from an unpruned vine; likewise it stands for the uncut hair of a Nazirite who has consecrated himself in a special vow to Yahweh (Num 6:2, 13, 18, 19, 20, 21). Some Heb. mss read a pl noun נזיריך "your untrimmed vines."

6.a. This form in MT is pl, while all the "you"s are sg.

6.b. In Sam this series of nouns is in the pl; the sg, taken as collective, is preferred as the harder reading. Cf. v 44.

9.a. עבר, "pass on, through," in the hiph with an acc having to do with sound means "proclaim, sound" (BDB, "עבר hiph 2.a.," 718).

9.b. LXX reads *ἐν πάσῃ τῇ γῇ ὑμῶν*, "in all your land," both here and at the end of the verse.

10.a. GKC §134o, n. interprets the form שְׁנַת, "year of . . . " as a connective form, not as a *nomen regens.*

10.b. דרור, (lit.) "flowing, running freely," means "liberty." In the latter sense it refers to the freeing of indentured servants from servitude to return to their inherited land. This word appears in Jer 34:8, 14; King Zedekiah proclaimed a release of Hebrew male and female slaves. Many scholars interpret this proclamation in light of Exod 21:2 or Deut 15:2. It was made to win Yahweh's favor during a crisis. Once the crisis subsided, the owners went back on their word and reclaimed their slaves. Another occurrence of this word is in Ezek 46:17; this text treats inalienable royal property, which may be leased out but only until the year of דרור; then it reverts to the prince (נשׂיא). Zimmerli (*Ezekiel 2*, 497) interprets this דרור to refer to the restitution of property in the fiftieth year, the year of Jubilee. Finally, Isa 61:1 speaks about the coming prophet who will proclaim דרור for prisoners. This will be the year of Yahweh's רצון, "pleasure," as well as the day of God's נקם, "vengeance." This day will inaugurate the ideal age. Cf. R. North, "דְּרוֹר *d^e rôr*," *TDOT* 3:265–69.

10.c. Cf. F. Horst, "Zwei Begriffe für Eigentum (Besitz): נחלה and נחזה," in *Verbannung und Heimkehr: Beiträge zur Geschichte und Theologie Israels im 6. und 5. Jahrhundrt v. Chr.*, FS W. Rudolph, ed. A. Kuschke (Tübingen: Mohr, 1961) 135–56.

14.a. Sam, LXX, Syr, and Vg have a sg verb; this form is in accord with the sg pronominal suffixes.

14.b. Keil and Delitzsch understand the sg suffix on עמיתך, "your fellow countryman," to have distributive force, i.e., for any particular Israelite.

14.c. The use of an inf abs of קנה, "buy," may be too difficult grammatically; a better reading may be תקנה if a preformative has fallen out (Elliger, 337); nevertheless, the inf abs may be used to continue a preceding finite verb (GKC §113z; Bertholet, 90).

14.d. Cf. n. 19:33.b.

16.a. The compound prep לפי means "according to the portion of, in proportion to" (BDB, "פה, 6.c.," 805).

17.a. LXX* reads *κύριον τὸν θεόν σου*, "the Lord your God."

17.b. LXX omits כי, "because."

17.c. Syr has a second person sg suffix to agree with the preceding occurrence of this word. This is an example of leveling the text.

18.a. LXX adds *πάντα*, "all."

18.b. LXX adds *πάσας*, "all."

20.a. Sometimes הן, "behold," carries the force of "if" (Joüon §167l).

20.b. Many Heb. mss, Sam^mss, LXX, Syr, and Vg read תבואתינו, "our harvests." The extent of support for this reading gives it weight.

21.a. Sam reads עשׂתה, but MT may preserve an older form of the 3rd fem sg pf (GKC §75m).

21.b. Sam and LXX read תבואתה, "its produce."

22.a. This is a rare example of the occurrence of the indicator of the acc את with the acc of time (Joüon §126i).

22.b. LXX reads *παλαιὰ παλαιῶν*, "old things of old things." Cf. 26:10.

23.a. The term הארץ, "the land," stands first for emphasis; it also signals a new section.

23.b. The phrase לצמתת, "in perpetuity," comes from the root צמת, "put an end to"; this word occurs only in this idiom. J. E. Hogg ("The Meaning of לצמתת in Lev. 25:23–30," *AJSL* 42 [1925/26] 210) understands צמתת to mean "'without right of redemption' or 'in derogation of the seller's right of redemption.'" Cf. J. Rabinowitz, *VT* 8 (1958) 95.

25.a. Some Heb. mss, Sam, LXX, and Syr read וכי, "and it." It is possible that the *waw* has fallen out of MT.

25.b. LXX adds *ὁ μετὰ σοῦ*, "who is with you," as in v 39. This is another example of leveling of the text.

25.c. מוך, "be low, depressed, run down, grow poor" (BDB, 551; KB, 526) occurs only in vv 25, 35, 39, 47 and 27:8; there is a term *mk* in Ugar meaning "sink, vanish" (*UT* #1473). Levine (175) suggests that it comes from the root מכך, "collapse," meaning that a person is reduced to poverty.

25.d. The prep מן, "from," has a partitive use, "of" (GKC §119w, n. 2).
25.e. The definite adj הקרב, "the one who is near," has superlative force in this context (Baentsch, 427).
27.a. עדף is an infrequent word in the OT. Here it means "excess, surplus" (BDB, 727). Elsewhere it is used in the qal for "surplus" of food (Exod 16:23), "excess" of a class of people (Num 3:46, 48, 49), and "excess" in the length of curtains (Exod 26:12, 13).
29.a. LXX omits ממכרו, "its sale."
30.a. In place of MT ketib לא, "no," Sam and the versions read the qere לו, "his," taking the antecedent of עיר, "city," which is usually fem, as a masc (PIR, 200–201). *BHS* proposes לָהּ, "hers."
31.a. 11QpaleoLev, Sam, LXX, Syr, Tg, and *Tg. Ps.-J.* read a pl verb to agree with the pl subj. However, the sg, also supported by *Tg. Neof.*, could be a distributive sg (GKC §145m).
31.b. LXX has λυτρωταὶ διὰ παντός = גאלת עולם, "an enduring right of redemption," as in v 32.
31.c. 11QpaleoLev does not have *waw*, "and"; this may be an error of haplography.
31.d. LXX and Tg read a pl verb, possibly for sense as in this Eng trans.
32.a. In MT this phrase is a *casus pendens*, which is resumed by the prefix of the verb תהיה, "it will be" (cf. n. 32.b.).
32.b. The verb תהיה is fem by attraction to the predicate גאלת עולם, "enduring right of redemption" (Joüon §150m; cf. n. 33.b.).
33.a. Vg has a negative before the verb, which Bertholet (91), Dillmann (670), and NEB accept. PIR (201), NEB, and JB, however, take this clause as a conditional clause. It is possible that the first clause is a general statement leading to the specific decree, so NIV. H. Möller offers a good explanation, namely that the אשר is connected not to the following יגאל, "he will redeem," but to the preceding גאלת עולם, "an enduring right of redemption" ("Lösungsvorschlag für eine Crux interpretum (Lev 25 33)," *ZAW* [1978] 411–12).
33.b. For MT בית ועיר, "a house and a city," *BHS* suggests reading בית עיר, "a house in a city," since in vv 32 and 33 the pl form בתי ערי, "houses in cities," occurs. LXX has a pl reading here. The *waw* breaks up a constr chain and produces an unwieldy compound subj. PIR works to make sense out of MT as it stands: "[he shall leave] the house [which has been sold] and [go] to the city of his possession." They add the comment: "A levitical possession is redeemed by a Levite from another Levite, who has as a Levite a city where a right of possession is reserved for him" (202).
33.c. For MT אחזתו, "his possession," LXX, *Tg. Ps.-J.*, and *Tg. Onq.*[mss] have אחזתם, "their possession"; this may be another case where the translators seek to make an intelligible trans.
33.d. The pronoun היא is fem sg because it is attracted to the fem sg predicate אחזתם, "their possession," instead of the masc pl subj בתי ערי הלוים, "the houses of the cities of the Levites" (GKC §145o, n.; Joüon §149c; cf. n. 32.a.).
34.a. LXX has pl terms, οἱ ἀγροὶ οἱ ἀφωρισμένοι, "the special fields."
34.b. For MT הוא, "it," Sam, 11QpaleoLev, *Tg. Neof.*, and Syr read a fem היא, "it," to agree in gender with אחזה, "possession."
34.c. For MT להם, "to them" = "their," a few Heb. mss read לכם, "to you" = "your"; 11QpaleoLev supports MT.
34.d. J. E. Hogg, *AJSL* 42 (1925/26) 210.
35.a. Sam and Heb. mss read this verb in the piel instead of hiph.
35.b. For MT גר, "a resident alien," LXX and Vg read כגר, "like a resident alien"; this may be to provide a better trans. as in this Eng trans. (so PIR, 202–3).
35.c. A couple of Heb. mss, Sam, and LXX add אחיך, "your brother," as in v 36.
36.a. Going back to the twelfth century, נשך has been described as interest deducted from the loan in advance and מ/תרבית as "increase" that is due as the loan is paid (E. Neufeld, *HUCA* 26 [1955] 355–57; E. A. Speiser, *Y. Kaufmann Jubilee Volume*, 44). This position is supported by taking נשך from a root נשך, "bite." S. Loewenstamm ("נשך and מ/תרבית," *JBL* 88 [1969] 78–80) questions this identification, pointing out that there is no evidence to suggest that נשך has any other meaning than "interest." If so, נשך, "interest," comes from another root נשך II (so KB, 689). How does נשך differ from מ/תרבית? Loewenstamm argues that תרבית represents interest on the loan of food supplies (Ezek 18:8, 13, 17; 22:12; Prov 28:8); the language of v 37 gives strong support to this proposal. Loewenstamm finds that Akk documents from Elam have two words for these different kinds of interest.
36.b. LXX adds ἐγὼ κύριος, "I am the Lord."
36.c. GKC §76i prefers to read וְחַי, "and he lives," the short form of the 3rd person pf qal, in place of MT וְחֵי, "and life of," as in v 35.
37.a. Sam has the spelling בתרבית in place of MT במרבית.
39.a. For MT תעבד בו, "you will make him do work," LXX reads δουλεύσει σοι, "he will serve you."

41.a. In place of MT מעמך, "from you[r midst]," LXX has τῇ ἀφέσει = ביובל, "in Jubilee."
43.a. פרך, means "harshness, severity" (BDB, 827); this root in Akk *parāku* (noun *parku*) means "obstruct, impede" (*AHw* 828–29) and in Aram "smash, crumble crush" (Jastrow, 1228–29). It stands for ruling over another as a tyrant, intentionally making that person endure brutal hardship and intolerable working conditions.
43.b. Cf. n. 17.a.
44.a. Cf. n. 6.a. PIR (203) interprets the sg forms as collectives.
45.a. Cf. n. 25.d.
45.b. LXX does not translate אשר עמכם, "who are [living] with (among) you."
45.c. This complex prep phrase is a *casus pendens,* which is resumed by the pronominal suffix on the prep מן, "from."
46.a. LXX omits בהם תעבדו, "you will make them serve."
47.a. A few Heb. mss, Sam[mss], LXX, and Syr read ותושב, "and a temporary resident." Sam reads ולתושב, "and for a temporary resident." According to PIR (203), these variants simplify the reading and conform this verse to other similar texts. Nevertheless, some sign such as a prep or a conj is needed to show that two different classes of aliens are referred to by גר, "alien," and תושב, "temporary resident," as the context suggests.
47.b. LXX omits או לעקר, "or to a member."
48.a. The prep אחרי usually governs the inf constr; the phrase אחרי אשר, "after that," generally stands before a finite verb except here and 2 Sam 5:9b, where the prep comes before the verb (BDB, 30 [pl 3]; Joüon §129p; GKC §130d).
49.a. LXX omits the first או, "or," but this may be only to provide a better reading in Gk.
49.b. LXX seems to read ואם, "and if," for MT או, "or."
51.a. Cf. n. 16.a.
52.a. Cf. n. 16.a.; n. 51.a.
53.a. Here the obj of רדה, "rule over," stands in the acc, but usually its obj is introduced by the prep ב as in vv 43 and 46. Here this verb functions as a virtual pass.

Form/Structure/Setting

Based on content, this speech has two major sections: (1) setting the calendar for the sabbatical year with some laws (vv 2bβ-7) and (2) setting the calendar for the year of Jubilee with several extensive laws (vv 8–55). From an analysis of the structure, however, there are two major sections divided differently: (1) the calendar for the sabbatical year and the year of Jubilee with some laws (vv 2bβ–22) and (2) legislation regulating the גאלה, "laws of redemption," pertaining to property and to debtor-slaves in relationship to the year of Jubilee (vv 23–55; cf. Sun, "Investigation," 499). As in most cases in this commentary, the structural signals are followed in considering the form of the speech.

The following structural outline is an expansion of the outline in the *Form/Structure* section on 25:1–26:46, being subordinate to "1. Legislation concerning seven-year cycles (25:2aβ–55)":

a. Calendar and laws for the sabbatical year and the year of Jubilee (vv 2aβ–22)
  1) Concerning the sabbatical year (vv 2aβ–7)
    a) Basic regulation (v 2aβ–b)
    b) Explication of the regulation (vv 3–7)
      (1) Description of normal agricultural activity for six years (v 3)
      (2) Regulations for rest from agricultural activity during the seventh year (vv 4–7)
  2) Concerning the year of Jubilee (vv 8–17)
    a) Basic regulation for the year of Jubilee (vv 8–12)
      (1) The calendar for the year of Jubilee (v 8)
      (2) Proclamation of the year of Jubilee (vv 9–10)

                (a) Proclamation proper (v 9)
                (b) Proclamation of liberty and command to return to patrimony (v 10)
            (3) Explication of the year of Jubilee (vv 11–12)
                (a) Identification of the year of Jubilee (v 11a)
                (b) Prohibition against sowing and harvesting with support (vv 11b–12a)
                (c) Permission to eat from the land's produce (v 12b)
        b) Concerning leasing of land in relationship to Jubilee (vv 13–17)
            (1) Basic statement about return to one's patrimony at Jubilee (v 13)
            (2) Regulations about leasing of land (vv 14–16)
            (3) Parenesis (v 17)
                (a) Prohibition and exhortation (v 17a)
                (b) Formula of Yahweh's self-introduction (v 17b)
    3) Parenesis (vv 18–19)
    4) Disputation about concerns of people (vv 20–22)
b. Laws on kinsman-redeemer in relationship to Jubilee (vv 23–55)
    1) Laws on selling/leasing of land (vv 23–34)
        a) Basic law (vv 23–24)
        b) Explication of basic law (vv 25–34)
            (1) Laws on redemption of a patrimony leased because of debt (vv 25–28)
            (2) Laws on sale of houses (vv 29–31)
                (a) Permitted in a walled city (vv 29–30)
                (b) Prohibited in unwalled villages (v 31)
            (3) Laws on sale of property belonging to Levites (vv 32–34)
    2) Laws about loans to poor Israelites (vv 35–38)
        a) Basic regulation (v 35)
        b) Laws against loaning money at interest (vv 36–37)
        c) Expanded formula of Yahweh's self-identification (v 38)
    3) Laws on slavery caused by debt (vv 39–55)
        a) Regarding an Israelite debtor-slave (vv 39–43)
            (1) Primary set of laws (vv 39–41)
                (a) Case (v 39a)
                (b) Regulations proper (vv 39b–41)
                    (i) Nature of service (vv 39b–40a)
                    (ii) Release at Jubilee (vv 40b–41)
            (2) Reason (vv 42–43)
                (a) Reason proper (v 42a)
                (b) Prohibitions (vv 42b–43a)
                (c) Exhortation (v 43b)
        b) Laws on Israelites' holding of slaves (vv 44–46)
            (1) Law proper (vv 44–46a)
                (a) Acquisition of slaves (vv 44–45a)
                (b) Classification of slaves as property and laws of inheritance of slaves (vv 45b–46a)
            (2) Prohibition against mistreatment of Israelite slaves (v 46b)
        c) Laws on the redemption of an Israelite debtor-slave held by a resident alien (vv 47–55)
            (1) Basic law (vv 47–54)
                (a) Case (v 47)
                (b) Ways of redemption from debt slavery (vv 48–54)
                    (i) Right of redemption and agents of redemption (vv 48–49)
                    (ii) Setting the redemption price (vv 50–52)

(iii) Standard of treatment for an Israelite slave with a prohibition (v 53)
(iv) Guaranteed release of Israelite slave at Jubilee (v 54)
(2) Reason (v 55)
(a) Reason proper (v 55a)
(b) Formula of Yahweh's self-introduction (v 55b)

The first section treats the sabbatical year. It is composed of two kinds of material: the calendar for the observance of the sabbatical year (v 2b) explicated by general laws (vv 3–4a) plus specific laws about leaving the land fallow (vv 4b–5, 6–7). The second section focuses on setting the time for the year of Jubilee (v 8) and the proclamation of its beginning (vv 9–10). It assumes that the fallow laws for a sabbatical year apply to this time period. There is a law against sowing and harvesting (v 11b) cast in the same basic, though abbreviated, form as the similar law for the sabbatical year (vv 4b–5a). Attached to this is legislation on returning to one's family property at Jubilee (vv 13–16). It concludes with a brief parenesis underscored with the exhortation to fear God and the formula of Yahweh's self-introduction (v 17).

Then the laws regarding the year of Jubilee and possibly those regarding the sabbatical year are supported by a parenesis (vv 18–19) in the same style as found in the core section of the laws on holy living (chaps. 18–20). The parenesis begins with the injunction to do God's decrees and to keep his judgments (cf. 18:4–5, 26; 19:37; 20:8, 22). It is supported by the twofold promise of dwelling securely in the land and of having abundance of food. The inclusion of a promise accords with other promises sprinkled throughout the laws on holy living; e.g., in 18:5 there is the general promise of life, and in 20:24 is the promise to possess the land of Canaan. Following is a disputation that addresses the people's concern about having enough food for a sabbatical year and the year following (vv 20–22). The reference to sowing in the eighth year (v 22) reveals that this disputation originally addressed a sabbatical-year cycle, not the year of Jubilee unless the theory that the two years fall together is valid. By its context, however, this disputation applies primarily to a sabbatical year and by extension to the year of Jubilee. The promise of God's special blessing on the produce of the fields in the sixth year (v 21) is germane given the people's apprehension about the potential financial hardship such observance might produce. In conclusion, the two units of this section are thus closely linked, for the year of Jubilee is a high sabbatical year.

Joined to the three sets of laws regarding the sale of property and debtor-slaves are laws on the rights of the sale and the redemption of property (גאלה; vv 25–34), laws regarding interest on loans to poor Israelites (vv 35–38), and laws concerning slavery resulting from debt (vv 39–55). These laws are interrelated with the year of Jubilee because that year is the terminal date for such contracts. Each of the three series of laws begins with the same case: כי ימוך אחיך, "if your brother becomes poor." This symmetry in style supports the conclusion that these three sets of laws have been arranged for this speech. These laws serve as an integral part of the liberating power of the year of Jubilee. Two brief pareneses are worked into the fabric of this material in order to motivate Israel to comply with these laws (vv 42, 55).

The primary reason that these laws have been incorporated into the legislation on the year of Jubilee is that debt was the greatest internal threat to the social foundation of the equality of all Israelites, based on the enduring right of every family to its patrimony. These laws sought to guard this egalitarian ideal amidst the forces of fortune and misfortune that over time caused some to become rich and others to become poor. The legislator did not try to preempt either the natural or the social forces from working; rather through cultic legislation he sought to prevent the rise of a slave class in Israel by having a set time when all debts were forgiven and every patrimony was returned to its original owner. That both releases took place simultaneously is important, for it enabled every released Israelite debtor-slave to return to his patrimony, free and clear, where he could again support his family. These laws, therefore, are not a disjunctive appendix to the laws of Jubilee, but an integral dimension of its program.

There are many signs that these laws on redemption have been adapted for their setting in the laws on holy living (chaps. 17–26). The laws about debt (vv 35–38) conclude with the formula of Yahweh's self–identification expanded with a relative clause referring to the Exodus (v 38; cf. *Excursus* at 18:1–2). Again in v 42 Israel is identified as Yahweh's servant whom he delivered out of Egypt. At the Exodus Yahweh revealed his merciful character, the trait that the Israelites are to display in their treatment of others, especially the less fortunate (cf. 19:9–10, 13–14). A similar statement at v 55 concludes this series of laws. In addition, there is the motivational statement ויראת מאלהיך, "you shall fear your God" (vv 36, 43b; cf. v 17). To this is joined the ethical injunction not to תרדה בפרך, "rule ruthlessly," over a servant (vv 43, 46, 53). It is tied to the motivation, as the second person singular form of the verb attests, and it is in accord with several laws in chap. 19 (e.g., vv 11, 14, 18). This ethical motivation fits in well with the ethos of the laws on holy living, especially the speech in chap. 19 (e.g., vv 9–18). These laws then are an integral part of the material on holy living.

The composition of this speech is marked by three distinctive styles: impersonal laws (vv 26–34, [41], 42, 48–54 [less 53bβ]), laws in the second person singular (vv 3–5, 6–7, 8–9a, 14a, 15–16, 17bα, 25, 35–37, 39–40, [41], 43–44a, 46bβ, 47, 53b), and material, both parenetic and legal, cast in the second person plural (vv 2aβ+b, 9b–13, 14b, 17a, 17bβ–24, 38, 44b, 45, 46a+bα, 55b). Literary critics use these variations in style as one means of identifying a variety of sources. In Noth's judgment (184), the mixture of styles gives evidence that this passage was the product of a long, gradual development, but for him the various stages are no longer discernible. As to dating this speech, Noth (185) concedes that directions for Jubilee and for the restoration of land to its owner might reach back into the era when Israel settled in Canaan. He concludes that this chapter reached its present form in the exile before the finalization of chap. 23, for here the year begins on the tenth of the seventh month (v 9; contra 23:24b–25). Kilian (*Literarkritische,* 147–48) finds in Lev 25 three strata. In addition, he finds evidence that a priestly author made a few editorial changes to the document consisting of the first two strata. Furthermore, he judges the legislation of redemption to be quite distinct from the material on the year of Jubilee (145–47). The latter came from a source unattested elsewhere in the Holiness Code. This person had to have worked after the time of Nehemiah, for the events reported in Neh 5 show no awareness of this Jubilee legislation. Elliger (347–48), likewise, reconstructs a very complex literary history for this speech, arguing that it went through five stages in its production. Material from two earlier hands was taken over by the first holiness redactor; that redactor, who is identifiable by the use of the second person masculine plural, added vv 1–2, 6aα, 9b, 10, 11aβ–12, 17b–19, 23–24, 55 and also inserted vv 3–5. This same redactor gave the framework to chap. 18. Based on that theory plus the characteristics of this hand and the mention of Mount Sinai in the opening formula, Elliger postulates that this speech originally introduced the Holiness Code. The next hand, the second redactor of the Holiness Code (see *Form/Structure/Setting* to chaps. 17–26) moved this speech to its present location and included a few additions (vv 41b, 42, 44b, 45, 46abβ, 47bγ, 49a, 50b–53). Finally some additional material became attached to this speech. Cholewiński (*Heiligkeitsgesetz*, 101–18) identifies three strata in this speech; these strata follow basically the literary styles presented above. In his judgment, the person who added the strata composed in the second person singular worked only here in the Holiness Code (105). The final redactor was the main redactor of the Holiness Code; he is known by second and third person plural forms, by the use of inclusios, and by the use of alternating patterns. This person undergirded the laws with a distinctive theological perspective. From another perspective, Sun ("Investigation," 549–50) concludes that the groups of laws in the singular (vv 3–7, 15–16, 25–34, 35–37, 39–43, 47–54) are homogeneous from a literary perspective and that the laws on the role of property and slavery are currently so tied to the observance of the year of Jubilee that they are no longer separable from it. While recognizing that vv 8–9a are a fragment of a longer text, he concludes that in the earliest texts the sabbatical year was already connected with the year of Jubilee. He, therefore, is convinced that only one redactional hand worked in chap. 25; this hand is identifiable by the use of the plural (vv 2aβb, 6*, 9b–10, 14, 17aαb [perhaps also v 17aβ], 18–19, 20–22, 23–24, 38, 47, 44–46, 55).

Working from these analyses, it is evident that this speech went through at least two editions. The first edition is discernible by the use of the second person singular forms at the structural seams. The calendrical material and the laws on the sabbatical year form a block. The calendar for the year of Jubilee, however, has two distinct layers; it begins in the second person singular (vv 8–9a) and shifts to the second person plural for the bulk of the material (vv 9b–13). This shift suggests that material from different sources has been joined. The legislation on redemption is cast in three distinctive styles. Both the laws on leasing land (vv 25–34) and the laws on redemption of an Israelite debtor-slave (vv 47–54) held by a resident alien are impersonal casuistic laws except for the statement of the case, which stands in the second person singular. The laws on making loans without interest to poor Israelites (vv 35–37) are formulated in the second person singular, while the laws on Israelites holding slaves (vv 44–46) are cast in the second person plural except for the lead line (v 44a). These different styles point to the likelihood that these sets of laws were taken from different portions of the priestly legal material. These sets of laws have been placed into a common legislation by having the case of each section formulated in the second person singular (vv 25, 35, 39); in the section on laws regarding the redemption of an Israelite debtor-slave, the case is formulated similarly.

A person who preferred the second person singular made the initial framework for the collection of these laws in the first edition. Since the calendar for the sabbatical year and the lead material on the calendar of Jubilee (vv 8–9a) stand in the first person, the oldest stage of this speech contained legislation on the sabbatical year and the year of Jubilee. Later, when this legislation became included as one of the speeches in the division on holy living, the speaker, who preferred the second person plural, included material to strengthen the rhetorical and ideological force of this speech. That person may have added the parenetic material (vv 17, 18–19), the formulae of Yahweh's self-identification (vv 38, 55), and the disputation (vv 20–22), tying this speech more tightly into the laws on holy living. To this person may belong the inclusion of additional regulations on the year of Jubilee (vv 9b–12). He could have found these laws in another source. At this stage the theology undergirding the fallow years was placed to frame the speech with inclusios. This produced the second edition.

Cholewiński (*Heiligkeitsgesetz,* 106–8) has found three pairs of inclusios: 2a$\beta\gamma$ ~ 17b–19, 23–24 ~ 38, and 42 ~ 55. These verses clearly express the theological premises underlying this legislation as motivation for the people to keep them. In the first pair Yahweh gives Israel the land, and the land gives Israel its produce. Therefore, Israel needs to obey Yahweh by letting the land rest every seventh year. In the second inclusio, Yahweh has given Israel the land of Canaan, and Israel is to give the land גאלה, "the right of redemption." In the third, since Yahweh has redeemed Israel out of Egypt, they have become his slaves; therefore, they are not to sell fellow Israelites as permanent slaves. These theological themes of Yahweh as the one who led Israel out of Egypt and as the one who gave her the land are interwoven in these inclusios. The second member of each of these sets also has the formula of Yahweh's self-introduction. Finally, given the predominance of the second person plural in chap. 26, this speaker is the one who joined these two blocks of material into a single speech.

Two additional issues need to be addressed in regard to these laws, namely the origin of the laws regarding Jubilee and the relationship of these laws to similar passages in the Pentateuch.

ORIGIN OF JUBILEE

Scholars are widely divided in accounting for the origin of the laws on Jubilee. Some assign them to Israel's earliest days (e.g., Jirku, "Jobeljahr," 172–79; Ginzberg, *JQR* 22 [1931/32] 364–91; Lewy, *Eretz Israel* 5 [1958] 29–30; van der Ploeg, *CBQ* 13 [1951] 169–71; van Selms, *IDBSup* 497); many others argue that they are a utopian ideal from a visionary circle of the post-exilic community (e.g., Pedersen, *Israel,* 1:89; de Vaux, *AI,* 1:175–77; Porter, 196–98; Snaith, 163; Westbrook, *ILR* 6 [1971] 224–26; Gnuse, *BTB* 15 [1985] 46). Kaufman argues that this law is a merger of an old tribal "jubilee" (יובל) with the practice of proclaiming liberty (דרור) by the kings into "a new fiftieth-year proclamation of Jubilee" ("Reconstruction," 283).

This debate is far from settled. There are several factors pointed out by the latter scholars to support a late origin of this legislation. First is the lack of any references to it in the earlier documents. 2 Chr 36:21 is cited as support, for it reports that the sabbatical year had not been observed for a long time. The references to דרור, the liberation of slaves and prisoners in Ezek 46:17 and Isa 61:1–3 may be connected to the ideology of Jubilee. If there is a tie, these references, assigned by most critical scholars to the post-exilic era, support dating the legislation of Jubilee to this same era. Second, the legislation of Jubilee is considered a reform of the deuteronomic laws on the release of debts and Hebrew slaves and thus is later. Third, since the implementation of the ideals of this legislation would cause great economic hardship to the nation in general and especially to the rich, many scholars view this legislation as a utopian ideal of the returning exiles, an ideal that was too exalted ever to be put into practice (e.g., de Vaux, *AI,* 1:177). Fourth, the social and economic abuses addressed by legislation of the Jubilee came much later than the simpler tribal society witnessed to in the Judges and 1 Samuel (Gnuse, *BTB* 15 [1985] 46). To find the setting that gave rise to this radical legislation, G. Wallis (*MIO* 15 [1969] 341–45) proposes that this legislation was composed by the exiles to regain the right to own land, which probably had been lost during exile, on their return to Israel.

While the case for a post-exilic date for this legislation is strong, three sets of arguments may be set forth for an early origin of the ideology of Jubilee. First is the presence of four rare terms; their unfamiliarity is an indicator that they come from an early stage of the Hebrew language. Most amazingly the precise meaning and etymology of the key term יובל, "Jubilee," is uncertain. While some, as van Selms, attempt to demonstrate that its literal meaning is "ram's horn" (*IDBSup* 496), North thinks that its meaning is only discernible from v 10 (*TDOT* 6:3). Thus there is no consensus on its basic meaning. The term פרך, "ruthless," is obscure; it occurs only in vv 43, 46, 53 and in the same way in Exod 1:13, 14. These facts suggest that it was an ancient word. While it does occur in Ezek 34:4, Ezekiel may be using it to allude to the harsh treatment of slaves mentioned in Lev 25 and Exod 1 (Cooke, *Ezekiel,* 374). The term מוך, "below, become poor," occurs only in vv 25, 35, 39, 47 and in 27:8. If it is a cognate to Ugar *mk,* "sink, vanish," it is an ancient word. לצמתת, "in perpetuity," occurs only in this idiom and only in vv 23 and 30. Rabinowitz (*VT* 8 [1958] 95) finds a parallel phrase *samid adi darīti,* "alienated for ever," in documents found at Ugarit. He goes on to argue from this connection between property laws attested at Ugarit and in Lev 25 that those of Lev 25 come from an early period.

Second, while there are only a few references to the year of Jubilee in the OT, namely Lev 27:16–25 and Num 36:4, they take for granted the existence of such legislation. Another allusion to this legislation is found in Yahweh's promise to deliver Jerusalem from the siege of Sennacherib (Isa 37:21–35); v 30 is cast in language that is very similar to that of Lev 25:5, 11, 22, drawing the audience's attention to either a sabbatical year or a year of Jubilee. Isaiah may be drawing on the tradition of Jubilee in the formulation of this sign in order to heighten its power. In addition, the plot of the story of Ruth requires this or similar legislation about גאלה, "the right of redemption of property" (cf. Leggett, *Levirate,* 292–95). Another tie may be found in the incident of King Zedekiah's freeing Hebrew slaves in 588 B.C. in an attempt to win God's favor during a time of natural catastrophe (Jer 34:8–22). Zedekiah was very likely seeking to comply with this or similar ancient legislation. The language used in Jeremiah makes a connection with several texts in the Pentateuch (W. Holladay, *Jeremiah 2,* Hermeneia [Minneapolis: Fortress, 1989] 238). חפשי, "free," relates to Exod 21:2, and the reference to the law on releasing Hebrew slaves accords with Deut 15:1 and 12. The use of the technical phrase קרא דרור, "proclaim liberty," establishes a direct tie with Lev 25:10 and with the dependent vv 40–41. It is clear that the Jeremiah passage is drawing on an ancient legal tradition understood widely, not one specific formulation of that tradition such as is found in Lev 25. Another possible reference to the obligation of a kinsman to redeem property may be the socio-economic background behind the obscure verse Ezek 11:15 (W. Brownlee, "The Aftermath of the Fall of Judah according to Ezekiel," *JBL* 89 [1970] 393; Leggett, *Levirate,* 89, n. 23; Zimmerli, *Ezekiel 1,* 261). These references to the sabbatical year and laws related to Jubilee, though sparse, indicate that there existed a legal tradition reaching back into Israel's early history that at least corresponded to the legislation regarding the sabbatical year and the year of Jubilee.

Third, other Middle Eastern nations in the second millennium practiced a general release that has some similarities to the debt and slave laws of Jubilee. At Nuzu property was transferred after *šūdûtu* or after *andurāru* (C. H. Gordon, *RB* 44 [1935] 34–41). This latter term may be directly related to דרור, "liberty." In the Akkadian period (2400–2200 B.C.) and the Old Babylonian period (1900–1600 B.C.) kings issued a royal decree, a *mīšnarum,* cancelling private and public debts, suspending taxes, releasing land held by creditors, and freeing enslaved free men, and this was the beginning of a variety of reforms (cf. Westbrook, *ILR* 6 [1971] 215–19). This practice usually took place in the first or second year of a king's reign. A king might issue one or more such decrees during his reign. By such edicts he sought to reestablish greater economic parity among the people. The effect of these decrees was temporary, as the persistent need to issue new ones attests. Nevertheless, their existence demonstrates that the second millennium B.C. offered a time when such laws of release were practiced (cf. M. Weinfeld, "Institutions in the Priestly Source," *Eighth World Congress of Jewish Studies,* 126–29; Lewy, *Eretz Israel* 5 [1958] 29). This legislation on Jubilee differs from the practice in Mesopotamia in that instead of relying on sporadic decrees issued by monarchs, it sets by law fixed intervals for the proclamation of liberty. Lewy (*Eretz Israel* 5 [1958] 29) contributes the insight that a state not governed by a king had to have a fixed interval in order that such a proclamation might be made. Westbrook, however, finds this difference to be so fundamental that he claims the parallels between the Israelite laws and the *mīšnarum* carry no weight in support of the claim that Jubilee was an early Israelite legislation (cf. Lemche, *VT* 26 [1976] 39–41). In light of Westbrook's argument it may be stated that the parallels with Mesopotamian legal practices offers some evidence, but not proof, that the year of Jubilee originated in the earlier days of Israel's origin.

Regarding the weight assigned in this debate to the lack of references to Jubilee by those who argue for a late date, it is not too surprising that there are so few references to the year of Jubilee in the OT, for it occurred only once every fifty years. The scarce biblical material covering the early period of Israel's history would have had little reason to mention the year of Jubilee unless some major event would be made more understandable in light of the laws of this year. Another reason for the lack of reference to this day in the historical works dealing with the Kingdom period is found in the statement of 2 Chr 36:21 that Israel had failed to observe the sabbatical years. While most scholars were skeptical about the observance of the sabbatical year, some studies have challenged that skepticism. Those who argue that Jubilee is a late legislation are similarly faced with the difficulty of the sparsity of references to it in late sources. This sparsity is a greater obstacle for their position for two reasons. First, there are more later sources, providing more opportunities for a reference to it. Second, if zealous visionaries of the post-exilic community designed this manifesto to counter the types of social sins that brought on the exile, surely there would be some reference to the inaugural observance of this year, especially since the post-exilic community became very zealous in observing laws distinctive to the Jewish community such as the Sabbath. To say that Jubilee was forgotten in the very period of its origin, as does Gnuse (*BTB* 15 [1985] 46), taxes the limits of credulity. Wacholder (*HUCA* 44 [1973/74] 153–84) has shown that the sabbatical year was a living observance from the post-exilic period to the fifth century A.D. He (154), nevertheless, finds no trace of observance of a year of Jubilee. Likewise, Sarna, from a thorough study of the release of slaves by Zedekiah, has concluded that 588/87 and 595/94 were sabbatical years in Judah ("Zedekiah's Emancipation," 148–49). Since skepticism about the sabbatical year has weakened, it is possible that evidence will be discovered to challenge the overwhelming skepticism about any observance of the year of Jubilee.

Paucity of references to a specific matter does not necessarily indicate its lack of importance, for many significant items in the cult are infrequently, if at all, mentioned in the OT outside their basic prescriptions, e.g., the shewbread, the reparation offering, and the Feast of Weeks (cf. *Form/Structure/Setting* to the history of chap. 16). Therefore, the dearth of references to Jubilee does not necessarily mean that this year was never celebrated, and it does not mandate that this legislation came from a late period.

A weighing of these various arguments finds them leaning toward the early origin of the sabbatical year and the year of Jubilee along with the legal framework regarding inalienability of a clan's property and debtor-slaves. The final formulation of this legislation took place after the settlement, for this legislation deals with a complex social issue that arose after Israel had become settled in Canaan, namely, the buying and selling of houses in walled and unwalled cities. These laws on the sale of houses in walled cities most likely made concessions to the needs of a mixed urban population of Canaanites and Israelites living side by side. Thus the sabbatical year and the visionary ideal of Jubilee were anchored in the ideology that gave birth to Israel, and the legislation was adapted to changing social conditions during Israel's history.

RELATIONSHIP TO PARALLEL TEXTS IN THE PENTATEUCH

Another important issue is the relationship of this legislation to other OT legislation about the sabbatical year, the release of slaves, and letting land lie fallow. Two OT texts, Exod 23:10–11 and Deut 15:1–11, have laws that relate to a fallow year, and two other texts prescribe the release of slaves.

The laws in Exod 23:10–11 are motivated by concern for the poor and for wild animals. To account for this motivation many interpreters, noting that nothing is said about this being a fixed year for the entire nation, argue that the goal of helping both the poor and the animals would have been achieved more beneficially if the fallow year rotated from field to field, that is, leaving some land fallow every year (e.g., Baentsch, *Exodus,* 206). The legislation in Lev 25:2–7, however, specifically decrees that all agricultural land is to lie fallow during the same seventh year. In that case Lev 25 presents a different program than Exod 23, assuming that this interpretation of Exod 23 is correct. But a comparison of Exod 23:10–11 with Lev 25:2–7 offers no discrepancies.

How does Deut 15:1–11 fit in with these two texts? This passage is primarily concerned with the release of debts. The key term is שמטה, "release," technically "remission of debt." This term does not appear in Lev 25, but it does occur in Exod 23:11. Wright (*EvQ* 56 [1984] 133) takes the position that the laws in Deut 15:1–11 assume the fallow year (134). It needs to be noted that nothing in Deut 15:1–11 expressly regulates agrarian practices. If Wright's position is correct, Deuteronomy adds to the practice of a fallow year the law that debts may not be collected during this year. Furthermore, the practice of שמטה is variously interpreted. One interpretation is that a holder of a pledge was to release that pledge in the seventh year. North (*Sociology,* 199) identifies the pledge to be a parcel of land or a valuable object, while others, such as Horst (*Privilegrecht,* 59–61), take the pledge to be a person. Another interpretation is that a person's entire debt was cancelled. But a group of scholars, such as Driver and White (179), Keil and Delitzsch (3:369), and Wright (*EvQ* 56 [1984] 135–36), do not think that the entire debt was cancelled, but only that payment on a debt was suspended for the year the land lay fallow. Craigie (*Deuteronomy,* 236) takes this position, noting that in the case of a debt of grain, suspension would be necessary during a fallow year, for such observance would not provide a farmer any means for making a payment for that year. If the position that only the payment on a debt was suspended is correct, the Jubilee laws regarding debts were much more radical and liberating for the poor than those in Deuteronomy.

Two other texts, Exod 21:2–6 and Deut 15:12–18, have laws on the release of slaves. According to Exodus, a Hebrew slave is to serve for six years and be released in the seventh. If one enters slavery with his wife, both may go out free. But if one marries during his time of bondage, his wife and children must be left behind. If that person, however, wishes to remain in slavery, he may do so, though with the loss of all rights to becoming free. Deut 15:12–18 restates these laws for a slave with the added stipulation that when a slave is set free, his master is to provide him with abundant provisions from his flocks, threshing floor, and wine vat. Many scholars interpret the six-year period to apply to each case and not to a universal seventh year (e.g., Craigie, *Deuteronomy,* 238; Gnuse, *BTB* 15 [1985] 45). The identification of the seventh year remains disputed. Working from another perspective, however, there are several points of contact between Deut 15 and Lev 25. In Deut 15:12, the Hebrew slave is designated אחיך, "your brother," as it is found in Lev 25:25, 35, 36, 39, 46, 47; cf. v 48. Both laws are tied to the history of the deliverance from Egypt (v 15; Lev 25:38, 42, 55). The promise of God's blessing is the motivation to keep these laws in Deuteronomy (vv 14b, 18b); a parallel is found in Lev 25 in the motivations to observe the sabbatical year and the year of Jubilee (vv 18–19, 20–22). These ties strongly indicate that laws in one tradition were influenced by the laws in another tradition (cf. Kilian, *Literarkritische,* 132).

Out of this comparison arises a hard question. If slaves were freed every seventh year, why is there any need for a release of slaves at the year of Jubilee? There have been several attempts to address this issue. One approach claims that the Leviticus laws were the product of an effort to reform the older laws. S. R. Driver, e.g., proposes that the six-year limit of servitude stipulated by the laws in Deuteronomy proved impractical and unenforceable (*Deuteronomy,* ICC, 185). To correct this situation the Jubilee laws extended the years of a slave's servitude and, in turn, required the master to treat his servant with kindness. Working from the same perspective, Ginzberg says that Lev 25 arose to help the rich by providing a longer, steady supply of labor (*JQR* n.s. 22 [1932] 349). Jubilee, then, instead of promoting the freedom of every Israelite citizen, in most cases would make debtor-slaves serve many more years.

A second approach accounts for the differences by applying traditio-historical criticism to the various texts. Lemche, e.g., takes a distinctive approach (*VT* 26 [1976] 49–51). He interprets יובל to mean "manumission year," "the year of release." Originally it did not convey any span of time; thus it was observed in the seventh year in accordance with Exod 21:2–6 and Deut 15:12–18. Lemche takes the position that the seven-year period applied to each slave and to the sale of each property. Over time the legislation of Lev 25 grew with the addition of the laws of the fallow year and attendant social laws. With the shift of the Jubilee laws from each case to a national program, the redactor made the year of Jubilee every seventh sabbatical year because of the economic impact of observing Jubilee. Lemche concludes that the legislation in Lev 25 is the process of a long history of growth and development; parts of this legislation were taken from the Book of the Covenant and from the sabbatical year laws in Deuteronomy. Such complex reconstructions, unfortunately, are impossible to substantiate or refute because of the sparsity of evidence.

A third approach works from the perspective that the laws address different social circumstances leading into servitude. Mendelsohn (*Slavery,* 89) posits that the slave addressed in Exodus-Deuteronomy was forced into servitude because of debt while the person of Lev 25 sold himself into bondage to cover his debts. This proposal stumbles over the inequality of the situation of a volunteer slave who would have to serve for decades up to a lifetime in contrast to the person who was forced into slavery having to serve only six years. Offering an explanation in the same direction, Wright (*EvQ* 56 [1984] 195–200) seeks to solve the riddle by pointing out that the different sets of laws address two different classes, namely a Hebrew (עברי) in Exodus/Deuteronomy and an Israelite in Leviticus. "Hebrew" means a social class of landless people who supported themselves by working for others. If a Hebrew fell into debt, he became a slave for six years. When he was released, he became חפשי, "free," i.e., a free person without title to land, but one who could continue to live as a day-laborer or a tenant farmer. By contrast, the laws of Lev 25 address an Israelite with a patrimony who, because of debt, had to submit to a master himself as a hired laborer while maintaining the right of redemption; i.e., at any time a kinsman might redeem him or he might purchase his own freedom. Wright's proposal faces the formidable obstacle that a landed Israelite would usually be subject to a much longer period of bondage than would a class of landless workers. There is another difficulty with his proposal, namely that under the covenant ideal these "Hebrews" had the notion that they too should have a patrimony.

A fourth approach to account for the tensions among the different texts emphasizes that these sets of laws on slaves vary in reference both to land and to time. The laws of Exodus and Deuteronomy do not directly address the issue of land, the issue central to the legislation in Leviticus. Those laws, furthermore, address time differently in that they most likely govern the length of servitude of each individual slave, while the laws in Leviticus concern the proclamation of liberty for all slaves at the same time. For Leviticus there was to be a year, every seventh sabbatical year, in which every Israelite family was free, living on its own patrimony. Thus this legislation particularly addressed the exception clause in the slave-release laws of Exodus and Deuteronomy wherein a slave has the right to bind himself to his master for life. Such a slave and no doubt his family, even if that slave had married and begotten children while in servitude, was to be released at the year of Jubilee. These laws, furthermore, addressed the situation of a person who chronically fell into heavy debt. There was a time when such a person would be completely forgiven of all debts. The year of Jubilee, therefore, had as its goal the restoration of all Israelites to the status of free citizens with a patrimony every fifty years just as when Joshua apportioned the land (Josh 13–19). Clearly then this legislation addressed a different dimension of the issue of debtor-slave than did the laws found in Exodus and Deuteronomy. The high goal of these laws guarded against the development of a class of perpetual Israelite slaves, rather than only offering a Hebrew freedom after seven years of servitude.

In conclusion, it is true that if the laws on the release of debts and slaves found in Exodus, Leviticus, and Deuteronomy are read on the same plane, there exist some contradictions among them, but every society has laws drawn up from differing perspectives and addressing differing situations that contain provisions that conflict in a strictly literalistic interpretation. This common phenomenon of a legal system is normally resolved by certain laws taking priority over other laws depending on the situation and the precedent of legal interpretation. Such would have been the situation in ancient Israel, for there is nothing unmanageable in applying these different sets of release laws. Conversely, the existence of these different sets of laws provided a stronger net of safety to protect the citizens of ancient Israel from becoming perpetual slaves.

Comment

1 This is the only introductory formula with the element בהר סיני, "at Mount Sinai." It joins with this same phrase in the summary statement at 26:46 to frame this speech. This introductory formula is different because it is the final speech in Leviticus save for the appendix (chap. 27). The mention of Moses' receiving these laws on Mount Sinai underscores the authority of this speech.

2 God, the owner of the land, gives it to Israel as her inheritance for entering into covenant with him. This truth is the foundation for these laws on the sabbatical year and the right of redemption of a family's patrimony. God is concerned that the land has periodic rest every seven years. Just as the people are to rest every seventh day, the land is to rest every seventh year. God wants his people to be free from continuous labor in order that they might enjoy the gift of the promised land and the grace of his blessing. Observance of this rest honors Yahweh, as the phrase שׁבת ליהוה, "sabbath to Yahweh," communicates (Rashi, 113). By such observance the people clearly acknowledge Yahweh's ownership of the land and boldly demonstrate their trust in him for their food supply.

4–7 In the sabbatical year all farming activity is to cease. A landowner is neither to sow his fields nor to prune his vines or fruit trees. Nor is one allowed to harvest that which grows of itself either in the fields or in the vineyards. At harvest time some will be tempted to harvest the grain and the fruit that have grown voluntarily. But the people are not to profit from the natural growth of the seventh year. Certainly all members of a household may eat from that produce, thanking God for their daily food, but they may not harvest the yield either to sell or to stockpile. Rather the landowners are to share this produce freely with their servants, their laborers, and their animals, both domestic and wild (cf. Exod 23:10–11). The list of people in v 6 means that no one living in Israel is excluded from gathering produce of the sabbatical year for eating.

8 Seven is a most sacred number. Therefore, seven sevens is even more sacred. The forty-ninth year is a sabbatical year; its greater sacredness is celebrated in the fiftieth year, called יובל, the "year of Jubilee" (v 10). On which year is considered to be the fiftieth year, see the *Excursus* on the year of Jubilee at v 13.

9–10 The year of Jubilee is to be proclaimed by a sounding of the שׁופר, "trumpet," i.e., a ram's horn, throughout the land. The language pictures heralds going throughout the land announcing that the trumpet has sounded (Elliger, 352). This took place on the tenth of Tishri, the seventh month, the Day of Atonement. The year of Jubilee appropriately begins on this day, for it is the most solemn day of the year when the whole nation receives forgiveness for all its sins. On this day דרור, "liberty," is proclaimed, i.e., all debts are cancelled, landowners who have leased their patrimony return to their land, and Israelite debtor-slaves are freed. At the beginning of the new Jubilee cycle every Israelite is to be a free citizen living on his patrimony. Thus this fiftieth year is especially consecrated (קדשׁ).

The meaning of יובל is far from clear. A frequently suggested meaning is "ram." In the phrase קרן היובל, "the horn of 'Jubilee'" (Josh 6:5), יובל seems to refer to a musical instrument (cf. Exod 19:13). Van Selms proposes that שׁופרות היובלים (Josh 6:4, 6, 8, 13) means "trumpets of rams' horns"; יובל, therefore, means "ram's horn" (*IDBSup* 496). North is not persuaded that יובל has anything to do with a horn (*TDOT* 6:1–2). Both in Josh 6:5 and in Exod 19:13 משׁך precedes the phrase and means "trumpet blast," leaving יובל undetermined in North's opinion. For North the meaning of יובל must be gained from this verse in Leviticus; here it is the name for the joyful homecoming that took place in the seventh sabbatical year (*TDOT* 6:3). The technical meaning of יובל is certain, but its etymology and general meaning remain hidden. יובל is used as a proper name in this text, for it appears in the declaratory formula היא יובל, "it is Jubilee," without the article.

11–12 All the restrictions regarding sowing and harvesting for the sabbatical year (vv 4–7) apply to the year of Jubilee. The year of Jubilee is declared to be holy. The permissibility of eating freely from the produce that grows that year is repeated for emphasis.

13 This verse repeats the message of v 10b.

Excursus: The Year of Jubilee

A puzzling question is which year or span of time was the year of Jubilee. This question is motivated by the great economic and social hardship that the observance of two successive fallow years would have caused. To answer this question, some creative proposals have been set forth.

One is that the year of Jubilee was a utopian ideal that was never designed for observance (cf. *Form/Structure/Setting* for a discussion of this position).

Another proposal interprets the year of Jubilee as a "leap year" of forty-nine days inserted into the calendar every forty-ninth year (Hoenig, *JQR* 59 [1969] 222–23;

Wenham, 319). This leap year was to realign the lunar calendar with the solar calendar. Such a leap year accounts for the disappearance of Jubilee from the calendars of the Second Temple, for the adoption of a solar-lunar calendar eliminated the need for these extra days (Hoenig, 236). To increase support for this position its advocates emend Lev 25:8 to read "the *days* [MT years] of the seven sabbaths of years, forty-nine, shall be for you a year" (first proposed by S. Zeitlin, "Some Stages of the Jewish Calendar," *SAJ Review* 8 [1929] 6–8; Hoenig, 222). Unfortunately for this position, such an emendation has no textual support. The most formidable obstacle to this position, though, is that forty-nine days are not sufficient to align the lunar and solar calendars. In a forty-nine-year period there would need to be some sixty-one days for a full alignment (cf. Gnuse, *BTB* 15 [1985] 47). Other, equally unsatisfying, proposals that try to interpret Jubilee as an intercalary year are recorded by North (*Sociology,* 125–29).

Several interpreters (cf. North, *Sociology,* 122–25) have sought to demonstrate that the seventh sabbatical year and the year of Jubilee, the fiftieth, are overlapping years of two different calendars, such as the liturgical and the civil calendars. The major difficulty is that any fallow year that did not begin in the fall would disrupt the agricultural sequence of two agricultural years and be very burdensome. The text says that the year of Jubilee begins in the fall, the seventh month. The language of the law against sowing and reaping in a sabbatical year likewise indicates that a fallow year began in the fall.

North has put forth an imaginative proposal (*Sociology,* 118–20). Discounting the importance of the fallow year, he develops his position on the premise that the intent of this legislation was for the relief of the poor. To meet the needs of the poor, fields observed sabbatical years on a rotating basis to provide some food each year for the underprivileged. That is, a landowner relinquished his claim on a harvest for the benefit of the poor (North, 118). Thus there was no common national sabbatical year or year of Jubilee. While this interpretation is very innovative, it runs counter to the legislation of Lev 25.

A proposal adopted by several contemporary scholars holds that the forty-ninth sabbatical year and the year of Jubilee are identical (e.g., van Selms, *IDBSup* 496; North, *Sociology,* 129–33). The forty-ninth year is the climax of a sequence of sevens: the seventh day, the seventh month, the seventh year, and the seventh sabbatical year (North, 132). The climactic forty-ninth year is called יובל, "Jubilee," or the fiftieth year. In the same general direction, but with a different slant, Kaufman ("Reconstruction," 278) posits that "Jubilee" is to be understood as a proclamation of liberty at a point in time during the seventh sabbatical year.

The position that the seventh sabbatical year and the year of Jubilee overlap somehow stands in accord with the promise of abundance to survive a year of Jubilee or a sabbatical year found in vv 20–22. By reason of the context, one would assume that this promise is for the year of Jubilee, but a close look at its content indicates that it is in accord with a sabbatical year. In that promise the questioner asks, "What shall we eat in the seventh year?" If there were two consecutive fallow years, one would expect the question to be either what shall we eat in the eighth year or what shall we eat during the two years of fallow. While this promise speaks of needing food for three years, its primary concern is for food in the seventh year. The conclusive evidence that this promise does not think of two successive fallow years is the reference to sowing seed in the eighth year. If the year of Jubilee were the fiftieth year, that would be the eighth year, and sowing would not be allowed. This promise recognizes that every fallow year impacts parts of three years. In that a sabbatical year began in the fall, the fallow impacted the seventh and eighth years, reaching into the ninth year. If the counting of years was by a calendar that began in the spring, the fallow year would have covered parts of years seven and eight, and the produce from seed sown in the fall of the eighth year would not be harvested until the beginning of the ninth year (Hoenig, *JQR* 59 [1969] 226–29). Not until the ninth year would a normal sowing and harvesting cycle be experienced. Moreover, working with this way of counting, two successive fallow years would impact parts of four calendar years. Therefore, this promise, if it relates to the year of Jubilee as the context suggests, is a strong indication that the year of Jubilee and the forty-ninth sabbatical year overlapped.

Although the text does speak of a fiftieth year, the ancient way of reckoning time does not exactly mesh with the modern way, especially when numbers are used symbolically. Every calendar offers difficulty in counting days; e.g., May 7 to May 10 is considered three days although it is part of four. Similarly, from Jubilee, the seventh sabbatical year, to the next Jubilee is fifty years (North, *Sociology*, 130). Texts stipulating that the Feast of Weeks begins on the fiftieth day after Passover face the same problem with numbering. Pentecost is the fiftieth day after Passover, the day after the seventh Sabbath. But the calendric description in Lev 23:16 identifies Pentecost as "the day after the seventh Sabbath," even though it begins its counting with the day after that Sabbath, not with that Sabbath; i.e., forty-nine exact days are counted as fifty days (North, 131). This difficulty for a modern way of counting was not necessarily a problem for the ancients, especially since they did not number the years consecutively. Furthermore, if the 490 years of Daniel 9:24 are ten Jubilees, then this passage supports the position that Jubilee was the seventh sabbatical year of a cycle. In this light the number fifty may be more emblematic rather than a specific calendar number. This last proposal may explain why the post-exilic community kept track of sabbatical years but did not make any reference to the year of Jubilee. E.g., Josephus records sabbatical years for a 126-year period, but he does not account for the year of Jubilee (*Ant.* 13.9.5; 14.10.6).

This position of equating the seventh sabbatical year and the year of Jubilee is a serious attempt to accept this legislation as being followed to some extent in some eras of ancient Israel's history, a legislation designed to promote liberty, not a national disaster. In trying to account for the relationship of the year of Jubilee to the seventh sabbatical year, it is important to note that there are no directions for the start of the sabbatical year. This lack stands in marked contrast to the explicit directions for announcing the year of Jubilee in the seventh month. This special way of announcing the year of Jubilee may be intended to mark this sabbatical year as distinct from other sabbatical years.

(This material has been prepared with help from Steve Wilkens, Ph.D.).

14–16 Buying and selling of property is determined by the number of years until the next year of Jubilee. Actually land may not be bought and sold; rather it may be leased for the period of time until the next Jubilee. The price for a piece of land is to be fixed according to the number of years until the next Jubilee. In a transaction involving redeemable land, the seller may buy it back at the price of the sale less the value of the harvests that have passed. The basic price remains the same so that the buyer does not profit at his poorer brother's expense by leasing a tract for a price driven lower by his brother's distress and then collecting a high price when the seller or his kinsman can reclaim the land (cf. Westbrook, *RIDA* 32 [1985] 98–100). The inability of a powerful person to demand the sale of a patrimony is attested in the account of Naboth's refusal to sell his land to King Ahab (1 Kgs 21:1–26). Under Israelite law, Ahab was powerless to acquire that vineyard as long as Naboth lived. There is a general command not to הונה, "mistreat" or "take advantage of" (cf. 19:33), עמית, "an associate" (cf. 5:21[6:2]), in making a lease on his family property. This prohibition means, among many things, that a leaser is not to drive such a hard bargain for the use of a fellow Israelite's land that he does not adequately lessen the burden of his associate's debt.

17 The exhortation not to take advantage of each other is repeated from v 14b and grounded on the cornerstone of Israelite faith, namely, each person's ירא, "fear," of his God (cf. 19:14). In fearing God, one places far greater value on personal relationships than on personal gain. This value begins with a personal relationship with God, as the reference to God as "your God" indicates. The importance of this exhortation is further strengthened with the formula of Yahweh's self-identification (cf. 18:2).

18–19 At this point comes an expanded exhortation to follow God's laws. This is a good rhetorical device by which the speaker seeks to win the audience's adherence to these specific standards. The exhortation is underlined with the promises that they will dwell securely on the land, stated twice for impact, and that they will have enough food to eat to satisfaction. Yahweh thus promises that he will protect his people from marauding bands that frequently present a threat to raid the countryside during harvest. Such raids impoverish the inhabitants, for in minutes raiders take away the fruit of months of labor. The experience of such raids demoralizes the people, causing them to hide what little they have in an attempt to survive; such was the state of affairs in the days of Gideon (Judg 6:1–6). By contrast, trust in God's promise of protection develops confidence.

20–22 The speaker directly addresses the people's question of what they will eat in the seventh year, the fallow year. By anticipating the congregation's primary question, the speaker skillfully maintains the initiative in overcoming the audience's resistance. Yahweh answers their question. He promises that he will bless the land in a very special way in the sixth year. The use of the word צוה, "command," before ברכתי, "my blessing," stresses Yahweh's determined will to give the people an abundant harvest. The old produce will be sufficient to be eaten for parts of three years, reaching into the ninth year until the new crop is harvested. Of course, the people themselves will have the responsibility of storing the heavy harvest and proportioning it wisely. It is debated whether this three-year period applies to the sabbatical year—years six, seven, and eight—or to the years of the Jubilee cycle, which seems to require two consecutive fallow years—years seven and eight—plus, the ninth year waiting for harvest. The former is the preferred position, for the text says that they will sow in the eighth year, which would be forbidden in the year of Jubilee if it is the fiftieth year, but not if it was the eighth year of a sabbatical-year cycle. The reference to the ninth year is realistic, for a sabbatical-year cycle would take a couple of years to recover the supplies depleted during the fallow year, especially given that harvests for different produce come at different times of the year. In this context, the promise, which is primarily for a sabbatical year, may also apply to a year of Jubilee.

23–24 Each family has its own inheritance, which may not be sold or bought לצמתת, "in perpetuity." Undergirding the principle of each family's right to occupy their inheritance stands the theology that God himself holds title to the land. The people then are גרים, "resident aliens," or תושבים, "tenants," with God. The phrase "with me" may carry the meaning "under my protection" (H. D. Preuss, "אֵת *ʾēth,*" *TDOT* 1:450). Just as an alien who is the guest of an Israelite comes under the protection of the head of the house, so too the families in Israel as resident aliens on the land owned by Yahweh come under his protection. The close relationship between Yahweh and the families in Israel as well as the security that this great God offers them is stressed here. The divine owner declares that every property held by the families of Israel as an inheritance given them under the covenant carries a גאלה, "right of redemption." Or to say it another way, no land held by an Israelite is to be exempted from the "right of redemption." No legal loopholes are to be devised to circumvent the intention of this law.

25 This law deals with a person who has מוך, "become poor," and has fallen so far into debt that he must sell his patrimony to survive. The meaning of the unusual term מוך is clarified by the companion expression in v 35, namely, מטה ידו, "he cannot support himself," (lit.) "his hand shakes," i.e., the person is no longer able to support his family (Hubbard, *Bulletin for Biblical Research* 1 [1991] 7). This metaphorical expression intimates the harsh effects that poverty has on a person. The first line of defense for one who is so poor is to sell a part of his inheritance to גאלו הקרב אליו, "his nearest kinsman." This person is to come (בא) and redeem (גאל) him. A גאל, "kinsman-redeemer's," duty was "to make a claim in the sense of resuming a claim or right which had lapsed or had been forfeited" (Neufeld, *RIDA* 8 [1961] 34). בא has a technical juristic force here, namely to act on one's responsibility as a kinsman for a relative who is in distress (Elliger, 355). The expression "the nearest kinsman" indicates that there was a successive line of responsibility to act as a kinsman for property sold (ממכר) by one's brother. The only OT reference to such a line of order is found in vv 48–49; it starts with brothers and then moves to uncles and cousins. This position is assuming that the line in those verses may be applied to this verse, but Porter (206) thinks that the circle of kinsmen in this case is much wider than in the case in v 49. Nevertheless, in support of making the connection between the two cases is the play on the terms אח, "brother," and גאל, "redeem, redeemer." Unfortunately further details about the line of succession have not been preserved. That there was such a line of successive redeemers is supported by the story of Ruth. Boaz responded to Ruth's request for him to act as a kinsman for her, but before he could act, a kinsman nearer than himself had to be given the opportunity to act as her redeemer (cf. Ruth 3:12; 4:1–6).

Scholars debate two issues in regard to this law. First, they ask whether this kinsman buys back land already sold to another party or whether he has a right of preemption on land up for sale by his relative (cf. Leggett, *Levirate,* 88–92). The cases covered by the following two laws certainly favor the former position. Conversely, the record of Jeremiah's exercising his right to purchase a piece of land owned by his cousin by buying it directly from him (Jer 32) supports the latter position. The transaction Boaz made for Ruth (Ruth 4) agrees with the procedure recorded in Jer 32. Leggett (91–92) holds that the former position was the primary intent of this law and that the prior right of purchase developed from it. Second is the issue whether the redeemed property comes under the control of its original owner or remains under the redeemer's control until the year of Jubilee. Most scholars take the former position, claiming that redemption by its very meaning implies that the land returns to its original owner. A few scholars, however, defend the latter position, arguing that the redeemer enters with the primary aim of keeping the property in the greater family and making the farming of that property viable, but not necessarily with the design of turning over the recovered property immediately into the hands of his brother (Pedersen, *Israel,* 1:84–88; D. Daube, *The NT and Rabbinic Judaism,* 273). A document from Ugarit supports this position, for it reads as though a person redeemed seven individuals and continued to hold their land until he was compensated for the price of their redemption (Yaron, *VT* 10 [1960] 89–90). Moreover, the law in v 35, which stipulates that a kinsman is to help a poor kinsman with loans, not gifts, is taken to support this position, because the kinsman in that case does not make an outright donation to his troubled brother. The other side asks in rebuttal how a redeemer served a distressed brother if he merely took over the property in place of the initial buyer. In addition, the cases covered by the following two laws certainly support the former interpretation. Wright (*God's People,* 122) thinks that both possibilities are permitted by this law depending on the particulars of each situation. Once a possession had been redeemed, it is quite conceivable that a clan could guide their kinsman in making his patrimony productive. However one understands these alternatives, the design of this law is to prevent land from passing out of a clan's hands. Furthermore, as Eichrodt states, these laws blocked land speculation in ancient Israel in order to increase the possibility of the Israelites' preserving their independence by controlling some property (*Theology of the OT,* 1:96–97).

26–27 The person who has leased out his patrimony retains the right to repossess his inheritance by paying off the indebtedness. A person may prosper after he has sold his land. Possibly he has a bumper crop on the land that remained under his control, or he saves wages from working as a hired laborer, or he receives a windfall such as an inheritance. The law protects the family owner from the purchaser's refusal to let the land return to its owner by demanding that the price for the repurchase of the land be set justly. The original price the owner had received is to be reduced by the value of the crops harvested from that land since its lease.

28 But if the owner never accumulates enough money to repurchase his land, it is returned to him, free and clear, in the year of Jubilee. He returns to work his inheritance. In this case Yahweh himself, through this legislation, acts as his kinsman (cf. Hubbard, *Bulletin for Biblical Research* 1 [1991] 8–13). In doing so, Yahweh continues to act on behalf of his oppressed people as he did in delivering them from Egyptian bondage. In Hubbard's view, "redemption amounts to an institutional Exodus in Israel" (11).

29–31 Houses in עיר חומה, "a walled city," do not carry a perpetual גאל, "right of redemption." They may be bought and sold. After such a house has been sold, it may be redeemed in the year immediately after its sale. Afterwards that house becomes the buyer's for as long as he wants. The year of Jubilee does not have any effect on the ownership of such a house. This exception in the laws of redemption coincides with the nature of life in a walled city. In these larger cities the population was racially mixed, and the populace did not live off the land. Canaanites and other resident aliens who lived in the cities were not covered by land inheritance laws of Israel; this exception thus gave them the right to buy and sell houses in Israelite walled cities. A house in a village (חצר), however, is treated as a field. Its deed carries גאלה, "a right of redemption." It may be leased, but it has to be returned to its owner at Jubilee.

32–34 Houses in Levitical cities also carry גאלת עולם, "an enduring right of redemption," because the Levites had no inheritance other than the gift of certain cities along with pasture land (Num 35:1–8; Josh 21). שׂדה מגרשׁ, "pasture land," may never be sold, for it is אחזת עולם, "an enduring possession." שׂדה מגרשׁ is land surrounding Levitical cities for the Levites to pasture their own flocks. Since the task of the Levites is to serve the people at the sanctuary and to teach them the law, they are not to be burdened with farming and shepherding. Their houses then are their primary possession. So the laws of redemption apply to their houses. These houses return to their original owner at Jubilee (Ezek 48:13–14). Priests are most likely included in the term Levites (Hoffmann, 2:343).

35–37 This brief set of laws addresses the issue of making loans to fellow Israelites faced with poverty. These laws prohibit the practice of charging interest on a loan to a fellow Israelite faced with poverty. Whenever a brother needs money, a member of the community is to החזיק, "support him" (lit. "strengthen"), as they would a resident alien or a stranger. The initial law requires making a loan to a fellow Israelite. It would have been likely that some would not make the loan to a poor member of the community if no interest could be charged. This law shows that one is not to be generous to a foreigner and shut up his compassion toward his fellow kinsman who is facing poverty. The issue is that no fellow Israelite is to profit from a brother's need for financial assistance. He is not to charge interest (נשך) on money or interest (תרבית) on a loan of seed or food (cf. Exod 22:24[25]; Deut 23:20–21[19–20]; see n. 36.a.). Thus interest charged on anything taken on credit is prohibited.

This prohibition is supported by the basic premise of biblical faith, the fear of God (cf. v 17). Devotion to God motivates the faithful to express compassion toward others, whether they are successful or poor. The inclusion of Yahweh's self-identification underscores the authority of these laws. This formulation acknowledges the covenant relationship by which Yahweh becomes the God of Israel and Israel the people of God. Yahweh delivered them from Egyptian bondage to give them the land of Canaan where they might worship him as their God (cf. v 2). This reference to the Exodus also communicates the principle that Yahweh requires and expects expressions of mercy from those to whom he has shown mercy.

The formulation of these laws against making loans at interest does not address the issue of loaning money at interest for a commercial enterprise. Neufeld concludes from this fact, plus the fact that this set of laws along with the law in Exod 22:24[25] focuses on the poor, that OT law did not object to commercial loans at interest (*HUCA* 46 [1955] 365; cf. Noth, 178–79). Gamoran (*JNES* 30 [1971] 127–34) discounts Neufeld's position. He stresses that the laws of Deut 23:19–20 are quite comprehensive in the prohibition of making loans with interest. Nevertheless, Neufeld may be correct in suggesting that these laws against interest may not cover all situations of lending money. Unfortunately there is insufficient information to resolve this matter. Certainly, though, the law is bold and clear against making loans at interest to the poor.

39–40 Beset by poor harvests, plagues, personal illness, marauding bands, or other difficult circumstances, a brother may become so מוך, "poor," that he has to sell himself in servitude to another person. This would have been especially true during the days of the judges, for the Israelites began their occupation of Canaan with limited capital and limited experience in farming. Losses inflicted by marauding bands were a recurring problem that caused these peasants great economic hardship and threatened many with the loss of their patrimony, as the Book of Judges attests. When an Israelite put himself in the service of another

Israelite, his master may put him to work, but not to those low menial tasks done by a slave. This includes any task that would have little value save to painfully humble his servant. Such cruelty is not to happen to an Israelite servant. The master thus is to treat his Israelite servant as שׂכיר, "a hired servant." שׂכיר does not mean that he will receive regular wages, though he might receive some remuneration in addition to shelter and food, but that he will be treated with the respect shown a hired worker and his tasks will be similar to those of a hired worker. In Jewish tradition a Jewish slave is to be employed at his own trade (Hoffmann, 2:349).

41–42 The Israelite slave is to work until the year of Jubilee. Then he and his sons are to return to משׁפחתו, "his clan," and אחזת אבתיו, "his ancestral possession." משׁפחה is used imprecisely in the OT; it is a group of father's houses and usually a subunit of a tribe. Gottwald (*The Tribes of Yahweh,* 257–67) identifies משׁפחה as a "protective association of extended families." Every Jubilee all Israelites return to the status of free citizens. According to Exod 21:2–6 and Deut 15:12–18, a Hebrew slave is to be released in the seventh year. But a Hebrew slave who has renounced his freedom at the seventh year forfeits any right to ever claim or demand his freedom again such as on the fourteenth anniversary of his servitude (cf. Hoffmann, 2:348–49). Many believe, however, that this proclamation of liberty at Jubilee includes those Israelites who have bound themselves to their master at the time of their seventh-year release (*b. Qidd.* 15a; Josephus, *Ant.* 4.8.28).

This law applies especially to the children of a slave who remained in servitude. They go free with their father at the year of Jubilee. In contrast to Exod 21:2–6, this law makes no distinction between children born before and those born during their father's servitude. At Jubilee the master has apparently no claim on those children born during servitude, nor can he use the children to coerce their father into a longer period of bond service. The motivation for this law is the remembrance that all Israelites are slaves to Yahweh (cf. v 55). Yahweh has purchased Israel's redemption from Egyptian servitude, and they have become his slaves. Therefore, no Israelite may be sold as a perpetual slave to another Israelite, for Yahweh is the owner of both the one selling himself and the one doing the buying.

43 A person who becomes the master of a fellow Israelite is not to רדה, "rule over," that one פרך, "ruthlessly." The root פרך means "grind down" (qal) and "crush, break in pieces, rub off" (piel; KB, 911). Used with a slave, it describes toil that breaks the body and grinds down the spirit. The appeal to follow this standard is the master's ירא, "fear," of God (cf. vv 17, 36).

44–46 Israelites are permitted to own slaves, both male and female. Such slaves are to be purchased from the surrounding nations, from resident aliens in Israel, and even from aliens that have been born in Israel. These slaves become perpetual servants. Since slaves are classified אחזה, "property" or "a possession," they are passed from father to son as part of the family's inheritance. Nevertheless, the law requires that an Israelite treat his slaves kindly. Given this permission to possess slaves, it is reiterated that a master may not rule over an Israelite slave ruthlessly (cf. v 43). Whereas this legislation frees the citizens of Israel from any fear of indigenous slavery, it also shows that the path to travel before the institution of slavery is universally condemned will be very long.

47–53 This section regulates the situation in which an Israelite who has become poor must sell himself to גר, "a resident alien," תושׁב, "a temporary resident," or a member of a resident alien's family. This set of laws is crucial to maintaining the freedom of the peasantry, for debt was the primary source of slaves in the ancient Middle East (Leggett, *Levirate,* 100). If an Israelite sells himself to a non-Israelite, that situation does not set aside his גאלה, "right of redemption." One of his kinsmen may redeem him. In this passage those who may act as next of kin are enumerated: אחיו, "one of his brothers," דדו, "one of his uncles," בן־דדו, "one of his cousins," or משאר בשרו ממשפחתו, "a near kinsman from his extended family" (cf. 18:6; vv 41–42). It is clear that the close family members are obligated to act as next of kin for another member of that family. Although the order of responsibility is not stated here, it may be assumed that the basis is the eldest to the youngest starting with the category of closest relative. No indication is made whether the uncles are on the father's and/or mother's side, and there is no indication whether or not obligations of kinsmen extended beyond cousins. In any case Gottwald states that "the *mishpāḥāh* is [understood] to be the widest social unity that had the obligation to do *gōʾēl* for any of its needy members" (*The Tribes of Yahweh,* 264). A debtor servant also retains the right to purchase his own freedom (cf. v 25) The price of such a servant's redemption is to be determined on the basis of the wages of a hired worker according to the length of time until the next Jubilee.

The standard by which an Israelite master is to govern an Israelite servant is the standard also for a resident alien's handling of an Israelite servant (cf. vv 43, 46). A foreign master is to treat his Israelite servant as a hired hand; he may not treat him בפרך, "harshly" (cf. v 43). If an Israelite who has been sold to a foreigner has not been redeemed, he and his children gain their full freedom at the year of Jubilee.

54–55 If a debtor-slave has not been גאל, "redeemed," by any of the ways provided for him to gain his freedom, he יצא, "goes out," in the year of Jubilee. Each Israelite slave takes his children with him into freedom. The use of the verb יצא is significant; as Hubbard (*Bulletin for Biblical Research* 1 [1991] 11) points out, it connects with the coming reference to Yahweh's having הוציא, "brought," his people and his עבדים, "servants," out from Egypt. This language means that the release at the year of Jubilee possesses the same quality as the exodus from Egypt. Each Jubilee, Yahweh acts again as Israel's great Redeemer (גאל). This legislation on Jubilee concludes with the affirmation that Israel is Yahweh's servant, whom he brought out from Egyptian bondage (cf. vv 38, 42). That all Israelites are Yahweh's servants is stressed by being stated in the expression of historical origin and then restated in the declaratory formula "they are my servants." This special legislation has its foundation in Israel's special saving history. Israel's faithful following of this legislation "perpetuates the first liberation—that from Egyptian slavery" (Hubbard, 11). Since all, even the highest officials, are Yahweh's servants, they are responsible to him for treating their servants as they wish to be treated and for making sure that they are released in the year of Jubilee. Furthermore, this legislation has its foundation in the holy character of Yahweh, their God, as the formula of self-introduction conveys (cf. 18:2).

Explanation

This speech sets forth the legislation for the sabbatical year and the year of Jubilee. Every seventh year was a sabbatical year. During that year the land was to rest by lying fallow. None of this year's growth could be harvested, stored, or sold. Nevertheless, all living in Israel, especially the poor and aliens, were permitted to gather freely from all that grew of itself for their daily needs. Animals, both domestic and wild, were free to graze in the fields.

The seventh sabbatical year or the year immediately following, i.e., the fiftieth year, was the year of Jubilee. During this year the land was to lie fallow. More importantly, liberty was to be proclaimed throughout the land. All Israelite slaves were freed, and every patrimony that had been leased out was returned to its owner. The goal of Jubilee was to maintain the solidarity of the various clans in Israel by keeping alive the ideal of the equality of all Israelite citizens under the covenant. From another perspective, this legislation sought to prevent the rich from amassing property into large estates (cf. Isa 5:8) and reducing the poor to landless tenant farmers. Thus it attacked head-on the dehumanizing powers of debt and landlessness (cf. W. Brueggemann, *Finally Comes the Poet: Daring Speech for Proclamation* [Minneapolis: Fortress, 1989] 102–4).

Observance of these laws obviously meant that the people would not profit as much, losing the produce of one year out of seven. During a sabbatical year they would have to rely heavily on Yahweh to provide their needs. Obedience to Yahweh thus required hard work blended with trust. Yahweh, however, did not lay a heavy obligation on his people without offering his grace. He promised to bless the land so that it would yield such an abundance in the sixth year that there would be enough food to carry the people through the sabbatical year and into the next year while they were waiting for the first harvest of the next seven-year cycle (vv 20–22). In addition, Yahweh promised to protect them so that they would dwell in safety (v 19). These promises address the major fears of inhabitants in small villages in ancient times, namely, poor crops and plundering by marauding bands. Yahweh thereby committed himself to make it possible for his people to keep these laws.

A major tenet of this legislation is the laws of redemption. These laws address the issues of maintaining ownership of a patrimony and personal freedom. This legislation regarding the redemption of land was founded on the premise that Yahweh owned the land that he had given to his people through the covenant. Israelite families were in essence his tenants who worked the land and lived off its increase. The belief in Yahweh's ownership of the land, therefore, produced in ancient Israel a distinctive economic system based on the perpetual right of a family to its patrimony. Each parcel of land distributed to a family under the covenant carried a right of redemption. Debt could never force a family to sell its land. But faced with financial hardship, they could lease it for the number of years until the next Jubilee. The right of redemption that went with a patrimony permitted the original owner to reclaim full control of his patrimony whenever he met the debt obligation. That is, the lessee could not hold back the land from returning to the lessor. The lessor was able to redeem the patrimony in any one of three ways. (1) A kinsman could pay off the debt. (2) Whenever this head of the family accumulated enough money, he could redeem it himself. (3) At the year of Jubilee a patrimony was automatically returned to its original owner free of debt. In the last scenario Yahweh himself was acting as the next of kin, liberating his kinsman's property (Hubbard, *Bulletin for Biblical Research* 1 [1991] 11).

An exception to the right of redemption of property was made for houses in walled cities. The reason for this difference may have been that these cities were heavily inhabited by Canaanites. In any case, a person owning a house in a walled city, unlike a farmer, was not dependent on that piece of property for his livelihood, nor was that house a part of the inheritance of land distributed to Israelites under the covenant. Whenever a person sells a house in a walled city, he had a year to reclaim that house. Afterwards the sale was irrevocable.

Houses in Levitical cities, i.e., those cities assigned to the Levites throughout the land, carry a right of redemption (Num 35:1–8). Since the Levites had no tribal inheritance and since these cities were Yahweh's gift to them, they could not sell their houses, but only lease them out until the year of Jubilee. Any unreclaimed house in a Levitical city was returned to its original owner at the year of Jubilee. Neither could the Levites sell the grazing land that accompanied their cities.

The legislation of redemption regulates the making of loans to the poor and the treatment and release of debtor-slaves. It addresses these issues because the major threat to the ideal of social equality of all Israelites was debt. Debt could separate a family from its land and rob a family of its freedom. The head of the family might have to sell family members and himself into servitude to keep them from starvation. These laws against taking interest on loans made to poor fellow citizens guarded against debts increasing swiftly and automatically. Compound interest on debts would drive more and more small landowners from their properties. To impede this force of indebtedness, these laws sought to keep the burden of debt at a lower, more manageable level.

The theological basis for these laws regarding debt is that Yahweh had delivered Israel from Egyptian bondage. Now all of them were his servants. That is, all members of the covenant were on equal footing as Yahweh's redeemed slaves.

During the course of life, nevertheless, an Israelite with a burdening debt had to meet his obligation. Such a person might sell himself into servitude. One who had already leased out his patrimony and faced greater debt, for example, would have been forced down this path. To prevent an Israelite family from becoming perpetual bond servants, these laws of redemption in regard to debtor-slaves were given. They offered an Israelite slave four ways to gain release from bondage. (1) At any time a kinsman could redeem him. (2) Whenever he had acquired sufficient funds, most likely through a windfall like an inheritance, he could purchase his own freedom. (3) A slave was freed at the end of six years of service, according to Exod 21:2 and Deut 15:12. At this time of release, however, a slave might agree to bind himself as a slave to his master for life (Deut 15:16–17). One reason an Israelite slave might take this step was that he feared to try to make a living on his own. The primary reason for such action, though, was the stipulation that if a debtor-slave married during his time of service and had children, his wife and children would not go free with him (Exod 21:4–6). In order to stay with his family, he could bind himself to this master; if he did so, his servitude was for life. That set of laws on debtor servants, standing alone, made it possible for a class of Israelite slaves to develop. (4) The final provision for the release of an Israelite slave, whether one was in the first cycle of servitude or voluntarily had oneself bound to a master, was the proclamation of liberty at the beginning of the year of Jubilee. This legislation set a limit to the length of servitude of an Israelite family, including a debtor-slave who had bound himself to a master. While nothing in the legislation is said about such a person's wife, it is assumed that she too was released. These four ways to freedom were guaranteed to an Israelite whether he had become the debtor-slave of a fellow Israelite or of a resident alien. That is, an alien master living in Israel had to abide by the same laws as did an Israelite.

This legislation, furthermore, regulated the way a master was to treat an Israelite debtor servant. Such a servant was to be treated as a hired servant, not as a bond slave. He was not to be treated harshly nor assigned demeaning tasks. If a landowner already owned slaves, he was not to number any Israelites among his slaves acquired from foreign nations or from resident aliens. Foreign slaves became part of an estate and were passed on as part of an inheritance.

Two motivations in this legislation encouraged Israel to proclaim the release: (1) the fear of Yahweh (v 17) and (2) the deliverance from Egypt (v 38). Each Israelite was to act in light of his fear, or reverence, for Yahweh. Motivated by such fear, a person was diligent to obey Yahweh's law. Whoever feared Yahweh honored whom Yahweh honored. Just as Yahweh loved and blessed his redeemed people, his people were to honor and love one another. No Israelite was to lord it over another Israelite ruthlessly. Furthermore, since Israel had been slaves in Egypt, Yahweh wanted them to remember his delivering them with a grateful heart. This attitude was concretely expressed by not treating fellow Israelites like bond slaves and by granting their freedom when any of the conditions for redemption from bondage had been met or at the year of Jubilee.

The principle of Jubilee promoted an ancient celebration of home-coming (North, *Sociology*, 158). The day when all disenfranchised Israelites returned to their patrimony would have been as joyful as the day when Joshua first divided up the land to each family in Israel (Josh 13–21). Such a program offered those beset with economic hardship and those in debt a genuine hope of a new day. Such former debtors began the new Jubilee cycle as free Israelites. Those forced into servitude by debt could work with a lighter heart, knowing that their day of release was coming. By establishing this legislation Yahweh revealed himself as "the powerful protector of the weak" (Hubbard, *Bulletin for Biblical Research* 1 [1991] 13). He erected a high barrier against the forces that produce a continuous cycle of poverty among his covenant people. This practice was one path to the peace Yahweh desired for them.

Yahweh gave Israel the sabbatical year and the year of Jubilee to curtail the human desire to accumulate more and more by interrupting the continuous activity of sowing and harvesting. Greed prevents a person from enjoying what he has, for it drives one to spend all one's energy on getting more. Conversely, if a person can learn to live with what one has and to take periodic times of rest away from work, that person has time to enjoy and appreciate what one has gained with a thankful attitude. In addition, Yahweh was teaching his people that the land, like people, needed rest. Here is an early expression of conservation. People must not overwork the land on which they depend for their livelihood by exhausting its fertility for immediate satisfaction. Rather they must manage their use of the land to maintain its fertility throughout the generations. Such management is an expression of trust in Yahweh to supply his people's needs.

The effect of the Jubilee legislation on ancient Hebraic society is impossible to measure in light of the sparse references to it in the OT. Its impact was no doubt much greater than that of some romantic manifesto that became lost in the pages of a cultic law code. The Book of Ruth clearly witnesses to the importance of the laws of kinsman redemption among the populace at the close of the era of the Judges (cf. 2:20; 3:9, 12, 13; 4:1–12, 14). The account of Naboth's vineyard indicates that in Northern Israel the crown disregarded the ancient ordinary laws even though citizens held tenaciously to them (1 Kgs 21:1–24). The laws about inalienable tribal inheritances and the restrictions against loaning money at interest may lie behind the social solidarity of the state of Judah and its ability to endure as a self-governing political state for several decades after the fall of Northern Israel. That these laws had not been completely forgotten in the South is demonstrated by two incidents recorded in Jeremiah: Zedekiah's proclamation of a release of Hebrew slaves during a time of extreme national danger (Jer 34:8–17) and Jeremiah's redemption of his uncle's field at Anathoth (Jer 32:6–15). This conjecture about the influence of these laws does not mean to say that they were followed to the letter; rather it is saying that they contributed to the solidarity of ancient Judean society, which was a factor in its surviving some 140 years longer than the nation of Northern Israel.

The Sabbath, the sabbatical year, and the year of Jubilee function in later Scriptures as typologies of the ideal age when Yahweh will reign supreme over the entire globe. Since the year of Jubilee marked the release of all Israelites from debt and servitude, it became a typology of the ideal age when everyone will be free from all debts, living on their Yahweh-given inheritance and zealously worshiping Yahweh. Three futuristic OT texts employ terms and images from the Jubilee as descriptive of the coming salvation. First, Isa 61:1–3 speaks of a coming prophet who will proclaim liberty, i.e., the year of Jubilee. It will be the year of Yahweh's favor and the day of vengeance. The faithful who have suffered oppression, bondage, and imprisonment will be freed. Mourners will be comforted. In the promised land the people will rebuild the ruins. Conversely, those who have amassed fortunes by greed will lose their ill-gotten gains and face divine punishment. At this great time Yahweh will put an end to the enslaving cycle of debt and poverty (Brueggemann, *Finally Comes the Poet,* 105). Second, the vision of Daniel in 9:24–27 sets the messianic age to begin in the year of the tenth Jubilee (49 x 10 = 490 years; A. Lacocque, *The Book of Daniel* [Atlanta: John Knox Press, 1979] 178). This great Jubilee will inaugurate an era when sin will cease, iniquity will have been fully atoned, eternal righteousness will have been brought in, and true worship of Yahweh will take place at the anointed holy place (v 24). Third, in an elaborate vision of an ideal Israel, Ezekiel applies the laws on the right of redemption of property specifically to the property of the prince who will lead the nation (46:16–18). Not only is his property protected by a right of redemption, but the head of the government, the prince, may not displace any of the people from their inheritance. The use of Jubilee as a typology for the messianic era continues in Judaism, e.g., *The Book of Jubilees* (cf. 1:29) and 11Q Melchizedek.

There are two uses of Jubilee as a typology in the interpretation of Jesus' ministry. The most important of these NT texts is the Lucan account of Jesus' visit to the synagogue in Nazareth. There he read the Scripture lesson from Isa 61:1–2 (Luke 4:16–30; Tannehill, BZNW 40 [1973] 51, 75). Luke casts this scene as programmatic of Jesus' mission. By reading from this OT passage, Jesus was claiming that he was the one anointed by the Spirit to preach good news to the poor, to proclaim release or forgiveness to captives and recovery of sight to the blind, to set at liberty the oppressed, and to proclaim the acceptable year of the Lord. Tannehill shows that these ideas, above all the proclamation of release, are definitive for the presentation of the work and teaching of Jesus in Luke-Acts. First, Jesus was anointed with the Spirit at his baptism (Luke 3:21–23), and Luke stresses Jesus' continued endowment with the Spirit (4:1, 14; cf. Acts 4:27; 10:38). Second, Luke employs the word used for preaching in the Isaianic passage ten times as compared to Matthew's use of it a single time and its absence from Mark. That Luke portrays Jesus as fulfilling this task is, therefore, evident in his use of this term in three summary statements of Jesus' work (4:43; 8:1; 20:1; Tannehill, 69–70). Third, Luke highlights Jesus' mission to the poor. Fourth, the term release/forgiveness, which is the name for Jubilee in LXX, functions as the key dimension of Jesus' earthly work in Luke-Acts (cf. Luke 7:36–50; 19:1–10; 24:47; Acts 2:38; 5:31; 10:43; 13:38; 26:18; Tannehill, 68). The sum of these points means that with Jesus' mission "the time of the Lord's favor" had arrived (Tannehill, 71). Furthermore, the reference to Jubilee in the scene at Nazareth establishes a tie with the vision of Daniel about the great Jubilee that will inaugurate the messianic age. Strobel (BZNW 40 [1973] 44–46, 49–50) demonstrates that in the days of Jesus there was the expectation that the final, tenth Jubilee prophesied by Daniel was about to take place. Luke builds on that expectation by recounting the scene at Nazareth when Jesus himself inaugurated the eschatological age at the time set by Yahweh in the prophecy of Daniel.

The second reference to Jubilee in relationship to Jesus' ministry occurs in his reply to John the Baptist's inquiry whether he was truly the Messiah (Luke 7:20–23; Matt 11:2–6). Jesus sent back to John a report stating that he had healed the blind, the lame, and the leprous, raised the dead, and preached to the poor. He cast his answer in the language of both Isa 35:5–7 and 61:1, eschatological texts filled with the imagery of the year of Jubilee. Thereby Jesus was claiming that he, the anointed messenger, was bringing in the age of Yahweh's favor.

That the purpose of the year of Jubilee was important to Jesus is further demonstrated by the fact that the goals of this legislation were central to his teaching. Jesus spoke against amassing treasures on earth for one's own personal glory, teaching that one's heart is where one's treasures are (Matt 6:19–21). He encouraged people to help one another, i.e., to accept the responsibility that other people are one's next of kin. If a person compels one to go a mile, that one must go two miles (Matt 5:40–42). Above all Jesus offered forgiveness to all who believed on him, and he taught that those who are forgiven must forgive others (Matt 6:14–15; Mark 11:25; Luke 17:4). In his kingdom all people are free and equal. The goal of the Jubilee legislation is becoming realized.

Another symbolic connection between Jubilee and the portrayal of the messianic era is the custom of announcing the year of Jubilee with a trumpet blast. There are frequent references in both testaments that the messianic era will begin with a blast of the trumpet. Isaiah prophesies that a trumpet will be blown, and the exiles from all lands will return to worship Yahweh on the holy mountain in Jerusalem (27:13). In Zech 9:9–17 a trumpet blast will announce the victorious, triumphant entry of the Messiah into Jerusalem and the start of an era of global peace. Using this imagery, the NT proclaims that the trumpet shall announce the return of Jesus Christ (1 Cor 15:52; 1 Thess 4:16; Matt 24:31).

This Jubilee manifesto has not been lost on the pages of a forgotten OT book. It has had a leavening effect on social thought in the West, as the inscription of the words of v 10, "proclaim liberty throughout the land," on the Liberty Bell attests. Jubilee holds out the ideal of an egalitarian society being realized in an era of social harmony. These ideals have often inspired leaders of democracy and great social reformers. This legislation, which encourages each family's ownership of land, has contributed to the Western ideal that every family has a right to own property. The view of land ownership herein, however, is revolutionary. It does not promote the ownership of private property in a way that allows the rich to amass large tracts of land, displacing the poor, nor does it permit the speculative buying and selling of land that feeds inflation, which in turn increases poverty. Neither does this manifesto promote a social or common ownership of land. Instead, this legislation prescribes a classless society in which each family has an inalienable ownership of a plot of land. It promotes responsible work that attends ownership of property, and at the same time it promotes responsible brotherhood of all Yahweh's people arising from their faith in Yahweh. Those who are more prosperous assist their poorer brothers, raising them to their own level, because they fear Yahweh. Kinsman helps kinsman, neighbor helps neighbor to face and to overcome economic hardship. Greed and covetousness are broken. This wonderful manifesto will continue to feed both the eschatological vision and utopian thinking until the kingdom of the Lord Jesus Christ is fully established.

2. *Some General Commandments on Faithful Worship (26:1–2)*

Translation

1 *"You shall not make for yourselves idols,*[a] *and you shall not set up an image*[b] *or a sacred pillar*[c] *for yourselves, and you shall not place a sculptured stone*[d] *in your land to bow down before it, because*[e] *I am Yahweh your God.* 2 *Keep my Sabbaths and revere my sanctuary. I am Yahweh.*

Notes

1.a. Cf. n. 19:4.a.

1.b. The root of פסל, "idol, image," means "hew into shape." פסל includes any image made out of a variety of materials, including wood (Isa 40:20; 44:17), stone (Hab 2:18–19), and metal (Judg 17:3–4; Isa 40:19). These materials could be overlaid with gold and silver and even set with precious stones.

1.c. מצבה comes from the root נצב, "stand, be stationed." It refers to a stone that had been set up as a pillar for a memorial or for a cultic object; often these pillars were set up near an altar or at a sanctuary. Since not all pillars set up were cultic, not all were condemned. In OT times people erected pillars of varying sizes to commemorate alliances, deaths, and important events. E.g., at Bethel Jacob set up a pillar and then anointed it (Gen 28:18; cf. 35:14); he also set up one for the formal agreement he reached with Laban (Gen 31:45–54). Moses set up twelve stones beside the altar at Mount Sinai, on which he made the sacrifices to seal the covenant (Exod 24:4; cf. Josh 4:20–24). On the other hand, peoples throughout the Middle East erected stones of varying heights, rough or partly dressed or shaped, with or without engravings, to a particular deity. Because these kinds of pillars were objects of worship, Israel was commanded not to set up sacred pillars (here; Deut 16:22) and to break down those that were standing (Exod 23:24; Deut 7:5; 12:3). At times Israel worshiped such pillars (2 Kgs 17:10; Hos 10:1), but her great reformers smashed them (2 Chr 14:2[3]; 2 Kgs 18:4; 2 Chr 31:1; 2 Kgs 23:14).

1.d. מַשְׂכִּית means "picture" in Prov 25:11. The phrase אבן מַשְׂכִּית means (lit.) "a stone with a relief" (KB, 605–6; cf. Y. Mansur, "אבן מַשְׂכִּית," *Leshonenu* 24 [1959/60] 181–82). Porter (207) thinks this is a boundary stone such as was used in Mesopotamia to mark off the boundaries of a field; on these stones, emblems of a god were engraved. This term may include these stones, but it was not limited to them (cf. Num 33:52). This is demonstrated by the term חדרי מַשְׂכִּית, "rooms of pictures," in Ezek 8:12. This means a room in which there were images; perhaps one or more of them were engraved in stone and set on pedestals, or perhaps along a wall there was a massive stone with reliefs of various gods, or portraits of these gods or scenes from the various myths about them may have been painted on the walls (cf. Levine, 181; Zimmerli, *Ezekiel 1,* 220–21).

1.e. LXX and Syr omit כי, "because."

Form/Structure/Setting

This brief group of laws establishes a bridge between the regulations on cyclical time and the following blessings and curses. In fact, the speaker has employed them to take the place of the standard introductory formula in order to connect the material in chap. 25 with that in chap. 26. The following structural outline of this brief bridge is an expansion of the outline in the *Form/Structure* section on 25:1–26:46, being subordinate to "2. Some general commandments (26:1–2)":

- a. Prohibitions against idolatry (v 1)
  - 1) Three prohibitions (v 1a)
  - 2) Formula of Yahweh's self-introduction (v 1b)
- b. Commandments for observance of the Sabbath and reverence of the sanctuary (v 2)
  - 1) Commandments proper (v 2a)
  - 2) Formula of Yahweh's self-introduction (v 2b)

The design of this brief unit carries great rhetorical force, for three terse, categorical prohibitions are followed by two short, categorical commands, and both sets of laws are underscored by the formula of Yahweh's self-introduction, the short formula being followed by the long formula. Laws similar to those in v 1 occur in 19:4, while the laws in v 2 repeat identically 19:30, and v 2aα occurs also in 19:3aβ. Kilian (*Literarkritische,* 158) posits that they have been placed here by the redactor of the Holiness Code, for they are for this redactor important ordinances worthy of repetition. Whether or not a redactor has placed them here, they do tie this speech into the laws on holy living.

A puzzling issue in dealing with the structure of chaps. 25–26 is the location of these two verses. Some scholars, e.g., Noth (193) and Levine (181–82), place these two verses with what precedes. From this perspective, the commandment on the Sabbath is united with the calendrical material on the sabbatical year in chap. 25. More importantly both units are predominantly laws. But these reasons are very general and far from compelling.

A more important reason is that these words prepare Israel for hearing the coming blessings and curses. They call to the audience's mind the covenant, for two of the commandments, the prohibition against worshiping idols and the command to observe the Sabbath, are part of the Decalogue (Exod 20:4, 8), which is the keystone of the Sinaitic covenant (Exod 19–24). Additionally the use of the formula of Yahweh's self-introduction likewise points to the covenant, for it heads the giving of the Decalogue (Exod 20:2; cf. *Excursus* at 18:2). This reason behind the design of these verses finds additional support in the reference to Mount Sinai in the opening introductory formula; this reference is proof that these laws have as their theological setting the Sinaitic Covenant (cf. Wright, *God's People,* 149). The blessings and curses that follow are an integral part of a covenant document, as will be demonstrated in the *Form/Structure/Setting* to 26:3–46. Thus the linkage between 26:1–2 and 26:3–45 is very strong. These laws, therefore, prepare the audience for hearing the blessings and curses that follow, for obedience to them will move Yahweh to bless his people as he promises, while breaking them will place Israel in jeopardy of being punished by the sequence of curses. Furthermore, there is a tie with the instructions for restoration of an exiled Israel in 26:40–45, for on returning to the promised land Israel will have to follow and observe these laws as the foundation for building a dynamic, renewed community obedient to Yahweh, her God. Significant supplemental support for this interpretation of the location of these verses comes from Kilian (*Literarkritische,* 158–59), for he finds a parallel with the covenant book in Exod. He notes that a prohibition similar to v 1 occurs toward the end of that book (Exod 23:24) and that Exod 23:25a*α*, the next line in the covenant book, parallels 26:3 in Yahweh's promise to bless those who serve him. This similar pattern in Exod 23 confirms taking 26:1–2 as the lead into the recounting of blessings and curses. This ideological accounting for the presence of this brief unit coincides with its rhetorical force.

Comment

1 This chapter opens with a reiteration of the commandment not to turn to idols, which stands in 19:4. This commandment is an elucidation on the second commandment of the Decalogue (Exod 20:4–6//Deut 5:8–10). The use of four terms for idols encompasses every type of idolatry: אלילים, "idols," פסל, "an image," מצבה, "a sacred pillar," אבן משכית, "a sculptured stone." פסל, "image," stands for divine figurines made out of a variety of materials. מצבה means stones of varying sizes set up as pillars. אבן משכית refers to stones with an engraving of a deity or a symbolic representation of a deity; they could be small, such as boundary stones, or massive stones erected as stele. The three prohibitions cast in the strong form underscore the demand that Israel is to worship Yahweh alone.

2 The fourth commandment of the Decalogue, on keeping the Sabbath (Exod 20:8–11), is restated; cf. 19:3, 30; 23:3. The next commandment is מקדשי תיראו, "revere my sanctuary," the place where Yahweh dwells; this commandment is found also at 19:30. Both the observance of the Sabbath and the reverence of the sanctuary acknowledge the supreme Lordship of Yahweh.

Explanation

Yahweh demands exclusive worship from his people. They are not to make any likeness of him in any medium. Other peoples crafted idols to represent their gods. They set up pillars in their honor. They engraved stones with representations of their deities and the stories of their exploits. Then they fell down before these cold monuments. Yahweh, conversely, is the Creator and cannot be represented in any medium of the created order. He is Spirit. He must be worshiped in spirit and in truth (John 4:24). Integral to the worship of Yahweh, the people must observe the Sabbath by resting from their earthly obligations and remembering Yahweh as their Creator and their Redeemer. To worship Yahweh in truth the people must revere, i.e., promote the sanctity of, the sanctuary, where Yahweh manifests his presence. Yahweh, the personal God, may be approached by his people through the sacrificial offerings he has prescribed and through the word, not through human-made objects representing him.

3. Blessings and Curses (26:3–46)

Bibliography

Baltzer, K. *The Covenant Formulary in Old Testament, Jewish, and Early Christian Writings.* Tr. D. Green. Philadelphia: Fortress, 1971. **Batto, B.** "The Covenant of Peace: A Neglected Ancient Near Eastern Motif." *CBQ* 49 (1987) 187–211. **Buis, P.** "Comment au septième siècle envisageait-on l'avenir de l'alliance? Étude sur Lev. 26,3–45." In *Questions disputées d'Ancien Testament: Méthode et Théologie.* Ed. C. Brekelmans. Bibliotheca Ephemeridum Theologicarum Lovaniensium 33. Leuven/Louvain: Leuven UP, 1974. 131–40. **Fensham, F. C.** "Malediction and Benediction in Ancient Near Eastern Vassal-Treaties and the Old Testament." *ZAW* 74 (1962) 1–9. **Frankena, R.** "The Vassal-Treaties of Esarhaddon and the Dating of Deuteronomy." *OTS* 14 (1965) 122–54. **Hillers, D. R.** *Treaty Curses and the Old Testament Prophets.* BibOr 16. Rome: Pontifical Biblical Institute, 1964. **Levine, B.** "The Epilogue to the Holiness Code: A Priestly Statement on the Destiny of Israel." In *Judaic Perspectives on Ancient Israel.* Ed. J. Neusner et al. Philadelphia: Fortress, 1987. 9–34. **Lipiński, E.** "*Nešek* and *Tarbīt* in the Light of Epigraphic Evidence." *Orientalia Lovaniensia Periodica* 10 (1979) 133–41. **Lohfink, N.** "Die Abänderung der Theologie des priestlichen Geschichtswerk im Segen des Heiligkeitsgesetzes. Zu Lev. 26,9.11–13." In *Wort und Geschichte.* FS Karl Elliger. Ed. H. Gese and H. Rüger. AOAT 8. Neukrichen-Vluyn: Neukirchener, 1973. 129–36. **McCarthy, D. J.** *Treaty and Covenant: A Study in Form in the Ancient Oriental Documents and in the Old Testament.* AnBib 21A. Rome: Biblical Institute Press, 1981. **Noth, M.** "'For All Who Rely on Works of the Law Are under a Curse.'" In *The Laws in the Pentateuch and Other Studies.* Tr. D. Ap-Thomas. Edinburgh: Oliver & Boyd, 1967. 118–31. **Paul, S. M.** *Studies in the Book of the Covenant in the Light of Cuneiform and Biblical Law.* VTSup 17. Leiden: Brill, 1970. **Waltke, B. K.** "The Phenomenon of Conditionality within Unconditional Covenants." In *Israel's Apostasy and Restoration.* FS R. K. Harrison. Ed. A. Gileadi. Grand Rapids: Baker Book House, 1988. 123–39.

Translation

3 *"If you walk in my decrees and faithfully keep*[a] *my commandments,* 4 *I shall send you*[a] *the rains*[b] *in their seasons, and the ground will yield its crops and the trees of the field their fruit.* 5 *Threshing*[a] *will continue for you until vintage*[b] *and vintage will continue until sowing.*[bc] *You will eat bread to satisfaction, and you will dwell securely in your land.* 6 *I shall give peace*[a] *in the land in order that you may lie down without being frightened.*[b] *I shall remove the wild beasts from the land. The sword will not pass*[c] *through your land.*[d] 7 *You will pursue your enemies, and they will fall by the sword before you.*

*8Five of you will chase a hundred and a hundred of you will chase ten thousand and
your enemies will fall by the sword before you. 9I shall turn[a] to you, I shall make you
fruitful, I shall increase your number, and I shall maintain my covenant with you.
10You will be eating from an earlier harvest long stored until you have to remove the old
to make room for the new harvest.[a]*

*11"I shall put my tabernacle[a] in your midst, and I shall not abhor[b] you. 12I shall walk
about among you. I shall be your God and you will be my people. 13I am Yahweh your
God, who brought you out of Egypt so that[a] you would no longer be slaves[b] to the
Egyptians.[c] I broke the bars of your yoke and enabled you to walk upright.[d]*

*14"But if you will not obey me and you will not do all[a] these commandments, 15and[a]
if you despise my decrees[b] and abhor my laws by not doing my commandments so that
you break my covenant, 16I shall surely do this to you: I shall inflict on you sudden
terror[a]—wasting disease,[b] fever,[c] diminishing[d] eyesight, and loss of appetite.[e] You will
sow your seed in vain, for your enemies will eat it. 17I shall set my face against you so
that you will be crushed by your enemies. Those who hate you will rule[a] over you. You will
flee though no one is pursuing you.*

*18"If in spite of these things you will not listen to me, I shall go on to discipline[a] you
seven times[b] for your sins. 19I shall break your strong pride. I shall make the sky like iron
for you and your land like bronze.[a] 20Your strength will be spent for nought, for your land
will not give its crops and the trees of the earth[a] will not yield their fruit.*

*21"If you defy[a] me[b] and you are not willing to listen to me, I shall increase your af-
flictions seven times according to your sins. 22I shall loose[a] wild beasts against you; they
will rob you of your children,[b] destroy your cattle, make you few in number, and your
roads will be deserted.*

*23"If in spite of these things you do not accept my[a] discipline and you continue to defy
me, 24then[a] even I shall defy you;[b] I, even I, shall smite you seven times[c] for your sins. 25I
shall bring the sword on you for vengeance, the vengeance prescribed by the covenant.[a]
When you gather in your cities, I shall send a pestilence[b] among you, and you will be
given into the hand[c] of your enemy. 26When I break your supply of bread, ten women
will bake your bread in one oven, and they will distribute your bread by weight. You will
eat, but you will not be satisfied.*

*27"If in spite of this you do not listen to me and you continue to defy me, 28I shall
angrily defy you; and I, even I, shall discipline you for your sins seven times. 29You will
eat the flesh of your sons, and you will eat the flesh of your daughters.[a] 30I shall destroy
your high places,[a] demolish your incense altars, and pile your corpses[b] on the corpses of
your idols;[c] I myself shall abhor you. 31I shall reduce your cities to ruins and make desolate your sanctuaries,[a] and I shall not delight in the soothing aroma of your sacrifices.
32I shall make the land[a] so desolate that your enemies who occupy it will be appalled at
it. 33I shall scatter you among the nations, and I shall unsheath my sword after you so
that your land will be laid waste and your cities will become[a] ruins. 34Then the land will
enjoy its sabbath years all the time that it lies desolate[a] and you are in the land of your
enemies; then the land will rest and enjoy[b] its sabbaths. 35All the time that it lies desolate[a]
it will have rest because it did not rest during the sabbath years when you dwelt on it.
36As for those among you who are left, I shall make their hearts timid in the land of their
enemies so that the sound of a blowing leaf will chase them. They will flee as though
fleeing from the sword, and they will fall though no one is chasing them. 37They will
stumble over each other as though fleeing from the sword[a] even though no one is chasing
them. You will not make a stand[b] before your enemies. 38You will perish among the*

nations. The land of your enemies will devour you. 39 *Those who are left among you will languish away*[a] *in the land of your*[b] *enemies because of their iniquity.*[c] *They will also languish away because of their fathers' iniquities added to theirs.*[d]

40 *"But if they will confess their iniquity and the iniquity of their fathers by their treacherous deeds which they have done against me and verily by which they have defied me—*41 *indeed, I will have defied them in that I will have brought*[a] *them into the land of their enemies—if perchance*[b] *their uncircumcised heart is humbled and they make compensation for their iniquity,* 42 *I shall remember my covenant*[a] *with Jacob,*[b] *and I shall remember also my covenant*[a] *with Isaac,*[b] *and verily my covenant*[a] *with Abraham,*[b] *and I shall remember the land.* 43 *For the land will be forsaken by them*[a] *and will enjoy*[b] *its sabbaths while it lies desolate*[c] *without them. They will make compensation for their iniquity because, even because,*[d] *they despised my laws and abhorred my decrees.* 44 *Yet in spite of this*[a] *when they are in the land*[b] *of their enemies, I shall not despise them or abhor them to destroy them completely, breaking my covenant with them, because I am Yahweh their God.* 45 *I shall remember for their sake the former covenant, when I brought them out of Egypt in the sight of the nations in order to be their God. I am Yahweh."*

46 *These are the decrees, laws, and instructions*[a] *which Yahweh established between himself and the Israelites at Mount Sinai through Moses.*

Notes

3.a. The two verbs, תשמרו, "you will keep," and ועשיתם, "you will do," are a hendiadys meaning "diligently, faithfully keep" (Levine, 182).

4.a. Sometimes the pronominal suffix on a verb functions like a dative (Joüon §129h).

4.b. The pl form of גשם, "rain," is very rare in the OT. It occurs only here and in Ezek 34:26; Ezra 10:9, 13; Ps 105:32.

5.a. The noun דיש, "(the process of) threshing," appears only in this verse; however, the verb דוש, "thresh," is well attested (e.g., Deut 25:4).

5.b. Joüon (§125h) accounts for the use of the particle את with an indefinite noun as a desire for clarity.

5.c. Sam reads the definite article on this word.

6.a. Batto (*CBQ* 49 [1987] 203–6) suggests that in this idiom נתן means "plant," and he seeks to show that this verse is part of the idyllic theme of peace on earth as a result of the divine covenant. He goes on to demonstrate that Jesus' words in Matt 10:34 and Luke 12:51 are formulated intentionally as the opposite of this verse.

6.b. This is a circumstantial clause introduced by a *waw* (Joüon §159d).

6.c. The idiom חרב תעבר, "a sword will pass through," appears elsewhere in the OT only in Ezek 14:17.

6.d. This sentence comes at the beginning of the verse in LXX.

9.a. פנה אל means "turn to, turn and look, look on graciously, regard" (2 Kgs 13:23; Ezek 36:9–10; Pss 25:16; 69:17[16]; 86:16; 119:132; BDB, 815).

10.a. The verbs are chiastically arranged.

11.a. In place of MT משכני, "my tabernacle," LXX^{BA} reads τὴν διαθήκην μου = בריתי, "my covenant."

11.b. געל, "abhor, detest," occurs nine times in the OT, and five of those occurrences are in this chapter, vv 15, 30, 43, 44; cf. Jer 14:19; Ezek 16:5, 45. Levine ("Epilogue," 14) finds that the basic image of this root is "physical spoilage or filth."

13.a. מן + inf constr expresses a negative consequence (Joüon §169h).

13.b. In place of MT מהית להם עבדים, LXX reads ὄντων ὑμῶν δούλων, "where you were slaves."

13.c. MT reads להם, "to them"; this trans. uses "Egyptians," the antecedent, for clarity.

13.d. The acc קוממיות expresses a quality about the subj (Joüon §126d). This term, which occurs only here, comes from the root קום, "rise, stand up." BDB (879) gives it the meaning "uprightness," but KB (1018) defines it in light of its adverbial function "in an upright bearing" (cf. GKC §86k).

14.a. LXX does not read כל, "all."

15.a. A few Heb. mss, Sam[mss], Syr, and Vg do not have a *waw*. LXX renders it ἀλλά, "but."

15.b. LXX renders בחקתי, "in my decrees," with the pronoun αὐτοῖς, "them."

16.a. According to Joüon (§102d) the substantive בהלה is used adverbially, "I shall inflict you, causing sudden terror." The root בהל means "dismay, terrify, make haste." Such a terror causes shuddering (Job 21:6). Terror produces confusion and panic, causing one to flee (Ps 48:6[5]; Jer 51:32). B. Otzen says that "the noun *behalah* denotes simply the terror associated or even identical with sudden death" ("בהל *bhl*," *TDOT* 2:5). Sam has the erroneous spelling בחלה.

16.b. השחפת occurs only here and in Deut 28:22; its meaning is taken to be "wasting disease, consumption."

16.c. קדחת, "fever," comes from the root "kindle"; this word occurs only here and in Deut 28:22.

16.d. כלה, "complete, bring to an end," in relationship to the eyes describes a disease that destroys one's eyesight (BDB, 428).

16.e. The root דוב, "pine away," may be another spelling of דאב, "become faint, languish" (BDB, 187). The phrase דאבון נפש, "languishing, faintness," occurs in Deut 28:65, a parallel passage. This word with נפש may mean "despondency," or if נפש is closer to its literal meaning of "throat," the phrase means "loss of appetite."

17.a. In place of MT ורדו, "and they will rule," LXX has καὶ διώξονται = ורדפו, "and they will pursue." PIR (204) explains the variant as assimilation to a parallel passage.

18.a. This piel inf constr has the ה sufformative (GKC §52p; Joüon §52c).

18.b. Often the idea of multiplication is expressed by the cardinal number standing alone (Joüon §142q).

19.a. נחושה, "bronze, copper," is a poetic spelling of נחשת (e.g., Job 20:24; Isa 45:2).

20.a. In place of הארץ, "the land," which is supported by 11QpaleoLev, several Heb. mss, LXX, and *Tg. Ps.-J.* read השדה, "the field." LXX also has the possessive pronoun ὑμῶν, "your." Elliger (363) accepts the variant reading, but PIR (204) understands the variant as an assimilation to a similar passage.

21.a. קרי, "meeting" (KB, 1065), occurs seven times in the OT, and all of these are in this chapter and only in the idiom with the verb הלך, "walk" (sometimes the prep ב, "in, with," precedes קרי [vv 24, 27]); this idiom means "to walk contrary, resist, oppose." Levine ("Epilogue," 15), however, takes קרי from קרר, "be cold"; then this idiom means (lit.) "to walk with coldness."

21.b. LXX does not have anything for עמי, "with me," but it does read μετὰ ταῦτα, "after these things," which is not in MT.

22.a. Sam and 11QpaleoLev read a qal instead of the hiph in MT.

22.b. Where MT has השדה ושכלה אתכם, "the field, and he will rob you of your children," LXX reads τὰ ἄγρια τῆς γῆς, "the fields of the earth."

23.a. Some Heb. mss, 11QpaleoLev, LXX, *Tg. Ps.-J.*, Syr, and Vg omit לי, "to me."

24.a. Sam reads גם, "also," in place of MT אף, "indeed," conforming to the wording later in the verse; 11QpaleoLev omits אף אני, "even I."

24.b. LXX reads θυμῷ πλαγίῳ, "with contrary anger" or "angrily hostile," as in v 28; LXX is leveling the text.

24.c. Cf. n. 18.b.

25.a. Levine ("Epilogue," 16) understands נקם to be synonymous with the oaths and adjurations of the covenant. Therefore, he renders the clause חרב נקמת נקם־ברית, "a sword enforcing the threats of the covenant."

25.b. דבר, "pestilence," is a fatal plague that befalls both people and animals (Jer 27:13; Ezek 33:27; Exod 9:3). In the LXX it is often rendered by θανατός, "death." According to Hab 3:5, pestilence and plague accompany God when he leaves his abode and comes to battle his foes on earth (cf. Mayer, "דֶּבֶר *debher*," *TDOT* 3:125–27).

25.c. *Tg. Ps.-J.* and *Tg. Neof.* read pl forms, "hands of your enemies."

29.a. This curse is much more graphically and heinously described in Deut 28:53–57 (cf. Isa 9:19–20; 49:26; Jer 19:9; Lam 4:10; Ezek 5:10; Zech 11:9).

30.a. במה, which is usually rendered "high place," comes from a Sem root meaning "back, ridge." Akk *bamtu* B means "chest, rib cage" (*CAD* 2:78–79; *AHw* [101] adds "slope, ridge, middle of back"), and Ugar *bmt* means "back" of an animal (K.-D. Schunck, "בָּמָה, *bāmāh*," *TDOT* 2:140). In Heb., במה sometimes means "back" (Deut 33:29) or "ridge, high ground" (Deut 32:13; Amos 4:13; Isa 58:14). But its most frequent use in the OT is for "a cultic (high) place." No structure has been found that may be unequivocally identified as a במה (M. Haran, *Temples*, 21). Haran believes that במה was an altar, but what distinguished it from other altars is unknown. From references in the OT he concludes that they were "simple, solid, and exposed constructions, located in the open" (23). At Megiddo and Nahariyah heaps of unhewn stones made in an oval shape and with a flat surface have been found (Haran, 21). Although these structures are earlier than Israel, they are the best candidates to date for a במה. Cf. Schunck, *TDOT* 2:139–45.

30.b. D. Neiman ("*PGR*: a Canaanite Cult-Object in the OT," *JBL* 67 [1948] 55–60) proposed that פגר means "a cult object, stele," but this proposal has not won acceptance.

30.c. גלולים is another term for idols (cf. v 1). Ezekiel relishes this term, using it some thirty-nine times (e.g., 16:36; 18:6, 12, 15). גלולים refers to large images shaped as either a human or an animal. This word appears to be a pejorative term, for it has been formed after the same pattern as שִׁקּוּץ, "detestable things." This formation is evidently intentional, for גלול and שִׁקּוּץ sometimes occur together (e.g., Deut 29:16[17]; Ezek 20:7, 8; 37:23). The etymology of גלול has not been determined beyond question. Some, such as Preuss and Zimmerli, connect it with גל, "dung, manure," so that גלולים means "things of dung, dung idols." This explanation is in accord with Ezekiel's emphasis on the uncleanness and the defilement caused by idolatry. Cf. H. D. Preuss, "גלולים *gillûlîm*," *TDOT* 3:1–5; W. Zimmerli, *Ezekiel 1*, 187.

31.a. Many Heb. mss, Sam, and Syr have מקדשכם, "one sanctifying you," in place of MT מקדשיכם, "your sanctuary."

32.a. LXX adds *ὑμῶν*, "your."

33.a. This is an example of a masc verb used with a fem subj (cf. Gen 41:27; Hoffmann, 2:373).

34.a. Instead of השמה, "lying desolate," Sam has אשמה. LXX reads the final ה as a pronominal sufformative. LXX is followed.

34.b. MT הרצת preserves the old form of the third sg pf (GKC §75m), but Sam has the spelling הרצתה.

35.a. Cf. n. 34.a.

37.a. The placing of the prep כ, "as, like," on the phrase מפני חרב, "before the sword," is explained by GKC (§118s, n. 2) as the putting of the prep on a word with a prep that has become viewed as a fixed form.

37.b. תקומה is a fem noun from the root קום, "arise"; it occurs only here. BDB (879) gives it the meaning "standing, power to stand" by relating it to a meaning of קום in qal, namely, "maintain oneself" (Josh 7:12, 13; Nah 1:6; Lam 1:14; Pss 1:5; 24:3). *TWOT* (2:794) renders it "the ability to stand and resist."

39.a. מקק, "rot, fester, decay," occurs only nine times in the OT. In Ps 38:6(5) it describes the festering of wounds, and in Zech 14:12 it pictures the rotting away of one's eyes, tongue, and flesh. It is applied metaphorically to the wasting away of those who rebel against God, because of their iniquity (here; Ezek 4:17; 24:23; 33:10).

39.b. Many Heb. mss, Sam, and the versions have the third person pronominal suffix instead of the second person. Elliger (363) accepts the variant, but PIR (204) understands the variant as assimilation to a parallel passage.

39.c. LXX reads *διὰ τὰς ἁμαρτίας ὑμῶν*, "through your sins." Apparently it had in its Vorlage חטאה, "sins," instead of עון, "iniquity."

39.d. LXX omits ואף בעונת אבתם אתם, "even because of the iniquities of their fathers added to theirs." Elliger (363) thinks MT may be a gloss. Furthermore, he views אתם, "with them = added to theirs," to be an error of dittography from אבתם, "their fathers."

41.a. In place of MT והבאתי, "and I shall bring," LXX has *καὶ ἀπολῶ* = והאבדתי, "and I shall cause to perish."

41.b. For MT או־אז, "or then," Syr has ואז ,"and then," and LXX *τότε* = אז, "then." או introduces an indirect question as in 1 Sam 20:10; it may be rendered "if perchance" (GKC §150i).

42.a. LXX omits the suffix; this may simply be to give a smoother Gk. reading. Syr adds עם, "with."

42.b. The syntax את־בריתי יעקוב, (lit.) "my covenant (with) Jacob," is unusual, for יעקוב is essentially a genitive. The sense is ברית יעקוב אשר לי, "the covenant of Jacob which I have" (Joüon §129a, n. 2; cf. Jer 33:20). GKC (§128d) tenuously offers the explanation that MT is an ellipsis for בריתי ברית יעקב, "my covenant, the covenant with Jacob"; but GKC is more confident with the proposal that the י pronominal suffix is a case of dittography. This same discussion applies to the two following, similar phrases.

43.a. In this example the prep מן introduces the agent of the action (Joüon §132d).

43.b. In place of MT ותרץ, "let it enjoy," Sam has והרצתה, "it will enjoy"; cf. n. 34.b. The rare occurrence of the jussive after the indicative expresses the reason (Joüon §116e).

43.c. השמה is the hoph inf constr of שמם, "be desolate" (cf. GKC §67y). Sam has the spelling באשמה; cf. n. 34.a.

43.d. The double conj occurs also in Ezek 13:10 and 36:3 without the *waw*. Sam does not read the *waw* here. BDB (775) renders יען וביען, "because and by the cause that." According to Cooke, the repetition of the conj adds a solemn emphasis (*Ezekiel*, 140).

44.a. *BHS* takes בדא in Tg^{mss} to equal בזאת, "by this," for MT ואף־גם־זאת, "even also this."

44.b. Sam has a pl form.

46.a. LXX has a sg form.

Form/Structure/Setting

The following structural outline is an expansion of the outline in the *Form/Structure* section on 25:1–26:46, being subordinate to "3. Blessings, curses, and restoration (26:3–45)":

- a. List of blessings (vv 3–13)
  - 1) Blessings proper (vv 3–12)
    - a) Condition (v 3)
    - b) Enumeration of blessings (vv 4–12)
      - (1) First blessing—fertile growing conditions (vv 4–5)
      - (2) Second blessing—peace throughout the land (vv 6–8)
      - (3) Third blessing—increase in prosperity (vv 9–10)
      - (4) Fourth blessing—God's presence among his people (vv 11–12)
  - 2) Expanded formula of Yahweh's self-introduction (v 13)
- b. List of Curses (vv 14–39)
  - 1) First curse—many plagues and defeat in battle (vv 14–17)
    - a) Condition (vv 14–15)
    - b) Curse proper (vv 16–17)
  - 2) Second curse—drought (vv 18–20)
    - a) Condition (v 18a)
    - b) Curse proper (vv 18b–20)
  - 3) Third curse—wild animals (vv 21–22)
    - a) Condition (v 21a)
    - b) Curse proper (vv 21b–22)
  - 4) Fourth curse—war, pestilence, famine (vv 23–26)
    - a) Condition (v 23)
    - b) Curse proper (vv 24–26)
  - 5) Fifth curse—dire conditions and exile (vv 27–39)
    - a) Curse proper (vv 27–33)
      - (1) Condition (v 27)
      - (2) Curses (vv 28–33)
        - (a) Basic statement of principle of Yahweh's intent to punish (v 28)
        - (b) Specific punishments (vv 29–33)
          - (i) Cannibalism practiced (v 29)
          - (ii) Desolation of land by Yahweh (vv 30–32)
          - (iii) Exile of people (v 33)
    - b) Purpose and results (vv 34–39)
      - (1) Land to lie fallow (vv 34–35)
      - (2) Plight of captives (vv 36–39)
        - (a) Plight described (vv 36–38)
        - (b) Reason (v 39)
- c. Restoration possible (vv 40–45)
  - 1) Condition—confession of sin (vv 40–41)
    - a) Confession proper (vv 40–41a)
    - b) Specific conditions (v 41b)

(1) Contrition of heart (v 41bα)
(2) Restitution (v 41bβ)
2) Restoration proper (vv 42–45)
a) Basis in Yahweh's remembrance of the covenant (v 42)
b) Parenthesis referring back to the fifth curse and condition of restoration (v 43)
(1) Land to lie fallow (v 43aα)
(2) Restitution (v 43aβ+b)
c) Restoration motivated by Yahweh's commitment to his people (vv 44–45)
(1) Yahweh's promise not to continue to spurn his people (v 44)
(a) Promise proper (v 44a)
(b) Formula of Yahweh's self-introduction (v 44b)
(2) Restatement of Yahweh's remembrance of covenant (v 45)
(a) Remembrance proper (v 45a–bβ)
(b) Formula of Yahweh's self-introduction (v 45bγ)

In this portion of the speech there are three sections: blessings (vv 3–13), curses (vv 14–39), and prescription for restoration (vv 40–45).

In the first section there are four blessings: proper rains in their seasons (vv 4–5), peace (vv 6–8), fertility (vv 9–10), and God's presence (vv 11–13). Porter (209–10) finds five blessings, for he identifies two blessings in vv 6–8—peace (v 6) and victory at war (v 7)—but the following discussion will demonstrate that this set of verses constitutes a single blessing. Each blessing, introduced by a perfect *waw* consecutive in the first person with Yahweh as the speaker, is based on the opening condition (v 3). Three blessings begin with the verb ונתתי, "and I shall give" (vv 4, 6, 11), while the third blessing (v 9) has four first person perfects in a row, each followed by the object "you" (pl), to emphasize that God will bless his people. This style counters Porter's finding two blessings in vv 6–8. Typically each blessing opens with a definitive promise by Yahweh and is continued by a description of what this divine action will mean for Israel. The fourth blessing is distinct in that the consequence constructed out of verbs in the second person plural is missing. In its place is the covenantal formula לכם לאלהים ואתם תהיו־לי לעם והייתי, "I shall be your God, and you will be my people." It is also distinct in that in contrast to giving Israel something tangible, Yahweh promises to dwell among his people. Nevertheless, this portion is part of the blessings, for it is introduced, as are the first and second blessings, with נתתי, "I shall give," and it expresses Yahweh's promise of his presence, the greatest promise that he ever makes (e.g., Exod 3:12).

The list of blessings concludes with an expanded formula of Yahweh's self-introduction amplified with a relative clause (cf. 19:36; 22:33; 23:43; 25:38, [42], 55). Attached to the formula are two statements with two *waw* consecutive imperfects that describe how Yahweh has lifted up the character of his people. Is this formula of self-introduction a part of the fourth blessing or does it conclude the series of blessings? The expanded description of Yahweh's delivering his people favors the latter position. The speaker included it here both to identify the God who promised to walk among his people and to tie these blessings into the laws on holy living.

The second section (vv 14–39) unfolds a sequence of curses that will befall the people should they disobey the law. There are five sets of curses. As is typical in covenants from the Middle East, the number of curses outweighs the number of blessings (cf. McCarthy, *Treaty and Covenant,* 176). Each of the curses is introduced with ואם, "and if," but with different elements added: ואם . . . ואם, "and if . . . and if" (vv 14, 15), ואם־עד־אלה, "and if in addition to these things" (v 18), ואם, "and if" (v 21), ואם־באלה, "and if in spite of these things" (v 23), ואם בזאת, "and if in spite of this" (v 27). Following the condition of failure to obey, the punishment Yahweh will impose on his people is usually introduced with a perfect *waw* consecutive. In the first curse, however, Yahweh's response is introduced with the emphatic formulation אף־אני אעשׂה־זאת, "I shall surely do this." In the last three curses Yahweh's response to Israel is introduced with והלכתי . . . (ב)קרי, "I shall walk contrary [to you] . . . " (vv 21 [תלכו], 24, 28). This expression establishes a sharp contrast with the promise in vv 11–12 that Yahweh would והתהלכתי, "walk about," among his people for their good and their honor.

The curses are arranged to express increasing severity. Several elements are employed to communicate that increasing ferocity. First is the variation in the lead formulation as listed above. Second is the repetition of the condition of Israel's disobedience before each set of curses. This repetition stands in marked contrast to the single mention of the condition of obedience at the head of the list of blessings. This style intimates that Israel's obstinacy toward Yahweh grows stronger. Third is the use of the term יסר, "discipline, punish." This verb signifies that the curses are disciplines designed to awaken the people to their wrongful ways. The use of יסר communicates that these disciplines are to have a corrective as well as a punitive purpose. Disciplines against unresponsive students must increase in the attempt to get through to them so that they will finally change their wrongful ways. Fourth is the use of the phrase "seven times for your sins" in the last four curses (vv 18, 21, 24, 28). This symbolic number communicates that Yahweh will dramatically increase the level of punishments at each new stage in response to Israel's continued sinning. Fifth, to highlight the purpose of the sequence of the curses and to stress their interrelatedness, they are arranged in an A:B:C::C:B pattern by the terms used for Yahweh's afflicting his people. The key wording of the last four curses is as follows: ויספתי ליסרה אתכם, "and I shall continue to discipline you" (v 18): ויספתי עליכם מכה, "and I shall increase on you smiting" (v 21): והכתי אתכם, "and I shall smite you" (v 24): ויסרתי אתכם, "and I shall discipline you" (v 28). Each level of punishment will be designed to awaken Israel to her waywardness so that she might repent before experiencing the ultimate curse.

In the third section (vv 40–45), the possibility of restoration of the remnant that survives the fifth curse is offered. This section amazingly lacks a distinct introduction. Nevertheless, the term והתודו, "and they will confess," is a bold shift from the description of Israel as unresponsive to Yahweh in the preceding section. On the other hand, the wording הלך עמי בקרי, "walk contrary to" (vv 40, 41; cf. vv 21, 23, 27, 28), ties this section directly into the middle section. At the center of this section is the rationale that Israel may be sent into captivity in order that the land may rest and thus enjoy its last sabbatical years (vv 41, 43). V 41 looks back to the fifth curse, and v 43 looks back specifically to vv 34–35. Although this is a rough literary style, the speaker wished to link this section closely to the preceding curse. The use of this rationale establishes a solid tie between this portion of blessings and curses and chap. 25 on the year of Jubilee. In addition, there is a link with chaps. 18 and 20, where it is said that Israel's sinning might so defile the land that it would spew them out. Moreover, the term זכר, "remember" (vv 42

[3x], 45), signifies that Yahweh will change direction based on his past promises. His redemptive remembering is grounded in the ברית, "covenant," a key term in this section (vv 42 [3x], 44, 45) as well as the legal framework for the blessings and curses (cf. vv 9, 15, and 25). Finally, Yahweh's forgiving, reclaiming grace is clearly pictured in the last two verses of this section (vv 44–45), and it is in harmony with his mercy that moves him both to bless his people and to discipline them in hope that they may repent.

The genre of this chapter is blessings and curses. This genre often comes at the end of covenants and law codes that have been found in the ancient Middle East, e.g., Code of Lipit-Istar (epilogue, *ANET* 161), Code of Hammurabi reverse 26–27 (*ANET* 178–80), Sefire Treaty, Shamshi-Adad Treaty, and Esarhaddon Treaty (cf. Weinfeld, *Deuteronomy and the Deuteronomic School* [Oxford, 1972] 151, 156–57; Hillers, *Treaty Curses,* 7–11). They promote the acceptance of a new set of laws, and in the case of a treaty they encourage the loyalty of the subjects (Weinfeld, 156). The curses, which invoke the gods to punish any violations of the agreement, are a standard part of such documents, for it is presupposed either that one party cannot continually monitor the other or that there is no viable earthly way to enforce the treaty. In Leviticus these blessings and curses are the conclusion of a legal corpus. The numerous references to the covenant (vv 9, 15, 25, 42 [3x], 44, 45) nevertheless indicate that the speaker views these laws as part of the covenant. This assumption explains why the laws in vv 1–2 reiterate laws from the Decalogue (Exod 20:2–17), the center of the Sinaitic covenant. These blessings and curses encourage and admonish the people to keep both the moral and the ceremonial law in order to be Yahweh's people.

A parallel text of blessings and curses is found in Deut 28. Both chapters belong to the same genre, and both come near the end of a document that is a corpus of laws and rituals given in the context of a covenant. Bertholet (97) finds several points of contact between these two texts. The most specific one is their use of the distinctive terms שחפת, "a wasting disease," and קדחת, "fever" (Lev 26:16; Deut 28:22), the only occurrences of these terms in the OT. Other points of contact listed by Bertholet are Lev 26:4 with Deut 28:12, v 6 with Deut 28:26 (אין מחריד, "none making afraid"), v 14 with Deut 28:15, v 16 with Deut 28:22 (cf. vv 33, 65), v 17 with Deut 28:25, v 19b with Deut 28:23, v 29 with Deut 28:53, and v 36 with Deut 28:65–67. Given the length of both Deut 28 and Lev 26, these limited references indicate that the interplay between the two documents is very limited. The curses in Deut 28, moreover, are formulated quite differently from those in Lev 26. Noth states that the curses in Deut 28 are longer and have a different accentuation than those in Lev 26. In Weinfeld's judgment (*Deuteronomy,* 151), the primary point of commonality between these two texts is that the blessings and curses function in both as part of a law code and a treaty. Based on these facts, it is evident that both chapters drew on the same general tradition and practice but that they originated independently (cf. Noth, 195).

There are, furthermore, many points of connection between Lev 26 and Amos, Jeremiah, and Ezekiel. The closest ties are with Ezekiel, e.g., Lev 26:3–13//Ezek 34:25–28; vv 11–12//Ezek 36:28; 37:24–27; vv 21–22//Ezek 5:17; 14:15, 21; vv 30–31// Ezek 6:3–6. In the count made by Colenso, as cited by Bertholet (94), there are at least twenty-two expressions that appear only in these two sources in the OT plus thirteen others that are common to them but not to any other book in the

Pentateuch. Levine comes to the position that this text "encapsulates diction that is virtually pervasive in Ezekiel" and thus comes from the same literary circles ("The Epilogue," 30). Kilian similarly accounts for the contact between these two sources by proposing that a member of Ezekiel's circle, one thoroughly ingrained in his master's style, composed Lev 26 (*Literarkritische,* 161–62). While these proposals are possible, it seems much more likely that Lev 26 was a source used by Ezekiel and the other prophets, for a single source can be drawn on by a variety of authors over a couple of centuries more readily than that source can come into existence by pulling material from such a diversity of sources.

Hurvitz supports the priority of Leviticus with solid linguistic evidence in *A Linguistic Study of the Relationship between the Priestly Source and the Book of Ezekiel: A New Approach to an Old Problem* (Paris: J. Gabalda, 1982) by tracing the linguistic development of selected data that relate to both the priestly material and Ezekiel. Several examples in his study relate to chap. 26. He finds that Lev 26:11–12, which is parallel to Ezek 37:26–27, uses התהלך, "walk to and fro," with Yahweh as its subject, but Ezekiel and other later Hebrew literature avoid this phraseology as being too anthropomorphic (Hurvitz, 102–3). The phrase ב √שכן, "dwell in, among" (v 11), occurs in classical Hebrew, but this expression is avoided in rabbinic literature. Ezekiel, however, employs the phrase על √שכן, "to dwell with, over," in 37:27. Hurvitz (111–12) views Ezekiel's phraseology to be in transition to the post-biblical term שכינה, "dwelling, divine presence." His next study concerns the use of the terms קום, "(lit.) rise, stand up," and עמד, "stand"; in classical Hebrew their usage is distinct, but in later Hebrew עמד penetrates into the semantic field of קום. הקים used with ברית, "covenant," means "maintain" as in Lev 26:9; but in 17:13–14 Ezekiel avoids הקים by creating a neologism with the expression לעמדה, "to maintain it," with ברית as the antecedent of the pronominal suffix. In addition, Hurvitz notes that in 13:6 Ezekiel uses the piel קִיֵּם, "establish, fulfill," the word that often displaces הקים, "establish," in later Hebrew (32–35). The final example from Lev 26 cited by Hurvitz is the use of געל, "spurn" (104–7). In Leviticus (vv 11, 30, 44) געל has Yahweh as its subject, but not in Ezekiel. In the parallel texts of Lev 26:43//Ezek 5:6, 26:30//6:3–5, and 26:11–12//37:26–27, Ezekiel actually avoids this word, possibly because of its harsh meaning. Levine ("The Epilogue," 25–30), however, takes issue with Hurvitz. He postulates that the writer of Lev 26 took over the use of געל from Jeremiah (14:19), for this writer used it as did Jeremiah to communicate that Israel had so rebelled against God that they had gone beyond the point of returning to him. Hurvitz finds that these linguistic data bear witness to Ezekiel's being composed later than the priestly material (94–97). In a debate of this nature one wishes for a third ancient document containing these terms in order that it could serve as a reference point. Nevertheless, the amount of evidence presented by Hurvitz in contrast to Levine's arguments on a single word favors the acceptance of Hurvitz's position. It is more likely then that Lev 26 preceded Ezekiel and that it represents the tradition on which Ezekiel and the other prophets drew to interpret for the people how God was working in their midst, calling them to repentance through a variety of disciplines. Only by grounding their preaching on the received tradition did the prophets have any hope that their message might be understood and then heeded by the people.

Many scholars, e.g., Thiel (*ZAW* 71 [1969] 65–67), however, argue that the specific nature of certain curses, especially vv 30–33, and the material about restoration came out of the historical experiences of the exile and the return from captivity. There are, conversely, many reasons for placing the origin of this chapter much earlier than the exile. (1) The genre of blessings and curses is very early. Mesopotamian law codes from the third and second millennium B.C. conclude with blessings and curses. (2) Reventlow (*Das Heiligkeitsgesetz,* 146–48, 150–57, 161) and Elliger (364–69) have exerted great effort to demonstrate that beneath these blessings and curses lies an older stratum that was composed in parallelism and 3 + 3 meter. If their findings have any validity, they support the position that these curses come from an early era. (3) The language of these blessings and curses is very general, composed of fixed phraseology, typical of curses found in treaties and other documents of the ancient Middle East. The language is so typical that none of the curses requires a historical situation to account for its presence in this list. One example is the reference to cannibalism (v 29). While some have argued that this curse presupposes the exile, such a curse is common in treaties that have survived from the ancient Middle East (e.g., Ashurnirari Treaty rev. 4. 10–11; Esarhaddon Treaty 448–51, 547–50, 57–72; Hillers, *Treaty Curses,* 62–63). The historical accounts of the exile support the position that this is a general curse, not one written back into the document from actual experience, for there is no evidence that the Israelites exiled in Babylon ever had to resort to such a terrible practice for survival. In fact, life in Babylon for many Jews was so tolerable that large numbers preferred to stay there rather than return to Palestine after Cyrus's edict of return. (4) Numerous OT passages, especially in the prophets, assume the people's knowledge that specific blessings accompany obedience to the law and specific curses disobedience. There are a few passages that assume the dogma that Yahweh warns or disciplines his people by a series of curses so that they may repent and escape the curse of captivity (e.g., Amos 4:6–11; Isa 9:7[8]–10:4); this is a distinctive feature of the presentation of curses in Lev 26. Such prophetic preaching did not create a new idea, nor did it take place in a vacuum. Rather by such bold preaching the prophet interpreted the contemporary situation in light of the received law in order to lead the people to repentance. With this kind of preaching, a prophet impacted his audience, because he based it on texts like Lev 26, which were accepted by the people as authoritative. (5) The ultimate curse of exile does not demand an exilic setting, for the existence of such a curse is widespread in documents from the ancient Middle East (e.g., Code of Hammurabi 26:71–80; 27:74; 28:20–24; Matiʾilu 4:6; Sepre I.A, 42; McCarthy, *Treaty and Covenant,* 173–74). (6) The idea of a remnant does not require a setting after the fall of Jerusalem, for such an understanding of how a tribe or a nation might survive after experiencing a devastating catastrophe was ancient and widespread, as Hasel has shown (*The Remnant:The History and Theology of the Remnant Idea from Genesis to Isaiah,* AUMSR 5 [Berrien Springs, MI: Andrews UP, 1980] 382–92). He discovered that the idea of a remnant appears very early in the literature from the Levant and that this theme appears in a wide variety of genres that treat the tragic devastation of a family, a tribe, or the earth's population (Hasel, 382–83). (7) Noticeably absent are specific curses against city life, the capital city, and commercial activity, the key cultural issues in Israel at the time of the exile. If this material were composed after the downfall of Jerusalem, references to these important areas of Israel's national life that were in conflict with genuine worship of Yahweh would be expected. Given these seven reasons, there is little difficulty in placing the origin of these blessings and curses early in Israel's history.

As for the marked difference in style between the blessings and curses and the rest of Leviticus, it may be accounted for by positing that the speaker drew freely on existing curse formulae, each one having a long tradition behind it. The creative contribution of this speaker lies in the way he organized this material. His imprint is vividly seen in the structure of this speech. He gives four blessings and then five curses. The sequential pattern of x, x + 1 is frequently found in ancient Middle Eastern literature (cf. W. Roth, "The Numerical Sequence x/x + 1 in the Old Testament," *VT* 12 [1962] 300–11), but the sequence of four/five is uncommon. In this way the speaker displayed a creative independence. In addition, the formulation of the curses into five graded levels of discipline comes from the speaker's shaping the curses to present a distinct theological perspective. Realizing the utterly gloomy picture painted by the fifth curse, the speaker proclaimed the possibility of restoration in the last section of this speech. In good homiletical style he prepared the audience to hear the blessings and curses by referring to two commandments that are in accord with the Decalogue. At the end of the sermon he extended hope to the people of the covenant with Yahweh's promise that he would not forsake his people, though they were in exile, and that out of the dust of the exile Yahweh could again make his people flourish on their own land.

The sermonic design of this speech, therefore, is the work of a creative author who drew on the received tradition that went back to Sinai. Its setting was a festival in which the covenant was remembered or renewed.

Comment

3 This verse begins the series of blessings that Yahweh promises to his people for their faithful observance of the covenant. If the people הלך, "walk," in his decrees and שׁמר, "keep," his commandments (cf. 18:4–5), Yahweh promises that he will bless them abundantly. This condition to the blessings is critical, for all these enumerated blessings flow out of the people's obedience to the revealed laws.

4–5 In the first blessing Yahweh promises to send the rains in their season. Heavy rains are needed in the fall (October-November) to water the newly planted soil, and gentle rains must fall in the late winter and early spring (March-April; Deut 11:14) to bring the ripening grains to an abundant yield. Rain at the right time increases the production of the crops wonderfully, but falling at the wrong time, rain can be very destructive. God's blessing will produce such an abundant harvest that the farmers will be fully occupied harvesting one crop until the next one ripens and so on until the time for sowing again. This imagery does not speak of a frantic lifestyle such as that in modern cities, but rather shows that Yahweh will so bless the fields that the people will not be idle, but gainfully occupied. With bumper harvests the people will have enough to eat until satisfaction. They will not have to ration their food. In addition to an abundant food supply, God promises that his people will dwell securely, enabling them to benefit from their hard labor.

6–8 Yahweh will give his people שׁלום, "peace," enabling them to שׁכב, "lie down," in the land unafraid. שׁכב carries the picture of flocks lying quietly and securely in an open field unafraid of wild animals (Keil and Delitzsch, 470; cf. v 22;

Exod 23:29). Since marauders will not take their harvest, they will be able to benefit from their own toil. Neither will Israel need to fear the sword passing through her land. Sword is a synecdoche for war. It pictures the pain and ravage inflicted by marching armies, and it calls to mind the fear that war produces among the people. The linkage of עבר, "pass through," with sword is unusual; it may picture an army marching through Canaan on its way to another place. This is especially true of Canaan; through the centuries many armies have marched through this land, a bridge between Asia, Africa, and Europe, on their way from one continent to another. Nevertheless, whenever Israel is threatened by enemies, she will be empowered by God to pursue and defeat those enemies. God so helps his people that he reverses the odds; five Israelite soldiers will put to flight a hundred of the enemy, and a hundred ten thousand (cf. Josh 23:10; Deut 32:30; Isa 30:17).

9–10 God will actively פנה אל, "look after," his people. He will make their fields fruitful, and he will multiply their own offspring. Thereby he will continue to fulfill his promise to Abraham, namely that he would multiply his offspring so greatly that he would become the father of a multitude of nations (Gen 17:2–6; cf. 15:5). Through these blessings Yahweh will הקים, "maintain," his covenant relationship with his people by providing abundantly for their needs. הקים is used for making a covenant, maintaining it, and fulfilling it (Levine, 183–84). Here it carries the middle meaning, and it stands in contrast to הפר, "break, nullify," in the following curses (v 15); for this same contrast see Ezek 16:59–62 (Yahweh-Israel) and Num 30 (father-daughter; husband-wife). This verse pictures a series of abundant harvests. The old that had been dried and stored will have to be moved aside so that the new harvest may have a place to dry out. Rashi (123, 123a) understands that the first part of v 10 describes the high quality of the grain (i.e., it is good enough to be food even into the third year after its harvest) and that the second part of this verse means that the fields will yield abundantly.

11–13 Yahweh himself promises to set his משכן, "tabernacle," among his people (cf. Exod 26; 36). There he will meet with his people, and his presence will be immanent (cf. Exod 29:45–56). In his mercy Yahweh provides a place where his people may come to him, but he does not make himself casually available. All approaches to him require appropriate recognition of his holiness. Thus this promise communicates the nearness of Yahweh to his people without negating his transcendence. Cross uses the term "covenant presence" to capture this idea (*Canaanite Myth,* 299). Yahweh's presence is not only found at the tabernacle; he also promises to be present among his people as the expression התהלך, "to walk about," communicates. התהלך means "to walk back and forth, up and down." Yahweh will watch over, care for, and bless every family. This wording for the promise makes a tie with the patriarchal traditions. Enoch, Noah, and Abraham walked with God (Gen 5:22, 24; 6:9; 17:1). In contrast God here promises to walk with Israel. Yahweh is seeking to realize the goal of the covenant, namely that he will be the God of this people and they will be his people. This goal also has a historical anchor in the great saving event of Israel's deliverance from Egyptian bondage. Yahweh brought them out of Egypt so that they never again should be in slavery. He broke the bars of the yoke that enslaved them (cf. Ezek 34:27; Nah 1:13). This bar is the heavy crosspiece resting on an oxen's back, forcing it to pull a heavy load. Not only has Yahweh freed his people; he causes them to קוממיות, "walk upright." Slaves are bent over under the heavy burdens they must bear. But Yahweh will heal the stoop produced by the heavy loads Israel carried while enslaved to the Egyptians. Not only will he ease the burden of his people; he will give them dignity so that they may walk upright, i.e., with confidence (cf. Deut 4:6–8). Yahweh desires that his people have honor and dignity.

14–15 At this juncture the speech turns to a series of curses. Each series is introduced by a condition pertaining to that series. In this series the contrary attitude of Israel increases from lack of obedience to outright rebellion. In the first curse the people שׁמע, "disobey," God by not doing all the מצות, "commandments." The inclusion of the dative לי, "to me," after שׁמע, "hear, obey," is unusual; it stresses that the people deliberately disobey Yahweh whom they know (cf. Rashi, 123b). Failure to obey the laws leads to negative attitudes. They מאס, "despise," God's חקת, "decrees," and געל, "abhor," his משׁפטים, "laws." מאס means "to treat lightly, disregard, despise, loathe" (cf. 2 Kgs 17:15; Isa 5:24; 30:12; 20:13, 16, 24; Jer 6:19; 8:9; Ezek 5:6; Amos 2:4; Job 5:17; 7:16; 9:21; 10:3; Prov 3:11). געל, "abhor, consider something as filth, dung," communicates the depth of their hostility to the law (H. F. Fuhs, "גָּעַל *gāʿal*," *TDOT* 3:47–48). This rare verb occurs five times in Lev 26 (vv 11, 15, 30, 43, 44); overall it occurs several times with מאס, "despise" (26:15, 43, 44; Jer 14:19; Sir 31:16). The people not only fail to obey God's laws; they abhor them (i.e., they are repulsed by them). With this attitude they cannot even force themselves to keep the laws. Truly they have הפר, "broken," the covenant (cf. Gen 17:14; Deut 31:16, 20; Jer 11:10; 31:32; 33:21; Ezek 16:59; 44:7). Breaking the covenant does not mean that they get out from under the covenant, but rather that they must be punished by the curses enumerated in that covenant. Yahweh's use of the pronoun "my" with decrees, laws, and covenant underscores Israel's intentional turning away from those essential elements that define their relationship with Yahweh.

16–17 The opening sentences stress that Yahweh will be active, not silent, unresponsive to his people's sinning. He asserts what he will do in response to his people's disgusting attitude and disobedience. Yahweh will set his face against them. His presence promised in the blessings (vv 11–13) will be turned from blessing to punishment. Out of mercy Yahweh will begin to discipline his people with lesser punishments. At first he will הפקיד, "visit," them with בהלה, "a sudden terror." בהלה depicts the feeling of frightful panic aroused by an unexpected, dreadful happening (cf. Ps 48:6[5]; Jer 51:32). The plagues enumerated after בהלה may be understood as a list of "sudden terrors": שׁחפת, "a wasting disease," קדחת, "fever," מכלות עינים, a disease that destroys one's eyesight, and מדיבת נפשׁ, "loss of appetite or languishing of one's strength." Anyone who suffers the swift loss of prowess caused by any one of these terrors, let alone all four, is terribly frightened, for such a one feels that death is looking over the shoulder. Added to this loss is the curse that farmers will sow לריק, "in vain," for their enemies will eat what they have sown. It is the height of anguish to work hard for months only to have the harvest taken away by a marauding band. To watch the fruits from months of toil evaporate in a moment causes the people to lose heart. This last curse is an abbreviated form of the type of curse which Hillers (*Treaty Curses,* 28–29) classifies as futility curses; in the protasis an activity is described, and in the apodosis the activity fails to reach its goal.

Yahweh expresses his firm resolve to punish his people. He will set his face against them. Because Yahweh will be against them, his protection will be removed, leaving Israel to be smitten by enemies. Their enemies will רדה, "rule," over them harshly (cf. 25:43). During such a time of oppression, the people will be so on edge that the slightest noise will cause them to hide themselves in whatever shelter they can find even though nothing is pursuing them.

18 The second series of curses comes in vv 18–20. If his people will not שׁמע, "listen," to Yahweh, i.e., that which Yahweh has tried to communicate through the curses, Yahweh will continue to יסר, "discipline," his unrepentant people seven times for their חטאת, "sins." The number seven is used figuratively to communicate a significant increase in the severity of the punishments that Yahweh will visit on them (cf. Isa 4:1; Ps 79:12). He will increase the punishment in response to Israel's continued disobedience, for it is his desire that the punishment awaken Israel to the waywardness of her ways. Yahweh is ever hopeful that his people will repent.

19–20 This time Yahweh will set about to break "the pride of your [Israel's] strength," גאון עזכם, i.e., "powerful pride" (cf. Ezek 33:28; Levine, 156). Pride is an enormous barrier between God and humankind. It prompts humans to trust in their own self-sufficiency and not in God (Ezek 7:24; 24:21 [מקדשׁי, "my sanctuary"]; 30:6, 18). National pride is fed by a nation's perceived strength (עז). It may reside in that nation's natural resources, such as fertile soil, or in its military might. Whenever a nation builds its confidence solely on the source of its strength, pride is fed. Here Israel's pride is in the fertility of their land. Their pride leads them to trust in the land for wealth and security, not in Yahweh their God. In response Yahweh will make the heavens as iron and the earth as bronze (cf. Deut 28:23, but the similes are inverted; also in Esarhaddon Treaty 528–32). Iron and bronze were the strongest metals in ancient times. The land will become so hard that it will be impenetrable. This metaphor speaks of a long, enduring drought. All the energy spent in plowing and sowing will be for nought. The land will not yield any crops, and the fruit trees will not bear fruit. Most of all, the ancients feared a drought or a famine of seven years (cf. Gen 41:25–35; C. H. Gordon, *Or* n.s. 22 (1953) 79–81).

21 Vv 21–22 present the third in the series of curses. If the people will continue to walk contrary to (קרי) or defy Yahweh and will not be willing to listen to him, Yahweh will increase his מכה, "smiting," them sevenfold for their continued sins (cf. v 18).

22 This time Yahweh will send חית השׂדה, "wild beasts," among them. The curse of devouring animals is found in other treaties (e.g., Sefire I.A.30–32; Sefire II.A.9; cf. Deut 28:38, 39, 42; Jer 8:17; Hillers, *Treaty Curses,* 54–55). These animals will cause havoc in the villages (cf. Exod 23:29). They will consume the children, leaving parents שׁכל, "childless." שׁכל pictures a mother bereaved of her children (cf. Ezek 5:17; 36:12–14). The loss of children is a terribly harsh curse on a family, especially the mother. These animals will thus depopulate villages, and they will also kill off the domesticated flocks. The survivors will be so afraid to travel that the roads will become desolate. Such a dreaded condition is described in 2 Kgs 17:25–26 for the region of Samaria after it fell to the Assyrians (cf. Ezek 14:15). Conversely Isa 11:6–9, 35:9 and Hos 2:20(18) speak of the glorious blessing in the age to come when animals will be at peace with people.

23–24 The fourth in this series of curses comes in vv 23–26. If Israel will not accept Yahweh's acts of discipline (נוסר) and they continue to walk contrary to or defy him (cf. v 21), Yahweh himself will walk contrary to or defy them and smite them sevenfold for their sins (cf. v 18). Whereas the highest point of Yahweh's blessing is his presence, the deepest agony of his cursing is when Yahweh turns against his people and plans their harm.

25–26 Yahweh will let them be defeated by their enemies. He will bring on them the חרב נקמת, "avenging sword." The destruction wrought is called נקם ברית, "vengeance of the covenant." Yahweh will not punish his people out of capricious anger; rather he will smite them rationally on the basis of the formal covenant agreement between them and himself. Levine (187) thinks נקם in this usage more accurately means "the threat of punishment," rather than vengeance. If he is correct, the phrase means "the threat of punishment prescribed by the covenant." Because of the threat of war, people will leave the countryside out of fear and gather together in cities for some security. Yahweh, however, will send דבר, "pestilence," a death-causing plague, among these dense refugee settlements. While they are weakened by the plague, their enemies will be able to break through the city's fortifications and capture the inhabitants. Furthermore, Yahweh will break the staff of bread (Ezek 4:16; 5:16; 14:13; Ps 105:16; Sir 48:2). It is possible that this metaphor builds on the use of a staff to aid in walking; bread, like a staff, is the basic support of life. Schult ("Marginalie zum 'Stab des Brotes,'" *ZDPV* 87 [1971] 206–8) believes that the metaphor may go back to a custom of carrying bread on a staff of wood in a variety of configurations. He mentions that he saw in Old Jerusalem two lads carrying bread baked in rings with a wooden pole supported on their shoulders. Twine held several of these rings together; the chain of bread was tied so as to hang from the pole; and there were several chains hanging from the pole. These lads were weighed down, carrying the bread from the baker to the store. But, under this curse, instead of a staff loaded down with rings of bread, there will be so little grain left that what is distributed to ten women will be so little that all the loaves they make will be able to be baked in one oven. This picture is a potent hyperbole. The loaves of bread will be so few that they will have to be rationed out by weight (cf. Ezek 4:16). The people will eat, but their hunger will not be assuaged.

27–28 The fifth in this series of curses is found in vv 27–39. If the people continue to fail to listen to Yahweh and continue to defy him, Yahweh will intensify his opposition. He will display his anger as he walks contrary to them. He will יסר, "discipline," them even seven times more harshly (cf. v 18).

29–33 Yahweh will bring on the people a famine so great that the people will resort to cannibalism. They will kill their own children for food. This curse is also found in Deut 28:53–57; Isa 49:26; Jer 19:9; Ezek 5:10; and Zech 11:9. That there were a few times Israelites felt compelled to resort to such a source of food is reported in 2 Kgs 6:28–29; Lam 2:20; 4:10; Josephus, *Ant.* 4.3.4ff.

In addition, Yahweh will turn mightily against their false places of worship. He will destroy their במות, "high places." במות were constructed on natural heights (Jer 48:35; Isa 15:2) or on artificial "mounds" made out of dirt or stone; essentially they were altars on which animal sacrifices and grain offerings were offered (M. Haran, "Temples and Cultic Open Areas as Reflected in the Bible," in *Temples and High Places in Biblical Times* [Jerusalem: The Nelson Glueck School of Biblical Archaeology of Hebrew Union College—Jewish Institute of Religion, 1981] 33–34). "Mounds" could be located in many places, such as in a valley (Jer 7:31; 19:5–6) or within a village (1 Kgs 13:32; 2 Kgs 17:9, 29). Many במות were equipped with an אשרה, "Asherah," a wooden pole, a symbol of the goddess of fertility, and one or more מצבות, "pillars" (Schunck, *TDOT* 2:142; cf. n. 1.c.). In the early days of Israel as a nation, some high places were legitimate (e.g., 1 Sam 9:16–24; 1 Kgs 3:4), but for the most part they were illegitimate places of worship; because they were local shrines, they became the locus of syncretistic worship, i.e., the inclusion of pagan fertility practices into the worship of Yahweh. The prophets condemned all במות (Amos 7:9; Hos 10:8; Jer 19:3–5). At some of these shrines even child sacrifice was practiced (Jer 7:31; 19:5–6; 32:35). Yahweh will also cut down their חמנים, "incense altars." These incense braziers are usually associated with "high places" in the OT (2 Chr 14:4[5]; 34:3–4). Archaeologists have found stone artifacts, cubic or elongated with a cup-like hollowed out place on the upper part, which de Vaux identifies as חמנים (*AI,* 2:286; cf. G. E. Wright, "Sin-Image or Altar of Incense?" *BA* 1 [1938] 9–10; K. Elliger, "Chammanim = Masṣeben?" *ZAW* 57 [1939] 256–65; idem, "Der Sinn des Wortes *chammān,*" *ZDPV* 66 [1942] 129–39; H. Ingholt, "Le Sens du Mot *Ḥammān,*" in *Melanges Syriens offerts à R. Dussaud* [Paris: Geuthner, 1939] 2:795–802). De Vaux thinks that חמנים were small enough to be placed on an altar (*AI,* 2:286). This term could have been applied also to incense burners made out of clay and in a variety of shapes (de Vaux, *AI,* 2:286–87). Beyse ("חמם *ḥmm,*" *TDOT* 4:476) identifies these incense altars as stele-like. One of these artifacts that has been found was dedicated to the Phoenician god Baal Hammon (Beyse, *TDOT* 4:476). This cult object may thus have taken its name from this deity. Beyse refers to another inscription (CIS, II,3 No. 3978 from Palmyra) that mentions a חמן dedicated to the sun-god. When this evidence is joined with other pieces of information, it may be postulated that these incense altars were particularly used in the cult of the sun-god (Beyse 4:476–77, but cf. Levine, "Epilogue," 17).

This text says that Yahweh will place their פגרים, "corpses," on the פגרי גלולים, "'corpses' of their idols." פגרי גלולים indicates that גלולים are large images in human form. Calling them "corpses" is most derogatory; they are lifeless objects. גלולים itself is a deprecatory term, expressing the small nature of idolatry. Yahweh casts human corpses on these dead idols. Putting corpses and bones on an idol or burning them on an altar permanently desecrated that object of worship (cf. Ezek 6:4b–5; 2 Kgs 23:14–16). Such a process was the most defiling. The very gods whom these people have trusted to protect them will be eternally defiled by the people's own dead bodies. Idols are utterly worthless! In this way Yahweh will demonstrate how he געל, "abhors" (cf. v 15), his people for their false worship practices. The depth of his feelings is captured with the use of נפשי, "my soul, my person."

Yahweh will cause war to reduce their cities to חרבה, "ruins," and will make their מקדשיכם, "sanctuaries," שמם, "desolate." חרבה, "waste places, ruins," is frequently used in the prophets to describe the cities, buildings, and land devastated by war (Isa 5:17; 44:26; 49:19; Jer 7:34; 25:18; Ezek 5:14). מקדש is a general term for anything that possesses sanctity, e.g., a tithe, cultic vessels, an altar, or a temple (Haran, *Temples,* 14–15). Here it refers to a place where the people worship whether or not a temple is present. But instead of the term מקדשי, "my sanctuary(ies)," as in v 2, here they are called מקדשיכם, "your sanctuaries," for the people have turned the sanctuaries where Yahweh was once worshiped in purity into places where they follow worship practices like those of their neighbors. The few sacrifices that they will try to offer up will not move him to have favor on them. Yahweh will not smell ריח ניחוח, "the soothing aroma," from their sacrifices (cf. 1:9); i.e., he will not be moved to act mercifully toward his people. Yahweh will make the land so desolate (השמה) that even Israel's enemies who come to dwell in her land will be astounded (שׁמם) at the horrendous sight of destruction. There is a play on the various meanings of the root שׁמם, "be desolate, appalled" (BDB, 1080–81). This root is used six times in vv 31–35 to communicate the deep feelings of horror that Israel will experience before the vast devastation of her homeland.

Yahweh will then scatter his people among the nations. He will chase them far and wide with a drawn sword in his hand (cf. Ezek 5:2, 12; 12:14). Exile is the ultimate punishment. National sovereignty will end. Exile will undo the goal of the covenant in giving an inheritance to the people of the covenant as Yahweh had promised to Abraham (Gen 12:7; 13:14–17). Driven from their land, the people will be unable to go up to worship Yahweh at the sanctuary where he dwells. This loss will threaten to destroy their understanding of God, the Lord who holds them together as the people of God. In a foreign land, keeping the law will be a heavy burden, even an impossibility in the case of some laws. Despondent and discouraged, they will face continuous threats. Exile is indeed the ultimate curse for a nation.

34–35 All the time Israel will be in exile, the land will lie fallow as in a sabbatical year (cf. 25:2–7). In fact, these years of rest for the land will compensate for all the sabbatical years the land was worked. This curse anticipates that Israel's failure to observe the sabbatical years will be symptomatic of her not keeping the law in general. Wright (*God's People,* 150) concurs, arguing that the issue of keeping the sabbatical years is a moral and socio-economic issue, not just a cultic issue. He says, "The focus of attention is not the land *per se,* but the land as the 'middle term' between Yahweh and Israel, the land as the tangible symbol and ground of his blessing and claim on them and their relationship to him" (*God's People,* 150). Israel's neglect of the sabbatical year springs from the same moral evil that has led to her neglect of social justice and acts of mercy, and it will reach beyond those neglects to the higher issue of her not maintaining the dynamic of her relationship with Yahweh (Wright, *God's People,* 151). This position is reinforced by the ideology expressed in vv 42–45.

36–39 The speech turns to describe the adverse circumstances of the survivors scattered among the nations. These people will become edgy, for Yahweh will make their hearts timid (מרך בלבבם; cf. Job 23:16). This curse is the direct opposite of the exhortation found in Deut 20:2–4 that the people are not to be timid because God himself fights for them. In their timidity, they will flee at the slightest sound, even when they hear the wind rustling the leaves of a tree. While fleeing in such panic, they will stumble over each other. They will not make a stand against their enemies. Many will perish in a foreign land. Others will מקק, "languish away," slowly in the land of their enemies. מקק means "fester" of wounds (Ps 38:6[5]). The noun of this root מק means "rot" (Isa 3:24; 5:24; BDB 596–97). In Zech 14:12 it describes the wasting away of the body, the flesh, the eyes, and the tongue. Here it pictures the slow but steady erosion of people's lives as they eke out a miserable existence in a foreign land (cf. Ezek 4:17; 24:23; 33:10). They will face such a miserable lot because of their sins compounded by the sins of their fathers. While an individual is accountable for himself before God (e.g.,

Ezek 18; 33), Yahweh will punish the nation for the accumulation of the sins of the generations.

40–41 Now a word of hope is extended to those dispersed among the nations. If Israel can come to realize that they are in bondage to another nation solely because of their iniquitous deeds and will repent of their iniquities and the iniquity of their fathers, they can move Yahweh to change their miserable circumstances. The use of עון, "iniquity," three times in these verses ties this word of restoration directly to the last curse for it occurs twice in v 39. They must acknowledge that they have acted מעל, "treacherously" (cf. 5:15), against God and that they have indeed defied him or walked קרי, "contrary" (cf. v 21), to him. מעל is a strong term for an act of sin; it speaks of treachery, the betrayal of God's trust. To make their confession genuine (cf. Dan 9:4–19; Ezra 9:6–15; Neh 9:6–37), they must get to the core reason for their sinning. They need to go beyond confessing specific rebellious deeds to acknowledging the attitude or disposition that has separated them from God. Their foul attitude must be exorcised by confession. Using another metaphor, their heart has become so hard that it has become encased in a hard growth like a foreskin. This condition requires surgery. The foreskin of the heart must be circumcised (Deut 10:16; 30:6; Jer 4:4; cf. Rom 2:28–29). When the hard core of stubbornness is removed, the people will have a tender heart, a heart bent on obeying God's word. The removal of this hard "foreskin" will also symbolize the renewal of the covenant, just as circumcision is the symbol of the covenant.

42 By stating that he will remember his covenant (זכר בריתי) with the patriarchs, Yahweh strongly and definitively affirms that he will come to rescue Israel from the hardship of the captivity. זכר ברית, "remember the covenant," is a special phrase pertaining to the covenant; it only stands with God as its subject (cf. W. Schottroff, *"Gedenken" im alten Orient und im Alten Testament* [1964] 202–16). In this idiom זכר, "remember," does not stand opposite of שכח, "forget," but of הפר, "break" (v 44; Jer 14:21; Schottroff, 206). Moreover, in this idiom it neither focuses on mental activity nor on great achievements of the past; rather it speaks of God's turning to act for the benefit of his people in the present. Nevertheless, this activity is congruent with past promises. The maker of the covenant acts to preserve the covenant when it is endangered by its human partner (Schottroff, 216–17). "God remembers" means that in a definite time Yahweh will carry out the covenant duties to which he has committed himself by entering history in a marvelous way for the redemptive benefit of his people (cf. Exod 2:24; Schottroff, 206). He will demonstrate the covenant pledge that "I am Yahweh, your God (e.g., 18:2; 19:2; Schottroff, 206). "Remember," thus, is a key term in Israel's worship of Yahweh. Its function in worship rests on the premise that Yahweh is continually true to his word and seeks to fulfill it (cf. B. S. Childs, *Memory and Tradition in Israel,* SBT 37 [London: SCM Press, 1962] 31–44). That is why in laments Israel beseeches God to remember, for his memory moves him to act on the basis of his past commitments (e.g., Pss 25:6; 74:2, 18).

This text states that the locus of Yahweh's memory is his covenant with Jacob, Isaac, and Abraham. He made a covenant with Abraham (Gen 15) based on his earlier promises (Gen 12:2–3), and he formally continued that covenant with Isaac (Gen 26:24) and Jacob (Gen 35:9–15). In this covenant God selected the offspring of Abraham to be his people, and he promised them a land as their inheritance. Several texts, thus, interpret Israel's saving history in light of God's remembering his promises to Abraham (e.g., Pss 105:42; 106:45). It is worth stressing that in the promise to Abraham that he would make his offspring into a great nation, Yahweh had the blessing of all nations in view. At the end of this text, Yahweh says that he will remember the land, i.e., the land of promise that will have been lying fallow. This phrase means that he will bring the survivors back to this land of promise in order that it might again be inhabited and that again it might be made productive.

43–44 Whenever the people will be taken into captivity, the land, being depopulated, will lie fallow (cf. vv 34–35). These years of fallow will compensate for the missed sabbatical years. The reason the people have to pay is underscored with the double conjunction יען וביען, "because, even because"; they have מאס, "rejected" or "despised" (cf. v 15), God's משפטים, "laws," and have געל, "abhorred" (cf. v 15), his חקות, "decrees" (cf. 18:4–5). Guilty without excuse, Israel must bear the heaviest punishment. This punishment for immorality bears witness that there is a moral relationship between the people and their land. If a people abuse their land, the land will demand rest before it can continue to support its people (cf. 18:24–30). Thus ecology and moral integrity are closely tied to each other.

Whereas God will become so angry at his people that he will send them into captivity (cf. Jer 25:11; 2 Chr 36:20–21), his anger will not burn so hotly and so long that he will מאס, "spurn," and געל, "abhor," them so as to utterly wipe (כלה) them out. He will not let his people become so amalgamated among the nations that every trace of their racial identity will be lost forever. If Yahweh's concern for Israel is genuine, how can he punish them so harshly? First, he punishes them in just measure. Second, he punishes them in increasing severity, with the design of each level of punishment being to turn them from their sinful ways. Third, he forewarns them before he punishes them; the prophet is his messenger to warn his people of the danger they face by reason of their disobedience to God's laws. Fourth, once Israel repents, Yahweh will redeem them and will bring them back to the promised land.

Yahweh, furthermore, reveals his grace in promising not to הפר, "break," his covenant with them. That is, he will continue to show them mercy by acting toward them in light of both the promises he spoke to Abraham (Gen 12:2–3) and the mission he gave his people at Sinai, namely, to be a holy people and a royal priesthood (Exod 19:5–6). Yahweh's promise of not breaking his covenant stands in tension with the statement in v 15, which says that Israel has broken the covenant. Is the covenant broken or isn't it? This difficulty in interpretation is common to the variety of covenants that can be made. Each one has its conditional and unconditional aspects. In this section two kinds of covenants are witnessed: a grant in which Yahweh, its author, makes a unilateral pledge to the forefather of Israel and a treaty in which Yahweh imposes obligations on Israel, a second party. The promises made by Yahweh in the grant are unconditional; nevertheless, those promises can be carried forward and experienced only by those who are committed to him (Waltke, "Phenomenon," 128). In regard to the Sinaitic covenant, since it is more like a treaty, the benefits that Yahweh confers therein are conditional, based on Israel's response, but the law of that covenant is irrevocable (Waltke, 133). In the scenario foreseen in these verses, Israel will have broken that covenant because she will have violated its stipulations. Therefore, she will be punished. Whenever she is being punished, she will not be directly benefiting from the promises made by the grant to Abraham. But her failure will not automatically mean that Yahweh will, on his part, abrogate that covenant, nor will he rescind the promises made to Abraham in the grant. In advance Yahweh renounces those options. Instead he promises that he will continue to bring about his promises to Abraham through a remnant who have humbled themselves and turned to him (cf. v 41). This great affirmation stands as the foundation of the hope that a dispersed Israel will someday return to the land of her inheritance.

45 This verse reiterates that Yahweh will remember the ברית ראשנים, "first covenant." This covenant is defined as the one that was made after Israel's deliverance from Egyptian bondage. ראשנים in Deut 19:14 (cf. Isa 61:4) refers to the first generation to occupy Canaan.

46 This verse is a summary statement attesting that the decrees, laws, and instructions in this legislation have come from Yahweh via Moses at Mount Sinai. This statement applies not only to the laws on holy living in chaps. 17–26, but also to the entire book as the use of these three terms attests. תורות, "instructions," occurs in 6:2(9), 7(14), 18(25); 7:1, 7, 11, 37; 11:46; 12:7; 13:59; 14:2, 32, 54, 57; 15:32, but not in chaps. 17–26. חק, "decree," occurs throughout Leviticus, but the masculine is found predominantly in chaps. 1–10 (6:11[18], 15[22]; 7:34; 10:11, 13, 14, 15; 24:9), while the feminine is favored in chaps. 16–26 (3:17; 7:36; 10:9; 16:29, 31, 34; 17:7; 18:3, 4, 5, 26, 30; 19:19, 37; 20:8, 22, 23; 23:14, 21, 31, 41; 24:3; 25:18; 26:3, 15, 43). The use of the masculine form thus establishes a clear tie with the first and second divisions of Leviticus. On the other hand, the use of משפטים, "laws," covers specifically chaps. 17–26 (24:22; 25:18; 26:15, 43), for its use in 5:10 and 9:16 is quite different. Moreover, God has given these laws openly before the nations (לעיני הגוים; v 45) in order that they might know who he is and how mightily he acts in the events of his people (cf. Ezek 20:9, 41).

Explanation

In the ancient Middle East blessings and curses were an integral part of a covenant and frequently of a law code. Since the contracting parties knew that it was impossible to monitor adherence to the multiple stipulations of a law code or a covenant, they called on the gods to bless the obedient and punish the disobedient. It was believed that the gods would richly bless each party that was obedient to the covenant. Conversely, should one party persist in failing to fulfill the stated obligations, the curses would be activated, either by the gods or by the offended leaders who acted on behalf of the gods. Given the apprehension that those who entered into a covenant had that the other party might not live up to its terms, it is not surprising that these documents often contain far more curses than blessings. The piling up of curses was designed to discourage a recalcitrant party from breaking the stipulations of the covenant by calling attention to the hardships that he would face.

The laws given by Yahweh in Leviticus conclude with blessings and curses. It is possible that this chapter provides this element of the Sinaitic covenant (Exod 19–24). To his obedient people Yahweh promised to send the rains appropriate to the seasons in order that the fields and orchards would yield an abundant harvest. In addition to plenty of food, he promised his people security both from natural forces like wild animals and from their enemies. He also promised to make them so fruitful that they would rapidly grow in numbers. With his blessing resting on them, they would be molded into a solid, unified confederation of tribes, able to overcome hardships and to defeat their foes. Most importantly, Yahweh, the personal God, promised to dwell among his people in the sanctuary that they had made for him and to go about among them.

In chaps. 25–26 the land served as the playing field where Israel put into practice the laws given her by God. The land was Yahweh's gift to her, and she had the responsibility to manage the land according to his precepts. A visible sign of her obedience to the law given at Sinai would be her letting the land rest every seventh day, every seventh year, and every seventh year times seven, the year of Jubilee. Yahweh gave her these seasons of rest in order that she might enjoy the abundance Yahweh had given her and that she might express complete trust in Yahweh for her food supply. Should she fail to observe these laws regarding the Sabbath, it would be symptomatic of her not keeping all the law given to her at Sinai. Her failure would indicate that she had not shown mercy to the unfortunate and had not pursued social justice. At the same time it would reveal that she had not been putting her complete trust in Yahweh. Thus the land became a theater for Israel to display to the nations her moral integrity and her devotion to Yahweh.

Whenever Israel failed to keep the covenant, Yahweh committed himself to chastise them. These curses, though, were not self-operating. They would begin only when Yahweh activated them, and he would direct their course. Yahweh's use of these curses was based on a definitive program. He would employ them in sets of increasing severity sevenfold in order to discipline his people and to motivate them to repent and seek his favor. Should the people persist in their rebellion against him, Yahweh, like a master teacher, would increase their discipline by unleashing on them harsher and harsher curses, ever hopeful that they might recognize their sinful ways and return to him.

The curses existed in a fivefold pattern of increasing severity: sudden terror, consumption, and fever (vv 16–17); drought (vv 19–20); wild beasts (v 22); defeat in war followed by pestilence and famine (vv 25–26); and devastation in war ending in exile (vv 29–33). Exile was the ultimate punishment, for Israel would be taken away from the land given to her under the terms of the covenant. Yahweh thereby would be forced to reverse his goal of creating a holy nation on the land he had provided for them. If he had to execute such a punishment, Yahweh's failure in creating a holy people like himself would be put on public display. Dispersed among pagan nations, the people would have to eke out their existence in the midst of foreigners who worshiped other gods in strange and loathsome ways and who lived by different moral standards. A tremendous loss for the Israelites would be that they would no longer have access to the sanctuary, where Yahweh was present among them and where they were free to make sacrifices, entreating his favor and help. In exile, unless Yahweh intervened, they would be threatened with the loss of their identity as the people of God.

The belief that Yahweh disciplines his people in order to keep them from continuing in their sinful paths is expressed compassionately in Deut 8:5 and Prov 3:11–12. This belief is reiterated in Heb 12:4–11, which says that God disciplines his children as a father in order that they might share in his holiness (also Rev 3:19). That is, as a parent God afflicts any of his children who err in order to keep those who are failing to obey him from ever leaving his family and coming under the ultimate curse of the covenant. Jealously he disciplines them, seeking to produce in them "the peaceful fruit of righteousness" (Heb 12:11).

In Lev 26 Yahweh held out hope to his people should they be taken into exile. Whenever they would be living in the land of their captors, if they acknowledged that they had walked contrary to him and repented of their sins, he promised to hear their cries and forgive their sins. He would act toward them in remembrance of his covenant with Abraham. He had initiated that covenant to bless all nations with salvation through his people (Gen 12:2–3). In coming again to his people he would invigorate them in order to work toward that global promise. In other words, while exile would terminate for a season the existence of Israel as a sovereign nation, it would not put an end to the continued existence of Israel as the people of God with a mission to all the nations. Here the theology of the remnant is founded on Yahweh's being true to the covenant and to his promises to Abraham. The experience of exile would humble the Israelite survivors, motivating them to turn back to God with fervent zeal. When the remnant repented and sought Yahweh, he would bring them back to the land in order that they might again become a holy nation. In summary, this ultimate curse of exile set before Israel the threat that persistent disobedience would cause her to forfeit her right to occupy the land of her inheritance for a season (cf. 18:24–28), but it did not threaten the annihilation of Israel, the seed of Abraham.

This speech on blessings and curses is a key to understanding other portions of the OT. The prophets often interpreted Israel's present experience and destiny in light of the covenant (e.g., Amos 3:2). They believed that an obedient Israel would be blessed by Yahweh. Conversely, they proclaimed forcefully that a disobedient Israel was being punished or disciplined. Two prophetic passages warn that Israel's woes had been increasing curses as disciplines for her continued sinning (Amos 4:6–12; Isa 9:7[8]–10:4). Prophets like Jeremiah warned the people, who had been disobedient for decades, that they were in danger of going into exile if they continued to be disobedient (e.g., Jer 13:24–27; 18:15–17; 19:3–9; cf. Amos 7:17; Hos 11:5–7; Ezek 5–7, 12, 21). Moreover, the prophets looked beyond exile to Israel's restoration (Amos 9:11–15; Hos 2:16[14]–3:5; 11:10–11). They uttered messages of hope that built her confidence. These words of hope helped to preserve the identity of Israel during the years of exile (e.g., Jer 30–33; Ezek 11:16–20; 16:53–63; 36–37).

The fact that blessings and curses are an essential part of covenant is evident in various NT texts. Jesus' Sermon on the Mount may be viewed as the messianic torah of the coming Kingdom of God. In Matt 5 Jesus began his penetrating sermon with ten beatitudes (vv 3–11). Beatitudes differ from blessings in that they describe a disposition or a circumstance that God will turn into great joy, while blessings are direct promises of God's favor. In these beatitudes Jesus is promising his disciples that when they endure hunger, poverty, mourning, and persecution, they need not despair, for out of their earthly poverty Jesus will be able to bless them in a way that will enrich their present lives and bear fruit abundantly in the age to come (cf. R. A. Guelich, *The Sermon on the Mount* [Waco, TX: Word Books, 1982] 109–11). The blessings that overcome the various distresses express the "newness" of the covenant that Jesus established; through these his disciples will have in this world a foretaste of the enchantment of the coming kingdom. In the parallel passage in Luke, Jesus delivers four beatitudes and four woes (Luke 6:20–26). The woes are pronounced against those who experience the many glories of this world, for they have made these the ultimate goal of their lives.

Why are there woes in Luke and not Matthew? Is it possible that because Matthew wrote to a Jewish audience, he assumed that they would implicitly understand that curses accompany blessings? The woes, though suppressed, are thus implied, for he wished to focus on the unique character of the kingdom of God proclaimed by Jesus. The use of only blessings in Matthew reveals that he aligned the presentation with the eschatological hope of the prophet Isaiah, especially Isa 61 (Guelich, 115–18). Luke, on the other hand, addressing a gentile audience, presented both beatitudes and woes in order to communicate that both are integral to the new covenant that Jesus inaugurated.

In his teaching, Jesus promised blessing to his faithful disciples and warned of the curses of judgment (Matt 5:19; cf. 6:23; 1 Cor 3:17; 14:38; 16:22). He became so distressed at the scrupulous, though hollow, religious practices of the scribes and the Pharisees that he delivered a series of curses against them (Matt 23:23–33; Luke 11:42–44). Jesus delivered these curses out of a troubled, broken heart, because God had sent the prophets, the wise, and the scribes to his people in order to warn them of their wrongful ways, but his people had not listened (Matt 23:34–35). Furthermore, Jesus bitterly lamented the fate of Jerusalem that was at hand for her having killed the messengers sent from God (Matt 23:37–38; Luke 13:34–35). Nevertheless, he saw the end of Jerusalem's desolation coming at the end of time, when she will say, "Blessed be he who comes in the name of the Lord" (Matt 23:39; Luke 13:36).

Paul recognized that the new covenant made by Jesus comes with blessings and curses. From this perspective he interpreted the state of the believers' welfare in the Corinthian church in relationship to their attitude in partaking of the Lord's Supper (1 Cor 11:23–34). Those who partook of the elements of the Eucharist unworthily became sick (v 30). The implication drawn from their illnesses is that their deceitful actions brought them under the curses that attend the new covenant. These illnesses served both as disciplines in the present time and as foretastes of the final judgment (v 32). Conversely, it is implied that all who partook worthily drank to themselves God's blessings.

As seen in his Epistle to the Galatians, Paul perceived that in the new covenant blessings and curses are still operational. Those who practice evil will be cursed and not inherit the Kingdom of God (5:19–21), and those who preach another gospel will be accursed (1:8–9). On the other hand, those who by faith glory in the cross of Jesus will be blessed with peace and mercy (6:14–16). In Gal 3:6–14 Paul expounded on the way that the blessings and curses given in the old covenant are applicable under the new covenant. He acknowledged that those who rely for salvation on the works of the law come under a curse since they are unable to keep all that is written (v 10). Conversely, through Christ all who believe have been redeemed from the curse of the law because Christ has taken each one's curse on himself by becoming "a curse for us" (v 13). Christ's work, therefore, makes it possible for the blessings that God gave to Abraham to be experienced by the Gentiles (vv 8,

14). Thus, because of Christ, all children of faith, Jew and Gentile, bond and free, female and male, will be richly blessed with and through Abraham (v 9).

In the somewhat obscure passage of Rom 9–11, Paul interpreted Israel's place in God's economy in light of the gospel being preached to the Gentiles. In his day the Jews were suffering from the wrath of God because of their disobedience and unbelief, while God showed mercy to the Gentiles. By reason of her unbelief, Israel had come under God's wrath (9:22–24). This meant sorrow and hardship for the Jews, but it did not mean that they have been cast away from God forever. Being faithful to his promises, God employed the distresses of his people for good. Paul looked beyond this time of the Jews' distress to the time when God will again enter history to bless his people with full salvation in the coming resurrection (11:11–12, 15, 26–32). God indeed is preserving a remnant as a manifestation of his grace (11:5–6). Furthermore, God has brought salvation to the world out of Israel's time of hardship (11:11–12). God has used the jealousy of the Gentile toward the Jew and the Jew toward the Gentile as a spur to move both Gentile and Jew to salvation. That the Gentiles have been blessed with access to full salvation for a season offers no grounds for their boasting (11:18), for they have been grafted into the tree, which has its roots in Abraham. If they fail to rejoice in God's goodness, they too will be pruned away (11:19–24). Moreover, Israel may take hope in the fact that her God's ability to use her suffering to advance his kingdom means that her season of judgment is limited; there will be a definite time when God will end her sorrow (J. Dunn, *Romans 9–16*, WBC 38B [Dallas: Word Books, 1988] 691). In that day Israel will be grafted back into the tree and prosper (11:23–25). Verily "all Israel will be saved" (11:26). In the end the promised blessings of the covenant will cease to be the privilege of any specific group; they will be the right of every believer (cf. Dunn, 668). Paul was far from devaluing the importance and place of Israel in saving history. Rather he was interpreting their present sorrow and oppression in light of the blessings and curses that attended their obedience or disobedience to the covenant. He probed into these difficult issues confident that in the end God's loyal love will be made visible to all (Dunn, 691).

In apocalyptic texts of both testaments, the end of the age is portrayed as a drama of a series of curses being released on the earth, bringing the earth to utter desolation (e.g., Isa 24; 34; 2 Pet 3; Rev 6:1–11:19; 15:1–16:21). Against the bleak backdrop of this terrible destruction, there is painted the glorious picture of a renewed earth where God will reign supreme (e.g., Isa 11:1–9; 35; 52:7–10; 54:11–17; Rev 21:1–22:5). Isaiah foresaw this wonderful era of peace as the restoration of Jerusalem to an unsurpassed glory (Isa 60–62). Jerusalem will become the center of a world government where Yahweh will reign supreme over all the nations, and peoples from all the nations will flow to Jerusalem to worship him and to learn his law (Isa 2:1–5; 60–62; cf. 4:2–5). Using another image, Isaiah looked for the time when there will be a new heaven and a new earth (Isa 65; 66). The author of Revelation employed a similar picture to describe the universal peace at the end of the ages. He saw a new Jerusalem descending from heaven where all those who have served God faithfully on earth will have access to the tree of life for eternity (Rev 21). There his people will bask in God's glorious light, joyfully worshiping him and drinking freely from the river's water of life (Rev 22:2). "There will be no more curse" (Rev 22:3a).

VI. Laws on Tithes and Offerings (27:1–34)

Bibliography

Cartledge, T. W. "Vow." *ISBE* rev. 4:998–99. **Keller, C. A.** "נדר *ndr* geloben." *THAT* 2:39–43. **Meyers, C.** "Procreation, Production, and Protection: Male-Female Balance in Early Israel." *JAAR* 51 (1983) 569–93, esp. 584–86. **Richards, K. H.** "Cobb's Living Historic Routes: A Response." *Semeia* 24 (1982) 99–106. **Wendel, A.** *Das israelitisch-jüdische Gelübde.* Berlin: Philo-Verlag, 1931.

Translation

[1]Yahweh said to Moses: [2]"Speak to the Israelites and say to them: If anyone wishes to perform[a] a vow of the value[b] of persons[c] to Yahweh, [3]the value of a male[a] between the ages of twenty and sixty[b] is fifty shekels of silver according to the sanctuary shekel. [4]And if the person is a female, her value is thirty shekels. [5]If the person is between the ages of five and twenty, the value of a male is twenty shekels and a female[a] is ten shekels. [6]If the person is between one month and five years old, the value of a male is five shekels of silver and the female[a] is three shekels of silver.[b] [7]If the person is sixty years old or older, the value of the male is fifteen shekels[a] and the female[b] is ten[c] shekels. [8]If one is poorer[a] than[b] the set value, he is to stand the person[c] before the priest, and the priest is to set the amount.[d] According to[e] what the person making the vow can afford[f] the priest is to set it.

[9]"If [what he vowed][a] is an animal which may be presented[b] as an offering[c] to Yahweh, whatever is given from it[d] becomes holy. [10]He may not exchange it[a] or make a substitute for it, either a good one for a bad one or a bad one for a good one. If he indeed[b] does substitute one animal for another, both it and the substitute[c] become[d] holy. [11]If [the item vowed][a] is any unclean animal, which[b] may not be presented[c] as an offering to Yahweh, he is to station[d] the animal before the priest. [12]The priest is to set its[a] value, either high or low. It is to be according to the valuation of[b] the priest. [13]If he really[a] wishes to redeem it,[b] he is to add 20 percent[c] to the value.

[14]"If a person dedicates his house as holy to Yahweh, the priest is to set its value, either high or low; just as the priest evaluates it, thus it will be established.[a] [15]If the one making the dedication[a] redeems his house, he is to add 20 percent to its price,[b] and it will become his.

[16]"If a person dedicates to Yahweh a part of[a] his patrimony, its value is to be set according to the amount of seed needed for it at the rate of fifty shekels of silver for a homer of barley seed. [17]If[a] he dedicates his field from[b] the year of Jubilee on, its value is established.[c] [18]But if he dedicates his field after the Jubilee, the priest[a] will compute its value according to the years that are left until the Jubilee, and its value is to be reduced proportionately. [19]If the one dedicating it really[a] wishes to redeem it, he[b] is to add 20 percent[c] to its value, and it becomes his legally.[d] [20]But if he does not redeem the field, or if he sells the field to someone else, it can never be redeemed. [21]When the field is released[a] in the Jubilee, it will become holy to Yahweh like a devoted[b] field; it will become the possession of the priest.

[22]"If one[a] consecrates to Yahweh a purchased field which is not part of[b] his patrimony, [23]the priest[a] will compute for him the proportionate[b] value[c] in relation to the next year of Jubilee; that person is to pay its value on that day; it is holy to Yahweh. [24]In[a] the

year of Jubilee the field will return to the person from whom he bought it, whose patrimony the land is. [25]*Every valuation will be made in the shekel of the sanctuary; the shekel is worth*[a] *twenty gerahs.*

[26]*"But*[a] *no one may dedicate a first-born*[b] *among*[c] *animals which already belongs to Yahweh as first-born; whether it is a cow or a sheep, it is Yahweh's.* [27]*If it is one of the unclean animals, he may reclaim*[a] *it for its value and add 20 percent to it.*[b] *If he does not redeem it, it is to be sold for its value.* [28]*But*[a] *nothing which a person devotes to Yahweh from all that he owns, whether it be a human,*[b] *an animal, or a field of his patrimony, may be sold or redeemed. Everything devoted, being most holy, belongs to Yahweh.* [29]*No human*[a] *devoted may be ransomed; that one must be put to death.*

[30]*"A tithe*[a] *of everything of the land, either yield of grain or fruit*[b] *from trees,*[c] *is Yahweh's; it is holy to Yahweh.* [31]*If one indeed*[a] *redeems any of his tithe,*[b] *he is to add 20 percent to it.*[c] [32]*As for the tithe*[a] *of the herd and the flock, a tenth one of all that pass under the shepherd's rod*[b] *will be holy to Yahweh.* [33]*He may not pick out the good from the poor*[a] *or make a substitution.*[b] *If he indeed*[c] *makes*[d] *a substitution, both the animal and its substitute*[e] *become holy and cannot be redeemed."*

[34]*These are the commandments which Yahweh gave to Moses on Mount Sinai for the Israelites.*

Notes

2.a. *BHS* proposes the form יְפַלֵּא (piel) as in 22:21 for MT יַפְלִא (hiph); cf. Num 6:2 for another occurrence of the piel used like a hiph. Levine (193), however, proposes that it comes from פלה, "set apart," rather than פלא, "be extraordinary, be distinct." Cf. n. 22:21.a.

2.b. On the frozen form ערכך, "value, valuation, equivalence," see n. 5:15.a.

2.c. For MT נפשׁת, "persons," LXX reads τῆς ψυχῆς αὐτοῦ = נפשׁו, "his person."

3.a. GKC (§128d) suggests that הזכר, "the male," after ערכך, "the value," may not be the gen, but the subj of the following clause, here and in vv 5–6. But since ערכך acts like a frozen term, MT is acceptable; cf. v 23.

3.b. Heb. expresses a person's age by the constr of בן, "sons of," or בת, "daughters of," followed by a number and a word for time, which may be omitted (cf. BDB, "בן," 9.a., 121–22).

5.a. The prep phrase לנקבה, "for a female," is elliptical for ערכך־הנקבה, "the value of a female" (cf. Baentsch, 438).

6.a. Cf. n. 5.a.

6.b. LXX* and Syr do not read כסף, "silver."

7.a. LXX adds ἀργυρίου, "silver."

7.b. Cf. n. 5.a.

7.c. In place of MT עשׂרה, "ten," a fem abs, some Heb. mss and Sam read עשׂרת, "ten," a fem constr, as in v 5.

8.a. Cf. n. 25:25.c.

8.b. This is a comparative use of the prep "from" (GKC §133a).

8.c. העמיד means "station (oneself)"; cf. 14:11; 16:7. LXX does not render the pronominal suffix on this verb. The antecedents of the pronoun of the subj and the pronominal suffix are not immediately clear. Baentsch (439), Dillmann (686), and Bertholet (439) identify the acc as the person who has made the vow and the subj as an indefinite "one," possibly a temple official. Another possible interpretation cited by Dillmann (686) is that the person making the vow presents the person vowed before the priest. It is possible that this vague language is used to cover both cases, that of a person who vows himself and that of a family member vowed by the head of the family.

8.d. העריך means "evaluate, assess"; it is a technical administrative term (e.g., 2 Kgs 23:35; Levine, 194).

8.e. על־פי means "according to the measure of, in accordance with" (BDB, "פה 6.d.," 805).

8.f. Cf. n. 5:7.a.

9.a. This phrase has been added to make clearer the Eng trans.

9.b. Several Heb. mss, Sam, Tg[mss], and Vg read a sg; cf. n. 11.a. MT is accepted, and the form is taken as a pl functioning as a virtual pass.

9.c. On קרבן see *Comment* on 1:2.

9.d. In place of ממנו, "from them," some Heb. mss, Sam[mss], LXX, and Syr read ממנה, "from it." While MT is the more difficult reading, the grammar clearly prefers the variant reading.

10.a. LXX does not have anything for לא יחליפנו, "he may not exchange it."

10.b. The inf abs before the impf stresses the fact that an exchange has surely taken place (cf. GKC §113n).

10.c. Sam has the spelling ותמירתו; cf. n. 33.e.

10.d. According to GKC §112y, והיה, "and it will come to pass," introduces the consequence in the future; the event itself is carried by יהיה, "it will be."

11.a. This phrase has been added to make clearer the Eng trans.

11.b. LXX renders ממנה, "from it," by a pl form.

11.c. A couple of Heb. mss, Sam, and Vg read a sg form; cf. n. 9.b.

11.d. Cf. n. 8.c.

12.a. Sam, minuscule mss of LXX, and Tg[mss] read a masc pronominal suffix in place of the fem suffix in MT. 11QpaleoLev supports MT.

12.b. In place of MT כערכך, "according to the valuation of," LXX and *Tg. Ps.-J.* read כאשר יעריך, "just as he evaluates."

13.a. Cf. n. 10.b.

13.b. 11QpaleoLev, Sam, a couple of mss of LXX, Tg[mss], and *Tg. Ps.-J.* read a masc pronominal suffix in place of the fem suffix in MT.

13.c. LXX, *Tg. Neof.*, Syr, and Vg do not render the suffix on this word in the MT (*The Paleo-Hebrew Leviticus Scroll,* 48).

14.a. קום, "arise, stand," may mean technically "be in force, be legally binding" (25:30; Gen 23:20; Levine, 213).

15.a. LXX and Vg read a pronominal suffix on the ptcp.

15.b. עליו, "on it," is not rendered in LXX[mss] and *Tg. Neof.*

16.a. The prep מן, "from," is used partitively to specify "a portion of" a field (cf. BDB, "מן 3.b.," 580).

17.a. Several Heb. mss, Sam, LXX, and Syr read a *waw* at the beginning of the verse. 11QpaleoLev supports MT.

17.b. This is an example of a temporal use of the prep מן, "from," in relation to the point of beginning (*IBHS* §11.2.11c).

17.c. Cf. n. 14.a.

18.a. LXX and Syr do not read a *waw.*

19.a. Cf. n. 13.a. LXX does not have any equivalent for the inf abs.

19.b. LXX, Syr, and Vg do not read a *waw.*

19.c. 11QpaleoLev reads את, the sign of the definite dir obj.

19.d. Cf. n. 14.a.

21.a. On this technical use of יצא, "go out," see 25:30–31.

21.b. חרם is "a thing or a person offered permanently and definitively to God or the sanctuary." Lohfink (*TDOT* 5:185) holds that חרם is either a concrete noun or a noun for an action; he is arguing against Brekelmans' position (*THAT* 1:636) that חרם is a noun expressing a quality like קדש, "holy." Lohfink explains the use of חרם here as an epexegetic gen.

22.a. A Heb. ms and Syr add איש, "a person"; this variant results from the influence of another passage (PIR, 205).

22.b. Cf. n. 16.a.

23.a. LXX does not read a *waw.*

23.b. Sam reads a pl form. מכסת, "computation, valuation, assessment," occurs only here and in Exod 12:4 (BDB, 493; KB, 550). It may be related to Akk *miksu,* "a share of crops due to another, customs, dues" (*CAD* 10:2:63).

23.c. GKC (§127i) suggests that it is better to read ערכך, "value," instead of MT הערכך, "the value." However, if ערכך is either a noun with the reduplication of the third radical or a frozen form with the pronominal suffix, the article is acceptable. Cf. n. 2.b.

24.a. LXX and Syr read a *waw.*

25.a. A couple of Heb. mss and Sam do not have יהיה, "it is (worth)."

26.a. LXX renders אך, an adverb that establishes a contrast with the preceding material (BDB, 36), by *καί*, "and."

26.b. Sam and LXX add כל, "all."

26.c. The prep ב has the sense "among" (GKC §119i).

27.a. LXX reads ἀλλάξει, "he exchanges." This reading suggests a Vorlage with a form of המיר instead of MT's ופדה, "and he reclaims/ransoms."

27.b. LXX adds καὶ ἔσται αὐτῷ ,"and it will be his"; cf. n. 31.b.

28.a. Cf. n. 26.a. This time the LXX uses δέ, a mild adversative.

28.b. The prep מן, "from," has partitive force (GKC §119w, n. 2).

29.a. Cf. n. 16.a.

30.a. LXX does not read a *waw.*

30.b. Many Heb. mss, Sam, LXX, Syr, and Vg read a *waw* on this word.

30.c. Elliger (390) thinks that עץ, "tree," means mostly "vines" in this text.

31.a. Cf. n. 13.a.

31.b. LXX and Vg place this word in the acc suggesting that they read מעשׂרו, "its tenth," instead of MT ממעשׂרו, "from its tenth"; Elliger (381) prefers the variant, but PIR (206) suggests that the variant may be an error of haplography. On מן, cf. n. 16.a.

31.c. Cf. n. 27.b.

32.a. The ordinal העשׂירי,"the tenth (part)," is used as a substantive for "the tithe" (cf. BDB, 798).

32.b. The article is used to designate the kind of staff that would come to the mind of the ancient audience (GKC §126q).

33.a. For the ָ under ל see Joüon §103c, n.

33.b. LXX has a shorter reading, ἀλλάξεις καλὸν πονηρῷ. *BHS* proposes that it equals תמיר טוב ברע, "you may exchange the good for the poor."

33.c. Cf. n. 10.b.

33.d. LXX reads a second person sg.

33.e. Cf. n. 10.c.

Form/Structure/Setting

The location of this speech on vows is puzzling. Why does it come after the chapter on blessings and curses, which, at least to a modern person, is an appropriate way to conclude the laws given in Leviticus? Those who take the position that this section of the Pentateuch records the revelation as it was given to Moses at Sinai hold that this was the order in which the law was given. Critical scholars, on the other hand, view it as an appendix. Wenham (336), however, suggests that this speech is the counterpart to the speech in chap. 26. In that speech Yahweh vows to bless or to curse his people depending on their response to his law. This speech, on the other hand, regulates the vows made by the people to Yahweh. Human vows are, moreover, often related to seasons of blessings and of curses, for it is during times of distress or abundance that people usually make vows.

These comments by Wenham open up the need to reassess the position of this speech. It could not have been placed before chap. 25, for the laws in vv 17–24 presuppose the legislation on the year of Jubilee. To place this speech right after chap. 25 was not desirable to the compiler, for he wished to present the material on blessings and curses immediately after the laws on the year of Jubilee. The location of the blessings and curses in Deuteronomy also indicates that ancient Jewish compilers did not favor ending a book with that genre. Furthermore, these laws on vows differ fundamentally from much of the preceding material in Leviticus in that they cover a purely voluntary situation. The other laws, however, for the most part, treat obligatory situations; thus they fittingly come after that type of legal material. From the perspective of the whole book, this location establishes a balance between these laws and the sacrificial laws of chaps. 1–7; i.e., just as Leviticus opens with regulations, it closes with regulations. These are small, but definitive, signs that this legislation is rightly placed in Leviticus.

The structure of this chapter is outlined as follows:

- I. Introductory formula (v 1)
- II. Speech (vv 2–33)
  - A. Commission to speak (v 2aα)
  - B. Speech proper (vv 2aβ–33)
    - 1. Concerning vows (vv 2aβ–13)
      - a. Of person (vv 2aβ–8)
      - b. Of animals (vv 9–13)
    - 2. Concerning dedications to the sanctuary (vv 14–25)
      - a. Of a house (vv 14–15)
      - b. Of a field (vv 16–24)
        - 1) Inherited land (vv 16–21)
        - 2) Purchased land (vv 22–24)
      - c. Statement on value of a shekel (v 25)
    - 3. Restrictions on objects that may be vowed (vv 26–33)
      - a. Concerning first-born (vv 26–27)
      - b. Concerning things devoted (vv 28–29)
        - 1) With regard to animals (v 28)
        - 2) With regard to humans (v 29)
      - c. Concerning tithes (vv 30–33)
        - 1) Of crops (vv 30–31)
        - 2) Of animals (v 32–33)
- III. Summary formula (v 34)

This outline reveals that the structure of this speech is uniform. Critical scholars for the most part accept the literary unity of vv 1–25 (Elliger, 382). This unit presents laws on vows (vv 1–13) and dedications to the sanctuaries (vv 14–25). To this is added a series of laws that restrict the objects that may be vowed, namely first-born (vv 26–27), anything that is devoted (vv 28–29), and tithes (vv 30–33). Usually critical scholars judge these three sections to be later appendices (e.g., Elliger, 385; Noth, 207). While it is possible that these qualifying vows were added much later, there is no compelling reason to hold this position.

Most critical scholars assign these laws to a late date. In the later period the sanctuary favored the conversion of materials vowed, consecrated, or tithed into currency in order that it might have the funds necessary to carry out the operation, maintenance, and equipment of the sanctuary (cf. Levine, 192). While these laws may have become the rule in the post-exilic community, however, that does not mean that they may not have been formulated earlier. Given Noth's judgment (204) that this legislation does not envision the wholesale conversion of sacrificial gifts into currency, which was the case in the late post-exilic period, this legislation may be assigned to a much earlier era, for it establishes only the possibility of such action.

The genre of this speech is regulations on vows and gifts to the sanctuary.

Comment

2–8 Anyone may make a vow of a person to Yahweh. In the neighboring cults such a vow was the means of devoting a person to the sanctuary for service, for participation in the cultic ritual, or for sacrifice, especially if the vow concerned a child (cf. 18:21; 20:2–5). The making and the fulfillment of such a vow in Israel, however, had to take a different course, because human sacrifice was banished, and the servants at the sanctuary, for the most part, were Levites. The dedication of Samuel to the sanctuary at Shilo was an exception (1 Sam 1:11), although it is conceivable that a dedicated person could have been made a part of the maintenance staff at the sanctuary. In any case, an Israelite who makes a vow of oneself or of a family member to God is to fulfill that vow by contributing to the sanctuary a predetermined payment. This practice is similar to that of the redemption of the first-born children (Exod 13:13; 34:20; Num 18:16). This law fixes the price for a person, not letting it fluctuate according to conditions of the market. The use of the unusual technical term ערכך, "value, price," establishes a definite tie with the legislative tradition behind 5:14–26[6:7]. Wenham argues that the price for a person seems to be set according to the price a person might fetch in the slave market (Wenham, *ZAW* 90 [1978] 264), but the price of slaves varied in different times and locations, as I. Mendelsohn (*Slavery in the Ancient Near East,* 117–18) observes. In this law the price was set on the basis of a person's strength, not on the basis of a person's intrinsic value as a human being. The price, therefore, varied according to age and gender. Since women were not considered to be able to work as hard as men, their price was less by a third to a half. The same was true of children and the elderly. The inclusion of children means that a head of the household might vow members of his family as well as himself. The price may be charted:

age	male	female
1 month to 5 years	5 shekels	3 shekels
5–20 years	20 shekels	10 shekels
20–60 years	50 shekels	30 shekels
60+ years	15 shekels	10 shekels

On the sanctuary shekel see v 25.

Pondering another understanding of the price, Noth (205) postulates that this amount is to be paid annually. It would be impossible for ordinary citizens to pay such a high sum annually, however, since wages of a laborer in those days were about a shekel a month, according to Wenham (388). If this wage figure is accurate, very few people could even afford to make this vow in the first place. It may be assumed that the practice of vowing oneself to God took place infrequently and under unique circumstances.

8 An exception to these valuations is made for anyone who has made the vow of a person but is too poor to pay the valuation as prescribed. Someone is to העמיד, "station," that person vowed, or the one who has vowed another member of his family is to station the one vowed before the priest. The priest is to assess the vowed person's worth and then set the price that he can afford. Rabbinic interpretation has established that the price set is to leave that person enough to live on, including a bed, a mattress, a cushion, and the tools needed for his trade (Rashi, 131a). This is another example of the law's merciful concern for the poor by providing alternatives so that they may fulfill the requirement of the law (e.g., 5:11; 14:21–22).

9–10 A person may make a vow in which he pledges to give an animal (בהמה), one from cattle, sheep, and goats (cf. 1:2), to Yahweh. Such a vowed animal becomes קדש, "holy." It will be presented as one of the offerings of the sanctuary

(קרבן; cf. 1:2). The person who vows may not substitute something else for what has been vowed (cf. Mal 1:8), nor may that one make an exchange, such as a רע, "bad," i.e., an animal of lesser value, for a טוב, "good," animal. If a person makes an exchange, the animal used in exchange and the original animal both become holy, i.e., the property of the sanctuary. Why would a person want to alter the object of a vow? Of course, there is the human tendency to make bold, generous promises during moments of distress or euphoria, only to change the mind quickly when the moment of enthusiasm passes. This exception may also be addressing the kind of vow in which a person identifies the pledge to the vow in a general way, e.g., the next born lamb; that person then is caught off guard when the pledge is disclosed. The prime example of this type of vow was that of Jephthah (Judg 11:30–31, 34–40). He vowed that he would give to Yahweh whatever would come forth from his household to meet him on his successful return from a campaign against his enemy. When he returned, his daughter was unfortunately the first one to run out to meet him. Grieving Jephthah kept his vow.

11–13 The law regulates the giving of an unclean animal as קרבן ליהוה, "a gift to Yahweh." Under certain types of vows defined above, a person does not know whether the animal that will fulfill the vow will be clean or unclean. If the vowed animal is unclean, the one making the vow must bring it, and the priest is to determine its value. His valuation is nonnegotiable. Since there is no possibility that the unclean animal could be sacrificed, its value could be converted into currency for the treasury of the sanctuary. Presumably the sanctuary sold the animal for this price (Noordtzij, 276). The one who has made the vow, however, has the opportunity גאל, "to redeem," the unclean animal by paying the set price plus 20 percent. Levine (193) comments that the person who made the vow was expected to redeem it.

14–15 This speech continues with regulations on items consecrated or dedicated (הקדיש) to Yahweh. הקדיש is a broader term than נדר, "vow." It stands for anything that is turned over to the sanctuary. The gift may fulfill a vow, or it may be a special, generous offering as an expression of one's devotion (cf. 22:2–3). Possibly some type of oath accompanied the dedication. In either case, that which is vowed or dedicated becomes holy. These laws cover the consecration of a house, a portion of a field which was one's patrimony, or a purchased field. If a person dedicates a house to Yahweh, the priest is to determine the value of that house. The house is most likely one in a walled city, which is not subject to the laws of the year of Jubilee (25:29–30). The price that the priest sets for the house is nonnegotiable. The one who dedicates the house may redeem it by paying the amount set by the priest plus 20 percent. Otherwise the house becomes the property of the sanctuary. In the latter case, the sanctuary may do with the gift as it pleases.

16–21 A person may dedicate to Yahweh a field that is part of his אחזה, "tribal inheritance." The value of that field is determined by two criteria. First, its value is set according to the amount of seed needed for sowing that parcel. A parcel that can be sown with a homer of barley seed is valued at fifty shekels until the year of Jubilee. The term חמר, "homer," is literally a donkey; thus it is a dry measure of the amount of seed which a donkey can carry. Cook (*ISBE* rev. 4:1051) estimates a homer to be 220 liters, 232 liquid quarts, or 199 dry quarts. An alternative interpretation from a minority viewpoint is that the homer of seed refers not to the amount sown, but the amount produced; then the parcel of land would be several times smaller (de Vaux, *AI,* 1:168; Wenham, 340 n.). Snaith (117) estimates that this amount sows about 3.75 acres. Second, the value of the field is determined by the number of years until the next Jubilee (cf. chap. 25). The value placed on land dedicated in the year of Jubilee stands, but the value of land dedicated after the year of Jubilee has to be set in proportion to the number of years to the next Jubilee, for a patrimony automatically reverted to the original owner at the year of Jubilee.

Apparently the owner continues to work a dedicated field, for the priests would not have had the manpower to work the fields dedicated to God. Given that the price of redemption is fixed, should a field produce a good yield or the price of barley be higher than set in v 16, the owner could then redeem his field for less than the real value of the crops, as Wenham points out (340). A person who dedicates a field has the opportunity to redeem that field by paying 20 percent above its current worth. If he redeems it, the transaction stands. The sanctuary benefits from the proceeds. This law strongly encourages a person to redeem a field of his inheritance before the year of Jubilee because land left unredeemed in the year of Jubilee becomes holy like a "devoted" (חרם) field (cf. below). In the context of giving something to God, חרם defines anything that is totally and irrevocably given over to the sanctuary (N. Lohfink, "חָרַם *ḥāram,*" *TDOT* 5:188). A devoted field becomes the אחזה, "inheritance," of the priests (cf. Num 18:14).

If the original owner does not redeem this field but sells it to another person, he also loses the right to redeem it. This stipulation raises the question of how a person could sell that which he has dedicated to the sanctuary. Could that person be employing a loophole in the law to increase his income on a field? Perhaps an owner comes to consider his dedication of a field an unwise move. Then he seeks some way to recover some value from his loss. He sells the field to another without informing the buyer that the field has been consecrated to Yahweh. The buyer retains the right to work that land until the year of Jubilee. The penalty for employing this conniving tactic is the owner's loss of that land. In the year of Jubilee this latter field, which has been twice sold, so to speak, becomes חרם, "devoted," i.e., under complete control of the sanctuary. Keil and Delitzsch (483–84) suggest an alternative explanation, one that does not ascribe any deception to the person who has dedicated the field. In their reconstruction, the owner of a dedicated field, being obligated to continue to cultivate that field, earns the money to pay the vow from the crops. He keeps the difference between the yield and the vow. Given the burden of working a field from which he does not keep the majority of the produce, the dedicator sells it to another to work the field and carry out the obligations. Levine (196) offers another interpretation. He thinks that the owner cannot sell consecrated land. Therefore, it is the priesthood who sells the land of a donor who, they perceive, does not intend to redeem it. The major difficulty with this interpretation is that it presupposes a different subject for "sell" than that for the preceding verb, "redeem"; the parallel construction does not allow for a shift in the subject of these verbs (Keil and Delitzsch, 414).

22–24 A person may dedicate a field that is מקנתו, "purchased property," i.e., a field that is not part of his tribal inheritance and that must be returned to its original owner at the year of Jubilee. The priest is to set the value of such a field according to the number of years until the next Jubilee. Then the person who dedicates it is to give that price to the priests. The amount he pays is to be paid in the official currency of the sanctuary. The price of this purchased property is to be determined according to the standards of the sanctuary. There is to be no debate. The donor has to make the payment right away, for the land, not being his patrimony, may not be used as collateral (Levine, 197). That sum becomes holy, but the field returns to its owner in the year of Jubilee.

25 These valuations must be paid in the shekel of the sanctuary, i.e., the currency accepted by the sanctuary. In ancient times there were no banks, and there was no minted currency. Since the Temples received offerings and gifts, they had standard weights for weighing silver and gold, which they accepted as currency. A שֶׁקֶל, "shekel," is the basic "weight" for currency, weighing around 11.4 grams or .4 ounce (E. Cook, *ISBE* rev. 4:1054). These shekels were put into standardized shapes before coinage became widespread under the Persian Empire (H. Perkin, "Money," *ISBE* rev. 3:403–4), but they were still weighed for accuracy. The sanctuary shekel was evaluated at twenty gerahs (Exod 30:13: Num 3:47; 18:16; Ezek 45:12).

26–27 At this point the legislation provides some exception to the foregoing laws. The first-born of humans and animals belong to Yahweh by his position as Lord of the people and their Redeemer (Exod 13:2; 34:19–20). A first-born animal may not be הקדיש, "consecrated," to Yahweh. It is already his. This means that a person may not use the ploy of paying a vow with a first-born animal, attempting to gain double spiritual benefit from the presentation of a single animal. The first-born of an unclean animal also belongs to God, but the owner has to redeem it by paying to the sanctuary its value plus 20 percent (cf. Exod 13:13; 34:20). If for some reason the owner cannot redeem the animal, the animal is to be sold. The proceeds from the sale go to the sanctuary.

28 The weightiest vow is called חרם, "the devoted or proscribed thing" (cf. vv 16–21). Anything, a person, an animal, or a field of one's inheritance, that becomes חרם, "devoted," קדש־קדשים הוא ליהוה, "is most holy to Yahweh," and may not be redeemed. That means it may not be used for any purpose other than at the sanctuary and by the priests. It belongs to the sanctuary forever. But how does something become devoted since that classification is "an imposed position" (Levine, 198)? From the context, חרם, "devoted," may refer to property that has been proscribed either by means of a direct oath or by means of fulfilling the obligation stated in an oath for failure to uphold that oath, i.e., "I shall do such and such if I do not live up to this oath." It is the oath that makes an object "devoted," according to Levine (199). He postulates that a person (אדם) who is devoted is a non-Israelite slave who has become the legal property of his master. Furthermore, he adds that since the background of these laws is not known, its full force is obscure. Finally Levine notes that the taking of such oaths in the late Second Temple period was common.

29 Another law regarding חרם, "the devoted or proscribed thing," is given. In most other passages the use of חרם describes something so taboo that it must be completely destroyed. Certain spoils taken in a holy war were so devoted (e.g., Josh 6:17; 7:1, 11–13, 15). If a person becomes so devoted, that one comes under the death penalty; there is no means of פדה, "redemption," for that person. How does a person in Israel come to be classified as "a devoted thing"? The law in

Exod 22:19[20] provides an explanation. It states that a person who sacrifices to a pagan god becomes devoted and falls under the death penalty. That party was most likely declared devoted by a judicial body. Another example is found in Deut 13:13–19(12–18); any group of wicked men who lead the community away from service to God become devoted to destruction.

30–33 All the tithe of the produce of the field and the fruit of the trees belongs to Yahweh (Deut 14:22–26). It is classified as קדשׁ ליהוה, "holy to Yahweh." It cannot be disposed of freely. Any of this tithe may be redeemed if its owner pays to the sanctuary its value plus 20 percent. This alternative is confined to the produce of the field, for the law does not prescribe any substitute for an animal that belongs to Yahweh by right (Elliger, 391).

All flocks are also to be tithed. How were the animals for the tithe determined? The precise method is not known. This language, however, suggests that the increment of a flock or a herd was passed through a line and every tenth member was pointed out by a שׁבט, "staff," like that of a shepherd, and then marked for dedication to the sanctuary. The shepherd's staff (שׁבט) is a club used as a weapon (Harrison, 238). One way of marking animals in antiquity was the use of a colored dye to make a stripe across their backs (cf. Jer 33:13; Ezek 20:37). Possibly this law means that each year every tenth animal of a flock or a herd is given to Yahweh, but such a tithe would be far too costly.

This law states that the shepherd may not arrange the line of animals so that the mark always falls on the poorer, weaker members of the flock. After an animal is marked, the shepherd may not make a substitution. The animal that is selected for the tithe becomes holy; it may not be redeemed. According to Num 18:21–32, the tithe belonged to the Levites, and they in turn were obligated to tithe their portion to the priests. Also see Deut 26:12–15.

34 Since an inclusive summary statement occurs at 26:46, this summary statement is primarily for this speech. Nevertheless, because of its position as the last verse of the Book of Leviticus, it also functions as the concluding statement to the book. This statement underscores the authority of these laws.

Explanation

A vow is an oath by which one binds oneself to take a specified course of action. The vow may be unconditional or conditional. In an unconditional vow a person expresses resolve to live according to certain standards, to take a defined course of action, or to maintain loyalty. There are several situations in which one is moved to make a vow. Marriage vows are an example of a pledge of loyalty. Similarly, by a vow a person may commit to accomplish a certain goal as an expression of devout zeal for Yahweh. David, e.g., vowed that he would not rest until he found a dwelling place for the Ark of the Lord. His goal was to make the worship of Yahweh central to the monarchy (Ps 132:2–5). By fulfilling this vow David demonstrated before the entire nation his deep loyalty to Yahweh. Furthermore, a vow may be an expression of gratefulness to Yahweh out of a thankful heart (cf. 1 Sam 1:21).

Another type of unconditional vow is a pledge to serve God in a special way. Usually those taking such a vow join a group that is serving God by a special form of discipline. The vow of the Nazirite, for example, exists for those who wish to express their total devotion to God through self-discipline (Num 6:1–12). This vow requires three specific abstinences: avoidance of juice from grapes and eating grapes, not cutting one's hair, and never contacting a corpse. It could be for a period of time (Num 6:13–20) or for life (case of Samson, Judg 13:7). Another example of total devotion to God was the practice of the Rechabites. This family committed itself to live by the distinct standards laid on them by their father (Jer 35:1–11). While there is no mention of a vow in this passage about them, the distinctiveness of their lifestyle suggests that it was sustained by vows. Their example illustrates how a father's house in Israel could bind itself together to live in a distinct way for the glory of God.

In a conditional vow a person commits to a specified course of action provided something favorable happens to the one who swears. Usually it is out of a strong sense of need or out of fear that a person seeks to motivate God to act in a redemptive way by pledging to present God with some kind of gift. By taking a vow, the supplicant underscores the urgency of the petition being made (Ps 66:13–14). The supplicant is seeking to motivate God to act right away. A vow is not made with the design to purchase God's intervention as though by a bribe. A prime example is Hannah's bewailing her barrenness (1 Sam 1:9–12). She prayed for a child, and she strengthened her petition by vowing to give her child back to Yahweh to live as a Nazirite; i.e., the child would become a servant of the sanctuary.

Not only an individual, but also the entire nation might make a vow. In the wilderness when Israel was confronted by a formidable foe, she vowed to obey the ordinance that required devoting the spoils of war to Yahweh, if Yahweh would deliver the enemy into her control (Num 21:2).

A vow is completely voluntary (Deut 23:23[22]). Only in the case of certain women is a vow restricted. Given that ancient Israel was a patriarchal society, a young woman's vow is subject to her father's approval (Num 30:3–5), and a married woman's vow is subject to her husband's approval (Num 30:6–8, 10–15).

Nowhere does God require the making of vows, and nowhere does he encourage their being made. Nevertheless, there is some evidence, such as Jonah 1:4 and Jer 44:25, that making vows was fairly common in the ancient Middle East (Cartledge, *ISBE* rev. 4:998). The Scriptures, however, caution against making rash utterances with the mouth (Lev 5:4; Eccl 5:1[2]). This caution assuredly addresses the making of vows. The classic case of a vow leading to a tragic end is Jephthah's vow to sacrifice whatever came out of his house on his triumphant return from battle, only to return to see his daughter running out to meet him (Judg 11:30–40). Deut 23:25[24] even says, "If you refrain from vowing, it will be no sin."

Once a vow has been made, the person who made it is obligated to the vow no matter the cost (Num 30:2; Deut 23:22–24[21–23]). That position is the firm exhortation and counsel of Scripture, for the person who fails to pay his vows falls under the hot wrath of God. Neither may one diminish the value of the vow nor usually make a substitution. No wonder the preacher says, "It is better that you should not vow than that you should vow and not pay" (Eccl 5:4[5]; cf. Prov 20:25).

The laws in this speech regulated the paying of vows and the dedication to God of a highly prized possession like a piece of land or a house. It recognized the human tendency, after making a vow in a moment of great excitement or under extreme duress, to seek to offer a substitute for the item or animal that was vowed after the surge of emotion has passed. This speech, therefore, regulates what might and might not be substituted for something vowed to God. It also addressed the sanctuary's need for funds in addition to goods and thus regulated the exchange of certain vows into money for the operation of the sanctuary. Provisions for fulfilling a vow by the payment of a sum to the sanctuary primarily applied to the type of vow in which a person pledged himself or another member of his family to Yahweh. It was possible that a person could fulfill such a vow by becoming a servant of the sanctuary, but given the servant role of the Levites, an ancient sanctuary had little need for more workers. Since in Israel a person could not be sacrificed, these vows regarding people could only be fulfilled by paying the sanctuary the amount specified in this law. This law then set the value for persons, dependent on the person's age and sex. It provided, however, an exception for one who is too poor to pay the established fee.

Should a person substitute another item or animal for the item or animal consecrated, both the original item and the substituted item become holy; i.e., they become the property of the sanctuary. A clean, sacrificial animal that had been vowed may not be redeemed, but an unclean animal that had been vowed may be redeemed. The priest determines the value of a redeemable animal, and the party redeems it by paying that price plus 20 percent. A house that had been dedicated may be redeemed in the same way. A field dedicated to the sanctuary before the year of Jubilee, however, must be redeemed by paying its worth until the Jubilee plus 20 percent. It had to be redeemed since a patrimony in Israel was inalienable. Should a person who had dedicated any part of his patrimony to the sanctuary sell that field, that family lost that patrimony to the sanctuary in the year of Jubilee. It also was possible to redeem the tithe of the harvest by paying its value plus 20 percent, but it was not possible to redeem the tithe of the flock.

This law stipulated that a person might not vow anything that already belonged to God by reason of another law. This includes vowing either a first-born animal, something devoted, or tithe, for the law had already defined these as God's due (Exod 13:2, 12; 22:30[31]; 34:19; Deut 14:22–23). No one was to manipulate the law to make himself appear to the community more zealous or devoted in his service of Yahweh than he really was.

Several OT references speak of fulfilling vows. In Nah 2:1[1:15], e.g., Judah is exhorted to keep her feasts and fulfill her vows as a sign of her devotion to Yahweh. A psalmist who has come through the darkest suffering says in confidence, "My vows I will pay before those who fear him" (Ps 22:26[25]; cf. Pss 56:13[12]; 63:2[1]; 76:12[11]; 116:13, 18–19). The primary way a vow was fulfilled was the presentation of a sacrifice to Yahweh (Ps 66:13–15). In fact, one of the offerings of well-being is named a vow offering (Lev 7:16; 22:17–25; 23:38; Deut 12:6, 11, 17); regulations regarding such an offering are given in Num 15:1–10.

Paying a vow is a joyous occasion. In fulfilling the conditions of the vow, the worshiper has a profound sense of living up to one's words. One psalmist exclaims joyfully and confidently, "You, O God, have heard my vows; you have given me the heritage of those who fear your name" (Ps 61:6[5]). In fact, the paying of vows is frequently made parallel to praising God (Pss 22:26[25]; 61:9[8]; 63:2[1]) or making a praise offering (Ps 50:14).

The NT does not offer any more regulations or insight into the making of vows. Two passages in Acts, though, recount events in which a vow played a major role. At Corinth Paul placed himself under a vow for a short duration; since he shaved his head at the end of the vow, possibly he had taken a Nazirite vow for a brief period (Acts 18:18). Acts 21:22–24 refers to four believers who had placed themselves under a vow similar to Paul's for a limited span of time. All in all it may be affirmed that the NT adopts the OT teaching on making and fulfilling vows. Furthermore, the lack of emphasis in the NT on making vows diminishes their importance for believers in Jesus.

Index of Authors Cited

Index of Principal Subjects